Gree

a Lonely Planet tra

David Willett
Rosemary Hall
Paul Hellander
Kerry Kenihan

Greece

2nd edition

Published by
Lonely Planet Publications
Head Office: PO Box 617, Hawthorn, Vic 3122, Australia
Branches: 155 Filbert St, Suite 251, Oakland, CA 94607, USA
                        10 Barley Mow Passage, Chiswick, London W4 4PH, UK
                        71 bis rue du Cardinal Lemoine, 75005 Paris, France

Printed by
Pac-Rim Kwartanusa Printing
Printed in Indonesia

Photographs by

Greg Alford	Brigitte Barta	Vicki Beale	Michelle Coxall	Bertold Daum
David Hall	Rosemary Hall	Paul Hellander	Ann Jousiffe	Kerry Kenihan
Leanne Logan	Linda Welters	David Willett		

Front cover: Blue door and pink pot, Santorini (Leanne Logan)
Main title page: George, an octopus fisherman from Paros, with one of his catch (Leanne Logan)
The Mainland title page: At the Acropolis, Athens (Vicki Beale)
The Islands title page: Kafeneio, Santorini (Brigitte Barta)

George Dalaras *Kalos tous* CD cover reproduced with kind permission of MINOS-EMI Greece.

First Published
February 1994

This Edition
March 1996
Reprinted with Update supplement November 1996

**Although the authors and publisher have tried to make the information as
accurate as possible, they accept no responsibility for any loss, injury or
inconvenience sustained by any person using this book.**

National Library of Australia Cataloguing in Publication Data

Willett, David
    Greece

    2nd ed.
    Includes index.
    ISBN 0 86442 354 3 (pbk.).

    1. Greece – Guide-books. I. Hall, Rosemary. Greece.
    II. Hellander, Paul D. III. Kenihan, Kerry, 1944- . IV. Title.
    V. Title: Greece. (Series: Lonely Planet travel guidebook).

914.950476

text & maps © Lonely Planet 1996
photos © photographers as indicated 1996
climate charts compiled from information supplied by Patrick J Tyson, © Patrick J Tyson, 1996

All rights reserved. No part of this publication may be reproduced, stored in a retrieval system or transmitted
in any form by any means, electronic, mechanical, photocopying, recording or otherwise, except brief extracts
for the purpose of review, without the written permission of the publisher and copyright owner.

David Willett

David is a freelance journalist based near Bellingen on the mid-north coast of New South Wales, Australia. He grew up in Hampshire, England, and wound up in Australia in 1980 after stints working on newspapers in Iran (1975-78) and Bahrain. He spent two years working as a sub-editor at the Melbourne *Sun* newspaper before trading a steady job for a warmer climate. Between jobs, David has travelled extensively in Europe, the Middle East and Asia. He coordinated this 2nd edition of *Greece*, and updated the introductory chapters as well as the chapters on Athens, Crete and the Saronic Gulf islands. He has previously updated Tunisia for LP's *North Africa* guide, and Sumatra for the *Indonesia* guide. He has also contributed to the *Mediterranean Europe* and *Africa* shoestring guides.

Rosemary Hall

Rosemary was born in Sunderland, England. She graduated in fine art, but fame and fortune as an artist eluded her, so she spent a few months bumming around Europe and India. After teaching in northern England, she decided to find work somewhere more exotic, finally landing a job in Basra, Iraq. After two years the Iraqi government refused to renew her work permit, so she settled in London, tried to make it again as a painter, did supply teaching and travelled in India and South-East Asia. She researched Iraq for Lonely Planet's *West Asia on a shoestring*. Rosemary wrote the 1st edition of *Greece* and updated the Dodecanese chapter for this edition.

Paul Hellander

Like a number of authors who ended up working for Lonely Planet, Paul came to Australia from England, having temporarily satiated his wanderlust along the way in over 30 countries. After leaving England, he spent five years seeking fame and fortune in Greece, but ended up being exported to Australia to teach Greek instead. He is a former lecturer in Modern Greek at Adelaide University and now runs an Internet-based translation agency in Adelaide. He was the language consultant for the 1st edition of *Greece* and is the author of Lonely Planet's *Greek Phrasebook*. Paul updated the chapters on Northern Greece, Central Greece, the North-Eastern Aegean islands and Evia & the Sporades for this edition of *Greece*. When he isn't writing, translating or travelling, Paul lives in cyberspace at sals@adelaide.dialix.com.au.

Kerry Kenihan

An Australian journalist since 1968, Kerry has contributed to (and edited) magazines, newspaper sections, a history book and a cookbook. She is the author of seven other books including psychology, sociology and travel books, novels and a biography, and the co-author of seven travel guides. She has been a specialist travel writer and radio broadcaster for 12 years and has lived in Greece twice. For this edition of *Greece* she updated the Peloponnese, Ionian islands and most of the Cycladic islands. Researching for LP saw her return (an unashamed Hellenophile) to Greece for the 12th time.

From the Authors

David Willett Thanks to my partner, Rowan, for being my extra eyes and ears, and thanks to our son Tom for his constant enthusiasm for ruins. Travelling wouldn't be much fun without the friends you meet on the road, especially Terry Maurer – the fisherwoman of Hania harbour, and Tolis.

Rosemary Hall Thanks to the staff at the GNTO in London and the EOT and municipal tourist offices in the Dodecanese for their help and assistance. Warm thanks for advice, help and hospitality to John & Rena Paradisos and Anna Rizos (Lipsi), Frank & Kath (Leros), Eva Angelos (Karpathos), Alexis Zikas (Kos), Katina Michenni (Patmos), Ron Ferguson (Rhodes), and Kostas and Stelios (Tilos). Thanks also to Hilda Jeschek, Robin Pridy and Franz Frimmersworzf for their companionship, particularly on walks on Kastellorizo and Nisyros. Thanks to David Willett for the good humour and support during our brief but valuable (to me) telephone chats. And last, but not least, thanks to all the LP staff involved with the production of the book, particularly Rowan McKinnon.

Paul Hellander In Greece, the following persons offered me practical assistance and moral support during a hectic three months of travel: Georgos Bagias (Epiros); Georgos & Anna Tsanaktsis, Haralambos & Evthymia Tsanaktsis, Lazaros Arapidis (Macedonia); Christos & Litsa Kotronis (Thessaly); Areti Billini (Athens); Maria Haristou, Antonis Konstantinidis, Antonis Godis (Thessaloniki & Halkidiki); Maria & Evangelia Aïvazidis, Apostolos Kyriakidis (Thrace) and Stratos Abatzis (Lesvos). Special thanks to Dimitra Kaplanelli of the Office of Tourism for the North-Eastern Aegean (Mytilini) for hospitality and assistance beyond the call of duty, and to the NEL shipping line of Lesvos for welcome transport assistance. Many thanks also to Giannis Livanidis of the Volos EOT, for much appreciated practical assistance and to the staff at the EOT offices in Ioannina, Thessaloniki, Kavala, Chios and Samos. Thanks also to my virtual friends and colleagues at MGSA-L and HELLAS, on the Internet, for their last-minute assistance.

Finally, heartfelt thanks to my wife, Stella, for giving me her blessing to undertake the task, for holding the fort while I was away and for carrying the bags around Samos, Ikaria and the Sporades. My work is dedicated to my two sons Byron and Marcus, both in Ioannina, who I hope will understand their father's crazy job one day.

Kerry Kenihan In Australia, my gratitude is to GNTO's George Masvoulas and Freda Tzoumacas; Olympic Airways; my computer-wise, supportive sons Myles and Quentin; their father, Geoffrey; and Paul Utry. Thanks to Wilf, Elizabeth and, especially, Gwen Tansley, who restored my health and productivity on my return; and to co-writer David Willett and LP's Rob van Driesum, Brigitte Barta and Michelle Stamp for their patience. In Greece, I am indebted to the EOT's Dr Miltiades Spyrou (Athens); Vassiliki Petronikolou (Patras); Syros EOT; and to Elenyi Spyronis, Sia Moraitou, Nikolaos Spiridonos, Toli Hioutzioumis and Nicky Rao in Athens. My thanks also to Kyrina Korda (Patras); Magda Grammenou (Corfu); Francesco (Ios); Nikos Kypreos (Paros); the municipalities of Lefkada and Kefallonia; and fellow traveller, Jillian Williams. I am grateful for Freda and Mike's care on my spiritual home, Kythira; also for that of Leonie Fisher (Santorini) and the old, goat-herd woman who saved my life after I fell from a cliff above Diakofto. I thank the Greek strangers and friends who welcomed me professionally and personally and those who helped when, through no fault of Greece, I was injured and ill.

This Book

This is the 2nd edition of LP's Greece guide. Rosemary Hall wrote the 1st edition. David Willett was the coordinating author of this edition, which has been updated, expanded and reorganised. David wrote the Athens, Crete, Saronic Gulf islands and introductory chapters. Paul Hellander wrote the Central

Greece, Northern Greece and North-Eastern Aegean islands chapters. He also devised the book's transliteration system and provided linguistic assistance. Rosemary Hall was responsible for the Dodecanese chapter and Kerry Kenihan looked after the Cyclades, Ionian and Peloponnese chapters. Ann Moffat of the Australian National University wrote the text for the art section.

From the Publisher

This book was edited by Brigitte Barta, Rowan McKinnon, Frith Pike, Jane Marks, Liz Filleul and Nick Tapp. Michelle Stamp coordinated the design, mapping and illustration. Andrew Smith, Marcel Gaston, Jacqui Saunders and Richard Stewart assisted with maps. Tamsin Wilson, Louise Keppie, Margaret Jung, and Trudi Canavan helped with the illustrations, and Peter Morris drew the cartoon. The cover was designed by Simon Bracken and Andrew Tudor. Sharon Wertheim did the indexing. Special thanks to Adrienne Costanzo for her help and advice, and to Dan Levin for sorting out the Greek script. Thanks also to our resident philosophy buff, Rowan McKinnon, for writing (with much help from Lord Bert) the philosophy asides.

Thanks to the many travellers who wrote in with comments about our last edition, and with tips about travel in Greece (apologies if we've misspelt your name):

A Panagiotopoulos (USA), A Bostock (D), AJ Bond UK, Amy Schuler (USA), Anthony Crawford (C), Bernard Jacks (USA), Bob & Patsy Campbell (USA), C & P Pilsworth (UK), Campbell Lyle (UK), Cheryl Tummons (USA), Colin Unsworth (UK), D Fletcher (UK), Debbie Keffer (C), Doug Myers (USA), E Thomas & R Brookes (UK), Elizabeth Goldsmith (USA), Emma Hill (UK), Fr Tony Noble (AUS), Frede Sneftrup Hansen (DK), Geoff Kent (AUS), H Seymoure (UK), Iain Booth (UK), J & R Stucker (USA), James Wilde (USA), Jan Tepper (USA), Jane Organ (UK), Janet Nowottny (UK), Jennifer Woznesensky (C), Jenny Chua Wong (HK), Joan Cooper (UK), Joan Weaver (USA), Judith Herzig (NZ), Ken Mirkin (USA), Kris Wyld (AUS), Kristian Larsen (DK), Leif Mortensen (DK), Liz Zavazal (C), Lucien Boissonnas (CH), Marilyn Milota (USA), Megan Cox (NZ), Nicholas Couis (AUS), Pamela Mertens (AUS), Phil Smith (UK), Rebecca Mowling (UK), Romanna Jakymec (USA), S & S Fellows (UK), Sandy Clendenen (USA), Sara Lodge (UK), Stephen & Georgia (AUS), Stephen Hopkins (UK), Sylvia Rose (UK), Tanya Papadopoulos (Aus), Tony & Cyd Del Prete (USA)

AUS – Australia, C – Canada, CH – Switzerland, D – Germany, DK – Denmark, NZ – New Zealand, UK – United Kingdom, USA – United States of America

Warning & Request

Things change – prices go up, schedules change, good places go bad and bad places go bankrupt – nothing stays the same. So if you find things better or worse, recently opened or long since closed, please write and tell us and help make the next edition better.

Your letters will be used to help update future editions and, where possible, important changes will also be included in an Update section in reprints.

We greatly appreciate all information that is sent to us by travellers. Back at Lonely Planet we employ a hard-working readers' letters team to sort through the many letters we receive. The best ones will be rewarded with a free copy of the next edition or another Lonely Planet guide if you prefer. We give away lots of books, but, unfortunately, not every letter/postcard receives one.

Contents

INTRODUCTION 13

FACTS ABOUT THE COUNTRY 15

History 15   Government 42   Arts 44
Mythology 34   Economy 42   Culture 51
Geography 39   Population 43   Religion 52
Climate 39   People 43
Flora & Fauna 40   Education 43

GREEK ART THROUGH THE AGES 53

FACTS FOR THE VISITOR 69

Visas & Embassies 69   Post & Telecommunications 78   Dangers & Annoyances 93
Documents 70   Time 80   Work 93
Customs 70   Electricity 80   Activities 94
Money 71   Laundry 80   Highlights 95
When to Go 72   Weights & Measures 80   Accommodation 97
What to Bring 73   Books 80   Food 99
Tourist Offices 74   Maps 84   Drinks 105
Useful Organisations 75   Media 84   Entertainment 106
Business Hours & Public   Film & Photography 85   Things to Buy 108
Holidays 76   Health 85
Cultural Events 76   Women Travellers 92

GETTING THERE & AWAY 109

Air 109   Sea 119   Leaving Greece 121
Land 116   Tours 121

GETTING AROUND 122

Air 122   Car & Motorbike 126   Boat 128
Bus 124   Bicycle 128   Local Transport 134
Train 125   Hitching 128   Tours 135
Taxi 126   Walking 128

ATHENS 139

History 141   Entertainment 187   **Attica** **203**
Orientation 143   Things to Buy 190   Coast Road to Cape Sounion .. 203
Information 145   Getting There & Away 190   Inland Road to Cape Sounion 205
Things to See 148   Getting Around 193   Cape Sounion 205
Activities 172   **Around Athens** .... **196**   Lavrio 206
Organised Tours 173   Piraeus 196   Rafina 206
Festivals 174   Dafni 201   Marathon Region 207
Places to Stay 174   Elefsina (Eleusis) 203   Vravrona (Brauron) 208
Places to Eat 181   Moni Kaissarianis 203

PELOPONNESE 209

Corinthia .... **213**   Loutraki 217   Argos 224
Corinth 213   Perahora 217   Around Argos 225
Ancient Corinth &   West of Corinth 217   Nafplio 226
Acrocorinth 215   **Argolis** .... **218**   Around Nafplio 229
Corinth Canal 216   Mycenae 219   Epidaurus 230
Isthmia 217   Ancient Mycenae 219   Ancient Troizen 231

Arcadia **232**	Neapoli 243	Around Pylos 259
Tripolis................................232	Elafonisi 243	**Elia** **260**
Around Tripolis 233	Gythio 243	Tholos to Pyrgos 260
Megalopoli......................... 233	**The Mani** **245**	Pyrgos..................................260
Around Megalopoli 233	Lakonian Mani 246	Olympia...............................261
Central Arcadia................. 234	Messinian Mani 250	Ancient Olympia.................262
Andritsena 235	**Messinia** **252**	Kyllini 265
Myli to Leonidio 236	Kalamata 252	Hlemoutsi Castle.................266
South of Leonidio 236	Around Kalamata 256	**Achaïa**...............................**266**
Lakonia **236**	Langada Pass 256	Patras..................................266
Sparta 236	Koroni 256	Diakofto 271
Mystras 238	Finikoundas 257	Zahlorou 272
Geraki 241	Methoni 257	Kalavryta............................273
Gefyra & Monemvassia 241	Pylos................................258	Around Kalavryta 274

CENTRAL GREECE 275

Sterea Ellada **275**	Messolongi 285	Agios Konstantinos 292
Athens to Thiva 275	Agrinio 286	**Thessaly** **292**
Thiva (Thebes) 277	South-West Coastal Resorts ... 287	Volos...................................296
Livadia............................... 278	Karpenisi 288	Pelion Peninsula.................300
Delphi 278	Around Karpenisi 288	Trikala 306
Ancient Delphi 279	Karpenisi to Agrinio 289	Around Trikala 308
Around Delphi 283	Lamia 289	Meteora 310
Delphi to Nafpaktos 284	Lamia to Karpenisi 291	Kastraki 312

NORTHERN GREECE..314

Epiros............................ **314**	Thessaloniki 335	Komotini 384
Ioannina 316	Around Thessaloniki........348	Alexandroupolis..................385
The Zagorohoria................ 323	Pella 348	Evros Delta..........................389
Metsovo 324	Mt Olympus 349	Alexandroupolis to
Preveza 331	Veria 354	Didymotiho 389
Around Preveza 333	Philippi 379	North of Didymotiho 390
Arta.................................... 334	**Thrace**............................**380**	
Macedonia..................... **335**	Xanthi 382	

SARONIC GULF ISLANDS 395

Aegina **396**	Poros Town 401	Around the Island..................406
Aegina Town 397	Around the Island 402	**Spetses** **406**
Around the Island 398	Peloponnesian Mainland ...402	Spetses Town.......................407
Moni & Angistri Islets 399	**Hydra** **402**	Around the Island................410
Poros............................... **399**	Hydra Town 404	

CYCLADES..411

Andros **413**	Ermoupolis 429	**Ios**....................................**444**
Gavrio 415	Galissas 431	Gialos, Ios Town & Milopotas
Batsi 415	Other Beaches 432	Beach...................................445
Andros Town 415	**Naxos & the Minor**	Around the Island................446
Around the Island 416	**Islands** **432**	**Folegandros** **447**
Tinos **416**	Naxos 432	Hora.....................................447
Tinos Town 417	Minor Islands 436	Around the Island................449
Around the Island 419	**Amorgos** **437**	**Sikinos** **449**
Mykonos **419**	Amorgos Town 438	**Santorini (Thira)**............**450**
Mykonos Town 421	Aegiali..............................438	Fira......................................451
Around the Island 423	Around the Island 438	Around the Island................454
Delos **424**	**Paros & Antiparos** **439**	Thirasia & Volcanic Islets 455
Ancient Delos 425	Paros.................................439	**Anafi** **455**
Syros.............................. **427**	Antiparos..........................443	**Milos** **456**

Plaka & Trypiti	458	Kythnos	461	Sifnos	464
Around Plaka & Trypiti	459	Merihas	462	Kamares	464
Around the Island	459	Around the Island	462	Apollonia	465
Kimolos	459	**Serifos**	**463**	Around the Island	465
Kea	**460**	Livadi	463		
Korissia	460	Serifos Town	464		
Around the Island	461	Around the Island	464		

CRETE 466

Central Crete	**470**	Kritsa	490	Agia Galini	504
Iraklio	471	Ancient Lato	490	Rethymno to Hania	505
Knossos	479	Spinalonga Peninsula	490	Hania	505
Myrtia	483	Spinalonga Island	491	Akrotiri Peninsula	512
Tylisos	483	Lassithi Plateau	491	Hania to Agia Roumeli via	
Arhanes	483	Around Sitia	494	Samaria Gorge	512
Gortyn	484	Zakros & Kato Zakros	494	Agia Roumeli	513
Phaestos	484	Ancient Zakros	495	Hora Sfakion	514
Agia Triada	484	Around Ierapetra	496	Around Hora Sfakion	514
Malia	486	**Western Crete**	**496**	Paleohora	515
Eastern Crete	**486**	Rethymno	496	Around Paleohora	518
Agios Nikolaos	486	Around Rethymno	501	Kastelli-Kissamos	519
Gournia	489	Rethymno to Plakias	501	Around Kastelli-Kissamos	521
Moni Faneromenis	490	Around Plakias	503		

DODECANESE 522

Rhodes	**524**	Mandraki	559	Lakki	583
Rhodes City	529	Around the Island	560	Platanos	583
Eastern Rhodes	536	**Astypalea**	**561**	Around Platanos	584
Western Rhodes	538	Astypalea Town	562	Krithoni & Alinda	584
Southern Rhodes	540	Livadia	563	Gourna	585
The Interior	541	Other Beaches	564	Northern Leros	585
Halki	**542**	**Symi**	**564**	Xirokambos	585
Emboreios	542	Symi Town	566	**Patmos**	**585**
Around the Island	543	Around the Island	567	Skala	587
Karpathos	**543**	**Kos**	**568**	Monasteries & Hora	589
Pigadia	544	Kos Town	570	North of Skala	589
Southern Karpathos	546	Around Kos Town	573	South of Skala	590
Northern Karpathos	548	Around the Island	573	**Lipsi**	**590**
Kassos	**550**	Mountain Villages	574	Lipsi Town	591
Phry	550	**Kalymnos**	**574**	Walks to the Beaches from	
Around the Island	552	Pothia	577	Lipsi Town	592
Kastellorizo	**552**	Around Pothia	579	**Arki & Marathi**	**593**
Kastellorizo Town	553	Vathy	580	Arki	593
Tilos	**555**	The West Coast	580	Marathi	594
Livadia	556	Telendos Islet	580	**Agathonisi**	**594**
Megalo Horio	558	Myrties to Emboreios	581	Agios Giorgios	595
Around Megalo Horio	558	Emboreios	581	Around the Island	595
Nisyros	**558**	**Leros**	**581**		

NORTH-EASTERN AEGEAN ISLANDS 597

Samos	**599**	Agios Kirykos to the North		**Inousses**	**623**
Samos Town (Vathy)	601	Coast	611	Inousses Town	623
Around Pythagorio	606	Evdilos	612	Island Walk	624
South-West Samos	607	West of Evdilos	612	**Psara**	**625**
West of Samos Town	607	Fourni Islands	614	**Lesvos (Mytilini)**	**625**
Ikaria & the Fourni		**Chios**	**614**	Mytilini	627
Islands	**608**	Chios Town	617	Around the Island	631
Agios Kirykos	610	Around the Island	619	**Limnos**	**635**

Myrina 637	Hora 642	Limenas 648
Around the Island 639	Sanctuary of the Great Gods 643	East Coast 651
Samothraki **640**	Around the Island 645	West Coast 651
Kamariotissa 642	**Thasos** **647**	

IONIAN ISLANDS 653

Corfu **655**	**Lefkada & Meganisi** **664**	Zakynthos Town 675
Corfu Town 657	Lefkada 664	Around the Island 678
Around the Island 661	Meganisi 668	**Kythira & Antikythira** **679**
Paxoi & Antipaxoi **663**	**Kefallonia & Ithaki** **668**	Kythira 679
Paxoi 663	Kefallonia 668	Antikythira 684
Antipaxoi 664	**Zakynthos** **675**	

EVIA & THE SPORADES 685

Evia **687**	**Skopelos** **693**	Islets around Alonnisos 701
Halkida 687	Skopelos Town 695	**Skyros** **701**
Central Evia 687	Glossa 696	Skyros Town 703
Northern Evia 688	Around the Island 697	**Magazia & Molos** **705**
Southern Evia 688	**Alonnisos** **697**	Around the Island 706
Skiathos **689**	Patitiri 699	
Skiathos Town 691	Old Alonnisos 700	
Around the Island 692	Beaches 700	

LANGUAGE GUIDE 707

GLOSSARY 714

APPENDIX – CLIMATE CHARTS 718

INDEX 719

Maps 719	Text 720

Map Legend

BOUNDARIES

- International Boundary
- Regional Boundary

ROUTES

- Freeway
- Highway
- Major Road
- Unsealed Road or Track
- City Road
- City Street
- Railway
- Underground Railway
- Tram
- Walking Track
- Walking Tour
- Ferry Route
- Cable Car or Chairlift

AREA FEATURES

- Parks
- Built-Up Area
- Pedestrian Mall
- Market
- Cemetery
- Forest
- Beach or Desert
- Rocks

HYDROGRAPHIC FEATURES

- Coastline
- River, Creek
- Intermittent River or Creek
- Rapids, Waterfalls
- Lake, Intermittent Lake
- Canal
- Swamp

SYMBOLS

○ CAPITAL	National Capital	
◎ Capital	Prefecture Capital	
◓ CITY	Major City	
● City	City	
● Town	Town	
● Village	Village	
■ ▼	Place to Stay, Place to Eat	
☎ ▮	Cafe, Pub or Bar	
✉ ☎	Post Office, Telephone	
❶ ⑤	Tourist Information, Bank	
⊜ ℗	Transport, Parking	
🏛 ⌂	Museum, Youth Hostel	
⌘ ▲	Caravan Park, Camping Ground	
✚ ✚	Church or Monastery, Cathedral	
☪ ✡	Mosque, Synagogue	
卍 卐	Buddhist Temple, Hindu Temple	
✚ ★	Hospital, Police Station	

♨ 🅱	Embassy, Petrol Station
✈ ✝	Airport, Airfield
Ⓜ 🏊	Metro Station, Swimming Pool
◆ ✿	Shopping Centre, Gardens
⚘ 🐘	Winery or Vineyard, Zoo
← A25	One Way Street, Route Number
🏛 ⚑	Stately Home, Monument
♜ ■	Castle, Tomb
⌒ ⌂	Cave, Hut or Chalet
▲ ※	Mountain or Hill, Lookout
🗼 ⤢	Lighthouse, Shipwreck
)(⊙	Pass, Spring
🦅 🐟	Beach, Surf Beach
∴	Archaeological Site or Ruins
	Ancient or City Wall
⟶ ⟵	Cliff or Escarpment, Tunnel
	Railway Station

Note: not all symbols displayed above appear in this book

Transliteration & Variant Spellings: an Explanation

The issue of correctly transliterating Greek is a vexed one. While the alphabet itself is not difficult to learn, and despite the fact that there are only 24 letters in the alphabet, giving a Latin alphabet rendition of Greek is fraught with inconsistencies and pitfalls.

The Greeks themselves are not very consistent when it comes to providing transliterated names on their signs, though things are gradually improving. The word 'Piraeus', for example has been variously represented by the following transliterations: Pireas, Piraievs and Pireefs; and when appearing as a street name (eg Piraeus Street) you will also find Pireos!

The legacy of various military dictatorships in Greece, the most recent foray being from 1967 to 1974, has left another linguistic minefield in its wake: that of diglossy, or two forms of the Greek language. There a purist form called Katharevousa and a popular form called Dimotiki. The Katharevousa form was never more than an artificiality and Dimotiki has always been spoken as the mainstream language, but this linguistic schizophrenia means there are often two Greek words for each English word. Thus, the word for 'baker' in everyday language is *fournos*, but the shop sign will more often than not say *artopoieion*. The product of the baker's shop will be known in the street as *psomi*, but in church as *artos*.

As if all that was not enough, there is also the issue of anglicised vs hellenised forms of place names; for example, Athina vs Athens; Patra vs Patras; Thiva vs Thebes; Evia vs Euboia – the list goes on and on! Toponymic diglossy (the existence of both an official and everyday name for a place) is responsible for Kerkyra – Corfu, Zante – Zakynthos, and Santorini – Thira. In this guide we have tended to provide modern Greek equivalents for town names, with one or two well-known exceptions, eg Athens and Patras. Where mention is made of ancient sites, settlements or people closely related to antiquity, we have attempted to stick to the more familiar classical names. Thus we have Thucydides instead of Thoukididis; Mycenae instead of Mykines.

Problems in transliteration have particular implications for vowels, especially given that Greek has six ways of rendering the vowel sound *ee*, two ways of rendering the *o* sound and two ways of rendering the *e* sound. In most instances in this book, *y* has been used for the *ee* sound when a Greek *upsilon* (υ, Υ) has been used, and *i* for Greek *ita* (η, H) and *iota* (ι, I). In the case of the Greek vowel combinations that make the *ee* sound, that is οι, ει and υι, an *i* has been used. For the two *e* Greek sounds, αι and ε, an *e* has been employed.

As far as consonants are concerned, the Greek letter *gamma* (γ, Γ) appears as *g* rather than *y* throughout this book. This means that *agios* (Greek for male saint) is used rather than *ayios*, and *agia* (Greek for female saint) rather than *ayia*. The letter *delta* (δ, Δ) appears as *d*, rather than *dh*, throughout this book, so *domatia* (Greek for rooms), rather than *dhomatia*, is used. The letter *fi* (φ, Φ) can be transliterated as either *f* or *ph*. Here, a general rule of thumb is that classical names are spelt with a *ph* and modern names with an *f*. So Phaistos is used rather than Festos, and Folegandros is used rather than Pholegandros. The Greek chi (ξ, X) has been more or less uniformly represented as *h* in order to give as close as possible an approximation of the pronunciation of the Greek. Thus, we have 'Haralambos' instead of 'Charalambos' and 'Polytehniou' instead of 'Polytechniou'. Bear in mind that the *h* is to be pronounced as an aspirated *h*, much like the *ch* in loch. The letter *kapa* (κ, K) has been used to represent that sound, except where well-known names from antiquity have adopted by convention the letter *c*, eg Polycrates, Acropolis.

Wherever reference to a street name is made, we have omitted the Greek word 'odos'. Words for avenue *(leoforos)* and square *(plateia)* have, however, been included to assist in differentiating types of locations.

For a more detailed guide to the Greek language, check out Lonely Planet's *Greek Phrasebook*.

Introduction

Greece has always attracted travellers, drawn by the fascination of some of Europe's earliest civilisations. Philosophers muse that to journey to Greece is to return home, for the legacy of ancient Greece pervades the consciousness of all Western nations. Greek Doric, Ionic and Corinthian columns adorn many of our buildings, and much of our greatest early literature drew on the Greek myths for inspiration. Some of our most evocative words are Greek – chaos, drama, tragedy and democracy, to name a few. Perhaps the greatest legacy is democracy itself.

While it was this underlying awareness of Greek culture that drew the wealthy young aristocrats of the 19th century to the country, the majority of today's visitors are drawn by Greece's beaches and sunshine. Island-hopping has become something of an initiation rite for the international singles set. Their numbers are dwarfed, however, by the millions of package holiday-makers who come to Greece every year in search of two weeks of sunshine by the sea.

Package tourism took off with the advent of cheaper airfares in the 1960s and gathered pace through the '70s and '80s. By the early 1990s, almost nine million visitors a year were pouring through the turnstiles, making tourism easily the most important industry in the country. The marked fall in numbers in the last couple of years is causing great concern. Greece is no longer the low-budget destination it once was, and it appears that the sunshine set are opting to head somewhere cheaper.

The ancient sites are an enduring attraction. The Acropolis needs no introduction as the most remarkable legacy of the classical period. At Knossos on Crete, you can wander around the ancient capital of one of Europe's oldest civilisations: the Minoan. The many Minoan, Mycenaean and classical Greek sites, and elaborate Byzantine churches, stand alongside the legacies left by foreign occupiers: towering Venetian, Frankish and Turkish castles, and crumbling, forgotten mosques.

Reminders of the past are everywhere. The Greek landscape is littered with broken columns and crumbling fragments of ancient walls. Moreover, there is hardly a meadow, river or mountaintop which is not sacred because of its association with some deity, and the spectres of the past linger still.

Greece has clung to its traditions more tenaciously than most European countries. Through hundreds of years of foreign occupation by Franks, Venetians, Turks and others, tradition and religion were the factors that kept the notion of Greek nationhood alive. Greeks today remain only too well aware of the hardships their forebears endured. Even hip, young Greeks defend these traditions and enthusiastically participate in many of them.

The traditions manifest themselves in a variety of ways, including regional costumes, such as the baggy pantaloons and

high boots worn by elderly Cretan men, and in the embroidered dresses and floral headscarves worn by the women of Olymbos, on Karpathos. Many traditions take the form of festivals, where Greeks express their *joie de vivre* through dancing, singing and feasting.

Festival time or not, the Greek capacity for enjoyment of life is immediately evident. If you arrive in a Greek town in the early evening in summer, you could be forgiven for thinking you've arrived mid-festival. This is the time of the *volta*, when everyone takes to the streets, refreshed from their siesta, dressed up and raring to go. All this adds up to Greece being one of Europe's most relaxed and friendliest countries. But Greece is no European backwater locked in a time warp. In towns and cities you will find discos as lively as any in Italy, France or Britain, and boutiques as trendy.

If you're a beach-lover, Greece, with its 1400 islands, has more coastline than any other country in Europe. You can choose between rocky outcrops, pebbled coves or long swathes of golden sand.

Greece's scenery is as varied as its beaches. There is the semitropical lushness of the Ionian and North-Eastern Aegean islands and southern Crete; the bare sun-baked rocks of the Cyclades; and the forested mountains, icy lakes and tumbling rivers of northern Greece. Much of this breathtaking landscape is mantled with vibrant wild flowers.

There is yet another phenomenon which even people cynical about anything hinting of the esoteric comment upon. It takes the form of inexplicable happenings, coincidences, or fortuitous occurrences. It could be meeting up with a long-lost friend, or bumping into the same person again and again on your travels; or missing the ferry and being offered a lift on a private yacht; or being hot, hungry, thirsty and miles from anywhere, then stumbling upon a house whose occupants offer hospitality.

Perhaps these serendipitous occurrences can be explained as the work of the gods of ancient Greece, who, some claim, have not entirely relinquished their power, and to prove it, occasionally come down to earth to intervene in the lives of mortals.

Facts about the Country

HISTORY

The geographical position of Greece at the crossroads of Europe and Asia has resulted in a long, complicated and turbulent history.

Stone Age

The discovery of a Neanderthal skull in a cave on the Halkidiki peninsula of Macedonia has confirmed the presence of humans in Greece 700,000 years ago. Bones and tools from Palaeolithic times have been found in the Pindos mountains.

The move to a pastoral existence came during Neolithic times (7000-3000 BC). The fertile area that is now Thessaly was the first area to be settled. The people grew barley and wheat, and bred sheep and goats. They used clay to produce pots, vases and simple statuettes of the Great Mother (the earth goddess), whom they worshipped.

By 3000 BC, people were living in settlements complete with streets, squares and mud-brick houses. The villages were centred around a large palace-like structure which belonged to the tribal leader. The most complete Neolithic settlements in Greece are Dimini (inhabited from 4000 to 1200 BC) and Sesklo, both near the city of Volos.

Bronze Age

Around 3000 BC, Indo-European migrants introduced the processing of bronze (an alloy of copper and tin) into Greece – the beginning of three remarkable civilisations: the Cycladic, Minoan and Mycenaean.

Cycladic Civilisation The Cycladic civilisation is divided into three periods: Early (3000-2000 BC), Middle (2000-1500 BC) and Late (1500-1100 BC). The most impressive legacy of this civilisation is the statuettes carved from Parian marble – the famous Cycladic figurines. Like statuettes from Neolithic times, they depicted images of the Great Mother. Other remains include bronze and obsidian tools and weapons, gold jewellery, and stone and clay vases and pots.

The peoples of the Cycladic civilisation were accomplished sailors who developed prosperous maritime trade links. They exported their wares to Asia Minor (the west of present-day Turkey), Europe and north Africa, as well as to Crete and continental Greece. The Cyclades islands were influenced by both the Minoan and Mycenaean civilisations.

Minoan Civilisation The Minoan civilisation of Crete was the first advanced civilisation to emerge in Europe, drawing its inspiration from two great Middle Eastern civilisations: the Mesopotamian and Egyptian. Archaeologists divide the Minoan civilisation, like the Cycladic, into three phases: Early (3000-2100 BC), Middle (2100-1500 BC) and Late (1500-1100 BC).

Many aspects of Neolithic life endured during the Early period, but by 2500 BC most people on the island had been assimilated into a new and distinct culture which we now call the Minoan, after the mythical King Minos. The Minoan civilisation reached its peak during the Middle period, producing pottery and metalwork of remarkable beauty and a high degree of imagination and skill. The Late period saw the civilisation decline both commercially and militarily against Mycenaean competition from the mainland, until its abrupt end around 1100 BC, when Dorian invaders and natural disasters ravaged the island.

Like the Cycladic civilisation, the Minoan was a great maritime power which exported goods throughout the Mediterranean. The polychrome Kamares pottery which flourished during the Middle period was highly prized by the Egyptians.

The first calamity to strike the Minoans was a violent earthquake in about 1700 BC, which destroyed the palaces at Knossos, Phaestos, Malia and Zakros. The Minoans

CHRONOLOGY OF MAJOR EVENTS

Period/Age	*Events*
Cycladic & Minoan civilisations 3000-1100 BC	**2800 BC** – marble figurines carved in Cyclades
	2000 BC – first palaces built on Crete
	1700 BC – Minoan palaces (Knossos, Phaestos, Malia & Zakros) rebuilt after earthquake
Mycenaean Age 1900-1100 BC	*c.* **1450 BC** – massive volcanic eruption on Thira; Minoan palaces destroyed
Dark Age 1200-800 BC	**1200 BC** – Dorians conquer Greece, introducing Iron Age technology
	1000 BC – first appearance of pottery with geometric patterns (the Geometric Age)
Archaic (Middle) Age 800-480 BC	**800 BC** – emergence of the independent city-states
	776 BC – first Olympic Games held
	c. **750 BC** – Homer thought to have composed the *Iliad* and the *Odyssey*
	490 BC – Persians defeated at the Battle of Marathon
Classical Age 480-338 BC	**461-429 BC** – Pericles presides over golden age of Athens; plays by Sophocles and Euripides written
	438 BC – Parthenon completed
	431-421 BC – First Peloponnesian War
	399 BC – Socrates sentenced to death
	338 BC – Philip of Macedon conquers Greece
	324 BC – death of Alexander the Great
	168 BC – Romans defeat Macedon at the Battle of Pydna
Roman Rule 146 BC to 324 AD	**67 AD** – Nero starts work on the Corinth Canal
	132 – Temple of Olympian Zeus completed in Athens
Byzantine Age 324-1453	**384** – Christianity becomes the official religion of Greece
	529 – Emperor Justinian closes schools of philosophy in Athens
	1204 – crusaders sack Constantinople
	1210 – Venetians occupy Crete
Ottoman Rule 1453-1829	**1453** – Ottoman Turks capture Constantinople
	1669 – Iraklio, Crete, surrenders to Turks after a 21-year siege
	1821 – Bishop Germanos raises the Greek flag at Patras, starting the War of Independence
Modern Greece 1829-present	**1829** – Turks accept Greek independence by the Treaty of Adrianople
	1893 – French company completes Corinth Canal
	1896 – First modern Olympics in Athens
	1923 – Compulsory population exchange with Turkey agreed at the Treaty of Lausanne
	1946-49 – Greek civil war
	1981 – Andreas Papandreou becomes Greece's first socialist leader when PASOK wins elections; Greece joins EC
	1990 – Konstantinos Mitsotakis' conservative ND party wins the general election
	1993 – Papandreou's socialist PASOK party back in power

KERRY KENIHAN

KERRY KENIHAN

ANN JOUSIFFE

BERTOLD DAUM

Top Left:	Evzone, Parliament Building, Athens
Top Right:	Flowers for sale off Plateia Syntagmatos, Athens
Bottom Left:	Flea market, Athens
Bottom Right:	The Parthenon, Acropolis, Athens

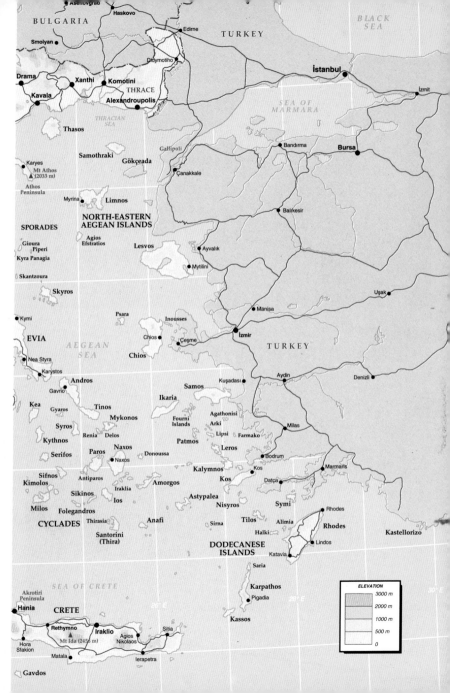

DAVID HALL

VICKI BEALE

ROSEMARY HALL

Top: The Theatre of Herodes Atticus, Acropolis, Athens
Left: The Parthenon, Acropolis, Athens
Right: Entrance to the Acropolis, Athens

rebuilt them to a more complex, almost laby-rinthine design with multiple storeys, sumptuous royal apartments, reception halls, storerooms, workshops, living quarters for staff and an advanced drainage system. The interiors were decorated with the celebrated Minoan frescoes, now on display in the archaeological museum at Iraklio.

The Minoans were also literate. Their first script resembled Egyptian hieroglyphics, the most famous example of which is the inscription on the Phaestos disc (1700 BC). They progressed to a syllable-based script which 20th-century archaeologists have dubbed Linear A, because it consists of linear symbols. Like the earlier hieroglyphics, it has not yet been deciphered, but archaeologists believe that it was used to document trade transactions and the contents of royal storerooms, rather than to express abstract concepts.

Some historians have suggested that the civilisation's decline after 1500 BC was accelerated by the effects of the massive volcanic explosion on the Cycladic island of Santorini (Thira), an eruption which vulcanologists believe was more cataclysmic than any on record. They theorise that the fall-out of volcanic ash from the blast may have been sufficient to cause a succession of crop failures – with resulting social unrest.

Mycenaean Civilisation The decline of the Minoan civilisation in the Late Minoan period coincided with the rise of the first great civilisation on the Greek mainland, the Mycenaean (1900-1100 BC), which reached its peak between 1500 and 1200 BC. Named after the ancient city of Mycenae, where the German archaeologist Heinrich Schliemann made his celebrated finds in 1876, it is also known as the Achaean civilisation after the Indo-European branch of migrants who had settled on mainland Greece and absorbed many aspects of Minoan culture.

Unlike Minoan society, where the lack of city walls seems to indicate relative peace under some form of central authority, Mycenaean civilisation was characterised by independent city-states such as Corinth,

Pylos, Tiryns and, the most powerful of them all, Mycenae. These were ruled by kings who inhabited palaces enclosed within massive walls on easily defensible hilltops.

The Mycenaeans' most impressive legacy is magnificent gold jewellery and ornaments, most of which can be seen in the National Archaeological Museum in Athens. The Mycenaeans wrote in what is called Linear B (unrelated to the Linear A of Crete), which has been deciphered as an early form of Greek. They also worshipped gods who were precursors of the later Greek gods.

Examples of Linear B have also been found on Crete, suggesting that Mycenaean invaders may have conquered the island, perhaps around 1500 BC, when many Minoan palaces were destroyed. Mycenaean influence stretched further than Crete: the Mycenaean city-states banded together to defeat Troy (Ilium) and thus to protect their trade routes to the Black Sea, and archaeological research has unearthed Mycenaean artefacts as far away as Egypt, Mesopotamia and Italy.

The Mycenaean civilisation came to an end during the 12th century BC when it was overrun by the Dorians.

Geometric Age
The origins of the Dorians remains uncertain. They are generally thought to have come from Epiros or northern Macedonia, but some historians argue that they only arrived from there because they had been driven out of Doris, in central Greece, by the Mycenaeans.

The warrior-like Dorians settled first in the Peloponnese, but soon fanned out over much of the mainland, razing the city-states and enslaving the inhabitants. They later conquered Crete and the south-west coast of Asia Minor. Other Indo-European tribes known as the Thessalians settled in what is now Thessaly. Of the original Greek tribal groups, the Aeolians fled to the north-west coast of Asia Minor; the Ionians sought refuge on the central coast and the islands of Lesvos, Samos and Chios, although they also

Geometric detail from an urn, 750 BC

held out in mainland Greece – in Attica and the well-fortified city of Athens.

The Dorians brought a traumatic break with the past, and the next 400 years are often referred to as Greece's 'dark age'. But it would be unfair to dismiss the Dorians completely; they brought iron with them and developed a new style of pottery, decorated with striking geometrical designs – although art historians are still out to lunch as to whether the Dorians merely copied the designs perfected by Ionians in Attica. The Dorians worshipped male gods instead of fertility goddesses and adopted the Mycenaean gods of Poseidon, Zeus and Apollo, paving the way for the later Greek religious pantheon.

Perhaps most importantly, the Dorian warriors developed into a class of landholding aristocrats. This worsened the lot of the average farmer but also brought about the demise of the monarchy as a system of government, along with a resurgence of the Mycenaean pattern of independent citystates, this time led by wealthy aristocrats instead of absolute monarchs – the beginnings of 'democratic' government.

Archaic Age

By about 800 BC, local agriculture and animal husbandry had become productive enough to trigger a resumption of maritime trading. New Greek colonies were established in north Africa, Italy, Sicily, southern France and southern Spain to fill the vacuum left by the decline of those other great Mediterranean traders, the Phoenicians.

The people of the various city-states were unified by the development of a Greek alphabet (of Phoenician origin, though the Greeks introduced vowels), the verses of Homer (which created a sense of a shared Mycenaean past), the establishment of the Olympic Games (which brought all the city-states together), and the setting up of central sanctuaries such as Delphi (a neutral meeting ground for lively negotiations), giving Greeks, for the first time, a sense of national identity. This period is known as the Archaic, or Middle, Age.

Most city-states were built to a similar plan, with a fortified acropolis (high city) at the highest point. The acropolis contained the cities' temples and treasury and also served as a refuge during invasions. Outside the acropolis was the agora (market), a bustling commercial quarter, and beyond it the residential areas.

The city-states were autonomous, free to pursue their own interests as they saw fit, which inevitably caused bickering and wars between them. As we have already seen, most city-states abolished monarchic rule in favour of an aristocratic form of government, usually headed by an archon (chief magistrate). Aristocrats were often disliked by the population because of their inherited privileges, and some city-states fell to rule by tyrants after Kypselos started the practice in Corinth around 650 BC. Tyrants seized their position rather than inheriting it, and were often perceived as having the welfare of ordinary citizens at heart by instituting improvements for the benefit of the majority.

Athens & Solon The seafaring city-state of Athens, meanwhile, was still in the hands of aristocrats, and a failed coup attempt by a would-be tyrant led the legislator Draco to draw up his infamous laws in 620 BC (hence the word 'draconian'). These were so harsh that even the theft of a cabbage was punishable by death.

Solon was appointed archon in 594 BC with a far-reaching mandate to defuse the mounting tensions between the haves and the have-nots. He cancelled all debts and freed those who had become enslaved because of their debts. Declaring all free Athenians equal by law, he abolished inherited privileges and restructured political power along four classes based on wealth. Although only the first two classes were eligible for office, all four were allowed to elect magistrates and vote on legislation in the general assembly, known as the ecclesia. His reforms have led him to be regarded as the harbinger of democracy.

Sparta Sparta, in the Peloponnese, was a very different kind of city-state. The Spartans were descended from the Dorian invaders and used the Helots, the original inhabitants of Lakonia, as their slaves. They ran their society along strict military rules laid down by the 9th-century legislator Lycurgus.

Newborn babies were inspected and, if found wanting, were left to die on a mountain top. At the age of seven, boys were taken from their homes to start rigorous training that would turn them into crack soldiers. Girls were spared military training but were forced to keep very fit in order to produce healthy sons. Spartan indoctrination was so

Sixth-century Spartan pottery design depicting a trading scene

effective that dissent was unknown and a degree of stability was achieved that other city-states could only dream of.

While Athens became powerful through trade, Sparta became the ultimate military machine. They both towered above the other city-states.

The Persian Wars The Persian campaign against Athens was sparked by a rebellion in the Persian colonies on the coast of Asia Minor. Emperor Darius spent five years suppressing the revolt, and became hellbent on revenge against Athens, one of the few states outside the area to support the rebels. He appealed to Sparta to attack Athens from behind, but the Spartans threw his envoy in a well.

A 25,000-strong Persian army reached Attica in 490 BC, but suffered a humiliating defeat when outmanoeuvred by an Athenian force of 10,000 at the Battle of Marathon.

Darius died in 485 BC before he could mount another assault, so it was left to his son Xerxes to fulfil his father's ambition of conquering Greece. In 480 BC Xerxes gathered men from every nation of his far-flung empire and launched a coordinated invasion by army and navy, the size of which the world had never seen. The historian Herodotus estimated that there were five million Persian soldiers. No doubt this was a gross exaggeration, but it was obvious Xerxes intended to give the Greeks more than a bloody nose.

The Persians dug a canal near present-day Ierissos so that their navy could bypass the rough seas around the base of the Mt Athos peninsula (where they had been caught out before), and spanned the Hellespont with pontoon bridges for their army to march over.

Some 30 city-states of central and southern Greece met in Corinth to devise a common defence (others, including Delphi, sided with the Persians). They agreed on a combined army and navy under Spartan command, with the Athenian leader Themistocles providing the strategy. The Spartan king Leonidas led the army to the pass at

Thermopylae, near present-day Lamia, the main passage into central Greece from the north. This bottleneck was easy to defend, and although the Greeks were greatly outnumbered they held the pass until a traitor showed the Persians a way over the mountains. The Greeks were forced to retreat, but Leonidas, along with 300 of his elite Spartan troops, fought to the death. The fleet which held off the Persian navy north of Euboea (Evia) had no choice but to retreat as well.

The Spartans and their Peloponnesian allies fell back on their second line of defence (an earthen wall across the Isthmus of Corinth), while the Persians advanced upon Athens. Themistocles ordered his people to flee the city: the women and children to Salamis, and the men to sea with the Athenian fleet. The Persians razed Attica and burned Athens to the ground.

Things did not go so well for the Persian navy. By skilful manoeuvring, the Greek navy trapped the larger Persian ships in the narrow waters off Salamis, where they became easy pickings for the more mobile Greek vessels. Xerxes, who watched the defeat of his mighty fleet from the shore, returned to Persia in disgust, leaving his general Mardonius and the army to subdue Greece. However, a year later the Greeks, under the Spartan general Pausanias, obliterated the Persian army at the Battle of Plataea. The Athenian navy sailed to Asia Minor and destroyed what was left of the Persian fleet at Mykale, freeing the Ionian city-states there from Persian rule.

Classical Age

After the defeat of the Persians, the disciplined Spartans once again retreated to their Peloponnesian 'fortress', while Athens basked in its role as liberator and embarked on a policy of blatant imperialism. In 477 BC it founded the Delian League, so called because the treasury was kept on the sacred island of Delos. The league consisted of almost every state with a navy, no matter how small, including many of the Aegean islands and some of the Ionian city-states in Asia Minor.

Ostensibly its purpose was twofold: to create a naval force to liberate the city-states that were still occupied by Persia, and to protect against another Persian attack. The swearing of allegiance to Athens and an annual contribution of ships (later just money) were mandatory. The league, in effect, became an Athenian empire.

Indeed, when Pericles became leader of Athens in 461 BC, he moved the treasury from Delos to the Acropolis and used its contents to begin a building programme in which no expense was spared. His first objectives were to rebuild the temple complex of the Acropolis which had been destroyed by the Persians, and to link Athens to its lifeline, the port of Piraeus, with fortified walls designed to withstand any future siege.

Under Pericles' leadership (461-429 BC), Athens experienced a golden age of unprecedented cultural, artistic and scientific achievement. With the Aegean Sea safely under its wing, Athens began to look westward for further expansion, bringing it into conflict with the city-states of the mainland. It also encroached on the trade area of Corinth, which belonged to the Spartan-dominated Peloponnesian League. A series of skirmishes and provocations led to the Peloponnesian Wars.

First Peloponnesian War One of the major triggers of the first Peloponnesian War (431-421 BC) was the Corcyra incident, in which Athens supported Corcyra (present-day Kerkyra or Corfu) in a row with its mother city, Corinth. Corinth, now under serious threat, called on Sparta to help. Sparta's power depended to a large extent on Corinth's wealth, so it rallied to the cause.

Athens knew it couldn't defeat Sparta on land, so it abandoned Attica to the Spartans and withdrew behind its mighty walls, opting to rely on its navy to put pressure on Sparta by blockading the Peloponnese. Athens suffered badly during the siege. Plague broke out in the overcrowded city, killing a third of the population – including Pericles, but the defences held firm. The blockade of the Peloponnese eventually began to hurt, and the two reached an uneasy truce.

The Sicilian Adventure Throughout the war Athens had maintained an interest in Sicily and its grain, which the soil in Attica was too poor to produce. The Greek colonies there mirrored the city-states in Greece, the most powerful being Syracuse, which had remained neutral during the war.

In 416 BC, the Sicilian city of Segesta asked Athens to intervene in a squabble it was having with Selinus, an ally of Syracuse. A hot-headed second cousin of Pericles, Alcibiades, convinced the Athenian assembly to send a flotilla to Sicily; it would go on the pretext of helping Segesta, and then attack Syracuse.

The flotilla, under the joint leadership of Alcibiades, Nicias and Lamachos, was ill-fated from the outset. Alcibiades was called back to Athens on blasphemy charges arising from a drinking binge in which he knocked the heads off a few sacred statues. Enraged, he travelled not to Athens but to Sparta and persuaded the surprised Spartans to go to the aid of Syracuse, which had been under siege from the Athenians for over three years. Nicias' health suffered and Lamachos, the most adept of the three, was killed. Sparta followed Alcibiades' advice and broke the siege in 413 BC, destroying the Athenian fleet and army.

Second Peloponnesian War Athens was depleted of troops, money and ships; its subject states were ripe for revolt, and Sparta was there to lend them a hand. In 413 BC the Spartans occupied Decelea in northern Attica and used it as a base to harass the region's farmers. Athens, deprived of its Sicilian grain supplies, soon began to feel the pinch. Its prospects grew even bleaker when Darius II of Persia, who had been keeping a close eye on events in Sicily and Greece, offered Sparta money to build a navy as long as the Spartans kept their promise to return the Ionian cities in Asia Minor to Persia.

Athens went on the attack and even gained

Barefooted Greek warriors

the upper hand for a while under the leadership of the reinstated Alcibiades, but its days were numbered once Persia entered the fray in Asia Minor, and Sparta regained its composure under the outstanding general, Lysander. Athens surrendered to Sparta in 404 BC.

Corinth urged the total destruction of Athens but Lysander felt honour-bound to spare the city that had saved Greece from the Persians. Instead he crippled it by confiscating its fleet, abolishing the Delian League and tearing down the walls between the city and Piraeus.

Spartan Rule The Peloponnesian Wars had exhausted the city-states, leaving only Sparta in a position of any strength. During the wars, Sparta had promised to restore liberty to the city-states who had turned against Athens, but Lysander now changed his mind and installed oligarchies (governments run by the super-rich) supervised by Spartan garrisons. Soon there was widespread dissatisfaction.

Sparta found it had bitten off more than it could chew when it began a campaign to reclaim the cities of Asia Minor from Persian rule. This brought the Persians back into Greek affairs, where they found willing clients in Athens and increasingly powerful

Thebes. Thebes, which had freed itself from Spartan control and had revived the Boeotian League, soon became the main threat to Sparta, while Athens regained some of its former power at the head of a new league of Aegean states known as the Second Confederacy – this time aimed against Sparta rather than Persia.

The rivalry culminated in the decisive Battle of Leuctra in 371 BC, where Thebes, under the leadership of the remarkable statesman and general Epaminondas, inflicted Sparta's first defeat in a pitched battle. Spartan influence collapsed, and Thebes filled the vacuum.

In a surprise about-turn Athens now allied itself with Sparta, and their combined forces met the Theban army at Mantinea in the Peloponnese in 362 BC. The battle was won by Thebes, but Epaminondas was killed. Without him, Theban power soon crumbled. Athens was unable to take advantage of the situation. The Second Confederacy became embroiled in infighting fomented by the Persians and when it eventually collapsed, Athens lost its final chance of regaining its former glory.

The city-states were now spent forces and a new power was rising in the north: Macedon. This had not gone unnoticed by the inspirational orator Demosthenes in Athens, who urged the city-states to prepare to defend themselves. Only Thebes took heed of his warnings and the two cities formed an alliance.

The Rise of Macedon

While the Greeks engineered their own decline through the Peloponnesian Wars, Macedon (geographically the modern nome, or province, of Macedonia) was gathering strength in the north. Macedon had long been regarded as a bit of a backwater, a loose assembly of primitive hill tribes nominally ruled by a king. The Greeks considered the people to be barbarians (those whose speech sounded like 'bar-bar', which meant anyone who didn't speak Greek).

The man who turned them into a force to

be reckoned with was Philip II, who came to the throne in 382 BC.

As a boy, Philip had been held hostage in Thebes where Epaminondas had taught him a thing or two about military strategy. After organising his rebellious hill tribes into an efficient army of cavalry and long-lanced infantry, Philip made several forays south and manipulated his way into membership of the Amphyctionic Council (a group of states whose job it was to protect the oracle at Delphi).

In 339 BC, on the pretext of helping the Amphyctionic Council sort out a sacred war with Amfissa, he marched his army into Greece. The result was the Battle of Khaironeia in Boeotia (338 BC), in which the Macedonians defeated a combined army of Athenians and Thebans. The following year, Philip called together all the city-states (except Sparta, which remained aloof) at Corinth and persuaded them to form the League of Corinth and swear allegiance to Macedonia by promising he would lead them in a campaign against Persia. The barbarian upstart had become leader of the Greeks.

Philip's ambition to tackle Persia never materialised, for in 336 BC he was assassinated by a Macedonian noble. His son, the 20-year-old Alexander, who had led the decisive cavalry charge at Khaironeia, became king.

Alexander the Great Alexander, highly educated (he had been tutored by Aristotle), fearless and ambitious, was an astute politician and intent upon fulfilling what his father had begun. Philip II's death had been the signal for rebellions throughout the budding empire, but Alexander wasted no time in crushing them, making an example of Thebes by razing it to the ground. After restoring order, he turned his attention to the Persian Empire and marched his army of 40,000 men into Asia Minor in 334 BC.

After a few bloody battles with the Persians, most notably at Issus (333 BC), Alexander succeeded in conquering Syria, Palestine and Egypt – where he was proclaimed pharaoh and founded the city of

Alexandria. Hellbent on sitting on the Persian throne, he then began hunting down the Persian king, Darius III, defeating his army in Mesopotamia in 331 BC. Darius III fled east while Alexander mopped up his empire behind him, destroying the Persian palace at Persepolis in revenge for the sacking of the Acropolis 150 years earlier, and confiscating the well-endowed royal treasury. Darius' body was found a year later: he had been stabbed to death by a Bactrian (Afghan) dissident.

Alexander continued east into what is now known as Uzbekistan, Bactria (where he married a local princess, Roxane) and northern India. His ambition was now to conquer the world, which he believed ended at the sea beyond India. But his soldiers grew weary and in 324 BC forced him to return to Mesopotamia, where he settled in Babylon and drew up plans for an expedition south into Arabia. The following year, however, he fell ill suddenly and died, heirless, at the age of 33. His generals swooped like vultures on the empire.

When the dust settled, Alexander's empire had fallen apart into three large kingdoms and several smaller states. The three generals with the richest pickings were Ptolemy, founder of the Ptolemaic dynasty in Egypt (capital: Alexandria), which died out when the last of the dynasty, Cleopatra, committed suicide in 30 BC; Seleucus, founder of the Seleucid dynasty which ruled over Persia and Syria (capital: Antiochia); and Antigonus, who ruled over Asia Minor and whose Antigonid successors would win control over Macedonia proper.

Macedonia lost control of the Greek city-states to the south, who banded together into the Aetolian League centred around Delphi and the Achaean League based in the Peloponnese; Athens and Sparta joined neither. One of Alexander's officers established the mini-kingdom of Pergamum in Asia Minor, which reached its height under Attalos I (ruled 241-196 BC) when it rivalled Alexandria as a centre of culture and learning. The island of Rhodes developed into a powerful mini-state by taxing passing ships.

Still, Alexander's formidable achievements during his 13 years on the world stage earned him the epithet 'the Great'. He spread Greek culture throughout a large part of the 'civilised' world, encouraged intermarriage and dismissed the anti-barbarian snobbery of the classical Greeks. In doing so, he ushered in the Hellenistic period of world history, in which Hellenic ('Greek') culture broke out of the narrow confines of the ancient Greek world and merged with the other proud cultures of antiquity to create a new, cosmopolitan tradition.

Roman Rule

While Alexander the Great was forging his vast empire in the East, the Romans had been expanding to their west and now also began making inroads into Greece. They found willing allies in Pergamum and Rhodes, who feared Syrian and Macedonian expansionism. The Romans defeated the Seleucid king, Antiochus III, in a three-year campaign and in 189 BC gave all of Asia Minor to Pergamum. Several wars were needed to subjugate Macedon, but in 168 BC Macedon

Alexander the Great (356 - 323 BC)

lost the decisive Battle of Pydnaa and it was turned into a Roman province 20 years later.

The Achaean League was defeated in 146 BC; the Roman consul Mummius made an example of the rebellious Corinthians by completely destroying their beautiful city, massacring the men and selling the women and children into slavery. Attalos III of Pergamum died without an heir in 133 BC, donating Asia Minor to Rome in his will. In 86 BC, Athens joined in a rebellion against the Romans in Asia Minor staged by the king of the Black Sea region, Mithridates VI. In return, the Roman statesman Sulla invaded Athens, destroyed its walls and took off with its most valuable sculptures.

Soon most of Greece was under Roman rule and the area became a battleground as Roman generals fought for supremacy. In a decisive naval battle off Cape Actium (31 BC) Octavian was victorious over Antony and Cleopatra and consequently became Rome's first emperor, assuming the title Augustus, the Grand One.

For the next 300 years Greece, as the Roman province of Achaea, experienced an unprecedented period of peace, the Pax Romana. The Romans had always venerated Greek art, literature and philosophy, and aristocratic Romans sent their offspring to the many schools in Athens. Indeed, the Romans adopted most aspects of Hellenistic culture, spreading its unifying traditions throughout their empire.

Christianity & the Byzantine Empire

The Pax Romana began to crumble in 250 AD when the Goths invaded Greece, the first of a succession of invaders spurred on by the 'great migrations', which included the Visigoths in 395, the Vandals in 465, the Ostrogoths in 480, the Bulgars in 500, the Huns in 540 and the Slavs after 600.

A new religion, Christianity, had a much more lasting impact. St Paul had made several visits to Greece in the 1st century AD and made converts in many places. The definitive boost to the spread of Christianity in this part of the world came with the conversion of the Roman emperors and the rise of the Byzantine Empire, which blended Hellenistic culture with Christianity.

In 324 Emperor Constantine I (also known as Constantine the Great), a Christian convert, transferred the capital of the empire from Rome to Byzantium, a city on the western shore of the Bosphorus, which was renamed Constantinople (present-day İstanbul). This was as much due to insecurity in Italy itself as to the growing importance of the wealthy eastern regions of the empire. By the end of the 4th century, the Roman Empire was formally divided into a western and eastern half. While Rome went into terminal decline, the eastern capital grew in wealth and strength, long outliving its western counterpart (the Byzantine Empire lasted until the capture of Constantinople by the Turks in 1453).

Emperor Theodosius I made Christianity the official religion in Greece in 394 and outlawed the worship of Greek and Roman gods, now branded as paganism. Athens remained an important cultural centre until 529, when Emperor Justinian forbade the teaching of classical philosophy in favour of Christian theology, then seen as the supreme form of intellectual endeavour. The Hagia Sophia (Church of the Divine Wisdom) was built in Constantinople and many magnificent churches were also built in Greece, especially in Thessaloniki, a Christian stronghold much favoured by the Byzantine emperors.

The Crusades

It is one of the ironies of history that the demise of the Byzantine Empire was accelerated not by invasions of infidels from the east, nor barbarians from the north, but by fellow Christians from the west – the Frankish crusaders. The stated mission of the crusades was to liberate the Holy Land from the Muslims, but in reality they were driven as much by greed as by religious fervour. By the time the First Crusade was launched in 1095, the Franks had already made substantial gains in Italy at the empire's expense and the rulers of Constantinople were understandably nervous about giving the crusaders safe passage when they passed through on their way to Jerusalem. The first three crusades passed by without incident, but the Fourth Crusade opted to travel by ship in order to save time. They struck a deal with Venice, the only state with enough ships to transport them. Venice had a score to settle with the Byzantines and managed to divert the crusaders' energies away from Jerusalem and towards Constantinople instead.

Constantinople was sacked in 1204 and the crusaders installed Baldwin of Flanders as head of the short-lived Latin Empire of Constantinople. Much of the Byzantine Empire was partitioned into feudal states ruled by self-styled 'Latin' (mostly Frankish) princes. Greece now entered one of the most tumultuous periods of its history. The Byzantines fought to regain their lost capital and to keep the areas they had managed to hold on to (the so-called Empire of Nicaea, south of Constantinople in Asia Minor), while the Latin princes fought among themselves to expand their territories.

Meanwhile, Venice had secured a foothold in Greece. Over the next few centuries they acquired all the key Greek ports, including the island of Crete, and became the wealthiest and most powerful traders in the Mediterranean.

Despite this disorderly state of affairs, Byzantium was not yet dead. In 1259, the Byzantine emperor Michael VIII Palaeologos recaptured the Peloponnese from the Frankish de Villehardouin family, and made the city of Mystras his headquarters. Many eminent Byzantine artists, architects, intellectuals and philosophers converged on the city for a final burst of Byzantine creativity. Michael VIII managed to reclaim Constantinople in 1261, but by this time Byzantium was a shadow of its former self.

The Ottoman Empire

Constantinople was soon facing a much greater threat from the East. The Seljuk Turks, a tribe from central Asia, had first appeared on the eastern fringes of the empire in the middle of the 11th century. They established themselves on the Anatolian plain by defeating a Byzantine army at Manzikert in 1071. The threat looked to have been contained, especially when the Seljuks were themselves overrun by the Mongols. By the time Mongol power was on the wane, the followers of Osman (who ruled from 1289 to 1326), better known as the Ottomans, had supplanted the Seljuks as the dominant Turkish tribe. The Muslim Ottomans rapidly expanded the areas under their control and by the mid-15th century were harassing the Byzantine Empire on all sides. Western Europe was too embroiled in the Hundred Years' War to come to the rescue, and in 1453 Constantinople fell to the Turks under Mohammed II (the Conqueror). Once more Greece became a battleground, this time fought over by the Turks and Venetians. Eventually, with the exception of the Ionian islands, Greece became part of the Ottoman Empire.

Much has been made of the horrors of the Turkish occupation in Greece. However, in the early years at any rate, Greeks probably marginally preferred Ottoman to Venetian or Frankish rule. The Venetians in particular treated their subjects little better than slaves. But life was not easy under the Turks, not least because of the high taxation they imposed. One of their most hated practices was the taking of one out of every five male children to become janissaries, personal bodyguards of the sultan. Many janissaries became infantrymen in the Ottoman army, but the cleverest could rise to high office – including grand vizier (chief minister).

Ottoman power reached its zenith under Sultan Süleyman the Magnificent (ruled 1520-66), who expanded the empire through the Balkans and Hungary to the gates of Vienna. His successor, Selim the Sot, added Cyprus to their dominions in 1570, but his death in 1574 marked the end of serious territorial expansion.

Although they captured Crete in 1670 after a 25-year campaign and briefly threatened Vienna once more in 1683, the ineffectual sultans that followed in the late-16th and 17th centuries saw the empire go into steady decline. They suffered a series of reversals on the battlefield, and Venice succeeded in holding onto the Peloponnese after a campaign in 1687 that saw them advance as far as Athens. The Parthenon was destroyed during the fighting when a shell struck a store of Turkish gunpowder.

Chaos and rebellion spread across Greece. Corsairs terrorised coastal dwellers, gangs of klephts (anti-Ottoman fugitives and brigands) roamed the mountains, and there was an upsurge of opposition to Turkish rule by freedom fighters – who fought each other when they weren't fighting the Turks.

Russian Involvement

Russia's link with Greece went back to Byzantine times, when the Russians had been converted to Christianity by Byzantine missionaries. The Church hierarchies in Constantinople and Kiev (later in Moscow) soon went separate ways, but when Constantinople fell to the Turks, the metropolitan (head) of the Russian Church declared Moscow the 'third Rome', the true heir of Christianity, and campaigned for the liberation of its fellow Christians in the south. This fitted in nicely with Russia's efforts to expand southwards and south-westwards into Ottoman territory – perhaps even to turn the Ottoman Empire back into a Byzantine Empire dependent on Russia.

When Catherine the Great became Empress of Russia in 1762, both the Republic of Venice and the Ottoman Empire were weak. She sent Russian agents to foment rebellion, first in the Peloponnese in 1770 and then in Epiros in 1786. Both were crushed ruthlessly – the latter by Ali Pasha, the governor of Ioannina, who proceeded to set up his own power base in Greece in defiance of the sultan.

Independence Parties In the 1770s and 1780s Catherine booted the Turks from the Black Sea coast and created a number of towns in the region which she gave Ancient Greek or Byzantine names. She offered Greeks financial incentives and free land to settle the region, and many took up her offer.

One of the new towns was Odessa, and it was there in 1814 that businessmen Athanasios Tsakalof, Emmanuel Xanthos and Nikolaos Skoufas founded the first Greek independence party, the Filiki Eteria (Friendly Society). The message of the society spread quickly and branches opened throughout Greece. The leaders in Odessa believed that armed force was the only effective means of liberation, and made generous monetary contributions to the freedom fighters.

There were also stirrings of dissent among Greeks living in Constantinople. The Ottomans regarded it as beneath them to participate in commerce, and this had left the door open for Greeks to become a powerful economic force in the city. These wealthy Greek families were called Phanariots. Unlike the Filiki Eteria, who strove for liberation through rebellion, the Phanariots believed that they could effect a takeover from within.

The War of Independence

Ali Pasha's private rebellion against the sultan in 1820 gave the Greeks the opportunity they had been waiting for. On 25 March 1821, Bishop Germanos of Patras hoisted the Greek flag at the monastery of Agia Lavra in the Peloponnese, an act of defiance that marked the beginning of the War of Independence. Fighting broke out almost simultaneously across most of Greece and the occupied islands, with the Greeks making big early gains. The fighting was savage, with atrocities committed on both sides. In the Peloponnese, 12,000 Turkish inhabitants were massacred after the capture of the city of Tripolitsa (present-day Tripolis) and Maniot freedom fighters razed the homes of thousands of Turks. The Turks retaliated with massacres in Asia Minor, most notoriously on the island of Chios, where 25,000 civilians were killed.

The fighting escalated and within a year the Greeks had captured Monemvassia, Navarino (modern Pylos), Nafplio and Tripolitsa in the Peloponnese, and Messolongi, Athens and Thiva (Thebes). Greek independence was proclaimed at Epidaurus on 13 January 1822.

The Western powers were reluctant to intervene, fearing the consequences of creating a power vacuum in south-eastern Europe, where the Turks still controlled much territory. Help came from the philhellenes – aristocratic young men, recipients of a classical education, who saw themselves as the inheritors of a glorious civilisation and were willing to fight to liberate its oppressed descendants. These philhellenes included Shelley, Goethe, Schiller, Victor Hugo, Alfred de Musset and Lord Byron. Byron arrived in Messolongi – an important centre of resistance – in January 1824 and died three months later of pneumonia.

The prime movers in the revolution were the klephts Theodoros Kolokotronis (who led the siege on Nafplio) and Markos Botsaris; Georgos Koundouriotis (a ship owner) and Admiral Andreas Miaoulis, both from Hydra; and the Phanariots Alexandros Mavrokordatos and Dimitrios Ypsilantis. Streets all over Greece are named after these heroes.

The cause was not lacking in leaders; what was lacking was unity of objectives and strategy. Internal disagreements twice escalated into civil war, the worst in the Peloponnese in 1824. The sultan took advantage of this and called in Egyptian reinforcements. By 1827 the Turks had captured Modon (Methoni) and Corinth, and recaptured Navarino, Messolongi and Athens.

At last the Western powers intervened, and a combined Russian, French and British fleet destroyed the Turkish-Egyptian fleet in the Bay of Navarino in October 1827. Sultan Mahmud II defied the odds and proclaimed a holy war. Russia sent troops into the Balkans and engaged the Ottoman army in yet another Russo-Turkish war. Fighting continued until 1829 when, with Russian troops at the gates of Constantinople, the sultan accepted Greek independence by the Treaty of Adrianople.

Birth of the Greek Nation

Meanwhile, the Greeks had begun organising the independent state they proclaimed several years earlier. In April 1827 they elected as their first president a Corfiot who had been the foreign minister of Tsar Alexander I, Ioannis Kapodistrias. Nafplio, in the Peloponnese, was selected as the capital.

With his Russian past, Kapodistrias believed in a strong centralised government. Although he was good at enlisting foreign support, his autocratic manner at home was unacceptable to many of the leaders of the War of Independence, particularly the Maniot chieftains who had always been a law unto themselves, and he was assassinated in 1831.

Amid the ensuing anarchy, Britain, France and Russia once again intervened and declared that Greece should become a monarchy and that the throne should be given to a non-Greek so that they would not be seen to be favouring one Greek faction. A fledgling kingdom was now up for grabs among the offspring of the crowned heads of Europe, but no-one exactly ran to fill the empty throne. Eventually the 17-year-old Prince Otto of Bavaria became king, arriving in Nafplio in January 1833. The new kingdom (established by the London Convention of 1832) consisted of the Peloponnese, Sterea Ellada, the Cyclades and the Sporades.

King Otho (as his name became) got up the nose of the Greek people from the moment he set foot on their land. He arrived with a bunch of upper-class Bavarian cronies, to whom he gave the most prestigious official posts, and he was just as autocratic as Kapodistrias. Otho moved the capital to Athens in 1834.

Patience with his rule ran out in 1843 when demonstrations in the capital, led by the War of Independence leaders, called for a constitution. Otho mustered a National Assembly which drafted a constitution calling for parliamentary government consisting of a lower house and a senate. Otho's cronies were whisked out of power and replaced by War of Independence freedom fighters, who bullied and bribed the populace into voting for them.

The Great Idea

By the middle of the 19th century the people of the new Greek nation were no better off materially than they had been under the Ottomans, and it was in this climate of despondency that the Megali Idea (Great Idea) of a new Greek Empire was born. This empire was to include all the lands that had once been under Greek influence with Constantinople as its capital. Otho enthusiastically embraced the idea, which increased his popularity no end.

Not with the Greek politicians, however, who still sought ways to increase their own power in the face of his autocratic rule. By the end of the 1850s, most of the stalwarts from the War of Independence had been replaced by a new breed of university graduates (Athens University had been founded in 1837). In 1862 they staged a bloodless revolution and deposed the king. But they weren't quite able to set their own agenda, because in the same year Britain returned the Ionian islands (a British protectorate since 1815) to Greece, and in the general euphoria the British were able to push forward young Prince William of Denmark, who became King George I (the Greek monarchy retained its Danish links from that time).

His 50-year reign brought stability to the troubled country, beginning with a new constitution in 1864 which established the power of democratically elected representatives and pushed the king further towards a ceremonial role. An uprising in Crete against Turkish rule was suppressed by the sultan in 1866-68, but in 1881 Greece acquired Thessaly and part of Epiros as the result of another Russo-Turkish war.

When Harilaos Trikoupis became prime minister in 1882, he prudently concentrated his efforts on domestic issues rather than pursuing the Great Idea. The 1880s brought the first signs of economic growth: the country's first railway lines and paved roads were constructed; the Corinth Canal (begun in 62 AD!) was completed – enabling Piraeus to become a major Mediterranean port; and the merchant navy grew rapidly.

However, the Great Idea had not been buried, and reared its head again after Trikoupis' death in 1896. In 1897 there was another uprising in Crete, and the hot-headed prime minister Theodoros Deligiannis responded by declaring war on Turkey and sending help to Crete. A Greek attempt to invade Turkey in the north proved disastrous – it was only through the intervention of the great powers that the Turkish army was prevented from taking Athens.

Crete was placed under international administration. The day-to-day government of the island was gradually handed over to Greeks, and in 1905, the president of the Cretan assembly, Eleftherios Venizelos, announced Crete's union (enosis) with Greece, although this was not recognised by international law until 1913. Venizelos went on to become prime minister of Greece in 1910 and was the country's leading politician until his republican sympathies brought about his downfall in 1935.

The Balkan Wars

Although the Ottoman Empire was in its death throes at the beginning of the 20th century, it was still clinging onto Macedonia. It was a prize sought by the newly formed Balkan countries of Serbia and Bulgaria, as well as by Greece, leading to the Balkan wars. The first, in 1912, pitted all three against the Turks; the second, in 1913, pitted Serbia and Greece against Bulgaria. The outcome was the Treaty of Bucharest (August 1913), which greatly expanded Greek territory by adding the southern part of Macedonia, part of Thrace, another chunk of Epiros, and the North-East Aegean Islands, as well as recognising the union with Crete.

In March 1913, King George was assassinated by a lunatic and his son Constantine became king.

WW I & Smyrna

King Constantine, who was married to the sister of the German emperor, insisted that Greece remain neutral when WW I broke out in August 1914. As the war dragged on, the Allies (Britain, France and Russia) put increasing pressure on Greece to join forces with them against Germany and Turkey. They made promises which they couldn't hope to fulfil, including land in Asia Minor. Venizelos favoured the Allied cause, placing him at loggerheads with the king. Tensions between the two came to a head in 1916, and Venizelos set up a rebel government, first in Crete and then in Thessaloniki, while the pressure from the Allies eventually persuaded Constantine to leave Greece in June 1917. He was replaced by his more amenable second son, Alexander.

Greek troops served with distinction on the Allied side, but when the war ended in 1918 the promised land in Asia Minor was not forthcoming. Venizelos took matters into his own hands and, with Allied acquiescence, landed troops in Smyrna (present-day İzmir) in May 1919 under the guise of protecting the half a million Greeks living in that city (just under half its population). With a firm foothold in Asia Minor, Venizelos now planned to push home his advantage against a war-depleted Ottoman Empire. He ordered his troops to attack in October 1920 (just weeks before he was voted out of office). By September 1921, the Greeks had advanced as far as Ankara.

The Turkish forces were commanded by Mustafa Kemal (later to become Atatürk), a general who belonged to the Young Turks, a group of army officers pressing for Western-style reforms. He believed that Turkey needed a modern government in place of the absolute sultanate, and the Greek invasion was just the cause he needed to rally support.

Kemal first halted the Greek advance outside Ankara in September 1921 and then routed them with a massive offensive the following spring. The Greeks were driven out of Smyrna and many of the Greek inhabitants were massacred. Mustafa Kemal was now a national hero, the sultanate was abolished and Turkey became a republic. The outcome of the failed Greek invasion and the revolution in Turkey was the Treaty of Lausanne of July 1923. This gave eastern Thrace and the islands of Imvros and Tenedos to Turkey, while the Italians kept the Dodecanese (which they had temporarily acquired in 1912 and would hold until 1947).

The treaty also called for a population exchange between Greece and Turkey to prevent any future disputes. The Great Idea, which had been such an enormous drain on the country's finances over the decades, was at last laid to rest. Almost 1.5 million Greeks left Turkey and almost 400,000 Turks left Greece. The exchange put a tremendous strain on the Greek economy and caused great hardship for the individuals concerned. Many Greeks abandoned a privileged life in Asia Minor for one of penury in shantytowns in Greece.

The Republic of 1924-35

The arrival of the refugees coincided with, and compounded, a period of political instability which was unprecedented even by Greek standards. In October 1920, King Alexander had died from a monkey bite, resulting in the restoration of his father, King Constantine. Constantine identified himself too closely with the war against Turkey, and abdicated after the fall of Smyrna. He was replaced by his first son, George II, but he was no match for the group of army officers who seized power after the war. A republic was proclaimed in March 1924 amid a series of coups and counter-coups.

A measure of stability was attained with Venizelos' return to power in 1928. He pursued a policy of economic and educational reforms, but progress was inhibited by the Great Depression. His anti-royalist Liberal Party began to face a growing challenge from the monarchist Popular Party, culminating in defeat at the polls in March 1933. The new government was preparing for the restoration of the monarchy when Venizelos and his supporters staged an unsuccessful coup in March 1935. Venizelos was exiled to Paris, where he died a year later. In November 1935 King George II was restored to the throne by a rigged plebiscite, and he installed the right-wing General Ioannis Metaxas as prime minister. Nine months later, Metaxas assumed dictatorial powers with the king's consent under the pretext of preventing a communist-inspired republican coup.

WW II

Metaxas' grandiose vision was to create a Third Greek Civilisation based on its glorious Ancient and Byzantine past, but what he actually created was more like a Greek version of the Third Reich. He exiled or imprisoned opponents, banned trade unions and the KKE (Kommunistiko Komma Ellados, the Greek Communist Party), imposed press censorship, and created a secret police force and a fascist-style youth movement. Metaxas is best known, however, for his reply of *ohi* (no) to Mussolini's request to allow Italians to traverse Greece at the beginning of WW II, thus maintaining Greece's policy of strict neutrality. The Italians invaded Greece, but were driven back into Albania.

A prerequisite of Hitler's plan to invade the Soviet Union was a secure southern flank in the Balkans. The British, realising this, asked Metaxas if they could land troops in Greece. He gave the same reply as he had given the Italians, but died suddenly in January 1941. The king replaced him with the timorous Alexandros Koryzis, who agreed to British forces landing in Greece and committed suicide when the Germans invaded.

German troops marched through Yugoslavia and invaded Greece on 6 April 1941. The defending Greek, British, Australian and New Zealand troops were seriously outnumbered, and the whole country was under Nazi occupation within a month. King George II and his government went into exile in Egypt. The civilian population suffered appallingly during the occupation, many dying of starvation. The Nazis rounded up more than half the Jewish population and transported them to death camps.

Numerous resistance movements sprang up. The three dominant ones were ELAS (Ellinikos Laïkos Apeleftherotikos Stratos), EAM (Ethnikon Apeleftherotikon Metopon) and EDES (Ethnikos Dimokratikos Ellinikos Syndesmos). Although ELAS was founded by communists, not all of its members were left wing, whereas EAM consisted of Stalinist KKE members who had lived in Moscow in the 1930s and harboured ambitions of establishing a postwar communist Greece. EDES (Ethnikos Dimokratikos Ellinikos Syndesmos) consisted of right-wing and monarchist resistance fighters. These groups fought one another with as much venom as they fought the Germans.

By 1943 Britain had begun speculating on the political complexion of postwar Greece. Winston Churchill wanted the king back and was afraid of a communist takeover, especially after ELAS and EAM formed a coalition and declared a provisional government in the summer of 1944. The Germans were pushed out of Greece in October 1944, but the communist and monarchist resistance groups continued to fight one another.

Civil War

On 3 December 1944, the police fired on a communist demonstration in Syntagma Square. The ensuing six weeks of fighting between the left and the right were known as the Dekemvriana (events of December), the first round of the civil war, and only the intervention of British troops prevented an ELAS-EAM victory. An election held in March 1946 and boycotted by the communists was won by the royalists, and a rigged plebiscite put George II back on the throne.

In October the left-wing Democratic Army (DA) was formed, which resumed the fight against the monarchy and its British supporters, marking the beginning of the second round of the civil war. The DA recruited thousands of members, and used guerrilla tactics to occupy land along the Albanian and Yugoslav borders under the leadership of Markos Vafiadis.

By 1947 the USA had replaced Britain as Greece's 'minder' and, inspired by the Truman Doctrine which aimed to contain the spread of Soviet influence, gave large sums of money to the anti-communist coalition government. The government made communism illegal and implemented the Certificate of Political Reliability (proof that the carrier was not left wing), which remained valid until 1962 and without which Greeks couldn't vote and found it almost impossible to get work. The extremely bitter civil war dragged on until October 1949, when Yugoslavia fell out with the Soviet Union and cut off the DA's supply lines. Vafiades was assassinated by a group of his Stalinist underlings and the DA capitulated.

More Greeks had been killed in the civil war than had been killed in WW II; thousands were homeless, many had been taken prisoner or exiled, and the DA had taken some 30,000 Greek children from northern Greece to Eastern-bloc countries, ostensibly for protection. The country was in an almighty mess politically and economically.

Reconstruction & the Cyprus Issue

A general election was held in 1950. The system of proportional representation resulted in a series of unworkable coalitions, and the electoral system was changed to majority voting in 1952 – which excluded the communists from future governments. The next election was a victory for the newly formed right-wing Ellinikos Synagermos (Greek Rally) party led by General Papagos, who had been a field marshal during the civil war. General Papagos remained in power until his death in 1955, when he was replaced by Konstantinos Karamanlis, the minister of public works.

Greece joined NATO in 1951, and in 1953 the USA was granted the right to operate sovereign bases in Greece. Intent on maintaining a right-wing government in Greece, the USA gave generous aid and even more generous military support. Living standards of Greeks improved during the 1950s, although it remained a poor country. The new tourist industry also began bringing in revenue.

Cyprus occupied centre stage in Greece's foreign affairs, and has remained there to this day. Since the 1930s, Greek Cypriots (four-fifths of Cyprus' population) had demanded enosis, while Turkey had maintained its claim to the island ever since the British occupied it in 1914 (it became a British

crown colony in 1925). After a new outbreak of communal violence between Greek and Turkish Cypriots in 1954, Britain stated its intention to make Cyprus an independent state.

The right-wing Greek EOKA (National Organisation of Cypriot Freedom Fighters) began guerrilla activities against the British administration. In 1959, however, Greece and Turkey accepted independence, and in August 1960 Cyprus became a republic with Archbishop Makarios as president and a Turk, Fasal Kükük, as vice president. This didn't really solve the issue, as the EOKA continued its activities while Turkish Cypriots clamoured for partition of the island, and the prospect of civil war remained.

Back in Greece, Georgos Papandreou, a former Venizelos supporter, founded the broadly based EK (Centre Union) in 1958, but an election in 1961 returned the ERE (National Radical Union), Karamanlis' new name for Papagos' Greek Rally party, to power for the third time in succession. Papandreou accused the ERE of ballot-rigging – probably true, but the culprits were almost certainly right-wing, military-backed groups (rather than Karamanlis) who feared communist infiltration if the EK came to power. Political turmoil followed, culminating in the murder, in May 1963, of Grigorios Lambrakis, the deputy of the communist EDA (Union of the Democratic Left). All this proved too much for Karamanlis, who resigned and left the country.

Despite the ERE's sometimes desperate measures to stay in power, an election in February 1964 was won by the EK. Papandreou wasted no time in implementing a series of radical changes. He freed political prisoners and allowed exiles to come back to Greece, reduced income tax and the defence budget, and increased spending on social services and education. Papandreou's victory coincided with King Constantine II's accession to the Greek throne, and with a renewed outbreak of violence in Cyprus which erupted into a full-scale civil war before the UN intervened and installed a peace-keeping force.

The Colonels' Coup

The right in Greece was rattled by Papandreou's tolerance of the left, fearing that this would increase the EDA's influence. The climate was one of mutual suspicion between the left and the right, each claiming that the other was plotting a takeover. Finally, Papandreou decided the armed forces needed a thorough overhaul, which seemed fair enough, as army officers were more often than not the perpetrators of conspiracies. King Constantine refused to cooperate with this, and Papandreou resigned. Two years of ineffectual interim governments followed before a new election was scheduled for May 1967.

The election was never to be. A group of army colonels led by Georgos Papadopoulos and Stylianos Patakos staged a coup d'état on 21 April 1967. King Constantine tried an unsuccessful counter-coup in December, after which he fled the country. A military junta was established with Papadopoulos as prime minister.

The colonels imposed martial law, abolished all political parties, banned trade unions, imposed censorship, and imprisoned, tortured and exiled thousands of Greeks who opposed them. Suspicions that the coup had been aided by the CIA remain conjecture, but criticism of the coup, and the ensuing regime, was certainly not forthcoming from either the CIA or the US government. In June 1972 Papadopoulos declared Greece a republic (confirmed by rigged referendum in July) and appointed himself president.

In November 1973 students began a sit-in at Athens' Polytechnic college in protest against the junta. On the night of 16 November, tanks stormed the building, injuring many and killing at least 20. On 25 November, Papadopoulos was deposed by the thuggish Brigadier Ioannidis, head of the military security police.

In an effort to muster public support, Ioannidis mounted a coup in Cyprus in July 1974. The plan was to assassinate Makarios and unite Cyprus with Greece, but Makarios got wind of the plan and escaped. The junta installed Nikos Sampson, a former EOKA leader, as president, and Turkey reacted by invading the island.

The junta, realising they'd made the ultimate blunder by putting Greece's claim to Cyprus in jeopardy, removed Sampson and threw in the towel. However, the Turks continued to advance until they occupied the northern third of the island, forcing almost 200,000 Greek Cypriots to flee their homes for the safety of the south.

After the Colonels

The army now called Karamanlis from Paris to clear up the mess in Greece. An election was arranged for November 1974 (won handsomely by Karamanlis' New Democracy party), and the ban on communist parties was lifted. Andreas Papandreou (son of Georgos) formed PASOK (the Panhellenic Socialist Union), and a plebiscite voted 69% against restoration of the monarchy.

(Former king Constantine, who now lives in London, didn't revisit Greece until the summer of 1993. The New Democracy government sent missile boats and a transport plane to follow his yacht. Nonetheless the ex-king said he and his family enjoyed the holiday, and he had no wish to overthrow the Greek constitution.)

Karamanlis' New Democracy (ND) party won the election in 1977, but his personal popularity began to decline. One of his biggest achievements before accepting the largely ceremonial post of president was to engineer Greece's entry into the European Community (now the European Union), which involved jumping the queue ahead of other countries who had waited patiently to be accepted. On 1 January 1981 Greece became the 10th member of the EC.

The Socialist 1980s

Andreas Papandreou's PASOK party won the election of October 1981 with 48% of the vote, giving Greece its first socialist government. PASOK promised removal of US air bases and withdrawal from NATO.

Seven years into government, these promises remained unfulfilled (although the US military presence was reduced), unemployment was high and reforms in education and welfare had been limited. Women's issues had fared better, though: the dowry system was abolished, abortion legalised, and civil marriage and divorce were implemented. The crunch came in 1988 when Papandreou's love affair with air hostess Dimitra Liani (whom he subsequently married) hit the headlines, and PASOK became

embroiled in a financial scandal involving the Bank of Crete.

In July 1989 an unlikely coalition of conservatives and communists took over to implement a *katharsis* (campaign of purification) to investigate the scandal. In September it ruled that Papandreou and four former ministers be tried for embezzlement, telephone tapping and illegal grain sales. The trial of Papandreou ended in January 1992 with his acquittal on all counts.

A Legend in Her Lifetime – Melina Merkouri

When she died on March 6, 1994 at the age of 68, tempestuous Greek actor and patriot turned fiery politician Melina Merkouri was mourned as the last of the goddesses of Greece. Cinemas closed in tribute, television stations screened exerpts of her movies and, on radio, recordings of her gravel-voiced songs were played all day.

Initially a stage actress, she had received acclaim at the 1955 Cannes Film Festival for her first and title film role in *Stella*. But she really achieved superstardom with her portrayal of the Piraeus prostitute Ilya in the film *Never on Sunday*, directed by Jules Dassin, whom she married.

When the chain-smoking Melina died in New York after complications following surgery to alleviate lung cancer, her body was returned to her beloved Greece for burial with prime ministerial honours. Born Amalia-Maria Merkouri into a family with strong political traditions, she turned to politics following the 1967 military coup in Greece. An outspoken opponent abroad of the junta dictatorship, she was stripped of her citizenship. Her property was seized and she survived three assassination attempts in exile.

After the fall of the dictatorship in 1974, Melina came back to her homeland. In 1977, she was elected to government. The first woman to hold a senior position in Greek parliament, Melina was appointed Minister of Culture in 1981 for eight years and again in 1993 when her PASOK party was returned to power.

Melina fought tirelessly to have the Elgin Marbles (reliefs taken from the Parthenon by Lord Elgin in 1803 and still housed in the British Museum) returned to Greece. She also campaigned for Greek women's rights, was active in initiating restoration of many heritage buildings in Piraeus and instigated the establishment of municipal theatre companies throughout the country.

Additionally, Melina was greatly responsible for the redevelopment of tourism in Greece after 1974; it was her idea to claim Athens as the first Cultural Capital of Europe, back in 1986.

Following her death, the Melina Merkouri Foundation was established in Athens to carry out her wishes to have a new Acropolis Museum built to maintain the values of Greek civilisation. Its staff will also continue to argue for the return of the Elgin Marbles. Stamps were produced in her honour in 1995. ∎

Melina Merkouri

The 1990s

An election in 1990 brought the ND back to power with a majority of only two seats, and with Konstantinos Mitsotakis as prime minister. Intent on redressing the country's economic problems – high inflation and high government spending – the government imposed austerity measures which included a wage freeze for civil servants and steep increases in public-utility costs and basic services. It also announced a privatisation programme aimed at 780 state-controlled enterprises; OTE (the telecommunications company), electricity and Olympic Airways were first on the list. The government also cracked down on tax evasion, which is still so rife it's described as the nation's favourite pastime.

The austerity measures sparked off a series of strikes in the public sector in mid-1990 and again in 1991 and 1992. The government's problems were compounded by an influx of Albanian refugees (see the People section later in this chapter), and the dispute over the use of the name Macedonia for the southern republic of former Yugoslavia (see the Macedonia information box in the Northern Greece chapter).

By late 1992 corruption allegations were being made against the government and it was claimed that Cretan-born Mitsotakis had a large, secret collection of Minoan art, and in mid-1993 there were allegations of government telephone tapping. Former Mitsotakis supporters began to cut their losses: in June 1993 Antonis Samaras, the ND's former foreign minister, founded the Political Spring party and called upon ND members to join him. So many of them joined that the ND lost its parliamentary majority and hence its capacity to govern.

An early election was held in October, which Andreas Papandreou's PASOK party won with 47% of the vote against 39% for ND and 5% for Political Spring. Through the majority voting system, this translated into a handsome parliamentary majority for PASOK. The victory was no surprise but the margin was, and it showed the deep level of dissatisfaction with the government's austerity measures. The people chose to ignore 74-year-old Papandreou's heart condition and generally poor health, and the scandals that had plagued the closing stages of his government in the late 1980s.

On assuming office, Papandreou appointed his wife as chief of staff, his son Georgos as deputy foreign minister, his wife's cousin as deputy minister of culture, and his personal physician as minister of health. He held true to his election promise to renationalise public transport, but baulked at further reversals of his predecessor's privatisation drive. The proposed sale of 40% of OTE was put on ice pending suitable market conditions. Tax reforms succeeded in reducing the huge public debt, but proved extremely unpopular.

Papandreou's health declined dramatically in late 1995. After a long hiatus during which Greece was effectively leaderless, Costas Simitis was appointed prime minister in early 1996. Simitis is regarded as an honest politician who has a real chance of turning around the economy.

The PASOK logo

MYTHOLOGY

Mythology was an integral part of the lives of all ancient peoples. The myths of ancient Greece are the most familiar to us, for they are deeply entrenched in the consciousness

The Twelve Deities

Name	Domain	Aegis
Zeus	supreme deity	thunderbolt
Hera	marriage, childbirth	cuckoo, peacock
Ares	war	armour
Hephaestus	fire, industry	hammer, anvil
Demeter	fertility	sheaf of wheat
Aphrodite	love, beauty	dove, girdle
Hestia	domesticity	hearth
Athena	wisdom	owl, armour
Poseidon	sea, earthquakes	trident
Apollo	sun, music, poetry	bow, lyre
Artemis	moon, hunting, chastity	she-bear, stag
Hermes	commerce	winged sandals

Olympian Creation Myth

According to mythology the world was formed from a great shapeless mass called Chaos. From Chaos came forth Gaea, the Mother Earth. She bore a son, Uranus, the Firmament, and their subsequent union produced three 100-handed giants and three one-eyed Cyclopes. Gaea dearly loved her hideous offspring, but not so Uranus, who hurled them into Tartarus (the underworld).

The couple then produced the seven Titans, but Gaea still grieved for her other children. She asked the Titans to take vengeance upon their father, and free the 100-handed giants and Cyclopes. The Titans did as they were requested, castrating the hapless Uranus, but Cronos (the head Titan), after setting eyes on Gaea's hideous offspring, hurled them back into Tartarus, whereupon Gaea foretold that he (Cronos) would be usurped by one of his own offspring.

Cronos married his sister Rhea, but wary of his mother's warning, he swallowed every child Rhea bore him. When Rhea bore her sixth child, Zeus, she smuggled him to Crete, and gave Cronos a stone in place of the child, which he duly swallowed. Rhea hid the baby Zeus in the Dikteon cave in the care of three nymphs.

On reaching manhood, Zeus, determined to avenge his swallowed siblings, became Cronos' cupbearer and filled his cup with poison. Cronos drank from the cup, then disgorged first the stone and then his children Hestia, Demeter, Hera, Poseidon and Hades, all of whom were none the worse for their ordeal. Zeus, aided by his regurgitated brothers and sisters, deposed Cronos, and went to war against the Titans who wouldn't acknowledge him as chief god. Gaea, who still hadn't forgotten her imprisoned, beloved offspring, told Zeus he would only be victorious with the help of the Cyclopes and the 100-handed giants, so he released them from Tartarus.

The Cyclopes gave Zeus a thunderbolt, and the three 100-handed giants threw rocks at the Titans, who eventually retreated. Zeus banished Cronos, as well as all of the Titans except Atlas (Cronos' deputy), to a far-off land. Atlas was ordered to hold up the sky.

Mt Olympus became home-sweet-home for Zeus and his unruly and incestuous family. Zeus, taking a fancy to Hera, turned himself into a dishevelled cuckoo whom the unsuspecting Hera held to her bosom, whereupon Zeus violated her, and Hera reluctantly agreed to marry him. They had three children: Ares, Hephaestus and Hebe. ∎

of Western civilisation. They are accounts of the lives of the deities whom the Greeks worshipped and of the heroes they idolised.

The myths are all things to all people – a rollicking good yarn, expressions of deep psychological insights, words of spine-tingling poetic beauty and food for the imagination. They have inspired great literature, art and music, by providing archetypes through which we can learn much about the deeper motives of human behaviour.

The myths we know are thought to be a blend of Dorian and Mycenaean mythology. Most accounts derive from the works of the poets Hesiod and Homer, produced in about 900 BC. The original myths have been chopped and changed countless times – dramatised, moralised and even adapted for ancient political propaganda, so numerous versions exist.

The Greek Myths, by Robert Graves, is regarded as being the ultimate book on the subject. It can be heavy going, though. *An Iconoclast's Guide to the Greek Gods* by Maureen O'Sullivan makes more entertaining reading.

The Twelve Deities

The main characters of the myths are the 12 deities, who lived on Mt Olympus – which the Greeks thought to be at the exact centre of the world.

The supreme deity was **Zeus**, who was also god of the heavens. His job was to make laws and keep his unruly family in order by brandishing his thunderbolt. He was also the possessor of an astonishing libido and vented his lust on just about everyone he came across, including his own mother. Mythology is littered with his offspring.

Zeus was married to his sister, **Hera** (see the Olympian Creation Myth information box), who was the protector of women and the family. Hera was able to renew her virginity each year by bathing in a spring. She was the mother of Ares and Hephaestus.

Ares, god of war, was a nasty piece of work. He was fiery-tempered and violent, liking nothing better than a good massacre. Athenians, who fought only for such noble ideals as liberty, thought that Ares must be a Thracian – whom they regarded as bloodthirsty barbarians.

Hephaestus was worshipped for his matchless skills as a craftsman. When Zeus decided to punish man, he asked Hephaestus to make a woman. So Hephaestus created Pandora from clay and water, and, as everyone knows, she had a box, from which sprang all the evils afflicting humankind.

The next time you have a bowl of corn

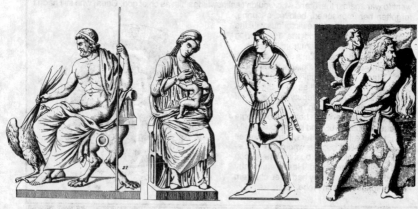

Zeus   Hera   Ares   Hephaestus

flakes, give thanks to **Demeter**, the goddess of earth and fertility. The English word 'cereal', for products of corn or edible grain, derives from the goddess' Roman name, Ceres. The Greek word for such products is *demetriaka*.

The goddess of love (and lust) was the beautiful **Aphrodite**. Her *tour de force* was her magic girdle which made everyone fall in love with its wearer. The girdle meant she was constantly pursued by both gods and goddesses – the gods because they wanted to make love to her, the goddesses because they wanted to borrow the girdle. Zeus became so fed up with her promiscuity that he married her off to Hephaestus, the ugliest of the gods.

In contrast **Hestia**, the goddess of the hearth, symbol of security, happiness and hospitality, was as pure as driven snow. She spurned disputes and wars and swore to be a virgin forever.

Athena, the powerful goddess of wisdom and guardian of Athens, is said to have been born (complete with helmet, armour and spear) from Zeus' head, with Hephaestus acting as midwife. Unlike Ares, she derived no pleasure from fighting, but preferred to use her wisdom to settle disputes peacefully. If need be, however, she went valiantly into battle.

Poseidon, the brother of Zeus, was god of the sea and preferred his sumptuous palace in the depths of the Aegean to Mt Olympus. When he was angry (which was often) he would use his trident to create massive waves and floods. His moods could also trigger earthquakes and volcanic eruptions. He was always on the lookout for some real estate on dry land and challenged Dionysos for Naxos, Hera for Argos and Athena for Athens.

Apollo, god of the sun, and **Artemis**, goddess of the moon, were the twins of Leto and Zeus. Many qualities were attributed to Apollo, for the Ancient Greeks believed that the sun not only gave physical light, but that its light was symbolic of mental illumination. Apollo was also worshipped as the god of music and song, which the ancients believed were heard only where there was light and security. Artemis was worshipped as the goddess of childbirth, yet she asked Zeus if he would grant her eternal virginity. She was also the protector of suckling animals, but loved to hunt stags!

Hermes was born of Maia, daughter of Atlas and one of Zeus' paramours. He had an upwardly mobile career. His first job was as protector of the animal kingdom. As the chief source of wealth was cattle, he therefore became the god of wealth. However, as civilisation advanced, trade replaced cattle as the main source of wealth, so Hermes

Demeter

Aphrodite

Hestia

Athena

became god of trade. However, a prerequisite for good trade was good commerce, so he became the god of commerce. To progress in commerce a merchant needed to be shrewd, so this attribute was assigned to Hermes. Later it was realised that to excel in commerce one needed to use the art of persuasion, so oratory was added to his portfolio.

Lesser Gods

After his brothers Zeus and Poseidon had taken the heavens and seas, **Hades** was left with the underworld (the earth was common ground). This vast and mysterious region was thought by the Greeks to be as far beneath the earth as the sky was above it. The underworld was divided into three regions: the Elysian Fields for the virtuous, Tartarus for sinners and the Asphodel Meadows for those who fitted neither category. Hades was also the god of wealth, in the form of the precious stones and metals found deep in the earth.

Some versions of mythology include **Dionysos**, the god of wine and revelry, in the first rank of the Olympians in place of Hestia. Dionysos was a son of Zeus by another of the supreme deity's dalliances. He had the job of touring the world with an entourage of fellow revellers spreading the word about the vine and wine.

Pan, the son of Hermes, was the god of the shepherds. Born with horns, beard, tail and goat legs, his ugliness so amused the other gods that eventually he fled to Arcadia where he danced, played his famous pipes and watched over the pastures, shepherds and herds.

Other gods included **Asclepius**, the god of healing; **Eros**, the god of love; and **Hypnos**, the god of sleep.

Mythical Heroes

Heroes such as **Heracles** and **Theseus** were elevated almost to the ranks of the gods. Heracles, yet another of Zeus' offspring, was performing astonishing feats of strength before he had left the cradle. His 12 labours were performed to atone for the murder of his wife and children in a bout of madness. The deeds of Theseus included the slaying of the Minotaur at Knossos.

Other heroes include **Odysseus**, whose wanderings after the fall of Troy are recorded in Homer's Odyssey, and **Jason**, who led his Argonauts to recover the golden fleece from Colchis (in modern Georgia).

Poseidon

Apollo

Artemis

Hermes

GEOGRAPHY

Greece, at the southern extremity of the Balkan peninsula, is the only member of the EU without a land frontier with another member. To the north, Greece has land borders with Albania, the Former Yugoslav Republic of Macedonia, and Bulgaria; and to the east with Turkey.

Greece consists of a peninsula and about 1400 islands, of which 169 are inhabited. The land mass is 131,900 sq km and Greek territorial waters occupy 400,000 sq km. The islands are divided into six groups: the Cyclades, the Dodecanese, the islands of the North-Eastern Aegean, the Sporades and the Saronic Gulf islands. The two largest islands, Crete and Evia, do not belong to any group. In Greece, no area is much more than 100 km from the sea. The much indented coastline has a total length of 15,020 km.

Roughly four-fifths of Greece is mountainous, with most of the land over 1500 metres above sea level. The Pindos mountains, which are an offshoot of the Dinaric alps, run north to south through the peninsula, and are known as the backbone of Greece. The mountains of the Peloponnese and Crete are part of the same formation. The highest mountain is Mt Olympus (2917 metres). Greece does not have many rivers, and none which are navigable. The largest are the Aheloös, Aliakmonas, Aoös and Arahthos, all of which have their source in the Pindos range in Epiros. The long plains of the river valleys, and those between the mountains and the coast, are the only lowlands. The mountainous terrain, dry climate and poor soil restricts agriculture to less than a quarter of the land. Greece is, however, rich in minerals, with reserves of oil, manganese, bauxite and lignite.

Ancient Greece was famous for its forests, but Epiros and Macedonia in northern Greece are now the only places where extensive forests remain. Goats have been among the main culprits, but firewood gathering, shipbuilding, housing and industry have all taken their toll on the forests. Forest fires are also a major problem, with an estimated 25,000 hectares destroyed by fire every year. The loss of forest cover has been accompanied by serious soil erosion problems, prompting the Ministry of Agriculture to launch a major reafforestation programme.

CLIMATE

Greece can be divided into a number of main climatic regions. Northern Macedonia and northern Epiros have a climate similar to the Balkans, with freezing winters and very hot, humid summers; while the Attic peninsula, the Cyclades, the Dodecanese, Crete, and the central and eastern Peloponnese have a more

---

The Evil Olive

It is a sad irony that the tree most revered by the Greeks is responsible for the country's worst ecological disaster. The tree is the olive. It was the money tree of the early Mediterranean civilisations, providing an abundance of oil that not only tasted great but could also be used for everything from lighting to lubrication. The ancient Greeks thought it was too good to be true and they concluded it must be a gift from the gods.

In their eagerness to make the most of this gift, native forest was cleared on a massive scale to make way for the olive. Landowners were urged on by decrees such as those issued in the 6th century BC by the archon of Athens, Solon, who banned the export of all agricultural produce other than olive oil and made cutting down an olive tree punishable by death.

Much of the land planted with olives was unsuitable hill country. Without the surface roots of the native forest to bind it, the topsoil of the hills was rapidly washed away. The olive tree could do nothing to help. It has no surface root system, depending entirely on its impressive tap root.

Thus, the lush countryside so cherished by the ancient Greeks was transformed into the harsh, rocky landscape that greets the modern visitor. ■

typically Mediterranean climate with hot, dry summers and milder winters.

Snow is very rare in the Cyclades (it snowed on Paros for the first time in 15 years in 1992), but the high mountains of the Peloponnese and Crete are covered in snow during the winter, and it does occasionally snow in Athens. In July and August, the mercury can soar to 40°C in the shade just about anywhere in the country. July and August are also the months of the meltemi, a strong northerly wind that sweeps the eastern coast of mainland Greece (including Athens) and the Aegean islands, especially the Cyclades. The wind is caused by air pressure differences between North Africa and the Balkans. The wind is a mixed blessing: it reduces humidity, but plays havoc with ferry schedules and sends everything flying – from beach umbrellas to washing hanging out to dry.

The western Peloponnese, western Sterea Ellada, south-western Epiros and the Ionian islands escape the meltemi and have less severe winters than northern Greece, but are the areas with the highest rainfall. The North-Eastern Aegean islands, Halkidiki and the Pelion peninsula fall somewhere between the Balkan-type climate of northern Greece and the Mediterranean climates. Crete stays warm the longest – you can swim off its southern coast from mid-April to November.

Mid-October is when the rains start in most areas, and the weather stays cold and wet until February – although there are also occasional winter days with clear blue skies and sunshine.

See the appendix at the back of this book for climatic figures.

FLORA & FAUNA

Greece is endowed with a variety of flora unrivalled in Europe. The wild flowers are spectacular. There are over 6000 species, some of which occur nowhere else, and more than 100 varieties of orchid. They continue to thrive because most of the land is too poor for intensive agriculture and has escaped the ravages of chemical fertilisers.

The regions with the most wild flowers are the mountains of Crete and the arid and mountainous Mani area of the Peloponnese. Trees begin to blossom as early as the end of February in warmer areas, and the wild flowers start to appear in March. During spring the hillsides are carpeted with flowers, which seem to sprout even from the rocks. Spring flowers include anemones, white cyclamens, irises, lilies, poppies, gladioli, tulips, countless varieties of daisy and many more. By summer, the flowers have disappeared from all but the northern mountainous regions. Autumn brings flowers too, especially crocuses.

You will not see many animals in the wild, due mainly to the popularity of hunting – both legal and illegal. Millions of animals are killed during the long 'open' season, from 20 August to 10 March, which encompasses the bird migratory period. The Hellenic Wildlife Hospital (☎ 0297-22 882), on the island of Aegina, reports that 80% of the animals it treats have been shot. It's legal to hunt only 35 of the 400-odd bird species found in Greece, but many birds brought to the hospital are protected or rare species.

One bird it should be impossible to mistake is the hoopoe, a member of the kingfisher family which has a prominent black-tipped crest and black-and-white striped wings. Greece has most species of woodpecker, wagtail, shrike and tit and some species of warbler, bee-eater,

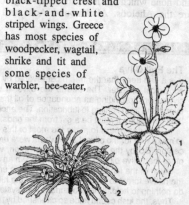

Mountain wild flowers: **1** *Ramonda nathaliae* **2** *Anchusa caespitosa*

lark, swallow, flycatcher, thrush and chat.

Out of a total of 408 species of migratory birds in Europe, 240 are found in Greece. One is the stork, which, although not endangered, is decreasing in number. Storks arrive in early spring from Africa, and return to the same nest year after year. The nests are built on electricity poles, chimney tops and church towers, and can weigh up to 50 kg; look out for them in northern Greece, especially in Thrace.

Lake Mikri Prespa, in Macedonia, has the richest colony of fish-eating birds in Europe, including egrets, herons, cormorants and ibises, as well as the Dalmatian pelican – Turkey and Greece are now the only countries in Europe where this bird is found. The wetlands at the mouth of the Evros River, close to the border with Turkey, are home to two easily identifiable wading birds – the avocet, which has a long upcurved beak, and the black-winged stilt, which has extremely long pink legs.

Upstream on the Evros River in Thrace, the dense forests and rocky outcrops of the 7200-hectare Dadia Forest Reserve play host to the largest range of birds of prey in Europe. Thirty-six of the 38 species can be seen here, and it is a breeding ground for 23 of them. Permanent residents include both the giant black vulture, whose wingspan reaches three metres, the griffon vulture and golden eagles. Europe's last 15 pairs of royal eagles nest on the river delta. The reserve is managed by the Worldwide Fund for Nature (☎ 01-363 4661). About 350 pairs (60% of the world's population) of the rare Eleonora falcon nest on the remote island of Piperi in the Sporades.

Greece's animals are hunted with the same enthusiasm as the birdlife. Potential victims include badgers, polecats, squirrels, rabbits, hares and foxes. Dormice probably don't warrant wasting a cartridge, nor the cute European suslik – a small ground squirrel. Looming much larger in the hunter's sights is the wild boar, still found in the mountains of the north. The wolf, an endangered species, is not protected in Greece as it is in other countries. It survives in small numbers

The grey wolf: it still survives in small numbers in the mountains of northern Greece

in the forests of the Pindos in Epiros as well as in the Dadia Reserve area.

The brown bear, Europe's largest land mammal, is also an endangered species. It survives in very small numbers in the Pindos mountains, the Peristeri range that rises above the Prespa Lakes and in the mountains which lie along the Bulgarian border. Other countries where the brown bear survives are France, Italy, Spain and Turkey.

One of the pleasures of island hopping in Greece is watching the dolphins as they follow the boats. Although there are many dolphins in the Aegean, the striped dolphins have recently been victims of murbilivirus – a sickness which affects the immune system. Research into the virus is being carried out in the Netherlands.

Europe's rarest mammal, the monk seal, was once very common in the Mediterranean, but it's now on the brink of extinction in Europe – it survives in slightly larger numbers in the Hawaiian islands. There are only about 350 left in Europe, all of which live in Greece. There are about 30 in the Ionian Sea and the rest are found in the Aegean. Until recently the seals were killed by fishermen because they damaged nets. The monk seal requires a gently sloping sandy beach on which to give birth; but unfortunately tourists 'require' these beaches for sunbathing, so fewer and fewer are available for the seals. The Hellenic Society for the Study & Protection of the Monk Seal (☎ 01-364 4164), Solomnou 35, Athens 10682, has a seal-rescue centre on Alonnisos, and the WWF funds seal-watch projects on Kefallonia, Ithaki and Lefkada.

The waters around Zakynthos and Kefallonia are home to the last large sea turtle colony in Europe, that of the loggerhead turtle. Each female turtle comes onto land to lay her eggs, which she buries in the sand. After hatching, the baby turtles have to make their way to the sea, but only a few make the distance, faced not only with natural hazards, but cars, discos and beach parties. For details on how you can avoid contributing to the loggerhead's demise, see the Ionian Islands chapter. Other reptiles you will come across in Greece are frogs, lizards and tortoises. For information on snakes in Greece, see the Health section in the Facts for the Visitor chapter.

Greece's national parks are Vikos-Aoös and Prespa national parks in Epiros, Olympus National Park on the borders of Thessaly and Macedonia, Parnassos and Iti national parks in Central Greece, Parnitha National Park in Attica and Samaria National Park in Crete. All of these have refuges and some have marked hiking trails. Greece also has a National Marine Park off the coast of Alonnisos in the Sporades.

Greece is – belatedly – becoming environmentally conscious, although, regrettably, it is often a case of closing the gate after the horse has bolted. The various societies for animal protection in Greece are listed in the *Athenian* magazine.

GOVERNMENT

Since 1975, democratic Greece has been a parliamentary republic with a president as head of state. The president and parliament, which has 300 deputies, have joint legislative power. The government is made up of a cabinet comprising a prime minister and 22 ministers.

Greece is divided into regions and island groups. The regions of the mainland are the Peloponnese, Central Greece (officially called Sterea Ellada), Epiros, Thessaly, Macedonia and Thrace. The island groups are the Cyclades, Dodecanese, North-Eastern Aegean, Sporades and Saronic Gulf, all in the Aegean Sea, and the Ionian, which is in the Ionian Sea. The large islands of Evia and Crete do not belong to any group. For administrative purposes these regions and groups are divided into prefectures or nomes (*nomoi* in Greek).

ECONOMY

Traditionally, Greece is an agricultural country, but the importance of agriculture to the economy has declined rapidly since WW II. Some 50% of the workforce is now employed in services (contributing 59% of GDP), 22% in agriculture (contributing 15%), and 27% in industry and construction (contributing 26%). Tourism is by far the biggest industry; shipping comes next. The nine million tourists who visit Greece each year contribute almost US$3 billion to the economy.

The previous government's austerity measures went down like a lead balloon, leading to a huge election victory for Andreas Papandreou's opposition PASOK party in the October 1993 general election. But this hasn't solved the problem; austerity measures are still needed if Greece is to comply with EU economic directives, which are a condition for achieving integration with the more affluent community members. The measures are also likely to push up unemployment, which is officially running at 8% but is unofficially estimated to be several per cent higher. Greece has the second-lowest income per capita of all the EU countries after Portugal.

Inflation and the state budget deficit have become a bigger problem than ever as the monetary unification of Europe draws near. Moves to reduce deficit financing have finally brought inflation below 10% for the first time in more than 20 years, but attempts to get the economy moving have been undermined by the escalating fighting in the Balkans that has cut Greece's major overland trade route to the rest of Europe. The economy grew by only 1.5% in 1994, well under the European average.

POPULATION

A census is taken every 10 years in Greece. The 1991 census recorded a population of 10,264,156 – an increase of 5.4% on the 1981 figure. Women outnumber men by more than 200,000. Greece is now a largely urban society, with 68% of the population living in cities. By far the largest is Athens, with more than 3.1 million people living in the greater Athens area. The population figures of other major cities are: Thessaloniki (740,000), Piraeus (196,000), Patras (172,800), Iraklio (127,600), Larisa (113,400) and Volos (106,100). Less than 15% of people live on the islands, the most populous of which are Crete (537,000), Evia (209,100) and Corfu (105,000).

PEOPLE

It is doubtful that any Greek alive today is directly descended from an ancient Greek. Contemporary Greeks are a mixture of all of the invaders who have occupied the country since ancient times. Today, there are a number of distinct ethnic minorities living in the country.

The country's small Roman Catholic population is of Genoese or Frankish origin. They live mostly in the Cyclades, especially on the island of Syros, where they make up 40% of the population. The Franks dominated the island from 1207 AD to Ottoman times.

About 300,000 ethnic Turks who were exempt from the population exchange of 1923 live in western Thrace. There are also small numbers of Turks on Kos and Rhodes which, along with the rest of the Dodecanese, did not become part of Greece until 1947.

There are small Jewish communities in several large towns. In Ioannina, Larisa, Halkidi and Rhodes, they date back to the Roman era, while in Thessaloniki, Kavala and Didymotiho, most are descendants of 15th-century exiles from Spain and Portugal.

In 1429, 20,000 exiled Jews arrived in Thessaloniki and by the 16th century they constituted the major part of the population. In 1941, the Germans entered Thessaloniki and herded 46,000 Jews off to Auschwitz, most never to return. They comprised 90% of Thessaloniki's Jews, and more than half the total number in Greece. The small number of Jews in Athens are mostly German Jews who came over with King Otho in the 1830s. Today there are only about 5000 Jews living in Greece.

Very small numbers of Vlach and Sarakatsani shepherds live a semi-nomadic existence in Epiros. They take their flocks to the high ground in summer and return to the valleys in winter. The Vlachs originate from the region which is now Romania; the origins of the Sarakatsani are uncertain.

You will come across Gypsies everywhere in Greece, but especially in Macedonia, Thrace and Thessaly. There are large communities of Gypsies in the Thracian towns of Alexandroupolis and Didymotiho.

The shedding of years of hardline Stalinism and isolation in Albania have left that country in turmoil and the people in a state of abject poverty. Consequently, thousands of Albanians have been crossing the poorly guarded border into Greece illegally. Police deported 90,000 in 1991, but many returned. In early 1993, police estimated there were about 130,000 illegal Albanians in Greece, but other sources put the number as high as 600,000. The Greek government claims that the Albanian authorities are encouraging this exodus, and the government in Tiranë accuses Greece of violating human rights in its treatment of the refugees.

EDUCATION

Education in Greece is free at all levels of the state system from kindergarten to tertiary. Primary schooling begins at the age of six, but most children attend a state-run kindergarten from the age of five. Private kindergartens are popular with those who can afford them. Primary school classes tend to be larger than those in most European countries – usually 30 to 35 children.

Primary school hours are short (8 am to 1 pm), but children get a lot of homework.

At 12, children enter the *gymnasio*, and at 15 they may leave school, or enter the *lykeio*, from where they take university-entrance examinations. Although there is a high percentage of literacy, many parents and pupils are dissatisfied with the education system, especially beyond primary level. The private sector therefore flourishes, and even relatively poor parents struggle to send their children to one of the country's 5000 *frontistiria* (intensive coaching colleges) to prepare them for the very competitive university-entrance exams. Parents complain that the education system is badly underfunded. The main complaint is about the lack of modern teaching aids in both gymnasia and lykeio.

Grievances reached a height in 1991, when lykeio students staged a series of sit-ins in schools throughout the country, and organised protest marches. In 1992, gymnasia pupils followed suit, and the government responded by making proposals which called for stricter discipline and a more demanding curriculum. More sit-ins followed, and in the end the government changed its plans and is still reassessing the situation.

ARTS

See the colour art section for a detailed look at the history of art and architecture in Greece.

Drama

Drama in Greece can be dated back to the contests staged at the Ancient Theatre of Dionysos in Athens during the 6th century BC for the annual Dionysia festival. During one of these competitions, Thespis left the ensemble and took centre stage for a solo performance regarded as the first true dramatic performance. The term Thespian for actor derives from this event.

Aeschylus (525-456 BC) is the so-called 'father of tragedy'; his best known work is the *Oresteia* trilogy. Sophocles (496-406 BC) is regarded as the greatest tragedian. He is thought to have written over 100 plays, of which only seven major works survive. These include *Ajax*, *Antigone*, *Electra*, *Trachiniae* and his most famous play, *Oedipus Rex*. His plays dealt mainly with tales from mythology and had complex plots. Sophocles won first prize 18 times at the Dionysia festival, beating Aeschylus in 468 BC, whereupon Aeschylus went off to Sicily in a huff.

Euripides (485-406 BC), another famous tragedian, was more popular than either Aeschylus or Sophocles because his plots were considered more exciting. He wrote 80 plays of which 19 are extant (although one, *Rhesus*, is disputed). His most famous works are *Medea*, *Andromache*, *Orestias* and *Bacchae*. Aristophanes (427-387 BC) wrote comedies – often ribald – which dealt with topical issues. His play *The Wasp* ridicules Athenians who resorted to litigation over trivialities; *The Birds* pokes fun at Athenian gullibility, and *Plutus* deals with the unfair distribution of wealth. You can see plays by the Ancient Greek playwrights at the Athens and Epidaurus festivals (see the Athens and Peloponnese chapters), and at various other festivals around the country.

Film

Greeks are avid cinema goers, although most of the films shown are North American or British. The Greek film industry is in the doldrums. This is largely due to inadequate government funding, which is compounded by the type of films the Greeks produce. Greek films have a reputation for being slow moving, with symbolism and ambiguity often used to convey complex themes. Although they are well made and the cinematography is often outstanding, they are too avant-garde to have mass appeal.

Greece's most acclaimed film director is Theodoros Angelopoulos, whose films include *The Beekeeper*, *Alexander the Great*, *Travelling Players*, *Landscapes in the Mist* and *The Hesitant Step of the Stork*. All have received awards at both national and international festivals.

THREE PILLARS OF WESTERN PHILOSOPHY

Socrates – 'Know thyself'

Very little is certain about Socrates because he committed none of his thoughts to paper. Historians and philosophers have constructed a picture of the man and his ideas mostly through the writings of Xenophon, in his *Memorabilia*, and more importantly, through the work of Plato, a one-time pupil of Socrates, in his 'dialogues'. Socrates is represented in Plato's dialogues both as a historical figure and as a character called 'Socrates' who articulated many of Plato's own ideas. As a result, the distinction between the ideas of the Platonic Socrates and Socrates himself is hard to make. Of all Plato's writings about Socrates, the only one that is considered reasonably historical is the *Apology* – an account of Socrates' speech at his own trial where he was sentenced to death as an enemy of the state. Plato was present at the trial, but it was some years later that he wrote the *Apology* based on his recollections. Socrates was already an old man when Plato came to him as a pupil, so there is much about the man that remains unknown.

Socrates was born around 470 BC in Athens and fought in the First Peloponnesian War as an infantry soldier. When serving in the trenches it is said that he would become transfixed in torpid states for up to 24 hours at a time, utterly lost in thought. The chaos of the war affected him greatly and thereafter he gave his life over to teaching in the streets, the marketplace and, particularly, the gymnasia – a mission that he believed was bestowed upon him by his god, the *daimon*. He was a man of very meagre means and most tales of Socrates have him dressed in rags and walking barefoot.

He was deeply religious and regarded mythology with disdain, claiming that tales of gods were merely the contrivance of poets. However, the *daimon's* existence was demonstrated in the perfect order of nature, in the universality of people's belief in the divine, and in the revelations that come in dreams and omens. Socrates not only believed that the soul was immortal, but that it was the very essence of an individual: his or her character and intellect – the *self*.

Socrates' method was dialectic, that is, he sought to illuminate truth by a process of question and answer. He would teach his pupils by responding to a question with another question, and then another, until the pupil came to answer his or her own inquiry. He believed that knowledge is inside everybody but that it needs to be revealed to them.

He was most concerned with moral questions and, for him, goodness was a fixed and knowable thing. It was the nature of people's actions and their character, rather than the nature of the world as revealed to the senses, that he spoke most about. He sought a 'way to live'. He believed that people are corrupted by putting the desires of the body and of the material world before the need to care for the soul, and that the condition of a person's soul is directly responsible for his or her happiness and well-being. The soul itself was seen as neither good nor bad, but well or poorly realised, and people's unhappiness was thought to result from their not knowing what happiness really is. Accordingly, actions that are unethical are in some sense involuntary – people are responsible for their wrong-doings, but they commit them because they have poor conceptions of themselves. However, those who know the true good will always act in accordance with it, for to do otherwise would be to knowingly choose sadness over happiness.

Socrates believed the duty of government was to look after the souls of the citizens of the state, and that a profound understanding of goodness should be an essential prerequisite for members of a government. He held that democracy was a flawed system because it left the state in the hands of the unenlightened and it valued all opinion as equal.

It's likely that Socrates did some work on what was to become Plato's theory of Ideas. The problem of how to define class-names, or 'universals' (nouns like 'tree' that cover whole classes of objects) had been touched on by previous thinkers, but Socrates' work was significant. (For a further discussion about the nature of class-names see the sections on Plato and Aristotle, below.)

In 399 BC, at the age of 70, Socrates was indicted for 'impiety'. He was charged with 'corruption of the young' and 'neglect of the gods whom the city worships and the practice of religious novelties'. He was contemptuous of the charges but was convicted and the prosecutors sought the death penalty. Under Athenian law, the accused was entitled to suggest a lesser penalty than that proposed by the prosecutors, and the judges would choose between the two – it seems unlikely that the death penalty would have been insisted upon. But Socrates incensed the court by suggesting a mere fine of 30 minae, and a larger majority than that which had found him guilty condemned him to death by the drinking of hemlock. He preferred to face death than to give credence to the charges by proposing a more substantial penalty. Socrates' friends had plans for his escape both before trial and during the 30 days that he was interned awaiting execution, but he would have none of it. He argued that the court was a legitimate one, and although the verdict was wrong, he was compelled to obey its rulings. The story of Socrates' day of his execution, when he explains that the soul must be immortal for 'universals' to exist, is told in Plato's *Phaedo*.

Socrates lived a life of deep conviction and died as a martyr. It is remarkable that a man born nearly 2500 years ago, who wrote nothing and of whom so little is known, should be revered as such a giant in the development of Western thought. ■

Plato – 'Until philosophers are kings...cities will never cease from ill, nor the human race'

Plato was born around 428 BC in Athens, or perhaps Aegina, in the early years of the First Peloponnesian War into an aristocratic and very well connected family. He was a student of Socrates who had a great influence upon him. In his early years, Plato had political ambitions but these waned in later life. He lived through turbulent times as a young man, through the Second Peloponnesian War and the fall of Athens. Plato was still a young man when Socrates was executed in 399 BC by the Athenian democrats. This, and the fact that his family were well connected in Periclean politics, caused Plato to despise democracy, and this theme ran through all of his work.

Around 387 BC Plato founded the Academy in Athens as an institute of philosophical and scientific studies. Although he is remembered as a great thinker, during his life he regarded the founding and administration of the Academy as his most important work. Aristotle came to the Academy at the age of 17 and remained there for nearly 20 years. Most of the important mathematical work of the 4th century BC, including major developments in geometry, was done at the Academy.

Plato was a prolific writer: in all there are 36 works, with some composed as appendices to others, although there is still debate as to the exact sequence in which they were written. Plato's writings take the form of dialogues and they read like scripts or dramas, complete with pathos and humour. He never introduced himself as a character in his dialogues, but he did use real people as speakers, including Socrates, Parmenides and Timaeus. These were all renowned thinkers in their own right, and it is not clear how much they (Socrates in particular) were used as vehicles for Plato's own musings and how well they represent themselves as genuine historical figures.

There are three main themes to Plato's work: metaphysics; ethics and politics; and aesthetics and mysticism. His greatest dialogue, the *Republic*, weaves these disparate elements into a more or less coherent whole.

Politically, Plato was an authoritarian. He, like all ancient Greeks, believed in a static universe where goodness and reality are fixed, unchanging qualities. The *Republic* is, in part, given over to Plato's view of the ideal state. He begins by dividing all people into three classes: the commoners, the soldiers and the rulers. He believed the state should seek to emulate the static perfection of heaven, and the rulers of this state should be those who best understand the nature of goodness and who are exponents of a certain moral and intellectual rigour. Furthermore, Plato thought that leisure was essential to wisdom and that only those who were free of the need to earn a livelihood were capable of enlightenment and thereby suitable as leaders of the perfect state. However, Plato also believed that the ego is the flaw in human nature and that both wealth and poverty are harmful. So, in the ideal state, rulers and citizens alike would act for the good of the whole rather than the benefit of one class. To this end, Plato declared that all people should live in modest houses and eat simple food – all extravagances would be forbidden; that women and men should be equal, should be given the same education and have the same prospects; that marriages should be arranged by the State and children should be removed from their parents at birth, never knowing their natural parents. He believed these initiatives, amongst others, would minimise personal possessive emotions so that public spirit would be the overwhelming thing that an individual felt. Plato made the distinction between 'ideal' and ordinary desires: an ideal desire is one that the desirer feels on behalf of all people and bears no relation to his or her own ego.

Plato was a pious man and his philosophical ideas reflected his conviction that there was a heaven, or rather a dwelling place of the gods that the soul could enter if the person had led a good life in accordance with the highest principles of philosophy. The notion of divine perfection was a central tenet in his thinking. The problem of class-ideas or 'universals' had been a conundrum for thinkers until Socrates – for example, 'woman' is greater, more real and more enduring than any individual woman. The problem was in determining the meaning of nouns like 'woman' or 'house' that can be applied to whole classes of individual instances, ie the meaning of 'woman' in its broadest sense is not this woman or that woman, or even these two women together. For Plato, the answer to this riddle was that objects in the world are merely appearances of perfect 'Ideas' or 'Forms'. These things were seen as singular, determinate and unchanging objects which could be apprehended by the intellect only. So, every tree that is perceivable is of the material world – it's born and it dies – and is merely a copy of the perfect tree created by God, and God's tree bears no relation to time or space. It is this idealised tree that determines the properties of 'treeness'. When a person describes something as beautiful, what they mean is that the Form 'beauty' has become present in that thing.

Knowledge, for most contemporary thinkers, is founded on perception. Plato, however, held that knowledge cannot be derived from the senses, and that true knowledge belongs to the realm of concepts. He argued that we perceive *through* our senses, not *with* them. It is the intellect that makes good of the information gathered through the senses. We know that smells and shapes are different, and yet there is no sense-organ that can perceive both. Furthermore, we have knowledge of concepts that are not derived from experience: perfect symmetry has no manifestation in the world we apprehend with our senses. Plato claimed that all knowledge is recollection – that it comes as revelation to the intellect. For him, each person has knowledge within, but they need to get at it, and this is achieved by philosophical instruction and through introspection.

Plato's ideas embraced a dualism that exists between reality and appearance, pure forms and sensible objects, intellect and sensory apprehension and, ultimately, soul and body. For him, the body and earthly desires impede wisdom, and wisdom is the soul transcending. ■

Aristotle – 'He who exercises his reason and cultivates it seems to be both in the best state of mind and most dear to the gods'

At the end of an extraordinary period of Greek thought came Aristotle, and his legacy cannot be overstated. It took 2000 years after his death until another great thinker came along who might be regarded as his equal: Descartes. Almost every significant philosophical advance since has been initiated by some reaction to an Aristotelian idea. In the case of logic (Aristotle's famous syllogisms), his work remained unsurpassed until the writings of German philosopher Gottlob Frege began to attract attention at the beginning of this century.

Aristotle was born in 384 BC in Stagira on the Halkidiki peninsula of Macedonia. His father was physician to the Macedonian King Amyntas III (father of Philip II and grandfather of Alexander the Great). Aristotle learned much about medicine from his father and studied the case histories in Hippocrates' *Epidemiai*. He would later become a great authority on biology. In 367 BC, Aristotle went to Athens to become a pupil of Plato at the Academy. He remained there for nearly 20 years, until Plato's death.

After Plato's death a rift appeared between Aristotle and the Academy. This was perhaps because Aristotle was overlooked as Plato's successor to head the Academy, a position that was filled by Speusippus, or possibly because of the strong anti-Macedonian sentiment that came over Athens after Philip had plundered the Greek city-state of Olynthus in 348 BC. Aristotle left the Academy and travelled widely with another graduate, Xenocrates. Over the next few years he immersed himself in biological studies – a departure from the theoretical work he had done at the Academy. He wrote in his treatise *On Generation of the Animals*: 'credit must be given to observation rather than theories, and to theories only in so far as they are confirmed by the observed facts'. This kind of methodology was at odds with that employed by Plato – who held that no knowledge could be gleaned from observations – and was the kind of approach that would be taken on by the empiricist philosophers of the 17th and 18th centuries.

In 343 BC, he was commissioned to tutor Alexander, then aged 13, and he stayed there for three years until Alexander was pronounced regent.

At nearly 50, Aristotle returned to Athens and, after the death of Speusippus, was once again denied the presidency of the Academy, this time in favour of Xenocrates, his old travelling companion. Shortly thereafter, under the protection of Alexander (who had just become king of the Greeks), he founded a rival institution, the Lyceum. He stayed in Athens for another 12 years, working and lecturing in philosophy and the sciences. He often strolled with his pupils as he taught them, and the Lyceum became known as the Peripatetic ('walking around') school.

Alexander the Great died in 323 BC, and Athens was again gripped by strong anti-Macedonian sentiments. Aristotle, with his Macedonian background, was swept up in this. Like Socrates, Aristotle was indicted on 'impiety', ostensibly over some of his writings, but the real motives were political, due to his connections with the Macedonian nobility. He fled Athens with some of his followers. One year later, aged 62 or 63, he died of a stomach condition.

Aristotle wrote voluminously on metaphysics, ethics, politics, logic and physics. Much of his writing has been lost. Of more than 170 manuscripts, only 47 remain.

He attacked Plato's theory that Ideas were separate from the material world. He regarded class-names as descriptive words, more like adjectives. Proper names, like 'Syntagma Square', signify a 'this', while class-names, or universals, like 'square', signify a 'such', indicating a kind of thing rather than a specific thing. For Plato, class-names referred to a single specific thing, the Idea or Form, but Aristotle held that this was simply wrong. For him, a universal derives its meaning from the fact that there are many individual instances of it. If there were no red things in the world, then the notion of 'redness' would be nonsensical.

However, Aristotle had his own metaphysic that is hard enough to grapple with. Central to this was his distinction between 'form' and 'matter'. In the case of a statue, the sculptor confers shape (the form) onto marble (the matter). The Aristotelian idea is that, more than merely determining shape, a thing's form is that which is unified about it – its *essence*. Matter without form is just potentiality, but by acquiring form its actuality increases; and change consists in giving form to matter. God has no matter, but is pure form and absolute actuality, and therefore unchanging (this conforms to the classical Greek idea of a static universe). Thus humans, by increasing the amount of form in the world, by building houses and bridges, are making it more divine.

Aristotle's main argument for God's existence was that there had to be something that initiated motion. He viewed the soul as 'the form of a material body having life potentially within it...soul is the actuality of the body'. And yet, Aristotle's view of the soul was quite different to Plato's and to the view that was to be espoused by Christianity. For Aristotle, the soul was inseparable from the body. However, he made a distinction between the irrational soul and the rational soul, or the *mind*. The irrational soul, it seemed, determined such things as the vagaries of taste and was inexorably connected to the body. Mind, however, was seen as divine and impersonal – provided they thought clearly, all people should agree on issues of pure reason like mathematics. Thus, the immortality of the mind was not a personal immortality. Rather, when exercising pure reason, people partake in the divine – in God's immortality.

Aristotle's considerable influence on the development of Western philosophy has been most keenly felt in the area of logic. He was the first thinker to look at structures of deductive arguments, or syllogisms. A syllogism is an argument in three parts: a major premise, a minor premise and a conclusion. He found that many deductive arguments could be expressed this way and also that they existed in recurring forms. For example, all people are mortal (major premise), Socrates is a person (minor premise), therefore Socrates is mortal (conclusion) – this form is called 'Barbara'. Or, all people are rational, some animals are people, therefore some animals are rational – this form is called 'Darii', and there are others. Notice that by replacing 'person' with 'A', 'mortal' with 'B' and 'Socrates' with 'C', then 'Barbara' can be expressed thus: all A's are B, C is an A, therefore C is a B. This is symbolic logic, and this is loosely where Frege and Bertrand Russell picked up Aristotle's thread more than 2000 years after his death. ■

Literature

The first, and greatest, ancient Greek writer was Homer, author of the *Iliad* and *Odyssey*. Nothing is known of Homer's life or where or when he lived, or whether, as it is alleged, he was blind. The historian Herodotus thought Homer lived in the 9th century BC, and no scholar since has proved nor disproved this.

Herodotus was the author of the first historical work about Western civilisation. His highly subjective account of the Persian Wars has, however, led him to be regarded as the 'father of lies' as well as the 'father of history'. The historian Thucydides was more objective in his approach, but took a high moral stance. He wrote an account of the Peloponnesian Wars, and also the famous *Melian Dialogue*, which chronicles the talks between the Athenians and Melians prior to the Athenian siege of Melos. Pindar (518-438 BC) is regarded as the pre-eminent lyric poet of ancient Greece. He was commissioned to recite his odes at the Olympic Games. The greatest writers of love poetry were Sappho and Alcaeus, both of whom lived on Lesvos in the 5th century. Sappho's poetic descriptions of her affections for other women gave rise to the term 'lesbian'.

In Byzantine times, poetry, like all of the arts, was of a religious nature. During Ottoman rule, poetry was inextricably linked with folk songs, which were not written down but passed on by word of mouth. Many of these songs were composed by the klephts, and told of the harshness of life in the mountains, and of their uprisings against the Turks.

Dionysios Solomos (1798-1857) and Andreas Kalvos (1796-1869), who were both born on Zakynthos, are regarded as the first modern Greek poets. Solomos' work was heavily nationalistic and his *Hymn to Freedom* became the Greek national anthem. At this time there were heated debates among writers, politicians and educators about whether the official language should be Demotiki or Katharevousa. Demotic was the spoken language of the people and Katharevousa was an artificial language loosely based on Ancient Greek. Almost all writers favoured demotic, and from the time of Solomos, most wrote only in that language. The highly acclaimed poet Constantine Cavafy (1863-1933) was less concerned with nationalism, being a resident of Alexandria, in Egypt; he wrote many love poems.

The best known 20th-century Greek poets are George Seferis (1900-71), who won the Nobel prize in 1963, and Odysseus Elytis (born 1911), who won the same prize in 1979. Seferis drew his inspiration from the Greek myths, whereas Elytis' work is surreal. Angelos Sikelianos (1884-1951) was another poet who drew inspiration from ancient Greece, particularly Delphi, where he lived. His poetry is highly evocative, and includes incantatory verses, emulating the Delphic oracle. Yiannis Ritsos is another highly acclaimed Greek poet; his work draws on many aspects of Greece – its landscape, mythology and social issues. The most celebrated 20th-century Greek novelist is Nikos Kazantzakis. See the Books & Maps section in the Facts for the Visitor chapter for a commentary on his works.

Music & Dance

The folk dances of today derive from the ritual dances performed in ancient Greek temples. One of these dances, the *syrtos*, is depicted on ancient Greek vases, and there are references to dances in Homer's works. Many Greek folk dances, including the syrtos, are performed in a circular formation; in ancient times, dancers formed a circle in order to seal themselves off from evil influences.

Each region of Greece has its own dances, but one dance you'll see performed everywhere is the *kalamatianos*, originally from Kalamata in the Peloponnese. It's the dance in which dancers stand in a row with their hands on one anothers' shoulders.

Singing and the playing of musical instruments have also been an integral part of life in Greece since ancient times. Cycladic figurines holding musical instruments resembling harps and flutes date back to

2000 BC. Musical instruments of ancient Greece included the lyre, lute, *piktis* (pipes), *kroupeza* (a percussion instrument), *kithara* (a stringed instrument), *aulos* (a wind instrument), *barbitos* (similar to a violin cello) and the *magadio* (similar to a harp).

If ancient Greeks did not have a musical instrument to accompany their songs, they imitated the sound of one. It is believed that unaccompanied Byzantine choral singing derived from this custom.

The bouzouki, which you will hear everywhere in Greece, is a mandolin-like instrument similar to the Turkish *saz* and *baglama*. It is one of the main instruments of *rembetika* music – the Greek equivalent of the American Blues. The name rembetika

may come from the Turkish word *rembet* which means outlaw. Opinions differ as to the origins of rembetika, but it is probably a hybrid of several different types of music. One source was the music which emerged in the 1870s in the 'low life' cafés called *tekedes* (hashish dens), of urban areas, and especially ports. Another source was the Arabo-Persian music played in sophisticated Middle Eastern music *(cafés amanedes)* in the 19th century. Rembetika was popularised in Greece by the refugees from Asia Minor.

The songs which emerged from the tekedes had themes concerning hashish, prison life, gambling, knife fights etc, whereas café aman music had themes which centred around erotic love. These all came

---

The Music of Georgos Dalaras

Georgos Dalaras is a musical phenomenon in Greece. With a successful career spanning over 26 years, and more than 40 albums of his own and participation in over 50 other albums, he is Greece's undisputed ambassador of song. Essentially unknown to the wider public outside his homeland, Georgos Dalaras nonetheless performs regularly to captive audiences in the USA, Australia, Israel and in many countries in Europe. Two of his albums became the first Greek records to go gold and platinum.

So who is Georgos Dalaras and why is he so popular? He is most famous for his remarkable voice and his commitment to the preservation of the popular Greek song in a commercial musical environment dominated by disco and techno. Georgos Dalaras is a political singer too, and managed to tread the fine line between acceptability and political-pariah status during the dark years of the military junta (1967-74).

In recent times his musical output has embraced the issue of the Turkish occupation of Cyprus with major concerts at Wembley Arena in 1992, the Palais des Congrès in Paris in 1993 and the Meadowlands Arena in New Jersey in 1994. He has participated in cultural and political festivals in Cuba and sang alongside Peter Gabriel and Sting for Amnesty International in 1988 at the Olympic Stadium in Athens.

More than anyone else, Georgos Dalaras was responsible for re-awakening respect for and interest in rembetika – Greek blues of the 1920s. While you're in Greece, try to catch one of his concerts. It will be a rare treat.

It is hard to suggest a representative work from his vast discography, but for a retrospective look at rembetika, have a listen to his double album *50 Chronia Rembetiko*. And the 1972 album *Mikra Asia*, a nostalgic tribute to the 1921 Asia Minor disaster, still stands the test of time as one of the masterpieces of contemporary Greek music. ∎

together in the music of the refugees, from which a subculture of rebels, called *manges*, emerged. The manges wore showy clothes even though they lived in extreme poverty. They worked long hours in menial jobs, and spent their evenings in the tekedes, smoking hashish and singing and dancing. Although hashish was illegal, the law was rarely enforced until Metaxas did his clean-up job in 1936. It was in a tekes in Piraeus that Markos Vamvakaris, now acknowledged as the greatest *rembetis*, was discovered by a recording company in the 1930s.

Metaxas' censorship meant that themes of hashish, prison, gambling and the like disappeared from recordings of rembetika in the late 1930s, but continued clandestinely in some tekedes. This polarised the music, and the recordings, stripped of their 'meaty' themes and language, became insipid and bourgeois; recorded rembetika even adopted another name – *laiko tragoudi* – to disassociate it from its illegal roots. WW II brought a halt to recording, but a number of composers emerged at this time. They included Apostolos Kaldaras, Yiannis Papaïoanou, Georgos Mitsakis and Manolis Hiotis, and one of the greatest female rembetika singers, Sotiria Bellou, appeared at this time.

During the 1950s and 1960s rembetika became increasingly popular, but less and less authentic. Much of the music was glitzy and commercialised, although the period also produced two outstanding composers of popular music (including rembetika) in Mikis Theodorakis and Manos Hatzidakis. The best of Theodorakis' work is the music which he set to the poetry of Seferis, Elytis and Ritsos.

During the junta years, many rembetika clubs were closed down, but interest in genuine rembetika revived in the 1980s – particularly among students and intellectuals. There are now a number of rembetika clubs in Athens.

Since independence, Greece has followed mainstream developments in classical music. The Athens Concert Hall has performances by both national and international musicians.

CULTURE

Traditional Lifestyle

Greece is steeped in traditional customs. Name days (celebrated rather than birthdays), weddings and funerals all have great significance. On someone's name day an open-house policy is adopted and refreshments are served to wellwishers who stop by to give gifts. Weddings are highly festive occasions, with dancing, feasting and drinking sometimes continuing for days.

Greeks tend to be more superstitious than other Europeans. Tuesday is considered an unlucky day because on that day the Byzantine Empire fell to the Ottomans. Many Greeks will not sign an important transaction, get married or begin a trip on a Tuesday. Greeks also believe in the 'evil eye', a superstition prevalent in many Middle Eastern countries. If someone is the victim of the evil eye, then bad luck will befall them. The bad luck is the result of someone's envy, therefore one should avoid being too complimentary about things of beauty, especially newborn babies. To ward off the evil eye, Greeks often wear a piece of blue glass, resembling an eye, on a chain around their necks.

Avoiding Offence

The Greeks' reputation for hospitality is not a myth. Greece is probably the only country in Europe where you may be invited into a stranger's home for coffee, a meal or even to spend the night. This can often lead to a feeling of uneasiness in the recipient if the host is poor, but to offer money is considered offensive. The most acceptable way of saying thank you is through a gift, perhaps to a child in the family. A similar situation arises if you go out for a meal with Greeks; the bill is not shared as in northern European countries, but paid by the host.

When drinking wine it is the custom to only half fill the glass. It is bad manners to empty the glass, so it must be constantly replenished. When visiting someone you will be offered coffee and it is bad manners to refuse. You will also be given a glass of water and perhaps a small serve of preserves.

It is the custom to drink the water, then eat the preserves and then drink the coffee.

Personal questions are not considered rude in Greece, and if you react as if they are you will be the one causing offence. You will be inundated with queries about your age, salary, marital status etc – expect commiserations if you are over 25 and not married!

If you go into a *kafeneio*, taverna, or shop, it is the custom to greet the waiters or assistant with *kalimera* (good day) or *kalispera* (good evening) – likewise if you meet someone in the street.

You may have come to Greece for sun, sand and sea, but if you want to bare all, other than on a designated nude beach, remember that Greece is a traditional country, so take care not to offend the locals.

Sport

Greek men are football and basketball mad, both as spectators and participants. If you happen to be eating in a taverna on a night when a big match is being televised, expect indifferent service.

RELIGION

About 98% of Greeks belong to the Greek Orthodox Church. Most of the remainder are either Roman Catholic, Jewish or Muslim.

Philippi, in Macedonia, is reputedly the first place in Europe where St Paul preached the gospel. This was in 49 AD, and during the next five years he preached also in Athens, Thessaloniki and Corinth.

The Greek Orthodox Church is closely related to the Russian Orthodox Church and together with it forms the third-largest branch of Christianity. Orthodox, meaning 'right belief', was founded in the 4th century by Constantine the Great, who was converted to Christianity by a vision of the Cross.

By the 8th century, there were a number of differences of opinion between the Pope

in Rome and the Patriarch of Constantinople, as well as increasing rivalry between the two. One dispute was over the wording of the Creed. The original Creed stated that the Holy Spirit proceeds 'from the Father', which the Orthodox Church adhered to, whereas Rome added 'and the Son'. Another bone of contention concerned the celibacy of the clergy. Rome decreed priests had to be celibate; in the Orthodox Church, a priest could marry before he became ordained. There were also differences in fasting: in the Orthodox Church, not only was meat forbidden during Lent, but wine and oil were also.

By the 11th century these differences had become irreconcilable, and in 1054 the Pope and the Patriarch excommunicated one another. Ever since, the two have gone their separate ways as the (Greek/Russian) Orthodox Church and the Roman Catholic Church.

During Ottoman times membership of the Orthodox Church was one of the most important criteria in defining a Greek, regardless of where he or she lived. The church was the principal upholder of Greek culture and traditions.

Religion is still integral to life in Greece, and the Greek year is centred around the festivals of the church calendar. Most Greeks, when they have a problem, will go into a church and light a candle to the saint they feel is most likely to help them. On the islands you will see hundreds of tiny churches dotted around the countryside. Most have been built by individual families in the name of their selected patron saint as thanksgiving for God's protection.

If you wish to look around a church, you should dress appropriately. Women should wear skirts that reach below the knees, and men should wear long trousers and have their arms covered. Regrettably many churches are kept locked nowadays, but it's usually easy enough to locate caretakers, who will be happy to open them up for you.

Greek Art
through the Ages

Greece has preserved its art and architecture over a period of some 4000 years. This heritage remains remarkably accessible and is part of modern Greek life today. It also draws people back to Greece again and again. Visitors come to search for ancient frescoes, marble temples, crusader castles, and Byzantine churches, icons and mosaics. There are also relics of Greece's more recent history: the monuments and art which recall the War of Independence, traditional village life and folk arts, and contemporary art.

There is a variety of museums, too, through which each region reveals its own story.

Wherever the search leads, the journey can be as rewarding as the goal.

Previous page: Fisherman; fresco from Akrotiri, Santorini (Thira), c. 1600 BC (National Archaeological Museum, Athens)

Right: Children boxing; fresco from Akrotiri, Santorini (Thira), c. 1600 BC

NATIONAL ARCHAEOLOGICAL MUSEUM, ATHENS

CYCLADES & MINOAN CRETE

The prehistoric art of Greece has been discovered only recently, notably in the Cyclades and on Crete. Smooth, flattish figurines, carved from the high-quality marble of Paros and Naxos in the middle of the 3rd millennium BC, caught the imagination of 20th-century artists and collectors because of their pared-down style.

Even more recently, in the 1960s and 1970s, excavations on Santorini (Thira) have revealed houses with frescoes preserved by the eruption of the island's volcano in the late 17th century BC. They were painted in fresco technique using yellow, blue, red and black pigments, with some details added after the plaster had dried. Plants and animals are depicted as well as men and women. Figures are usually shown in profile or in a combination of profile and frontal views. Stylistically, the frescoes are similar to the paintings of Minoan Crete, which are less well preserved. Some of these frescoes are now in the National Archaeological Museum in Athens, while others, such as the narrative frieze showing ships and harbour towns, will be displayed in a new museum on Santorini.

Minoan culture, dating from the third millennium until around 1400 BC, is named after the legendary King Minos, whose wife gave birth to the Minotaur.

In 1899 Sir Arthur Evans began excavations of the huge palace and residential complex at Knossos and over the next 30 years substantially reconstructed it, restoring many of its very fragmentary frescoes *in situ*. Similar palaces on Crete, usually of two storeys and built around a large courtyard, have since been excavated at Phaestos, Agia Triada, Malia, Gournia and Zakros.

Left: Marble figurine of a woman; Early Cycladic, c. 2800-2300 BC

Right: Marble figurine of a seated figure proposing a toast; Early Cycladic, c. 2800-2300 BC

NICHOLAS P GOULANDRIS FOUNDATION & MUSEUM OF CYCLADIC ART

NICHOLAS P GOULANDRIS FOUNDATION & MUSEUM OF CYCLADIC ART

ANN JOUSIFFE

Ceramics are ubiquitous on Greek sites, especially after the introduction of wheel-made pottery in about 2000 BC. Minoan pottery is often characterised by a high centre of gravity and beak-like spouts. Painted decoration was applied as a white clay slip (a thin paste of clay and water) or one which fired to a greyish black or dull red. Flowing designs with spiral or marine and plant motifs were used. The Archaeological Museum in Iraklio has a wealth of Minoan material, including frescoes and intricately carved seals.

MYCENAEAN GREECE

In the 1870s Heinrich Schliemann, after excavating at Troy near the entrance to the Dardanelles, had turned to the mainland Greek sites of Mycenae and Tiryns. This mainland Greek-speaking Mycenaean culture superseded the Minoan culture on Crete and flourished from around 1600 to 1200 BC. Characteristic of these sites are walls of massive, 'Cyclopean' stonework, such as at Tiryns, and palaces with a megaron (reception room) which had a central hearth and a roof supported by four internal columns.

Prestigious beehive-shaped stone tombs covered by a mound of earth have been found not only at Mycenae, where two large ones are romantically known as the tombs of Agamemnon and Clytaemnestra, but also at Pylos and elsewhere.

Mycenaean pottery shapes include a long-stemmed goblet and a globular vase with handles resembling a pair of stirrups. Decorative motifs are similar to those on Minoan pottery but rather stiffer. Small terracottas of women with a circular body or with arms upraised are known to modern scholars as phi (ϕ) and psi (ψ) figurines from their resemblance to these letters of the Greek alphabet. Such artefacts have been found over a wide area around the Mediterranean, indicating extensive trade. Spectacular Mycenaean gold masks, diadems, cups and dress ornaments; dagger blades with battle scenes inlaid in gold and silver; carved ivory and seal-stones; and pottery occupy the central hall of the Archaeological Museum in Athens.

The Mycenaean palaces were burnt and the culture was largely destroyed for reasons unknown around 1200 BC. This is also the traditional date given for the Greek sacking of Troy, but Homer's epics, given written form first in the 8th century BC, reflect an earlier stage of Mycenaean culture.

PROTOGEOMETRIC & GEOMETRIC POTTERY

The archaeological record picks up again around 1000 BC with substantial pots decorated with blackish-brown horizontal lines around the circumference, hatched triangles, and compass-drawn concentric circles. This Protogeometric style was followed by the more crowded decoration of geometric patterning, often in bands or panels, and with stylised animal friezes. Some geometric pots from around 750 BC, used as grave markers in the Dipylon cemetery in Athens, have panels depicting the corpse on a bier surrounded by stick-like figures tearing at their hair in mourning. Terracotta figurines of horses suggest an equestrian aristocracy. By the 7th century BC, Corinth was producing pottery with added white and purple-red clay slip and friezes of lions, goats and swans, with details incised and a background fill of rosettes.

Facing page: The palace at Knossos, Crete

ARCHAIC PERIOD

In the 6th century BC the first large stone temples were built, like that at Corinth with its unusual monolithic columns. The first life-size marble statues, the stiff nude male kouros and draped female kore, were carved with an obvious debt to Egyptian sculpture. Athens took over from Corinth in pottery production using red clay with a high iron content. A thick colloidal slip made from this clay produced a glossy black surface which contrasted with the red and was enlivened with added white and purple-red. Details were incised through the slip before firing. Scenes from Greek mythology, especially showing Heracles and his labours or Dionysos, the god of wine, replaced animal motifs. The ability to draw three-quarter views of the human figure on vases, and presumably also on lost wooden panels, coincided with the steady development of naturalism in sculpture, as seen in the reliefs from the 6th-century BC temple-like treasuries at Delphi. By 480 BC, after the sacking of Athens' Acropolis by the Persians, naturalism was being achieved for the first time in European art. This period, through to the death of Alexander the Great in 323 AD, is known as 'classical'.

Left: Theseus fights the Minotaur; Attic black-figure belly amphora, c. 540 BC

Right: Triptolemos on his wheeled and winged throne; Attic red-figure column krater, by the Nausikaa Painter, 450-445 BC

Bottom: Detail from Eastern Greek Caeretan hydria; 520-51 BC

NICHOLAS P GOULANDRIS FOUNDATION & MUSEUM OF CYCLADIC ART

NICHOLAS P GOULANDRIS FOUNDATION & MUSEUM OF CYCLADIC ART

NICHOLAS P GOULANDRIS FOUNDATION & MUSEUM OF CYCLADIC ART

CLASSICAL PERIOD

The art of classical Greece shows an obsession with the human figure and with drapery. At first the classical style was rather severe, as with the bronze charioteer at Delphi, the Zeus from Artemision in the Athens Archaeological Museum, and the sculpture from the temple at Olympia. Sculptors sought ideal proportions for the human figure. New poses were explored and the figures became increasingly sinuous, with smaller heads in relation to the body. The nude female figure first appeared in the 4th century BC as Aphrodite.

Apart from the 5th-century marble relief sculpture on the temples and some very moving Attic tombstones, little original work of the classical period survives. Most free-standing classical sculpture described by ancient writers was made of bronze and survives only as marble copies made by the Romans. In the last century, however, some classical

NATIONAL ARCHAEOLOGICAL MUSEUM, ATHENS

Grave stele of a woman with her maid; Attic, early 4th century BC

bronzes, lost when they were being shipped abroad in antiquity, have been recovered from the sea.

Europeans first drew on Roman works for their knowledge of Greek architecture. The three major Greek styles were known from the tiers of columns on the Colosseum in Rome. Whereas the rather plain Doric and the Ionic voluted capitals were more commonly used in Greece, for example on the colonnades surrounding temples, Romans preferred the Corinthian capitals based on the acanthus leaf. Thus, when the Romans finally completed the large temple of Olympian Zeus in Athens, it was in the Corinthian order.

It was only after the publication in the 18th century of engravings made from measured architectural drawings of monuments like the Parthenon and Erechtheion on the Acropolis that a genuine Greek Revival style was possible in Europe. It is the 5th-century temples such as the Parthenon, Erechtheion and Temple of Athena Nike on the Acropolis of Athens, and the temples at Olympia and on Aegina, that epitomise classical Greek art.

The classical period was also the time when the Greek tragedies of Aeschylus, Sophocles and Euripides and the comedies of Aristophanes were written and first performed in the theatre built into the slope of Athens' Acropolis. The ancient theatres at Dodoni, Megalopolis, Epidaurus and Argos are larger, the latter seating about 20,000; most are still used for summer festivals and have excellent acoustics.

The Parthenon, Athens;
5th century BC

ANN JOUSIFFE

HELLENISTIC PERIOD

During the Hellenistic period (323-31 BC) sculpture often showed greater realism than the classical. It was able to express suffering and old age, and delighted in the grotesque. In this period, too, when the empire won by Alexander was centred on Macedon in Northern Greece, Antioch in Syria, and Alexandria in Egypt, portraiture first came into its own in sculpture and on coins. There are also traces of paintings on tombstones at Volos and on the walls of some of the temple-like tombs of Macedonia. Gold was again available at this time in some quantity, as can be seen from the furnishings of Philip of Macedon's tomb, now in the Archaeological Museum in Thessaloniki, and from the exquisite jewellery of the period.

Cities of the eastern Mediterranean became increasingly wealthy and Delos, which had been a sacred island, developed as a cosmopolitan commercial centre in the 2nd century BC judging from the remains of lavish houses with floor mosaics, a theatre and sanctuaries for Eastern cults as well as for Apollo.

NATIONAL ARCHAEOLOGICAL MUSEUM, ATHENS

Statuette of a boy playing with a goose; marble, 3rd century BC

ROMAN PERIOD

In the Hellenistic and Roman period Athens, with its marble from Mt Pendeli, continued to produce sculpture, largely for export. It received prestigious buildings such as the theatre donated by Herodes Atticus (now lacking a roof but again used for concerts and drama) and large colonnaded stoas were added to frame the Agora.

From the middle of the 2nd century BC, when Rome gained control of Greece, Corinth became an important Roman city with fountains, baths and gymnasia which have been excavated in recent years. Athens obtained a new commercial agora (now known as the Roman Agora) in the time of Augustus, at the end of the 1st century BC, and a century and a half later the emperor Hadrian endowed the city with a library and built an elegant arch which still stands between the old and new parts of the city.

In the northern town of Philippi there are substantial architectural remains of large early Christian churches, and early mosaics have survived in the Church of St Dimitrios in Thessaloniki.

BYZANTINE PERIOD

During the Byzantine period, through to 1453, Constantinople was the most important Greek-speaking city. The Parthenon in Athens was converted into a church and smaller churches were built throughout Greece, especially from the 10th century on. Usually they had a central dome supported by four arches on piers and flanked by vaults, with smaller domes at the four corners and three apses to the east. The external brickwork, which alternates with stone, is sometimes set in patterns. The churches were usually decorated with frescoes on a dark-blue ground with a bust of Christ in the dome; the four Gospel-writers in the pendentives supporting the dome; the Virgin and Child in the apse; then scenes from the life of Christ (Annunciation, Nativity, Baptism, Entry into Jerusalem, Crucifixion and Transfiguration); and, below that, at the lowest level, figures of the saints. In the later centuries the scenes involve more detailed narratives, including cycles of the life of the Virgin and the miracles of Christ.

Judas' Betrayal of Christ; mosaic from the monastery church at Dafni, 11th century

DAFNI MONASTERY & THE GREEK MINISTRY OF CULTURE

Three 11th-century churches – at Dafni, at Moni Osiou Louka near Delphi, and at Nea Moni on Chios – retain their mosaic wall decoration with tesserae of coloured glass for the figures, and glass with gold leaf for the background. At Kastoria, in Epiros, and in the Mani there are small chapels of simple design; some at Kastoria have scenes painted on the exterior walls. At Mt Athos and on Patmos, where the first monasteries were built in the 10th century, the monastic buildings as well as the churches survive, though much has changed through centuries of continuous use and a number of fires. At Meteora, in Central Greece, the monasteries are built high on precipitous rocks and for centuries were almost inaccessible. In addition to their frescoes, all these monasteries retain some of their ecclesiastical treasures, including manuscripts, vestments, icons and silver. Marble reliefs from the earliest churches and early icons are a special feature of the Byzantine Museum in Athens.

After the temporary fall of Constantinople to a crusading army in 1204, much of Greece became the fiefdoms of Western aristocrats. The most notable of these was the Villehardouin family, who built castles in the Peloponnese at Hlemoutsi, Nafplio, Kalamata and Mystras. At Mystras

BENAKI MUSEUM, ATHENS

The Virgin Enthroned, with a border of scenes from the life of Christ and portraits of saints; icon of the Cretan school, 16th century

BYZANTINE MUSEUM, ATHENS

BYZANTINE MUSEUM, ATHENS

BYZANTINE MUSEUM, ATHENS

BENAKI MUSEUM, ATHENS

they also built a palace which became, for two centuries prior to the Turkish conquest, a court of the Byzantine imperial family, second only to Constantinople. The now empty frescoed churches and two-storey houses on the steep hillside of Mystras convey the spirit of this late Byzantine administrative and intellectual centre which also had strong links with Renaissance Italy. The Byzantines also held onto Monemvassia with its castle and churches on the south-eastern tip of the Peloponnese, while the Venetians built castles on the south-western tip at Koroni and at Methoni. Byzantines, Franks and Venetians all contributed in turn to building the fortress above Corinth.

The Venetian settlements on Crete and other islands were long-lasting as they profited from supplying the ships which ferried crusaders to the Holy Land and from trading with Constantinople and the Ottomans.

The Byzantine fortress at Lindos on Rhodes, like the town of Rhodes itself, was taken over by the Knights of St John of Jerusalem. These medieval towns and most of the great enceintes have been carefully restored.

BENAKI MUSEUM, ATHENS

Facing page:
Top left: The Archangel Michael; icon, 14th century

Top right: St John the Theologian on Patmos dictating the Book of Revelations to Prochoros; icon, 17th to 18th century

Bottom left: St Constantine the Great and St Helena; icon, 18th century

Bottom right: The Presentation of Christ in the Temple and the Baptism of Christ in the River Jordan by John the Baptist; icon of the Cretan school, 16th century

This page:
Left: Gold pendant with enamels and pearls, from Patmos; 18th century

TURKISH OCCUPATION

Few of the wooden houses of the Ottoman period survive and there are now only a few mosques, mostly in the north, but also in Athens. Kavala, Xanthi and Didymotiho near the Turkish border retain some of this architecture.

In Ioannina the local ruler Ali Pasha maintained an idiosyncratic court in the late 18th and early 19th centuries in what had been the Byzantine fortress. One of the mosques by the lake is now a museum housing Epirote costumes of this period.

The numerous folk museums of Greece, such as those at Kastoria and Thessaloniki, illustrate the culture of Greeks under Turkish rule which, in northern Greece, lasted into the 20th century.

MODERN GREECE

After the War of Independence, Greece continued the neoclassical style, dominant in Western European architecture and sculpture at the turn of the century, thus providing a sense of continuity with its ancient past. This neoclassical style is apparent in Nafplio, initially the capital, and in Athens, notably in the Doric and Ionic ensemble of the National Library and the university. Notable, too, are the old royal palace, the Polytehnio, and the mansions which are now the Byzantine, Benaki and Kanellopoulos museums. Architects working in this style were mainly Germans or Greeks: C and T von Hansen, E Ziller, L Kaftanzoglu, Leo von Klenze and S Kleanthes. In many towns the archaeological museums, town halls, law courts and mansions exhibit the same

Blind Eros and Two Sirens; *painting on wood by Agapios Manganaris of Sifnos;1825*

BYZANTINE MUSEUM, ATHENS

PAUL HELLANDER

BENAKI MUSEUM, ATHENS

BENAKI MUSEUM, ATHENS

Top: Painted ceiling, Kastoria Folk Museum

Middle: Embroidery from Ioannina; 18th century

Bottom: Cushion embroidered with a forked-tailed Gorgon in the centre; from Crete, 18th to 19th century

restrained form of neoclassicism. The cemetery of Ermoupolis, on Syros, and the First Cemetery of Athens are virtual museums of 19th-century Greek sculpture, again in the classical tradition.

With the German Otho on the Greek throne, the Munich school of art, working in the traditions of classicism and romanticism, was the main influence on Greek painters after independence. During the 19th century, however, Greek artists trained in various centres of Europe, including Rome and Paris. Andreas Kriezis specialised in portraits and nautical themes, and Dionysios Tsokos and Theodoros Vryzakis often focused on the War of Independence. Nikiphoros Lytras, Konstantinos Volanakis and Nicholas Gyzis, in the second half of the century, chose genre scenes and their paintings became more pictorial than descriptive. Gyzis' historical paintings were more visionary, coinciding with the fascination with the Great Idea of a new Greek empire. The settings, costumes and historical subjects of many of these 19th-century paintings express Greek conditions of the time.

From the first decades of the 20th century, artists like Konstantinos Parthenis and Konstantinos Kaleas and, later, George Bouzianis were able to use the heritage of the past and at the same time assimilated various developments in modern art. These paintings are best studied in the National Art Gallery in Athens where there is also some sculpture and works of the naive painters and water colourists, notably Panayiotis Zographos.

Naive painters are also represented in folk-art museums. Theses artists often paint directly onto wood panels, as with icons, and choose subjects like ships, wedding festivities, portraits and village life. Painted shop signs and painted wooden ceiling and wall panels and frescoes in houses are special genres.

Weaving and embroidery display regional characteristics. They survive in some quantity from the 17th century on. Geometric and stylised animal and bird motifs on a natural linen ground are most common in needlework, the designs laid out by counting threads. On the mainland, embroidery was applied particularly to dress, and on the islands to household articles like bed curtains, cushion covers and towels. Rich reds, greens, browns, deep blues and pale yellows predominate.

Floral designs, pastel colours and freehand patterns usually reflect Turkish influence, as in Epiros or the islands near Turkey. Italian influence occurs in Crete and in white embroideries and drawn-thread work. Ecclesiastical vestments and altar cloths are also richly embroidered. The conservatism of designs may be linked to the desire to preserve local traditions in the face of Turkish rule.

Ceramics, woodcarving and metal work have achieved rather less prominence. Wooden chests and icon screens and sanctuary doors in churches were often elaborately carved and there was a folk tradition of carved figures on ships' prows. Silversmiths produced liturgical vessels and crosses, ornate Gospel covers, icon frames, and sword sheaths. The Benaki Museum in Athens has the finest collection of decorative arts from medieval and modern Greece as well as some from earlier centuries.

Ann Moffatt, Australian National University, Canberra

Further reading:

Greek Art and Archaeology by J G Pedley, Cassell, London, 1992
The Greek Museums by M Andronicos et al, Athens, 1975

Facts for the Visitor

VISAS & EMBASSIES

Nationals of Australia, Canada, all EU countries, Israel, Japan, New Zealand, Norway, Iceland, Switzerland and the USA can stay in Greece for up to three months without a visa. Greek embassies have a list of other nationalities allowed in without a visa. The list changes, but includes nationals of the European principalities of Monaco and San Marino and most South American countries. Those not on the list, such as South Africans, can expect to pay about US$20 for a three-month visa.

Greek Embassies

The following is a selection of Greek diplomatic missions abroad:

Albania
  Rruga Frederik Shiroka, Tiranë (☎ 342 90)
Australia
  9 Turrana St, Yarralumla, Canberra ACT 2600 (☎ 062-73 3011)
Bulgaria
  Klement Gottwald 68, Sofia (☎ 02-44 3770)
Canada
  76-80 Maclaren St, Ottawa, Ontario K2P OK6 (☎ 613-238 6271)
Cyprus
  Byron Boulevard 8-10, Nicosia (☎ 02-44 18802)
Denmark
  Borgergade 16, 1300 Copenhagen K (☎ 33 11 4533)
Egypt
  18 Aisha el Taymouria, Garden City, Cairo (☎ 02-355 1074)
France
  17 Rue Auguste Vacquerie, 75116 Paris (☎ 01-47.23.72.28)
Germany
  Koblenzer Str 103, 5300 Bonn 2 (☎ 228-83010)
Ireland
  1 Upper Pembroke St, Dublin 2 (☎ 01-767 254/255)
Israel
  35 Shaul Hameleck St, PO Box 33631 (☎ 03-695 9704)
Italy
  Via S Mercadante 36, Rome 00198 (☎ 06-854 9630)

Japan
  16-30 Nishi Azabu, 3-chome, Minato-ku, Tokyo 106 (☎ 03-340 0871/0872)
New Zealand
  5-7 Willeston St, Wellington (☎ 04-473 7775)
Netherlands
  Dr Kuiper 10, The Hague (☎ 070-363 87 00)
Norway
  Nobels Gate 45, 0244 Oslo 2 (☎ 22 44 2728)
South Africa
  Reserve Bank Building, St George's Rd, Capetown (☎ 21-24 8161)
Spain
  Avenida Doctor Arce 24, Madrid 28002 (☎ 01-564 4653)
Sweden
  Riddargatan 60, 11457 Stockholm (☎ 08-663 7577)
Switzerland
  Jungfraustrasse 3, 3005 Bern (☎ 31-352 1637)
Turkey
  Ziya-ul-Rahman Caddesi 9-11, Gaziosmanpaşa 06700, Ankara (☎ 312-446 5496)
UK
  1A Holland Park, London W11 3TP (☎ 0171-229 3850)
USA
  2221 Massachusetts Ave NW, Washington DC 20008 (☎ 202-667 3169)

Visa Extensions

If you wish to stay in Greece for longer than three months, apply at a consulate abroad or at least 20 days in advance to the Aliens' Bureau (☎ 01-770 5711), Leoforos Alexandras 173, Athens. Take your passport and four passport photographs along. You may be asked for proof that you can support yourself financially, so keep all your bank exchange slips (or the equivalent from a post office). These slips are not always automatically given – you may have to ask for them. The Aliens Bureau is open from 8 am to 1 pm on weekdays. Elsewhere in Greece apply to the local police authority. You will be given a permit which will authorise you to stay in the country for a period of up to six months. Many travellers overcome this red tape by briefly visiting Turkey and then re-entering Greece.

Turkish-Occupied North Cyprus

Greece will refuse entry to people whose passport indicates that they have visited Turkish-occupied North Cyprus since November 1983. This can be overcome if, upon entering North Cyprus, you ask the immigration officials to stamp a piece of paper (loose-leaf visa) rather than your passport. If you enter North Cyprus from the Greek Republic of Cyprus (only possible for a day visit), an exit stamp is not put into your passport.

Foreign Embassies in Greece

All foreign embassies in Greece are in Athens and its suburbs. There are consulates of various countries in Thessaloniki, Patras, Corfu, Rhodes and Iraklio. See the relevant chapters for details. Foreign embassies in Athens (telephone code 01) include:

Albania
    Karahristou 1, Athens 115 21 (☎ 723 4412)
Australia
    Dimitrou Soutsou 37, Athens 115 21
    (☎ 644 7303)
Bulgaria
    Stratigou Kallari 33A, Psyhiko, Athens 154 52
    (☎ 647 8105)
Canada
    Genadiou 4, Athens 115 21 (☎ 725 4011)
Cyprus
    Herodotou 16, Athens 106 75 (☎ 723 7883)
Egypt
    Leoforos Vasilissis Sofias 3, Athens 106 71
    (☎ 361 8612)
France
    Leoforos Vasilissis Sofias 7, Athens 106 71
    (☎ 361 1663)
Germany
    Dimitriou 3 & Karaoli, Kolonaki, Athens 106 75
    (☎ 728 5111)
Ireland
    Leoforos Vasileos Konstantinou 7, Athens 106
    74 (☎ 723 2771)
Israel
    Marathonodromou 1, Psyhiko, Athens 154 52
    (☎ 671 9530)
Italy
    Sekeri 2, Athens 106 74 (☎ 361 7260)

Japan
    Athens Tower, Leoforos Messogion 2-4, Athens
    115 27 (☎ 775 8101)
Netherlands
    Vasileos Konstantinou 5-7, Athens 106 74
    (☎ 723 9701)
New Zealand (Honorary Consulate)
    Semitelou 9, Athens 115 28 (☎ 771 0112)
South Africa
    Kifissias 60, Maroussi, Athens 151 25
    (☎ 689 5330)
Turkey
    Vasilissis Georgiou B 8, Athens 106 74
    (☎ 724 5915)
UK
    Ploutarhou 1, Athens 106 75 (☎ 723 6211)
USA
    Leoforos Vasilissis Sofias 91, Athens 115 21
    (☎ 721 2951)

DOCUMENTS

To enter Greece you need a valid passport or, for EU nationals, travel documents (ID cards). You must produce your passport or EU travel documents when you register in a hotel or pension in Greece. You will find that many accommodation proprietors will want to keep your passport during your stay. This is not a compulsory requirement; they need it only long enough to take down the details.

If you want to rent a car or motorbike, you will need an International Driving Permit or, if you are from an EU country, an EU driving licence. An International Driving Permit can be obtained before you leave home or from the ELPA (Greek Automobile Touring Club) on production of a national driving licence, passport and photograph. See the Useful Organisations in this chapter for contact details. For information on student cards see the information box later in this chapter.

CUSTOMS

There are no longer duty-free restrictions within the EU. This does not mean, however, that customs checks have been dispensed with: random searches are still made for drugs.

Arrival & Departure

Upon entering the country from outside the EU, customs inspection is usually cursory for foreign tourists. There may be spot-checks, but you probably won't have to open your bags. A verbal declaration is usually all that is required.

You may bring the following into Greece duty free: 200 cigarettes or 50 cigars; one litre of spirits or two litres of wine; 50 grams of perfume; 250 ml of eau de cologne; one camera (still or video) and film; a pair of binoculars; a portable musical instrument; a portable radio or tape recorder; a typewriter; sports equipment; and dogs and cats (with a veterinary certificate).

Importation of works of art and antiquities is free, but they must be declared on entry, so that they can be re-exported. Import regulations for medicines are strict; if you are taking medication, make sure you get a statement from your doctor before you leave home. It is illegal, for instance, to take codeine into Greece without an accompanying doctor's certificate.

An unlimited amount of foreign currency and travellers' cheques may be brought into Greece. If, however, you intend to leave the country with foreign banknotes in excess of US$1000, you must declare the sum upon entry. You may import 100,000 dr and export up to 20,000 dr.

Restrictions apply to the importation of sailboards into Greece. See the Activities section later in this chapter for more details.

It is strictly forbidden to export antiquities (anything over 100 years old) without an export permit. This crime is second only to drug smuggling in the penalties imposed. It is an offence to remove even the smallest article from an archaeological site.

The place to apply for an export permit is Antique Dealers & Private Collections Section, The Archaeological Service, Polignotou 13, Athens.

Vehicles

Cars can be brought into Greece for four months without a carnet; only a green card (international third-party insurance) is required. Your vehicle will be registered in your passport when you enter Greece in order to prevent you leaving the country without it.

MONEY

Banks will exchange all major currencies in either cash, travellers' cheques or Eurocheques. To get Eurocheques you need a European bank account and usually have to wait at least two weeks to receive the cheques. The best known travellers' cheques in Greece are Thomas Cook and American Express. A passport is required to change travellers' cheques, but not cash.

Commission charged on the exchange of banknotes and travellers' cheques varies not only from bank to bank but from branch to branch. It's less for cash than for travellers' cheques. The lowest charges levied are 200 dr for cash (banknotes only; no coins) with a value of up to 20,000 dr, and 400 dr for cash with a value above 20,000 dr.

For travellers' cheques the commission levied is 350 dr up to 20,000 dr; 450 dr for amounts between 20,000 and 30,000 dr; and a flat rate of 1.5% is levied on amounts over 30,000 dr. No commission is charged on Eurocheques.

All post offices have exchange facilities for banknotes, travellers' cheques and Eurocheques, and charge less commission than banks. It is often quicker to change money at a post office than in a bank. Many travel agencies and hotels will also change money, travellers' cheques and Eurocheques at bank rates, but their commission charges are higher.

All major credit cards and Eurocheques are acceptable, but only in the larger, more expensive establishments. Some C-class hotels accept credit cards, but D and E-class hotels rarely do. Most up-market restaurants also accept credit cards. Visa, Access (MasterCard) and Eurocard are the most widely accepted credit cards.

You can get a cash advance on a Visa card at the Commercial Bank of Greece and on Access (MasterCard) at the National Bank of Greece. Most branches of these banks – and others – have 24-hour automatic teller machines (ATMs), some of which can give you direct access to your bank account at home if you have a Maestro-Cirrus card. Some banks also have 24-hour automatic exchange machines which accept banknotes of most European countries as well as Australian, Canadian and US dollars, and Japanese yen.

There are restrictions on the amount of drachmas you may bring in or take out of Greece. See the Customs section earlier in this chapter for details.

International Transfers

If you run out of money or need more for whatever reason, you can instruct your bank back home to send you a draft. Specify the city and the bank as well as the branch that you want the money sent to. If you have the choice, select a large bank and ask for the international division.

Money sent by telegraphic transfer (which usually involves a charge of US$20 or more, but ask) should reach you within a week; by mail, allow at least two weeks. When it arrives, it will most likely be converted into drachmas – you can take it as it is or buy travellers' cheques. US citizens can also use Western Union, which has offices in Athens, Piraeus and Thessaloniki.

Currency

The unit of currency is the drachma. Coins come in denominations of five, 10, 20, 50 and 100 dr. Bank notes come in 50, 100, 500, 1000, 5000 and 10,000 dr. The larger notes can be difficult to change in remote areas.

Exchange Rates

Australia	A$1	=	177.59 dr
Canada	C$1	=	173.38 dr
Japan	¥100	=	226.16 dr
Germany	DM1	=	164.62 dr
New Zealand	NZ$1	=	152.72dr
USA	US$1	=	233.06dr
UK	UK£1	=	368.12 dr

Costs

Greece is no longer dirt cheap. A rock-bottom daily budget would be 4000 dr. This would mean hitching, staying in youth hostels or camping, staying away from bars, and only occasionally eating in restaurants or taking ferries. Allow at least 8000 dr per

day if you want your own room and plan to eat out regularly as well as travelling about and seeing the sights. You will still need to do a fair bit of self-catering. If you really want a holiday – comfortable rooms and restaurants all the way – you will need closer to 12,000 dr per day. These budgets are for individuals. Couples sharing a double room can get by on less.

Prices vary quite a lot between islands, particularly for accommodation. Hydra and Mykonos are the most expensive; the cheapest tend to be the less well-known ones.

Most museums are free for card-carrying students and teachers from the EU. An International Student Identification Card (ISIC) gets you admission for half price, as does a pensioner card. Otherwise visits to sites and museums quickly cut into your budget. Most small museums charge 400 dr, and major sites and museums cost between 1200 and 2000 dr. They are free on Sunday and public holidays, except for tour groups.

Tipping

In restaurants the service charge is included in the bill but it is the custom to leave a small amount. The practice is often just to round off the bill. Likewise for taxis – a small amount is appreciated.

Bargaining

Bargaining is not as widespread in Greece as it is further east. Prices in most shops are clearly marked and non-negotiable. The same applies to restaurants and public transport. It is always worth bargaining over the price of hotel rooms or domatia, especially if you are intending to stay a few days. You may get short shrift in peak season, but prices can drop dramatically in the off season. Souvenir shops and market stalls are other places where your negotiating skills will come in handy. If you feel uncomfortable about haggling, walking away can be just as effective – you can always go back.

WHEN TO GO

Spring and autumn are the best times to visit Greece. Winter is pretty much a dead loss

Student Cards

An ISIC (International Student Identity Card) is a plastic ID-style card with your photograph. These cards are widely available from budget travel agencies (take along proof that you are a student). In Athens you can get one from the International Student & Youth Travel Service (ISYTS; ☎ 01-323 3767), 2nd floor, Nikis 11.

Some travel agencies in Greece offer discounts on organised tours to students. However, there are no student discounts for travel within Greece, but Olympic Airways gives a 25% discount on domestic flights which are part of an international flight. Turkish Airlines (THY) gives 55% student discounts on its international flights. There are flights from Athens to İstanbul and İzmir. Most shipping lines to Cyprus, Israel and Egypt from Piraeus give a 20% student discount and a few of the lines from Greek to Italian ports do so. If you are under 26 years but not a student, the FIYTO (Federation of International Youth Travel Organisation) card gives similar discounts. Many budget travel agencies issue FIYTO cards including the International Student & Youth Travel Service, Nikis 11, Athens (☎ 01-323 3767); London Explorers Club, 33 Princes Square, Bayswater, London W2 (☎ 0171-792 3770) and SRS Studenten Reise Service, Marienstrasse 23, Berlin (☎ 030-2 83 30 93). ■

outside the major cities. Most of Greece's tourist infrastructure goes into hibernation from the end of November until the beginning of April – hotels and restaurants are closed and bus and ferry services are either drastically reduced or plain cancelled.

The cobwebs are dusted off in time for Easter, when the first tourists start to arrive. Conditions are perfect between Easter and mid-June, when the weather is pleasantly warm in most places, but not too hot; beaches and ancient sites are relatively uncrowded; public transport operates on close to full schedules; and accommodation is cheaper and easier to find.

Mid-June until the end of August is the high season. It's party time on the islands and everything is in full swing. It's also very hot – in July and August the mercury can soar to 40°C in the shade just about anywhere in the country; the beaches are crowded, the ancient sites are swarming with tour groups and in many places accommodation is booked solid.

The season starts to wind down after August and conditions are ideal once more until the shutdown at the end of November. Before ruling out a winter holiday entirely, it's worth considering going skiing (see the Activities section later in this chapter for details).

WHAT TO BRING

Sturdy shoes are essential for clambering around ancient sites and wandering around historic towns and villages, which tend to have lots of steps and cobbled streets. Footwear with ankle support is preferable for trekking, although many visitors get by with trainers.

A day pack is useful for the beach, and for sightseeing or trekking. A compass is essential if you are going to trek in remote areas, as is a whistle, which you can use should you become lost or disorientated. A torch (flashlight) is not only needed if you intend to explore caves, but comes in handy during occasional power cuts. If you like to fill a washbasin or bathtub (a rarity in Greece), bring a universal plug as Greek bathrooms rarely have plugs.

Many camp sites have covered areas where tourists without tents can sleep in summer, so you can get by with a lightweight sleeping bag and foam bedroll. Whether or not you are going to self-cater, a plastic food container, plate, cup, cutlery, bottle opener, water container and an all-purpose knife are useful, not only for picnics, but for food you take with you on long boat trips.

You will need only light clothing – preferably cotton – during the summer months. But if you're going to climb Mt Olympus (or any other high mountain) you will need a sweater and waterproof jacket, even in July and August. During spring and autumn you'll need a light sweater or jacket in the evening. In winter take a heavy jacket or coat, warm sweaters, winter shoes or boots, and an umbrella.

In summer a sun hat and sunglasses are essential (see the Health section later in this chapter). Sunscreen creams and suntan oil are expensive, as are moisturising and cleansing creams. Film is not wildly expensive, especially in larger towns and tourist areas, but the stock tends to hang around for a while in remoter areas.

If you read a lot, it's a good idea to bring along a few disposable paperbacks to read and swap.

TOURIST OFFICES

Tourist information is handled by the Greek National Tourist Organisation, known by the initials GNTO abroad and EOT (Ellinikos Organismos Tourismou) in Greece.

Local Tourist Offices

The address of the EOT's head office is Amerikis 2, Athens 105 64 (☎ 1-322 3111). There are about 25 EOT offices throughout Greece. Most EOT staff speak English, but they vary in their enthusiasm and helpfulness. All of the offices have maps, glossy brochures and information on transport and accommodation. In addition to EOT offices, there are also municipal tourist offices which serve the same function.

Tourist Police

The tourist police work in cooperation with the regular Greek police and EOT. Each tourist police office has at least one member of staff who speaks English. Hotels, restaurants, travel agencies, tourist shops, tourist guides, waiters, taxi drivers and bus drivers all come under the jurisdiction of the tourist police. If you think that you have been ripped off by any of these businesses or their staff, report it to the tourist police and they will investigate. If you need to report a theft or loss of passport, then go to the tourist police

first, and they will act as interpreters between you and the regular police.

The tourist police also fulfil the same functions as the EOT and municipal tourist offices, dispensing maps and brochures, and giving information on transport. They can often help you to find accommodation.

Greek Tourist Offices Abroad

GNTO offices abroad include:

Australia
   51 Pitt St, Sydney NSW 2000 (☎ 02-241 1663)
Canada
   1300 Bay St, Toronto, Ontario M5R 3K8
   (☎ 416-968 2220); 1233 Rue de la Montagne,
   Suite 101, Montreal, Quebec H3G 1Z2
   (☎ 514-871 1535)
France
   3 Ave de l'Opéra, Paris 75001
   (☎ 01-42.60.65.75)
Germany
   Neue Mainzerstrasse 22, 6000 Frankfurt
   (☎ 69-237 735); Pacellistrasse 2, W 8000
   Munich 2 (☎ 89-222 035); Abteistrasse 33, 2000
   Hamburg 13 (☎ 40-454 498); Wittenplatz
   3A, 10789 Berlin 30 (☎ 30-217 6262)
Italy
   Via L Bissolati 78-80, Rome 00187
   (☎ 06-474 4249); Piazza Diaz 1, 20123 Milan
   (☎ 02-860 470)
Japan
   Fukuda Building West, 5F 2-11-3 Akasaka,
   Minato-Ku, Tokyo 107 (☎ 03-350 55 911)
Netherlands
   Leidsestraat 13, Amsterdam NS 1017
   (☎ 020-625 4212)
Norway
   Ovre Slottsgate 15B, 0157 Oslo 1 (☎ 2242 6501)

Greek National Tourist Organisation logo

Switzerland
    Loewerstrasse 25, CH 8001 Zürich
    (☎ 01-221 0105)
UK
    4 Conduit St, London W1R ODJ
    (☎ 0171-499 9758)
USA
    Olympic Tower, 645 5th Ave, New York, NY
    10022 (☎ 212-421 5777); Suite 160, 168 North
    Michigan Ave, Chicago, Illinois 60601
    (☎ 312-782 1091); Suite 2198, 611 West 6th St,
    Los Angeles, California 92668
    (☎ 213-626 6696)

USEFUL ORGANISATIONS

Most of the organisations of interest to travellers have their headquarters in Athens.

Accommodation

The Athens International Youth Hostel (☎ 01-523 4170) is affiliated with the International Youth Hostel Federation (IYHF). The address is Victor Hugo 16, Athens 104 37. You may can buy an IYHF card here, although you can stay without a card at most Greek youth hostels.

Student Travellers

Apart from selling tickets for air, sea and road travel, the International Student & Youth Travel Service (☎ 01-323 3767), 2nd floor, Nikis 11, Athens, also issues student cards – if you have documents proving you are a student.

Tourist Assistance Programme

The programme operates in conjunction with various Greek consumer associations to help people who are having trouble with any tourism-related service. Legal advice is available in English, French and German. The main office (☎ 01-330 0673) is at Valtetsiou 43-45 in Athens. In Iraklio, Crete, contact the Consumers Association of Crete (☎ 081-240 666), Milatou 1 and Agiou Titou, and in Volos contact the Consumers Association of Volos (☎ 0421-39 266), Haziagari 51.

Mountaineering Clubs

Ellinikos Orivatikos Syndesmos (EOS – Greek Alpine Club; ☎ 01-321 2429/2355) is the largest and oldest Greek mountaineering and trekking organisation. Its headquarters are at Plateia Kapnikareas 2, Athens – on Ermou, 500 metres west of Syntagma. The headquarters of the Hellenic Federation of Mountaineering Clubs (☎ 01-323 4555; fax 01-323 7666) is at Karageorgi Servias 7, Athens – on the edge of Syntagma. Both of these organisations are underfunded and staffed by volunteers, but if you call or visit between 7 and 9 pm on a weekday evening, there should be someone there.

Automobile Associations

ELPA (☎ 01-779 1615), the Greek automobile club, has its headquarters on the ground floor of Athens Tower, Messogion 2-4, Athens 115 27. The ELPA offers reciprocal services to members of national automobile associations on production of a valid membership card. If your vehicle breaks down, dial ☎ 104.

Gay & Lesbian Travellers

Greece is a popular destination for gay travellers. The address of the Greek Gay Liberation Organisation is PO Box 2777, Athens GR 100 22. The monthly magazine *To Kraximo* has information about the local gay scene, but is published entirely in Greek. The *Spartacus International Gay Guide*, published by Bruno Gmünder (Berlin), is a good international directory of gay entertainment venues in Europe.

For lesbians, the comprehensive international guide *Women Going Places* (Women Going Places Productions) is recommended.

Disabled Travellers

If mobility is a problem and you wish to visit Greece, the hard fact is that most hotels, museums and ancient sites in Greece are not wheelchair accessible. This is partly due to the uneven terrain of much of the country, which, with its abundance of stones, rocks and marble, presents a challenge even for able-bodied people.

If you are determined, then take heart in the knowledge that disabled people do come to Greece for holidays. But the trip needs careful planning, so get as much information as you can before you go. The British-based Royal Association for Disability and Rehabilitation (RADAR) publishes a useful guide called *Holidays & Travel Abroad: A Guide for Disabled People*, which gives a good overview of facilities available to disabled travellers in Europe. Contact RADAR (☎ 0171-637 5400) at 25 Mortimer St, London W1N 8AB.

Lavinia Tours (☎ 031-23 2828; fax 031-21 9714), Egnatia 101 (PO Box 111 06), Thessaloniki 541 10, specialises in arranging travel for disabled travellers. The managing director, Eugenia Stravropoulou, has travelled widely both in Greece and abroad in her wheelchair.

BUSINESS HOURS & PUBLIC HOLIDAYS

Banks are open Monday to Thursday from 8 am to 2 pm, and Friday from 8 am to 1.30 pm. Some banks in large towns and cities open from 3.30 to 6.30 pm in the afternoon and on Saturday morning.

All post offices are open Monday to Friday from 7.30 am to 2 pm. In the major cities they stay open until 8 pm, and open on Saturday from 7.30 am to 2 pm.

The opening hours of OTE offices (for long-distance and overseas telephone calls) vary according to the size of the town. In smaller towns they are usually open every day from 7.30 am to 3 pm; from 6 am until 11 pm in larger towns; and 24 hours in major cities like Athens and Thessaloniki.

In summer, shops are open from 8 am to 1.30 pm and from 5.30 to 8.30 pm on Tuesday, Thursday and Friday, and from 8 am to 2.30 pm on Monday, Wednesday and Saturday. They open 30 minutes later in winter. These times are not always strictly adhered to. Many shops in tourist resorts are open seven days a week. *Periptera* (street kiosks) are open from early morning until late at night. They sell everything from bus tickets and cigarettes to hard-core pornography. Opening times of museums and archaeological sites vary, but most are closed on Monday.

All banks and shops and most museums and ancient sites close during public holidays. National public holidays in Greece are:

1 January – New Year's Day
6 January – Epiphany
February – First Sunday in Lent
25 March – Greek Independence Day
March/April – Good Friday
(Orthodox) Easter Sunday
1 May – Spring Festival/Labour Day
15 August – Feast of the Assumption
28 October – Ohi Day
25 December – Christmas Day
26 December – St Stephen's Day

CULTURAL EVENTS

The Greek year is a succession of festivals and events, some of which are religious, some cultural, others an excuse for a good knees-up, and some a combination of all three. The following is by no means an exhaustive list, but it covers the most important events, both national and regional. If you're in the right place at the right time, you'll certainly be invited to join the revelry.

January

Feast of Agios Vasilios (Feast of St Basil) The year kicks off with this festival on 1 January. A church ceremony is followed by the exchanging of gifts, singing, dancing and feasting; the New Year pie *(vasilopitta)* is sliced and the person who gets the slice containing a coin will supposedly have a lucky year.

Epiphany Epiphany (the Blessing of the Waters), on 6 January, commemorates Christ's baptism by St John and is celebrated throughout Greece with religious ceremonies, when waters (seas, lakes and rivers) are blessed and crosses immersed in them. The largest ceremony takes place at Piraeus.

Gynaikratia 8 January is a day of role reversal in villages in the prefectures of Rodopi, Kilkis and Seres in northern Greece. Women spend the day in kafeneia (cafés) and other social centres where men usually congregate, while the men stay at home to do housework.

February-March

Carnival The Greek carnival season is the three weeks before the beginning of Lent (the 40-day period before Easter which is traditionally a period of fasting). The carnivals are ostensibly Christian pre-Lenten celebrations, but many derive from pagan festivals. There are many regional variations, but fancy dress, feasting, traditional dancing and general merrymaking prevail. The Patras carnival is the largest and most exuberant, with elaborately decorated chariots parading through the streets. The most bizarre carnival takes place on the island of Skyros where the men transform themselves into grotesque 'half-man, half-beast' creatures by donning goat-skin masks and hairy jackets. Other carnivals worth catching are those at Athens, Veria, Zakynthos, Kefallonia, and at Naoussa in Macedonia.

Shrove Monday (Clean Monday) On the Monday before Ash Wednesday (the first day of Lent), people take to the hills throughout Greece to have picnics and fly kites.

March

Independence Day The anniversary of the hoisting of the Greek flag by Bishop Germanos at Moni Agias Lavras is celebrated on 25 March with parades and dancing. Germanos' act of revolt marked the onset of the War of Independence. Independence Day coincides with the *Feast of the Annunciation*, so is also a religious festival.

March-April

Easter In the Greek Orthodox religion, Easter is the most important festival. Emphasis is placed on the Resurrection rather than on the Crucifixion, so it is a joyous occasion. The festival commences on Good Friday with the procession of a shrouded bier (representing Christ's funeral bier) through the town or village. On Saturday evening the Resurrection mass takes place. At midnight, packed churches are plunged into darkness to symbolise Christ's passing through the underworld.

The ceremony of the lighting of candles which follows is the most significant moment in the Orthodox year, for it symbolises the Resurrection. Its poignancy and beauty are spellbinding. If you are in Greece at Easter you should endeavour to attend this ceremony, which ends with the setting off of fireworks and candle-lit processions through the streets. The Lenten fast ends on Easter Sunday with the cracking of red-dyed Easter eggs and an outdoor feast of roast lamb followed by Greek dancing. The day's greeting is *Hristos anesti* ('Christ is risen'), to which the reply is *Alithos anesti* ('Truly He is risen'). On both Palm Sunday (the Sunday before Easter) and Easter Sunday, St Spiridon (the mummified patron saint of Corfu) is taken out for an airing and joyously paraded through the town. He is paraded again in Corfu town on 11 August.

*Feast of Agios Georgos*The feast day of St George, Greece's patron saint, and patron saint of shepherds, takes place on 23 April or the Tuesday following Easter (whichever comes first). It is celebrated at several places, but with particular exuberance in Arahova, near Delphi.

May

May Day On the first day of May there is a mass exodus from towns to the country. During picnics, wild flowers are gathered and made into wreaths to decorate houses.

Anastenaria This fire-walking ritual takes place on 21 May in Langadas near Thessaloniki. Villagers clutching icons dance barefoot on burning charcoal. See the Northern Greece chapter for more details about this ritual.

June

Navy Week This naval festival is celebrated in June in fishing villages and ports throughout the country. Volos and Hydra have unusual versions of these celebrations: in Volos there is a re-enactment of the departure of the *Argo*, for legend has it that Iolkos (from where Jason and the Argonauts set off in quest of the Golden Fleece) was near the city. Hydra commemorates Admiral Andreas Miaoulis, who was born on the island and was a hero of the War of Independence. There is a re-enactment of one of his naval victories, accompanied by feasting and fireworks.

Feast of St John the Baptist This feast day on 24 June is widely celebrated. Wreaths made on May Day are kept until this day, when they are burned on bonfires.

July

Feast of Agia Marina (Feast of St Marina) This feast day is celebrated on 17 July in many parts of Greece, and is a particularly important event on the Dodecanese island of Kassos.

Feast of Profitis Ilias This feast day on 20 July is celebrated at hilltop churches and monasteries dedicated to the prophet, especially in the Cyclades.

August

Assumption Greeks celebrate Assumption Day (15 August) with family reunions. The whole population seems to be on the move either side of the big day, so it's a good time to avoid public transport. The island of Tinos gets particularly busy because of its miracle-working icon of Panagia Evangelistria. It becomes a place of pilgrimage for thousands, who come to be blessed, healed or baptised, or just for the excitement of being there. Many are unable to find hotels and sleep out on the streets.

September

Genesis tis Panagias (the Virgin's Birthday) The day is celebrated on 8 September throughout Greece with religious services and feasting.

Exaltation of the Cross This is celebrated on 14 September throughout Greece with processions and hymns.

October

Feast of Agios Dimitrios This feast day is celebrated in Thessaloniki on 26 October with wine drinking and revelry.

Ohi (No) Day Metaxas' refusal to allow Mussolini's troops to traverse Greece in WW II is commemorated on 28 October with remembrance services, military parades, folk dancing and feasting.

December

Christmas Day Although not as important as Easter, Christmas is still celebrated with religious services and feasting. Nowadays much 'Western' influence is apparent, including Christmas trees, decorations and presents.

Summer Festivals & Performances

There are cultural festivals throughout Greece in summer. The most important are the Athens Festival (June to September), with drama and music performances in the Theatre of Herodes Atticus, and the Epidaurus Festival (July to September), with drama performances in the ancient theatre at Epidaurus. Others include the Philippi and Thasos Festival (July and August); the Renaissance Festival in Rethymno (July and August); the Dodoni Festival in Epiros (August); the Olympus Festival at Katerini and Litohoro (August); the Hippocratia Festival on Kos (August); and the Patras Arts Festival (August and September).

Summer is also the time for wine festivals where, for a nominal admission charge, you can drink as much as you like. The biggest ones are held at Rethymno and Alexandroupolis.

Thessaloniki hosts a string of festivals and events during September and October, including the International Trade Fair and the Feast of Agios Dimitrios (details on the latter in the list above).

The nightly son et lumière (sound and light) shows in Athens and Rhodes run from April to October. The Corfu show runs from May to September.

Greek folk dances are performed in Athens from mid-May to September and in Rhodes from May to October.

POST & TELECOMMUNICATIONS

Post offices *(tahydromio)* are easily identifi-

able by means of the yellow signs outside. Regular post boxes also are yellow. The red boxes are for express mail only.

Postal Rates

The postal rate for postcards and airmail letters to destinations within the EU is 90 dr for up to 20 grams and 180 dr for up to 50 grams. To other destinations the rate is 120 dr up to 20 grams and 220 dr for up to 150 grams. Post within Europe takes five to eight days and to the USA, Australia and New Zealand, nine to 11 days. Periptera (kiosks) also sell stamps, plus a 10% surcharge.

Express mail costs an extra 350 dr and should ensure delivery in three days within the EU. Valuables should be sent registered post, which costs an extra 280 dr.

Sending Mail

Do not wrap a parcel until it has been inspected at a post office. In Athens, take your parcel to the Parcel Post Office (☎ 01-322 8940) in the arcade at Stadiou 4, and elsewhere to the parcel counter of a regular post office.

Receiving Mail

Mail can be sent poste restante (general delivery) to any main post office. The service is free of charge, but you are required to show your passport. Ask your friends and relatives to write your family name in capital letters and underline it, and to mark the envelope 'poste restante'. It is a good idea to ask the post-office clerk to check under your first name as well if letters you are expecting cannot be located. After one month, uncollected mail is returned to the sender. If you are about to leave a town and expected mail hasn't arrived, ask at the post office to have it forwarded to your next destination, c/-poste restante. See the Post & Telecommunications section in the Athens chapter for addresses of post offices which hold poste restante mail.

Parcels are not delivered in Greece; they must be collected from the parcel counter of a post office – or, in Athens, from the Parcel Post Office.

Telephone

The Greek telephone service is maintained by the public corporation known as Organismos Tilepikoinonion Ellados, which is always referred to by the acronym OTE (pronounced O-tay). The system is modern and efficient. Public telephones all use phonecards, which are widely available from outlets such as periptera, corner shops and tourist shops. They cost 1300 dr for 100 units, 6000 dr for 500 units, and 11,500 dr for 1000 units. A local call costs one unit. The 'i' at the top left of the push-button dialling panel brings up the operating instructions in English. Don't remove the card before you are told to do so – you may lose the remaining credit.

Direct-dial long-distance and international calls can be made from public phones. It is also possible to use various national card schemes, such as Telecom Australia's Telecard, to make international calls. You will still need a phonecard to dial the scheme's access number, which will cost you one unit. International calls can also be made from OTE offices. They contain cubicles equipped with meters. A counter clerk tells you which cubicle to use, and payment is made afterwards. Villages and remote islands without OTE offices almost always have at least one metered phone for international and long-distance calls – usually in a shop, kafeneio or taverna.

Another option is to use a periptero telephone. Almost every periptero has a metered telephone which can be used for local, long-distance and direct-dial international calls. There is a small surcharge, but it is considerably less than that charged by hotels.

Reverse-charge (collect) calls can be made from an OTE office. The time you have to wait for a connection can vary considerably, from a few minutes to two hours. If you are using a private phone to make a reverse-charge call, dial the operator (domestic ☎ 151; international ☎ 161).

To call overseas direct, dial the Greek overseas-access code (00), followed by the country code for the country you are calling, then the local area code (dropping the leading zero if there is one) and then the number. The table below lists some frequently used country codes and per-minute charges:

Country	Code	Cost per minute
Australia	61	295 dr
France	33	135 dr
Germany	49	135 dr
Ireland	353	135 dr
Italy	39	135 dr
Japan	81	500 dr
Netherlands	31	135 dr
New Zealand	64	500 dr
Turkey	90	135 dr
UK	44	135 dr
USA & Canada	1	295 dr

Off-peak rates are 25% cheaper. They are available to Africa, Europe, the Middle East and India from 10 pm to 6 am; to the Americas, Asia and Oceania between 8 pm and 5 am.

Fax, Telex & Telegraph

Telegrams can be sent from any OTE office;

larger offices have telex facilities. Main city post offices have fax machines.

TIME

Greece is two hours ahead of GMT/UTC and three hours ahead on daylight-saving time, which begins at 12.01 am on the last Sunday in March, when clocks are put forward one hour. Clocks are put back an hour at 12.01 am on the last Sunday in September.

So, when it is noon in Greece it is also noon in İstanbul, 10 am in London, 11 am in Rome, 2 am in San Francisco, 5 am in New York and Toronto, 8 pm in Sydney, and 10 pm in Auckland.

ELECTRICITY

Electricity is 220 volts, 50 cycles, and plugs are the standard continental type with two round pins. All hotel rooms have power points and most camping grounds have supply points.

LAUNDRY

Large towns and some islands have laundrettes, which charge from 1500 dr to 2500 dr to wash and dry a load whether you do it yourself or have it service-washed. Hotel and room owners will usually provide you with a washtub if requested.

WEIGHTS & MEASURES

Greece uses the metric system. Liquids – especially barrel wine – are often sold by weight rather than volume: 959 grams of wine, for example, is equivalent to 1000 ml.

Remember that, like other continental Europeans, Greeks indicate decimals with commas and thousands with points.

BOOKS

Most books are published in different editions by different publishers in different countries. As a result, a book might be a hardcover rarity in one country while it's readily available in paperback in another. Fortunately, bookshops and libraries search by title or author, so your local bookshop or library is best placed to advise you on the availability of the following recommendations.

People & Society

Of the numerous festivals held in Greece, one of the most bizarre and overtly pagan is the carnival held on the island of Skyros. The definitive book on the subject is *The Goat Dancers of Skyros* by Joy Coulentianou.

The Cyclades, or Life Amongst the Insular Greeks by James Theodore Bent (first published 1885) has stood the test of time and is still the greatest English-language book about the Greek islands. It relates the experiences of the author and his wife during a year of travelling around the Cyclades in the late 19th century. Sadly, the book is out of print. (The Hellenic Book Service may have a second-hand copy; see the Bookshops section later in this chapter.)

Time, Religion & Social Experience in Rural Greece by Laurie Kain Hart is a fascinating account of village traditions – many of which are alive and well beneath the tourist veneer. *Portrait of a Greek Mountain Village*, by Juliet du Boulay, is in similar vein, based on the author's experiences in an isolated village.

A Traveller's Journey is Done and *An Affair of the Heart* , by Dilys Powell, wife of archaeologist Humfry Payne, are very readable, affectionate insights into village life in the Peloponnese during the 1920s and 1930s when Payne was excavating there.

Road to Rembetica: Music of a Greek Subculture – Songs of Love, Sorrow and Hashish by Gail Holst is an exploration of the intriguing subculture which emerged from the poverty and suffering of the refugees from Asia Minor.

The Colossus of Maroussi by Henry Miller is now regarded as a classic. With senses heightened, Miller relates his travels in Greece at the outbreak of WW II with feverish enthusiasm. Another book which will whet your appetite if you are contemplating a holiday in Greece is *Hellas: A Portrait of Greece* by Nicholas Gage.

Vanishing Greece by Clay Perry, with an introduction by Patrick Leigh Fermor, is a large and expensive book with magnificent photographs of the landscapes and people of rural Greece. But the message of the book is a sad one: that the rural culture of Greece, little changed since Homer's time, is fast vanishing.

History & Mythology

A Traveller's History of Greece by Timothy Boatswain & Colin Nicholson is probably the best choice for the layperson who wants a good general reference on the historical background of Greece. It gives clear and comprehensive coverage from Neolithic times to the present day. *Modern Greece: A Short History* by C M Woodhouse is in a similar vein, although it has a right-wing bent; Woodhouse makes no attempt to hide his glee at the fall of PASOK in 1990. The book covers the period from Constantine the Great to 1990.

Mythology is an intrinsic part of life in ancient Greece, and some knowledge of it will enhance your visit to the country. One of the best publications on the subject is *The Greek Myths* by Robert Graves (two volumes) which relates and interprets the adventures of the main gods and heroes worshipped by the ancient Greeks. Maureen O'Sullivan's *An Iconoclast's Guide to the Greek Gods* presents entertaining and accessible versions of the myths. The two volumes of Homer's *Odyssey* and *Iliad* translated by E V Rien are possibly the best translations of these epics – Homer's account of the Trojan War and Odysseus' (known as Ulysses in Latin) subsequent adventures. *Ovid's Metamorphoses* translated by A D Melville is a beautiful poetic interpretation of the Greek myths. Ovid (Publius Ovidius Naso) was a Roman who lived in the 1st century BC.

Women in Athenian Law and Life by Roger Just is the first in-depth study of the role of women in ancient Greece.

The Argonautica Expedition by Theodor Troev encompasses Greek mythology, archaeology, travel and adventure. It relates the voyage undertaken by the author and his crew in the 1980s following in the footsteps of Jason and the Argonauts. The aim of the expedition was to investigate the possibility that maritime and cultural links had existed between what is now the Georgian coast and other points in the ancient world.

Mary Renault's novels provide an excellent feel for ancient Greece. *The King Must Die* and *The Bull from the Sea* are vivid tales of Minoan times.

Mistras and Byzantine Style and Civilisation by Sir Steven Runciman and *Fourteen Byzantine Rulers* by Michael Psellus are both good introductions to the Byzantine Age – a period in the country's history which is often overlooked by visitors to Greece.

Farewell Anatolia and *The Dead are Waiting* by Dido Soteriou are two powerful novels focusing on the population exchange of 1923. Soteriou was born in Asia Minor in 1909 and was herself a refugee.

The Villa Ariadne by Dilys Powell is centred around the dwelling of the title, which was built by Sir Arthur Evans and still stands near Knossos. Many people who were prominent in the shaping of modern Crete were either residents or guests at this house at one time or another, so the book is a very readable account of recent Cretan history. Crete played a pivotal role during WW II and many books have been written about this period of the island's history. *The Cretan Runner* by Georgios Psychoundaki (translated by Patrick Leigh Fermor) is a graphic account of this traumatic time – the author was active in the island's resistance movement.

In a similar vein, *The Jaguar* by Alexander Kotzias is a moving story about the leftist resistance to the Nazi occupation of Greece. Although a novel, it is packed with historical facts. *Greek Women in Resistance* by Eleni Fountouri is a compilation of journals, poems and personal accounts of women in the resistance movement from the 1940s to 1950s. The book also contains poignant photographs and drawings.

Eleni by Nicholas Gage is an account by the author of his family's struggle to survive the horrors of the civil war, and his mother's death at the hands of the communists. It was made into a film in 1985.

The third volume of Olivia Manning's Balkan trilogy, *Friends & Heroes* has Greece as its setting. It is based on the author's own experiences as the wife of a British Council lecturer, and is a riveting account of the chaos and confusion among the émigré community fleeing the Nazi invasion of Europe. *The Flight of Ikaros* by Kevin Andrews is another classic. The author relates his travels in Greece during the 1940s civil war. *Greece in the Dark* by the same author is a perceptive account of his life in Greece during the junta years.

Poetry

Sappho: A New Translation by Mary Bernard is the best translation of this great ancient poet's works.

Collected Poems by George Seferis, *Selected Poems* by Odysseus Elytis and *Collected Poems* by Constantine Cavafy are all excellent translations of Greece's greatest modern poets.

Novels

The most well-known and widely read Greek author is the Cretan writer Nikos Kazantzakis, whose novels are full of drama and larger-than-life characters. His most famous works are *The Last Temptation, Zorba the Greek, Christ Recrucified* and *Freedom or Death*. The first two have been made into films.

The Mermaid Madonna and *The Schoolmistress with the Golden Eyes* are two passionate novels by the writer Stratis Myrivilis. Their settings are two villages on the island of Lesvos, the writer's birthplace. *When the Tree Sings* by Stratis Haviaras is a beautifully lyrical and impressionistic novel inspired by the author's experiences as a young boy in Greece during the traumatic 1940s.

The Australian journalists George Johnston and Charmian Clift wrote several books with Greek themes during their 19 years as expatriates, including Johnston's novel *The Sponge Divers*, set on Kalymnos, and Clift's autobiographical *A Mermaid Singing*, which is about their experiences on Hydra. Most evocative is Johnston's award-winning *Clean Straw For Nothing*, second in a trilogy, which was followed by the tragic *A Cartload of Clay*. The last two are classified as fiction but many close to Johnston and Clift believed the books mirrored their lives in Greece, England and Australia.

The experiences of Australian writer Gillian Bouras are recounted in her books about living in Greece – *A Foreign Wife* and *Aphrodite and the Others*. Fellow Australian Beverley Farmer has two collections of beautifully written short stories, *Home Time* and *Milk*, many of which are about the experiences of foreigners who endeavour to make their home in Greece.

Travel Literature

During the 19th century many books about Greece were written by philhellenes who went to the country to help in the struggle for self determination. *Travels in Northern Greece* by William Leake is an account of Greece in the last years of Ottoman rule. Leake was the British consul in Ioannina during Ali Pasha's rule. The English painter and writer Edward Lear of *The Owl and the Pussy Cat* fame spent some time in Greece in the mid-19th century and wrote *Journeys of a Landscape Painter* and *A Cretan Diary*.

Lawrence Durrell, who spent an idyllic childhood on Corfu, is the best known of the 20th-century philhellenes. His evocative books *Prospero's Cell* and *Reflections on a Marine Venus* are about Corfu and Rhodes respectively. His coffee-table book *The Greek Islands* is one of the most popular books of its kind. Even if you disagree with Durrell's opinions, you will probably concede that the photographs are superb. *My Family and Other Animals* by Gerald Durrell is a hilarious account of the Durrell family's chaotic and wonderful life on Corfu – Gerald and Lawrence were brothers.

Patrick Leigh Fermor, another ardent philhellene, is well-known for his exploits in rallying the Cretan resistance in WW II. He now lives in Kardamyli in the Peloponnese. His highly acclaimed book *The Mani* is an account of his adventures in the Mani peninsula during the 1950s, when many traditional customs were still in evidence. By the same author, *Roumeli* relates travels in northern Greece. *Deep into Mani* by Peter Greenhalgh & Edward Eliopoulis is a journey through the Mani some 25 years after Fermor's book about the area was written. If you are going to explore the Mani, this book (as well as those by Fermor) will greatly aid your appreciation of the region, which is one of the most strikingly beautiful in Greece.

Travels in the Morea by Nikos Kazantzakis is a highly readable account of the great writer's travels through the Peloponnese in the 1930s.

Under Mount Ida: A Journey into Crete by Oliver Burch is a compelling portrayal of this diverse and beautiful island – full of insights into its landscape, history and people.

If you are planning a trip to Mt Athos, and wish to get the most out of the experience, some preliminary reading is essential. The most informative and interesting accounts are *The Station* by Robert Byron and *Athos: the Holy Mountain* by Sidney Loch.

Travel Guides

The ancient Greek traveller Pausanias is acclaimed as the world's first travel writer. *The Guide to Greece* was written in the 2nd century BC. Umpteen editions later, it is now available in English in paperback.

For archaeology buffs, the *Blue Guides* are hard to beat. They go into tremendous detail about all the major sites, and many of the lesser known ones. They have separate guides for Greece and Crete. In contrast, *Ebdon's Odyssey* by John Ebdon is a highly entertaining and irreverent account of travels in Greece.

Lonely Planet's *Trekking in Greece* by Marc S Dubin is an in-depth guide to Greece's mountain paths, complemented with excellent maps.

Museum Guides

Museums and Galleries of Greece and Cyprus by Maria Kontou, of the Ministry of Culture, lists 165 museums in Greek and English with about 1000 photographs to illustrate exhibits which relate to visual arts, natural history, navigation, science, technology and the theatre.

Botanical Field Guides

The Flowers of Greece & the Aegean by William Taylor & Anthony Huxley is the most comprehensive field guide to Greece. The Greek writer, naturalist and mountaineer George Sfikas has written many books on wildlife in Greece, some of which have been translated into English. Amongst them are *Wildflowers of Greece*, *Trees & Shrubs of Greece*, *Medicinal Plants of Greece* and *Wildflowers of Mt Olympos*.

Children's Books

Greek publishers Malliaris-Paedia put out a good series of books on the myths, retold in English for young readers by Aristides Kesopoulos. The titles are *The Gods of Olympus and the Lesser Gods*, *The Labours of Hercules*, *Theseus and the Voyage of the Argonauts*, *The Trojan War and the Wanderings of Odysseus*, and *Heroes and Mythical Creatures*.

Robin Lister's retelling of *The Odyssey* is aimed at slightly older readers (ages eight to 10), but makes compelling listening for younger children when read aloud.

Bookshops

The bookshops in Greece which have the most comprehensive selections of foreign-language books (including English) are in Athens and Thessaloniki (see these sections). All other major towns and tourist resorts have bookshops which sell some foreign-language books. Imported books are expensive – normally two to three times the recommended retail price in the UK and the US. Larger shops, such as Compendium in Athens, have some good deals, including the Penguin classics for 800 dr each. The Greek publisher Efstathiadis specialises in English translations of books by Greek authors as well as books about Greece by foreign authors. Many hotels have small collections of second-hand books to read or swap.

Abroad, the best bookshop for new and second-hand books about Greece, written in both English and Greek, is the Hellenic Book Service, 91 Fortress Rd, Kentish Town, London NW5 1AG (☎ 0171-267 9499). It stocks almost all of the books recommended here, and will take mail or telephone orders.

MAPS

Unless you are going to trek or drive, the maps given out by the EOT will probably suffice, although they are not 100% accurate. On islands where there is no EOT there are usually tourist maps for sale for around 300 dr, but again, these are not very accurate.

If you are going to trek, then the best available topographical survey maps of Greece are the *Karta Nomos* (1:200,000), published by the Ethniki Statistiki Ypiresia (National Statistical Office). There are 52 sheets; each covers a single administrative area. Relief is shown by colour tints with contours at 200-metre intervals. All names are given in Greek script only. The maps may be bought at the Athens Statistical Service Office, Lykourgou 14, 3rd floor, near Omonia (show your passport). The maps are available at Stanfords, 12-14 Long Acre, London, WC2E 9LP (☎ 0171-836 1321; fax 0171-836 0189). Lonely Planet's *Trekking in Greece* has over 40 contoured sketch maps which should suffice for most of the standard treks.

Under present Greek government regula-

tions, larger scale topographic surveys published by the military authorities are not available to the general public. All is not lost, however. The bimonthly EOS magazine *Korfes* publishes a series of walking maps (1:50,000) based on the military topographical maps. Copies of these maps may be purchased in Greece at the EOS office (☎ 01-246 1528), Plateia Kentriki 16, Aharnes (a satellite suburb north of Athens). Before trekking out to Aharnes, it's probably worth checking if the maps are also available from the head office of the EOS (☎ 01-321 2429/2355) at Plateia Kapnikareas 2, Athens – on Ermou, 500 metres west of Syntagma. The maps cover the most popular trekking and climbing areas in Greece. Recent editions have names in both Greek and Latin script; earlier ones have names in Greek only. These maps are also available at Stanfords.

The best motoring map of the Greek mainland is the Bartholomew/RV Euromap (1:800,000), and for the islands and the Peloponnese, the 15 Freytag & Berndt maps.

MEDIA
Newspapers & Magazines

Greeks are great newspaper readers. There are 15 daily newspapers, of which the most widely read are *Ta Nea*, *Kathimerini*, and *Eleftheros Typos*.

English-language newspapers are the daily (except Monday) *Athens News* (200 dr) which carries world news and Greek news, and the *Weekly Greek News* (250 dr), which carries predominantly Greek news. Both are widely available in Athens and at major resorts.

The *Athenian* (600 dr) is a high-quality monthly magazine with articles on politics, travel and the arts, as well as carrying gallery and museum listings. Its *Athenian Organiser* page at the back has a long list of useful telephone numbers for museums, galleries, libraries and cultural organisations. *Athenscope* (300 dr) is a weekly listings magazine for the Athens entertainment scene.

Foreign newspapers are also widely available, although only between April and October in smaller resort areas. They include almost every British newspaper, the *Herald Tribune*, the *European* and international magazines such as *Time*, *Newsweek* and the *Economist*. The papers reach Athens (Syntagma) at 1 pm on the day of publication on weekdays, and at 7 pm on weekends. They are not available until the following day in other areas.

Radio & TV

Greece has two state-owned radio channels, ET 1 and ET 2. ET 1 runs three programmes, two of them devoted to popular music and news, and a third playing classical music mostly. It has a news update in English at 7.30 am from Monday to Saturday, and at 9 pm from Monday to Friday. It can heard on 91.6 MHz and 105.8 MHz on the FM band, and 729 KHz on the AM band. ET 2 broadcasts popular music mainly. Local radio stations are increasing at such a rate that the mountains around Athens have so many radio masts that they look like pin cushions. Athens International FM (93.4 MHz) broadcasts the BBC World Service live 24 hours a day, interspersed with occasional Greek news and music programmes. The broadcast area covers Aegina and much of Attica as well as Athens and Piraeus. Elsewhere, the best short-wave frequencies for picking up the World Service are:

GMT	Frequency
3 am to 7.30 am	9.41 MHz (31-metre band)
	6.18 MHz (49-metre band)
	15.07 MHz (19-metre band)
7.30 am to 6 pm	15.07 MHz (19-metre band)
	12.09 MHz (25-metre band)
	15.07 MHz (19-metre band)
6.30 pm to 11.15 pm	12.09 MHz (25-metre band)
	9.41 MHz (31-metre band)
	6.18 MHz (49-metre band)

As far as Greek TV is concerned, quantity rather than quality is the operative word. There are nine TV channels and various pay-TV channels. All the channels show English and US films, and soapies, with Greek sub-titles. A bit of channel-swapping normally finds something in English.

FILM & PHOTOGRAPHY

Major brands of film are widely available, although they can be expensive in smaller towns. In Athens, expect to pay about 1500 dr for a 36-exposure roll of Kodak Gold ASA 100; less for other brands. As elsewhere in the world, developing film is a competitive business. Most places want from 60 to 80 dr per print, plus a 400 dr service charge.

Never photograph a military installation or anything else that has a sign forbidding photography. Greeks usually love having their photos taken but, of course, it's polite to ask first. Because of the brilliant sunlight in summer, it's a good idea to use a polarising lens filter.

HEALTH

Citizens of EU countries are covered for free treatment in public hospitals within Greece on presentation of an E111 form. Enquire at your national health service or travel agent in advance. Emergency treatment is free to all nationalities in public hospitals. In an emergency, dial 166. There is at least one doctor on every island in Greece and larger islands have hospitals. Pharmacies can dispense medicines which are available only on prescription in most European countries, so you can consult a pharmacist for minor ailments.

All this sounds fine, but although medical training is of a high standard in Greece, the health service is underfunded and one of the worst in Europe. Hospitals are overcrowded, hygiene is not always what it should be and relations are expected to bring in food for the patient – which could be a problem for a tourist. Conditions and treatment are better in private hospitals, which are expensive. All this means that a good health-insurance policy is essential.

Predeparture Planning

Travel health depends on your predeparture preparations, your day-to-day health care while travelling and how you handle any medical problem or emergency that does develop. While the list of potential dangers can seem quite frightening, with a little luck, some basic precautions and adequate information, few travellers experience more than upset stomachs.

Health Insurance A travel-insurance policy to cover theft, loss and medical problems is a good idea. There is a wide variety of policies available and your travel agent will be able to make recommendations. The travel policies handled by STA Travel and other student travel organisations are usually good value. Some policies offer lower and higher medical-expense options but the higher options are chiefly for countries such as the USA which have extremely high medical costs. Check the small print:

- Some policies specifically exclude 'dangerous activities' which can include scuba diving, motorcycling, even trekking. If such activities are on your agenda, you don't want that sort of policy.
- A locally acquired motor-cycle licence may not be valid under your policy.
- You may prefer a policy which pays doctors or hospitals direct rather than you having to pay on the spot and claim later. If you have to claim later make sure you keep all documentation. Some policies ask you to call back (reverse charges) to a centre in your home country where an immediate assessment of your problem is made.
- Check that the policy covers ambulances or an emergency flight home. If you have to stretch out you will need two seats and somebody has to pay for them!

Medical Kit It's wise to carry a small, straightforward medical kit. The kit should include:

- Aspirin or paracetamol (acetominophen in the USA) – for pain or fever.
- Antihistamine (such as Benadryl) – useful as a decongestant for colds and allergies, to ease the itch from insect bites or stings, and to help prevent motion sickness. Antihistamines may cause sedation and interact with alcohol so care should be taken when using them.
- Antibiotics – useful if you're travelling well off the beaten track, but they must be prescribed and you should carry the prescription with you.

- Kaolin preparation (Pepto-Bismol), Imodium or Lomotil – for stomach upsets.
- Antiseptic such as Betadine, which comes as a solution, impregnated swabs or ointment, and an antibiotic powder or similar 'dry' spray – for cuts and grazes.
- Calamine lotion – to ease irritation from bites or stings.
- Bandages and Band-aids – for minor injuries.
- Scissors, tweezers and a thermometer (note that mercury thermometers are prohibited by airlines).
- Insect repellent, sunscreen and chap stick.

Ideally antibiotics should be administered only under medical supervision and should never be taken indiscriminately. Take only the recommended dose at the prescribed intervals and continue using the antibiotic for the prescribed period, even if the illness seems to be cured earlier. Antibiotics are quite specific to the infections they can treat. Stop immediately if there are any serious reactions and don't use the antibiotic at all if you are unsure that you have the correct one.

Warning Codeine, which is commonly found in headache preparations, is banned in Greece; check labels carefully, or risk prosecution. There are strict regulations applying to the importation of medicines into Greece, so obtain a certificate from your doctor which outlines any medication you may have to carry into the country with you.

Health Preparations Make sure you're healthy before you start travelling. If you are embarking on a long trip, make sure your teeth are OK. If you wear glasses or contact lenses, take a spare pair and your prescription in case of loss. While poets since time immemorial have waxed lyrical about the dazzling light of Greece, on a more practical level, too much sunlight, whether it's direct or reflected (glare), can damage your eyes. It is very important to wear good sunglasses. Make sure they're treated to absorb ultraviolet radiation – if not, they'll do more harm than good as they'll dilate your pupils and make it easier for ultraviolet light to damage the retina.

If you require a particular medication, take

an adequate supply, as it may not always be available in remote areas. The same applies to oral contraceptives. It will be easier to obtain replacements if the prescription has the generic rather than the brand name, which may not be available locally.

A medical-emergency pendant containing relevant details of your health history is worth having if your medical condition is not easily recognisable (heart trouble, diabetes, asthma, allergic reactions to antibiotics, etc).

Immunisations These are an entry requirement for Greece only if you're coming from an area where yellow fever is endemic.

Basic Rules
Food & Water Tap water is safe to drink in Greece, but if you prefer mineral water, it is widely available. You might experience mild intestinal problems if you're not used to copious amounts of olive oil; however, you'll get used to it and current research says it's good for you.

If you don't vary your diet, are travelling hard and fast and missing meals, or simply lose your appetite, you can soon start to lose weight and place your health at risk. Fruit and vegetables are good sources of vitamins and Greece produces a greater variety of these than almost any other European country. If your diet isn't well balanced or if your food intake is insufficient, it's a good idea to take vitamin and iron pills.

Everyday Health Normal body temperature is 98.6°F or 37°C; more than 2°C higher indicates a 'high' fever. The normal adult pulse rate is 60 to 80 per minute (children 80 to 100, babies 100 to 140). You should know how to take a temperature and a pulse rate. As a general rule the pulse increases about 20 beats per minute for each °C rise in fever.

Respiration (breathing) rate is also an indicator of illness. Count the number of breaths per minute: between 12 and 20 is normal for adults and older children (up to 30 for younger children, 40 for babies). People with a high fever or serious respiratory illness (like pneumonia) breathe more quickly than normal. More than 40 shallow breaths a minute may indicate pneumonia.

Medical Problems & Treatment
Potential medical problems can be broken down into several areas. Firstly there are the problems caused by extremes of temperature, altitude or motion. Then there are diseases resulting from poor environmental sanitation, insect bites or stings, and animal or human contact. Simple cuts, bites and scratches can also cause problems.

Environmental Considerations
Sunburn By far the biggest health risk in Greece comes from the intensity of the sun. You can get sunburnt surprisingly quickly, even through cloud. Use a sunscreen and take extra care to cover areas which don't normally see sun – eg your feet. A hat provides added protection, and you should also use zinc cream or some other barrier cream for your nose and lips. Calamine lotion is good for mild sunburn. Greeks claim that yoghurt applied to sunburn is soothing.

Prickly Heat Prickly heat is an itchy rash caused by excessive perspiration trapped under the skin. It usually strikes people who have just arrived in a hot climate and whose pores have not yet opened sufficiently to cope with greater sweating. Keeping cool and bathing often may help until you acclimatise.

Heat Exhaustion Dehydration or salt deficiency can cause heat exhaustion. Take time to acclimatise to high temperatures and make sure you get sufficient liquids. Wear loose clothing and a broad-brimmed hat. Do not do anything too physically demanding. Salt deficiency is characterised by fatigue, lethargy, headaches, giddiness and muscle cramps and in this case salt tablets may help. Vomiting or diarrhoea can deplete your liquid and salt levels. Anhydrotic heat exhaustion, caused by an inability to sweat, is quite rare. Unlike the other forms of heat exhaustion, it is likely to strike people who have been in a hot climate for some time, rather than newcomers.

Heat Stroke This serious, and sometimes fatal, condition can occur if the body's heat-regulating mechanism breaks down and body temperature rises to dangerous levels. Long, continuous periods of exposure to high temperatures can leave you vulnerable to heat stroke. You should avoid excessive alcohol or strenuous activity when you first arrive in a hot climate.

The symptoms are feeling unwell, not sweating very much or at all and a high body temperature (39°C to 41°C). Where sweating has ceased the skin becomes flushed and red. Severe, throbbing headaches and lack of coordination will also occur, and the sufferer may be confused or aggressive. Eventually the victim will become delirious or convulse. Hospitalisation is essential, but meanwhile get victims out of the sun, remove their clothing, cover them with a wet sheet or towel and fan continually.

Fungal Infections Fungal infections, which occur with greater frequency in hot weather, are most likely to occur on the scalp, between the toes or fingers (athlete's foot), in the groin (jock itch or crotch rot) and on the body (ringworm). You get ringworm (which is a fungal infection, not a worm) from infected animals or by walking on damp areas, like shower floors.

To prevent fungal infections wear loose, comfortable clothes, avoid artificial fibres, wash frequently and dry carefully. If you do get an infection, wash the infected area daily with a disinfectant or medicated soap and water, and rinse and dry well. Apply an antifungal cream or powder – Tinaderm is widely available. Try to expose the infected area to air or sunlight as much as possible and wash all towels and underwear in hot water as well as changing them often.

Hypothermia Too much cold is just as dangerous as too much heat, particularly if it leads to hypothermia. Although everyone associates Greece with heat and sunshine, the high mountainous regions can be cool, even in summer. There is snow on the mountains from November to April. On the highest mountains in the north, snow patches can still be seen in June. Keeping warm while trekking in these regions in spring and autumn can be as much of a problem as keeping cool in the lower regions in summer.

Hypothermia occurs when the body loses heat faster than it can produce it and the core temperature of the body falls. It is surprisingly easy to progress from very cold to dangerously cold due to a combination of wind, wet clothing, fatigue and hunger, even if the air temperature is above freezing. It is best to dress in layers; silk, wool and some of the new artificial fibres are all good insulating materials. A hat is important, as a lot of heat is lost through the head. A strong, waterproof outer layer is essential, as keeping dry is vital. Carry basic supplies, including food containing simple sugars to generate heat quickly and lots of fluid to drink. A space blanket is something all travellers in cold environments should carry.

Symptoms of hypothermia are exhaustion, numb skin (particularly toes and fingers), shivering, slurred speech, irrational or violent behaviour, lethargy, stumbling, dizzy spells, muscle cramps and violent bursts of energy. Irrationality may take the form of sufferers claiming they are warm and trying to take off their clothes.

To treat mild hypothermia, first get the person out of the wind and/or rain, remove their clothing if it's wet and replace it with dry, warm clothing. Give them hot liquids – not alcohol – and some high-kilojoule, easily digestible food. Do not rub victims, instead allow them to warm themselves slowly. This should be enough to treat the early stages of hypothermia. The early recognition and treatment of mild hypothermia is the only way to prevent severe hypothermia, which is a critical condition.

Lightning Recent fatalities have highlighted the dangers of trekking in exposed areas during electrical thunderstorms. If you are caught in a thunderstorm, seek shelter, preferably in a low-lying area.

Motion Sickness Sea sickness can be a problem. The Aegean is very unpredictable and gets very rough when the meltemi wind blows. Eating lightly before and during a trip will reduce the chances of motion sickness. If you are prone to motion sickness, try to find a place that minimises disturbance – near the wing on aircraft, close to midships on boats, near the centre on buses. Fresh air usually helps; reading and cigarette smoke don't. Commercial motion-sickness preparations, which can cause drowsiness, have to be taken before the trip; when you're feeling sick, it's too late. Ginger is a natural preventative and is available in capsule form.

Jet Lag Jet lag is experienced when a person travels by air across more than three time zones (each time zone usually represents a one-hour time difference). It occurs because many of the functions of the human body (such as temperature, pulse rate and emptying of the bladder and bowels) are regulated by internal 24-hour cycles called circadian rhythms. When we travel long distances rapidly, our bodies take time to adjust to the 'new time' of our destination, and we may experience fatigue, disorientation, insomnia, anxiety, impaired concentration and loss of appetite. These effects will usually be gone within three days, but there are ways of minimising the impact of jet lag:

- Rest for a couple of days prior to departure; try to avoid late nights and last-minute dashes for travellers' cheques, passport etc.
- Try to select flight schedules that minimise sleep deprivation; arriving late in the day means you can go to sleep soon after you arrive. For very long flights, try to organise a stopover.
- Avoid excessive eating (which bloats the stomach) and alcohol (which causes dehydration) during the flight. Instead, drink plenty of non-carbonated, non-alcoholic drinks such as fruit juice or water.
- Avoid smoking, as this reduces the amount of oxygen in the aeroplane cabin even further and causes greater fatigue.

- Make yourself comfortable by wearing loose-fitting clothes and perhaps bringing an eye mask and ear plugs to help you sleep.

Infectious Diseases

Diarrhoea A change of water, food or climate can all cause the runs; diarrhoea caused by contaminated food or water is more serious. Despite all your precautions you may still get a mild bout of travellers' diarrhoea, but a few rushed toilet trips with no other symptoms is not indicative of a serious problem. Moderate diarrhoea, involving half-a-dozen loose movements in a day, is more of a nuisance. Dehydration is the main danger with any diarrhoea, particularly for children where dehydration can occur quite quickly. Fluid replacement remains the mainstay of management. Weak black tea with a little sugar, soda water, or soft drinks allowed to go flat and diluted 50% with water are all good.

Viral Gastroenteritis This is caused not by bacteria but, as the name suggests, by a virus. It is characterised by stomach cramps, diarrhoea, and sometimes by vomiting and/or a slight fever. All you can do is rest and drink lots of fluids.

Tetanus This potentially fatal disease is difficult to treat but is preventable with immunisation. Tetanus occurs when a wound becomes infected by a germ which lives in the faeces of animals or people, so clean all cuts, punctures or animal bites. Tetanus is also known as lockjaw, and the first symptom may be discomfort in swallowing, or stiffening of the jaw and neck; this is followed by painful convulsions of the jaw and whole body.

Rabies Rabies is caused by a bite or scratch by an infected animal. It's rare, but is found in Greece. Dogs are the most noted carriers, but any bite, scratch or even lick from a warm-blooded, furry animal should be cleaned immediately and thoroughly. Scrub with soap and running water, and then clean with an alcohol or iodine solution. If there is any possibility that the animal is infected, medical help should be sought immediately. Even if the animal is not rabid, all bites should be treated seriously as they can become infected or can result in tetanus. A rabies vaccination is now available and should be considered if you are in a high-risk category – eg if you intend to explore caves (bat bites can be dangerous) or work with animals.

Sexually Transmitted Diseases Sexual contact with an infected sexual partner spreads these diseases. Gonorrhoea and syphilis are the most common of these diseases; sores, blisters or rashes around the genitals, discharges or pain when urinating are common symptoms. Symptoms may be less marked or not observed at all in women. Syphilis symptoms eventually disappear completely but the disease continues and can cause severe problems in later years. The treatment of gonorrhoea and syphilis is with antibiotics.

There are numerous other sexually transmitted diseases, for most of which effective treatment is available. However, there is no cure for herpes and there is also currently no cure for AIDS.

Abstinence is the only 100% guarantee of avoiding sexually transmitted diseases, but condoms are also effective. Condoms (*kapotes* in Greek – ka-PO-tes) are widely available. They are sold in pharmacies and periptera.

There are no STD clinics in Greece, but the Andreas Syngros Hospital (☎ 01-723 9611), Dragoumi 5, Athens (behind the Hilton Hotel), specialises in the treatment of STDs. Treatment is free, but telephone to find out when the out-patient clinic is open. Elsewhere go to the local hospital.

HIV/AIDS HIV, the Human Immunodeficiency Virus, may develop into AIDS, Acquired Immune Deficiency Syndrome. HIV is a major problem just about everywhere, including Greece. Any exposure to blood, blood products or bodily fluids can put the individual at risk. While transmission in industrialised countries is predominantly through contact between homosexual or bisexual males, or via contaminated needles shared by IV drug users, Greece has recorded a large increase in the number of women contracting HIV through heterosexual activity in the last two years.

Apart from abstinence, the most effective preventative is to practise safe sex using condoms. It is impossible to detect the HIV-positive status of a healthy-looking person without a blood test.

HIV/AIDS can also be spread through infected blood transfusions, but this is a problem mainly in developing countries which cannot afford to screen blood for transfusions. It can also be spread by dirty needles – vaccinations, acupuncture, tattooing and ear or nose piercing can be potentially as dangerous as intravenous drug use if the equipment is not clean. If you do need an injection, ask to see the syringe unwrapped in front of you.

Fear of HIV infection should never preclude treatment for serious medical conditions. Although there may be a risk of infection, it is very small indeed.

Insect-Borne Diseases

Typhus Tick typhus is a problem from April to September in rural areas, particularly areas where animals congregate. Typhus begins with a fever, chills, headache and muscle pains, followed a few days later by a body rash. There is often a large painful sore at the site of the bite and nearby lymph nodes are swollen and painful. There is no vaccine available. The best protection is to check your skin carefully after walking in danger areas such as long grass and scrub. A strong insect repellent can help. (See the Cuts, Bites & Stings section below for information about ticks.)

Cuts, Bites & Stings

Cuts & Scratches Skin punctures can easily become infected in hot climates and may be difficult to heal. Treat any cut with an antiseptic such as Betadine. Where possible avoid bandages and Band-aids, which can keep wounds wet.

Bedbugs & Lice Bedbugs live in various places, but particularly in dirty mattresses and bedding. Spots of blood on bedclothes or on the wall around the bed are signs that you'd better find another hotel. Bedbugs leave itchy bites in neat rows. Calamine lotion may help.

All lice cause itching and discomfort. They make themselves at home in your hair (head lice), your clothing (body lice) or in your pubic hair (crabs). You catch lice through direct contact with infected people or by sharing combs, clothing and the like. Powder or shampoo treatment will kill the lice and infected clothing should then be washed in very hot water.

Bee & Wasp Stings Although there are a lot of bees and wasps in Greece, their stings are usually painful rather than dangerous. Calamine lotion will give relief and ice packs will reduce the pain or swelling.

Jelly Fish, Sea Urchins & Weever Fish Watch out for sea urchins around rocky beaches; if you get some of their needles embedded in your skin, olive oil will help to loosen them. If they are not removed they will become infected. Be wary also of jellyfish, particularly during the months of September and October. Although they are not lethal in Greece, their stings can be painful. Dousing in vinegar will deactivate any stingers which have not 'fired'. Calamine lotion, antihistamines and analgesics may reduce the reaction and relieve the pain. Much more painful than either of these, but thankfully much rarer, is an encounter with the weever fish. It buries itself in the sand of the tidal zone with only its spines protruding, and injects a painful and powerful toxin if trodden on. Soaking your foot in very hot water (which breaks down the poison) should solve the problem. It can cause permanent local paralysis in the worst instance.

Leeches Leeches are found in damp forest litter as well as in swampy areas. Salt or a lighted cigarette end will persuade them to let go. Don't pull them off, as the bite could become infected. Leeches inject an anti-coagulant which can cause a bite to bleed quite profusely for a while. The itching that follows can last for up to a week.

Mosquitoes These can be a nuisance in Greece, but most people get used to mosquito bites after a few days as their bodies adjust and the itching and swelling become less severe. Avoid bites by covering bare skin and using an insect repellent. Apply vinegar to bites. Insect repellents and mosquito coils are widely available. Some, but by no means all, places to stay have insect screens on windows. One of the most effective deterrents is a small two-pronged electronic device on which a thin tablet is placed. Some hotels supply these, or they can be purchased in shops.

Scorpions Avoid walking barefooted on beaches, particularly at night on pebbled shores, as disturbed scorpions can sting. If stung, seek medical help immediately.

Snakes Greece's only poisonous snake is the adder, but it is so rare that you hardly ever hear of anyone being bitten. Snakes like to sunbathe on dry stone walls, so take care if you need to climb over one of these. Don't put your hands into holes and crevices, and be careful when collecting firewood. In the unlikely event of snakebite, keep the victim calm and still, wrap the bitten limb tightly, as you would for a sprained ankle, and then attach a splint to immobilise it. Then seek medical help. Tourniquets and sucking out the poison are now comprehensively discredited.

Ticks If you plan to spend your time on beaches or in bars, ticks won't be a problem. Ticks are found mainly in grasslands and scrub areas and are associated with animals. They hang around on grasses and branches waiting for a host to brush past. The season is from April to September. It's wise to examine yourself and your clothes after walking through likely tick areas. If you find a tick, a dousing with alcohol will encourage it to let go. It should then be pulled off with tweezers, taking care to ensure you remove all of it. Tick bites normally result in no more than an itchy swelling that lasts for three or four days, but can also spread tick typhus (see the section on Insect-Borne Diseases).

Sheepdogs These dogs are trained to guard penned sheep from bears, wolves and thieves. They are often underfed and sometimes ill-treated by their owners. They are almost always all bark and no bite, but if you are going to trek into remote areas, you should consider having rabies injections (see Rabies). You are most likely to encounter these dogs in the mountainous regions of Epiros and Crete. Wandering through a flock of sheep over which one of these dogs is vigilantly (and possibly discreetly) watching is simply asking for trouble.

Women's Health
Gynaecological Problems Poor diet, lowered resistance due to the use of antibiotics for stomach upsets and even the contraceptive pill can lead to vaginal infections when travelling in hot climates. Maintaining good personal hygiene, and wearing skirts or loose-fitting trousers and cotton underwear will help to prevent infections.

Yeast infections, characterised by a rash, itch and discharge, can be treated with a vinegar or lemon-juice douche, or with yoghurt. Nystatin, miconazole or clotrimazole suppositories are the usual medical prescription. Trichomoniasis is a more serious infection; symptoms are a discharge and a burning sensation when urinating. Male sexual partners must also be treated, and if a vinegar-water douche is not effective medical attention should be sought. Metronidazole (Flagyl) is the prescribed drug.

Pregnancy Most miscarriages occur during the first three months of pregnancy, so this is the most risky time to travel as far as your own health is concerned. Miscarriage is not uncommon, and can occasionally lead to severe bleeding. The last three months should also be spent within reasonable distance of good medical care. A baby born as early as 24 weeks stands a chance of survival, but only in a good modern hospital. Pregnant women should avoid all unnecessary medication. Additional care should be taken to prevent illness, and particular attention should be paid to diet and nutrition. Alcohol and nicotine, for example, should be avoided.

Women travellers often find that their periods become irregular or even cease while they're on the road. Remember that a missed period in these circumstances doesn't necessarily indicate pregnancy.

Tampons Tampons are available in pharmacies and supermarkets in major towns. Recognisable brands include OB and Tampax. These will not be found in small villages where only sanitary napkins may be sold, so ensure you have adequate supplies.

WOMEN TRAVELLERS
Many women travel alone in Greece and, as the crime rate is low, they are often safer than they would be in most European countries. This does not mean that you should be lulled into complacency; bag snatching and rapes do occur, but with no more frequency than elsewhere.

The biggest nuisance to foreign women travelling alone are the guys the Greeks have nicknamed *kamakia*. The word means 'fishing tridents' and refers to the kamaki's favourite pastime, which is 'fishing' for foreign women in order to have a sexual encounter which they can boast to their friends about.

A kamaki will approach and ask something like 'Where do you come from?' or 'Do you like Greece?'. A woman looking at a map gives him a good reason to approach and offer help. Ignoring him at this stage does not always work because a kamaki enjoys a challenge. He'll follow you for a while, but give up eventually. Unfortunately, in your efforts to shake him off, you've probably walked in the opposite direction to the way you wanted to go, and are hopelessly lost, so out will come the map again...

Dressing conservatively helps to a certain extent to keep kamakia at bay, as does looking as if you know where you are going, even if you haven't got a clue. However, these men are very much in the minority, and are a hassle rather than a threat. The majority of Greek men treat foreign women with respect, and are genuinely helpful.

DANGERS & ANNOYANCES
Theft
Crime, especially theft, is low in Greece, but unfortunately it is on the increase. The worst area is Omonia in Athens – keep track of your valuables here and at the flea market which gets very crowded. The vast majority of thefts from tourists are still committed by other tourists, and not by Greeks. Bearing this in mind, the biggest danger of theft is probably in dormitory rooms in hostels and at camp sites. So make sure you do not leave valuables unattended in such places. If you are staying in a hotel room, and the windows and door do not lock securely, ask for your valuables to be locked in the hotel safe – hotel proprietors are happy to do this.

Bar Scams
A warning needs to be given to solo male travellers about an unpleasant practice which is currently largely confined to Athens, although there have been cases in other cities. The practice follows this pattern: a male traveller enters a bar and buys a drink; the owner then offers him another drink. Women appear, more drinks are provided and the visitor relaxes as he realises that the women are not prostitutes, just friendly Greeks. The crunch comes at the end of the evening when the traveller is presented with an exorbitant bill.

Drugs
Greek drug laws are the strictest in Europe. Greek courts make no distinction between possession and pushing. The minimum sentence for even a small quantity of dope is seven years.

WORK
Unemployment in Greece is high so the chances of a foreigner finding lucrative employment are slim. If you wish to take up permanent employment in Greece then the most widely available option is to teach English. A TEFL (Teaching English as a Foreign Language) certificate or a university degree is an advantage but not essential. In the UK, look through the *Times Educational Supplement* or Tuesday's edition of the *Guardian* newspaper – in other countries, contact the Greek embassy. EU nationals don't need a work permit; however, if they intend to stay longer than three months, they will require a residency permit. Nationals of other countries do require a work permit.

Another possibility is to find a job teaching English once you are in Greece. You will see language schools everywhere. Strictly speaking, you need a licence to teach in these schools, but many will employ teachers without one. The best time to look around for such a job is late summer.

If you are an EU national, it's worth contacting the employment agency Working Holidays, Pioneer Tours (☎ 01-322 4321), Nikis 11, Athens. Penny Economou, the manager, is friendly and helpful and speaks excellent English. This agency offers hotel, bar, fruit picking and au pair work. EU nationals can also make use of the OAED (Organismos Apasholiseos Ergatikou Dynamikou), the Greek National Employment Service, in their search for a job. The OAED has offices throughout Greece.

Another alternative is to look through the classifieds of the English-language newspapers, or put an advertisement in one yourself. The notice board at the Compendium bookshop in Athens sometimes advertises jobs. The other option is to look for non-taxable casual work – ask around restaurants and bars in tourist areas. In autumn and winter many foreigners are employed in harvesting and agricultural work. From November to

February, there is work picking oranges in the Peloponnese, especially around the towns of Argos and Nafplio. Crete has the longest season, and the greatest number of crops, so work is available there from November to May. Try the Arhanes region in late summer for work during the grape harvest. Youth hostels are good places to make enquiries about casual work. The UK Employment Service puts out a free booklet entitled *Working in Greece*.

ACTIVITIES
Windsurfing
Windsurfing is the most popular water sport in Greece. Hsrysi Akti on Paros, and Vasiliki on Lefkada vie for the best windsurfing beaches. According to an Australian magazine, Vasiliki is one of the best places in the world to learn the sport, but you'll see sailboards for hire on almost every beach, except the least developed ones. Hire charges range from 1500 to 2000 dr an hour. If you are a novice, most places which rent equipment also give instruction.

Sailboards may only be brought into Greece if a Greek national residing in Greece guarantees that it will be taken out again. To find out the procedure for arranging this, contact the Hellenic Windsurfing Association, Filellinon 7, Athens (☎ 01-323 0330).

Water Skiing
Islands with water-ski centres are Chios, Corfu, Crete, Kythira, Lesvos, Poros, Skiathos and Rhodes.

Snorkelling & Diving
Snorkelling is enjoyable just about anywhere along the coast off Greece. Especially good places are Monastiri on Paros, Velanio on Skopelos, Paleokastritsa on Corfu, Telendos islet (near Kalymnos) and anywhere off the coast of Kastellorizo.

Diving is a another matter. Any kind of underwater activity using breathing apparatus is strictly forbidden other than under the supervision of a diving school. This is to protect the many antiquities in the depths of the Aegean. There are diving schools on the islands of Corfu, Crete (at Rethymno), Evia, Mykonos and Rhodes, and Halkidiki and Glyfada (near Athens) on the mainland. At Glyfada, contact the Aegean Dive Shop (☎ 01-894 5409), Pandoras 31, Glyfada.

Trekking
More than half of Greece is mountainous. It could be a trekkers' paradise, but there is one drawback. Like all organisations in Greece, the EOS (Ellinikos Orivatikos Syndesmos), the Greek Alpine Association, is grossly underfunded. Most EOS staff are volunteers who have full-time day jobs. Consequently, many of the paths in Greece are overgrown and inadequately marked. Don't be put off by this, however, as the most popular routes are well walked and maintained. For trekking in more remote places, see Lonely Planet's *Trekking in Greece*.

On small islands it's fun to discover pathways for yourself. You are unlikely to get into danger as settlements or roads are never far away. You will encounter a variety of paths: *kalderimi* are cobbled or flagstone paths which link settlements and date back to Byzantine times. Sadly, many have been bulldozed to make way for roads. Donkey and mule paths are identifiable by droppings and brown dust on the paths. They are used by farmers, are easy to

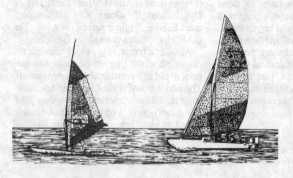

walk along, and usually lead to a settlement, field or farm. Goat tracks are also useful, as goats follow contours and zigzag up slopes – they never charge straight uphill. They can be very narrow and tricky to negotiate, but widen as they approach 'home' – a compound or enclosure.

There are also a number of companies running organised treks. One of the biggest is *Trekking Hellas* (☎ 01-323 4548; fax 01-325 1474), Filellinon 7, Athens 105 57. It offers a range of treks and other wilderness activities all over Greece.

Skiing

Greece provides some of the cheapest skiing in Europe. There are 16 resorts dotted around the mountains of mainland Greece, mainly in the north. The main skiing areas are Mt Parnassos, 195 km north-west of Athens, and Mt Vermio, 110 km west of Thessaloniki. There are no foreign package holidays to these resorts; they are used mainly by Greeks. Most have all the basic facilities and are a pleasant alternative to the glitzy resorts of northern Europe. The season depends on snow conditions but runs approximately from January to the end of April. For further information pick up a copy of *Greece: Mountain Refuges & Ski Centres* from an EOT office. Information may also be obtained from the Hellenic Skiing Federation (☎ 01-524 0057; fax 01-524 8821), PO Box 8037, Omonia, Athens 100 10.

Language Courses

If you are serious about learning the language, an intensive course at the start of your stay is a good way to go about it. Most of the courses are in Athens, but there are also courses on the islands in summer.

The Athens Centre (☎ 01-701 2268; fax 01-701 8603), Arhimidous 48, has a very good reputation. Its courses cover five levels of proficiency from beginners to advanced. There are five immersion courses a year for beginners, packing 60 hours of class time into three weeks for 75,000 dr. The centre runs additional courses at the Anargyrios and Korgialenios College on the island of Spetses in June and July. Their Athens location is a fine neoclassical building in the quiet residential suburb of Mets.

XEN (the YWCA) (☎ 01-362 4291; fax 01-362 2400), Amerikis 11, runs six-week beginners' courses starting in February, May, and October. The courses involve 40 hours of class time and cost 40,000 dr.

Other places in Athens offering courses are the Hellenic American Union (☎ 01-362 9886), Massalias 22, and the Hellenic Language School, Zalongou 4 (☎ 01-362 8161; fax 01-363 9951). The Hellenic Language School also offers courses in Hania, Crete, during June, July and August.

The Hellenic Culture Centre (☎ & fax 01-647 7465, or 0275-61 482) runs courses on the island of Ikaria from June to October. Three-week beginners' courses are 125,000 dr, and there are also two-week courses for 95,000 dr. The centre can also arrange accommodation.

Courses in Modern Greek and Greek Civilisation are conducted at Corfu's Ionian University in July and August. Details are available at Deligiorgi 55-59 (☎ 01-522 9770) in Athens, or from the Secretariat of the Ionian University (☎ 0661-22 993/994) at Megaron Kapodistria 49, Corfu town.

Information about language courses is also available from EOT offices and Greek embassies.

Other Courses

XEN (see above) also has courses in cookery, painting, photography, jewellery-making and Greek dancing.

The Dora Stratou Dance Company (☎ 01-324 4395) holds a series of folk-dancing workshops for amateurs during July and August. The *Weekly Greek News* carries information about this and other workshops.

HIGHLIGHTS
Ancient Sites

Greece has more ancient sites than any other country in Europe. Don't miss the well-known ones such as the Acropolis, Delphi, Delos, Epidaurus, Knossos, Mycenae and Olympia, but also seek out some of the lesser known ones, where you will encounter only a handful of other visitors. These include the Sanctuary of the Great Gods on Samothraki, Ancient Dion near Mt Olympus, Dodoni near Ioannina and Lato near Agios Nikolaos on Crete.

Historic Towns

Two of Greece's most spectacular medieval cities are the deserted Byzantine city of Mystras and the still-inhabited Byzantine city of Monemvassia. Both cities are in the Peloponnese.

The old town of Rhodes is the finest surviving example of a fortified medieval town. The Kastro quarter of Naxos town, on Naxos, where archways span the narrow stepped alleyways of whitewashed Venetian houses, is tranquil and beautiful. The *hora* (main village) of Folegandros is one of the prettiest of the archetypal Cycladic towns; with its dazzling white cubic architecture and narrow winding streets. The 13th-century village of Pyrgi, on Chios, is visually the most unusual village in Greece – the exterior walls of the houses are decorated with striking black-and-white geometrical patterns. Mesta, also on Chios, is an evocative fortified medieval village. The old quarter of the Thracian town of Xanthi has the best preserved houses from the Turkish era.

Museums

First on everyone's list should be the National Archaeological Museum in Athens. Its vast collection includes the celebrated finds unearthed by Heinrich Schliemann at Mycenae, and the Minoan frescoes from Akrotiri, on the island of Santorini (Thira). The Archaeological Museum in Thessaloniki houses treasures from the graves of the Macedonian royal family. Iraklio's Archaeological Museum houses finds from the Neolithic to the Roman periods, but its star attraction is the Minoan collection.

The Cycladic Art Museum in Athens wins top marks for presentation as well for its collection of early Cycladic art. Other outstanding museums are Nafplio's Popular Art Museum and the Folklore Museum in Thessaloniki.

Hotels

It is the islands that provide some of the finest settings. It's hard to imagine anywhere more romantic than Anemomilos Apartments, perched above the sea on a precipice on Folegandros in the Cyclades. The white-walled apartments are traditionally Cycladic with laced-cotton curtains on the windows.

The Captain's House in Emboreios, Halki, in the Dodecanese, is an outstanding place to stay: a turn-of-the-century ex-admiral's house with antique furniture, a tranquil garden and charming owners. If you want to splurge, Symi is the best place in the Dodecanese. The Hotel Aliki ranks first among a number of beautifully restored 19th-century mansions.

The Hotel Laureate, on Lesvos, could be classified as one of the island's treasures. It offers beautifully furnished studio apartments in a converted mansion that could easily have been plucked out of the English countryside.

Hydra, in the Saronic Gulf, has a remarkably high standard of accommodation across the board, none better than the very stylish Hotel Orloff.

Restaurants

Some of the best food in Athens costs a mere 250 dr and comes wrapped in a piece of greaseproof paper – the fabulous gyros at Savas, on Mitropoleos near Plateia Monastirakiou. You can lash out and pay 300 dr for the chicken version. Still in Athens, the inconspicuous Taverna Avli, tucked away in the unfashionable area near the railway stations at Proussis 21, turns out food of unusual imagination and variety.

There are some gems dotted around the Greek islands. A meal at the Restaurant Morias sta Mesta is an experience to treasure. The restaurant is located on a romantic little square in the medieval town of Mesta on Chios. Outstanding in the Cyclades are the Mokka Restaurant at Livadi, Serifos, and the Restaurant I Trata at Paroikia, Paros, which both offer superb seafood prepared according to island recipes.

If you make it to Karpathos, don't miss the delicious appetisers at Kalimera Ellas Ouzeria. The local speciality, galakto-boureko, served at O Michalaras Special Cakes Café, is something to look out for on Kalymnos.

Back on the mainland, a treat lies in store for anyone venturing into the back blocks of Epiros. The unassuming Skaraveos Restaurant in Arta serves superb home cooking.

Beaches

Out of high season, especially if you have your own transport, Sithonia, the middle prong of the Halkidiki peninsula, is worth exploring for its long stretches of fine sandy beach. In the Peloponnese, the western coast of the Messini peninsula, from Kyparissia to Methoni, is studded with sandy beaches. Zaga beach, at Koroni, on the eastern side of the same peninsula, is one of the most gorgeous – and longest – beaches in Greece.

The islands of Paros, Naxos, Ios and Mykonos have the best beaches in the Cyclades. Unfortunately a lot of people know this, so finding a secluded spot requires legwork. The coasts of Thasos and Limnos, both in the North-Eastern Aegean group, boast many sandy beaches. Other exceptional beaches are those on the small island of Elafonisi, near Neapoli in the Peloponnese; Porto Katsiki and Vasiliki on Lefkada, in the Ionian group; Psili Ammos on Patmos, Armenistis on Ikaria and Eristos on Tilos, in the Dodecanese group; and Pahia Ammos on Samothraki and Skala Eresou on Lesvos, in the North-Eastern Aegean group.

ACCOMMODATION

There is a range of accommodation available in Greece to suit every taste and pocket. All places to stay are subject to strict price controls set by the tourist police. By law, a notice must be displayed in every room, which states the category of the room and the price charged in each season. The price includes 4.5% community tax and 8% VAT.

Accommodation owners may add a 10% surcharge for a stay of less than three nights, but this is not mandatory. A mandatory charge of 20% is levied if an extra bed is put into a room. During July and August, accommodation owners will charge the maximum price, but in spring and autumn, prices will drop by up to 20%, and perhaps by even more in winter. These are the times to bring your bargaining skills into action.

Rip-offs rarely occur, but if you suspect you have been exploited by an accommodation owner, report it to either the tourist police or regular police and they will act swiftly.

Camping

There are almost 350 camping grounds in Greece. A few are operated by the EOT, but most are privately run. Very few are open outside the high season (April to October). The Greek Camping Association (☎ 01-346 5262) publishes an annual booklet listing all of the country's camp sites and their facilities. The association's address is Solonos 102, GR-196 80 Athens.

Camping fees are highest from 15 June to the end of August. Most camping grounds charge from 920 to 1000 dr per adult and 550 to 600 dr for children aged four to 12. There's no charge for children aged under four. Tent sites cost from 630 to 860 dr for small tents, and from 750 to 1320 dr per night for large tents. Caravan site rates range from 1080 to 1620 dr.

Between May and mid-September it is warm enough to sleep out under the stars, although you will still need a lightweight sleeping bag to counter the pre-dawn chill. It's a good idea to have a foam pad to lie on and a waterproof cover for your sleeping bag.

Camping other than at official sites is illegal, but the rule is not always strictly enforced. If you do decide to take a chance on this, make sure you are not camping on private land, and clear up all rubbish when you leave. If you are told to move by the police, do so without protest, as the law is occasionally enforced in this matter. Freelance camping is more likely to be tolerated on islands which don't have camp sites. It's wise to ask around before freelance camping anywhere in Greece.

Hostels

There is only one youth hostel in Greece affiliated to the International Youth hostel Federation (IYHF), the superb Athens International Youth Hostel (☎ 01-523 4170). You don't need a IYHF card to stay there; temporary membership costs 500 dr per day.

Most youth hostels in Greece are run by the Greek Youth Hostel Organisation (☎ 01-751 9530), Damareos 75, 116 33 Athens. There are affiliated hostels in Athens (two), Litohoro (Mt Olympus), Mycenae, Olympia, Patras and Thessaloniki on the mainland, and on the islands of Corfu, Crete, Ios, Naxos, Santorini, and Tinos. There are six on Crete – at Iraklio, Malia, Myrthios, Plakias, Rethymno and Sitia.

Other hostels belong to the Greek Youth Hostels Association (☎ 01-323 4107), Dragatsaniou 4, 105 59 Athens. It has hostels in Delphi and Nafplio on the mainland, and on the islands of Corfu, Crete (Hersonisos and Iraklio) and Santorini.

Whatever their affiliation, the hostels are mostly very casual places. Their rates vary from 1000 to 1500 dr and you don't have to be a member to stay in any of them. Few have curfews.

Athens has a number of private hostels catering to budget travellers. Standards vary enormously – from clean, friendly places to veritable fleapits. Most charge from 1500 to 2000 dr for dorm beds.

There are XEN (YWCA) hostels for women only in Athens and Thessaloniki.

Mountain Refuges

There are 55 mountain refuges dotted around the Greek mainland, Crete and Evia. They range from small huts with outdoor toilets and no cooking facilities to comfortable modern lodges. They are run by the country's various mountaineering and skiing clubs. The EOT publication *Greece: Mountain Refuges & Ski Centres* has details about each refuge. Prices range from 1200 to 2000 dr per person, depending on the facilities.

Domatia

Domatia are the Greek equivalent of the British bed and breakfast, minus the breakfast. Once upon a time domatia comprised little more than spare rooms in the family home which could be rented out to travellers in summer; nowadays, many are purpose-built appendages to the family house. Some come complete with fully equipped kitchens. Standards of cleanliness are generally high. The décor runs the gamut from cool grey marble floors, coordinated pine furniture, pretty lace curtains and tasteful pictures on the walls, to ones so full of kitsch, you are almost afraid to move in case you break an ornament.

They remain a popular option for budget travellers. Domatia are classified A, B and C. Expect to pay 3500 to 5000 dr for a single, and 5000 to 8000 dr for a double, depending on the class, whether bathrooms are shared or private, and the season. In some domatia, you may be charged between 300 and 400 dr for hot water. Domatia are found throughout the mainland (except in large cities) and on almost every island which has a permanent population. Most domatia are available only between April and October.

From June to September domatia owners are out in force, touting for customers. They meet buses and boats, shouting 'Room, room!', and often carry photographs of their rooms. In peak season, it can prove a mistake not to take up an offer – but be wary of owners who are vague about the location of their accommodation. 'Close to town' can turn out to be way out in the sticks. If you are at all dubious, insist they show you the location on a map.

Farmstays

You can guarantee that you will wind up out in the sticks if you take up any of the accommodation options available through the Ministry of Agriculture's agrotourism scheme, which offers rooms in farm houses in remote rural areas. The scheme was set up to provide extra income for farmers, thereby hopefully encouraging them to stay on their farms rather than moving to the city.

It's ideal for people with their own transport who want to get out and see rural Greece. The Ministry of Agriculture (☎ 01-524 8555), Aharnon 2, 104 39 Athens (just north of Plateia Vathis), publishes a brochure called *Agrotourism: Holidays in the Countryside* which lists more than 250 farms. The majority are in central Greece, the northwest and the Peloponnese, but there are also places on many of the islands including Chios, Crete, Evia, Karpathos, Kefallonia, Kythira, Limnos, Lesvos, Samos, Samothraki and Skopelos.

Like domatia, farmstays are classified A, B or C according to their facilities. They charge similar prices. Some also offer meals.

Hotels

Hotels in Greece are divided into six categories: deluxe, A, B, C, D and E. Hotels are categorised according to the size of the room, whether or not they have a bar, and the ratio of bathrooms to beds, rather than standards of cleanliness, comfort of the beds and friendliness of staff – all elements which may be of greater relevance to guests. As one would expect, deluxe, A and B-class hotels have many amenities, private bathrooms and constant hot water. C-class hotels have a snack bar, rooms have private bathrooms, but hot water may only be available at certain times of the day. D-class hotels may or may not have snack bars, most rooms will share bathrooms, but there may be some with private bathrooms, and they may have solar-heated water, which means hot water is not guaranteed. E classes do not have a snack bar, bathrooms are shared and you may have to pay extra (300 or 400 dr) for hot water, or there may be none at all.

Prices are controlled by the tourist police and the maximum rate that can be charged for a room should be displayed on a board behind the door. The classification often is not much of a guide to price. Rates in D and E-class hotels generally are comparable with domatia. Expect to pay between 6000 and 9000 dr for a single in high season in C class, 9000 to 12,000 dr for a double and 10,000 to 14,000 dr for a triple. Prices are about 2000 dr higher across the board in a B class, and a further 2000 dr higher in A class – although there are enough exceptions to prove the rule many times over.

Pensions

Pensions in Greece are virtually indistinguishable from hotels. They are classed A, B or C. An A-class pension is equivalent in amenities and price to a B-class hotel, a B-class pension is equivalent to a C-class hotel and a C-class pension is equivalent to a D or E-class hotel.

Apartments

Self-contained family apartments are available in some hotels and domatia. There are also a number of purpose-built apartments, particularly on the islands, which are available for either long or short-term rental. Prices vary considerably according to the amenities offered. In Athens, the classified sections of the *Athens News* and *Weekly Greek News* both advertise apartments. The notice board at Compendium Bookshop in Athens is also worth a look. The tourist police may be able to help in other major towns. In rural areas and islands, ask in a kafeneio.

Traditional Settlements

Traditional settlements are old buildings of architectural merit that have been renovated and converted into tourist accommodation. These are terrific places to stay, but they are expensive – most are equivalent in price to an A or B-class hotel. The EOT publishes a leaflet with details of these places and you may reserve a room through them. There are traditional settlements on the islands of Santorini, Psara and Chios, on the peninsulas of the Mani and Pelion, and in Monemvassia.

FOOD

Greek food does not enjoy a reputation as one of the world's great cuisines. Maybe that's because many travellers have experienced Greek cooking only in tourist resorts. The old joke about the Greek woman who, on summer days, shouted to her husband 'Come and eat your lunch before it gets hot' is based on truth. Until recently, food was invariably served lukewarm – which is how Greeks prefer it. Most restaurants that cater to tourists have now cottoned on that foreigners expect cooked dishes to be served hot, and improved methods of warming meals (including the dreaded microwave) have made this easier. If it is not hot, ask that it be served *zesto* or order grills, which have to be cooked to order. Greeks are fussy about fresh ingredients, and frozen food is rare.

Greeks eat out regularly, regardless of socioeconomic status. Despite a flagging economy, enjoying life remains of paramount importance, and a large part of this enjoyment comes from eating and drinking with friends.

By law, every eating establishment must display a written menu including prices. Bread will automatically be put on your table and usually costs between 100 and 200 dr, depending on the restaurant's category. If you don't want bread, you must specify this when ordering. If it comes to the table, you will be billed for it.

Tavernas

The taverna is usually a traditional place with a rough-and-ready ambience, although some are more up-market, particularly in Athens, resorts and big towns. In simple tavernas, a menu is usually displayed in the window or on the door, but not all have menus and you may be invited into the kitchen to peer into the pots and point to what you want. This is not merely a privilege for tourists; Greeks also do it because they want to see the taverna's version of the dishes on offer. Some tavernas don't open until 8 pm, and then stay open until the early hours. Some are closed on Sunday.

Restaurants

A restaurant *(estiatorio)* is more sophisticated than a taverna, with damask tablecloths, smartly attired waiters and printed menus at each table – often with an English translation. Ready-made food is usually displayed in a *bain-marie* and there may be a charcoal grill. Some restaurants offer breakfast and remain open all day while others serve lunch between 1 and 3 pm and dinner from 8 pm to 1 am. Some close on Sunday. Restaurants specialising in spit roasts and charcoal-grilled food – usually lamb, pork or chicken – are called *psistaria*.

Ouzeria

An *ouzeri* serves ouzo. Greeks believe it is essential to eat when drinking alcohol so, in traditional establishments, your drink will come with a small plate of titbits or mezedes – perhaps olives, a slice of feta and some pickled octopus. Ouzeria are becoming trendy and are increasingly offering menus with larger choices of appetisers and main courses.

Galaktopoleia

A *galaktopoleio* (literally 'milk shop') sells dairy produce including milk, butter, yoghurt, rice pudding, cornflour pudding, custard, eggs, honey and bread. It may also sell home-made ice cream in several flavours. Look for the sign *pagoto politiko* displayed outside. Most have seating and serve coffee and tea. They are inexpensive for breakfast and usually open from very early in the morning until evening.

Zaharoplasteia

A *zaharoplasteio* (pâtisserie) sells cakes (both traditional and Western), chocolates, biscuits, sweets, coffee, soft drinks and, possibly, bottled alcoholic drinks. They usually have some seating.

Kafeneia

Kafeneia are often regarded by foreigners as the last bastion of male chauvinism in Europe. With bare light bulbs, nicotine-stained walls, smoke-laden air, rickety wooden tables and raffia chairs, they are frequented by middle-aged and elderly Greek men in cloth caps who while away their time fiddling with worry beads, playing cards or backgammon or engaged in heated political discussion. It was once unheard of for women to enter kafeneia but, in large cities, this situation is changing.

In rural areas, Greek women are rarely seen inside kafeneia. When a female traveller enters one, she is inevitably treated courteously and with friendship if she manages a few Greek words of greeting. If you feel inhibited about going into a kafeneio, opt for outside seating. You'll feel less intrusive. Kafeneia originally only served Greek coffee but, now, most also serve soft drinks, Nescafé and beer. They are generally fairly cheap, with Greek coffee for about 150 dr and Nescafé with milk for 250 dr or less. Most kafeneia are open all day every day, but some close during siesta time (roughly from 3 to 5 pm).

Other Eateries

Infiltrations from other countries include pizzerias, creperies and *gelaterias* (which sell Italian-style ice cream in various flavours). You'll also find the occasional Chinese, Japanese and Indian restaurant in Athens and Thessaloniki but authenticity of cuisine cannot be guaranteed and prices tend to be high.

Meals

Breakfast Most Greeks have Greek coffee and perhaps a cake or pastry for breakfast. Budget hotels and pensions offering breakfast provide it continental style (rolls or bread with jam, and tea or coffee) and up-market hotels serve breakfast buffets (Western and continental styles). Otherwise, restaurants and galaktopoleia serve bread with butter, jam or honey; eggs; and the budget travellers' favourite, yoghurt *(yiaourti)* with honey. In tourist areas, many menus offer an 'English' breakfast – which means bacon and eggs.

Lunch This is eaten late – between 1 and 3 pm – and may be either a snack or a complete meal. The main meal can be lunch or dinner – or both. Greeks enjoy eating and often have two large meals a day.

Dinner Greeks also eat dinner late. Many people don't start to think about food until about 9 pm, which is why some restaurants don't bother to open their doors until after 8 pm. In tourist areas dinner is often served earlier.

A full dinner in Greece begins with appetisers and/or soup, followed by a main course of either ready-made food, grilled meat, or fish. Only very posh restaurants or those pandering to tourists include Western-style desserts on the menu. Greeks usually eat cakes separately in a galaktopoleio or zaharoplasteio.

Greek Specialities

Mezedes In a simple taverna, possibly only three or four *mezedes* (appetisers) will be offered – perhaps taramasalata (fish-roe dip), tzatziki (yoghurt, cucumber and garlic dip), olives and feta (sheep's or goat's milk cheese). Ouzeria and restaurants usually offer wider selections.

Mezedes include *ohtapodi* (octopus), *garides* (shrimps), *kalamaria* (squid), dolmades (stuffed vine leaves), *melitzano-salata* (aubergine or eggplant dip) and *mavromatika* (black-eyed beans). Hot mezedes include *keftedes* (meatballs), *fasolia* (broad white beans), *loukanika* (little sausages), *tyropitta* (cheese pie), *spana-kopitta* (spinach pie), *bourekaki* (tiny meat pie), *kolokythakia* (deep-fried zucchini), *melitzana* (deep-fried aubergine) and *saganaki* (fried cheese). It is quite acceptable to make a full meal of these instead of a main course. Three plates of mezedes are about equivalent in price and quantity to one main course. You can also order a *pikilia* (mixed plate).

Soups & Salads Soup is a satisfying starter or, indeed, an economical meal in itself with bread and a salad. *Psarosoupa* is fish soup with vegetables, made piquant when egg and lemon sauce *(avgolemano)* is added. Greek bouillabaisse *(kakavia)* is laden with seafood and more expensive – but heavenly. Economical *fasolada* (bean soup) is also a meal in itself. *Avgolemano soupa* (egg and lemon soup) is usually prepared from a chicken stock. And, if you're into offal, don't miss the traditional Easter soup *mayiritsa* at this festive time.

The ubiquitous (and no longer inexpensive) Greek or village salad *horiatiki salata* is a side dish for Greeks, but many drachma-conscious tourists make it a main dish. It consists of peppers, onions, olives, tomatoes and feta cheese, sprinkled with oregano and dressed with olive oil and lemon juice. A tomato salad often comes with onions, cucumber and olives, and, with bread, makes a satisfying lunch. In winter, try the cheaper *radikia salata* (dandelion salad).

Main Courses The most common main courses are moussaka (layers of eggplant or zucchini, minced meat and potatoes topped with cheese sauce and baked), *pastitsio* (baked cheese-topped macaroni and béchamel, with or without minced meat), dolmades (stuffed vine leaves) and *yemista* (stuffed tomatoes or green peppers). Other main courses include *giouvetsi* (casserole of lamb or veal and pasta), *stifado* (meat stewed with onions), *soutzoukakia* (spicy meatballs in tomato sauce, also known as Smyrna sausages) and *salingaria* (snails in oil with herbs). *Melizanes papoutsakia* is baked eggplant stuffed with meat and tomatoes, and topped with cheese, which looks, as its Greek name suggests, like a little shoe. Spicy *loukanika* (sausage) is a good budget choice and comes with potatoes or rice. Lamb fricassee, cooked with lettuce *arni fricassée me maroulia* is usually filling enough for two to share.

Fish is usually sold by weight in restaurants but is not as cheap nor as widely available as it used to be. The Mediterranean has been overfished – sometimes legally, to satisfy a growing demand from restaurateurs in big cities – and sometimes illegally by dynamiting. Calamari (squid), deep fried in batter, remains a tasty option for the budget traveller at 900 to 1300 dr for a generous serve. Other reasonably priced fish (about 1000 dr a portion) are *marides* (whitebait), sometimes cloaked in onion, pepper and tomato sauce, and *gopes*, which are similar to sardines. More expensive are ohtapodi (octopus), *bakaliaros* (cod), *xifias* (swordfish) and *glossa* (sole). Ascending the price scale further are *lithrinia* (bass) and *barbounia* (red mullet). *Astakos* (lobster) is topnotch at about 10,000 dr per kg.

Fish is mostly grilled or fried. More imaginative fish dishes include shrimp casserole and mussel or octopus saganaki (fried with tomato and cheese) and psarosoupa (fish soup). As Greece has few rivers and lakes, freshwater fish are not widely available although reasonably priced *pestrofa* (trout) is found in Epiros, from Lake Pamvotis in Ioannina, the Aoös River in Zagoria, and also from the Prespa Lakes in Macedonia.

Regional Dishes Greek food is not all moussaka and souvlakia. Every region has its own specialities and it need not be an expensive culinary adventure to discover some of these. Corfu, for example, which was never occupied by the Turks, retains traditional recipes of Italian, Spanish and ancient Greek derivations. Corfiot food is served in several restaurants and includes *sofrito* (lamb or veal with garlic, vinegar and parsley), *pastitsada*, (beef with macaroni, cloves, garlic, tomatoes and cheese) and *burdeto* (fish with paprika and cayenne). Look for poultry and venison in the Peloponnese, citrus-flavoured dishes in Argolis (along with succulent fresh oranges and lemons), and eggplant dishes in Argos and try the famed olives when in Kalamata. Only in Epiros will you find freshwater crustaceans, trout, carp and eel, cooked to special recipes. Game is inevitably on the menu in Thessaly and Macedonia.

Santorini's baby tomatoes flavour distinctive dishes, not least a rich soup as thick and dark as blood. The *myzithra* (soft ewe's milk cheese) of Ios is unique, and the lamb pies of Kefallonia and Crete are worth searching for. Andros' specialty, *froutalia*, (spearmint-flavoured potato and sausage omelette) is good value. Rhodes' special, baked omelette is loaded with meat and zucchini. Spetses'

A Greek Feast
Greek dishes are easy to prepare at home. Here's a simple lunch or dinner to share with friends.

Tzatziki (Cucumber & Yoghurt Dip)
Peel and grate a medium cucumber. Add a breakfast cup of yoghurt, a tablespoon of olive oil, a pinch of salt, a teaspoon of vinegar, 1½ teaspoons of freshly chopped dill and a minced garlic clove and refrigerate for two hours. Garnish with an olive and serve with fresh crusty bread or as a companion to vegetables or fried fish.

Soupa Avgolemono (Egg & Lemon Soup)
Add 6½ tablespoons of uncooked rice to six cups of boiling chicken, fish or beef stock, then cover and simmer until the rice is tender. Beat two eggs, adding a pinch of salt and the juice of a large lemon. Add stock to this mixture slowly, so that it doesn't curdle, then pour the mixture into a pot for reheating. Stir and ensure it does not boil.

Soutzoukakia (Sausages from Smyrna)
This hearty dish originated in Smyrna (İzmir) in the days of Greek occupation and has subsequently been adopted by the cooks of Thessaloniki. Soak two slices of white bread in a half cup of water, mash and add three garlic cloves, finely chopped, half a teaspoon of pepper and a dessertspoon of cumin.

Add 500g (1lb) of minced lamb or beef and a beaten egg, mix well and form into small sausages. Place in an oiled roasting pan and bake in a medium to hot oven until the sausages brown on the base side. Turn the sausages and add 500 g (1lb) of tomatoes, a dollop of butter and teaspoon of sugar and return to the oven for about 15 minutes – or until the tomatoes are soft and the soutzoukakia are brown on the other side. Serve with fried potatoes or rice, and salad.

Halvas tou Fournou (Baked Halva)
Here's a delightful dessert that is simple to make. Sift a half cup of flour with two teaspoons of baking powder and a pinch of salt. Add two cups of semolina and a cup of finely chopped nuts. Cream ¾ of a cup of butter or margarine with a cup of sugar and add three beaten eggs and grated lemon peel. Combine the mixtures well, then pour into a greased, square, 25-cm (10-inch) pan. Bake in a medium oven until golden. Boil three cups of water with three cups of sugar, and add four cloves and a half stick of cinnamon, then pour it over the rest of the dessert. Leave it to stand until the cinnamon and clove mixture has been absorbed, then serve with or without cream, warm or cold. It's filling and keeps for days.

Recipes serve four people. ■

baked fish is renowned. Soutzoukakia, while available nationally, are best in Thessaloniki where most cooks dare to add the cumin needed to give them oomph.

If you're out in the countryside and the loud bangs disturbing you are not caused by children setting off firecrackers in celebration of Easter or Independence Day, it will be shooting season. Be prepared to be offered pigeon, partridge, duck and hare (sometimes written on the menu as rabbit).

Desserts & Cakes Greek cakes and puddings include baklava (layers of filo pastry filled with honey and nuts), *loukoumades* (puffs or fritters with honey or syrup), *kataïfi* (chopped nuts inside shredded wheat pastry or filo soaked in honey), *rizogalo* (rice pudding), *loukoumi* (Turkish delight), halva (made from semolina or sesame seeds) and *pagoto* (ice cream). Tavernas and restaurants usually only have a few of these on the menu. The best places to go for these delights are galaktopoleia or zaharoplasteia.

Vegetarian Food

Greece has few vegetarian restaurants. Unfortunately, many vegetable soups and stews are based on meat stocks. Fried vegetables are safe bets as olive oil is always used – never lard. The Greeks do wonderful things with artichokes *(anginares)*, which thrive in Greece. Stuffed, served as a salad, as a mezes, (particularly with raki in Crete) and as the basis of a vegetarian stew, the artichoke warrants greater discovery by visitors. Vegetarians who eat eggs can be assured that an economical omelette can be whipped up anywhere. Salads are cheap, fresh, substantial and nourishing. Other options are yoghurt, rice pudding, cheese and spinach pies, and nuts. Creperies also offer tasty vegetarian selections.

Lent, incidentally, is a good time for vegetarians because the meat is missing from many dishes.

Fast Food

Western-style fast food has arrived in Greece in a big way. Fans of McDonald's will find their favourite burger in a number of locations in Athens and major towns. There are also a host of similar franchises like Wendy's and Goody's, as well as chicken and pizza chains.

It's hard, though, to beat the eat-on-the-street Greek offerings. Foremost among them are the *gyros* and the souvlakia. The gyros is a giant skewer laden with slabs of seasoned meat which grills slowly as it rotates and the meat is trimmed steadily from the outside; souvlakia are small individual kebab sticks. Both are served wrapped in pitta bread, with salad and lashings of tzatziki.

Snacks Favourite Greek snacks include pretzel rings sold by street vendors, *tost* (toasted sandwiches), tyropitta, *bougatsa* (custard-filled pastry), spanakopitta and *sandouits* (sandwiches). Street vendors sell various nuts and dried seeds such as pumpkin for 200 to 400 dr a bag. Chestnuts are roasted on the roadsides in the autumn.

Fruit

Greece grows many varieties of fruit. Most visitors will be familiar with *syka* (figs), *rodakina* (peaches), *stafylia* (grapes), *karpouzi* (watermelon), *milo* (apples), *portokalia* (oranges) and *kerasia* (cherries).

Many will not, however, have encountered the *frangosyko* (prickly pear). Also known as the Barbary fig, it is the fruit of the opuntia cactus, recognisable by the thick green spiny pads that form its trunk. The fruit are borne around the edge of the pads in late summer and autumn and vary in colour from pale orange to deep red. They are delicious but need to be approached with extreme caution because of the thousands of tiny prickles (invisible to the naked eye) that cover their skin. Never pick one up with your bare hands as the needles can easily become embedded in your skin. They must be peeled before you can eat them. The simplest way to do this is to trim the ends off with a knife and then slit the skin from end to end.

Another fruit that will be new to many people is the *mousmoula* (loquat). These small, brown fruit are among the first of summer, reaching the market in mid-May. The flesh is juicy and pleasantly acidic.

Self-Catering

Eating out in Greece is as much an entertainment as a gastronomic experience, so to self-cater is to sacrifice a lot. If, however, you are on a low budget you will need to make the sacrifice – for breakfast and lunch at any rate. All towns and villages of any size have well-stocked supermarkets, fruit and vegetable stalls, bakeries, and a weekly *laïki agora* market.

Many towns also have huge indoor food markets which feature fruit and vegetable stalls, butchers, dairies and delicatessens, all under one roof.

Only in isolated villages and on remote islands is food choice limited. There may only be one all-purpose shop – a *pantopoleio* which will stock meat, vegetables, fruit, bread and tinned foods.

DRINKS
Nonalcoholic Drinks

Coffee & Tea Greek coffee is the national drink. It is a legacy of Ottoman rule and, until the Turkish invasion of Cyprus in 1974, the Greeks called it Turkish coffee. It is served with the grounds, without milk, in a small cup. Connoisseurs claim there are at least 30 variations of Greek coffee, but most people know only three – *glyko* (sweet), *metrio* (medium) and *sketo* (without sugar).

The next most popular coffee is instant, called Nescafé (which it usually is). Ask for

Greek coffee: finely ground coffee is boiled with water and sugar and served in tiny cups

Nescafé *me ghala* (pronounced 'me GA-la') if you want it with milk. In summer, Greeks drink Nescafé chilled, with or without milk and sugar – this version is called *frappé*.

Espresso and filtered coffee are served only in trendy cafés. Cappuccino is often seen on menus but tends to be the Viennese rather than the Italian version. Or at least, the Greek version of a Viennese cappuccino, which is a strange concoction of black instant coffee with synthetic cream floating on top. You'll pay through the nose for it – more than 500 dr. If you want an Italian cappuccino, ensure it's what the café serves before you order. Tea is inevitably made with a tea bag.

Fruit Juice Packaged fruit juices are available everywhere. The Life range is especially good. It includes peach, *sanguini* (blood orange), Ruby grapefruit, Williams pear and Valencia orange. Fresh orange juice is not hard to find, but doesn't come cheap.

Milk Milk is expensive – a litre costs about 400 dr. Fresh milk can be hard to find on the islands and in remote areas. UHT milk is available almost everywhere, as is condensed milk.

Soft Drinks Coca-Cola, Pepsi, Seven-Up, Sprite and Fanta are available everywhere in cans and bottles.

Water Tap water is safe to drink in Greece but, if you prefer it, bottled spring water is sold widely in 750-ml and 1.5-litre plastic bottles. If you're happy with tap water, fill a container with it before embarking on ferries where the price of bottled water is inflated. Bottled sparkling mineral water is rarely seen.

Alcohol

Beer All the beers produced in Greece are brewed under licence by off-shoots of major northern European breweries. The most popular beers are Amstel and Heineken. Amstel is cheaper than Heineken, and bottles are cheaper than cans. Supermarkets are the cheapest place to buy beer. A 500-ml bottle of Amstel costs about 170 dr (including 25 dr deposit on the bottle), while a 500-ml can costs about 210 dr. Amstel also produces a low-alcohol beer and a bock, which is dark, sweet and strong.

Other beers brewed locally are Henniger, Kaiser, Kronenbourg and Tuborg. Imported lagers, stouts and beers are found in tourist spots such as music bars and discos. You might even spot Newcastle Brown, Carlsberg, Castlemaine XXXX and Guinness.

Wine According to mythology, the Greeks invented or discovered wine and it has been produced in Greece on a large scale for more than three thousand years.

The modern wine industry, though, is still very much in its infancy. Until the 1950s, most Greek wines were sold in bulk and were seldom distributed any further afield than the nearest town. It wasn't until the advent of industrialisation (and the resulting rapid urban growth) that there was much call for bottled wine. Quality control was unheard of until 1969, when appellation laws were introduced as a precursor to applying for membership of the European Community, and wines have improved significantly since then. The big private wineries have introduced new technology, and cooperative wineries and some smaller growers are following suit.

Don't expect Greek wines to taste like French wines. The varieties grown in Greece are quite different. Some of the most popular and reasonably priced labels include Rotonda, Kambas, Boutari, Calliga and Lac des Roches. Boutari's Naoussa is worth looking out for. It's a dry red wine from the Naoussa area of north-west Macedonia.

More expensive, but of good quality, are the Achaïa-Clauss wines from Patras. The most expensive wines are the Kefallonian Robola de Cephalonie, a superb dry white, and those produced by the Porto Carras estate in Halkidiki. Good wines are produced on Rhodes (famous in Greece for its champagne) and Crete. Other island wines worth sampling are those from Samos (immor-

talised by Lord Byron), Santorini, where rosé is memorable, Kefallonia and Paros. *Aspro* is white, *mavro* is red and *kokkinelli* is rosé.

Strong Liquor Ouzo is the most popular aperitif in Greece. Distilled from grape stems and flavoured with anise, it is similar to the Middle Eastern *arak*, Turkish *raki* and French Pernod. Clear and colourless, it turns white when water is added. A 700-ml bottle of a popular brand like Ouzo 12, Olympic or Sáns Rival costs about 1000 dr. In an ouzeri, a glass costs from 250 to 400 dr. It will be served neat, with a separate glass of water to be used for dilution.

The second-most popular spirit is Greek brandy, which is dominated by the Metaxa label. Metaxa comes in a wide choice of grades, starting with three star – a high-octane product without much finesse. You can pick up a bottle in a supermarket for about 1500 dr. The quality improves as you go through the grades: five star, seven star, VSOP, Golden Age and finally the top-of-the-range Grand Olympian Reserve (4400 dr). Other reputable brands include Cambas and Votrys.

The Cretan speciality is raki, a fiery clear spirit that is served as a greeting (regardless of the time of day).

If you're travelling off the beaten track, you may come across *chipura*. Like ouzo, it's made from grape stems but without the anise. It's an acquired taste, much like Irish poteen and packing a similar punch. You'll most likely encounter chipura in village kafeneia or private homes.

There have been reports, mainly from Ios and Paros, about hooch (flavoured to taste like well-known spirits) being sold in place of the genuine article. Beware of citrus-flavoured shots, often given or sold cheaply, to give one a thirst for more strong, straight stuff.

ENTERTAINMENT

All of the large cities have cinemas, theatres, classical concerts, rock gigs, discos and jazz clubs. Discos abound in resort areas.

Retsina

A holiday in Greece would not be the same without a jar or three of retsina, the famous – some might say notorious – resinated wine that is the speciality of Attica and neighbouring areas of Central Greece.

Your first taste of retsina may well leave you wondering whether the waiter has mixed up the wine and the paint stripper, but stick with it – it's a taste that's worth acquiring. Soon you will be savouring the delicate pine aroma, and the initial astringency mellows to become very moreish. Retsina is very refreshing consumed chilled at the end of a hot day, when it goes particularly well with tzatziki.

Greeks have been resinating wine, both white and rosé, for millennia. The ancient Greeks dedicated the pine tree to Dionysos, also the god of wine, and held that land that grew good pine would also grow good wine.

No-one seems quite sure how wine and pine first got together. The consensus is that it was an inevitable accident in a country with so much wine and so much pine. The theory that resin entered the winemaking process because the wine was stored in pine barrels does not hold water, since the ancients used clay amphora rather than barrels. It's more likely that it was through pine implements and vessels used elsewhere in the process. Producers discovered that wine treated with resin kept for longer, and consumers discovered that they liked it.

Resination was once a fairly haphazard process, achieved by various methods such as adding crushed pine cones to the brew and coating the insides of storage vessels. The amount of resin also varied enormously. One 19th-century traveller wrote that he had tasted tested a wine 'so impregnated with resin that it almost took the skin from my lips'. His reaction was hardly surprising; he was probably drinking a wine with a resin content as high as 7.5%, common at the time. A more sophisticated product awaits the modern traveller, with a resin content no higher than 1% – as specified by good old EU regulations. That's still enough to give the wine its trademark astringency and pine aroma.

The bulk of retsina is made from two grape varieties, the white *savatiano* and the red *roditis*. These two constitute the vast majority of vine plantings in Attica, Central Greece and Evia. Not just any old resin will do; the main source is the Aleppo pine *(Pinus halepensis)*, which produces a resin known for its delicate fragrance.

Retsina is generally cheap and it's available everywhere. Supermarkets stock retsina in a variety of containers ranging from 500-ml bottles to five-litre casks and flagons. Kourtaki and Cambas are both very good, but the best (and worst) still flows from the barrel in traditional tavernas. Ask for *heema*, which means 'loose'. ■

Cinemas show films in the original language (usually English) with Greek subtitles. In summer, many of the indoor cinemas close and are replaced by outdoor cinemas which show reruns mainly.

Folk Dancing

The pre-eminent folk dancers in Greece are the ones who perform at the Dora Stratou Theatre on Filopappos hill in Athens, where performances take place nightly in summer. Another highly commendable place is the Old City Theatre, Rhodes City, where the Nelly Dimoglou Dance Company performs during the summer months. Folk dancing is an integral part of all festival celebrations and there is often impromptu folk dancing in tavernas.

Spectator Sports

Soccer (football) is the most popular sport in Greece. The season lasts from September to the middle of May and matches are played on Wednesday and Sunday, and are often televised. Entry to a match costs around 1200 dr. Fixtures and results are given in the *Weekly Greek News*.

THINGS TO BUY

Greece produces a vast array of handcrafts. The Centre of Hellenic Tradition, at Pandrossou 36, Plaka, Athens, has a good range.

Antiques

It is illegal to buy, sell, possess or export any antiquity in Greece (see the Customs section earlier in this chapter). However, there are antiques and 'antiques'; a lot of items only a century or two old are regarded as junk, rather than part of the national heritage. These items include handmade furniture and odds and ends from rural areas in Greece, ecclesiastical ornaments from churches and items brought back from far-flung lands. Good hunting grounds for this 'junk' are Monastiraki and the flea market in Athens and the Piraeus market held on Sunday morning (see the Piraeus section in the Athens chapter).

Ceramics

You will see ceramic objects of every shape and size – functional and ornamental – for sale throughout Greece. The best places for high quality handmade ceramics are Athens, Rhodes and the islands of Sifnos and Skyros.

If you have taken a fancy to an ancient vase in a museum collection, there are artists in Greece who produce hand-painted replicas of museum items (see the Agios Nikolaos section in the Crete chapter). There are a lot of places selling plaster copies of statues, busts, grave steles, etc.

Leather Work

You will see leather goods for sale throughout Greece; most are made from leather imported from Spain. The best place for buying leather goods is Hania, on Crete. However, bear in mind that the goods are not as high quality or as good value as those available in Turkey.

Jewellery

You could join the wealthy North Americans who spill off the cruise ships onto Mykonos to indulge themselves in the high-class gold jewellery shops there. But although gold is good value in Greece, and designs are of a high quality, it is priced beyond the capacity of most tourists' pockets. If you prefer something more reasonably priced, go for filigree-silver jewellery. Ioannina is the filigree-jewellery centre of Greece, but you will see it for sale in shops throughout the country.

Bags

Tagari bags are woven wool bags – often brightly coloured – which hang from the shoulder by a rope. If you think they are a bit passé (a relic from the hippie era), minus the rope they make attractive cushion covers.

Getting There & Away

Most travellers arrive in Greece by air or by sea, especially since the fighting in the Balkans cut the main road and rail routes.

Whichever way you're travelling, make sure you take out travel insurance. This covers you not only for medical expenses and luggage theft or loss, but also for cancellations or delays in your travel arrangements under certain circumstances (you might fall seriously ill two days before departure, for example). Make sure you declare any existing medical conditions, because these are the cause of most disputes over travel-insurance claims. The kind of cover you get depends on your insurance and type of ticket, so ask both your insurer and your ticket-issuing agency to explain where you stand. Ticket loss is also (usually) covered by travel insurance. Make sure you have a separate record of all your ticket details – or better still, a photocopy. Buy travel insurance as early as possible. If you buy it just before you fly, you may find that you're not covered for such problems as delays caused by industrial action.

Paying for your ticket with a credit card sometimes provides limited travel insurance, and you may be able to reclaim the payment if the operator doesn't deliver. In the UK, for instance, credit-card providers are required by law to reimburse consumers if a company goes into liquidation and the amount in contention is more than UK£100. Ask your credit-card company what it's prepared to cover.

AIR

Greece has 16 international airports, but only those at Athens, Thessaloniki, Iraklio (Crete), Rhodes and Corfu take scheduled flights. Athens handles the vast majority of flights, including all intercontinental traffic.

Thessaloniki has direct connections to Brussels, Copenhagen, Dusseldorf, Frankfurt, İstanbul, Cyprus, London, Milan, Munich, Nuremberg, Paris, Stockholm, Tiranë, Vienna and Zürich. Most of these flights are with Greece's national airline, Olympic Airways, or the flag carrier of the country concerned. Iraklio has Olympic Airways flights to Rome and Vienna, while Transavia flies to Amsterdam, and Lufthansa to Frankfurt. From the middle of June, Olympic Airways has direct links from Corfu to Milan and Rome.

Greece's other international airports are at Mykonos, Santorini (Thira), Hania (Crete), Kos, Karpathos, Samos, Skiathos, Hrysoupolis (for Kavala), Preveza (for Lefkada), Kefallonia and Zakynthos. These airports are used exclusively for charter flights, mostly from the UK, Germany and the Scandinavian countries. Charter flights also fly to all of Greece's other international airports. Athens is one of the major centres in Europe for budget airfares.

In Greece, as with everywhere else, always remember to reconfirm your onward or return bookings by the specified time – usually 72 hours before departure on international flights. If you don't, there's a real risk that you'll turn up at the airport only to find that you've missed your flight because it was rescheduled, or that the airline has given the seat to someone else. Lonely Planet has received several letters from people who've found themselves in this predicament.

There is an airport tax of 5700 dr on all international departures. This is paid when you buy your ticket, not at the airport.

Buying a Plane Ticket

If you are flying to Greece from outside Europe, the plane ticket will probably be the most expensive item in your budget, and buying it can be an intimidating business. There will be a multitude of airlines and travel agents hoping to separate you from your money, and it's well worth taking time to research the options. Start early: some of the cheapest tickets have to be bought months in advance, and some popular flights sell out early.

Discounted tickets fall into two distinct categories: official and unofficial. Official discount schemes include advance-purchase tickets, budget fares, Apex, Super-Apex and a few other variations on the theme. These tickets can be bought both from travel agents and direct from the airline. They often have restrictions on them – advance purchase is the usual one. Others are restrictions on the minimum and maximum period you must be away, such as a minimum of 14 days and a maximum of one year.

Unofficial tickets are simply discounted tickets that the airlines release through selected travel agents. Don't go looking for discounted tickets straight from the airlines because they are available only through travel agents. Airlines can, however, supply information on routes and timetables, and their low-season, student and senior citizens' fares can be very competitive.

Return tickets always work out much cheaper than two one-way tickets; in some cases, *cheaper* than a one-way ticket.

Round-the-World (RTW) tickets have become very popular in recent years. The airline RTW tickets are often real bargains, and can work out to be no more expensive than an ordinary return ticket. Prices start at about UK£850, A$1800 or US$1300 depending on the season. The official airline RTW tickets are usually put together by a combination of two airlines, and permit you to travel anywhere on their route systems so long as you don't backtrack. Other restrictions are that you (usually) must book the first sector in advance and cancellation penalties then apply. There may be restrictions on how many stops you are permitted, and usually the tickets are valid for 90 days up to a year from the date of the first outbound flight. An alternative type of RTW ticket is one put together by a travel agent using a combination of discounted tickets.

Air Travel Glossary

Apex Apex, or 'advance purchase excursion' is a discounted ticket which must be paid for in advance. There are penalties if you wish to change it.

Baggage Allowance This will be written on your ticket: usually 20 kg to go in the hold, plus one item of hand luggage.

Bucket Shop An unbonded travel agency specialising in discounted airline tickets.

Bumped Just because you have a confirmed seat doesn't mean you're going to get on the plane – see Overbooking.

Cancellation Penalties If you have to cancel or change an Apex ticket there are often heavy penalties involved; insurance can sometimes be taken out against these penalties. Some airlines impose penalties on regular tickets as well, particularly against 'no show' passengers. See the Getting Around chapter for details of cancellation penalties levied on domestic Olympic Airways flights.

Check In Airlines ask you to check in a certain time ahead of the flight departure (usually 1½ hours before international flights). If you fail to check in on time and the flight is overbooked the airline can cancel your booking and give your seat to somebody else.

Lost Tickets If you lose your airline ticket, an airline will usually treat it like a travellers' cheque and, after enquiries, issue you with another one. Legally, however, an airline is entitled to treat it like cash and if you lose it then it's gone forever. Take good care of your tickets.

No Shows No shows are passengers who fail to show up for their flight, sometimes due to unexpected delays or disasters, sometimes due to simply forgetting, sometimes because they made more than one booking and didn't bother to cancel the one they didn't want. Full-fare passengers who fail to turn up are sometimes entitled to travel on a later flight. The rest of us are penalised (see Cancellation Penalties).

Overbooking Airlines hate to fly empty seats and since every flight has some passengers who

Generally, you can find discounted tickets at prices as low, or even lower, than Apex or budget tickets. Phone around the travel agents for bargains.

Charter Flights

Charter-flight tickets are usually the cheapest of all – and the most restrictive. These tickets are for seats left vacant on flights which have been block booked by package-tour companies. However, conditions apply on charter flights to Greece. A ticket must be accompanied by an accommodation booking. This is normally circumvented by issuing accommodation vouchers which are not meant to be used – even if the hotel named on the voucher actually exists. The law requiring accommodation bookings was introduced in the 1980s to prevent budget travellers flying to Greece on cheap charter flights and sleeping rough on beaches and in parks. It hasn't worked.

The main catch for travellers using charter flights involves visits to Turkey. If you fly to Greece with a return ticket on a charter flight, you will forfeit the return portion if you visit Turkey. Greece is one of several popular charter destination countries which have banded together to discourage tourists from leaving the destination country during the duration of the ticket. The countries involved want to ensure that people don't flit off somewhere else to spend their tourist dollars. The result is that if you front up at the airport for your return charter flight with a Turkish stamp in your passport, you will be forced to buy another ticket.

This does not apply if you take a day excursion into Turkey, because the Turkish immigration officials do not stamp your passport. Neither does it apply to regular or excursion-fare flights.

Charter-flight tickets are only valid for up to four weeks, and usually have a minimum-stay requirement of at least three days. Sometimes it's worth buying a charter return

---

fail to show up (see No Shows) airlines often book more passengers than they have seats. Usually the excess passengers balance those who fail to show up but occasionally somebody gets bumped. If this happens, guess who it is most likely to be? The passengers who check in late.

Reconfirmation At least 72 hours prior to departure time of an onward or return flight you must contact the airline and 'reconfirm' that you intend to be on the flight. If you don't do this the airline can delete your name from the passenger list and you could lose your seat. You don't have to reconfirm the first flight on your itinerary or if your stopover is less than 72 hours. It doesn't hurt to reconfirm more than once.

Restrictions Discounted tickets often have various restrictions on them – advance purchase is the most usual one (see Apex). Others are restrictions on the minimum and maximum period you must be away, such as a minimum of 14 days or a maximum of one year. See Cancellation Penalties.

Tickets Out An entry requirement for many countries is that you have an onward or return ticket, in other words, a ticket out of the country. If you're not sure what you intend to do next, the easiest solution is to buy the cheapest onward ticket to a neighbouring country or a ticket from a reliable airline which can later be refunded if you do not use it.

Transferred Tickets Airline tickets cannot be transferred from one person to another. Travellers sometimes try to sell the return half of their ticket, but officials can ask you to prove that you are the person named on the ticket. This is unlikely to happen on domestic flights, but on an international flight tickets may be compared with passports.

Travel Periods Some officially discounted fares, Apex fares in particular, vary with the time of year. There is often a low (off-peak) season and a high (peak) season. Sometimes there's an intermediate or shoulder season as well. At peak times, when everyone wants to fly, not only will the officially discounted fares be higher but so will unofficially discounted fares or there may simply be no discounted tickets available. Usually the fare depends on your outward flight – if you depart in the high season and return in the low season, you pay the high-season fare. ■

even if you want to stay for longer than four weeks. The tickets can be so cheap that you can afford to throw away the return portion.

The best place to look for cheap charter deals is the travel sections of major newspapers. More information on charter flights is given later in this chapter under specific point-of-origin headings.

Courier Flights

Another option (sometimes even cheaper than a charter flight) is a courier flight. This deal entails accompanying freight or a parcel which will be collected at the destination. You might also be able to fly one way. The drawbacks are that your time away may be limited to one or two weeks, your luggage is usually restricted to hand luggage (the parcel or freight you carry comes out of your luggage allowance), and you may have to be a resident of the country which operates the courier service and apply for an interview before they'll take you on.

Travel Agents

The travel pages of the national newspapers and magazines (like *Time Out*) are where travel agents promote their special deals. Before you make a decision, there are a number of questions you need to ask about the ticket. Find out the airline, the route, the duration of the journey, the stopovers allowed, any restrictions on the ticket and – above all – check the price. Ask whether the fare quoted includes all taxes and other possible inclusions.

You may discover when you start ringing around that those impossibly cheap flights, charter or otherwise, are not available – but the agency just happens to know of another one that 'costs a bit more'. Or the agent may claim to have the last two seats available for Greece for the whole of July, which they'll hold for a maximum of two hours. Don't panic – keep ringing around.

If you are flying to Greece from the USA, South-East Asia or the UK, you will probably find that the cheapest flights are being advertised by obscure agencies whose names haven't yet reached the telephone directory – the proverbial bucket shops. Many such firms are honest and solvent, but there are a few rogues who will take your money and disappear, only to reopen elsewhere a month or two later under a new name. If you feel suspicious about a firm, don't give them all the money at once – leave a small deposit and pay the balance when you get the ticket. If they insist on cash in advance, go somewhere else or be prepared to take a big risk. Once you have booked the flight with the agency, ring the airline to check that you have a confirmed booking.

It can be easier on the nerves to pay a bit more for the security of a better known travel agent. Firms such as STA, which has offices worldwide, Council Travel in the USA or Travel CUTS in Canada offer good prices to Europe (including Greece), and are unlikely to disappear overnight.

The fares quoted in this book are intended as a guide only. They are approximate only and are based on the rates advertised by travel agents at the time of going to press.

Travellers with Special Needs

If you've broken a leg, you're a vegetarian or require a special diet, you're travelling in a wheelchair, taking a baby or whatever, let the airline staff know as soon as possible – preferably when booking your ticket. Check that your request has been registered when you reconfirm your booking (at least 72 hours before departure) and again when you check in at the airport.

Children under two years of age travel for 10% of the standard fare (or free, on some airlines) as long as they don't occupy a seat. But they do not get a baggage allowance. 'Skycots' should be provided by the airline if requested in advance; these will take a child weighing up to about 10 kg. Olympic Airways charges half-fare for accompanied children aged between two and 12 years, while most other airlines charge two-thirds.

To/From the UK

British Airways, Olympic Airways and Virgin Atlantic operate daily, direct flights between London and Athens. The pricing is very competitive, with all three offering return tickets for under UK£200 in high season, plus UK£21 tax. These prices are for midweek departures; you will pay about UK£40 more for weekend departures. At these prices, there are no longer savings to be made by taking a connecting flight via Timbuktu with some obscure airline. There are connecting flights to Athens from Edinburgh, Glasgow and Manchester.

British Airways also has daily flights from London to Thessaloniki, stopping in Turin for an hour *en route*, while Olympic Airways has four direct flights a week. The British Airways flight is slightly cheaper, with a return ticket costing UK£191 (plus UK£21 tax) for midweek departures and UK£224 for weekend departures. Most scheduled flights from London leave from Heathrow airport, but a few leave from Gatwick.

London is Europe's major centre for discounted fares. The following are the addresses of some of the most reputable agencies selling discount tickets:

Campus Travel
  52 Grosvenor Gardens, SW1
  (☎ 0171-730 3402); tube stn: Victoria
STA
  86 Old Brompton Rd, SW7
  (☎ 0171-937 9921); tube stn: South Kensington
Trailfinders
  194 Kensington High St, W8
  (☎ 0171-938 3232); tube stn: High St Kensington

The listings magazines such as *Time Out*, the Sunday papers, the *Evening Standard* and *Exchange & Mart* carry ads for cheap fares. Also look through the Yellow Pages for travel agents' ads and look out for the free magazines and newspapers widely available in London, especially *TNT*, *Southern Cross* and *Trailfinder* – you can pick them up outside the main train and tube stations. Some travel agents specialise in flights for students aged under 30 and travellers aged under 26 (you need an ISIC card or an official youth card). Whatever your age, you should be able to find something to suit your pocket. You can also telephone the Air Travel Advisory Bureau (☎ 0171-636 5000) for

information about current charter-flight bargains.

Most British travel agents are registered with ABTA (Association of British Travel Agents). If you have paid for your flight to an ABTA-registered agent who then goes out of business, ABTA will guarantee a refund or an alternative. If an agency is registered with ABTA, its ads will usually say so.

In areas of London with large numbers of ethnic Greeks, there are travel agencies which specialise in package holidays and charter flights to Greece. Their prices may well be as competitive as those offered by the more centrally located agencies, and their staff are usually very helpful. Two agencies worth trying are:

Anemone
  109 Myddleton Rd, N22 (☎ 0181-889 9207)
Hermes Travel
  8 Wordsworth Parade, Green Lanes, N8
  (☎ 0181-881 0268)

Typical charter fares to Athens from London are UK£70/129 one way/return in the low season and UK£99/189 in the high season. These prices are for advance bookings. Even in high season it's possible to pick up last-minute deals for as little as UK£59/99. Many travel agencies also offer charter flights to the islands as well as to Athens. Most island destinations cost about UK£109/209 in high season.

Charter flights to Greece also fly from Birmingham, Luton, Manchester and Newcastle. Look in the Yellow Pages and local press for ads.

In Athens, budget fares to London start from as low as 23,700 dr – including the airport tax.

To/From Europe

Athens is linked to every major city in Europe by either Olympic Airways or the flag carriers of each country.

Though London is the discount capital of Europe, Amsterdam, Frankfurt, Berlin and Paris are also major centres for cheap airfares.

To/From France From Paris, return discount charter flights to Athens cost around 1230FF in low season and about 1900FF in high season. Reliable travel agents include:

Council Travel
    22, Rue des Pyramides, 75001 Paris
    (☎ 01-44.55.55.44)
FUAJ (Fédération Unie des Auberges de Jeunesse)
    22, Rue Pajol, 75018 Paris (☎ 01-44.89.87.27)
Look Voyages
    19, Rue Villedo, 75001 Paris (☎ 01-44.58.59.60)
Nouvelles Frontières
    87, Blvd de Grenelle, 75015 Paris
    (☎ 01-41.41.58.58)
OTU (Organisation du Tourisme Universitaire)
    39, Ave Georges Bernanos, 75005 Paris
    (☎ 01-44.41.38.50, 01-43.29.90.78)
Selectour Voyages
    29, Rue de la Huchette (☎ 01-42.85.40.84)
Voyages et Découvertes
    21, Rue Cambon (☎ 01-42.96.16.80)

To/From Germany For cheap air tickets in Frankfurt, try SRID Reisen (☎ 069-43 01 91), Berger Strasse 118. In Berlin, Alternativ Tours (☎ 030-8 81 20 89), Wilmersdorfer Strasse 94 (U-Bahn: Adenauerplatz), specialises in discounted fares to just about anywhere in the world. SRS Studenten Reise Service (☎ 030-2 83 30 93), at Marienstrasse 23 (U-Bahn and S-Bahn: Friedrichstrasse), offers flights with discounted student (aged 34 or less) or youth (aged 25 or less) fares. Travel agents offering unpublished cheap flights advertise in *Zitty*, Berlin's fortnightly entertainment magazine.

To/From the Netherlands Reliable travel agents in Amsterdam include:

Budget Air
    Rokin 34 (☎ 020-627 12 51)
ILC Reizen
    NZ Voorburgwal 256 (☎ 020-620 51 21)
Malibu Travel
    Damrak 30 (☎ 020-623 68 14)
NBBS
    Rokin 38 (☎ 020-626 25 57)

From Athens to Europe Budget fares from Athens to a host of European cities are widely advertised by the travel agents around Syntagma. Typical one-way fares include:

Destination	One-Way Fare
Amsterdam	38,700 dr
Copenhagen	52,700 dr
Frankfurt	54,200 dr
Geneva	52,700 dr
Hamburg	52,700 dr
Madrid	52,700 dr
Milan	52,200 dr
Munich	49,200 dr
Paris	52,200 dr
Rome	42,200 dr
Zürich	52,700 dr

These fares include the airport tax.

To/From Turkey
Olympic Airways, Turkish Airlines and Thai International share the İstanbul-Athens route, with at least one flight a day. Fares are US$243 one way (50% student discount available).

Turkish Airways flies twice a week from İzmir to Athens. The fare is US$219 one way (50% student discount) and US$395 return. There are no direct flights from Ankara to Athens; all flights go via İstanbul.

To/From Cyprus
Olympic Airways and Cyprus Airways share the Cyprus-Greece routes. From Larnaca, there are daily flights to Athens (CY£94/163 one way/return) and five a week to Thessaloniki (CY£180/343). In summer, Cyprus Airways also flies three times a week to Iraklio and Rhodes. All of these flights have a 55% student discount.

From Paphos, Cyprus Airways flies to Athens once a week in winter, and twice a week in summer (CY£163/294).

To/From Albania
Olympic Airways flies twice a week from Tiranë to Athens (US$188/341 one way/return), going via Ioannina once a week (US$148/269), and once a week to Thessaloniki (US$148/269). Student discounts of 25% are available.

To/From the USA

The North Atlantic is the world's busiest long-haul air corridor, and the flight options to Europe – including Greece – are bewildering. These include advance-purchase fares, budget fares, Apex, Super-Apex and charter flights. New York has the most direct scheduled flights to Athens. Delta Airlines, Olympic Airways and Trans World Airlines all have daily flights. The fare on Olympic Airways is US$1040 one way. Apex fares range from US$900 to US$1400, depending on the season and how long you want to stay away.

Boston is the only other east-coast city with direct flights to Athens. Olympic Airways has a flight every Saturday. Fares are the same as from New York.

There are no direct flights to Athens from the west coast. Olympic Airways has six flights a weeks via New York for US$1630.

There are connecting flights to Athens from many other US cities, stopping at New York's John F Kennedy airport. Most European national airlines fly from New York (and some from other cities) to their home countries, and then on to Athens. These connections usually mean a stopover of three or four hours.

For flight bargains, scan the *New York Times*, *LA Times*, *Chicago Tribune* and *San Francisco Chronicle Examiner*. All of these publish weekly travel sections in which you'll find any number of travel agents' ads. Council Travel and STA have offices in major cities nationwide. Access International in New York offers discounts to Europe from 50 cities in the USA.

One-way fares can work out very cheap on a stand-by basis. Airhitch (☎ 212-864 2000) specialises in this sort of thing, and can get you to Europe one way for US$169 from the east coast, US$269 from the west coast and US$229 from elsewhere in the USA.

Courier flights are another possibility. Discount Travel International in New York (☎ 212-362 3636) offers New York-London return fares for US$399 in high season, US$299 in low season. Council Travel (☎ 212-661 1450) also handles courier

flights from New York, while its Los Angeles office (☎ 213-463 0655) has flights to Paris and Amsterdam for US$370. Call two or three months in advance, at the beginning of the calendar month.

If courier flights to Athens are not available, take a flight to London from where there are many cheap flights to Greece. The *Travel Unlimited* newsletter, PO Box 1058, Allston, MA 02134, publishes details of the cheapest airfares and courier possibilities for destinations all over the world from the USA and other countries, including the UK. It's a treasure-trove of information. A single monthly issue costs US$5, and a year's subscription costs US$25 (US$35 outside the USA).

From Athens to the USA The budget travel agents around Syntagma offer the following one-way fares to the USA (prices include airport tax): Atlanta 112,700 dr; Chicago 110,700 dr; Los Angeles 127,700 dr; and New York 74,700 dr.

Travel agents in Athens who sell low-priced tickets to the USA include Consolas Travel (☎ 01-321 9228), Eolou 100, and Periscope (☎ 01-322 1515/4874), Filellinon 22. Consolas Travel also has an office in Iraklio (☎ 081-288 847).

To/From Canada

Olympic Airways has two flights a week from Toronto to Athens via Montreal. Return Apex fares cost C$1098 in low season and C$1498 in high season. There are no direct flights from Vancouver, but there are connecting flights via Toronto, Amsterdam, Frankfurt and London on Canadian Airlines, KLM, Lufthansa and British Airways.

Budget flights are also available from Canada. Travel CUTS has offices in all major cities including Toronto (☎ 416-798 2887), Vancouver (☎ 604-681 9136) and Edmonton (☎ 403-488 8487). Scan the budget travel agents' ads in the *Toronto Globe & Mail*, the *Toronto Star* and the *Vancouver Province*.

For courier flights originating in Canada, contact FB On Board Courier Services in

Toronto (☎ 416-675 4133) and Vancouver (☎ 604-278 1266). Prices to London return are C$570 from Vancouver.

At the time of writing, budget travel agencies in Athens were advertising flights to Toronto for 100,700 dr and to Montreal for 72,700 dr, including the airport tax.

To/From Australia

There are two Olympic Airways flights a week from Sydney and Melbourne to Athens. Return excursion fares range from A$2249 in the low season to A$2899 in high season, but there are normally special deals available which bring the price down to about A$1730 in low season and A$2199 in high season. Olympic Airways has offices in Melbourne (☎ 03-9629 2411, toll free 008-331 448) and Sydney (☎ 02-251 1047, toll free 1800-221 663).

It's worth checking out special deals offered by other airlines. Some include free side trips within Europe. KLM and Alitalia are two likely candidates.

STA and Flight Centres International are two of Australia's major dealers in cheap fares. The Sunday tabloid newspapers are the best place to look for cheap flights, as well as the Thursday travel sections of the *Sydney Morning Herald* and the Saturday edition of the Melbourne *Age*.

From Athens to Australia A one-way ticket from Athens to Sydney or Melbourne costs 153,700 dr, including the airport tax.

To/From New Zealand

There are no direct flights from New Zealand to Athens, though there are connecting flights via Sydney, Melbourne, Bangkok and Singapore on Olympic Airways, United Airlines, Qantas Airways, Thai Airways and Singapore Airlines.

LAND
To/From Turkey

Bus There are two buses a day between Athens and İstanbul (22 hours), travelling via Thessaloniki (7½ hours) and Alexandroupolis (14½ hours). The buses are run by

the Hellenic Railways Organisation (OSE) and leave the Peloponnese train station in Athens at 8 am and 7 pm. In İstanbul, they use the Anadolu Terminalı (Anatolia Terminal) at the Topkapı *otogar* (bus station), leaving at 10 am and 6.30 pm. One-way fares from Greece are 16,600 dr from Athens, 10,900 dr from Thessaloniki and 5850 dr from Alexandroupolis. Students qualify for a 15% discount and children under 12 travel for half fare. See the Getting There & Away sections for each city for information on where to buy tickets. (See the Alexandroupolis Getting There and Away section for alternative ways of getting to Turkey by public transport.)

Citizens of most Western countries, including Australia, Canada, New Zealand and the USA, don't need a visa for stays of up to three months. British passport-holders will have to hand over UK£5 for a Turkish visa at the border. It cannot be obtained in advance.

You may not be allowed into Turkey if your passport is due to expire within three months.

Train There are daily trains between Athens and İstanbul (13,250 dr), via Thessaloniki (8370 dr), Alexandroupolis (5000 dr) and many more places *en route*. The service is incredibly slow and the train gets uncomfortably crowded. There are often delays at the border and the journey can take up to 35 hours. You'd be well advised to take a bus. Inter-Rail passes are valid in Turkey, but Eurail passes are not.

Car & Motorbike The crossing points are at Kipi, 43 km north-east of Alexandroupolis, and at Kastanies, 139 km north-east of Alexandroupolis. Kipi is much the more convenient if you're heading for İstanbul, but the route through Kastanies goes via the fascinating towns of Soufli and Didymotiho, in Greece, and Edirne (ancient Adrianople) in Turkey.

Hitching If you want to hitchhike to Turkey, try to get a lift from Alexandroupolis right through to Turkey as you cannot hitchhike across the border.

To/From Bulgaria

Bus There are OSE buses running between Athens and Sofia (15 hours; 9400 dr) every day except Monday, leaving at 5 pm in both directions. The OSE also operates three buses a day between Thessaloniki and Sofia (7½ hours; 3500 dr) and three a week between Alexandroupolis and Plovdiv (7000 dr). There is also an OSE bus service from Patras to Plovdiv, via Ioannina, Thessaloniki and Sofia. Student and child discounts are available.

Train There is a daily train running between Sofia and Athens (18 hours; 9000 dr) via Thessaloniki (nine hours; 4510 dr).

Car & Motorbike The Bulgarian crossing is at Promahonas, 145 km north-east of Thessaloniki and 50 km from Serres.

Hitching If you want to hitchhike to Bulgaria, try to get a lift from Thessaloniki or Serres straight through to Sofia. Lifts can be hard to come by beyond Serres.

To/From Albania

Bus There is a daily OSE bus from Athens to Tiranë and vice versa, via Ioannina and Gjirokastër. The bus departs Athens at 9 pm, from Larisis Station and arrives in Tiranë the following day at 5 pm. This bus departs Ioannina at 7.30 am and passes through Gjirokastër at 10.30 am. It departs from Tiranë is at 7 am. At the time of writing there was a bus connection between Korçë (Korytsa in Greek) and Thessaloniki, running via Florina.

Car & Motorbike There are two crossing points between Greece and Albania. The main one is 60 km north-west of Ioannina. Take the main Ioannina-Konitsa road and turn left at Kalpaki. This road leads to the border town of Kakavia. The other border crossing is at Krystallopigi, 14 km west of Kotas on the Florina-Kastoria road.

Kapshtica is the closest town on the Albanian side. It is possible to take a private vehicle into Albania, although it's not a great idea. Always carry your passport in areas near the Albanian border.

To/From FYROM

Train There are local trains from Skopje, capital of the Former Yugoslav Republic of Macedonia (FYROM), to the town of Gevgelija, near the Greek border. From Gevgelija, there are three trains a day to Thessaloniki. Two of them are international services originating in Belgrade.

There are no trains between Florina and FYROM, although there may be trains to Skopje from the FYROM side of the border.

Car & Motorbike There are two border crossings with FYROM. One is at Evzoni, 68 km north of Thessaloniki. This is the main highway to Skopje which continues to Belgrade, capital of Serbia. The other border crossing is at Niki, 16 km north of Florina. This road leads to Bitola, and continues to Ohrid, once a popular tourist resort on the shores of Lake Ohrid.

To/From Europe

Overland travel between Western Europe and Greece is now a thing of the past. Airfares are so cheap that land transport cannot compete – even if it were possible to travel through the war zone that was once Yugoslavia. Buses that used to travel through Yugoslavia now go through Italy and take a ferry across to Greece.

Travelling from the UK to Greece through Europe means crossing various borders, so check whether any visas are required before setting out. Australians, for example, will need a visa to travel through France.

Bus Fear of flying is about the only reason anyone would opt to go to Greece by bus instead of by plane. If you like the idea of spending days on a bus instead of hours on a plane, there are a couple of companies willing to oblige.

Olympic Bus operates the only year-round

service, leaving London at 6.30 pm on Friday and travelling via Brussels, Frankfurt, Munich, Innsbruck, Venice and Brindisi. It reaches Athens at 5 pm on Monday – more than 70 hours later. The return service leaves Athens at 12 pm on Tuesday. Olympic's London office (☎ 0171-837 9141) is at 70 Brunswick Centre, London WC1 1AE. At the time of writing, one-way/return fares from London had been slashed to UK£50/100. Athens bookings are handled by Iason Tours (☎ 01-324 4633), Eolou 100, near Omonia.

The only other service still operating out of the UK is run by Eurolines. It does the trip in just 51 hours, taking the short route across France and northern Italy to Ancona, and then taking the ferry from to Igoumenitsa via Corfu. The buses run only during August and September, when they leave London's Victoria Coach Terminus on Friday at 9 am. Fares are UK£126/218 one way/return. Eurolines (☎ 0171-730 0202) is at 52 Grosvenor Gardens, Victoria, London SW1.

Train Unless you have a Eurail pass or are aged under 26 and eligible for a discounted fare, travelling to Greece by train is prohibitively expensive. The full fare one way/return from the London is UK£226/416, or UK£169/308 if you're under 26.

Greece is part of the Eurail network, and Eurail passes are valid on ferries operated by Adriatica di Navigazione and Hellenic Mediterranean Lines that ply between the Italian port of Brindisi and Corfu, and between Igoumenitsa and Patras.

The passes can only be bought by residents of non-European countries and are supposed to be purchased before arriving in Europe. They can, however, be bought in Europe as long as your passport proves that you've been there for less than six months. In London, head for the French National Railways office (☎ 0171-493 9731) at 179 Picadilly, W1.

If you are starting your European travels in Greece, you can buy your Eurail pass from the Hellenic Railways Organisation offices at Karolou 1 and Filellinon 17 in Athens, and at Patras and Thessaloniki stations.

Greece is also part of the Inter-Rail pass system, but the pass for those aged over 26 is not valid in France, Italy and Switzerland – rendering it useless if you want to use the pass to get to Greece. The Inter-Rail youth pass for those under 26 is valid throughout Europe, and can be used. The pass costs UK£249 and is valid for a month.

When weighing up the options, you should consider the cost of other cheap-ticket deals. Travellers aged under 26 years can pick up BIJ (Billet International de Jeunesse) tickets, which cut fares by up to 50%. Various agents issue BIJ tickets in Europe, including Eurotrain (☎ 0171-730 3402), 52 Grosvenor Gardens, London SW1. In Athens, BIJ tickets are issued by Voyages Wasteels Hellas (☎ 01-324 0622/2038/3039), Xenofontos 14, near Syntagma.

Cheap deals aside, rail services from Western Europe to Greece have been severely disrupted by events in former Yugoslavia. The direct route to most Western European cities was via Belgrade, but this service was suspended at the time of writing. The most straightforward alternative route is to take a train to Italy and then a ferry to Greece from Brindisi.

A more complicated and longer route is to get a train to Budapest, then another one to Bucharest, from where there are trains to Thessaloniki and Athens, via Sofia, thus doing a big loop around the trouble spots.

Car & Motorbike Once again the troubles in former Yugoslavia have put paid to the most direct route for motorists driving from Western Europe to Greece. The route coming from the UK was Ostend, Brussels, Salzburg and then down the Yugoslav highway through Zagreb, Belgrade and Skopje and crossing the border to Evzoni. An alternative route was to take the longer, scenic road down the coast, via Split and Dubrovnik. The inland route added up to 3150 km and 50 hours non-stop driving.

The alternative is to drive to an Italian port and get a ferry to Greece. Coming from the

UK, this means driving through France, where petrol costs and road tolls are exorbitant. In Italy, petrol prices have been deregulated, so they are not as expensive as they used to be, but you must pay tolls on the autostrade.

SEA

To/From Turkey

There are five regular ferry services between Turkey's Aegean coast and the Greek islands. Tickets for all ferries to Turkey must be bought a day in advance. You will almost certainly be asked to turn in your passport the night before the trip. You'll get it back the next day before you board the boat. Port taxes for departures to Turkey are about 4000 dr. (See the relevant sections under individual island entries for more information about the following trips.)

Rhodes to Marmaris Small Turkish car ferries run between Rhodes and Marmaris daily (except Sunday) between April and October and less frequently in winter. Prices vary, so shop around. There are also hydrofoils to Marmaris daily (weather permitting) from April to October. They are currently cheaper, costing 6000/12,000 dr one way/return.

Chios to Çeşme There are daily boats (except Monday) between Chios and Çeşme from mid-July to mid-September. In spring and autumn there are three boats a week – on Tuesday, Thursday and Sunday. In winter there is just one boat a week, on Thursday, if the weather permits and there are sufficient passengers to make the trip worthwhile. Tickets cost 12,000/16,000 dr one way/return, including port taxes.

Kos to Bodrum There are daily ferries in summer from Kos town to Bodrum (ancient Halicarnassus) in Turkey. Boats leave at 8 am and return at 4 pm. The journey takes one hour and costs 13,000 dr return (including the port taxes). Many travel agents around Kos town sell tickets.

Lesvos to Ayvalık There are daily boats running between Lesvos and Ayvalık from late May to September. During the rest of the year there are boats once or twice a week, weather permitting. Tickets cost 14,000 dr one way/return.

Samos to Kuşadası In summer there are daily boats to Kuşadası (for Ephesus) from Samos town. There is no scheduled service in winter, but this may change. Tickets cost 6000/9500 dr one way/return (plus 4000 dr Greek port tax and 3000 dr Turkish port tax).

Crete to Kuşadası Marlines operates a summer service between Iraklio on Crete and Kuşadası as an extension of its Ancona-Iraklio run. Boats leave Iraklio at 10 pm on Monday for the 14-hour trip. The deck-class fare is 12,400 dr in high season. Return boats from Kuşadası leave at 7 pm on Wednesday.

To/From Italy

Events in former Yugoslavia mean that ferries to Greece from Italy are more popular than ever, so the earlier you make a reservation the better. There are ferries to Greece from the Italian ports of Ancona, Bari, Brindisi, Otranto, Ortona, Trieste and Venice. For more information about these services, see the Patras, Igoumenitsa, Corfu and Kefallonia sections.

In the UK, reservations can be made on almost all of these ferries at Viamare Travel Ltd (☎ 0171-431 4560; fax 0171-431 5456), Graphic House, 2 Sumatra Rd, London NW6 IPU.

The prices listed below are for one-way deck class in the high season (July and August). Deck class on these services means exactly that. If you want a reclining, aircraft-type seat, you'll be up for another 10 to 15% on top of the listed fares.

Ancona to Patras The ferry operators in Ancona all have booths at the *stazione marittima* (ferry terminal), off Piazza Candy, where you can pick up timetables and price lists and make bookings.

Superfast Ferries are the fastest and most

convenient, but easily the most expensive. They have boats sailing in each direction every day and do the trip in just 20 hours for L142,000. Marlines (☎ 71-20 25 66) has four boats a week (36 hours, L110,000), stopping at Igoumenitsa. Minoan Lines (☎ 71-5 67 89) operates daily ferries to Igoumenitsa, Corfu, and Patras (34 hours, L120,000), while ANEK runs three ferries per week on the same route (33 hours, L112,000).

Ancona to Iraklio Marlines has a weekly boat from Ancona to Iraklio on Crete from the end of June until mid-September. The service takes 51 hours and costs L227,000 for deck class in high season. Boats continue to Kuşadası in Turkey. At the time of writing, the service left Ancona at 6 pm on Saturday.

Bari to Corfu, Igoumenitsa & Patras ANEK, Arkadia Lines, Marlines and Ventouris Ferries all operate on this route, charging about L68,000 to Corfu and Igoumenitsa and L86,000 to Patras.

Bari to Kefallonia Ventouris Ferries has boats to Kefallonia every second day during July and August for L86,000.

Brindisi to Corfu, Igoumenitsa & Patras The route from Brindisi to Patras (18 hours) via Corfu (nine hours) and Igoumenitsa (10 hours) is the cheapest and most popular of the various Adriatic crossings.

The major companies operating ferries from Brindisi are: Adriatica di Navigazione (☎ 831-52 38 25), Viale Regina Margherita 13 (open from 9 am to 1 pm, 4 to 7 pm), and on the 1st floor of the stazione marittima, where you must go to check in; Hellenic Mediterranean Lines (☎ 831-52 85 31), Corso Garibaldi 8; Fragline (☎ 831-56 03 50), Corso Garibaldi 88; and AK Ventouris (☎ 831-52 48 69), represented by Agenzia Angela Gioia at Via Consiglio 55.

Adriatica and Hellenic are the most expensive, but they are the best. They are also the only lines which officially accept Eurail passes. If you want to use your Eurail pass, it is important to reserve some weeks in advance, particularly in summer. Even with a booking in summer, you must still go to the Adriatic or Hellenic embarkation office in the stazione marittima to have your ticket checked.

Both lines charge L73,500 for deck-class passage to Corfu, Igoumenitsa or Patras in high season, while Fragline charges L50,000. AK Ventouris charges L43,000 to Igoumenitsa and L71,500 to Patras. Prices are about 30% less in the low season. The cheapest cabin accommodation costs around L30,000 more than deck class in low season, and L45,000 more in high season. Fares for cars range from L57,500 to L90,000 in the high season.

Charitos Lines runs catamarans from Brindisi to Corfu and Igoumenitsa between July and mid-September. The fare is L36,000/72,000 in low/high season and the trip takes 3½ hours.

Brindisi to Kefallonia Hellenic Mediterranean has daily services to the port of Sami on Kefallonia from the beginning of July through to mid-September. The trip takes 13½ hours and costs L73,500 for deck class.

Trieste to Patras ANEK Lines has two boats a week travelling via Igoumenitsa. The trip takes 33 hours and costs L124,000 for deck class.

Venice to Patras Minoan Lines has boats from Venice every day from the beginning of April through to mid-October. Boats leave Venice at 6 pm and arrive in Patras at 10 am two days later, calling in at Corfu on the way. The fare is L131,500 for deck class.

To/From Cyprus & Israel

Salamis Lines operates a weekly year-round service connecting Piraeus and Rhodes with Limassol on Cyprus and the Israeli port of Haifa. The service leaves Haifa at 8 pm on Sunday and Limassol at 1 pm on Monday, reaching Rhodes at 9 am on Tuesday and Piraeus at 7 am on Wednesday. Approximate deck-class fares from Haifa are US$105 to

Rhodes and US$110 to Piraeus. The fares from Limassol are US$70 to Rhodes and US$75 to Piraeus. Bookings in Haifa are handled by Allalouf Shipping (☎ 04-671 743), 40 Hanamal St, and in Limassol by Salamis Tours (☎ 05-355 555) at Salamis House, 28 October Ave.

There are two additional services in summer. Vergina Lines has a boat leaving Haifa at 8 pm on Sunday and Limassol at 12 pm on Monday bound for Iraklio on Crete and Piraeus. Poseidon Lines leaves Haifa at 8 pm on Thursday and Limassol at 1 pm on Friday, calling at Rhodes as well as Crete on the way to Piraeus.

For more information about these services, see the Piraeus, Iraklio and Rhodes sections.

TOURS

If a package holiday of sun, sand and sea doesn't appeal to you, but you would like to holiday with a group, there are several companies which organise special-interest holidays.

The UK-based Explore Worldwide (☎ 0252-31 9448) organises reasonably priced, small-group holidays which include visits to many of the country's ancient sites. Island Holidays (01764-670107) specialises in cultural holidays on Crete.

If you want to go trekking, get in touch with Exodus Expeditions (☎ 0181-675 5550) at 9 Weir St, London. Exodus also has an Australian office (☎ 02-251 5430) at Suite 105, Level 105, 1 York St, Sydney. The company is represented in New Zealand by Adventure World (☎ 09-524 5118) in Auckland, and in Canada by Gap Adventures (☎ 416-535 6600) in Toronto. For more information on trekking, see the Organised Treks section in the Getting Around chapter.

If you wouldn't mind a holiday of sun, sand and sea, but don't like crowded, tacky resorts, UK companies specialising in package holidays to unspoilt areas of Greece include: Laskarina (☎ 0162-982 4881), Greek Islands Touring Club (☎ 01932-22 0416), Simply Ionian (☎ 0181-995 1121) and Simply Crete (☎ 0181-994 4462).

For information on sailing holidays in Greece, see the relevant section in the Getting Around chapter.

LEAVING GREECE
Departure Tax

There is no departure tax as such, but there is an airport tax of 5700 dr for all international departures. The money goes, in theory, to a good cause – the funding of the new international airport at Athens. The tax is paid when you buy your ticket, not on departure. Port taxes vary from 1500 to 3000 dr, depending on the port.

Getting Around

AIR

Greece has an extensive domestic air network. The majority of flights are handled by Olympic Airways and its offshoot, Olympic Aviation. Olympic lost its monopoly on domestic routes in 1993, but no serious competition has emerged. Several companies have tried but most have failed. The only newcomer to show any sign of permanence is Air Greece, which offers a cheaper alternative to Olympic on some of the major routes, such as Athens-Thessaloniki, Athens-Rhodes and Athens-Iraklio.

Olympic Airways has offices wherever there are flights, as well as in other major towns. The head office in Athens (☎ 01-966 6666) is at Leoforos Syngrou 96. The airline accepts the following credit cards: American Express, Visa, MasterCard, Diners Club and Eurocard.

Olympic Airways domestic tickets are nontransferable. If a passenger cancels a reservation between eight and 24 hours prior to departure, a cancellation charge of 30% of the fare is imposed. If the cancellation occurs within eight hours of departure or the passenger does not show up for the flight, the cancellation charge is 50% of the fare. Different conditions may apply for special fares – check when you buy your ticket. Travel insurance will generally cover you if you have to cancel due to ill health or an emergency, but check your policy.

The free-baggage allowance on domestic flights is 15 kg, except when the domestic flight is part of an international journey. The international free-baggage allowance is then extended to the domestic sector. A free-baggage allowance of 20 kg applies if tickets for domestic travel are sold and issued outside Greece. Olympic offers a 25% student discount on domestic Olympic Airways flights, but only if the flight is part of an international journey.

Domestic passengers are also funding the building of Athens' new international airport. The airport tax for domestic flights is 3000 dr, which is paid as part of the ticket. All prices quoted in this book include this tax.

Mainland Flights

Athens is far and away the busiest of the nine airports on the Greek mainland. The only mainland route that doesn't involve Athens is the Thessaloniki-Ioannina service (six per week, 50 minutes, 10,000 dr). See the table in this section for details of flights to mainland cities from Athens.

Mainland Intercity Flights
One-way fares (including airport taxes), frequency and duration of flights from Athens are:

City	Flights/Week	Duration	Fare
Alexandroupolis	10	55 mins	16,000 dr
Ioannina	15	70 mins	15,800 dr
Kalamata	8	50 mins	11,800 dr
Kastoria	6	75 mins	16,400 dr
Kavala	10	60 mins	15,800 dr
Kozani	6	70 mins	14,800 dr
Preveza	7	60 mins	11,800 dr
Thessaloniki	41	50 mins	19,400 dr

Mainland to Island Flights

Olympic Airways operates a busy schedule to the islands in summer. Athens has flights to a total of 22 islands, with services to all the island groups as well as to three destinations on Crete – Hania, Iraklio and Sitia. There are flights from Thessaloniki to Hania and Iraklio on Crete, to Lesvos (Mytilini)

Summer flights from Athens & Thessaloniki to the Greek Islands

This table lists one-way fares (including airport taxes) from **Athens**, the frequency of flights and their duration.

Island	Flights/Week	Duration	Fares
Astypalea	3	65 mins	19,000 dr
Chios	35	50 mins	13,000 dr
Corfu	24	50 mins	18,000 dr
Crete (Hania)	25	45 mins	17,000 dr
Crete (Iraklio)	40	45 mins	19,200 dr
Crete (Sitia)	4	85 mins	21,000 dr
Karpathos	4	80 mins	24,600 dr
Kassos	1	130 mins	24,600 dr
Kefallonia	13	60 mins	15,800 dr
Kos	15	50 mins	18,600 dr
Kythira	20	50 mins	12,800 dr
Leros	10	65 mins	20,000 dr
Lesvos (Mytilini)	26	45 mins	14,800 dr
Limnos	25	60 mins	12,800 dr
Milos	21	45 mins	12,600 dr
Mykonos	42	45 mins	16,200 dr
Naxos	15	45 mins	17,200 dr
Paros	52	45 mins	16,000 dr
Rhodes	35	55 mins	23,000 dr
Samos	32	60 mins	14,800 dr
Santorini (Thira)	46	50 mins	17,800 dr
Skiathos	20	40 mins	14,600 dr
Skyros	7	45 mins	13,800 dr
Syros	19	35 mins	13,000 dr
Zakynthos	14	55 mins	15,400 dr

This information is for flights between 14 June and 26 September. Outside these months, the numbers of flights to the islands drops dramatically – especially to Mykonos, Paros, Skiathos and Santorini (Thira).

One-way fares (excluding airport taxes), frequency and duration of flights from **Thessaloniki** are:

Island	Flights/Week	Duration	Fares
Chios	2	50 mins	21,000 dr
Corfu	3	50 mins	18,000 dr
Crete (Hania)	2	105 mins	27,600 dr
Crete (Iraklio)	6	110 mins	27,600 dr
Lesvos (Mytilini)	9	60 mins	18,800 dr
Limnos	7	50 mins	13,000 dr
Mykonos	3	75 mins	23,000 dr
Rhodes	2	70 mins	29,800 dr
Santorini (Thira)	3	90 mins	25,000 dr

and Limnos in the North-Eastern Aegean group, and to Rhodes in the Dodecanese. See the table on the previous page for details. In spite of the number of flights, it can be hard to find a seat during July and August. Early bookings are recommended.

Flight schedules are greatly reduced in winter, with only a few services to smaller islands.

Inter-Island Flights

There are year-round, inter-island flights between Rhodes and Iraklio, Karpathos, Kassos, Kastellorizo and Kos; between Karpathos and Kassos; between Limnos and Lesvos (Mytilini); and between Sitia (Crete) and Karpathos. The one-way fares, frequencies and duration of flights are listed in the table below.

BUS

All long-distance buses on both the mainland and the islands are operated by KTEL (Koino Tamio Eispraxeon Leoforion), a collective of private bus companies. Drivers take great pride in their buses, staking out a little territory where they sit and adorning it with icons, pin-ups, psychedelic love hearts and plastic mobiles. Bus fares are fixed by the government.

The bus network is comprehensive and major routes have frequent services. With the exception of towns in Thrace, which are reached by buses from Thessaloniki, all of the large towns on the mainland, including those in the Peloponnese, are served by frequent buses from Athens. The islands of Corfu, Kefallonia and Zakynthos can also be reached directly from Athens by bus, and the fare includes the price of the ferry ticket.

Villages in remote areas are often served by only one or two buses a day. These operate for the benefit of school children and people going into the nearest town to shop, rather than for tourists. These buses leave the villages very early in the morning and return early in the afternoon. On islands where the capital is inland rather than a port, buses normally meet the boats. Some of the very remote islands have not yet acquired a bus, but most have some sort of motorised transport – even if it is only a bone-shaking, three-wheeled truck.

In large and medium-size towns there is usually a central, covered bus station with seating, waiting rooms, toilets, a shop selling snacks and drinks, and a snack bar selling pies, cakes and coffee. In some larger towns and cities, there may be more than one bus station, each serving different destinations.

Inter-Island Flights

Islands	Flights/Week	Duration	Fares
Chios – Lesvos (Mytilini)	2	25 mins	9400 dr
Iraklio – Mykonos	2	60 mins	18,000 dr
Iraklio – Rhodes	4	45 mins	19,000 dr
Iraklio – Santorini (Thira)	3	40 mins	13,400 dr
Karpathos – Kassos	4	15 mins	5800 dr
Karpathos – Rhodes	28	40 mins	11,800 dr
Karpathos – Sitia	1	25 mins	10,600 dr
Kassos – Rhodes	7	40 mins	11,800 dr
Kassos – Sitia	1	55 mins	7600 dr
Kastellorizo – Rhodes	7	45 mins	10,000 dr
Kos – Rhodes	3	30 mins	12,000 dr
Lesvos (Mytilini) – Limnos	7	35 mins	12,600 dr
Mykonos – Rhodes	3	60 mins	18,000 dr
Mykonos – Santorini (Thira)	6	30 mins	12,800 dr
Rhodes – Santorini (Thira)	4	60 mins	18,000 dr

In small towns and villages the 'bus station' may be no more than a bus stop outside a kafeneio or taverna which doubles up as a booking office – here a timetable will be displayed and tickets will be sold. In remote areas, the timetable may be in Greek only, but in most booking offices timetables are in both Greek and Roman script. The timetables give both the departure and return times – useful if you are making a day trip – and the times will be given using the 24-hour-clock system.

When you buy a ticket you will be allotted a seat, and the seat number will be noted on the ticket. The seat number is indicated on the back of each seat of the bus, not on the back of the seat in front; this causes confusion among Greeks and tourists alike. You can board a bus without a ticket and pay on board, but on a popular route, or during high season, this may mean that you have to stand. Keep your ticket for the duration of the journey as it will be checked several times *en route*.

It's best to turn up at least 20 minutes before departure to make sure you get a seat. Buses often leave a few minutes before their scheduled time of departure – another reason to give yourself plenty of time. Check the destination with the driver before you board the bus, and check that your luggage has been placed in the appropriate hold.

The buses are comfortable. Not all are air-conditioned, but they all have either curtains or blinds which you can pull down for shade. Buses do not have toilets on board and they don't have refreshments available, so make sure you are prepared on both counts. Buses stop about every three hours on long journeys. Smoking is prohibited on all buses in Greece; only the chain-smoking drivers dare to ignore the no-smoking signs.

Bus fares are reasonably priced, with a journey costing approximately 1000 dr per 100 km. Fares and journey times on some of the major routes are: Athens-Thessaloniki, 7½ hours, 6800 dr; Athens-Patras, three hours, 3000 dr; and Athens-Volos, five hours, 4350 dr; Athens-Corfu, 11 hours, 7450 dr (including boat ticket).

TRAIN

The Greek Railways Organisation, OSE (Organismos Sidirodromon Ellados), is gradually getting its act together and modernising its creaky rolling stock, but train travel in Greece is still viewed by most people as a poor alternative to road travel.

For starters, the rail system is not huge. There are essentially two main, standard-gauge lines: Athens to Thessaloniki and Thessaloniki to Alexandroupolis. The Peloponnese system uses a narrow-gauge track, as does the Volos to Kalambaka line.

There are also two distinct levels of service: the slow, stopping-all-stations services that crawl around the countryside, and the faster, modern intercity trains that link most major cities.

Travel by the former is cheaper than by bus, but it is painfully slow and certainly not more comfortable. There seems to be no effort to upgrade the dilapidated rolling stock on these services. Unless you are travelling on a very tight budget, they are best left alone – except on shorter runs such as Athens-Halkida and Volos-Kalambaka. Sample journey times and fares include Athens-Thessaloniki, eight hours, 5160/3440 dr (1st/2nd class); Athens-Patras, five hours, 2370/1580 dr; and Athens-Volos, seven hours, 3930/2620 dr.

The intercity network, which links Athens with Thessaloniki, Volos and Alexandroupolis and Athens with the Peloponnese, is a better way to travel. The services are not necessarily express – the Greek terrain is too mountainous – but the trains are modern and comfortable. There are 1st and 2nd-class smoking/non-smoking seats and there is a café-bar on board. On some services, meals can be ordered and delivered to your seat. There is a comfortable night service between Athens and Thessaloniki – especially if you travel in a 1st-class sleeper – on which you can also transport your vehicle.

Ticket prices for intercity services are subject to a distance loading on top of the normal fares. This ranges from a 400-dr supplement for up to 100 km to 3700 dr for over 751 km. Seat reservations should be made as far in advance as possible, especially in summer.

Eurail and Inter-Rail cards are valid in Greece, but it's not worth buying one if Greece is the only place you plan to use it. You're much better off buying a tourist rail pass, which are available for individual passengers, as well as for families and groups of up to five people. They are valid for 10, 20 or 30 days and entitle the holder to make an unlimited number of journeys on all the rail routes. An individual pass costs 13,100 dr for 10 days, 19,670 dr for 20 days and 26,220 dr for 30 days. Whatever pass you have, you must have a reservation. You cannot board a train without one.

Senior cards are available to passengers over 60 years of age on presentation of their IDs or passports. They cost 15,600 dr for 1st-class travel and 10,400 dr for 2nd class, and are valid for one year from the date of issue. The cards entitle passengers to a 50% reduction on train travel plus five free journeys per year. Free journeys may not be taken 10 days before or after Christmas or Easter, or between 1 July and 30 September.

Tickets can be bought from OSE booking offices in a few major towns, otherwise from train stations. There is a 20% discount on return tickets, and a 30% discount for groups of 10 or more.

TAXI

Taxis are widely available in Greece except on very small or remote islands. They are reasonably priced by European standards, especially if three or four people share costs. Flagfall is 200 dr and then 113 dr per km outside a built-up area. Additional costs (on top of the per-km rate) are 300 dr from an airport, 160 dr from a train or bus station and 55 dr for each piece of luggage. Intercity taxis do not have meters, so you should always settle on a price before you get in.

CAR & MOTORBIKE

No-one who has travelled on Greece's roads will be surprised to hear that the country's road-fatality rate is the highest in Europe. More than 2000 people die on the roads

every year, with overtaking listed as the greatest cause of accidents. Stricter traffic laws were introduced in 1992 (see the following section) and they would appear to have had some effect in reducing the toll, but Greek roads remain a good place to practise your defensive-driving techniques.

Heart-stopping moments aside, your own car is a great way to explore off the beaten track. Bear in mind that roads in remote areas are often either dirt or poorly maintained asphalt. Get a good road map before you set off.

There are six stretches of highway in Greece where tolls are levied. They are Athens-Corinth, Corinth-Patras, Athens-Lamia, Lamia-Larisa, Larisa-Thessaloniki and Thessaloniki-Evzoni. Most charge 400 dr for a car.

Almost all islands are served by car ferries, but they are expensive. Sample prices for small vehicles include: Piraeus to Mykonos, 14,400 dr; Piraeus to Crete (Hania and Iraklio), 15,200 dr; Piraeus to Rhodes, 18,600 dr; and Piraeus to Lesvos, 17,300. The charge for a large motorbike is about the same as the price of a 3rd-class passenger ticket.

Petrol in Greece is expensive, and the further you get from a major city the more it costs. Prices vary from petrol station to petrol station. Super can be found as cheaply as 196 dr per litre at big city discount places, but 205 to 215 dr is the normal range. You may pay closer to 220 dr per litre in remote areas. The price range for unleaded – available everywhere – is from 185 to 201 dr per litre. Diesel costs about 140 dr per litre. See the Documents section in the Facts for the Visitor chapter for information on licence requirements for EC nationals and travellers from other countries.

Road Rules

In Greece, as throughout Continental Europe, you drive on the right and overtake on the left. Outside built-up areas, traffic on a main road has right of way at intersections. In towns, vehicles coming from the right have right of way. Seat belts must be worn in front seats, and in back seats if the car is fitted with them. Children under 12 years are not allowed in the front seat. It is compulsory to carry a first-aid kit, fire extinguisher and warning triangle, and it is forbidden to carry cans of petrol. Helmets are compulsory for motorcyclists if the motorbike is 50 cc or more.

Outside residential areas the speed limit is 120 km/h on highways, 90 km/h on other roads and 50 km/h in built-up areas. The speed limit for motorbikes up to 100 cc is 70 km/h and for larger motorbikes, 90 km/h.

Drivers exceeding the speed limit by 20% are liable for a fine of 10,000 dr; and by 40%, a 30,000 dr fine. Other offences and fines include:

- driving on the wrong side of the road – 20,000 dr
- going through a red light – 50,000 dr
- violating right of way at a crossroads – 20,000 dr
- overcrowding a vehicle – 10,000 dr
- use of undipped headlights in towns – 10,000 dr
- illegal reversing – 5000 dr

Drink-driving laws are strict – a blood-alcohol content of 0.05% is liable to incur a penalty, and over 0.08% is a criminal offence.

The police can issue traffic fines, and payment cannot be made on the spot – you will be told where to pay.

If you are involved in an accident and no-one is hurt, the police will not be required to write a report, but it is advisable to go to a nearby police station and explain what happened. A police report may be required for insurance purposes. If an accident involves injury, a driver who does not stop and does not inform the police may face a prison sentence.

See the Useful Organisations section in the Facts for the Visitor chapter for information about the Greek Automobile Club (ELPA).

Rental

Car If the deadly driving has not put you off getting behind a wheel in Greece, then perhaps the price of hiring a car will. Rental cars are widely available, but they are more expensive than in most other European countries. Most of the big multinational car-hire companies are represented in Athens and large towns, on large islands and at international airports. The smaller islands often have only one car-hire outlet.

The multinationals are, however, the most expensive places to hire a car. High-season weekly rates with unlimited mileage start at about 105,000 dr for the smallest models, such as a 900-cc Fiat Panda. The rate drops to about 85,000 dr per week in winter. To these prices must be added VAT of 18%, or 13% on the islands of the Dodecanese, the North-Eastern Aegean and the Sporades. Then there are the optional extras, such as a collision-damage waiver of 3000 dr per day (more for larger models), without which you will be liable for the first 1,500,000 dr of the repair bill (much more for larger models). Other costs include a theft waiver of at least 700 dr per day and personal-accident insurance. It all adds up to an expensive exercise. The major companies offer much cheaper prebooked and prepaid rates.

Local companies offer some good deals for those prepared to shop around. They are normally more open to negotiation, especially if business is slow. Their advertised rates are about 25% cheaper than those offered by the multinationals.

If you want to take a hire car to another country or onto a ferry, you will need advance written authorisation from the hire company. Unless you pay with a credit card, most hire companies will require a minimum deposit of 20,000 dr per day. See the Getting Around sections for cities and islands for details of places to rent cars.

The minimum driving age in Greece is 18 years, but most car-hire firms require you to be at least 23 years old, although a few will rent vehicles to 21-year-olds.

Motorbike Mopeds and motorcycles are available for hire wherever there are tourists to rent them. In many cases their maintenance has been minimal, so check the machine thoroughly before you hire it – especially the brakes: you'll need them!

Greece is not the best place to initiate yourself into motorcycling. Apart from the reckless drivers with whom you will be sharing the road, the roads are hilly and they are badly maintained in remote areas. Every year many tourists have motorcycle accidents in Greece. Take care!

Rates range from around 3000 dr per day for a moped or 50 cc motorbike to 5000 dr per day for a 250 cc motorbike. Out of season these prices drop considerably, so use your bargaining skills. By October it is sometimes possible to hire a moped for as little as 1200 dr per day. Most motorcycle hirers include third-party insurance in the price, but it is wise to check this. This insurance will not include medical expenses; see the following warning.

Warning If you are planning to hire a motorcycle or moped, check that your travel insurance covers you for injury resulting from a motorbike accident. Many insurance companies don't offer this cover. Check the fine print!

Purchase

Greece has no automotive industry and imported cars are heavily taxed. Several firms in Athens are authorised to buy and sell tax-free cars in transit. One is Auto Imports at Liossion 220. Other possibilities are Transco (☎ 01-959 4827), Syngrou 336, and Kyriakos (☎ 01-922 2746), Syngrou 144. You will pay at least 400,000 dr for a decent, second-hand, small car.

BICYCLE

Cycling has not caught on in Greece, which isn't surprising considering the hilly terrain. Tourists are beginning to cycle in Greece, but if you decide to do so you'll need strong leg muscles. You can hire bicycles in most tourist places, but they are not as widely available as cars and motorbikes. Prices range from 1000 to 3000 dr per day, depending on the type and age of the bike. Bicycles are carried free on ferries.

HITCHING

Hitching is never entirely safe in any country in the world, and we don't recommend it. Travellers who decide to hitch should understand that they are taking a small but potentially serious risk. People who do choose to hitch will be safer if they travel in pairs and should let someone know where they are planning to go.

Some parts of Greece are much better for hitching than others. Getting out of major cities tends to be hard work, and Athens is notoriously difficult. Hitching is much easier in remote areas and on islands with poor public transport. On country roads, it is not unknown for someone to stop and ask if you want a lift even if you haven't stuck a thumb out. You can't afford to be fussy about the mode of transport – it may be a tractor or a spluttering old truck.

Greece has a reputation for being a relatively safe place for women to hitch, but it is still unwise to do it alone. It's better to hitch with a companion, preferably a male one.

WALKING

Unless you have come to Greece just to lie on a beach, the chances are you will do quite a bit of walking. You don't have to be a trekker to start clocking up the kilometres. The narrow, stepped streets of many towns and villages can only be explored on foot, and visiting the archaeological sites involves a fair amount of legwork. See the What to Bring, Health and Trekking sections in the Facts for the Visitor chapter for more information about walking.

BOAT
Ferry

For most people, travel in Greece means island hopping. Every island has a ferry service of some sort, although in winter services to some of the smaller islands are fairly skeletal. Services start to pick up again from April onwards, and by July and August there are countless services criss-crossing the Aegean. Ferries come in all shapes and sizes, from the giant 'superferries' that work the major routes to the small ageing open ferries that chug around the backwaters.

Prices are fixed by the government, and are determined by the distance travelled rather than by the facilities of a particular boat. There can be big differences in the size, comfort and facilities of boats offering rival services on a given route, but the fares will be the same. The small differences in price you may find at ticket agencies are the results of some agents sacrificing part of their designated commission to qualify as a 'discount service'. The discount is seldom more than 50 dr.

The hub of Greek's ferry network is Piraeus, the port of Athens. Ferries leave here for the Cyclades, Dodecanese, the North-Eastern Aegean and Saronic Gulf islands and Crete. Athens' second port is Rafina, 70 km away from the city and connected by an hourly bus service. There are ferries from Rafina to several of the Cyclades, and to Evia. The port of Lavrio, in southern Attica, offers the only ferry link from the mainland to the Cycladic island of Kea. There are regular buses from Athens to Lavrio.

Ferries for the Ionian islands leave from the Peloponnese ports of Patras (for Kefallonia, Ithaki, Paxoi and Corfu) and Kyllini (for Kefallonia and Zakynthos); from Astakos (for Ithaki and Kefallonia) and Mytikas (for Lefkada and Meganisi), both in Sterea Ellada; and from Igoumenitsa in Epiros (for Corfu).

Ferries for the Sporades islands leave from Volos, Thessaloniki, Agios Konstantinos, and Kymi on Evia. The latter two ports are easily reached by bus from Athens. Some of the North-Eastern Aegean islands have connections with Thessaloniki as well as Piraeus. The odd ones out are Thasos which is reached from Kavala, and Samothraki, which can be reached from Alexandroupolis year round and also from Kavala in summer. See the table in this section, as well as the relevant port and island sections throughout the book.

Ferry timetables change from year to year and season to season, and ferries are subject to delays and cancellations at short notice

due to inclement weather, strikes or boats simply conking out. No timetable is infallible, but the comprehensive weekly list of departures from Piraeus put out by the EOT in Athens is as accurate as humanly possible. The guys to go to for the most up-to-date ferry information are the local port police (*limenarheio*), whose offices are usually on or near the quayside.

If you're going to do a lot of island hopping and you enjoy poring over timetables, you may want a copy of the *Greek Travel Pages*. This weighty tome is published monthly, primarily for the tourist industry, and has timetable for the major routes as well as lots of other travel facts. You can pick up a copy from Eleftheroudakis bookshop, Nikis 4, Athens, for 4000 dr. If you don't want to spend this much money, a travel agency may let you browse through their copy.

Throughout the year there is at least one ferry a day from a mainland port to the major island in each group, and during the high season (from June to mid-September) there are considerably more. Ferries sailing from one island group to another are not so frequent, and if you're going to travel in this way you'll need to plan carefully, otherwise you may end up having to backtrack to Piraeus.

The large ferries usually have four classes: 1st class has air-con cabins and a posh lounge and restaurant; 2nd class has smaller cabins and sometimes a separate lounge; tourist class gives you a berth in a shared four-berth cabin and 3rd (deck) class gives you access to a room with 'airline' seats, a restaurant, a lounge/bar and, of course, the deck.

Deck class remains an economical way to travel (see the accompanying table of fares), while a 1st-class ticket can cost almost as much as flying on some routes. Children under four travel for free, while children between four and 10 pay half fare. Full fares apply for children over 10. Unless you state otherwise, when purchasing a ticket, you will automatically be given deck class. As deck class is what most tourists opt for, it is those prices which will be quoted in this

Major Ferry Routes from Ports in Mainland Greece

This table shows the high-season deck-class prices at the time of writing. It should be considered a guide only; fares can change at short notice and sailing times can also vary, according to how many islands are visited *en route* and prevailing weather conditions. For more up-to-date information, contact the EOT or local port police.

Cyclades

	Piraeus	Rafina
Andros	–	2 hours (2000 dr)
Tinos	5 hours (3600 dr)	3½ hours (2750 dr)
Mykonos	5½ hours (3700 dr)	4¼ hours (3300 dr)
Syros	4 hours (3300 dr)	4¼ hours (3300 dr)
Naxos	6 hours (3600 dr)	–
Paros	5 hours (3300 dr)	–
Ios	7½ hours (4700 dr)	–
Folegandros	9-10 hours (4500 dr)	–
Santorini	9 hours (4300 dr)	–
Serifos	4½ hours (2900 dr)	–
Sifnos	5½ hours (3000 dr)	–

Crete

	Piraeus
Iraklio	12 hours (4900 dr)
Hania	11 hours (4600 dr)
Rethymno	12 hours (5000 dr)

Dodecanese Islands

	Piraeus
Rhodes	14-18 hours (6700 dr)
Astypalea	16 hours (5100 dr)

North-Eastern Aegean Islands

	Piraeus
Samos	13 hours (4800 dr)
Chios	8 hours (4200 dr)
Lesvos	12 hours (5300 dr)

Ionian Islands

	Igoumenitsa	Patras	Killini
Corfu	1½ hours (700 dr)	10 hours (4500 dr)	–
Kefallonia	–	4 hours (2500 dr)	2¾ hours 2200 dr
Ithaki	–	6 hours (3100 dr)	–
Zakynthos	–	–	1½ hours (1000 dr)

Sporades

	Volos	Agios Konstantinos
Skiathos	3-4 hours (2300 dr)	3½ hours (3000 dr)
Skopelos Town	4½ hours (2800 dr)	4½ hours (3500 dr)
Alonnisos	6 hours (3200 dr)	6 hours (3900 dr)

Saronic Gulf Islands

	Piraeus
Aegina	1½ hours (1000 dr)
Poros	3 hours (1400 dr)
Hydra	3½ hours (1700 dr)
Spetses	4½ hours (2200 dr)

Evia

	Glyfa	Arkitsa	Oropou	Agia Marina	Rafina
Agiokambos	30 minutes (300 dr)	–	–	–	–
Loutra Edipsou	–	one hour (700 dr)	–	–	–
Eretria	–	–	30 minutes (300 dr)	–	–
Nea Styra	–	–	–	40 minutes (500 dr)	–
Marmari	–	–	–	–	1½ hrs (900 dr)
Karystos	–	–	–	–	one hour (1400 dr)

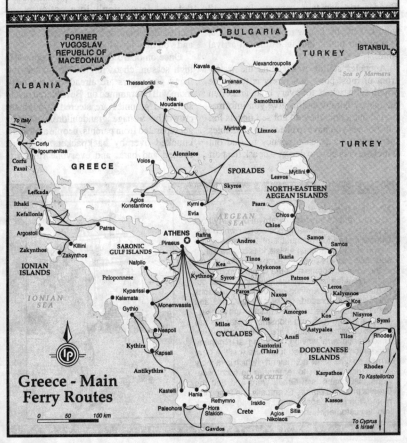

Greece - Main Ferry Routes

0   50   100 km

book. The ticket prices include embarkation tax, a contribution to NAT (the seaman's union) and 8% VAT.

Given that ferries are prone to delays and cancellations, do not purchase a ticket until it has been confirmed that the ferry is leaving, as getting a refund usually proves to be either impossible or a lot of hassle. If you need to reserve car space, however, you may need to pay prior to the day of departure.

Travelling time can vary considerably from one ferry to another, depending on how many islands are called in at on the way to your destination. For example, the Piraeus-Rhodes trip can take between 14 and 18 hours depending on the route. Before buying your ticket, check how many stops the boat is going to make, and its estimated arrival time.

Agencies selling tickets line the waterfront of most ports, but rarely is there one which sells tickets for every boat, and often an agency is reluctant to give you information about a boat they do not sell tickets for. This means you have to check the timetables displayed outside each agency to find out which ferry is next to depart – or ask the port police. In high season, a number of boats may be due at a port at around the same time, so it is not beyond the realms of possibility that you might get on the wrong boat. The crucial thing to look out for is the name of the boat; this will be printed on your ticket, and in large English letters on the side of the vessel.

If for some reason you haven't purchased a ticket from an agency, makeshift ticket tables are put up beside a ferry about an hour before departure. Tickets can also be purchased on board the ship, after it has sailed. If you are waiting at the quayside for a delayed ferry, don't lose patience and wander off. Ferry boats, once they turn up, can demonstrate amazing alacrity – blink and you may miss the boat.

Once on board the fun really begins – in high season, chaos reigns. No matter how many passengers are already on the ferry, more will be crammed on. Bewildered black-shrouded grannies are steered through the crowd by teenage grandchildren, children get separated from parents, people almost get knocked over by backpackers, dogs get excited and bark, and everyone rushes to

Meeting the Ferry

At a few remote islands, the arrival of a ferry boat is a once or twice-weekly occurrence which provides a lifeline for the inhabitants. Witnessing the arrival of a ferry at such an island is an interesting spectacle, as it is one of the most exciting events of the week. It seems as if the whole population – including at least one tail-wagging dog – turns out to meet the ferry. Arriving and departing relations are warmly embraced, sacks of vegetables and crates of drinks are unloaded quickly and haphazardly, and high-tech and industrial appliances are carried off with the utmost care. All this takes place amid frantic arm waving, shouting and general pandemonium in the rush to ensure that the ferry arrives on time at the next island – which invariably it does not. It serves to remember on such occasions that chaos is a Greek word and that the Greeks invented drama. Eventually, the task completed, the ferry departs and the island slips back into its customary tranquillity. ∎

procure a seat. As well as birds in cages and cats in baskets there is almost always at least one truck of livestock on board – usually sheep, goats or cattle – who will vociferously make their presence known.

Greeks travelling third class usually make a beeline for the lounge/snack bar, whereas tourists often make for the deck where they can sunbathe. In high season, you need strong nerves and lungs to withstand the lounge/snack bar, which usually has at least two TVs turned on full blast, tuned to different channels and crackling furiously from interference. A couple of other people will have ghetto blasters pumping out heavy metal, and everyone will be engaged in loud conversation. Smoke-laden air adds the final touch to this delightful ambience. Unlike other public transport in Greece, smoking is not prohibited on ferries.

On overnight trips, backpackers usually sleep on deck in their sleeping bags – you can also roll out your bag between the 'airline' seats. If you don't have a sleeping bag, claim an 'airline' seat as soon as you board. Leave your luggage on it – as long as you don't leave any valuables in it. The noise on board usually dies down around midnight so you should be able to snatch a few hours' sleep. Outside the high season, ferries can be very subdued places, and sometimes it may seem as if you are the only passenger on board.

The food sold in the snack bars ranges from mediocre to inedible, and the choice is limited to packets of biscuits, sandwiches, very greasy pizzas and cheese pies. Most large ferries also have a self-service restaurant where the food is OK, and reasonably priced with main courses starting at around 900 dr. If you are budgeting, have special dietary requirements, or are at all fussy about what you eat, then take some food along with you.

Inter-Island Boat

In addition to the large ferries which ply between the large mainland ports and island groups, there are smaller boats which link two, three or four islands in a group, and occasionally, an island in one group with an island in another. These boats always used to be caïques – sturdy old fishing boats – but gradually these are being replaced by new purpose-built boats, which are usually called express or excursion boats. Tickets tend to cost more than those for the large ferries, but the boats are very useful if you're island hopping.

Taxi Boat

Taxi boats are small boats which transport people to places which are inaccessible or difficult to get to by land. Most islands have at least one of these boats; some owners charge a set price for each person, others charge a flat rate for the boat, and this cost is divided by the number of passengers. Either way, prices are usually quite reasonable.

Hydrofoil

Hydrofoils are an alternative to ferries for reaching some of the islands. They take half the time and cost twice the price, and do not take cars or motorbikes. Some routes operate only during high season, and according to demand, and all are prone to cancellations if the sea is at all rough. A well-established service links Piraeus and the Saronic Gulf islands. Some hydrofoils continue from the Saronic Gulf islands to Porto Heli, Tolo and Nafplio in the Peloponnese and some to Leonidio, Kyparissi, Monemvassia, Neapoli (all in the Peloponnese) and then on to the island of Kythira.

Another well-established service (summer only) is between Thessaloniki and the Sporades; some call in at Moudania on the Halkidiki peninsula. From Moudania there are hydrofoils to Alonnisos which continue on to either Volos or Agios Konstantinos. The Sporades are also served by hydrofoils from Volos and Agios Konstantinos.

The Dodecanese has a well-established service between Rhodes and Kos and a high-season service between Rhodes, Leros and Samos. Other high-season hydrofoils link Rhodes with Halki, Tilos, Nisyros, Karpathos and Kastellorizo; and Rafina with the Cycladic islands of Andros, Tinos, Mykonos and Naxos. Some examples of hydrofoil prices are: Agios Konstantinos to Skopelos (5324 dr) and Alonnisos (5577 dr); and from Piraeus to Hydra (2700 dr) and Spetses (3000 dr). Tickets cannot be bought on board hydrofoils – you must buy them in advance from an agent.

Catamaran

Catamarans are the new guys on the inter-island travel scene. Catamarans operate alongside hydrofoils on some of the hydrofoil routes. The Flying Cats (as the company calls them) operated by Ceres offer VIP class as well as economy travel. Economy fares are the same as for hydrofoils, while an extra 7500 dr gets you a plush, red-leather seat and free drinks in the VIP lounge.

Yacht

Despite the disparaging remarks about yachting among backpackers, yacht is *the* way to see the Greek islands. Nothing beats the peace and serenity of sailing the open sea, and the freedom of being able to visit remote and uninhabited islands.

The free EOT booklet *Sailing the Greek Seas*, although long overdue for an update, contains lots of information about weather conditions, weather bulletins, entry and exit regulations, entry and exit ports and guidebooks for yachters. You can pick up the booklet at any GNTO/EOT office either abroad or in Greece.

If you are not rich enough to buy a yacht there are several other options open to you. You can hire a bare boat (a yacht without a crew) if two crew members have a sailing certificate. Prices start at US$1300 per week for a 28-footer that will sleep six. It will cost an extra US$700 per week for a skipper. Yacht-charter companies operating in and around Athens and Piraeus include:

Aegean Yachts
    Poseidonos 10, Glyfada, Attica (☎ 01-893 2001)
Alfa Levante Yachts
    Vasilissis Sofias 12, Athens (☎ 01-721 9360)
Fine Yachting & Travel
    Koundouriotou 145, Piraeus (☎ 01-412 0414)

Ghiolman Yachts
    Filellinon 7, Athens (☎ 01-323 3696)
G M Yachting
    Makariou 2, Alimos, Attica (☎ 01-981 5619)
Hermes
    Stadiou 4, Athens (☎ 01-323 5270)
Koutsoukelis Yachting
    Stadiou 5, Athens (☎ 01-322 7011)
Seahorse
    Alkyonidon 83, Voula, Attica
    (☎ 01-895 2212/6733)
Seaways Sailing
    Irakeos 23, Glyfada, Attica (☎ 01-963 3356)

There are many more yacht-charter companies in Greece; the EOT can give you some addresses. Also check the Dodecanese chapter in this book.

Ghiolman Yachts (see above) also offer a range of yachting holidays for those who just want to go sailing without the hassle of chartering a yacht. The possibilities include a week sailing the Sporades for US$700, or US$900 in July and August, and two weeks in the Aegean for US$1100/1300.

A number of UK-based holiday companies also offer holidays sailing around the Greek islands. You can book holidays with them either excluding or including the airfare to Greece. Some of these include:

Greek Islands Touring Club
    66 High St, Walton-on-Thames,
    Surrey KT12 1BU (☎ 01932-220416)
Tenrag Yacht Charters
    Bramling House, Bramling, Canterbury,
    Kent CT3 1NB (☎ 01227-721874)
World Expeditions
    7 North St, Maidenhead,
    Berkshire SL6 6BP (☎ 01628-74174)

LOCAL TRANSPORT
To/From the Airport

Olympic Airways operates buses to a few domestic airports (see individual entries). Where the service exists, buses leave the airline office about 1½ hours before departure. In many places, the only way to get to the airport is by taxi. This means that in at least one case (Karpathos to Kassos) you will fork out more for the taxi than the flight. Check-in is an hour before departure for domestic flights.

Transport to and from international airports in Greece is covered in the Getting Around section of the relevant city.

Bus

Most Greek towns are small enough to get around on foot. The only places where you may need to use local buses are Athens, Piraeus and Thessaloniki. The procedure for buying tickets for local buses is covered in the Getting Around section for each city.

Metro

Athens is the only city in Greece with an underground system. At the moment, the service is restricted to a single line running from the port of Piraeus to the northern suburb of Kifissia, with 21 stations in between. A new line, scheduled for completion in 1998, will greatly expand the network. There will be stops at Syntagma and at Larisis train station.

Taxi

The taxi drivers of Athens are legendary for their ability to part locals and tourists alike from their drachma – see the Dangers & Annoyances section in the Athens chapter. If you have a complaint about a taxi driver, take the cab number and report your complaint to the tourist police. Taxi drivers in other towns in Greece are, on the whole, friendly, helpful and honest.

Taxis in towns and cities have meters. The flagfall is 200 dr. Each km costs 58 dr from 5 am to midnight, and double that from midnight to 5 am. Additional charges are 300 dr from an airport, 160 dr from a train or bus station, and 55 dr for each piece of luggage.

TOURS

Tours are worth considering only if your time is very limited, in which case there are countless companies vying for your money. The major players are CHAT, GO Tours and Key Tours, all based in Athens and offering almost identical tours. They include Delphi (two days, 27,500 dr); ancient Corinth, Mycenae and Epidaurus (two days, 27,500 dr); Delphi and Meteora (three days, 69,500 dr); and ancient Corinth, Mycenae, Epidaurus, Sparta, Mystras, ancient Olympia and Delphi (five days, 120,000 dr). These prices include twin-share accommodation and half board. For details of these companies, see Organised Tours in the Activities section of the Athens chapter.

Organised Treks

Trekking Hellas, Filellinon 7, Athens 105 57 (☎ 01-325 0853; fax 323 4548) is a well-established company which specialises in treks and other adventure activities for small groups. It offers a wide range of treks lasting from three days to a week and graded from introductory to challenging. Prices range from 24,000 dr per person for a three-day introductory trek around Mystras, to 112,000 dr for a challenging seven-day trek around Mt Olympus. Other activities include rafting (three days, 36,000 dr) and mountain biking (three days, 39,000 dr).

Other tours are recommended throughout the book.

Athens Aθήνα

The perpetual 'high' which the novelist Henry Miller experienced during his travels in Greece did not flag when he came to the capital. In the *Colossus of Maroussi* Miller waxed lyrical about the extraordinary quality of the city's light and rhythm. Few visitors today, however, share his bubbling enthusiasm. Most beat a hasty retreat after the obligatory visit to the Acropolis and the National Archaeological Museum. Despite its glorious past and its influence on Western civilisation, it is a city which few fall in love with. Modern Athens is a vast concrete urban sprawl that suffers badly from the curse of the industrial age, pollution.

To appreciate Athens, it's important to be aware of the city's traumatic history. Unlike most capital cities, Athens does not have a history of continuous expansion; it is one characterised by glory, followed by decline and near annihilation, and then resurgence in the 19th century – when it became the capital of independent Greece.

The historical event which, more than any other, shaped the Athens of today was the compulsory population exchange between Greece and Turkey that followed the signing of the Treaty of Lausanne in July 1923. The population of Athens virtually doubled overnight, necessitating the hasty erection of concrete apartment blocks to house the newcomers.

The expansion of Athens in all directions began at this time, and accelerated during the 1950s and 1960s when the country began the transition from an agricultural to an industrial nation. Young people began to flock to the city from the islands and rural areas, and this trend has continued ever since.

Yet Athens has many redeeming qualities. The city is bounded on three sides by Mt Parnitha (1413 metres), Mt Pendeli (1109 metres) and Mt Hymettos (1026 metres). The latter was once famed for its violet sunsets – these days normally obliterated by the city's appalling pollution. At least one of these mountains can be glimpsed from almost every street in the city. Within the city there are no less than eight hills, of which the most prominent are Lykavittos (277 metres) and the Acropolis (156 metres).

These hills are a pleasant place to escape from the traffic-congested streets. Athens improves considerably when viewed from a height, and there are stunning views over the city to the glistening waters of the Saronic Gulf – its boundary on the fourth side.

Travelling east, Athens is the last European city in the Mediterranean. King Otho and the middle class which evolved after Independence might have been intent upon making Athens European in every sense of the word, but the influence of Asia Minor is still immediately evident – the coffee, the raucous street vendors on every square and the bustling outdoor markets.

Some of the older parts of the city have a ramshackle Third World feel about them, in contrast with the elegant neoclassical mansions in more salubrious areas.

One of the most endearing aspects of the city is the congeniality of the local people in

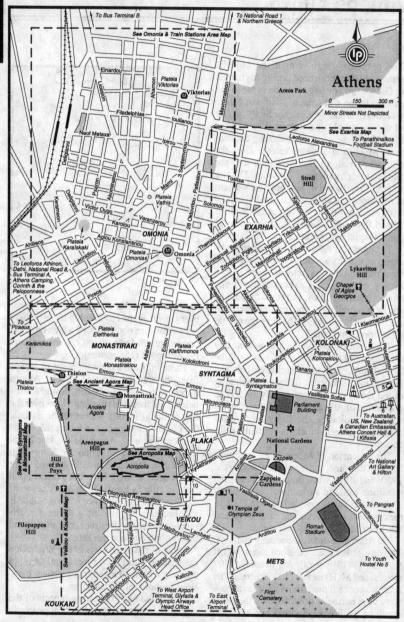

Athens

0   150   300 m
Minor Streets Not Depicted

To Bus Terminal B
To National Road 1 & Northern Greece
See Omonia & Train Stations Area Map
Einardou
Plateia Viktorias
Viktorias
Areos Park
Filadelphias
Ioulianou
See Exarhia Map
Neof Metaxa
Ipirou
To Panathinaikos Football Stadium
Leoforos Alexandras
3 Septemvriou
Plateia Vathis
Tositsa
Strefi Hill
EXARHIA
Solomou
28 Oktovriou - Patission
Veranzerou
OMONIA
Agiou Konstantinou
Plateia Karaiskaki
Plateia Omonias
Omonia
Lykavittos Hill
Pireos
To Leoforos Athinon, Dafni, National Road 8, Bus Terminal A, Athens Camping, Corinth & the Peloponnese
Panepistimiou (El Venizelou)
Akadimias
Chapel of Agios Georgios
Kleomenous
To Piraeus
Plateia Eleftherias
Keramikos
Plateia Klafthmonos
KOLONAKI
MONASTIRAKI
Plateia Monastirakiou
Kolokotroni
Plateia Kolonakiou
SYNTAGMA
Plateia Thisiou
Thision
See Ancient Agora Map
Ermou
Monastiraki
Ermou
Plateia Syntagmatos
Vasilissis Sofias
Ancient Agora
Mitropoleos
Parliament Building
To Australian, US, New Zealand & Canadian Embassies, Athens Concert Hall & Kifissia
Areopagus Hill
PLAKA
National Gardens
See Acropolis Map
Acropolis
To National Art Gallery & Hilton
Hill of the Pnyx
Zappeio
Zappeio Gardens
Dionysiou Areopagitou
Temple of Olympian Zeus
To Pangrati
Filopappos Hill
VEIKOU
Roman Stadium
METS
To Youth Hostel No 5
First Cemetery
KOUKAKI
To West Airport Terminal, Glyfada & Olympic Airways Head Office
To East Airport Terminal

1	St George Lycabettus Hotel
2	Athenian Inn
3	Benaki Museum
4	Goulandris Museum of Cycladic & Ancient Greek Art
5	UK Embassy
6	Byzantine Museum
7	War Museum
8	Church of Agios Dimitrios
9	Monument of Filopappos
10	Choregic Monument of Lysicrates
11	Arch of Hadrian

contrast to the anonymity one feels in many Western capitals. Within a week of staying in Athens the chances are you'll be passing the time of day, or stopping for a chat, with new acquaintances.

Perhaps most significant of all is that wherever you are in the centre of the city the Acropolis, with its transcendent and compelling aura, stands proudly on the skyline. It serves as a constant reminder that whatever trials and tribulations might have befallen the city, its status as the birthplace of Western civilisation is beyond doubt.

HISTORY
Early History
The early history of Athens is inextricably interwoven with mythology, making it impossible to disentangle fact from fiction. What is known is that the hilltop site of the Acropolis, endowed with two bounteous springs, drew some of Greece's earliest Neolithic settlers. When a peaceful agricultural existence gave way to the war-orientated city-states, the Acropolis provided an ideal defensive position: its steep slopes formed natural defences on three sides and it was an excellent vantage point from which to spot potential danger coming from either land or sea.

By 1400 BC, the Acropolis had become a powerful Mycenaean city. Unlike the cities of Mycenae, Pylos and Tiryns, it survived the Dorian assault on Greece in 1200 BC. It couldn't, however, escape the dark age that enveloped Greece for the next 400 years, and very little is known of this period.

After its emergence from the dark age in the 8th century BC, a period of peace followed, both for Athens and the surrounding united towns. During this time the city became the artistic centre of Greece, excelling in ceramics. The geometric designs of vases from the dark ages evolved into a narrative style, depicting scenes from everyday life and from mythology. This pottery subsequently became known as the Proto-Attic style.

By the 6th century BC, Athens was ruled by aristocrats, generals and the archon (chief magistrate). A person's position in the hierarchy depended on their wealth, which was gained either from commerce or agriculture. Labourers and peasants had no say at all in the functioning of the city – until the reform-oriented Solon became archon in 594 BC.

Solon did much to improve the lot of the poor and is regarded as the harbinger of Athenian democracy. His most significant reforms were the annulment of all debts and the implementation of trial by jury. Continuing unrest over the reforms created the pretext for the tyrant Peisistratos, formerly head of the military, to seize power in 560 BC.

Peisistratos built up a formidable navy, much to the consternation of other city-states, and extended the boundaries of Athenian influence on land. He was a patron of the arts as well as a general. He inaugurated the Festival of the Great Dionysia, which was the precursor of Attic drama, and commissioned many splendid sacred and secular buildings – most of which were destroyed by the Persians on the eve of the Battle of Salamis in 480 BC.

Peisistratos was succeeded by his son Hippias, who was very much a tyrant. Athens managed to rid itself of this oppressor in 510 BC only by swallowing its pride and accepting the help of Sparta. Hippias wasn't finished, and headed off to Persia to stir up trouble, returning with Darius 20 years later to be defeated at the Battle of Marathon.

Athens' Golden Age
After Athens had finally repulsed the

Athena & the Olive Tree

According to mythology, Cecrops, a Phoenician, came to Attica, where he founded a city on a huge rock near the sea. The gods of Olympus proclaimed that the city should be named after the deity who could produce the most valuable legacy for mortals. Athena and Poseidon contended. Athena produced an olive tree, symbol of peace and prosperity. Poseidon struck a rock with his trident and a horse sprang forth, which symbolised all the qualities of strength and fortitude for which he was renowned. Athena was the victor, for the gods proclaimed that her gift would better serve the citizens of Athens than the arts of war personified by Poseidon's gift. ■

challenge of the Persian Empire at the battles of Salamis and Plataea (again, with the help of Sparta), its power knew no bounds.

In 477 BC Athens established a confederacy on the sacred island of Delos and demanded tributes from the surrounding islands to protect them from the Persians. It was little more than a standover racket because the Persians were no longer much of a threat. The treasury was moved to Athens in 461 BC and Pericles (ruled from 461 to 429 BC) used the money to transform the city. The period has become known as Athens' golden age, the pinnacle of the classical age.

Most of the monuments on the Acropolis today date from this time. Drama and literature flourished in the form of the tragedies written by Aeschylus, Sophocles and Euripides. The sculptors Pheidias and Myron and the historians Herodotus, Thucydides and Xenophon also lived at this time.

Rivalry with Sparta

Arch rival Sparta wasn't prepared to sit back and allow Athens to revel in glory. The increasing jockeying for power between the two led to the outbreak of the Peloponnesian Wars in 431 BC. The warring dragged on until 404 BC when Sparta gained the upper hand. Athens was never to return to its former glory. The 4th century BC did, however, produce three of the West's greatest orators and philosophers: Socrates, Plato and Aristotle. The degeneracy into which Athens had fallen was perhaps epitomised by the ignominious death sentence passed on Socrates for the crime of corrupting the young with his speeches.

Athens' days of glory were now numbered. In 338 BC, along with the other city-states of Greece, Athens was conquered by Philip II of Macedon. After Philip's assassination, his son Alexander the Great, a cultured young man, favoured Athens over other city-states. After his untimely death, Athens passed in quick succession through the hands of several of his generals.

Roman & Byzantine Rule

After the Romans conquered Greece in 31 BC, Athens continued to be a major seat of learning, and many wealthy young Romans attended Athens' schools. Anybody who was anybody in Rome at the time spoke Greek. The Roman emperors, particularly Hadrian, graced Athens with many grand buildings.

After the subdivision of the Roman Empire into east and west, Athens remained an important cultural and intellectual centre until the Emperor Justinian closed its schools of philosophy in 529 AD. The city then declined into nothing more than an outpost of the Byzantine Empire.

Between 1200 and 1450, Athens was invaded by Franks, Catalans, Florentines and Venetians – all opportunists preoccupied only with grabbing for themselves principalities from the crumbling Byzantine Empire.

Ottoman Rule & Independence

Athens was captured by the Turks in 1456, and nearly 400 years of Ottoman rule followed. The Acropolis became the home of the Turkish governor, the Parthenon was converted into a mosque and the Erechtheion was used as a harem.

In the early stages of the War of Independence (1821-27), fierce fighting broke out in the streets of Athens, with the city changing hands several times between Turks and Greek liberators. In 1834 Athens had superseded Nafplio as the capital of independent Greece and King Otho set about transforming the sparsely populated, war-scarred town into something worthy of a capital. Bavarian architects created a city of imposing neoclassical buildings, tree-lined boulevards, flower gardens and squares. Sadly, many of these buildings have been demolished. The best surviving examples are on Vasilissis Sofias.

The 20th Century

Athens grew steadily throughout the latter half of the 19th and early 20th centuries, and enjoyed a brief heyday as the 'Paris of the eastern Mediterranean'. This came to an abrupt end in 1923 with the Treaty of Lausanne. This treaty resulted in nearly a million refugees from Turkey descending on Athens – an event which marked the beginning of its much-maligned concrete sprawl.

Athens, along with the rest of Greece, suffered appallingly during the German occupation of WW II. During this time more Athenians were killed by starvation than by the enemy. This suffering was perpetuated in the civil war that followed.

The industrialisation programme that was launched during the 1950s, with the help of US aid, brought another population boom as

people from the islands and mainland villages headed to Athens in search of work.

The colonels' junta (which ruled from 1967 to 74), with characteristic insensitivity, tore down many of the crumbling old Turkish houses of Plaka and the imposing neoclassical buildings of King Otho's time. Subsequent governments have become steadily more conservation-conscious, and these days old buildings of architectural merit are being restored. The sleazy bars, nightclubs and strip joints of Plaka have been closed down and many of its streets have become pedestrian ways.

ORIENTATION
City Centre

Although Athens is a huge, sprawling city, nearly everything of interest to travellers is located within a small area bounded by Plateia Omonias to the north, Plateia Monistirakiou to the west, Plateia Syntagmatos to the east and the Plaka district to the south. The city's two major landmarks, the Acropolis and Lykavittos hill, can be seen from just about everywhere and are useful for getting one's bearings. The streets are clearly signposted in Greek and English. If you do get lost, it's very easy to find help. A glance at a map is often enough to draw an offer of assistance. Anyone you ask will be able to direct you to Syntagma.

Plateia Syntagmatos (Πλατεία Συντάγματος) Syntagma is the heart of the modern city of Athens. It is flanked by luxury hotels, banks, airline offices and expensive coffee shops and is dominated by the old royal palace. It was from the palace balcony that the constitution *(syntagma)* was declared on 3 September 1843. The building has housed the Greek parliament since 1935.

Syntagma is a pleasant introduction to the city, despite the manic speed at which the traffic zooms around it. At its centre is a large, paved square, planted with orange, oleander and cypress trees. If you're arriving on the airport bus and want to stay in Plaka, Syntagma is the place to get off. The stop is opposite the National Gardens, just before the square. Syntagma will have its own metro stop when the new line is finished.

Plaka (Πλάκα) Plaka is the old Turkish quarter of Athens and virtually all that existed when Athens was declared the capital of independent Greece. Its narrow, labyrinthine streets nestle into the north-eastern slope of the Acropolis, and most of the city's ancient sites are close by. Plaka is touristy in the extreme. Its main streets, Kydathineon and Adrianou, are packed solid with restaurants and souvenir shops and there is an abundance of accommodation to suit every budget. It is the most attractive and interesting part of Athens and the majority of visitors make it their base. The most convenient trolleybus stop is on Filellinon, near the junction with Kydathineon.

Plateia Monastirakiou (Πλατεία Μονα–στηρακίου) Monastiraki is in the heart of the city's market district. The central meat and fish market is on Athinas, opposite the fruit and vegetable market, halfway between Monastiraki and Omonia. Shops along the streets bordering the markets sell cheeses, nuts, herbs, honey, dried fruits and cold meats. On Eolou most shops sell cut-price clothing and street vendors offer items such as sheets, towels, tablecloths and underwear.

The famous flea market is to the south-west on Ifestou; while Areos, to the south, is the favourite hang-out of a colourful bunch of freaks and travellers selling Indian paraphernalia. Ermou and Mitropoleos, which run almost parallel between Monastiraki and Syntagma, offer somewhat more up-market shopping. Ermou is lined with fashion and textile shops and Mitropoleos is the best place in Athens to buy carpets and flokati rugs. Athens Cathedral dominates the large square halfway along Mitropoleos.

Monastiraki is the metro stop for Plaka.

Plateia Omonias (Πλατεία Ομόνιας) Omonia is more of a transport hub than a square. The major streets of central Athens all meet here. The two most important streets are El Venizelou and Stadiou, which run

parallel south-east to Syntagma, one km away. Athens University is halfway along El Venizelou, which is more commonly known as Panepistimiou (university). Athinas heads south from Omonia to Plateia Monistirakiou; Pireos runs south-west to Piraeus; Agiou Konstantinou goes west towards the railway stations; and 3 Septemvriou heads north – although the major street heading north is 28 Oktovriou-Patission, which starts 50 metres along Panepistimiou from the square. South of Panepistimiou, the street becomes Eolou and runs almost to the foot of the Acropolis. Omonia is a stop on the Metro system, as well as being on almost every trolleybus route.

The square is not a pleasant place to hang out (see Dangers & Annoyances, below). A lot of homeless people sleep rough in the underground hall and passages connected to the Metro station. Their numbers have been boosted by refugees from the fighting in the Balkans. Junkies seem to prefer Plateia Vathis, 300 metres to the north-west.

Beyond the City Centre
Around Syntagma Amalias is the main street heading south from the eastern side of Syntagma. Next to it are the National Gardens – a park of subtropical trees and ornamental ponds – and then the more formally laid-out Zappeio gardens. Amalias skirts the Arch of Hadrian and the Temple of Olympian Zeus and leads into Syngrou, which runs all the way to the coast at Faliro. Buses from the airport and Piraeus approach Syntagma along Amalias.

Vasilissis Sofias runs east from Syntagma, skirting the northern edge of the National Gardens. It is one of Athens' most imposing streets, laid out by the Bavarian architects brought in by King Otho. Its neoclassical buildings now house a collection of museums, embassies and government offices. To the north of Vasilissis Sofias, at the foot of Lykavittos hill, is the opulent residential district of Kolonaki with its ultra-trendy boutiques, expensive coffee shops and private art galleries. Kolonaki has long been the favoured address of Athenian socialites. More recently it has become a popular area with gays, who frequent its sophisticated bars.

Around Plaka South of the Acropolis is Filopappos hill, and flanking it are the pleasant residential districts of Veïkou and Koukaki. To the east, on the other side of Syngrou, is the district of Mets, which still has some delightful old Turkish houses. North-east of Mets is Pangrati. Both are pleasant residential neighbourhoods.

West of Plateia Monastirakiou Ermou becomes a lot tattier west of Plateia Monastirakiou. This is Athens at its most clapped out, with a ramshackle Third World feel. There are lots of second-hand shops with a bizarre array of bric-a-brac overflowing onto the pavements. This stretch of Ermou is closed to traffic on Sunday for the famous markets.

North of Omonia Venturing north from Omonia the seediness gradually recedes and, beyond Plateia Vathis, gives way to a respectable, if characterless, neighbourhood. Athens' two train stations are at the western edge of this area, on Deligianni. The National Archaeological Museum is on the eastern side, on 28 Oktovriou-Patission. The area's main square is Plateia Viktorias, near which is the red-light district on Filis.

Just south of the National Archaeological Museum is the Athens Polytehnio. This establishment has university status, with faculties of fine arts and engineering, whereas most students at Athens University read law or medicine. The Polytehnio has a long tradition of radical thinking and alternative culture, and led the student sit-in of 1973 in opposition to the junta.

Squashed between the Polytehnio and Strefi hill is the student residential area of Exarhia. It's a lively area with graffiti-covered walls and lots of cheap restaurants catering for the crowds of Bohemian-looking professors and rebellious-looking students.

INFORMATION
Tourist Offices
EOT's head office (☎ 322 3111) at Amerikis 2 does not deal with enquiries from the general public. The organisation's public face is a small information window (☎ 322 2545) in the National Bank of Greece building on Syntagma Square. It is a very unsatisfactory and impersonal arrangement which requires you to talk into a microphone to someone on the other side of a heavy plate-glass window, who responds in kind. They can slide photocopied information sheets out to you, provided you know what to ask for. It's worth asking for their free map of Athens, which has most of the places of interest clearly marked and also shows the trolleybus routes. Unfortunately the map is designed to last the length of the average tourist stay – about a day – before it falls to bits. There's also a notice board with transport information, including a very useful timetable of the week's ferry departures from Piraeus.

The EOT window is open Monday to Friday from 8 am to 6 pm and Saturday from 9 am to 2 pm.

The EOT office (☎ 979 9500) at the East Air Terminal is open Monday to Friday from 9 am to 7 pm and Saturday from 10 am to 5 pm.

Tourist Police
The head office (☎ 902 5992) of the tourist police is at Dimitrakopoulou 77, Veïkou. It is open 24 hours a day, but it's quite a trek from the city centre – take trolleybus No 1, 5 or 9 from Syntagma. The tourist police also have a 24-hour information service (☎ 171). You can call them for general tourist information or in an emergency – someone who speaks English is always available.

They will also act as interpreters for any dealings you might have with the crime police (☎ 770 5711/5717), Leoforos Alexandras 173, or the traffic police (☎ 523 0111), Agiou Konstantinou 28, near Omonia.

Money
Most of the major banks have branches

around Syntagma, open Monday to Thursday from 8 am to 2 pm and Friday from 8 am to 1.30 pm. The National Bank of Greece and the Credit Bank, on opposite sides of Stadiou at Syntagma, both have 24-hour automatic-exchange machines.

American Express (☎ 324 4975/4979), Ermou 2, Syntagma, is open Monday to Friday from 8.30 am to 4 pm, and Saturday from 8.30 am to 1.30 pm. It also has a free poste-restante service for card-holders. Non-members can use the service, but there's a collection fee of 600 dr per item. Thomas Cook (☎ 322 0155) has an office at Karageorgi Servias 4, open Monday to Friday from 8.30 am to 8 pm, Saturday from 9 am to 6.30 pm and Sunday from 10 am to 2.30 pm.

In Plaka, Acropole Foreign Exchange, Kydathineon 23, is open from 9 am to midnight every day. It does, however, charge a hefty 2.5% commission. Ergobank, at the junction of Adrianou and Kydathineon, has a 24-hour automatic-exchange machine.

The banks at both the East and West airport terminals are open 24 hours a day, although you may have trouble tracking down the staff late at night.

Post & Telecommunications

Athens' central post office (☎ 321 6023) is at Eolou 100, Omonia (postcode 10 200), just east of Plateia Omonias. Unless specified otherwise, poste restante will be sent here. If you're staying in Plaka, it's far more convenient to get your mail sent to the poste restante at the large post office on Syntagma (on the corner of Mitropoleos; postcode 103 00). Both are open Monday to Friday from 7.30 am to 8 pm and Saturday from 7.30 am to 2 pm.

Parcels for abroad that weigh over two kg must be taken to the parcel post office (☎ 322 8940), Stadiou 4. The office is in the arcade that runs between Amerikis and Voukourestiou. Parcels should be taken along unwrapped for inspection.

The OTE office, 28 Oktovriou-Patission 85, is open 24 hours a day. There are also offices at Stadiou 15 and on the southern corner of Plateia Omonias; both of these offices are open from 7 am to 11.30 pm daily. There is also an office at Athinas 50.

The telephone code for Athens is 01. Some useful telephone numbers include:

general telephone information	(☎ 134)
numbers in Athens & Attica	(☎ 131)
numbers elsewhere in Greece	(☎ 132)
international telephone information	(☎ 161 or 162)
international telegrams	(☎ 165)
domestic operator	(☎ 151 or 152)
domestic telegrams	(☎ 155)
wake-up service	(☎ 182)

If you simply cannot live without your mobile phone, they can be rented from Trimtel Mobile Communications (☎ 729 1964), Menandrou 9.

Foreign Embassies

See Visas & Embassies in the Facts for the Visitor chapter for a list of foreign embassies in Athens.

Cultural Centres

Following is a list of international cultural centres in Athens:

British Council
    Plateia Eterias (also known as Plateia Kolonakiou) 17 (☎ 363 3215)
French Institute of Athens
    Sina 31 (☎ 362 4301)
Goethe Institute
    Omirou 14-16 (☎ 360 8114)
Hellenic-American Union
    Massalias 22 (☎ 362 9886)

These cultural centres hold concerts, film shows and exhibitions from time to time. Major events are listed in various English-language newspapers and magazines.

Travel Agencies

The bulk of the city's travel agencies are around Omonia and Syntagma squares, but only the agencies at Syntagma deal in discounted air tickets. There are lots of them just south of the square on Filellinon, Nikis and Voulis. The International Student & Youth Travel Service (ISYTS) (☎ 323 3767), Nikis

11 (2nd floor), is the city's official student and youth travel service, specialising in tickets for domestic and international air, sea and land travel. It also issues International Student Identity Cards (ISICs) and has information on cheap accommodation. Magic Bus (☎ 323 7471), Filellinon 20, specialises in discount air fares. It has some very good last-minute deals on charter flights. It no longer operates its own buses to Europe (see the Getting There & Away chapter).

Bookshops

Athens has three good English-language bookshops. The pick of them is Compendium (☎ 322 1248), upstairs at Nikis 28. It has a second-hand section as well as a good selection overall. The place is also child-friendly, and holds a children's story hour on the second and fourth Saturday of every month at 11 am. The English-language notice board outside has information about jobs, accommodation and courses in Athens. Compendium also stocks some Lonely Planet guides, as does Eleftheroudakis (☎ 322 9388) at Nikis 4. Pantelides Books (☎ 362 3673), Amerikis 11, stocks a range of feminist books as well as paperbacks, travel guides, maps etc.

Ippokratous, in the student suburb of Exarhia, is packed solid with bookshops. The foreign-language bookshop *(xenoglosso vivliopoleio)* at No 10-12 stocks books in French, Italian and German as well as English.

The second-hand bookshop at Ifestiou 24 in the flea market is an amazing place: a dusty cavern with piles of books everywhere – stacked to the ceiling in places. One of these stacks is devoted to books in English, dumped totally at random. You'll find everything from bundles of Marvel comics to books on neurology.

French, German, English, Italian and Spanish books are available at Kauffmann (☎ 322 2160), Stadiou 28, and The Booknest (☎ 323 1703), Panepistimiou 25-29.

International newspapers reach the periptera on Syntagma same day at 1 pm on weekdays and 7 pm on weekends.

Laundries

Plaka has a very convenient laundrette at Angelou Geronta 10, just off Kydathineon near the outdoor restaurants. It is also the cheapest, charging 1500 dr to wash and dry five kg. Others are at Psaron 9 near Plateia Karaïskaki (2500 dr), at Kolokinthous 41 on the corner of Leonidou (both in Omonia), and at Erehthiou 9 in Koukaki (2000 dr).

Luggage Storage

The service at Pacific Travel (☎ 324 1007), Nikis 26, is cheap, reliable and convenient – about all you can ask for. It charges 300 dr per day, 600 dr per week and 1800 dr per month; and opening hours are Monday to Saturday from 7 am to 8 pm, Sunday and holidays from 7 am to 2 pm. Many Athens hotels will store luggage free for guests, although a lot them do no more than pile bags in a hallway.

Emergency

For the fire brigade ring ☎ 199. For emergency medical treatment ring the tourist police (☎ 171) and they will tell you the location of the nearest hospital. Hospitals give free emergency treatment to tourists. For hospitals with out-patient departments on duty call ☎ 106; for the telephone number of an on-call doctor ring ☎ 105 (from 2 pm to 7 am); for a pharmacy open 24 hours call ☎ 107; and for first-aid advice phone ☎ 166. US citizens can ring ☎ 721 2951 for emergency medical aid.

Dangers & Annoyances

Pickpockets It seems that the Sunday market on Ermou is the favourite stamping ground for pickpockets and bag thieves. Plateia Omonias has a reputation for similar activity, but this type of crime is much rarer than in most European cities.

Slippery Surfaces Many of Athens' pavements and other surfaces underfoot are made of marble and become incredibly slippery when wet, so if you are caught in the rain, be very careful how you tread.

Hotel Touts It is the normal procedure for owners of student hostels in Athens to employ touts to meet tourists who have arrived by train. Most of the hostels recommended in the Places to Stay section in this chapter do this, and it often saves a lot of hassle to take up an offer. Before doing so, however, ask to see the hostel leaflet. This will have a picture of the hostel, information about the facilities offered and (very importantly) a map showing its location. Be very suspicious of a tout who cannot show you a leaflet. It's a good idea to agree upon a price in writing before taking up an offer.

Taxi Drivers Athens residents will tell you that their taxi drivers are the biggest bunch of bastards in the world. It seems that they have as much trouble getting a fair deal as tourists do. Most of the rip-off stories involve cabs picked up from the airport or from Bus Terminal A at Kifissou. A favourite trick is to set the meter on night rate (tariff 2) during the day. They should be charging the day rate (tariff 1) between 6 am and midnight. Every now and again, the police conduct well-publicised clamp-downs. At the time of research, one cabby was caught at the airport with a handy remote-controlled device that could make the meter spin round at 2000 dr per minute!

If you are catching a cab to Athens from the airport, agree on the price before you get in. If the driver still attempts to charge you more, ask to see the official tariff list (which every driver must keep in the cab) and point out the error. If there is still a dispute over the fare, take the driver's number and report it to the tourist police.

Taxi Touts Taxi drivers working in league with some of the overpriced C-class hotels around Omonia are a problem that many have to contend with. The scam involves taxi drivers picking up late-night arrivals, particularly at the airport and Bus Terminal A, and persuading them that the hotel they want to go to is full – even if they have a booking. The taxi driver will pretend to phone the hotel of choice, announce that it's full and

suggest an alternative. You can ask to speak to the hotel yourself, or simply insist on going where you want.

THINGS TO SEE
Walking Tour
This walk takes in most of Plaka's main sites. It takes about 45 minutes without detours. Plaka is a fascinating place to explore, full of surprises tucked away in the labyrinthine streets that weave over the undulating terrain.

The walk begins at the former royal palace, now the **parliament building**, which flanks the eastern side of Syntagma. The palace was designed by the Bavarian architect Von Gartner and was built in 1836-42. The building remained the royal palace until 1935, when it became the seat of the Greek parliament. (The royal family moved to a new palace on the corner of Vasileos Konstantinou and Herod Atticus, which became the presidential palace upon the abolition of the monarchy in 1974.)

Plateia Syntagmatos has been a favourite place for protests and rallies ever since the rally that led to the granting of a constitution on 3 September 1843, declared by King Otho from the balcony of the royal palace. In 1944 the first round of the civil war began here after police opened fire on a rally organised by the communists. Known as the Dekembriana (events of December), it was followed by a month of fierce fighting between the communist resistance and the British forces. In 1954 the first demonstration demanding the *enosis* (union) of Cyprus with Greece took place here. At election time, political parties stage their rallies in the square and most protest marches end up here.

The parliament building is guarded by the much photographed *evzones* (guards traditionally from the village of Evzoni in Macedonia). Their somewhat incongruous uniform of short kilts and pom-pom shoes is the butt of much mickey-taking by sightseers. Their uniform is based on the attire worn by the klephts, the mountain fighters who battled so ferociously in the War of Independence. Every Sunday at 11 am the evzones perform a full changing-of-the-guard ceremony.

Standing with your back to the parliament building you will see ahead of you, to the right, the **Hotel Grande Bretagne**. This, the grandest of Athens' hotels, was built in 1862 as a 60-room mansion to accommodate visiting dignitaries. In 1872 it was converted into a hotel and became the place where the crowned heads of Europe and eminent politicians stayed. The Nazis made it their headquarters during WW II. The hotel was the scene of an attempt to blow up the British prime minister, Winston Churchill, on Christmas Eve 1944 while he was in Athens to discuss the Dekembriana fighting. A bomb was discovered in the hotel sewer.

At the time of writing, it was not possible to cross over Amalias and walk through the middle of the square because of the metro

Choregic Monument of Lysicrates

works. Instead, cross Amalias and follow Othonos, on the southern flank of the square, down to Mitropoleos, which starts at the post office. Take the first turn left into Nikis, and walk up to the crossroads with Kydathineon, a pedestrian walkway and one of Plaka's main thoroughfares.

Turn right and a little way along you will come to the **Church of Metamorphosis** on Plateia Satiros; opposite is the **Museum of Greek Folk Art**. Continue along here, and after Plateia Filomousou Eterias (more commonly known as Plateia Plakas), the square with the outdoor tavernas, take the first turn left into Adrianou, another of Plaka's main thoroughfares. At the end, turn right, and this will bring you to the square with the **Choregic Monument of Lysicrates**. (The name *choregos*, was given to the wealthy citizens who financed choral and dramatic performances.) This monument was built in 334 BC to commemorate a win in a choral festival. An inscription on the architrave states:

Lysicrates of Kykyna, son of Lysitheides, was Choregos; the tribe of Akamantis won the victory with a chorus of boys; Theon played the flute; Lysiades of Athens trained the chorus; Euainetos was archon.

The reliefs on the monument depict the battle between Dionysos and the Tyrrhenian pirates, whom the god had transformed into dolphins. It is the earliest known monument using Corinthian capitals externally. It stands in a cordoned-off archaeological site which is part of the **Street of Tripods**. It was here that winners of ancient dramatic and choral contests dedicated their tripod trophies to Dionysos. In the 19th century, the monument was incorporated into the library of a French Capuchin convent, in which Byron stayed in 1810-11 and wrote *Childe Harold*. The convent was destroyed by fire in 1890. Recent excavations around the monument have revealed the foundations of other choregic monuments.

Facing the monument, turn left and then right into Epimenidou. At the top of the steps, turn right into Stratonos, which skirts

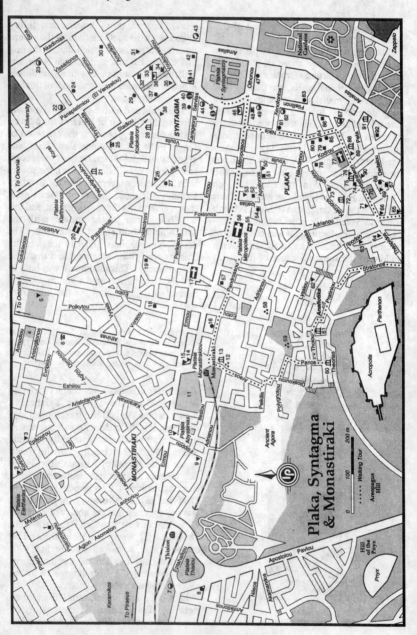

Plaka, Syntagma
& Monastiraki

PLACES TO STAY

1	Hotel Capri
18	Hotel Tempi
19	Hotel Carolina
27	Hotel Achilleas
30	XEN
42	Hotel Grande Bretagne
51	Hotel Omiros
52	John's Place
57	Hotel Plaka
73	Hotel Nefeli
74	Student & Travellers' Inn
78	Acropolis House Pension
79	Kouros Hotel
80	Hotel Myrto
84	George's Guesthouse
86	Festos Youth & Student Guesthouse
92	Hotel Solonion

PLACES TO EAT

2	Olympic Restaurant
3	O Telis Psistaria
4	Fruit & Vegetable Market
5	Meat Market Tavernas
9	Epiros Taverna
10	Taverna Abyssinia
14	Grigoris & Savas
15	Sigalas Taverna
26	Orient Restaurant
31	Apotsos Ouzeri
32	Floca Coffee Shop
33	Zonar's
34	Brazil Coffee Shop
35	Wendy's
38	Far East Restaurant
42	GB Corner Restaurant
48	Neon Café
50	Galaktopoleio

53	Peristeria Taverna
62	Eden Vegetarian Restaurant
63	Ouzeri Kouklis
64	Taverna O Thespis
65	Diogenes Taverna
66	Taverna Damigos
67	Tristato Café
69	Taverna Acropol
71	Plaka Psistaria
76	The Cellar & Galaktopoleio
89	Taverna Saita
90	Michiko Japanese Restaurant

OTHER

5	Meat & Fish Market
6	OTE
7	Buses to Peania & Koropi
8	Pit Poule
11	Flea Market
12	Library of Hadrian
13	Museum of Traditional Greek Ceramics
16	Centre of Hellenic Tradition
17	Church of Kapnikarea
20	Church of Agii Theodori
21	City of Athens Museum
22	Buses to Dafni & Elefsina
23	Buses to Moni Kaissariannis
24	OSE
25	OTE
28	National Historical Museum
29	Pantelides Books
36	Parcel Post Office
37	Festival Box Office
39	Thomas Cook

40	EOT & National Bank of Greece
41	Credit Bank
43	Egyptian Consulate
44	Buses to Airport
45	American Express
46	Post Office
47	Olympic Airways
49	Bus 040 to Piraeus
54	National Welfare Organisation's Folk Art Gallery
55	Church of Agios Eleftherios
56	Athens Cathedral
58	Tower of the Winds
59	Roman Agora
60	Paul & Alexandra Kanellopoulos Museum
61	Museum of the University
68	Self-Service Laundrette
70	Plateia Plakas
72	Centre of Folk Arts & Traditions
75	Children's Museum
77	Church of Metamorphosis
81	International Student & Youth Travel Service and Pioneer Tours
82	Buses to Cape Sounion
83	EOS
85	Compendium Books
87	Trolleybus Stop for Plaka
88	Museum of Greek Folk Art
91	Jewish Museum

the Acropolis. A left fork after 150 metres leads to the highest part of Plaka, an area called Anafiotika. The little whitewashed cube houses are the legacy of the people from the small Cycladic island of Anafi who were used as cheap labour in the building of Athens after Independence. It's a beautiful spot, with brightly painted olive-oil cans brimming with flowers bedecking the walls of the tiny gardens.

The path winds between the houses and comes to some steps on the right, at the bottom of which is a curving pathway leading downhill to Pratiniou. Turn left at Pratiniou and veer right after 50 metres into Tholou. The yellow-ochre building with brown shutters at No 5 is the old university, built by the Venetians. The Turks used it as public offices and it was Athens University from 1837 to 1841. It is now the **Museum of the University**, and its displays include some wonderful, old anatomical drawings and gruesome-looking surgical instruments. It is open Monday and Wednesday from 2.30 to 7 pm, and Tuesday, Thursday and Friday from 9.30 am to 2.30 pm. Admission is free.

At the end of Tholou, turn left into Panos. At the top of the steps on the left is a restored 19th-century mansion which is now the **Paul & Alexandra Kanellopoulos Museum**. Retracing your steps, go down Panos to the ruins of the **Roman Agora**, then turn left into Polygnotou and walk to the crossroads. Opposite, Polygnotou continues to the **Ancient Agora**. At the crossroads, turn right and then left into Poikilis, then immediately right into Areos. On the right are the remains of the **Library of Hadrian** and next to it is the **Museum of Traditional Greek Ceramics**, open Wednesday to Monday from 10 am to 2 pm. Admission is 500 dr. The museum is housed in the Mosque of Tzistarakis, built in 1759. After Independence it lost its minaret and was used as a prison.

Ahead is **Plateia Monastirakiou**, named after the small church. To the left is the metro station and the **flea market**. Plateia Monastirakiou is Athens at its noisiest, most colourful and chaotic. It teems with street vendors selling nuts, coconut sticks and fruit.

Turn right just beyond the mosque into Pandrossou. This street is a relic of the old Turkish bazaar. Today it is full of souvenir shops, selling everything from cheap kitsch to high-class jewellery and clothes. The street is named after King Cecrop's daughter, Pandrosos, who was the first priestess of Athens. At No 89 is Stavros Melissinos, the 'poet sandalmaker' of Athens who names the Beatles, Rudolph Nureyev and Jackie Onassis among his customers. Fame and fortune have not gone to his head, however – he still makes the best-value sandals in Athens, costing between 2400 and 3700 dr per pair.

Pandrossou leads to **Plateia Mitropoleos** and the **Athens Cathedral**. The cathedral has little architectural merit, which isn't surprising considering that it was constructed from the masonry of over 50 razed churches and from the designs of several architects. Next to it stands the much smaller, and far more appealing, **Church of Agios Eleftherios**, which was once the cathedral. Turn left after the cathedral, and then right into Mitropoleos and follow it back to Syntagma.

The Acropolis

Athens exists because of the Acropolis, the most important ancient monument in the Western world. Crowned by the Parthenon, it stands sentinel over Athens, visible from almost everywhere within the city. Its monuments of Pentelic marble gleam white in the midday sun and gradually take on a honey hue as the sun sinks. At night they are floodlit and seem to hover above the city. No matter how harassed you may become in Athens, a sudden unexpected glimpse of this magnificent sight cannot fail to lift your spirits. Inspiring as these monuments are, they are but faded remnants of Pericles' city, and it takes a great leap of the imagination to begin to comprehend the splendour of his creations. Pericles spared no expense – only the best materials, architects, sculptors and artists were good enough for a city dedicated to the cult of Athena, tutelary goddess of Athens. The city was a showcase of colossal buildings, lavishly coloured and gilded, and of gargantuan statues, some of bronze, others of marble plated with gold and encrusted with precious stones.

The crowds that swarm over the Acropolis need to be seen to be believed, especially on Sunday when admission is free (except for guided tours). It's best to get there as early as possible. You need to wear shoes with good soles because the paths around the site are uneven and very slippery.

Between April and October, the Acropolis archaeological site (☎ 321 0219) is open Monday to Friday from 8 am to 6.30 pm; and Saturday, Sunday and holidays from 8.30 am to 2.30 pm. The Acropolis **museum** is open Tuesday to Friday from 8 am to 6.30 pm; Saturday, Sunday and holidays from 8.30 am to 2.30 pm; and Monday from 11 am to 6.30 pm. In winter, both site and museum close at 5 pm instead of 6.30 pm. The combined admission fee is 2000 dr (free on Sunday and public holidays).

There is only one entrance to the Acropolis, but there are several approaches to this entrance. The main approach from the north is along the path that is a continuation of Dioskouron in the south-west corner of

Plaka. From the south, you can either walk or take bus No 230 along Dionysiou Areopagitou to just beyond the Theatre of Herodes Atticus where a path leads to the entrance.

History The Acropolis (high city) was first inhabited in Neolithic times. The first temples were built during Mycenaean times in homage to the goddess Athena. All the buildings on the Acropolis were reduced to ashes by the Persians on the eve of the Battle of Salamis (480 BC).

People lived on the Acropolis until the late 6th century BC, but in 510 BC the Delphic oracle declared that it should be the province of the gods. When Pericles set about his ambitious rebuilding programme, he transformed the Acropolis into a city of temples which has come to be regarded as the zenith of classical Greek achievement.

All four of the surviving monuments of the Acropolis have received their fair share of battering through the ages. Ravages inflicted upon them during the years of

foreign occupation, pilfering by foreign archaeologists, inept renovation following Independence, visitors' footsteps and earthquakes have all taken their toll. The year 1687 was a particularly bad one. The Venetians attacked the Turks and opened fire on the Acropolis, causing an explosion in the Parthenon, where the Turks were storing gunpowder. The resulting fire blazed for two days, damaging all of the buildings.

However, the most recent menace, acid rain, caused by industrial pollution and traffic fumes, is proving to be the most irreversibly destructive. It is dissolving the very marble of which the monuments are built. Major renovation work is taking place in an effort to save the monuments for future generations.

Beulé Gate & Monument of Agrippa Once you've bought your ticket for the Acropolis and have walked a little way along the path, you will see on your left the Beulé Gate, named after the French archaeologist, Ernest Beulé, who uncovered it in 1852. The eight-

The Acropolis in classical times

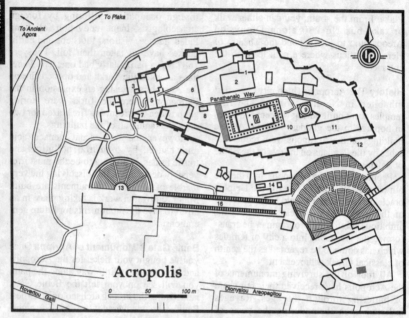

Acropolis

1	Erechtheion	9	Altar of Rome & Augustus
2	Porch of the Caryatids	10	Parthenon
3	Monument of Agrippa	11	Museum
4	Beulé Gate	12	Wall of Cimon
5	Propylaia	13	Theatre of Herodes Atticus
6	Athena Promachos	14	Asclepion
7	Temple of Athena Nike	15	Ancient Theatre of Dionysos
8	Entrance Court	16	Stoa of Eumenes

metre pedestal on the left, halfway up the zigzag ramp leading to the Propylaia, was once topped by the Monument of Agrippa, a bronze statue of the Roman general riding a chariot. It was erected in 27 BC to commemorate victory in a chariot race at the Panathenaic games.

Propylaia The Propylaia formed the towering entrance to the Acropolis in ancient times. Built by Mnesicles in 437-432 BC, its architectural brilliance ranks with that of the Parthenon. It consists of a central hall, with two wings on either side. Each section had a gate, and in ancient times these five gates were the only entrances to the 'upper city'. The middle gate (which was the largest) opened onto the Panathenaic Way. The western portico of the Propylaia must indeed have been imposing, consisting of six double columns, Doric on the outside and Ionic on the inside. The fourth column along has been restored. The ceiling of the central hall was painted with gold stars on a dark blue background. The northern wing was used as a picture gallery (*pinakotheke*) and the south wing was the antechamber to the Temple of Athena Nike.

The Propylaia is aligned with the Parthenon – the earliest example of a building designed in relation to another. It remained intact until the 13th century when various occupiers started adding to it. It was badly damaged in the 17th century when a lightning strike set off an explosion in a Turkish gunpowder store. Heinrich Schliemann paid for the removal of one of its appendages – a Frankish tower – in the 19th century. Reconstruction took place between 1909 and 1917 and there was further restoration after WW II. Once you're through the Propylaia, there is a stunning view of the Parthenon ahead.

Panathenaic Way The Panathenaic Way, which cuts across the middle of the Acropolis, was the route taken by the Panathenaic procession. The procession was the climax of the Panathenaia, the festival held to venerate the goddess Athena. The origins of the Panathenaia are uncertain. According to some accounts it was initiated by Erichthonius; according to others, by Theseus. There were two festivals: the Lesser Panathenaic Festival took place annually on Athena's birthday, and the Great Panathenaic Festival was held every fourth anniversary of the goddess' birth.

The Great Panathenaic Festival began with dancing and was followed by athletic, dramatic and musical contests. The Panathenaic procession, which took place on the final day of the festival, began at the Keramikos and ended at the Erechtheion. Men carrying animals sacrificed to Athena headed the procession, followed by maidens carrying rhytons (horn-shaped drinking vessels). Behind them were musicians playing a fanfare for the girls of noble birth who followed, proudly holding aloft the sacred peplos (a glorious saffron-coloured shawl). Bringing up the rear were old men bearing olive branches. The grand finale of the procession was the placing of the peplos on the statue of Athena Polias in the Erechtheion.

Temple of Athena Nike On the right after leaving the Propylaia, there is a good view back to the exquisitely proportioned little Temple of Athena Nike (to which visitors have no access). It stands on a platform perched atop the steep south-west edge of the Acropolis, overlooking the Saronic Gulf. The temple, designed by Callicrates, was built of Pentelic marble in 427-424 BC. The building is almost square, with four graceful Ionic columns at either end. Its frieze, of which only fragments remain, consisted of scenes from mythology on the east and south sides, and scenes from the Battle of Plataea

Greek Marble

So you thought Italy produced the world's best marble? Wrong, say the Greeks. The Italians import enormous amounts of raw marble from Greece.

Greece has, in fact, been renowned for its fine marble since ancient times. For example, the most impressive legacy of the Cycladic civilisation is the figurines sculpted from the islands' magnificent white marble. The Temple of Athena Nike, in the Acropolis, was built entirely of Pentelic marble – from Attica – between 427 and 424 BC. Paros is famous for its pure white marble which was once considered the world's finest – the Venus de Milo was carved from it and Napoleon's tomb is a Parian marble creation.

In addition to yielding excellent white marble, Greece is also renowned for its pink marble (found around Ioannina and Volos) and green marble (from the island of Timos).

Today, Greek marble is sliced and used for floors, staircases, gravestones, fireplaces, tables and bartops. Unsliced pieces are made into pots, lamp bases, candlesticks and whole sinks for bathrooms or kitchens. Highly polished leftovers are made into figurines, marble eggs, or stones set in gold or silver as pieces of jewellery. ■

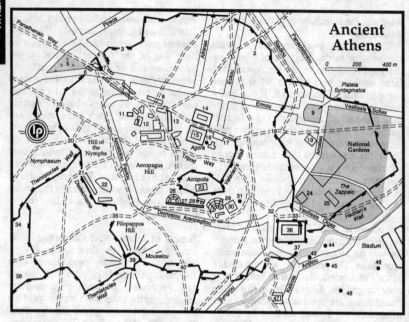

Ancient
Athens

0   200   400 m

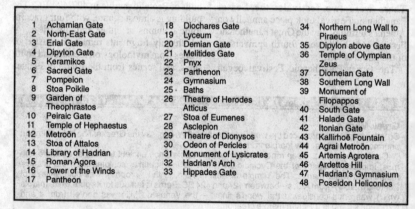

1	Acharnian Gate	18	Diochares Gate	34	Northern Long Wall to Piraeus
2	North-East Gate	19	Lyceum	35	Dipylon above Gate
3	Eriai Gate	20	Demian Gate	36	Temple of Olympian Zeus
4	Dipylon Gate	21	Melitides Gate		
5	Keramikos	22	Pnyx	37	Diomeian Gate
6	Sacred Gate	23	Parthenon	38	Southern Long Wall
7	Pompeion	24	Gymnasium	39	Monument of Filopappos
8	Stoa Poikile	25	Baths		
9	Garden of Theophrastos	26	Theatre of Herodes Atticus	40	South Gate
10	Peiraic Gate	27	Stoa of Eumenes	41	Halade Gate
11	Temple of Hephaestus	28	Asclepion	42	Itonian Gate
12	Metroön	29	Theatre of Dionysos	43	Kallirhoë Fountain
13	Stoa of Attalos	30	Odeon of Pericles	44	Agrai Metroön
14	Library of Hadrian	31	Monument of Lysicrates	45	Artemis Agrotera
15	Roman Agora	32	Hadrian's Arch	46	Ardettos Hill
16	Tower of the Winds	33	Hippades Gate	47	Hadrian's Gymnasium
17	Pantheon			48	Poseidon Heliconios

(479 BC) and Athenians fighting Boeotians and Persians on the other sides. Parts of the frieze are in the Acropolis Museum. The platform was surrounded by a marble parapet of relief sculptures; some of these are also in the museum, including the beautiful one of Athena Nike fastening her sandal.

The temple housed a statue of the goddess Athena. In her right hand was a pomegranate (symbol of fertility) and in her left a helmet (symbol of war). The temple was dismantled in 1686 by the Turks, who positioned a huge cannon on the platform. It was carefully reconstructed between 1836 and 1842, but was taken to pieces again in 1936 because the platform was crumbling. The platform was reinforced and the temple rebuilt.

Statue of Athena Promachos In ancient times, only the pediment of the Parthenon was visible from the Propylaia; the rest was obscured by numerous statues and two sacred buildings.

Continuing ahead along the Panathenaic Way you will see, to your left, the foundations of pedestals for the statues which once lined the path. One of them, about 15 metres beyond the Propylaia, is the foundation of the gigantic statue of Athena Promachos (*promachos* means 'champion'). The nine-metre-high statue was the work of Pheidias, and symbolised Athenian invincibility against the Persians. The helmeted goddess held a shield in her left hand and a spear in her right. The statue was carted off to Constantinople by Emperor Theodosius in

426 AD. By 1204 it had lost its spear, so the hand appeared to be gesturing. This led the inhabitants to believe that the statue had beckoned the crusaders to the city, so they smashed it to pieces.

Parthenon You have now reached the Parthenon, the monument which more than any other epitomises the glory of ancient Greece. The name Parthenon means 'virgin's apartment'. It is the largest Doric temple ever completed in Greece, and the only one to be built completely (apart from its wooden roof) of Pentelic marble. It is built on the highest part of the Acropolis, halfway between the eastern and western boundaries.

The Parthenon had a dual purpose – to house the great statue of Athena which had been commissioned by Pericles, and to serve as a treasury for the tribute money which had been moved from Delos. It was built on the site of at least four earlier temples, all dedicated to the worship of Athena. It was designed by Ictinus and Callicrates, under the surveillance of Pheidias, to be the pre-eminent monument of the Acropolis.

The Parthenon

Building began in 447 BC and was completed in time for the Great Panathenaic Festival of 438 BC.

The temple consisted of eight fluted Doric columns at either end and 17 at each side. To achieve perfect form, its lines were ingeniously curved to counteract inharmonious optical illusions. Thus the foundations are slightly concave and the columns slightly convex, to make both look straight. Supervised by Pheidias, the sculptors Agoracritos and Alcamenes worked on the pediments and the sculpted sections of the frieze (metopes). All of the sculptures they created were brightly coloured and gilded. There were 92 metopes, 44 statues and a frieze which went all the way around.

The metopes on the eastern side depicted Athenians fighting giants (*gigantions*), and on the western side Theseus leading the Athenians into battle against the Amazons. Those on the southern side represented the contest of the Lapiths and Centaurs at the marriage feast of Pierithoös. An Ionic frieze 159.5 metres long ran all around the Parthenon. Much of it was damaged in the explosion of 1687, but the greatest existing part (just over 75 metres) consists of the much publicised Elgin Marbles, now in the British Museum.

The ceiling of the Parthenon, like that of the Propylaia, was painted blue and gilded with stars. At the eastern end was the cella (inner room of a temple), the holy of holies, into which only a few privileged initiates could enter. Here stood the statue for which the temple was built – the *Athena Polias* (Athena of the City), which was considered one of the wonders of the ancient world. The statue was designed by Pheidias and completed in 432 BC. It was made of gold plate over an inner wooden frame, and stood almost 12 metres high on its pedestal. The face, hands and feet were made of ivory, and the pupils of the eyes were fashioned from jewels. The goddess was clad in a long dress of gold with the head of Medusa carved in ivory on the breast. In her right hand, she held a statuette of Nike – the goddess of victory – and in her left a spear; at the base

of the spear was a serpent. On her head she wore a helmet, on top of which was a sphinx with griffins in relief at either side. In 426 BC the statue was taken to Constantinople and disappeared. There is a Roman copy (the Athena Varvakeion) in the National Archaeological Museum.

Erechtheion Although the Parthenon was the most impressive monument of the Acropolis, it was more of a showpiece than a sanctuary. That role fell to the Erechtheion, built on the part of the Acropolis that was held most sacred. It was here that Poseidon struck the ground with his trident and that Athena produced the olive tree. The temple is named after Erichthonius, a mythical king of Athens. It housed the cults of Athena, Poseidon and Erichthonius.

If you follow the Panathenaic Way around the northern portico of the Parthenon, you will see the Erechtheion to your left. It is immediately recognisable by the six larger-than-life maidens who take the place of columns to support its southern portico, its much-photographed **Caryatids**. They are so called because the models for them were women from Karyai (modern-day Karyes) in Lakonia.

The Erechtheion was part of Pericles' plan for the Acropolis, but the project was postponed after the outbreak of the Peloponnesian Wars, and work did not start until 421 BC, eight years after his death. It is thought to have been completed in 406 BC.

The Erechtheion is architecturally the most unusual monument of the Acropolis. Whereas the Parthenon is considered the supreme example of Doric architecture, the Erechtheion is considered the supreme example of Ionic. It was ingeniously built on several levels to counteract the unevenness of the ground. It consists of three basic parts – the main temple, the northern porch and the southern porch – all with different dimensions.

The main temple is of the Ionic order and is divided into two cellas: one is dedicated to Athena, the other to Poseidon; thus the temple represents a reconciliation of the two deities after their contest. In Athena's cella stood an olive-wood statue of Athena Polias holding a shield on which was a gorgon's head. It was this statue on which the sacred peplos was placed at the culmination of the Panathenaic Festival. The statue was illuminated by a golden lantern placed at its feet.

The northern porch consists of six graceful Ionic columns; on the floor are the fissures supposedly cleft by Poseidon's trident. This porch leads into the **Temenos of Pandrossos**, where, according to mythology, the sacred olive brought forth by Athena grew. To the south of here was the **Cecropion** – King Cecrop's burial place.

The southern porch is that of the Caryatids, which prop up a heavy roof of Pentelic marble. The ones you see are plaster casts – the originals (except for one removed by Lord Elgin) are in the site's museum.

The Caryatids, which support the southern portico of the Erectheion

Acropolis Museum The museum at the south-east corner of the Acropolis houses a collection of sculptures and reliefs from the site. The rooms are organised in chronological order, starting with finds from the temples that predated the Parthenon and were destroyed by the Persians. They include the pedimental sculptures of Heracles slaying the Lernaian Hydra and of a lioness devouring a bull, both in Room I. The kore (maiden) statues in Room IV are regarded as the museum's prize exhibits. Most date from the 6th century BC and were uncovered from a pit on the Acropolis where they were buried by the Athenians after the Battle of Salamis. They were votives dedicated to Athena, each once held out an offering to the goddess. The earliest of these kore statues are quite stiff and formal in comparison with the later ones, which have flowing robes and elaborate headdresses.

Room VIII contains the few pieces of the Parthenon's frieze that escaped the clutches of Lord Elgin. They depict the Olympians at the Panathenaic procession. It also holds the relief of Athena Nike adjusting her sandal. Room IX is home to four of the five surviving Caryatids, safe behind a perspex screen. The fifth is in the British Museum.

Southern Slope of the Acropolis

The entrance to the southern slope of the Acropolis is on Dionysiou Areopagitou. The site (☎ 322 4625) is open every day from 8.30 am to 2.30 pm. Admission is 500 dr.

Theatre of Dionysos The importance of theatre in the life of the Athenian city-state can be gauged from the dimensions of the enormous Theatre of Dionysos on the south-eastern slope of the Acropolis.

The first theatre on this site was a timber structure erected sometime during the 6th century BC, after the tyrant Peisistratos had introduced the Festival of the Great Dionysia to Athens. This festival, which took place in March or April, consisted of contests where men clad in goatskins sang and performed dances. Everyone attended, and the watching of performances was punctuated by feasting, revelry and generally letting rip.

During the golden age in the 5th century BC, the annual festival had become one of the major events on the calendar. Politicians would sponsor the production of dramas by writers such as Aeschylus, Sophocles and Euripides, with some light relief provided by the bawdy comedies of Aristophanes. People came from all over Attica, their expenses met by the state – if only present-day governments were as generous to the arts!

The theatre was reconstructed in stone and marble by Lycurgus between 342 and 326 BC. The auditorium had a seating capacity of 17,000 spread over 64 tiers of seats, of which about 20 survive. Apart from the front row, the seats were built of Piraeus limestone and were occupied by ordinary citizens, although women were confined to the back rows. The front row consisted of 67 thrones built of Pentelic marble, which were reserved for festival officials and important priests. The grandest was in the centre and reserved for the Priest of Dionysos, who sat shaded from the sun under a canopy. The seat can be identified by well-preserved lion-claw feet at either side. In Roman times, the theatre was also used for state events and ceremonies as well as for performances.

The reliefs at the rear of the stage, mostly of headless figures, depict the exploits of Dionysos and date from the 2nd century BC. The two hefty, hunched-up guys who have managed to keep their heads are *selini*. Selini were worshippers of the mythical Selinos, the debauched father of the satyrs whose chief attribute seems to have been an out-sized phallus. His favourite pastime was charging up mountains in lecherous pursuit of nymphs. He also happened to be Dionysos' mentor.

Asclepion & Stoa of Eumenes Directly above the Theatre of Dionysos, wooden steps lead up to a pathway. On the left at the top of the steps is the Asclepion, which was built around a sacred spring. The worship of Asclepius, the physician son of Apollo, began in Epidaurus and was introduced to

Athens in 429 BC at a time when plague was sweeping the city.

Beneath the Asclepion is the Stoa of Eumenes, a long colonnade built by Eumenes II, King of Pergamum (197-159 BC), as a shelter and promenade for theatre audiences.

Theatre of Herodes Atticus The path continues west from the Asclepion to the Theatre of Herodes Atticus, built in 161 AD. Herodes Atticus was a wealthy Roman who built the theatre in memory of his wife Regilla. It was excavated in 1857-58 and completely restored in 1950-61. There are performances of drama, music and dance here during the Athens Festival. The theatre is open to the public only during performances.

Panagia Hrysospiliotissa If you retrace your steps back to the Theatre of Dionysos, you will see an indistinct rock-strewn path leading to a grotto in the cliff face. In 320 BC, Thrasyllos turned the grotto into a temple dedicated to Dionysos. Today it is the tiny Panagia Hrysospiliotissa (Chapel of our Lady of the Cavern). It is a poignant little place with old pictures and icons on the walls. Above the chapel are two Ionic columns which are the remains of Thrasyllos' temple.

Ancient Agora

The Agora (market) was Athens' meeting place in ancient times. It was the focal point of administrative, commercial and political life, not to mention social activity. All roads led to the Agora, and it was a lively, crowded place. Socrates spent a lot of time here expounding his philosophy, and in 49 AD St Paul disputed daily in the Agora, intent upon winning converts to Christianity.

The site was first developed in the 6th century BC. It was devastated by the Persians in 480 BC, but a new agora was built in its place. It was flourishing by Pericles' time and continued to do so until 267 AD, when it was destroyed by the Herulians, a Gothic tribe from Scandinavia. The Turks built a residential quarter on

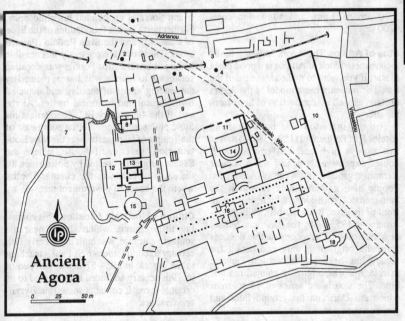

Ancient Agora

0   25   50 m

1	Stoa Poikile
2	Stoa of Basileios
3	Entrance
4	Mosaic showing reconstruction of Agora
5	Altar of the Twelve Gods
6	Stoa of Zeus Eleutherios
7	Temple of Hephaestus
8	Temple of Apollo
9	Temple of Ares
10	Stoa of Attalos
11	Stoa of the Giants
12	New Bouleuterion
13	Metroön
14	Odeon of Agrippa
15	Tholos
16	Middle Stoa
17	Sewer
18	Church of the Holy Apostles

the site, but this was demolished by archaeologists after Independence. If they'd had their way the archaeologists would have also knocked down the whole of Plaka, which was also Turkish. The area has been excavated to classical and, in parts, Neolithic levels.

Nowadays, the Agora looks like a huge bombsite. To visualise how it must have looked in classical times requires an even greater feat of imagination than that needed when visiting the Acropolis. Exceptions to

the ruined look of the place are the Temple of Hephaestus, the Stoa of Attalos and the Church of the Holy Apostles.

The site is bounded by Areopagus hill in the south, the Athens-Piraeus metro line to the north, Plaka to the east and Leoforos Apostolou Pavlou to the west. There are several entrances, but the most convenient of these is the southern entrance at the western end of Polygnotou (see the Walking Tour section earlier). The Ancient Agora (☎ 321 0185) is open from Tuesday to Sunday from

8.30 am to 3 pm, and admission costs 1200 dr.

Stoa of Attalos The Agora Museum in the reconstructed Stoa of Attalos is a good place to start if you want to make any sense of the site. The museum has a model of the Agora upstairs as well as a collection of finds from the site.

The original stoa was built by King Attalos II of Pergamum (159-138 BC). It was two storeys high and had two aisles. It housed expensive shops and was a popular stamping ground for wealthy Athenians. People also gathered here to watch the Panathenaic procession, which crossed in front of the stoa. It was authentically reconstructed in 1953-56 by the American School of Archaeology. The reconstruction deviates from the original in only one detail; the façade has been left in natural Pentelic marble, but was originally painted red and blue. The stoa has a series of 45 columns which are Doric on the ground floor and Ionic on the upper gallery.

Temple of Hephaestus This temple at the western edge of the Agora was surrounded by foundries and metalwork shops, and was dedicated to Hephaestus, god of the forge. It was one of the first buildings of Pericles' rebuilding programme and is the best preserved Doric temple in Greece. It was built in 449 BC by Ictinus, one of the architects of the Parthenon. It has 34 columns and the frieze on the eastern side depicts nine of the Twelve Labours of Heracles. In 1300 AD it was converted into the **Church of Agios Georgios**. The last service held here was on 13 December 1834 in honour of King Otho's arrival in Athens.

Unlike the Parthenon, the monument does not evoke a sense of wonder, but is nevertheless a pleasant place to wander around. The garden that surrounds the temple has been reconstructed to resemble the Roman garden that existed there in antiquity.

To the north-east of the Temple of Hephaestus are the foundations of the **Stoa of Zeus Eleutherios**, one of the places

where Socrates expounded his philosophy. Further north are the foundations of the **Stoa of Basileios** and the **Stoa Poikile** (Painted Stoa). These two are presently inaccessible to the public. The Stoa Poikile was so called because of its murals, which were painted by the leading artists of the day and depicted mythological and historical battles. At the end of the 4th century BC, Zeno taught his Stoic philosophy here. To the south-east of the Temple of Hephaestus was the **New Bouleuterion**, or council house, where the Senate (originally created by Solon) met. To the south of here was the circular **Tholos** where the heads of government met.

Church of the Holy Apostles This charming little church, which stands near the southern entrance, was built in the early 11th century to commemorate St Paul's teaching in the Agora. In 1954-57 it was stripped of its 19th-century additions and restored to its original form. It contains some fine Byzantine frescoes.

The Keramikos

The Keramikos was the city's cemetery from the 12th century BC to Roman times. It was discovered in 1861 during the construction of Pireos, the street which leads to Piraeus. Despite its location on the seedier part of Ermou, beyond Monastiraki, it is one of the most green and tranquil of Athens' ancient sites.

The entrance to the site (☎ 346 3552) is at Ermou 148. It is open Tuesday to Sunday from 8 am to 3 pm, and admission is 500 dr.

Sacred & Dipylon Gates The first place to check out once you have entered the site is the small knoll ahead and to the right from the entrance. Here you will find a plan of the site. A path leads down to the right from the knoll to the remains of the city wall, which was built by Themistocles in 479 BC, and rebuilt by Konon in 394 BC. The wall is broken by the foundations of two gates.

The first, the Sacred Gate, spanned the Sacred Way and was the one by which pilgrims from Eleusis entered the city during the annual Eleusian procession. The Dipylon Gate, to the north-east of the Sacred Gate, was the city's main entrance and was where the Panathenaic procession began. It was also the stamping ground of the city's prostitutes, who gathered there to offer their services to jaded travellers.

From a platform outside the Dipylon Gate, Pericles gave his famous speech extolling the virtues of Athens and honouring those who died in the first year of the Peloponnesian Wars. The speech stirred many more to battle – and to their deaths.

Between the Sacred and the Dipylon gates are the foundations of the **Pompeion**. This building was used as a dressing room for participants in the Panathenaic procession.

Street of Tombs The Street of Tombs leads off the Sacred Way to the left as you head away from the city. This avenue was reserved for the tombs of Athens' most prominent citizens. The surviving stele are now in the National Archaeological Museum, and what you see are replicas. They consist of an astonishing array of funerary monuments, and their bas-reliefs warrant more than a cursory examination.

Ordinary citizens were buried in the areas bordering the Street of Tombs. One very well-preserved stele shows a little girl with her pet dog. You will find it by going up the stone steps on the northern side of the Street of Tombs. The site's largest stele, that of sisters Demetria and Pamphile, is on the path running from the south-east corner of the street of tombs. Pamphile is seated beside a standing Demetria.

Oberlaender Museum The site's Oberlaender Museum is named after its benefactor, Gustav Oberlaender, a German-American stocking manufacturer. It contains steles and sculpture from the site, as well as an impressive collection of vases and terracotta figurines. The museum is to the left of the site entrance.

Roman Athens
Tower of the Winds & Roman Agora These are next to one another to the east of the Ancient Agora and north of the Acropolis.

The well-preserved Tower of the Winds was built in the 1st century BC by a Syrian astronomer named Andronicus. The octagonal monument of Pentelic marble is an ingenious construction which functioned as a sundial, weather vane, water clock and compass. Each side represents a point of the compass, and has a relief of a figure floating through the air, which depicts the wind associated with that particular point. Beneath each of the reliefs are the faint markings of sundials. The weather vane, which disappeared long ago, was a bronze Triton that revolved on top of the tower. The Turks, not ones to let a good building go to waste, allowed dervishes to use the tower.

The entrance to the Roman Agora is through the well-preserved **Gate of Athena Archegetis**, which is flanked by four Doric columns. It was erected sometime in the 1st century AD and financed by Julius Caesar.

The rest of the Roman Agora appears to the layperson as little more than a heap of rubble. To the right of the entrance are the foundations of a 1st-century public latrine. In the south-east area are the foundations of a propylon and a row of shops.

The site (☎ 321 0185) is open Tuesday to Sunday from 8.30 am to 3 pm. Admission is 500 dr.

City of Hadrian The Roman emperor Hadrian had a great affection for Athens. Although, like all Roman emperors, he did his fair share of spiriting the city's classical artwork to Rome, he also embellished the city with many monuments influenced by classical architecture. Grandiose as these monuments are, they lack the refinement and artistic flair of their classical predecessors.

Hadrian's Library This library is to the north of the Roman Agora. The building, which was of vast dimensions, was erected in the 2nd century AD and included a cloistered courtyard bordered by 100 columns. As well as books, the building housed music and lecture rooms and a theatre. The library is at present inaccessible to visitors.

Arch of Hadrian This lofty monument of Pentelic marble – now blackened by the effluent of exhausts – stands where traffic-clogged Vasilissis Olgas and Amalias meet. It was erected by Hadrian in 132 AD, probably to commemorate the consecration of the Temple of Olympian Zeus (see below). The inscriptions show that it was also intended as a dividing point between the ancient city and the Roman city. The north-west frieze bears the inscription, 'This is Athens, the Ancient city of Theseus'; while the south-east frieze states 'This is the city of Hadrian, and not of Theseus'.

Temple of Olympian Zeus This is the largest temple in Greece and took over 700 years to build. It was begun in the 6th century BC by Peisistratos, but was abandoned for lack of funds.

Various other leaders had stabs at completing the temple, but it was left to Hadrian to complete the work in 131 AD. The temple is impressive for the sheer size of its 104 Corinthian columns (17 metres high with a base diameter of 1.7 metres), of which 15 remain – the fallen column was blown down in a gale in 1852. Hadrian put a colossal statue of Zeus in the cella and, in typically immodest fashion, placed an equally large one of himself next to it.

The site (☎ 922 6330) is open Tuesday to Sunday from 8.30 am to 3 pm. Admission is 500 dr.

Roman Stadium The last Athenian monument with Roman connections is the Roman Stadium, which lies in a fold between two pine-covered hills between the neighbourhoods of Mets and Pangrati. The stadium was originally built in the 4th century BC as a venue for the Panathenaic athletic contests. A thousand wild animals are said to be have been slaughtered in the arena at Hadrian's inauguration in 120 AD. Shortly after this, the seats were rebuilt in Pentelic marble by Herodes Atticus. After hundreds of years of disuse the stadium was completely restored in 1895 by wealthy Greek benefactor, Georgios Averof. The following year the first Olympic Games of modern times were held here. It is a faithful replica of the Roman Stadium, comprising seats of Pentelic marble for 70,000 spectators, a running track and a central area for field events.

Byzantine Athens
Churches Byzantine architecture in Athens is fairly thin on the ground. By the time of the split in the Roman Empire, Athens had shrunk to little more than a provincial town and Thessaloniki had become the major city.

The monastery at Dafni (see Around Athens), 10 km west of the city, is the most important Byzantine building. Athens has a number of churches, of which the 11th-century **Church of Agios Eleftherios** on Plateia Mitropoleos is considered the finest. It was once the city's cathedral, but is now overshadowed by the much larger new cathedral. It is built partly of Pentelic marble and decorated with an external frieze of symbolic beasts in bas-relief.

The **Church of Kapnikarea**, halfway down Ermou, is another small 11th-century church. Its dome is supported by four large Roman columns. The **Church of Agii Theodori**, just off Plateia Klafthmonos on Stadiou, has a tiled dome and the walls are decorated with a terracotta frieze of animals and plants. Other churches worth peering into are the **Church of the Holy Apostles** (see Ancient Agora, earlier) and the **Church of Agios Dimitrios** (see West of the Acropolis in the Hills of Athens section, later).

Museums
National Archaeological Museum This museum (☎ 821 7717), opened in 1874, stands supreme among the nation's museums. Despite all the pilfering by foreign archaeologists in the 19th century, it still has the world's finest collection of Greek antiquities. It is so crammed with treasures that to do the place justice you need to visit several times. If time is very short, at least ensure

you visit the magnificent Hall of Mycenaean Antiquities and the Thira Exhibition, which contains the celebrated collection of Minoan frescoes unearthed at Akrotiri on the island of Thira (Santorini). The following is intended as only a brief description of the general layout of the museum, focusing on some of the most important, spectacular, intriguing or quirky exhibits. A number of the rooms were closed at the time of writing. Several guidebooks to the museum are on sale in the foyer. There are comprehensive explanations in English in each room.

The museum is at 28 Oktovriou-Patission 44 and is open Tuesday to Friday from 8 am to 7 pm; Saturday, Sunday and holidays from 8.30 am to 3 pm and on Monday from 12.30 to 7 pm. It closes at 5 pm instead of 7 pm between November and March. Admission is 2000 dr (free on Sunday and public holidays). To reach the museum take trolleybus No 2, 4, 5, 9, 11, 12, 15 or 18 from Amalias.

Hall of Mycenaean Antiquities

This museum's *tour de force* is the Hall of Mycenaean Antiquities where gold gleams at you from everywhere. The chief exhibits are from the six shaft graves of Grave Circle A at Mycenae. Shaft graves were rectangular pits about six metres deep. The pit bottom was covered with pebbles, and stone walls measuring about 1.5 metres high were built around the sides. After the body and treasures were placed in the pit, it was covered with tree trunks which rested upon the top of the stone wall. The pit was then filled with soil. Graves one to five were excavated by Heinrich Schliemann in 1874-76 and the sixth by Panagiotes Stamatakis in 1886-1902. Just beyond case 25 are four grave steles, two on each side. On the back of the one nearest case 25 are two pictures of Grave Circle A; one shows a reconstruction of the site. The five cases beyond the steles – numbers 3, 4, 23, 24 and 27 contain the most valuable finds from these shaft graves. Most famous of all is the golden **Mask of Agamemnon** in case 3. It has subsequently been proven that the death mask belonged to a king who died three centuries before Agamemnon.

In the centre of the hall, cases 28 and 29 contain objects from the third grave, including gold sheets which covered the bodies of two royal babies. On the left, cases 5 and 6 contain finds from Grave Circle B (from 1650 to 1550 BC) which was outside the citadel at Mycenae. In case 5 is an unusual rock-crystal vase in the shape of a duck: its head and neck are gracefully turned back to form a handle. On the right, against the blue partition, is the head of a woman, possibly a sphinx or goddess, carved in limestone with brightly painted lips, eyes and fringe. It is a rare example of a Mycenaean sculpture in the round and dates from the 13th century BC. On the other side of the partition are fragments of frescoes from the palace at Mycenae which reveal a strong Minoan influence.

Case 30, also in the centre, contains miscellaneous finds from Mycenae, including a delightful ivory carving of two voluptuous-looking women and a child, who may represent Demeter, Persephone and Iacchus. On the right, just beyond here, is the famous **Warrior Vase** which, along with the Mask of Agamemnon, Schliemann rated as one of his greatest finds. It depicts men leaving for war and a woman waving them goodbye.

The rest of the hall is devoted to other Mycenaean sites. On the left, case 9 contains tablets with inscriptions in Cretan Linear B script. In case 15, on the right, are objects from Tiryns, including the famous **Tiryns Treasure**. The treasure is believed to have been looted by a tomb robber, who then reburied it and failed to retrieve it. Back in the centre, case 32 contains the famous gold cups from the beehive-shaped tomb at Vaphio which depict the taming of wild bulls. These magnificent cups are regarded as among the finest examples of Mycenaean art.

Towards room 21, at the far end of the hall, on the right-hand wall, is an explanation in English of the three different types of Mycenaean graves: shaft graves, chamber tombs and tholos tombs. The latter are the

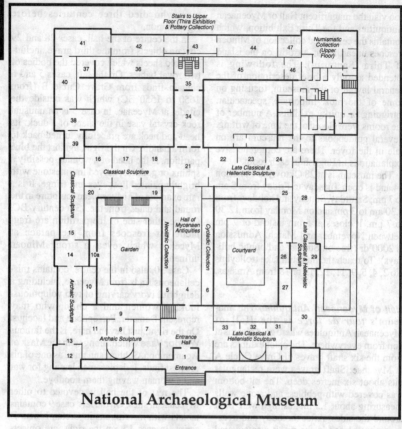

National Archaeological Museum

(Floor plan labels:)

Stairs to Upper Floor (Thira Exhibition & Pottery Collection)

Numismatic Collection (Upper Floor)

Classical Sculpture

Archaic Sculpture

Neolithic Collection

Garden

Hall of Mycenaean Antiquities

Cycladic Collection

Courtyard

Late Classical & Hellenistic Sculpture

Late Classical & Hellenistic Sculpture

Late Classical & Hellenistic Sculpture

Archaic Sculpture

Entrance Hall

Entrance

most elaborate and impressive, and the entrance to one of them, the **Treasury of Atreus**, has been reconstructed around the doorway at this end of the hall. To the right are some slabs which decorated the façade of this treasury.

Cycladic Collection Room 6, to the right of the Hall of Mycenaean Antiquities, is devoted to Cycladic art. At the western end is the largest Cycladic figurine ever found. It is almost life-size and was found on the island of Amorgos. On the top wall are fragments of frescoes, including one of a delicately painted seascape with flying fish. On the right are cases of pottery painted with lovely free-flowing designs depicting flowers, fish and birds.

Cases 56, 57 and 58 contain attractive ceramic 'frying pans' from early Cycladic cemeteries on Syros. They are black with intricate inlaid patterns in white. In case you're wondering why on earth these people took frying pans to the grave with them, they are so called merely because of their shape. Their function remains obscure. On the wall, in English, there are several possible explanations.

Neolithic Collection Room 5, to the left of the Hall of Mycenaean Antiquities, contains Neolithic finds – mainly from Thessaly. There is also a case of pottery, figurines and jewellery from Troy, including a beautiful necklace of delicate gold beads. These finds were presented to the museum by Sophie Schliemann, wife of Heinrich.

Archaic Sculpture Rooms 7 to 14, entered from the left side of the vestibule, contain archaic sculpture. The main feature of room 7 is the huge sepulchral amphora (a jar with two handles and a narrow neck) dating from 760 BC and found in the Keramikos. It is considered the most masterful example of the geometric style of pottery.

The chief exhibit in room 8 is the huge kouros found at Sounion (600 BC). This was a votive offering found in the Temple of Poseidon at Cape Sounion. To the right of the entrance to room 9 is the torso of a kore figure with elaborately folded drapery. Opposite is the Nike from Delos (550 BC) which, unlike the stiff formalised poses of earlier sculptures, looks as if it's dancing a jig, despite being minus hands and feet. To the left, at the end of the room, is a graceful tomb statue of a young girl called Phrasikleia (540 BC). Traces of colour can still be seen on its surface; check out the elegant sandals.

Room 10 contains gravestones from the 6th century and two well-preserved sphinxes, one from Piraeus (540 BC) and the other from Sparta (570 BC). In Room 11 is the torso of another colossal kouros (540 BC), found at Megara in Attica. Also in this room are some grave steles, including a particularly well-preserved one of the warrior Aristion which still has traces of colour remaining.

Room 13 is dominated by the sepulchral kouros named Croesus. To the left of this sculpture is the base of a kouros found in the Keramikos; it has reliefs on three sides. One side shows four clothed youths provoking a fight between a cat and dog; another shows naked youths wrestling; and the third shows youths playing a ball game. There is another plinth behind the screen. One of its sides shows naked youths playing a game which looks similar to hockey, while the other two sides depict chariot scenes.

Room 14 is given over to provincial stele monuments. The gravestone by Alxenor is one of the finest in the room and bears an endearing, if egocentric, inscription by the artist: 'Alxenor the Naxian made me. Admire me'.

Classical Sculpture The bronze statue of **Poseidon of Artemision** (450 BC) in room 15 is one of the highlights of the museum. The statue was hauled from the sea off Cape Artemision in 1928, and shows Poseidon poised to hurl his trident (now missing). More than any other statue of Poseidon, it conveys the god's strength and unlimited power.

Just within the door of this room is a beautiful and well-preserved relief from Eleusis (440 BC). It depicts Demeter, accompanied by her daughter Persephone, giving Triptolemos an ear of wheat to sprout.

Room 16 contains classical grave monuments, most of which were found in Attica. Rooms 17 and 19 contain classical votive sculpture. Room 20 consists mostly of Roman copies of classical Greek statues. At the far end is the statue of Varvakeion Athena, which was made in about 200 BC. It is the most famous copy – much reduced in size – of the statue of Athena Parthenos by Pheidias. Room 18 contains late 5th and early 4th-century sepulchral monuments.

Late Classical & Hellenistic Sculpture In room 21, the central hall, your eye will be drawn to another outstanding piece – the 2nd-century bronze statue of the Horse and Jockey of Artemision, which was found with the statue of Poseidon. It is a remarkably animated sculpture; especially impressive is the jockey's anxious expression.

There is an unusual grave monument (540 BC) in the centre of room 24 consisting of a floral column which supports a cauldron decorated with griffins.

Room 25 is mostly devoted to charming diminutive reliefs of nymphs. They are not individually labelled, but there is an explanation in English of their role. On the left, just before room 26, is a highly unusual votive relief of a snake and a huge sandal on which is carved a worshipping figure. It dates from 360 BC and is believed to depict the Hero of the Slipper who was worshipped near the Theatre of Dionysos. Rooms 26 and 27 contain more votive reliefs.

Room 28 contains some extremely realistic funerary monuments, particularly the Grave Monument of Aristonautes (330 BC) found in the Keramikos. The large sepulchral relief of a boy attempting to restrain a frisky horse is a powerful and unprecedented piece of realist sculpture, especially the leg muscles of both the horse and boy, and the magnificent drapery. It was found near Larisis Station in 1948, and dates from the second half of the 3rd century. The famous Ephebos of Antikythira (340 BC) stands in the centre of the room. The amazingly lifelike eyes are almost hypnotic. Behind this statue, to the right, is the head of a bronze statue – probably of the Elean boxer Satyros. He certainly looks a nasty piece of work in contrast to the calm 'other world' expressions on the faces surrounding him.

Room 29 is dominated by the statue of Themis (the goddess of justice). Behind her is a head of Alexander the Great which has graffitied cheeks (added later). Next to him is a head of the orator Demosthenes, looking very perplexed. Also of note is the statue of the Gallic warrior whose animated aggression is in marked contrast to the serene repose of Themis.

The comic masks on the right in room 30 provide some light relief, although some of their expressions are as menacing as they are funny. A little way down in the middle of the room is a delightful and sensitive sculpture of a naked boy with his hand on a goose – note his gentle smile and the apparent softness of his skin. Dominating the room is yet another statue of the sea god, Poseidon (140 BC), which was found on Milos in 1877. Behind this statue is the bronze head of a very melancholy-looking guy; it was found on Delos. To the right is an amusing sculpture of Pan making amorous advances towards Aphrodite, who is about to clobber him with her sandal.

Room 34 is built to simulate an open-air sanctuary and displays objects from the **Sanctuary of Aphrodite** which existed near Dafni. Room 36 houses the **Karapanos Collection**, which includes a chariot from the Roman period. Room 37 is the first bronze room to be opened. A case on the left shows casting techniques; another shows burial offerings. In the middle is a bronze statue of a youth (337 BC) which was found in the Bay of Marathon.

Thira Exhibition The hall at the top of the stairs houses the celebrated frescoes unearthed by Spyridon Marinatos at the Minoan settlement of Akrotiri on Santorini (Thira) in the late 1960s.

The frescoes are more varied and better preserved than the Minoan frescoes found on Crete. Extremely beautiful and harmonious in both colour and form, they give a comprehensive insight into the everyday life of the Minoans. Scenes depicted in the frescoes include two boxing youths, a youth holding two strings of fish, and women performing religious rites. The most unusual is the one which shows a flotilla of ships sailing from one coastal town to another. The frescoes will remain here until a suitable museum has been built on Santorini.

Pottery Collection On leaving the Thira exhibition, turn left to reach the first of the pottery rooms. These house the world's most comprehensive collection of ancient Greek pottery. The collection traces the development from the Bronze Age, through the Protogeometric and Geometric periods to the beginning of simple decorative motifs.

Flora, fauna and human figures first featured on pottery in the 8th century BC, and mythical scenes appeared a century later. The 6th century BC saw the emergence of the famous Attic black-figured pottery. By the middle of the 5th century, the pots with black figures had been superseded by red-figured pottery, which reached the peak of perfection during Pericles' rule.

Numismatic Collection The numismatic exhibit, at the left at the top of the stairs and through room 56, was closed at the time of writing. The vast collection comprises 400,000 coins from ancient Greek, Hellenic, Roman and Byzantine times. Only a fraction of the collection is on display at any one time. Coins to look out for are the **owl coins** of classical Athens and the **Macedonian coins**.

The numismatic collection is normally open Tuesday to Sunday from 8.30 am to 3 pm and entry is 500 dr.

Benaki Museum This museum contains the sumptuous and eclectic collection of Antoine Benaki, the son of an Alexandrian cotton magnate named Emmanual Benaki. These exhibits were accumulated during Antoine's 35 years of avid collecting in Europe and Asia. In 1931 he turned the family house into a museum and presented it to the Greek nation.

The ground floor is devoted to ancient and medieval arts. It includes Bronze Age finds from Mycenae and Thessaly; two early works by El Greco; ecclesiastical furniture brought from Asia Minor by refugees; pottery, copper, silver and woodwork from Egypt, Asia Minor and Mesopotamia; and a reconstruction of a Muslim reception hall.

The 1st floor is devoted to the 17th to 19th centuries, and includes a reconstruction of a 17th-century room from a Rhodes mansion. Also on display are some Byron memorabilia, relics from the War of Independence, letters of Eleftherios Venizelos (who was a close friend of Emmanual Benaki) and the poet George Seferis, exquisite embroidery from the islands and Chinese ceramics. In the basement is a stunning collection of Greek regional costumes.

The museum is on the corner of Vasilissis Sofias and Koumbari. At the time of writing, it was closed for a complete refit and was not scheduled to reopen until mid-1997. The museum shop (☎ 362 7367) remains open Monday to Friday from 8.30 am to 3 pm selling books, cards and replicas.

Goulandris Museum of Cycladic & Ancient Greek Art This private museum (☎ 801 5870) houses a collection of Cycladic art which is second in importance only to that displayed at the National Archaeological Museum. The museum was custom-built for the collection and the finds are beautifully displayed, lit and labelled. Although the exhibits cover all periods from Cycladic to Roman times, the emphasis is on the Cycladic from 3000 to 2000 BC. The 230 exhibits include the folded-arm, marble figurines which inspired many 20th-century artists with their simplicity and purity of form.

The museum has now taken over the 19th-century mansion next door, which it uses for temporary exhibitions. The entrance to the museum is at Neofytou Douka 4, just around the corner from Vasilissis Sofias. It is open Monday, Wednesday, Thursday and Friday from 10 am to 4 pm, and on Saturday from 10 am to 3 pm. Admission is 400 dr.

Byzantine Museum This museum (☎ 723 1570) has a large collection of Christian art from the 4th to 19th centuries, housed in the Villa Ilissia, an attractive, mock-Florentine mansion at Vasilissis Sofias 22.

Unfortunately the museum will be operating at half-capacity until 1998, as the wing to the right of the courtyard is being completely rebuilt. This wing housed many of the finest frescoes and icons; some are in storage, others have been moved temporarily to Thessaloniki.

The downstairs rooms in the surviving wing are given over to re-creations of churches, starting with a very solemn basilica from the 5th to 7th centuries. The reconstruction of an 11th-century Byzantine church is beautiful in its simplicity, in contrast to the elaborate decorations of the post-Byzantine church next door. The bishop's throne in this room was brought to Athens by refugees from Asia Minor. The upstairs rooms contain icons and frescoes.

The museum is open Tuesday to Sunday from 8.30 am to 3 pm. Admission is 500 dr.

Museum of Greek Folk Art This museum (☎ 322 9031) houses a superb collection of secular and religious folk art, mainly from the 18th and 19th centuries. On the 1st floor is embroidery, pottery, weaving and puppets. On the 2nd floor is a reconstructed traditional village house with paintings by the primitive artist Theophilos of Lesvos (Mytilini). Greek traditional costumes are displayed on the 3rd and 4th floors.

The museum is at Kydathineon 17, Plaka, and is open Tuesday to Sunday from 10 am to 2 pm. Admission is 500 dr.

National Art Gallery The emphasis in this gallery (☎ 721 1010) is on Greek painting and sculpture from the 19th and 20th centuries. There are also 16th-century works and a few works by European masters, including paintings by Picasso, Marquet and Utrillo and Magritte's sculpture *The Therapist*.

Paintings by the primitive painter Theophilos are displayed on the mezzanine floor and 20th-century works are on the 1st floor. The 2nd floor has mostly 19th-century paintings, with one room of earlier works. It has four El Greco paintings, including *The Crucifixion* and *Symphony of the Angels*.

Greek sculpture of the 19th and 20th centuries is effectively displayed in the sculpture garden and sculpture hall, which are reached from the lower floor. There are several works by Giannolis Halepas (1851-1937), one of Greece's foremost sculptors.

The gallery is at Vasileos Konstantinou 50 (opposite the Hilton Hotel) and is open Wednesday to Saturday and Monday from 9 am to 3 pm and Sunday from 10 am to 2 pm. Admission is 500 dr.

War Museum This museum (☎ 729 0543) is a relic of the colonels' junta. Greece seems to have been at war since time immemorial, and a look around helps to get the country's history in perspective. All periods from the Mycenaean to the present day are covered,

and displays include weapons, maps, armour and models of battles.

The museum is at Vasilissis Sofias 24, just beyond the Byzantine Museum, and it's open Tuesday to Saturday from 9 am to 2 pm. Entry is free.

Centre of Folk Arts & Traditions There's no entry charge for this small museum (☎ 324 3987) either. It has a good display of costumes, embroideries, pottery and musical instruments.

It's at Angelika Hatzimihali 6 and is open Tuesday and Thursday from 9 am to 9 pm and on Wednesday, Friday and Saturday from 9 am to 1 pm and 5 to 9 pm.

Paul & Alexandra Kanellopoulos Museum This museum (☎ 321 2313) houses the small but fascinating private collection of the Kanellopoulos family. Exhibits include pieces from Cycladic, Minoan and classical times; Attic vases; Byzantine jewellery and embroideries; Persian jewellery from the 5th century BC; icons; and coins.

The museum is on the corner of Theorias and Panos, Plaka. It's open Tuesday to Friday from 8.30 am to 3 pm. Admission is 400 dr.

National Historical Museum This museum (☎ 323 7617) specialises in memorabilia from the War of Independence, including Byron's helmet and sword. There is also a series of paintings depicting events leading up to the war. It also has Byzantine and medieval exhibits, and a collection of photographs and royal portraits.

The museum is housed in the old parliament building at Plateia Kolokotroni, Stadiou. Theodoros Deligiannis, who succeeded Trikoupis as prime minister of Greece, was assassinated on the steps of the building in 1905. It's open Tuesday to Sunday from 9 am to 1.30 pm, and admission is 500 dr.

City of Athens Museum This museum (☎ 324 6164) occupies the palace where King Otho and his consort Amalia lived for a few years during the 1830s. It contains some of the royal couple's furniture, costumes and personal mementoes, as well as paintings, prints and models of Athens in the 19th century.

The museum is at Paparigopoulou 7 and is open on Monday, Wednesday, Friday and Saturday from 9 am to 1.30 pm. Admission is 400 dr.

Jewish Museum The museum (☎ 323 1577) traces the history of the Jewish community in Greece back to the 3rd century BC through an impressive collection of religious and folk art and documents. It includes a reconstruction of a synagogue.

The museum is housed on the 3rd floor of a 19th-century building at Amalias 36. It's open Sunday to Friday from 9 am to 1 pm and entry is free.

Theatre Museum Aspiring Thespians may be interested in visiting this museum (☎ 362 9430), which contains theatre memorabilia from the 19th and 20th centuries. Exhibits include photographs, costumes, props and reconstructions of the dressing rooms of Greece's most celebrated 20th-century actors.

The museum is at Akadimias 50. Opening times are Monday to Friday from 9 am to 3 pm. Admission is 150 dr.

Hills of Athens

Lykavittos Hill The name Lykavittos means 'hill of wolves' and derives from ancient times when the hill was in remote countryside and wolves menaced the sheep that grazed there. Today, it is no longer remote or inhabited by wolves, but rises out of a sea of concrete to offer the finest views in Athens. Pollution permitting, there are panoramic views of the city, the Attic basin, the surrounding mountains and the islands of Salamis and Aegina. A path leads to the summit from the top of Loukianou. Alternatively, you can take the funicular railway from the top of Ploutarhou (400/800 dr, one way/return).

There is an expensive café halfway up the path and another at the top, as well as a restaurant looking down towards the Acropolis. Also on the summit is the little **Chapel of Agios Giorgios**. The chapel is floodlit at night and from the streets below looks like a vision from a fairy tale. The open-air **Lykavittos Theatre**, to the north-east of the summit, is used for performances of jazz and rock during the Athens Festival.

West of the Acropolis The low hill of the **Areopagus** lies between the Acropolis and the Ancient Agora. According to mythology, it was here that Ares was tried by the council of the gods for the murder of Halirrhothios, son of Poseidon. The council accepted his defence of justifiable deicide on the grounds that he was protecting his daughter, Alcippe, from unwanted advances.

It became the place where murder trials were heard before the Council of the Areopagus. By the 4th century, its jurisdiction had been extended to cover treason and corruption. In 51 AD, St Paul delivered his famous 'Sermon to an Unknown God' from Areopagus hill and gained his first Athenian convert, Dionysos, who became patron saint of the city.

The hill is linked to the Acropolis by a saddle and can be climbed by steps cut into the rock. There are good views of the Ancient Agora from the summit. The rock is very slippery, so wear suitable shoes.

Filopappos hill, also called the Hill of the Muses, is clearly identifiable to the west of the Acropolis by virtue of the **Monument of Filopappos** at its summit. The monument was built in 114-116 AD in honour of Julius Antiochus Filopappos, who was a prominent Roman consul and administrator. There are small paths all over the hill, but the paved path to the top starts next to the Dionysos Taverna on Dionysiou Areopagitou. The pine-clad slopes are a pleasant place for a stroll and offer good views of the plain and mountains of Attica and of the Saronic Gulf.

After 250 metres, the path passes the **Church of Agios Dimitrios**, which contains some fine frescoes. It was sensitively restored in 1951-57. Above here is the rocky

ATHENS

Hill of the Pnyx. This was the meeting place of the Democratic Assembly in the 5th century BC. Among the great orators who addressed assemblies here were Aristides, Demosthenes, Pericles and Themistocles.

To the north-west of the Hill of the Pnyx is the **Hill of the Nymphs** on which stands an observatory built in 1842. It is open to visitors on the last Friday of each month.

Parks

Athens is sadly lacking in parks. Only three are large enough to be worthy of a mention and a visit.

National Gardens These gardens are a delightful shady refuge during the summer months and are the favourite haunt of Athens' many stray cats. They were formerly the royal gardens and were designed by Queen Amalia.

The garden contains subtropical trees, ornamental ponds with waterfowl, and a **botanical museum** which houses interesting drawings, paintings and photographs. There are entrances to the gardens from Vasilissis Sofias and Amalias.

Zappeio Gardens These gardens are laid out in a network of wide walkways around the Zappeio, which was built in the 1870s with money donated by the wealthy Greek-Romanian benefactor, Konstantinos Zappas. Until the 1970s, the Zappeio was used mainly as an exhibition hall. It was used for Council of Europe meetings during Greece's presidency of the EC.

Areos Park This pleasant park is north of the National Archaeological Museum on Leoforos Alexandras. It is a large park with wide, tree-lined avenues, one of which has a long line of statues of War of Independence heroes.

Athens' First Cemetery Athens' First Cemetery (Proto Nekrotafeion Athinon) is not strictly a park, but it bears more than a passing resemblance to one. In the absence of real parks, any patch of greenery is welcome. Athenian families who come to attend the graves of loved ones certainly seem to take this attitude, turning duty into an outing by bringing along a picnic. It's a peaceful place to stroll around and is the resting place of many famous Greeks and philhellenes.

The cemetery is 600 metres south-east of the Temple of Zeus at the end of Anapafseos. You'll know you're getting close when you see all the stone masons and flower shops. Other shops sell cemetery paraphernalia, ranging from life-size figures of Christ to miniature picture frames – used to put photographs of the deceased on the gravestones.

The cemetery is well kept and most of the tombstones and mausoleums are lavish in the extreme. Some are kitsch and sentimental, others are works of art created by the foremost Greek sculptors of the 19th century, such as the *Sleeping Maiden* by Halepas, which is the tomb of a young girl. Someone places a red rose in her hand every day.

Among the cemetery's famous residents are the writers Rangavis (1810-92) and Soutsos (1800-68); the politician Harilaos Trikoupis (1832-96); the archaeologists Heinrich Schliemann (1822-90) and Adolph Furtwängler (1853-1907); the benefactors Antoine Benaki, Georgios Averof and Theodoros Syngros; and War of Independence heroes Sir Richard Church (1784-1873), Kolokotronis (1770-1843), Makrygiannis and Androutsos. Schliemann's mausoleum is decorated with scenes from the Trojan War. Located near the entrance is a memorial – poignant in its simplicity – to the 40,000 citizens who died of starvation during WW II.

ACTIVITIES
Skiing

The nearest ski fields to Athens are on Mt Parnassos, where the season lasts from mid-December to March or April. The ski department (☎ 324 1915) at Klaoudatos, the big department store on Athinas, organises excursions to the resort of Kalaria. Their buses leave from the stadium in Athens every morning at 5.40 am and get to Kalaria at

8.30 am. They return at 4 pm. Tickets are 5000 dr, including a lift pass. An extra 2500 dr gets you all the gear – skis, bindings, boots and poles.

Tennis

Getting a game of tennis usually involves wangling your way into one of the exclusive clubs, such as the Athens Tennis Club (☎ 923 2872), next to the Temple of Olympian Zeus at Vasilissis Olgas 2.

Golf

Golf is expensive, but it's not quite so complicated to get a game. The Glyfada Golf Club (☎ 894 6820), near the airport, is the only course. Green fees are 11,000 dr on weekdays, 15,000 dr on weekends and public holidays. You'll be up for another 2300 dr for a bag of clubs, and 700 dr for a buggy.

Other Sports Clubs

Addresses of other sports clubs include:

Gliding
  Gliding Club of Athens, Pafsaniou 8
  (☎ 723 5158)
Horse Riding
  Horse Riding Club of Athens, Gerakas
  (☎ 661 1088)
  Horse Riding Club of Greece, Paradissos
  (☎ 682 6128)
Jogging
  Hash House Harriers Jogging Club, Kifissia
  (☎ 621 9821)

Bird-Watching

Keen bird-watchers may like to contact the Hellenic Ornithological Society (☎ 361 1271), Benaki 53, Athens.

Bridge

Players of the world's most popular card game can contact the Greek Federation of Bridge Clubs (☎ 321 0490), Evripidou 6.

Language Courses

If you are serious about learning Greek, an intensive course at the start of your stay is a good way to go about it. Most of the courses are in Athens, but there are also courses on the islands in summer.

The Athens Centre (☎ 701 2268; fax 701 8603), Arhimidous 48, has a very good reputation. Its courses cover five levels of proficiency from beginners to advanced. There are five immersion courses a year for beginners, packing 60 hours of class time into three weeks for 75,000 dr. The centre occupies a fine neoclassical building in the quiet residential suburb of Mets.

XEN (the YWCA) (☎ 362 4291; fax 362 2400), at Amerikis 11, runs six-week beginners' courses starting in February, May, and October. Courses involve 40 hours of class time and cost 40,000 dr.

Other places in Athens offering courses are the Hellenic American Union (☎ 362 9886), Massalias 22, and the Hellenic Language School, Zalongou 4 (☎ 362 8161; fax 363 9951).

Private lessons are advertised sometimes on the notice board outside the Compendium bookshop, Nikis 28.

Children's Activities

The Children's Museum, Kydathineon 14, is more of a play group than a museum. It has a games room and a number of 'exhibits', such as a mock-up of a metro tunnel, for children to explore.

It's open on Monday and Wednesday from 9.30 am to 1.30 pm, Friday from 9.30 am to 1.30 pm and from 5 to 8 pm, and on weekends from 10 am to 1 pm. Entry is free. Parents have to stay and supervise their children.

ORGANISED TOURS

The three main companies running organised tours around Athens are CHAT (☎ 322 3137), Stadiou 4; GO Tours (☎ 322 5951/5955), Voulis 31-33; and Key Tours (☎ 923 3166/3266), Kaliroïs 4. You will find their brochures everywhere, all offering similar tours and prices. They include a half-day sightseeing tour of Athens (7700 dr), which does nothing more than point out all the major sights; and Athens by Night (10,500 dr), which takes in the son et lumière (sound-and-light show) before a taverna dinner with folk dancing.

The companies also have one-day tours to Cape Sounion (5800 dr); Delphi (14,500 dr, 16,500 dr with lunch); the Corinth Canal, Mycenae, Nafplio and Epidaurus (same prices); and one-day cruises to Aegina, Poros and Hydra (15,000 dr including lunch).

Future Travel and Tourism (☎ 323 3131; fax 323 1894), at level four, Kolokotroni 9, specialises in tailor-made tours for either individuals or groups.

FESTIVALS

Athens Festival The state-sponsored Athens Festival is the city's most important cultural event, running from mid-June to the end of September. It includes classical-music concerts and dance performances by national and international orchestras and dance companies.

The main attraction is the performance of ancient Greek dramas at the Theatre of Herodes Atticus. The plays are performed in modern Greek, but somehow it doesn't seem to matter if you don't understand. The setting is superb, backed by the floodlit Acropolis, and the atmosphere is electric. There are also performances at the Lykavittos Theatre, the open-air amphitheatre in Piraeus, and the Theatre of Epidaurus – special buses run here from Athens (see also the Nafplio and Epidaurus sections in the Peloponnese chapter).

Tickets sell out quickly, so try to buy yours as soon as possible. They can be bought at the festival box office (☎ 322 1459), in the arcade at Stadiou 4. Opening times are Monday to Friday from 8.30 am to 1.30 pm and from 6 to 8.30 pm. Tickets may also be purchased on the day of the performance at the theatre box offices, but queues tend to be very long. There are student discounts for most performances on production of an ISIC.

Alternative Athens Festival A privately sponsored alternative festival runs concurrently with the established festival. It features jazz and rock artists at venues including the Lykavittos Theatre, the Panathinaïkos Football Stadium on Leoforos Alexandras and the clubs listed under Live Music in the Entertainment section later in this chapter. Tickets for these performances can be purchased at the box offices of the respective venues and at major music shops. The EOT does not give out a programme for the alternative festival, but events are listed in the English-language newspapers as well as being widely advertised on posters.

PLACES TO STAY

Athens is a noisy city and Athenians keep late hours, so an effort has been made to select hotels in quiet areas, pedestrian precincts or side streets. All the prices quoted here are for the high season. Most places offer considerable discounts in the off season.

Plaka is the most popular place to stay. Most of the sights are close by and it's convenient for every transport connection other than the railway station. It has a very good choice of accommodation right across the price spectrum, from travellers' hostels to smart mid-range hotels and pensions. Not surprisingly, rooms fill up quickly in July and August, so it is wise to make a reservation. If you haven't booked, a telephone call can save a fruitless walk.

The other main hotel area is around Plateia Omonias, but the options are not very attractive. They all seem to be either cheap bordellos where you won't get a wink of sleep, or characterless modern C-class places. An added drawback to the Omonia region is the general seediness after dark. There are, however, a few good budget places in the streets north of Omonia.

Koukaki, south of the Acropolis, is a quiet residential suburb with some good pensions and mid-range hotels.

If you arrive in the city late and cannot find anywhere to stay, don't be tempted to sleep out. It is illegal and could be dangerous. You would be better off going to one of the many all-night cafés, some of which are recommended in Places to Eat later.

Bottom End

Camping There are no camp sites in central Athens. The EOT's *Camping in Greece* brochure lists all 17 sites in Attica. The nearest to the city centre is *Athens Camping* (☎ 581 4114), Leoforos Athinon 198, seven km from the centre. It has hot water, a mini-market and snack bar and is open year-round. To get there, take bus No 880 or 860 to Elefsina from outside the Academy of Arts on Panepistimiou. From Piraeus, take bus No 802 or 845. These buses can also drop you at *Dafni Camping* (☎ 581 1562/1563), a good shady site next to the famous monastery three km further on.

If you prefer to be by the sea, there are several camp sites on the coast road to Cape Sounion (see the Coast Rd to Sounion and Cape Sounion sections later).

Hostels There are a few places around Athens making a pitch for the hostelling market by tagging 'youth hostel' onto their names. There are some truly dreadful dumps among them.

There is only one youth hostel worth bothering with and that's the excellent IYHF-affiliated *Athens International Youth Hostel* (☎ 523 4170), Victor Hugo 16. Location is the only drawback, otherwise the place is almost too good to be true. It occupies the former C-class Hotel Victor Ougo, which has been completely renovated – it even has double-glazed windows. The spotless rooms, all with private bathroom, sleep two to four people and come complete with sheets and pillow cases. Rates are 2000 dr per person, including continental breakfast, for those with an IYHF card. If you don't have a card, you can either pay 2600 dr to join or 500 dr for a daily stamp. There is no curfew. The manager is a friendly guy called Akis, who speaks good English and is a mine of information about Athens.

After this, the average C-class hotel looks decidedly tatty. The sleazy *Athens Inn Youth Hostel* (☎ 524 6906), on the opposite side of the road at No 13, certainly does. It charges 1500 dr for dorm beds and 4000 dr for a double.

Even this place looks good, however, alongside the squalid *Youth Hostel No 2* (☎ 644 2421) at Drossi 1. The hostel is a long way from the centre of town – 1.5 km east of Oktovriou-Patission, along Alexandras. It's above the Restaurant Babis, a rembetika club, and is open only from May to September. Facilities are extremely primitive. It charges 1500 dr for dorm beds.

Standards aren't a lot better at *Youth Hostel No 5* (☎ 751 9530), Damareos 75, even though it's apparently a member of the Greek Youth Hostel Organisation. Maybe the cleaner just hadn't called for a few weeks because the place is not without its admirers. It charges 1500 dr per night for dorm beds, and 50 dr for a coin-operated hot shower. The hostel is to the east of the old Athens stadium, 1.5 km from Syntagma. Trolleybuses No 2 and 11 can drop you just around the corner on Frinis. Get off at the Filolaou stop, just past Damareos.

Hotels – Plaka, Syntagma & Monastiraki

The *Student & Travellers' Inn* (☎ 324 4808), right in the heart of Plaka at Kydathineon 16, is hard to look past. It's a friendly, well-run place with beautiful polished floors and spotless rooms. It has beds in four-person dorms for 2000 dr, while singles/doubles/triples are 4500/6000/7500 dr with shared bathroom. English breakfast is served in the vine-covered courtyard at the back for 1050 dr, and there's a small Athenian bar lined with prints of 19th-century Athenian scenes.

The huge timber spiral staircase at *George's Guest House* (☎ 322 6474) speaks of grander times at Nikis 46, but it's a friendly place with dorms for 2000 dr, and doubles/triples for 5000/6000 dr with shared bathroom.

The *Festos Youth & Student Guesthouse* (☎ 323 2455), Filellinon 18, has been a popular place with travellers for a long time despite its noisy situation on one of the busiest streets in Athens. Dorm beds are 2000 dr, but they pack eight into a room. It charges 2500 dr per person in private rooms with shared bathroom. Traffic noise mingles with noise from the bar on the 1st floor, which has a happy hour between 5 and 7 pm, when large beers are 300 dr. It also serves meals and has at least one vegetarian item on the menu.

The *XEN* (YWCA) (☎ 362 4291), Amerikis 11, is an option for women only. It has singles/doubles with shared bathroom for 3500/6000 dr, and for 4500/6500 dr with private bathroom. There are laundry facilities and a snack bar which charges 700 dr for continental breakfast. Annual membership costs 600 dr.

The rooms at *John's Place* (☎ 322 9719), Patröou 5, are very basic but clean. Singles/doubles/triples with shared bathroom are 4000/6000/9000 dr. Patröou is on the left heading down Mitropoleos from Syntagma.

Another cheap option is the E-class *Hotel Solonion* (☎ 322 0008), Tsagari 11-13. The place looks dilapidated but the rooms are clean enough. It charges 3500/5000 dr for singles/doubles with shared bathroom. This one of the few places in Plaka where no English is spoken. Tsagari is the second street on the right after Filellinon heading south on Amalias.

There are a couple of much better hotels close to the Plaka near Plateia Monastirakiou. The D-class *Hotel Tempi* (☎ 321 3175), Eolou 29, is a cheery place on the pedestrian precinct part of Eolou. The rooms at the front have balconies overlooking a little square with a church and a flower market. Rates are 4200/6800/9000 dr with shared bathroom, or 7800 dr for doubles with private bathroom. The washing machine is an added attraction.

The *Hotel Carolina* (☎ 331 1784) is close by at Kolokotroni 55 with singles/doubles with shared bathroom for 4400/7700 dr, or 5500/8800 dr with private bathroom. Ask for a room overlooking the pedestrian precinct on Kalamiotou. The rooms at the other end are above a bar that belts out rock music until 3 am.

The *Hotel Capri* (☎ 325 2091/2085) is well away from the rest of the tourist hotels at Psaromiligou 6, near Plateia Eleftherias, but that's not necessarily a bad thing. Some of the main sites of ancient Athens are close

by – the Keramikos is just down the road. There a couple of good restaurants nearby. Its prices are very competitive at 3500/5000/6500 dr for singles/doubles/triples with bathroom. The hotel is five minutes' walk from Thision metro station, the stop before Monastiraki coming from Piraeus. From the station, cross Ermou and follow Agion Asomaton to Psaromiligou, then turn right.

Hotels – Veïkou & Koukaki This isn't exactly backpacker territory, but the *Marble House Pension* (☎ 923 4058 or 922 6461), Zini 35A, Koukaki, is one of Athens' better budget hotels. Monica, the French manager, is friendly and helpful, and rates for the immaculate rooms are 5300/7800 dr for singles/doubles with shared bathroom and 6600/8900 dr with private bathroom. The pension is on a quiet cul-de-sac off Zini. To get there, catch trolleybus No 1, 5, 9 or 18 from Syntagma to the Zini stop on Veïkou, turn left into Zini and the cul-de-sac is the first turn-off on the left.

Hotels – Omonia & Surrounds This section includes the student district of Exarhia and the area around the train stations as well as Omonia.

The *Hostel Aphrodite* (☎ 881 0589), Einardou 12, is one of the best budget places in Athens. It is very clean, with dazzling, white walls and good-sized rooms, many with balconies. It has dorm beds for 1500 dr, singles/doubles/triples with shared bathroom for 4000/5000/6000 dr as well as doubles with private bathroom for 6000 dr.

The lively basement bar is a good place to compare notes with fellow travellers until the wee small hours. In the morning, it becomes the breakfast room, turning out a range of set breakfasts.

English-speaking staff are helpful and knowledgeable about Athens. Einardou is a small street off Mihail Voda, about 1.5 km north of Plateia Omonias. Trolleybus No 1 goes up Mihail Voda, although the route is not shown on the EOT map. Get off at the Proussis stop, just south of Einhardou. Paloma Tours' 20-day ferry passes to the

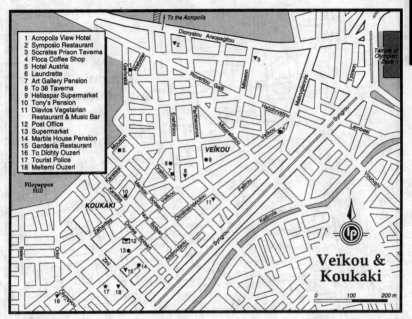

1 Acropolis View Hotel
2 Symposio Restaurant
3 Socrates Prison Taverna
4 Floca Coffee Shop
5 Hotel Austria
6 Laundrette
7 Art Gallery Pension
8 To 38 Taverna
9 Hellaspar Supermarket
10 Tony's Pension
11 Diavlos Vegetarian
   Restaurant & Music Bar
12 Post Office
13 Supermarket
14 Marble House Pension
15 Gardenia Restaurant
16 To Dichty Ouzeri
17 Tourist Police
18 Meltemi Ouzeri

Veïkou &
Koukaki

Cyclades can be bought here. The hostel is only 10 minutes' walk from Larisis Station. The nearest metro station is Viktorias, five minutes' walk away at Plateia Viktorias.

The *Hostel Argo* (☎ 522 5939), Victor Hugo 25, isn't in quite the same league, but the owner is cheerful and the rooms are clean. Beds in four-person dorms are 2000 dr, and singles/doubles are 3500/5000 dr with shared bathroom. There is a bar and breakfast room, and also a washing machine.

The *Hotel Mystras* (☎ 522 7737/1807), Kerameon 26, is the closest budget hotel to the Peloponnese train station. It's another place that's well set up for travellers; it has a bar, breakfast room, ticket service and an efficient laundry. The spacious singles/doubles/triples are 4000/5000/6000 dr with private bathroom. Some rooms have a shower instead of a bath and cost 200 dr less.

Another option nearby is the *Hotel Rio* (☎ 522 7075), Odysseos 13. It has dorm beds for 2000 dr and singles/doubles/triples for

4500/6000/6600 dr with private bathroom. Walk down Kerameon and turn left into Odysseos and the hotel is on the right.

The *Museum Hotel* (☎ 380 5611/5613), Bouboulinas 16, is a long-established hotel behind the National Archaeological Museum. The rooms are plain but comfortable, and reasonably priced at 5000/7000/8400 dr with private bathroom.

Exarhia is off the beaten track as far as hotels go, but there are a couple of good places tucked away at the base of Strefi hill. The *Hotel Orian* (☎ 382 7362/7116/0191) and *Hotel Dryades* (with the same owner and telephone numbers) are 50 metres apart on Anexartisias, which skirts the western side of the hill. They are managed by a friendly guy who speaks good English. The Orion is clean and well kept with singles/doubles for 4500/6000 dr with shared bathroom, while the Dryades charges 6000/8000 dr for rooms with private bathroom. The hotels are to the left at the top of the steps leading off

Omonia & Train Stations Area

0   125   250 m

PLACES TO STAY		27	Pitta Pan & Café Brettania	18 19	Public Toilets First-Aid Centre
1	Hostel Aphrodite	33	Vegetarian Fast Food	20	Minion Department
3	Oscar Hotel	35	Ideal Restaurant		Store
13	Hotel Mystras			22	National Theatre
14	Hotel Rio	**OTHER**		23	OSE
16	Hostel Argo			24	Traffic Police
17	Athens International	5	OTE	25	Laundrette
	Youth Hostel	6	Buses to Marathon &	26	Buses to Bus
34	Titania Hotel		Rafina		Terminal A
		7	Mavromateon Terminal	28	Bus 049 to Piraeus
PLACES TO EAT			(Buses to Lavrion &	29	OTE
			Cape Sounion)	30	Marinopoulos
2	Taverna Avli	8	National Archaeological		Supermarket
4	Dafni Taverna		Museum	31	Central Post Office
11	O Vaggelis Taverna	9	Polytehnio	32	Buses to Airport
12	O Makis Psistaria	10	Rodon Club	36	Klaoudatos
21	Neon Café	15	Laundrette		Department Store

Emmanual Benaki at the junction with Kalidromiou. You can save yourself a long uphill trek by catching a bus No 230 from Amalias to the Kalidromiou stop on Harilou Trikoupi, which runs parallel to Benaki.

The *Hotel Exarchion* (☎ 360 3296/1256/ 8684) is right at the heart of student territory on Plateia Exarhion. It's a modern hotel and the light, airy rooms have large French windows which open out onto balconies. Singles/doubles are 5500/7700 dr with private bathroom. The square is surrounded by bars, clubs and restaurants and can be noisy at night, so ask for a room at the back.

Middle
Plaka The *Acropolis House Pension* (☎ 322 2344/6241), Kodrou 6-8, is a beautifully preserved 19th-century house which retains many original features. The rooms are attractively furnished and have 24-hour hot water. The hotel is centrally heated and some rooms also have air-conditioning. Singles/doubles/ triples with private bathroom are 9100/ 10,900/14,300 dr. There are also singles/ doubles with shared bathroom for 7500/ 9000 dr. Breakfast costs 1150 dr per person.

The *Kouros Hotel* (☎ 322 7431), Kodrou 11, looks extremely promising, but guests appear to be regarded as a bloody nuisance. It's a shame, because it's an old house with

beautiful moulded ceilings and loads of character. It charges 5000/10,000/15,000 dr for rooms with shared bathroom. Kodrou is on the northern edge of Plaka, five minutes' walk from Syntagma, and is the southern (pedestrian) extension of Voulis, which leads into Kydathineon.

New owners have almost finished a major renovation job at the *Hotel Myrto* (☎ 322 7237 or 323 4560), nearby at Nikis 40. It has immaculate singles for 10,000 dr and doubles from 15,000 dr with en suite bathroom, as well as doubles with shared bathroom for 10,000 dr. All rooms come with central heating, air-con and TV, and breakfast is included. The modern Hotel Nefeli (☎ 322 8044/8045), Iperidou 16, is a popular place. It has singles/doubles for 11,000/ 12,000 dr, including breakfast. To get there from Syntagma, head south down Voulis and turn right into Iperidou.

Outside Plaka, the *Hotel Achilleas* (☎ 323 3197), Leka 21, is a very comfortable modern hotel with large, airy rooms. Rooms on the top floor open onto garden terraces. It charges 10,900/14,000/17,000 dr for singles/ doubles with breakfast. To get there from Syntagma, head west along ·Ermou, turn right into Voulis and you'll see Leka leading off diagonally to the left.

The Achilleas is a stablemate of the *Hotel Plaka* (☎ 322 2096), the best of a cluster of

B and C-class hotels on busy Mitropoleos. The hotel is at the junction with Kapnikareas and it offers a very similar deal to the Achilleas.

The *Hotel Omiros* (☎ 323 5486/5487), Apollonos 15, is a B-class hotel with large, comfortable air-con singles/doubles for 9000/12,500 dr. Apollonos runs roughly parallel to Mitropoleos, one street closer to Plaka.

Veïkou & Koukaki The *Art Gallery Pension* (☎ 923 8376/1933), Erehthiou 5, Veïkou, is a small, friendly place run by the brother-and-sister team of Ada and Yannis Assimakopoulos. It has comfortable singles/doubles for 13,000/15,000 dr with balcony and private bathroom. To get there, take trolleybus No 1, 5, 9 or 18 from Syntagma to the Drakou stop on Veïkou. Erehthiou runs north from Veïkou towards the Acropolis.

Tony's Pension (☎ 923 6370/0561), Zaharitsa 26, Koukaki, is another clean, well-maintained pension. It offers singles/doubles/triples for 8500/9600/12,000 dr with private bathroom. Tony also has well-equipped two-person studio apartments nearby for long or short-term rental. Short-term prices are the same as for rooms at the pension. Take the trolleybus to the Drakou stop on Veïkou, head north-west along Drakou, and Zaharitsa is the second on the left.

The *Hotel Austria* (☎ 923 5151; fax 924 7350), Mouson 7, is situated in a quiet spot on the slopes of Filopappos hill with good views over the city from its roof garden. The place is spotless, but the rooms are on the spartan side for 13,900/17,900 dr. Mouson is on the left at the top of Drakou.

There are indeed views of the Acropolis from many of the rooms at the *Acropolis View Hotel* (☎ 921 7303/3035; fax 923 0705), just south of the Theatre of Herodes Atticus at Webster 10. The best views are from the roof terrace. Some of the rooms look out over Filopappos hill. Rates are 14,000/18,700 dr for air-con singles/doubles with buffet breakfast. Bus No 230 from Syn-

tagma stops at the Theatre of Herodes Atticus, two minutes' walk away.

Around Omonia Omonia is not really the place to be looking for up-market accommodation – you can do much better for your money elsewhere.

There are a couple of exceptions. The new *Oscar Hotel* (☎ 883 4215), on the corner of Samou and Filadelphias opposite Larisis Station, is a smart B-class hotel that has a roof garden with small swimming pool. Singles/doubles here cost 14,000/20,000 dr, including breakfast.

The *Titania Hotel* (☎ 330 0111; fax 330 0700), with an imposing façade at Panepistimiou 52, is a very comfortable modern hotel that has just had a complete refit. The large singles/doubles are 17,700/23,700 dr, including breakfast. All the rooms have satellite TV. There are great views over the city from the rooftop bar at night.

Kolonaki This posh area predictably doesn't have any budget accommodation or, indeed, much accommodation at all. It does, however, have the B-class *Athenian Inn* (☎ 723 8097/9552/8756; telex 224 092 INN GR; fax 721 5614), Haritos 22. It's a small but distinguished place on a quiet street in the heart of Kolonaki that was reputably a favourite of Lawrence Durrell. It has a cosy intimacy which is often lacking in hotels of this category. The rooms are unpretentious but comfortable with air-con and pretty pictures of island scenes on the walls. It charges 14,400/21,500/26,800 dr for single/doubles/triples, including breakfast. Haritos is five blocks north of Vasilissis Sofias, and just north-east of Plateia Kolonakiou.

Top End
If you are wealthy, *the* place to stay in Athens is – and always has been – the deluxe *Hotel Grande Bretagne* (☎ 331 4444; fax 322 8034), on Syntagma. Built in 1862 to accommodate visiting heads of state, it ranks among the grand hotels of the world. No other hotel in Athens can boast such a rich history (see the Walking Tour section

earlier). It has undergone much expansion since it first became a hotel in 1872, but still has an old-world grandeur. The elegantly furnished rooms have air-con, minibar, satellite TV and video. Their singles/doubles are US$250/295, and suites start at US$500.

St George Lycabettus Hotel (☎ 729 0711; fax 729 0439), Kleomenous 2, has a prime location at the foot of Lykavittos hill. It looks a bit tatty on the outside, but it's deluxe inside. The big attraction here is that you can lie in bed at night and gaze at the floodlit Acropolis – or satellite TV, if you prefer. The roof garden surrounds a good-sized swimming pool. Prices depend on the view from the window. It charges 46,900/55,900 dr for a single/double with a view of the Acropolis, and 44,300/51,900 dr for a view of Lykavittos hill. The price includes a buffet breakfast. The hotel is at the western end of Kleomenous, on the edge of Plateia Dexamenis.

Hilton-hoppers will find their favourite (☎ 725 0201; fax 725 3110) at Vasilissis Sofias 46, opposite the National Art Gallery. The Athens version is a vast concrete edifice. From the outside, it looks more like a 1950s housing project than a luxury hotel. Inside, no expense has been spared. It has lashings of marble and bronze, public areas with enormous chandeliers and carpets which were especially designed by eminent Greek artists. Singles/doubles are US$248/285, plus tax, while suites start from US$450.

The posh leafy suburb of Kifissia has a number of luxury hotels. The A-class *Theoxenia Hotel* (☎ 801 2751/2765), on the corner of Filadelpheos and Kolokotroni, charges 20,000/26,000 dr for singles/doubles. Facilities include a swimming pool. Likewise the A-class *Semiramis Hotel* (☎ 808 8101), Harilaou Trikoupi 48, where the rates are 24,600/35,500 dr. The deluxe *Pentelikon Hotel* (☎ 808 0311; fax 801 0314), Deligianni 66, is an exquisite place built in traditional style with a swimming pool and a lovely garden. All of the beautifully furnished rooms have minibar and satellite TV. The rates are 53,000/64,000 dr for singles/doubles and 115,000 dr for suites.

PLACES TO EAT

Plaka is the part of town where most visitors wind up eating. The streets are lined with countless restaurants, tavernas, cafés, pâtisseries and gyros stalls.

There's more to Athens eating than Plaka though. There are a lot of good places in the Exarhia area, where prices are more in line with the average student's pocket. The waiters may not speak any English, but you'll find good food and good prices. Every neighbourhood of Athens has its good eating places. These are often small, friendly, unpretentious tavernas tucked away on side streets.

Inexpensive

Plaka For most people Plaka is the place to be. It's hard to beat the atmosphere of dining out beneath the floodlit Acropolis.

You do, however, pay for the privilege – particularly at the outdoor restaurants around the square on Kydathineon. It's the setting you're paying for, not the food, which is hard to get excited about. The best of the bunch is the *Taverna Acropol*, which prices its menu more realistically and is popular with Greek family groups. Stuffed tomatoes are 1100 dr, moussaka is 900 dr and there's fresh seafood by the kilo. The Acropol is on the opposite side of the Plateia Plakas to Kydathineon.

One of the best deals in the Plaka is the *Plaka Psistaria*, Kydathineon 28, with a range of gyros and souvlaki to eat there or take away.

Another place that is worth seeking out is the *Ouzeri Kouklis*, Tripodon 14, an old-style ouzeri with an oak-beamed ceiling, marble tables and wicker chairs. It serves only mezedes, which are brought round on a large tray so you can take your pick. They include flaming sausages (ignited at your table) and cuttlefish for 800 dr, as well as the usual dips for 400 dr. The whole selection, enough for four hungry people, costs 6400 dr. Draught red wine is 800 dr and ouzo is 1000 dr. The ouzeri is open for lunch and dinner and it gets very busy later in the evening. Tripodon is the first street on the right off Thespidos (the

ATHENS

continuation of Kydathineon) as you climb up the hill from Adrianou.

Vegetarian restaurants are thin on the ground in Athens. The *Eden Vegetarian Restaurant*, Lyssiou 12, is one of only three. (The others are in Koukaki and Omonia and are discussed later.) The Eden has been around for years, substituting soya products for meat in tasty vegetarian versions of moussaka (1250 dr) and other Greek favourites. The restaurant was previously at Flessa 3. Lyssiou leads off to the left at the northwestern end of Tripodon.

With such an emphasis on outdoor eating in summer, it's no great surprise that the three cellar restaurants on Kydathineon are closed from mid-May until October. They are also three of Plaka's cheapest places. You can expect to pay about 1500 dr per person for a main dish washed down with half a litre of draught retsina. They include the *Taverna Damigos*, at No 41, which claims to be the oldest taverna in Plaka, opened in 1865 by the Damigos family. Unfortunately, the family photographs that bedeck the walls are much more interesting than the food. The *galaktopoleio* next door, at No 43, has takeaway crêpes, both savoury and sweet. Prices start at 450 dr. The taverna known as *The Cellar* is downstairs at No 10. It looks promising with its colourful murals of carousing Athenians, but the food is a bit pale. The *galaktopoleio* at No 10 serves breakfast. In the evening, the tables outside are a popular spot for a beer.

The third of the cellar places is the *Taverna Saita*, at No 21, near the Museum of Greek Folk Art. It is more rough and ready but turns out tastier food.

Peristeria Taverna, next to John's Place at Patröou 5, is the best of the Plaka cheapies and is open all year. Chicken, moussaka and meatballs are all 1000 dr and draught retsina is 600 dr. Patröou is the fourth street on the left down Mitropoleos from Syntagma.

The old-fashioned *galaktopoleio* nearby, at Apollonos 11, is another of the very few places serving breakfast. It turns out bacon and eggs for 800 dr; or coffee, toast and jam for 550 dr.

Monastiraki There are some excellent cheap eats around Plateia Monastirakiou, particularly for gyros fans. The two restaurants opposite each other at the bottom end of Mitropoleos offer good food – and great theatre. It's astonishing to watch the speed at which these places work; the waiters run to keep up with demand. *Savas*, at Mitropoleos 86, has a slightly better selection than the other one. It has a takeaway stall serving gyros with a choice of chicken (300 dr), pork or minced beef (both 250 dr), and a restaurant (there's a shop in between) with seating in the square opposite. The restaurant charges an extra 60 dr per gyros, but also has salads and side dishes such as baked peppers. *Grigoris*, at Mitropoleos 88, serves good coffee a lot cheaper than anywhere else around. Greek coffee is 170 dr, filter coffee is 230 dr, espresso 280 dr and cappuccino 300 dr.

An old Athens taverna with loads of atmosphere is the cavernous *Sigalas Taverna*, Plateia Monastirakiou 2. The taverna, established in 1879, has huge barrels of retsina lining its walls. Tzatziki, aubergine dip and taramasalata are all 440 dr, and moussaka and stuffed tomatoes are both 950 dr. The taverna is open from 6 am to 2 am every day. The taverna is on the right at the bottom of Mitropoleos – it's the building with the four old-fashioned, wrought-iron lamps outside.

The best taverna food in this part of town is at the *meat market*, 400 metres along Athinas from Plateia Monastirakiou, on the right. The place must resemble a vegetarian's vision of hell, but the food is great and the tavernas are open 24 hours a day, except Sunday. They serve traditional meat dishes such as patsas (tripe soup), podarakia (pig-trotter soup) as well as less exotic dishes such as stifado and meatballs. Soups start at 600 dr, and main dishes at 1000 dr.

Opposite the meat market is the main *fruit & vegetable market*, where you'll find the widest range of whatever's in season and the best prices. The stretch of Athinas between the meat market and Plateia Monistirakiou is the place to shop for nuts and nibblies.

O Telis psistaria, at the junction of

Evripidou and Epikourou near Plateia Eleftherias, is famous for its only dish – pork
chops and chips. A huge pile of chips topped
by three or four chops costs 1100 dr. The
Olympic Restaurant, nearby on Plateia Eleftherias, is a very good cheap taverna. It has
spaghetti with tomato sauce for 350 dr and
soups for 540 dr as well as delicious macaroni with octopus for 1100 dr. To get to these
restaurants, head north along Athinas from
Plateia Monastirakiou and turn left onto
Evripidou before the meat market.

There are a couple of good places to eat in
the flea market. *Epiros Taverna*, Filippou 16,
has cheap ,tasty food. The outdoor tables are
great in summer for watching the market's
hustle and bustle.

The *Taverna Abyssinia*, on the western
side of nearby Plateia Abyssinias, does a
roaring trade on Sunday market days when
it has live folk music.

Syntagma Fast-food is the order of the day
at busy Syntagma. The self-serve salad bar
at *Wendy's*, at the junction of Stadiou and
Voukourestiou, is one of the best deals
around with a choice of about 20 salads.
Vegetarians beware – many of the salads
have meat in them. You can pile enough on
a small plate (680 dr) to constitute a meal. A
large serve is 920 dr.

The *Neon Café*, at the south-western
corner of Plateia Syntagmatos, is a stylish
self-service cafeteria. It has spaghetti or
fettucine with a choice of sauces for 780 dr,
moussaka for 1350 dr and roast beef for 1680
dr. It is probably the only eating place in
Athens with a non-smoking area.

It's very hard to ignore the delicious
aromas emanating from the *Brazil Coffee
Shop* on Voukourestiou (between Panepistimiou and Stadiou). It has Greek coffee for
250 dr, filter coffee for 350 dr and espresso
for 500 dr, plus cakes and croissants priced
from 250 dr.

Veïkou & Koukaki The *Gardenia Restaurant*, Zini 31, at the junction with
Dimitrakopoulou, claims to be the cheapest
taverna in Athens. I wouldn't doubt it. A plate

of gigantes beans is 450 dr, chicken and
potatoes 550 dr, and moussaka is 650 dr. A
large Amstel beer costs 230 dr, and a litre of
draught retsina is 400 dr. What's more, the
food is good and the service is friendly. The
owner is an effervescent woman called Gogo
who speaks English.

On the opposite side of the road at Zini 26
is *Meltemi Ouzeri*, Zini 26, a pleasant spot
with white, stucco walls, marble-topped
tables and blue-painted wooden chairs, all of
which give the place a Cycladic-island feel.
In summer, an outside eating area is shielded
from the traffic by large pot plants. There is
a wide choice of delicious mezedes priced
from 450 dr, or you can try a mixed plate for
1000 dr.

To 38 Taverna, Veïkou 38, is another
good-value establishment. The restaurant is
lively, rough and ready, and very popular. A
generous serving of crisp fried cod costs
1200 dr, and a plate of cuttlefish cooked with
spinach is 920 dr. There is no name on the
door, only the number. There's a barber's
shop next door. It is open in the evening from
8 pm, but is closed from 1 June to 15 September.

The *Diavlos Vegetarian Restaurant &
Music Bar*, Drakou 9, has the most extensive
vegetarian menu in town, with more than 50
dishes to choose from. These include home-
made pies with chips and salad (from 1000
dr), croquettes and fritters (1000 dr), soya
moussaka (1300 dr) and tofu curry with rice
(1500 dr). Diavolos is open every day from
10 am to 3 am. The place tends to be deserted
until the rembetika music starts at about
11 pm.

Omonia The *Vegetarian Fast Food* restaurant, Panepistimiou 55, offers a choice of
three dishes from its buffet for 700 dr, as well
as portions of wholemeal pizza and pies for
400 dr. You can wash your meal down with
a fresh carrot juice for 300 dr. There is also
a well-stocked health-food shop, which
carries a small range of biodynamic produce.

The choice of fast-food outlets at Plateia
Omonias includes *Pitta Pan*, which brings
McDonald's-style marketing slickness to the

ATHENS

humble gyros and souvlaki. Their basic-model pork gyros sells for 355 dr and a plain souvlaki goes for 295 dr. Pitta Pan is on the corner of the square between Athinas and Pireos.

Right next to Pitta Pan is the *Café Brettania*, which is one of the nicest things about Omonia. The décor is pleasant, with marble tables and wrought-iron chairs; the food is great and the waiters are courteous. It has a large variety of beverages: cappuccino is 480 dr and soft drinks are 250 dr. The café is open 24 hours a day, with free entertainment provided by a clientele that gets more and more weird as the night progresses.

The *Neon Café* occupies a beautiful neo-classical building on the corner of Dorou, on the opposite side of the square. It is a stable-mate of the Neon at Syntagma and serves the same fare.

Exarhia Exarhia has lots of ouzeria and tavernas to choose from, and prices are tailored to suit the pockets of the district's student clientele. It's quite a long hike to the area from Syntagma. The alternative is to catch a No 230 bus from Amalias or Panepistimiou to Harilaou Trikoupi and walk across. It is, however, only a short walk from the National Archaeological Museum to lively Plateia Exarhion. The square (triangle actually) is lined with cafés and snack bars, many with seating under shade.

The café behind the National Archaeological Museum, at Bouboulinas 34, has a mixed plate of mezedes for two people for 1200 dr and toasted sandwiches with a large choice of fillings priced from 250 dr. The café is closed on Sunday.

Most of the better eating places are south of Plateia Exarhion. The *Ouzeri Refenes*, Emmanual Benaki 51, is a friendly place run by a woman from the island of Ikaria. The customers all seem to be fellow islanders. The mixed plate of mezedes is very good value for 1000 dr, and beers are 300 dr. The *Ouzeri I Gonia* is another good place a bit further up the hill at Arahovis 59, on the corner of Emmanual Benaki. It has a good

range of tasty mezedes priced between 500 and 950 dr, and ouzo is 600 dr a bottle.

The *Taverna Barbargiannis*, Emmanual Benaki 94 on the corner of Dervenion, serves a delicious thick chicken soup for 950 dr that comes with a generous portion of chicken on the side. It also serves a tasty bean soup for 650 dr as well as a selection of meat dishes for under 1200 dr.

Another good place is the *Taverna Rozalia*, Valtetsiou 58. In summer, it has outdoor seating in the garden opposite under a tangle of trees and vines. It has a large range of mezedes priced from 450 dr, but casseroles are the speciality. The pork in lemon sauce and the beef in wine both cost 1500 dr and come in individual clay pots.

Gargadovas Taverna, Isavron 29B, serves mezedes to serious night owls. There is no menu; the night's offerings are brought round on a tray for you to take your pick. All are priced from 400 to 800 dr. It's open from 9.30 pm to 6 am, closed on Sunday.

Walls lined with old prints, marble-top tables, raffia chairs and polished timber floors create a very Bohemian atmosphere at *Taverna Efimero*, Methonis 58. Mezedes range in price from 400 to 650 dr, and main courses start at 950 dr.

Taverna Ta Bakiria, Mavromihali 119, has a lovely traditional décor with brass and copper trays and ceramic dishes hanging on the walls. It serves a good range of grilled meats, and very tasty casseroles delicately flavoured with herbs. Wine is priced from 1200 to 1600 dr.

Around the Train Stations Wherever you choose to eat in this area you will find the lack of tourist hype refreshing – it's a million miles from the strategically placed menus and restaurant touts of Plaka.

O Makis Psistaria, at Psaron 48 opposite the church, is a lively place serving hunks of freshly grilled pork or beef, plus chips, for 1200 dr. Just north of Plateia Vathis, *O Vaggelis Taverna*, Liossion 21 (the entrance is around the corner on Sahini), is an unpretentious traditional taverna with garden seating in summer. Main dishes are priced

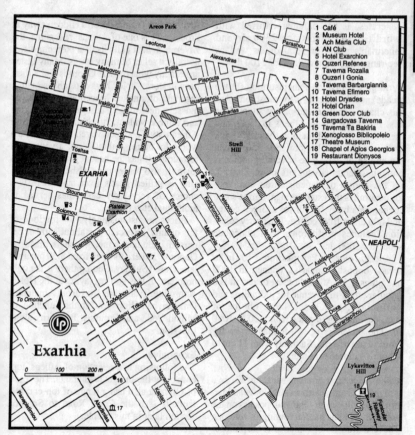

1	Café
2	Museum Hotel
3	Ach Maria Club
4	AN Club
5	Hotel Exarchion
6	Ouzeri Refenes
7	Taverna Rozalia
8	Ouzeri I Gonia
9	Taverna Barbargiannis
10	Taverna Efimero
11	Hotel Dryades
12	Hotel Orian
13	Green Door Club
14	Gargadovas Taverna
15	Taverna Ta Bakiria
16	Xenoglosso Bibliopoleio
17	Theatre Museum
18	Chapel of Agios Georgios
19	Restaurant Dionysos

Exarhia

from 900 to 1250 dr, and a litre of retsina is 600 dr.

The *Dafni Taverna*, further north at Ioulianou 65, offers equally good value with very tasty gigantes beans for 700 dr and moussaka for 950 dr. In summer, there's outdoor seating in the small courtyard.

Mid-Range

Plaka *Tristato Café*, in Plaka on the corner of Dedalou and Angelou Geronta, is a 1920s-style coffee shop which is very popular with young Athenians. Coffees are 700 dr and

there is a large selection of tempting cakes for 700 dr.

The *Taverna O Thespis*, at the top end of Thespidos, has a great setting on the lower slopes of the Acropolis with seating under the trees in the small square outside. The speciality here is bekri meze (beef in a spicy tomato sauce) for 2150 dr. Thespidos is the south-western extension of Kydathineon, beyond Adrianou, that leads uphill towards the Acropolis.

The *Diogenes Taverna*, Plateia Lysikratous 1 at the southern end of Sellev, has outdoor seating near the Monument of

Lysicrates. It has calamari stuffed with swordfish and clams for 2300 dr and fisherman's pilaf for 1600 dr, as well as free-range chicken souvlaki for 2100 dr.

Syntagma *Floca*, on Panepistimiou (in the arcade) near Syntagma, is the most central of this chain of coffee-and-pastry shops. The first Floca opened in Athens in 1939, and there are now 14 of them in the city. Greek coffee is 450 dr, filter coffee is 550 dr and the choice of chocolate-covered goodies is enough to tempt anyone off a diet. *Zonar's*, on the corner of Panepistimiou and Voukourestiou, is the establishment coffee shop. It charges a hefty 600 dr for a Greek coffee and 800 dr for filter coffee. The pastry selection includes profiteroles with chocolate sauce for 1000 dr.

Apotsos Ouzeri, Panepistimiou 10 (in an arcade opposite Zonar's), opened in 1900 and plans to be Athens' oldest ouzeri. It is a popular lunch-time venue for journalists and politicians, and has a large choice of mezedes ranging in price from 400 to 1000 dr. The ouzeri is open Monday to Friday from 11 am to 5 pm, Saturday from 11 am to 4 pm. It's closed on Sunday.

Veïkou *Socrates Prison*, Mitseon 20, is a delightful taverna with an Art Nouveau interior and 19th-century Parisian posters on the walls. It also has garden seating in summer. The restaurant is not named after the philosopher, but after the owner (also called Socrates) who reckons the restaurant is his prison. It has an imaginative range of mezedes from 450 dr and main dishes from 1250 dr. The restaurant is closed from 10 to 31 August.

To Dichty, near the corner of Veïkou and Olympiou, is an up-market ouzeri with a nautical bent. Its walls are decked out with fishing nets, plastic lobsters and lifebuoys. The range of mezedes includes peppers with regato cheese (600 dr), fried savoury octopus (1200 dr), mussels with fried cheese (1500 dr) and cuttlefish cooked in red wine (1300 dr). It's open Monday to Saturday from 6 pm to 2 am.

Around the Train Stations Hidden away at Proussis 21 is one of Athens' real gems, the *Taverna Avli*. It calls itself a *mezedopoleio*, literally a seller of many tastes. Many tastes are exactly what owners Georgos and Krissa have in store – spicy Mykonos cheese salad, saganaki of smoked Macedonian cheese or mussels, deep-fried 'sausages' of aubergine and minced walnut, zucchini fritters, North African-style chopped vegetable salad and a whole lot more. Although not a vegetarian restaurant, it has the best vegetarian food in town. It also serves meat dishes. The speciality is grilled goat's liver, and there is a choice of very tasty casseroles served in individual clay pots.

Prices are astonishingly low for food of this quality. Expect to pay about 2500 dr per person including wine, which is made by Georgos' father. It's open from 8.30 pm until late, closed Sunday. Getting there is the only problem, unless you're staying at the Hostel Aphrodite. Trolleybus No 1 from Amalias or Omonia can drop you at the junction of Mihail Voda and Proussis. It returns along Liossion.

Expensive

The following is a selection of Athens' top-end, blow-the-budget restaurants. The resort of Glyfada also has a range of top-end restaurants (see the Coast Road to Sounion section later in this chapter).

Plaka & Syntagma The Hotel Grande Bretagne's *GB Corner* restaurant has a set menu for 6000 dr for both lunch and dinner. It serves international dishes as well as local specialities such as Athenian tripe soup.

Asian food is at the luxury end of the scale in Athens. The *Michiko Japanese Restaurant* (☎ 322 0980), Kydathineon 27, is housed in Plaka's largest surviving mansion. It has a shady front garden with seating around an ornamental pool. The menu includes a range of three-course meals priced from 5500 dr.

The *Orient Restaurant*, Leka 26, has an extensive menu of Szechwan, Cantonese and Korean dishes, including a range of set menus for 5000 dr. The *Far East Restaurant*, in the arcade at Stadiou 7, has a spacious, elegant oriental interior and serves Korean, Japanese and Chinese cuisine at similar prices.

Monastiraki The menu at *Pit Poule* (☎ 342 3665), Apostolou Pavlou 51 on the corner of Poulopoulou, serves French Mediterranean food. Budget on upwards of 12,000 dr per person, excluding wine. It's open from 8 pm every day except Sunday.

Omonia The *Ideal Restaurant* (☎ 461 4604), Panepistimiou 46 (next to the Ideal Cinema), is a long-established favourite with Athenians. The interior is Art Deco and the menu has a mixture of Greek, Turkish and European dishes with daily specials. Expect to pay upwards of 6000 dr per person, excluding wine.

Veïkou *Symposio* (☎ 922 5321), south of the Acropolis at Erehthiou 46, is one of Athens' most elegant restaurants. It occupies a beautifully restored 1920s house, and offers a menu loaded with caviar, foie gras and smoked salmon. The salad of smoked salmon, prawns and caviar with vodka dressing (2800 dr) gives a fair indication of what's in store. The wine list is similarly top of the range. You can reckon on paying at least 10,000 dr per person, excluding wine. It's open from 8 pm until late, closed Sunday. Reservations are recommended.

Kolonaki There's no finer view in Athens than that offered by the *Restaurant Dionysos*, at the top of Lykavittos hill – accessible by the funicular railway. It has set menus for 4200 and 5900 dr as well as à la carte. It's open from 9 am until midnight.

Ilissia The Athens Hilton, in the district of Ilissia, just east of Kolonaki, has several restaurants. *Ta Nissia Restaurant*, which specialises in mezedes and fish dishes, is very popular with well-heeled Athenians. Dinner here will cost around 7500 dr.

ENTERTAINMENT
Cinema
Athenians are avid cinema-goers. Most cinemas show recent releases from Britain and the USA in English. The two areas with the highest concentration of cinemas are the main streets running between Syntagma and Omonia and the Patission and Plateia Amerikis area.

The major cinemas in central Athens are the *Apollon* (☎ 323 6811), Stadiou 19; *Astor* (☎ 323 1297), Stadiou 28; *Asty* (☎ 322 1925), Koraï 4; *Elly* (☎ 363 2789), Akadimias 64; *Ideal* (☎ 382 6720), Panepistimiou 46; and *Titania* (☎ 381 1147), on the corner of Panepistimiou and Themistokleous. The Asty shows mostly avant-garde films; the others show mostly first-run films (usually from Britain or the USA with Greek subtitles). Shows start at approximately 7, 9 and 11 pm.

Outside the central area, the *Ilion* (☎ 881 0602), on the corner of Troias 34 and 28 Oktovriou-Patission, shows mainly foreign-language (not English or Greek) films. The *Greek Cinema Club* (☎ 361 2046), Kanaris 1, Kolonaki, regularly shows avant-garde films, both Greek and international. All the major cinemas have listings in the *Athens News*, *Athenscope* and the *Weekly Greek News*. Admission costs between 1200 and 1500 dr.

Many of the indoor cinemas close between the end of May and mid-September, when the action moves to outdoor cinemas on the coast. They show mainly re-runs of old favourites. Going to the outdoor cinema tends to be a social occasion more than anything, so there's a lot of audience noise. There are two showings per evening: the early show starts around dusk and the late show at about 11 pm.

Theatre
Athens has a dynamic theatre scene, but, as you'd expect, most performances are in Greek. If you're a theatre buff you may enjoy a performance of an old favourite, provided you know the play well enough. The *Weekly Greek News* has a cursory listing, but the

listings in *Athenscope* are more comprehensive. They both state when a performance is in English – which happens occasionally.

Greek Folk Dancing

In summer, performances of Greek folk dances are given by the *Dora Stratou Dance Company* at their own theatre (☎ 324 4395) on Filopappos hill. The company was formed many years ago and has gained an international reputation for authenticity and professionalism. Performances are held nightly at 10.15 pm from May to October, with additional performances at 8.15 pm on Wednesday and Sunday. Tickets may be bought at the door and cost 1500 dr. The theatre is signposted from the western end of Dionysiou Areopagitou. The troupe occasionally holds dance workshops, which are advertised in the *Weekly Greek News*.

Concerts, Opera, Ballet & Contemporary Dance

There are frequent classical-music concerts, by both international and Greek performers, at the *Athens Concert Hall* (Megaron Mousikis) (☎ 728 2333), Vasilissis Sofias (next to the US Embassy). Dance performances and jazz concerts are also held here. The *Pallas Theatre* (☎ 322 4434), Voukourestiou 1, also has performances of classical music. The *Olympia Theatre* (☎ 361 2461) has performances of both ballet and opera by the National Opera (Ethniki Lyriki Skini) (☎ 361 2461), Akadimias 59. Dance performances are also given at the *Politechno Theatres* (☎ 651 4746), opposite the Alphaville cinema on Mavromihali, and at *Athens College Theatre* (☎ 647 4676), Stefanou Delta, Psyhiko.

If anything big is happening, posters will be displayed, and tickets will be for sale at the box office in the arcade at Stadiou 4. The English-language newspapers, *Athenscope* and the *Athenian* publish listings.

Son et Lumière

Athens' endeavour at this spectacle is not one of the world's best, but it is an enduring and integral part of the Athens tourist scene.

There are shows in English every night at 9 pm from the beginning of April until the end of October at the theatre on the Hill of the Pnyx (☎ 322 1459). There are shows in French at 10 pm every night except Tuesday and Friday, when the show is in German. During the performance, the monuments of the Acropolis are lit up in synchronisation with the accompanying music, sound effects, and historical narration. The lights are the most exciting part of the performance. Tickets cost 1500 dr. The Hill of the Pnyx is west of the Acropolis off Dionysiou Areopagitou. Bus No 230 from Syntagma will get you there.

Music Bars

Steven's Pub, Dionysiou Areopagitou 3 on the corner of Tzireon, is a good place to meet other travellers. Draught beer is 600 dr a pint and cocktails are 1200 dr. Western pop music is played and there's a small dance floor.

Over in Mets, *Stadio*, on the corner of Markou Mousourou and Ardittou, is a favoured venue of Athenian sophisticates. There's a roof terrace in summer with good views of the Acropolis. There's no cover charge but drinks are expensive.

Booze, next to the Hotel Carolina at Kolokotroni 57, has a huge collection of alternative rock music from around the world. It's open every day, except Sunday, from 11 pm until 3 am. Admission is 1000 dr, which includes your first drink.

In Kolonaki, *The Cave*, at Haritos 6, looks like a real cave with a few strategically placed helmets for added authenticity. Music is techno and jazz only. Cocktails start at 1300 dr and beer is 800 dr.

The highest concentration of music bars is in Exarhia. The *Green Door Club*, Kalidromiou 52 at the junction with Emmanual Benaki, is one of the most popular. If you want to hear some good music and have a conversation at the same time, then try the *Passenger Club*, 1st Floor, Mavromihali 168. The music is mellow (mostly jazz and R&B), with no hard rock or heavy metal. Cocktails are priced from 1200 dr, spirits are 1000 dr and beer 800 dr.

Two bars to stay clear of are *Club 11*, Nikis 11, and *Paper Moon*, Nikis 1. Both employ touts to roam Syntagma and Plaka, targeting male tourists with talk of beautiful girls. The girls then persuade suckers to buy them ludicrously overpriced drinks.

Gay Bars
A popular bar with gays (male) is *Alexander Club*, Anagnostopoulou 44, Kolonaki. It's a relaxed, friendly place and is open every night from 9 pm to 2 am throughout the year. Another popular gay place is *Granazi Bar*, Lembesi 20, which is south of Hadrian's Arch and east of Syngrou.

Discos
Discos operate in Athens only between October and April. In summer, the action moves to the coastal suburbs of Ellinikon and Glyfada. There are more discos around the Mikrolimano in Piraeus.

The closest disco to Plaka is *Disco Absolut*, Filellinon 23, where anyone over 25 may well feel geriatric. The *Wild Rose*, in the arcade at Panepistimiou 10, is also popular.

Aerodhromio, opposite the airport (East Terminal) at Ellinikon, has an open-air dance floor. Admission at most places ranges from 1000 dr on weekdays to 3000 dr on Friday and Saturday nights. The price often includes one free drink. Subsequently, expect to pay about 600 dr for soft drinks, 1000 dr for a beer and 1500 dr for spirits. Discos don't start to get busy until around midnight.

Live Music
The best place to hear rock music is the *Rodon Club* (☎ 524 7427), Marni 24, which has bands most Fridays and Saturdays. It often has international bands. Gigs are listed in *Athenscope*. Other venues are the *Ach Maria Club* (☎ 363 9217), Solomou 20; and the *AN Club*, Solomou 13-15, in Exarhia. The *Rock Club*, at Emmanual Benaki 3 – formerly a gay bar called The Factory, also has bands occasionally. If anything exciting is going on at any of these places you'll see posters all over Exarhia.

Rembetika Clubs
Athens has a good number of rembetika clubs, but most close down from May to September. Performances in these clubs start at around 11.30 pm; most places do not have a cover charge but drinks are expensive – sometimes as much as 3000 dr for spirits. Clubs open up and close down with great rapidity – telephone to check if a club is still open. The biggest concentration of clubs is in and around Exarhia.

Taxima (☎ 383 9919), Isavron 29, is a well-established, friendly club in a traditionally furnished neoclassical house. The club is closed on Sunday. *Frangosyriani* (☎ 380 0693), Arahovis 57, is reputedly one of the most authentic clubs. It's closed on Tuesday and Wednesday. *Kavouras* (☎ 381 0202), Themistokleous 64, is another club in a neoclassical house. It's closed on Sunday. *Minore* (☎ 823 8630), Notara 34, is popular with young people and there's lots of dancing. It's open Friday to Sunday.

A more central club is the *Rembetiki Stoa Athanaton* (☎ 321 4362), at Sofokleous 19, next to the central meat market. Unusually, for a rembetika club, it's open in the afternoon from 3 to 6 pm and reopens from midnight until 6 am. It's closed on Sunday.

Spectator Sports
Soccer Six of the 18 teams in the Greek Soccer League's first division are from Athens. They are AEK, Apollon, Athinikos, Olympiakos, Panathinaïkos and Panionios. Two other Athenian clubs, Ethnikos and Ionikis, fluctuate between the first and second divisions. AEK plays at the Nea Philadelphia Stadium; Apollon at Rizoupolis; Athinikos at Vyronas; Panionios at Nea Smyrni; and Panathinaïkos at the Panathinaïkos Stadium, Leoforos Alexandras 160, just north of Lykavittos hill.

Olympiakos and Ethnikos play at the Karaïskaki Stadium in Piraeus on alternate weeks. Olympiakos is the most popular team – the Greek equivalent of Manchester United – and its main rival is wealthy Panathinaïkos, which won both the first division championship and Greek Cup in 1995. First division matches are played on Sunday and cup matches on Wednesday. They are often televised. Entry to a match costs an average of 1200 dr.

The soccer season lasts from September to the middle of May. Fixtures and results are given in the *Weekly Greek News*.

Horse Racing Horse races are held three times a week at the Faliro Ippodromo (☎ 941 7761) at the southern end of Syngrou. Bus No 126 from Syntagma will take you there. Meetings are normally held on Monday, Wednesday and Friday, starting at about 2 pm.

THINGS TO BUY
Flea Market
This market is the first place which springs to most people's minds when they think of buying things in Athens. The flea market is the commercial area which stretches both east and west of Plateia Monastirakiou and consists of shops selling goods running the whole gamut from high quality to trash. However, when most people speak of the Athens flea market, they are referring to the outdoor flea market which takes place on Sunday morning. This market spills over into Plateia Monastirakiou and all the way down Ermou to the entrance to the Keramikos.

A visit to Athens isn't complete without a visit to this market. All manner of things are on sale – new, second-hand, third-hand and fourth-hand. There's everything from clocks to condoms, binoculars to bouzoukis, tyres to telephones, giant evil eyes to jelly babies, and wigs to welding kits. Wandering around the market, you'll soon realise that Greece is top of the league of European countries when it comes to mass-produced kitsch. If you're looking for a plastic jewellery box with a psychedelic picture of the Virgin Mary on the lid, which plays 'Never on a Sunday' when you open it, you might just be in luck at the flea market.

Flokati Rugs
Most of Athens' flokati-rug shops are on or around Mitropoleos. Karamihos Mazarakis

Flokati, at Voulis 31-33, has the largest selection of rugs.

Traditional Handcrafts
The National Welfare Organisation's Hellenic Folk Art Gallery, on the corner of Apollonos and Ipatias, Plaka, is a good place to go shopping for handcrafts. It has top-quality merchandise and the money goes to a good cause – the preservation and promotion of traditional Greek handcrafts. It has a wide range of knotted carpets, kilims, flokatis, needle-point rugs and embroidered cushion covers as well as a small selection of pottery, copper and woodwork. The shop is open Tuesday to Friday from 9 am to 8 pm, Monday and Saturday from 9 am to 3 pm, and is closed on Sunday. The organisation has another branch at Vassilis Sofias 135, at the junction with Alexandras.

The Centre of Hellenic Tradition, Pandrossou 36, Plaka, has a display of traditional and modern handcrafts from each region of Greece. Most of the items are for sale.

Mado, next to the Lysicrates monument on Sellev, Plaka, is a workshop that turns out beautiful, handwoven wall-hangings. Many depict island scenes.

Good-quality leather sandals may be bought from Stavros Melissinos, Pandrossou 89 (see the Walking Tour section earlier).

GETTING THERE & AWAY
Air
Athens is served by Ellinikon airport, on the coast nine km south-east of the city. There are two terminals with separate entrances 1.5 km apart: the West Terminal for all Olympic Airways flights (domestic and international) and the East Terminal for all other flights.

The facilities are dreadful at both terminals, and are the subject of constant complaint by hotel and tour operators as well as travellers. Nothing is likely to change, however, until the new international airport at Spata (21 km east of Athens) is completed. That's not scheduled to happen until 1998. Ellinikon will then handle only domestic flights.

For Olympic Airways flight information ing ☎ 936 3363 and for all other airlines ring ☎ 969 9466/9467. The head office of Olympic Airways (☎ 926 9111) is at Leoforos Syngrou 96. The most central Olympic Airways branch office (domestic: ☎ 926 7235; international: ☎ 926 7489) is at Othonos 6, Plateia Syntagmatos. For information about domestic flights from Athens see the Getting Around chapter. There is luggage storage (open 24 hours; 700 dr per piece) at the East Terminal, opposite the domestic arrivals.

Athens is one of Europe's major centres for buying discounted air tickets. There are dozens of travel agents on Filellinon, Nikis and Voulis which sell low-priced air tickets to Europe and the USA. See the Travel Agencies section under Information at the beginning of this chapter for some recommendations. Airline offices in Athens include:

Aeroflot	(☎ 322 0986)
Air Canada	(☎ 322 3206)
Air France	(☎ 323 8507/8509)
Air India	(☎ 360 2457)
Alitalia	(☎ 995 9200/9208)
American Airlines	(☎ 325 5061)
British Airways	(☎ 325 0601)
Continental Airlines	(☎ 324 9300)
Cyprus Airways	(☎ 324 6965)
CSA-Czech Airlines	(☎ 323 0174)
Delta Airlines	(☎ 323 5242)
El Al	(☎ 323 0116/0118)
Egypt Air	(☎ 323 8907/8908)
Garuda Indonesia	(☎ 360 6198)
Gulf Air	(☎ 322 0881)
KLM	(☎ 988 0177)
Lufthansa	(☎ 771 6002)
Qantas Airways	(☎ 323 9063/9066)
Singapore Airlines	(☎ 323 9111/9115)
South African Airways	(☎ 361 5111)
Thai Airways	(☎ 364 7610)
Turkish Airlines	(☎ 322 1035)
TWA	(☎ 322 6451)
Virgin Atlantic	(☎ 924 9100/9104)

Bus

Athens has two main intercity bus stations. Terminal A is north-west of Omonia at Leoforos Kifissou 100 and has departures to the Peloponnese, the Ionian islands and western Greece. Terminal B is north of Omonia off Liossion and has departures to central and northern Greece as well as to Evia. The EOT gives out an intercity bus schedule.

Terminal A To get there, take bus No 051 from the junction of Zinonos and Menandrou, near Omonia. Buses run every 15 minutes from 5 am to midnight. The table below shows the destination, journey time, fare and frequency of buses departing from this terminal:

Destination	Duration	Fare	Frequency
Argos	2 hours	1900 dr	hourly
Astakos	5 hours	4250 dr	3 daily
Corfu	11 hours	7450 dr	5 daily
		(with boat ticket)	
Corinth	1½ hours	1250 dr	half-hourly
Epidaurus	2½ hours	1950 dr	2 daily
Gythio	4½ hours	3750 dr	5 daily
Igoumenitsa	8½ hours	6900 dr	4 daily
Ioannina	7½ hours	6000 dr	9 daily
Kalamata	4½ hours	3500 dr	12 daily
Kavala	10 hours	9200 dr	3 daily
Kefallonia	8 hours	6200 dr	5 daily
Lefkada	5½ hours	5100 dr	4 daily
Loutraki	1½ hours	1250 dr	11 daily
Monemvassia	6½ hours	4550 dr	2 daily
Nafplio	2½ hours	2100 dr	hourly
(via Mycenae)		1750 dr	
Olympia	5½ hours	4650 dr	4 daily
Patras	3 hours	3000 dr	half-hourly
Pyrgos	5 hours	4350 dr	10 daily
Sparta	4½ hours	3050 dr	9 daily
Thessaloniki	7½ hours	6800 dr	10 daily
Zakynthos	7 hours	4895 dr	4 daily
		(with boat ticket)	

Terminal B The EOT information sheet misleadingly lists the address of the terminal as being Liossion 260, which turns out to be a small workshop. Liossion 260 is where you should get off the No 024 bus that runs from outside the main gate to the National Gardens on Amalias. From Liossion 260, turn right onto Gousiou and you'll see the terminal at the end of the road on Agiou Dimitriou Oplon. The table following shows the destination, journey time, fare and frequency of buses departing from this terminal:

Destination	Duration	Fare	Frequency
Agios Konstantinos	2½ hours	2450 dr	hourly
Delphi	3 hours	2400 dr	5 daily
Edipsos	3¼ hours	2200 dr	7 daily
Halkida	1½ hours	1100 dr	half-hourly
Karpenisi	6 hours	3950 dr	2 daily
Kymi	3½ hours	2400 dr	7 daily
Lamia	3¼ hours	2800 dr	hourly
Levadia	2 hours	1900 dr	hourly
Trikala	5½ hours	4450 dr	7 daily
Volos	6¼ hours	4350 dr	9 daily

Buses for nearly all destinations in Attica leave from the Mavromateon terminal at the junction of Alexandras and 28 Oktovriou-Patission, 250 metres north of the National Archaeological Museum. Buses for southern Attica leave from this terminal, while buses to Rafina and Marathon leave from the bus stops 150 metres north on Mavromateon.

Train
Trains for northern Greece, Evia and Europe leave from Larisis Station, Deligianni. Selected destinations, journey times, fares and frequency are:

Destination	Duration	Fare	Frequency
Alexandroupolis	14 hours	6300 dr** 9450 dr*	3 daily
Halkida	1½ hours	880 dr**	16 daily
Larisa	5 hours	2460 dr** 3690 dr*	14 daily
Thessaloniki	8 hours	3440 dr** 5160 dr*	10 daily
Volos	7 hours	2620 dr** 3930 dr*	5 daily
Xanthi	12 hours	5520 dr** 8280 dr*	3 daily

*1st class   **2nd class

Four of the trains to Thessaloniki are express intercity services which take six hours and cost more than twice the standard fare – 7140 dr in 2nd class, 8860 dr in 1st class. The 7 am service from Athens is express right through to Alexandroupolis, arriving at 7 pm. It will get you to Larisa in four hours and to Xanthi in 10½ hours. There also are two express trains a day to Volos, taking 4¾ hours. These other express services also cost about double the standard fare.

Couchettes are available on overnight services to Thessaloniki, priced from 1400 dr in 2nd class and 5400 dr in 1st class.

All trains for the Peloponnese leave from Peloponnese Station, which is on Sidirodromon. Selected destinations, journey times, fares and frequency are:

Destination	Duration	Fare	Frequency
Corinth	1¾ hours	780 dr** 1170 dr*	14 daily
Kalamata	6½ hours	2160 dr** 3240 dr*	4 daily
Kyparissia	6 to 8 hours	2560 dr** 3840 dr*	5 daily
Mycenae	2½ hours	900 dr** 1350 dr*	5 daily
Nafplio	3½ hours	1400 dr**	2 daily
Patras	3½ to 4½ hours	1580 dr** 2370 dr*	8 daily
Pyrgos	5 to 7 hours	2160 dr** 3240 dr*	6 daily
Tripolis	four hours	1500 dr** 2250 dr*	3 daily

*1st class   **2nd class

The two stations are very close to one another. To reach them take trolleybus No 1 from Syntagma. The stop is the same for both stations, but to get to Peloponnese Station cross over the metal bridge at the southern end of the Larisis Station.

There is baggage storage at Larisis Station; open from 6.30 am to 9.30 pm and the cost is 300 dr per piece. More information on services is available from the following OSE offices: Filellinon 17 (☎ 323 6747); Sina 6 (☎ 362 4402); and Karolou 1 (☎ 524 0647). These offices also handle advance bookings.

Car & Motorbike
National Road 1 is the main route north from Athens. It starts at Nea Kifissia. To get there from central Athens, take Vasilissis Sofias from Syntagma. National Road 8, which begins beyond Dafni, is the road to the Peloponnese. Take Agiou Konstantinou from Omonia.

The northern reaches of Syngrou, just south of the Temple of Olympian Zeus, are packed solid with car-rental firms. Local companies offer much better deals than their international rivals. Just Rent a Car (☎ 923 9104), Syngrou 43, is one of the best. Other outlets include:

Avis
    Amalias 48 (☎ 322 4951)
Budget
    Syngrou 8 (☎ 921 4771)
Eurodollar Rent a Car
    Syngrou 29 (☎ 922 9672)
Hertz
    Syngrou 12 (☎ 922 0102)

Campervans can be hired from Camper Caravans (☎ 323 0552), Nikis 4, and motorbikes are available from Motorent (☎ 923 4939), Falirou 5 (parallel to and east of Syngrou); and from Papavassiliou Eleftherios (☎ 325 0677), Asomaton 6, Thision.

Hitching

Athens is the most difficult place in Greece to hitchhike from. Your best bet is to ask the truck drivers at the Piraeus cargo wharves for a ride. Otherwise, for the Peloponnese, take bus No 860 or 880 from Panepistimiou to Dafni, where National Road 8 begins. For northern Greece, take the metro to Kifissia, then a bus to Nea Kifissia and walk to National Road 1.

GETTING AROUND
To/From the Airport

Express-line bus No 91 operates 24 hours a day between central Athens and the East and West terminals. The buses are blue and have their destination marked on the front in English. Coming from the airport, the service starts at the West Terminal and calls at the East Terminal before heading for the city. It stops at Stiles, just south of the Temple of Olympian Zeus (for Veïkou and Koukaki); at Amalias, opposite the National Gardens (for Syntagma); and at the northern end of Stadiou (for Omonia). Going to the airport, the main stops are on Stadiou (opposite Emmanual Benaki) and Syntagma (outside the Bank of Macedonia-Thrace).

The buses run every 30 minutes between 6 am and 9 pm, every 40 minutes from 9 pm until 12.20 am, and then hourly until 6 am. The night (early morning) buses leave Stadiou at 1.30, 2.30, 3.30, 4.30 and 5.30 am, arriving at Syntagma five minutes later. The fare is 160 dr, 200 dr from midnight to 6 am. Tickets can be bought from booths adjacent to the stops or on the bus. During rush hour the journey can take up to an hour. At other times, it should take about 30 minutes.

Passengers for the West Terminal also have the option of taking the Olympic Airways buses, which leave from the Olympic Airways terminal at Syngrou 96 (every 30 minutes, 6.30 am to 8.20 pm, 160 dr). Bus No 133 from Syntagma to Agios Kosmas (every 15 minutes, 5.40 am to midnight, 75 dr), and bus No 122 from Stadiou or Syntagma to Voula (every 15 minutes, 5.30 am to 11.30 pm, 75 dr) can drop you outside the terminal on Leoforos Poseidonos.

There are also express buses from both airport terminals to Plateia Karaïskaki in Piraeus. Buses leave the East Terminal at 6, 8.10, 9.10, 11.10 and 11.55 am, and at 1.30, 2.20, 3.50, 4.35, 6.25, 7.10 and 9.25 pm, calling at the West Terminal on the way to Piraeus. They leave Piraeus at 5, 7, 8, 9.50 and 10.50 am, and at 12.20, 1.10, 2.40, 3.30, 5.20, 6.05 and 8.20 pm.

A taxi to or from either airport terminal to central Athens costs about 2000 dr.

Bus & Trolleybus

Since most of Athens' ancient sites are within easy walking distance of Syntagma and many of the museums are close by on Vasilissis Sofias near Syntagma, the chances are that you won't have much need for public transport.

The blue-and-white buses that serve Athens and the suburbs operate every 15 minutes from 5 am until midnight. There are also green buses operating 24 hours a day between the city centre and Piraeus, every 20 minutes from 6 am until midnight and then hourly. Bus No 040 runs from Filellinon to Akti Xaveriou in Piraeus, and No 049 runs from the northern end of Athinas to Plateia Themistokleous.

Trolleybuses also operate from 5 am until midnight. The free map handed out by EOT shows most of the routes.

There is a flat fare of 75 dr throughout the city on both buses and trolleybuses. Tickets must be purchased before you board, either at a transport kiosk or a periptero. Most, but not all, periptera sell tickets. The same tickets can be used on either buses or trolleybuses. Tickets can be bought in blocks of 10, but there is no discount for bulk buying. Tickets must be validated using the red ticket machine as soon as you board a bus or trolleybus. Plain-clothed inspectors make spot checks, and the penalty for travelling without a validated ticket is 1500 dr. Monthly travel cards also are available for buses and trolleybuses. They are valid from the first day of each month to the last and cost 3750 dr.

Metro

Athens' metro is simple to understand and you cannot get lost as there is only one line, which is divided into three sections: Piraeus to Omonia, Omonia to Perissos and Perissos to Kifissia. The stations are: Piraeus, Faliro, Moshato, Kalithea, El Venizelou/Tavros, Petralona, Thision, Monastiraki, Omonia, Plateia Viktorias, Attiki, Agios Nikolaos, Kato Patissia, Perissos, Pefkakia, Nea Ionia, Iraklio, Irini, Maroussi, Kat and Kifissia. The line runs underground between Monastiraki and Attiki. The price of a ticket for travel within one or two sections is 75 dr and 100 dr for three sections. There are ticket machines and ticket booths at all stations. The machines for validating tickets are at the platform entrances. As with bus tickets, the penalty for travelling without a validated ticket is 1500 dr. The trains run every five minutes between 5 am and midnight.

A new metro system is under construction and is scheduled to open in 1998.

Taxi

Athens' taxis are yellow. If you see an Athenian standing in the road bellowing and waving their arms frantically, the chances are they will be trying to get a taxi at rush hour. Despite the large number of taxis careering around the streets of Athens, it can be incredibly difficult to get one.

To hail a taxi, stand on a pavement and shout your destination as they pass. If a taxi is going your way the driver may stop even if there are already passengers inside. This does not mean the fare will be shared: each person will be charged the fare shown on the meter. If you get in one which does not have other passengers, make sure the meter is switched on.

The flagfall is 200 dr, with a 160 dr surcharge from ports, railway and bus stations and a 300 dr surcharge from the airport. After that, the day rate (tariff 1 on the meter) is 58 dr per km. The rate doubles between midnight and 5 am (tariff 2 on the meter). Baggage is charged at the rate of 55 dr per item over 10 kg. The fare should be less than 400 dr for most journeys in central Athens. It sometimes helps if you can point out your destination on a map – many taxi drivers in Athens are extremely ignorant of their city.

If it is absolutely imperative that you get somewhere on time (eg to the airport), and you want to go by taxi, it is advisable to book a radio taxi – you will be charged 300 dr extra, but it's worth it. The radio taxis operating out of central Athens include:

Athina 1	(☎ 921 7942)
Enotita	(☎ 645 9000)
Ermis	(☎ 411 5200)
Ikaros	(☎ 513 2240)
Kosmos	(☎ 420 0042)
Parthenon	(☎ 582 1292)
Proödos	(☎ 643 3400)
Sata	(☎ 862 5407)

For more information about Athens' taxi drivers, including their legendary reputation and how they are (hopefully) mending their ways, see the Taxi section in the Getting Around chapter.

Car & Motorbike

Athens has a reputation as a nightmarish place to drive in, but it's probably no worse than negotiating your way around any other strange major city. The traffic jams at least offer an opportunity to work out where you're going! The most confusing aspects of driving in Athens are the one-way system that operates on most streets in central Athens, and the pedestrian precincts around Eolou and Plaka. Private vehicles are also barred from Ermou and Karageorgi Servias west of Syntagma under a trial scheme designed to reduce traffic pollution around Plaka. Other streets are expected to be added. Main routes through the city are clearly marked.

Athenian drivers have a cavalier attitude towards driving laws. Contrary to what you will see, parking *is* illegal alongside kerbs marked with yellow lines, where street signs prohibit parking and on pavements and pedestrian malls.

Athens has numerous small car parks, but these are totally insufficient for the large number of cars used in the city. There is an underground car park opposite the meat market on Athinas, with entry from Sokratous, and a multistorey car park is under construction on Amerikis.

For details of car and motorcycle-rental

Traffic Chaos

If your first introduction to Greece is Athens, the chances are you will soon be cursing cars like you've never done before. Despite the fact that Greeks have the second-lowest GDP per capita of all EU countries, there are more cars per head of population in Athens than in any other Mediterranean city.

The problems of traffic congestion and pollution have been testing the ingenuity of politicians and town planners for years. Ironically, the measures adopted to date have succeeded only in increasing the number of vehicles on the road.

The first measures came in 1980, when the famous odds and evens number-plate legislation was introduced. It banned odd and even plates from the city centre on alternate days. This, it was calculated, would halve the number of cars in the city centre. Instead, it resulted in many families purchasing a second car with the requisite odd or even number plate.

The next attempt, at the beginning of 1993, was more sophisticated – but equally ill fated. It was decreed that all cars in use in central Athens must be fitted with catalytic converters. This was promoted by a 1991 regulation reducing import taxes on cars with catalytic converters, as long as the owner scrapped a vehicle at least 15 years old. Many low-income families then became car owners for the first time by buying an old banger and trading it in for a new 'clean' car.

Recent attempts at restricting traffic have aimed at reducing the impact of vehicle emissions on the Acropolis and Plaka. The tactic of closing certain streets around Plaka to private vehicles was hailed as a great success after a brief trial in May and June 1995.

The great hope for a long-term solution to the problem is the new metro system, due for completion in 1998. In the meantime, the works merely worsen the situation. ■

agencies in Athens, see the previous Getting There & Away section.

Bicycle
The sports department of Klaoudatos, the large department store on Athinas, near Omonia, hires out good mountain bikes for 3000 dr per day.

Around Athens

PIRAEUS Πειραιάς
Piraeus (in Greek Pi-re-AS) is the port of Athens, the main port of Greece and one of the major ports of the Mediterranean. It's the hub of the Aegean ferry network, the centre for Greece's maritime export-import and transit trade and the base for its large merchant navy. Nowadays, Athens has expanded sufficiently to meld imperceptibly into Piraeus. The road linking the two passes through a grey, urban sprawl of factories, warehouses and concrete apartment blocks. Piraeus is as bustling and traffic-congested as Athens. It's not a place in which many visitors want to linger; most come merely to catch a ferry.

History
The histories of Athens and Piraeus are inextricably linked. Piraeus has been the port of Athens since classical times, when Themistocles transferred his Athenian fleet from the exposed port of Phaleron (modern Faliro) to the security of Piraeus. After his victory over the Persians at the Battle of Salamis in 480 BC, Themistocles fortified Piraeus' three natural harbours. In 445 BC Pericles extended these fortifying walls to Athens and Phaleron. The Long Walls, as they were known, were destroyed as one of the peace conditions imposed by the Spartans at the end of the Peloponnesian Wars, but were rebuilt in 394 BC.

Piraeus was a flourishing commercial centre during the classical age, but by Roman times it had been overtaken by Rhodes, Delos and Alexandria. During medieval and Turkish times it diminished to a tiny fishing village, and by the time of Independence it was home to less than 20 people. Its resurgence began in 1834 when Athens became the capital of independent Greece. By the beginning of this century it had superseded the island of Syros as Greece's principal port. In 1923 its population was swollen by the arrival of 100,000 refugees from Turkey. The Piraeus which evolved from this influx had a seedy but somewhat romantic appeal with its bordellos, hashish dens and rembetika music – all vividly portrayed in the film *Never on a Sunday*.

These places have long since gone and beyond its façade of smart, new shipping offices and banks, much of Piraeus is now just plain seedy. The exception is the eastern quarter around Zea Marina and Mikrolimano, where the seafront is lined with seafood restaurants, bars and discos.

Orientation
Piraeus is 10 km south-west of central Athens. The largest of the three harbours is the Great Harbour (Megas Limin), on the western side of the Piraeus peninsula. All ferries leave from here. Zea Marina (Limin Zeas), on the other side of the peninsula, is the port for hydrofoils to the Saronic Gulf islands (except Aegina) as well as being the place where millionaires moor their yachts. North-east of here is the picturesque Mikrolimano (small harbour), which is brimming with private yachts.

The quickest and easiest way of getting to Piraeus from central Athens is by metro, which terminates at the north-eastern corner of the Great Harbour on Akti Kalimassioti. Most ferry departure points are a short walk from here. A left turn out of the metro station leads after 250 metres to Plateia Karaïskaki, which is the terminus for buses to the airport. Jutting out into the harbour behind the square is Akti Tzelepi with its mass of ticket agencies. Continuing south around the harbour from Plateia Karaïskaki, the waterfront becomes Akti Poseidonos as far as Plateia Themistokleous, and then Akti Miaouli as it skirts the southern edge of the harbour. The

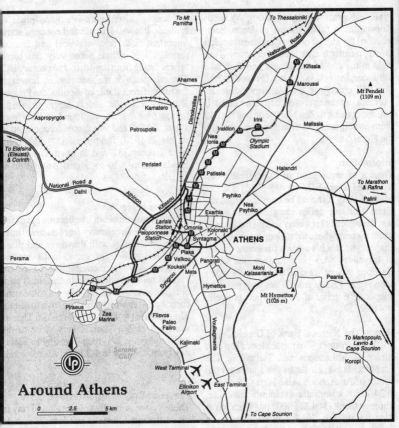

To Mt
Parnitha

To Thessaloniki

National Road 1

Kifissia

Maroussi

Ahames

Mt Pendeli
(1109 m)

Kamatero

Aspropyrgos

Irini

Petroupolis

Iraklion

Melissia

Nea
Ionia

Olympic
Stadium

To Elefsina
(Eleusis)
& Corinth

Peristeri

Patissia

Halandri

National Road 8

Dafni

Athinon

Kifissou

Psyhiko

To Marathon
& Rafina

Palini

Larisis
Station

Exarhia

Nea
Psyhiko

Omonia

Peloponnese
Station

Kolonaki

Syntagma

ATHENS

Perama

Plaka

Pangrati

Moni
Kaissarianis

Peania

Velvou

Koukaki

Mets

Syngrou

Hymettos

Mt Hymettos
(1026 m)

Piraeus

Zea
Marina

Flisvos
Paleo
Faliro

Vouliagmenis

Saronic
Gulf

Kalimaki

To Markopoulo,
Lavrio &
Cape Sounion

Koropi

West Terminal

Around Athens

Ellinikon
Airport

East Terminal

To Cape Sounion

0   2.5   5 km

waterfront on the northern edge of the harbour is Akti Kondyli, which is ahead and to the right from the metro entrance.

The departure points for the various ferry destinations are shown on the map of Piraeus. Note that there are two departure points for Crete. Ferries for Iraklio leave from the western end of Akti Kondyli, but ferries for other Cretan ports occasionally dock there as well. It's a long way to the other departure point for Crete on Akti Miaouli, so check where to find your boat when you buy your ticket. All ferries display a clock face showing their departure time, and have their

ports of call written in English above their bows.

Piraeus also has railway stations for both northern Greece and the Peloponnese. The station for the Peloponnese is one block north of the metro, and the station for northern Greece is at the western end of Akti Kondyli.

There are buses (No 904 or 905) to Zea Marina from the bus stop next to the metro. If you want to walk, it takes about 30 minutes. Head up Vasileos Georgiou Androutsou from Plateia Themistokleous and turn right onto Vasileos Konstantinou at

Plateia Koraï. Continue along Vasileos Konstantinou (also known as Iroön Polytehniou) for almost one km, and then turn left down Afendouli after the Hotel Savoy. Turn right at the end of Afendouli, and then take the second street on the left (Freatidas) and you will emerge at the Maritime Museum, overlooking the hydrofoil departure point. If you are coming to Zea Marina on bus No 040 from Syntagma, get off at the stop opposite the Hotel Savoy.

Information
Thanks to some kind of bureaucratic bad joke, the Piraeus EOT (☎ 413 5716) is at Zea Marina. Why it should be here and not at the Great Harbour defies imagination. Doubtless the office is kept busy telling millionaire yacht owners where to stock up on caviar and champagne, but it's useless for the thousands of travellers who pour through the Great Harbour every day. The office is open Monday to Friday from 8 am to 3 pm. The telephone number of Piraeus' port police is ☎ 417 2657.

Money The National Bank of Greece is just north of Plateia Themistokleous on the corner of Antistaseos and Tsamadou. The Emporiki Bank, closer to the square on the corner of Antistaseos and Makras Stoas, has a 24-hour automatic-exchange machine. Thomas Cook (☎ 422 5000) has a branch at Akti Poseidonos 26. It's open Monday to Friday from 8.30 am to 8 pm, Saturday from 9 am to 6.30 pm and Sunday from 10 am to 2.30 pm.

Post & Telecommunications The main post office is on the corner of Tsamadou and Filonos, just north of Plateia Themistokleous. It's open Monday to Friday from 7.30 am to 8 pm and Saturday from 7.30 am to 2 pm. The OTE is just north of here at Karaoli 19 and is open 24 hours. The postcode for Piraeus is 185 01 and the telephone code is 01.

Archaeological Museum
If you have time to spare in Piraeus, the archaeological museum is a good place to spend it. It's well laid out and contains some important finds from classical and Roman times. These include some very fine tomb reliefs dating from the 4th to 2nd century BC. The star piece of the museum is, however, the magnificent statue of Apollo, the Piraeus Kouros. It is the oldest larger-than-life hollow bronze statue yet found. It dates from about 520 BC and was discovered, buried in rubble, in 1959. The museum (☎ 452 1598) is at Trikoupi 31 and is open Tuesday to Sunday from 8.30 to 3 pm. Admission is 500 dr.

Maritime Museum
The maritime museum's collection spans the history of the Greek navy from ancient times to the present day with drawings and plans of battles, models of ships, battle scenes, uniforms and war memorabilia. There are various nautical oddments in the small park outside the museum, including a submarine conning tower which children love to climb. The museum (☎ 451 6822) is on Akti Themistokleous at Zea Marina, very close to the hydrofoil quay. It's open Tuesday to Saturday from 8.30 am to 1.30 pm. Admission is 200 dr.

Places to Stay – bottom end
There's no reason why anyone should stay in Piraeus when Athens is so close. If you do get stuck, don't attempt to sleep out – Piraeus is the most dangerous place in Greece to do so.

Most of the cheap hotels are geared more towards accommodating sailors than tourists. The *Hotel Acropole* (☎ 417 3313), Gounari 7, is one of the few which caters for backpackers. It has dorm beds for 2000 dr, and tidy but plain single/double rooms with shared bathroom for 6000/8000 dr. Gounari is the main thoroughfare running inland from Plateia Karaïskaki. The hotel is just a little way up on the left, and is very close to public transport.

The C-class *Hotel Delfini* (☎ 412 9779), nearby at Leoharous 7, is a bit smarter with ingles/doubles for 7000/10,000 dr with rivate bathroom.

Places to Stay – middle

The best hotels are to be found around the Mikrolimano. There are three good B-class options on Vasilissis Pavlou, which runs around the hillside above the harbour. The pick of them is the plush *Hotel Mistral* (☎ 411 7675) at No 105. It charges 17,000/22,000 dr for very comfortable air-con rooms with great views over the harbour below. The rates include buffet breakfast, and facilities include a roof garden with res-

taurant, bar and swimming pool. The *Hotel Castella* (☎ 411 4735/4737), at No 75, has singles/doubles with air-con for 16,000/25,000 dr, including breakfast. It also has views of the harbour, as does the *Hotel Cavo d'Oro* (☎ 412 2210), at No 19, where air-con singles/doubles are 14,000/20,000.

Places to Eat

If all you want is a quick bite before catching a ferry, then there are several reasonably priced places on Akti Poseidonos and along Gounari. The tiny *Restaurant I Folia*, opposite Plateia Karaïskaki on Akti Poseidonos,

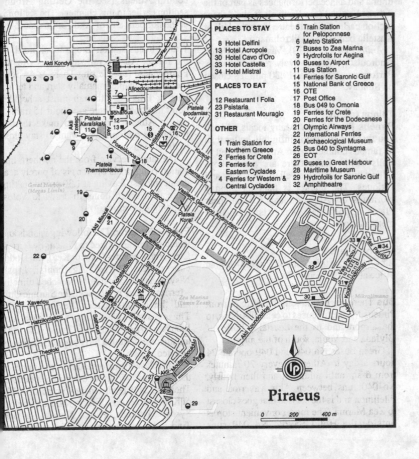

PLACES TO STAY
8 Hotel Delfini
13 Hotel Acropole
30 Hotel Cavo d'Oro
33 Hotel Castella
34 Hotel Mistral

PLACES TO EAT
12 Restaurant I Folia
23 Psistaria
31 Restaurant Mouragio

OTHER
1 Train Station for Northern Greece
2 Ferries for Crete
3 Ferries for Eastern Cyclades
4 Ferries for Western & Central Cyclades
5 Train Station for Peloponnese
6 Metro Station
7 Buses to Zea Marina
9 Hydrofoils for Aegina
10 Buses to Airport
11 Bus Station
14 Ferries for Saronic Gulf
15 National Bank of Greece
16 OTE
17 Post Office
18 Bus 049 to Omonia
19 Ferries for Crete
20 Ferries for the Dodecanese
21 Olympic Airways
22 International Ferries
24 Archaeological Museum
25 Bus 040 to Syntagma
26 EOT
27 Buses to Great Harbour
28 Maritime Museum
29 Hydrofoils for Saronic Gulf
32 Amphitheatre

Piraeus

0   200   400 m

does a bowl of gigantes beans for 500 dr, calamari for 600 dr and moussaka for 780 dr.

The setting around the Mikrolimano is rather more relaxed, with a string of seafood restaurants right on the waterfront. The *Restaurant Mouragio*, Akti Koumoundourou 60, has a good range and reasonable prices. Expect to pay about 2500 dr per person, plus drinks.

Over at Zea Marina, the *psistaria* at Akti Moutsoupoulou 24 is a good place to fill up.

Entertainment
The Piraeus *open-air amphitheatre* features drama and dance performances as part of the Athens Festival (see Festivals in the Athens section earlier). The theatre is on the Hill of Kastella behind the Mikrolimano.

Anifori (☎ 411 5819), Vasileos Georgiou Androutsou 47, is a lively rembetika club. Performances begin at 10.30 pm. It's closed on Sunday.

Things to Buy
Piraeus Flea Market Many locals will tell you that this market is infinitely better than its famous counterpart in Athens. As well as stalls selling junk, there are small shops selling high-quality jewellery, ceramics and antiques. The market is held on Sunday mornings on Alipedou and Skilitsi, near Plateia Ippodamias, which is behind the metro station.

Getting There & Away
Air Olympic Airways (☎ 452 0968) has an office at Akti Miaouli 27.

Bus There are no intercity buses to or from Piraeus. There are buses to central Athens, to the airport and to the coastal suburbs of Glyfada and Voula, south of the airport.

Green buses No 040 and 049 operate 24 hours a day to Athens – every 20 minutes from 6 am until midnight and then hourly. No 040 runs between Akti Xaveriou and Filellinon and is the service that goes closest to Zea Marina. The most convenient stop is outside the Hotel Savoy. No 049 runs

between Plateia Karaïskaki and Platei Omonias. The fare is 75 dr for both services

Buses to the airport leave from the south western corner of Plateia Karaïskaki. The depart from Piraeus at 5, 7, 8, 9.50 an 10.50 am; and at 12.20, 1.10, 2.40, 3.30 5.20, 6.05 and 8.20 pm. The fare is 160 d Blue bus No 110 runs from Platei Karaïskaki to Glyfada and Voula every 1 minutes (75 dr). It stops outside the airport West Terminal.

Metro The metro is the fastest and easies way of getting from the Great Harbour t central Athens (see the Getting Aroun section earlier in this chapter). The station i at the northern end of Akti Kalimassioti.

Train Piraeus station is one block north o the metro. All the railway services to th Peloponnese (see Getting There & Away i the Athens chapter) actually start and termi nate at Piraeus, although most schedule don't mention it. There are about 15 trains day to Athens – enough to make them reasonable option if you want to stay clos to the stations.

The single service from the northern lin station (via Larisis Station) is of purely aca demic interest, leaving at 1.30 pm and takin more than seven hours to crawl to Volos stopping all stations.

Ferry – domestic The following islands an island groups are linked to Piraeus by ferries Crete, the Cyclades (except Kea), the Dode canese (Kastellorizo, Agathonisi, Lipsi Nisyros and Tilos cannot be reached directly – ferries change in Rhodes), the Saronic Gul and the North-Eastern Aegean (excep Thasos and Samothraki; for Psara and Inousses ferries change on Chios). The EOT in Athens gives out a ferry schedule which is updated weekly.

The following information applies only to the high season from June to mid-September There are daily ferries to the Cycladic islands of Kythnos, Serifos, Sifnos, Milos, Kimolos Syros, Mykonos, Paros, Naxos, Ios and Tinos; and two or three ferries a week to

Iraklia, Shinoussa, Koufonisi, Donoussa, Amorgos, Folegandros, Sikinos, and Anafi. In the shoulder season (April, May and October) ferry schedules are reduced to some extent and in winter they are reduced drastically.

There are daily ferries to the Dodecanese islands of Rhodes, Kos, Kalymnos, Leros and Patmos; and two or three a week to Astypalea, Karpathos, and Kassos. Daily ferries also operate to the North-Eastern Aegean Islands of Chios, Lesvos (Mytilini), Ikaria and Samos. Limnos has two or three connections a week. The Saronic Gulf islands are linked by daily ferries all year. Crete has a host of ferry connections. There are two a day to Iraklio year-round and at least one a day to Hania; as well as three or four a week to Rethymno, two or three a week to Kastelli (via Monemvassia, Neapoli, Gythio, Kythira and Antikythira) and one a week to Agios Nikolaos.

Ferry ticket prices are fixed by the government. All ferries charge the same for any given route, although the facilities on board differ – quite radically at times. The small differences in prices charged by agents are the result of agents sacrificing part of their allotted commission to increase sales. These discounts seldom amount to more than 50 dr. Agents cannot charge more than the fixed price. If you want to book a cabin or take a car on board a ferry, it is advisable to buy a ticket in advance in Athens. Otherwise, wait until you get to Piraeus; agents selling ferry tickets are thick on the ground around Plateia Karaïskaki. If you're running short of time, you can buy your ticket quayside from the tables set up next to each ferry. It costs no more to buy your ticket at the boat, contrary to what some agents might tell you.

See Boat in the Getting Around chapter and the Getting There & Away sections for each island for more information.

Ferry – international There are three ferries a week in summer to Limassol in Cyprus and Haifa in Israel, one a week in winter. Salamis Lines operates the F/B *Nissos Kypros* all year-round via Rhodes. It leaves Piraeus on

Thursday at 7 pm and Rhodes on Friday at 4 pm, arriving at Limassol at 10 am on Saturday and Haifa at 7 am on Sunday. In summer, Vergina Ferries runs the F/B *Vergina* to Cyprus and Haifa via Iraklio on Crete, leaving Piraeus on Thursday at 7 am, while Poseidon Lines operates the F/B *Sea Harmony* via Rhodes and Crete. The high season runs from 15 June until 13 September. Deck-class fares from Piraeus to Limassol are 14,300/16,500 dr in low/high season, and 22,000/24,200 dr to Haifa. The fares from Crete and Rhodes are virtually the same, although Rhodes is halfway to Cyprus. All three lines offer 20% student (up to 28 years), youth (up to 25 years) and return-ticket discounts.

Hydrofoil There are year-round, daily hydrofoils from Zea Marina to the Saronic Gulf islands of Aegina, Hydra, Poros and Spetses. Some of these also call at Ermioni, Porto Heli, Leonidio, Tolo, Nafplio, Monemvassia and Neapoli in the Peloponnese and the island of Kythira. In addition, there are hourly hydrofoils from Akti Tzelepi (at the Great Harbour) to Aegina. You can buy tickets at the kiosks adjacent to the departure points. For more information see Hydrofoil in the Getting Around chapter and the Getting There & Away sections in the island chapters.

Getting Around

Bus Bus No 040 (a green one) goes from Vasileos Konstantinou to Syntagma every 20 minutes during the day and hourly during the night. This bus can take up to 45 minutes to get from Athens to Piraeus; the metro is quicker.

DAFNI Δαφνί
Moni Dafniou

This monastery, 10 km north-west of Athens along the busy road to Corinth, is Attica's most important Byzantine monument. It is built on the route of the Sacred Way and on the site of an ancient Sanctuary of Apollo. Its name derives from the daphne laurels which were sacred to Apollo.

ATHENS

The monastery's 11th-century church contains some of Greece's finest mosaics. These were created at a time when the artistic and intellectual achievements of Byzantium had reached unprecedented heights. The monastery was sacked in 1205 by the renegades of the Fourth Crusade who had earlier captured Constantinople. It was rebuilt and occupied by monks until the time of the War of Independence, after which it was used as army barracks and as a hospital for the mentally ill. Much restoration has taken place since.

The mosaics on the church walls depict saints and monks, the ones on the dome depict apostles, prophets and guardian archangels. Exquisite though these mosaics are, they fade into insignificance once the visitor has gazed upon the Christos Pantokrator (Christ in Majesty) which occupies the centre of the dome. Even a confirmed atheist cannot help but be impressed by this masterpiece of Byzantine art. The monastery (☎ 581 1558) is open daily from 8.30 am to 3 pm, and entry is 800 dr.

Places to Stay

Dafni Camping (☎ 581 1563), 200 metres from the monastery, charges 900 dr per person and 700 dr per tent for good shady sites.

Getting There & Away

Bus Nos 860 and 880 from Panepistimiou, just north of Sina, will drop you at the Venzini stop right outside the monastery, as will Nos 853, 862 and 873 from Plateia Eleftherias, off Pireos. The buses run very 20

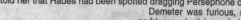

The Abduction of Persephone

The story of the abduction of Persephone to the underworld and her subsequent return is the mythological explanation for the changing of the seasons and the cycle of life, death and rebirth.

According to one version of the myth, Hades, the god of the underworld, fell in love with Persephone, daughter of Demeter, the goddess of wheat and fertility. Zeus was placed in a tricky spot when he was asked to give his consent to their marriage. He didn't want to upset his big brother by saying no, but he knew that Demeter doted on Persephone and would not want to lose her to the underworld. He ended up saying nothing, so Hades just went ahead and grabbed Persephone, swooping down on her while she was picking flowers in a field near Eleusis. A distraught Demeter searched everywhere for her daughter, but to no avail. Eventually she came in disguise to Eleusis and was taken in by King Celeus. His son, Triptolemus, recognised her and told her that Hades had been spotted dragging Persephone off.

Demeter was furious, sensing that her fellow gods and goddesses had been holding out on her. In revenge, she cursed the soil so that nothing would grow while her daughter was kept from her. Zeus was forced into a diplomatic shuffle to negotiate Persephone's release, which was obtained on the condition that she had not eaten anything while in the underworld, for no-one can return to the world of the living after tasting the food of the dead. The diplomatic shuffle became ever more desperate after it was discovered that Persephone had eaten a seed of the pomegranate that Hades had given her as a token of his love. It was finally agreed that Persephone could spend nine months of the year with her mother on earth, and the other three months in the underworld. Demeter lifted her curse, apart from the three-month period when Persephone had to return to the underworld. During this time the earth's soil became infertile again. In thanks to King Celeus and Triptolemus, Demeter gave permission for her principal temple in Greece to be built at Eleusis. ■

minutes and take about 30 minutes in reasonable traffic. Don't catch the buses to Dafni from Syntagma, which go to a suburb of the same name to the south-east.

ELEFSINA (ELEUSIS) Ελευσίνα

The ruins of ancient Eleusis are in the modern industrial town of Elefsina, 12 km further along the road from Moni Dafniou and on the same bus route.

The ancient city of Eleusis was built around the **Sanctuary of Demeter**. The site dates back to Mycenaean times, when the cult of Demeter began.

The cult became one of the most important in ancient Greece. By classical times it was celebrated with a huge annual festival, which attracted thousands of pilgrims wanting to be initiated into the Eleusian mysteries. They walked in procession from the Acropolis to Eleusis along the Sacred Way, which was lined with statues and votive monuments. Initiates were sworn to secrecy on punishment of death, and during the 1400 years that the sanctuary functioned no-one did divulge its secrets. The sanctuary was closed by the Roman emperor Theodosius in the 4th century AD.

Although the sanctuary was the most important in ancient Greece after Delphi, the modern site is not particularly inspiring. Most of it is overgrown, and an industrial complex occupies the western edge. A visit to the site's **museum** first will help you to make some sense of the ruins. Both the site and museum are open Tuesday to Sunday from 8.30 am to 3 pm. Admission is 500 dr.

MONI KAISSARIANIS

Μονή Καισσαριανής

This 11th-century monastery, five km east of Athens is set amid pines, plane and cypress trees on the slopes of Mt Hymettos. The air is permeated with the aroma of herbs which grow on the mountain.

The source of the river Ilissos is on the hill above the monastery. Its waters were once believed to cure infertility and were sacred to Aphrodite; a temple dedicated to her stood nearby. The spring feeds a fountain on the eastern wall of the monastery, where the water gushes from a marble ram's head (this is a copy – the 6th-century original is in the National Archaeological Museum).

Surrounding the courtyard of the monastery are a mill, bakery, bathhouse and refectory. The church is dedicated to the Presentation of the Virgin and is built to the Greek-cross plan. Four columns taken from a Roman temple support its dome. The 17th-century frescoes in the narthex are the work of Ioannis Ipatos. Those in the rest of the church date from the 16th century, and were painted by a monk from Mt Athos.

The monastery is best visited during the week – it's swarming with picnickers at weekends. The grounds are open until sunset and the monastery buildings are open Tuesday to Sunday from 8.30 am to 3 pm; admission is 800 dr. To get to the monastery take bus No 224 from Plateia Kaningos (at the north end of Akadimias), or from the junction of Akadimias and Sina, to the terminus. From here it's a walk of about 30 minutes to the monastery.

Attica Αττική

Attica, a *nomos* of Sterea Ellada, contains more than just the capital and its port of Piraeus. There are several places of interest, most of which can be reached by the orange buses which depart from the Mavromateon bus terminal.

COAST ROAD TO CAPE SOUNION

This road skirts Attica's Apollo coast. It's a beautiful coastline of splendid beaches and stunning sea vistas which has been spoilt by overdevelopment. Many of the beaches are either EOT pay beaches or belong to hotels. The beaches have boats and water-sports equipment for hire, tennis and volleyball courts and children's playgrounds.

The first resort you'll encounter travelling south is **Glyfada**, Attica's largest resort. The place is overrun with package tourists in summer, and they are joined by half the

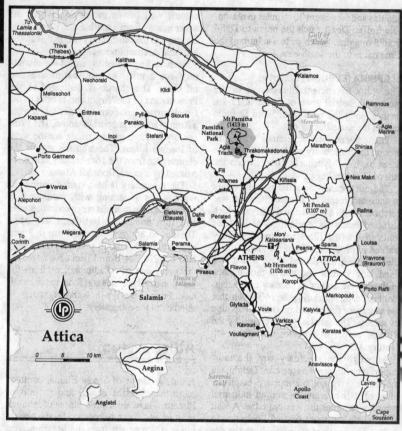

Attica

0 5 10 km

population of Athens at weekends. In addition, Glyfada has a permanent population of wealthy expatriates. Loads of bars and discos and noisy air traffic complete the picture – you'd be better off staying on the bus.

If you want to stay in Glyfada, the *Hotel Ilion* (☎ 894 6011) has clean singles/doubles with private bathroom for 4900/5900 dr. The hotel is at Kondyli 4, on the corner of Plateia Bizaniou, which is where the No 120 bus from Syntagma terminates. Konstantinoupoleos, which runs parallel to Kondyli one block south, is packed with bars and tavernas.

Tzavelas Taverna, away from the main pack at the junction of Konstantinoupoleos and Lazaridi Sabba, has the best prices. *Tiller's Pub*, at No 9, is the favourite haunt of the expatriate community. It turns out a huge English breakfast of bacon, eggs, sausage and beans for 1100 dr. The *Joker Club*, opposite, has live bands on most nights.

The beach-resort belt continues south through Voula, Vouliagmeni and Varkiza. There are camp sites by the beach at both Voula (☎ 01-895 2712) and Varkiza (☎ 01-897 4329). The coast south of Varkiza to

Cape Sounion is dotted with the weekenders of well-to-do Athenians, but it's still possible to find stretches of beach with hardly a soul in sight. Cape Sounion, 70 km from Athens, is at the south-eastern tip of Attica.

Getting There & Away
Blue city buses can take you as far south as Varkiza for 75 dr. There are buses from Syntagma to Glyfada (No 120) and Voula (No 122). The Voula buses are much faster and also stop at Glyfada. The buses going to Vouliagmeni and Varkiza (Nos 116 & 117) leave from south of the Zappeio gardens on Vasilissis Olgas. If your destination is Sounion, take one of the *paraliako* (coastal) buses which leave hourly, on the half-hour, (two hours, 1000 dr) from the Mavromateon bus terminal. The buses also stop on Filellinon, on the corner of Xenofondos, 10 minutes later, but by this time they're usually very crowded.

INLAND ROAD TO CAPE SOUNION
The inland road to Cape Sounion passes through the Mesogeia (middle land) region, renowned for the fine olives and grapes grown on its red soil. **Peania**, a village 18 km east of Athens in the eastern foothills of Mt Hymettos, was the birth place of the orator Demosthenes (384-322 BC). Little remains of the ancient town. Visitors come today not for the ruins, but to look around the **Vorres Museum** (☎ 01-664 2520/4771), which houses folkloric items, prints and pictures, and an impressive collection of contemporary Greek paintings. Modern sculptures stand in the courtyard. The museum is a fair hike from the bus stop on Peania's main square, Plateia Vasileos Konstantinou. Walk down Demosthenous (which has the New Democracy building on the corner and the post office next to it) and turn right onto Dimihounta at the bottom. Walk to the top of Dimihounta, and turn left onto Diadohou Konstantinou – where you'll soon find a reassuring sign pointing straight ahead to the museum. The museum is only open on weekends from 10 am to 2 pm. Admission is 500 dr.

The **Koutouki cave** (☎ 01-664 2108), four km west of Peania on the slopes of Mt Hymettos, has an impressive array of stalactites and stalagmites that are very effectively lit. The cave is signposted from Peania. It is open daily from 10 am to 5.30 pm. Admission is 500 dr. It's a good idea to telephone first to check that the cave is open.

The largest of the villages of Mesogeia is **Koropi**, a lively market town seven km south of Peania that is noted for its retsina. Its Church of the Transfiguration, on the road to Markopoulo, is one of the oldest churches in Attica and contains the remains of 10th-century frescoes. The road continues to **Markopoulo**, an unremarkable town except for its bakers and churches. It is said that the best bread in Attica is baked here, and several of its small churches contain attractive 17th-century frescoes. The road south continues to Lavrio and Cape Sounion.

Getting There & Away
There are Athens suburban blue buses to Peania and Koropi from Eptahalkou, just south of the metro line at Thision. Bus Nos 125, 307 and 308 all terminate at Koropi. Markopoulo is on the route of the *mesogiaki* (inland) buses bound for Sounion from the Mavromateon terminal in Athens. They leave hourly, on the hour, and take 2¼ hours to get to Sounion (900 dr).

CAPE SOUNION Ακρωτήριο Σούνιο
Temple of Poseidon
The ancient Greeks chose their temple sites carefully, with the prime considerations being a site's natural beauty and its appropriateness to the god in question. Nowhere is this more evident than at Cape Sounion, where the Temple of Poseidon stands on a craggy spur that plunges 65 metres to the sea. The temple was built in 444 BC at the same time as the Parthenon. It is constructed of local marble from Agrilesa and its slender columns – of which 16 remain – are Doric. It is thought that the temple was built by Ictinus, the architect of the Temple of Hephaestus in Athens' Ancient Agora.

The temple looks gleaming white when

viewed from the sea and is discernible from a long distance away. It gave great comfort to sailors in ancient times: they knew that once they'd spotted it, they were nearly home. The views from the temple are equally impressive. On a clear day, you can see Kea, Kythnos and Serifos to the south-east, and Aegina and the Peloponnese to the west. The site also contains scanty remains of a propylon, a fortified tower and, to the north-east, a 6th-century temple to Athena.

You'll have to visit early in the morning before the tourist buses arrive if you wish to indulge the sentiments of Byron's lines from *Don Juan*:

Place me on Sunium's marbled steep,
Where nothing save the waves and I,
May hear our mutual murmurs sweep...

Byron was so taken by Sounion that he carved his name on one of the columns – many others have followed suit.

The site is open Monday to Saturday from 9 am to sunset and on Sunday from 10 am to sunset. Admission is 800 dr.

Places to Stay & Eat

There are two camp sites at Cape Sounion. They are *Camping Vakchos* (☎ 0292-39 571/262) and *Sounio Beach Camping* (☎ 0292-39 358/718). Both are on the road to Lavrio.

The café at the site is expensive, so it's a good idea to bring along something to eat and drink. The nearest tavernas are at Sounio beach on the way to Lavrio.

Getting There & Away

You can take either the inland or coastal bus to Cape Sounion. See the Coast Road to Sounion and the Inland Road to Sounion sections for more information.

LAVRIO Λαύριο

Lavrio is an unattractive industrial town on the east coast of Attica, 10 km north of Sounion. It is only worth a mention because it is the departure point for ferries to the island of Kea. The town has definitely seen

better days. In ancient times its silver mines, worked by slaves, helped to finance Pericles' building programme. The island of Makronisos, opposite the port, was used as a place of exile during the civil war. If you have time to spare you could visit the **mineralogical museum** (☎ 0292-26 270), Plateia Iroön Polytehniou. It's open Wednesday, Saturday and Sunday from 10 am to noon. Admission is 50 dr.

Getting There & Away

Bus There are buses every 30 minutes to Lavrio from the Mavromateon terminal in Athens (1½ hours, 800 dr).

Ferry Goutos Lines runs the F/B *Myrina Express* from Lavrio to Kea (1610 dr) and Kythnos (2230 dr). From mid-June, there are ferries to Kea every morning and evening from Monday to Friday, and up to six a day at weekends. Three ferries a week continue to Kythnos. In winter there are ferries to Kea every day except Monday, returning every day except Wednesday. One service a week continues to Kythnos. The EOT in Athens gives out a timetable for this route.

The ticket office at Lavrio is opposite the quay.

RAFINA Ραφήνα

Rafina, on Attica's east coast, is Athens' main fishing port and second-most important port for passenger ferries. The port is much smaller than Piraeus and less confusing – and fares are about 20% cheaper, but you have to spend an hour on the bus and 380 dr to get there.

The port police (☎ 0294-22 888) occupy a kiosk near the quay, which is lined with fish restaurants and ticket agents. The main square, Plateia Plastira, is at the top of the ramp leading to the port. Rafina's post code is 190 09.

There's no reason to hang about in Rafina and there are frequent bus connections with Athens. If, however, you want to stay the night and catch an early ferry or hydrofoil, there are a couple of reasonable hotels. The D-class *Hotel Koralli* (☎ 0294-22 477), on

Plateia Plastira, has singles/doubles/triples for 5000/7300/10,200 dr. The C-class *Hotel Avra* (☎ 0294-22 780) overlooks the port just south of the square. It has large singles/doubles with sea views for 10,000/14,000 dr, including breakfast.

Getting There & Away

Bus There are 29 buses a day from the Mavromateon terminal in Athens to Rafina (one hour, 380 dr) between 5.45 am and 10.30 pm. The first bus leaves Rafina at 5.50 am and the last at 10.15 pm.

Ferry Strintzis Lines and Agoudimos Lines both operate ferries to the Cycladic islands of Andros (two hours, 2000 dr), Tinos (3½ hours, 2750 dr) and Mykonos (4¼ hours, 3300 dr). There are ferries every morning at 8 am and every afternoon between 4.15 and 6.30 pm. The Agoudimos Lines ferry leaving at 6.30 pm on Sunday also calls at Syros (4¼ hours, 3300 dr).

There are also frequent ferries to the ports of Karystos and Marmari on the island of Evia. There are three services a day to Marmari (915 dr) and two to Karystos (1415 dr). Both take about an hour.

Hydrofoil Hermes Hydrofoils and Ilio Lines both have daily services to the Cyclades. Flying Hermes hydrofoils operate every day to Andros (70 minutes, 4100 dr), Tinos (two hours, 6200 dr) and Mykonos (2½ hours, 7300 dr). They leave at 7.45 am on Tuesday, Thursday, Friday and Sunday, and at 8.30 am on other days. Every Thursday, Hermes has a 7.45 am service to Syros (2¼ hours, 6200 dr); Paros (three hours, 6600 dr); Naxos (3¾ hours, 6745 d); Iraklia (4¾ hours, 6900 dr); Shinoussa (five hours, 6905 dr); Koufonisi (5¼ hours, 6900 dr); Katapola (six hours, 8000 dr); Aegiali (6½ hours, 8000 dr); and Donoussa (7¼ hours, 6900 dr).

Ilio Lines has hydrofoils at 8 am every day to Tinos and Mykonos. On Thursday, the service continues to Paros, Sifnos and Serifos. It also has a service leaving Rafina

on Monday at 5.45 am to Santorini (Thira) (6½ hours, 8020 dr) via Syros, Tinos, Mykonos, Paros, Naxos and Ios.

MARATHON REGION

Marathon Μαραθώνας

The plain surrounding the unremarkable small town of Marathon, 42 km north-east of Athens, is the site of one of the most celebrated battles in world history. In 490 BC, an army of 9000 Greeks and 1000 Plataeans defeated the 25,000-strong Persian army, proving that the Persians were not invincible. The Greeks were indebted to the ingenious tactics of Miltiades, who altered the conventional battle formation so that there were fewer soldiers in the centre, but more in the wings. This lulled the Persians into thinking that the Greeks were going to be a pushover. They broke through in the centre, but were then ambushed by the soldiers in the wings. At the end of the day, 6000 Persians lay dead and only 192 Greeks. The story goes that after the battle a runner was sent to Athens to announce the victory. After shouting *Enikesame!* ('We won!') he collapsed in a heap and never revived. It is the origin of today's marathon foot race.

Marathon Tomb

This burial mound stands 350 metres from the Athens-Marathon road, four km before the town of Marathon. In ancient Greece, the bodies of those who died in battle normally were returned to their families for private burial, but as a sign of honour the 192 men who fell at Marathon were cremated and buried in this collective tomb. The mound is 10 metres high and 180 metres in circumference. The tomb site is signposted from the main road and is open Tuesday to Sunday from 8.30 am to 3 pm. The **museum**, nearer to the town, has the same opening hours. The admission fee of 500 dr covers both sites.

Lake Marathon

This huge dam, eight km west of Marathon, was Athens' sole source of water until 1956. The massive dam wall, completed in 1926, is faced with the famous Pentelic marble that was used to build the Parthenon. It's an awesome sight, standing over 50 metres high and stretching more than 300 metres. It is thought to be the only dam in the world with marble walls.

Ramnous Ραμνούς

The ruins of the ancient port of Ramnous are 15 km north-east of Marathon. It's an evocative, overgrown and secluded little site, standing on a plateau overlooking the sea. Among the ruins are the remains of a Doric **Temple of Nemesis** (435 BC), which once contained a huge statue of the goddess. Nemesis was the goddess of retribution and mother of Helen of Troy. There are also ruins of a smaller 6th-century temple dedicated to Themis, goddess of justice. The site is open Tuesday to Sunday from 8.30 am to 3 pm and admission is 500 dr.

Shinias Σχοινιάς

The long, sandy, pine-fringed beach at Shinias, south-east of Marathon, is the best in this part of Attica. It's also very popular, particularly at weekends. *Camping Marathon* (☎ 0294-55 587) is on the way to the beach.

Getting There & Away

There are hourly buses from the Mavromateon terminal to Marathon (1¼ hours, 600 dr). The tomb, the museum and Shinias beach are all within short walking distance of bus stops (tell the driver where you want to get out). There are no buses to Lake Marathon or Ramnous; you need your own transport.

VRAVRONA (BRAURON) Βραυρώνα

The ruins of the ancient city of Brauron lie just outside the modern coastal town of Vravrona (pronounced Vra-vr-ON-a), 40 km east of Athens. Brauron belonged to King Cecrop's league of 12 cities. King Cecrops was the mythical founder of Athens. Remains dating back to 1700 BC have been found at the site, but it is best known for the **Sanctuary of Artemis**. According to mythology, it was to Brauron that Iphigenia and Orestes brought the *xoanon* (sacred image) of Artemis that they removed from Tauris. The site became a sanctuary to Artemis during the time of the tyrant Peisistratos, who made the worship of Artemis the official religion of Athens.

The cult centred around a festival, held every five years, at which girls aged between five and 10 performed a ritual dance that imitated the movements of a bear. The ruins of the dormitories where the girls stayed can be seen at the site. The sanctuary's Doric temple, of which only a small section still stands, was built in the 5th century BC on the site of an earlier temple that was destroyed by the Persians. The site's **museum** (☎ 0299-27 020) houses finds from the sanctuary and the surrounding area. Both site and museum are open Tuesday to Sunday from 8.30 am to 3 pm. Admission is 500 dr.

Getting There & Away

Getting to Vravrona by public transport is a challenge. There are no direct buses, but the 5.50 am bus to Markopoulo from the Mavromateon terminal in Athens connects with the 6.50 am bus from Markopoulo to Vravrona (180 dr). There is a bus back to Markopoulo at 2.30 pm.

Peloponnese Πελοπόννησος

The Peloponnese (Pe-lo-PO-nis-os in Greek) is the southernmost section of the Balkan peninsula. The construction of the Corinth Canal through the Isthmus of Corinth in the late 19th century effectively severed it from the mainland, and now the only link is the bridge that spans the canal. Indeed, the Peloponnese has every attraction of an island – and better public transport.

It's a region of outstanding natural beauty, with lofty, snow-crested mountains, valleys of citrus groves and cypress trees, cool springs and many fine beaches. The landscape is diverse and there are the legacies left behind by the many civilisations which took root in the region. Ancient Greek sites, crumbling Byzantine cities and Frankish and Venetian fortresses are found in profusion. The best-known attraction is the ancient site at Olympia. Less well known is that the beaches of the Messinian Mani, south of Kalamata, are some of the finest in Greece. The rugged Mani peninsula has additional attractions – the remnants of the many fortified tower houses that were built as refuges from clan wars from the 17th century onwards.

With your own transport, two weeks is sufficient to visit the major attractions. On public transport, allow at least three weeks, or be selective about your destinations. Ideally, the Peloponnese warrants a month's wandering, such is the variety of its magnificent natural and ancient splendours. Accommodation prices quoted in this section are for high season (July and August). Expect to pay less at other times and certainly try bargaining. The EOT publishes a brochure called *Agrotourism: Holidays in the Countryside* that has a lot of accommodation options in the Peloponnese.

History & Mythology

The name Peloponnisos derives from the mythological hero, Pelops, and from the word for island, nisos. Literally translated, it

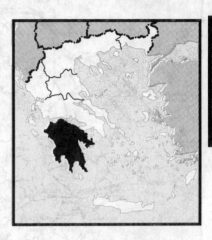

means 'island of Pelops'. The region's medieval name was the Morea (*mouria* is Greek for mulberry tree), perhaps because mulberry trees grow so well in the area.

The deities may have resided on Mt Olympus, but they made frequent jaunts into the Peloponnese. It is a region rich in myths, and Pelops features in many of them.

Since ancient times, the Peloponnese has played a major role in Greek history. When the Minoan civilisation declined after the 1450 BC, the focus of power in the ancient Aegean world moved from Crete to the hill-fortress palaces of Mycenae and Tiryns in the Peloponnese. As elsewhere in Greece, the 400 years following the Dorian conquests in the 12th century BC are known as the dark age. When the region emerged from it in the 7th century BC, Sparta, Athens' arch rival, had surpassed Mycenae as the most powerful city in the Peloponnese. The period of peace and prosperity under Roman rule (146 BC to around 250 AD) was shattered by a series of invasions by Goths, Avars and Slavs.

The Byzantines were slow to make inroads into the Peloponnese, and were not

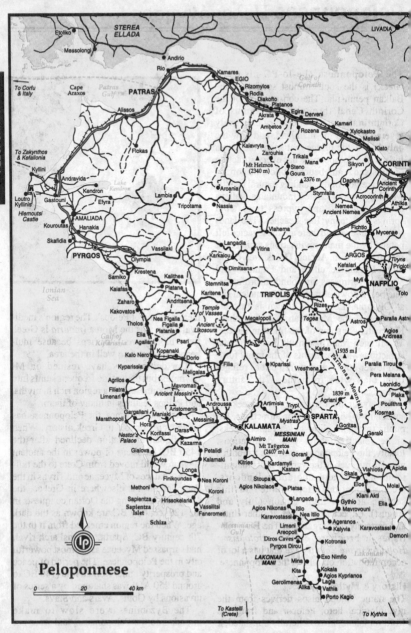

Peloponnese

0   20   40 km

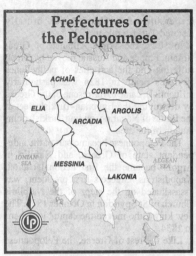

firmly established until the 9th century. In 1204, after the fall of Constantinople to the crusaders, the crusader chiefs William de Champlitte and Geoffrey de Villehardouin divided the region into 12 fiefs, which they parcelled out to various barons of France, Flanders and Burgundy. These fiefs were overseen by de Villehardouin, the self-appointed Prince of Morea (as the region was then called).

The Byzantines gradually won back the Morea. Although the empire as a whole was now in terminal decline, a glorious renaissance took place in the Morea, centred on Mystras, which Byzantine Emperor Michael VIII Paleologus made the region's seat of government.

The Morea fell to the Turks in 1460 and hundreds of years of power struggles between the Turks and Venetians followed. The Venetians had long coveted the Morea and had succeeded in establishing trading ports at Methoni, Pylos, Koroni and Monemvassia.

The War of Independence began in the Peloponnese. Bishop Germanos of Patras raised the flag of revolt near Kalavryta on 25 March 1821. The Egyptian army, under the leadership of Ibrahim Pasha, brutally restored Turkish rule in 1825.

In 1827, the Triple Alliance of Great Britain, France and Russia, moved by Greek suffering and the activities of philhellenes (Byron's death in 1824 was particularly influential), came to the rescue of the Greeks by destroying the Egyptian-Turkish fleet at the Battle of Navarino, ending Turkish domination of the area.

The Peloponnese became part of the independent state of Greece, and Nafplio in Argolis became the first national capital. Kapodistrias, Greece's first president, was assassinated on the steps of the Nafplio's Church of St Spyridon in October 1831. The new king Otho moved the capital to Athens in 1834.

Like the rest of Greece, the Peloponnese suffered badly during WW II. The town clock of Kalavryta, in the central north, is forever stopped at 2.34, the time when on 13 December 1943, at which the Germans began a massacre of all the males aged over 15 in reprisal for resistance activity.

The civil war (1944-49) brought widespread destruction and, in the 1950s, many villagers migrated to Athens, Australia, Canada, South Africa and the USA. More recently, the towns of Corinth and Kalamata have suffered devastating earthquakes. Both are still recovering.

Getting There & Away

Air Kalamata, in the south-west, has the only (domestic) airport in the Peloponnese.

Bus There are buses from Athens to most

Pelops

Pelops was the son of the conniving Tantalos, who invited the gods to a feast and served up the flesh of his son to test their power of all-knowing. Of course, the omniscient gods knew what he had done and refrained from eating the flesh. However, Demeter, who was in a tizz over the abduction of her daughter, Persephone, by Hades, accidentally ate a piece of Pelops' shoulder. Fortunately, the gods reassembled Pelops, and fashioned another shoulder of ivory. Tantalos was suspended from a fruit tree overhanging a lake, and was punished with eternal tantalising thirst.

Pelops took a fancy to the beautiful Hippodameia, daughter of Oinomaos, king of Elia. Oinomaos, who was a champion chariot racer, was told by an oracle that his future son-in-law would bring about his death. Oinomaos announced that he would give his daughter in marriage to any suitor who defeated him in a chariot race, but that he would kill those who failed – a fate which befell many suitors. Pelops took up the challenge and bribed the king's charioteer, Myrtilos, to take a spoke out of a wheel of the king's chariot. The chariot crashed during the race and Oinomaos was killed, so Pelops married Hippodameia and became king of Elia. The couple had two children, Atreus and Thyestes. Atreus became king of Mycenae and was the father of that kingdom's greatest king, Agamemnon. Pelops' devious action is blamed for the curse on the Royal House of Atreus which ultimately brought about its downfall. ∎

Ancient coin depicting a chariot race

towns in the Peloponnese. For details, see Getting There & Away in the Athens chapter. There are also connections to Patras from Ioannina in northern Greece and from the Ionian island of Lefkada. Both run via the ferry that operates between Andirio, in Sterea Ellada, and Rio, nine km east of Patras. If you don't have your own transport, travelling by bus is a pleasant way to explore the Peloponnese. Services are adequate to all but the most remote areas.

Train The rail network in the Peloponnese is run on narrow-gauge lines. The two main lines are: Athens, Corinth, Diakofto, Patras, Pyrgos, Kyparissia, Kalamata; and Athens, Corinth, Mycenae, Argos, Tripolis, Kalamata. There are also four branch lines: Diakofto to Kalavryta (rack-and-pinion); Pyrgos to Olympia; Pyrgos to Katakolo; and Kavasila to Kyllini.

Car & Motorbike If you are travelling from Athens to the Peloponnese with your own vehicle, you have the choice of the New National Road (a toll highway) or the slower Old National Road which hugs the coast and has fine sea views. Coming from north-west Greece, you can get to the Peloponnese on the Andirio-Rio ferry.

Ferry Patras is one of Greece's major ports with ferries to Corfu and Brindisi, Bari, Ancona, Trieste and Venice in Italy. Kyllini, south-west of Patras, has ferry connections with Kefallonia and Zakynthos. Ferries for Crete (Kastelli-Kissamos) and Piraeus leave from Monemvassia, Gythio and Kalamata. Most stop at Kythira and Antikythira.

Hydrofoil In July and August, hydrofoils plying between Piraeus and the Saronic Gulf islands call in at some of the ports on the east coast of the Peloponnese, including Porto Heli, Tolo, Nafplio, Monemvassia and Neapoli and also Kythira. See the Saronic Gulf Islands chapter for details.

Corinthia Κορινθία

Corinthia occupies a strategic position adjoining the Isthmus of Corinth. The region was once dominated by the mighty ancient city of Corinth, now one of the main attractions. Few travellers opt to linger long, although there are several minor sites in the pretty hinterland west of Corinth that are worth a detour if you have your own transport.

CORINTH Κόρινθος
Modern Corinth (in Greek CO-rin-thos, population 23,000), six km west of the Corinth Canal, is the fairly dull administrative capital of Corinthia prefecture. The town was rebuilt here after it was destroyed by an earthquake in 1858. The new town was wrecked by another, equally violent earthquake in 1928 and badly damaged again in 1981.

The modern town is dominated by concrete buildings erected to withstand future earthquakes, but it has a pleasant harbour, friendly people, tasty food and warrants an overnight stay because of its proximity to ancient Corinth and Nemea. Old Corinth is a mere village near the ancient site.

Orientation & Information
It is not difficult to negotiate Corinth. The post office is at Adimantou 33. The OTE is on the corner of Kolokotroni and Adimantou. Corinth's telephone code is 0741 and the postcode is 201 00. The National Bank of Greece is at Ethnikis Antistaseos 7.

Corinth has no EOT. The helpful tourist police (☎ 23 282), at Ermou 51, are open daily from 8 am to 2 pm and 5 to 8 pm. The regular police (☎ 22 143) are in the same building.

Folkloric Museum
This museum, to the east of the wharf, focuses on bridal and festive costumes from the past three centuries. There are costumes from the islands and the mainland, as well as metalwork, embroidery, gold and silver

PELOPONNESE

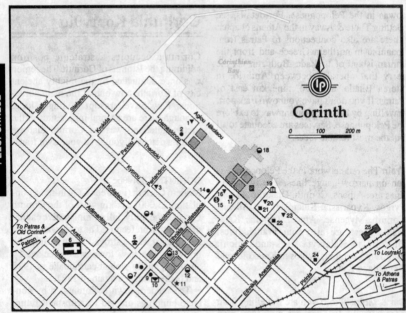

Corinth

0   100   200 m

PLACES TO STAY		OTHER		10	Post Office
17	Belle-Vue Hotel	2	Cinema	11	Tourist Police & Police
21	Hotel Corinthos	4	Bus Stop for Lecheon	12	Bus Station for Ancient
22	Hotel Konstantatos		(Blue Dolphin		Corinth, Loutraki &
24	Hotel Apollon		Camping)		Nemea
		5	OTE	13	Taxi Rank
PLACES TO EAT		6	Agios Pavlos Church	14	Town Hall
		7	Bus Station for Athens,	15	National Bank of
1	Taverna O Anaxagoras		Nafplion, Sparta,		Greece
3	Food Market		Kalamata & Tripolis	18	Bay-Cruise Boats
16	Kanita Restaurant	8	Gregorios Lagos Car	19	Folkloric Museum
20	Taverna O Thodorakis		Rental	25	Train Station
23	Restaurant To 24 Hours	9	Rent a Car		

objects, and carvings, both secular and ecclesiastical. The museum is open daily, except Monday, from 8.30 am to 1 pm. Admission is 400 dr.

Places to Stay – bottom end
Corinth Beach Campground (☎ 27 967/968) is about three km west of the town centre.

Buses to ancient Corinth can drop you off at the camp site. The *Blue Dolphin Campground* (☎ 25 766/767) is three km from ancient Corinth, on the beach. Take the bus to Lecheon from the stop on Koliatsou, just off Ethnikis Antistaseos.

The *Belle-Vue Hotel* (☎ 22 088), at Damaskinou 41, is old but clean and has single/double/triple rooms for 2700/4200/4500 dr with shared bathroom. The *Hotel Apollon* (☎ 22 587) Pirinis 18, near the train station, has neat singles/doubles, all with shower, for 4000/5500 dr.

Places to Stay – middle
The C-class *Hotel Corinthos* (☎ 26 701/702/703), Damaskinou 26, has pleasant singles/doubles for 10,000/15,000 dr with bathroom and balcony. The well-furnished (complete with stuffed fox in the lounge) C-class *Hotel Konstantatos* (☎ 22 120 or 25 311), also on Damaskinou, has singles without bath for 6000 dr and rooms with private facilities for 9000/11,500 dr. Air-con doubles are 16,000 dr.

Places to Eat
The lively *Taverna O Thodorakis* is back from the waterfront and serves sardines for 750 dr and big, salted-fish cutlets with feta for 900 dr. Greek salad is 850 dr and barrel wine is 250 dr. The taverna is open in the evenings. *Taverna O Anaxagoras*, Agiou Nikolaou 31, at the opposite end of the waterfront, specialises in mezedes, priced from 300 to 400 dr. Daily dishes can include the prized barbouni (red mullet). The taverna is open for lunch and dinner all year round.

The *Kanita Restaurant*, Damaskinou 41, facing the harbour, is open all day. It serves generous helpings of traditional dishes including mezedes for 400 dr and main meals from 800 dr. *Restaurant To 24 Hours* on Agiou Nikolaou (near the train station) is more expensive but, as the name suggests, it never closes. Corinth's *food market* is on the corner of Kyprou and Periandrou.

Getting There & Away
Bus Corinth has two intercity bus terminals. One is on the corner of Aratou and Ethnikis Antistaseos. Buses leave here every hour for Nafplio (1¼ hours, 750 dr) via Mycenae (45 minutes, 500 dr) and Argos (one hour, 950 dr). Nine buses go to Tripolis (1½ hours, 1250 dr); eight a day to Sparta (three hours, 1950 dr); and seven to Kalamata (four hours, 2650 dr). Tickets are bought on the bus.

Corinth's other bus terminal is on the corner of Ermou and Koliatsou. Buses leave half-hourly for Athens (1½ hours, 1250 dr) and Loutraki (20 minutes, 220 dr), hourly buses go to ancient Corinth (20 minutes, 140 dr), and seven buses a day go to Nemea (one hour, 650 dr).

Train There are 14 trains (fast and slow) a day going to Athens (two hours, 780 dr). On the line which skirts around the north and west coasts, there are nine trains per day to Patras (3½ hours, 1000 dr); six to Pyrgos (5½ hours, 2100 dr); and four to Kyparissia (6½ hours) and Kalamata (7½ hours, 1650 dr). On the inland line, three trains a day run to Argos (one hour, 510 dr), Tripolis (2½ hours, 980 dr) and Kalamata (5½ hours, 1650 dr).

Car Car-hire outlets in Corinth include Rent a Car (☎ 25 573), at Adimantou 39, and Gregorios Lagos (☎ 22 617), at Ethnikis Antistaseos 42.

ANCIENT CORINTH & ACROCORINTH
The sprawling ruins of ancient Corinth are seven km south-west of modern Corinth. Towering 575 metres above them is the massive, fortified bulk of Acrocorinth.

Allow a day to see both ancient Corinth and Acrocorinth. Most people come on day trips from modern Corinth, but there are tavernas and a few domatia in the village near the ancient site. Look for the signs. Acrocorinth has a restaurant.

The site (☎ 0741-31 207) and its museum are open daily, except Monday, from 8 am to 6 pm, 7 pm in summer. Admission to the site (including the museum) is 1200 dr.

History
During the 6th century BC, Corinth was one of ancient Greece's richest cities, with a population of 750,000. It owed its wealth to its strategic position on the Isthmus of Corinth, which meant it was able to build twin ports, one on the Aegean Sea (Kenchreai) and one on the Ionian Sea (Lecheon). From these ports it traded throughout the Mediterranean.

It survived the Peloponnesian Wars and flourished under Macedonian rule, but it was sacked by the Roman consul Mummius in 146 BC for revolting against Roman rule. In 44 BC, Julius Caesar began rebuilding the city and again it became a prosperous port.

During Roman times, when Corinthians weren't clinching business deals, they were paying homage to the goddess of love, Aphrodite, in a temple dedicated to her (which meant they were having a rollicking time with the temple's sacred prostitutes, both male and female). St Paul, perturbed by the Corinthians' wicked ways, spent 18 fruitless months preaching here.

Getting There & Away

Buses to ancient Corinth leave Corinth hourly on the hour, returning on the half hour. There are no direct buses to Acrocorinth. You can drive, otherwise it's a strenuous 1½-hour walk. Begin in the early morning before it gets too hot. Taxis charge from 2000 dr one way from ancient Corinth to Acrocorinth.

Ancient Corinth

Exploring the Site Earthquakes and sackings by a series of invaders have left little standing in ancient Corinth. The remains are mostly from Roman times. An exception is the 5th-century BC, Doric **Temple of Apollo**, the most prominent ruin on the site. To the south of this temple is a huge **agora**, or forum, bounded at its southern side by the foundations of a **stoa**. This was built to accommodate the bigwigs who were summoned here in 337 BC by Philip II, to sign oaths of allegiance to Macedon. In the middle of the central row of shops is the **bema**, a marble podium from which Roman officials addressed the people.

At the eastern end of the forum are the remains of the **Julian Basilica**. To the left (north) is the **Lower Peirene fountain** – the Upper Peirene fountain is on Acrocorinth. According to mythology, Peirene ·wept so much when her son Kenchrias was killed by Artemis that the gods, rather than let all the precious water go to waste, turned her into a

fountain. In reality, it's a natural spring which has been used since ancient times and still supplies old Corinth with water. The water tanks are concealed in a fountain house with a six-arched façade. Through the arches are the remains of frescoes.

West of the fountain, steps lead to the **Lecheon road**, which used to be the main thoroughfare to the port of Lecheon. On the right (east) side of the road is the **Peribolos of Apollo**, a courtyard flanked by Ionic columns. Some have been restored. Nearby is a **public latrine**. Some seats remain. The site's **museum** houses statues, mosaics, figurines, reliefs and friezes.

Acrocorinth Ακροκόρινθος

Earthquakes and invasions compelled the Corinthians to retreat to Acrocorinth, a sheer bulk of limestone which was one of the finest natural fortifications in Greece. The original fortress was built in ancient times and was coveted and strengthened by streams of invaders. The ruins are a medley of imposing Roman, Byzantine, Frankish, Venetian and Turkish ramparts, harbouring remains of Byzantine chapels, Turkish houses and mosques.

On the higher of Acrocorinth's two summits is the **Temple of Aphrodite** where the sacred courtesans, who so raised the ire of St Paul, catered to the desires of the insatiable Corinthians. Little remains of the temple, but the views are tremendous. The site is open Tuesday to Sunday from 8.30 am to 6 pm. Admission is 500 dr.

CORINTH CANAL

The concept of cutting a canal through the Isthmus of Corinth to link the Ionian and Aegean seas was first proposed by the tyrant Periander, founder of ancient Corinth. The enormity of the task defeated him, so he opted instead to build a paved slipway across which sailors dragged small ships on rollers – a method used until the 13th century.

In the intervening years, many leaders, including Alexander the Great and Caligula, toyed with the canal idea, but it was Nero who actually began digging in AD 67. In true megalomaniac fashion, he struck the first blow himself using a golden pickaxe. He then left it to 6000 Jewish prisoners to do the hard work. The project was soon halted by invasions of the Gauls. Finally, in the 19th century (1883-93), a French engineering company completed the canal.

The Corinth Canal, cut through solid rock, is over six km long and 23 metres wide. The vertical sides rise 90 metres above the water. The canal did much to elevate Piraeus' status as a major Mediterranean port. It's an impressive sight, particularly when a ship is passing.

Getting There & Away

The canal can be reached on a Loutraki bus from modern Corinth to the canal bridge. Any bus or train between Corinth and Athens will also pass over the canal. In summer, you can board a cruise vessel to take you from Corinth harbour through the awesome canal and possibly on to the Saronic Gulf islands. A sign on the wharf or the crew will give details.

ISTHMIA Ισθμία

At the south-eastern end of the canal is the site of ancient Isthmia. The remains of the **Sanctuary of Poseidon**, a defensive wall, and **Roman theatre** are of interest mainly to archaeological buffs. As with Nemea, Delphi and Olympia, ancient Isthmia was renowned as one of the sites of the Panhellenic Games, and the site's excellent **museum** (open daily except Tuesday) contains various ancient athletic exhibits. The modern village of Isthmia lies a short distance to the east of the ancient site.

LOUTRAKI Λουτράκι

Loutraki (population 7000), six km north of the Corinth Canal, lounges between a pebbled beach and the tall cliffs of the Gerania mountains. Once a traditional spa town patronised by elderly and frail Greeks, it remains a major producer of bottled mineral water. The town was devastated by the 1981 earthquake; and subsequent reconstruction has resulted in its reincarnation as

a tacky resort with modern, characterless hotels. Loutraki hardly warrants an overnight stay. But pause, *en route* from Corinth to Perahora, to taste the celebrated water which gushes from a fountain on the main street.

Getting There & Away

Half-hourly buses run from Corinth to Loutraki (20 minutes, 220 dr) and there are eight buses a day from Athens (1½ hours, 1250 dr). From Loutraki, buses leave every hour for Perahora (20 minutes, 220 dr).

PERAHORA Περαχώρα

The village of Perahora (population 1495), 13 km north of Loutraki, stands on a plateau inland from the sea. The road continues west to the lovely **Lake Vouliagmeni**, a lagoon linked to the sea by a narrow channel. Several inexpensive fish tavernas and a few domatia are on its shore.

Beyond the lake are the ruins of **ancient Perahora** which were excavated by Humfry Payne from 1930 to 1933. Payne was accompanied by his wife, Dilys Powell, who describes her stay in the area in her book *An Affair of the Heart*. At the site are the ruins of an agora, a stoa and an 8th-century temple in a **Sanctuary to Hera**. A visit is worthwhile for views of surrounding mountains.

Getting There & Away

There are hourly buses from Loutraki to Perahora (20 minutes, 220 dr). In July and August, there is one return bus a day from Vouliagmeni.

WEST OF CORINTH

The coastline stretching west from Corinth towards Patras is dotted with a series of fishing villages and cement resorts facing the Gulf of Corinth. Places such as **Derveni** (which has a sandy beach), **Kamari, Xylokastro**, and **Kiato** are popular mainly with Greek holiday-makers and groups from northern Europe. Beach buffs will be mostly uninspired. But consolation comes with clear and unpolluted water, friendly villages, inexpensive fresh fish and occasional hotels set on small bays surrounded by pencil pines. There are several interesting minor sites inland that are worth a detour if you have the time.

Ancient Sikyon Σικυών

Ancient Sikyon, known as the City of Pumpkins, possibly because of the plump, terracotta pottery once produced here, is six km south of Kiato. Founded in 2nd millenium BC by the Ionians and later conquered by the Dorians, it became an important cultural centre focusing on wax painting, sculpture and pottery. It was crushed by various forces and finally destroyed by earthquake in 23 AD.

Its **museum** (☎ 0742-28 900), housed in a restored Roman baths, is open Monday to Sunday from 8.30 am to 9 pm. Admission is free. It contains vases from various periods, terracotta statuettes from Archaic to Roman times and a Praxiteles-styled marble head of Apollo. The museum was temporarily closed at the time of writing, so check the latest situation with Corinth's tourist police. Nearby is a partially preserved **gymnasium** from Hellenistic and Roman times and the remains of the **Temple of Artemis**.

Getting There & Away You can either take a taxi to the site from Kiato, or walk. There are regular trains to Kiato from Corinth and Patras.

Stymfalia Στυμφαλία

If you've got your own transport, the 36-km drive from Kiato to Stymfalia is worth the effort for the scenery as much as anything else. Little remains of the ancient site apart from the ruins of three temples. The site is next to a marshy lake of the same name, which was the home of the mythical, man-eating Stymfalian birds that Heracles was ordered to shoo away as the sixth of his labours. The birds were depicted in sculptures on the Temple of Artemis Stymfalia. Finds from the site are on display in the museum at Sikyon.

Nemea Νεμέα

Ancient Nemea lies four km north-east of the modern village of the same name. According to mythology, it was here that Heracles carried out the first of his 12 labours – the slaying of the lion which had been sent by Hera to destroy Nemea. The lion became the constellation Leo – each of the 12 labours is related to a sign of the zodiac.

Like Olympia, Nemea was not a city but a sanctuary and venue for the biennial Nemean games, held in honour of Zeus. These games became one of the great Panhellenic festivals. Only three columns of the 4th-century-BC, Doric **Temple of Zeus** remain. Other ruins include a bathhouse and hostelry. The site's **museum** is excellent and includes models of the site and English explanations.

At the **stadium**, 500 metres back on the road, you can see the athletes' starting line and distance markers. The site and museum (☎ 0746-22 739) are open Tuesday to Sunday from 8.30 am to 3 pm. Admission to both is 500 dr.

Getting There & Away Nemea is 35 km south-west of Corinth, which has seven buses a day to Nemea (one hour, 650 dr). Ask the driver to drop you at the site, four km before the village. There are also buses from Argos (460 dr), in Argolis.

Argolis Αργολίδα

The Argolis peninsula, which separates the Saronic and Argolic gulfs in the north-east, is a veritable treasure trove for archaeology buffs. The town of Argos, from which the region takes its name, is thought to be the longest continually inhabited town in Greece. Argolis was the seat of power of the Mycenaean Empire that ruled Greece from 1600 to 1200 BC. The ancient cities of Mycenae, Tiryns, Argos and Epidaurus are the region's major attractions.

MYCENAE Μυκήνες

The modern village of Mycenae (in Greek Mi-KI-nes) is 12 km north of Argos, just east of the main Argos-Corinth road. It has little to commend it other than its proximity to the ancient site, two km to the north. The village is geared towards the hordes of package tourists visiting ancient Mycenae. There is accommodation along its single street. There's no bank, but there is a post office with a currency-exchange service at the ancient site. Mycenae's telephone code is 0751. The postcode is 212 00.

Places to Stay – bottom end

The two camping grounds at Mycenae are *Camping Mycenae* (☎ 76 247), near the bus stop in Mycenae village, and *Camping Atreus* (☎ 76 221), near the Corinth-Argos road.

Mycenae's *YHA hostel* (☎ 76 255) is above the Restaurant Iphigenia on the main road. Beds are 1000 dr per person and a Hostelling International card is required. It's a small hostel, so ring first to check it's not full.

Places to Stay – middle

The charming C-class *Belle Helene Hotel* (☎ 76 255) has doubles/triples with breakfast for 7000/10,000 dr. The renowned amateur archaeologist Heinrich Schliemann (see under Ancient Mycenae) stayed here while excavating. Other famous guests have included Claude Debussy and Virginia Woolf. The bus stop is outside. Further up, the friendly *Hotel Klitemnistra* (☎ 76 451) has an airy restaurant and singles/doubles/triples for 4000/6000/7000 dr. The B-class *La Petit Planete* (☎ 76 240), on Leoforos Tsounta, charges 8900/13,200 dr for singles/doubles and also has a restaurant and bar.

Places to Eat

Restaurants cater for day-trippers. The best value is to be found at the *Hotel Klitemnistra Restaurant*, which serves good three-course meals for between 1300 and 1500 dr.

Getting There & Away

Bus Mycenae is served by three buses per day from Nafplio (one hour, 460 dr) and six per day from Argos (30 minutes, 200 dr). Most buses stop at the village and the ancient site. Otherwise, take an hourly Corinth-Argos bus which will leave you on the main road with a three-km uphill walk to the site.

Train The Mycenae train station is at Fichtio, two km from the village. It is on the Corinth-Kalamata line.

ANCIENT MYCENAE

In the barren foothills of Mt Agios Ilias (750 metres) and Mt Zara (600 metres) stand the sombre and mighty ruins of ancient Mycenae, vestiges of a kingdom which, for 400 years (1600-1200 BC), was the most powerful in Greece, holding sway over the Argolid (the modern-day prefecture of Argolis) and influencing the other Mycenaean kingdoms.

The site (☎ 0751-76 585) is open daily from 8 am to 7 pm. Admission to the citadel and the Treasury of Atreus is 1500 dr. After exploring, revive yourself with Argolis orange juice, sold from a van opposite the mobile post office.

History & Mythology

Mycenae is synonymous with Homer and Schliemann. In the 9th century BC, Homer told in his epic poems, the *Iliad* and the *Odyssey*, of 'well-built Mycenae, rich in gold'. These poems were, until the 19th century, regarded as gripping and beautiful legends. In the 1870s, the amateur archaeologist Heinrich Schliemann (1822-90), despite derision from professional archaeologists, struck gold, first at Troy then at Mycenae.

In Mycenae, myth and history are inextricably linked. According to Homer and Aeschylus's *Oresteia*, the city of Mycenae was founded by Perseus, the son of Danaë and Zeus. Perseus' greatest heroic deed was the killing of the hideous snake-haired Medusa, whose looks literally petrified the beholder. Eventually, the dynasty of Perseus

The Life of Heinrich Schliemann

Heinrich Schliemann is often dismissed as being too eccentric and monomaniacal to be taken seriously in the dry, academic world of archaeology – someone who was driven more by impulse than carefully correlated facts. Despite his inaccurate dating of his finds, Schliemann must be acknowledged as the archaeologist who proved that the kingdom of Mycenae had existed and was not merely a product of Homer's imagination.

The life of Heinrich Schliemann was as dramatic, fantastic and eventful as any of Homer's tales. He was born in the Baltic German state of Mecklenburg in 1822. His father was a feckless womaniser and drunkard whose long-suffering wife died when Schliemann was only nine years old. Forced to leave school at 14, Schliemann got a job stacking crates in a local grocery shop. Five years later he'd had enough, and set off to seek his fortune. He walked to Hamburg and got a job as a ship's boy on a vessel bound for Venezuela. The ship was wrecked off the Dutch Frisian island of Texel, but against all odds Schliemann survived and wandered into Amsterdam half-naked, half-dead and destitute.

With a thirst for both knowledge and money, he worked for various trading companies in Holland and studied obsessively in his spare time. Languages were one of his passions; he learnt modern European languages in six weeks, but Ancient Greek took him a while longer. By the age of 24 he was working for an international Dutch trading company, and in 1846 he was appointed their representative in St Petersburg. Already fluent in English, Portuguese, French, Dutch, Spanish and Italian, he was now able to add Russian to his repertoire.

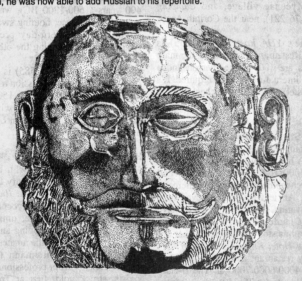

The death mask Schliemann mistakenly thought to be that of Agamemnon

was overthrown by Pelops, a son of Tantalus. The Mycenaean Royal House of Atreus was probably descended from Pelops, although myth and history are so intertwined, and the genealogical line so complex, that no-one really knows. Whatever the bloodlines, by Agamemnon's time the House of Atreus was the most powerful of the Achaeans (Homer's

Over the next 20 years Schliemann made a considerable amount of money in various business enterprises. One particularly lucrative one was as a private banker in California during the gold rush. By the time he was 40, he had so much money in the bank he decided it was time to indulge a fantasy which had obsessed him for many years. Since his time in Amsterdam, he had steeped himself in Greek mythology and was convinced that Homer's epics were, albeit loosely, based on fact. In 1868 he decided to prove this, but wanted a sympathetic partner to help him. He wrote to a friend, a bishop in Athens, asking him to find him a suitable wife. The bishop came up with a number of likely candidates, including 17-year-old Sophia Engastromenos (later the family name was changed to Kastomenos). When they met, Schliemann asked her a number of questions. The two crucial ones were: Could she recite some of Homer by heart? And, would she like to travel? The highly intelligent Sophia passed the test, they were married and she was whisked off to Hissartik (ancient Ilium, alias Troy) in Asia Minor to assist Schliemann in his excavations. In his overenthusiasm Schliemann dug too deep and uncovered treasures which belonged to a pre-Homeric period, not that of King Priam as he believed. The same happened in Mycenae, where he excavated next. The gold mask which he unearthed and excitedly proclaimed as the death mask of Agamemnon actually belonged to a king who lived three centuries earlier.

His marriage to Sophia was a happy one: she accompanied him in all his expeditions, ever-supportive, hard-working and enthusiastic. Marriage did not, however, diminish Schliemann's eccentricities and obsessions – the Schliemanns' house, on El Venizelou in Athens (built by the esteemed German architect, Ernst Ziller) was named Iliou Melathron (Palace of Troy) and their son and daughter were called Agamemnon and Andromache.

Appropriately, his mausoleum in Athens' First Cemetery, designed by Ziller, is adorned with scenes from the Trojan War.

One of the biggest archaeological mysteries of postwar years has been the whereabouts of Priam's Treasure – Schliemann's name for the treasures he uncovered at Troy has stuck even though they belong to a much earlier king. Schliemann donated the gold to Berlin, where it went on display in the Ethnological Museum. In 1945 when the Red Army occupied Berlin the collection disappeared. Some people believed the gold had been melted down, others that it had been sold on the black market by Soviet soldiers. Another rumour was that it was stored in a vault at the Pushkin Museum in Moscow, although Russia repeatedly denied this. Then in August 1993 Russia's Minister for Culture Yevgeni Siderov stated that he had seen and touched the treasures which had indeed been hidden in Russia on orders from the Kremlin at the end of WW II.

Talks have been taking place between Bonn and Moscow over the many artworks which disappeared during WW II, and Schliemann's gold will be amongst those discussed. Presently the Russians, Germans, Turks and Greeks are all laying claims to Priam's Treasure. ■

Heinrich Schliemann

name for the Greeks). It eventually came to a sticky end, fulfilling the curse which had been cast because of Pelops' misdeeds.

The historical facts are that Mycenae was

first settled by Neolithic people in the 6th millennium BC. Between 2100-1900 BC, during the Old Bronze Age, Greece was invaded by people of Indo-European stock

PELOPONNESE

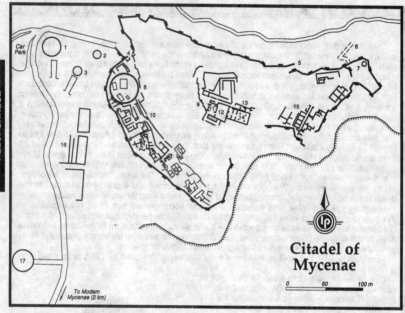

Citadel of Mycenae

0   50   100 m

To Modern
Mycenae (2 km)

1	Grave Circle B	7	Secret Cistern	13	Agamemnon's Death
2	Tomb of Clytaemnestra	8	Grave Circle A		Chamber
3	Tomb of Aegisthus	9	Agamemnon's Palace	14	Megaron
4	Lion Gate	10	Houses	15	Artisans' Quarters
5	Postern Gate	11	Throne Room	16	Merchants' Houses
6	Drain	12	Great Court	17	Treasury of Atreus

who had crossed Anatolia via Troy to Greece. The invaders brought an advanced culture to the then-primitive Mycenae and other mainland settlements. This new civilisation is now referred to as the Mycenaean, named after Mycenae, its most powerful kingdom. The other kingdoms included Pylos, Tiryns, Corinth and Argos in the Peloponnese. Evidence of Mycenaean civilisation has also been found at Thiva (Thebes) and Athens.

The city of Mycenae consisted of a fortified citadel and surrounding settlement. Due to the sheer size of the walls of the citadel

(13 metres high and seven metres thick), the ancient Greeks believed they must have been lifted by a Cyclops, one of the giants described by Homer in the *Odyssey*.

Archaeological evidence indicates that the palaces of the Mycenaean kingdoms were destroyed around 1200 BC. It was long thought that the destruction was the work of the Dorians, but later evidence indicates that the decline of the Mycenaean civilisation was symptomatic of the general turmoil around the Mediterranean at the time. The great Hittite Empire in Anatolia, which had reached its height between 1450 and

1200 BC, was now in decline, as was the Egyptian civilisation. The Mycenaeans, Hittites and Egyptians had all prospered through their trade with each other, but this had ceased by the end of the 1200s. Many of the great palaces of the Mycenaean kingdoms were destroyed 150 years before the Dorians arrived. Whether the destruction was the work of outsiders or due to internal division between the various Mycenaean kingdoms remains unresolved.

Exploring the Site

The **Citadel of Mycenae** is entered through the **Lion Gate**, so called because of the relief above the lintel of two lionesses supporting a pillar. This motif is believed to have been the insignia of the Royal House of Atreus.

Inside the citadel, you will find **Grave Circle A** on the right. This was the royal cemetery and contained six grave shafts. Five were excavated by Schliemann in 1874-76 and the magnificent gold treasures he uncovered are in Athens' National Archaeological Museum. In the last grave shaft, Schliemann found a well-preserved gold death mask with flesh still clinging to it. Fervently, he sent a telegram to the Greek king stating 'I have gazed upon the face of Agamemnon'. The mask turned out to be that of an unknown king who had died some 300 years before Agamemnon.

To the south of Grave Circle A are the remains of a group of houses. In one was found the famous **Warrior Vase** which Schliemann regarded as one of his greatest discoveries.

The main path leads up to Agamemnon's

The Trojan War & the Fall of the House of Atreus

In his epic poems, the *Iliad* and the *Odyssey*, Homer related the events of a crucial period in Mycenaean history – the Trojan War and its aftermath. Homer called Troy 'Ilium' (hence the epic's title, the *Iliad*). The 10-year war took place around 1250 BC between the Achaeans and the Trojans, during the reign of Mycenae's King Agamemnon and Troy's King Priam.

Agamemnon's brother, Menelaus, king of Sparta, had suffered great humiliation when his beautiful wife, Helen, was abducted by Paris, the son of King Priam. Menelaus sought the advice of Nestor, king of Pylos, the oldest and wisest of the Mycenaean kings, who told him that nothing less than a combined force of all the armies of Greece would be sufficient to get Helen back. So, accompanied by Agamemnon, Menelaus visited all the princes and heroes in the land to ask for their assistance. Amongst them were Odysseus, king of Ithaca (Ithaki), Patroclus, Achilles and Nestor. Agamemnon, as the most powerful and richest king in Greece, headed the Greek expedition to Troy. Fighting on the Trojan side were Paris, his brother Hector and Priam. The war dragged on for 10 years, during which time Hector killed Patroclus, Achilles killed Hector and Paris killed Achilles, and still there was no end in sight. Odysseus then came up with the idea of the wooden horse filled with soldiers.

While all this was going on in Troy, back in Mycenae, Agamemnon's wife, Clytaemnestra, had taken a lover, Aegisthus. On his return to Mycenae, Agamemnon was greeted lovingly by his wife (despite his being accompanied by his Trojan concubine, Cassandra). However, later while he was taking a bath, Clytaemnestra, assisted by her lover, stabbed him to death. Orestes, her son, then avenged the murder of his father by murdering her, and so the Mycenaen Royal House of Atreus came to its dramatic end. ■

The Trojan horse: the trick that brought Troy's downfall

palace, centred around the **Great Court**. The rooms to the north were the private royal apartments. One of these rooms is believed to be the chamber in which Agamemnon was murdered. Access to the **throne room**, west of the Great Court, would originally have been via a large staircase. On the south-eastern side of the palace is the **megaron** (reception hall).

On the northern boundary of the citadel is the **Postern Gate** through which, it is said, Orestes escaped after murdering his mother. In the far north-eastern corner of the citadel is the **secret cistern**. It can be explored by torchlight, but take care – the steps are slippery.

Until the late 15th century BC, the Mycenaeans put their royal dead into shaft graves. They then devised a new form of burial – the tholos tomb, shaped like a beehive. The approach road to Mycenae passes to the right of the best preserved of these, the **Treasury of Atreus** or tomb of Agamemnon. A 40-metre-long passage leads to this immense beehive-shaped chamber. It is built with stone blocks that get steadily smaller as the structure tapers to its central point. Further along the road on the right is **Grave Circle B**, and nearby are the tholos tombs of Aegisthus and Clytaemnestra.

Getting There & Away
Buses depart several times daily for both ancient and modern Mycenae from Nafplio and Argos. See the Getting There & Away section under (modern) Mycenae for details.

ARGOS Αργος
Argos (AR-ghos, population 24,000) is the oldest continuously inhabited town in Greece, but vestiges of its past glory lie mostly beneath the uninspiring modern town. The ruins that have been excavated are perhaps only of interest to aficionados, but Argos is a convenient base from which to explore the sites of Argolis and has a refreshing lack of tourist hype. It is also a major transport hub for buses. Argos is a good place to find a job picking oranges.

Orientation & Information
Argos' showpiece and focal point is the magnificent central square, Plateia Agiou Petrou, with its Art Nouveau lights, citrus and palm trees and the impressive Agios Petros church. Beyond, Argos deteriorates into an unremarkable working town.

The central square is 500 metres from the train station. To reach the square, walk up Filellinon to a five-road intersection. Continue straight ahead along Makariou, past a junction with a large church on the left, until the road forks at the OTE. The left fork, which is Vasileos Georgiou, leads to Plateia Agiou Petrou.

Argos has two bus stations. The Athens bus station is very near the central square. From the ticket office, turn right and then second right onto Vasilissas Olgas which leads to Plateia Agiou Petrou, passing the archaeological museum on the right. The Arcadia-Lakonia bus station is at Pheothonos 24. To get there from the Athens bus station, turn left from the ticket office, take the first right and then the first left onto Pheothonos. The bus station is along here on the right.

The post office is at Danaou 16. This street runs off the central square next to the Hotel Telessila. The OTE office is at Nikitara 8, off the east side of the central square.

Argos' postcode is 212 00 and the telephone code is 0751. The National Bank of Greece is along Nikitara from the central square. Argos' hospital (☎ 24 455/456; emergency 166) is on Corinth, off the north side of the central square. There is neither EOT nor tourist police in Argos. Regular police can be contacted on ☎ 100.

Archaeological Museum
Even if you're only passing through Argos, try to pause long enough to visit the archaeological museum, near the central square on Vasilissas Olgas. The collection includes some outstanding Roman mosaics and sculptures; Neolithic, Mycenaean and Geometric pottery; and bronze objects from the Mycenaean tombs. The museum (☎ 68 819)

is open Tuesday to Sunday from 8.30 am to 3 pm. Admission is 500 dr.

Roman Ruins

There are Roman ruins on both sides of Tripolis, the main Argos-Tripolis road. From the central square, walk along Danaou and turn right onto Theatron to get there. On the west side of the road is an enormous **theatre** which could seat up to 20,000 people (more than at Epidaurus). It dates from classical times but was greatly altered by the Romans. Nearby are the remains of a 1st-century AD **odeion** (indoor theatre) and **Roman baths**. The site is open every day from 8.30 am to 3 pm. Admission is free.

It's 45 minutes of hard slog by footpath from the theatre up to the **Fortress of Larissa**, a conglomeration of Byzantine, Frankish, Venetian and Turkish architecture, standing on the foundations of the city's principal ancient citadel.

The **Sanctuary of Apollo & Athena** and the nearby remains of a **Mycenaean necropolis**, where some chamber tombs and shaft graves have been excavated, lie to the north of the Roman ruins. The hill to the north-east of these ruins is the site of a small, ancient citadel and an early Bronze Age settlement, now crowned by the chapel of Agios Elias. To reach these ruins from the Roman ruins, walk north along Tripolis and turn left at the intersection with Tsokri. From the central square, walk up Vasileos Konstantinou, which becomes Tsokri.

Places to Stay

The cheapest hotel in Argos is the D-class *Hotel Theoxenia* (☎ 67 808), Tsokri 31, where airy single/double/triple rooms are 3000/6000/8000 dr with shared bathroom. From the central square walk up Vasileos Konstantinou, which becomes Tsokri.

The C-class *Hotel Telessila* (☎ 68 317, 66 249) on the central square, has singles/doubles with shared facilities for 2750/4400 dr, or 3850/5500 dr with bathroom. North-east of the central square, the D-class *Hotel Palladion* (☎ 67 807, 28 235 or 22 968), Vasilissas Sophias, has reasonable

singles/doubles/triples for 4000/6000/7500 dr with private bathroom. The C-class *Hotel Mycenae* (☎ 68 754), on the central square, has large, comfortable rooms for 7700/12,000/15,000 dr. An apartment for four, including breakfast, is 24,000 dr.

Places to Eat

The restaurants on the central square are either relatively expensive or serve fast food. Head for the back streets for traditional, cheap fare. A few simple *ouzeria* are between the main square and the train station. Argos' *food market* is on Vasileos Konstantinou.

Getting There & Away

Bus The Athens bus station has buses every half-hour to Nafplio (30 minutes, 200 dr); hourly buses to Athens (two hours, 1900 dr); six buses a day to Mycenae (25 minutes, 200 dr); and two buses a day to Nemea (one hour, 460 dr). The fare to Corinth is 950 dr.

From the Arcadia-Lakonia bus station, nine buses a day go to Tripolis (1¼ hours, 900 dr); and eight via Tripolis to Sparta (2½ hours, 1200 dr). To Leonidio it's three hours and costs 1200 dr.

Train Four trains leave for Athens (three hours, 1040 dr) via Mycenae (10 minutes, 105 dr), Nemea (45 minutes, 200 dr) and Corinth (one hour, 510 dr). Three trains a day go to Kalamata (3½ hours, 1260 dr) via Tripolis (one hour, 950 dr).

AROUND ARGOS

About seven km from Argos off the main road to Tripolis is the pretty village of **Kefalari**. It is surrounded by vineyards which sprawl out either side of the two-km dirt road that climbs up to the **Pyramid of Helenekion** (or Pyramid of Kenchreai). It was built in 4 BC to commemorate a victory over Sparta and evolved into a fort. It stands – fenced, crude and crumbling – on a hilltop by a church. It's hardly worth the walk, but the deviation to Kefalari is. The village centrepiece is the substantial and beautiful **Church of the Virgin & Child Life-Giving Spring**. Framed by trees and bougainvillea, beneath grottos sacred to Dionysos and Pan on the slope of Mt Haon, it spans a gushing mountain stream. Visitors can soak up the tranquillity at open-air summer tavernas. Buses headed for Kefalari leave from Argos' Arcadia-Lakonia bus station. Back on the road to Tripolis, *Lerna Camping* (✆ 0751-47 520/521) at the nearby village of **Myli**, close to Nafplio, offers a tranquil alternative to staying in Nafplio or Argos. (See also the south-east section for details of the scenic coastal route from Myli to Leonidio).

NAFPLIO Ναύπλιο

Nafplio (NAF-pli-o, population 10,000), 12 km south-east of Argos on the Argolic Gulf, is capital of the prefecture of Argolis and has been a major port since the Bronze Age. So strategic was its position that it had three fortresses – the massive principal fortress of Palamidi, the smaller İç Kale ('inner castle' in Turkish) and the diminutive Bourtzi on an islet north of the old town.

Nafplio is one of Greece's prettiest towns. In the old town, narrow streets with elegant Venetian houses and gracious neoclassical mansions are dominated by the towering Palamidi Fortress.

Removed from the spotlight as capital of Greece after Kapodistrias' assassination by the Maniot chieftains, Konstantinos and Georgos Mavromihalis, Nafplio settled into a more comfortable role as a peaceful seaside resort. With good bus connections, the city is an absorbing base from which to explore many ancient sites.

Like Argos, Nafplio can offer casual work on local orange or apricot orchards.

Orientation

The old town occupies a narrow promontory with the İç Kale fortress on the southern side and the promenades of Bouboulinas and Akti Miaouli on the north side. The principal streets of the old town are Amalias, Vasileos Konstantinou, Staïkopoulou and Kapodistriou. The old town's central square is Plateia Syntagmatos (Syntagma Square), at the western end of Vasileos Konstantinou. The bus station is on Syngrou, the street separating the old town from the new. The main street of the new town is 25 Martiou, an easterly continuation of Staïkopoulou.

Information

Nafplio's post office is on Syngrou, and the OTE is on the northern side of 25 Martiou. Nafplio's postcode is 211 00 and the telephone code is 0752. The National Bank of Greece is on Plateia Syntagmatos. The municipal tourist office (✆ 24 444) is on 25 Martiou, opposite the OTE and diagonally opposite the helpful tourist police (✆ 28 131) at the southern end of Syngrou. Follow the road as it curves right.

Palamidi Fortress

This vast citadel stands on a 215-metre-high rock. Within the outer walls are three separate Venetian fortresses, built between 1711 and 1714 but seized by the Turks only a year after completion. Above each of the gates of the citadel is the Venetian emblem of the Lion of St Mark. During the War of Independence, the Greeks, under the leadership of the venerable klepht chief, Theodoros Kolokotronis, besieged the citadel for 15 months before the Turks surrendered. In the new town, north of the OTE, stands a splendid equestrian statue of Kolokotronis, who was known as the Grand Old Man of the Morea.

The fortress affords marvellous views. The energetic can tackle the seemingly endless steps (about 1000) that lead there from south-east of the bus station. Climb early and take water. There's also a road to the fortress. A taxi costs about 1000 dr one way. The fortress (✆ 28 036) is open Monday to Friday from 8 am to 5 pm in winter (until 7 pm in summer), and weekends from 8 am to 5 pm. Admission is 800 dr.

Museums

Nafplio's **Popular Art Museum** (✆ 28 379) won the European Museum of the Year award in 1981 for its superior displays of traditional textile-producing techniques (with in-depth explanations in English) and folk costumes. The museum is in the old

PELOPONNESE

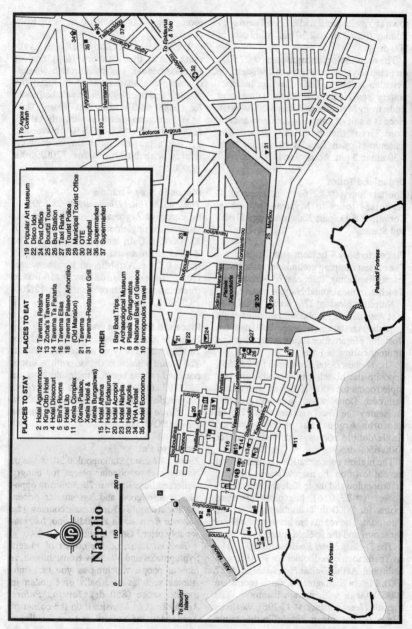

Nafplio

0   150   300 m

PLACES TO STAY

2 Hotel Agamemnon
3 King Otto Hotel
4 Hotel Dioscouri
5 Elini's Rooms
6 Hotel Lito
11 Xenia Complex
   (Xenia Palace,
   Xenia Hotel &
   Xenia Bungalows)
15 Hotel Athena
17 Hotel Epidaurus
20 Hotel Acropol
23 Hotel Nafplia
33 Hotel Argolis
34 YHA Hostel
35 Hotel Economou

PLACES TO EAT

12 Taverna Retsina
13 Zorba's Taverna
14 Taverna Ta Fanaria
16 Taverna Ellas
18 Taverna Palaeo Arhontiko
   (Old Mansion)
21 Taverna
31 Taverna-Restaurant Grill

OTHER

1 Bay Boat Trips
7 Archaeological Museum
8 Platia Syntagmatos
9 National Bank of Greece
10 Iannopoulos Travel
19 Popular Art Museum
22 Disco Idol
24 Post Office
25 Bourtzi Tours
26 Bus Station
27 Taxi Rank
28 Tourist Police
29 Municipal Tourist Office
30 OTE
32 Hospital
36 Supermarket
37 Supermarket

To Argos &
Corinth

To Epidaurus
& Tolo

Palamidi Fortress

Ic Kale Fortress

To Bourtzi
Island

town at Ypsilandou 1 and is open Tuesday to Sunday from 9 am to 2.30 pm. Admission is 500 dr.

The **archaeological museum** (☎ 27 502) on Plateia Syntagmatos is in an 18th-century Venetian building. The collection includes pottery from Neolithic to classical times, and finds from Mycenae and Tiryns. The prize piece is a suit of bronze Mycenaean armour from Tiryns that is virtually intact. The museum is open Tuesday to Sunday from 8.30 am to 3 pm. Admission is 500 dr.

Organised Tours
Bourtzi Tours (☎ 22 691), at Syngrou 4, organises tours to Mystras; Mycenae, Corinth and Delphi; Kalavryta; and Hydra and Spetses.

Places to Stay – bottom end
The closest camping grounds are at the beach resorts, including Tolo, east of Nafplio (see Beaches in the Around Nafplio section).

Nafplio's pleasant *YHA hostel* (☎ 27 754) is at Argonafton 15, about 20 minutes' walk from the bus station. Beds are 1000 dr and a Hostelling International card is required. The summer curfew is 1 am.

The D-class *Hotel Economou* (☎ 23 955), opposite the hostel, has agreeable double/ triple rooms for 8000/10,000 dr with shared bathroom. Doubles with bathroom are 8000 dr. Nearby, the *Hotel Argolis* (☎ 27 721), on Leoforos Argous, has clean, balconied single/double rooms with bathroom for 4500/6500 dr.

The highest concentration of domatia is in the old town on the narrow streets between Staïkopoulou and the İç Kale fortress. *Elini's Rooms* (☎ 27 036), has pine-furnished rooms for 7000 dr a double with private bathroom. The rooms are between the Hotel Dioscouri and the İç Kale fortress.

The D-class *Hotel Epidaurus* (☎ 27 541), on Ypsilandou, has doubles for 9000 dr with bathroom. At the C-class *Hotel Athena* (☎ 27 695), Plateia Syntagmatos, small rooms are 8000/9500 dr with private bathroom. The friendly *Hotel Acropol* (☎ 17 796), Vasilissis Olgas 9, has clean single/double/triple

rooms for 5700/7900/9500 dr with bathroom.

The D-class *Hotel Lito* (☎ 28 093) Zygomata 28 at the southern (top) end of Farmakopoulou, has comfortable singles/ doubles with shared bathroom for 6500/ 8000 dr and doubles with private bathroom for 10,000 dr. The *King Otto Hotel* (☎ 27 585), Farmakopoulou 3, is similarly priced. *Hotel Nafplia* (☎ 28 167/910), Navarinou 11, has a bar and quiet singles/doubles/ triples with bathroom for 7700/9500/ 11,000 dr.

Places to Stay – middle
The C-class *Hotel Dioscouri* (☎ 28 550), on the corner of Zygomata 6 and Vyronos, has immaculate single/double rooms for 10,000/ 13,700/17,000 dr, including breakfast. The B-class *Hotel Agamemnon* (☎ 28 021/022; fax 28 022), at Akti Miaouli 3 on the waterfront, offers mandatory half-board (breakfast and lunch or dinner) for 12,200/ 19,300/25,600 dr.

Places to Stay – top end
Nafplio's *Xenia Complex* (☎ 28 991/992; fax 28 987) has three types of accommodation. The *Xenia Palace* is deluxe with a disco, pool and private beach. Singles/doubles are 28,000/32,000 dr. The A-class *Xenia Hotel* has singles/doubles for 18,000/28,000 dr, and *Xenia Bungalows* has singles/doubles for 27,000/40,000 dr.

Places to Eat
Zorba's Taverna, Staïkopoulou 30, is one of Nafplio's most popular places for hungry Hellenophiles. *Taverna Ta Fanaria*, opposite, is also good and has similar prices, starting at about 900 dr for main courses. The *Taverna Retsina*, on Kapodistriou, has reasonably priced Greek dishes.

Taverna Ellas, on the corner of Plateia Syntagmatos and Vasileos Konstantinou, is fun for people-watching as you tuck into staples such as meatballs or chicken in tomato sauce (850 dr). *Taverna Palaeo Arhontiko* (Old Mansion), on the corner of Ypsilandou and Sofroni, is open for dinner only and serves squid, swordfish and dishes of German origin.

The simple *Taverna-Restaurant Grill*, at 25 Martiou 11 in the new town, serves wine from the barrel and has long had a reputation for hearty home-cooked lunches and grills at night. Prices are reasonable.

Entertainment

From mid-June to the end of August, ancient Greek dramas are performed at the *Theatre of Epidaurus* (30 km from Nafplio) in conjunction with the Athens Festival. Tickets can be bought in Nafplio at Bourtzi Tours (☎ 22 691), Syngrou 4. Tickets go on sale 10 days before each performance. For more information, see the Epidaurus section. On performance evenings, Bourtzi Tours runs buses to Epidaurus from Nafplio, as does the KTEL bus syndicate, which operates excursions from Nafplio bus station.

A young crowd hangs out at the eateries and bars around Plateia Kapodistriou off Syngrou. *Disco Idol* is on the corner of Syngrou and Flessa. There are several music bars on Bouboulinas and one on 25 Martiou.

Take a boat trip to Bourtzi islet for coffee or return to a past, romantic era on a horse-drawn carriage ride around the old town. Boats leave for the islet (500 dr) at the eastern end of the old town waterfront by the car park. Bargain for your carriage ride.

Getting There & Away

Bus There are hourly buses from Nafplio to Athens (2½ hours, 2100 dr); half-hourly buses to Argos (30 minutes, 200 dr); hourly buses to Tolo (30 minutes, 200 dr); three a day to Porto Heli (two hours, 1200 dr); and three a day to Mycenae (one hour, 460 dr), Epidaurus (40 minutes, 460 dr) and Galatas (two hours, 1300 dr). Other destinations include Ligourio (40 minutes; 460 dr), Tripolis (1¼ hours; 900 dr) and Corinth (1¼ hours, 750 dr).

Car & Motorbike A reliable motorbike-hire outlet is Moto Rent (☎ 27 183 or 25 642), Tsilikanidou 3, in the new town. Sun Drive (☎ 59 797) rents cars from its office in Tolo.

Hydrofoil Every day except Sunday during July and August there are hydrofoils from Nafplio to Zea Marina (four hours, 5090 dr) via Tolo (20 minutes, 650 dr), Porto Heli (50 minutes, 1900 dr), Spetses (one hour, 2200 dr), Ermioni (1½ hours, 2400 dr), Hydra (two hours, 2500 dr), Poros (2½ hours, 3400 dr), Methana (three hours, 4300 dr) and Aegina (three hours, 4400 dr). You can buy tickets from Iannopoulos Travel (☎ 27 456 or 28 054) on Plateia Syntagmatos.

AROUND NAFPLIO
Beaches

The nearest sandy beach to Nafplio is **Karathona beach**, at the far side of the Palamidi Fortress. There is no access from the fortress. To get there, walk (one hour) or take a bus from 25 Martiou, which doubles back to the coast. It's also possible to walk around the base of the headland.

Further around the coast, a line of beaches begins with **Asini**, nine km from Nafplio, followed by **Tolo**, **Drepano**, **Plaka**, **Kadia** and **Iria**. Tolo, 11 km from Nafplio, is the most developed of these, with water-sports equipment for hire.

Places to Stay Most hotels along this coast are block-booked by package-holiday companies, but there's a plethora of prominently signposted camping grounds.

Near Asini beach is *Kastraki Camping* (☎ 59 386/387); at Tolo is *Lido I* (☎ 59 489), *Lido II* (☎ 59 396), *Sunset Camping* (☎ 59 566), *Stars* (☎ 59 226), *Tolo Plaz* (☎ 59 133) and *Xeni* (☎ 59 338); at Plaka is *Plaka Beach* (☎ 92 294/395), *Argolis Beach* (☎ 92 228) and *Triton* (☎ 92 228). The telephone code for these camp sites is 0752.

At Iria beach, 27 km from Nafplio, is *Poseidon* (☎ 0753-91 341) and *Iria Beach Camping* (☎ 0753-91 253).

Getting There & Away There are hourly buses from Nafplio to Tolo (30 minutes, 200 dr) via Asini.

Ancient Asini Ασίνη

The ruins of ancient Asini, on a rocky headland one km inland from Asini beach, offer a diversion from sun seeking. There are the remains of an acropolis, Mycenaean tombs, Roman baths and Venetian fortifications.

Tiryns Τίρυνθα

The ruins of Homer's 'wall-girt Tiryns' are four km north-west of Nafplio. The walls of Tiryns are the apogee of Mycenaean architectural achievement (or paranoia), being even more substantial than those at Mycenae. In parts, they are 20 metres thick. The largest stones are estimated to weigh 14,000 kg. Within the walls there are vaulted galleries, secret stairways, and storage chambers. Frescoes from the palace are in Athens' National Archaeological Museum. Tiryns' setting is less awe-inspiring than Mycenae's but it's less visited. The site (☎ 0752-27 502) is open Monday to Friday from 8 am to 7 pm, and weekends from 8.30 am to 3 pm. Admission is 500 dr. The ruins stand to the right of the Nafplio-Argos road. Any Nafplio-Argos bus can drop you outside the site.

EPIDAURUS Επίδαυρος

Epidaurus (Ep-EE-dav-ros), 30 km east of Nafplio, is one of the most renowned of Greece's ancient sites. Epidaurus was a sanctuary of Asclepius, the god of medicine. The difference in the atmosphere here, compared with that of the war-orientated Mycenaean cities, is immediately obvious. Henry Miller wrote in *The Colossus of Maroussi* that Mycenae 'folds in on itself', but Epidaurus is 'open, exposed...devoted to the spirit'. Epidaurus seems to emanate joy, optimism and celebration.

History & Mythology

Legend has it that Asclepius was the son of Apollo and Coronis. While giving birth to Asclepius, Coronis was struck by a thunderbolt and killed. Apollo took his son to Mt Pelion where the physician Chiron instructed the boy in the healing arts.

Apollo was worshipped at Epidaurus in Mycenaean and Archaic times but, by the 4th century BC, he had been superseded by his son. Epidaurus became acknowledged as the birthplace of Asclepius. Although there were sanctuaries to Asclepius throughout Greece, the two most important were at Epidaurus and on the island of Kos. The fame of the sanctuary spread, and when a plague was raging in Rome, Livy and Ovid came to Epidaurus to seek help.

It is believed that licks from snakes were one of the curative practices at the sanctuary. Asclepius is normally shown with a serpent, which – by renewing its skin – symbolises rejuvenation. Other treatments provided at the sanctuary involved diet instruction, herbal medicines and occasionally even surgery, The sanctuary also served as an entertainment venue. Every four years the Festival of Asclepieia took place at Epidaurus. Dramas were staged and athletic competitions were held.

Theatre

Today, the 3rd-century theatre, not the sanctuary, pulls the crowds to Epidaurus. It is one of the best preserved of classical Greek buildings, renowned for its amazing acoustics. A coin dropped in the centre can be heard from the highest seat. Built of limestone, the theatre seats up to 14,000 people. Its entrance is flanked by restored Corinthian pilasters. The Festival of Epidaurus takes place each year in July and August. See the Entertainment section for details.

Museum

The museum, between the sanctuary and the theatre, houses statues, stone inscriptions recording miraculous cures, surgical instruments, votives and partial reconstructions of the sanctuary's once-elaborate tholos. After the theatre, the tholos is considered to have been the site's most impressive building and fragments of beautiful, intricately carved reliefs from its ceiling are also displayed.

Sanctuary

The vast ruins of the sanctuary are less crowded than the theatre. In the south is the huge **katagogeion** which was a hostelry for pilgrims and patients. To the west is the large **banquet hall** in which the Romans built an **odeion**. It was in this building that the Festival of Asclepieia took place. Opposite is the **stadium**, venue for the festival's athletic competitions.

To the north are the foundations of the **Temple of Asclepius** and next to them is the **abaton**. The therapies practised here seemed to have depended on the influence of the mind upon the body. It is believed that patients were given a pep talk by a priest on the powers of Asclepius then put to sleep in the abaton to dream of a visitation by the god. The dream would hold the key to the healing process.

East is the **Sanctuary of Egyptian Gods**, which is an indication that the cult of Asclepius was an adaptation of the cult of Imhotep. Imhotep was worshipped in Egypt for his healing powers. To the west of the Temple of Asclepius are the remains of the **tholos**, built in 360-320 BC. The function of the tholos is unknown.

Set among the green foothills of Mt Arahneo, the air redolent with herbs and pine trees, it's easy to see how the sanctuary would have had a beneficial effect upon the ailing. Considering the state of Greece's current health system, perhaps the centre should be resurrected.

Places to Stay & Eat

Although most visitors make a day trip to Epidaurus, there is accommodation there. The B-class *Xenia Hotel* (☎ 0753-22 003/004/005) at the site charges 13,200/20,200 dr for singles/doubles. The village of Ligourio, four km north of Epidaurus on the main road to Nafplio, offers cheaper options. The *Hotel Koronis* (☎ 0753-22 267) and the *Hotel Asklepios* (☎ 0753-22 251) are both on the Nafplio-Epidaurus road and charge around 5000/6000 dr for single/double rooms with shared facilities and, at the latter, 7000 dr a double with bath.

The *Restaurant Oasis*, on the main road in Ligourio, serves reasonably priced Greek food.

Entertainment

Ancient dramas are performed at the Epidaurus theatre during the Festival of Epidaurus, from 26 July to 30 August each year. Performances start at 9 pm, and tickets can be bought in Epidaurus (☎ 0753-22 006) at the site office on Thursday, Friday and Saturday from 9.30 am to 1 pm and 6 to 9 pm. They can also be bought from the Athens Festival box office (see the Entertainment section in the Athens chapter), or from Bourtzi Tours in Nafplio (see the Nafplio section in this chapter). Prices vary according to seating. Student discounts are available. At festival time, there are special buses from Athens (2½ hours, 2000 dr one way).

Getting There & Away

Three buses a day leave Nafplio for Epidaurus (40 minutes, 460 dr) running via Ligourio (also 460 dr).

ANCIENT TROIZEN Τροιζήν

Troizen (also known as Trizin), 49 km southeast of Ligourio, was an Ionian colony, the birthplace of Theseus and a refuge for Athenian women and children during the Persian invasion beginning in 480 BC. It shared many traditions and cults with Athens. The site is a few minutes' walk from the picturesque, mountain-clinging village of **Trizin**, also called Trizina.

The **Sanctuary of Hippolytos** is the first ruin you come across, followed by the remains of the city wall with an Hellenic tower. Small stones in the upper construction indicate Frankish rebuilding. A further 10 minutes' climbing brings you to the **Devil's Bridge**, a natural extension across the deep Gefyron gorge.

Buses from Nafplio to the seaside village of **Galatas** (two hours, 1300 dr) can drop you at the turn-off to Trizin, from where it's a steep climb to the site. The alternative is to continue to Galatas, which has camping facilities, and take a taxi back to Trizin. Galatas and Trizin can also be visited from the island of Poros (see the Saronic Gulf Islands chapter).

Arcadia Αρκαδία

The picturesque rural prefecture of Arcadia occupies much of the central Peloponnese. Its name evokes images of grassy meadows, forested mountains, gurgling streams and shady grottos. It was a favourite haunt of Pan, who played his pipes, guarded herds and frolicked with nymphs in this sunny, bucolic idyll.

Almost encircled by high mountains, Arcadia was remote enough in ancient times to remain largely untouched by the battles and intrigues of the rest of Greece. It was the only region of the Peloponnese not conquered by the Dorians. It remains a backwater, dotted with crumbling medieval villages, remote monasteries and Frankish castles, visited only by determined tourists. Few tourists make it either to the 100-odd km of unspoilt coastline on the Argolic gulf, running from the pretty town of Myli in the north to Leonidio.

TRIPOLIS Τρίπολη

The violent recent history of Arcadia's capital, Tripolis (TRI-po-lee, population 22,000), is in stark contrast with the surrounding rural idyll. In 1821, during the War of Independence, the town was captured by Kolokotronis and its 10,000 Turkish inhabitants massacred. The Turks retook the town three years later, and burnt it to the ground before withdrawing in 1928.

Tripolis itself is not a place to linger long, but it's a major transport hub for the Peloponnese. It also has some impressive neoclassical buildings and Byzantine churches, a large park and wonderful window-shopping for consumer goods. This is a good place to buy flokati rugs, made in nearby mountain villages.

Orientation & Information

The town's central square is Plateia Vasileos Georgiou. From the train station, walk along Lagopati and turn left onto Venizelou. You'll pass the Arkadias bus station on Plateia Kolokotroni. Buses leave for Athens, Argos, Pyrgos and various Arcadian villages. Buses for Kalamata, Pylos, Monemvassia and Gythio leave from the Messinia and Lakonia bus terminals on the main square. Tickets for Sparta, Mystras, Monemvassia and Gythio are available at the travel agency-kafeneio opposite the station. The neighbouring fast-food place sells tickets to Kalamata and Pylos.

The post office and OTE are north then west off Plateia Vasileos Georgiou. Tripolis' postcode is 221 00. The telephone code is 071. The National Bank of Greece is on Oktovriou 25, off Ethnikis Antistaseos. The tourist police (☎ 22 4847) are on the main square, almost next to the regular police (☎ 22 2411) on Ethnikis Antistaseos. The municipal tourist office (☎ 23 9392) is in the town hall on the same street.

Places to Stay

The cheapest hotel is the E-class *Hotel Ikinouria* (☎ 24 1004), on Ligouriou, which has singles/doubles for 2000/4000 dr. Ligouriou, which runs off Plateia Kolokotroni, is the road to Sparta. The hotel is on the left. The C-class *Galaxy Hotel* (☎ 22 5195/5196/5197), on the main square, has pleasant singles/ doubles for 5000/6700 dr. The B-class *Hotel Arkadia* (☎ 22 5551/ 5552/5553), on Plateia Kolokotroni, has single/double/triple rooms with bath, TV and phone for 7500/12,000/14,400 dr. The comfortable *Hotel Anactoricon* (☎ 22 2545), at Ethnikis Antistaseos 48, has singles/doubles with TV and bathroom for 7300/8800 dr.

Places to Eat

A plethora of cafés and restaurants on and around Plateia Kolokotroni and Plateia Vasileos Georgiou present reasonably priced, traditional fare.

Getting There & Away

Bus From the Arkadias bus station, 13 buses a day go to Athens (2¼ hours, 2400 dr); eight to Megalopoli (40 minutes, 550 dr); three to both Pyrgos (three hours, 2250 dr) and Argos (1¼ hours, 900 dr); and two to both Dimitsana (one hour, 1000 dr) and Andritsena (1½ hours, 1250 dr). On weekdays, one bus goes daily to Stemnitsa (1 hour; 850 dr). For Karitena (850 dr), take the Andritsena bus. There are also buses to Patras (four hours, 2550 dr), Corinth (1½ hours, 1250 dr), Monemvassia (3½ hours, 2380 dr) and Olympia (four hours, 1750 dr).

From the Messinia and Lakonia bus terminals, nine buses a day travel to Sparta (1½ hours, 850 dr); six to Kalamata (two hours, 1300 dr); and two to Pylos (three hours, 2000 dr). The fare to Nafplio is 900 dr and the ride takes 1¼ hours.

Frequent local buses (blue) leave from Plateia Kolokotroni for Tegea (90 dr).

Train Tripolis is on the main Athens-Kalamata line, with four trains a day travelling to Athens (four hours, 1500 dr) via Argos (1½ hours, 950 dr) and Corinth (2½ hours, 1000 dr). All but one train stops at intermediate stations (see the Getting Around section at the beginning of this chapter). Three trains a day go to Kalamata (three hours, 840 dr).

AROUND TRIPOLIS
Ancient Tegea Αρχαία Τεγέα
Ancient Tegea, eight km south-east of Tripolis, was the most important city in Arcadia in classical and Roman times. Tegea was constantly bickering with its arch rival, Mantinea, and fought a long war with Sparta, to which it finally capitulated and became allied in the Peloponnesian Wars. It was laid waste in the 5th century AD but rebuilt by the Byzantines, who called it Nikli. The ruins of the city lie scattered around the modern village of Tegea (also called Alea).

The bus from Tripolis stops outside Tegea's **museum**, which houses thrones, statues and reliefs from the site, including fragments of the pediment from the 4th-century BC, Doric **Temple of Athena Alea**. The temple's pediment was regarded as one of the greatest artworks of its time. The museum has erratic opening times: Tuesday to Sunday, supposedly from 8.30 am to 3 pm.

Try calling first (☎ 55 6153). Admission is 300 dr.

Standing on the site of an ancient theatre, the **Church of Episkopi** in Tegea, once a forum for match-making, has a festival on Assumption Day, 15 August.

MEGALOPOLI Μεγαλόπολη
Despite its name, Megalopoli (Me-gha-LO-po-lee, which means 'great city'), there's little left that reflects its former grandeur. It was founded in 371 BC as the capital of a united Arcadia nestled in a leafy valley on the banks of the Elisson River. The modern town is dominated by its large hydroelectric plant, but it is surrounded by rolling orchard country with mountain backdrops. Megalopoli is an important transport hub astride the main route from Tripolis to Kalamata and Pyrgos.

Places to Stay & Eat
There are six modest hotels to choose from on the streets leading off Plateia Polyviou, including the *Hotel Paris* (☎ 0791-22 410) on Agiou Nikalaou. It has tidy singles/doubles/triples with facilities for 4000/6500/7500 dr.

Friendly Greek-Australians Andrew and Peter run *Ithrakos Snack Bar* on the square. Beyond the sandwich ingredients is a kitchen where good fish and a small selection of Greek dishes are prepared. Ask for grandfather's excellent local wine.

Getting There & Away
There are eight buses a day to Athens (4½ hours, 2800 dr), via Tripolis (30 minutes, 550 dr) and Kalamata (one hour, 850 dr); and two to Andritsena (1¼ hours, 700 dr).

AROUND MEGALOPOLI
Poetically described as the first city which saw the sun, **Ancient Likosoura**, the holy city of the Arcadians is regarded as Greece's oldest ruin. A small **museum** has copies of statues from the nearby **Sanctuary of Despina and Demeter**. The originals are housed in the National Archaeological Museum in Athens. The site is 10 km west

of Megalopoli, just past the village of **Lykeo** where the museum caretaker lives. The route passes through oak woods, and there are beautiful mountain views.

CENTRAL ARCADIA

The area to the west of Tripolis is a tangle of medieval villages, precipitous ravines and narrow winding roads, woven into valleys of dense vegetation beneath the slopes of the Menalon mountains. This is the heart of the Arcadia prefecture, an area which has some of the most breathtaking scenery in the Peloponnese. Driving or trekking, the possibilities for discovering remote settlements and idyllic camping and picnic spots are endless. The area's most enticing villages – Karitena, Stemnitsa and Dimitsana – are within easy reach of Tripolis by public transport. All are on the 37-km stretch of road which runs from the Pyrgos-Tripolis road in the north to the Megalopoli-Andritsena road in the south.

There's no organised camping in the area but unofficial camping is OK. The region is high above sea level and nights are chilly, even in summer.

Karitena Καρίταινα

High above the Megalopoli-Andritsena road is the splendid medieval village of Karitena (Kar-IT-ena, population 320), aptly called the 'Toledo of Greece'. A stepped path leads from the central square to the village's 13th-century **Frankish castle** atop a massive rock.

Karitane's 13th-century **Church of Agios Nikolaos** has well-preserved frescoes. The church is locked. Ask around and someone will direct you to the caretaker. From the church, a path leads down to the **Frankish bridge** which spans the River Lousios (a tributary of the Alfios). The bridge features on the 5000 dr note. Karitena has domatia. North of Karitena, the road runs to the east of the Lousios gorge. After 10 km, south of the small village of Elliniko, a dirt track to the left leads in 1½ hours of walking to the site of **Ancient Gortys**, which can also be reached by hardy vehicle. It's on the west side of the gorge, approached via a bridge. Gortys was an important city from the 4th century BC. Most ruins date from Hellenistic times, but to the north are the remains of a **Sanctuary to Asclepius**.

Getting There & Away Most buses from Megalopoli, Pyrgos and Tripolis to Andritsena (1½ hours, 850 dr) detour three km to Karitena. A few will leave you on the main road, from where it's an arduous uphill walk to the village. The staff at the bus station you leave from will be able to tell you where the bus will stop. It takes four hours to Karitena from Athens and the fare is 3650 dr. Ascertain the drop-off point at Athens' Terminal A.

Stemnitsa Στεμνίτσα

Stemnitsa (Stem-NIT-sa) is 15 km north of Karitena, at an altitude of 1000 metres. If you're driving, take the first turn left down from Karitena and follow the sign to Dimitsana, not Stemnitsa – if you want to save a few km. Stemnitsa is on the way, a spectacular village of stone houses and Byzantine churches. North of the village, a path to the left leads to **Moni Agiou Ioannitou Prodromou**. The walk takes about an hour. A monk will show visitors the chapel's splendid 14th and 15th-century frescoes. From here, paths lead to the deserted monasteries of **Paleou** and **Neou Philosophou** and also south along the riverbank to the site of ancient Gortys. The monks at Prodromou can direct you.

Stemnitsa has one hotel, the charming C-class *Hotel Triokolonion* (☎ 0795-81 297). It has singles/doubles/triples/quads with bathroom for 5500/7800/10,000/11,250 dr. It also serves good food.

Getting There & Away On weekdays, there's a daily bus from Tripolis, via Hrissovitsi, to Stemnitsa (one hour; 850 dr).

Dimitsana Διμιτσάνα

Built amphitheatrically on two hills at the beginning of the Lousios gorge, Dimitsana (Dim-it-SAN-a, population 650), 11 km north of Stemnitsa, is a lovely medieval village. Despite its remoteness, Dimitsana played a significant role in the country's struggle for self-determination. Its Greek school, founded in 1764, was one spawning ground for the ideas leading to the uprisings against the Turks. Its students included Bishop Germanos of Patras and Patriarch Gregory V, who was hanged by the Turks in retaliation for the massacre in Tripolis. The village also had a number of gunpowder factories and a branch of the secret Filiki Eteria ('friendly society') where Greeks met to discuss the revolution (see the History section in the Facts about the Country chapter for more details of the Filiki Eteria).

From the heady days before independence, Dimitsana has become a sleepy village where the most exciting event is the arrival of the daily Tripolis bus. Apart from the beauty of the village and its surroundings, tourists will appreciate the **folk museum** and **library**, on Nikolaou Makri (open daily from 8 am to 2 pm, free admission) and the **Moni Aimialon**, three km south on the road to Stemnitsa (open daily from 9 am to 2 pm).

Dimitsana's one hotel, the C-class *Hotel Dimitsana* (☎ 0795-31 518), has singles/doubles at 8000/11,900 dr with bathroom. The hotel is south of the village, on the main road coming from Stemnitsa. The EOT has renovated the *Kazakos Traditional Settlement* (☎ 0795-31 660), near Plateia Agia Kyriaki.

Getting There & Away Two buses a day come from Tripolis to Dimitsana (one hour, 1000 dr).

ANDRITSENA
The village of Andritsena (Ανδρίτσαινα, population 900), 81 km west of Tripolis, is perched awesomely 765 metres up a mountainside. Crumbling stone houses with rickety wooden balconies flank its narrow cobbled streets and a stream gushes through its central square. Here, old men sit outside the Apollon Kafeneio, shaded by an enormous plane tree.

The post office, OTE and bank are all near the central square. Andritsena's postcode is 270 61 and the telephone code is 0626. The village's only concession to tourism is its small **folk museum**, which is usually open daily from 11 am to 1 pm and 5 to 6 pm. Admission is free. However, most people come to Andritsena to visit the Temple of Vasses, 14 km away.

Temple of Vasses
The Temple of Vasses, 14 km south of Andritsena, stands at an altitude of 1200 metres on a hill overlooked by Mt Paliavlakitsa. The road from Andritsena climbs steadily along a mountain ridge, through increasingly dramatic scenery, to Greece's most isolated temple.

Well preserved, it was built in 420 BC by the people of nearby Figalia, who dedicated it to Apollo Epicurus (The Helper) for delivering them from pestilence. Designed by Ictinus, the architect of the Parthenon, it combines Doric and Ionic columns and a single Corinthian column – the earliest example of this order. The site is not enclosed and admission is free.

There are no buses to Vasses. In summer, it's usually possible to find people in the square to share a taxi for about 3000 dr.

From Vasses, a dirt road continues for 11 km to the village of **Perivolia**, from where a track leads in two km to the village of **Ano Figalia**, which is built on the site of ancient Figalia (see the Elia section for more details).

Places to Stay & Eat
Andritsena has one hotel, the *Theoxenia Hotel* (☎ 22 219/235/270). Rates are 8000/10,000 dr for singles/doubles, including breakfast.

Andritsena's few eateries are on the central square. Meals are also served at the Theoxenia Hotel.

Getting There & Away
There are two buses a day to Andritsena from Athens Bus Terminal A (four hours, 3650 dr). There are also services from Megalopoli

(1¼ hours, 700 dr), Pyrgos (1½ hours) and Tripolis (1½ hours, 1250 dr).

MYLI TO LEONIDIO

There are lots of opportunities to explore on the scenic coast road that runs south from the pretty town of Myli, 46 km east of Tripolis, to Leonidio.

The opening 34-km leg from Myli to **Astros** is a delight. Astros, notable for its dahlias and roses, is perched above **Paleos Astros**, which has a kastro and camping by the beach four km downhill. From Astros, a good road hugs the coast, curving above tiny pebble-beached villages. Along the way there are some shady camping grounds, domatia, studios and tavernas. The first settlement of any consequence is the isolated seaside village of **Paralia Tyrou**, also known as **Tyrosapounakia**, which has several hotels and tavernas. Above the village, clifftop windmills stand arrogantly against the sky.

Leonidio is a further 20 km south of Paralia Tyrou. The town's tiny Plateia 25 Martiou is an archetypal, unspoiled, whitewashed Greek village square, set around a shady tree. The OTE is visible from the square, and the friendly police (☎ 0757-22 222) are close at hand on Kiloso. The cosy kafeneio on the square serves terrific mezedes. Apartments are available in town, but most of the accommodation is in the nearby seaside villages of **Lakos**, **Plaka** and **Poulithra** where *Hotel Cacas* (☎ 51 269) and *Katavros Hotel* (☎ 51 214) have singles/doubles for about 5000/7000 dr. *Restaurant Akroyali* serves excellent seafood. There are buses going down the coast to Leonidio from Argos (three hours, 1200 dr), or catch them from stops along the way.

SOUTH OF LEONIDIO

It's possible to continue south from Leonidio over the rugged Parnon mountains to the town of Geraki in Lakonia, 48 km away. The road is one of the most dramatic in the Peloponnese. It is little more than a mountain path as far as **Kosmas**, then the road twists around precipitous rock faces that plunge into the gorges below. Almost every hairpin bend reveals another forlorn roadside shrine erected in memory of a hapless soul who didn't quite make it. The landscape appears almost deserted, until a flock of sheep or goats and a startled shepherd cross your way. The final leg is no more than a gentle coast down to Geraki.

From here you can head 40 km west to Sparta, or continue south through **Vlahiotis**, **Molai** and **Sykia** to Monemvassia.

Lakonia Λακωνία

The modern region of Lakonia occupies almost identical boundaries to the powerful kingdom ruled by King Menelaus in Mycenaean times. Menelaus ruled from his capital at Sparta, which was later to achieve much greater fame as the arch rival of Athens in classical times. The Spartans who fought Athens were the descendants of the Dorians, who had arrived in about 1100 BC after the decline of the Mycenaean empire. Little remains of ancient Sparta, but the disappointment is more than compensated for by the glorious Byzantine churches and monasteries at Mystras, just to the west. Another place not be missed is the evocative, medieval town of Monemvassia, in the south-east.

English speakers can thank the Lakonians for the word laconic – brief of speech, which many Lakonians still are.

SPARTA Σπάρτη

If the city of the Lacedaemonians were destroyed, and only its temples and the foundations of its buildings left, remote posterity would greatly doubt whether their power were ever equal to their renown.

Thucydides

Sparta (in Greek SPAR-ti, population 12,900), in the south-east, is the capital of Lakonia prefecture. Ancient Sparta produced no great artists, writers, historians, philosophers or monuments of beauty. It is renowned for the privations its citizens were compelled to endure. Most people come to Sparta to visit Mystras, six km away.

Orientation

You won't get lost in Sparta. It was constructed in 1834 on a grid system, and has two main thoroughfares. Paleologou runs north to south through the town, and Lykourgou runs east to west. They intersect in the middle of town. The central square, Plateia Kentriki, is one block west of the intersection. The bus station is on Vrasidou. To get to the central square from here, turn left onto Paleologou and then right onto Lykourgou.

Information

The post office is at Kleomvrotou 12, one block north of the intersection. The OTE is between Lykourgou and Kleomvrotou, one block east of Paleologou. Sparta's postcode is 231 00. The telephone code is 0731. Sparta's EOT (☎ 24 852) is in the town hall

on the main square. The friendly tourist police (☎ 26 229) are at Hilonos 8, one block east of the museum. The National Bank of Greece is on the right side of Paleologou (when you face north).

Exploring Ancient Sparta

To witness the accuracy of Thucydides' prophecy, wander around ancient Sparta's meagre ruins. Walk north along Paleologou. At the top is a large statue of a belligerent King Leonidas, standing in front of a football stadium. Left of the stadium, a path leads to the southern gate of the **acropolis**. Pathways from here lead to forlorn ruins amid olive groves. Away to the left is to the 2nd or 3rd-century BC **theatre**, the site's most discernible ruin. Along the road to Tripolis, a path leads to the **Sanctuary of Artemis Orthia**. Like most of the deities in Greek mythology, the goddess Artemis had many aspects, one of which was Artemis Orthia. In earliest times, this aspect of the goddess was

A Spartan Existence

The bellicose Spartans sacrificed all the finer things in life for military expertise. Male children were examined at birth by the city council and those deemed too weak to become good soldiers were left to die of exposure. Those fortunate enough to survive babyhood were taken away from their mothers at the age of seven to undergo rigorous military training.

The training seems to have consisted mainly of beatings and deprivations of all kinds. They were forced to go barefoot, even in winter, and were starved so that they would have to steal food for survival. If discovered, they were punished not for the crime, but for allowing themselves to get caught: another lash of the whip.

Although girls were allowed to stay with their mothers, they also underwent tough physical training so that they would give birth to healthy sons. ■

Statue of a barefooted Spartan warrior

honoured through human sacrifice. The Spartans gave this activity away for the slightly less gruesome business of flogging young boys in honour of the goddess.

Museum & Gallery

Sparta's **archaeological museum** (☎ 28 575), east of Paleologou, includes votive sickles which Spartan boys dedicated to Artemis Orthia, heads and torsos of various deities, a statue of Leonidas, masks and a stele. The museum is open Tuesday to Saturday from 8.30 am to 3 pm and Sunday from 8.30 am to 2.30 pm. Admission is 500 dr.

The **John Coumantaros Art Gallery**, Paleologou 123, has an impressive collection of 19th and 20th-century French and Dutch paintings and also holds changing exhibitions of works by contemporary Greek painters. It's open Tuesday to Saturday from 9 am to 3 pm and Sunday from 10 am to 2 pm. Admission is free.

Places to Stay

Camping Mystras (☎ 22 724) and *Camping Castleview* (☎ 93 384) both on the Sparta-Mystras road, have good facilities and charge similar rates. The friendly D-class *Hotel Cecil* (☎ 24 980), Paleologou 125, has cosy rooms with shared facilities for 4000/6500/8000 dr. A double with a bathroom costs 7500 dr.

The C-class *Laconia Hotel* (☎ 28 951), Paleologou 61, has singles/doubles/triples for 6000/9000/10,500 dr. The C-class *Hotel Maniatis* (☎ 22 665, 29 991; fax 29 994), Paleologou 72, has immaculate rooms with air-con and telephone. Rates are 9000/11,500/13,800 dr. Visible from Paleologou at Thermopylon 84 is the marbled *Hotel Apollon* (☎ 22 491) which charges 7700/9700/11,700 dr for balconied rooms with bathroom and phone.

Places to Eat

Next to the Hotel Maniotis, the elegant *Dias Restaurant* looks expensive but its prices for many Greek dishes are reasonable. The *Diethnes Restaurant*, Paleologou 105, is long-established and serves tasty, traditional food.

For a splurge, make for *Dionysos Taverna* which has moved from town and gone up-market in a shaded location one km from Sparta on the Mystras road. There are *supermarkets* and *fast-food outlets* on Paleologou.

Getting There & Away

From Sparta's bus station on Vrasidou, there are nine buses a day to Athens (4½ hours, 3050 dr) via Corinth (three hours, 1950 dr); five to Gythio (one hour, 650 dr); four to Neapoli (four hours, 2100 dr) and Tripolis (1¼ hours, 850 dr); two a day to Kalamata (2½ hours, 800 dr) via Artemissia (500 dr); and one a day to Gerolimenas (three hours, 1550 dr). There are also buses to Geraki (45 minutes, 500 dr) and to Monemvassia (2½ hours, 1500 dr).

Frequent buses for the camping grounds, Dionysos Taverna and Mystras (30 minutes, 175 dr) leave from a bus stop round the corner from Lykourgou, on Agisilaou. The EOT gives schedules and the main bus station has times written on its board.

MYSTRAS Μυστράς

The captivating ruins of the once awesome town of Mystras (Mis-TRAS), crowned by an impregnable fortress, spill from a spur of Mt Taÿgetos.

History

The fortress of Mystras was built by Guillaume de Villehardouin in 1249. When the Byzantines won back the Morea from the Franks, Emperor Michael VIII Paleologus made Mystras its capital and seat of government. It soon became populated by people from the surrounding plains seeking refuge from the invading Slavs. From this time, until the last despot, Dimitrios, surrendered to the Turks in 1460, a despot of Morea (usually a son or brother of the ruling Byzantine emperor) lived and reigned at Mystras.

While the empire plunged into decline elsewhere, Mystras enjoyed a renaissance under the despots. A school of humanistic philosophy was founded by Gemistos Plethon (1355-1452). His enlightened ideas attracted intellectuals from all corners of Byzantium. After Mystras was ceded to the Turks, Plethon's pupils moved to Rome and Florence where they made a significant contribution to the Italian Renaissance. Art and architecture also flourished, evidenced in the splendid buildings and vibrant frescoes of Mystras.

Mystras declined under Turkish rule. It was captured by the Venetians in 1687 and thrived again with a flourishing silk industry and a population of 40,000. It was recaptured

by the Turks in 1715, and from then on it was downhill all the way. It was burned by the Russians in 1770, by the Albanians in 1780 and by Ibrahim Pasha in 1825. By the time of Independence, it was in a very sorry state; virtually abandoned and in ruins. Since the 1950s, much restoration has taken place.

Exploring the Site

A day is needed to do Mystras justice. Wear sensible shoes, bring plenty of water and begin at the upper entrance to the site to walk down, rather than uphill. The site is divided into three sections – the **kastro** (the fortress

PELOPONNESE

Mystras

0   50   100 m

Kastro (621 m)

Upper Entrance

Agia Sofia

UPPER TOWN

Agios Nikolaos

Small Palace

Nafplio Gate

Convent of Pantanassa

Monemvassia Gate

Taxiarhes

House of Frangopoulos

Palace of the Despots

Aphentiko

Monastery of Perivleptos

Agios Hristoforos

Laskaris Mansion

LOWER TOWN

Vrontokhion Monastery

Agios Georgios

Agios Theodoros

Vaulted Passage

Evangelistria

To Neos Mystras & Sparta

Marmara Fountain

Museum

Episcopal Palace

Mitropolis (Cathedral of Agios Dimitrios)

on the summit), the **upper town** (hora) and the **lower town** (kato hora).

Kastro & Upper Town From opposite the upper-entrance ticket office, a path (sign-posted 'kastro') leads up to the fortress. It was built by the Franks and extended by the Turks. The path descending from the ticket office leads to **Agia Sofia**, which served as the palace church – some frescoes survive. Steps descend from here to a T-junction. A left turn leads to the **Nafplio Gate**, which was the main entrance to the town. Near the gate is the huge **Palace of the Despots**, a complex of several buildings constructed at different times. The vaulted audience room, the largest of its buildings, was added in the 14th century. Its façade was painted, and its window frames were very ornate, but hundreds of years of neglect have robbed it of its former opulence.

From the palace, a winding, cobbled path leads down to the **Monemvassia Gate**, the entrance to the lower town.

Lower Town Through the Monemvassia gate, turn right for the well-preserved, 14th-century **Convent of Pantanassa**. The nuns who live here are Mystras' only inhabitants. The building has beautiful stone-carved ornamentation on its façade and the capitals of its columns. It's an elaborate, perfectly proportioned building – never overstated. Exquisite, richly coloured 15th-century frescoes are among the finest examples of late Byzantine art. There is a wonderful view of the pancake-flat and densely cultivated plain of Lakonia from the columned terrace on the northern façade.

The path continues down to the **Monastery of Perivleptos**, which is built into a rock. Its 14th-century frescoes are equal to those of Pantanassa and have been preserved virtually intact. Each scene is an entity – enclosed in a simple symmetrical shape. The overall effect is of numerous icons, placed next to one another, relating a visual narrative. The church has a very high dome. In the centre is the Pantokrator, surrounded by the apostles, and the Virgin flanked by two angels.

As you continue down towards the Mitropolis, you will pass **Agios Georgios**, one of Mystras' many private chapels. Further down and above the path on the left is the **Laskaris Mansion**, a typical Byzantine house where the ground floor was used as stables and the upper floor was the residence.

The **Mitropolis** (Cathedral of Agios Dimitrios) consists of a complex of buildings enclosed by a high wall. The original church was built in the 13th century but was greatly altered in the 15th century. The church stands in an attractive courtyard surrounded by stoas and balconies. Its impressive ecclesiastical ornaments and furniture include a carved marble iconostasis, an intricately carved wooden throne and a marble slab in the floor on which is carved a two-headed eagle (symbol of Byzantium). This is located exactly on the site where Emperor Constantine XI was crowned. The church also has some fine frescoes. The adjoining **museum** houses fragments of sculpture and pottery from Mystras' churches.

Beyond the Mitropolis is the **Vrontokhion Monastery**. This was once the wealthiest monastery of Mystras, the focus of cultural activities and the burial place of the despots. Of its two churches, **Agios Theodoros** and **Aphentiko**, the latter is the most impressive, with striking frescoes.

In summer, Mystras is open every day from 8 am to 6 pm and in winter from 8 am to 3.30 pm. Admission is 1200 dr. Students from EU countries are admitted free on production of an ISIC card. Outside the lower entrance to Mystras is a *kantina* (mobile café), which sells snacks and fresh orange juice.

Places to Stay

Most people visit Mystras on a day trip from Sparta. There is limited accommodation in the village of Nea Mystras, near the site. The B-class *Hotel Byzantion* (☎ 0731-93 309), near the central square, has singles/doubles/triples for 6000/8000/10,000 dr. There are *domatia* on the road opposite the hotel.

Getting There & Away

Frequent buses go to Mystras from Sparta (see the Getting There & Away section for Sparta). A taxi from Sparta to Mystras' lower entrance costs 1000 dr, 1500 dr to the upper entrance.

GERAKI Γεράκι

Geraki (Ye-RA-kee), 40 km east of Sparta, is an unsung Mystras. While the latter is on almost everyone's list of 'must sees' in the Peloponnese, the medieval city of Geraki crumbles in obscurity on a remote hillside. The modern village of Geraki was built over the site of ancient Geronthrai which dates back to Mycenaean times. Fragments of the walls remain to the north and east of the village in an open site. The ruins of the medieval city lie four km to the east, about 50 minutes' walk along a road from the modern village.

The city was one of the 12 Frankish fiefs of the Peloponnese. The fortress was built by Jean de Nivelet in 1245 but was ceded to the Byzantines in 1262. It is reached by a steep path and has breathtaking views of the surrounding plain and mountains. The site is open and unattended but its 15 small chapels are locked. Ask in the village taverna for the caretaker who will give you the keys to the most important churches. People in the village square can suggest domatia.

Getting There & Away

If you are driving, the road to Geraki is signposted to the right a little way out of Sparta along the Tripolis road. Several buses a day come from Sparta to the modern village (45 minutes, 500 dr).

GEFYRA & MONEMVASSIA

Γέφυρα και Μονεμβασία

Monemvassia (Mon-em-vas-EE-a), 99 km from Sparta, is a massive rock which rises dramatically from the sea off the east coast. It is reached by a causeway from the mainland village of Gefyra (also called Nea Monemvassia). In summer, Gefyra and Monemvassia brim with tourists, but the extraordinary impact of the first encounter with the medieval town of Monemvassia – and the delights of exploring it – override the effects of mass tourism. The poet Yiannis Ritsos, who was born and lived for many years in Monemvassia, wrote of it: 'This scenery is as harsh as silence'.

From Gefyra, Monemvassia is a huge rock topped by a fortress with a few scattered buildings at sea level. But cross the causeway and walk along the curving road by the sea for 20 minutes and you will come to a narrow tunnel in a massive fortifying wall. The tunnel is L-shaped so you cannot see the other side. You emerge into the magical town of Monemvassia, concealed until that moment. Unlike Mystras, Monemvassia's houses are inhabited, mostly by weekenders from Athens.

History

The island, appropriately called the Gibraltar of Greece, was part of the mainland until it was separated by a devastating earthquake in 375 AD. Its name means 'single entry' (*moni* – single, *emvasia* – entry), as there is only one way to the medieval town. During the 6th century, barbarian incursions forced the inhabitants of the surrounding area to retreat to this natural rock fortress. By the 13th century, it had become the principal commercial centre of Byzantine Morea <196> complementary to Mystras, the spiritual centre. It was famous throughout Europe for its highly praised Malvasia (also called Malmsey) wine.

Later came a succession of invasions from Franks, Venetians and Turks. During the War of Independence, its Turkish inhabitants were massacred on their surrender following a three-month siege by the Greek army.

Orientation & Information

All practicalities can be dealt with in Gefyra. The main street is 23 Iouliou which skirts around the coast and leads to the causeway. The bus station is on 23 Iouliou, a short walk from the causeway. The post office is on the left side of Spartis coming from the causeway. The National Bank of Greece is next door. The OTE is at the top of 28 Oktovriou,

PELOPONNESE

which is a turn-off to the right from 23 Iouliou. Monemvassia's postcode is 230 70. The telephone code is 0732.

There are no tourist police and no EOT in Monemvassia or Gefyra. However, Greek-Australian Peter Derzolis, the manager of Malvasia Travel Agency (☎ 61 752/432, after hours 752 445), up from the bus station, is extremely helpful and sells ferry and air tickets. He also has a currency-exchange service, can arrange accommodation, and rents out cars and motorbikes.

Medieval Town

The narrow, cobbled main street is lined with souvenir shops and tavernas, flanked by winding stairways which weave between a complex network of stone houses with walled gardens and courtyards. The main street leads to the central square and the **Cathedral of Christ in Chains**, dating from the 13th century. Opposite is the **Church of Agios Pavlos**, built in 956 AD and now a small **museum**. Above it is the **Church of Mirtidiotissa**, virtually in ruins, but still with a small altar and a defiantly flickering candle. Overlooking the sea is the recently restored, whitewashed 16th-century **Church of Panagia Hrysaphitissa**.

The **fortress** and the upper town are reached up the signposted steps to the left, shortly after entering the old town. The upper town is now a vast and fascinating jumbled ruin, except for the **Church of Agia Sophia**, which perches on the edge of a sheer cliff.

Places to Stay – bottom end

Camping Paradise (☎ 61 680) is a pleasant, well-shaded camping ground, next to a beach with a minimarket, bar and disco. It is 3.5 km south of Gefyra.

Gefyra has numerous *domatia*. Look for signs on the approach road from Molai and also on 28 Oktovriou beyond the bus station.

The basic E-class *Hotel Akrogia* (☎ 61 360) is opposite the National Bank of Greece. Single/double rooms with shower are 5000/7000 dr. The D-class *Hotel Aktaion* (☎ 61 234), by the causeway, charges

4000/8000 dr for singles/doubles with bathroom.

The friendly *Hotel Glyfada* (☎ 61 752/432, after hours 61 445) on the beach is signposted on the left as you approach Gefyra and within strolling distance. The rooms are spacious, with private facilities, telephone, refrigerator, cutlery and crockery. Rates for singles/doubles/triples/quads are 5000/6500/8000/11,000 dr. There is a restaurant operating in summer.

The C-class *Hotel Minoa* (☎ 61 224/398/209), up from the causeway, has large well-furnished rooms. Rates are 7200/9000 dr for singles/doubles and 10,800/16,000 dr for triples/quads.

Places to Stay – middle & top end

There are no budget places in Monemvassia. The best places are expensive, impeccably restored, traditional settlements. They include *Malvasia Guest Houses* (☎ 61 113/435/323), with singles/doubles/triples for 7500/10,000/14,000 dr (including breakfast); and *Byzantino* (☎ 61 254/351/562; fax 61 331), with doubles/triples for 12,500/15,500 dr and a suite costing 19,300 dr.

The EOT traditional settlement *Kellia*, meaning 'cells', (☎ 61 520), is above the sea next to the Panagia Hrysaphitissa. Former monastery cells have been converted to delightful doubles/triples for 14,800/18,600 dr, including breakfast. To rent a room in a private house, enquire through Malvasia Travel Agency. You should expect to pay around 10,000 dr a double. Staying in Monemvassia is a memorable experience, and the mystery of the town increases under night stars.

Places to Eat

Gefyra In Gefyra, *Taverna Nikolas* serves tasty, reasonably priced dishes. *T' Agnantio Taverna*, also on the main road, is also recommended.

Monemvassia In Monemvassia, *To Kanoni*, on the right of the main street, has an imaginative and extensive menu. There are more *tavernas* on the main street.

Getting There & Away
Bus Most bus services to and from Monemvassia involve a change of bus in the small town of Molai, but it is possible to buy a ticket to your final destination. Four buses depart daily for Athens (6½ hours, 4550 dr) via Sparta (two hours, 1500 dr) and Tripolis (3½ hours, 2400 dr); and one bus a day (summer only) goes to Gythio (1½ hours, 1300 dr). An express bus to Athens departs at 4.10 am (5½ hours, 3250 dr) and stops briefly at Geraki (1500 dr).

Ferry The F/B *Theseus*, which also services Piraeus, Neapoli, Elafonisi, Gythio and Crete, is the only ferry which calls in at Monemvassia (see the Getting There & Away section for Gythio). Buy tickets from Angelakos Travel (☎ 61 219) by the petrol station, left across the causeway.

Hydrofoil In summer, five Flying Dolphins weekly skim to Kythira (one hour, 4400 dr) and Leonidio (one hour, 2900 dr) and three a week to Piraeus (four hours, 6500 dr) via Kyparissi (north of Monemvassia), Spetses and Hydra.

Getting Around
Car & Motorbike These can be rented from Malvasia Travel Agency (☎ 61 752/432) up from the bus station. The medieval town of Monemvassia is inaccessible to cars and motorbikes but parking is available outside the tunnel to the town.

NEAPOLI Νεάπολη
Neapoli (Ne-A-po-lee) is the southernmost port of the Peloponnese on the tip of the easternmost peninsula. It's a major jumping-off point for the island of Kythira. Frequent caïques make the crossing to the small island of Elafonisi, which lies west of Neapoli and north of Kythira. Domatia are available.

Getting There & Away
Bus Four buses come daily to Neapoli from Sparta (four hours, 2100 dr). Caïques can take visitors on a five-minute trip to Elafonisi from the village of **Viglafia**, about 10 minutes by taxi north-west of Neapoli via Agios Nikolaos village.

Ferry The F/B *Martha* leaves Neapoli every day for Agia Pelagia on Kythira, with additional trips on Monday, Wednesday, Friday, and Sunday. The F/B *Theseus* includes Neapoli on its meander down the Peloponnese coast *en route* to Crete (see the Gythio Getting There & Away section).

Hydrofoil In summer, hydrofoils leave daily except Monday for Piraeus via Spetses, Hydra and Poros.

ELAFONISI Ελαφονήσι
Elafonisi island sees few foreign tourists but it's popular with Greeks who pop over from the mainland for fish lunches in summer, particularly on a Sunday. The island's main attractions, apart from the seafood, are its superb beaches – which the Greeks liken to the those of the South Seas. They're not exaggerating. Elafonisi's telephone code is 0732.

The island has no hotels but there are pensions – the *Elafonisos* (☎ 49 268) and *Liaros* (☎ 49 271/272) – and a few *domatia*. There is no official camping ground, but it may be possible to camp unofficially.

Getting There & Away
Caïque In summer, caïques ply between Elafonisi, Neapoli and Viglafia several times a day. The F/B *Theseus* calls in late on Thursday.

GYTHIO Γύθειο
Once the port of ancient Sparta, Gythio (YI-thee-o, population 4200) is the gateway to the Lakonian Mani. It's an attractive fishing town with a bustling waterfront of 19th-century, pastel-coloured buildings, behind which crumbling old Turkish houses clamber up a steep, wooded hill.

Orientation & Information
The bus station is at the northern end of the town. To reach the waterfront of Akti Vasileos Pavlou, walk straight ahead with the

PELOPONNESE

park on your left. The town's central square, Plateia Mavromihali, is halfway along the waterfront. The quay is opposite this square. Beyond it, the waterfront road veers left, then right. A little way along, a causeway leads to Marathonisi islet.

The post office is on Ermou. From the bus-station office, turn right (walking away from the park) then veer right onto Herakles. Walk past the OTE office on the corner of Herakles and Kapsali and take the second turn to the left onto Ermou. The post office is on the right. Gythio's postcode is 232 00. The telephone code is 0733.

The National Bank of Greece is up from the wharf and bus station. A health clinic and pharmacy (☎ 22 001/002/003) is on the waterfront between Plateia Mavromihali and the causeway.

There are no tourist police nor EOT. The regular police (☎ 22 100) are on the waterfront between the bus station and Plateia Mavromihali.

Things to See & Do

According to mythology, the tranquil pine-shaded **Marathonisi islet** is ancient Cranae where Paris (prince of Troy) and Helen (wife of Menelaus) consummated that affair which caused a bit of a ruckus back in Mycenaean times. The islet's 18th-century tower once belonged to the wild Mavromihalis family, the Maniot rebels who played a part in the assassination of Kapodistrias, Greece's first president, in Nafplio. The tower now houses a small **museum**, open 9 am to 1 pm and 3 to 9 pm, focusing on Mani history. The islet is perfect for a picnic.

Gythio has an **ancient theatre**, but don't expect another Epidaurus – this one is minuscule yet well preserved. To reach it, follow the directions for the post office, continue along Ermou and turn right on to Arheou Theatrou. Walk to the end of here and turn left. The theatre is on the right by an army camp.

Swimming is safe on six km of sandy beaches which extend from the village of **Mavrovouni** two km south of Gythio.

There's some surfing to be had on the rising tide around here, but bring your own board.

Places to Stay – bottom end

There are four camping grounds near Gythio, all on the coast on the road to Areopoli. They are *Meltemi* (☎ 22 833 or 23 260), *Gythion Beach* (☎ 23 441), *Mani Beach* (☎ 23 450/451) and *Kronos* (☎ 24 124). There are bus stops at all camping grounds except Kronos, which is three km from the nearest bus stop.

Koutsouris Rooms to Rent (☎ 22 321) has cosy rooms with small kitchen and bathroom. Singles/doubles/triples are 4000/5000/6000 dr. Guests relax in a garden with citrus trees and tortoises. Walk up Tzannibi Gregoraki, turn right at the church with the clock tower, and the rooms are on the left.

The *Bougainvillaea Rooms* (no telephone), Herakles 22 (next to the OTE and buried beneath bougainvillea), is outstanding. The owner, Greek-Canadian Kim Brummel, has various double rooms from 4000 to 6000 dr.

On the waterfront, between Plateia Mavromihali and the causeway, the *Saga Pension* (☎ 23 220), with car park, has immaculate rooms with facilities for 5000/6000/7000 dr.

Left of the wharf on Vasileos Georgiou, the *Hotel Leonides* (☎ 22 389) has doubles with bathroom for 8000/9000 dr. Just up from here is the *Hotel Gythion* (☎ 23 777). It has doubles/triples with facilities for 8000/10,000 dr.

Places to Stay – middle

The superior *Cavo Grosso Bungalows* (☎ 22 774/897 or 23 488/823), two km south of Gythio, is 300 metres from Mavrovouni beach. Each two-room bungalow has its own bathroom, lounge and breakfast-making facilities. The rates in July and August are 17,000 dr for two, 20% more for each extra person, with small children staying for free. In the off season, doubles go for 14,300 dr. Catch the Areopoli bus and ask the driver to drop you off at the signposted turn-off to Cavo Grosso.

Places to Eat

Most waterfront tavernas are tourist traps. The workers' café-like *Petakos Taverna* serves excellent, herbed, home-style dishes. Walk north along the waterfront on the road signposted to Skala. The restaurant is in the town's stadium on the right. The *Saga Pension Restaurant* (see Places to Stay), on the waterfront, serves tasty traditional, reasonably priced food.

There is a *supermarket* between the bus station and the OTE, and a laïki agora on Ermou on Tuesday and Friday mornings.

Mavrovouni village has three quite reasonable *tavernas*, a *supermarket* and *bakery*. There are five more *fish tavernas* along the beach.

Getting There & Away

Bus Six buses a day go to Areopoli (30 minutes, 400 dr); five to Athens (5½ hours, 3750 dr) via Sparta (one hour, 650 dr); four to the camping grounds along the Areopoli road; four to Kalamata, two via Sparta and two via Itilo and Limeni (30/40 minutes, 400 dr); three to the Diros caves (one hour, 550 dr); two to Gerolimenas (two hours, 900 dr); and one to Monemvassia (1½ hours, 1280 dr).

Ferry The F/B *Martha* and F/B *Theseus* call at Gythio. In theory, *Theseus* is expected to arrive from Kalamata and continue to Agia Pelagia, Kythira (three hours, 900 dr), Antikythira (2200 dr), and Kastelli-Kissamos on Crete (3600 dr) once a week.

On its return, the *Theseus* calls in at Gythio from where it goes to Agia Pelagia, Neapoli (four hours, 1400 dr); Monemvassia (five hours, 2300 dr); and Piraeus (13 hours, 3900 dr). The *Martha* arrives from Kythira on Monday, Wednesday and Sunday, and returns Monday, Tuesday and Saturday (900 dr). Services are subject to change, mainly because of the sea's unpredictability. For tickets and details, go to the helpful Rozakis Travel Agency (☎ & fax 22 229/207), on the waterfront before Plateia Mavromihali. The port police (☎ 22 750/207) are on the waterfront before the causeway.

Getting Around

Car & Motorbike Gythio has no car-hire outlets. Motorbikes can be rented from Super Cycle Moto (☎ 24 407/001), a little way up Tzannibi Gregoraki from Plateia Mavromihali.

The Mani Η Μάνη

The region referred to as the Mani covers the central peninsula in the south of the Peloponnese. For centuries, the Maniots were a law unto themselves, renowned for their fierce independence and resentment of any attempt to govern them.

Today, the Maniots are regarded by other Greeks as independent, royalist and right wing. But don't be deterred from visiting the region by descriptions of the Maniots as hostile, wild and hard people. Contact with the outside world and lack of feuding have mellowed them. The Maniots are as friendly and hospitable as Greeks elsewhere, despite the fierce appearance of some older people who dress like the Cretans and offer fiery raki as a gesture of hospitality. But the music and dance of the two differ.

The Mani is generally divided into the Messinian Mani (also called the outer Mani) and the Lakonian (or inner) Mani. The Messinian Mani starts south-east of Kalamata and runs south between the coast and the Taÿgetos mountains, while the Lakonian Mani covers the rest of the peninsula south of Itilo. Such was the formidable reputation of the inhabitants of the remote inner Mani that foreign occupiers thought they were best left alone.

The Mani has no significant ancient sites, but it well compensates with medieval and later remains, bizarre tower settlements – particularly in the inner Mani – and some magnificent churches, all enhanced by the distant presence of the towering peaks of the

PELOPONNESE

Taÿgetos mountains. The Diros caves in the south are awesome.

History

The people of the Mani regard themselves as direct descendants of the Spartans. After the decline of Sparta, citizens loyal to the principles of Lycurgus, founder of Sparta's constitution, chose to withdraw to the mountains rather than serve under foreign masters. Later, refugees from occupying powers joined these people who became known as Maniots, from the Greek word *mania*.

The Maniots claim they are the only Greeks not to have succumbed to foreign invasions. This may be somewhat exaggerated but the Maniots have always enjoyed a certain autonomy and a distinctive lifestyle. Until independence, the Maniots lived in clans led by chieftains. Fertile land was so scarce that it was fiercely fought over. Blood feuds were a way of life and families constructed towers as hide-outs.

The Turks failed to subdue the Maniots, who eagerly participated in the War of Independence. But, after 1834, although reluctant to relinquish their independence, they became part of the new kingdom.

For a background of the Mani, try to obtain copies of *Mani* by Patrick Leigh Fermor, *Deep into Mani* by Eliopoulis & Greenhold and *The Architecture of Mani* by Ioannis Saïtis, a chief architect of Vathia. The latter should be available at bookshops in Athens or London.

LAKONIAN MANI

Grey rock, mottled with defiant clumps of green scrub and the occasional stunted olive or cypress tree characterises the bleak mountains of inner Mani. The lower slopes are terraced for, wherever possible, this unyielding soil has been cultivated. A curious anomaly is the profusion of wild flowers which mantle the valleys in spring, exhibiting nature's resilience by sprouting from the rocks.

The indented coast's sheer cliffs plunge into the sea and rocky outcrops shelter pebbled beaches. This wild and barren landscape is broken only by austere and imposing stone towers, mostly abandoned, but still standing sentinel over the region. Restoration of Maniot buildings is increasing and many refugee Albanians, who are fine stonemasons, have been engaged on these projects.

To explore the Lakonian Mani, head from Gythio to Areopoli and then south to Gerolimenas, loop round and return to Areopoli via Kotronas. You can then continue north from Areopoli to Itilo and continue to the Messinian Mani.

Areopoli Αρεόπολη

Areopoli (Ar-e-O-po-lee, population 980), capital of the Mani, is aptly named after Ares, the god of war. Dominating the central square is a statue of Petrobey Mavromihalis, who proclaimed the Maniot insurrection against the Turks. Konstantinos and Georgos Mavromihalis, who assassinated Kapodistrias, Greece's first president, belonged to the same family. The town retains many other reminders of its rumbustious past.

In the narrow, cobbled streets of the old town, grim tower houses stand proudly vigilant. Stroll around during siesta time when the heat and silence make it especially evocative.

Also have a look at the unusual reliefs above the doors of the **Church of Taxiarhes**, on Kapetan Matapan, which depict feuding archangels and signs of the zodiac.

Orientation & Information The bus stop is in front of the Nicolas Corner Taverna on Plateia Athanaton, the central square. The post office and OTE are on the corner of the central square and Kapetan Matapan, the main thoroughfare through the old town. Areopoli's postcode is 230 62. The telephone code is 0733, which covers all the villages of the Lakonian Mani. For the National Bank of Greece, walk along Kapetan Matapan and turn right at the first church on to P Mavromihali. The bank is along on the left. It is open only on Tuesday and Thursday, from 9 am to noon. Areopoli has neither an EOT nor tourist police.

Places to Stay – bottom end The cheapest rooms are at *Perros Bathrellos* (☎ 51 205), 70 metres along Kapetan Matapan, on the left, above a nameless taverna. Look for the domatia sign. Basic but clean single/double/triple rooms with shared facilities cost 4000/5000/6000 dr.

Along Kapetan Matapan towards the Church of Taxiarhes, a sign directs you left to *Tsimova Rooms* (☎ 51 301). George Versakos, who runs the place, has cosy rooms, filled with ornaments, family photos and icons, in a 300-year-old renovated tower. Rates are 6000/11,000/14,000 dr for doubles/triples/quads with bathroom. A two-roomed apartment with kitchen is 15,000 dr. George will show you around his mini-museum of daggers, pistols, a stele and ancient coins.

In the new town, the *Hotel Mani* (☎ 51 269/190) has comfortable singles/doubles/triples/quads with bathroom for 6000/7000/8000/10,000 dr. The hotel is beyond the National Bank. On the main square, the *Hotel Kouris* (☎ 51 340) has spotless singles/doubles/triples with bathroom for 6000/8000/10,000 dr.

Places to Stay – middle At the end of Kapetan Matapan, a sign points right to the *Kapetanakas Tower* (☎ 51 233), a traditional settlement. It is austerely authentic, in keeping with the spirit of the traditional Mani. Doubles/triples are 13,200/16,000 dr with bathroom.

Places to Stay – top end At the Church of Taxiarhes, a sign points to the right to the *Londas Pension* (☎ & fax 51 012), which is a 200-year-old tower. The rooms have white-washed stone walls and beamed ceilings. Doubles/triples here are 17,000/23,000 dr, including breakfast.

Places to Eat The *Nicolas Corner Taverna*, open all day on the central square, serves tasty Greek staples. The nameless *taverna* below the rooms of Perros Bathrellos, on Kapetan Matapan (see Places to Stay), is also commendable. The *Europa Psistaria* on the central square serves good grilled food. A *supermarket* is at the beginning of Kapetan Matapan.

Getting There & Away The bus office (☎ 51 229) is inside the Nicolas Corner Taverna. There are four buses a day to Gythio (30 minutes, 400 dr); three to Itilo (20 minutes, 200 dr) via Limeni; two buses to Gerolimenas (30 minutes, 500 dr) via Pyrgos Dirou; two buses to the Diros caves (15 minutes, 180 dr); one to Lagia (40 minutes, 550 dr) via Kotronas; and three a week (on Monday, Wednesday and Friday) to Vathia (40 minutes, 650 dr).

Limeni Λιμένι
From Areopoli, a coastal road continues three km north to Limeni (Li-ME-nee), past the new *Limeni Village Bungalows* complex (☎ 51 111/112). It has Maniot tower replicas and overlooks the sleepy harbour. Rates for singles/doubles/triples are 11,000/13,000/16,000 dr and the facilities include a pool, bar and restaurant. The village proper has *domatia* and a taverna.

Itilo & Neo Itilo Οίτυλο και Νέο Οίτυλο
Itilo (IT-ee-lo), 11 km north of Areopoli, was the medieval capital of the Mani. To travel between Lakonian and Messinian Mani, you must change buses at Itilo.

The village is now a crumbling and tranquil backwater, severed in two by a ravine which was traditionally regarded as the border between outer and inner Mani. Above the ravine is the massive 17th-century **Castle of Kelefa** from which the Turks attempted to constrain the Maniots. You can't miss it on a hill above the road from Neo Itilo. Nearby, the **Monastery of Dekoulou** has colourful frescoes in its church. Neo Itilo, four km before, is a quiet secluded bay with superb views and a pebbled beach.

Places to Stay & Eat In Neo Itilo, the *Galarie Pension* (☎ 59 390), on the right heading for Itilo, has doubles/triples with large balcony, bathroom and beautiful furniture for 12,000/13,000 dr. To the left off the same road, is the plush C-class *Hotel Itilo* (☎ 59 222) which has rates from 17,000 dr including breakfast. A swimming pool and hydro-massage facilities are being installed. Excluding the last two weeks of July and all of August, a 35% discount applies for stays of one week or more. There are also *domatia* are on the right.

Between Neo Itilo and Itilo at the small, unprepossessing village of Karavostassi, people who eat at *O Faros Fish Restaurant* can camp freely. On Itilo's outskirts, *Xenonas Studios* (☎ 59 388) offers superb valley views, a pool and facilities to cater for breakfast. Double/triple units with bathroom are 15,000/18,000 dr. Coming from Nea Itilo, the studios are on the right before you get to Itilo. Ask the driver to drop you outside.

Try the fairly priced *Garden Taverna* on Nea Itilo's central square by the bus stop. In summer there's a *taverna* near the Hotel Itilo.

Getting There & Away Three buses a day go to Areopoli (30 minutes, 200 dr) and three to Kalamata (2 hours, 1000 dr). The Areopoli-Itilo bus stops at Neo Itilo. A bus form Limeni to Itilo takes 20 minutes and costs 200 dr.

Diros Caves Σπήλαιο Διρού

These extraordinary caves can be reached by taking a turn-off at the village of Pyrgos Dirou, notable for its towers, eight km south of Areopoli. The caves are four km onwards.

The caves were inhabited by Neolithic people but abandoned after an earthquake. They were rediscovered in 1900. Systematic exploration was undertaken by the speleologists Ioannis and Anna Petrochilos in 1949. Experts believe the caves may extend as far north as Sparta.

Tourists glide along the caves' subterranean river in small boats. The half-hour trip through narrow tunnels and immense caverns is awe inspiring. Myriad clusters of stalactites and stalagmites have fittingly poetic names such as the Palm Forest, Crystal Lily and the Three Wise Men. The last part of the trip is on foot.

The caves are open daily from 8 am to 6 pm from June to September, and from 8 am to 4.30 pm from October to May. Admission is 2300 dr. In summer there are queues so plan on arriving early. If you arrive after 4 pm you may not get in. For information, call ☎ 52 222/223.

Places to Stay & Eat Most people visit the caves on day trips from Areopoli or Gythio, but there is accommodation closer to the caves at Pyrgos Dirou and on the road to the caves. Just out of Pyrgos Dirou on the left, the *Greek Kitchen* offers free camping to diners. At *Kambinara Domatia & Restaurant* (☎ 52 256), tidy doubles/triples with shared bathroom are 5000/7000 dr. The rooms are two km from the caves on the right coming from Pyrgos Dirou. The nearest hotel is the D-class *To Panorama* (☎ 52 280), one km from the caves on the right. Comfortable doubles with private bathroom are 7000 dr.

The restaurant at Kambinara Domatia & Restaurant excels in grilled food. There is a reasonably priced *restaurant* at the caves.

Pyrgos Dirou to Gerolimenas

Journeying south down Mani's west coast from Pyrgos Dirou to Gerolimenas, the barren mountain landscape is broken only by deserted settlements of mighty towers. From one of these, Stavri, reached by turning right from the main road, you can trek in 40 to 50 minutes over rough terrain to the **Castle of Maina**, on the Tigani promontory. This Frankish castle was built by William II de Villehardouin in 1248. Back on the main road, **Kita**, with a plethora of towers, is worth a stroll. Although 17 km separates Pyrgos Dirou and Gerolimenas, there is only one place to stay in between: the *Tsitsiris Castle Guest House* (☎ 56 297) at Stavri. This is a traditional settlement in a wonderfully restored tower house, its rooms have air-con and telephones. Single/double/triple rates, including breakfast are 11,600/15,400/ 20,300 dr. The guesthouse has an atmospheric restaurant and bar. Signposted from the main road, it's a two-km, uphill walk from the turn-off. Taxis are available at Gerolimenas.

Gerolimenas Γερολιμένας
Gerolimenas (Ye-ro-li-ME-nas) is a tranquil fishing village built around a small, sheltered bay on the south-western tip of the peninsula. It's irresistible with the omnipresent gentle, rhythmic sound of waves lapping the pebbled shore. The village has a post office with a currency-exchange service (open Monday to Friday from 8 am to 2 pm), but no bank or OTE.

Walk to Ano Boutari & Kato Boutari From the village, walk back along the road towards Pyrgos Dirou. About 100 metres beyond the Hotel Akroyali, a road off to the right (Mantoivaloi) leads two km to the almost deserted village of Ano (upper) Boutari. The **Church of Agios Stratigos** has some well-preserved frescoes mostly dating from the 12th century. Further on at the village of Kato (lower) Boutari, the **Anemodoura Tower**, built around 1600, is thought to be one of the earliest Maniot towers.

Places to Stay & Eat The E-class *Hotel Akrotenaritis* (☎ 54 254) has singles/ doubles/triples for 2200/4500/6500 dr with shared bathroom. The hotel is by the bus stop. The D-class *Hotel Akroyali* (☎ 54 204), overlooking the beach, charges 4500/7000/ 8500/11,000 dr for rooms with private bathroom and 15,000 dr for four-person apartments. Student discounts apply. The wife of one of the family owners, Mrs Theodorakakis, has studied the history of Greek architectural restoration. Her unusual stone-tablet motif copies are for sale. The hotel organises summer fishing trips.

Both hotels have similarly priced *restaurants* and there is a waterfront *taverna* which offers barbecued seafood. There is a *super-market* on the road which runs behind the Hotel Akroyali.

Getting There & Away There are buses to Sparta (three hours, 1550 dr); to Gythio (two hours, 900 dr); and to Areopoli (30 minutes, 500 dr).

Gerolimenas to Port Kagio
South of Gerolimenas, the road continues four km to the small village of Alika, where it divides. One road leads east to Lagia and the other south to Vathia and Porto Kagio. The southern road follows the coast, passing pebbly beaches. It then climbs steeply inland to Vathia (VA-thee-a), the most dramatic and awesome of all traditional Mani villages, comprising a cluster of closely packed tower houses perched on a lofty rock.

Beyond Vathia, the road continues to climb, affording intoxicating views. Twelve km from Alika, the road descends to the indented coastline with rocky outcrops sheltering more pebbled beaches. A turn-off to the right leads to two sandy beaches at Marmari on the coast. The road continues to the fishing village of Porto Kagio on the shore of an almost circular bay.

Places to Stay & Eat The only accommodation at Vathia is at another wonderful traditional settlement. *Vathia Towers* (☎ 52 222/224) is austere and dramatic. Single/ double/triple/quad rooms here cost around 10,000/14,000/16,000/17,500 dr.

Porto Lagio has one place to stay, the *Akroteri Domatia* (no telephone), overlooking the beach. Immaculate, marbled rooms with balcony and bathroom cost 8000 to 11,000 dr a double, depending on size and position. Three village *tavernas* specialise in fish dishes.

Lagia to Kotronas
Approached from Alika, Lagia, at 400 metres above sea level, is formidable. It was once the chief town of the south-eastern Mani. Now, the village is permeated with a strange aura of insularity and brooding, as if

the ghosts of old Mani still linger in its deserted towers.

From Lagia, the road winds down with spectacular views of the little fishing harbour of **Agios Kyprianos** – a short diversion from the main road. The next village is **Kokala**, busy, friendly and with two pebbled beaches. The bus stop is in front of Synantisi Taverna.

After Kokala, the road climbs again. After four km, there are more beaches at the sprawling village of **Nyfi**. A turn-off to the right leads to the sheltered beach of **Alipa**. Continuing north, a turn-off beyond Flomochori descends to **Kotronas**.

Places to Stay Lagia has no accommodation but there are possibilities in Kokala. *Marathos Domatia*, above the taverna on the beach nearest to Lagia, has doubles for 4500 dr with shared bathroom and 6000 dr with private facilities. Further along the road, *Pension Kokala* (☎ 58 307) has comfortable double/triple rooms for 6000/7000 dr.

On a hill overlooking the sea is *Papa's Rooms* (☎ 58 290), named after the owner, jovial Papageorgis, the local priest. The double/triple/quad rooms here cost 10,000/12,000/14,000 dr, but Papa, like most Greek owners, is not averse to bargaining. Go up the dirt track (drivable) opposite Synantisi Taverna in the centre of the village by the bus stop to find the rooms.

At Nyfi, *Pension Nifi* (☎ 58 242) has pleasant doubles with shared bathroom for 4500 dr. The pension doesn't have a sign, but it's a distinctive cream and brown building, above a taverna on the right at the beginning of the village.

Places to Eat In Kokala, the *Marathos Taverna* on the beach, below rooms of the same name, has reasonably priced food. Further along the road, *Restaurant Monaxia*, signposted on the right, is a quality place.

Kotronas Κοτρώνας
Around Kotronas (Ko-tr-O-nas) the barrenness of the Mani gradually gives way to relative lushness, with olive groves and

cypress trees. Kotronas bustles compared to the Mani's half-deserted tower villages. Its main thoroughfare leads to the waterfront where the bus turns around. To the left is a bay with a small, sandy beach.

The post office is on the right of the main thoroughfare as you go towards the sea. The islet off the coast is linked by a causeway. Walk inland along the main thoroughfare and turn left at the fork. Take the first left and walk to a narrow road, which soon degenerates into a path, leading to the causeway. On the island are ruins surrounding a small well-kept church.

Places to Stay & Eat The *Adelfia Pension* (☎ 53 209) is the unmissable pink, yellow, blue, and red building on the right of the main road towards the sea. Rates for cheery single/double/triple rooms are 3000/4000/4500 dr with shared bathroom. Above a taverna overlooking the beach, the *Kotroni Domatia* (☎ 53 269/246) has doubles with shared bathroom for 4200 dr.

The well-equipped *Kotronas Bay Bungalows* (☎ 53 400) each accommodate up to four people and cost 16,000 dr. There is a restaurant. To reach them, turn left at the waterfront and follow the road skirting the bay.

The *Kotroni Taverna*, below the Kotroni Domatia, has tasty, reasonably priced grills. There are two *minimarkets* and a *bakery* on the main street.

MESSINIAN MANI
The Messinian Mani, or outer Mani, lies to the north of its Lakonian counterpart, sandwiched between the Taÿgetos mountains and the west coast of the Mani peninsula. Kalamata lies at the northern end of the peninsula. The indented coast is scattered with superb beaches at the feet of guardian mountains. There are glorious views between the villages of Kambos and Almyro and on the ascent to Kardamyli and the village of Stavropigi. There are many camp sites along this stretch of coast, unlike the inner Mani.

Stoupa Στούπα

Stoupa, 10 km south of Kardamyli, is experiencing a metamorphosis from a fishing village to a holiday resort for discriminating package tourists intent on discovering the unspoilt Greece. Although not as picturesque as Kardamyli, it has three lovely beaches. It was the founding place of the ancient kingdom of Kefktron. Like Kardamyli, Stoupa also has literary connections. Nikos Kazantzakis lived here for a time and based the protagonist of his novel *Zorba the Greek* on Alexis Zorbas, who worked as a coalmine supervisor in Pastrova, near Stoupa.

Orientation & Information Stoupa is one km west of the main Areopoli-Kalamata road. From the bus turnaround point, with your back to the mountains, walk straight ahead to reach the sea. To the right is the larger of Stoupa's two main beaches – a glorious crescent of golden sand. The road which skirts around this beach continues over the headland to the other beach.

Stoupa's development as a resort has been so rapid that its amenities have yet to catch up. With no bank, post office nor OTE, Katerina's supermarket, to the left of the main beach, has a currency-exchange service and an OTE telephone. Stoupa's postcode is 540 54 and the telephone code is 0721. Stoupa has no EOT or tourist police.

Places to Stay & Eat Avoid Stoupa in July and August when accommodation is monopolised by package-tour operators. *Camping Delfinia* (☎ 77 318) is a nicely maintained camping ground near Kaminia beach, two km the Kardamyli side of Stoupa. It has a restaurant, minimarket, playground and also apartments. *Camping Kala Goria* (☎ 77 319), above Stoupa's small beach, is well kept, with a children's playground, minimarket and bar. *Camping Kalogria* (☎ 77 319) is near the beach.

If you are two or more, seek out Thanasis, who you will find in a small office (more like a hole in the wall without a telephone) at the beginning of the large beach. The wacky Thanasis is the champion of independent and out-of-season travellers, renting a variety of houses in Stoupa. None are purpose-built and he doesn't let to tour groups. The houses are available year-round for short and long-term rental and cost from 7000 dr for two.

Petros Nikolareas Furnished Apartments (☎ 77 063) has comfortable double/triple apartments for 7000/9000 dr. Facing the sea from the bus stop, take the road which forks to the left. The rooms are on the right. A bit more expensive are the clean and spacious *Maistreli Apartments* (☎ 77 595). From the bus stop, walk ahead towards the sea. The apartments are on the left.

The C-class *Stoupa Hotel* (☎ 54 308/485) has double/triple rooms with bathroom and balcony for 7500/8700 dr. The hotel, with a bar, is on the right side of the approach road to Stoupa.

Stoupa has many restaurants and tavernas, particularly by the beaches. Prices for top seafood and traditional dishes range from reasonable to expensive. The *Ipocampus Taverna*, on the road from the bus stop to the sea, is recommended for seafood and grills.

Getting There & Away Stoupa is on the main Itilo-Kalamata bus route. Some buses will let you off at the bus turnaround in the village. Others will drop you on the main road from where it's a 1.5-km walk to the beaches.

Kardamyli Καρδαμύλη

Kardamyli (Kar-da-MEE-lee, population 350) was one of the seven cities offered to Achilles by Agamemnon. It features an atmospheric and derelict old quarter, and a picturesque new village where the buildings have remained faithful to traditional styles.

Orientation & Information Kardamyli is on the main Areopoli-Kalamata road. The central square, Plateia 25 Martiou 1821, is at the northern end of the main thoroughfare. The bus stops are opposite the centre of the village. The post office is beyond the bus stops, on the left, as you walk south towards Stoupa. To get to Kardamyli's pebble-and-stone beach, walk back along the road towards Kalamata and look for the sign pointing left, beyond the bridge. To reach Old or Upper Kardamyli, turn right before the bridge.

There is no OTE, but Morgan Holidays (☎ 73 520; fax 73 190), 150 metres south of the bus stop, on the left, has a metered telephone. Kardamyli's postcode is 240 22. The telephone code is 0721. There are no tourist police and no EOT, but the staff at Morgan Holidays are helpful.

Taÿgetos Gorge (Χαράδρα Ταΰγετου) The bridge at the beginning of the village, coming from Kalamata, crosses the mouth of the Taÿgetos gorge. You can trek up the gorge for 2½ hours to reach the deserted **Monastery of the Saviour**. Alternatively, you can trek down the gorge in four to five hours. Take the 6.15 am bus from Kardamyli to the mountain village of Exahori. Opposite the bus stop, a path leads to the vicinity of the village of Kolibetseïka, from where a path leads down into the gorge. These treks are strenuous. Strong footwear is essential and take plenty of water.

Places to Stay & Eat *Melitsina Camping* (☎ 73 461) has wheelchair access and a restaurant and bar. Numerous domatia signs are along Kardamyli's main road and the area offers several farm-stay options. Olivia Koumounakou (☎ 73 326/623) rents immaculate *domatia*. Doubles with private bathroom for 7500 dr. Opposite are the equally agreeable *apartments* (closed in August) of Statis Bravacos (same telephone numbers as Olivia's rooms), where doubles are also 7500 dr. Walk towards Stoupa, turn right opposite the post office and look for two white houses.

Continuing to this road's end, a right turn will reveal a charming stone building which is *Lela's Taverna & Rooms* (☎ 73 541). A little name-dropping won't go amiss. Lela is the former housekeeper of author Patrick Leigh Fermor, who still lives in the village. Doubles with bathroom are 10,000 dr.

At the Kalamata end of town, Stavros and Katina Papadea (☎ 73 445) have *domatia*

including large doubles for 8500 dr. Walk along the main road towards Kalamata and turn left at the sign for Kardamyli beach towards a distinctive red-brick building on the right. Back on the main road, continuing towards Kalamata, you will come to *Castle Pension* (☎ 73 226/396) on the right. The pension is a beautiful stone building which has wrought-iron balconies. Its double/triple rooms with bathroom and kitchen cost 8900/ 11,000 dr.

Lela's Taverna & Rooms, with a sea view, serves food that gets glowing reports from locals and tourists. Self-caterers will find all needs at *Kardimilis Market*. There is a *supermarket* on the road to Kalamata.

Getting There & Away Kardamyli is on the main Itilo-Kalamata (two hours, 1000 dr) bus route.

Getting Around Morgan Holidays has car and mountain-bike hire.

Around Kardamyli
A fascinating excursion south of Kardamyli is to the lesser-known village of **Proastio** on a slope of Mt Taÿgetos. Time seems to stand still in this Maniot village of churches with their notable bell towers. On the outskirts is a quaint stone bridge. The village affords magnificent bay views.

Messinia Μεσσηνία

The farmland of Messinia, in the south-west, is some of the richest in Greece – famous for its plump Kalamata olives. It's a region of verdant plains and gentle hills covered with orchards and vineyards. It also has some of the best beaches in the country, set against the backdrop of the dramatic Taÿgetos mountains, their peaks capped with snow in winter.

KALAMATA Καλαμάτα
Kalamata (population 33,000) is Messinia's capital and the second-largest city in the

eloponnese. 'Calamitous Kalamata' aptly sums up this hapless city. The old town was almost totally destroyed by the Turks during the War of Independence and rebuilt unimaginatively by French engineers in the 1830s. On 14 September 1986, Kalamata was devastated by an earthquake which registered 6.2 on the Richter scale. Twenty people died, hundreds were injured and over 10,000 homes were destroyed. The destruction is still evident.

The most pleasant parts of Kalamata are the pebble-and-shingle beach, the kastro and the old houses around its base. Tó reach the latter, walk up Ypapandis from Plateia 25 Martiou. Kalamata's archaeological museum and folk museum were both severely damaged in the earthquake and remain closed.

Orientation

The old town around the kastro is picturesque, and the waterfront along Navarinou is lively – but it's a long (three km), hot walk between the two. The main streets linking the old town with the waterfront are Faron and Aristomenous. On Aristomenous are the two large squares of Plateia Georgiou and Plateia Konstantiadokou.

The train station is at the end of Sidirodromikou Stathmou. The bus station is inconveniently located at the north-western edge of town. To get to the local bus terminal from here, walk south along Artemidos and cross the third bridge over the River Nedon. Continue straight ahead to Plateia 25 Martiou. A No 1 bus goes to the waterfront.

Information

Kalamata's municipal tourist office (☎ 21 959) is on Makedonias (the road signposted to Athens). The tourist police (☎ 23 187), Aristomenous 46, are open daily from 8 am to 2 pm. The regular police and the EOT are in the same building.

The post office is at Iatropoulou 4. To get there, take Sidirodromikou Stathmou, which branches off Plateia Georgiou, turn right onto Iatropoulou and it's on the left. It's open Monday to Friday from 7.30 am to 2 pm. The

OTE, open 24 hours, is on the western side of Aristomenous, north of Plateia Georgiou. Kalamata's postcode is 241 00. The telephone code is 0721.

Several banks are on Aristomenous, including the National Bank of Greece opposite the OTE. Another branch is on the waterfront on the corner of Ariti and Navarinou. Euphoria, at Faron 210, sells English-language newspapers and books. There is a laundrette on the waterfront on the corner of Mezonos 2.

Kastro

Looming over the town is the 13th-century kastro. Remarkably, it survived the 1986 earthquake. There are excellent views from the battlements. The kastro is the setting for an annual summer festival, which includes cultural events such as contemporary musical performances and plays.

Things to See & Do

Greece is not big on providing children's entertainment, but south of the station, Kalamata's shady, open-air **train museum**, with play equipment, offers hours of pleasure for kids and train lovers among original steam engines and carriages. Admission is free and you can picnic.

A **diving school** (☎ 94 330) operates from Faron 207. Summer nightlife in piano bars, discos and tavernas vibrates mainly along the waterfront. The four-km-long beach is safe for swimming.

Places to Stay – bottom end

Camping Patista (☎ 29 525), *Elite Camping* (☎ 27 368), *Camping Fare* (☎ 29 520) and *Maria's Sea & Sun Camping* (☎ 41 314) are along the waterfront east of town. Maria's, edging onto the beach four km from town on Navarinou, is the pick of the bunch with welcome shade from tamarisk trees. The camping ground has a minimarket, bar, restaurant and two-person bungalows. All of the camping grounds can be reached by bus No 1.

Near the train station, the D-class *Hotel George* (☎ 27 225), on the corner of Dagre

PELOPONNESE

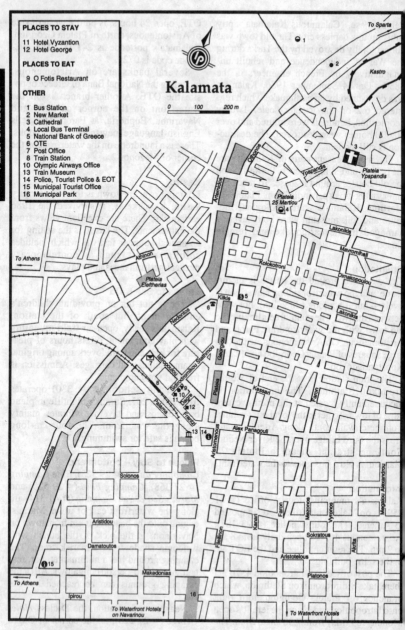

PLACES TO STAY
11 Hotel Vyzantion
12 Hotel George

PLACES TO EAT
9 O Fotis Restaurant

OTHER
1 Bus Station
2 New Market
3 Cathedral
4 Local Bus Terminal
5 National Bank of Greece
6 OTE
7 Post Office
8 Train Station
10 Olympic Airways Office
13 Train Museum
14 Police, Tourist Police & EOT
15 Municipal Tourist Office
16 Municipal Park

Kalamata

0   100   200 m

To Sparta

To Athens

To Athens

To Waterfront Hotels
on Navarinou

To Waterfront Hotels

Kastro

Plateia
Ypapandis

Plateia
25 Martiou

Lakonikis

Mavromihali

Kolokotroni

Dimakopoulou

Lakonikis

Kilkis

Kessani

Faron

Alex Panagouli

Faron

Kanari

Mezonos

Vyronos

Megalou Alexandrou

Sokratous

Aristotelous

Platonos

Aftotia

Makedonias

Iplrou

Solonos

Aristidou

Damatoutos

Plateia
Eleftherias

Athinon

Artemidos

Nedontos

Otonos

Ypapandis

Iatropoulou

Sidirodromikou Stathmou

Georgiou

Plateia

Palama

Frantzi

Aristomenous

Artemidos

Eias Nedas

and Frantzi 5, has tidy single/double rooms for 3500/4000 dr. Near the waterfront, the D-class *Hotel Nevada* (☎ 82 429), Santa Rosa 9, has clean singles/doubles/triples for 3400/4900/6800 dr with shared bathroom. Opposite, the homely *Hotel Avra* (☎ 82 759), Santa Rosa 10, has doubles/triples with shared facilities for 6000/7000 dr. For these hotels, walk up Faron from the waterfront and take the first left onto Santa Rosa.

The cheapest waterfront hotel is the D-class *Hotel Plaza* (☎ 82 590), Navarinou 117, where clean rooms with balcony and shared facilities are 5000/7500/9000 dr.

Places to Stay – middle

The traditionally furnished *Hotel Vyzantion* (☎ 86 824/825, 83 251), Sidirodromikou Stathmou 13, has singles/doubles with bathroom for 6000/8000 dr. On the waterfront, the spacious C-class *Haikos Hotel* (☎ 88 902/924/946/968; fax 23 800), Navarinou 115, offers nicely furnished rooms for 9900/12,000/14,500 dr.

Places to Stay – top end

The B-class *Filoxenia Hotel* (☎ 23 166/167/168) overlooks the beach at the eastern end of Navarinou. It has a restaurant, bar, pool and disco. Mandatory half-board (breakfast and lunch or dinner) rates are 15,150/22,300 dr for singles/doubles. The A-class *Hotel Elite Village* (☎ 25 015, 22 434 or 85 303; fax 84 369), Navarinou 2 has restaurants, bars, a pool and disco. Single/double rooms are 18,300/25,500 dr for half-board.

Places to Eat

There are numerous fast-food joints in Kalamata. For traditional ambience, try *O Fotis Restaurant* on Sidirodromikou Stathmou, close to the train station. *Restaurant Tampaki*, at Navarinou 41 and its next-door neighbour on the waterfront both serve traditional fare and good seafood at reasonable prices.

Self-caterers should visit Kalamata's large *food market* across the bridge from the bus station. Kalamata is noted for its olives, olive oil, figs, raki and *mastica* (a surprisingly smooth mastic-based liqueur).

Things to Buy

Kalamata silk mantillas or kerchiefs, still woven Byzantine-style by nuns at the Convent of Agios Konstantinos and Agia Eleni, are on sale at the base of the kastro.

Getting There & Away

Air There are daily flights from Kalamata's airport (☎ 69 442) to Athens (11,800 dr). The Olympic Airways office (☎ 22 376/724) is at Sidirodromikou Stathmou 17.

Bus There are 12 buses a day from Kalamata to Athens (4½ hours, 3500 dr) via Megalopoli (1 hour; 850 dr), Tripolis (2 hours; 1300 dr) and Corinth (4 hours; 2650 dr), as well as nine a day to Koroni (1½ hours, 750 dr) and Pylos (1½ hours, 750 dr). Five buses a day leave for Methoni (1½ hours, 850 dr), three of which continue to Finikoundas (two hours, 1000 dr). There are four to Itilo (two hours, 1000 dr); two to Patras (four hours, 3350 dr) via Pyrgos (two hours, 1900 dr); and two to Sparta (2½ hours, 800 dr) via Artimisia (360 dr) and Mavromati (1½ hours, 450 dr).

Train Kalamata is the end of the line for both branches of the Peloponnese railway. Daily, four trains trundle to Athens (seven hours, 2160 dr) via Tripolis (2½ hours, 840 dr); Argos (four hours, 1260 dr) and Corinth (5¼ hours, 1650 dr). On the other branch line, four trains a day go to Athens (11 hours, 2860 dr) via Kyparissia (two hours, 590 dr), Pyrgos (3¼ hours, 860 dr) and Patras (six hours, 1500 dr).

Ferry The F/B *Theseus* sails for Kastelli-Kissamos on Crete three times weekly in summer and twice in winter. The eight-hour voyage costs from 4100 dr (deck class). Tickets are available from Spyros Maniatis (☎ 20 704) on the west side of the customs office by the port.

Getting Around

To/From the Airport Kalamata's airport is 10.5 km west of the city. There is no airport shuttle bus. A taxi costs about 1000 dr.

Bus The No 1 is Kalamata's only local bus. It travels frequently between Plateia 25 Martiou and the Filoxenia Hotel, at the eastern end of the waterfront, making its way south along Aristomenous and Faron. The flat fare is 110 dr.

Car & Motorbike There are lots of places to hire cars and motorbikes from on the waterfront and on Faron. It pays to compare prices.

AROUND KALAMATA

The coast south-west of Kalamata boasts superb beaches, both sandy and pebbled, by attractive seaside villages. They include Petalidi (which has three camping grounds), Kalamaki, Hrani, Agios Andreas (which, locals assert, was built on an ancient Temple of Apollo) and Koroni.

LANGADA PASS

The 59-km road from Kalamata to Sparta is one of the most stunning routes in Greece, twisting and turning as it cuts through the Taÿgetos mountains by way of the Langada pass. It's a lonely road, but in the middle of nowhere, on a hairpin bend, it can yield a surprise – an old man, his donkey tethered, patiently waiting for motorists to stop and buy honey from his stall. The highest point of the pass is 1524 metres, after which it begins descending through the **Langada gorge** to the village of Trypi. To the north of this gorge is where the ancient Spartans threw babies too weak or deformed to become good soldiers. It is possible to travel by bus along this route, but you'll need to change buses in Artimisia.

There are two D-class hotels in tranquil Trypi. The *Keadas Hotel* (☎ 0731-98 222) has singles/doubles for 4500/6800 dr. The *Hotel Trypi* (☎ 0731-25 387) is similarly priced. Drivers and hikers will find delightful picnic areas on the Kalamata side of the pass.

KORONI Κορώνη

Koroni (Ko-RO-nee, population 1420) is 35 km south-east of Methoni and 43 km south-west of Kalamata. It's a delightful medieval town, built on a promontory, with pastel-tiled Venetian houses reaching uphill to its castle. The castle, most of which is taken up by the **Timios Prodromos Convent**, is tame compared with Methoni's, but it's a tranquil place for a stroll with views of the Messinian gulf and the Taÿgetos mountains. Koroni's main attraction is its **Zaga beach**, a long sweep of golden sand.

Orientation & Information

Facing the church, turn left from the bus station to get to Koroni's main street, passing the post office on the way. The OTE is on the left side of the main street coming from the bus terminal. Koroni has neither an EOT nor tourist police. Koroni's postcode is 240 04. The telephone code is 0725.

To get to Zaga beach, ascend the steps to the right of the church opposite the bus stop, turn left on to Maisonos and look for the beach sign pointing left. The entrance to the castle is on the way to the beach. For the harbour, turn right from the bus station, take the first right and turn right again at the waterfront.

Places to Stay & Eat

Camping Koroni (☎ 22 119) is a good camping ground with a restaurant, bar, minimarket, pool, kitchen and wash room. Rates are 1200 dr per person and 1000/1200 dr per small/big tent. It's on the road coming from Kalamata on the left. Buses stop outside.

The *Koroni Pension* (☎ 22 385/448) is above the Symposium restaurant, and both are owned by an amiable Greek-American named George. Spacious, clean rooms with bathroom are 7000/8000 dr and there's a communal kitchen. The pension is on the main street.

At the beginning of Zaga beach, Andreas Koutsoukos (☎ 22 262) rents fine *domatia* above his taverna. Double/triple/quad rates are 6000/7500/10,000 dr. The rooms have

ROSEMARY HALL

BERTOLD DAUM

DAVID HALL

ROSEMARY HALL

Top: Gerolimenas Bay, the Mani, Peloponnese
Left: The Corinth Canal, Peloponnese
Right: Entrance to the stadium, Olympia, Peloponnese
Bottom: The fortress, Methoni, Messinia, Peloponnese

KERRY KENIHAN

KERRY KENIHAN

ROSEMARY HALL

ROSEMARY HALL

Top Left: Maniot house, Monemvassia, Lakonia, Peloponnese
Top Right: The village priest of Diakofto, Peloponnese
Bottom Left: Taÿgetos Gorge near Kardamyli, Messinia, Peloponnese
Bottom Right: The main street, Monemvassia, Lakonia, Peloponnese

air-con, telephone, refrigerator, hot plates, electric mosquito zappers and bathroom.

One of Koroni's nicest restaurants is *Symposium*, on the main street, owned by the same George. Moussaka or meatballs with two vegetables are 1100 dr, as is a combination seafood plate.

Getting There & Away

There are nine buses a day to Kalamata (1½ hours, 750 dr) and two to Finikoundas.

FINIKOUNDAS Φοινικούντας

Finikoundas, midway between Koroni and Methoni, is a fishing village rapidly developing into a holiday resort with a reputation for good windsurfing. Currently it is visited more by backpackers than package tourists. With no archaeological sites nor cultural diversions, the beach is it – unless you're into migratory birds, which are a short caïque trip away on the nearby islet of **Sapientza**. From the bus stop, walk straight ahead to reach the waterfront.

Places to Stay

Camping Ammos (☎ 0723-71 262), two km west of Finikoundas, is a pleasant camping ground with water-sports facilities. There are numerous *domatia* in the village and two appealing mid-range hotels. *Hotel Finikoundas* (☎ 71 308), by the bus stop, has single/double/triple rooms for 8500/11,000/13,000 dr. Turn left at the waterfront to find the *Hotel Porto* (☎ 71 457), with similar rates.

Getting There & Away

Three buses a day go to Kalamata (2 hours; 1000 dr) via Methoni (30 minutes, 280 dr) and Pylos; and two a day to Koroni. If the lousy bus service tempts you to take a taxi, the fares are 2000 dr to Methoni and 2500 dr to Koroni.

METHONI Μεθώνη

Methoni (Meth-ON-ee, population 1500), 12 km south of Pylos, was another of the seven cities offered to Achilles by Agamemnon. Homer described it as 'rich in vines'.

Today, it's a pretty seaside town, with a sandy beach that's crowded in summer, and a magnificent 13th-century fortress. This vast fortification, uncharacteristically, does not perch on a hill but is on a promontory, surrounded on three sides by the sea and separated from the mainland by a moat. This medieval port town, which stood within the fortress walls, was the Venetians' first and longest-held possession in the Peloponnese, and a stopover point for pilgrims *en route* to the Holy Land. In medieval times, the twin fortresses of Methoni and Koroni were known as 'the Eyes of the Serene Republic'.

Orientation & Information

Methoni consists of two main streets. Arriving by bus from Pylos, facing straight ahead, you will see a fork in the road. The left fork leads to the beach, and the right is Methoni's shopping street. The post office and OTE are adjacent to each other on the left side of the beach road. The National Bank of Greece is on the right of the shopping street.

There are no tourist police and no EOT in Methoni. The regular police (☎ 22 316) are on a side street off the beach road. Look for the sign before the post office and OTE.

Fortress

This splendid fortress, a supreme example of military architecture, is vast and romantic. Allocate at least half a day to explore it thoroughly. Within the walls are a Turkish bath, a cathedral, houses, a cistern, parapets and underground passages. See how many Lion of St Mark insignias you can spot. A short causeway leads from the fortress to the diminutive octagonal Turkish castle on an adjacent islet. Bring a torch to explore the interior. The site is open Monday to Saturday from 8 am to 7 pm and on Sunday from 8 am to 6 pm. Admission is free. Facing the sea at the start of the beach, turn right to reach the castle entrance.

Places to Stay – bottom end

Camping Methoni (☎ 31 228) is a reasonable camping ground 600 metres beyond the

PELOPONNESE

Methoni Beach Hotel, which is at the beginning of the beach.

The *domatia* of Dimitrios Tsonis (☎ 31 640/588), above Cafeteria George, are spotless. Double/triple rates are 6000/6700 dr, with use of a communal kitchen. Family apartments are also available. Take the right fork from the bus stop. The domatia are on the left. There are other *domatia* on this and the beach roads.

Methoni Beach Hotel (☎ 31 455) is at the beginning of the beach and charges B-class rates.

Places to Stay – middle

The *Albatros Hotel* (☎ 31 160/170), next to the post office, has rooms with private facilities, refrigerator and balcony. Rates are 8000/9500/11,500. The C-class *Hotel Castello* (☎ 31 300/280) is beautifully furnished. Each room has a balcony overlooking rose and dahlia gardens with views of the fortress. Doubles with breakfast are 9000 dr and family apartments are 15,000 dr. Walk down the beach road towards a sign pointing left. The hotel is closed in August.

The B-class *Hotel Amalia* (☎ 31 129/193/195/233), stands in splendid isolation on a hill with wonderful views of Methoni and the fortress. Rates for balconied rooms with breakfast are 10,000/13,000/15,500 dr. The hotel is 250 metres up a drivable dirt road beginning beyond the camping ground.

Places to Eat

The *Restaurant Oinouses*, on the beach, serves tasty food at reasonable prices. The *Louise* is a good restaurant on the shopping street.

Getting There & Away

A bus timetable is pinned on the door of the newsagent down from the bus stop. There are five buses a day to Kalamata (1½ hours, 850 dr), seven to Pylos (15 minutes, 175 dr) and four to Finikoundas (30 minutes, 280 dr). No buses go direct to Koroni – change at Finikoundas.

PYLOS Πύλος

Pylos (PI-los, population 2800), on the coast 51 km south-west of Kalamata, presides over the southern end of an immense bay. On this bay on 20 October 1827, the British, French and Russian fleets, under the command of Admiral Codrington, fired at point-blank range on Ibrahim Pasha's Turkish and Egyptian fleet, sinking 53 ships and killing 6000 men, with negligible losses on the Allies' side.

It was known as the Battle of Navarino (the town's former name), and was decisive in the War of Independence, but it was not meant to have been a battle at all. The presence of the Allied fleet was intended merely to coax Ibrahim Pasha and his fleet into leaving, but things got out of hand. George IV, on hearing the news, described it as a 'deplorable misunderstanding'.

With its huge natural harbour almost enclosed by the Sfaktiria islet, a delightful tree-shaded central square, two castles and surrounding pine-covered hills, Pylos is one of the most picturesque towns in the Peloponnese.

Orientation & Information

The bus station is on the central square, Plateia Trion Navarhon, at the bottom of the road from Kalamata, and back from the waterfront. The post office is on Nileos. To reach it, have your back to the bus station, and turn left. Take the first right away from the square to reach the OTE. The National Bank of Greece is on the central square. There are no tourist police and no EOT in Pylos. The regular police (☎ 22 316) are between the square and the waterfront. Pylos' postcode is 240 01. The telephone code is 0723.

Castles

Pylos has two castles at each side of the bay. **Paleokastro** is six km north of Pylos at the other side of the bay, but it's in such ruin that it's hardly worth visiting. In contrast, **Neo Kastro** is in town and in good nick. It was used as a prison until this century. Within its walls are a citadel, a mosque converted into a church and a courtyard surrounded by dungeons. Soon, a marine archaeological museum will open at the castle to house finds from wrecks of the Turkish and Egyptian ships. Underwater exploration in the bay is being funded by UNESCO. The castle is open daily, except Monday, from 8 am to 3 pm. Admission is 400 dr, extra for cameras. It's free on Sunday and public holidays. To reach the castle entrance, walk up the road from the central square signposted to Methoni and follow the sign pointing right.

Boat Tours

You can ask around the waterfront for fishermen to take you around the Bay of Navarino and the island of Sfaktiria. The price usually depends on the number of passengers, but reckon on about 3000 dr. On the trip around the island, stops can be made at memorials to admirals of the Allied ships. Boats may pause so you can see wrecks of sunken Turkish ships, discernible in the clear waters.

Places to Stay – bottom end

The nearest camping ground to Pylos is *Navarino Beach Camping* (☎ 22 761), eight km north of Pylos on Gialova beach. Take a Kyparissia bus from Pylos.

There are several *domatia* on the approach road to Pylos. Look for signs. The pleasant D-class *Hotel Navarino* (☎ 22 564) has singles/doubles/triples with shared bathroom for 7500/10,000/12,000 dr. From the bus station, walk to the waterfront, turn left and the hotel is on the left.

The C-class *Hotel Galaxy* (☎ 22 780), on Plateia Trion Navarhon, has reasonable rooms for 7700/11,000/12,000 dr. The C-class *Arvaniti Hotel* (☎ 23 050/341), on Nileos beyond the post office, is a better choice with spacious rooms for 7500/9000/10,800 dr.

Places to Stay – middle

The tastefully decorated C-class *Hotel Karalis Beach* (☎ 22 960) has rooms for 9000/15,000 dr. The hotel is below the castle, almost overhanging a rocky beach. Turn left from the central square onto the waterfront

and continue for 200 metres. The C-class *Karali Hotel* (☎ 23 021/2), Kalamatas 26, is another luxurious place, with rooms for 10,000/17,000 dr. It's on the Kalamata-Pylos road, on the left approaching Pylos.

Places to Eat

Ta Adelfia, below the Hotel Navarino, has outdoor seating with a bay view. *Gregory's Restaurant* has tasty, reasonably priced dishes and garden seating. The *National Restaurant*, next to a kafeneio off the square on the waterfront, serves good staples. The *kafeneio* presents tasty mezedes with ouzo (200 dr).

After a meal, order coffee and cake on the square and watch the world go by. There are *supermarkets*, *fruit & vegetable stalls*, a *baker* and *psistaria* on lively Ipiskoupou. Turn right at the bus station and climb the wide steps straight ahead.

Getting There & Away

Nine buses a day go to Kalamata (1½ hours, 750 dr); six to Kyparissia (two hours, 900 dr), via Nestor's Palace (30 minutes, 280 dr) and Hora (35 minutes); five to Methoni (15 minutes, 175 dr); four to Finikoundas (45 minutes) and two to Athens (seven hours, 4250 dr). To Tripolis, it's three hours and costs 2000 dr. Buy tickets on the bus.

Getting Around

Motorbike & Car Both can be hired from Kassimiotis Rent-a-Motorbike-or-Car (☎ 22 393). It's on the left as you approach the square.

AROUND PYLOS
Nestor's Palace

This is supposedly Homer's 'sandy Pylos' where Telemachos (with Athena disguised as Mentor) was warmly welcomed when he came to ask of the wise old King Nestor the whereabouts of his long-lost father, Odysseus, King of Ithaca.

The palace, originally a two-storey building, is the best preserved of all Mycenaean palaces. Its walls stand a metre high, giving

PELOPONNESE

a good idea of the layout of a Mycenaean palace complex. The main palace, in the middle, was a vast building of many rooms. The largest, the **throne room**, was where the king dealt with state business. In the centre was a large, circular hearth surrounded by four ornate columns which supported a 1st-floor balcony. Some of the fine frescoes discovered here are in the museum in the nearby village of Hora (see the following section). Rooms surrounding the throne room include the sentry box, pantry, waiting room, a vestibule and, most fascinating, a bathroom with a terracotta tub still in place.

The most important finds were about 1200 Linear B script tablets, the first discovered on the mainland. Some are in Hora's museum. The site was excavated later than the other Mycenaean sites, between 1952 and 1965. An excellent guidebook by Carl Blegen, who led the excavations, is sold at the site for 500 dr.

Nestor's Palace is 17 km north of modern Pylos. It is open daily from 8.30 am to 3 pm, Sunday from 9.30 am to 2.30 pm. Admission is 500 dr.

Hora Χώρα
Hora's fascinating little **archaeological museum**, three km north-east of Nestor's Palace, houses finds from the site and other Mycenaean artefacts from Messinia. The prize pieces are the frescoes from the throne rooms at Nestor's Palace. The museum is open Monday, Wednesday and Saturday from 8.45 am to 3 pm and Sunday from 8.30 am to 3 pm. Admission is 500 dr.

Getting There & Away
The Kyparissia bus from Pylos stops at Nestor's Palace and Hora.

Elia Ηλία

Elia is a most fertile region, watered by the River Alfios, the 'Sacred Alph' in Samuel Taylor Coleridge's *Kubla Khan*. Valleys are graced with vine, orange and olive groves,

clusters of cherry and walnut trees and fields of corn, wheat and vegetables. The prime attraction is the site of ancient Olympia.

THOLOS TO PYRGOS
Heading north into Elia from Messinia, the mountains to the east give way to interrupted plains fringed by golden-sand beaches. Interspersed by pebbled shores and rocky outcrops, these beaches stretch right around Elia's coastline. The best beaches in the south are at **Tholos**, where there's a camping ground, and at **Kakovatos** and **Kouroutas**. There's seaside accommodation in each village, but most of it is in uninspiring, concrete buildings.

A sign outside Tholo points to the mountain village of **Nea Figalia**, 14 km inland. From here, it's a further 20 km to the tranquil site of **Ancient Figalia**, set high above the River Nedron almost at its source. Laurels, cypresses and citrus trees are clustered around the ruins of this ancient Arcadian marketplace with towers; a small acropolis; an agora; and a temple to Dionysos, the wine pourer. A rough road leads east from Nea Figalia to Andritsena (see the Arcadia section).

PYRGOS Πύργος
The capital of Elia prefecture is Pyrgos (population 24,000), 98 km south-west of Patras and 24 km from Olympia. It's an unattractive agricultural town with little of interest except its municipal theatre and market. It is, however, the connecting point for buses and trains to Olympia. The bus and train stations are about 100 metres apart, the former on Manolopoulou and the latter a short walk away. If you must stay overnight, try the C-class *Hotel Olympos* (☎ 0621-23 650/651/652), on the corner of Vasileos Pavlou and Karkavitsa; or the *Hotel Pantheon* (☎ 0621-97 468), Themistokleous 7. Both are near the train station and charge around 8000 dr a double.

Getting There & Away
Bus There are 16 buses a day to Olympia (30 minutes, 300 dr) on weekdays, 14 on Satur-

day, and nine on Sunday. There are 10 buses a day to both Athens (five hours, 4350 dr) and Patras (two hours, 1500 dr); seven a day to Lehena (one hour; 860 dr); four to Kyparissia (one hour; 860 dr); three each to Kyllini (50 minutes; 850 dr), Tripolis (four hours, 2250 dr), Kalamata (two hours, 1900 dr) and Andritsena (1½ hours; 1250 dr).

Train Seven trains a day chug to Patras (two hours, 820 dr); six a day to both Athens (seven hours) and Kyparissia (1¼ hours) five to Olympia (36 minutes, 210 dr); and four to Kalamata (3¼ hours, 860 dr). To Corinth, it's 5½ hours (2100 dr).

OLYMPIA Ολυμπία

Ancient Olympia lies half a km east of the modern village of Olympia (O-lim-BEE-a). Modern Olympia panders unashamedly to tourists. Its main street is lined with souvenir and coffee shops and restaurants. Despite the commercialism, it's pleasantly laid-back. The village is nestled in a hollow amid stately cypress trees, grassy meadows and bright wild flowers; and encircled by the soft, green foothills of Mt Kronion. Nikos Kazantzakis wrote that there was 'no landscape which so perseveringly invites peace and reconciliation'.

The ancient site is the major attraction (see the following Ancient Olympia section) but you can visit the **Historical Museum of the Olympic Games** in town. Although most of the labelling is in French, the collection of commemorative stamps and literature covering the games needs little explanation. The museum is at the western end of the village, two blocks south of Praxitelous Kondyli. It is open Tuesday to Sunday from 8.30 am to 3 pm. Admission is 500 dr.

Orientation

The modern village lies along the main Pyrgos-Tripolis road, known as Praxitelous Kondyli. In the town centre, Douma, branching off Praxitelous Kondyli, leads to the train station. The bus stops for Pyrgos and Tripolis are opposite one another on Praxitelous

Kondyli, a little east of the turn-off for the train station.

Information

Olympia's outstanding municipal tourist office (☎ 23 100/173) is on Praxitelous Kondyli, by the bus stops. The staff offer a good map of the village, have comprehensive information on bus, train and ferry schedules (from Kyllini and Patras) and can change currency. It is open daily from 8.30 am to 10 pm in July and August and until 8.15 pm in winter. There are no tourist police. The regular police (☎ 22 100) are behind the tourist office.

To get to the post office, walk along Praxitelous Kondyli towards ancient Olympia from the bus stops and take the first turn right. The OTE is on Praxitelous Kondyli, beyond the turn-off for the post office. Olympia's postcode is 270 65. The telephone code is 0624. The National Bank of Greece is on the corner of Praxitelous Kondyli and Stefanopoulou. The hospital (☎ 22 222) is signposted from the church at the western end of the village.

Places to Stay – bottom end

The nearest camping ground to Olympia is *Camping Diana* (☎ 22 314/425), 250 metres from the village. This is a good place with a pool and costs 1000 dr per person and 700 dr for a small tent. Students receive a 10% reduction. A sign by the National Bank of Greece points the way. Other camping grounds near Olympia are *Camping Olympia* (☎ 22 745), one km along the road to Pyrgos; and *Camping Alphios* (☎ 22 950), one km from Praxitelous Kondyli, signposted from the Pyrgos side of the village.

Olympia's *YHA hostel* (☎ 22 580), Praxitelous Kondyli 18, has dorm beds for 1300 dr, including hot shower. There is no curfew and no Hostelling International card is required.

There are several places with *domatia*. *The Pension Achilleys* (☎ 22 562), Stefanopoulou 4, has cosy singles/doubles/triples with shared facilities for 3,500/5000/7500 dr. Walking towards Pyrgos, turn left at the

PELOPONNESE

National Bank of Greece, and the pension is on the right. A little further along and to the left is the airy *Pension Posidon* (☎ 22 567), Stefanopoulou 9. Singles/doubles with shared bathroom are 4000/5000 dr.

The D-class *Hotel Hermes* (☎ 22 577) has pleasant rooms with facilities for 4000/5500/7000 dr. Coming from Pyrgos, the hotel is on the right 500 metres before the village. Just before the church is the C-class *Hotel Oinomaos* (☎ 22 056). It has light and spacious rooms with facilities for 4000/6000/8000 dr. The *Hotel Pelops* (☎ 22 543), next to the church at Barelas 2, has tasteful rooms with private facilities and phone for 6000/8500/10,000 dr.

Places to Stay – middle

The luxurious A-class *Hotel Andonios* (☎ 22 348/349), complete with bar and restaurant, commands panoramic views from the balconies above the village's south side. Rates are 16,500/27,500 dr for units with bathroom, air-con, TV and radio. To reach the hotel, take the road by the side of the church at the Pyrgos end of the village.

Places to Stay – top end

The sprawling A-class *Hotel Amalia* (☎ 22 190/1), on the Pyrgos-Olympia road, has a restaurant, pool and roof garden. Singles/doubles/triples with breakfast are 19,000/28,000/33,000 dr. Also A-class is the *Best Western Hotel Europa International* (☎ 22 650/700/306; fax 23 166), close to the ancient site. Facilities include a bar, restaurant, pool, tennis court and horse riding. Singles/doubles with breakfast are 15,000/25,500 dr.

Places to Eat

Restaurants in Olympia cater mainly for bus groups, so don't expect too much. *Taverna O Barba Fotis*, next to the Hotel Hermes, retains its traditional-taverna ambience. The *Pension Posidon*, on Stefanopoulou, has a summer-only outdoor grill taverna. *Taverna Praxitelous*, next door to the police station, is a local favourite. At the *Hotel Pelops*,

platters featuring 14 different traditional treats are reasonably priced.

Self-caterers will find *supermarkets* along Praxitelous Kondyli and *greengrocers* and a good *baker* on Spilopoulou, near the church.

Entertainment

The *Touris Club*, up the hill past the hospital, caters for visitors seeking traditional fun. Open for groups year-round, and individuals between 1 February and 30 October, the club seats 1000 for lunch or dinner, which is followed at about 9 pm by costumed dancing from all parts of Greece. One can relax by the pool by day for the price of a drink. An ouzo (800 dr) comes with excellent mezedes.

Getting There & Away

Bus Four buses a day arrive from Athens (5½ hours, 4650 dr) returning via Pyrgos. There are numerous services to Pyrgos (30 minutes, 300 dr) – 15 on weekdays, 12 on Saturday and nine on Sunday. Three buses a day travel to Tripolis (four hours, 1750 dr).

Train There are five trains a day travelling to Pyrgos (36 minutes, 210 dr).

ANCIENT OLYMPIA

Ancient Olympia was a complex of temples, priests' dwellings and public buildings. It was also the venue of the Olympic Games, which took place every four years. During these games the city-states were bound by *ekeheiria* (a sacred truce) to stop beating the hell out of one another, and compete in races and sports instead. City-states contravening this three-month truce were heavily fined.

The site is open Monday to Friday from 8 am to 7 pm and Saturday and Sunday from 8.30 am to 3 pm. Admission is 1200 dr (free on Sunday and public holidays).

History & Mythology

The origins of Olympia date back to Mycenaean times. The Great Goddess, identified with Rea, was worshipped here in the 1st millennium BC. By the classical era, Rea had been superseded by her son Zeus. A small regional festival, which probably

PELOPONNESE

included athletic events, was introduced in the 11th century BC. The first official quadrennial Olympic Games were held in 776 BC. By 676 BC, they were open to all male Greeks, reaching their height of prestige in 576 BC. The games were held in honour of Zeus, popularly acclaimed as their founder. They took place at the time of the first full moon in August.

The athletic festival lasted five days and included wrestling, chariot and horse racing, the pentathlon (wrestling, discus and javelin throwing, long jump and running), and the pancratium (a vicious form of fisticuffs).

Originally only Greek-born males were allowed to participate, but later Romans were permitted. Slaves and women were not allowed to enter the sanctuary as participants or spectators. Women trying to sneak in were thrown from a nearby rock.

The event served purposes besides athletic competition. Writers, poets and historians read their works to a large audience, and the citizens of various city-states got together.

Traders clinched business deals and city-state leaders talked in an atmosphere of festivity that was conducive to resolving differences through discussion, rather than battle.

The games continued during the first years of Roman rule. By this time, however, their importance had declined and, thanks to Nero, had become less edifying. In 67 AD, Nero entered the chariot race with 10 horses, ordering that other competitors could have no more than four. Despite this advantage, he fell and abandoned the race. He was still declared the winner by the judges.

The games were held for the last time in 394 AD before they were banned by Emperor Theodosius I as part of a purge of pagan festivals. In 426 AD, Theodosius II decreed that the temples of Olympia be destroyed.

The modern Olympic Games were instituted in 1896 and, other than during WW I and WW II, have been held every four years in different cities around the world ever since. The Olympic flame is lit at the ancient site and carried by runners to the city where the games are held.

Exploring the Site

Ancient Olympia is signposted from the modern village. The entrance is beyond the bridge over the Kladeos River (a tributary of the Alfios). Thanks to Theodosius II and various earthquakes, little remains of the magnificent buildings of ancient Olympia, but enough remains to sustain an absorbing visit in an idyllic, leafy setting. The first ruin encountered is the **gymnasium**, which dates from the 2nd century BC. South of here is the partly restored **palaestra**, or wrestling school, where contestants practised and trained. The next building was the **theokoleon** (the priests' house). Behind it was the workshop where Pheidias sculpted the gargantuan chryselephantine **statue of Zeus**, one of the Seven Wonders of the Ancient World. The workshop was identified by archaeologists after the discovery of tools and moulds. Beyond the theokoleon is the

The ancient Greeks used circular stones or plates for discus throwing

leonidaion, an elaborate structure which accommodated dignitaries.

The **altis**, or **Sacred Precinct of Zeus**, lies to the left of the path. Its most important building was the immense 5th-century Doric **Temple of Zeus** in which stood Pheidias' statue. The 12-metre-high statue was later removed to Constantinople by Theodosius II, where it was destroyed by a fire in 475 BC. The temple consisted of 13 lateral columns and six at either end. None are standing.

The **stadium** lies to the east of the altis and is entered through an archway. Little survives of the 200-metre track, although the start and finish lines and the judges' seats remain. The stadium seated at least 30,000 spectators. Slaves and women spectators had to be content to watch from the Hill of Cronos. South of the stadium was the **hippodrome**, where the chariot contests thrilled the crowds.

To the north of the Temple of Zeus was the

pelopion, a small, wooded hillock with an altar to Pelops. It was surrounded by a wall and the remains of its Doric portico can be seen. Many artefacts, now displayed in the museum, were found buried on the hillock.

North is the 6th-century Doric **Temple of Hera**, the site's most intact structure. Hera was worshipped along with Rea until the two were superseded by Zeus.

To the east of this temple is the **nymphaeum**. This monument was erected by the wealthy Roman banker Herodes Atticus in 156-160 AD. Typical of buildings financed by Roman benefactors, it was grandiose, consisting of a semicircular building with Doric columns flanked at each side by a circular temple. The building contained statues of Herodes Atticus and his family. Despite its elaborate appearance, the nymphaeum had a practical purpose: it was a fountain house supplying Olympia with fresh spring water.

From the nymphaeum, a row of 12 **trea-**

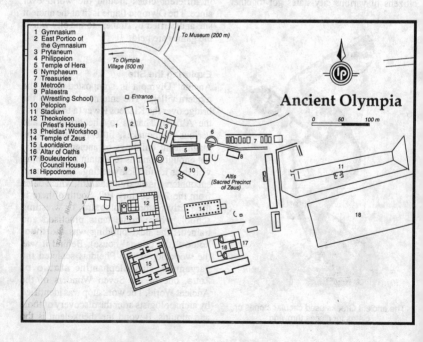

1 Gymnasium
2 East Portico of the Gymnasium
3 Prytaneum
4 Philippeion
5 Temple of Hera
6 Nymphaeum
7 Treasuries
8 Metroön
9 Palaestra (Wrestling School)
10 Pelopion
11 Stadium
12 Theokoleon (Priest's House)
13 Pheidias' Workshop
14 Temple of Zeus
15 Leonidaion
16 Altar of Oaths
17 Bouleuterion (Council House)
18 Hippodrome

To Museum (200 m)

To Olympia Village (500 m)

Entrance

Ancient Olympia

0   50   100 m

Altis (Sacred Precinct of Zeus)

suries stretched to the stadium. These looked like miniature temples. Each was erected by a city-state for use as a storehouse. These buildings marked the northern boundaries of the altis. The remains are reached by ascending a flight of stone steps.

At the bottom of these steps are the scant remains of the 5th-century BC **metroön**, a temple dedicated to Rea, the mother of the gods. Apparently the ancients worshipped Rea in this temple with orgies.

To the west of the Temple of Hera are the foundations of the **philippeion**, a circular construction with Ionic columns built by Philip of Macedon to commemorate the Battle of Khaironeia (338 BC), where he defeated a combined army of Athenians and

The 4th-century statue Hermes of Praxiteles now resides in the museum at Olympia

Thebans. The building contained statues of Philip and his family.

North of the Philippeion was the **prytaneum**, the magistrate's residence. Here, winning athletes were entertained and feasted.

South of the Temple of Zeus is the **bouleuterion** (council house), where competitors swore to obey the rules decreed by the Olympic Senate.

Museum

The museum is 200 metres north of the site, on the opposite side of the road. The star piece is the 4th-century Parian marble statue of **Hermes of Praxiteles**, a masterpiece of classical sculpture from the Temple of Hera. Hermes was charged with taking the infant Dionysos to Mt Nysa. The statue portrays the god in repose.

Other important exhibits are a sculptured **Head of Hera** and the pediments and metopes from the Temple of Zeus. The eastern pediment depicts the chariot race between Pelops and Oinomaos. The western pediment shows the fight between the Centaurs and Lapiths and the metopes depict the Twelve Labours of Heracles.

The museum is open Tuesday to Friday from 8 am to 7 pm, Saturday and Sunday from 8.30 am to 3 pm, and Monday from 11 am to 7 pm. Admission is 1200 dr.

Horse-drawn-carriage rides around the site and museum are expensive at 5000 dr but romantic if the mood and pocket agree.

KYLLINI Κυλλήνη

The shabby little port of Kyllini (Ki-LEE-ni), 78 km south-west of Patras, is the jumping-off point for ferries to Kefallonia and Zakynthos. If you get stuck in Kyllini, the tourist/port police (☎ 0623-92 211) at the quay will recommend accommodation. Kyllini is near the first of a succession of excellent beaches stretching south.

Getting There & Away

Bus & Train One bus a day leaves Patras for Kyllini (1½ hours, 1000 dr). At least three buses a day come from Pyrgos (50 minutes,

850 dr). Supposedly, seven trains a day run on the Kyllini branch line (35 minutes), but this is subject to more delays and cancellations than are normal in Greece.

Alternatively, you can get a bus from Patras to Lehena (on the main Patras-Pyrgos road) and then take a local bus to Kyllini (20 minutes, 100 dr). You can also take a taxi from Lehena to Kyllini, which costs around 2000 dr.

Boat Depending on the season, between three and seven boats a day go to Zakynthos (1½ hours, 1040 dr) and two boats daily to Poros on Kefallonia (1½ hours, 2000 dr).

HLEMOUTSI CASTLE

Six km south of Kyllini, this castle was completed by the Franks in 1223 AD. Destroyed in 1430, it was later rebuilt by the Turks to withstand artillery fire. The castle's battlement-fortification walls, hexagonal keep, vaulted galleries and rock location make it one of Morea's most impressive medieval constructions, with a round tower by the entry gate and a western bastion dating from its Turkish period. The castle can be reached in a roundabout way from **Gastouni**, but it's easier to visit direct from Kyllini.

Achaïa Αξαΐα

Achaïa owes its name to the Achaeans, an Indo-European branch of migrants who settled on mainland Greece and brought forth the Mycenaean civilisation. When the Dorians arrived, the Achaeans were pushed into this north-western corner of the Peloponnese.

The coast of Achaïa consists of a string of resorts which are more popular with Greeks than with tourists. Inland are the high peaks of Mt Panahaïko, Mt Erymanthos (where Heracles captured the Erymanthian boar) and Mt Helmos.

The village of Diakofto, 55 km west of Patras, is the starting point for a ride on the fantastic rack-and-pinion railway to Zah-

lorou and Kalavryta. Overnight stops at Zahlorou and Kalavryta are highly recommended.

PATRAS Πάτρα

Achaïa's capital, Patras (in Greek PA-tra, population 172,800), is Greece's third-largest city and the principal port for boats to and from Italy and the Ionian islands. It sees many tourists in transit but few stay – which is a pity. The higher you climb up the steep hill behind the teeming, somewhat seedy waterfront, the better Patras gets.

The city was destroyed by the Turks during the War of Independence, but under Kapodistrias was rebuilt on a modern grid plan of wide, arcaded streets, large squares and ornate neoclassical buildings. Some look in dire need of a facelift, but many are now being restored.

Orientation

Patras' grid system means easy walking. The waterfront is known as Iroön Polytehniou at the north-eastern end, Othonos Amalias in the middle and Akti Dimeon to the west. Customs is at the Iroön Polytehniou end, and the main bus and train stations are on Othonos Amalias. Most of the agencies selling ferry tickets are on Iroön Polytehniou and Othonos Amalias. The main thoroughfares of Agiou Dionysiou, Riga Fereou, Mezonos, Korinthou and Kanakari run parallel to the waterfront. A small, popular square, Plateia Trion Symahon, faces the train station. The main square is Plateia Vasileos Georgiou, up from the waterfront along Gerakostopolou. South along Mezonas, almost to the intersection with Pantanassis, is the **muncipal library** which houses an art gallery. On the square is a small replica of Milan's *La Scala*, the **municipal theatre**. The prettiest and largest square is Plateia Ypsila Alonia in the upper city at the end of Kanari. Bordered by pines and cafés, it is where locals relax. Sisini runs north from the square to triangular Plateia Agiou Georgiou, surrounded by dilapidated neoclassical residences.

Information

Tourist Offices The EOT (☎ 361 653/358/359) is outside customs. Helpful English-speaking staff offer information on transport schedules and give out a map. It is open daily from 7 am to 9.30 pm. The tourist police (☎ 22 0902/0903), opposite, are also courteous, and are open 24 hours a day.

Money The National Bank of Greece is on Plateia Trion Symahon. In summer, the opening times are Monday to Thursday from 8 am to 2 pm and 6 to 8.30 pm, Friday from 8 am to 1.30 pm and 6 to 8.30 pm, and weekends from 11 am to 1 pm and 6 to 8.30 pm. In winter, it is closed on weekends. American Express is represented by Albatros Travel (☎ 22 0993/4609), Othonos Amalias 48.

Post & Telecommunications The main post office is on the corner of Zaïmi and Mezonos. It is open Monday to Friday from 7.30 am to 8 pm; Saturday from 7.30 am to 2 pm; and Sunday from 9 am to 1.30 pm. A mobile post office outside the customs office is open Monday to Saturday from 8 am to 8 pm and Sunday from 9 am to 6 pm. Patras' postcode is 260 01.

The main OTE office is on the corner of Dimitriou Gounari and Kanakari in the western part of the city. It is open 24 hours. There is also an OTE at customs, open daily from 7.30 am to 6.30 pm and 7.30 to 10.30 pm. Patras' telephone code is 061.

Foreign Consulates There is a German consulate (☎ 22 1943) at Mezonos 98, and a British consulate (☎ 27 6403) at Votsi 2.

Bookshops The Press Agency Bookstore (☎ 27 7396), Agiou Nikolaou 32, sells English-language books, newspapers and magazines. For books only, try Vivlio Paleo Clio (☎ 22 5659) on Patreos 27.

Laundry There are two self-service laundrettes. The most central is on Korinthou at the corner of Zaïmi. The other is east of the waterfront at the top of Kilkis on Korinthou.

They are open weekdays from 9 am to 9 pm, on Saturday from 9 am to 1 pm and closed on Sunday. In August, opening hours are from 8 am to 3 pm and 5 pm to 9 pm.

Emergency A first-aid centre and ambulance station (☎ 27 7386) is on the corner of Karolou and Agiou Dionysiou.

Kastro

The medieval Venetian kastro, built on the ruin of an ancient acropolis, dominates the city. Set in an attractive pencil-pined park, it is reached by climbing steps at the end of Agiou Nikolaou. The views of the Ionian islands of Zakynthos and Kefallonia are rewarding.

Archaeological Museum

The small museum (☎ 27 5070) is well laid out, and the collection of finds from the Mycenaean, Hellenic and Roman periods is labelled in English. Exhibits include funerary objects; sculptures; figurines; a mosaic; and an ivory-framed, blue-glass disc found in a Roman house in Patras.

Facing shady Plateia Olgas, a favourite spot for families and tame, hungry pigeons, the museum is at Mezonos 42. Opening times are Tuesday to Sunday from 8.30 am to 3 pm. Admission is 400 dr.

Achaïa Clauss Winery

This picturesque, hillside winery, nine km south-east of Patras, was founded in 1854 by the Bavarian Baron von Clauss. It produces some of Greece's finest wine, particularly reds. The Mavrodaphne (black daphne), first produced in 1861, was named after the object of the baron's unrequited love – she died of tuberculosis.

The winery is open for a free tour and welcome sample from 7.30 am to 1 pm and from 4 to 7 pm (10 am to 4.30 pm off season). Take bus No 7 from the corner of Kolokotroni and Kanakari to get there.

About one km from the winery is the Church of Agios Konstantinos, which overlooks the pretty village of Saravali.

PELOPONNESE

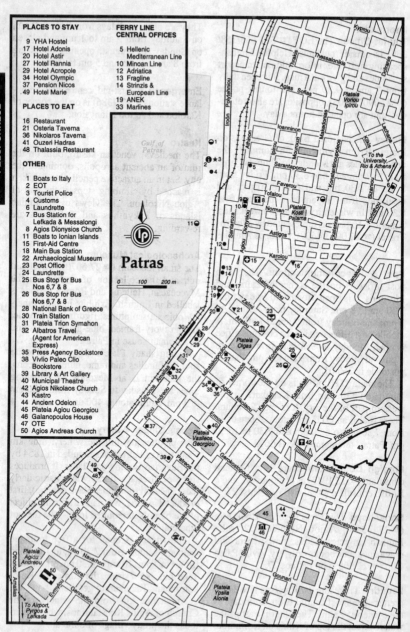

PLACES TO STAY

9 YHA Hostel
17 Hotel Adonis
20 Hotel Astir
27 Hotel Rannia
29 Hotel Acropole
34 Hotel Olympic
37 Pension Nicos
49 Hotel Marie

PLACES TO EAT

16 Restaurant
21 Osteria Taverna
36 Nikolaros Taverna
41 Ouzeri Hadras
48 Thalassia Restaurant

OTHER

1 Boats to Italy
2 EOT
3 Tourist Police
4 Customs
6 Laundrette
7 Bus Station for
  Lefkada & Messalongi
8 Agios Dionysios Church
11 Boats to Ionian Islands
15 First-Aid Centre
18 Main Bus Station
22 Archaeological Museum
23 Post Office
24 Laundrette
25 Bus Stop for Bus
  Nos 6,7 & 8
26 Bus Stop for Bus
  Nos 6,7 & 8
28 National Bank of Greece
30 Train Station
31 Plateia Trion Symahon
32 Albatros Travel
  (Agent for American
  Express)
35 Press Agency Bookstore
38 Vivlio Paleo Clio
  Bookstore
39 Library & Art Gallery
40 Municipal Theatre
42 Agios Nikolaos Church
43 Kastro
44 Ancient Odeion
45 Plateia Agiou Georgiou
46 Galanopoulos House
47 OTE
50 Agios Andreas Church

**FERRY LINE
CENTRAL OFFICES**

5 Hellenic
  Mediterranean Line
10 Minoan Line
12 Adriatica
13 Fragline
14 Strinzis &
  European Line
19 ANEK
33 Marlines

Patras

0   100   200 m

Other Things to See & Do

There are a couple of places worth checking around Plateia Agiou Georgiou. **Galanopoulos House**, built in 1930 for a wealthy merchant, exemplifies 19th-century, European eclectic architecture, combining Art Nouveau and neoclassicism.

Behind Plateia Agiou Georgiou there is an **ancient odeion** (theatre) which predates the odeion of Herodus Atticus in Athens. The odeion was restored after WW ll.

Festivals

It is claimed that the **Patras Carnival** is the world's biggest non-commercial (unlike Rio's) celebration. Euphoria and high spirits are shared as floats and about 50,000 people in fancy dress parade the streets for many of the 40 days from 17 January (St Anthony's Day). The **International Patras Festival of the Arts** is held from July until September on an annual theme featuring music (from classical to jazz), art exhibitions, theatre and other events. EOT can supply details. Patras celebrates Independence Day on 25 March with colourful parades and much music.

Places to Stay – bottom end

Kavouri Camping (☎ 42 8066/2145), two km east of customs, is the closest camping ground. Take bus No 1 from Agios Dionysios church. There are two more camping grounds at Rio, nine km north-east of Patras. *Rio Camping* (☎ 99 1585/1450/3388) and *Rio Mare* (☎ 99 2263) can both be reached on bus No 6 from Kanakari.

At the time of writing, the Patras *YHA hostel* was planning to move from Iroön Polytehniou 68, 1.5 km east of the customs building, to a neoclassical building at Tofalou 2, nearer the port. Restoration work had yet to be completed, so call ☎ 42 7278 to find out where to go. Dorm beds are 1500 dr, roof space is 1000 dr and breakfast is 500 dr. A Hostelling International card is not needed. The new building faces Agios Dionysios church.

Up from the waterfront on the corner of Patreos and Agiou Andreou 121, *Pension Nicos* (☎ 62 3757) is a ramshackle but cheery place geared for backpackers. Nicos' singles/doubles are 2500/3000 dr, triples/quads with shared facilities are 4500/5500 dr and doubles/triples with bathroom are 5500/6000 dr. The *Hotel Olympic* (☎ 22 4103) is a bit on the gloomy side, but is centrally located at Agiou Nikolaou 45. Single/doubles with bath are 6000/8800 dr. Hotels (not these) in the low-budget range tend to double as bordellos, but many are clean if you can tolerate the noise of comings and goings.

Places to Stay – middle

Facing Plateia Olgas, the B-class *Hotel Rannia* (☎ 22 0114/0537/0435), at Riga Fereou 53, has clean rooms with bathroom for 7000/11,300 dr. Another respectable option is the *Hotel Acropole* (☎ 27 9809/9810/9811), Othonos Amalias 39, with rooms with shower for 8000/10,000 dr. *Hotel Marie* (☎ 33 1302/1324), on Dimitriou Gounari 6, charges 5000/7000 dr. *Hotel Adonis* (☎ 22 4213/4235), Zaïmi 9, opposite the bus station, has well-furnished single/double/triple air-con rooms for 11,950/14,400/18,100 dr, including breakfast.

Places to Stay – top end

The best place in town is the *Hotel Astir* (☎ 277 502, 276 311; fax 271 644), near the bus station on Agiou Andreou 16. A block deep, it also faces the port. Sunset reflections on islands and night movements of brightly lit ships are magic from suites and the poolside roof-garden. There are bars, a Greek/French restaurant, bridge room, sauna, and convention and garage facilities. Singles/doubles/triples are 17,000/22,500/27,000 dr. Reduced rates apply for adult and student groups. The *Achaïa Beach* (☎ 99 1801) is at coastal Paralia Proastiou, three km southwest of Patras, complete with a bar, restaurant, pool and nightclub. Singles/doubles are 12,300/15,400 dr, including breakfast. On the same stretch of coast, *To Tzaki Hotel* (☎ 42 8303/8325; fax 42 6750) has a bar, restaurant and TV lounge. Doubles are 23,000 dr, including breakfast. Nine km north-east of Patras at Rio is the *Hotel Porto*

Rio (☎ 99 2102) with two restaurants, a nightclub, two pools, tennis courts and a health studio. Singles/doubles are 19,000/26,000 dr, including breakfast.

Places to Eat

The waterfront eateries seem to specialise in overpriced souvlaki, moussaka and English breakfasts. Takeaway and budget sit-down meals improve from Agiou Andreou upwards. *Nikolaros Taverna*, Agiou Nikolaou 50, and the nameless restaurant at Riga Fereou 3, both serve good traditional food. The green-shuttered *Osteria Taverna*, Aratou 5, near the Hotel Astir, has three intimate rooms shared by students, diplomats and TV stars who enjoy international, home-Greek, vegetarian and special fare such as bureka – a filling starter of minced meat, eggplant and cheeses (1000 dr). The seafood platter (3500 dr) is enough for two generous servings. A liqueur (made to a secret recipe) comes free with the bill, not necessarily to soften the blow. *Thalassia Restaurant*, Agiou Andreou 128, specialises in seafood, with mains from 1500 to 3000 dr. At *Ouzeri Hadras*, Parteniou 2, left past Agios Nikolaos church, a three-dish meal for two for 2000 dr includes fried cheese, omelette, special spetsofaï (sausages in a rich, red-wine sauce), bread and house wine. Old, non-commercial Greek recordings are played in white-washed traditional surroundings.

Fish is much cheaper here than in Athens. Self-caterers will find good whitebait from 250 dr a kilo and superb barbouni (red mullet) for 1200 dr a kilo at shops and stalls.

Entertainment

Performances from comedy to ancient Greek tragedy are staged at the municipal theatre. Patras also has a lively nightclub and disco scene.

Getting There & Away

Many first-time visitors to Greece assume that the best way to get from Patras to Athens is by bus. The bus is faster, but is more expensive and drops you off a long way from the city centre at Terminal A on Kifissou. It will cost at least 1000 dr for a taxi to the inner city if the connecting bus is full, and there is no public transport after midnight. The train takes you close to the city centre, within easy walking distance of good accommodation.

Bus The main bus station on Othonos Amalias has buses every half-hour to Athens (three hours, 3000 dr); 10 a day to Pyrgos (two hours, 1500 dr); four a day to both Ioannina (four hours, 1500 dr) and Kalavryta (1250 dr); three a day to Thessaloniki (9½ hours, 6850 dr) and Delphi; two a day to Kalamata (four hours, 3350 dr) and Tripolis (four hours, 2550 dr); and one a day, in summer only, to Kyllini (1½ hours, 1000 dr). There are four buses a day to the Ionian island of Lefkada (2250 dr), leaving from a small bus station on the corner of Faverou and Konstantinopoleos.

Take bus No 6 from Kanakari for the Rio-Andirio ferry (30 minutes, 180 dr). For buses to Amfissa (1850 dr), Arta (2500 dr) and Zakynthos (1175 dr), buy tickets at Flamingo Travel, Othonos Amalias 44. The buses leave from in front of the train station opposite.

Train There are at least seven trains a day to Athens (five hours, 1580 dr), via Diakofto (one hour, 510 dr) and Corinth (2½ hours, 1000 dr); seven a day to Pyrgos (two hours, 820 dr); and four trains a day to Kalamata (six hours, 1500 dr).

The intercity trains to Athens take 3½ hours and cost 2600 dr.

Ferry – domestic There are daily ferries from Patras to the Ionian islands of Kefallonia (four hours, 2500 dr), Ithaki (six hours, 3050 dr) and Corfu (10 hours, 4500 dr). See also the section on International Ferries, below. Patras' port police are on ☎ 34 1002.

There is also a ferry that connects Rio, nine km north-east of Patras, and Andirio (for Lefkada) every 15 minutes between 7am and 11 pm (15 minutes, 100 dr; car 1000 dr).

Ferry – international In summer, there are numerous daily ferries from Patras to the Italian ports of Brindisi (18 hours), Bari (17½ hours) and Ancona (20-36 hours). Most services stop at Igoumenitsa and Corfu. It is possible to stop over on some vessels in Corfu free of charge, so long as you specify this when you buy your ticket. There are also daily sailings to Venice and two a week to Trieste. See the Getting Around chapter for more details of services.

Prices vary according to the journey time and the luxury level of the boat, so shop around. At the time of writing, the cost of low/high season one-way, deck-class tickets on most lines to Brindisi was 7000/10,000 dr. Inter-Rail pass holders travel free on most boats to Brindisi, but must pay 1500 dr port tax. Expect to pay 14,400/16,800 dr to Ancona; 11,500 dr to Bari; 16,100/17,400 dr to Trieste; and 15,800/18,400 to Venice. Most companies offer discounts for return travel. Ferries to Italy leave from two points on the waterfront (see the Patras map).

The addresses and routes of the central offices or representatives of the ferry lines operating out of Patras are:

Adriatica
    Othonos Amalias 8 (☎ 42 2138): Brindisi via Igoumenitsa and Corfu
ANEK
    Othonos Amalias 25 (☎ 22 6053): Trieste via Corfu, Igoumenista and Ancona
Fragline
    Othonos Amalias 5 (☎ 27 7676): Brindisi via Igoumenitsa and Corfu
Hellenic Mediterranean
    On the corner of Sarantoporou & Athinon (☎ 65 2521): Brindisi via Kefallonia and Ortona via Igoumenitsa and Corfu
Marlines
    Othonos Amalias 56 (☎ 22 6666): Ancona via Igoumenitsa and Corfu, and Limassol via Crete and Rhodes
Minoan
    On the corner of Norman 1 & Athinon (☎ 42 1500): Ancona or Venice via Igoumenitsa and Corfu
Strintzis & European Lines
    Othonos Amalias 14 (☎ 62 2602): Ancona and Bari or Venice via Igoumenitsa and Corfu
Superfast Ferries
    Othonos Amalias 12 (☎ 62 2500): Ancona direct

Ventouris
    Othonos Amalias 85 (☎ 27 9995): Brindisi via Igoumenitsa

Getting Around

Bus Local bus Nos 6, 7 and 8 leave from bus stops on either side of Aratou (see map).

Car Car-hire outlets include Europcar (☎ 62 1360), Agiou Andreou 6; Avis (☎ 27 5547), Othonos Amalias 7 and Hertz (☎ 22 0990), Karolou 2.

DIAKOFTO Διακοφτό

Diakofto (Dee-a-kof-TO, population 2500), 55 km from Patras and 80 km from Corinth, is a serene village, tucked between steep mountains and the sea amid lemon and olive groves.

Orientation & Information

Diakofto's layout is easy to figure out. The train station is in the middle of the village. To reach the waterfront, cross the railway track and walk down the road ahead. Turn right and you will come to pebbly Egali beach after one km.

For the central square, walk along the road opposite the station and veer right. Turn right here to reach the post office on the left. The National Bank of Greece is further along on the right and the OTE is 300 metres beyond here, on the left. There is no EOT in Diakofto and no tourist police. Diakofto's postcode is 251 00 and the telephone code is 0691.

Diakofto-Kalavryta Railway

This rack-and-pinion railway runs through the spectacular Vouraïkos gorge, ascending 700 metres in 22.5 km. It was built by an Italian company between 1885 and 1895 and it is a remarkable feat of engineering. The original steam engines were replaced in the early 1960s by diesel cars, but the old steam engines can still be seen outside Diakofto and Kalavryta stations. The line crosses narrow bridges and goes through tunnels and along precariously overhanging ledges. Down below, the Vouraïkos River tumbles over massive boulders, and the surrounding countryside is a riot of wild flowers in spring. The journey from Diakofto to Kalavryta, stopping *en route* at Zahlorou, takes about 1½ hours. See the following Getting There & Away section for departure times.

It's possible to walk through the gorge along the track. But ensure that you don't enter a tunnel at the same time as a train. A few flat, grassy areas along the route are ideal for camping. Campers who eat at the Zahlorou's Romantza Restaurant can use its shower. Water should be carried, although water and meals are available at Zahlorou, the halfway point.

Places to Stay
Next to Egali beach, *Eleon Beach Camping* (☎ 41 539) is not far from Diakofto and signposted in the village. Diakofto's D-class *Hotel Lemonies* (☎ 41 229/ 41 821) has pleasant doubles/triples with bathroom for 6000/7500 dr. The hotel is on the right halfway down the road to the sea. *Hotel Helmos* (☎ 41 236), also D-class, on the central square, has rooms for 3300/5000/6700 dr.

Diakofto's nicest accommodation is at the C-class *Chris Paul Hotel* (☎ 41 715/855; fax 42 128), managed by the friendly Greek-Australians John and Maria. The air-con singles/doubles/triples are 8700/13,000/16,000 dr including breakfast. The hotel, with pool and bar, is near the train station and is well signposted.

Places to Eat
Soulekas Psistaria, just beyond the National Bank, has succulent and cheap souvlaki, chicken and salads. Another good souvlaki-chicken place is *Zorthofos*, across the train line from the village. The more up-market, seafront *Kohili Taverna* is on the left at the bottom of the road leading from the station. It's closed in November.

Getting There & Away
Bus Most Patras-Athens buses will drop you off on the New National Highway, from where you can walk to Diakofto. But ensure your request is understood or you may be dumped on the National Road well away from the turn-off. Some buses go into the village. Enquire at Athens Terminal A or the Patras bus station.

Train Diakofto is on the main Athens-Patras line.

Rack-&-Pinion Railway Departure times from Diakofto are 6, 9, 10.50 and 11.50 am; and 1.50 and 4.20 pm. The journey to Zahlorou takes 50 minutes and costs 400 dr. To Kalavryta from Diakofto, it takes about 1½ hours. The return trip costs 1150 dr. For 100 dr more one way, you can ride first class. The seats are the same but stunning views from the rear of the train on ascent and the front on descent are worth the extra.

ZAHLOROU Ζαχλωρού
The picturesque and unspoilt settlement of Zahlorou, the halfway stop on the Diakofto to Kalavryta train line, straddles both sides of the river and railway line. Many people take the train to this point and walk back to Diakofto.

Moni Megalou Spileou
Μονή Μεγάλου Σπήλαιου
A steep three-km path (signposted) leads from Zahlorou to the Moni Megalou Spileou (Monastery of the Great Cavern). The original monastery was destroyed in 1934 when gunpowder stored during the War of Independence exploded. The new monastery houses illuminated gospels, relics, silver crosses, jewellery and the miraculous icon of the Virgin Mary which, like numerous icons in Greece, is said to have been painted by St Luke. It was supposedly discovered in the nearby cavern by St Theodore and St Simeon in 362 AD. A monk will show visitors around. Modest dress is required of both sexes – no bare arms or legs.

Places to Stay & Eat
The quaint D-class *Hotel Romantzo* (☎ 22 758) is by the train station. Doubles with shared bathroom are 7000 dr. Next door, the clean, modern *Messinia Rooms to Rent*

(☎ 22 789) has rooms with bathroom that are fairly priced. You can sleep on the roof for free and have a hot shower for 900 dr. Both places have restaurants.

Getting There & Away
The rack-and-pinion railway stops at Zahlorou on the way to Kalavryta at 6.50, 9.50 and 11.40 am and 12.40, 2.40 and 5.10 pm. On the return journey, it stops at 8.40 and 11.40 am and 1.45, 2.40, 4.30 and 7 pm.

You can drive to Zahlorou on a dirt road leading off from the Diakofto-Kalavryta road.

KALAVRYTA Καλάβρυτα
At an elevation of 756 metres, Kalavryta (Ka-LA-vri-ta, population 2000) is a cool mountain resort with copious springs and shady plane trees. Two relatively recent historical events have assured the town a special place in the hearts of all Greeks. The revolt against the Turks began here on 25 March 1821 when Bishop Germanos of Patras raised the banner of revolt at the monastery of Agia Lavra, six km from Kalavryta. And, on 13 December 1943, in one of the worst atrocities of WW II, the Nazis set fire to the town and massacred all its male inhabitants over 15 years old in a reprisal against resistance activity. The total number killed in the region was 1436. The hands of the cathedral clock stand eternally at 2.34, the time the massacre began.

Orientation & Information
Opposite the train station, a large building was being converted into a museum at the time of writing. Kalavryta is the founder member of the Union of Martyred Towns. To the right of the museum-to-be is Syngrou. After one block, it becomes 25 Martiou. To the left is Konstantinou. The central square, Plateia Eleftherias, is between these two streets, two blocks up from the train station. The bus station is on the left side of Kallimani. From the train station, walk up Syngrou and turn right at Hotel Maria onto Kallimani. The post office is on the main square and the OTE is on Konstantinou.

Kalavryta's postcode is 250 01 and the telephone code is 0692. The National Bank of Greece is on 25 Martiou, just before the central square. Kalavryta has no EOT or tourist police.

Martyrs' Monument
This huge cross on a hill of pine and cypress trees above the town is an imposing, poignant shrine to those who were massacred. Follow the signpost from the station. It will lead to 13 Dekemvriou. Beyond the cemetery, on the left, a paved path and steps lead to the shrine.

Places to Stay
There is no camping here, but five km north – on the return to Zahlorou, is a basic camping ground by the train line. Most Kalavryta hotels do not offer single rooms in high season, winter ski season nor at Easter. Negotiate prices other times.

The cheapest hotel in Kalavryta is the D-class *Hotel Paradissos* (☎ 22 303), on Kallimani, with attractive doubles/triples with bathroom for 9000/12,000 dr. The *Hotel Maria* (☎ 22 296), Syngrou 2, has comfortable doubles with bathroom and breakfast for 16,000 dr.

The traditionally decorated, B-class *Hotel Filoxenia* (☎ 22 422), on Kallimani has singles/doubles/triples/quads with bathroom, minibar and TV for 9700/14,900/19,200/23,000 dr. Walk one block up Syngrou from the train station and you'll come to Hotel Maria on the right. To reach the other two hotels, turn right at Hotel Maria onto Kallimani.

Behind the train station, the B-class *Villa Kalavrita* (☎ 22 712/845) is another traditionally presented hotel. Double/triple/quad rooms with bathroom are 17,000/20,000/24,000 dr for half-board (breakfast and lunch or dinner).

Places to Eat
To Tzaki Taverna, opposite the church, is large and cheerful. Main meals are reasonably priced. *Taverna Stani*, up from Hotel Maria has excellent staples. While listening

to locals erupt into spontaneous weekend song, lash out on house specialities of goat in white sauce (1800 dr) or roast lamb in vine leaves (2000 dr). Each dish is enough for two people.

Food shops are on 25 Martiou. Enjoy the colourful Saturday *market* down from the ski centre (see the Around Kalavryta section).

Getting There & Away
Bus Five buses a day depart for Patras (1250 dr) and two for Athens (2650 dr).

Train The narrow-gauge train to Diakofto (via Zahlorou) leaves at 7.10 and 10.10 am; and 12.15, 1.10, 3 and 5.30 pm.

Taxi Kalavryta's taxi rank (☎ 22 127) is on the central square.

AROUND KALAVRYTA
Moni Agias Lavras
The original 10th-century monastery was burnt by the Nazis. The new monastery has a small museum where the banner standard is displayed along with other monastic memorabilia. There is no bus to the monastery so walk the six km from Kalavryta or take a taxi.

Limni Kastrion Cave
This cave, also known as the Cave of the Lakes, 16.5 km south of Kalavryta near the village of Kastria, is two km long and has 13 subterranean lakes linked by waterfalls and a profusion of stalactites hanging high above. The cave is usually open daily from 9.30 am to 4.30 pm, although it is advisable to call first (☎ 0692-31 633). One bus a day goes to Kastria. Check the schedule at the bus station. A taxi to the cave from Kalavryta will cost about 6000 dr return.

Ski Centre
The ski centre (elevation 1650-2100 metres), with nine pistes and one chair lift, is 14 km

east of Kalavryta on Mt Helmos. It has a cafeteria and first-aid centre but no overnight accommodation. The ski centre has an office in Kalavryta (☎ 22 661; fax 22 415), at the top of 25 Martiou. Opening times are Monday to Friday from 7 am to 3 pm. Several outlets on Konstantinou rent skis for approximately 3000 dr per weekday, and 3500 dr on weekends. There are no buses to the centre from Kalavryta. A taxi will cost around 6000 dr.

Mt Helmos Refuge
The EOS-owned *B Leondopoulos Mountain Refuge* is situated at 2100 metres on Mt Helmos. A marked footpath leads to the refuge from the ski centre (one hour). Another leads from the village of Ano Loussi (1½ hours), on the way to Kastria. If you would like to stay in the refuge, or want more details on walks or climbs on Mt Helmos, talk to the ski-centre staff in Kalavryta.

Mavroneri Waterfall
This waterfall, which plunges into a ravine on the northern side of Mt Helmos, is one of a several places in Greece claiming to be the source of the River Styx, across which the dead must journey before they can enter Hades.

It is possible to trek to the waterfall from the EOS refuge of B Leondopoulos on Mt Helmos (two hours) or from the village of Peristera (five hours). Peristera is one of a cluster of remote mountain villages lying west of a road which runs south from Akrata, about 10 km east of Diakofto.

With your own transport, (you may need chains in winter), you may explore this remote region. Buses are infrequent. For more information about trekking to the waterfall, contact the Egio branch of the EOS (☎ 0691-25 285), on the corner of Sotiriou Pontou and Aratou. Egio is on the coast, 13 km west of Diakofto.

Central Greece

Steeped in history and battles, central Greece is a land of mountains and plains whose attractions, with some exceptions, are subtle rather than obvious. From the rugged mountains of the South Pindos to densely populated Attica, from the sleepy wetlands of the south-west to the verdant Pelion, central Greece covers a wide range of varied landscapes and two major areas: Thessaly and Sterea Ellada. Three major attractions draw travellers to this ancient land – the oracle of Delphi, the amazing rock forest of Meteora and its monasteries and the lush Pelion peninsula with its traditional stone houses.

Sterea Ellada
Στερεά Ελλάδα

Sterea Ellada is bordered by Thessaly and Epiros to the north and the narrow gulfs of Corinth and Patras in the south. The region acquired the name Sterea Ellada (mainland Greece) in 1827, because it was the only continental portion of the newly formed Greek state – the Peloponnese was classed as an island. To the west is the region of Aetolo-Akarnania where England's most famous philhellene bard, Lord Byron, died at Messolongi while assisting in the Greek War of Independence.

To the east is the large island of Evia, which is separated from the mainland by a narrow gulf, and is a jumping-off point for the Sporades islands. Evia is covered in the Sporades chapter.

ATHENS TO THIVA

If you have your own transport and intend travelling from Athens to Delphi you have a choice of two routes: the main highway or the old mountain road to Thiva; the latter is a turn inland just west of Elefsina (Eleusis). Along the way you can take a turn-off left to the 4th-century BC **Fortress of Aigosthena**, and have a swim at nearby **Porto Germeno**, on the north coast of the Gulf of Corinth. The fortress is well preserved, with its towers still standing. Within the walls are two Byzantine churches.

Porto Germeno is a pleasant low-key resort with a pebble beach, inexpensive fish tavernas and one hotel, the C-class *Hotel Egosthenion* (☎ 0263-41 226). Singles/doubles go for 7000/9000 dr.

Back on the Thiva road, two km beyond the turn-off for the Fortress of Aigosthena and Porto Germeno, you will see the **Fortress of Eleutherai** to the right. This fortress also dates from the 4th century BC, but is less impressive than Aigosthena. The fortress stands at the entrance to the pass over Mt Kythairon. According to mythology, baby Oedipus was left to perish on this mountain.

If you are a battle buff you may like to make the five-km detour to the remains of **Plataea**, which once overlooked the plain where the famous Battle of Plataea (479 BC) took place. The ruins are reached by turning left at Erythres.

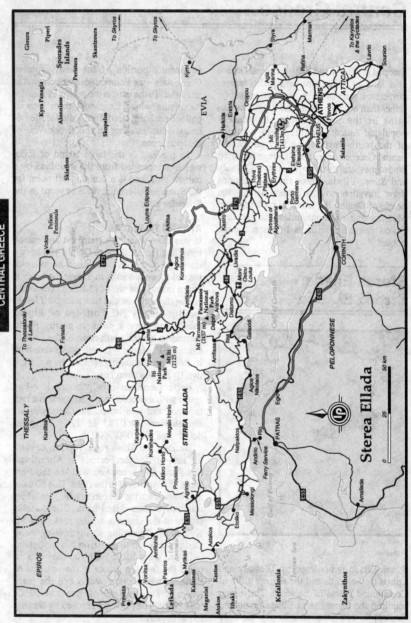

CENTRAL GREECE

Sterea Ellada

THIVA (THEBES) Θήβα

Thiva (THEE-va, population 19,000), 87 km north-west of Athens, figured prominently in history and mythology, and the two are inextricably linked. The tragic fate of its royal dynasty, centred around the myth of Oedipus, rivalled that of Mycenae.

Present-day Thiva is a drab provincial town with few vestiges of its past glory as a city-state.

Thiva's telephone code is 0262 and its postcode is 322 00.

History

After the Trojan War, Thebes became the dominant city of the district of Boeotia. In 371 BC the city was victorious in a battle against Sparta, which had hitherto been invincible. In 336 BC Thebes was sacked by Alexander the Great for rebelling against Macedonian control: 6000 Thebans were killed and 30,000 taken prisoner.

Archaeological Museum

Thiva has an impressive archaeological museum (☎ 27 913). The collection includes pottery from prehistoric and Mycenaean times, Linear B tablets found in the Mycenaean palaces and some Mycenaean clay coffins, which are unique to mainland Greece.

The museum is open Tuesday to Sunday from 8.30 am to 3 pm. Admission is 500 dr. It's at the northern end of Pindarou, which runs parallel to Epaminondou, where the bus station is located.

Places to Stay – bottom end

If you get stuck in Thiva there are three hotels to choose from. The D-class *Dionyssion Melathron* (☎ 27 855), at Dimokritou 7, has singles/doubles with shared bathroom for 4000/4500 dr and 5000/6000 dr with private bathroom.

The C-class *Neobe Hotel* (☎ 27 949),

CENTRAL GREECE

Oedipus Rex

Laius, ruler of Thebes, had been warned by the Delphic oracle that any child born to his wife, Jocasta, would murder him. When, despite this, Jocasta gave birth to Oedipus, Laius took him away, drove a nail through his feet (hence the name 'Oedipus', which means 'swollen foot') and left him on Mt Cithaeron. However, Oedipus did not perish – a shepherd found him and took him to Corinth, where Oedipus was adopted by King Polybus and his wife, Periboea.

As a young man, Oedipus consulted the oracle about his future and heard to his dismay that he would kill his father and marry his mother. Unaware that Polybus and Periboea were not his real parents, Oedipus fled, determined not to let the oracle's prophecy come true. While heading towards Thebes, Oedipus entered into an argument with a stranger and became so enraged that he killed him, not realising that the man was Laius, his real father. At the entrance to the city of Thebes, Oedipus came upon the Sphinx, a monster who posed a riddle to all passers-by and devoured those who could not answer it. Having been outwitted by Oedipus, who guessed correctly, the Sphinx killed herself.

As a reward for having destroyed this vexatious creature, the Thebans proclaimed Oedipus their king and gave him the hand in marriage of the recently widowed Queen Jocasta, thereby fulfilling the oracle's prophecy. Following their union, Thebes was besieged by a plague so Oedipus consulted the oracle once more, which said he should banish the murderer of Laius. The renowned prophet Tiresias appeared at Oedipus' court at this time and revealed the gods' wishes: the plague would end only at the death of the man who had killed his father and married his mother. Only now did Oedipus and Jocasta discover the truth. Jocasta hanged herself; Oedipus blinded himself and went into exile and eventually died in Colonus in Attica.

The riddle, in case you're wondering, was 'What creatures have four legs in the morning, two at midday, and three in the evening, and are at their weakest when they have the most?' The answer is people – they crawl on all fours as babies, walk upright when mature and use a cane in old age. ■

Epaminondou 63, has singles/doubles with shared bathroom for 4500/7000 dr and rooms with private bathroom for 5000/7500 dr.

Places to Stay – middle
The C-class *Meletiou Hotel* (☎ 27 333; fax 23 334), at Epaminondou 58, has singles/doubles for 9000/15,000 dr.

Getting There & Away
Bus Hourly buses operate from both Athens (1½ hours, 1170 dr) and Livadia (45 minutes, 720 dr).

Train There are 10 services to and from Athens daily (1½ hours, 780 dr), as well as nine services northwards.

LIVADIA Λειβαδιά
Livadia (population 18,000) is on the Athens-Delphi road, 45 km north-west of Thiva. The town flanks both sides of a gorge through which the River Erkinas flows. A 14th-century Frankish castle overlooks Livadia from Profitis Elias hill.

The town's main claim to fame is as the site of the oracle of Trophonios. According to legend, the ordeal one had to go through in order to consult this oracle resulted in a permanent look of fright. First, the pilgrim drank from the fountain of Lethe (Waters of Forgetfulness) and then of the Mnemosyne (Waters of Remembrance). They were then lowered into a hole in a cave and left there for days on end to commune with the oracle.

Springs, which are supposedly the original Lethe and Mnemosyne, can be seen in a very attractive park. The pleasant *Xenia Restaurant* in the park is signposted from the Athens-Delphi road, just south of the town.

Livadia's telephone code is 0261 and its postcode is 321 00.

Places to Stay
The D-class *Hotel Erkyna* (☎ 28 227), Lappa 6, has rooms for 4200/6400 dr with shared bathroom.

The C-class *Hotel Philippos* (☎ 24 931/932; fax 24 934), on Athinon, has singles/doubles for 9900/13,800 dr.

The B-class *Levadia Hotel* (☎ 23 611; fax 28 266), at Plateia L Katsoni 4, has singles/doubles for 13,600/19,500 dr.

Getting There & Away
Bus Frequent buses run from Livadia to Athens, Thiva, Delphi and Distomo (for Moni Osiou Louka).

Train There are 13 services to and from Athens daily (1½ hours, 1470 dr), as well as to most destinations north.

DELPHI Δελφοί
If the ancient Greeks hadn't chosen Delphi as their navel of the earth and built the Sanctuary of Apollo here, someone else would have thought of a good reason to make this eagle's eyrie village a tourist attraction. Its location on a precipitous cliff edge is spectacular and despite its overt commercialism and the constant passage of tour buses through the narrow streets of the modern village, it still has a special feel. Modern Delphi (population 2,400) is 178 km north-west of Athens and is the base for exploring one of Greece's major tourist sites.

Orientation & Information
Almost everything you'll need in Delphi is on Vasileon Pavlou & Frederikis. The bus stop is here next to the Taverna Kastri at the Itea side of town. The post office, OTE and the National Bank of Greece are also on this street. Ancient Delphi is 1.5 km along the main road to Arahova.

Delphi's municipal tourist office (☎ 82 900) is at the Arahova end of Vasileon Pavlou & Frederikis. Opening times are Monday to Saturday from 8 am to 2 pm, with additional opening hours of 6 to 8 pm during July and August. In summer the bank is open from 6 to 7.30 pm in addition to normal hours.

Delphi's telephone code is 0265; the postcode is 330 54.

Places to Stay – bottom end
Delphi's nearest and best camp site is

Apollon Camping (☎ 82 750/762), 1.5 km west of modern Delphi. *Delphi Camping* (☎ 28 944/363) is four km down the Delphi-Itea road.

Finding a room in Delphi does not present any problems, as hotels are plentiful.

The *YHA hostel* (☎ 82 268), Apollonos 31, is one of Greece's best. It is run by a helpful and courteous woman from New Zealand, and has double rooms for 6000 dr and dorm beds for 1500 dr. The hostel is open from March to November. Apollonos runs north of Vasileon Pavlou & Frederikis.

Places to Stay – middle

Most of Delphi's hotels are on Vasileon Pavlou & Frederikis. The D-class *Hotel Athina* (☎ 82 239), Vasileon Pavlou & Frederikis 55, has nicely furnished singles/ doubles for 4000/6000 dr with shared bathroom and 5200/7000 dr for doubles with private bathroom.

The C-class *Hotel Pan* (☎ 82 294; fax 82 320), at No 53, has pleasant rooms for 5000/7500 dr with private bathroom. The refurbished C-class *Hotel Hermes* (☎ 82 318; fax 82 639), Vasileon Pavlou & Frederikis 29, has spacious, tastefully furnished singles/doubles/triples for 8000/ 12,000/15,000 dr with private bathroom and breakfast. This hotel has spectacular views down to the Gulf of Corinth. The very pleasant C-class *Hotel Parnassos* (☎ 82 321; fax 82 621) at No 32 is similarly priced and is run by a Greek-Australian couple who make visitors from down under very welcome.

Places to Stay – top end

Delphi's most luxurious hotel is the A-class *Hotel Amalia* (☎ 82 101/102/103; fax 82 290), at Apollonos 1. The hotel has a bar, café, restaurant and swimming pool. Rates are 19,000/28,000 dr for singles/doubles.

Another plush place is the A-class *Hotel Vouzas* (☎ 82 232/234; fax 82 033 or 01-982 3772), Vasileon Pavlou & Frederikis 1. Singles/doubles here are 19,500/27,600 dr. The hotel has a bar, restaurant and roof garden.

Places to Eat

The *Taverna Vakhos*, Apollonos 31, next door to the youth hostel, serves tasty Greek staples at a reasonable price and offers an unparalleled view over the deep valley and olive groves below. However, the tables with a view can get booked out by tour groups.

Down on the main street is a string of establishments catering mainly to the tourist traffic and offering set menu choices for around 2500 dr. Look out for *Lefas* and the *Sun Flower*. Most offer good views along with the food. The *Arachova* is a smaller, more economical place that you may want to look out for. It is also a bit more genuine-looking.

Getting There & Away

Bus There are seven buses a day from Delphi to Amfissa (30 minutes, 260 dr); six to Itea (30 minutes, 260 dr) and Arahova (20 minutes, 150 dr); five to Athens (three hours, 2400 dr); one direct bus to Patras (1350 dr) and two via Itea. For Thiva, take a bus to Livadia, from where there are frequent buses. The bus to/from Athens gets very crowded in the summer, so turn up early to buy a ticket.

Train The nearest train station to Delphi is in Livadia (47 km away), which is on the Athens-Thessaloniki line. Taking the train is only worth considering if you have a rail pass.

ANCIENT DELPHI

To the majority of people, Delphi, of all the ancient sites in Greece, is the one with the most potent 'spirit of place'. Built on the slopes of Mt Parnassos, overlooking the Gulf of Corinth and extending into a valley of cypress and olive trees, Delphi's allure lies both in its stunning setting and its awe-inspiring ruins. The ancients regarded Delphi as the centre of the world, for according to mythology Zeus released two eagles at opposite ends of the world and they met here.

The site is open Monday to Friday from 7.30 am to 7.15 pm and weekends from

8.30 am to 2.45 pm. Admission is 1200 dr (free on Sunday and public holidays).

History

Delphi reached its height in the 4th century BC as a sanctuary dedicated to Apollo, when multitudes of pilgrims bearing expensive votive gifts came to ask advice of its oracle. The Delphic oracle was believed to be Apollo's mouthpiece, and was the most powerful in Greece. Battles were fought, marriages took place, journeys were embarked upon and business deals clinched on the strength of its utterances.

Following battles between the city-states, the oracle was showered with treasures by the victors and accused of partiality by the vanquished. Not surprisingly, the sanctuary became a hotbed of chicanery, coveted for its priceless treasures. It eventually brought about Greece's demise at the hands of the Macedonians.

Delphi was protected by a federation of Greek states called the Amphyctionic Council. However, the surrounding territory belonged to the city of Krisa, which took advantage of this by charging visitors an exorbitant fee for the privilege of disembarking at its port of Kirrha. This angered the city-states, especially Athens, who called upon the Amphyctionic Council to do something about it. The result was the First Sacred War (595-586 BC), which resulted in the council destroying Krisa and its port.

The council now took control of the sanctuary, and Delphi became an autonomous state. The sanctuary enjoyed great prosperity, receiving tributes from numerous benefactors, including the kings of Lydia and Egypt. Struggles for its control ensued, and Delphi passed from one city-state to another, resulting in further sacred wars.

The Third Sacred War was precipitated by a dispute between Thebes and the district of Phocis, in 356 BC, over control of the sanctuary. Philip II, the king of Macedon, seized

CENTRAL GREECE

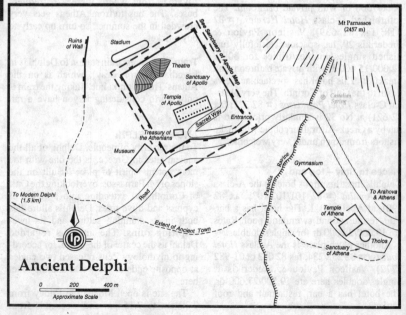

Ancient Delphi

0   200   400 m

Approximate Scale

The Delphic Oracle

During early Mycenaean times, the earth goddess, Gaea, was worshipped at Delphi, and it is believed the oracle originated at that time. Later Delphi became a sanctuary to Themis, then Demeter and later Poseidon, but by the end of the Mycenaean period, Apollo had replaced the other deities. The oracle was a priestess over 50 years of age, who sat on a tripod at the entrance to a chasm which emitted vaporous fumes. When the priestess inhaled these fumes, they induced a frenzy. Her seemingly unintelligible utterances in answer to a pilgrim's question were translated into verse by a priest.

In summer Apollo was worshipped at Delphi, but in winter, he and the oracle took a rest and Dionysos stepped into his place. As everywhere, the god of wine was honoured with merrymaking and feasting, which must have come as a welcome relief from the serious business of trying to comprehend the oracle's cryptic and grave messages. ∎

the opportunity to exert power over the city-states by acting as arbitrator in this war. He brought an end to the conflict and, in 346 BC, the sanctuary again came under the protection of the Amphyctionic Council. Philip now took Phocis' place in the council, which had probably been his intention all along.

The Fourth Sacred War broke out in 339 BC when the Amphyctionic Council declared war on Amfissa because it had staked a claim to the sanctuary. The council appealed to Philip for help. Philip saw this as an opportunity to bring his formidable army into Greece and, in so doing, not only destroyed Amfissa, but fought, and defeated, a combined army of Athenians, Thebans and their allies in the Battle of Khaironeia, in Boeotia (north-west of Athens). Philip had now achieved his ambition – control of Greece.

In 191 BC Delphi was taken by the Romans and the oracle's power dwindled. It was consulted on personal, rather than political issues. Along with the country's other pagan sanctuaries, it was abolished by Theodosius in the late 4th century AD.

Exploring the Site

The **Sanctuary of Apollo** is on the left of the main road as you walk towards Athens. From the entrance, at the site of the old **Roman agora**, steps lead to the **Sacred Way**, which winds up to the foundations of the Doric **Temple of Apollo**.

Once you have entered the site, you will pass on your right the pedestal which held the statue of a bull dedicated by the city of Kerkyra (Corfu). Further along are the remains of monuments erected by the Athenians and Lacedaemonians. The semicircular structures on either side of the Sacred Way were erected by the Argives (people of Argos). The one to the right was the **King of Argos Monument**, which was built in the 4th century BC.

In ancient times the Sacred Way was lined with treasuries and statues given by grateful city-states, including Thebes, Siphnos, Sikyon, Athens and Knidos, in thanks to Apollo for helping them win battles. The **Athenian treasury** has been reconstructed. To the north of this treasury are the foundations of the **bouleuterion** (council house).

The 4th-century BC Temple of Apollo dominated the entire sanctuary. Inside the cella was a gold statue of Apollo and a hearth where an eternal flame burned. On the temple architrave were inscriptions of the wise utterings of Greek philosophers, such as 'Know Thyself' and 'Nothing in Excess'. The chasm from which the priestess inhaled the intoxicating vapours has not been found; all that is known is that it was somewhere within the temple.

Above the temple is the well-preserved 4th-century BC **theatre**, which was restored by the Romans. From the top row of seats there are magnificent views. Plays were per-

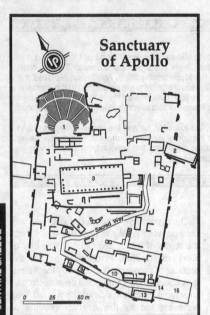

Sanctuary of Apollo

1 Theatre
2 Stoa of Attalos
3 Temple of Apollo
4 Bouleuterion (Council House)
5 Athenian Treasury
6 Knidos Treasury
7 Thebes Treasury
8 Siphnos Treasury
9 Sikyon Treasury
10 King of Argos Monument
11 Votive offering of Lacedaemonians
12 Site of Bull of Kerkyra
13 Votive offering of Athens
14 Main Entrance
15 Roman Agora (Market Place)

0 25 50 m

formed here during the Pythian Festival, which, like the Olympic Games, was held every four years. From the theatre another path leads up to the **stadium**, the best preserved in all of Greece.

From the Sanctuary of Apollo, walk towards Arahova and you will come to the **Castalian spring** on the left, where pilgrims had to cleanse themselves before consulting the oracle. Opposite is the **Sanctuary of Athena** (free admission), where Athena Pronaia was worshipped. This is the site of the 4th-century **tholos**, the most striking of Delphi's monuments. It was a graceful circular structure comprising 20 columns on a three-stepped podium – three of its columns have been re-erected. The purpose of the tholos is unknown.

Museum

Ancient Delphi managed to amass a considerable treasure-trove, and this is reflected in its magnificent museum collection. Most labels are in Greek and French only, with the exception of some of the major exhibits.

On the landing is the **omphalos**, a sculpted cone which once stood at what was considered the centre of the world – the spot where the eagles released by Zeus met. In the second room along from here are two 6th-century **kore figures**. To the right of this room are displayed parts of the frieze from the **Siphnian treasury**, which depicts the battle between the gods and the giants, and the gods watching the fight over the corpse of Patroclus during the Trojan War.

In the rooms to the left are fragments of metopes from the **Athenian treasury** depicting the Labours of Hercules, the Exploits of Theseus and the Battle of the Amazons. Further on you can't miss the large **Acanthus Column**, with three women dancing around it. In the end room is the celebrated life-size **Bronze Charioteer**, which commemorates a victory in the Pythian Games of 478 or 474 BC.

The museum (☎ 0265-82 313) is open Tuesday to Friday from 7.30 am to 7.15 pm; weekends and public holidays from 8.30 am to 2.45 pm and Monday from 12 to 6.15 pm. Admission is 1200 dr.

Getting There & Away

Buses between Arahova and modern Delphi will drop you off at the site. See Getting There & Away under modern Delphi for details.

AROUND DELPHI

Mt Parnassos Παρνασσός Ορος

There are two ski centres on Mt Parnassos, both with overnight accommodation. The largest is the EOT centre at Fterolakkas (1750 metres), which also has facilities higher up at Kelaria (1950 metres). For more information contact the EOT in Delphi or Athens or the ski centre (☎ 22 689/694/695). The centre is 24 km from Arahova and 17 km from Amfikleia. The Athens department store Klaoudatos organises trips to this ski centre. For more information, see Skiing in the Activities section of the Athens chapter.

The second centre is at Gerondovrahos. For more information contact Athens Ski-Lovers Club (☎ 01-643 3368), Sarantapihou 51, Athens, or Nikos Georgakos (☎ 0267-31 391) in Arahova. The centre is 25 km from Arahova and 34 km from Delphi.

Getting There & Away

There is no public transport to either centre – you'll need to take a taxi or hitch from Delphi or Arahova.

Arahova Αράχωβα

Arahova (Ar-A-ho-va, population 2800, altitude 960 metres) is built on a rocky spur of Mt Parnassos, 12 km from Delphi on the main Athens-Delphi road. The main street is flanked by shops selling embroideries, handwoven goods, flokati rugs and various other souvenirs. The town is also noted for its cheese, honey and a pleasant, unresinated red wine.

Despite this overt flaunting of its assets to passing tourists, Arahova is a charming town and an alternative base to modern Delphi from which to visit the ancient site. In the little alleys bordering the main street, stone houses cling to the steep hillside. The **Festival of Agios Georgios** is held in the town on St George's Day (23 April). However, if this date falls during Lent, the festival is postponed until Easter Tuesday. It's a joyous occasion celebrated with feasting and folk dancing.

Arahova is also a trendy ski resort and for Greeks is very much the 'in' place to be seen during the skiing season. Prices in winter reflect this trend.

Orientation & Information

The town's main thoroughfare is Delphon which snakes its way through three squares. The bus station is at the Celena Café opposite the central square. The EOT office (☎ 31 630/692) is on the eastern side of the town on Delphon.

Opening hours are 8 am to 3.30 pm and 8 am to 10 pm on Friday and Saturday. The post office and OTE are on Plateia Xenias, one block west of the central square. Arahova's telephone code is 0267 and the postcode is 320 04.

Places to Stay & Eat

The D-class *Hotel Apollon* (☎ 31 427), Delphon 20, has pleasant, spotless singles/doubles for 4000/6300 dr, with shared bathroom. The centrally located and very trendy C-class *Arahova Inn* (☎ 31 353; fax 31 134) is one of the town's more popular hotels. Rooms cost 9000/14,000 dr in low (summer) season, but 13,900/19,800 dr in high (winter) season. The hotel also has a bar, restaurant and central heating.

The older B-class *Hotel Xenia* (☎ 31 230; fax 32 175), Plateia Xenias, also has a bar, restaurant and central heating. The rates are 8500/12,000 dr.

The town has some rooms to rent in private houses where you pay around 6000 dr a double, depending on the season. For information about these enquire at the Celena Café.

Lining Delphon are three restaurant/ tavernas that you might want to look out for. *To Agnantio* and *Taverna O Sakis* both offer standard fare and have good views from the restaurant. In between is an unnamed *taverna*, which offers similar food without the views.

Getting There & Away

The five buses a day which run between Athens and Delphi stop at Arahova. In addition there are some local buses to Delphi (20 minutes, 250 dr). A taxi from Arahova to Delphi will cost 1500 dr.

CENTRAL GREECE

Moni Osiou Louka
Μονή Οσίου Λουκά

The Moni Osiou Louka (Monastery of St Luke Stiris) is eight km east of the village of Distomo, which lies just south of the Athens-Delphi road. Its principal church contains some of Greece's finest Byzantine frescoes.

The monastery is dedicated to a local hermit who was canonised for his healing and prophetic powers. The monastic complex includes two churches. The interior of the main one of **Agios Loukas** is a glorious symphony of marble and mosaics. There are also icons by Michael Damaskinos, the 16th-century Cretan icon painter.

In the main body of the church the light is partially blocked by the ornate marble window decorations. This creates striking contrasts of light and shade which greatly enhance the atmosphere. The crypt where St Luke is buried also contains fine frescoes. The other church, **Theotokos** (Church of St Mary), built in the 10th century, has a less impressive interior.

The monastery is in an idyllic setting, with breathtaking vistas from its leafy terrace. There is a taverna in the monastery grounds. The monastery is open from 8 am to 2 pm daily and also from 4 to 6 pm from May to September. Admission is 600 dr, and modest dress is required (no shorts).

Places to Stay Moni Osiou Louka is a hassle to get to by public transport, so if you get stuck, there are a couple of budget hotels in Distomo, including the D-class *Hotel America* (☎ 0267-22 079), J Kastriti 1, where singles/doubles are 3500/6000 dr with private bathroom. Nearby, the D-class *Hotel Koutriaris* (☎ 0267-22 268), on the central square of Plateia Ethnikis Antistasis, has singles/doubles for 4400/5600 dr with shared bathroom.

Getting There & Away There is one direct bus a day from Athens which leaves Bus Terminal B at 10.30 am (3½ hours, 1690 dr). Otherwise you can take the Delphi bus from Athens and ask the driver to stop at the turn-off for Distomo, from where you can take a taxi nine km to the monastery. From Livadia there are 11 buses a day to Distomo (45 minutes, 520 dr) and one to the monastery at 1.30 pm (one hour, 715 dr). There are hourly buses to Athens from Livadia (two hours, 1430 dr).

DELPHI TO NAFPAKTOS
The 80-km route from Delphi westwards along the Gulf of Corinth is via the much less travelled, but no less attractive drive as far as Nafpaktos, where there is an imposing Venetian fortress. This route skirts the north shore of the Gulf of Corinth, passing a number of seaside towns and villages before meeting the important ferry boat link at Andirio. Boats here run every half hour or so. The coast is more popular as a holiday destination with Greeks than with foreign tourists.

The market town of **Itea**, 10 km down the road to the coast, is less attractive and more commercial. From Itea an alternative road branches left for two km to **Kira**. This was ancient Kirrha, the port of Delphi, which was destroyed by the Amphyctionic Council in the First Sacred War (595-586 BC). Kira has a good beach and two camp sites, *Kaparelis Camping* (☎ 0265-32 330) and *Ayannis Camping* (☎ 0265-32 555).

Galaxidi, a bit further along the road, is perhaps the prettiest town along this coast. It was a prosperous caïque-building centre in the 19th century, and some fine stone mansions survive from this time.

Its naval museum houses models of ships, marine paintings and paraphernalia from the War of Independence (1821-26).

Galaxidi has a number of hotels, and *Galaxidi Camping* (☎ 0265-41 530) is just west of town.

Nafpaktos, just inside the region of Aetolo-Akarnania and nine km east of Andirio, is a little resort with an attractive harbour, a good beach and a well-preserved Venetian castle. It sits in a lush region with a backdrop of pine-covered mountains. Nafpaktos was known as Lepanto in medieval times and it was here in 1571 that the famous naval battle of Lepanto took place.

Nafpaktos has several hotels as well as

two camp sites between it and Andirio: *Platanitis Beach* (☎ 0634-31 555) and *Dounis Beach* (☎ 0634-31 565). There is another camp site, *Doric Camping* (☎ 0266-31 722), further east along the coast at **Agios Nikolaos**. If you are looking for a hotel here, try the nifty C-class *Akti* (☎ 0634-28 464; fax 24 171) near the eastern promenade. Singles/doubles are 7000/10,500. There are also a couple of more expensive hotels nearby.

Getting There & Away

The Delphi-Patras bus goes along this stretch of coast. There are five buses a day from Itea to Nafpaktos and vice versa, stopping at the coastal towns along the way, and six buses a day from Delphi to/from Itea.

MESSOLONGI Μεσολόγγι

Most people come to Messolongi for historical or sentimental reasons, rather than to seek a lively holiday spot. Its location is rather melancholy, as it lies between the outlets of the rivers Aheloös and Evinos, on the shores of an uninspiring and seemingly endless lagoon. It is Messolongi's connection with the War of Independence and the role played by Britain's philhellene bard Lord Byron that gives the town its historic reputation. The siege by the Turks and ultimate self-sacrificial exodus of the men, women and children of Messolongi in 1826 was recognised as one of the most heroic deeds of the war and was immortalised in Dionysios Solomos' epic poem *I Eleftheri Poliorkimeni* (The Free Besieged).

History

Lord Byron arrived in Messolongi in 1824, already a famous international philhellene, with the intention of lending his weight, reputation and money to the independence cause. After months of vainly attempting to organise the motley Greek forces who spent much time squabbling among themselves, Byron's efforts came to nought. He contracted a fever, no doubt hastened on by the unsanitary and damp conditions of what was,

at the time, a miserable outpost, and died, his immediate aims unfulfilled, on 19 April 1824.

Ironically, his death spurred on internationalist forces to precipitate the end of the War of Independence and Byron became a Greek national hero. One hundred years after Byron's death saw many male children, now men in their seventies, christened with the name Byron, or Vyronas in Greek. There is hardly a Greek town or city without a Vyronos street.

Orientation & Information

Messolongi is the capital of the prefecture of Aetolo-Akarnania, though it is only a small town. The town is laid out in a roughly rectangular grid and the two main streets, running more or less parallel along its length are Eleftheron Poliorkimenon and Spyrou Moustakli. Both bring you to the main square, Plateia Markou Botsari. The OTE and post office are both within shouting distance of the square.

Messolongi's phone code is 0631 and its postcode is 302 00.

Things to See

All arrivals to Messolongi enter via the **exodus gate** through which the besieged residents of Messolongi attempted to escape on the night of 22-23 April 1826, only to be caught and slaughtered by a mercenary force nearby. The gate is narrow and dangerous for traffic, so beware if you are entering by car.

Just beyond the gate, to the right, is the **Garden of the Heroes** translated incorrectly as Heroes' Tombs on the road sign. This memorial garden was established on the orders of the then governor of Greece, Yiannis Kapodistrias who, in 1829, issued the following decree:

...within these walls of the city of Messolongi lie the bones of those brave men, who fell bravely while defending the city...it is our duty to gather together, with reverence, the holy remains of these men and to lay them to rest in a memorial where our country may, each year, repay its debt of gratitude

Aegina, 14 May 1829

You will find the Greek text of this decree on the marble slab to the right as you enter the garden. Within the leafy grounds of the garden you will find memorials to many other philhellenes as well. Beneath the statue of **Lord Byron**, which features prominently in the garden, is buried the heart of the poet. A much larger and more modern bronze statue of Byron outside the garden now overshadows the smaller sculpted one inside. The garden is open from 9 am to 8 pm (it closes earlier in winter).

On the main square and housed in the town hall is a **museum** dedicated to the revolution. There is also a collection of Byron memorabilia, although its credibility is a bit stretched at times. Bone up on your War of Independence history beforehand, in order to get a full feel for the importance of these historic events. Museum opening times are 8 am to 1.30 pm and 4 to 6 pm.

Places to Stay

There isn't much choice here. The D-class *Avra* (☎ 22 284) is as central as you can get and is quite homey, with doubles/triples for 7000/8000 dr. The B-class *Theoxenia* (☎ 22 493) is out of town somewhat on the lagoon side and has rooms in the 7000/9000 dr price bracket. The B-class *Liberty* (☎ 24 831; fax 24 832), close to the Garden of the Heroes, is rather large and impersonal and has rooms for 6700/8900/10,700 dr.

Places to Eat

No bright culinary spots are to be found in Messolongi. The best place to look is the street running off the main square, Harilaou Trikoupi. *To Elliniko* is one option and the *Psistaria Taverna Melachri* further along on the same side is another. There are fast-food joints scattered along here as well, and in the side-streets you will find one or two reasonable cafeterias. Both major hotels have restaurants attached.

Getting There & Away

The bus station is on Mavrokordatou 5. This street forms one side of the main square. From here buses go to Athens, Patras and most destinations north, though you may need to change at Agrinio.

AGRINIO Αγρίνιο

You could be excused for missing Agrinio in your haste to and from Epiros, since its appeal does not lie in any immediate tourist attraction. A city of 34,000 inhabitants, Agrinio was, according to mythology, built by King Agrio, son of Thestias. During the Turkish occupation it was called Vrahori. Along with Larisa, this town shares the unenviable record of being the hottest town in Greece. Today it is the administrative centre of the prefecture of Aetolo-Akarnania. Set on the rim of a broad and fertile agricultural plain, it is an important service centre for the whole region and welcomes the few travellers who choose to stay here.

Orientation & Information

The town is set just east of the main north-south highway that links Epiros with the ferry crossing at Andirio. Plateia Dimokratias is the heart of the town, with Papastratou running north from the square and Harilaou Trikoupi running south and eventually linking up with the main highway.

The post office is on Agiou Hristoforou, 100 metres north-east of the main square. The OTE office is in Papakosta, just off the south side of the square. Most buses arrive at the bus station on Harilaou Trikoupi, 200 metres south of the square. Just up from the bus station heading towards the square on your left is a town map, which is useful if you can read Greek. Buses from Karpenisi arrive at a separate terminal on Ethnikis Antistasis in the south-east corner of town. The police station (☎ 0641-22 766) is on the corner of Papakosta and Alexopoulou, 150 metres south of the OTE.

Agrinio's phone code is 0641 and the postcode is 301 00.

Places to Stay

Agrinio is a town more used to business reps than tourists, so prices tend to be a bit on the high side. There's no harm in asking for a discount though. Should you choose to stay in Agrinio, there is the D-class *Akropol* (☎ 23 738), Ilia Iliou 6, with functional singles/doubles with shared bathroom for 4800/7300 dr.

The C-class *Lito* (☎ 23 043) is on Plateia Dimokratias and has very nice rooms with air-con for 8400/11,500 dr.

The B-class *Hotel Galaxias* (☎ 23 551; fax 22 380) at Kazantzi 19, just above the Astro restaurant, has rooms for 8800/10,600/14,500 dr. The B-class *Esperia* (☎ 23 033; fax 44 641) is at Harilaou Trikoupi 31 and is the nearest to the bus station. This hotel was wary of giving out prices, but they would be in much the same category as the Galaxias.

Places to Eat

There is not a great deal to choose from and the choice is mainly limited to fast-food outlets, psistarias and ouzeria. One exception is the *Astro Restaurant* which is just off the main square on Salakou. Here you will find good, ready-made food served in a pleasant environment. *Pizza Roma* just south of the square on Harilaou Trikoupi is a well-run restaurant offering pizza and other dishes.

Getting There & Away

Buses run regularly to and from Agrinio, including the following more important destinations. Athens (almost hourly departures, 4½ hours, 4000 dr), 10 a day to Ioannina (three hours, 2350 dr), two a day to Karpenisi (3½ hours, 1700 dr) and eight to Patras (two hours, 1250 dr).

SOUTH-WEST COASTAL RESORTS
Amfilohia

This attractive little place at the south-eastern corner of the Gulf of Ambracia attracts a small holiday crowd. Most visitors are merely passing through, since it is on the main highway between Epiros and the south. It is a lively town of 5000 inhabitants and although it would probably not warrant a long-term stay, it is an amenable enough stopover point. Swimming is OK, but you

might want to try a bit further north up the gulf at Krikellos. There is a long, curving promenade with many restaurants and cafés to relax in. If you are here in August or September, look out for the strange luminescence of the water at night.

There are five recognised hotels to choose from, of which the *Oscar* (0642-22 155/867) is probably your best choice; singles/doubles there are 6500/9000 dr. There is also a small camping site *Stratis Beach Park* at Katafourko beach, north of Amfilohia, with a bar, restaurant, supermarket and shaded sites.

Vonitsa

The town of Vonitsa is popular enough with local holiday-makers, but doesn't have any real beach scene to speak of, since it is on the still waters of the Gulf of Ambracia. It is quiet and pleasant and conveniently located for the town of Preveza and the Aktio airport. The route through Vonitsa from Preveza is a quicker way through to the main north-south highway to the Peloponnese. There is one D-class and four C-class hotels to choose from.

Mytikas

The small village of Mytikas is built on the gulf of the same name. This place has yet to feel the effect of mass tourism since it is mainly confined to Greeks and the few foreign visitors who find their way here. The beach is pebbly but uncommercialised and there are only a couple of hotels and a few tavernas. You can take a local caïque to the little islands of Kalamos and Kastos, if the isolation of Mytikas is not enough for you.

Astakos

Slightly more up-market, Astakos is another place for a quiet, hassle-free holiday. It can also be used as a more convenient stepping-stone for access to the Ionian islands, via Ithaki. There is one C-class establishment, the *Cavo Mytikas* (☎ 0646-81 323; fax 81 244) and some rooms in summer. Restaurants and tavernas cater mainly to local tastes.

CENTRAL GREECE

KARPENISI Καρπενήσι

Karpenisi (population 10,000, altitude 960 metres) is in the foothills of Mt Tymfristos (2315 metres), 82 km west of Lamia. The town is not especially attractive but lies in a beautiful, well-wooded region which the EOT brochures tout as the 'Switzerland of Greece'. There are many opportunities for trekking and, if you have your own transport, you can explore some delightful mountain villages. Bear in mind that Karpenisi is built on a steep hill. Motorists should take note that Karpenisi also has a pay and display parking system. The minimum cost is 100 dr for one hour. Display your ticket on the dashboard.

Karpenisi's telephone code is 0237 and its postcode is 361 00.

Activities

If you are keen to participate in some kind of organised adventure sport activity, get in contact with Trekking Hellas (☎ 25 940; fax 25 940) at Zinopoulou 7, on the main square. They organise group activities in trekking, kayaking, canyoning and rafting.

Places to Stay

Karpenisi has one D-class hotel, the *Hotel Panellinion* (☎ 22 330), Spyrou Tsitsara 9, where singles/doubles are 4500/5500 dr with shared bathroom. The C-class *Hotel Galini* (☎ 22 914), R Fereou 3, has rooms for private bathroom for 5000/8200 dr. In the same class but decidedly better, the *Hotel Helvetia* (☎ 22 465), Zinopoulou 33, has lovely rooms for 7600/9500 dr. The *Anesis Hotel* (☎ 22 840; fax 22 305), Zinopoulou 50, has rooms for 8800/9500 dr with private bathroom.

The B-class and rather grungy *Mont Blanc* (☎ 22 322), known in Greek as Lefko Oros, Ethnikis Antistasis 2, has drab rooms for 7000/9000 dr. For a real splurge, head for the A-class *Hotel Montana* (☎ 25 000; fax 25 009), on a hill above the town. You may be tempted to choose this first when you consider the mediocre quality of most of the other hotels in town. Mind you, a double with breakfast will set you back 25,000 dr.

The Mt Tymfristos refuge of *Takis Flengas* (☎ 0237-22 002), at 1840 metres, can be reached along a 12-km road from Karpenisi, or is a 2½-hour walk along a path. If you wish to stay at the refuge, contact the Karpenisi EOS (☎ 0237-23 051), Georgiou Tsitsara 2, Karpenisi.

Places to Eat

There are no real gastronomic delights here. Apart from a few fast-food places along the two main streets leading down from the main square, of which the *Three Star Restaurant* on A Karpenisioti has some redeeming qualities, there is not much choice other than psistarias. Of this nondescript bunch, *Restaurant Triandafyllis*, opposite the OTE, is probably better than most.

Getting There & Away

There are two buses a day from Athens to Karpenisi (six hours, 3200 dr) and another two to Lamia (1½ hours, 1200 dr) There are also two buses a day to and from Agrinio in Aetolo-Akarnania (3½ hours, 1700 dr).

AROUND KARPENISI

From Karpenisi a scenic mountain road leads south for 37 km to the village of **Proussos**. Along the way you'll pass several picturesque villages. The charming village of **Koryshades** has well-preserved mansions and is five km south-west of Karpenisi, reached by a turn-off right along the Proussos road. **Mikro Horio** and **Megalo Horio** are 12 km further along the road.

The **Monastery of the Virgin of Proussiotissa**, just before the village of Proussos, has a miracle-working icon. There are more icons, wood carvings and ecclesiastical ornaments in the monastery's 18th-century church. A small number of monks live at the monastery and pilgrims flock there in August for the Feast of the Assumption.

Places to Stay

The D-class *Hotel Antigone* (☎ 0237-41 395), at Megalo Horio, has single/double rooms with private bathroom for 4300/8000 dr. The *Agathidis Pension* (☎ 0237-91 248),

GREG ALFORD

GREG ALFORD

ROSEMARY HALL

Top: View from Ancient Delphi, Sterea Ellada
Bottom Left: Ancient Delphi, Sterea Ellada
Bottom Right: Agios Stefanos (St Stephen Convent), Meteora, Thessaly

ROSEMARY HALL

DAVID HALL

LINDA WELTERS

Top: The mosaic courtyard at the ancient site of Pella, Macedonia
Left: Monastery of Dionysiou, Mt Athos Peninsula, Macedonia
Right: Man in foustanella, Metsovo, Epiros

at Proussos, has rooms with private bathroom for 6000/8500 dr. The A-class pension *Dryas* (☎ 0237-41 131) at Megalo Horio is your most comfortable option. A double room with breakfast will cost you 16,000 dr.

KARPENISI TO AGRINIO

Two buses a day run along this tortuous (but sealed) road across the mountains and villages of the Agrafa to Agrinio in Aetolo-Akarnania. During the Tourkokratia (the period of Turkish occupation of Greece), the villages of this region were considered too remote to be recorded for taxation purposes, so they were classified as *agrafa* (unrecorded). The bus covers the distance in a slow 3½ hours and it is quite a spectacular drive. The beauty of this trip is the emptiness of the countryside, through which the road climbs and twists downwards as far as the first main centre of habitation, the twin villages of **Anatoliki** and **Dytiki Frangista**, just before which is the modern taverna *Sotira* with a children's play park and, surprisingly, a swimming pool. The road then crosses the long bridge over the artificial Lake Kremasta into Aetolo-Akarnania, climbs high over the last ridge and eventually winds down through small farm holdings into Agrinio. If you suffer from motion sickness, think twice before making this trip.

LAMIA Λαμία

Lamia is the capital of the prefecture of Fthiotida and is an attractive town at the western end of the Maliakos gulf, built in the form of an amphitheatre along the foothills of Mt Orthys. Lamia rarely figures on people's itineraries, but it deserves a look-in. Like most towns that are not dependent on tourism for their livelihood, Lamia is a vibrant and lively place all year round. It is famous for its lamb on the spit, its *kourabiedes* (almond shortcake) and its *xynogala* (sour milk).

To the east of Lamia is the narrow pass of Thermopylae, where, in 480 BC, Leonidas and 300 Spartans managed to temporarily halt the Persian advance of Xerxes and his 30,000 strong army.

Orientation

The main cluster of activity in Lamia is centred around Plateia Eleftherias, Plateia Laou and Plateia Parkou, where most public services can also be found. The main bus stations are towards the end of Satovriandou. This is the street that leads south from Plateia Parkou and then dips down a hill by the primary school building. The local railway station is south of the centre on Konstantinoupoleos, close to the bus terminals. Drivers should be aware that a pay and display parking system is in force in the central area. Parking costs 100 dr per hour. Look out for the black-and-orange (short-term, two hours) and green-and-white (long-term, 24 hours) parking zone signs.

Information

The EOT office is at Plateia Laou 3 (☎ 0231-30 065; fax 30 066) and is open Monday to Friday from 7 am to 2.30 pm. The OTE is on Plateia Eleftherias and the post office is on Athanasiou Diakou, south from Plateia Eleftherias. You will find most banks on, or near, Plateia Parkou. Lamia's telephone code is 0231 and its postcode is 351 00.

Things to See & Do

Lamia's **frourio**, or fort, is worth a hike up just for the views. The **Gorgopotamos railway bridge** is a fairly famous landmark in recent Greek history. It is seven km southeast of Lamia. It was blown up by the united national forces on 25 November 1944 to delay the German advance and was considered one of the greatest acts of sabotage of the time. If you are heading south by train to Athens, you will cross the reconstructed bridge over a deep ravine, shortly after leaving Lianokladi station.

Thermopylae (Thermopyles in modern Greek) is 18 km from Lamia on the main Athens highway. A large statue of Leonidas marks the spot where the Persian army was delayed on its way to Thessaly, but where Leonidas and his brave Spartans ultimately

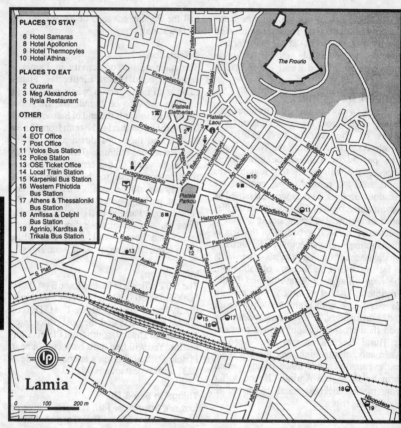

PLACES TO STAY

6 Hotel Samaras
8 Hotel Apollonion
9 Hotel Thermopyles
10 Hotel Athina

PLACES TO EAT

2 Ouzeria
3 Meg Alexandros
5 Ilysia Restaurant

OTHER

1 OTE
4 EOT Office
7 Post Office
11 Volos Bus Station
12 Police Station
13 OSE Ticket Office
14 Local Train Station
15 Karpenisi Bus Station
16 Western Fthiotida
  Bus Station
17 Athens & Thessaloniki
  Bus Station
18 Amfissa & Delphi
  Bus Station
19 Agrinio, Karditsa &
  Trikala Bus Station

The Frourio

Lamia

0   100   200 m

---

perished. Today the pass is much wider than it was in antiquity because of a gradual silting up of the land on the sea side.

Places to Stay

The hotel scene on Lamia does not allow for much choice or great quality. Since Lamia is not a tourist town, its hotel owners don't seem to make much effort to make their establishments attractive. The D-class *Thermopyles* (☎ 21 366) at Rozaki Angeli 36 has unassuming but OK singles/doubles for 7000/8800 dr. Directly opposite at Rozaki

Angeli 47 is the more presentable *Athina* (☎ 27 700) with rooms for much the same price.

The C-class *Apollonion* (☎ 22 668) on Plateia Parkou doesn't offer much more in facilities and comfort than the above hotels apart from a phone and a TV. Rooms here go for 9000/11,000.

One exception to the rule of mediocrity is the C-class *Hotel Samaras* (☎ 28 971; fax 42 704). It is on the corner of Karagiannopoulou and Ath Diakou and has well-appointed rooms with TV and air-con (both with remote control) for 9900/12,000 dr.

Try asking for a better room rate out of season: most hotels will have lower rates than the prices listed here.

Places to Eat & Drink

If you like lamb on the spit, you can't go wrong here. Karaïskaki, a tree-shaded pedestrian street, is full of psistarias with the rather grotesque sight of whole roast lambs in their windows. Two point-and-choose places offering reasonable ready-made food are the *Meg Alexandros* on Plateia Laou and the *Ilysia* round the corner on Kalyva Bakogianni. The English-language menu at this second place is a killer!

A cluster of little ouzeria are hidden away at the bottom of some steps leading from Plateia Eleftherias to Androutsou. Take your pick.

Plateia Eleftherias is a rather up-market place for the younger set, who patronise the swish cafeterias that border the square. Plateia Laou is a little more sedate, with its kafeneia, and overall has a more relaxed feel to it, especially since the square is shaded by large plane trees. Similarly, Plateia Parkou has outdoor cafés, but they are a bit more impersonal.

Getting There & Away

Bus The scene here is a tad confusing. There are a few terminals, all within walking distance of each other, but all serving different destinations.

The main terminal for Athens and Thessaloniki buses is on Papakyriazi, which runs off Satovriandou. There are almost hourly buses for Athens (three hours, 2800 dr) and two a day (three on weekends) for Thessaloniki (four hours, 3800 dr).

Further down the hill and on the corner of Konstantinoupoleos is the bus station for western Fthiotida, which includes the village of Ypati in its route.

The Karpenisi ticket agency is on Markou Botsari 3, again close by. There are four buses a day to Karpenisi (1½ hours, 1150 dr). There are another two sub-stations on Thermopylon, 100 metres south of the

railway line: one for Agrinio, Karditsa and Trikala and the other for Amfissa and Delphi. Finally, buses for Volos leave from a small station at the end of Rozaki Angeli.

Train Lamia has a very inconveniently located main railway station seven km west of the town centre at Lianokladi. The intercity trains all stop at Lianokladi. Train tickets can be pre-purchased from the OSE office at Averof 7. The No 7 bus, whose destination is Stavros, links the Lianokladi station with the Lamia town centre.

The small train station in town has only two trains a day linking Lamia with Lianokladi from the branch line terminus at Stylida (14 km east of Lamia) – hardly a reliable transport option, though the train does go on to Athens.

LAMIA TO KARPENISI

If you have the time, an exploration of the mountainous region west of the city of Lamia is worthwhile. The attractive village of **Ypati**, 25 km past Lamia and eight km south of the Karpenisi-Lamia road, has the remains of a fortress and is the starting point for treks on Mt Iti (2152 metres).

This mountain is the focus of the Iti National Park, established in 1966. It's a verdant region with forests of fir and black pine. According to mythology, Mt Iti was the place where the dying Heracles built his own funeral pyre and was burned to death. While the mortal elements in Heracles perished, the immortal Heracles joined his divine peers on Mt Olympus.

From Ypati it's a four-hour walk along a marked path to the mountain's *Trapeza Refuge* (1850 metres). For information about this refuge contact the Lamia EOS (☎ 0231-26 786), Ipsilandou 20, Lamia.

Ypati has two hotels. The D-class *Hotel Panellinion* (☎ 0231-59 640) is open in July and August only and has singles/doubles with shared bathroom for 3700/5000 dr. The D-class *Hotel Panorama* (☎ 0231-59 222) has rooms with shared bathroom for 4000/4500 dr and doubles with private bathroom for 4800 dr. This hotel operates from April to October only. Ypati is served by frequent buses from Lamia.

From the Ypati turn-off the road is fast and relatively flat and runs along the valley of the River Sperhios. After Makri, the road begins to climb through forested hills and really climbs at the village of Tymfristos, winding slowly upwards to a pass at the summit of which you enter the prefecture of Evrytania. This road gets quite a bit of snow in winter.

A new road then winds down fairly quickly to Karpenisi, avoiding the village of Agios Nikolaos.

AGIOS KONSTANTINOS
Αγιος Κωνσταντίνος

Agios Konstantinos, on the main Athens-Thessaloniki route, is one of the three mainland ports which serve the Sporades islands (the other two are Thessaloniki and Volos).

There are a number of hotels in the town, however, with judicious use of buses from Athens to the port, you will probably not need to stay overnight before catching a Sporades-bound ferry or hydrofoil. If you get stuck, try the *Hotel Poulia* (☎ 0235-31 663). Rates are 3500/4500 dr for singles/doubles. A more comfortable option is the A-class *Motel Levendi* (☎ 0235-32 251; fax 32 255), where singles/doubles are 13,800/15,200 dr.

Getting There & Away
Bus Buses depart hourly for Agios Konstantinos from Athens Terminal B bus station (2½ hours, 2450 dr).

Ferry There are one or two daily ferries from Agios Konstantinos to Skiathos (3½ hours, 2980 dr) and one or two to Skopelos town (5½ hours, 3480 dr) and Alonnisos (six hours, 3850 dr).

Hydrofoil Hydrofoils depart up to three times daily for Skiathos (1½ hours, 5300 dr), Skopelos town (2½ hours, 7070 dr) and Alonnisos (three hours, 7420 dr).

Thessaly Θεσσαλία

Thessaly is the proud possessor of two of Greece's most extraordinary natural phenomena: the giant rock pinnacles of Meteora and the riotously fertile Pelion peninsula. On a more modest scale it also has the beautiful Vale of Tembi. Travelling north from Thessaly to Macedonia, whether by road or train, you will pass through this 12-km-long valley, which is a narrow passageway between Mt Olympus and Mt Ossa. The road and railway line share the valley with a river, whose richly verdant banks contrast dramatically with the sheer cliffs on either side. If you have your own transport there are viewpoints at the most scenic spots.

The valley has also been a favoured place for invaders of Greece. The Persian king Xerxes gained access to central Greece via Tembi in 480 BC, as did the Germans in 1941.

LARISA Λάρισα
Larisa is not the kind of place you would choose as your prime holiday destination, but it is worth more than a passing glance. Larisa occupies a position as an important

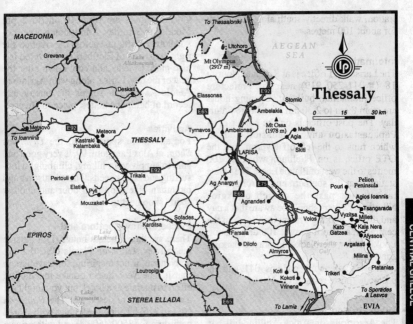

CENTRAL GREECE

transport hub and since it is pretty well central to the Thessaly region, it is likely that you are going to find yourself at least passing through here, if only fleetingly on the train heading either north or south. Despite its seeming initial lack of promise, Larisa is nonetheless a lively and sophisticated Greek town, almost bereft of tourists, and is a very important service centre for the whole of the vast agricultural plain of Thessaly. It is a vibrant student town, as the bustling cafeterias around the central area testify. It is also a strategic military and air force base, given the more forgiving and flat terrain of the land around Larisa, in comparison with much of Greece.

Larisa has been inhabited for over 8000 years and its multifarious and fascinating past is only gradually being uncovered, since in recent years fast-growing residential development has tended to disguise what historical remains lie beneath the modern city.

Orientation

Larisa is built on the east bank of the River Pinios, which eventually flows through the Vale of Tembi to the sea. Its main square is called Plateia Laou. The railway station is on the southern side of town and the main bus station on the northern side. To get to the town centre from the railway station, bear left onto the road outside the station towards a busy intersection and then turn to the right from the intersection, along Alex Panagouli. This street leads directly north to Plateia Laou.

Kyprou and Nikitara run across the south end of this square and Eleftheriou Venizelou and 31 Avgoustou across the north end. Plateia Ethnarhou Makariou (more commonly known as Plateia Tahydromiou) and Plateia Michael Sapka are the other two squares around which most of the social life revolves. The streets around these squares are mainly a pedestrian zone.

To get to Plateia Laou from the main bus

station, walk directly south along Olympou for about 100 metres.

Information

The Larisa EOT office is at Koumoundourou 18 (☎ 041-250 919) near the prefecture office (nomarhia) building. Opening hours are from 8 am to 2.30 pm Monday to Saturday. The post office is on the corner of A Papanastasiou and Athanasiou Diakou which runs to the left off Kyprou, and the OTE office is on Filellinon which is 100 metres to the west of Plateia Laou. The police station is at the southern end of A Papanastasiou, just past the church of Agios Nikolaos. Drivers should be aware that a pay and display parking system is in force in the central area. Parking costs 100 dr per hour. Look out for the black-and-orange parking zone signs.

Larisa's telephone code is 041 and its postcode (poste restante) is 410 01.

Things to See

The **Acropolis** on Agios Ahillios hill has archaeological evidence that indicates this area had been settled since the Neolithic Age (6000 BC), but was used as the ancient settlement's Acropolis during classical times, when the temple of **Polias Athina** once existed. The Acropolis is now the site of the **kastro**. Nearby are the excavations of a newly discovered **ancient theatre** which, when fully excavated, could rival that of the theatre at Epidaurus. The excavation site is on the corner of A Papanastasiou and Eleftheriou Venizelou. It is not particularly impressive at the moment and to fully uncover it will mean demolishing a good section of the neighbouring streets.

The **folkloric museum** at Mandilara 74 (☎ 239 446) has an interesting collection of tools and utensils from the pre-industrial age, beginning with exhibits showing how crops were sown and grown. There are Greek traditional costumes, displays about nomads and semi-nomads and, in the reception area, some samples of weaving and bronze ware from Tyrnavos, a town not far from Larisa.

Opening hours are from 10 am to 2 pm Monday to Saturday. Admission is free.

Alkazar Park, just across the river on the right at the end of Eleftheriou Venizelou is a nice place to relax and cool down after the heat of the day. Larisa, along with Agrinio in Aetolo-Akarnania, shares the unenviable record of being the hottest place in Greece.

Activities

For adventure sports fans, the *Olympios Shop*, at Alex Panagouli 99, is very good and able to supply your hiking, climbing, windsurfing and skiing needs. There is also a good mountain bike shop next door and another sports shop next to that.

Places to Stay – bottom end

There are three D-class hotels right outside the railway station on Plateia OSE that are convenient, if not inspiring, for travellers in transit. The *Neon* doesn't make much of an effort to operate as a hotel, but you might get a room if you're desperate. The *Pantheon* (☎ 236 726) has singles/doubles with shared bathroom for 3500/4600 dr and with private bathroom for 4600/5900 dr. The *Diethnes* (☎ 234 210), next door, is an old-fashioned place with functional rooms with shared bathroom for 3400/4600 dr.

Places to Stay – middle

The C-class *Hotel Atlantic* (☎ 287 711; fax 230 022) is reasonable enough and has rooms for 6000/8000 dr. It is on the south side of Plateia Laou. The older C-class *Hotel Anesis* (☎ 227 210) is relatively central, at Megalou Alexandrou 25, and has small rooms for 6000/7700 dr.

Places to Stay – top end

Larisa has a couple of overpriced B-class hotels where you may well get up to 50% discount at non-peak times. The *Astoria* (☎ 252 791; fax 229 097) at Protopapadaki 4 is as central as you can get and there's a lively nightlife in the immediate area. Rooms here go for 16,900/23,100 dr. The *Grand Hotel* (☎ 257 111; fax 557 888) at Papakyriazi 14, on the opposite corner of the

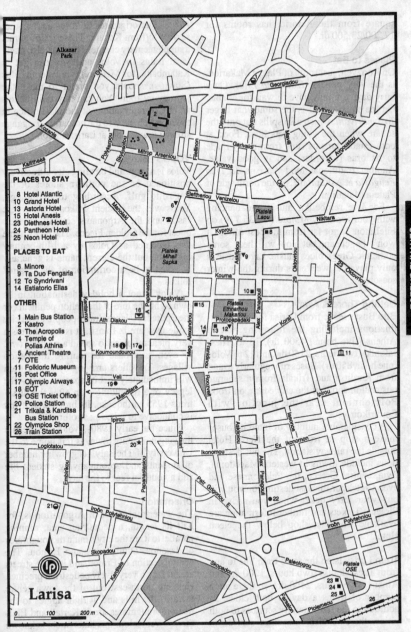

PLACES TO STAY

8 Hotel Atlantic
10 Grand Hotel
13 Astoria Hotel
15 Hotel Anesis
23 Diethnes Hotel
24 Pantheon Hotel
25 Neon Hotel

PLACES TO EAT

6 Minore
9 Ta Duo Fengaria
12 To Syndrivani
14 Estiatorio Ellas

OTHER

1 Main Bus Station
2 Kastro
3 The Acropolis
4 Temple of
  Polias Athina
5 Ancient Theatre
7 OTE
11 Folkloric Museum
16 Post Office
17 Olympic Airways
18 EOT
19 OSE Ticket Office
20 Police Station
21 Trikala & Karditsa
  Bus Station
22 Olympios Shop
26 Train Station

CENTRAL GREECE

Larisa

0   100   200 m

square from the Astoria, has rooms for 17,200/23,500 dr.

Places to Eat

On Roozvelt, just south of Plateia Makariou, is the very popular *Estiatorio Ellas.* On a busy day, you may have to wait for a table. On the square itself is the somewhat larger *To Syndrivani*, which also spills out onto the square when the going gets busy. Food at both establishments runs from ready-made to tis oras (to order) and is good value. Another traditional food place is *Ta Duo Fengaria* at Asklipiou 7, on the north side of Plateia Makariou.

For live rembetika music and dancing with your food, try *Minore* (☎ 536 779) on Filellinon 3, not far from the post office. It won't be cheap, but you will hear some authentic Greek blues music. Live music is only played at weekends during the winter season.

Getting There & Away

Bus Buses leave from Larisa for many destinations including the following: six to Athens (five hours, 4500 dr), 13 to Thessaloniki (two hours, 2150 dr) and 12 to Volos (one hour, 850 dr). Buses run regularly to and from Karditsa and Trikala from a separate bus station south of the city centre on Iroön Polytehniou, near the junction with Embirikou.

A considerable number of intercity buses make a stop in front of the Neon Hotel outside the railway station. The bus destinations include towns in western Macedonia, Evia, central Greece, the Peloponnese and even Crete. For this last destination you will buy your ferry ticket when you arrive in Piraeus. Tickets and further information are available from the shop below the Neon Hotel.

Train Larisa is on the main train line to and from Thessaloniki (two hours, 1200 dr) and Athens (five hours, 2460 dr), so there are a number of trains a day to both cities. In addition to the five intercity services to both cities, there is also one extra service to

Athens that originates in Volos and another service to/from Kozani. These trains attract a supplementary charge. There are also many local trains to Volos and you can get to Kalambaka (for Meteora), via Paleofarsalos (Stavros), should you prefer to make the journey by train. You can buy train tickets and make reservations at the OSE office in town on Veli, next to the nomarhia. Luggage storage is available at Larisa station.

VOLOS Βόλος

Volos is a large and bustling city attractively positioned on the northern shores of the Pagasitic gulf. According to mythology, Volos was the ancient Iolkos from where Jason and the Argonauts set sail on their quest for the Golden Fleece. The city's name was recorded as Golos by a 14th-century historian, but the current name is generally believed to be a corruption of the original Iolkos.

Volos is not a holiday destination in its own right: the lure of the Pelion peninsula or the Sporades islands draws people to the city while they are in transit. It is nonetheless a very pleasant place to spend a night or two, or even as a base for touring the Pelion villages. Travellers arriving by bus or train will immediately feel its spaciousness – the legacy of a rebuilding plan after the disastrous 1955 earthquake. Its broad waterfront is conducive to relaxing strolling.

Since the early 1980s, Volos has been a thriving university town, as it is home to the University of Thessaly. Its growing number of students and accompanying student life add a youthful feel to the city.

Orientation

The waterfront street of Argonafton is, for half its length, a pedestrian area; running parallel to it are the city's main thoroughfares of Iasonos, Dimitriados and Ermou. The central section of Ermou and its side streets are, in fact, a very lively pedestrian precinct. Heading north-east out of the town centre towards the hills and at right angles to the main thoroughfares are K Kartali and Eleftheriou Venizelou: this latter street is known

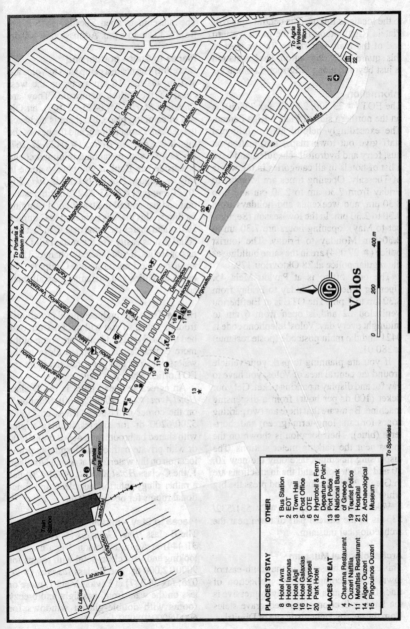

PLACES TO STAY

8 Hotel Avra
9 Hotel Iasonas
10 Hotel Aigli
16 Hotel Galaxias
17 Hotel Kypseli
20 Park Hotel

PLACES TO EAT

4 Charama Restaurant
7 Ouzeri Naftilia
11 Metaftsis Restaurant
14 Algeo Ouzeri
15 Pingoulinos Ouzeri

OTHER

1 Bus Station
3 EOT
5 Town Hall
6 OTE
12 Hydrofoil & Ferry
   Departure Point
13 Port Police
18 National Bank
   of Greece
19 Tourist Police
21 Hospital
22 Archaeological
   Museum

to the locals as Iolkou. The central square of Plateia Riga Fereou is at the north-western end of the main waterfront. To the west of this square is the train station. The bus station is just beyond, along Grigoriou Lambraki.

Information

The EOT (☎ 23 500, 24 233; fax 24 750) is on the northern side of Plateia Riga Fereou. The exceedingly helpful and multilingual staff give out town maps, information on bus, ferry and hydrofoil schedules, and have a list of hotels in all categories in the whole of Thessaly. Opening times are Monday to Friday from 7.30 am to 2.30 pm and 6 to 8.30 pm, and weekends and holidays from 9.30 to 2.30 pm. In the low-season (September to May), opening hours are 7.30 am to 2.30 pm Monday to Friday. The tourist police (☎ 27 094) are in the same building as the regular police at 28 Oktovriou 179.

The post office is at Pavlou Mela 45. Opening times are Monday to Friday from 8.30 am to 3 pm. The OTE is at Eleftheriou Venizelou 22 and is open from 6 am to midnight every day. Volos' telephone code is 0421 and the main postcode (poste restante) is 380 01.

If you are planning to park your vehicle around the central area of Volos, you have to pay for and display a parking ticket. Get your ticket (100 dr per hour) from a dispensing machine. Be aware that there are two parking zones for cars: long-term (green) and short-term (blue). Their location is shown on the maps near the parking meter stations. The dispensing machines take only the new 20, 50 and 100-dr coins and the instructions are in Greek. Put in the money and press the big white button.

Volos' General Hospital (☎ 24 531/532/ 533) is in the eastern part of town near the archaeological museum.

Archaeological Museum

This excellent museum, in the south-east of town, has a comprehensive collection of finds from the area. Especially impressive is the large collection of painted grave steles from the nearby Hellenistic site of Dimitrias.

The museum is open Tuesday to Sunday from 8.30 am to 3 pm. Admission is 400 dr.

Places to Stay – bottom end

Camping The nearest camp sites to Volos are at Kato Gatzea, 18 km away, on the west coast of the Pelion peninsula. They are *Camping Marina* (☎ 0423-22 167), an OK sort of camping place, but there is no beach to speak of. Further along, and the best of the bunch is *Camping Hellas* (☎ 0423-22 267; fax 22 492) with restaurant, minimarket and beachside bar. Book if you plan to come in July or August. Not far behind is *Sikia Fig Tree Camping* (☎ 0423-22 279), with restaurant and bar and all the usual good camping facilities. This place is right next to Camping Hellas and shares the same beach. In fact you could just as easily use the restaurant facilities of Hellas, if you fancied a change. There are also some domatia at Sikia Camping. The buses to Milies and Platanias pass all three sites.

Hotels There are eighteen hotels to choose from in Volos, so you will not miss out on a bed too easily. Listed below are some of the more central hotels, clustered close to the waterfront. You can get a full list from the EOT office when you arrive.

An agreeable cheap hotel is the D-class *Hotel Avra* (☎ 25 370 or 28 980), Solonos 5, on the corner of Iasonos. Rates are 3600/ 5200/6200 dr for singles/doubles/ triples with shared bathroom, and 4600/ 6400/7700 dr with private bathroom. Despite its prime location on the waterfront at Agiou Nikolaou 1, the C-class *Hotel Kypseli* (☎ 24 420) has a rather dingy interior, but clean and functional rooms for 6600/9000 dr.

Places to Stay – middle

The B-class *Hotel Galaxias* (☎ 20 750; fax 31 444) at Agiou Nikolaou 3 is a modern-looking and very clean hotel with rooms for 9000/12,000 dr. The B-class *Iasonas* (☎ 26 075; fax 24 347) at Pavlou Mela 1, more or less on the waterfront, has light and breezy rooms with double-glazed windows for 6000/8000/10,000 dr.

Places to Stay – top end

On the waterfront at Argonafton 24 is one of Volos' longest established hostelries, the B-class *Aigli* (☎ 24 471; fax 33 006); it has an impressive neoclassical façade and a warm interior. Rooms here are an equally impressive 11,400/17,500 dr including breakfast. Volos' fanciest hotel is the B-class *Park Hotel* (☎ 36 511; fax 28 645), Deligiorgi 2. The stylish rooms have air-con, direct-dial telephone, radio and balcony. Rates are 8900/13,000 dr including breakfast.

Places to Eat

Since Volos is considered the ouzeri capital of Greece, it would be a shame not to eat and drink as the locals do.

Some typical mezedes are spetsofaï (chopped sausages and peppers in a rich sauce); ohtapodi (octopus); htypiti (a mixed feta cheese and hot pepper dip); and fried calamari.

There is a cluster of ouzeria along the Argonafton waterfront of which the most popular seem to be *Naftilia* at the western end, and the *Pingouinos* and the *Aigeo* towards the middle. There are, of course, many ouzeria throughout the city itself, so half the fun may well be in seeking out your own favourite place. Bear one thing in mind: eating and drinking at an ouzeri can get a bit expensive if you don't keep a track of what you are eating and drinking.

For more traditional restaurant fare, try the *Metaftsis* on Argonafton, near the ferry boat pier, or the *Charama Restaurant*, Dimitriados 49, which serves very tasty dishes.

Getting There & Away

Bus From the bus station there are nine buses a day to Athens (five hours, 4350 dr); 12 a day to Larisa (one hour, 900 dr); four a day to Thessaloniki (three hours, 2950 dr); two to Trikala (two hours, 2100 dr) and two a day to Lamia (1½ hours, 2000 dr). There may be more buses in summer.

Buses to the major villages of the Pelion peninsula are as follows: 11 a day to Kala Nera, of which seven continue to Afyssos; 10 a day to Makrynitsa (via Portaria); seven

CENTRAL GREECE

The Ouzeri

The ouzeri is not purely a Volos institution, but Volos is famous throughout Greece for the quality and quantity of its ouzeria. The institution came about as a result of refugees from Asia Minor who established themselves in Volos after the exchange of populations in 1922, when Greeks and Turks were forced to swap homelands. Most of the refugees who came to Volos were seafarers who would gather on the harbour at lunchtime and drink *tsipouro* accompanied by various mezedes (tasty titbits). As the eating and drinking progressed, the demand for all the more exotic and different mezedes grew and so too did the repertoire of the establishment serving them. Seafood mezedes were the mainstay of this eating and drinking routine. An ouzeri (strictly speaking, a *tsipouradiko*), if you have not already come across one, is like a little restaurant where you eat from various plates of mezedes and drink little bottles of

tsipouro. When you have finished one round of mezedes or tsipouro, you order some more and so on, until you are full, or can't stand up. Tsipouro is a distilled spirit like ouzo, but stronger. You can dilute it with water, if you want to last a little longer. It costs 400 dr a pop. ■

to Vyzitsa (via Milies); six to Milina (via Argalasti and Horto), three of which continue to Platanias; three a day to both Zagora (via Hania) and Agios Ioannis (via Tsangarada). Buses also run to many of the smaller villages, but often only two or three times a day. Check the board at the bus station.

Train There are 15 trains a day to Larisa (540 dr). Two direct intercity trains a day go to Athens (the *Trikoupis* at 6.24 am and the *Thessalia* at 5.24 pm, 3970 dr) and three local trains go to Thessaloniki, with a connection at Larisa. However, there are many connections a day to both Thessaloniki and Athens from Larisa. You can make reservations for these connections and the Athens or Thessaloniki intercity trains from the surprisingly well-equipped on-line booking office at the station. Four trains a day go to Kalambaka (four hours, 1140 dr) via Trikala, for travellers wishing to get to Meteora.

Ferry There are daily ferries from Volos to Trikeri (Pelion; 1½ hours, 1180 dr); Skiathos (three hours, 2130 dr); Glossa (Skopelos; 3½ hours, 2850 dr); Skopelos town (4½ hours, 2850 dr); Alonnisos (five hours, 2940 dr); and twice weekly to Kymi in Evia (eight hours, 6870 dr).

Hydrofoil In summer, there are five or six daily hydrofoils to Skiathos (one hour, 4630 dr); Glossa (1½ hours, 5660 dr); Skopelos town (two hours, 6000 dr); and Alonnisos (three hours, 6700 dr). Additional services operate to Evia and some of the Sporades services stop at Trikeri and Trikeri island.

Getting Around
Cars can be rented from European Car Rental (☎ 24 381; fax 24 192), at Iasonos 83, and from Avis (☎ 20 849; fax 32 360), at Argonafton 41.

PELION PENINSULA Πήλιον Ορος
The well-watered Pelion peninsula lies to the east and south of Volos. It consists of a mountain range, of which the highest peak is

Mt Pliassidi (1651 metres). The inaccessible eastern flank consists of high cliffs which plunge dramatically into the sea. The gentler western flank coils around the calm sea of the Pagasitic gulf, and is fringed by sand and pebble beaches.

The interior is a green wonderland where trees heavy with fruit vie with wild olive groves, forests of horse chestnut, oak, walnut, eucalyptus and beech trees to reach the light of day.

The villages tucked away in this profuse foliage are characterised by whitewashed, half-timbered houses with overhanging balconies and grey slate roofs, and cobbled mule paths winding around their vibrant gardens. Flagstone squares harbouring little Byzantine churches and sculpted fountains shaded by enormous gnarled plane trees are another feature of these settlements.

If you have your own transport you can see a great deal of the peninsula in one day, but bear in mind that driving here is a tortuous affair with so many bends and turns. If you're travelling by bus, allow for two or three days: no single bus route goes around the whole peninsula, so it isn't possible to tour the coast and inland villages in a single day.

Many of the places to stay in the Pelion are traditional mansions which have been tastefully converted into pensions. They are wonderful places to spend a night or two, but they don't come cheap.

The Pelion has an enduring tradition of regional cooking. Be sure to try some of the local specialities, such as fasolada (bean soup), *kouneli stifado* (rabbit stew), spetsofaï and *tyropsomo* (cheese bread).

History & Mythology
In mythology the Pelion was inhabited by centaurs – reprobate creatures who took delight in deflowering virgins.

The Turkish occupation did not extend into the inaccessible central and eastern parts of the Pelion, and as a result the western coastal towns were abandoned in favour of mountain villages. In these remote settlements, culture and the economy flourished;

Pelion Peninsula

THESSALY

To Larisa

0   5   10 km

AEGEAN

THESSALY

To Sporades

CENTRAL GREECE

silk and wool were exported to many places in Europe. Like other remote areas in Greece it became a spawning ground for ideas which culminated in the War of Independence.

Getting There & Away

Buses to the villages of the Pelion leave from the Volos bus station (see Volos' Getting There & Away section).

Volos to Makrynitsa

Taking the north-eastern route from Volos, the road climbs to the villages of **Anakasia** and **Ano Volos**. The former is four km north-

east of Volos. In its central square is the **Theophilos Museum**, housed in an 18th-century mansion. The museum features the works of the primitive painter Theophilos (1866-1934), who lived for many years in Volos. It's open Monday to Friday from 8 am to 2 pm. Admission is free.

Portaria, the next village, is 13 km north-east of Volos. True to form, its plateia has a splendid old plane tree, and the little 13th-century **Church of Panagia of Portaria** has fine frescoes. A fork to the left in the village leads to Makrynitsa, 17 km north-east of Volos.

CENTRAL GREECE

Makrynitsa Μακρυνίτσα

Makrynitsa (Mak-rin-IT-sa), clinging to a mountainside at an elevation of 750 metres, is aptly called the Balcony of Pelion. The traditional houses were built with three storeys at the front and only one at the back, giving the impression they are stacked on top of one another. It is one of the loveliest of the Pelion villages, but is also the most touristy. However, as it is closed to traffic, it remains tranquil. There's a car park at the entrance to the village and if you've come by bus this is where you will alight. To get to the central square walk straight ahead along the cobbled main street. The square has an old hollow plane tree, a sculpted marble fountain and the little church of Agios Ioannis.

Places to Stay
The *Domatia Makropoulou* (☎ 99 016/073) is one of the cheapest places to stay in Makrynitsa. The simply furnished, spotless doubles/triples are 7300/8600 dr. Walk up the path by the side of Restaurant Galini, on the central square, continue along the path and you will come to the domatia on the right. On the way you will pass the *Archontiko Diomidi* (☎ 99 430; fax 99 114), a traditional mansion featuring lots of wall-hangings, brass and ceramic ornaments and carved-wood furniture. Rates are 7500 dr for a double.

The *Pension Xiradaki* (☎ 99 250) is a beautiful old stone mansion, with minimal but tasteful traditional décor. Single/double/triple/quad rates are 8000/14,100/17,400/18,900 dr, with breakfast. Look for the pension sign pointing left on the main street. This establishment also runs another two arhontika, the *Mousli* and the *Sislianou*, where room prices are the same.

The *Kentavros Xenonas* (☎ 99 075) is a spotless place near the main square and has exquisite double rooms for 11,000 dr which drop to 7700 dr in the summer. The *Hotel Achillefs* (☎ 99 177; fax 99 140), which is on the main square, has single/double rooms for 8500/11,000 dr.

Bookings for all establishments are recommended in high season.

Places to Eat
Try the reasonably priced *Restaurant Galini* on the central square for excellent spetsofaï, fasolada and kouneli stifado. The *Pantheon* nearby on the square has a much better view, but offers much the same fare. Meals at both establishments should cost around 2000 dr with wine.

Makrynitsa to Tsangarada
Back on the main Volos-Zagora route the road continues to the modern village of **Hania**, where there's a *YHA hostel* (☎ 0421-24 290) which only opens in July and August. Just two km from here is the ski resort of **Agriolefkes**, where there is a ski centre (☎ 39 136) with three downhill runs and one cross-country run. Information can be obtained either from the EOT in Volos or the Volos EOS (Greek Alpine Club) at Dimitriados 92 (☎ 25 696).

From Hania the road zigzags down through chestnut trees to a road junction. The left turn leads to **Zagora** (population 3000), the largest of the Pelion villages and a major fruit-growing centre. Zagora is a long, strung-out village, as the approach along the main road will testify, and is not as dependent on tourism as other villages in the area. The very successful Zagora agricultural cooperative was founded in 1916 and has been instrumental in promoting the growing and export of fruit (mainly apples) as a means of sustaining growth in the village region. The cooperative has its own restaurant, cafeteria and minimarket complex in town called *Milon tis Eridos* (apple of discord). Just down past the turn-off to Horefto, you will pass, on the left, the **Ellinomousio**, a museum dedicated to Rigas Fereos, one of the intellectual instigators of the War of Independence. The museum is open daily from 9.30 am to 1.30 pm and 5.30 to 8.30 pm.

Horefto, eight km downhill from Zagora, is a popular resort with a long sandy beach. The main beach is OK, but there are a couple of better beaches, within walking distance, north and south of the main village. There is a reasonable camp site here, but at the time of writing there was disruptive work taking place in front of the camp site to create a little harbour for the anticipated Flying Dolphin hydrofoil service from Volos. At the moment, Horefto takes some getting to by road because of the terrain, but don't expect the peace to last if the hydrofoil service makes a start.

North of Zagora, **Pouri**, another charming village, spills down a steep mountainside. This is the last of the central Pelion villages and is worth the detour from Zagora to have a look.

Back at the road junction, the right turn-off takes you through a series of villages to Tsangarada. This route is one of the most scenically spectacular in the Pelion.

The most delightful of the villages is **Kissos**, which is built on steep terraces. Its 18th-century Church of Agia Marina has fine frescoes. From Kissos, a six-km road leads down to the coastal resort of **Agios Ioannis** which is popular enough, though it wouldn't rank among the best. It is connected to Thessaloniki and the Sporades by a summer Flying Dolphin service.

Tsangarada Τσαγκαράδα

Tsangarada (Ts-an-ga-RA-da), nestling in oak and plane forests, is an extremely spread-out village comprising the four separate communities of Agioi Taxiarhes, Agia Paraskevi, Agios Stefanos and Agia Kyriaki. The largest is Agia Paraskevi, which is just north of the main Volos-Milies-Tsangarada road. The bus stops near the central square of Plateia Paraskevis. The plane tree on this square is reputedly the largest and oldest in Greece – locals claim it is 1500 years old. No doubt this is an exaggeration, but whatever its age it's a magnificent specimen with a girth of 14 metres.

The small seaside resort of **Mylopotamos**, with a sheltered beach, is eight km down the road from Tsangarada. The beach here has earned an EU Blue Flag award for cleanliness, so enjoy and respect it.

There is a very good *Tour & Travel Map* of Tsangarada that you should ask for from the EOT office in Volos, with all the details

you could want and a very good description of the area's attractions.

Places to Stay There are several domatia on the main road near Plateia Paraskevis. The *Konaki Pension* (☎ 0426-49 481), further along the road on the right (beyond the turn-off for Mylopotamos), is a traditional mansion with singles/doubles for 12,000 dr, including breakfast. Further along on the opposite side of the road, the *Paradisos Pension* (☎ 49 209; fax 49 551) is a lovely place run by the friendly and enthusiastic Rigakis brothers. The pension's immaculate and cosy single/double/triple rooms are 8700/12,000/13,700 dr. If you'd rather be on the coast, then Mylopotamos has a few domatia.

Places to Eat The *Paradisos Restaurant* (at the pension of the same name) is excellent. Their home-made apple and cherry preserve is ambrosia to anyone with a sweet tooth.

Volos to Milies & Vyzitsa

After leaving Volos, the west-coast road passes through the touristy villages of **Agria**, **Kato Lehonia** and **Ano Lehonia**. Several roads off to the left lead to one of the most beautiful areas of Pelion; the road from Ano Lehonia to **Vlasios** is particularly lovely. A right turn leads to the seaside resorts of **Platanidia**, **Malakio** and **Kato Gatzea**. After the tortuous driving along the roads of the eastern Pelion villages, this stretch of road is a blessing.

Further along the coast road at **Kala Nera**, 19 km from Volos, there is a turn-off to the left for Tsangarada. A little way along here, another turn-off to the left leads through apple orchards to the spread-out village of Milies (the Greek word for apple trees).

Milies Μηλιές

Built in the late 16th century, Milies (Mi-li-ES) was a rich agricultural centre, prospering on olive oil, fruit and silk production. Like most of the Pelion it enjoyed semi-autonomy and, largely due to its excellent school, it played a major role in the intellectual and cultural awakening that led to Greek independence.

Milies was the birthplace of Anthinos Gazis (1761-1828), the man who raised the Thessalian revolt in 1821. Shortly after independence a railway line was built between Volos and Milies and the town became a prosperous centre of commerce. *Little Smokey*, the steam train which used to chug along this route, retired long ago, but there is talk of reintroducing a train as a tourist attraction. Whether this is a feasible option is debatable, since it would mean some serious realignment of the old track which is clearly visible under the surface of the main Volos-Gatzea road. Meanwhile, the train station and line are still there, and the latter is delightful to walk along. You can walk down the track as far as the main Volos road.

To reach the station from Milies' central square, turn left at the clock tower as you face towards Vyzitsa (the next village along), then walk across the car park and take the cobbled path by the side of Aigli Taverna. The station is worth a look even if you aren't going to walk along the tracks. It has a curious ghost-town feel about it. Here you will find an abandoned station and tracks, left just as they were when the last train whistled its way down to Volos over 20 years ago.

If you are driving, look for the left turn-off to the station just before you reach the main village turn-off. While you are at the station, look out for the memorial to the 29 residents of Milies who were executed by the Germans in 1942.

The **Milies folk museum**, which houses a display of local crafts, is on the right beyond the central square.

Places to Stay The A-class *Palios Stathmos* (☎ 0423-86 425), by the station in Milies, is an old stone house with traditional furnishings. Doubles go for 9500 dr, including breakfast.

Places to Eat The setting of the *Palios Stathmos Restaurant* is idyllic and the food is tasty and reasonably priced. Just up the road from the station is the *Chryso Milo* restaurant, while up in the main village, the *Panorama* psistaria offers a range of local foods. On the road to Vyzitsa you will come across the *Taverna to Aloni*, on a bend in the road. However, the gastronomic highlight of Milies is the scrumptious tyropsomo. You can buy it at the Korbas bakery on the main Volos-Tsangarada road, just before the Milies turn-off.

Vyzitsa Βυζίτσα
Just two km beyond Milies is the peaceful little village of Vyzitsa (altitude 550 metres). Vyzitsa is a photographer's delight. Proclaimed a state heritage village by EOT, here you will find a model Pelion community. It is less touristy than Makrynitsa and in many ways is more attractive. Cobbled pathways wind between its traditional slate-roof houses. To reach Vyzitsa's shady central square walk 50 metres up a cobbled path to your right from the main parking area.

Places to Stay Vyzitsa has several domatia where doubles average 7500 dr – have a look for the signs. The *Karagiannopoulos Mansion* (☎ 0423-86 373) is a beautiful place – the lounge has a carved-wood ceiling and stained-glass windows. Rates are 10,300 dr for a double and 13,900 dr for a suite, both with breakfast. The mansion is on the road coming from Milies.

The *Kontos Mansion* (☎ 86 793) is equally appealing, and is the village's largest mansion. Rates here are 10,000/14,700 for singles/doubles and 19,400/22,400 dr for triples/quads. The pension is signposted to the right from the bus terminal, which is in the main parking area. The *Thetis Xenonas* (☎ 86 111), more or less on the main arrival area and with accompanying café, has doubles for 10,600 including breakfast.

Places to Eat The *Thetis Café*, just beyond the bus terminal, is a serene place, with tables and chairs on a patio shaded by walnut trees. On the main square, nestled in between two enormous plane trees, you have a choice of three establishments, of which *Georgaras* seems to be the most popular. The other two are *Drosia* and *Balkonaki*.

South to Platanias

Continuing south from Kala Nera the bus goes as far as Platanias. Although not as fertile as the northern part of the peninsula, the southern part of the Pelion is still attractive, with pine-forested hills and olive groves. Before heading inland once more, the road skirts the little coastal village of Afyssos, winds upwards through to the large unexceptional inland farming community of Argalasti, and then forks – the left fork continues inland, the right goes to the coastal resorts of Horto and Milina. From Milina the road heads inland and then south to Platanias. If you are really keen, you can now comfortably drive onwards from Milina, or take a twice-daily bus from Volos, all the way to the end of the desolate-looking peninsula to Trikeri and finally to Agia Kyriaki.

Afyssos

This up-market resort features a long and attractive promenade, but it tends to get pretty busy in the summer. There is one A-class hotel, the *Maïstrali* (☎ 0423-33 472), with doubles in the 13,000 dr range, and several domatia/pension places, if you do really prefer the hustle and bustle of the place.

Horto & Milina

These are the next two villages down that you will meet, if you take the right fork after Argalasti at Metohi. Horto is very low-key and small, while Milina is larger and probably offers a better balance of amenities. Both are on a quiet part of the peninsula with clean water but no spectacular beaches. There are two camp sites at Mirina, the *Olizon* (☎ 0423-65 236) and the *Kentauros* a little further on. Of the two, Olizon is probably a better choice.

Just beyond Milina at **Mavri Petra** is an appealing roadside taverna called *Flavios*. Set on a wide bay with fishing boats at anchor, it is a pleasant culinary oasis. Sardines, chips and salad with draught retsina should cost you under 2000 dr.

Trikeri

The road from Milina to Trikeri now becomes more and more desolate and the vegetation more stunted as rock takes over. Apart from one or two small sections, the road is sealed all the way and is wide and fast, with little to distract your attention other than the odd house-cum-taverna or goat pen. There is an end-of-the-world feel about this part of the Pelion and Trikeri may come as a surprise when you discover this lively and historically important little community perched on the hill top, keeping guard over the straits that separate the mainland from Evia.

Donkeys outnumber cars here and the residents pride themselves on their tradition as seafarers, fighters against the Turks in the War of Independence and as upholders of traditional customs and dress. The week following Easter is one of continual revelry as dancing takes place every day and women try to outdo each other in their local costume finery.

Agia Kyriaki

This is the last stop on the Pelion peninsula, a winding five-km drive down the hill, or a fast 15-minute walk down a stone path. This is a fishing village without the tourist trappings and most people only see it during a five-minute stopover on the Flying Dolphin from, or to, the Sporades. Here you will find bright, orange-coloured fishing boats put to good use by a lively, hard-working community.

Rooms are available at *Lambis Domatia* (☎ 0423-91 587/343), just out of Agia Kyriaki at **Mylos**. Follow a dirt road for about 500 metres and look for the Greek sign. Walk down the path and then look for the EOT sign on the wall, on your left. Haralambos Karapetis, an expat Australian-Greek, should be able to accommodate you as well. Ask around Mylos to be directed to Haralambos.

There are a couple of reasonable-looking places to eat on the waterfront, but the *Mouragio* has that more authentic fish taverna look, with tables right next to the water.

Palio Trikeri

If you really must go that one step further to get away from it all, then head for this little island just off the coast and inside the Pagasitic gulf. The Flying Dolphin is supposed to make a stop here four times a week, but you may have to ask to make sure. It's the same story with the regular ferries, except they may stop less frequently. Alternatively, you can twist someone's arm at Agia Kyriaki to take you down a farm track to the end of the headland, where they will whistle or shout to get someone to come over from the island to take you over on a caïque.

The *Palio Trikeri* domatia-cum-restaurant (☎ 0423-91 432) can probably offer you accommodation and food as can *Harikleia Brouzou-Roumbakia* (0423-91 031), which, similarly, has domatia with an attached restaurant.

Platanias Πλατανιάς

Platanias (Plat-ani-AS) is a popular resort with a good sand and pebble beach. It's a fun place to spend a day or two, even though it's quite developed. Les Hirondelles Travel Agency (☎ 71 231) rents a variety of watersports equipment, such as canoes

Places to Stay

Kastri Beach Camping (☎ 0423-71 209) is at Kastri beach, five km east of Platanias. Look for the sign pointing left on the approach road to Platanias. *Louisa Camping* (☎ 0423-71 260) is just 500 metres before Platanias.

A cheap hotel in Platanias is the D-class *Hotel Platanias* (☎ 0423-65 565), where pleasant singles/doubles/triples are 5200/ 6500/7800 dr with private bathroom. Turn left at the waterfront to reach the hotel. Another agreeable option is the D-class *Hotel des Roses* (☎ 65 568), by the bus terminal. Rates are 4500/5500 dr with shared

bathroom; doubles with private bathroom are 6500 dr.

The C-class *Hotel Drosero Akrogiali* (☎ 71 210/211) has doubles/triples for 6500/ 8200 dr with private bathroom. Turn right at the waterfront to reach this hotel.

Places to Eat

To Steki Restaurant has a large choice of well-prepared dishes. A meal here will cost you about 1800 dr with wine or beer. Turn left at the waterfront to reach this place.

Getting There & Away

Bus See the Getting There & Away section under Volos for bus services to Platanias.

Hydrofoil Hydrofoils sail daily in summer from Platanias to Skiathos (2569 dr), Glossa (2570 dr), Skopelos town (3870 dr), and Alonnisos (3870 dr). Tickets can be purchased from Les Hirondelles Travel Agency (☎ 71 231).

Getting Around Les Hirondelles Travel Agency rents motorbikes of varying sizes.

TRIKALA Τρίκαλα

Trikala (TRI-ka-la, population 48,000) is ancient Trikki, the reputed birthplace of Asclepius, the god of healing. It's a bustling agricultural town, through which flows the River Litheos, and is a major hub for buses. While Trikala's attractions hardly warrant a special trip, the chances are if you're exploring central Greece you'll eventually pass through here *en route* to somewhere else.

Orientation

Trikala's main thoroughfare is Asklipiou, the northern end of which is a pedestrian precinct. Facing the river, turn left from the bus station to reach Plateia Riga Fereou at the northern end of Asklipiou. The train station is at the opposite end of Asklipiou, 600 metres from Plateia Riga Fereou.

To reach the central square of Plateia Iroön Polytehniou turn right at Plateia Riga Fereou and cross the bridge over the river.

Information

Trikala does not have an EOT or tourist police; the regular police (☎ 32 777) are on the corner of Kapodistriou and Asklipiou. The National Bank of Greece is on the central square. The post office is at Saraphi 13; turn left at the central square and it's a little way along on the left. To reach the OTE walk along the left side of the central square and turn left onto 25 Martiou. The OTE is a little way along here on the right at the far side of a small square.

Trikala's telephone code is 0431 and the postcode is 421 01 (poste restante).

Things to See

The **River Litheos** which bisects the town is crossed by 10 bridges, half of which are for pedestrians only. The central iron bridge was built in France in 1886. At the time of writing the **Fortress of Trikala** was closed for restoration. In any case it's worth a wander up to the gardens which surround it for the views – and there's a pleasant café. Walk 400 metres up Saraphi from the central square and look for the sign pointing right. To get to Trikala's old **Turkish quarter** of Varousi, take a sharp right at the sign for the fortress. It's a fascinating area of peaceful narrow streets and fine old houses with overhanging balconies. If you keep on walking through Varousi and up the hill, you will come to the monastery of **Profitis Ilias**. It is a pleasant tree-lined walk after the town centre and you will eventually reach a **zoo** of sorts, if you keep on walking. The zoo is open from 8 am to 8 pm. If you don't mind looking at a collection of sad-looking animals – including an incongruous pair of lions – it's a pleasant enough place to spend an hour or so. Entrance is free.

At the other side of town is the **Koursoun Tzami**, a Turkish mosque built in the 16th century by Sinan Pasha, the same architect who built the Blue Mosque in Istanbul. This mosque has recently been the subject of a EU-funded restoration project and should have been restored to its former glory – minus the top of the minaret – by the time you read this. It will be used as a community

concert hall. From the bus station, turn right, follow the river and you'll reach the mosque in 300 metres.

Places to Stay – bottom end

Trikala isn't a tourist centre so finding accommodation is easy. The cheapest place is the gloomy – despite a rejuvenating face-lift of the façade – D-class *Hotel Panellinio* (☎ 27 644) on Plateia Riga Fereou. Rates are 3000/4000/5500 dr for singles/doubles/triples with shared bathroom. Practically on top of the bus station is the nice D-class *Litheon* (☎ 20 690; fax 37 390) which is being gradually renovated and has rooms for 6900/8700/11,000 dr.

The C-class *Hotel Palladion* (☎ 28 091/ 37 260), Vyronos 4, is another agreeable cheapie, with well-maintained rooms for 5000/1700 dr with shared bathroom. The hotel is behind Plateia Riga Fereou's Hotel Achillion.

Places to Stay – middle

The C-class *Hotel Dina* (☎ 74 777; fax 29 490), at Karanasiou 38, has immaculate rooms with air-con, telephone and balconies for 8200/11,000 dr. The hotel is 60 metres down from Plateia Riga Fereou, on the right. The palatial, but not particularly inspiring, B-class *Hotel Achillion* (☎ 28 291), on Plateia Riga Fereou, has rooms for 8800/12,000/15,000 dr.

Places to Stay – top end

The B-class *Hotel Divani* (☎ 27 286), Dionysiou 13 on Plateia Kitrilaki (Ethnikis Antistaseos), overlooking the river, is Trikala's best hotel, with inflated but negotiable prices. Rooms are 17,600/22,000 dr.

Places to Eat

Quality fast-food joints have sprung up all over Trikala, so if you really want your hamburger and fried chicken fix, you can't go wrong. For ready-made food at a reasonable kind of place, try *O Kostaras* on Plateia Kitrilaki. There are other eateries on this square in the warm months too.

Taverna o Babis near Hotel Dina is good

for an evening out, as is the *Pliatsikas* restaurant on Ioulietas Adam. Diagonally opposite, you might want to try *Yali Kafene*, a hip kind of ouzeri joint. *To Kellari* on Karanasiou is also worth a visit. Finally, the outdoor café *To Frourio* at the fortress is very pleasant, with an ornamental pond where extremely vigorous fountains play – watch how you go or you'll get a soaking.

Getting There & Away

Bus From Trikala's bus station there are 20 buses a day to Kalambaka (30 minutes, 340 dr); 14 to Larissa (one hour, 950 dr) seven to Athens (5½ hours, 4450 dr); six to Thessaloniki (5½ hours, 2950 dr); four to Volos (3½ hours, 2100 dr); and two to Ioannina (3½ hours, 2350 dr).

Train Trikala is on the narrow-gauge Volos-Kalambaka line. There are 10 trains a day in each direction, though only three eastbound trains go through to Volos. Connections to the main Athens-Thessaloniki line at Paleofarsalos, also called Stavros by locals, need to be planned with some care, otherwise you may be in for a long wait. Check the timetable (in Greek) at Trikala station, or get your ticket beforehand at the Trikala OSE office in town, 21 Avgoustou 1 (☎ 27 457), on the east side of Plateia Iroön Polytehniou.

AROUND TRIKALA

About 18 km from Trikala is the little village of **Pyli**, which means 'gate' – and rightly so, for just beyond Pyli is a spectacular narrow gorge leading into one of Greece's more attractive wilderness areas and one that is currently embroiled in a vigorous ecological debate. Industrial progressives, despite the protests of the ecological lobby and the local inhabitants, have been building a large, 135-metre-high dam near Mesohora village on the upper Aheloös River. Once completed, the area behind the dam, which includes two villages and three settlements, will be flooded, thereby bringing about the destruction of the area's native flora and fauna. If that isn't bad enough, the dam builders also want to divert part of the flow of the Aheloös

River to the plain of Thessaly, thus radically reducing the natural water flow of the river to the wetlands of Messolongi in Aetolo-Akarnania. This, it is claimed, would result in the destruction of the natural habitat of the bird life in the region. The debate has even reached the hallowed halls of the European Parliament and is still under heated discussion.

The area beyond Pyli is gradually being opened up to tourism. It is now possible to drive comfortably and on a very scenic, sealed road from Pyli to Arta (three hours), via Stournareïka and Mesohora and the disputed upper Aheloös dam. This provides a much-needed alternative route across the south Pindos ranges to and from Epiros. You can also travel the scenic loop through to Kalambaka and back, via the villages of Elati and Hrysomilia.

There is a small, but locally popular skiing centre at **Pertouli**, 30 km beyond Pyli. Here you will find forested, alpine scenery, reminiscent of Switzerland. Equipment can be hired here and the centre has a cosy, family atmosphere. Buses for Pertouli leave from the main bus station in Trikala.

For some time now, kayaking enthusiasts have been coming to the **Tria Potamia** area, which is 15 km north of Mesohora, to ride the waters of the Aheloös River. The sport is not as organised as it is in Konitsa in northern Epiros, but nonetheless it attracts a growing number of white-water jockeys. How long this activity will last, once the dam is plugged, is anyone's guess.

KALAMBAKA Καλαμπάκα

Kalambaka (population 12,000) is almost entirely modern, having been devastated by the Nazis in WW II. Its chief claim to fame is its proximity to Meteora. It takes a whole day to see all of the monasteries of Meteora, so you'll need to spend the night either in Kalambaka or the village of Kastraki, which is closer to the rocks. First-time visitors to Kalambaka will be amazed at the vertical rocks that guard the northern flank of the town. It is an unusual sight and gives

Kalambaka a special feel. The rocks are spectacularly illuminated at night.

Orientation

The central square is the hub of the town and the main thoroughfares of Rodou, Trikalon, Ioanninon, Kastrakiou and Vlahavas radiate from it. Kalambaka's other large square is Plateia Riga Fereou – Trikalon connects the two.

The bus station is on the right side of Rodou if you're walking from the central square. Most incoming buses stop on the central square to let passengers alight. To get to the train station from the central square walk along Trikalon, take the right fork after Plateia Riga Fereou, turn right at Kondili and the station is opposite the end of this road.

Information

There is no EOT in Kalambaka. The tourist police (☎ 22 109/813) are at Hatzipetrou 10, near the bus station.

The National Bank of Greece is on Plateia Riga Fereou. The post office and OTE are both on Ioanninon.

Kalambaka's telephone code is 0432 and the postcode is 422 00.

Places to Stay – bottom end

There are several camp sites in the area. *Theopetra Camping* (☎ 81 405/406), is the first site you come across if you're coming from Trikala. *Camping Philoxenia* (☎ 24 446) with good shade and a children's play area – including a water slide – is next on the right and *Rizos International* (☎ 22 239) is last. *Camping Kalambaka* (☎ 22 309) is on a road off to the right just before you enter Kalambaka.

There is no shortage of rooms in Kalambaka and you may well be approached as you arrive by train or bus. Choose with care. Look for the EOT-approved sign, wherever possible. *Koka Roka Rooms* (☎ 24 554), at the beginning of the path to Agia Triada Monastery, is a bit of an institution among travellers and has an impressive visitors' book. The few rooms are clean and nicely furnished and cost 6000 dr for doubles with

private bathroom. The owner is a friendly Greek-Australian. From the central square, walk 500 metres to the top of Vlahava, and you'll come to the rooms on the left.

Kalambaka's cheapest hotel is the D-class *Hotel Astoria* (☎ 22 213/23 557), G Kondili 93. The clean pine-furnished single/double/triple rooms cost 4000/5000/7000 dr. The hotel is on the road opposite the train station. The D-class *Hotel Meteora* (☎ 22 367; fax 26 550), Ploutarhou 14, is a charming and cosy place, with rooms for 6000/7500/9000 dr with private bathroom. The price includes breakfast. From the central square, walk along Kastrakiou, and Ploutarhou is the second turn right.

The C-class *Aeolic Star* (☎ 22 325; fax 23 031) on Ath Diakou 4 has clean, compact rooms for 6000/8500 dr. It is just north of the main square. The C-class *Hotel Odysseon* (☎ 22 320; fax 22 320), on Kastrakiou, heading out to Kastraki, has light, spacious rooms; rates are 8000/10,000/12,000 dr including breakfast. The *Hotel Helvetia* (☎ 23 041; fax 25 241), which is nearby at Kastrakiou 45, has very pleasant rooms for 7500/9000 dr.

Places to Stay – middle

The B-class *Hotel Famisi* (☎ 24 117/22 163; fax 24 615), Trikalon 103, has singles/doubles for 13,500/20,600 dr. All the rooms have balconies, a radio and direct-dial telephone. The hotel has a restaurant and bar.

Places to Stay – top end

A top-end choice in town is the A-class *Hotel Divani* (☎ 22 584; fax 23 638), the first hotel you come to on the left as you enter Kalambaka from Trikala. Rooms here are 18,000/22,000 dr and include breakfast.

Places to Eat

For standard look-and-point fare, the *Diethnes* restaurant is your best bet. It is on the corner of Trikalon on Plateia Riga Fereou.

The *Koka Roka Taverna*, below Koka Roka Rooms (see Places to Stay), serves tasty low-priced food in a warm and homey

CENTRAL GREECE

environment. Two enterprising young men now run the *Taverna Stathmos*, Kondili 56, which is the street directly opposite the railway station. It is open all day and operates as an ouzeri at lunch time, offering some wonderful original mezedes. At night it is a very good psistaria with some original recipes. Ask to try their stuffed steaks. Your host, Vasilis, is a Greek-Australian and will make you feel most welcome. Prices are very reasonable.

Getting There & Away
Bus From Kalambaka there are frequent buses to Trikala and to the surrounding villages and three through buses to Ioannina (three hours, 1750 dr). Five buses a day run to Metamorphosis (via Kastraki); they leave from Kalambaka's central square. There are buses to other destinations from Trikala.

Train Kalambaka is the western terminus of the narrow-gauge line to Volos. There are 10 departures a day, though only three trains go through to Volos. Connections with the main Athens-Thessaloniki line at Paleofarsalos (Stavros) need to be planned with some care, otherwise you may be in for a long wait. Check the timetable (in Greek) at the station.

Getting Around
Motorbikes can be hired from the *Hobby Shop* (☎ 25 562; fax 25 562) at Patriarhou Dimitriou 28. This is the main Kastraki road and the shop is on the right as you head out of Kalambaka. A 50-cc motorbike rental will cost you 3500 dr. They also offer a full motorbike service, and rent bicycles (1500 dr a day) and skiing gear (3000 dr a day for the full outfit). The owner also speaks English. There is another rental shop called *Moto Service* (☎ 23 526), on Meteoron. From the central square, walk along Ioanninon, turn right at the post office and the outlet is on the right.

METEORA Μετέωρα
Meteora (Me-TE-ora) is an extraordinary place. The massive pinnacles of smooth rocks with holes in them like Emmenthal cheese are ancient and yet, paradoxically, could be a setting for a science fiction story. The monasteries are the icing on the cake in this already strange and beautiful landscape.

Each monastery is built around a central courtyard surrounded by monks' cells, chapels and a refectory. In the centre of each courtyard stands the *katholikon* (main church).

History
The name Meteora derives from the adjective *meteoros*, which means suspended in the air. The word 'meteor' is from the same root. Many theories have been put forward as to the origins of this 'rock forest', but it remains a geological enigma.

From the 11th century, solitary hermit monks lived in the caverns of Meteora. By the 14th century, Byzantine power was on the wane and incursions into Greece were on the increase, so monks began to seek peaceful havens away from the bloodshed. The inaccessibility of the rocks of Meteora made them an ideal retreat, and the less safe the monks became, the higher they climbed, until eventually they were living on top of the rocks.

The earliest monasteries were reached by climbing articulated, removable ladders. Later, windlasses were used so monks could be hauled up in nets, and this method was used until the 1920s. A story goes that when apprehensive visitors enquired how frequently the ropes were replaced, the monks' stock reply was 'When the Lord lets them break'. These days access to the monasteries is by steps hewn into the rocks. Some windlasses can still be seen (you can have a good look at one at Agia Triada), but they are now used for hauling up provisions.

Monasteries
The monasteries are linked by asphalt roads, but the area is best explored on foot on the old paths, where they still exist. Strict dress codes are enforced. Women must wear skirts below their knees, men must wear long trousers and arms must be covered.

A dirt track leads in 15 minutes from

Kastraki (see below) to the **Monastery of Agios Nikolaos Anapafsas**. To reach it walk to the end of the main road in Kastraki which peters out to a dirt track. After about 10 minutes the path crosses a stream bed. Immediately after the stream, scramble up a steep slope towards the monastery which you will see perched on a rock high up on your left. You will come out on the main road just to the right of the path leading to the monastery. A slightly longer but more straightforward route is to follow the main road from Kastraki.

The Monastery of Agios Nikolaos Anapafsas was built in the 15th century. The superlative frescoes in its katholikon were painted by the monk Theophanes Strelizas from Crete. Especially beautiful is the one of Adam naming the animals. The monastery is open every day from 9 am to 6 pm. Admission is 400 dr.

On leaving the monastery, turn left onto the road and five minutes along, just before the road begins to wind, take a path off to the left. The start of the path is not marked, so look out for the sign with the white chevron on the bend. The path starts here. In five minutes you will come to a fork. Take the left fork and soon you will come to a T-junction at the base of the rocks. Turn left here and after about 20 minutes of zigzag climbing you will reach **Metamorphosis** (Grand Meteora), the best known of the monasteries.

The majestic and imposing Metamorphosis is built on the highest rock at 613 metres above sea level. Founded by St Athanasios in the 14th century, it became the richest and most powerful of the monasteries, thanks to the Serbian emperor Symeon Uros, who turned all his wealth over to the monastery and became a monk. Its katholikon has a magnificent 12-sided central dome. Its striking, although gory, series of frescoes entitled *Martyrdom of Saints* depicts the persecution of Christians by the Romans. The monastery is open from 9 am to 1 pm and 3.20 to 6 pm, but is closed on Tuesday. Entrance is 600 dr. There is a cantina selling snacks outside.

From Metamorphosis turn right on the road to reach the nearby **Varlaam**. It has fine

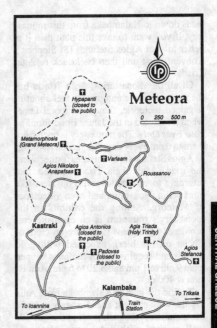

late Byzantine frescoes by Frangos Kastellanos. Varlaam is open from 9 am to 1 pm and 3.30 to 6 pm (closed on Friday). Admission is 400 dr.

On leaving Varlaam walk back to the main road and veer right. In about 15 minutes you will come to a fork: the right fork has a signpost to Roussanou and the left to Agios Stefanos. The best approach is to take the left fork and in about 10 minutes you will come to a signpost pointing right to Roussanou. A 10-minute walk along this path will lead to **Moni Roussanou**; access is across a vertiginous bridge. The katholikon features more gory frescoes. Roussanou is open from 9 am to 6 pm every day. Admission is 400 dr.

After Roussanou you have the choice of either a short walk to the Agios Nikolaos-Metamorphosis road or going back along the path and continuing along the road to Agia Triada. If you decide to do this you will reach Agia Triada in about 45 minutes (you may be able to hitch a lift on this stretch). A path

CENTRAL GREECE

leads down to Kalambaka from this monastery. If you want to take this path then it is better to visit Agios Stefanos (St Stephen's Convent) first and then backtrack to Agia Triada.

Of all the monasteries, **Agia Triada** has the most primitive and remote feel about it. It gained meteoric, though temporal fame, when it featured in the James Bond film *For Your Eyes Only*. The monastery is open from 9 am to 6 pm every day. Admission is 400 dr.

Agios Stefanos is 30 minutes further along the road. After Agia Triada it feels like returning to civilisation, with business-like nuns selling souvenirs and even videotapes of Meteora. Among the exhibits in the monastery's **museum** is an exquisite embroidered Epitaphios (a picture on cloth of Christ on his bier), executed with gold threads and sequins. Agios Stefanos is open from 9 am to 1 pm and 3.20 to 6 pm. Admission is 400 dr.

To find the path to Kalambaka from Agia Triada, walk straight ahead when you leave the monastery; the path is off to the left. It's well marked with red arrows, dots and slashes. The monks will tell you this walk takes 10 minutes, but unless you're James Bond or have the agility of a mountain goat, it'll take you around 30 minutes. On the walk there are tremendous views of the rocks at close quarters, where you see not only their dramatic contours but the details of their strata, too. The path ends near the Koka Roka Taverna in Kalambaka.

Activities

Meteora Adventures (fax 0432-23 134) runs a rock-climbing school for beginners, and rock-climbing packages in the Meteora region for both beginner and advanced climbers. The summer school is located at the entrance of Vrachos Camping in Kastraki. For further information contact Meteora Adventures, attention Jane Balistreri & Michael Klein, Kastraki, PO Box 4, 422 00 Kalambaka. Meteora is a mecca for rock climbers and if you are one of those people whose feet are firmly and permanently planted on terra firma, you will not cease to be amazed at the daily spectacle of fly-like climbers inching their way up those almost vertical pillars of rock that dot Meteora.

KASTRAKI Καστράκι

The small village of Kastraki, with its 1500 residents, nestles at the foot of the rocks, two km from Kalambaka. Its location right under the rocks is most impressive and the view all around the village has an other-world feel about it, since there is really no other place in Greece quite like it. Despite its small size, more than a million people pass through here each year, so it can feel a bit crowded at times. As an alternative base for exploring the Meteora monasteries, or climbing the rocks themselves, Kastraki is a much better choice than Kalambaka.

There is a nice walk from Kastraki to Kalambaka along the base of the rocks. From the main square take the steps down and follow the road opposite up the hill. Turn right at the top and follow the road until you reach the junction with the main road after about 10 minutes' walking. There are a couple of scenically located benches along the way, if you feel like taking in the views for a few minutes. Kalambaka is a brisk 15-minute walk away.

Places to Stay

Camping If you decide to stay here *Vrachos Camping* (☎ 0432-22 293; fax 23 134), on the left as you enter the village, has excellent facilities and a swimming pool. The sites are reasonably level and many are powered. The toilet blocks are new and there is a communal eating area. Kastraki also has a couple of other camping sites should this one be full: the *Meteora Garden* and *Boufidis Camping*.

Hotels *Zozas Pallas* (☎ 24 408; fax 25 344) has very luxurious singles/doubles/triples for 4000/8000/10,000 dr with private bathroom. The rooms are on the left (west) side of the Kalambaka-Kastraki road. One hundred metres further up towards the village is the newer establishment *Spanias Rooms* (☎ 26 966), with ample car parking and a relaxed and spacious environment. Rooms at Spanias go for 5500/7000/8000 dr. Both Zozas and Spanias have a bar and cafeteria and both are more like hotels than your average domatia. There are more domatia, too numerous to mention, scattered throughout the village.

The C-class *Hotel France* (☎ 24 186; fax 24 186), opposite Vrachos Camping, is run by a French-speaking Greek man and his wife who can fill you in on some 'hidden' walks around the rocks. Really good singles/doubles/triples here go for 5000/7000/9000 dr. The hotel also has a restaurant and bar.

Places to Eat

There is no shortage of eating places here, but prices reflect Kastraki's popularity as a tourist destination. Opposite Vrachos Camping is the unmarked *Dellas Psistaria*, which serves standard fare at a reasonable price. Further up the main road to the monasteries is the *Philoxenia Restaurant* which is open year-round. Their speciality is moussaka. It's on the main road, so you'll have to put up with the passing tourist traffic. There are a number of places around the main village square area, away from the traffic. Look out for the *Gardenia* or the *Platania*.

NORTHERN GREECE

Northern Greece comprises the regions of Epiros, Macedonia and Thrace. With thickly forested mountains and tumbling rivers, these areas resemble the Balkans more than they do other parts of Greece. Northern Greece offers great opportunities for trekking, but it is an area where you don't have to go into the wilds to get off well-worn tourist tracks, for its towns are little visited by foreign holiday-makers. Unlike the unglamorous and noisy towns of the Peloponnese and central Greece, many of which serve as transport hubs to get out of quickly, most towns in northern Greece have considerable appeal, with atmospheric old quarters of narrow streets and wood-framed houses.

Epiros Ηπειρος

Epiros occupies the north-west corner of the Greek mainland. To the north is Albania, to the west is the Ionian Sea and Corfu. Its port of Igoumenitsa is a jumping-off point for ferries to Corfu and Italy. The high Pindos

mountains form the region's eastern boundary, separating it from Macedonia and Thessaly.

The road from Ioannina to Kalambaka cuts through the Pindos mountains and is one of the most scenically spectacular in Greece, particularly the section between Metsovo and Kalambaka, which is called the Katara pass. In northern Epiros the Vikos-Aoös National Park is a wilderness of lofty mountains, cascading waterfalls, precipitous gorges, fast-flowing rivers and dense forests harbouring villages of slatestone houses. These settlements are known as the Zagorohoria villages (Zagoria).

The beaches fronting the Ionian Sea are popular with Greeks, and with visiting Italians and Germans. The oracle at Dodoni predates the more illustrious oracle of Delphi.

History

In early times Epiros' remote mountainous terrain was divided into tribes which were unaffected by, and oblivious to, what was happening in the rest of the country. Eventually one tribe, the Molossi, became so powerful that it dominated the whole region, and its leader became king of Epiros. The most renowned of these was King Pyrrhus (319-272 BC), whose foolhardy fracas in Italy against the Romans gave rise to the phrase 'Pyrrhic victory' – a victory achieved at too great a cost.

King Pyrrhus came to an undignified end. After unsuccessful attempts to gain control of Macedonia and parts of Rome he decided to have a go at Argos. As he entered the city, an old woman threw a tile from her rooftop which hit him on the head and killed him.

Epiros fell to the Turks in 1431, although its isolation ensured it a great degree of autonomy. It became part of independent Greece in 1913 when the Greek army seized it from the Turks during the second Balkan War. During WW II many Greeks took to the

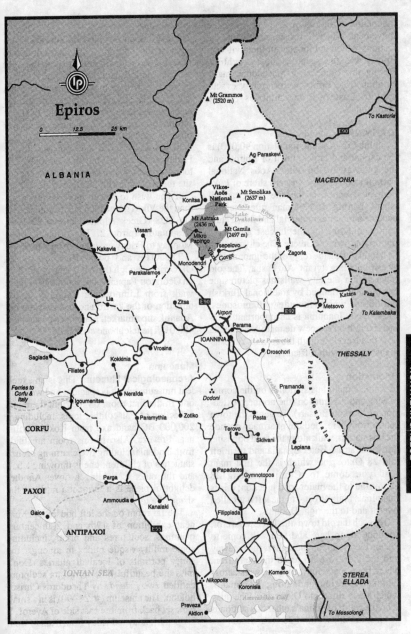

mountains of Epiros in a strong resistance movement. When the resistance split into the factions which culminated in the civil war, Epiros was the scene of heavy fighting. During this time, as in Macedonia, many children from Epiros were forcibly evacuated to Eastern-bloc countries by the communists.

IOANNINA Ιωάννινα

Ioannina (Yo-AN-ina; population 90,000) is the capital and largest town of Epiros, and the gateway to the Vikos-Aoös National Park. It stands on the western shore of Lake Pamvotis, which is the site of a tranquil island. During the Ottoman rule Ioannina became a major commercial and intellectual centre and one of the largest and most important towns in Greece. The city reached its height during the reign of the ignominious swash-buckling tyrant Ali Pasha. The old town within the city walls has picturesque narrow lanes flanked by traditional Turkish buildings, which include two mosques. These days, Ioannina is an important commercial hub on the new de facto Via Egnatia now that travel through the former Yugoslavia is fraught with difficulty.

Orientation

Ioannina's main bus station is on the corner of Sina and Zosimadon (the northern extension of Markou Botsari). To get to the town centre from here, find the pharmacy outside the bus station, walk along the road opposite, turn right at the Hotel Egnatia and then left into 28 Oktovriou which is the first main road you come to. Continue along 28 Oktovriou to the major road junction; this is Ioannina's main street – to the left it is called Averof and to the right Dodonis.

To reach the old town turn left into Averof, continue along here and you will come to Plateia Georgiou; on the right is the gateway into the old town. To reach the quay from where boats leave for the island, walk across Plateia Georgiou and along Karamanli, which veers right into Dionysiou. The quay is on the right. Ioannina's other bus station is at Vizaniou 28, south of 28 Oktovriou.

Information

The EOT is on Napoleonda Zerva 2. Turn right at the bottom of 28 Oktovriou into Dodonis and you will come to it on the right set back on a square. Most people come to Epiros to trek in the mountains, and Ioannina is a good place to get information or arrange an organised trek. For example, the EOT has information on the Vikos gorge trek. The office is open all year round from 7.30 am to 2.30 pm and 5.30 to 8.30 pm Monday to Friday, and 9 am to 2 pm on a Saturday. The tourist police (☎ 25 673 or 26 226) are opposite the post office on 28 Oktovriou.

If you wish to trek in more remote areas than the Vikos gorge then talk to someone at the EOS (Greek Alpine Club; ☎ 22 138), Despotatou Ipirou 2. The office is open Monday to Friday evenings from 7 to 9 pm.

The OTE and post office are on 28 Oktovriou, though there is a new post office on Georgiou Papandreou, about a 10-minute walk from Limnopoula Camping in the direction of the kastro and just past the big Atlantik supermarket. Ioannina's postcode is 450 01. The telephone code is 0651.

Museums

Archaeological Museum This is an excellent museum which is spacious and well laid out. In the first room on the right there is a collection of Palaeolithic tools, including a 200,000 BC hand axe from Kokkinopolis, near Preveza. Also in this room are finds from Dodoni including two charming bronze statuettes of children; one is throwing a ball and the other is holding a dove. Another delightful piece is a terracotta rattle in the shape of a tortoise.

The far room on the left houses a permanent exhibition of 19th and 20th-century paintings, sculptures and prints, including some mildly risqué nudes in amongst the stuffy portraits of local dignitaries. Don't miss the beautiful little terracotta sculpture entitled *Two Friends* by Theodoros Chrisohoïdou. The museum (☎ 24 490) is in a small park set back from the east side of Averof. It is open Monday to Friday from 8 am to 7 pm all year round. Admission is 400 dr, or 220 dr with student card.

Popular Art Museum This museum (☎ 26356), also known as the Municipal Museum, is housed in the Aslan Pasha mosque, in the old town. Its eclectic collection includes some local costumes and photographs of old Ioannina. It's open Monday to Friday from 8 am to 3 pm and weekends from 9 am to 3 pm. Admission is 500 dr, or 200 dr with student card.

Folkloric Museum This museum is located at Michael Angelou 42 and is open only on Monday from 5.30 pm to 8 pm and Wednesday from 10 am to 1 pm. Admission is 100 dr. This museum contains a small display of local costumes, embroidery and cooking utensils.

Vrellis Wax Museum This museum is a mini Madame Tussaud's, but with an emphasis on modern Greek history. At the time of writing it was about to be relocated from the small village of Mouzakeï to a new building in Bizani, 14 km out of Ioannina, on the road to Athens.

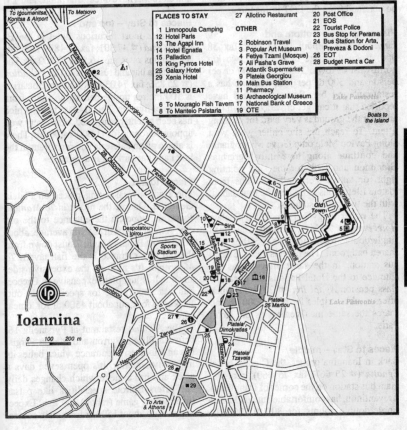

PLACES TO STAY	27 Allotino Restaurant	20 Post Office
1 Limnopoula Camping	**OTHER**	21 EOS
12 Hotel Paris		22 Tourist Police
13 The Agapi Inn	2 Robinson Travel	23 Bus Stop for Perama
14 Hotel Egnatia	3 Popular Art Museum	24 Bus Station for Arta,
15 Palladion	4 Fetiye Tzami (Mosque)	Preveza & Dodoni
18 King Pyrros Hotel	5 Ali Pasha's Grave	26 EOT
25 Galaxy Hotel	7 Atlantik Supermarket	28 Budget Rent a Car
29 Xenia Hotel	9 Plateia Georgiou	
	10 Main Bus Station	
PLACES TO EAT	11 Pharmacy	
6 To Mouragio Fish Tavern	16 Archaeological Museum	
8 To Manteio Psistaria	17 National Bank of Greece	
	19 OTE	

Ioannina

0   100   200 m

To Igoumenitsa, Konitsa & Airport
To Metsovo
To Arta & Athens
Old Town
Lake Pamvotis
Boats to the Island

NORTHERN GREECE

Organised Treks

Robinson Travel (☎ 29 402; fax 27 071), 8 Merarhias Grammou 10, specialises in treks to remote areas of Epiros. These eight, 10, 12 and 15-day treks cost approximately 10,000 dr per day inclusive.

Every Sunday between October and June the Ioannina EOS (see Information) organises a one-day trek in the Pindos mountains. Anyone is welcome and the cost is approximately 1500 dr per person.

Festivals

During July and August a festival of ancient drama takes place at the restored theatre at the nearby site of Dodoni. Information may be obtained from the EOT in Ioannina.

Places to Stay – bottom end

Limnopoula Camping (☎ 25 265; fax 38 060) is on the edge of the lake, two km north-west of town. The cost is 800 dr per person and 500 dr per tent. The site has a restaurant and bar. Some travellers have reported that it can get crowded in summer and that the ground is very hard for pitching a tent. To reach the site either walk west along Pavlou Mela onto Griva Mavrogianni and continue along here into Merarhias Grammou and look for the sign pointing right, or take a Perama-bound bus from Plateia Eleftherias. Alight at the roundabout with the two petrol stations.

The rather dingy but functional D-class *Hotel Paris* (☎ 20 541), Tsirigoti 6, has clean single/double rooms for 4000/6500 dr with shared bathroom. The hotel is near the main bus station. In the same alleyway as the entrance to the Hotel Paris is the cheap E-class pension *Agapi Inn* (☎ 20 541) which offers doubles/triples for 4000/6000 dr, and shares the same management as the Hotel Paris.

Places to Stay – middle

Back in Ioannina proper, the C-class *Hotel Egnatia* (☎ 25 667; fax 75 060), near the main bus station on the corner of Dangli and Aravantinou, has comfortable but unadorned single/double rooms for 8000/11,000 dr,

with private bathroom. The C-class *King Pyrros Hotel* (☎ 27 652), Gounari 3, charges 6000/8000 dr for rooms with a private bathroom; some rooms have TV. Gounari is opposite the clock tower on Averof. At Tsirigoti 10, near the Agapi Inn, is the comfortable and family-oriented C-class *Dioni* (☎ 27 864; fax 27 032) which has rooms for 7500/10,700 dr with TV and direct-dial phone. On King Pyrros square, nestled away in the far right corner, as you face the square from Dodonis is the decidedly pleasant and modern C-class *Galaxy Hotel* (☎ 25 432; fax 25 032) with rooms for 9000/13,000 dr. The Galaxy has fine views and all rooms have direct-dial phone and TV.

Places to Stay – top end

Ioannina's most luxurious hotel is the B-class *Xenia* (☎ 47 301; fax 47 189), Dodonis 33. Rooms rates are 16,500/23,300 dr. The hotel has a bar and restaurant. The *Palladion* (☎ 25 856; fax 74 034), at Markou Botsari 1, is 100 metres up the pedestrian street from the Hotel Egnatia. This B-class hotel, which has been recently renovated, offers very well appointed rooms for 11,000/14,000 dr. There is also a plush cafeteria and restaurant in the hotel and car parking is available.

Places to Eat

There are several eating places on Plateia Georgiou. One of the nicest is *To Manteio Psistaria*, opposite the entrance to the old city. A meal here will cost, on average, about 2000 dr. At Plateia Mavili 7, just down from the old city entrance is the fish tavern *To Mouragio*. It's a bit on the expensive side, since fish is just plain expensive in Greece, but is a good place for special night out. Expect to fork out about 4500 dr for a meal here.

The *Allotino* restaurant at Pyrsinella 16, between Plateia Pyrrou and Plateia Pargis, has an unobtrusive entrance which belies its impressive interior. It's open seven days a week and has a menu which changes daily and offers Epirote specialities like patsas (tripe soup), game (rabbit) and fish. Expect to part with about 1500 dr for a main course.

NORTHERN GREECE

Flokati

There are few better souvenirs of a visit to Greece than the luxuriant woollen flokati rugs produced in the mountain areas of central and northern Greece. They make beautiful, cosy floor coverings.

The process by which these rugs are produced has changed little over the centuries. The first step is to weave a loose woollen base. Short lengths of twisted wool are then looped through it, leaving the two ends on top to form the pile – the more loops, the denser the pile. At this point, the rug looks like a scalp after stage one of a hair transplant – a series of unconvincing little tufts. The twisted threads can easily be pulled through.

A transformation takes place during the next stage, the 'waterfall treatment'. The rugs are immersed in fast, running water for between 24 and 36 hours, unravelling the twisted wool and shrinking the base so that the pile is held fast. They can then be dyed.

The main production areas are the villages of Epiros, around the town of Tripolis in the Peloponnese and around the towns of Trikala and Karditsa in Thessaly. All these villages have plenty of the running water required for the waterfall treatment.

The rugs are sold by weight. A rug measuring 150 x 60 cm will cost from 10,000 to 40,000 dr, depending on the length and density of the pile. ∎

Things to Buy

Ioannina has for a long time been a centre for the manufacture of filigree silver. Shops selling this type of jewellery line Averof and Karamanli. Prices start at around 4000 dr for rings and earrings. You can also buy various wood carvings and other tourist-oriented items from the same area. Epiros is also famous for its flokati rugs, also known as *velenzes*.

Getting There & Away

Air There are at least two flights a day to Athens (15,800 dr) and flights to Thessaloniki (10,000 dr) on Friday, Saturday, Sunday and Monday. The Olympic Airways office (☎ 26 218) is on the right side of Dodonis as you walk towards the EOT.

Bus From the main bus station there are nine buses a day to Igoumenitsa (2½ hours, 1500 dr); nine to Athens (7½ hours, 6000 dr) and 11 to Konitsa (two hours, 950 dr); five to Thessaloniki (seven hours, 5000 dr); four to Metsovo (1½ hours, 900 dr); two to Trikala (3½ hours, 2250 dr) and one to Parga (three hours, 1500 dr). Buses to the Zagorohoria also leave from this bus station. The schedule is as follows: Papingo villages (Monday, Wednesday and Friday at 5.30 am and 2.30 pm, Sunday 9.30 am; two hours, 900 dr); Tsepelovo (Monday to Friday at 6 am and 3 pm, with an additional bus in summer at 9 am on Monday, Wednesday and Friday; 1½ hours, 750 dr); Monodendri (Monday to Friday at 5.30 am and 4.15 pm; 1½ hours, 600 dr).

From Ioannina's other bus station, at Vizaniou 28, there are 10 buses a day to Arta (2½ hours, 1500 dr); and two buses a day to Patras (4½ hours, 3500 dr). Buses also leave here for Preveza, Parga and Dodoni (see the Dodoni Getting There & Away section for details).

Car Budget Rent a Car (☎ 43 901) is at Dodonis 109, though they have a booth at Ioannina airport to meet all incoming flights.

To/From Albania See the Getting There & Away chapter for information on going to/from Albania from Ioannina.

Getting Around

To/From the Airport Ioannina's airport is five km north-west of town on the road to Perama. Take bus No 7, which runs every 20 minutes from the bus stop just south of Averof, near the clock tower. Bus Nos 1 and 2 run less frequently, but they also go past the airport.

Bus & Taxi The local bus service covers most parts of Ioannina. Buses from the lakefront usually take you up to the main square. Buy your ticket before you board the bus. There is a ticket kiosk near the Olympic Airways office. If you plan to use the bus system more than once, it is a good idea to purchase books of tickets, to save your being caught without a return ticket. Within the central area a single-trip ticket costs 85 dr. If you have a travelling companion, it is probably cheaper to take a taxi.

AROUND IOANNINA
The Island Το Νησί

This traffic-free island is a serene place to wander around. It has four monasteries and a whitewashed village which was built in the 17th century by refugees from the Mani in the Peloponnese. It is now permanent home to about 90 families. If you wish to stay here, there are also some domatia.

The **Moni Panteleimonos**, where Ali Pasha was killed, houses a small museum. The museum was damaged when a tree fell on it during a storm and in July 1992 Greek culture minister Anna Psarouda-Benaki ordered the funding of 55 million drachmas for repairs. This caused an outcry amongst Greek feminists who stated it was inappropriate for a woman minister to support a museum which commemorates a man who put women into sacks and drowned them. The museum has been rebuilt using the original stones. Entry is 100 dr and is usually open as long as the ferry is running.

The monastery is signposted, as are all the other monasteries on the island.

Places to Stay & Eat Sotirios Dellas (☎ 81 894) rents pleasant *domatia* for 4500/5500 dr. From the quay walk straight ahead along Monahon Nektariou for about 100 metres till you come to a square where the primary school is located. You will see a sign on your right leading you to the Saraï, a small square where Sotirios has his rooms. Look for the EOT sign. Another possibility are the nearby *domatia* of Varvara Varvaka (☎ 81 596). Rates are about the same price as at Sotirios', but are always negotiable.

For a memorable meal in a lakeside setting, head for the *Gripos* restaurant. It is to the right as you disembark from the ferry, is very good and serves exquisite grilled trout. The *Pamvotis* restaurant, to the left of the quay is owned by the same proprietor and

---

Ali Pasha

Ali Pasha, one of the most flamboyant characters of recent Greek history, was born in 1741 in the village of Tepelini in Albania. In 1787 the Turks made him Pasha of Trikala and by 1788 he ruled Ioannina. His life was a catalogue of brigandage, murder, warfare and debauchery.

Tales abound about Ali. He supposedly had a harem of 400 women, but as if that were not enough he was also enamoured of Kyra Frosyni, his eldest son's mistress. When she rejected his amorous overtures, she and 15 other women were put into sacks and tipped into the lake.

Ali's sons seem to have taken after their father: one was a sex maniac who was in the habit of raping women; the other had the more innocuous hobby of collecting erotic literature.

Ali's lifelong ambition was to break away from the Ottoman Empire and create an independent state. In 1797 he collaborated with Napoleon, but in 1798 he wrested Preveza from the French. In 1817 he courted the British, who rewarded him with Parga.

In 1822 Sultan Mahmud II decided he had had enough of Ali's opportunistic and fickle alliances and sent his troops to execute him. The 82-year-old Ali took refuge on the 1st floor of the guesthouse of Agios Panteleimon monastery on the island, but was killed when the troops fired bullets at him through the ceiling from below. Ali was then beheaded, and his head paraded around Epiros before being buried in Constantinople (İstanbul) – the rest of his body was buried in Ioannina. ∎

NORTHERN GREECE

is equally good and more likely to be open in the low season.

Getting There & Away There are boats every half-hour to the island (10 minutes, 150 dr). They usually run every hour in winter and every half-hour in summer. They leave from near the gate to the fortress, 50 metres west of Plateia Mavili.

Perama Cave Σπήλαιο Περάματος
This cave (☎ 0651-81 521), four km north of Ioannina, is one of the largest in Greece. It was discovered in 1940 by locals searching for a hiding place from the Nazis, and explored by the speleologists Ioannis and Anna Petrohilos, who also explored the Diros caves in the Peloponnese. The Perama cave is second in Greece only to the Diros caves in its astonishing array of stalactites and stalagmites. It consists of many chambers and passageways and is 1100 metres long. It's open from 8 am to 8 pm. Admission is 800 dr; 400 dr if you have a student card.

Getting There & Away Take bus No 8 from near the clock tower for the village of Perama. The buses run every 20 minutes.

Dodoni Δωδώνη
Dodoni, 21 km south-west of Ioannina and lying in a fertile valley at the foot of Mt Tomaros, is Epiros' most important ancient site.

The site's opening times change frequently, so enquire at the EOT in Ioannina. Admission is 400 dr.

History An earth goddess was worshipped here as long ago as 2000 BC. She spoke through an oracle which was reputedly the oldest in Greece. By the 13th century BC Zeus had taken over and it was believed he spoke through the rustling of leaves from a sacred oak tree. Around 500 BC a temple to Zeus was built, but only the foundations and a few columns of this and other smaller temples remain. The oracle was the most important in Greece until it was superseded by the Delphic oracle.

Exploring the Site The site's colossal 3rd-century BC **theatre**, an ambitious project overseen by King Pyrrhus, has been restored, and is now the site of the Festival of Ancient Drama (see under Festivals in the Ioannina section for details). To the north of the theatre a gate leads to the **acropolis**; part of its once substantial walls are still standing. To the east of the theatre are the foundations of the **bouleuterion** (council house) and a small temple dedicated to Aphrodite. Close by are the scant remains of the **Sanctuary of Zeus**. This sacred precinct was the site of the oracle of Zeus and the sacred oak.

Christianity also left its mark on Dodoni, as evidenced by the remains of a 6th-century Byzantine basilica, which was built over the remains of a sanctuary dedicated to Heracles.

Places to Stay The *Pension Andromahi* (☎ 82 296) is in the village of Dodoni, near the site.

Getting There & Away The bus service to Dodoni is pretty abysmal considering it's Epiros' major ancient site. There are buses from Ioannina on Monday, Tuesday, Wednesday, Friday and Saturday at 6.30 am and 4.30 pm. There are no buses on a Thursday and only one bus on a Sunday at 6 pm, which returns at 6.45 pm.

Buses leave from Ioannina's Vizaniou bus station for the village of Dodoni, and return at 7.30 am and 5.30 pm. An alternative is to get a Zotiko bus which stops 1.5 km from the site. This bus leaves the Bizaniou bus station on Monday, Wednesday and Friday at 5.30 am and 2 pm and returns at 7.15 am and 4.30 pm. If your interest in archaeology is not enough to get you out of bed at dawn, then a taxi will cost around 4500 dr return plus 600 dr per hour of waiting time.

THE ZAGOROHORIA Ζαγοροχώρια
The 44 Zagoria villages lie north of Ioannina in the region of Zagoria. The villages are collectively known as the Zagorohoria. This area offers some breathtaking vistas and is drawing more and more visitors. As with many inaccessible mountainous areas in

Greece, the Zagorohoria maintained a high degree of autonomy in Turkish times, so their economy and culture flourished.

An outstanding feature of the villages is their architecture. The houses are built entirely of slate from the surrounding mountains – a perfect blending of nature and architecture. With their winding, cobbled and stepped streets the villages could have leapt straight out of a Grimms' fairy tale. Some of the villages are sadly depopulated, with only a few elderly inhabitants, whilst others, like Papingo, Monodendri and Tsepelovo, are beginning to thrive on the new-found tourism in the area.

Good roads connect most of the villages, and with a car you can see many of them in one day.

The Vikos-Aoös National Park encompasses much of the area. Within the park is the Tymfi massif which is part of the north Pindos range and comprises Mt Astraka, Mt Gamila and Mt Tsouka Rossa, the Vikos gorge and the Aoös River gorge. It's an area of outstanding natural beauty and is becoming popular with trekkers. So far it is untouched by mass tourism, but several companies organise treks in the region, including the British-based Exodus Expeditions and Robinson Travel Agency in Ioannina.

The area is thickly forested; hornbeam, maple, willow and oak predominate, but there are also fir, pine and cedar trees. Bears, wolves, wild boars, wild cats, wild goats and the rare Rissos quadruped roam the mountains. Vlach and Sarakatsani shepherds still live a seminomadic existence taking their flocks up to high grazing ground in the summer and returning to the valleys in the autumn.

The telephone code (excluding Konitsa) for the Zagorohoria is 0653. For information about buses to these villages, see Ioannina's Getting There & Away section.

Vikos Gorge Χαράδρα του Βίκου

The focal point of the region is the 10-km-long Vikos gorge, which begins at the village of **Monodendri** (elevation 1090 metres), at the southern end of the gorge. Monodendri is 38 km north of Ioannina, and is reached by taking a right-hand turn from the main Ioannina-Konitsa road.

The Vikos gorge is the most trekked gorge in Greece, after the Samaria gorge on Crete. It doesn't require any special expertise but it is a strenuous walk of around 7½ hours ending at the twin villages of either **Megalo Papingo** or **Mikro Papingo**. Climbing boots are the best footwear, but trainers will suffice. You can tackle the gorge from either end, but if you have come by car, you will have to arrange a lift back to your vehicle via the long road route. Before you come to Monodendri visit the EOT or the EOS in Ioannina. They whom will give you a map of the gorge, and answer any questions you may have. Whatever you do, come prepared for some serious walking; this is not a Sunday afternoon stroll in the park.

At the far end of Monodendri there is a spectacular view down into the gorge from the 15th-century **Moni Agias Paraskevis**. The descent into the gorge is down a steep marked path between the village and the monastery. Once in the gorge, it's a four-hour walk to the end, from where a trail up to the right leads, in 2½ hours, to the settlement of Mikro Papingo. The larger settlement of Megalo Papingo is two km west of here, but the track splits into two at the base of the climb. Klima spring, about halfway along the gorge, is the only source of water, so take plenty along with you.

If you come by road to Papingo, the view is awe-inspiring as you approach the village from the bed of the **Voïdomatis River**, after you have passed through **Aristi**, the last village before Papingo. There are no less than 15 hairpin bends that switchback in rapid succession up to the ledge where the Papingo villages nestle under the looming hulk of Mt Gamila. As you wind your way up, there are breath-stopping views into the Vikos gorge on your right.

Papingo is popular with wealthy Greeks, attested to by the large number of Athens and Thessaloniki-registered Mercedes-Benzs and BMWs that make the trip up, so be prepared to pay for services accordingly. Trekkers with less lavish means can buy some food items, though it might be a good idea to stock up on provisions from Ioannina before you come, since there are limited supplies in the Papingo villages.

Places to Stay & Eat Monodendri's choicest accommodation is the lovely traditional *Monodendri Pension & Restaurant* (☎ 61 233), where doubles are 8100 dr. The restaurant serves reasonably priced, well-prepared food. The pension is in the middle of the village. Another pleasant place is the *Vikos Pension* (☎ 61 232), with doubles for 8750 dr. There are also rooms available in private houses – enquire at the restaurant.

Megalo Papingo has domatia and a couple of hostelries. The *Xenonas tou Kouli* (☎ 41 138, 41 115) has six rooms in various combinations costing from 7000 to 12,000 dr for singles/quadruples. There is a minimarket and café-bar as well. It is best to book in advance. The owners of this place also serve as official EOS tour guides. The *Xenonas Kalliopi* (☎ 41 081) on the south side of the village has eight rooms, again in various combinations ranging in price from 8000/12,000 dr for singles/triples. There is also a small restaurant-bar here serving home cooking and the regional specialities, pittes, which are oven-baked pies made from filo pastry and various delicious fillings.

Mikro Papingo has one nice place to stay – the *Xenonas Dias* (☎ 41 257/ 41 892) with 12 rooms for 9500/11,000/13,000 dr for doubles/triples/quads. There is also a little restaurant for breakfast and meals and the place is open all year round.

For a special treat, try *Nikos Tsoumanis Restaurant*. He offers local pittes, among other regular fare and has a good wine selection. Expect to pay between 3000 and 4000 dr.

Mt Gamila to Tselepovo

From Mikro Papingo there is a good marked path to the *Gamila Refuge* (1950 metres) (also called Rodovoli Refuge) which is owned by the EOS in Megalo Papingo (☎ 41 138/230), from whom you must get the key. Water is available at the refuge and, if it is fully booked, you can camp on the front porch.

From this refuge there are marked trails to Drakolimni (dragon) lake (1½ hours) and to the village of Tsepelovo (four hours). For rock climbers there are over 20 routes up Mt Astraka. The EOS in Ioannina gives out a leaflet detailing these.

Tsepelovo Τσεπέλοβο

Tsepelovo is a delightful Zagoria village, 51 km north of Ioannina. There are many opportunities for scenic day walks from the village.

Places to Stay The *Gouris Pension* (☎ 81 214/288) is an immaculate place where doubles cost 7000 dr. The enterprising owner, Alexis Gouris, also runs a grocery shop and restaurant in the village. He speaks excellent English and is very knowledgeable about treks in the area, and will happily pass on information to tourists. From the village bus stop, take the road leading uphill to the left from the square to reach Alexis' shop and rooms. Alexis' new 55-bed B-class hotel, the *Hagiati* (☎ 0653-81 301), is located just outside the village and has a swimming pool. Its furnished apartments go for 10,500 dr.

KONITSA Κόνιτσα

Konitsa (KO-nit-sa, population 4000), 64 km north of Ioannina, is the largest settlement in the area. It's a lively market town and is a good base from which to explore the northern Zagorohoria. In recent times, it has become a centre of sorts for kayaking and trekking in the Vikos-Aoös National Park. Konitsa is built amphitheatrically on a hillside, and the view over the Voïdomatis valley, as the sun sets over the mountains in Albania is quite a sight. A serpentine road leads up to Konitsa's centre from the main Ioannina-Kozani road.

Information

The bus station is on the central square, where you will also find the post office and

NORTHERN GREECE

the National Bank of Greece. There is no EOT or tourist police. Konitsa's postcode is 441 00 and the telephone code is 0655.

Things to See & Do

Museums There is a small **folkloric museum** just above To Dentro guesthouse. The opening hours are erratic, so check with the staff at the guesthouse. Opposite the town hall near the main square there is a **natural history museum** organised by the Konitsa Hunting Club!

Walk to Stomio Monastery (Μονή Στομίου) This scenic walk along the Aoös River gorge takes about 1½ hours. Cross the stone bridge at the beginning of the town (coming from Ioannina), turn left and follow the Aoös River to the waterfall. Cross the bridge and follow the path up to the monastery. Occasionally there is a lone monk in residence here who shows visitors around the monastery, but even if you find it locked, the walk is worth it for the tremendous views.

Adventure Sports Paddler (☎ & fax 23 101), at Averof 16, organises kayaking, rafting, canyoning, paragliding and trekking expeditions. Ask for Nikos Kyritsis, or call 22 385 and ask for Mihalis Oikonomou.

Places to Stay & Eat

To Dentro Guesthouse (☎ 22 055 or 23 001; fax 22 055), 500 metres before the town centre on the Ioannina road, is Konitsa's best deal. Look out for the bright orange coloured exterior on the last bend of the road up to the main square. It has beautifully furnished, spotless doubles/triples for 6000/9000 dr with private bath. Ioannis, the owner, can advise on local walks. To Dentro also has the best restaurant in town. Spaghetti bolognese is a good bet and trout is an equally good choice, but make sure you ask for their speciality; grilled feta with chilli and tomato.

If To Dentro is full, the *Hotel Tymfi* (☎ 22 035), next to the bus station, has functional but clean doubles/triples for 6600/9200 dr. The *Hotel Pindos* is a rather dilapidated-looking place. Technically it's open, but

don't bet on it. Down near the old bridge is the *Potamolithos* (☎ 23 304) which is a stone-clad hostel offering domatia. This place is very conveniently placed for the Aoös River gorge walks. Look for the wooden sign 100 metres along the Konitsa turn-off road.

There are plenty of other rooms for rent in high season. If you have time to pick and choose, look for the ones with the yellow-and-blue EOT sign.

There is a fast-food joint and a *psistaria* on the main square. There is also a small *supermarket* on the main market street behind the post office.

Getting There & Away

From Monday to Friday there are seven buses to Ioannina (two hours, 950 dr) from Konitsa; and on weekends there are four buses. Two buses a day from Ioannina to Kozani (2460 dr) pass through here. If you want to go further, go to Kozani first, then take another bus onwards from there. There are also buses from Ioannina to Thessaloniki that pass through Konitsa once a week in winter (Monday, 4450 dr), and twice a week (Monday and Friday) in summer.

METSOVO Μέτσοβο

The village of Metsovo (MET-sov-o, population 2800, elevation 1116 metres) sprawls down a mountainside just south of the Katara pass, at the junction of Epiros, Thessaly and Macedonia, 58 km from Ioannina and 90 km from Trikala. The inhabitants are descendants of Vlach shepherds, most of whom have hung up their crooks to make a living in the tourist trade.

Metsovo has many tourist trappings: locals dressed in traditional costumes, local handcrafts, regional cuisine, stone-built mansions, invigorating air, a superb mountain setting and good conditions for skiing. Some visitors find the village twee and artificial, while others are enamoured of its considerable charm.

Despite its peasant origins, Metsovo attracts an urban set and there is a wide choice of high quality hotels and restaurants.

Shepherds in the Metsovo region still lead a seminomadic existence

If are on your way by road across the Pindos range, make a stop at Metsovo for a day or two and sample its ambience.

History

Originally a small settlement of shepherds, the inhabitants of Metsovo were granted many privileges in Ottoman times as reward for guarding the mountain pass upon which Metsovo stands. This pass was the only route across the Pindos range, and the Metsovite guards' vigilance facilitated the passage of Ottoman troops. These privileges led to Metsovo becoming an important centre of finance, commerce, handcraft production and sheep farming. A school was established in the town in 1659 at a time when Greek-language schools were not allowed in other parts of the country.

Metsovo's privileges were abolished in 1795 by that spoilsport, Ali Pasha. In March 1854 it suffered considerable damage from Ottoman troops led by Ali Pasha. But Metsovo was very lucky in that it had many prosperous benefactors: locals who had gone on to achieve national and international recognition. The most famous of them were Georgios Averof (1815-99) and Mihalis Tositsas (1885-1950). Both bequeathed large amounts of money to Metsovo. This was used to restore the town to its former glory and to finance several small industries.

Orientation & Information

Orientation in Metsovo is easy as there is only one main thoroughfare. Coming from Kalambaka, turn-off to the left from the Katara pass to reach Metsovo. The main thoroughfare loops down to the central square, passing many restaurants, hotels and souvenir shops. A maze of stone pathways winds between the fine, traditionally built houses.

The bus stop is on the central square in front of Café Diethnes. The post office is on the right side of the main thoroughfare, when you're walking from the central square. To reach the OTE, walk along the road opposite the bus station, keep veering right and you will come to the OTE on the right. The building is a bit inconspicuous, so keep your eyes open. Metsovo's postcode is 442 00 and the telephone code is 0656. The National Bank of Greece is on the far side of the central square and there are another two banks as well.

The new Pindos vehicle tunnel to Metsovo from Malakasi has been completed on the Thessaly side of the Katara pass, but bureaucracy has so far prevented the completion of a connecting road, so the Katara pass is still the only approach option from the east.

There is no EOT or tourist police. The regular police (☎ 41 233/222) are on the

NORTHERN GREECE

right, a little way along the road opposite the bus stop.

Things to See

The restored **Tositsas mansion** has been turned into a folk museum, and is a faithful reconstruction of a wealthy 19th-century Metsovite household, with exquisitely handcrafted furniture, artefacts and utensils. The museum is about halfway up the main street. Opening times are Friday to Wednesday from 8.30 am to 1 pm and 4 to 6.30 pm. Wait at the door until the guide opens it and lets you in (every half-hour). Admission is 450 dr.

The 14th-century **Moni Agiou Nikolaou** stands in a gorge below Metsovo. Its chapel has post-Byzantine frescoes and a beautiful carved-wood iconostasis. The monastery is a 30-minute walk from Metsovo and is signposted to the left, just beyond the Hotel Athine.

The **Averof Gallery** was financed by Georgios Averof's three children. It houses a permanent collection of 19th and 20th-century works by Greek painters and sculptors. To reach the gallery turn left at the far side of the central square and the gallery is on the right. It's open Tuesday to Sunday from 9 am to 1.30 pm and 5 to 7.30 pm. Admission is 300 dr.

Activities

Coming from Kalambaka, Metsovo's ski centre (☎ 41 211) is on the right-hand side of the main Kalambaka-Ioannina highway, just before the turn-off for the town. There is a taverna at the centre and an 82-seat ski lift, two downhill runs and a five-km cross-country run. Ski hire is available in Metsovo.

Places to Stay – bottom end

There is no shortage of accommodation in Metsovo, with no less than 14 hotels and abundant domatia. Metsovo's hotels, predictably, have a folksy ambience, right down to the town's one E-class establishment. The E-class *Hotel Athine* (☎ 41 332), on the central square, is old but clean, and the woven rugs on the floors add a homely touch.

Double/triple rooms cost 7000/9000 dr with private bathroom. Allied to the Athine are the *Filoxenia* domatia (☎ 41 725) just behind the central park area and close to the art gallery. Singles/doubles cost 8000/11,000 dr, while 15,000 dr will get you a suite for four persons with one of the most spectacular views in town. The D-class *Hotel Acropolis* (☎ 41 672) has traditional furniture, wooden floors and ceilings, and very colourful wall-hangings. Rates here are 7500/9500 dr for doubles/triples with private bathroom. Look out for it on the right at the beginning of the road down to Metsovo.

Places to Stay – middle

The *Hotel Galaxias* (☎ 41 202; fax 41 124) is the closest hotel to the bus stop and is just behind it. Very nice singles/doubles cost 8000/12,500 dr. The C-class *Hotel Egnatia* (☎ 41 263/900; fax 41 485) has cosy rooms with balcony and wood-panelled walls. Room rates here are 10,000/12,000 dr. The hotel is on the right side of the main road as you approach the central square.

On the opposite side, further up the hill, the C-class *Hotel Bitouni* (☎ 41 217; fax 41 545) has immaculate rooms and a charming lounge with a flagstone floor, brass plates, embroidered cushions and carved wooden coffee tables. Rates here are 10,000/12,000/ 17,000 dr for doubles/singles/suites.

Places to Stay – top end

The *Hotel Apollon* (☎ 41 844/833; fax 42 110) is Metsovo's newest hotel. The gorgeous carpeted rooms cost 10,500/14,200/ 24,400 dr for singles/doubles/suites. For a touch of luxury, 24,200 dr will get you an attic suite for two, with hydromassage bath and minibar. To reach the hotel, walk along the road opposite the bus station and look for the sign pointing right.

Places to Eat

The *Athine Restaurant* (in the hotel of the same name; see Places to Stay) has tasty, reasonably priced food. The *Restaurant Galaxias* next to its associated hotel is a very good choice. Try the local pittes and hilopittes (pasta) with veal, accompanied by fine rosé for around 2000 dr. *Taverna To Spitiko*, on the left side of the main street coming from the central square, serves low-priced local dishes; a mixed cheese plate for two people is 1500 dr.

The 1st-floor *Taverna Metsovitiko Saloni* is an up-market establishment with a beautiful interior of traditional carved-wood furniture and colourful wall-hangings. The restaurant is just up from the post office.

Things to Buy

Craft shops selling both high-quality stuff and kitsch are ubiquitous in Metsovo. The old-fashioned food shop opposite the bus stop sells local cheeses, for which the town is famous.

Getting There & Away

From Metsovo there are six direct buses to Ioannina (800 dr) and two or three to Trikala (1200 dr). In summer there is also a direct bus to Athens (5000 dr). To catch a Thessaloniki bus you will have to walk up to the main road and wave the bus down. These buses normally come from Ioannina.

IGOUMENITSA Ηγουμενίτσα

Once a sleepy little outpost, the west-coast port of Igoumenitsa (Ig-ou-men-IT-sa, population 6000), 100 km from Ioannina, is where you get ferries to Corfu and Italy. There is little of attraction to keep you here, but if you are travelling to or from Greece by ferry and using Igoumenitsa as your entry or exit point, then you are likely to be spending some time here, if only to have a meal or wait out a few hours for a boat or bus. There is actually a very nice beach and taverna at **Drepanos**, about five km north of town, if you feel like a relaxing swim and a meal.

Orientation

The ferries for Italy and the domestic ferries for Corfu leave from two separate quays quite close to one another on the waterfront of Ethnikis Antistasis. To get to the bus station turn left from both ferry quays, walk along Ethnikis Antistasis, turn right into 23 Fevrouariou and two blocks inland turn left into Kyprou. The bus station is a little way along on the left.

Information

The EOT (☎ 22 227), on the waterfront and inside the Italian quay area, is open every day from 7 am to 2.30 pm. The tourist police office (☎ 22 222) is on the waterfront almost opposite the Corfu quay. The post office and OTE are next to each other on Evangelistrias. Igoumenitsa's postcode is 461 00 and the telephone code is 0665. The Ionian Bank is conveniently situated on the corner of El Venizelou.

Places to Stay & Eat

Ferries leave Igoumenitsa in the morning and evening these days so you may not have to stay overnight here before your departure. Walk two blocks up El Venizelou from the waterfront, turn right at Kyprou, cross over the road and you'll come to the D-class *Hotel Lux* (☎ 22 223), with singles/doubles for 3500/4800 dr with shared bathroom and 4700/5400 dr with private bathroom.

The D-class *Egnatia* (☎ 23 648/455) has comfortable rooms for 5510/9700 dr with private bathroom. Cross over Kyprou from El Venizelou and the hotel is on the right. A little way along the road to Parga (signposted from the waterfront), the C-class *Hotel Epirus* (☎ 22 504 or 23 474) has very pleasant rooms for 7000/9800 dr with private bathroom.

If you really can't be bothered walking too far and don't mind paying for a bit more comfort, the *Jolly Hotel* is right outside the Italian ferry terminal. It has air-conditioned and soundproofed rooms for 10,900/21,100 dr. All rooms have direct-dial phone and TV.

To Astron Restaurant, El Venizelou 9, and the *Restaurant Martinis-Bakalis*, on the corner of 23 Fevrouariou and Grigoriou Lambraki, serve reasonably priced, tasty food. The locals eat here so you can be assured of good value.

Getting There & Away

Bus From Igoumenitsa's bus station there

are nine buses to Ioannina (two hours, 1500 dr); five to Parga (one hour, 900 dr); five to Athens (eight hours, 6900 dr); two to Preveza (2½ hours, 1700 dr); and one to Thessaloniki (eight hours, 6450 dr).

Ferry & Catamaran – to/from Corfu There are ferries every hour to Corfu between 5 am and 10 pm (1½ hours, 700 dr). Agencies opposite the quay sell tickets. Match the name of the boat that you are planning to leave on with the name on the appropriate ticket office. Most of the ferries to/from Italy also stop at Corfu.

Ferry & Catamaran – to/from Italy There are six to eight ferries a day from Igoumenitsa to Brindisi (11 hours, 5000/9000 dr in low/high season) for a standard deck-class ticket. There are between two and four ferries a day to Bari (13 hours, 5850/9000 dr in low/high season); two to three ferries a day to Ancona (24 hours, 14,400/16,800 dr in low/high season); two ferries a week to Otranto (nine hours, 5000/9000 dr in low/high season); and three a week to Ortona (24 hours, 13,500/16,500 dr in low/high season). Some of the ferries to Ancona go direct, but all of the others go via Corfu (two hours) where some lines allow you to stop over free of charge. Boats leave in the morning between 6 and 8 am and in the evening. You should turn up at the port at least two hours before departure. Timetables are subject to change and demand is high in summer. Book ahead if you can.

All of the central ticketing offices are on Ethnikis Antistaseos. Hellenic Mediterranean (for Ortona) are at No 32 (☎ 25 682 or 22 180; Adriatica (for Brindisi) are at No 58 a (☎ 22 952/679); ANEK (for Ancona) are at No 34 (☎ 22 104/158); and Marlines (also for Ancona) are at No 42 (☎ 23 301/911). For other lines, go to Chris Travel Agency at No 60 (☎ 25 351/352/353).

A catamaran service operates, in the summer months, between Igoumenitsa and Brindisi via Corfu (every second day, 3½ hours, 10,000 dr) and between Igoumenitsa and Trieste (twice a week, 24 hours,

17,400 dr). The price is the same if you board the catamaran in Corfu.

PARGA Πάργα

Parga, 77 km north of Preveza and 48 km south of Igoumenitsa, spills down to a rocky bay, flanked by coves, and islets. Add to this a Venetian kastro and the long pebble and sand Valtos beach and you have somewhere truly alluring. So it will come as no surprise to be told that it's overrun with tourists in midsummer and that hotels, domatia and travel agents have swamped the once serene fishing village. Despite this, it is still an very attractive place for a day or two and is Epiros' number-one tourist resort. Try and visit Parga in early or late summer. If you are travelling along this coast, it would be a shame to miss this gem.

Orientation & Information

The bus station is at Alexandrou Baga 18 and the post office is in the same building. Turn left at the bus station and walk straight ahead at the crossroads into Vasila and you will come to the National Bank of Greece and the OTE; continue along this street to reach the waterfront. Parga's postcode is 480 60 and the telephone code is 0684. There is no EOT, but there is now a tourist-police department in the same building as the regular police (☎ 31 222) which is shared with the post office and the bus station.

Nekromanteio of Aphyra

Just about every travel agent in Parga advertises trips to the Nekromanteio of Aphyra. This involves taking a boat ride down the coast to the Aheron River (believed to be the ancient River Styx) and then up the navigable river as far as the Nekromanteio itself which you approach on foot. If you have your own transport, take the Preveza road as far as the village of Mesopotamos and look out for the sign to the Nekromanteio, one km off the main road. Entrance is 500 dr or 300 dr for those with a student card.

The Nekromanteio is a truly fascinating place, if you have time to spend and ponder over the mysteries of the ancient rituals of

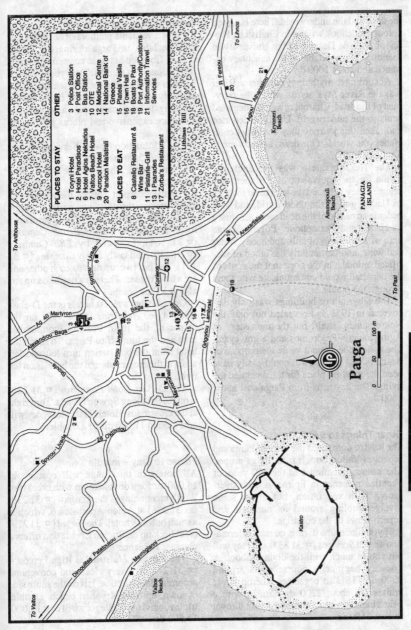

PLACES TO STAY
1 Toryni Hotel
2 Hotel Paradisos
6 Hotel Agios Nektarios
7 Valtos Beach Hotel
9 Acropol Hotel
20 Pansion Maistrali

PLACES TO EAT
8 Castello Restaurant & Wine Bar
11 Pistaria-Grill
13 I Psarades
17 Zorba's Restaurant

OTHER
3 Police Station
4 Post Office
5 Bus Station
10 OTE
12 Medical Centre
14 National Bank of Greece
15 Plateia Vasila
16 Town Hall
18 Boats to Paxi
19 Port Authority/Customs
21 Information Travel Services

Parga

the dead and the underworld. There is a good colour guidebook written in English by Professor Sotirios Dakaris of the University of Ioannina. It's available at the sanctuary entrance and costs 1000 dr.

According to mythology the Aheron River was the River Styx across which the ferryman of the dead, Charon, rowed the departed souls to the underworld. Until the departed had taken this journey they could not enter Hades (the world of the dead) and so were in a state of limbo.

The Nekromanteio was the ancients' venue for the equivalent of a modern-day séance. They believed the spot to be the gate of Hades, god of the underworld, and so it became an oracle of the dead and a sanctuary to Hades and Persephone. Pilgrims came here with offerings of milk and honey, water and wine, and particularly the blood of sacrificed animals; in the hope that the souls of the departed would communicate with them through the oracle.

The labyrinth of buildings was only discovered in 1958 and revealed not only the Nekromanteio itself, but the monastery of Agios Ioannis Prodromos and a graveyard. The eerie underground vault, the purpose of which is still not known, could easily have been the meeting place for the dead and the living. The day trips from Parga cost about 1500 dr.

Other Things to See & Do

The **kastro** dominates the town of Parga and separates **Valtos beach** from Parga proper. The kastro, a reminder of the 400 years of Venetian presence in Epiros, is a bit overgrown with vegetation, but offers some lovely rambling around its ramparts and superb views of the coastline.

If you like scuba diving, contact Information Travel Services (☎ 31 833) and they will put you in touch with the diving school. A one-day beginner's course costs around 9500 dr. ITS also organises Aheron River cruises for about 2200 dr. Cruises with a beach barbecue and unlimited drinks thrown in cost 5500 dr.

Places to Stay – bottom end

There is a veritable plethora of accommodation available in Parga during the tourist season, from top hotels to camping grounds; from domatia to studios. Take your pick – if you can get in during the low season. Avoid mid-July to the end of August, if you are not planning to stay more than a week here. Rates are expensive and places are hard to find.

Try Information Travel Services, Agiou Athanasiou 5, towards the far south end of the waterfront. They can help you find accommodation.

For the cheapest option, there are three camp sites on the coast just north of Parga, all signposted from the Parga-Igoumenitsa road. The first is *Lihnos Beach Camping* (☎ 31 161), followed by *Elia Camping* (☎ 31 130), and lastly *Enjoy Camping* (☎ 31 171). The last two are next to each other and are a bit crowded. There is a newer camp site also at Valtos beach.

One of Parga's nicest hotels is the D-class *Hotel Agios Nektarios* (☎ 31 150) on the corner of the main Preveza-Igoumenitsa road and the turn-off to Parga. To reach the hotel from the bus station turn left and left again at the crossroads and the hotel is on the right.

The D-class *Hotel Paradisos* (☎ 31 229) is on the left along Spyrou Livada. Turn right at the crossroads. Hotels in this category will cost around 11,000 dr for a double.

Places to Stay – middle

All hotels in this range will cost about 14,000 dr for a double room with breakfast. Worth mentioning is the *Acropol* (☎ 31 239; fax 31 236) at Agion Apostolon 6, which is a small but cosy hotel. The *Toryni* (☎ 31 219) is set back up on Spyrou Livada and offers a pleasant ambience.

The *Pansion Maïstrali* at Riga Fereou 4 (☎ 31 275) is a very clean and convenient accommodation option. It is on the south side of town, up from Kryoneri beach. Double/triple rooms in this category will cost 12,000/14,500 dr.

NORTHERN GREECE

Places to Stay – top end

The B-class *Valtos Beach Hotel* (☎ 31 610; fax 31 904), on the beach at Valtos, has singles/doubles for 11,347/13,616 dr, with breakfast. The hotel has a café and restaurant. The B-class *Parga Beach Hotel* (☎ 31 410/293; fax 31 412), on Parga beach, has rates of 8800/14,200 dr.

The *Lihnos Beach Hotel* (☎ 31 257; fax 31 157) has rates of 9000/13,000 dr. The last two hotels mentioned both have a bar, restaurant and tennis court. Valtos beach is just north of Parga and Lihnos beach is just to the south.

Places to Eat

Not surprisingly, there are plenty of places to eat, many of them touting tourist menus and English breakfasts, if that is what you want. In high season, tourist prices are all the rage.

Zorba's Restaurant is open all year round and caters for locals as well as visitors. It is on the waterfront, 50 metres to the right as you face the pier, by the statue of Ioannis Dimoulitsas. It offers good food, draught wine and has a picturesque location.

For a couple of cheap and tasty options, try the *I Psarades*, just back from the seafront on Plateia Vasila, or the *Psistaria-Grill* at Alexandrou Baga 4, 100 metres down from the bus station.

The *Castello Restaurant & Wine Bar* at Agion Apostolon 4, part of the Acropol Hotel, is a rather fancy European-style restaurant. It is very professionally run by its Swiss-trained manager and the outdoor section is very enticing.

Getting There & Away

Bus From Parga's bus station there are four buses a day to Igoumenitsa (one hour, 900 dr), six to Preveza (two hours, 1100 dr), one to Ioannina (three hours, 1800 dr) and four to Athens (seven hours, 6100 dr).

Excursion Boat The small Ionian islands of Paxoi and Antipaxoi lie just 20 km off the coast. In summer there are daily excursion boats to Paxoi (3000 dr) from Parga. The excursions are widely advertised by Parga's travel agents.

PREVEZA Πρέβεζα

Preveza (PRE-ve-za), built on a peninsula between the Ionian Sea and the Gulf of Ambracia, is a primarily functional place where ferries ply back and forth across the narrow strait to Aktion, but it is also a popular holiday destination for Greek tourists and German and Austrian tour groups which fly in to the airport at Aktion. Most people coming to Preveza are either heading out to the resorts at Parga, or to the beach resorts north of the town. Preveza is a pleasant town in its own right, but is undergoing quite a bit of renovation in its old town centre, resulting in a few temporary inconveniences such as unsealed roads, and scaffolding on buildings. A leisurely stroll through its narrow streets is nonetheless a pleasure.

Orientation & Information

If you arrive by bus, you will alight at the bus station on Irinis which is the main commercial thoroughfare. Turn left from the bus station along Irinis and walk about 500 metres, bearing left, until you reach the harbour. The EOT, post office and National Bank of Greece are in a row on the waterfront – turn left as you reach the quay. The Olympic Airways office (☎ 28 343) is on Spiliadou on the new harbour front.

If you arrive by plane, there is an Olympic Airways bus that will take you to the Aktion ferry and across to Preveza proper. The ferry ticket costs extra. Alight at the ferry terminal on the Preveza side of the harbour.

Preveza's telephone code is 0682 and the postcode is 481 01.

Festivals

In July each year there is an International Choral Festival with up to 20 or more international choirs taking part. Preveza's own choir has won considerable international acclaim. For detailed information, check with Preveza's municipal tourist office

NORTHERN GREECE

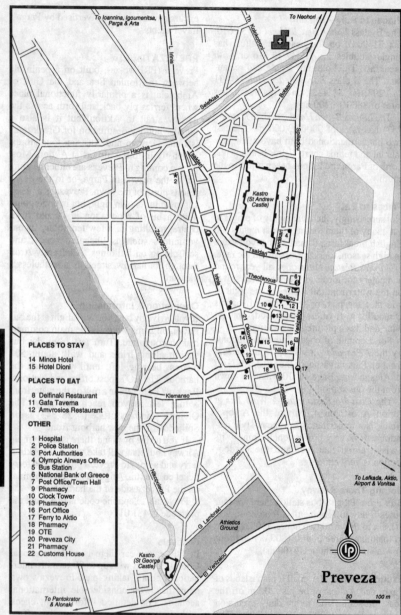

NORTHERN GREECE

PLACES TO STAY

14 Minos Hotel
15 Hotel Dioni

PLACES TO EAT

8 Delfinaki Restaurant
11 Gafa Taverna
12 Amvrosios Restaurant

OTHER

1 Hospital
2 Police Station
3 Port Authorities
4 Olympic Airways Office
5 Bus Station
6 National Bank of Greece
7 Post Office/Town Hall
9 Pharmacy
10 Clock Tower
13 Pharmacy
16 Port Office
17 Ferry to Aktio
18 Pharmacy
19 OTE
20 Preveza City
21 Pharmacy
22 Customs House

Preveza

0   50   100 m

(☎ 28 120; fax 27 553) which is housed in the town hall.

At the beginning of August, you may come across a mildly whimsical sardine festival. The Nikopolia Festival is an umbrella event for various musical and theatrical presentations held in August at Nikopolis. Again, check with the municipal tourist office for details.

Places to Stay

If you wish to camp, you have a choice of four camping grounds, the best of which is *Camping Kalamitsi* (☎ 22 192; fax 28 660) which has 116 sites. This site boasts a large pool, restaurant, laundry facilities, communal fridges and a minimarket. It has grassed tent sites and ample shade. The beach is ideal for snorkelling or just lazing about. It's four km along the main Preveza-Igoumenitsa road.

Nearest the bus station is the C-class *Preveza City* (☎ 27 370; fax 23 872) at Irinis 81-83, 200 metres from the bus station on the left in the direction of the waterfront. It has clean singles/doubles/triples for 6800/8800/ 10,500 dr. The spartan C-class *Minos Hotel* (☎ 28 424) at 21 Oktovriou 11 has singles/ doubles for 7740/10,200 dr. Within the town precinct, the C-class *Hotel Dioni* (☎ 27 123 or 24 304) is a good, but somewhat pricey choice. The hotel is on a quiet square, Plateia T Papageorgiou, and has singles/doubles/ triples for 10,500/ 14,800/19,000 dr. The bar has a pool table.

Places to Eat

The main road along the waterfront has a large number of drinks and snacks places, but there are a few places in the back streets worth investigating. Along the street leading to the clock tower of the St Haralambos church from the waterfront, there are two places worth checking. The *Gafa* taverna specialises in sardines and the *Amvrosios* next to it offers similar fare.

The *Delfinaki* (☎ 26 130), at Sapountzaki 4, is a tastefully modern, but a bit touristy, taverna. It serves some excellent home-made specialities. The baked peppers stuffed with cheese are worth tasting. A complimentary watermelon-skin sweet or coffee is offered after the meal in the summer months.

Getting There & Away

Air There are at least five flights a week in the low season and daily flights in the high season from Preveza airport to Athens (20 minutes, 11,800 dr). The airport is sometimes called Lefkada or Aktion. The Olympic Airways office (☎ 28 343) is on the corner of Spiliadou and Balkou. The airport is seven km south of Preveza and the Olympic Airways bus to the airport costs 300 dr, plus the Aktion ferry fare.

Bus From the intercity bus station there are eight buses a day to Ioannina (two hours, 1600 dr); five to Parga (two hours, 1100 dr) and Arta (one hour, 800 dr); two to Igoumenitsa (2½ hours, 1700 dr); four to Athens (six hours, 5950 dr) and one to Thessaloniki (eight hours, 6350 dr).

Ferry The Preveza-Aktion ferry plies to and fro every half-hour (70 dr per person; 660 dr per car).

AROUND PREVEZA

Nikopolis Νικόπολη

In 31 BC, Octavian (later Emperor Augustus of Rome) defeated Mark Antony and Cleopatra in the famous Battle of Actium (present-day Aktion). To celebrate this victory, Octavian built Nikopolis, which means 'city of victory' and populated it by forcible resettlement of people from surrounding towns and villages. It was plundered by Vandals and Goths in the 5th and 6th centuries, but rebuilt by Justinian. It was sacked again by the Bulgars in the 11th century, after which nobody bothered to rebuild it.

Little is left of the walls built by Augustus, but the Byzantine walls and a theatre survive, and there are remains of temples to Mars and Poseidon (an appropriate choice of gods for the warmongering Octavian), an aqueduct, Roman baths and a restored Roman odeion.

NORTHERN GREECE

The immense site sprawls over both sides of the Preveza-Arta road.

There is an **archaeological museum** at the Nikopolis site (☎ 41 336) open every day except Monday from 8.30 am to 3 pm. It has exhibits from the ancient citadel. Admission is 400 dr. Other exhibits may be viewed at the Ioannina Archaeological Museum. The Preveza-Arta buses stop at the site.

Beaches

Preveza's beaches are strung out for some 30 km from just north of the town all along the **Bay of Nikopolis**. The beaches at **Monolithi** 10 km out of Preveza and **Kastrosykia** 15 km from Preveza, are particularly popular.

ARTA Αρτα

Arta (population 18,000), the second-largest town of Epiros, is 76 km south of Ioannina and 50 km north-east of Preveza. Arta is easy to miss if you're speeding on your way to Athens, or locations further south, which is a pity, because Arta is worth a visit. After the barren agricultural scene of Ioannina and further north, it is a refreshing break to come across grove upon grove of orange plantations, as you leave the Louros valley and reach the open plains and wetlands of the north Ambracian gulf.

The town is built over the ancient city of Ambracia which King Pyrrhus of Epiros made his capital in the 4th century BC. In the 14th century the Frankish despot of Epiros made it his seat of government. The town has a wealth of Byzantine monuments of which the locals are justifiably proud.

The town today is a bustling supply centre for the north Ambracia region and is a pleasant place to stroll around.

Orientation & Information

The main bus station is on the Ioannina-Athens road on the east side of town and just outside the town walls. From the bus station, walk about 200 metres to your right and look for the Xenia hotel sign. Turn left into Krystalli and you will come onto Arta's main street Nikiforou Skoufa. Half of this street is for pedestrians only.

The OTE is on the main square, Plateia Ethnikis Antistasis, which is halfway along Skoufa. The post office is on Amvrakias, about a five-minute walk from the OTE in the general direction of the fortress walls. Arta's telephone code is 0681 and the postcode is 471 01.

Things to See

The town's most distinguished feature is its fine 18th-century **Bridge of Arta**, which crosses the River Arahthos. This bridge, famous in Greek demotic poetry to everyone in Greece, is probably Arta's most photographed monument. Legend has it that the master builder, who was having difficulty in preventing the bridge from being washed away every time he tried to complete it, was advised to entomb his wife in the stonework of the central arch. The bridge is still standing, although it has had a facelift or two in recent times and is now used by local pedestrians.

Arta also has several churches of note: the 13th-century **Church of Panagia Parigoritissa**, overlooking Plateia Skoufa, just south of the central square of Plateia Kilkis, is a well-preserved and striking building. The churches of **Agios Vasilios** and **Agia Theodora** have attractive ceramic decorations on their exterior walls. Both of these churches are just west of the main thoroughfare of Pyrrou, which runs south from the fortress to Plateia Kilkis.

Places to Stay & Eat

The town has two C-class hotels. The *Hotel Cronos* (☎ 22 211; fax 73 795), Plateia Kilkis, has singles/doubles for 7700/9910 dr with private bathroom. The *Hotel Amvrakia* (☎ 28 311; fax 31 544) has rooms for 7700/8800 dr with private bathroom. The Amvrakia is at Priovolou 13; this street is one block east of Pyrrou. The quieter B-class *Xenia* (☎ 27 413; fax 70 315) is in a quiet and pleasant setting inside the grounds of the fortress. Rooms here with private bathroom are a good value 6060/8370 dr.

There are several restaurants on Plateia Kilkis and you can always get a snack at the cafeterias on Plateia Ethnikis Antistasis. The Amvrakia Hotel has an associated restaurant next to it called the *Skaraveos*. This is a delightful little place decorated 'with a woman's touch', according to the proprietor. Here you can get some genuine and tasty home cooking for around 1700 dr.

On the Arta side of the Bridge are two establishments, the *Oasi* and the *Protomastoras*, the latter meaning 'chief builder' and named in honour of the ill-fated original architect of the bridge. Of the two, the Protomastoras gets more points for location.

Getting There & Away

There are 10 buses a day to Ioannina (2½ hours, 1500 dr) and five buses a day between Preveza and Arta (one hour, 800 dr).

Macedonia Μακεδονία

Macedonia is the largest prefecture in Greece, and its capital, Thessaloniki, is Greece's second city.

With abundant and varied attractions it's surprising that more travellers don't find their way here. Tucked up in the left-hand corner are the beautiful Prespa lakes, one of Europe's most important bird sanctuaries. To the south, Mt Olympus, at 2917 metres Greece's highest peak, rises from a plain just six km from the sea. The unsung towns of Veria, Edessa and Florina unfold their charms to only the occasional visitor. For archaeological buffs there is Alexander the Great's birthplace of Pella; the sanctuary of Dion, where Alexander made sacrifices to the gods; Vergina, where the Macedonian kings (apart from Alexander) were buried; and Philippi, where the battle which set the seal on the future of the western world was fought. Macedonia is also the site of the Monastic Republic of Athos.

THESSALONIKI Θεσσαλονίκη

Thessaloniki (Thess-alo-NI-ki, population 750,000) was the second city of Byzantium and is the second city of modern Greece. However, being second does not mean that Thessaloniki lies in the shadow of, or tries to emulate, the capital. It is a sophisticated city with a distinct character of its own. It has a lively nightlife, good restaurants and, although it doesn't have the impressive ancient monuments of the capital, it has several good museums, a scattering of Roman ruins and superlative Byzantine churches.

Thessaloniki sits at the top of the wide Thermaic gulf. The oldest part of the city is the Kastra, the old Turkish quarter, whose narrow streets huddle around a Byzantine fortress on the slopes of Mt Hortiatis.

Thessaloniki is best avoided during festival time (September and October), as accommodation is almost impossible to find, and prices are increased by at least 20%. At other times finding a room should not present any problems.

History

Like almost everywhere in Greece, Thessaloniki has had not only its triumphs but more than its fair share of disasters. As with Athens, an awareness of these helps greatly in one's appraisal of the city.

NORTHERN GREECE

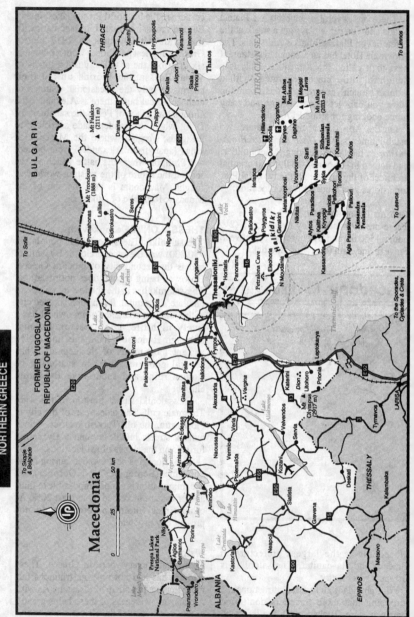

Macedonia

What's in a name?

An awful lot if you are Greek and the name is Macedonia. In January 1992, the Yugoslav Republic of Macedonia declared its full independence. After this pronouncement the Greek government protested vociferously, insisting that the new country change its name before the European Community granted it recognition. In May 1992, Greece stated it would recognise the republic's independence and cooperate with it to ensure stability in the region, so long as its name did not include the word Macedonia. In response, the EC recognised Macedonia in June 1992, provided it adopted another name. Amongst the Greek people, the issue has resulted in a surge of unprecedented nationalism with slogans throughout the country declaring 'Macedonia is Greek, always was, is, and always will be'.

The Greeks' objections to the name Macedonia are twofold. They believe that it is an infringement of their cultural heritage, and they read into it undercurrents of territorial claims. The 'Greekness' of Alexander the Great, the greatest of Macedonian kings, is indisputable. After all, it was he who spread Greek culture to India and the Middle East, and in so doing established Greek as the international language of the ancient world. Whether Alexander the Great's ancestors were Greek is a different matter. The ethnic origins of the ancient Macedonians has, since the beginning of recorded history, been a conundrum, for it seems that Macedonia has always been a mélange of languages and nationalities.

After Alexander's death, Macedonia continued to be part of Greece, until, with the rest of the country, it came under Roman domination. When the Roman Empire split in the 4th century, Macedonia, traversed by the Via Egnatia (the long straight road which linked Rome to Byzantium), became a powerful region with a relatively stable population. This stability came to an end in the 7th century when the region was invaded by Serbs, who were followed by Bulgars and Muslims. During Byzantine times, Samuel, a Slav Macedonian king, fought against the Byzantines, and his army made inroads into Macedonia. In the 14th century the Serb Stefan Dusan (who ruled from 1331 to 1355) occupied all of Macedonia, except Thessaloniki. This occupation was short-lived as it was quickly superseded by the Ottoman conquest.

The Greeks' concern about claims on the territory of Macedonia stem from the late 19th century, when the Ottoman Empire was on the point of collapse. At this time, countries welling over with nationalistic fervour were poised to pick up the spoils. The Serbs made no secret of the fact that they coveted Macedonia, but a much greater threat came from King Ferdinand of Bulgaria.

This volatile situation culminated in the two Balkan wars (1912-13). In the first Balkan war, the Serbs, Bulgarians and Greeks fought the Turks, and in the second round the Serbs and Greeks fought the Bulgarians. The second Balkan war was ended by the Treaty of Bucharest, which ceded more than half of Macedonia to Greece and divided the rest between Serbia and Bulgaria. In both world wars Bulgaria fought against Greece and in WW II parts of Macedonia were occupied by Bulgaria, which implemented a policy of enforced 'Bulgarianisation'. After the victory of the Allies in WW II, the threat from Bulgaria was replaced by one from Yugoslavia.

In April 1945, Tito proclaimed the Socialist Republic of Macedonia. Greece is convinced that Tito did this to strengthen the southern flank of his territory and that his ultimate ambition was to create an independent Macedonian state which would include the Greek province of Macedonia, and the Bulgarian region of Macedonia known as Pirin. Greece says it was too busy fighting the civil war to protest at the time, a situation that Tito was only too aware of. In 1952 a Macedonian grammar was published in Tito's republic and in 1968 the republic acquired the autocephalous Macedonian church. To Greece, these factors added credence to its suspicions.

Greece continued to protest against the name Macedonia throughout 1992 and into 1993. Then in April 1993, Macedonia was admitted to the UN under the temporary name of the Former Yugoslav Republic of Macedonia (FYROM), which doesn't exactly trip off the tongue.

To this day there are people in Greek villages on the borders of Bulgaria and the new republic who speak Macedonian. This is one of the south Slavonic group of languages, which is a dialect of Bulgarian, with some Turkish, Greek, Albanian and Vlach words. An offshoot of the present nationalistic fervour is that a minority of these people are demanding greater autonomy for Macedonian-speaking Greeks within Greece. The country is not without other ethnic minorities. Could it be that Greece, in its much ado about Macedonia, has inadvertently opened a Pandora's box? ■

The city was named Thessaloniki in 316 BC by the Macedonian general, Kassandros, after his wife, daughter of Philip II and half-sister of Alexander the Great. While Philip was successfully expanding his territory in Thessaly, his wife gave birth to their daughter. When he arrived home Philip announced that the child would be called Thessaloniki, which means 'Victory in Thessaly'.

After the Roman conquest in 168 BC, Thessaloniki became capital of the province of Macedonia. Thessaloniki's geographical location on the Thermaic gulf and its position on the Via Egnatia helped to promote its development. It was also an important staging post on the trade route to the Balkan region.

The Roman emperor Galerius made it the imperial capital of the eastern half of the Roman Empire, and after the empire split it became the second city of Byzantium, and flourished as both a spiritual and economic centre. Inevitably, its strategic position brought attacks and plunderings by Goths, Slavs, Muslims, Franks and Epirots. In 1185 it was sacked by the Normans, and in 1204 was made a feudal kingdom under Marquis Boniface of Montferrat. In 1246 it was reunited with the Byzantine Empire. After several sieges it finally capitulated to Ottoman rule when Murad II staged a successful invasion in 1430.

Along with the rest of Macedonia, Thessaloniki became part of Greece in 1913. In August 1917 a fire broke out in the city and, as there was no fire brigade, the flames spread quickly, destroying 9500 houses and rendering 70,000 inhabitants homeless. The problem of homelessness was exacerbated by the influx of refugees from Asia Minor after the 1923 population exchange. During the late 1920s the city was carefully replanned and built on a grid system with wide streets and large squares.

In 1978 Thessaloniki experienced a severe earthquake. Most of the modern buildings were not seriously damaged, but the Byzantine churches suffered greatly and most are still in the process of being restored.

Orientation

Thessaloniki's waterfront of Leoforos Nikis stretches from the port in the west, to the White Tower (Lefkos Pyrgos) in the east. North of the White Tower are the exhibition grounds where Thessaloniki's annual International Trade Fair is held. The university campus is north of here. The city's other principal streets of Mitropoleos, Tsimiski and Ermou run parallel to Nikis. Egnatia, the next street up, is the city's main thoroughfare and most of Thessaloniki's Roman remains are between here and Agiou Dimitriou. The city's two main squares are Plateia Eleftherias, and Plateia Aristotelous, both of which abut the waterfront.

The central food market is between Egnatia, Irakliou, Aristotelous and Dragoumi. Plateia Eleftherias is one of the city's local bus terminals, although the main terminal is at Plateia Dikastirion. The train station is on Monastiriou, a westerly continuation of Egnatia. The city does not have one general intercity bus station; there are several terminals for different destinations. The airport is 16 km south-east of the city.

Kastra, the old Turkish quarter, is north of Athinas and just within the ramparts.

Information

Tourist Office The EOT (☎ 271 888), Plateia Aristotelous 8, is open Monday to Friday from 8 am to 8 pm and Saturday from 8 am to 2 pm.

Tourist Police The tourist police (☎ 548 907) are at Egnatia 10, but the entrance to the building is around the corner on the left side of Tandalidou. The office is open from 7.30 am to 11 pm from October to March, and 24 hours from April to September.

Money The National Bank of Greece, Plateia Dimokratias, is open Monday to Friday from 8 am to 2 pm and 6 to 8 pm, on Saturday from 8 am to 1.30 pm and on Sunday from 9.30 am to 12.30 pm. Another branch, at Tsimiski 12, opens on weekends for the benefit of people wishing to change currency.

American Express (☎ 269 521) is at Tsimiski 19 and is open from Monday to Thursday from 8.30 am to 2 pm and on Friday from 8 am to 1.30 pm. Services are for card-holders only.

Business Hours Commercial shops are open during the following hours: Monday, Wednesday and Saturday from 8.30 am to 2.30 pm; Tuesday, Thursday and Friday from 8.30 am to 2.30 pm and 5 pm to 8.30 pm. They're not open on Sunday. Department stores and supermarkets are open during the following hours: Monday to Friday from 8 am to 8 pm and Saturday from 8 am to 3 pm. They're also closed on Sunday.

Post & Telecommunications The main post office is at Tsimiski 45. It's open Monday to Friday from 7.30 am to 8 pm, Saturday from 7.30 am to 2.15 pm and Sunday from 9 am to 1.30 pm. Thessaloniki's postcode is 541 01.

The OTE is at Karolou Dil 27 and is open 24 hours a day. Thessaloniki's telephone code is 031.

Foreign Consulates Foreign consulates in Thessaloniki include:

Bulgaria
    N Manou 12 (☎ 829 210)
France
    Evzonon 27 (☎ 838 418)
Germany
    Karolou Dil 4a (☎ 236 315)
Hungary
    Danaïdou 4 (☎ 547 395; fax 530 988)
Netherlands
    Komninon 26 (☎ 227 477; fax 283 794)
Romania
    Leoforos Nikis 13 (☎ 225 451; fax 225 428)
Turkey
    Ag Dimitriou 151 (☎ 209 964; fax 204 438)
Yugoslavia
    Vass Olgas 76, (☎ 831 059)
UK
    El Venizelou 8 (☎ 278 006 or 269 984)
USA
    Leoforos Nikis 59 (☎ 266 121)

Australia, New Zealand and Canada are represented by the British Consulate.

Mt Athos Permits After you've obtained a letter of recommendation from your consulate, permits to the monastic region of Mt Athos can be obtained from the Ministry of Macedonia & Thrace (☎ 270 092), on Plateia Diikitiriou. Mt Athos is out of bounds for women. For further information about applying for permission to visit this area, see the section on Mt Athos later in the chapter.

Bookshops Molho, Tsimiski 10, has a comprehensive stock of English-language books, magazines and newspapers. Malliaris Kaisia, at Aristotelous 9, also has many English-language publications.

Laundry Wash & Go, just north of Agiou Dimitriou, is a trendy place with magazines and a soft-drink machine. Walk up Tritis Septemvriou, turn left into Agiou Dimitriou and look for the sign pointing right. It's open Monday to Saturday from 9 am to 2.30 pm and 4.30 to 8.30 pm; Sunday from 9 am to 4.30 pm.

Bianca Laundrette, on Antoniadou, has a more utilitarian ambience. Walk up D Gournari from the Arch of Galerius and Antoniadou is off to the right. It's open Monday to Friday from 8 am to 2 pm. Both laundrettes charge around 1200 dr a load to wash and dry.

Emergency There is a first-aid centre (☎ 530 530) at Nav Kountourioti 6, near the port. The largest public hospital is Ippokration (☎ 830 024), Konstantinoupoleos 49.

Things to See
Archaeological Museum In 1977 one of Greece's most eminent archaeologists, Professor Andronikos, was excavating at Vergina near Thessaloniki when he found an unlooted tomb which turned out to be that of King Philip II of Macedon. The spectacular contents of this tomb, now on display in this museum, are comparable to the grave treasures of Mycenae.

Among the exhibits are exquisite gold jewellery, bronze and terracotta vases, tiny ivory reliefs of intricate detail and a solid

NORTHERN GREECE

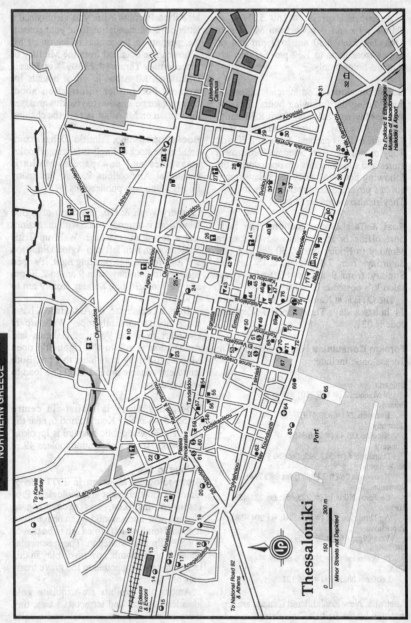

Thessaloniki

PLACES TO STAY

21	Capsis Hotel
29	ABC Hotel
39	YHA Hostel
54	Hotel Atlas
55	Hotel Averof
57	Hotel Atlantis
58	Hotel Acropol
68	Tourist Hotel
69	Electra Palace Hotel
73	Continental Hotel

PLACES TO EAT

23	Life Restaurant
37	Brothers' Taverna
42	Patsas Ilias
43	Ta Spata Psistaria
48	Ouzeri Aristotelous
49	Babel Snack Bar
50	O Loutros Fish Taverna
53	Saul Modiano
56	Ta Nea Ilisia
72	Olymbos Naousa Restaurant
77	Ta Nisia Taverna

OTHER

1	Kavala Bus Station
2	Church of Agia Ekaterini
3	Monastery of Vlatadon
4	Church of Osios David
5	Church of Nikolaos Orfanos
6	Turkish Consulate
7	Atatürk's House
8	Show Avantaz (Nightclub)
9	Church of Agios Dimitrios
10	Ministry of Macedonia & Thrace
11	Church of the Dodeka Apostoli
12	Alexandroupolis Bus Station
13	Train Station
14	Airport Bus Terminal
15	Ioannina Bus Station
16	Athens & Trikala Bus Station
17	Florina Bus Station
18	Pella, Kastoria, Volos & Edessa Bus Station
19	Katerini Bus Station
20	Veria Bus Station
22	Langadas Bus Station
24	Local Bus Station
25	Roman Agora
26	Church of Panagia Ahiropoiitos
27	Church of Agios Georgios
28	Arch of Galerius
30	En Chordais Music Store
31	International Exhibition Fairground
32	Archaeological Museum
33	White Tower
34	Aristotelion Cinema
35	Society for Macedonian Studies Art Gallery
36	Cinema Pallas
38	Plateia Navarinou
40	Club Privé
41	Church of Agia Sofia
44	Train Tickets Office (OSE)
45	OTE
46	EOS (Climbing Club)
47	Main Post Office
51	National Bank of Greece
52	American Express
59	Tourist Police
60	Commercial Bank
61	National Bank of Greece
62	Olympic Airways Office
63	Hydrofoil Departure Point
64	First-Aid Centre
65	Ferry Departure Point
66	Nomikos Lines
67	Plateia Eleftherias
70	UK Consulate
71	Doucas Tours
74	Plateia Aristotelous
75	EOT
76	Olympian Cinema
78	Museum of the Macedonian Struggle
79	Entasis (Music Bar)
80	US Consulate

gold casket with lion's feet, embossed with the symbol of the royal house of Macedonia, which contained the bones of Philip II. The most mind-boggling exhibit is the bones themselves, which are carefully laid out to reconstruct an almost complete skeleton. There is something very strange about looking at someone who until that moment was just a name in a history book.

The opening hours of the museum (☎ 830 538) are Monday from 12.30 to 7 pm; Tuesday to Friday from 8 am to 7 pm; and weekends and holidays from 8.30 am to 3 pm. In winter, it opens from 11 am to 5 pm on Monday; on the other days, it opens at the same time as in summer but closes at 5 pm. Admission costs 1500 dr. The museum is opposite the entrance to the exhibition grounds. To get there either walk east along Tsimiski or take bus No 3.

Folkloric & Ethnological Museum of Macedonia This museum (☎ 830 591), housed in a beautiful 19th-century mansion, is one of the best of its kind in Greece. As well as elaborate costumes and intricate embroidery, the collection also includes traditional agricultural and craft tools.

The upstairs exhibition is titled 'Thessaloniki 1913 to 1919'. Life in the city at that time is presented through photographs taken by Fred Boissonas, a pioneer photographer and philhellene. The exhibition also includes eyewitness accounts (translated into English) of the fire of 1917.

The museum is at Vasilissis Olgas 68, and

is open daily from 9.30 am to 4 pm. It's closed on Thursday. Admission is 200 dr. It is 15 minutes' walk from the archaeological museum, or you can take eastbound bus No 5, 7 or 33 and get off at the Fleming stop.

White Tower This 15th-century tower is both the city's symbol and most prominent landmark. During the 18th century it was used as a prison for insubordinate janissaries, the elite troops of forcibly converted Christian boys, who became servants of the sultan. In 1826, at the order of Mahmud II, many of the janissaries were massacred in this tower and thereafter it became known as the bloody tower. After independence it was whitewashed as a symbolic gesture to expunge its function during Turkish rule. The whitewash has now been removed and it has been turned into a very fine **Byzantine Museum** (☎ 267 832), with splendid frescoes and icons.

In the pleasant museum café a 30-minute audiovisual show is shown every hour between 10 am and 4 pm (except at 2 pm).

The opening hours of the museum are Monday from 12.30 to 7 pm, Tuesday to Friday from 8 am to 7 pm, weekends and holidays from 8.30 am to 3 pm, and Monday from 11 am to 5 pm. Admission is 800 dr.

Other Museums The **Museum of the Macedonian Struggle** (☎ 229 778) outlines the story of the liberation of Macedonia from the Ottomans and the threat of Bulgarian nationalism. The museum is at Proxenou Koromila 23, in what was the Greek consular building when Macedonia was still part of the Ottoman Empire. Proxenou Koromila runs parallel to, and between, Mitropoleos and Nikis. Opening times are Tuesday to Saturday from 9 am to 2 pm; and Wednesday and Saturday from 5 to 7 pm. It is closed on Monday. Admission is free.

The **Society for Macedonian Studies Art Gallery** has a permanent collection consisting of some 200 paintings, drawings and engravings by eminent 20th-century Greek artists. The gallery is on the 6th floor of the same building as the State Theatre of Northern Greece and the Aristotelion cinema. It is

open Sunday to Friday from 9 am to 2 pm, but is closed in August. Admission is free.

Kemal Atatürk, the founder of the Republic of Turkey, was born in Thessaloniki in 1881. The Turkish timber-framed house where he was born and spent his childhood has been faithfully restored and is now a museum called **Atatürk's House**.

A visit is a bit of a cloak-and-dagger affair, but is worth the effort. You must ring the bell of the Turkish Consulate building (around the corner on Agiou Dimitriou); you will be asked to show your passport, and then someone will show you around. The museum is open every day from 2 to 6 pm. Admission is free.

Roman & Byzantine Thessaloniki Thessaloniki has few remaining Roman ruins, but its churches represent every period of Byzantine art and architecture, and were once the city's foremost glory. Not withstanding the extensive damage they have received due to fire and earthquakes, and their conversion to mosques; a visit to the most renowned ones is still worthwhile. You can see the Roman remains and the major churches in a circular walk.

The **Roman agora**, in the upper part of Plateia Dikastirion, is reached by crossing Egnatia from Aristotelous. Excavations began in the 1970s and are still in progress, so the site is cordoned off from the public. So far the odeion and two stoas have come to light.

From the north-east corner of this site, walk up Agnostou Stratioti, cross over Olympou, walk straight ahead, and you will see the 5th-century **Church of Agios Dimitrios** on the opposite side of the road.

Dimitrios was born in the city in the 3rd century and became an eminent scholar, and an early convert to Christianity. He was martyred on the orders of Galerius, who was not a Christian and who was ruthless in his persecution of those who were. Several claims of appearances of Dimitrios' ghost in warrior-like guise at apposite moments during sieges caused the enemy to flee in terror. This, coupled with claims of miracu-

NORTHERN GREECE

lous cures at the site of his martyrdom, gained him a sainthood. The church is Greece's largest and was built on the site where he was martyred.

The church was converted into a mosque by the Turks who plastered over the interior walls. When it was restored to the Christians again, it was discovered to have the finest mosaics of all the city's churches.

The frescoes and the building received extensive damage in the fire of 1917. However, five 8th-century mosaics have survived and can be seen on either side of the altar. The church is open to the public Sunday to Friday from 9.30 am to 2.30 pm and 5.30 to 9.30 pm, and from 9.30 am to 3 pm on Saturday.

On leaving the church turn left and walk along Agiou Dimitriou till you come to Dragoumi, which leads off to the right. Walk down here until you reach Filippou, and you will see ahead the 3rd-century **Church of Agios Georgios**, the oldest of Thessaloniki's churches. It is a Roman brickwork rotunda, which was originally intended as a mausoleum for Galerius, but never fulfilled this function. Constantine the Great transformed it into a church. The minaret from its days as a mosque remains. At the time of writing the church was closed for restoration, opening only for occasional services.

Walk a little way around the church and turn right into D Gounari, and you will see ahead the imposing **Arch of Galerius**, which was erected in 303 AD to celebrate the emperor's victories over the Persians in 297 AD. Its eroded bas-reliefs depict battle scenes with the Persians. Turn right into Egnatia, and then left to reach the 8th-century **Church of Agia Sofia**, on Agias Sofias, which emulates its renowned namesake in İstanbul. The dome has a striking mosaic of the Ascension.

On leaving the Church of Agia Sofia, retrace your steps back to Egnatia, cross the road, and continue a little way up Agias Sofias to the **Church of the Panagia Ahiropoiitos**, on the right. This church, built in the 5th century, is an early example of basilican form; some mosaics and frescoes

remain. The name means 'made without hands' and derives from the 12th century, when an icon supposedly miraculously appeared in the church. So many icons in Greece have appeared miraculously, one wonders if perhaps God is a frustrated artist.

Several of the smaller churches are also worth a look. They include the 13th-century **Church of Agia Ekaterini**, the **Church of the Dodeka Apostoloi** (Church of the Twelve Apostles) and the 4th-century **Church of Nikolaos Orfanos**, which has exquisite frescoes. The little 5th-century **Church of Osios David**, in Kastra, was allegedly built to commemorate Galerius' daughter, Theodora, whose clandestine baptism took place while her father was on one of his campaigns.

Kastra & the Ramparts The Turkish quarter of Kastra is all that is left of 19th-century Thessaloniki. The original ramparts of Kastra were built by Theodosius (379-475), but were rebuilt in the 14th century.

Kastra's streets are narrow and steep, with lots of steps, flanked by timber-framed houses, with overhanging upper storeys and tiny whitewashed dwellings with shutters. From Kastra there are stunning views of modern Thessaloniki and the Thermaic gulf. To get here, either take bus No 22 or 23 from Plateia Eleftherias; or walk north along Agias Sofias, which becomes Dimadou Vlatadou after Athinas. At the top turn right into Eptapyrgiou.

Organised Tours

Doucas Tours (☎ 269 984; fax 286 610), El Venizelou 8, has a half-day tour of Thessaloniki for around 5000 dr. Their full-day 'Alexander the Great Tour' visits Pella, Vergina, Veria, Edessa, Kavala and Philippi. This tour costs 11,000 dr. Other tours include Meteora for 10,500 dr and a cruise around the Athos peninsula.

Festivals

Thessaloniki hosts a string of festivals in September and October, which are held in the exhibition grounds. The first is the International Trade Fair, which is followed by a cultural festival which includes film shows, Greek song performances and culminates in the celebration of St Dimitrios' Day on 26 October, followed by military parades on Ohi Day on 28 October.

Places to Stay – bottom end

There are no camp sites close to Thessaloniki; the nearest ones are on the crowded beaches at Perea and Agia Triada, 20 and 22 km away respectively. Take bus No 67, 69 or 72 from Plateia Dikastirion.

Thessaloniki's *YHA hostel* (☎ 225 946), Alex Svolou 44, has dorm beds for 1800 dr. The doors are locked between 11 am and 7 pm, and there is an 11 pm curfew. An IYHF card is required.

The E-class *Hotel Atlantis* (☎ 540 131), Egnatia 14, has pokey, but clean double/triple rooms for 4500/6500 dr with shared bathroom. The D-class *Hotel Acropol* (☎ 531 670), Tandalidou 4, is Thessaloniki's best budget hotel. It's clean, quiet and owned by a friendly English-speaking family. The single/double rooms cost 5000/7500 dr with shared bathroom. The hotel is just beyond the tourist police.

Another quiet option is the D-class *Hotel Averof* (☎ 538 498), Leontos Sofou 24, around the corner from Egnatia. The attractive pine-furnished rooms cost 4500/7500/9000 dr with shared bathroom. The D-class *Hotel Atlas* (☎ 537 046), Egnatia 40, has clean, carpeted singles/doubles for 5500/7500 dr with shared bathroom (shower 400 dr); doubles with private bathroom are 8000 dr. This is a nice hotel, but the rooms at the front get a lot of traffic noise.

The D-class *Tourist Hotel* (☎ 270 501 or 284 768), Mitropoleos 21, has pleasant rooms and a spacious lounge with comfortable armchairs and a TV. The cost is 10,000 dr for a double room. Walk east along Egnatia, turn left into El Venizelou, walk to Plateia Eleftherias, turn left into Mitropoleos and the hotel is at the end of the block on the left, at the corner of Komninon.

The C-class *Continental Hotel* (☎ 277 563), at Komninon 5, has singles/doubles/

triples for 5400/7600/9100 dr with shared bathroom, or 6800/10,000/11,200 dr with private bathroom. All of the rooms have a refrigerator and the ones with private bathroom have colour TV and air-con. The hotel has an idiosyncratic lift which should be donated to an industrial archaeological museum. To reach this hotel, turn right at the Tourist Hotel.

Places to Stay – middle

The C-class *ABC Hotel* (☎ 265 421; fax 276 542), Angeliki 41, has 102 rooms all with private bathroom, telephone and balcony. Singles/doubles here cost 10,900/16,500 dr including breakfast. The hotel is at the eastern end of Egnatia. Further east the modern B-class *Hotel Queen Olga* (☎ 824 621; fax 868 581), Vasilissis Olgas 44, has cosy rooms with a warm mellow décor and private bathroom, radio, colour TV, minibar and air-con. The rates are 14,000/18,200 dr. This hotel has a car park. Travelling east, the hotel is on the right. A little further along, on the opposite side of the road, is the B-class *Hotel Metropolitan* (☎ 824 221; fax 271 467), at Vasilissis Olgas 65. It has attractively furnished rooms with bathroom, telephone and radio. Singles/doubles/triples cost 11,900/ 15,500/ 18,600 dr including breakfast. All of the middle-range hotels recommended so far have bars and restaurants.

The B-class *Capsis Hotel* (☎ 521 421; fax 510 555), Monastiriou 28, 200 metres east of the train station, is the city's largest hotel. It has two standards of rooms: business-class singles/doubles with TV, radio, telephone and air-con cost 19,600/25,000 dr; standard rooms are plainer but have everything except the telephone and cost 13,000/19,000 dr. The hotel has a roof garden, pool, health studio, sauna, hairdressers, boutiques, bars and restaurants.

Places to Stay – top end

Thessaloniki's A-class *Electra Palace Hotel* (☎ 232 221; fax 235 947), Plateia Aristotelous 5a, has an impressive façade in the style of a Byzantine palace. The interior is a tasteful combination of Byzantine and modern décor. All rooms have a telephone, air-con, minibar, colour TV, three-channel music radio and a hair dryer. The cost for singles/doubles is 20,550/24,000 dr including breakfast. The hotel has two restaurants and a bar.

Thessaloniki's only deluxe-class hotel is the *Macedonia Palace Hotel* (☎ 837 520/620/720; telex 412162 MP GR), Megalou Alexandrou. The hotel lacks the grandeur of some of Athens' luxury hotels. From the outside it could be mistaken for a large apartment block, but inside it has lots of black and grey marble, giving it a touch of cool tranquil elegance. Singles/doubles here cost 24,000/31,250 dr and suites are 62,500 dr. The hotel overlooks the sea just beyond the White Tower.

Places to Eat – inexpensive

There are lots of fast-food places and snack bars in Thessaloniki where you can get a gyros, pizza or cheese pie for around 300 dr. *Babel Snack Bar*, Komninon 18, is a good place for a snack or breakfast with reasonably priced crêpes, pies, toasted sandwiches and filter coffee.

The bright and busy *Life Restaurant*, Filippou 1, on the corner of Syngrou and Filippou, offers a rarity in Greece – instant service. The menu is large and the food well prepared: moussaka, pastitsio and spaghetti are all around the 1000 dr mark. The restaurant is open every day for lunch and dinner. Another popular place with similarly priced Greek staples is *Ta Nea Ilisia* on Leontis Sofou, opposite the Hotel Averof.

For a lively evening out you could try the long-established *O Loutros Fish Taverna*, in an old Turkish hammam (bathhouse) on Komninon, near the flower market. Don't be misled by the rough-and-ready ambience – this taverna has a cult following. If you go there you'll be rubbing shoulders with politicians, professors and actors. Excellent fish dishes cost around 1000 to 1200 dr. The taverna is always crowded and there are often spontaneous renderings of rembetika music, usually on Tuesday and Thursday evenings.

For an ethnic experience go to the *Patsas*

Ilias tripe shop at Egnatia 102, where you can have a bowl of hearty tripe soup; other reasonably priced Greek staples are also available. At the popular *Ta Spata Psistaria*, Aristotelous 28, a tasty meal of gyros, chips, aubergine salad, fried zucchini and retsina will cost about 2000 dr.

The *Olymbos Naoussa Restaurant*, Leoforos Nikis 5, is a time-honoured restaurant whose dilapidated grandeur is offset by sparkling white damask tablecloths and napkins. It was once the city's premier restaurant and still has a loyal following amongst the older generation. It's a little pricier than the restaurants so far recommended but still manages to squeeze in to the bottom end of the market. Try the egg and lemon soup, the delicately herb-flavoured rice with mussels, or the chicken casserole. It is only open for lunch and is closed at weekends.

Brothers' Taverna (Taverna Ta Aderfia), at Plateia Navarinou 9, is another place which is always packed. It has a pleasing ambience, with enlarged pictures of old Thessaloniki on the walls; their very tasty kebabs cost around 1300 dr. However, latest reports from Thessaloniki suggest that one brother has recently left and the restaurant is now called *Taverna tis Pyxarias*. Name change notwithstanding, the restaurant still has a good reputation and is worth checking out.

Places to Eat – moderate & expensive

The *Ouzeri Aristotelous* has first-rate mezedes, which include cuttlefish stuffed with cheese, fried eggplant with garlic and whitebait in sauce. The restaurant, which has a Parisian ambience with marble-top tables, is in an arcade off the left side of Aristotelous as you walk towards the waterfront – look for the wrought-iron gate at the entrance to the arcade. It's open Monday to Saturday from 12.30 to 4.30 pm and from 8.30 pm to 3 am, and is closed on Sunday.

Ta Nisia Taverna, Koromila 13, is another wonderful place. It has white stucco walls, a wood-beamed ceiling, lots of plants, and pretty plates on the walls. The unusual and imaginative mezedes include cuttlefish with spinach in wine and little triangles of pastry filled with eggplant. The restaurant is open for lunch and dinner, but is closed on Sunday.

The *Saul Modiano* is one of Thessaloniki's most elegant restaurants, with purple velvet-upholstered chairs. Its imaginative dishes start at 1900 dr. Unlike most Greek restaurants, the elegance doesn't end when you enter the loo – the women's bathroom provides cotton-wool buds, make-up remover pads, perfume, and hand and body lotion. The restaurant is in an arcade off the northern side of Irakliou, between I Dragoumi and El Venizelou; the arcade is next to Stoa Fast Food Café.

Entertainment

Discos & Music Bars *Mylos* (☎ 525 968), Andreou Georgiou 56, is a huge old mill which has been converted into an entertainment complex with an art gallery, restaurant, bar and live-music club (classical and rock). Andreou Georgiou is off the map in a grim part of town. Either take a westbound bus No 31, or walk down 26 Oktovriou from Plateia Vardari to Andreou Georgiou, which is off to the right next to the petrol station at 26 Oktovriou 36. Mylos is a spruce cream and terracotta building, 250 metres along on the right.

Live bouzouki and Greek folk are played at *Show Avantaz*, Agiou Dimitriou 156 (opposite the Turkish Consulate). There is no cover charge but spirits cost 1400 dr. The club is open from 11 pm to 4 am nightly, but closes from June to September.

One of Thessaloniki's biggest winter discos is *Traffic* on Tritis Septemvriou, two blocks down from Egnatia on the right. *L'Apogée* at Ethnikis Andistasis 16 and *Troll*, almost next door, are lively winter discos in the eastern part of town (off the map) – any taxi driver will be able to take you there.

Thessaloniki's summer discos are out towards the airport – the hippest are *Swing* and *Amnesia*. Back in the centre *Club Privé*, formerly known as Loft, Pavlou Mela 40, is a popular music bar with arty décor. *Entasis*, Koromila 29, is a gay and lesbian bar.

Cinema Thessaloniki's cinemas showing first-run English-language films include the *Olympian* on Plateia Aristotelous, *Aristotelion*, opposite the White Tower, and *Cinema Pallas*, at Nikis 69. *Natali* is an open-air summer cinema on Megalou Alexandrou.

Things to Buy

Thessaloniki's women have a reputation for being the most chic in Greece, so, to supply a demand, Thessaloniki has many clothes and shoe shops selling ultra-fashionable gear. Bargains can be found along Egnatia and the shops around the indoor food market, and you can pick up high-quality stuff on Tsimiski. Also look out for vendors on Tsimiski, some of whom sell trendy handmade jewellery at reasonable prices.

If you are seriously interested in Greek or Middle-Eastern music, you can buy some genuine traditional musical instruments at En Chordais (☎ 282 248) which is hidden away somewhat at L Margariti. Looking westwards, turn left just past McDonald's on Egnatia and head down this street for about 200 metres. L Margariti runs off to the left. Kyriakos Kalaïtzidis, the owner of En Chordais, is also an accomplished musician and runs a music school, should you have a burning desire to learn the oud, the *toumberleki* (lap drum), or Byzantine choral music.

Getting There & Away

Air The Olympic Airways office (☎ 230 240) is at Nav Koundourioti 3. The airport phone number is ☎ 425 011.

Domestic There are at least seven flights a day to Athens (19,400 dr), six a week to Limnos (13,000 dr), four a week to Ioannina (10,000 dr) and two a week to both Iraklio (27,600 dr) and Rhodes (29,800 dr). There are three flights per week to Corfu (18,000 dr), Mykonos (23,000 dr) and Santorini (25,000 dr).

International There are international flights between Thessaloniki and the following destinations:

Budapest	four a week
Cyprus	five a week
Frankfurt	two a day
London	11 a week
Munich	two a day
Paris	one a week
Vienna	nine a week

Bus – domestic Most of Thessaloniki's bus terminals are close to the train station. Frequent buses for Athens and Trikala leave from Monastiriou 65 and 67, opposite the train station. Buses for Alexandroupolis leave from Koloniari 17 behind the train station. Buses for Pella, Edessa, Volos and Kastoria leave from Anageniseos 22 and for Florina from Anageniseos 42. Ioannina buses leave from Hristou Pipsou 19 (off Giannitson). Buses for Veria leave from 26 Oktovriou 10.

The Katerini bus station is at Promitheos 10, on a corner with Sapphous, a turn-off right (heading west) just beyond the Veria station. Kavala buses leave from Langada 59. This is the main road north out of Thessaloniki starting at Plateia Vardari.

All buses for the Halkidiki peninsula leave from Karakassi 68 which is in the eastern part of the city and off this book's map but on the EOT map. To reach the Halkidiki terminal take bus No 10 to the Botsari stop (near Markou Botsari).

Bus – international Greek Railways (OSE) runs buses to the following destinations: Sofia, three times daily (3500 dr); İstanbul, at 3 am daily, excluding Wednesday (10,900 dr); and Korçë (Korytsa) in Albania, Monday, Tuesday, Friday and Saturday at 8 am (5100 dr). Buses leave from the station forecourt and tickets can be bought in the station. These services, however, are subject to frequent changes.

Train – domestic All domestic trains leave from the station on Monastiriou (☎ 51 517/516). There are four trains a day to Athens (7½ hours, 5160/3440 dr in 1st/2nd class), four to Kozani (four hours, 1500/2250 dr) with connections to Florina (3¼ hours, 1350/2010 dr). There are three trains a day

to Alexandroupolis (4500/3000 dr) and three trains to Volos (4½ hours, 2460/1640 dr).

There are five additional express intercity services to Athens (six hours, 8860/7140 dr; two services to Alexandroupolis (5½ hours, 6280/4880 dr) and one service to Kozani (3¼ hours, 3250/2340 dr). Note that tickets to all destinations and intermediate stations using the intercity services attract a supplement which is worked out on a sliding scale, depending on the distance travelled. There is also one dedicated night-sleeper train to Athens. A limited number of sleepers are also available on ordinary overnight services.

Tickets may be bought at the train station or the OSE office (☎ 276 382), Aristotelous 18. The station has a National Bank of Greece, a post office, an OTE and a restaurant which is open 24 hours. Luggage storage is 250 dr per piece, per day.

Train – international There are currently five international services operating out of Thessaloniki. There are two intercity trains a day to Belgrade; one which departs at 6.09 am, and the *Akropolis* which leaves at 8.53 pm (7600 dr). The *Hellas Express* goes to Budapest (via Belgrade), with connections to other destinations in Eastern and Western Europe. This train leaves at 8.15 am (22,990 dr). There is one train for İstanbul leaving at 3.25 pm (8370 dr). Finally, there is one intercity train a day to Sofia, leaving at 2.27 pm (4510 dr). These times are subject to seasonal changes.

Car The ELPA (Greek Automobile Club; ☎ 426 319) is at Vasilissis Olgas 228. Cars may be hired from Budget Rent a Car (☎ 274 272), Angelaki 15; and InterRent-Europcar (☎ 826 333), G Papandreou 5, among others.

Ferry A ferry sails on Saturday throughout the year to Lesvos (15 hours, 7000 dr), Limnos (eight hours, 4200 dr) and Chios (18 hours, 7200dr). In summer there are boats on Monday and Friday to Iraklio, on Crete (7600 dr). Both go via Paros and Santorini; the one on Friday also stops at Tinos and Mykonos.

NORTHERN GREECE

The telephone number of Thessaloniki's port police is ☎ 53 1504. Ferry tickets may be purchased from Nomikos Lines (☎ 524 544/522/736), Koundourioti 8.

Hydrofoil In summer there are more or less daily hydrofoils to the Sporades islands of Skiathos (3½ hours, 10,800 dr), Skopelos (4¾ hours, 12,100 dr) and Alonnisos (5¼ hours, 12,100 dr). These also stop at Nea Moudania and Agios Ioannis on the Pelion peninsula. Hydrofoil tickets can be purchased from Egnatias Tours (☎ 223 811), Kambouniou 9.

Getting Around

To/From the Airport Thessaloniki's airport is 16 km south-east of town. There is no Olympic Airways transfer service. Public bus No 78 plies to and from the airport; it leaves in front of the train station and costs 130 dr. A taxi to or from the airport costs between 1000 and 1500 dr.

Bus Orange articulated buses operate within the city, and blue buses and orange single buses operate both within the city and out to the suburbs. The local bus station is on Filippou and there is a flat fare of 75 dr within the city.

On the articulated orange buses you buy a ticket from the conductor sitting next to the door. On the driver-only buses you buy the ticket from a machine on the bus, which is not very user friendly. It will take five, 10, 20 and 50 drachma coins, but does not give change and does not take the older coins. If you do not have the exact coins, drop your fare in the box next to the driver. There are three different tickets for the three zones: 75 dr within the city, 100 dr for the suburbs and 115 dr for outlying villages. Books of 12 tickets are available and monthly travel cards cost 3000 dr.

Taxi Thessaloniki's taxis are blue and white and the procedure for hailing one is the same as in Athens – stand on the edge of the pavement, and bellow your destination at every one which passes. For a radio taxi telephone ☎ 217 218.

AROUND THESSALONIKI

Langadas Λαγκαδάς

The village of Langadas, 12 km north-east of Thessaloniki, is famous for the fire-walking ritual *anastenaria* which takes place on 21 May, the feast day of St Constantine and his mother, St Helena. The fire walkers, or *anastenarides* (groaners) believe the ritual originated in the village of Kosti (an abbreviation of Konstantinos) in eastern Thrace. The story is that in 1250 AD the Church of St Constantine caught fire and the villagers, hearing groans from the icons, entered the church, retrieved them, and escaped unscathed. The icons were kept by the families concerned, and descendants and devotees honoured the saint each year by performing the ritual. In 1913 when the village was occupied by Bulgarians the families fled to the villages of Serres, Drama and Langadas, taking the icons with them.

The anastenarides step barefoot onto burning charcoal. Holding the icons and waving coloured handkerchiefs, they dance whilst emitting strange cries, accompanied by drums and lyres. They believe they will not be burned, because God's spirit enters into them. Each year new fire walkers are initiated.

The church condemns the ritual as pagan, and indeed the celebration seems to have in it elements of the pre-Christian worship of Dionysos. If you would like to see this overtly commercial but intriguing spectacle, it begins at 7 pm – turn up early to get a ringside seat. Frequent buses leave for Langadas from the terminal at Irinis 17, near Langada in Thessaloniki.

PELLA Πέλλα

Pella (PE-la), most famous as the birthplace of Alexander the Great, lies on the plain of Macedonia astride the Thessaloniki-Edessa road. Its star attraction is its marvellous mosaics. King Archelaos (who ruled 413-399 BC) moved the Macedonian capital from Aigai to Pella, although Aigai remained the royal cemetery.

The mosaics, most of which depict mythological scenes, are made from naturally coloured stones and the effect is one of subtle and harmonious blends and contrasts. They were discovered in the remains of houses and public buildings, on the north (right, coming from Thessaloniki) side of the road. Some are *in situ* and others are housed in the museum. Also on the north side of the road there is a courtyard laid out with a black and white geometric mosaic, and six re-erected columns.

The **museum**, which is at the southern side of the site, is one of Greece's best on-site museums. In Room 1, there's a reconstruction of a wall from a house at Pella, and a splendid circular table inlaid with intricate floral and abstract designs, which it is thought belonged to Philip II. In Room 2 are the mosaics which have been lifted from the site.

The site and museum (☎ 0382-31 160/278) are open Tuesday to Saturday from 8.30 am to 3 pm. Admission to the site (including museum entry) is 400 dr. There is a drinking fountain outside the museum, and a kafeneio next to the north side of the site.

Getting There & Away

There are frequent buses to Pella from Thessaloniki (40 minutes, 525 dr). If you use the bus and wish to visit Pella and Vergina in one day, after visiting Pella, take a Thessaloniki bus back along the main road, and get off at Halkidona, from where you can pick up a bus to Vergina.

MT OLYMPUS Ολυμπος Ορος

Mt Olympus, chosen by the ancients as the abode of their gods, is Greece's highest and most awe-inspiring mountain. It has around 1700 plant species, some of which are rare and endemic. The lower slopes are covered with forests of holm oak, arbutus, cedar and conifers; the higher ones with oak, beech and black and Balkan pine. The mountain also maintains a varied bird life. In 1937 it became Greece's first national park.

In August 1913, Christos Kakalos, a native of Litohoro; and the Swiss climbers, Frederic Boissonas and Daniel Baud-Bovy were the first mortals to reach the summit of Mytikas (2917 metres), Mt Olympus' highest peak.

Litohoro Λιτόχωρο

The village of Litohoro (Li-TO-ho-ro, altitude 305 metres) is the place to make for if you wish to climb Olympus. The village developed in the 1920s as a health resort for the tubercular; later it settled comfortably into its role as 'base camp' for climbing Olympus. The approach to Litohoro along the main road is picture-postcard stuff on a fine day. Directly in front of you as you make the final approach to the village, the gorge of the Enipeas River parts to reveal the towering peaks of Olympus. The ancients sure knew how to choose an abode for their gods.

In recent years Litohoro has once again begun to promote its health-resort image. This has resulted in difficulties in finding a hotel room in July and August, particularly at weekends.

Orientation Litohoro's main road is Agiou Nikolaou, which, if you are coming from Thessaloniki or Katerini, is the road by which you will enter the village; it leads up to the central square of Plateia Kentriki. On the right side of this road is a large army camp. The road to Prionia, where the main trail up Olympus begins, is a turn-off to the right, just before the central square. Leading off to the left from the main square, up the hill is 28 Oktovriou where you will find most of the provisions stores.

The bus terminal is on Plateia Kentriki, to the right as you face the sea.

Information The post office is on Plateia Kentriki. The OTE is on Agiou Nikolaou, almost opposite the turn-off for Prionia. Litohoro's postcode is 602 00 and the telephone code is 0352.

The National Bank of Greece is on Plateia Kentriki. The police station (☎ 81 100/101) is on the corner of the road to Prionia. There

NORTHERN GREECE

is a health centre (☎ 22 222) five km away, at the turn-off for the village from the main coastal highway.

There is an EOT office in a little white building with wooden eves on Agiou Nikolaou, just before the turn-off for Prionia.

The EOS (☎ 81 944) in Litohoro has helpful English-speaking staff who give information about Olympus and a free pamphlet giving details of some of the treks. To get to this office, when you are facing inland on Agiou Nikolaou, turn left opposite the Mirto Hotel and follow the signs. The office is open Monday to Friday from 9 am to 1 pm and 6 to 8.30 pm, and on Saturday from 9 am to 1 pm. It's closed on Sunday. The EOS has three refuges on Olympus.

The SEO (Association of Greek Climbers; ☎ 82 300) also gives information, but you are more likely to find someone who speaks English at the EOS. To get to the SEO, walk along the road to Prionia and take the first turn left and first left again. The SEO office is open from 6 to 10 pm every day, and has one refuge on Olympus.

Places to Stay There's a plethora of camp sites along the coast around the turn-off for Litohoro. They include *Olympios Zeus* (☎ 22 115/116/117), *Olympos Beach* (☎ 22 112 or 81 437) and *Minerva* (☎ 22 177/178). All of these sites have good facilities and a taverna, snack bar and minimarket. These sites all have the same telephone area code as Litohoro: 0352.

Litohoro's clean, well-run *YHA hostel* (☎ 82 176) charges 1300 dr for a dormitory bed and 500 dr for linen. Motorbike rental is 5000 dr, bicycle rental is 1500 dr, various items of mountain-clothing are for hire from 500 to 1000 dr and left-luggage storage is 450 dr. Maps and books on Olympus are on sale at the hostel.

The warden, Kostas Irandos, is an experienced mountaineer. He doesn't suffer fools, but if you are a serious trekker and genuinely interested in Olympus he is an invaluable source of information. You will find the hostel by following the signs from Plateia Kentriki.

Litohoro's cheapest hotel is the clean, well-kept D-class *Hotel Markesia* (☎ 81 831/832), which costs 4500/6000 dr for singles/doubles with private bathroom. However, this place only opens from June onwards. From Plateia Kentriki, facing inland, turn left into 28 Oktovriou and the hotel is along here on the left. The rather gloomy-looking C-class *Hotel Aphrodite* (☎ 81 415), on Plateia Kentriki, has OK rooms for 6000/7500/8500 dr with private bathroom. Directly opposite the main entrance of the Aphrodite is the newer and much brighter and breezier *Hotel Enipeas*, with doubles/triples for 7000/8500 and probably the best views in town of Olympus from their balconies.

Litohoro's poshest hotel is the C-class *Mirto Hotel* (☎ 81 398; fax 82 298), where all the rooms have a telephone, private bathroom and balcony. Singles/doubles cost 7000/8500 dr. The hotel, which is on Agiou Nikolaou, near the central square, has a cosy wood-panelled Tyrol-style TV lounge-cum-bar.

Places to Eat There is a selection of places to eat both on the main square and on the approach road coming up from the army barracks. The choice ranges from fast to traditional. *Olympos Taverna*, on Agiou Nikolaou opposite the Park Hotel, is reasonably good value. *Deas Psistaria*, next to the OTE, has generous portions of charcoal grill chicken for a reasonable price. *To Pazari*, just down from the Hotel Markesia on 28 Oktovriou, specialises in fish dishes. On the main square itself, the *Olympus Café* serves nice mezedes and ready-made food.

Getting There & Away There are 18 buses a day between Litohoro and Katerini (25 min, 360 dr). There are eight a day between Thessaloniki and Litohoro (one hour, 1350 dr). There are three buses a day from Litohoro to Athens (5½ hours, 6000 dr). Thessaloniki-Athens and Thessaloniki-Volos buses will drop you off on the main highway, from where you can catch the Katerini-Litohoro bus.

Litohoro train station is on the Athens-Volos-Thessaloniki line (10 trains a day) but the station is close to the coast, nine km from Litohoro, so you must walk from the station to the main road (150 metres) to catch the Katerini-Litohoro bus.

Getting Around Motorbikes and bicycles can be hired at the Litohoro YHA hostel. (See Places to Stay for details.)

Mt Olympus Trails

The following trails by no means exhaust the possibilities on Olympus, but they are the ones which (between June and September) can be tackled by anyone who is fit – no mountaineering experience or special equipment is required. It takes two days to climb Olympus, spending one night at a refuge. However, if you are a keen trekker you'll want to spend longer exploring the mountain – it really deserves more than a couple of days.

You will need to take warm clothing as it can become very cold and wet, even in August. Sunblock cream is also essential as much of the climbing is above the tree line. Climbing boots are the most suitable footwear, but sturdy shoes or trainers will suffice. A good topographical map of the region is essential. The relevant Korfes map of the Olympus region is probably the best available. Maps can be obtained from the youth hostel in Litohoro, or write to the EOS (☎ 01 246 1528) – Aharnes, Kentriki Plateia, 136 71 Aharnes . The Olympus map sells for around 2000 dr but the legend and place names are only in Greek.

Do your homework before you begin the trek by talking with someone at the EOS or SEO (see Information in the previous section on Litohoro). Let them know how long you plan to trek and when you will return. Bear in mind that Olympus is a high and challenging mountain – it has claimed its share of lives.

For more comprehensive trekking information on Mt Olympus, including detailed trail descriptions, see Lonely Planet's *Trekking in Greece*.

Litohoro to Prionia The most popular trail up Olympus begins at Prionia (Πριόνια), a tiny village 18 km from Litohoro. It has a car park, basic taverna and a source of water, but no telephone and there is no bus service. The EOS-owned *Dimitris Boundolas Refuge* (Refuge D) is halfway along the Litohoro-Prionia road at Stavros (930 metres). It is open from April to November. If you plan to do the six-hour trek from Diastavrosi to the SEO refuge you may wish to stay here.

Most people either opt to drive, hitch or take a taxi (5500 dr) to Prionia, but if you have sufficient stamina, you can trek there along an 18-km marked trail, which follows the course of the Enipeas River. The strenuous four-hour trek is over sharply undulating terrain but offers glorious views. It begins beyond the cemetery in Litohoro and ends just before the taverna at Prionia. Just one km before Prionia you can look at the ruined **Moni Agiou Dionysou** which was built at the beginning of the 16th century and blown up by the Turks in 1828. It was rebuilt only to be blown up again in 1943 by the Nazis who believed resistance fighters were using it as a hide-out.

Prionia to Spilios Agapitos The trail begins just beyond the taverna in Prionia. You'll have to fill up with water here as it is the last source before Refuge A at Spilios Agapitos (Σπήλαιος Αγαπητός). The trail is well maintained and well used – there is no chance of getting lost and you will meet other trekkers along the way. It is possible to go up on a mule (6000 dr) – contact the EOS for details. The trail is a steep path which passes first through thick forests of deciduous trees and then through conifers. It takes around 2½ hours to reach the refuge.

Refuge A (☎ 0352-81 800) can accommodate up to 90 people. It has cold showers and serves very good meals from 6 am to 9 pm, both to guests and to people just popping in. The warden, Kostas Zolotas, speaks fluent English, is an experienced mountaineer and will be able to answer any questions you may have. The cost of staying at the refuge, which is open from May to October, is 1560 dr a

NORTHERN GREECE

night (1170 dr for Alpine Club members). If you wish to stay during July and August it is advisable to make a reservation either through the EOS in Litohoro or Thessaloniki, or by telephoning the refuge.

Refuge A to Mytikas (via Kaki Skala) The path to Mytikas (Μύτικας) begins just behind Refuge A. Fill up your water bottles because there is no source of water beyond here. The last of the trees thin out rapidly; the path is still marked by red slashes and once again it is easy to follow. After one to 1½ hours you will come to a sign pointing right to the SEO refuge. To reach Mytikas continue straight ahead. The path now zigzags over the scree for another hour before reaching the summit ridge. From the ridge there is a 500 metre drop into the chasm of Kazania (the cauldron).

Just before the drop, in an opening to the right, is the beginning of Kaki Skala (Κακή Σκάλα; bad stairway), which leads, after 40 minutes of rock scrambling, to the summit of Mytikas. The route is marked by red slashes on the rocks. It is perhaps surprising that no-one has yet coined the nickname 'the original Stairway to (Olympian) Heaven', given the divine destination of the Kaki Skala. The route keeps just below the drop into Kazania, although at a couple of places you can look down into the cauldron – a dramatic sight. If you have never done rock scrambling before, take a look at Kaki Skala and decide then and there if you want to tackle it. Many turn back at this stage, but just as many novices tackle Kaki Skala. If you decide against it, all is not lost, for if you turn left at the summit ridge, an easy path leads in 15 to 20 minutes to Skolio (Σκολιό) peak (2911 metres), Mt Olympus' second highest peak.

Mytikas to Giossos Apostolides (SEO Refuge) After you've admired the breathtaking views from Mytikas, signed the

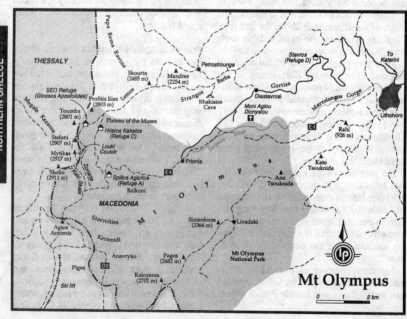

summit book and said a prayer of thanks to the gods for helping you up, and another, asking them to help you down, you are faced with the choice of returning to Refuge A via Kaki Skala, or continuing on to the *SEO Refuge* of Giossos Apostolides (Γιόσος Αποστολίδης). At 2720 metres this is the highest refuge in the whole of the Balkans and has a stunning panorama of the major peaks of Olympus. The refuge has beds for 90 people and meals are served. It has no showers or natural drinking water, but bottled water is sold; it is much less visited than Refuge A. The EOS *Refuge C*, called Hristos Kakalos (Χρήστος Κάκαλος), is nearby, and has beds for 18 people. It is open only during July and August.

Neither of these refuges has a telephone. To get to them you can return via Kaki Skala to the path signposted to the SEO Refuge; this path is called Zonaria (Ζωνάρια)and leads to the refuge in one hour. Alternatively, you can descend Mytikas via Louki couloir, which begins just north of the summit and is another 45-minute rock scramble. A few experienced climbers claim Louki couloir is easier than Kaki Skala, but the general consensus is that it's more difficult. It is certainly

more sheer and prone to rock falls – more of a danger to those climbing up, than to those descending. At the bottom of Louki couloir you meet up with the Zonaria path. Turn left onto the path and you will reach the SEO lodge in 20 minutes.

SEO Refuge to Diastavrosi The refuge is on the edge of the Plateau of the Muses and from here a well-maintained path leads, in 4½ hours, to Diastavrosi (Διασταύρωση), on the Prionia-Litohoro road. From the plateau the path goes along a ridge called Lemos (Λαιμός; neck) with the Enipeas ravine on the right and the Papa Rema ravine on the left. After one hour you arrive at Skourta summit (2485 metres) and from here it is 1½ hours to **Petrostrounga** (the stony sheepfold). The next stretch of path leads through woodland to a small meadow known as **Barba** and from here it is 40 minutes to Diastavrosi, which is 14 km from Litohoro.

Ancient Dion Δίον

Recently discovered ancient Dion is an extensive, well-watered site at the foot of Mt Olympus, just north of Litohoro and 16 km south of Katerini. It was the sacred city of the Macedons, who gathered here to worship the Olympian gods. Alexander the Great made sacrifices to the Olympic gods here, before setting off to conquer the world.

Dion's origins are unknown but there is evidence that an earth goddess of fertility was first worshipped here. Later, other gods were worshipped, including Asclepius, the god of medicine. The most interesting discovery so far is the evocative **Sanctuary to Isis**, the Egyptian goddess, in a lush low-lying part of the site.

Its votive statues were found virtually intact with traces of colour remaining. Copies of these statues have been placed in the positions of the originals, which are now in the site's museum. Also worth seeking out is the magnificent well-preserved mosaic floor, dating from 200 AD, which depicts the **Dionysos Triumphal Epiphany**. During the Olympus Festival, which takes place

NORTHERN GREECE

during August, plays are performed at the reconstructed theatre at the site.

The site's **museum** (☎ 0351-53 206) is well laid out with a large collection of statues and offerings from ancient Dion; labelling is in English and Greek. On sale at both the site and the museum is a pamphlet in English about Dion. It costs 300 dr and without this the site will have little meaning, for as yet labelling and signposts are nonexistent.

The site is open daily from 8 am to 7 pm, but closes in winter at 3 pm. Admission is 500 dr. The museum's opening times are Tuesday to Friday from 8 am to 7 pm and Monday from 12.30 to 7 pm. Admission is 400 dr.

Places to Stay As it is a bit of a hassle to get to Dion, you may wish to stay overnight in the modern village. The pleasant C-class *Dion Hotel* (☎ 53 336) is on the main road in (modern) Dion, near the bus stop. Singles/doubles with private bathroom are 6500/7000 dr.

Getting There & Away There are no buses from Litohoro to Dion; you must first go to Katerini from where there are 12 buses a day (150 dr). The Dion bus terminal is 400 metres from Katerini's intercity bus station. To reach it, walk out of the intercity bus station, cross the road, and walk along Karaïskaki, which is signposted to the centre. Continue along here for 150 metres and you will come to a crossroad; turn left into Pangari Tsaldari.

Walk a little way along here to a T-junction and turn right – the road is still called Tsaldari. Walk 100 metres along here and you will come to a five-road intersection. Cross over the road to Restaurant Olympos, make a right turn and take the second turn left into Kosma Ioannou. Continue up here for 40 metres and you will come to the Dion bus station on the left, opposite the Orfeas cinema.

Once you're in the village of modern Dion, both the site and museum are clearly signposted.

VERIA Βέροια

Most people merely pass through Veria (VER-ia, population 37,000), 75 km west of Thessaloniki, *en route* to the ancient site of Vergina. But Veria, capital of the prefecture of Imathia, is a fascinating town with over 70 churches that is called 'Little Jerusalem' by some people. There are many rather dilapidated houses from the Turkish era, but a government preservation order is in force and most of them are now undergoing gradual restoration. Mineral springs are located all over the town and the local tap water is said to be very good. Veria is also the centre of a vast peach-growing industry and wines made from grapes grown on the escarpment from Veria to Edessa are among Greece's most well-known exports.

Orientation & Information

The town's two main squares, Plateia Antoniou and Plateia Raktivan – more commonly known as Plateia Orologiou – are one km apart. Connecting them are the town's two main thoroughfares: the modern Venizelou which halfway along becomes Mitropoleos, and the traditional Vasileos Konstantinou (also called Kentrikis). To reach Plateia Antoniou from the intercity bus station, walk out of the rear end of the station onto Iras, turn right and immediately left into Malakousi, and the square is a little way along here with Venizelou and Vasileos Konstantinou both running off to the left. The train station is three km from the town centre on the old road to Thessaloniki.

The post office is at Mitropoleos 33 and the OTE at No 45. Veria's postcode is 591 00 and the telephone code is 0331.

The National Bank of Greece is on the corner of Mitropoleos and Ippokratous. There is no tourist office or tourist police. The regular police (☎ 22 391/233) are next door to the post office on Mitropoleos.

Things to See

The most interesting part of Veria is the old Turkish quarter. For a short walk around this area, begin by walking down Vasileos Konstantinou from Plateia Antoniou. The narrow and winding Vasileos Konstantinou is the commercial street of old Veria, flanked by old-fashioned tailor shops, bookbinders, kafeneia and antique shops. Halfway along on the right is a huge ancient-looking plane tree where in 1430 the Turks, after taking Veria, hanged the archbishop Arsenios. Directly opposite the plane tree is the dilapidated **old cathedral** which dates from the 12th century. A rather incongruous and now decapitated minaret bears testament to its usage as a mosque during the Turkish era. To reach the residential part of the old Turkish quarter, turn right at the plane tree into Goudi and just wander among the old streets with their many abandoned houses.

The **archaeological museum** is in this part of town on Leoforos Anixeos, which snakes its way to the left across the escarpment from the end of Elias. It contains some finds from the tombs of Vergina and Levkadia. The museum is open from 8.30 am to 3 pm from Tuesday to Sunday. Admission is 400 dr. To reach it, take any of the roads running east from Venizelou, which will bring you to Leoforos Anixeos.

St Paul the Apostle visited Veria twice on his second and third voyages (49-52 and 53-58 AD). Veria was known as Beroea in the New Testament and there is now a shrine at Mavromihali 1 where Paul is believed to have held his sermons. Mavromihali runs off Plateia Orologiou and leads to the Papakia district (see Places to Eat).

Places to Stay – bottom end

The best value of Veria's few hotels is *Hotel Veroi* (☎ 22 866; fax 20 014) on Plateia Orologiou. The hotel is very clean with large, comfortably furnished single/double rooms with balcony, costing 6500/9000 dr with private bathroom.

At the *Hotel Villa Elia* (☎ 26 800/1/2), Elias 16, room rates are 10,750/13,200 dr with private bathroom. Both Elias and Megalou Alexandrou are left turns off Venizelou, coming from Plateia Antoniou.

Places to Stay – middle

The best of Veria's hotels is the B-class *Hotel Macedonia* (☎ 66 946/924/968; fax 66 902), Kontogiorgaki 50. The spacious, tastefully furnished rooms are 10,000/13,500/16,200 dr with private bathroom. To reach the hotel walk along Venizelou, turn left into Elias and then right at the Top Café, into Paster. Kontogiorgaki is the continuation of Paster. The hotel is at the end of this street on the right.

Places to Eat & Drink

Veria is famous for is revani, a sweet syrupy cake which can be found throughout most of the town. The town is also famous for its infamous bean concoction, fasolada, usually cooked in the oven. Give it a go, if you can put up with the inevitable side-effects.

For uncomplicated easy-to-order eating, seek out the *mayiria* – literally 'cook houses'. These are pre-McDonald's, Greek fast-food joints and can be found in most towns. Look and point and you'll be eating within two minutes. The long-established *Estiatorion-Kosmas Sarafopoulos* on Kentrikis (Vasileos Konstantinou) 100 metres around the corner and down the hill from the Hotel Veroi. This place is popular with locals. There is a similar, but slightly more modern, place next to the Kozani bus terminal on Plateia Orologiou called the *Menou*.

For more relaxed eating in a pleasant location, head for the Papakia district. Follow Mavromihali, near the Kozani bus station, up the hill for about 200 metres. Here is a pleasant square with waterfalls, little streams and three places to eat. The *Saroglou* is a slightly pretentious place, but very popular. Next to it is the traditional *Kostalar*, in business since 1939, and across the road is the unassuming *Yiannis Psarotaverna*. Take your pick.

For that special treat, go to the *Gri Gri* at Kapetan Agra 4. This is an ouzeri, but is refreshingly modern, well-presented and has some exquisite specialities. Try their htypiti (feta cheese and chilli dip), or the mydia saganaki (pan-fried mussels in chilli sauce).

Bar/pub life is focussed on Elias and in the older quarter bordered by Elias and Mitropoleos. The *Elia Restaurant & Cafeteria* at the end of Elias has the best view in town, but the most inflated prices. The view and shade offered, it should be said, on a hot day more than compensate for the price you pay.

Getting There & Away

Bus Frequent buses leave from Veria's intercity bus station for Thessaloniki (1100 dr), Athens (7000 dr), Edessa (750 dr) and the ancient site of Vergina (240 dr). Buses for Kozani (900 dr) depart from a separate bus station on Plateia Orologiou and through buses to/from Ioannina will stop on this square also.

Train There are eight trains a day, in both directions, along the Thessaloniki-Kozani/Florina line. Two additional intercity services to and from Kozani pass through Veria twice a day. One goes to Athens and the other to Thessaloniki. Suburban buses ply regularly between the town centre and the station and normally meet arriving trains. Tickets can be purchased from the kiosk at the station. Tickets for other routes, including intercity trains, can be purchased from Filippidis Travel, on Mitropoleos.

VERGINA Βεργίνα

The ancient site of Vergina (Ver-GEE-na), 11 km south-east of Veria, is ancient Aigai, the first capital of Macedon. The capital was later transferred to Pella, but Aigai continued to be the royal burial place. Philip II was assassinated here in 336 BC at the wedding reception of his daughter, Cleopatra.

To fully appreciate the significance of the discoveries, you need to visit Thessaloniki's archaeological museum, where the magnificent finds of Philip II's tomb are displayed, along with Philip II himself! Unfortunately, Philip's tomb is off limits to visitors as it is still being excavated.

The ruins of ancient Vergina are spread out, but well signposted from the modern village of the same name. The **Macedonian tomb**, 500 metres uphill from the village, has a façade of four Ionic half-columns. Inside is a marble throne. Continue 400 metres further up the road to reach the ruins of an extensive palatial complex, built as a summer resi-

dence for King Antigonos Gonatas (278-240 BC). The focal point of the site is a large Doric peristyle which was surrounded by pebble mosaic floors. One of the mosaics, with a beautiful floral design, is well preserved and *in situ*. A large oak tree on the highest point of the site affords some welcome shade.

Both this site (☎ 0331-92 337) and the Macedonian tomb are open Tuesday to Saturday from 8 am to 3 pm and Sunday from 8.30 am to 3 pm, and are open to 7 pm in summer. Entrance to the sites is currently 400 dr, but there was talk of hiking the price up to 1200 dr at the time of writing.

There is a café opposite the Macedonian tomb and for those who wish to stay overnight, there is a choice of the *Pansion Vergina*, or *Ikos* domatia, both on the same road as the tombs.

EDESSA Εδεσσα

Edessa (population 16,000) is the capital of the prefecture of Pella. Extolled by Greeks for its many waterfalls, it is little visited by foreign tourists. Edessa is a truly delightful town with a presence of water and greenery unlike the majority of towns in Greece. Little streams and bridges and cool and shady parks dot the whole of Edessa which, being a small town, is very easy and pleasant to discover on foot. The town is perched precariously on a ledge overlooking the seemingly endless agricultural plain below and is the most northern of the Mt Vermion escarpment centres.

Until the discovery of the royal tombs at Vergina, Edessa was believed to be the site of the ancient Macedonian city of Aigai.

Orientation

Edessa's intercity bus station is on the corner of Filippou and Pavlou Mela. To reach the town centre, cross over Filippou and walk straight ahead along Pavlou Mela to the T-junction, and turn right into Egnatia. Almost immediately the road forks: the left fork continues as Egnatia; the right fork is Dimokratias. These two streets, along with Filippou, are the town's main thoroughfares.

The train station is opposite the end of 18 Oktovriou. To reach the town centre from here, walk straight ahead up 18 Oktovriou for 400 metres to a major road junction. From here the biggest waterfall is signposted sharp left; veer right for Dimokratias.

Information

There is no EOT or tourist police; the regular police are on Iroön Polytehniou, which runs between Filippou and Dimokratias. Since there are no tourist police, don't depend on the ordinary police for any tourist assistance.

The National Bank of Greece is at Dimokratias 1. The post office is at Dimokratias 26. The OTE is on Agiou Dimitriou. To reach it turn right from Pavlou Mela, by the Hotel Pella, and you will find it off to the left. Edessa's postcode is 582 00 and the telephone code is 0381.

Things to See

Edessa's main attraction is its **waterfalls**. There are a number of little ones (usually artificial) dotted around the town, but the biggest waterfall, called *katarraktes* (waterfalls), plunges dramatically down a cliff to the agricultural plain below. There are actually two falls: one that drops more or less vertically and another, a little way to the left, that tumbles and twirls, zigzag fashion, down the cliff face.

The whole set-up is actually very nice, if you discount the tacky tourist stalls on the street. There is a pleasant park area with little walkways and stairways that take you down and behind the large falls – mind your step, the steps near the falls can get slippery – and there are some caves towards the bottom of the falls themselves. The cliff is mantled with abundant vegetation and there are wonderful views of the vast plain which extends all the way to Thessaloniki.

Places to Stay – bottom end

The C-class *Hotel Alfa* (☎ 22 221; fax 24 777) in Egnatia has double-glazed and soundproofed rooms for 6000/10,500 dr. It is much nicer than the D-class *Hotel Pella*

(☎ 23 541), which is right next door at Egnatia 26, and has single/double rooms for 7100/9000 dr with private bathroom and is a reasonably cheap place to stay.

The D-class *Hotel Elena* (☎ 23 218; fax 23 951), Plateia Timenidon, has light and airy rooms for 7000/9100/10,200 dr with private bathroom. From the bus station turn right at Filippou, walk three blocks to the road junction with signposts to the waterfalls and Florina, turn right into Arch Panteleimonos and you will see the hotel a little way along there on the left.

Places to Stay – middle

Edessa's best hotel is the B-class *Hotel Katarraktes* (☎ 22 300; fax 27 237) at Karanou 18, where rates are 9700/9100/10,200 dr. The hotel has comfortable, traditionally furnished rooms with private bathroom and balcony. Follow the signposts for the katarraktes, and look for the hotel on the left, just before the waterfalls.

Places to Eat & Drink

There is no shortage of fast-food joints around the central area, so you won't starve. If you want real Greek food, check out the following places.

Close to the bus station and on the same street as the Hotel Pella and Hotel Alfa, at Egnatia 20 is the *Estiatorion Omonia* (the sign is in Greek only). The food is cheap and good and this is a long-established eating place with ready-made dishes for you to point at and choose from. A meal with draught wine will cost about 2000 dr.

Closest to the bus station is a nameless *taverna/psistaria* at Filippou 26, diagonally opposite the bus station. This place is convenient, though a little uninspiring. Another traditional place is *Taverna Roloï* (clock tavern), at Agiou Dimitriou 5, near the OTE and on the street leading to the clock tower. Behind the clock tower is *Pavlos Taverna* which looks a bit old and decrepit, but is probably worth trying.

For more up-market eating, there is any number of tavernas and psistarias right up by

NORTHERN GREECE

the waterfalls. Since this is a very touristy spot, expect tourist prices.

The younger set's bar and café life is centred on the little brick-paved street Angeli Gatsou, which starts just opposite the post office and by the little bridge.

Getting There & Away

Bus From the main bus station there are 15 buses to Thessaloniki (one hour and 40 minutes, 1300 dr), six a day to Veria (one hour, 750 dr) and three a day to Athens (eight hours, 7350 dr). Four buses a day go to Florina and Kastoria from a second bus station, marked by a bus sign on the corner of Egnatia and Pavlou Mela.

Train There are eight trains a day both ways on the Thessaloniki-Kozani/Florina line, plus an additional two intercity services. The stretch between Edessa and Amynteo is particularly beautiful as it skirts the western shore of Lake Vegoritida. The journey is meant to take 1½ hours, but Greek trains being what they are, it can sometimes take longer.

FLORINA Φλώρινα

The mountain town of Florina (FLO-ri-na, population 12,500) is the capital of the prefecture of Florina. Tourists used to come to Florina only because it was the last town in Greece before the former Yugoslav border. Now its economy is seriously compromised by the continuing political troubles with its neighbour to the north. Despite the recent changes, it's a lively town, and a pleasant place for an overnight stopover if you are touring the area.

If you enjoy your stay in Florina you're in good company. Greece's most famous film director, Theodoros Angelopoulos, loves Florina (although it is not his birthplace). Two of his films, *Alexander the Great* and *The Hesitant Step of the Stork* were made on location here.

Florina is the only place from which you can take a bus to the Prespa lakes and there is also a low-key skiing resort at Vigla, just west of Florina on the Prespa lakes road.

Orientation & Information

Florina is laid out in a long curving shape, much like a boomerang, and is divided by the river that flows along the length of the town. The main street is Pavlou Mela, which leads to the central square of Plateia Georgiou Modi. Half of Pavlou Mela is a pedestrian mall. To reach this street from the train station, walk straight ahead keeping the archaeological museum to your left. Bear left and you are on Pavlou Mela. From Plateia Georgiou Modi, turn right into Stefanou Dragoumi to reach the intercity bus station which is 250 metres up the street. Bear right at the end of the street, cross the road and look for the KTEL office, opposite the national stadium. If you turn left from Plateia Georgiou Modi, into 25 Martiou, you will reach the river. Megalou Alexandrou is the continuation of Pavlou Mela on the other side of the square.

The post office is at Kalergi 22; walk along Stefanou Dragoumi towards the bus station and Kalergi is off to the left. The OTE is at Tyrnovou 5. As you walk along Pavlou Mela from the train station, Tyrnovou is a turn-off to the left. The gaudily coloured National Bank of Greece is about 50 metres up Megalou Alexandrou on the right and the Commercial Bank is just behind it. Florina's postcode is 531 00 and the telephone code is 0385.

There is no EOT or tourist police; the telephone number of the regular police is ☎ 22 100.

Things to See & Do

The **archaeological museum** is housed in a modern building near the train station. It is well laid out, even though it feels a little bare. Only the labels downstairs are in English. The curator will show you around but his English is limited. Downstairs there is pottery from the Neolithic, early Iron Age and Bronze Age and grave steles and statues from the Roman period. Upstairs there are some Byzantine reliefs and fragments of frescoes, and finds from an as yet unidentified town built by Philip II, discovered on the nearby hill of Agios Panteleimonas. The

NORTHERN GREECE

museum is open every day from 8.30 am to 3 pm. Admission is 500 dr.

Close to the archaeological museum and easily mistaken for a railways building, is the **Florina Artists' Gallery**. It is open from Wednesday to Saturday (5 to 8 pm) and houses a collection of local artists' works.

Old Florina occupied both river banks, and many Turkish houses and neoclassical mansions survive. The town has a thriving artistic community, and the Society for the Friends of Art of Florina has restored one of the neoclassical mansions on the river bank, which is now the **Museum of Modern Art**, Leoforos Eleftherias 103. The museum houses a permanent collection of works by contemporary Greek artists and hosts frequent exhibitions.

It is open from 5 to 8 pm every day and from 10 am to 1 pm on Sunday. Admission is free. To reach the museum walk down 25 Martiou, cross the bridge over the river and turn right. Walk for about 200 metres. Even if you are not interested in art, this is a pleasant walk along the river bank.

If you feel energetic, there is a pleasant walk up to the Tottis Hotel (see Places to Stay) and cafeteria from where you can enjoy an unparalleled view of Florina. From the little **Church of Koimisis Theotokou** there is an established path that snakes up the hill. The blue and white church is on the south side of the river, just above Plateia Sholion. Walk down 25 Martiou, cross the river and turn left. Walk about 200 metres and you will come across the square, and the church above it.

Places to Stay – middle

The nearest hotel to the train station is the C-class *Hotel Ellenis* (☎ 22 671; fax 22 815), Pavlou Mela 39. It's pleasantly clean, if somewhat basic. The single/double room rates are 6500/9000 dr with private bathroom. Coming from the train station the hotel is on the left.

Up a notch, the C-class *Hotel Antigone* (☎ 23 180; fax 45 620), Arianou 1, has slightly jaded but pleasant rooms for 7200/9500 dr. Turn right into Stefanou Dragoumi, from Plateia Georgiou Modi, and the hotel is 200 metres along on the left, close to the bus station.

The B-class *Hotel Lingos* (☎ 28 322/323), Tagmatarhou Naoum 1, just north of Plateia Georgiou Modi, has comfortable, but essentially functional rooms for 8500/13,900 dr.

Places to Stay – top end

For a room with a magnificent view, the B-class *Hotel Tottis* (☎ 22 645; fax 29 523) is hard to beat. Overlooking Florina from the flanks of Panteleimonas hill, the rooms in this hotel have a grand panorama over all of Florina. Rooms here cost 10,600/16,900 dr. Take a taxi to get there, or, if you want to walk, see the Things to See & Do section.

The B-class *King Alexander* (☎ 23 501; fax 29 643), also in an elevated position above town at Leoforos Nikis 68, has luxurious rooms for 10,000/15,000 dr.

Places to Eat

Florina has an array of eating places, from fast food to traditional, centred round the Pavlou Mela/Plateia Modi area, so you can't go far wrong. Florina is famous for its large red peppers – piperies Florinis – some hot and some sweet. Make sure you try them out.

The *Taverna Takis*, 25 Martiou 18, serves tasty grilled food which is reasonably priced, despite the taverna's elegant ambience. A meat dish with salad and wine will cost about 2000 dr. *Restaurant Olympos*, Megalou Alexandrou 22 (on the right as you walk from Plateia Modi) has a good choice of well-prepared low-priced ready-made food. This restaurant is only open at lunch time, but is a very good choice. Lunch with wine here will cost about 1800 dr.

If you are waiting for a bus, or have just arrived by bus, the *Tria Adherfia*, 70 metres to the left as you exit the bus station ticket office is unpretentious, clean and convenient. If you're arriving on a late train and you fancy a pizza, try *Romana Pizza* on the corner of Pavlou Mela and Sidirodromikou Stathmou. It's the first eating place you come to after leaving the station.

Of all the fast-food joints *Delirio*, on the

corner of Pavlou Mela and Arhimandritou Papathanasiou is the best of the bunch.

Getting There & Away

Bus – domestic From the main bus station there is one bus a day to Athens (leaving at 8.30 am, 9 hours, 8000 dr), six buses a day to Thessaloniki (3 hours, 2450 dr), seven to Kozani (1¾ hours, 1350 dr), three to Kastoria (via Amynteo, two hours, 1600 dr) and two to Agios Germanos (for the Prespa lakes, 1½ hours, 800 dr), at 6.45 am and 2.30 pm.

If you are planning to enter FYROM from Florina, there are three buses a day to the border town of Niki (30 minutes, 280 dr).

Bus – international There is a bus to Korçë (Korytsa in Greek) in Albania run by the Greek Railways Organisation (OSE), that operates on Monday, Tuesday, Friday and Saturday. The bus leaves Florina train station at 11.50 am and the one-way ticket costs 2500 dr. This bus originates in Thessaloniki. (See also the introductory Getting There & Away chapter for details on transport to Albania).

Train – domestic Florina is at the end of the Thessaloniki-Edessa-Amynteo line. There are five to seven trains a day (depending on the season) in both directions. The approximate journey time from Thessaloniki is four hours, but it can take longer. You can also take the train to Kozani, via Amynteo.

Train – international There is currently no through service to Bitola, or beyond, in FYROM. See also the introductory Getting There & Away chapter for details on getting to FYROM from Florina.

PRESPA LAKES

In the mountainous north-west corner of Greece, at an altitude of 850 metres, are the two lakes of Megali Prespa and Mikri Prespa. The lakes are separated by a narrow strip of land. The area is one of outstanding natural beauty and is little visited by foreign tourists. The road from Florina crosses the Pisoderi pass and winds its way through thick forests and lush meadows with grazing cattle; if you have your own transport, there are lots of picnic tables.

Mikri Prespa has an area of 43 sq km and is located almost entirely in Greece, except for the south-western tip which is in Albania. Megali Prespa is the largest lake in the Balkans; the biggest part is in FYROM (1000 sq km); 38 sq km is in Greece and a small part in the south-west is in Albania. Much of the shore of Megali Prespa is of precipitous rock, which rises dramatically from the chilly blue water. The Prespa area became a national park in 1977. There is an excellent information centre in Agios Germanos.

Mikri (little) Prespa is a wildlife refuge of considerable interest to ornithologists. It is surrounded by thick reed beds where numerous species of birds, including cormorants, pelicans, egrets, herons and ibis, nest. The lake's islet of **Agios Ahillios** has ancient Byzantine remains. The boat operator will take you across and back for about 2000 dr for a boatload of four people. Phone ☎ 0385-46 112 to call the ferryman, otherwise get someone to beep the car horn loudly from the little jetty, which is one km down the turn-off road to Pyli.

Getting There & Away

Bus The only town with a direct bus link to the lakes is Florina. There are two buses on weekdays to Agios Germanos village, 16 km east of Psarades. The buses leave Florina at 7.45 am and 2.30 pm. These buses stop at the road junction between the two lakes: the left fork leads to Koula beach and Psarades, and the right fork leads to the villages of Lemos and Agios Germanos. Another bus bound for Pyli meets the second bus twice a week on Tuesday and Thursday. If you get this bus, ask to be let off at Koula beach, which is five km from Psarades.

From here you have the choice of either hitching a lift to Psarades, a long uphill walk, or asking someone at the taverna at Koula beach to telephone for a taxi (☎ 51 247) – they will willingly do this. The bus for Florina leaves Agios Germanos at 6.45 am

NORTHERN GREECE

and 3.45 pm on weekdays. On a Saturday there is only one bus at 7.45 am and there is none on Sunday.

Taxi If you decide to use a taxi for part of or the whole journey, prices from Psarades are approximately 1800 dr to Lemos (to pick up the bus to Florina), 6000 dr to Florina and 7000 dr to Kastoria.

Agios Germanos Αγιος Γερμανός
This village of 260 residents serves as the main transport hub for the Prespa region and, although it is a little way back from the lakes themselves, it is an attractive village and a convenient base. There are some good walks to be made from the village and there is always a taxi (☎ 0385-51 207) handy, should you need to move further afield. The village is primarily an agricultural settlement and is renowned for its bean crops. The mounds of cut cane you will see in springtime as you enter the village are used entirely for supporting the bean plants.

Orientation & Information Agios Germanos contains a bus terminus and the only post office in the Prespa basin. There are no banking facilities. The telephone code for the Prespa area is 0385 and the post code is 530 77. The phone number of the local police is ☎ 51 203.

Things to See There are two churches that may be of interest to fans of Byzantium: **Agios Athanasios** and **Agios Germanos**, named after the patron saint of the village.

For friends of nature, the Prespa Information Centre (☎ 51 452; fax 51 452), which is on the right just before you enter the village proper, is a very well presented display and resource centre for information on the Prespa National Park. There is some excellent material in Greek, but not too much in English. Nonetheless, the photographs, maps and diagrams are pretty self-explanatory.

A number of foreign visitors hike up into the hills to see the Sarakatsani shepherds. These are an itinerant group, considered a Greek minority, and can be found in the hills

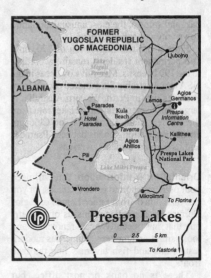

tending their sheep during the summer months.

Places to Stay & Eat There aren't too many places to stay and eat in Agios Germanos, but the well-run and comfortable *Agios Germanos Hostel* (☎ 51 320) is run by the local women's cooperative and is at the top end of the village. Follow the signs. Doubles/triples here cost 6200/7000 dr. *Les Pelicans* (☎ 51 442) is an EOT-approved domatia place and is just below the main square.

There is a restaurant of sorts on the main square. Otherwise, *Lefteris Taverna*, opposite the hostel, is about the nearest place in the village to an established eatery. There is also one ouzeri and one kafeneio.

Psarades Ψαράδες
The village of Psarades, on Megali Prespa, 70 km from Florina, is a revelation. It's positioned within a small inlet of Megali Prespa and is Greece's last village before the tri-national border point out on Megali Prespa lake. Psarades is a delectable little village with traditional stone houses, which are subject to a National Trust preservation order; old fishing boats made of cedar and

NORTHERN GREECE

oak; and some of the most unusual miniature cows you will see in Greece.

From a pre-war population of 770, only 143 permanent residents remain, according to the 1991 census. Many live overseas in the USA and Australia. Six hundred people from Psarades live in Perth, Western Australia. A large marble memorial on the lake front from the Macedonian Association of Chicago, attests to the strong bonds between Psarades and its former residents overseas.

Orientation & Information You will need your own transport to get to Psarades, or you can take a taxi from either Lemos or Agios Germanos. The village consists of a lakefront that has recently been renovated and looks smart and modern. Numerous modern restaurants and fish tavernas line the lake front.

There is no bank or post office, but Philippos Papadopoulos, the owner of the grocery shop on the village square, will exchange cash. So too, will Lazaros Hristianopoulos at the Syntrofia taverna. There is no OTE but one or two of the tavernas have metered telephones. Germanos Papadopoulos, the owner of Taverna Paradosi, speaks excellent English having spent many years in Canada. He'll be happy to give information about the village.

Things to See & Do It will be hard to resist taking a **boat trip** out onto Megali Prespa, since Psarades is Greece's only village with anchorage on this lake. More specifically, you should strive to be taken to the three *askitiria* (places of solitary worship) that can only be visited by boat. All three are out past the Roti headland to the left. The first one, Metamorphosi, dates from the 13th century. There are only a few remnants of the rich painting that once decorated this site and two sections from the wood-carved *temblon* (votive screen), the rest of which is in the Florina museum. The second is called Mikri Analipsi and is from the 14th or 15th century. Access to this one is a little difficult. The third and probably the best one is called Panagia Eleousa. A typical trip will cost you about 750 dr for the short tour and 1250 dr for the full tour, assuming that there are at least four persons per boatload.

More or less opposite the village, there are rock paintings of the **Panagia Vlahernitisa** (1455-56) and of **Panagia Dexiokratousa** (1373) along with some inscriptions. These are included in the boat tour mentioned above.

The church of **Kimisis Theotokou** in the village itself dates from 1893 and is decorated on the outside with the double-headed eagle of the Byzantine Empire. There is also an inscription that refers to the old name of the village, Nivitsa.

Places to Stay If you plan on coming to the area in the high season without a reservation, think twice, as the region is getting very popular.

There is no official camp site but you may be able to camp freelance at Koula beach on the southern shore of Megali Prespa, five km east of Psarades.

Psarades' only official, EOT-approved *domatia* are the clean, comfortable rooms of Lazaros & Eleni Hristianopoulos (☎ 0385-46 107), which cost 5000 dr for singles and doubles. The rooms are above the family taverna (Syntrofia), at the far end of the village. Several other families rent rooms unofficially, so if the Christianopoulos' rooms are full, you will be directed to another place to stay.

The *Hotel Psarades* (☎ 46 015) is right opposite the village of Psarades. They have excellent rooms for 5600/7000/8400 dr. All have views over the village. There is also a bar and restaurant here.

Places to Eat Five tavernas line the waterfront at Psarades. They all dish up excellent fresh fish, straight from the lake. Lazaros Hristianopoulos from the *Syntrofia* taverna is a very amenable host and his trout and house wine are to be recommended. The *Paradosi* is probably the only eating place open out of season, though Lazaros will look after you if you are staying at his domatia.

NORTHERN GREECE

If you fancy the walk and can do without the lakeside ambience, the restaurant at the Hotel Psarades is reasonably up-market.

KASTORIA Καστοριά

Kastoria (Kas-to-ri-A, population 17,000) lies between Mt Grammos and Mt Vitsi in western Macedonia, 200 km west of Thessaloniki. It is regarded by many Greeks as their most beautiful town. Indeed its setting is exemplary, occupying the isthmus of a promontory which projects into the tree-fringed Lake Orestiada, surrounded by mountains.

Its architecture is also outstanding, featuring many Byzantine and post-Byzantine churches and numerous 17th and 18th-century mansions, known as *arhontika*, because they were the homes of the archons – the town's leading citizens. In Kastoria the arhontika were the dwellings of rich fur merchants.

The town has a long tradition of fur production. Jewish furriers (refugees from Europe) came to Kastoria because of the large numbers of beavers living by the lake. They carried out their trade with such zeal that by the 19th century the beaver was extinct in the area. The furriers then began to import scraps of fur. Whatever your feelings are about the fur trade, you are not going to escape them in Kastoria; every street has some kind of office or business associated with the fur trade.

Pedestrians and motorists take note: Kastoria is very hilly.

Orientation

Kastoria's main bus station is one block inland from the south lakeside, on 3 Septemvriou. To reach the town centre from here, with your back to the station office turn left and keep walking, bearing right just past the soccer stadium, to Plateia Davaki which is one of the city's main squares. Mitropoleos, the town's main commercial thoroughfare, runs south-east from here to the other main square of Plateia Omonias.

Information

Kastoria's EOT (☎ 0467-24 484) is in the town hall on Ioustinianou, which runs north-east from Plateia Davaki. The staff are helpful and give out lots of brochures, maps and information.

The National Bank of Greece is on 11 Noemvriou, just north of Plateia Davaki. The post office is at the northern end of Leoforos Megalou Alexandrou, which skirts the lakeside. The OTE is on Agiou Athanasiou which runs off Plateia Davaki just north of Mitropoleos. Kastoria's postcode is 521 00 and the telephone code is 0467.

The phone number for the regular police is ☎ 83 333.

Byzantine Churches

Many of the numerous churches in Kastoria were originally private chapels attached to the arhontika houses. Almost all of the churches are locked, and gaining access to them is something of a Byzantine experience in itself. The key man (literally) for the ones around Plateia Omonias is Hristos Philikas. If you can track him down he will be happy to open them up for you – ask around the kafeneia on the square. Another possibility is the Byzantine Museum's curator who may be able to contact someone who can show you some of the churches.

Even if you don't manage to get a look inside any churches, all is not lost, for some of them have external frescoes. One such church is the **Taxiarhia of the Metropolis**, on Plateia Pavlou Mela, south of Plateia Omonias, which has a 13th-century fresco of the Madonna and Child above the entrance. Inside the church is the tomb of Pavlos Melas, a Macedonian hero who was killed by Bulgar terrorists during the struggles which culminated in the Balkan Wars. Melas' life is documented in Thessaloniki's Museum of the Macedonian Struggle. Many streets in Macedonia are named Pavlou Mela in memory of this hero.

Museums

The **Byzantine Museum** houses outstanding icons from many of the town's churches.

NORTHERN GREECE

It will help you to appreciate the churches if you visit this museum first. It is adjacent to the Xenia du Lac Hotel on Plateia Dexamenis. The museum is open from 8.30 am to 3 pm every day except Monday. Admission is 500 dr.

Most of the surviving **arhontika** are in the southern part of the town in the area called Doltso. The most important ones are the Emmanouil, Basara, Natzi, Skoutari, Papia, Vergoula and Papaterpou mansions – named after the families who once lived in them. These are closed to the public.

One of the arhontika has been converted into the **Kastorian Museum of Folklore**. A visit to the museum should be considered a must. The 530-year-old house belonged to the wealthy Neranzis Alvazis family. It is sumptuously furnished and has displays of ornaments, kitchen utensils and tools. The museum is open every day from 10 am to 12 pm and again from 3 to 5 pm. Admission is 200 dr. The guidebook at the museum is a bit steep at 1000 dr, but there is a good guided tour (in Greek, with a less informed version in English). There are postcards and other souvenirs on sale, including some music cassettes of traditional Kastorian folk music.

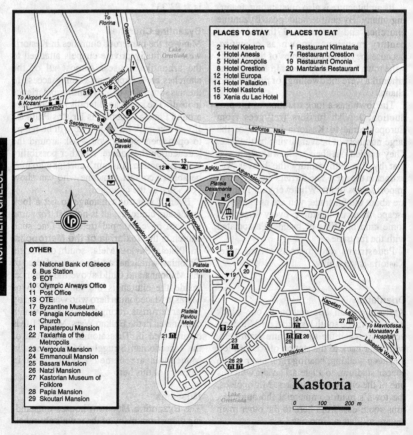

PLACES TO STAY	PLACES TO EAT
2 Hotel Keletron	1 Restaurant Klimataria
4 Hotel Anesis	7 Restaurant Orestion
5 Hotel Acropolis	19 Restaurant Omonia
8 Hotel Orestion	20 Mantziaris Restaurant
12 Hotel Europa	
14 Hotel Palladion	
15 Hotel Kastoria	
16 Xenia du Lac Hotel	

OTHER
3 National Bank of Greece
6 Bus Station
9 EOT
10 Olympic Airways Office
11 Post Office
13 OTE
17 Byzantine Museum
18 Panagia Koumbledeki Church
21 Papaterpou Mansion
22 Taxiarhia of the Metropolis
23 Vergoula Mansion
24 Emmanouil Mansion
25 Basara Mansion
26 Natzi Mansion
27 Kastorian Museum of Folklore
28 Papia Mansion
29 Skoutari Mansion

Kastoria

0   100   200 m

Lakeside Walk

A pretty tree-shaded nine-km road skirts the promontory. The lake is fringed by reeds which are the habitat of frogs and turtles and many species of birds. On the lake you will see many species of water fowl and the great crested grebe.

Just under halfway is the **Moni Mavriotissas**. Father Gabriel, the resident monk, will give you a guided tour. Next to the monastery is the 11th-century **Agia Maria** and the 16th-century **Church of St John the Theologian**. Both churches are liberally festooned with frescoes and icons, and are usually open. Beside the monastery there is a reasonably priced restaurant, which is the only source of refreshment on the walk. To begin the walk, take the road to the hospital (see the Kastoria map).

Places to Stay – bottom end

There is a free *camp site* in the grounds of the Moni Mavriotissas.

The C-class *Hotel Acropolis* (☎ 83 737), Grammou 14, has tidy rooms for 4200/4800/5800 dr for singles/doubles/triples without bathroom. You can pay a supplement for rooms with a bathroom.

Places to Stay – middle

The C-class *Hotel Keletron* (☎ 22 676), 11 Noemvriou 52 (a north-easterly continuation of Grammou), has comfortable rooms for 5000/6400 dr with private bathroom.

The renovated C-class *Hotel Anesis* (☎ 83 908; fax 83 768), Grammou 10, has clean and comfortable rooms for 6500/8500/10,200 dr with private bathroom. To reach this hotel from the bus station, face the lake and turn left, then take the first left into Filikis Eterias, then turn right at the T-junction and the hotel is on the left.

The C-class *Hotel Kastoria* (☎ 29 453), Nikis 122, has adequately furnished rooms with private bathroom for 6500/7500/10,500 dr. It's in a prime location overlooking the lake at the north-eastern edge of town, but nonetheless has a sort of run-down feel about it.

The *Hotel Orestion* (☎ 22 257), Plateia Davaki 1, is a superior C-class with very pleasant rooms for 8700/10,600/12,700 dr with private bathroom. In a similar vein is the *Hotel Europa* (☎ 23 826; fax 25 154) at Agiou Athanasiou 12, just up from Plateia Davaki.

Places to Stay – top end

Kastoria's A-class *Xenia du Lac Hotel* (☎ 22 565; fax 26 391), Plateia Dexamenis 11, is a quaintly old-fashioned kind of place despite its A rating. It's in a quiet part of town and singles/doubles are good value at 8800/15,400 dr with private bathroom.

Kastoria can be a busy town, so if you can't find a room at any of the above, there are another six hotels out on the main road between Kastoria and Kozani.

Places to Eat

One of the town's best restaurants is the bright and modern *Restaurant Omonia* on Plateia Omonias, with meals for under 1500 dr. Nearby the *Mantziaris Restaurant*, Valala 8, is also good and reasonably cheap, with meals for about 1100 dr.

Restaurant Klimataria, Orestion 6, is an old-fashioned, no-frills restaurant with a large choice of ready-made food. A meal here consisting of fasolada, salad and retsina costs around 1200 dr. To reach the restaurant, walk along 11 Noemvriou towards the lake. In the same part of town, *Restaurant Orestion*, Ermou 37, is an unpretentious little place which dishes up tasty low-priced ready-made food. It is closed on Saturday evenings and on Sunday. A meal here will cost around 1400 dr.

Getting There & Away

Air The airport is 10 km south of Kastoria. Between May and October, there are four flights a week from Kastoria to Athens (16,400 dr) on Sunday, Tuesday, Wednesday and Friday. The Olympic Airways office (☎ 22 275 or 23 125) is at Leoforos Megalou Alexandrou 15.

Bus From Kastoria's main bus station there are five buses a day to Thessaloniki (four

NORTHERN GREECE

hours, 3100 dr), five a day to Kozani (two hours, 1450 dr) and two to Athens (nine hours, 8050 dr). With the exception of the first bus, all Thessaloniki-bound buses go via Amynteo and Edessa. The first (6.30 am) bus goes via Kozani and Veria. There are more buses in summer.

HALKIDIKI Χαλκιδική

The Halkidiki peninsula is a large blob to the south-east of Thessaloniki, from which three long 'fingers' extend from the peninsula into the Aegean. The two large lakes of Koronia and Volvi separate the peninsula from the rest of Macedonia.

Halkidiki boasts 500 km of coastline, with superb sandy beaches surrounded by calm, aquamarine sea. Unfortunately, these assets have been ruthlessly exploited and the two fingers of Kassandra and Sithonia consist of either luxurious holiday complexes for the rich and famous, or package-tourist ghettos. The easternmost promontory of Halkidiki is the Monastic Republic of Mt Athos (Holy Mountain).

Halkidiki is not a place for budget or independent travellers as virtually all accommodation is booked solid throughout the summer. If you are camping a visit is more practicable: Halkidiki has many camp sites which, even if they are bursting at the seams, are unlikely to turn you away. The free *Guide to Halkidiki*, available at the Thessaloniki EOT, lists most of these sites. This guide aptly describes Halkidiki as one of 'the most dymanically [sic] developing areas of the country'.

Northern Halkidiki

The **Petralona cave**, 56 km south-east of Thessaloniki in northern Halkidiki, has stalactites and stalagmites and is where the 700,000-year-old Neanderthal skull (evidence of one of Europe's earliest inhabitants) was found. The cave is open daily from 9 am to 7 pm (5 pm in winter). Admission is 700 dr. Doucas Tours (see Organised Tours in the Thessaloniki section) sometimes have tours to the caves.

The **archaeological museum** at Poly-gyros, the capital of Halkidiki, houses finds from the peninsula's ancient sites including the Sanctuary of Zeus at Aphytis and the ancient city of Acanthos. The museum is open Tuesday to Sunday from 8.30 am to 3 pm. Admission is 500 dr.

Getting There & Away A bus goes to Petralona cave (one hour, 900 dr) at 1 pm every day, but does not return the same day. To get back to Thessaloniki you must walk or hitch to the village of Eleohoria, five km south, from where you can pick up a bus to Thessaloniki. All buses to the Sithonia 'finger' stop at Polygyros.

Kassandra Peninsula

The Kassandra peninsula is less beautiful than the Sithonian peninsula. Its commercialism is horrendous and, even if you're not averse to package tourists, roaring motorbikes, fast-food joints and discos, you're unlikely to find accommodation. However, if you have a tent, there are lots of well-advertised camp sites. Free camping is not allowed and there are large signs alerting you to the fact.

Getting There & Away There are 13 buses to Kallithea (1½ hours, 1400 dr) on the east coast; 11 buses to Pefkohori (two hours, 1800 dr), also on the east coast, via Kryopigi and Haniotis; seven buses to Paliouri (two hours, 2050 dr) and three buses to Agia Paraskevi 2½ hours, 1800 dr), both on the southern tip. All the buses leave from the bus terminal at Karakassi 68 in Thessaloniki.

Sithonian Peninsula

Sithonia is an improvement on Kassandra. The landscape *en route* is quite spectacular with sweeping vistas of thickly forested hills.

An undulating road makes a loop around Sithonia, skirting wide bays, climbing into the pine-forested hills and dipping down to the resorts. Travelling down the west coast there are good stretches of sandy beach between **Nikitas** and **Paradisos**. Beyond here, **Neos Marmaras** is Sithonia's biggest resort, with a very crowded beach. The gigantic monstrosity of Porto Carras sits at one side of the bay. This is a luxury holiday complex for 3000 guests built by the wine-producing magnate John G Carras and modelled on Spanish Marbella – ugh.

Beyond Neos Marmaras the road climbs into the hills from where dirt roads lead down to several beaches and camp sites. **Toroni** and **Koufos** are small resorts at the south-western tip. The latter is a picturesque little place with a good beach. The southern tip of Sithonia is still relatively isolated and is scenically the most spectacular region of Halkidiki (excluding the Athos peninsula) – rocky, rugged and dramatic. As the road rounds the south-eastern tip, Mt Athos comes into view across the gulf, further adding to the spectacular vistas.

Kalamitsi The resort of Kalamitsi is the most delightful corner of the Sithonian peninsula. This little enclave has a gorgeous sandy beach, a couple of tavernas, some rooms, two camp sites, boat-hire facilities, and it isn't commercialised. In short, it is one of Sithonia peninsula's hidden delights. *O Giorgakis* (☎ 0375-41 013), just above the restaurant of the same name, is a stone's throw from the beach. Fully equipped studios here will cost from 8000 to 12,000 dr depending on facilities.

Continuing up the east coast, the bus does a little two-km detour inland to the pleasant village of **Sikia**, which has less tourist hype than the coastal resorts. Back on the coast, the resort of Sarti is next along the route.

Sarti Sarti has not succumbed entirely to the package-tourist industry and has a good laid-back atmosphere. From its beach there are splendid views of Mt Athos. The town is not all that spectacular and tends to cater for local tourism.

Sarti consists of two streets: one is the waterfront and the other is parallel and one block inland. The bus terminal is on the latter – a timetable is pinned to a nearby tree. There is no tourist office but the staff of Koutras Travel (☎ 0375-41 553), near the bus terminal, are helpful and speak English. The agency organises half-day mule treks in the mountains for 4000 dr, and Mt Athos cruises for 2000 dr.

Places to Stay If you decide to stay, *Sarti Beach Camping* (☎ 0375-41 450; fax 94 211) is not only a camp site, but a holiday complex with a variety of accommodation. The camp site itself is well shaded, but offers little greenery. At their hotel, doubles with private bathroom go for 8000 dr. Three and four-person bungalows are 13,000 and 15,000 dr respectively. Motorbikes can be rented at this camp site; 50-cc models cost 3500 dr. Travelling north it's on the right side of the main approach road – buses stop outside.

On the opposite side of the road *Hotel-Villa Phyllis* (☎ 0375-94 055) has a friendly Greek-Australian owner and pleasant double/triple rooms for 9000 dr. There are many domatia further north along this road.

Places to Eat The *Pergola Café Restaurant* in Sarti is a great place where you can have a drink, a snack or a full meal; it's open all day till late evening. Their pergola plate has a bit of everything – meatballs, calamari, souvlaki – and is generally good value. From the bus stop turn left opposite Koutras Travel and you'll see the restaurant on the right – painted purple, grey and orange.

Getting There & Away Buses to Halkidiki leave from the bus terminal at Karakassi 68 in Thessaloniki. There are four buses a day to Nea Marmaras (2½ hour,s 2050 dr); and three buses to Sarti (3½ hours, 2850 dr). Most of the Sarti buses do a loop around the Sithonian peninsula enabling you to see the magnificent southern tip.

Secular Athos (Athos Peninsula)
Most of the easternmost portion of the three prongs of the Halkidiki peninsula is occupied by the Athonite monasteries. You will probably only want to pass through secular Athos on your way to see the monasteries. The beaches are admittedly very fine in parts, but they have long been developed for

the package-tour industry. Soulless resorts based on large hotels with no interest in, or of interest to, independent travellers are dotted along the coast. **Ierissos** is one of the few real towns, notable mainly for being the terminus for the irregular boat serving the east-coast monasteries, but you can't enter Athos this way. The **canal,** dug across the peninsula by the Persian king Xerxes in the 5th century BC for his invading fleet, is featured proudly on most maps, but it was filled in centuries ago and there's precious little for the untrained eye to see.

Ouranopolis (Ουρανόπολη) The village of Ouranopolis is at the end of secular Athos. The most obvious feature of the village is the 14th-century **tower** built to guard what was then a dependency of Vatopediou monastery. A building in a side street, one block back from the waterfront, is, despite appearances, actually early 20th century. It once housed a monastic copper works (now a pharmacy). Most of the rest of the village was founded in 1922 by refugees from Asia Minor.

As well as the ferry for pilgrims to Athos, boats from here run tourist trips along the coast of Mt Athos for those unwilling or unable (because of their gender) to set foot there. Ouranopolis' postcode is 630 75 and the telephone code is 0377.

Places to Stay & Eat There are domatia and a few hotels, including the D-class *Hotel Galini* (☎ 71 217), one block back from the coast road. It has singles/doubles for 6000/7500 dr with shared facilities – you take breakfast in the family's dining room behind the small grocer's shop they run beneath the hotel rooms.

The D-class *Hotel Akrogiali* (☎ 71 201), on the waterfront, has singles/doubles for 4950/7800 dr. The prominent B-class *Xenia* (☎ 71 202) has more up-market singles/ doubles for 6000/11,000 dr. The hotel has a bar and restaurant.

There are a number of restaurants facing the sea on the beach; between these and the road, not far away from the tower, *O Kokki-*

nos is reasonably priced and has good fish dishes.

Agion Oros (Mt Athos)

This semiautonomous monastic area, also known as Holy Mountain, occupies most of the Athos peninsula. To set foot here is to step back in time – literally by 13 days, because the Athonite community still uses the Julian calendar – and metaphorically by 500 years, as this is a remnant of the Byzantine Empire, which otherwise ended with the fall of Constantinople in 1453.

Setting foot here, however, is not straightforward. Foreign men are allowed to stay in the monasteries for four nights (extendible up to six) after completing some formalities (see Obtaining a Permit later in this section). Visitors walk from monastery to monastery, enjoying the landscape (Athos is also called the Garden of the Virgin Mary) on the way, experiencing a little of the ascetic life of the monks. Despite some of the rigours associated with a visit to the Holy Mountain, this unique experience can be a very enriching one.

Women cannot enter the area at all. The closest approach they can make to the monasteries is to view them from one of the round-trip cruises. Boats carrying women must keep at least 500 metres offshore.

History Hermits gravitated to Mt Athos from the very early years of the Byzantine Empire. The first monastery on Athos, Megisti Lavra, was founded between 961 and 963 AD by St Athanasius with support from the emperor, Nikephoros II Phokas. The next emperor, John Tsimiskes, gave Athos its first charter. The Athonite community flourished under the continuing support of the Byzantine emperors, who issued decrees reinforcing its status. The most notorious decree was that made under Constantine IX Monomahos barring access to women, beardless persons and female domestic animals. This is still in force, except that it is no longer a requirement to be bearded. Hens (for eggs) are tolerated; birds are apparently too lowly to be included in the ban.

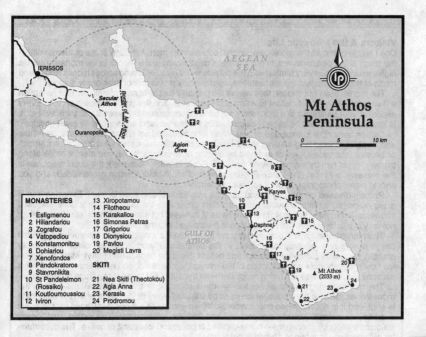

MONASTERIES

1 Esfigmenou
2 Hiliandariou
3 Zografou
4 Vatopediou
5 Konstamonitou
6 Dohiariou
7 Xenofondos
8 Pandokratoros
9 Stavronikita
10 St Pandeleimon (Rossiko)
11 Koutloumoussiou
12 Iviron
13 Xiropotamou
14 Filotheou
15 Karakallou
16 Simonas Petras
17 Grigoriou
18 Dionysiou
19 Pavlou
20 Megisti Lavra

SKITI

21 Nea Skiti (Theotokou)
22 Agia Anna
23 Kerasia
24 Prodromou

NORTHERN GREECE

Monasteries continued to be founded, particularly when Christians from outside the area came in during the first crusades. By 1400 there were said to be 40 monasteries, including foundations by Bulgarians, Russians and Serbian princes. The Athos community submitted to Turkish rule after the fall of Constantinople, but managed to retain its semi-independent status. The last monastery to be founded was Stavronikita, in 1542. The community declined over the centuries and today there are 20 ruling monasteries.

In the Greek War of Independence (1821-29) many monasteries were plundered and entire libraries burned by Turkish troops. Fires have in any case been a common occurrence during the centuries, due to the candles and oil lamps used in the wooden buildings. The present constitution of Athos dates from 1924. It was guaranteed by the 1975 Greek constitution, and recognises Athos as a part of Greece (all the monks, regardless of their origin, must become Greek nationals), with the Iera Synaxis (holy council; composed of one representative from each of the 20 monasteries) responsible for all of the internal administration.

Obtaining a Permit Only 10 foreign adult males may enter Mt Athos per day, but unrestricted numbers of Greek men may enter. Start the procedure early, particularly for summer visits, when you may have to wait weeks for a place – make a reservation. Athos can get quite crowded at weekends.

You can start the process in Athens or Thessaloniki, but you are supposed to complete the paperwork in the city in which you started it. As you have to be in Northern Greece anyway, it is simplest to start in Thessaloniki.

Ordained clergymen should have an introduction from their bishop, and need permission to visit Athos from the Ecumenical Patriarchate of Constantinople – apply

Visitors & the Monastic Life

Don't imagine that all the monks are simple, otherworldly men. Although some of the hermits in the south of the peninsula are, to put it politely, weird, many of the monks in the monasteries are highly educated men very familiar with the outside world – you will come across monks who spend much of their life outside the monasteries, as university professors or missionary doctors.

The monks have not chosen their way of life primarily for the benefit of visitors. Your reception will vary from correct but distant to warm and hospitable, and this partly depends on you. Every aspect of your behaviour in a monastery will be under close scrutiny (even if you think everyone is ignoring you) and will be eagerly discussed by the monks (who are apparently great gossips).

Certain behaviour is expected of you. Wear long trousers, not shorts, everywhere on Athos, and it's polite to wear long-sleeved shirts. Inside the monasteries, do not wear a hat, do not smoke or behave inconsiderately (for example by singing or whistling). When you meet a monk along the way, greet him by saying 'evloíte' (ev-lo-YEE-teh, literally 'bless me'); the usual response is the blessing 'o kyrios' (the Lord). Photography is often forbidden within monasteries, and you should never photograph a monk without his permission.

Remain dressed on the way to and from the washrooms, and even in them. Exposing skin is a big no-no, so attempt to wash with your shirt on, unless the guest quarters have enclosed showers. Do not swim within sight of a monastery, however hot and sweaty you feel after walking; not only is this forbidden, but raw sewage is discharged into the sea.

The monasteries have a common ground plan; from the outside, each resembles a fortified castle having one gateway for access. In the central courtyard is the katholikon (monastery church), frequently blood-red in colour, and behind this is the trapeza (refectory). Most monasteries now accommodate only a fraction of the monks they once did, and have abandoned derelict sections; some of these are being renovated with the aid of EU funds for heritage protection.

The monastic day begins at sunset, which is midnight in the Byzantine time kept in the monasteries (distrust the clocks, which must be adjusted every day). This is when the outer gate is shut, and it is not reopened until daybreak. When you reach a monastery, head for the guest quarters, arhontariki (usually signposted), and find the guestmaster. The monks traditionally welcome visitors by offering them home-distilled tsipouro and loukoumi, or coffee. The guestmaster will show you to a two to 10-bed guest room.

Visitors are not expected to participate completely in the monastic religious life, and some monasteries do not permit the non-Orthodox within the church; however, you should, if permitted, attend the morning and evening services which usually precede the mealtimes (it's bad form to sneak straight into the refectory for the food).

Services are indicated by a monk walking round the monastery striking a simandro, a large wooden plank, with a mallet in a distinctive rhythm. The only music permitted is that of the human voice (heavenly in some monasteries, diabolical in others), and the liturgical language used is an archaic form of Greek. The apparently endless repetition of some sections has a hypnotic effect.

Religious practice on Athos derives from the 14th-century Hesychast movement, according to which the divine light radiated at the Transfiguration can be perceived by certain practices of meditation and repetitive chanting.

at the Metropolis of Thessaloniki, Vogatsikou 5 (☎ 031-227 677).

Applying in Thessaloniki You need a letter of recommendation from your consulate. There are a number of foreign consulates listed under the Thessaloniki section. The British Consulate also acts for Australians, Canadians and New Zealanders.

The British consular hours are Monday to Friday from 9 am to 2 pm. The US consular hours are Tuesday and Thursday from 9 am to noon. Try telephoning the US Consulate (☎ 266 121, 260 716) if you need your letter of recommendation urgently.

The British charge the highest consular fees in Greece for letters of recommendation – UK£15 payable in drachma. Pious but poor Canadians should therefore use their embassy in Athens (if this doesn't require a

If the non-Orthodox are permitted in the church, they will usually be confined to the exonarthex, the outer porch (the double narthex is a peculiarity of the Athos churches). When there is no service in progress some monasteries make a point of showing non-Orthodox visitors the church interior – most of them are stuffed with more relics and icons than you can shake a censer at.

The monks dine twice a day, or only once on the frequent fasting days. The simple vegetarian meals rely heavily on produce from the monastery gardens, but are occasionally supplemented by fish. Common accompaniments to the cooked vegetables include home-baked bread, olives, eggs and cheese. Some monasteries serve very palatable wine with the meals, an uncharacteristic epicurean touch.

In some monasteries, non-Orthodox visitors eat separately from the monks, at others they eat with them, in which case you must stop eating as soon as the monks rise and leave, no matter how much food remains. On fasting days the monks normally provide some light refreshment for their guests.

Older books classify the monasteries into coenobite or idiorhythmic type, depending on whether communal life is centrally or more loosely organised. This distinction is now obsolete: the last idiorhythmic monastery, Pandokratoros, became coenobite on 8 June 1992 (Byzantine calendar), along with much feasting and celebration.

The lives of monks who live in *skites* – clusters of houses around a church – are not as strict as those of the monks who reside in the monasteries. Monks in the skites have more free time, and produce most of the Athos artefacts sold in Daphne and Karyes. One of the houses acts as the guest quarters, and visitors are received hospitably. Some *kelloi* – literally cells, but more like small farmhouses, and usually accommodating two to four monks – also receive guests. The hermits, of course, usually keep to themselves.

The accommodation offered by the monasteries can be spartan, the food frugal, and you won't meet any women, but you will have been in exalted company. The Byzantine emperor John VI Cantacuzenus on his enforced abdication in 1354, became a monk on Athos for the rest of his life. Rasputin, the Mad Monk (an unfair name, as technically speaking he wasn't a monk) walked here in 1891 from Siberia, a journey of 2000 miles. ■

David Hall

NORTHERN GREECE

special journey). The US Consulate doesn't levy a charge.

Take your letter of recommendation to the Ministry of Macedonia & Thrace (open from 11 am to 1.45 pm, Monday to Friday) on Plateia Diikitiriou (follow El Venizelou up from the waterfront). In Room 218 (1st floor, east wing), Directorate of Political Affairs, the staff exchange your letter of recommendation for a permit to enter Athos on a

particular date. This completes the paperwork, as it is no longer necessary to get a further note from the Aliens' Police.

In busy seasons, the ministry may give you a date for your visit several weeks or even months away. You can reserve a place from countries outside Greece either via your consulate or by contacting directly the Ministry of Macedonia & Thrace (☎ 031-270 092), Directorate of Political Affairs,

Room 218, Plateia Diikitiriou, Thessaloniki, 541 23.

Applying in Athens First obtain your letter of recommendation (ask for a *note verbale*) from the consular section of your embassy. Consular fees for this (payable in drachma) are: British UK£15; US gratis; Canadian C$10; Australian A$25

Take your letter of recommendation to the Ministry of Foreign Affairs, Zalakosta 2, to obtain a permit, or *diamonitirion*, to enter Athos on a specific date. No further paperwork is required.

It is also possible to make an advance reservation for a particular date through your embassy.

Orientation & Information There is no land access from secular Greece; all visitors enter the Athonite community by boat from Ouranopolis to Daphne, the small port of Athos. This has a port-authority building, police and customs, post office, a couple of general stores selling food and religious artefacts made on Athos, and a café. There is no OTE office, but one of the shops has a telephone with a meter. The only other town is Karyes, the administrative capital, which includes the headquarters building of the Holy Epistasia (holy council), an inn, post office, OTE office, doctor and a couple of shops. There are no tourist police, but there is a regular police station in Karyes.

The remaining settlements are the 20 monasteries plus four skites (SKI-tess), and the isolated dwellings of hermits – the total population of monks and resident laymen is about 1600. In addition to Karyes and Daphne, police are based at St Pandeleimon, Megisti Lavra, Agia Anna, Zografou and Hiliandariou.

The landscape is dominated in the south by the white peak of Mt Athos itself; the northerly part is densely wooded. Wildlife abounds; the small population of monks and absence of any industry (apart from some logging) have virtually turned the area into a reserve.

Leave video cameras behind – they're prohibited on Athos.

Exploring Athos Once you have obtained your diamonitirion (permit to stay in the monasteries), you are free to roam. There are few proper roads, and not many vehicles – you get around on foot, following the old paths, or by boat.

A caïque leaves Agia Anna every day at 9.45 am for Daphne, serving intermediate west-coast monasteries or their arsenals (landing stages for monasteries not immediately by the sea), returning from Daphne every afternoon. A more irregular caïque serves points on the east coast (theoretically three times a week, weather permitting on this exposed coast) between Ierissos and Mandraki, the harbour for Megisti Lavra. Another service around the south connects Mandraki and Agia Anna. The caïques are inexpensive; for example, at the time of writing the trip from Daphne to Dionysiou cost 250 dr.

Unless you travel exclusively by boat, you need to be reasonably fit and prepared to walk for several hours a day in the heat. Carry water with you; and, as food often becomes an obsession among visitors, take extra supplies, such as biscuits and dried fruit. (Chocolate, the hiker's usual emergency supply of calories, is a dumb thing to carry in hot weather.)

Other useful things to take include a torch (flashlight), compass, the best map of Athos you can find (a 1:50,000 map showing contours is available through Stanfords of London; ☎ 0171-836 1321), a whistle (in case you get lost), a small shaving mirror (not all monastic washrooms have mirrors) and mosquito coils.

You can only spend one night in each monastery. Some of the heavily visited ones near Karyes request that you telephone them in advance to be sure of a place (the numbers are displayed in the Holy Epistasia, where you wait for the diamonitirion), but this can be a frustrating experience, as the telephone is not answered for many hours of the day during periods of rest and meditation. You

NORTHERN GREECE

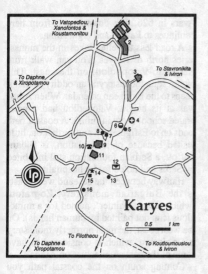

1	Skiti Agiou Andreou
2	Athonia School
3	Administrator
4	Hospital
5	Iosafeon
6	Bus stop
7	Guesthouse
8	WC
9	Government House (Kyvernio)
10	OTE
11	Protaton
12	Post Office
13	Dionysios Fournas
14	Police
15	Guesthouse
16	Bakery

must reach the monastery before sunset, as the gate is then shut, and not opened for anyone.

In **Karyes** you should see the 10th-century **Protaton**, the basilican church opposite the Holy Epistasia, which contains a number of treasures including paintings by Panselinos, the master of the Macedonian School. Karyes itself is a strange place – like a ghost town, with many derelict buildings testifying to a former, grander era. If you've had a long day, you may decide to stay at the monastery of **Koutloumoussiou** in Karyes. Otherwise, you should now decide on your itinerary.

A popular route is to head for one of the monasteries on the east coast, and then to continue to Megisti Lavra, returning to Daphne on the west coast. This can involve some lengthy walks unless you use the caïques, but these can be unreliable on the east coast.

From Karyes, you can walk to **Stavronikita** or **Iviron** on the coast, to continue by caïque, or coastal paths (easier to follow than the inland paths). Alternatively, from Karyes you can walk to **Filotheou** along a pleasant shady path (spring water available)

in about 3½ hours. About 30 minutes further on is **Karakallou**. Beyond here the old Byzantine path has been converted into a road, and you face a 5½-hour walk along it (unless a monastic vehicle gives you a lift) to **Megisti Lavra**.

Not only is this the oldest monastery on Athos, it is also the only one to remain undamaged by fire during its history. Its 10th-century structure protects a number of treasures, including frescoes by Theophanes of Crete and the tomb of St Athanasios, the founder.

A caïque leaves Megisti Lavra at about 3 pm for the skiti Agia Anna. Alternatively, you can follow the path around the wilderness of the south end of the peninsula. You come first to the skiti of **Kerasia**, and subsequently to **Agia Anna**, either of which (although Agia Anna has a better reputation for hospitality) can be used as a base for climbing Mt Athos (2033 metres).

This climb should not be undertaken lightly, and it is wise not to attempt it alone. It also wouldn't hurt to inform someone of your plans before setting off. Remember that it will be cold at the top, and you will need to take food and water. Water is available from a well at the chapel of Panagia (Virgin Mary), a short distance below the summit. You can return to Daphne by caïque from Agia Anna.

An alternative route is to head from Karyes to see the architecturally interesting monasteries on the west coast, including the spectacular Simonas Petras, clinging to a cliff like a Tibetan lamasery. From Karyes you climb over the central spine of the hills and head down again. You'll come first to **Xiropotamou**, which has newly renovated guest rooms (still lit by oil lamps) and serves good food and wine to guests separately from the monks. A path leads from here to Daphne; you can follow the coastal path from here or take the daily caïque leaving at 12.30 pm for Agia Anna calling at Simonas Petras, Grigoriou, Dionysiou and Pavlou. Alternatively, from Karyes you could head for Filotheou and then take a path to Simonas Petras from there.

Simonas Petras, also called Simopetra, is an awesome sight from its sea-level arsenal. From here it's a stiff climb to the monastery. The monastery's outside walls are surrounded by wooden balconies – as you walk along these from the guest rooms to the washroom, you can see the sheer drop beneath your feet. Swallows nest in the eaves and delight in taking vertiginous swoops to the sea. You can't normally get outside the monasteries to experience Athos at night – standing on these balconies in the dark, listening to the swallows and staring down towards the light of a solitary fishing boat is a magical experience.

From Simonas Petras you can descend to a coastal path which branches off the path to the arsenal at a small shrine. The path brings you to **Grigoriou**, which has a very pleasant position by the sea, and a comfortable guesthouse by the harbour outside the main monastery building. This has electric light and the rare luxury of showers.

The coastal path from here onwards is quite strenuous, as it climbs and descends three times before coming to **Dionysiou**, another cliff-hanger of a monastery resembling Simonas Petras in some ways. One of the treasures of its katholikon (main church), in a separate chapel, is an age-blackened icon claimed as the oldest in Athos. It is said to have been carried round the walls of Constantinople to inspire its successful defence against a combined siege by the Persians and

Avars in 626. The coastal path from here continues to Pavlou and Agia Anna.

A road less travelled takes in the monasteries north of Karyes. You can walk from Karyes to **Vatopediou**, on the coast. This picturesque monastery is an oddity in that it keeps to the European calendar. When Athos was at its height, Vatopediou had a celebrated school (now in ruins). A coastal path leads on to Esfigmenou, and further on, little visited because of its isolation, is **Hilian-dariou**, a Serbian foundation still inhabited by Serbs and noted for its hospitality.

Halfway between the east and west coasts is the Bulgarian monastery, **Zografou**, (which means 'painter', named for a miraculous icon not painted by human hands). On the west coast, the most northerly monastery is **Dohiariou**, which is considered to have some of the best architecture on Athos.

Coming south on the coastal path you reach **Xenofondos** and then **St Pandelei-mon**, the Russian monastery – which welcomes visitors with tea. This enormous building used to accommodate over 1000 monks, who came in swarms from Russia in the 19th century. Most of the distinctive Russian-style buildings date from that period and many are now derelict. The monastery was once renowned for the quality of its singing; which has been through a low point in the recent past, but is happily picking up again. These west-coast monasteries or their arsenals are served by the Ouranopolis-Daphne ferry.

Many alternative routes are possible using the network of old Byzantine paths – most of which have been recently marked by the Thessaloniki Mountaineering Club, but unmarked logging tracks make it amazingly easy to get lost in the woods. Monks' paths which cross vehicle tracks and lead directly to (or away from) monasteries are marked at the roadside by small crosses.

Getting There & Away Entry is by boat from Ouranopolis, which is accessible by bus from Thessaloniki's Halkidiki terminal at Karakassi 68. There are seven buses a day (2½ hours, 2080 dr). The first bus (6 am)

from Thessaloniki arrives in time for the boat; otherwise you need to stay overnight in Ouranopolis. This gives you a chance to buy easily carried food, and find somewhere to store unwanted gear (probably for a fee). Take only the bare minimum to Athos, as you'll have to lug it round all the time.

You may prefer to store unneeded baggage in Thessaloniki – when you return from Athos to Ouranopolis, the bus to Thessaloniki is waiting for the boat, and you may miss it while recovering luggage. Also, you might want to leave Athos via the west-coast boat to Ierissos – no big advantage if all your worldly goods are in Ouranopolis.

Entering Athos The boat, usually the small car ferry *Axion Esti*, leaves Ouranopolis at 9.45 am for Daphne (730 dr). You must surrender your Athos entry permit and passport on boarding. The journey takes about two hours; some intermediate stops are made for monks and other residents, but you can't get off before Daphne. Once there, an apparently clapped-out bus waits to take you to Karyes for 455 dr.

In the main square of Karyes, walk up the steps of the Holy Council building (flying the flag of the Byzantine Empire) and wait for the Byzantine bureaucracy to return your passport and issue your diamonitirion – this costs 2000 dr, but the monasteries do not expect any further donations for accommodating you for the next four nights. The diamonitirion can be extended (for a further two days) in Karyes at the end of the four days.

Leaving Athos The daily boat to Ouranopolis leaves Daphne at noon – there is a fairly rigorous customs check to ensure that you're not walking off with any antiquities (even visiting clerics have been known to snaffle valuable relics). The morning caïque from Agia Anna arrives in Daphne in ample time for the Ouranopolis boat. The irregular east-coast caïque provides an alternative exit to Ierissos.

KAVALA Καβάλα

Kavala (Ka-VA-la, population 57,000), 163 km east of Thessaloniki, is one of the most attractive of Greece's large cities. It spills gently down the foothills of Mt Symbolon to a commodious harbour. The old quarter of Panagia nestles under a massive Byzantine fortress.

Modern Kavala is built over ancient Neopolis, which was the port of Philippi. Mehmet Ali (1769-1849), who became Pasha of Egypt and founder of the last Egyptian royal dynasty, was born in Kavala. Like Athens and Thessaloniki, its population was almost doubled by the population exchange with Asia Minor.

Orientation

Kavala's focal point is Plateia Eleftherias. The town's two main thoroughfares, Eleftheriou Venizelou and Erythrou Stavrou run west from here parallel with the waterfront Ethnikis Antistasis. The old quarter of Panagia occupies a promontory to the southeast of Plateia Eleftherias. To get to the old quarter, walk east along Eleftheriou Venizelou from Plateia Eleftherias, turn left at the T-junction and take the first right (signposted Panagia and the castle).

The intercity bus station is on the corner of Mitropoleos Kavalas and Filikis Eterias, near the Thasos ferry quay.

One of the town's most prominent landmarks is an imposing aqueduct which was built during the reign of Süleyman the Magnificent (1520-66).

Information

Tourist Office The EOT (☎ 222 425) is on the west side of Plateia Eleftherias. The helpful staff give out a map of the town, have information on transport and have a list of the town's hotels with prices. They also have information on the summer drama festivals at Philippi and Thasos.

Opening times of the office are Monday to Friday from 7 am to 2.30 pm. If staffing allows, the office is also open from 5 to 8 pm and on Saturday from 8 am to 1 pm. It's closed on Sunday.

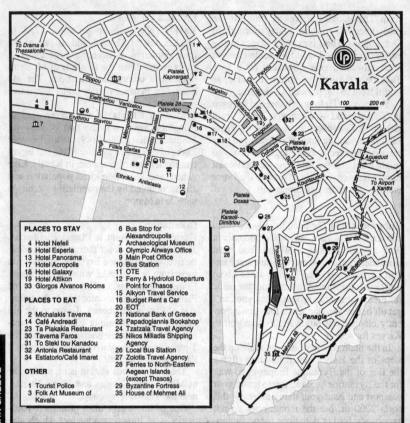

PLACES TO STAY

4 Hotel Nefeli
5 Hotel Esperia
13 Hotel Panorama
17 Hotel Acropolis
18 Hotel Galaxy
19 Hotel Attikon
33 Giorgos Alvanos Rooms

PLACES TO EAT

2 Michalakis Taverna
14 Café Andreadi
23 Ta Plakakia Restaurant
30 Taverna Faros
31 To Steki tou Kanadou
32 Antonia Restaurant
34 Estiatorio/Café Imaret

OTHER

1 Tourist Police
3 Folk Art Museum of Kavala
6 Bus Stop for Alexandroupolis
7 Archaeological Museum
8 Olympic Airways Office
9 Main Post Office
10 Bus Station
11 OTE
12 Ferry & Hydrofoil Departure Point for Thasos
15 Alkyon Travel Service
16 Budget Rent a Car
20 EOT
21 National Bank of Greece
22 Papadogiannis Bookshop
24 Tzatzala Travel Agency
25 Nikos Miliadis Shipping Agency
26 Local Bus Station
27 Zolotis Travel Agency
28 Ferries to North-Eastern Aegean Islands (except Thasos)
29 Byzantine Fortress
35 House of Mehmet Ali

Tourist Police The tourist police (☎ 222 905) are in the same building as the regular police at Omonias 119.

Money The National Bank of Greece is on the corner of Omonias and Dragoumi. There are many other banks in this area, but none have extended opening hours.

Post & Telecommunications The main post office is on the corner of Mitropoleos Kavalas and Erythrou Stavrou and is open Monday to Friday from 7.30 am to 8 pm. Kavala's postcode is 655 01. The OTE is at the corner of Antistasis and Averof. It is open from 6 am to midnight in summer and 6 am to 11 pm in winter. Kavala's telephone code is 051.

Bookshops The Papadogiannis Bookshop at Omonias 46 on the corner of Amynta stocks international newspapers and magazines. It also has a few English-language paperbacks – if you're a Barbara Cartland fan, you could be in luck.

Panagia Παναγία
The pastel-coloured houses in the narrow

tangled streets of the Panagia quarter are less dilapidated than those of Thessaloniki's Kastra and the area is less commercialised than Athens' Plaka.

Its most conspicuous building is the Imaret, a huge structure with 18 domes, which overlooks the harbour from Poulidou. In Turkish times the Imaret was a hostel for theology students. It has recently been restored and is now a pleasant café and restaurant (see Places to Eat). Within the café are some cabinets displaying memorabilia from Mehmet Ali's time. The carefully restored Turkish house where Mehmet Ali was born is now open to the public. If you ring the bell the caretaker will show you around; along with other rooms, you will see Ali's harem. The house is at the southern end of Poulidou. Nearby is an equestrian statue of Ali.

Museums
Kavala's **archaeological museum** houses well-displayed finds from ancient Amphipolis, between Thessaloniki and Kavala. Amphipolis was a colony of Athens, and a gold-rush town with mines on Mt Pangaeum. The finds include sculpture, jewellery, grave steles, terracotta figurines and vases. The museum is at the western side of town on Erythrou Stavrou. It's open Tuesday to Sunday from 8.30 am to 3 pm. Admission is 500 dr, but is free on Sunday and public holidays.

The **Folk Art Museum of Kavala** is also worth a visit. On the ground floor are pictures and sculptures by contemporary Greek artists including a large collection of works by Polygnotos Vagis (1894-1965), who was born in Potamia on Thasos, and emigrated to the USA where he gained an international reputation.

On the upper floor is a superb folk-art collection with costumes, jewellery, handcrafts, household items and tools. The museum is at Filippou 4.

Places to Stay – bottom end
Irini Camping (☎ 229 785) is two km east of Kavala on the coast road, and *Alexandros*

Camping (☎ 316 347) is further along the road at Nea Kavala. *Batis Kavala Camping* (☎ 243 051) is three km west of Kavala at Batis beach. Finally out at Keramoti, 37 km from Kavala there is *Keramoti Camping* (☎ 0591-51 279). They all charge in the region of 600 dr per person and 450 dr per tent per night.

The best deal for budget travellers and perhaps the nicest environment in Kavala to spend the night are the cosy *rooms* in the beautiful 300-year-old house rented by Giorgos Alvanos (☎ 228 412 or 221 781), Anthemiou 35, in Panagia. Single/double rates are 3000/4000 dr.

The *Hotel Attikon* (☎ 222 257), Megalou Alexandrou 8, is pretty dire and sleazy and is only included here because there is a dearth of budget accommodation in Kavala. Singles/doubles are 3000/4000 dr with shared bathroom. *Hotel Acropolis* (☎ 223 543), Eleftheriou Venizelou 53, is marginally better and has singles with shared bathroom for 4000 dr and doubles with private bathroom for 7500 dr. Take the lift to reception as you enter the building.

The C-class *Hotel Panorama* (☎ 224 205), Eleftheriou Venizelou 26 C, has reasonable singles/doubles for 5500/7500 dr with shared bathroom and 7500/9500 dr with private bathroom. Near the waterfront the *Hotel Nefeli* (☎ 227 441; fax 227 440), Leoforos Erythrou Stavrou 50, has pleasant singles/doubles for 11,000/14,000/16,800 dr with private bathroom. The C-class *Hotel Esperia* (☎ 229 621/625; fax 220 621), Erythrou Stavrou 42, is similarly priced.

Places to Stay – middle
The B-class *Hotel Galaxy* (☎ 224 812; fax 226 754), Eleftheriou Venizelou 27, is Kavala's best hotel, with spacious, attractively furnished single/double rooms for 14,000/19,000 dr. All rooms have air-con, refrigerator, telephone, radio and private bathroom.

There are many mid-range hotels on the stretch of coast just south-west of Kavala. The B-class *Blue Bay Hotel* (☎ 21 800; fax 21 755) is on the beach at Nea Iraklitsa. It

NORTHERN GREECE

has a restaurant, bar, roof garden and swimming pool. Rates are 8000/10,000 dr for singles/doubles and 14,100 dr for bungalows. The B-class *Egeon Strand Hotel* (☎ 21 897/898; fax 21 947), also on Nea Iraklitsa beach, has singles/doubles for 8000/11,000 dr. It doesn't have a swimming pool but has a sauna, solarium, gymnasium and hydromassage.

Places to Stay – top end
The most luxurious hotel in the vicinity of Kavala is the A-class *Tosca Beach Hotel* (☎ 224 765/768; fax 243 986) which has doubles for 11,800 dr and suites for 21,800 dr. The hotel is five km south-west of Kavala at Myrmigia beach.

Always bear in mind that the list prices given here may be heavily discounted out of season, sometimes by as much as 55%.

Places to Eat
Kavala's restaurant scene is a vast improvement on its accommodation. *Ta Plakakia Restaurant*, Doïranis 4, near Plateia Eleftherias, is a conveniently located eating place with a huge choice of low-priced dishes. The *Michalakis Taverna*, Kassandrou 3, on Plateia Kapnergati, is more up-market. Don't be put off by their tacky murals and folksy wall-hangings – the food is good. Prices at these two places range from 1500 dr to 2000 dr for a meal.

There are three popular restaurants on Poulidou, opposite the Imaret. The first is *Taverna Faros*; their fried mussels are delectable. Another one, *To Steki tou Kanadou*, has a wide-ranging fish menu and other seafood specialities. Try their mussels in tomato sauce. *Antonia Restaurant*, next door, is also recommended by locals and is equally well patronised. Prices at these three are similar and slightly upper market in range. Expect to part with at least 2000 dr for a meal. For a unique eating environment, try the *Estiatorio Imaret* in the Imaret itself, further up Poulidou on the right. This is probably Kavala's most atmospheric eating location. The price of a meal here is also in the 2000 dr bracket.

The *Café Andreadi*, on a side street off Eleftheriou Venizelou, has good cheese pies and custard pies and filter coffee. If you don't want a meal, then the café in the Imaret is in a lovely serene setting around a courtyard of fruit trees. Here you can play backgammon or other board games to while away an hour or so.

If you want to concoct a picnic there are fruit vendors everywhere and a food market between Spetson and Omonias.

Getting There & Away
Air Kavala shares Hrysoupolis Airport with Xanthi. There is one flight a day to Athens (15,800 dr) at 6.30 pm and additional flights in summer on Tuesday, Thursday and Saturday at 6.30 am. The airport is 29 km south-east of Kavala.

Bus From the intercity bus station there are half-hourly buses to Xanthi (one hour, 800 dr); hourly buses to Keramoti (one hour, 700 dr) and hourly services to Thessaloniki (two hours, 2500 dr). For Philippi take one of the frequent Drama buses and ask to be let off at the ancient site of Philippi (20 minutes, 300 dr).

Buses for Alexandroupolis (2½ hours, 2200 dr), which originate in Thessaloniki, do not leave from the intercity bus station, but from outside the Dore Café (☎ 227 601), Erythrou Stavrou 34, from where you can get departure times and buy a ticket.

To/From Turkey There are daily OSE buses that originate in Thessaloniki and depart from Kavala at 5.30 pm. Tickets cost 9450/16,050 for a single/return. Student and youth discounts apply to student cardholders. You can buy tickets from Alkyon Travel Service (☎ 836 251 or 222 533) on Eleftheriou Venizelou, next door to the Hotel Panorama.

Train The nearest train station to Kavala is at Drama, 30 km away. Drama is on the Thessaloniki-Alexandroupolis line and there are eight trains a day in either direction. There is a frequent bus service between

Kavala and Drama. Train tickets can be bought in advance from Alkyon Travel which also acts as an OSE agency.

Car Budget Rent a Car (☎ 228 785) is on the 1st floor of Eleftheriou Venizelou 35, opposite the Hotel Panorama. You can also rent a car from the Europcar agency at Alkyon Travel Service on Eleftheriou Venizelou.

Ferry There are ferries every hour from Kavala to Skala Prinou on Thasos (1¼ hours, 600 dr, or 3600 dr for driver and car). There is also a service every hour or so in summer (35 minutes, 350 dr, or 2500 dr for driver and car) from the small port of Keramoti, 46 km south-east of Kavala, to Limenas.

In summer there are ferries from Kavala to Samothraki (four hours, 2810 dr). Times and frequency vary month by month. Buy tickets and check the latest schedule at Zolotas Travel Agency (☎ 835 671) near the entrance to the Aegean islands ferry departure point.

There are ferries to Limnos (4½ hours, 3100 dr), Agios Efstratios (six hours, 3100 dr) and Lesvos (11½ hours, 5100 dr) with a further summer service to Patmos (19 hours, 8700 dr), via Chios and Samos. Some services also go through to Rafina (in Attica) and Piraeus. You can buy tickets and get the latest schedules from Nikos Miliades Shipping Agency (☎ 226 147; fax 838 767), Karaoli-Dimitriou 36.

Hydrofoil There are seven hydrofoils a day to Limenas (30 minutes, 1400 dr), five or six per day to Skala Prinou (1820 dr) and a further two per day to Potos (2800 dr), via Kallirahi, Maries and Limenaria. Purchase tickets at the departure point at the port. There are hydrofoil connections to Lesvos, Plomari (Lesvos) and Chios twice a week on average; with a further service including Limnos, once a week. Contact Skouroglou Travel (☎ 831 528) for the latest schedule and fares. Hydrofoil fares, in general, tend to be twice the equivalent regular ferry fare.

Hydrofoil tickets for the Limnos-Lesvos-Chios run and islands further south can also be bought from Miliades Shipping Agency.

Getting Around

To/From the Airport There is no Olympic Airways bus to the airport. A public bus leaves from the intercity bus station at 6.20 pm every evening.

PHILIPPI Φίλιπποι

The ancient site of Philippi (FEE-li-pee) lies 15 km inland from Kavala astride the Kavala-Drama road. The original city was called Krenides. Philip II seized it from the Thasians in 356 BC because it was in the foothills of Mt Pangaion, and there was 'gold in them thar' hills', which he needed to finance his battles to gain control of Greece.

During July and August the Philippi Festival is held at the site's theatre. Information about this can be obtained from the EOT in Kavala. The site (☎ 051-516 470) and museum (☎ 051-516 251) are open Tuesday to Sunday from 8.30 am to 3 pm. Admission to each is 500 dr.

History

A visit to Philippi is worthwhile more for the significance of the events which happened there than for what can actually be seen, so some knowledge of its history is essential. Philippi is famous for two reasons: it was the scene of one of the most decisive battles in history, and it was the first European city to accept Christianity.

By the 1st century AD, Greece had become the battleground for factions of the Roman republic, and Philippi was coveted for its strategic position on the Via Egnatia. Julius Caesar's death at the hands of the republicans Cassius and Brutus had created a power vacuum. Eager to fill this gap, the two most powerful armies of Rome (with 80,000 men per side) met in battle on the plain of Philippi. One side was led by the imperial Mark Antony (great nephew of Julius Caesar) and Octavian, and the other by Julius Caesar's assassins. Octavian was the victor, causing Cassius and Brutus to commit suicide. The battle set the seal on the future

NORTHERN GREECE

of a new Rome which was to be imperialist (and as things turned out, Christian as well).

Octavian, after this victory, waged another famous battle (the Battle of Actium) in 31 AD, where he fought his former ally Mark Antony and Antony's consort, Cleopatra. Again, Octavian was the victor (and again the defeated committed suicide) and so now in control, he established an autocracy, and became Augustus, first emperor of Rome.

Neopolis (present-day Kavala), the port of Philippi, was the landing stage in Europe for travellers from the Orient. And so it was here that St Paul came in 49 AD to embark upon his conversion of the pagan Europeans. His overzealous preaching landed him in prison – a misadventure which would be repeated many times in the future.

Exploring the Site

Despite Philippi being the first Christian city in Europe, its people didn't have much luck in their church-building endeavours. The 5th-century **Basilica A** was the first church built in the city, but it was wrecked by an earthquake shortly after completion. The remains of this church can be seen on the north side of the site (on the left coming from Kavala), near the road and to the east of the theatre.

Their next attempt was the 6th-century **Basilica B**, on the southern side of the site, next to the large and conspicuous forum. This church was an ambitious attempt to build a church with a dome, but the structure was top heavy and collapsed before it was dedicated. In the 10th century its sole remaining part, the narthex, was made into a church – several of its Corinthian columns can be seen.

Philippi's best preserved building is the **theatre**, which isn't Roman but was built by Philip II. Also in good nick are 50 marble latrines at the southern end of the forum. The site's **museum**, on the north side, houses both Roman and Christian finds from Philippi, and also Neolithic finds from the nearby site of Dikili Tach.

Getting There & Away

Buses between Kavala and Drama will let passengers off at the ancient site (20 minutes, 220 dr).

Thrace Θράκη

Thrace is the north-eastern region of Greece and the backwater of the mainland. If you ask Greeks from elsewhere what it has to offer, chances are most will reply 'nothing', and some will add in words weighted with meaning 'and Turks live there'. The Turkish population of Thrace, along with the Greek population of Constantinople and the former Greek islands of Imvros (Gökçe Ada) and Tenedos (Bozca Ada) were exempt from the 1923 population exchange. This phenomenon alone sets the area apart from the rest of Greece. The landscape is dotted with the slender minarets of mosques and villages of Turkish-style red-roofed houses. There is also a more pronounced Turkish influence in the food, and a greater proliferation of Eastern-style bazaars and street vendors.

Besides being of ethnographical interest the region has some picturesque towns and a varied landscape. It has a long coastline interspersed with wetlands and a hinterland

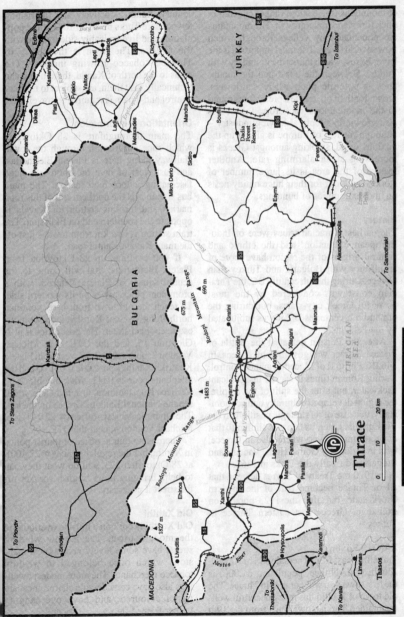

of mountains (the Rodopi range) covered in thick forest and undergrowth. The mountains are punctuated by valleys through which flow several rivers. The most important is the River Evros, which marks the boundary with Turkey. Between the coast and the mountains is a fertile plain where sunflowers, grown for their oil, create a pretty foreground to the mountainous backdrop. Tobacco is also grown, to supply a thriving industry – although the rest of Europe is giving up the noxious weed, smoking amongst Greeks is increasing at an alarming rate. Another feature of the area is its large number of storks. Look out for their huge untidy nests on high extremities of buildings.

History

The earliest Thracian tribes were of Indo-European extraction, and the ethnic and cultural origins of the region have more of an affinity with Bulgaria and Turkey than Greece. During the 7th century BC, the Thracian coast was conquered by the most powerful Greek city-states, but during the 6th and 5th centuries BC it was subjugated by the Persians.

After the Persian defeat at the Battle of Plataea, Thrace was governed by Athens. In 346 BC Philip II of Macedon gained control. During Roman times it was an insignificant backwater, but after the split of the empire, the region developed culturally and economically, because of its strategic position on the Via Egnatia. Later, its fate was similar to that of pretty much everywhere else in Greece, with invasions by Goths, Huns, Vandals and Bulgars and finally the Turks in 1361.

In 1920 the Treaty of Sèvres decreed that all of Thrace become part of the modern Greek state, but after the 1923 population exchange, Greece lost eastern Thrace to Turkey.

XANTHI Ξάνθη

Travelling east from Thessaloniki or Kavala, Xanthi (KSAN-thee, population 31,000) is the first town you will come to in Thrace. The old town of Xanthi has many beautiful well-maintained Turkish dwellings from the 19th

century. Xanthi is a lively and flourishing town where Turks make up 10% of the population, and live amicably side by side with the Greeks. The town is the centre of Thrace's tobacco-growing industry. The areas to the north of Xanthi, though you can technically visit them, are subject to military control and a pass is required to travel here.

Orientation & Information

The main thoroughfare is 28 Oktovriou, which runs north-south through the town. Halfway along here is Plateia Eleftherias, and just west of here on Iroön is a huge fascinating indoor food market. The main bus station is at the northern end of this food market and the bus station for Kavala is opposite the southern end on Eklission. The train station is two km from town – just off the main Kavala-Xanthi road.

If you continue up 28 Oktovriou from Plateia Eleftherias, you will come to the central square of Plateia Kentriki, with a prominent clock tower on its western side. To reach the old town from here, continue north along Vasileos Konstantinou, a picturesque cobbled street. The post office is at A Giorgiou 16, and the OTE is at Michael Vogdou 2; both streets lead west from Plateia Kentriki. Xanthi's postcode is 671 00 and the telephone code is 0541. Walk one block up Vasileos Konstantinou, turn right and you'll see the National Bank of Greece on the left. The Olympic Airways office (☎ 22 944) is at Michael Vogdou 4, near the OTE.

There is no tourist office or tourist police in Xanthi, but the regular police (☎ 22 100), at 28 Oktovriou 223, will do what they can to help, bringing in an English speaker off the street if necessary.

Old Xanthi

Old Xanthi is built on a hillside overlooking the modern town. The narrow winding streets have some lovely neoclassical mansions which once belonged to wealthy tobacco merchants. The more modest dwellings also have considerable charm; most are pastel coloured, and have overhanging timber-framed floors.

Two of the old town's mansions which adjoin one another have been converted into a **museum**. They were built for the Koumtzogli brothers, who were tobacco magnates. The museum is well laid out and exhibits include traditional agricultural and household implements, carpets, embroidery and jewellery. While you're in the museum cast your eyes upwards to the ceilings, which are amazing. Some made are of carved wood, others are painted with intricate designs. Also don't miss the antique toilet upstairs (no longer useable). The toilet's bowl is decorated both inside and out with elaborate floral designs.

Labelling of exhibits is in Greek, but the friendly curator, Deodoros Tserpistolis, will do his best to explain things, although his English is limited. The museum is at Antika 7 and is open every day from 11 am to 1 pm every day. Admission is 200 dr.

Places to Stay – bottom end

The rather sleazy D-class *Lux Hotel* (☎ 22 341 or 23 004), Georgiou Stavriou 18, near Plateia Kentriki, has singles/doubles for 3500/4000 dr with shared bathroom. If you're coming from Vasileos Konstantinou, turn right at the National Bank of Greece to reach the hotel.

The town's two clean and comfortable C-class hotels are much better options. The *Hotel Dimokritus* (☎ 25 111; fax 25 537), 28 Oktovriou 41, near Plateia Kentriki, has rates of 7000/8300/10,000 dr with private bathroom. The *Hotel Xanthippion* (☎ 77 061; fax 77 076), 28 Oktovriou 212, has singles/doubles for 7000/9000 dr with private bathroom. This hotel has a car park, and is at the southern end of town.

Places to Stay – middle

Xanthi's best hotel is the modern B-class *Hotel Nestos* (☎ 27 531; fax 27 535). The rooms go for 13,000/16,200 dr with private bathroom. The hotel is one km south of the town centre. Coming from Kavala by road, it's on the right as you enter the town. This hotel also has a car park.

Places to Eat & Drink

Locals rate the *Klimataria Restaurant* on Plateia Kentriki as the town's best eating place. It has a large selection of ready-made food: stuffed peppers, stuffed aubergines and chicken stew all cost around 1000 dr.

Students hang out at *Taverna Xanthi* which has outdoor eating in a walled garden. This restaurant only opens in the summer. Walk to the top of Vasileos Konstantinou and you will see a sign on a wall pointing left to the taverna. Turn left and you will find the restaurant immediately, though not obviously, to your left. A meal will cost about 1400 dr.

Close by, just where Paleologou begins to climb to old Xanthi, are two ouzeria, the *Kivotos* and the *Arhontisa*. Give them a try, if you can manage to order one or two mezedes in Greek. Keep track of what you are eating and drinking or the bill might be higher than you'd anticipated. Expect to pay over 2000 dr if you eat and drink at an ouzeri.

On Vasileos Konstantinou there are many zaharoplasteia selling Turkish cakes and confectionery. One of the best of these is *Anestis*, at the northern end of the street, on the right.

There is a leafy square with a range of cafés and zaharoplasteia where you might want to while away an hour or so with a newspaper or a book. Walk east from Plateia Kentriki along Panagi Tsaldari for 100 metres and turn left into Ydras. Follow this street for about 300 metres until you come across the square.

Getting There & Away

Air Xanthi shares Hrysoupolis Airport with Kavala in Macedonia (see the Kavala section for flight details). The airport is 47 km away.

Bus From the main bus terminal there are eight buses a day to Komotini (45 minutes, 750 dr) and seven to Thessaloniki (four hours, 2950 dr). There are no direct buses to Alexandroupolis; you must change buses at Komotini. Seven buses a day go to Kavala (one hour, 850 dr).

NORTHERN GREECE

The Muslim Minorities Question

The issue of the Muslim minorities in Greece is a touchy and sensitive matter. Greek Muslims number over 100,000 and consist of Turkish-speaking Muslims, Pomaks and Gypsies, known locally as *athinganoi*. The Treaty of Lausanne (1923) settled the boundaries of modern Turkey and resolved the territorial disputes raised in Anatolia by WW I. At the end of the war the Allies imposed the Treaty of Sèvres (1920) on the defeated Ottoman Empire; it effectively dismembered the empire, leaving only Anatolia (minus a Greek enclave at Smyrni, or İzmir) under Turkish rule. This settlement was rejected by the Turkish nationalists led by Mustafa Kemal (later Kemal Atatürk). Although they accepted the loss of Iraq, Syria, Arabia, and other non-Turkish areas, they objected to the loss of Smyrna to Greece. After driving the Greek troops out of Smyrna and ousting the sultan, Kemal's government was able to force the negotiation of a new treaty, which was finally concluded at Lausanne, Switzerland, on 24 July, 1923.

According to the Treaty of Lausanne, Turkey regained not only Smyrna but also eastern Thrace and some of the Aegean islands. It also resumed control of the Dardanelles (internationalised under the previous treaty) on the condition that they be kept demilitarised and open to all nations in peacetime. A separate agreement between Turkey and Greece provided for the exchange of minority populations. In the exchange, whole communities of Greeks and Turks were forcibly relocated to new homelands, with the exception of the Turks of central Thrace and the Greeks of İstanbul (Constantinople).

It is the result of this incomplete exchange of populations that is today causing Greece a considerable headache. Officially, there are no Turkish minorities in Greece but 'Muslim Greeks'. However, any visitor to Komotini and the villages around this town in central Thrace could easily be mistaken in believing that they were in Turkey. The Turkish language is widely spoken and it is hard to miss the women dressed in Muslim attire.

Paradoxically and in a country where individual TV satellite dishes cost a small fortune, there is not a Turkish-speaking village that does not sprout a forest of these expensive antennae, ostensibly for the purpose of receiving Turkish TV (and propaganda?) and apparently paid for indirectly by the Turkish government, via its consulate in Thessaloniki. This 'Turkish Trojan Horse' positioned deep within Greece's vulnerable eastern flank causes jitters whenever the term 'Turkish minority' is raised. An unofficial visit in May 1995 by the Turkish minister for information Yıldırım Aktuna, caused a storm, when the said minister boldly called for greater self-determination for Greece's Turkish-speaking Muslims.

How Greece will handle this delicate issue in a region already beset by ethnic conflicts, will be a subject of close scrutiny by all Balkan watchers. ■

Train There are six trains a day to both Alexandroupolis (860 dr) and Thessaloniki (2160 dr). The Thessaloniki-bound intercity trains leave Xanthi at 8.40 am and 5.56 pm. The equivalent services to Alexandroupolis depart at 11.24 am and 5.56 pm. These trains attract a ticket supplement. The 8.54 pm eastbound train goes to İstanbul.

Train tickets may be purchased either at the station; or from the OSE agent, Tarpidis Tours (☎ 22 277 or 27 840), at Tsaldari 5, which is in the Agora Nousa (an indoor shopping precinct) just east of Plateia Kentriki. A taxi to the train station will cost you about 600 dr.

Getting Around

To/From the Airport There are no Olympic Airways buses to Hrysoupolis. A taxi costs 6000 dr. Alternatively you can take a Kavala-bound bus to the town of Hrysoupolis, and take a taxi to the airport which is 12 km away.

KOMOTINI Κομοτηνή

Komotini (population 35,000), 57 km east of Xanthi, is the capital of the prefecture of Rodopi. Its population is half Greek and half Turkish. It lacks the character of Xanthi and is unremarkable except for its outstanding **archaeological museum** (☎ 0531-22 411), Simeonidi 4, which houses well-displayed

DAVID HALL

DAVID HALL

Top: Onion domes of the Russian monastery St Pandeleimon, Athos, Macedonia
Bottom: View of Mt Athos, Macedonia

GREG ALFORD

ANN JOUSIFFE

DAVID WILLETT

Top: View of Poros, Saronic Gulf islands
Left: The day's catch
Right: Selling fish from the boat at the harbour, Poros, Saronic Gulf islands

finds from little-known ancient sites in Thrace, most notably Abdera and Maronia.

The latter was Homer's Ismaros, where Odysseus obtained the wine which he used to intoxicate the Cyclops Polyphemus. Whilst in this drunken state, Polyphemus had a stake driven into his one remaining eye by villagers who sought revenge for his misdeeds. (The scant remains of the ancient site of Maronia are near the modern village of Maronia, 31 km south-east of Komotini.) The museum is well signposted and opening times are Tuesday to Sunday from 9 am to 5 pm. Admission is 500 dr.

The **Museum of Folk Life & History** (☎ 25 975; fax 37 145), at Agiou Georgiou 13, is worth a visit, if you are in between buses. Housed in the Peïdi Mansion, the display has samples of homewares, manuscripts and costumes. The more important displays are labelled in English also. A useful book on the history of Komotini and the Rodopi prefecture is available for 1000 dr. Entrance to the museum is free.

Komotini's telephone code is 0531 and its postcode is 691 00.

Places to Stay

The nearest camp site to Komotini is *Fanari Komotinis Camping* (☎ 0535-31 217/270). The site is by the sea near the village of Fanari, about 26 km south-west of Komotini.

If you get stuck in Komotini, finding a place to stay shouldn't be too much of a problem. Among the possibilities are the E-class *Hotel Hellas* (☎ 22 055), Dimokritou 31, where singles/doubles with shared bathroom are 3800/5500 dr. The *Pension Olympos* (☎ 37 690; fax 37 693), Orfeos 37, has singles/doubles with private bathroom for 8000/9500 dr. The *Democritus Hotel* (☎ 22 579; fax 23 396), Plateia Vizynou 8, has singles/doubles for 8500/11,100 dr with private bathroom.

Komotini's best hotel is the B-class *Chris & Eve Mansion* (☎ 29 777; fax 26 979). This is a posh place with a swimming pool, sauna and gymnasium. Rates are 11,500/15,400 dr for singles/doubles. Suites are also available.

The blinding of the Cyclops Polyphemus

The hotel is three km from Kavala on the Komotini-Alexandroupolis road.

Getting There & Away

Bus There are frequent buses from Komotini to Xanthi (45 minutes, 750 dr) and Alexandroupolis (70 minutes, 950 dr). Eight buses a day travel between Kavala and Komotini (45 minutes, 1550 dr). There are also eight buses a day to Thessaloniki (4½ hours, 3700 dr).

Train There are six trains a day to both Alexandroupolis (590 dr) and Thessaloniki (2500 dr). The Thessaloniki-bound intercity trains leave from Komotini at 8.11 am and 5.25 pm. The equivalent services to Alexandroupolis depart at 11.53 am and 6.25 pm. These trains attract a ticket supplement. The 9.33 pm eastbound train goes to İstanbul.

ALEXANDROUPOLIS Αλεξανδρούπολη

Alexandroupolis (Alex-and-ROU-pol-is, population 34,000), the capital of the prefecture of Evros, is a modern, dusty and prosaic town with a heavy military presence. Most travellers come here simply to transit east to Turkey, or to catch the ferry to Samothraki. Still, Alexandroupolis' maritime ambience and its liveliness all year round make it a pleasant stopover.

Alexandroupolis' hotels get surprisingly full, since Greek holiday-makers from northern Evros flock here in July and August. Their numbers are swelled by overlanders,

NORTHERN GREECE

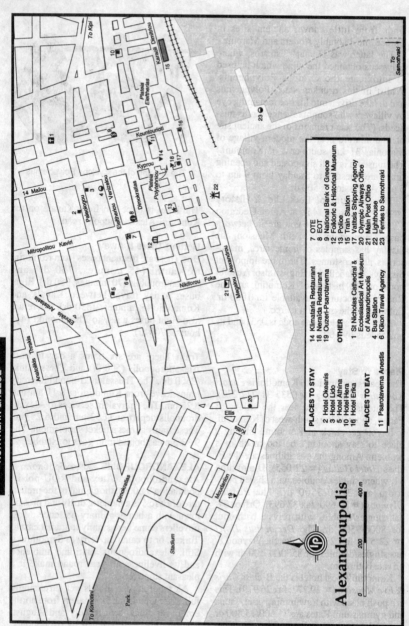

Alexandroupolis

0   200   400 m

PLACES TO STAY

2 Hotel Okeanis
3 Hotel Lido
5 Hotel Athina
10 Hotel Hera
16 Hotel Erika

PLACES TO EAT

11 Psarotaverna Anestis

14 Klimataria Restaurant
18 Neraida Restaurant
19 Ouzeri-Psarotaverna

OTHER

1 St Nicholas Cathedral &
   Ecclesiastical Art Museum
   of Alexandroupolis
4 Bus Station
6 Kikon Travel Agency
7 OTE
8 EOT
9 National Bank of Greece
12 Folkloric & Historical Museum
13 Police
15 Train Station
17 Vatitsis Shipping Agency
20 Olympic Airways Office
21 Main Post Office
22 Lighthouse
23 Ferries to Samothraki

NORTHERN GREECE

who descend upon the town *en route* to Turkey. During these months try to continue your journey to Samothraki or Turkey; otherwise, reserve accommodation in advance.

Orientation

The town is laid out roughly on a grid system, with the main streets running east-west, parallel with the waterfront, where the lively evening volta (promenade) takes place. Karaoli Dimitriou is at the eastern end of the waterfront, with Megalou Alexandrou at the western end. The town's most prominent landmark is the large 19th-century lighthouse on the middle of the waterfront. The two main squares are Plateia Eleftherias and Plateia Polytehniou. Both are just one block north of Karaoli Dimitriou.

The railway station is on the waterfront just south of Plateia Eleftherias and east of the port where boats leave for Samothraki. The intercity bus station is at Eleftheriou Venizelou 36, five blocks inland. The local bus terminal is on Plateia Eleftherias.

Information

The municipal tourist office (☎ 24 998) is in the town hall on Dimokratias. The helpful staff dispense maps and have information on accommodation and transport.

The main post office is on the waterfront on the corner of Nikiforou Foka and Megalou Alexandrou. The OTE is on the corner of Mitropolitou Kaviri and Eleftheriou Venizelou. Alexandroupolis' postcode is 681 00 and the telephone code is 0551.

The National Bank of Greece is at Dimokratias 246. The police (☎ 26 418) are at Karaïskaki 6. The port police telephone number is ☎ 26 468.

Ecclesiastical Art Museum of Alexandroupolis

This outstanding museum is one of the best of its kind in the country. It contains a priceless collection of icons and ecclesiastical ornaments brought to Greek Thrace by refugees from Asia Minor. Unfortunately due to a cutback in government funding, the museum is unable to keep regular opening

hours, but if you ring the bell of the offices next door, someone will show you around. Entrance is free. The museum is in the grounds of the St Nicholas Cathedral.

Folkloric & Historical Museum

By mid-1995 a new folkloric and historical museum will have opened on the corner of Dimokratias and Kanari in a brand-new, swish building. Organised by the Society of the Friends of Antiquities of the Evros Prefecture, the displays promise to offer an insight into life and culture of Eastern Thrace. No further details were available at the time of research.

Places to Stay

Camping Alexandroupolis (☎ 28 735) is on the beach two km west of the town. It's a clean, well-run site with good facilities. Take a local bus from Plateia Eleftherias to reach the site.

The *Hotel Lido* (☎ 28 808), Paleologou 15, is an outstanding D-class hotel with comfortable single/double/triple rooms for 2500/2600/5000 dr with shared bathroom, and 5200/6000 dr for doubles/triples with private bathroom. The hotel is one block north of the bus station. The *Hotel Erika* (☎ 34 115; fax 34 117), is a very superior D-class place where room rates are a rather high 8100/10,800/13,500 dr. All rooms have private bathroom, telephone, TV and balcony. The hotel is on the corner of Karaoli Dimitriou and Kountourioti.

The C-class *Hotel Okeanis* (☎ 28 830; fax 34 118) on Paleologou 20, almost opposite the Lido, has excellent, spacious rooms for 7000/9000 dr. C-class *Hotel Hera* (☎ 23 941; fax 34 222) on Leoforos Dimokratias 179, closer to the railway station, has nice, but smaller rooms for 8800/11,000 dr.

One other option for groups of two or more is the *Apartment Hotel Athina* (☎ 34 492; fax 37 301) at Paleologou 53. Here you can be self-contained with air-con and modern kitchen facilities. Doubles here go for 14,700 dr and suites for three to five people are 18,000 dr. Prices are negotiable and are usually lower than the published rates.

Places to Eat

The *Neraïda Restaurant*, on Kyprou where it widens to form a small square is a good choice and has a range of standard fare and some local specialities for 1400 to 1800 dr. In a similar vein and with similar prices, but with an English language menu that takes some beating, is the *Klimataria* which is diagonally opposite the Neraïda. Kyprou begins opposite the Samothraki ferry pier.

For a special treat at night, try a couple of restaurants not on the usual tourist beat. The *Psarotaverna Anestis* on Athanasiou Diakou 5, one street east of Kyprou, looks very unassuming, but has a fine choice of mezedes, especially fish dishes. Mydia saganaki (chilli mussels) are highly recommended.

Towards the western end of the promenade, past all the noisy cafeterias, is a new place called, somewhat unoriginally, *Ouzeri-Psarotaverna*. Look out for the fish sign. The food here is exquisite and is prepared by one of Alexandroupolis' best restaurateurs, Vasilis Palakidis. Shellfish and fish are, naturally, the specialities of the house. Expect to pay 3000 dr and upwards for a meal, especially if you order fish.

Getting There & Away

Air The Olympic Airlines office (☎ 26 361) is at Ellis 4. Alexandroupolis has a domestic airport, which is seven km east of town, near the village of Loutra. The airport serves Athens only, with a daily flight at 7.30 pm and a further flight at 6.30 am four times a week in summer. The cost is 16,000 dr.

Bus From Alexandroupolis' bus station there are frequent buses to Soufli, Didymotiho, Orestiada (two hours, 950 dr) and Komotini (one hour 10 minutes, 950 dr). There are five buses a day to Thessaloniki (six hours, 4600 dr) via Kavala. There are no direct buses to Xanthi; you must change buses in Komotini.

For what it's worth, there is one daily bus to Athens (12 hours, 11,000 dr).

To/From Turkey There are daily OSE buses to İstanbul, leaving at 9.30 am. The journey takes between five and seven hours and tickets cost 5850 dr. There are currently no private buses running to Turkey, but Kikon Travel Agency (☎ 25 455; fax 34 755), Eleftheriou Venizelou 68, organises three-day, all-in tours to İstanbul for 25,000 dr.

Otherwise, you can take a bus from the intercity bus station to Kipi (five departures a day, 600 dr) the border town, which is 43 km from Alexandroupolis. You cannot walk across the border but it is easy enough to hitch across – you may be lucky and get a lift all the way to İstanbul. Otherwise take a bus from İpsala (five km beyond the border) or from Keşan (30 km beyond the border).

To/From Bulgaria There is a private bus service to Plovdiv (6500 dr) and Sofia (7000 dr) which departs from Alexandroupolis on Tuesday, Friday and Sunday at 8.30 am. Return dates and times from Bulgaria are the same. Contact Kikon Travel Agency (☎ 25 455; fax 34 755), Eleftheriou Venizelou 68, for details.

Train There are five trains a day to Thessaloniki (seven hours, 5160/3440 dr in 1st/2nd class), including one which continues on to Athens and intermediate stations (14 hours, 9450/6300 dr). Two of these are intercity services; the *Alexandros* terminates in Thessaloniki and the other, the *Vergina*, terminates in Athens. There are also six trains a day to Pythio via Didymotiho and Orestiada.

To/From Turkey There is one train a day to İstanbul, which leaves Alexandroupolis at 11.06 pm. Tickets cost around 5000 dr and the journey can take 10 hours. The train is hot and crowded in summer; the bus is a marginally better choice.

To/From Bulgaria There is one service a day to Svilengrad with an ongoing connection to Plovdiv and Sofia. The ticket costs 2370 dr as far as Svilengrad and the trip takes four

NORTHERN GREECE

hours. The train leaves Alexandroupolis at 11.06 pm.

Ferry In July and August there are a number of sailings a day to Samothraki. In spring and autumn there are two sailings a day and in winter, one. Tickets and latest details may be obtained from Vatitsis Shipping Agency (☎ 26 721, 23 512 or 22 215), Kyprou 5 (opposite the port). Tickets cost 2200 dr and the trip takes two hours. There is another ticket office on the corner of Kyprou and Karaoli Dimitriou.

Hydrofoil Hydrofoil (Flying Dolphin) services now operate during the summer months, linking Alexandroupolis with Chios, via Limnos and Lesvos. Tickets to Chios (5½ hours) cost 13,000 dr. To Lesvos (3½ hours) the price is 9000 dr. Contact Kikon Travel Agency 5 455; fax 34 755), Eleftheriou Venizelou 68.

Getting Around

To/From the Airport There is no airport shuttle bus. Take a Loutra-bound bus from Plateia Eleftherias. A taxi to the airport will cost about 1000 dr.

EVROS DELTA Δέλτα Εβρου

The Evros delta, 20 km south-east of Alexandroupolis, is ecologically one of Europe's most important wetlands. Three hundred species of birds have been recorded including the last 15 surviving pairs of royal eagles; and more than 200,000 migrating waterfowl spend part of their winter here. Unfortunately the wetlands are in a highly sensitive area due to their proximity to Turkey, and permission from the security police in Alexandroupolis is technically required in order to visit. Contact the regular police or the Feres municipal tourist office (☎ 0555-22 211) for further information on organised tours.

ALEXANDROUPOLIS TO DIDYMOTIHO

North-east of Alexandroupolis the road, railway line and River Evros run close together, skirting the Turkish border. This is a highly sensitive area with many signs prohibiting photography. It's also a lush and attractive region with fields of wheat and sunflowers, and forests of pine trees.

Feres, 29 km north-east of Alexandroupolis, has the interesting 12th-century Byzantine Church of Panagia Kosmosoira. It is signposted from the main road.

Continuing north, the little town of **Soufli**, 67 km north-east of Alexandroupolis and 31 km south of Didymotiho, has lots of character. It has retained a number of its Turkish wattle-and-daub houses and is renowned in Greece for its production of silk. This is because the mulberry tree, upon which the silkworms feed, used to thrive in the region. Unfortunately, most of the mulberry trees have been chopped down to make way for crops, but the town still has one silk factory.

Soufli has an interesting **silk museum** with a display of silk-producing equipment. The museum is signposted from the town's main through road, but opening times are subject to change.

If you decide to spend the night in Soufli the D-class *Egnatia Hotel* (☎ 0554-22 124), Vasileos Georgiou 225, has singles/doubles for 3300/5300 dr with shared bathroom. The most up-market place to stay is the C-class *Hotel Orpheas* (☎ 0554-22 922; fax 22 305), on the corner of Vasileos Georgiou and Tsimiski. Rates are 8262/10,972 dr with private bathroom.

Soufli is on the Alexandroupolis to Didymotiho bus and train routes.

DIDYMOTIHO Διδυμότειχο

Didymotiho (Did-im-OT-iho, population 8500) is the most interesting of the towns north of Alexandroupolis, although few tourists venture here. The town's name derives from the double walls which once enclosed it (*didymo* – 'twin', *tihos* – 'wall'). In Byzantine times it was an important town. When it fell to the Turks in 1361, Murad I made it the capital. In 1365 he transferred the capital to Adrianople (present-day Edirne). The town's most prominent landmark is a large mosque, with a pyramidal shaped roof, on Plateia Kentriki. Fifteen per cent of the town's population is Turkish and there are also a number of Gypsies.

Orientation & Information

Orientation is easy in this small town, as almost everything you need is on or near Plateia Kentriki, the central square, which you can't miss because of the mosque. The OTE and the National Bank of Greece are on Plateia Kentriki and the post office is just north of here. Walk along Vasileos Alexandrou, and take the first left into Kolokotroni, and it's on the right. Didymotiho's telephone code is 0553 and the postcode is 683 00.

To get to Plateia Kentriki from the bus station, walk along the road straight ahead, and turn right into Venizelou, which is the town's main thoroughfare – the square is at the end of here. From the railway station turn left, and keep walking to 25 Maïou, and continue along here to Venizelou. There is no tourist office or tourist police.

Things to See

Didymotiho is yet another place to wander in. With the mosque on your left, walk straight ahead from Plateia Kentriki to the picturesque, tree-shaded Plateia Vatrahou (Frog Square in English), so named because of its frog-shaped fountain. Continue straight ahead up Metaxa. In this area there are many Turkish timber-framed houses. Continue uphill to the **Cathedral of Agios Athanasios**. Next to the cathedral are some well-preserved sections of the town's Byzantine walls.

If you walk back down Metaxa, and turn left into Vatatzi, you will come to the **folk museum** on the right. This outstanding museum has displays of Thracian costumes; 19th and early 20th-century agricultural equipment and household implements; and a reconstructed kitchen from a 1920s house. The museum is open Wednesday and Thursday from 5 to 8 pm and on weekends from 10 am to 2 pm. Call ☎ 0554-22 154, if you wish to visit out of hours.

Construction of the mosque on Plateia Kentriki was started by Murad I and finished by his son, Bayazıt, in 1368. It is the oldest

and largest mosque in Europe. Its minaret, which has two intricate ornate balconies, has lost its top, all the windows are smashed and the walls are crumbling. It is still obvious, however, that it must once have been a fine building.

Places to Stay

Didymotiho has two hotels. The tidy D-class *Hotel Anesis* (☎ 0553-24 850) has single/double rooms for 6100/7300 dr with private bathroom. The hotel is on the left side of Vasileos Alexandrou, coming from Plateia Kentriki. The other option is the posh B-class *Hotel Plotini* (☎ 0553-23 400; fax 0553-22 251), Agias Paraskevis 1, one km south of town on the road to Alexandroupolis – approaching the town it's on the left. Rooms here go for a reasonable 6500/10,000 dr.

Places to Eat

Fast-food and cheap souvlaki places are on Venizelou. One of the best places to eat is *Estiatorio O Kostas* on Venizelou, 100 metres on the right down from the main square. Patsas is their speciality. *Zythestiatorio Kipsilaki*, opposite the OTE, is also good. Both have ready-made food, and charge about 1400 dr for a meal with wine, at lunch time.

Didymotiho has some fine old kafeneia. The one at the top of Kolokotroni looks as if it's jumped straight out of the museum opposite. The one on Plateia Vatrahou has tables and chairs set under shady plane trees.

Getting There & Away

There are many buses a day from Alexandroupolis to Didymotiho (two hours, 900 dr). There are also at least three trains a day from Alexandroupolis (three hours, 700 dr).

NORTH OF DIDYMOTIHO

From Didymotiho the road continues for another 20 km to **Orestiada** (population 13,000). This town was built in the 1920s to house refugees who came from Turkey during the population exchange. It's a modern town with little character. If you get stuck it has a couple of budget hotels. The cheapest one is the D-class *Hotel Acropolis* (☎ 0552-22 277), Vasileos Konstantinou 48, where singles/doubles are 3400/6000 dr with private bathroom. The C-class *Hotel Vienna* (☎ 0552-22 578; fax 22 258), Orestou 64, has rates of 9000/11,200 dr with private bathroom.

The best hotel in this area is the *Hotel Electra* (☎ 0552-23 540; fax 23 133), at A Pantazinou 50. The rooms here cost 7000/ 10,600 dr.

It's another 19 km to **Kastanies**, Greece's northern road-border point into Turkey. Unless you're planning to continue to Turkey there's little point coming here.

If you cross the border into Turkey the first town you'll arrive at is the eastern Thracian town of **Edirne**, nine km from Kastanies. The town (formerly called Adrianoupolis) is overlooked by most tourists and retains much of its traditional character. If you want to cross the border here by bus the municipal tourist offices in Alexandroupolis will provide you with information.

NORTHERN GREECE

The Islands

Saronic Gulf Islands
Νησιά του Σαρωνικού

The five islands of the Saronic Gulf are the closest group to Athens. The closest, Salamis, is little more than a suburb of the sprawling capital. Aegina is also close enough to Athens for people to commute to work. Along with Poros, the next island south, it is a popular package-holiday destination. Hydra, once famous as the rendezvous of artists, writers and beautiful people, manages to retain an air of superiority and grandeur. Spetses, the most southerly island in the group, receives an inordinate number of British package tourists.

Spetses has the best beaches, but these islands are not the place to be if long stretches of golden sand are what you seek. With the exception of the Temple of Aphaia, on Aegina, the islands have no significant archaeological remains.

The islands are a very popular escape for Athenians. Accommodation can be nigh on impossible to find between mid-June and mid-September, and weekends are busy all year round. If you plan to go at these times, it's a good idea to reserve a room in advance.

The islands have a reputation for high prices, which is a bit misleading. What is true is that there are very few places for budget travellers to stay – no camp sites and only a couple of cheap hotels. There are a lot of good places to stay if you are happy to be paying 10,000 dr or more for a double. Midweek visitors can get some good deals. Food is no more expensive than anywhere else.

The Saronic Gulf is named after the mythical King Saron of Argos, a keen hunter who drowned in the gulf's waters pursuing a deer that had swum out to sea to escape.

Getting There & Away
Ferry There are at least 12 ferries a day sailing from Piraeus' Great Harbour to Aegina town (1½ hours, 700 dr). Many continue to Methana, in the Peloponnese (two hours, 900 dr), and Poros (3½ hours, 1200 dr); two or three continue from Poros to Hydra (4½ hours, 1500 dr), Ermioni, in the Peloponnese (five hours, 1800 dr), and Spetses (5½ hours, 1800 dr); and one continues from Spetses to Porto Heli (Peloponnese; 5¾ hours, 1800 dr).

Hydrofoil The Ceres Group operates a busy schedule to the islands and nearby Peloponnesian ports with its fleet of Flying Dolphin hydrofoils. Services to Hydra, Poros and Spetses leave from Zea Marina at Piraeus; and services to Aegina leave from the Great Harbour. See individual island entries for details.

Ceres also operates high-speed catamarans on some routes. These Flying Cats, as the company calls them, have both economy and VIP classes. Economy fares are the same as for hydrofoils. VIP class costs an extra 7500 dr, and gets you a plush red-leather seat, free drinks and headphone music.

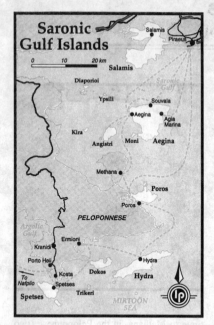

Saronic Gulf Islands

0   10   20 km

Getting Around

There is a comprehensive network of ferries and hydrofoils between the Saronic Gulf islands. See individual island entries for details.

Aegina Αίγινα

Unassuming Aegina (E-yee-na, population 11,000) was once a major player in the Hellenic world, thanks largely to its strategic position at the mouth of the Saronic Gulf. It began to emerge as a commercial centre in about 1000 BC. By the 7th century BC, it was the premier maritime power in the region and amassed great wealth through its trade with Egypt and Phoenicia. The silver 'turtle' coins minted on the island at this time are thought to be the first coins produced in Europe. The Aeginetan fleet made a major

contribution on the Greek side at the Battle of Salamis.

All this didn't go down too well with Athens, which felt uneasy about its neighbour's maritime prowess. Athens attacked the island in 459 BC, and a defeated Aegina was forced to pull down its city walls and surrender its fleet. It did not recover.

The island's other brief moment in the spotlight came in 1827-29, when it was declared the temporary capital of partly liberated Greece. The first coins of the modern Greek nation were minted here.

Aegina has since slipped into a humbler role as Greece's premier producer of pistachio nuts. The writer Nikos Kazantzakis was fond of the island and wrote *Zorba the Greek* while living in a house in Livadi, just north of Aegina town.

According to mythology, Aegina is named after the daughter of the river god, Asopus, who was abducted by Zeus and taken to the island. Aegina's son by Zeus, Aeacus, was the grandfather of Achilles of Trojan War fame.

Getting There & Away

Ferry In summer there are at least 12 ferries a day from Aegina town to Piraeus (1½ hours, 800 dr) as well as services from Agia Marina and Souvala. There are at least three boats a day to Poros (1½ hours, 700 dr) via Methana (40 minutes, 700 dr), and Poros (70 minutes, 700 dr) and a daily boat to Hydra (two hours, 1100 dr) and Spetses (three hours, 1700 dr). The ferry companies have ticket offices at the quay.

Hydrofoil The easiest way of getting to Aegina is on the hydrofoils that operate almost hourly from 7 am to 8 pm between Aegina town and the Great Harbour at Piraeus (35 minutes, 1500 dr). Two others go to Zea Marina (1500 dr). Four hydrofoils a day go to Methana (20 minutes, 1400 dr) and Poros (40 minutes, 1900 dr). Two continue to Hydra (1¼ hours, 2200 dr), Ermioni (1½ hours, 2800 dr) and Spetses (two hours, 2900 dr); and one keeps going to Porto Heli (2½ hours, 3300 dr). There is only one service on Sunday from Aegina to the other islands. It goes right through to Porto Heli.

There's a service from Aegina to Kythira (five hours, 11,300 dr) every Wednesday via Methana, Poros, Hydra, Ermioni, Spetses, Leonidio (2¾ hours, 4000 dr) and Monemvassia (four hours, 6000 dr). This service doesn't operate between 1 July and 9 September.

Hydrofoil tickets are sold at the quay in Aegina town.

Getting Around

There are frequent buses from Aegina town to Agia Marina (30 minutes, 300 dr), going via Paleohora and the Temple of Aphaia. Other buses go to Perdika (15 minutes, 175 dr) and Souvala (20 minutes, 250 dr). Sklavenas Motors (☎ 22 892), 50 metres past the Hotel Plaza, hires out mountain bikes as well as motorbikes.

AEGINA TOWN

Aegina town, on the west coast, is the island's capital and main port. The town is a charming and bustling, if slightly ramshackle, place; its harbour is lined with colourful caïques. Several of the town's

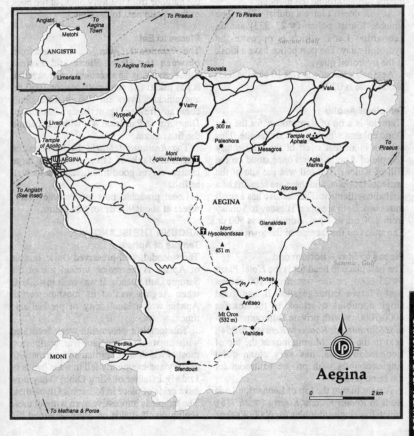

crumbling neoclassical buildings survive from its days as the Greek capital.

Orientation & Information

The ferry dock and nearby small quay used by hydrofoils are on the western edge of town. A left turn at the end of the quay leads to Plateia Ethnegersias, where you'll find the bus terminal and post office. The town beach is 200 metres further along. A right turn at the end of the quay leads to the main harbour. The OTE is off Aiakou, which heads inland next to the port authority building. The National Bank of Greece is on the waterfront just past Aiakou, and the Credit Bank is 150 metres further around the harbour.

Aegina doesn't have a tourist office. The amiable tourist police (☎ 23 333) are on Leonardou Lada, which is opposite the hydrofoil quay. The port police have a kiosk at the hydrofoil quay.

Aegina's postcode is 180 10 and the telephone code is 0297.

Temple of Apollo

'Temple' is a bit of a misnomer for the one Doric column which stands at this site. This column is all that's left of the 5th-century Temple of Apollo which once stood on the Hill of Koloni. The hill was the site of the ancient acropolis, and there are remains of a Helladic settlement. The site also has a small **museum**. Both are open Tuesday to Sunday from 8.30 am to 3 pm. Admission is 500 dr. The site is on the far side of the town beach.

Places to Stay – bottom end

The best place to head for is the *Hotel Plaza* (☎ 25 600), on the waterfront 100 metres past Plateia Ethnegersias. It has good singles/doubles overlooking the sea for 4000/7000 dr with private bathroom. *Antonios Marmarinos Rooms to Rent* (☎ 22 954), next to the Hotel Marmarinos at the top of Leonardou Lada, has very clean quiet singles/doubles with private bathroom for the same prices.

A right turn at the top of Leonardou Lada leads to *Rooms to Rent Electra* (☎ 26 715), which has singles/doubles for 6000/8000 dr.

Places to Stay – middle

The most interesting rooms in town are at the *Eginitiko Arkhontiko* (☎ 24 968), 100 m from the harbour at the junction of Aiakou and Thomaïdou. This fine 19th-century sandstone arhontiko has beautifully furnished singles/doubles for 7700/11,000 dr, and a splendid, ornate two-room suite for 22,000 dr. The only drawback here is the church bells ringing next door.

The *Xenon Pavlou Guest House* (☎ 22 795) is friendly and popular, even if the prices are a trifle steep at 7000/9000/11,000 for singles/doubles/triples with private bathroom. The guest house is on the far side of the harbour from the ferry dock, at the back of the square next to the church.

Places to Eat

The *Restaurant Lekka*, on the waterfront between the Hotel Plaza and Plateia Ethnegersias, is an excellent small taverna. It has baked fish with potatoes for 1050 dr, and chicken livers for 700 dr. Fish don't come any fresher than at the tiny *Restaurant Dionysos*, at Pan Irioti 47, which is behind the fish market.

The *Restaurant Maridaki*, between the National Bank of Greece and the large church, serves good traditional fare as well as fish.

Local pistachio nuts are on sale everywhere at about 900 dr for 500 grams.

AROUND THE ISLAND
Temple of Aphaia

The splendid, well-preserved Doric Temple of Aphaia is the major ancient site of the Saronic Gulf islands. It was built in 480 BC when Aegina was at its most powerful. Aphaia was a local deity of pre-Hellenic times.

The temple's pediments were decorated with outstanding Trojan War sculptures, most of which were spirited away in the 19th century and eventually fell into the hands of Ludwig I (father of King Otho). They now have pride of place in Munich's Glyptothek. The temple is impressive even without these sculptures. It stands on a pine-covered hill and commands imposing vistas of the Saronic Gulf and Cape Sounion.

The site (☎ 32 398) is open Monday to Friday from 8.15 am to 7 pm and Saturday and Sunday from 8.30 am to 3 pm. Admission is 800 dr. Aphaia is 12 km east of Aegina. Buses to Agia Marina stop at the site.

Paleohora Παλαιοχώρα

The ruins of Paleohora, on a hillside 6.5 km east of Aegina town, are a fascinating place to explore. The town was the island's capital from the 9th century to 1826, when pirate attacks forced the islanders to flee the coast and settle inland. (It didn't do them much good when the notorious pirate Barbarossa arrived in 1537, laid waste to the town and took the inhabitants off into slavery.)

The ruins are spread all over the hillside, and are far more extensive than at first appearance. The only buildings left intact are the churches. There are more than two dozen of them, in various states of disrepair, dotted around the hill. There are beautiful frescoes in some of them.

In the valley below Paleohora is **Moni Agiou Nektariou**, an important place of pilgrimage. The monastery contains the relics of a hermit monk, Anastasios Kefalas, who died in 1920. When his body was exhumed in 1940 it was found to have mummified – a sure sign of sainthood in Greek Orthodoxy, especially after a lifetime of performing miracle cures. Kefalas was canonised in 1961 – the first Orthodox saint of the 20th century. The enormous new church that has been built to honour him is a spectacular sight beside the road to Agia Marina. A track leads south from here to the 16th-century **Moni Hrysoleontissas**, in a lovely mountainous setting.

The bus from Aegina town to Agia Marina stops at the turn-off to Paleohora, otherwise it's a pleasant walk from Aegina town.

Beaches

Beaches are not Aegina's strong point. The east coast town of **Agia Marina** is the island's premier tourist resort, but the beach is no great shakes – if you can see it for package tourists. There are a couple of sandy patches that almost qualify as beaches between Aegina and Perdika, at the southern tip of the west coast.

MONI & ANGISTRI ISLETS

Νήσος Μονή & Νήσος Αγκίστρι

The Moni and Angistri islets lie off the west coast of Aegina, opposite Perdika. Moni, the smaller of the two, is a 10-minute boat ride from Perdika – frequent boats do the trip in summer. It's small, rocky and uninhabited, but gets some day-trippers from Aegina, and is popular with freelance campers.

Angistri is much bigger with around 500 inhabitants. There's a sandy beach at the port and other smaller beaches around the coast. Both package-holiday tourists and independent travellers find their way to Angistri. There are tavernas, hotels and domatia on the island. In summer, five caïques a day do the 25-minute trip from Aegina town to Angistri.

Poros Πόρος

The island of Poros (POR-ros, population 4000) is little more than a stone's throw from the mainland. The slender passage of water that separates it from the Peloponnesian town of Galatas is only 360 metres wide at its narrowest point.

Poros was once two islands, Kalavria and Sferia. These days they are joined by a narrow isthmus, cut by a canal for small boats and rejoined by a road bridge. The vast majority of the population lives on the small volcanic island of Sferia, which is more than half-covered by the town of Poros. Sferia hangs like an appendix from the southern coast of Kalavria, a large, well-forested island that has all the package hotels. The town of Poros is not wildly exciting, but it can be used as a base for exploring the ancient sites of the adjacent Peloponnese.

Getting There & Away

Ferry There are eight ferries a day to Piraeus (three hours, 1400 dr), via Methana and

Aegina; and at least one a day to Hydra (one hour, 700 dr), Ermioni, Spetses (two hours, 1300 dr) and Porto Heli. The ticket agencies are opposite the ferry dock.

Small boats shuttle constantly between Poros and Galatas (70 dr) on the mainland. They leave from the quay opposite Plateia Iroön.

Hydrofoil There are up to 10 hydrofoils a day from Poros to Zea Marina (3000 dr), as well as two a day to the Great Harbour at Piraeus. Direct services takes an hour; those via Methana and Aegina take 1½ hours.

There are four hydrofoils a day to Aegina (40 minutes 1900 dr), up to nine to Hydra (30 minutes, 1000 dr) and eight to Spetses (one hour, 1700 dr). Four of these continue to Porto Heli (1½ hours, 1900 dr). There are less frequent services to Ermioni, Leonidio and Tyros. Additional services to Geraka, Kythira, Monemvassia, Nafplio, Neapoli and Tolo don't operate between 1 July and

10 September. The Flying Dolphin agency is on Plateia Iroön, and has a timetable of departures outside.

Getting Around

The Poros bus operates almost constantly along a route that starts near the hydrofoil dock on Plateia Iroön in Poros town. It crosses to Kalavria and goes east along the south coast as far as Moni Zoödohou Pigis, then turns around and heads west as far as Neorion beach. The fare to the monastery is 150 dr.

Motor Stelios, on the waterfront next to the Hotel Latsi in Poros town, has 50-cc mopeds for hire for 3000 dr per day, good mountain bikes for 1500 dr and regular bikes for 1000 dr.

Some of the boats operating between Poros and Galatas switch to ferrying tourists to beaches in summer. Operators stand on the waterfront and call out their destinations.

POROS TOWN

Poros town is the island's only settlement. It's a pretty place of white houses with terracotta-tiled roofs, and there are wonderful views over to the mountains of Argolis. It is a very popular weekend destination for Athenians as well as for package tourists and cruise ships.

Orientation & Information

The ferry dock is at the western tip of Poros town, overlooked by the striking blue-domed clock tower. A left turn from the dock puts you on the waterfront road leading to Kalavria. The OTE building is on the right after 100 metres. A right turn at the ferry dock leads along the waterfront facing Galatas. The first square (triangle actually) is Plateia Iroön, which is where the hydrofoils dock. The bus leaves from next to the kiosk at the eastern end of the square.

The next square along is Plateia Karamanou, home of the post office. The National Bank of Greece is 500 metres further along the waterfront. The Credit Bank, on Plateia Iroön, is more convenient.

Poros does not have a tourist office. The tourist police (☎ 22 462/254) are 300 metres past the National Bank on the waterfront. Poros' postcode is 180 20 and the telephone code is 0298.

Suzi's Laundrette Service, next to the OTE, charges 1800 dr to wash and dry a 5-kg load.

Places to Stay – bottom end

The nearest camp site to town is *Camping Kyragelo* (☎ 24 520), 600 metres east of Galatas on the mainland. It's open from May to October and charges 800 dr per person and 400 dr per tent. It also has a few basic double rooms for 3000 dr.

Poros itself has very little cheap accommodation. The cheapest rooms are at the *Hotel Aktaion* (☎ 22 281) on Plateia Iroön, which charges 3500/6000/7500 dr for basic singles/doubles/triples with shared bathroom.

The *Hotel Latsi* (☎ 22 392), 600 metres from the ferry dock on the road to Kalavria,

has doubles with shared bathroom for 5000 dr as well as singles/doubles/triples for 6000/8000/11,000 dr with private bathroom.

If things are not too hectic, you may be offered a room by one of the domatia owners when you get off the ferry. Otherwise, head left along the waterfront and turn right before Motor Stelios – next to the Hotel Latsi. There are several domatia on the streets around here.

Places to Stay – middle

The place to be for a room with a view is the charming *Villa Tryfon* (☎ 22 215 or 25 854), on top of the hill overlooking the port. The double rooms are 9000 dr, and all have private bathroom and kitchen facilities as well as great views over to Kalavria. To get there, turn left from the ferry dock and take the first right up the steps 20 metres past the Agricultural Bank of Greece. Turn left at the top of the steps on Aikaterinis Hatzopoulou Karra, and you will see the place signposted up the steps to the right after 150 metres. It's behind the Arhontiko Taverna.

The Seven Brothers Hotel (☎ 23 412), Plateia Iroön, is a smart C-class hotel with large, comfortable singles/doubles for 9500/12,100 dr.

The travel agents opposite the ferry dock also handle accommodation. They include Hellenic Sun Travel (☎ 22 636; fax 25 653) and Family Tours (☎ 23 743; fax 24 480).

Places to Eat

O Pantelis Taverna is a lively, unpretentious place next to the markets on the back street running between Plateia Iroön and Plateia Karamanou.

If you're prepared to spend a bit more, the up-market *Taverna Sotiri*, 100 metres before the police station, on the waterfront facing Galatas, is the place. The food is excellent, but the place gets very busy after 9 pm.

The *Arhontiko Taverna* is a friendly, efficient place with very competitive prices, such as 1500 dr for a huge swordfish steak with garlic sauce. The taverna is off the street behind the OTE building – see directions to Villa Tryfon (which is behind it) above.

Entertainment

The *Livitri Bar*, on Dimosthenous, specialises in revelry of the Greek-dancing, plate-smashing kind. It's open from 11 pm until late between April and November.

AROUND THE ISLAND

Poros has a paucity of places of interest and its beaches are no great shakes. **Kanali beach**, on Kalavria just east of the bridge, is a mediocre pebble beach. **Neorion beach**, three km west of the bridge, is marginally better.

The best beach is reputedly at **Russian bay**, 1.5 km past Neorion.

The 18th-century **Moni Zoödohou Pigis** has a beautiful gilded iconostasis which came from Asia Minor and is decorated with paintings from the gospels. The monastery is in an attractive, verdant setting four km east of Poros town.

From the road below the monastery you can strike inland to the 6th-century **Temple of Poseidon**. The god of the sea and earthquakes was the principal deity worshipped on Poros. There's very little left of this temple, but the walk is worth doing for the scenery on the way. From the site there are superb views of the Saronic Gulf and the Peloponnese.

The orator Demosthenes committed suicide here in 322 BC, after failing to shake off the Macedonians, who were after him for inciting the city-states to rebel.

From the ruins you can continue along the road, which eventually winds back to the bridge. The road is drivable, but it's also a fine walk.

PELOPONNESIAN MAINLAND

The Peloponnesian mainland opposite Poros can easily be explored from the island.

A couple of km south-east of **Galatas** are the vast citrus groves of **Lemonodasos**. You can quench your thirst with a glass of fresh lemonade.

About nine km to the north-west of Galatas is the ancient site of **Troizen**, legendary birthplace of Theseus. Take a bus to Dhamala, six km from Galatas, and walk to the site from there. Alternatively, a Methana-bound bus will let you off at Agios Georgios, from where it is a three-km walk inland to the site.

Camping Kyragelo is about one km north-west of Galatas (see Places to Stay). There are also a couple of hotels and domatia in town.

Getting There & Around

Small boats do the five-minute run between Galatas and Poros (70 dr) every 10 minutes. A couple of buses a day depart for Nafplio (two hours, 1300 dr) and can drop you off at the ancient site of Epidaurus (see the Peloponnese chapter for details on this site).

The district around Galatas is ideal for exploring by bicycle. These can be hired on the seafront in Galatas.

Hydra Υδρα

Hydra (EE-dhra, population 3000) is the Saronic Gulf island with the most style. The gracious stone, white and pastel mansions of Hydra town are stacked up the rocky hillsides that surround the fine natural harbour. The first foreigners to be seduced by the beauty of Hydra were the film makers who began arriving in the 1950s; the island was used as a location for the film *Boy on a Dolphin*, among others. The artists and writers moved in next, followed by the celebs, and nowadays it seems the whole world is welcomed ashore.

If you've been in Greece for some time you may fall in love with Hydra for one reason alone: the absence of kamikaze motorcyclists. Hydra has no motorised transport except for sanitation and construction vehicles. Donkeys (hundreds of them) are the only means of transport.

The name Hydra suggests that the island once had plenty of water. Legend has it that the island was once covered with forests, which were destroyed by fire. Whatever the story, these days the island is almost totally barren and imports its water from the Peloponnese.

History

Like many of the Greek islands, Hydra was ignored by the Turks, so many Greeks from the Peloponnese settled on the island to escape Ottoman suppression and taxes. The population was further boosted by an influx of Albanians. Agriculture was impossible, so these new settlers began building boats. By the 19th century, the island had become a great maritime power. The canny Hydriots made a fortune by running the British blockade of French ports during the Napoleonic Wars. The wealthy shipping merchants built most of the town's grand old arhontika from the considerable profits. It became a fashionable resort for Greek socialites, and lavish balls were a regular feature.

Hydra made a major contribution to the War of Independence. Without the 130 ships supplied by the island, the Greeks wouldn't have had much of a fleet with which to blockade the Turks. It also supplied leadership in the form of Georgios Koundouriotis, who was president of the emerging Greek nation's national assembly from 1822 to 1827, and Admiral Andreas Miaoulis, who commanded the Greek fleet. Streets and squares all over Greece are named after these two. A mock battle is staged during the Miaoulia Festival held in honour of Admiral Miaoulis in late June.

Getting There & Away

Ferry Ventouris Lines has ferries to Piraeus (3½ hours, 1700 dr) from Monday to Thursday at 3.55 and 6 pm; Friday at 2.55 and 6 pm; Saturday at 2.55, 4.30 and 6 pm; and Sunday at 2, 3.55 and 6 pm. They go via Poros (800 dr), Methana and Aegina (1200 dr). There are daily boats to Spetses (one hour, 800 dr) at 11.30 am, and additional boats on Friday at 7.30 pm, and on Saturday and Sunday at 11.50 am.

The ticket office is close to the ferry dock, about 50 metres up Tombazi. Departures are shown on a board outside.

Hydrofoil There are between eight and 15 Flying Dolphin hydrofoils a day to Zea Marina (3800 dr). Direct services take 1¼ hours, services via Poros (30 minutes, 1000 dr), Methana (45 minutes, 1800 dr) and Aegina (1¼ hours, 2200 dr) take a shade

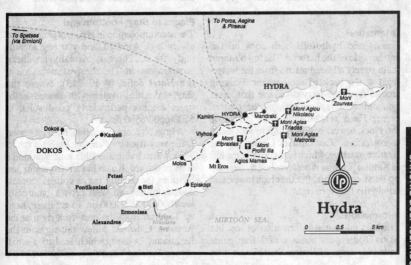

over two hours. There are up to nine hydro-foils a day to Poros, but only a couple via Methana and Aegina – at the beginning of the season just one a week. There are also between six and 11 hydrofoils a day to Spetses (30 minutes, 1400 dr), half of which call at Ermioni (25 minutes, 1300 dr) – adding 20 minutes to the trip. Many of the services to Spetses continue to Porto Heli (50 minutes, 1500 dr). The Flying Dolphin agent is on the first street to the right off Tombazi, about 150 metres from the port.

Getting Around
In summer, there are caïques from Hydra town to the island's beaches. Trips to most destinations cost about 250 dr. There are also water taxis which will take you anywhere you like. A water taxi to Kamini costs 1200 dr, and 1500 dr to Mandraki and Vlyhos.

The donkey owners clustered around the port charge 2000 dr to transport your bags to the hotel of your choice.

HYDRA TOWN
Most of the action in Hydra town is concentrated around the waterfront cafés and shops, leaving the upper reaches of the narrow, stepped streets deserted – and a joy to explore.

Orientation
Ferries and hydrofoils both dock on the eastern side of the harbour. The town's three main streets all head inland from the waterfront at the back of the harbour. Walking around from the ferry dock, the first street you come to is Tombazi, at the eastern corner. The next is Miaouli, on the left before the clock tower, which is the town's main thoroughfare. The third is Lignou, at the western extreme, which leads up over the hill to Kamini. Lignou is best reached by heading up Votsi, on the left after the clock tower, and taking the first turn right.

Information
There is no tourist-information office, but Saitis Tours puts out a useful free guide called *Holidays in Hydra*. Saitis Tours is on

the waterfront near Tombazi. The post office, clearly signposted nearby, is just back from the waterfront on a small side street; and the OTE is about 100 metres up Votsi. Hydra's postcode is 180 40 and the telephone code is 0298. The National Bank of Greece is on the waterfront before Miaouli. The tourist police (☎ 52 205) are opposite the OTE on Votsi.

Things to See
The peaceful streets of Hydra are a great place for a stroll. Several of the town's arhontika are worth seeking out, even if you can only look at them from the outside. They include the **Georgios Koundouriotis mansion** to the west of the harbour. Koundouriotis was a wealthy shipowner as well as a War of Independence leader, and the mansion houses a large portrait collection. The mansion is owned by the Ministry of Defence, which appears to be renovating it. Apparently it will be open to the public in 1996, but they've been saying that for years – ditto the almost-completed **naval museum** on the eastern side of the harbour.

Moni Panagias, behind the waterfront clock tower, is now used as offices but it has a peaceful courtyard and quite lavish ecclesiastical decorations inside its church.

Places to Stay – bottom end
The accommodation in Hydra is generally of a very high standard, and you pay accordingly for it. There is virtually no cheap accommodation. The cheapest rooms are at the *Hotel Sofia* (☎ 52 313), where the singles/doubles/triples with shared bathroom are not particularly good value at 5500/6600/8800 dr.

A little bit more expensive, but a lot better, is the very friendly *Pension Theresia* (☎ 53 983), which has quaint little rooms around a leafy courtyard. It also has a refrigerator and facilities for making tea or coffee. Singles/doubles/triples, all with private bathroom, are 7000/9000/11,000 dr. To get there, head up Tombazi from the port, fork right at the Amalour Café and follow the signs to the Restaurant Doukas, which lead to a small square. Pension Theresia is on the left of the

SARONIC GULF ISLANDS

square – the entry is around the corner on a side street.

Some of the rooms at *Savvas*, 150 metres from the port on Lignou, are a bit on the dingy side, but are fair value at 7000/9000 dr for singles/doubles with shared bathroom.

Places to Stay – middle

The *Hotel Hydra* (☎ 52 102) has a great setting overlooking the town from the west. It has large, comfortable singles/doubles for 9400/14,000 dr with en suite bathroom, and for 7100/9700 dr with private bathroom. It's a fair haul to get there – up more than 100 steps from Lignou, but the views over the town and harbour are worth it.

Finding the *Hotel Leto* (☎ 53 385) involves no more than a gentle stroll up Miaouli. It's a stylish place with beautiful polished timber floors. Singles are 11,000 dr, and doubles start from 13,500 dr. Prices include a buffet breakfast. The Leto is about 250 metres from the port. Follow Miaouli to the far side of the small park and then turn left up some steps into a narrow alleyway. You'll see the hotel on the right after 50 metres.

A little bit further up Miaouli is the *Hotel Miranda* (☎ 52 230), originally the mansion of a wealthy Hydriot sea captain. It has been beautifully renovated and converted into a very smart hotel. Singles/doubles are 14,000/16,500 dr with breakfast, and a two-room suite is 27,000 dr.

Places to Stay – top end

The two hotels at the top of the comfort scale both offer something special. The *Hotel Orloff* (☎ 52 564; fax 53 532) is a beautiful old mansion with a cool, vine-covered court-yard at the back. The furnishing is elegant without being overstated, and each of the 10 rooms has a character of its own. Singles/doubles are 16,000/24,000 dr, which includes a buffet breakfast – served in the courtyard in summer.

The *Hotel Bratsera* (☎ 53 971; fax 53 626) is a converted sponge factory. The architects have left the rich stonework and solid timbers to speak for themselves, and

have added some nice touches like doors made up from old packing cases. Doubles are priced from 26,000 to 31,000 dr, and four-bed suites are 42,000 dr.

The Bratsera has the town's only swimming pool. It's for guests only, but you'll qualify if you eat at their restaurant (see below).

Places to Eat – inexpensive

Hydra has one of the best budget tavernas around. The owners of *The Terrace*, as the signless restaurant opposite Pension Antonios is known, are people who really care about their food. Check out their beetroot salad – a bowl of baby beets and boiled greens with a dollop of cold, very garlicky, mashed potato on top. The flavours complement each other perfectly. You can eat well here for 1500 dr per person, including a jug of retsina, but get there early or you'll have a long wait.

The *Garden Restaurant*, on Sahtouri, is a

Sailing out of Hydra town

good psistaria with a large range of grilled food at reasonable prices. As suggested by the name, the setting is a pleasant walled garden. To get there, turn left at the Amalour Café and you'll see it on the right after about 300 metres.

Lulu's, 50 metres from the port on Miaouli, is a popular taverna but the food is no better than average.

Places to Eat – moderate

The *Veranda Restaurant*, halfway up the steps to the Hotel Hydra, occupies a terrace with great views over the town and harbour. The food is Mediterranean with a sprinkling of Italian dishes. A meal for two with wine will cost about 7000 dr.

The *Moita Restaurant*, close to the OTE on Miaouli, has an interesting menu that features such items as green salad with bacon, and warm goat's cheese drizzled with honey-thyme vinaigrette (1600 dr). You can reckon on spending about 9000 dr for two, with wine.

The *Bratsera Restaurant* has a small menu that includes Asian-influenced dishes such as chicken and rice with spicy plum sauce (2500 dr) and pork with ginger (2800 dr).

Entertainment

Kavos, with its sign made up of nautical oddments, is a popular disco just west of town on the coastal path to Kamini; but there is no point in heading out there before 11 pm. The *Amalour*, 100 metres up Tombazi, is a more sophisticated café-bar that sells a wide range of fresh juices as well as alcohol. For rock music, head to the *Pirate* at the western end of the waterfront.

AROUND THE ISLAND

It's a strenuous but worthwhile one-hour walk up to **Moni Profiti Ilia**, starting from Miaouli. Monks still inhabit the monastery, which has fantastic views down to the town. It's a short walk from here to the convent of **Moni Efpraxias**.

The beaches on Hydra are a dead loss, but the walks to them are enjoyable. **Kamini**, about 30 minutes' walk along the coastal path from town, has rocks and a very small pebble beach. **Vlyhos**, 20 minutes further on, is an attractive village with a slightly larger pebble beach, two tavernas and a ruined 19th-century stone bridge. There are domatia at Vlyhos as well as *Antigoni's Apartments* (☎ 53 228), which has self-catering apartments to sleep four for 12,000 dr, and to sleep six for 20,000 dr.

From here, walkaholics can continue to the small bay at **Molos**, or take a left fork before the bay to the inland village of **Episkopi**. There are no facilities at Episkopi. A seasonal café may be open at Molos but don't bank on it – take sustenance with you.

An even more ambitious walk is the three-hour stint to **Moni Zourvas**, in the north-east of the island. Along the way you will pass **Moni Agias Triados** and **Moni Agiou Nikolaou**.

A path leads east from Hydra town to the pebble beach at **Mandraki**. The beach is the exclusive reserve of the *Hotel Miramare* (☎ 52 300; fax 52 301), which has doubles with breakfast for 17,000 dr. There's a range of watersport equipment for hire, including sailboards (2500 dr per hour) and canoes (1000 dr).

Spetses Σπέτσες

Pine-covered Spetses (SPET-ses, population 3700), the most distant of the group from Piraeus, withstood the tourist onslaught longer than its neighbours. However, those days are long gone and Spetses is now a favourite of British package-tour operators.

Spetses' history is similar to Hydra's. It became wealthy through shipbuilding, ran the British blockade during the Napoleonic Wars and refitted its ships to join the Greek fleet during the War of Independence. Spetsiot fighters achieved a certain notoriety through their pet tactic of attaching small boats laden with explosives to the enemy's ships, setting them on fire and beating a hasty retreat.

The island was known in antiquity as

Pityoussa (pine-covered), but the original forest cover disappeared long ago. The pine-covered hills that greet the visitor today are a legacy of the far-sighted and wealthy philanthropist Sotirios Anargyrios.

Anargyrios was born on Spetses in 1848 and emigrated to the United States, returning in 1914 an exceedingly rich man. He bought two-thirds of the then largely barren island and planted the Aleppo pines that stand today. He also financed the island's road system, and commissioned many of the town's grand buildings, including the Hotel Possidonion. He was a big fan of the British public (private) school system, and established Anargyrios & Korgialenios College, a boarding school for boys from all over Greece. British author John Fowles taught English at the college from 1950-51, and used the island as a setting for his novel *The Magus*.

Getting There & Away

Ferry There is at least one ferry a day to Piraeus (4½ hours, 2200 dr), via Hydra (800 dr), Poros (1400 dr), Methana (1400 dr) and Aegina (1800 dr). Two companies operate the service on alternate days. Ventouris Lines tickets are sold by Meledon Travel on the seafront, and Eftikia Lines tickets from Alasia Travel next door.

Between July and September, there are ferries from Spetses to Kosta, 25 minutes away on the mainland. The ferries depart at 7.15 and 10 am, and at 1 and 4.30 pm; they return half an hour later. Get your ticket (150 dr) on the boat. Water taxis do the trip in 10 minutes for 2500 dr. The port police (☎ 72 245) are opposite the quay.

Hydrofoil There are between five and 10 Flying Dolphins a day to Zea Marina (4200 dr). Direct services take 1¾ hours, but most go via Hydra (30 minutes, 1400 dr) and/or Poros (70 minutes) and take about 2½ hours. In high season, there are five hydrofoils a week to Aegina (two hours, 2900 dr), dropping to one a week the rest of the time. You can get out to Kythira (2½ hours, 8200 dr)

five times a week in high season via Monemvassia (80 minutes, 3500 dr).

Getting Around

Spetses has two bus routes. There are three or four buses a day from Plateia Agias Mamas to Agioi Anargyri (550 dr return), via Agia Marina and Xylokeriza. Departure times are displayed on a board by the bus stop. There are hourly buses to Ligoneri (100 dr) from in front of the Hotel Possidonion.

No cars are permitted on the island. Unfortunately this ban has not been extended to motorbikes, resulting in there being more of the critters here than just about anywhere else.

The colourful horse-drawn carriages are a pleasant but expensive way of getting about. Prices are displayed on a board where the carriages gather by the port.

Boat Water taxis (☎ 74 885) go anywhere you care to nominate from Dapia harbour. A trip to Agia Marina costs 3500 dr and to Agioi Anargyri it's 7000 dr. In summer, there are caïques from the harbour to Anargyri (1000 dr return) and Zogheria (700 dr return).

SPETSES TOWN

Spetses town sprawls along almost half the north-east coast of the island, reflecting the way in which the focal point of settlement has changed over the years.

There's evidence of an early Helladic settlement near the Old harbour, about 1.5 km east of the modern commercial centre and port of Dapia, and Roman and Byzantine remains have been unearthed in the area behind Moni Agiou Nikolaou, halfway between the two.

The island is thought to have been uninhabited for almost 600 years before the arrival of Albanian refugees fleeing fighting between the Turks and the Venetians in the 16th century. They settled on the hillside just inland from Dapia, the area now known as Kastelli.

The Dapia district has a few impressive

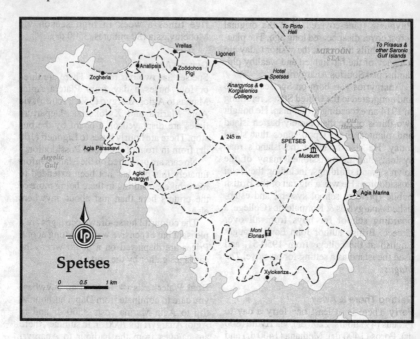

arhontika dotted about, but the prettiest part of town is around the old harbour .

Orientation & Information

The quay at Dapia harbour serves both ferries and hydrofoils. A left turn at the end of the quay leads east along the waterfront on Sotirios Anargyris, passing through the square where the horse-drawn carriages wait. The road is flanked by a string of uninspiring, concrete C-class hotels, and emerges after 200 metres on Plateia Agias Mamas, next to the town beach. The bus stop for Anargyri is next to the beach. The post office is on the street running behind the hotels; coming from the quay, turn right at the Hotel Soleil and then left.

The waterfront to the right of the quay is also called Sotirios Anargyris. It skirts the small Dapia harbour, passes the grand Hotel Possidonion and continues west around the bay to the Hotel Spetses. The OTE is behind the Dapia Harbour, next to the National Bank of Greece.

There is no tourist office on Spetses. The tourist police (☎ 73 100) are based in the police station – on the left as you walk up N Spetson from the quay – from June to September. N Spetson leads inland from the south-western corner of the square which has the horse-drawn carriages. The road at the south-eastern corner leads to the main square, known as Plateia Orologiou. Spetses' postcode is 180 50 and the telephone code is 0298.

Things to See

The **old harbour** is a delightful place to explore. The harbour is ringed by old Venetian buildings, and filled with boats of every shape and size – from colourful little fishing boats to sleek luxury cruising yachts. The ship builders of Spetses still do things the traditional way and the shore is dotted with the hulls of emerging caïques. The walk from

SARONIC GULF ISLANDS

Dapia harbour takes about 20 minutes. **Moni Agiou Nikolaou** straddles a headland at the halfway mark.

The **museum** is housed in the arhontiko of Hadzigiannis Mexis, a ship owner who became the island's first governor. It has a collection of ships' figureheads mounted on the walls, but most of the collection is devoted to folkloric items and portraits of the island's founding fathers. It's open Tuesday to Sunday from 8.30 am to 3 pm. Admission is 500 dr. The museum is clearly signposted from Plateia Orologiou.

The **Hotel Possidonion**, on the seafront just west of the Dapia, is worth a look even if you can't afford to stay there (see Places to Stay). The **Sotirios Anargyris mansion** is on the eastern side of the square behind the OTE, opposite the **Bouboulina mansion**.

Organised Tours

Meledon Travel (☎ 74 497) organises trips around the island by caïque for 2300 dr, including wine and commentary. Meledon Travel is on the waterfront east of the quay.

Places to Stay – bottom end

There is very little budget accommodation, as is the case throughout the Saronic islands. The nearest camp site is at Kosta on the mainland. Hotels and domatia are spread out all over the town and can be hard to find. You may be met at the quay if things are quiet, otherwise you can try one of the travel agents, most of which have rooms on their books.

Meledon Travel acts as an agent for one of the best deals in town, *Orloff Apartments* (☎ 72 246), which is about 1.5 km from the quay on the road to Agia Marina. To walk there from the quay, turn left along the waterfront to Plateia Agias Mamas, fork right and stay on the main road. The sign on the door is very discreet, invisible almost, but it's opposite the Hotel Mimosa. The Orloff has a good choice of rooms spread around the shady grounds. Most of the rooms come with private bathroom and kitchen, and singles/doubles/triples are 6000/8000/9000 dr. There are a few doubles without kitchen for 6000 dr.

Places to Stay – middle

The road to the Orloff leads past the *Hotel Kamelia* (☎ 72 415), signposted to the right at the supermarket 100 metres past Plateia Agias Mamas. It's a charming place surrounded by citrus trees and boasts a brilliant burgundy bougainvillea (depending on the season). Spotless singles/doubles with private bathroom are 8000/9000 dr.

Another good place is the pretty, whitewashed *Villa Kristina* (☎ 72 218), on Ikoniou, which is a left turn off Spetson about 300 metres beyond the police station. It has singles/doubles with private bathroom for 7200/9000 dr, as well as four-person studios for 14,000 dr.

Lascarina Bouboulina

Spetses contributed one of the most colourful figures of the War of Independence, the dashing heroine Lascarina Bouboulina. Her exploits on and off the battlefield were the stuff of legend. She had been widowed twice by the time the war began. Both her shipowning husbands had been killed by pirates, leaving her a wealthy woman. She used her money to commission her own fighting ship, the *Agamemnon*, which she led into battle during the blockade of Nafplio. She was featured on the old 50-dr note – a dramatic portrayal showing her directing cannon fire. She was also known for her fiery temperament and her countless love affairs. Her death was in keeping with her flamboyant lifestyle – she was shot during a family dispute in her Spetses home.

The Bouboulina mansion is on the western side of the square behind the OTE building. It houses a small museum, which is open from Tuesday to Sunday from 9 am to 5 pm; admission is 700 dr. ∎

The *Hotel Khemis* (☎ 73 725), on the corner of Plateia Agias Mamas, has a bit more character than some of its waterfront neighbours. Its singles/doubles are also better value at 8000/10,400 dr.

Places to Stay – top end

The A-class *Hotel Possidonion* (☎ 72 308/006; fax 72 208) lives on in crumbling Edwardian grandeur. Fortunately, the interior is in better shape than the exterior. Doubles are 22,000 dr and worth checking out if you feel ready for a splurge. Its companion in the top bracket, the *Hotel Spetses* (☎ 72 602/604; fax 72 494), has good views but otherwise is nothing out of the ordinary. Doubles are 23,800 dr with a sea view, 19,500 dr without.

Places to Eat

The *Restaurant Stelios*, between Plateia Mamas and the post office, is a popular taverna that pitches for the tourist trade with a series of set menus. Prices start at under 2000 dr for three courses and a jug of wine. The *Taverna O Roussos*, on Plateia Mamas, also has solid taverna fare at prices that won't break the bank.

Fish fans will enjoy the excellent *Restaurant Patralis*, a 10-minute walk from Dapia on the way to the Hotel Spetses. It has a great setting, a good menu and fish supplied by the restaurant's own boat. The fish à la Spetses (1500 dr), a large tuna or swordfish steak baked with vegetables and lots of garlic, goes down perfectly with a cold beer.

If character is what you are after, you won't find a better place than *Byzantino*, halfway to the old harbour. The early 19th-century port-authority building has been converted into a stylish restaurant specialising in mezedes. Reckon on about 7000 dr for two, with drinks.

AROUND THE ISLAND

Spetses' coastline is speckled with numerous coves with small pine-shaded beaches. A 24-km road (part sealed, part dirt) skirts the entire coastline, so motorbike is the ideal way to explore the island.

The beach at **Ligoneri**, west of town, has the attraction of being easily accessible by bus. **Agia Marina**, to the south of the old harbour, is a small resort with a crowded beach. **Agia Paraskevi** and **Anargyris**, on the south-west coast, have good, albeit crowded, beaches; both have water sports of every description. A large mansion between the two beaches was the inspiration for the Villa Bourani in *The Magus*.

The small island of **Spetsopoula** to the south of Spetses is owned by Stavros Niarchos.

Cyclades Κυκλάδες

The Cyclades are the archetypal Greek islands – rugged outcrops of rock dotted with brilliant white buildings offset by vividly painted balconies and bright blue church domes, all bathed in dazzling light and fringed with golden beaches lapped by aquamarine seas.

Goats and sheep are raised on the mountainous, barren islands, as well as some pigs and cattle. Naxos alone is sufficiently fertile to produce crops for export. Many islanders still fish, but tourism is becoming the dominant source of income.

Some of the Cyclades, like Mykonos, Santorini (Thira) and Ios, have been eager to embrace tourism, and their shores are spread with sun lounges, umbrellas and watersports equipment. Others, such as Andros, Syros, Kea, Kythnos, Serifos and Sifnos, are less visited by foreigners, but are popular weekend and summer retreats for Athenians, thanks to their proximity to the mainland.

Tinos is not a holiday island but the country's premier place of pilgrimage – a Greek Lourdes. Other islands, such as Anafi and the tiny islands east of Naxos, are little more than clumps of rock with tiny depopulated villages and few tourists.

The islands of the Cyclades are small and closely grouped, making them ideal for an island-hopping holiday.

It's best to avoid these islands in July and August, when accommodation can be hard to find. Most places are open only from April to October. Accommodation prices quoted in this section are for the July/August high season. Expect to pay less at other times. Consult the Ministry of Agriculture's brochure *Agrotourism: Holidays in the Countryside*, available from major EOT offices, for details of holidays in rural communities on Kea and Syros.

The Cyclades are more prone to the northwesterly *meltemi* wind than other island groups, but this provides a welcome respite from the heat.

History

The Cyclades have been populated since at least 5000 BC. Around 3000 BC, Phoenician colonists settled on the islands and their advanced culture heralded the Cycladic civilisation. During the Early Cycladic period (3000-2000 BC), people on Milos lived in houses, built boats and mined obsidian which was exported throughout the Mediterranean. It was during this time that the famous Cycladic marble statues were sculpted.

In the Middle Cycladic period (2000-1500 BC), the islands were occupied by the Minoans. Around the 15th century BC, at the beginning of the Late Cycladic period (1500-1100 BC), the Cyclades passed to the Mycenaeans. The Dorians followed but, by the 8th century BC, Archaic culture was burgeoning.

After the Greek victory over Persia, the Cyclades became part of the Delian League and were incorporated into the Athenian empire, thus suffering the onerous annual tax imposed by Athens.

In 190 BC, the islands were conquered by

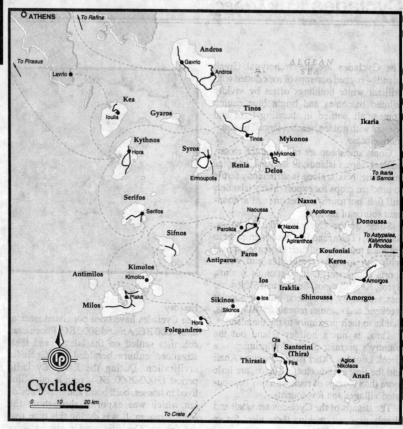

Cyclades

0   10   20 km

---

the Romans and trade links were established with many parts of the Mediterranean, bringing prosperity.

In 1204, the Franks gave the Cyclades to Venice, which parcelled the islands out to opportunistic aristocrats. Most powerful was Marco Sanudo (self-styled Duke of Naxos), who acquired Naxos, Paros, Amorgos and Folegandros.

The islands came under Turkish rule in 1453. Neglected by the Ottomans, they became backwaters, prone to pirate raids – hence the labyrinthine character of their towns. The mazes of narrow lanes were designed to disorientate attackers. On some islands, people moved inland to escape pirates.

The Cyclades' participation in the War of Independence was minimal but they became havens for people fleeing from islands where insurrections against the Turks had led to massacres.

The fortunes of the islands have been revived by the tourism boom that began in the 1970s. Until then, many islanders lived in abject poverty and many more gave up the battle and headed for the mainland in search of work.

Getting There & Away

For specific details, see sections under individual islands.

Air Milos, Mykonos, Naxos, Paros, Syros and Santorini have daily connections with Athens. Mykonos and Santorini have three flights a week to Iraklio and four to Rhodes.

Ferry There are frequent services to and from Piraeus and between subgroups of islands within the group. The most frequently visited islands – Mykonos, Naxos, Paros, Ios and Santorini – all have daily connections with Piraeus and each other. Mykonos also has daily links with Rafina.

There are also regular links between the islands and Crete. In summer, there are boats between Santorini and Iraklio (Crete) every day except Friday, and a weekly service between Santorini and Agios Nikolaos. Ios and Naxos have twice-weekly links with Iraklio.

Paros, the ferry hub of the Aegean, has daily connections with Piraeus in summer and an almost daily service to the North-Eastern Aegean island of Samos, via Ikaria. Mykonos and Naxos have once-weekly connections with Samos. Andros, the most northerly of the group, is served only from Rafina. Tinos, to the south-east of Andros, has good connections with Piraeus and Rafina. Syros has at least two ferries a day to Piraeus.

Kea, Kythnos, Serifos, Sifnos and Milos are known as the Western Cyclades. Kythnos, Serifos, Sifnos and Milos are served daily from Piraeus and Kea by daily ferries from Lavrio. Getting from the Western Cyclades to other islands is not so easy. The most frequent connection is on a small daily Paros-Sifnos ferry.

The less visited islands of Amorgos, Sikinos and Folegandros have four or five ferries a week to Piraeus; Anafi has only two or three. Sikinos and Folegandros have a once-weekly connection with Crete's Agios Nikolaos.

Paloma Tours (☎ 01-822 8198 or 823 3744), Marnis 4, Athens, opposite the National Archaeological Museum, sells a 20-day island pass which offers unlimited travel from Piraeus to the islands of Paros, Naxos, Ios and Santorini for 8500 dr – less than the price of a return trip to Santorini. The passes are available from mid-June to October. They are also available in Athens from the Hostel Aphrodite and the Student & Travellers' Inn (see Places to Stay in the Athens chapter).

Hydrofoil There are daily hydrofoil services between Rafina and Andros, Tinos and Mykonos; and one or two services a week to other islands. The services are prone to cancellation in rough weather. Kea and Kythnos have hydrofoil links with Piraeus (Zea Marina). Hydrofoil fares are about twice as much as ferry fares.

Getting Around

Air The only inter-island flights are between Mykonos and Santorini.

Bus The standard of bus services varies according to the size of the island and its popularity as a tourist destination. The most popular islands have good bus services; the less visited islands have less frequent services; and the tiny islands of Anafi, Donoussa, Koufonisi, Shinoussa and Iraklia have no public transport at all.

Car, Motorbike & Bicycle There are cars for hire on Andros, Tinos, Milos, Syros, Mykonos, Naxos, Paros, Ios, Santorini and Sifnos. Motorbike and moped hire is possible on most other islands, and bicycle hire is available on a few. For details, see the sections on individual islands.

Andros Ανδρος

Andros (AND-ros) is the most northerly of the Cyclades and the second largest after Naxos. It is also one of the most fertile, islands producing citrus fruit and olives. The island is unusual in that it has retained its pine forests and mulberry woods. More distinctive features are its dovecotes (although Tinos has more) and elaborate stone walls.

Getting There & Away

Ferry There are two ferries a day from the port of Gavrio to Rafina (two hours, 2000 dr), Tinos (1700 dr), Mykonos, and four or five a week travelling via Tinos to Syros (2½ hours). In summer, there are daily connections with Santorini. The telephone number of the port police in Gavrio is 71 213.

Hydrofoil There are daily hydrofoils from

Rafina to Andros (70 minutes, 4000 dr), continuing to Tinos and Mykonos. Most services stop at the main port of Gavrio, but there are occasional services to the ports of Andros town and Batsi. There is a weekly service from Batsi to Syros, Paros and Naxos and beyond; and a weekly service from Gavrio to Paros, Sifnos and Serifos.

Getting Around

Theoretically, six buses a day link Gavrio and Andros town, via Batsi but they tend to run only when ferries arrive.

Andros

0   2.5   5 km

GAVRIO Γαύριο

Gavrio, on the west coast, is the main port of Andros. The capital, Andros town, is on the east coast. Nothing much happens in Gavrio, but in high season it may be easier to find accommodation here than at the resort of Batsi or in Andros town, and there are lovely beaches nearby.

Orientation & Information

The ferry quay is in the middle of the waterfront and the bus stop is next to it. Turn right from the quay and walk along the waterfront for the OTE, turn left for the post office. Andros' telephone code is 0282. The postcode is 845 00. Andros doesn't have a tourist office or tourist police.

Places to Stay – bottom end

The island's only camp site, *Camping Andros* (☎ 71 444), is 300 metres from the harbour along the Batsi road. It has a restaurant, minimarket, bar and pool. If you decide to stay in town, look for domatia signs along the waterfront or try the *Hotel Galaxy* (☎ 71 005/228) to the left of the quay. It has clean doubles/triples with bath for 6000/9200 dr.

Places to Stay – middle

The B-class *Andros Holiday Hotel* (☎ 71 384), overlooking the beach, is regarded as Gavrio's best. It has a restaurant, bar, tennis court, sauna, jacuzzi and gym. Room rates here are 13,000/16,500/20,000 dr for a single/double/triple.

Places to Eat

The reasonably priced *Restaurant O Valmas* is one of Gavrio's best. Turn right from the quay, then left one block before the Batsi road.

BATSI Μπατσί

Batsi, eight km south of Gavrio, is Andros' major resort. The attractive town encircles a bay with a fishing harbour at one end and a nice sandy beach at the other.

Places to Stay & Eat

Scan the waterfront for domatia signs. The *Karanassos Hotel* (☎ 41 480), 50 metres from the beach, has singles/doubles with bath for 7600/9700 dr. The *Scouna Hotel* (☎ 41 165/240), overlooking the beach, has pleasant rooms for 8000/11,000 dr. *Likio Studios* (☎ 41 050/811) is set back from the beach amid masses of geraniums. Its spotless studios cost 14,000 dr for a double, or 22,000 dr for a two-bedroom apartment which sleeps four. All studios have cooking facilities. The owner meets ferries year-round if phoned.

Cavo d'Oro (☎ 41 776) at the beach end of the waterfront is a pizzeria with domatia (8000 dr for doubles with bath). It specialises in Andros' famed fourtalia, an omelette made with potatoes and home-made sausages. On the waterfront, *Esthesis Restaurant* has good food at reasonable prices as well as live music, including rembetika. Dishes include country sausage with capsicum, beefburger stuffed with cheese, and divine shrimp saganaki.

Sweet-toothed travellers should seek out the island's speciality, karydhaki – Andros walnuts cooked with honey, sugar, cinnamon and cloves.

ANDROS TOWN

Andros town is on the east coast, 35 km east of Gavrio. The town's setting along a narrow peninsula, is more striking than the town itself, although there are some fine old neo-classical mansions and a tiny central square shaded by trees.

Orientation & Information

The bus station is on Plateia Goulandri. To the left, as you face the sea, is the main pedestrian thoroughfare where you'll find the post office, OTE and National Bank of Greece. Walk along here towards the sea for Plateia Kaïri, the central square, beyond which is the headland. Steps descend to beaches from both sides of the square. The street traversing the promontory ends at Plateia Riva where there is a bronze statue of an unknown sailor. The ruins of a Venetian fortress stand at the tip of the headland.

Museums

Andros town has two outstanding museums, both endowed by Vasilis Goulandris, a wealthy ship owner and Andriot. The **archaeological museum** is north of Plateia Kaïri. Its contents include the 1st-century BC Hermes of Andros made of Parian marble and finds from Andros' two ancient cities of Zagora and Paleopolis. The museum is open Tuesday to Sunday from 8.30 am to 3 pm. Admission is 500 dr.

The **museum of modern art** has a collection of 20th-century Greek and European paintings. It's open Wednesday to Monday from 10 am to 2 pm and 6 to 9 pm.

Places to Stay & Eat

The best value is at the *Hotel Egli* (☎ 22 303), off the right side of the main road as you head towards the sea, between the two squares. Doubles with bathroom are 6500 dr with breakfast, and rooms for four are 12,000 dr with breakfast.

Restaurant Stathmos, on Plateia Goulandri by the bus station, has tasty low-priced fare. The *Parea Taverna* on the central square has a commanding beach view and daily specials for 600 to 1000 dr.

AROUND THE ISLAND

About 2.5 km from Gavrio, the **Agios Petros tower** is an imposing circular watchtower, dating at least from Hellenistic times – possibly earlier. It's a 30-minute walk to the tower from Camping Andros. Look for the signpost for Agios Petros, also the name of a village.

Along the coast road from Gavrio to Batsi is a turn-off left leading five km to the 12th-century **Moni Zoödohou Pigis**. A few nuns still live here. Between Gavrio and Paleopolis bay are several nice beaches – **Agios Kyprianos**, (where a former church is now a beachfront taverna), **Delavoia** (nudist), **Green beach** and **Aneroussa**. The *Aneroussa Beach Hotel* (☎ 41 044/045), open from May to October, offers singles/ doubles/ triples for 13,000/16,500/20,000 dr.

Paleopolis, nine km south of Batsi on the coast road, is the site of ancient Andros,

where the Hermes of Andros was found. There is little to see, but the mountain setting is lovely. Beyond Paleopolis, the main road strikes inland for Andros town. From the village of Mesaria, it's a strenuous two-hour walk to the 12th-century **Moni Panahrandou**, the island's largest and most important monastery.

The pretty blue-green bay at **Korthion**, in the south-east, remains almost untouched by tourism. Its *Hotel Korthion* (☎ 61 218/118), on the shore, has inexpensive singles/ doubles with bath and breakfast for 3000/ 6000 dr. The hotel can arrange windsurfing and jet-skiing.

Tinos Τήνος

Tinos (TEE-nos, population 9500) is green and mountainous, like nearby Andros. The island is a place of pilgrimage for the Greek Orthodox, so it's hardly surprising that churches feature prominently among the attractions. The celebrated Church of Panagia Evangelistria dominates its capital, while more modest churches, unspoilt hill villages and ornate whitewashed dovecotes are rural attractions. Tinos also has a large Roman Catholic population – the result of its long occupation by the Venetians. The Turks didn't succeed in wresting the island from the Venetians until 1715, long after the rest of the country had surrendered to Ottoman Turkey.

Getting There & Away

Ferry Several ferries go to Piraeus daily (five hours, 3600 dr) via Syros (900 dr) and two go daily to Rafina (3½ hours, 2800 dr) via Andros (1700 dr). Coming from Rafina, the ferry continues from Tinos to Mykonos. Tinos' port police (☎ 22 348) are on the waterfront near the quay.

Hydrofoil There are daily services to Rafina (two hours, 6175 dr) via Andros, as well as daily services to Mykonos, Paros, Naxos and Santorini – calling once a week at Amorgos,

DAVID HALL

DAVID HALL

ANN JOUSIFFE

Top: The statue of Cleopatra, Delos, Cyclades
Bottom Left: What's on the menu? Naxos town, Cyclades
Bottom Right: Santorini (Thira), Cyclades

VICKI BEALE

DAVID HALL

ANNA ΛΜ 385

DAVID HALL

Top: Paros, Cyclades
Middle: Fira, Santorini (Thira), Cyclades
Bottom: Mykonos town, Mykonos, Cyclades

Koufonisi, Iraklia and Shinoussa. There are two services a week to Syros and one a week to Serifos and Sifnos.

Getting Around
There are frequent buses from Tinos town to Kionia and several a day to Panormos and Kambos. Motorbikes and cars can be hired along Tinos town's waterfront.

TINOS TOWN
Tinos town, the island's capital and port, is picturesque with a lively waterfront and little streets with shops and stalls catering for pilgrims and tourists. The huge Church of Panagia Evangelistria presides over the action from its elevated position in the centre of town.

Orientation & Information
The ferry quay is in the middle of the waterfront. Leoforos Megaloharis, straight ahead, is the route pilgrims take to the church. The

narrow Evangelistrias, to the right facing inland, also leads to the church. The post office is at the south-eastern end of the waterfront; to reach it turn right from the quay. The OTE is on the right side of Leoforos Megaloharis.

The National Bank of Greece is on the waterfront beyond Evangelistrias. The bus station is to the right of the quay. The town beach of Agios Fokas is a 20-minute walk south from the waterfront.

Tinos has no tourist office or tourist police. The regular police (☎ 22 255) are right from the ferry quay and left at the Hotel Possidonion. Look for the sign.

Tinos' postcode is 842 00. The telephone code is 0283.

Church of Panagia Evangelistria
This church is a neoclassical marble confection of white and cream, with a high bell tower. The ornate façade has graceful white upper and lower colonnades. The final

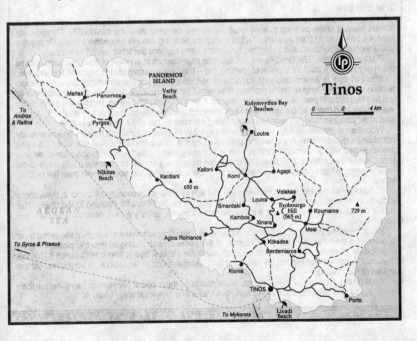

approach is up carpeted steps, doubtless a relief to pious souls choosing to crawl up. Enter for an ecclesiastical extravaganza; including the miracle-working icon draped with gold, silver, jewels and pearls, and surrounded by gifts from those hopeful of its powers.

A lucrative trade in candles, icon copies, incense and evil-eye deterrents is carried out on Evangelistrias. The largest candles cost around 5000 dr, and after an ephemeral existence burning in the church, the wax remains are gathered, melted down and resold.

Not only the frail, elderly and dying make the pilgrimage here. On the feasts of the Annunciation and Assumption and during Advent, Tinos also swarms with children. It is considered auspicious to be baptised at the church, a privilege costing nothing but a donation though many of these are very large. Hotels are crammed during pilgrimages, but most people sleep out because they can't find nor afford a room.

Within the church complex, several **museums** house religious artefacts, icons, and secular artworks. Below the church, a crypt marks the spot where the icon was found. Next to it is a mausoleum to the sailors killed on the *Elle*, a Greek cruise ship blown up in Tinos port on 15 August 1940, allegedly by an Italian submarine. The church and museums are open from 8 am to 8 pm.

Archaeological Museum

The archaeological museum (☎ 22 670), below the church on Leoforos Megaloharis, contains a mosaic, Roman sculptures, a 1st-century sundial designed by Andronicus of Kyrrhos and impressive clay *pithoi* (large

---

The Evil Eye

When travelling through Greece – particularly in the rural areas – you may notice that some bus drivers keep a chain bearing one or two blue stones dangling over the dashboard. Or you may spot a small, plastic blue eye attached to the cross hanging around someone's neck. Or maybe you'll wonder why there is a string of blue beads hanging from the front fender of a tractor.

Puzzle no longer. The Greeks are not sporting blue colours in support of their favourite soccer team or to show a particular political leaning. No – they are wearing blue to ward off the evil eye.

The evil eye is associated with envy, and can be cast – apparently unintentionally – upon someone or something which is praised or admired (even secretly). So those most vulnerable to the evil eye include people, creatures or objects of beauty, rarity and value. Babies are particularly vulnerable, and those who admire them will often spit gently on them to repel any ill effects. Adults and older children who are worried about being afflicted by the evil eye will wear blue.

Who then is responsible for casting the evil eye? Well, most culprits are those who are already considered quarrelsome or peculiar in some way by the local community. And folk with blue eyes are regarded with extreme suspicion – no doubt more than partly because being blue-eyed is a trait Greeks associate with Turks... All these quarrelsome, peculiar or blue-eyed folk have to do is be present when someone or something enviable appears on the scene – and then the trouble starts.

If, during your travels, someone casts the evil eye on you, you'll soon know about it. Symptoms include dizziness, headaches, a feeling of 'weight' on the head or of tightening in the chest. The locals will be able to point you in the direction of someone, usually an old woman, who can cure you.

What happens next is usually along these lines: the curer will make the sign of the cross over a glass of water; then she will pray silently, at the same time dropping oil into the glass. If the oil disappears from the surface, it proves that you have the evil eye – and it also cures it, for the 'blessed' water will be dabbed on your forehead, stomach and at two points on your chest (at the points of the crucifix).

Apparently, the cure works. But you know the old adage about prevention being better than cure. If you're worried about the evil eye, don't take any chances: wear blue. ■

jars). Opening times are Tuesday to Sunday from 8 am to 3 pm. Admission is 500 dr.

Places to Stay

Avoid Tinos at pilgrimage times, unless you want to join the huddled masses who sleep anywhere.

Camping Tinos (☎ 22 344 or 23 548) is a nice site with good facilities south of the town. Follow the sign on the waterfront.

Look for domatia signs along Evangelistrias and other streets leading inland from the waterfront. *Manthos' Rooms* (☎ 22 675), at Ioannou Voulgari 7, has rooms surrounding a vine-covered patio. To get there, turn right from the ferry quay and left at the supermarket into Zanaki Alavanou. Ioannou Voulgari is six streets up. Doubles are 6000 dr, or 7000 dr with bathroom. New studios with balconies are also available. Ask about the home-made lemonade.

Hotel Eleana (☎ 22 561) has well-kept doubles/triples with bathroom for 9000/12,000 dr. From the quay, turn right and then left at the Hotel Possidonion. The hotel is opposite the Church of Agios Ioannis.

The C-class *Hotel Meltemi* (☎ 22 881/882/883), on Megaloharis, has airy singles/doubles for 7800/11,600 dr with bathroom and breakfast. The C-class *Hotel Delfinia* (☎ 22 289), on the waterfront, has pleasant singles/doubles for 7500/10,000 dr with bathroom. The C-class *Oasis Hotel* (☎ 23 055 or 22 455), on Evangelistrias, offers doubles for 10,000 dr.

The B-class *Hotel Tinion* (☎ 22 261) has spacious doubles for 12,000 dr with bathroom. The hotel is *en route* to the camp site which is signposted from the waterfront. The *Hotel Aigli* (☎ 22 240), opposite the quay, has doubles with bath starting at 15,000 dr.

Places to Eat

To get to *Kypos Taverna* turn right from the quay, and then left at the Hotel Possidonion. Then take the third turn left. A full meal with retsina will cost about 2600 dr. There are also several places along the waterfront.

AROUND THE ISLAND

At **Kionia**, four km north-west of Tinos town, are several small beaches, the nearest overlooked by the Tinos Beach Hotel. The site of the **Sanctuary of Poseidon and Amphitrite**, before the hotel, dates from the 4th century BC. The Tiniots worshipped Poseidon because they believed he banished the snakes which once inundated the island.

At **Porto**, eight km east of Tinos town, is a sandy, uncrowded beach. Out of Loutra, **Kolymvythra bay**, on the north coast, has two lovely sandy beaches. Further along the coast is a small beach at **Panormos bay** from where distinctive green marble quarried in nearby **Marlas** and **Panormos** was once exported. Panormos is a picturesque village where sculptors still carve the marble. Figurines and other marble artefacts are on sale. Take the bus to Panormos village from where it's a pleasant three-km walk to the bay.

The ruins of the **Venetian Fortress of Exobourgo**, on a 565-metre hill, stand sentinel over a cluster of unspoilt hill villages. At the fortress, built on an ancient acropolis, the Venetians made their last stand against the Turks. The ascent can be made from several villages. The shortest is from Xinara. Take a Kambos bus. It's a steep climb, but the views are worth it.

Mykonos Μύκονος

Mykonos (MEE-kon-os, population 5000) is the most visited and expensive of all Greek islands and has the most sophisticated nightlife. It is the undisputed gay capital of Greece. The days when Mykonos was the favourite rendezvous for the world's rich and famous may be over, but Mykonos probably still has more poseurs per square metre than any other Mediterranean resort. Depending on your temperament, you'll be captivated or take one look and stay on the ferry. Barren, low-lying Mykonos would never win a Greek-island beauty competition, but it has good beaches and is the jumping-off point for the sacred island of Delos.

Getting There & Away

Air Mykonos has at least eight flights a day to Athens (16,200 dr), six weekly to Santorini (12,800 dr) and several a week to Rhodes (18,000 dr) and Iraklio on Crete (18,000 dr). The Olympic Airways office (☎ 22 327) is on Plateia Agios Loukas.

Ferry Mykonos has daily connections with Rafina (4¼ hours, 3300 dr), via Tinos and Andros; Piraeus (5½ hours, 3700 dr), via Tinos and Syros; and to Naxos (1400 dr); Paros (1600 dr); Ios (2700 dr) and Santorini (2800 dr). Around two ferries a week operate between Mykonos and Amorgos. There is a once-weekly connection with Samos via Ikaria.

The port police (☎ 22 218) are on the waterfront, above the National Bank of Greece.

Hydrofoil There are daily hydrofoils connecting Mykonos with Ios, Paros, Naxos and Santorini, as well as with Rafina via Andros and Tinos.

Excursion Boats These boats leave for Delos (30 minutes, 1500 dr return) between 8 and 10 am and return between noon and 2 pm. Every day, except Monday, between May and September, guided tours are conducted in English, French and German for 6500 dr. Tickets are available from several waterfront outlets. Delos can also be reached from Ornos.

Getting Around

To/From the Airport Mykonos' airport is about three km south-east of the town centre. A shuttle bus operates between the airport and the town.

Bus Mykonos has an excellent bus service. Mykonos town has two bus stations: the

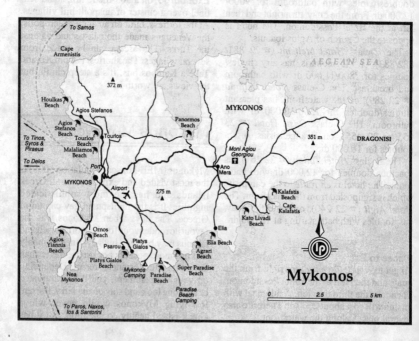

Mykonos

northern bus station has frequent departures to Agios Stefanos (via Tourlos), Ano Mera, Elia, Kato Livadi and Kalafatis, while the southern bus station has buses to Agios Yiannis, Psarou, Platys Gialos, Paradise beach and the airport.

Car & Motorbike Most car and motorbike-rental firms are around the southern bus station. The biggest is Pegasus Rent-a-Car (☎ 23 760) with vehicles from 12,600 to 24,500 dr per day and motorbikes from 5000 dr per day.

Caïque Caïques leave Mykonos town for Super Paradise, Agrari and Elia beaches and from Platys Gialos to Paradise, Super Paradise, Agrari and Elia beaches.

MYKONOS TOWN

Mykonos town, the island's port and capital, is the epitome of the warren-like Cycladic villages. Some visitors are enamoured, others find it claustrophobic. It can be very hard to find your bearings, and just when you think you've got it worked out, you'll find yourself back at square one. Throngs of pushy people add to the frustration. But even the most disenchanted could not deny that Mykonos town is beautiful – a conglomeration of chic boutiques, houses with brightly painted balconies and geraniums, clematis and bougainvillea growing against whiter than white walls. Mykonos is also a great place to people-watch – not Greeks but the holiday-makers of the world at their most eccentric. Sometimes, you may wonder if you'll ever meet a Greek.

Orientation

The waterfront is to the right of the ferry quay (facing inland) beyond the tiny town beach. The central square is Plateia Manto Mavrogenous (usually called Taxi Square), south along the waterfront.

The northern bus station is behind the OTE office (see Information), while the southern bus station is on the road to Ornos. The quay for boats to Delos is at the western end of the waterfront. South of here is

Mykonos' famous row of windmills, in sad disrepair, and the Little Venice quarter, where balconies hang over the sea.

Information

Mykonos has no tourist office. When you get off the ferry, you will see a low building with four numbered offices. No 1 is the Hotel Reservation Department (☎ 24 540), open from 8 am to midnight; No 2 is the Association of Rooms & Apartments (☎ 26 860), open from 10 am to 6 pm; No 3 has camping information (☎ 22 852); and No 4 houses the tourist police (☎ 22 482), who have variable opening times.

The National Bank of Greece is on the waterfront. Two doors away from the bank, Delia Travel (☎ 22 322) represents American Express. The Mykonian Hygeia (☎ 094-33 8292 or 35 1253) is a medical clinic; it's up from the southern bus station on the road to Ornos.

The post office is between the town beach and the central square, and the OTE is north of the beach. Mykonos' postcode is 846 00. The telephone code is 0289.

Museums & Galleries

Mykonos town has four museums. The **archaeological museum**, near the quay, houses pottery from Delos and some grave steles and jewellery from the island of Renia (the necropolis of Delos). Chief exhibits are a pithos featuring a Trojan War scene in relief and a statue of Heracles. It's open Tuesday to Sunday from 8 am to 3 pm. Admission is 500 dr, free on Sunday.

The **marine museum** has well-displayed nautical paraphernalia. It's open 10.30 am to 1 pm and 6.30 to 9 pm daily. Admission is 200 dr.

The excellent **folklore museum**, which is housed in an 18th-century sea captain's mansion, features a large collection of memorabilia, a reconstructed 19th-century kitchen and a bedroom with a four-poster bed. There's also a rather macabre stuffed pelican, the erstwhile Petros, who was run over by a car in 1985. He was hastily replaced by Petros II, whom you'll probably

Mykonos' windmills

meet while wandering. Petros I crash-landed on Mykonos during a mid-1950s storm. The islanders regarded him as a lucky omen because his arrival heralded Mykonos' status as the premier Cycladic resort. The museum, near the Delos quay, is open Monday to Saturday from 5.30 to 8.30 pm. Entrance is free.

On the road to Ornos is the **Windmill Cultural Museum**. Entrance is free but opening times are erratic.

The **municipal art gallery** (☎ 27 190) on Matogianni is open daily from 10 am to 6 pm, but don't rely on these times.

Church of Panagia Paraportiani

Of Mykonos' many churches, the Panagia Paraportiani is the most famous. It is actually four little churches amalgamated into one – a white, lumpy asymmetrical building which seems to have been cobbled together without rhyme or reason, and yet the result is one of great beauty. The interplay of light and shade on the multifaceted structure creates subtle nuances. It's a photographer's delight.

Organised Tours

Excursion boats run day trips to the sacred island of Delos. See the Mykonos Getting There & Away section for details.

Places to Stay – bottom end

Mykonos has two camping grounds: *Para-*

dise Beach Camping (☎ 22 582) on Paradise beach and *Mykonos Camping* (☎ 24 578), on Paraga beach (10 minutes' walk from Platys Gialos beach). Both sites have good facilities, and Paradise Beach Camping also has a diving school. Minibuses from the camping grounds meet ferries.

Mykonos' hotel prices will make your jaw drop. They're about double most places in Greece, although the standard of service doesn't always match the price. If you arrive without a reservation between June and September and are offered suitably priced accommodation, take it. Otherwise seek the assistance of organisations mentioned in the Information section. Also, if you choose domatia from owners meeting ferries, ask if they charge for transport. Some do.

The old-world D-class *Hotel Apollon* (☎ 22 223), on the waterfront, is run by two genteel elderly women. Rates are 7000/10,000 dr for singles/doubles with bathroom. The D-class *Hotel Carboni* (☎ 22 217), on Andronikou Matogianni, has attractive doubles with bathroom and breakfast for 14,000 dr. The D-class *Hotel Phillipi* (☎ 22 294), Kalogera 32, has immaculate singles/doubles/triples for 7400/13,000/18,000 dr with bathroom. The hotel has a delightful garden. Nearby, *Rooms Chez Maria* (☎ 22 480) has traditional touches. Doubles/triples are 12,000/13,000 dr.

Places to Stay – middle

The C-class *Hotel Delos* (☎ 22 517), is next to the post office. Rates are 14,800/17,000 dr for doubles/triples with bathroom. The *Hotel Delphines* (☎ 24 505), on Matogianni, is nicely furnished and has singles/doubles/triples for 13,000/16,500/20,000 dr. Little Venice's only seafront accommodation is *Voula's Apartments & Rooms* (☎ 22 951/157). Its balconied rooms are above a club and taverna so bring earplugs if you're not prepared to be part of the partying. Doubles/triples with bath and basic cooking facilities are 18,000/20,000 dr. Voula meets boats and does not charge for transport.

The *Hotel Kouneni* (☎ 22 301), in the town centre on Matogianni, has a charming garden and singles/doubles with bath and breakfast for 16,000/21,000 dr.

Places to Stay – top end

The A-class *Hotel Leto* (☎ 22 207), facing the town beach, has been host to guests including Greece's king and international celebrities. Single/double/triple rooms here cost 24,000/27,000/33,000 dr including breakfast. For more top-end hotel listings, see the Beaches and Ano Mera sections.

Places to Eat

The high prices charged in many Mykonos' eating establishments are not always indicative of quality or quantity. *Nico's Taverna*, up from the Delos quay, is popular, although service can be brusque when it's busy, and prices are higher than at waterfront cafés. Here, you may get favori, raw sea urchin doused in oil and vinegar.

Ta Kiopia Restaurant is fair value, with a full meal including retsina costing about 3000 dr. *Taverna Antonini*, on Plateia Manto Mavrogenous, offers well-prepared Greek staples for 500 to 2800 dr. The *Sesame Kitchen*, next to the marine museum, serves mostly vegetarian dishes at reasonable prices. The best value and view in Little Venice is at *Scarpa Restaurant* where seafood and service are tops.

The town has several supermarkets and fruit stalls, particularly around the southern bus station.

Entertainment

The nightlife on Mykonos leaves all other Greek islands in the shade. New places come and go but the following are perennials. The *Windmill Disco* and *Scandinavian Bar*, near the Panagia Paraportiani, vie to sell the cheapest drinks. Both are rowdy and get crowded. The *Irish Disco*, nearby, is also popular. *Pierro's Bar*, near Matogianni, used to be exclusively gay but now a mixed crowd spills into the street. *Mercedes*, near the archaeological museum, is an expensive, sophisticated disco with an older clientele.

The atmospheric waterfront *Thalami Bar* features Greek music.

For classy ambience try *Montparnasse Bar* or *Kastro Bar*, both in Little Venice. They play classical music at sunset. The *Gallery Bar* is agreeable and civilised. If you're roomless or an insomniac, head for the *Yacht Club*, by the quay, which is open 24 hours.

The *Hard Rock Café*, about four km along the Ano Mera road, is an astonishing complex serving Greek and US food. It has a nightclub and offers free use of a pool between noon and 4 am. A pink courtesy bus shuttles ragers to the café complex from the Yacht Club every half-hour between noon and 4 am.

Things to Buy

Nothing is cheap on Mykonos but it offers beautiful cotton and lace curtains, and museum copies of early Mykonian and Cycladic designs. Look, too, in Little Venice for feather-soft handknits of angora wool which is spun outside a few shops by old women.

Greek gold is much in evidence, particularly at Lalaounis off the waterfront by the taxi square. In Little Venice, Panagiotis Galatis, makes quality Byzantine-style jewellery, and icon replicas fashioned from old wood collected from all over Greece. His father, Yiannis, has a gallery opposite the southern bus station. In Little Venice, Karamichos Mazarakis sells handwoven rugs with Mykonian motifs.

AROUND THE ISLAND
Beaches

The nearest beaches to Mykonos town are **Malaliamos** and the tiny, crowded **Tourlos**, two km to the north. **Agios Stefanos**, two km beyond here, is larger but as crowded. Beyond **Ornos** is **Agios Yiannis**, the attractive beach where the movie *Shirley Valentine* was filmed. Unless you're pushed for time, jump on a bus to **Platys Gialos**, on the south-west coast. The beach is long and sandy but inevitably crowded. From here, caïques call at the island's best beaches further around the south coast. They are **Paradise**, **Super Paradise**, **Agrari** and **Elia**. Nudism is accepted on all these beaches. Super Paradise is where you'll find the hunks without trunks – it's the nudist gay beach. Elia is the last caïque stop, so is the least crowded. The next beach along, **Kato Livadi**, is also relatively uncrowded.

Beaches on the north coast are prone to the meltemi wind. The best is **Panormos beach**, reached along a road or a path just before Ano Mera.

Places to Stay – top end There are many places for splurge around the coast. Above Ornos is the converted *Church of St Konstantine* with traditionally furnished apartments for between two and five people for 20,000 dr. A festival is still held here in the property grounds on 21 May and 25 November. It's owned by the proprietor of *Voula Xidaki Apartments* (☎ 22 951 or 24 787), above Agios Ioannis beach, where sparkling doubles/triples/quads cost 16,000/20,000/24,000 dr.

The A-class *Petinos Beach* (☎ 22 913), above the beach at Platys Gialos, has a bar, pool and water-sports equipment. Doubles are 35,000 dr. Nearby, under the same management, is the *Hotel Petinos* (☎ 24 310) with doubles for 20,100 dr. The A-class *Princess of Mykonos* (☎ 23 806 or 24 713) at Agios Stefanos, was once a Jane Fonda hang-out. Singles/doubles are 36,000/40,800 dr.

Ano Mera Ανω Μέρα

The stark village of Ano Mera, seven km east of Mykonos town, is the island's only inland settlement. On its pretty central square is the 6th-century **Moni Panagias Tourlianis**, which has a fine stone carved bell tower, an ornate wood iconostasis carved in Florence in the late 1700s and 16th-century icons of the Cretan School. There's a small **museum**.

One of the island's best hotels, the A-class *Ano Mera Hotel* (☎ 71 215) has a pool, restaurant and disco. Singles/doubles/triples with breakfast are 20,600/23,500/28,200 dr.

Delos Δήλος

Despite its diminutive size, Delos is one of the most important archaeological sites in Greece, and certainly the most important in the Cyclades. The Cyclades are so named because they form a circle *(kyklos)* around Delos. Lying a few km off the west coast of Mykonos, the sacred island of Delos is the mythical birthplace of Apollo and Artemis.

History

Delos was first inhabited in the 3rd millennium BC. In the 8th century BC, the annual Delia festival was established on the island to celebrate the birth of Apollo. For a long time, the Athenians coveted Delos, seeing its strategic position as one from where they could control the Aegean. By the 5th century BC, it had come under their jurisdiction.

After Athens defeated the Persians, it established the Delian League in 477 BC, and its treasury was kept on the island. It carried out a number of 'purifications', decreeing that no-one could be born or could die on Delos, thus strengthening its control over the island by removing the native population.

Delos reached the height of its power in Hellenistic times, becoming one of the three most important religious centres in Greece and a flourishing centre of commerce. It traded throughout the Mediterranean and was populated with wealthy merchants, mariners and bankers from as far away as Egypt and Syria. These inhabitants built temples to the various gods worshipped in their countries of origin, although Apollo remained the principal deity.

The Romans made Delos a free port in 167 BC which brought even greater prosperity. But, by then, it had become debased and was the most lucrative slave market in the Mediterranean. In 88 BC, it was sacked by Mithridates and 10,000 of the island's inhabitants were massacred. From then on, Delos was prey to pirates and, later, also to looters of antiquities.

Getting There & Away

See Excursion Boats under Mykonos for schedules and prices.

ANCIENT DELOS
Orientation & Information

The small modern quay is south of the Sacred Harbour.

Many of the most significant finds from Delos are in the National Archaeological Museum in Athens. The on-site museum has a modest collection.

Overnight stays on Delos are forbidden, and the boat schedule allows only three hours there. Bring water and food as the island's cafeteria is poor value. Wear a hat and sensible shoes. Entrance to the site costs 1500 dr (including entrance to the museum).

Exploring the Site

Following is an outline of some significant archaeological remains on Delos. For further site details, buy a guidebook at the ticket office.

If you have the energy, climb Mt Kythnos (113 metres), to the south-east of the harbour to see the layout of Delos. There are terrific views of surrounding islands on clear days.

The path is reached by walking through the **theatre quarter**. Delos' wealthiest inhabitants built their houses here in the precincts of the **Theatre of Delos**. The houses surrounded peristyled courtyards. Mosaics, apparently a status symbol, were the most striking feature of each house.

These colourful mosaics were exquisite art works, mostly representational and offset by intricate geometric borders. The most lavish dwellings were the **House of Dionysos**, named after its mosaic depicting the wine god riding a panther; and the **House of Cleopatra**, where headless statues of the two owners were found. These are now in the museum. The **House of the Trident** was one of the grandest houses. The **House of the Masks**, probably a hostelry for actors, has another mosaic of Dionysos resplendent astride a panther. The **House of the Dolphins** has another exceptional mosaic.

The theatre dates from 300 BC and had a large cistern, the remains of which can be seen. It supplied much of the town with water. The houses of the wealthy had their own cisterns – essential appendages as Delos was almost as parched and barren then as it is today.

On the descent from Mt Kythnos, explore the **Sanctuaries of the Foreign Gods**. Here, at the **Shrine to the Samothracian Great Gods**, the Kabeiroi (the twins Dardanos and Aeton) were worshipped. At the **Sanctuary of the Syrian Gods** are remains of a theatre. Here, an audience watched orgies held in honour of the Syrian deities. There is also an area where Egyptian deities, including Serapis and Isis, were worshipped.

The **Sanctuary of Apollo**, to the north of the harbour, contains temples dedicated to him. It is also the site of the much photographed **Terrace of the Lions**. These proud beasts, carved from marble, were offerings from the people of Naxos that were presented to Delos in the 7th century BC. Their function was to guard the sacred area. To the east of them is the **Sacred Lake** (dry since 1925) where, according to legend, Leto gave birth to Apollo and Artemis.

Leto with the twins Apollo and Artemis

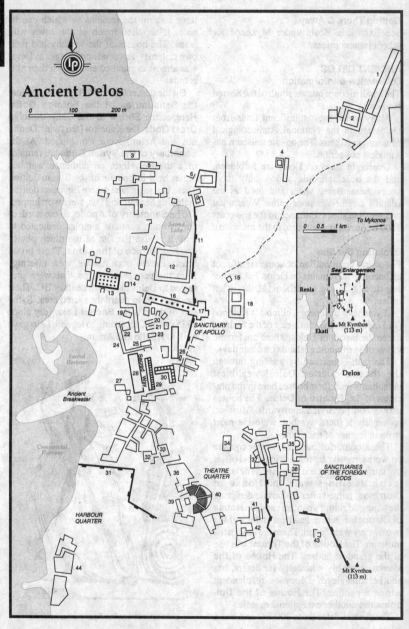

Ancient Delos

0   100   200 m

Sacred
Lake

Sacred
Harbour

Ancient
Breakwater

Commercial
Harbour

HARBOUR
QUARTER

SANCTUARY
OF APOLLO

Sacred Way

THEATRE
QUARTER

SANCTUARIES
OF THE FOREIGN
GODS

Mt Kynthos
(113 m)

To Mykonos

0   0.5   1 km

See Enlargement

Renia

Ekati

Mt Kynthos
(113 m)

Delos

1	Stadium
2	Gymnasium
3	House of Comedians
4	Sanctuary of Archegetes
5	House of Diadumenos
6	Lake House
7	Hill House
8	Institution of the Poseidoniasts
9	Palaestra
10	Terrace of the Lions
11	Roman Wall
12	Agora of the Italians
13	Stoa of Poseidon
14	Dodekatheon
15	Tourist Pavillion
16	Stoa of Antigonas
17	Sanctuary of Dionysos
18	Museum
19	Temple of Artemis
20	Poros Temple
21	Temple of the Athenians
22	Keraton
23	Temple of Apollo
24	Stoa of the Naxiots
25	House of the Naxiots
26	Monument of the Bulls
27	Agora of the Competialists
28	Stoa of Philip V
29	South Stoa
30	Agora of the Delians
31	Wall of the Triarus
32	House of Cleopatra
33	House of Dionysos
34	House of Hermes
35	Sanctuary of the Syrian Gods
36	House of the Trident
37	Shrine to the Samothracian Great Gods
38	Shrine to the Egyptian Gods
39	Cistern
40	Theatre of Delos
41	House of the Dolphins
42	House of the Masks
43	Sacred Cave
44	Warehouses

Syros Σύρος

Many tourists come to Syros (SEE-ros, population 25,000) merely to change ferries. This is a pity because its capital, Ermoupolis, named after Hermes, god of trade, is a beautiful city whose inhabitants have not become tourist-weary.

Syros' economy depends little on tourism, and though its ship-building industry has declined, it has textile factories, dairy farms and a horticultural industry supplying the rest of the Cyclades with plants and flowers. It's also the summer home of several celebrities such as French actress Catherine Deneuve.

History

In the Middle Ages, Syros was the only Greek island with an entirely Roman Catholic population, the result of conversions by the Franks who took over the island in 1207. This gave it the support and protection of the West (particularly the French) during Ottoman times.

Syros remained neutral during the War of Independence and thousands of refugees from islands ravaged by the Turks fled here. They brought their Orthodox religion and built a new settlement on a hill (now called Vrodado) and the port town of Ermoupolis. After Independence, Ermoupolis became the commercial, naval and cultural centre of Greece. Today, Syros' Catholic population is 40% and the Orthodox, 60% of the total. The city's large ornate churches and neoclassical mansions (many now being restored) are testimonies to its former grandeur.

Getting There & Away

Air Syros has at least two flights a day to Athens (13,000 dr). The Olympic Airways office (☎ 22 634) is on Akti Papagou.

Ferry Syros has at least two ferries a day to Piraeus (four hours, 3300 dr), Tinos and Mykonos; at least one to Paros (1300 dr) and Naxos; at least four a week to Amorgos; and one a week to Rafina (4¼ hours, 3300 dr). Syros' port police (☎ 22 690 or 28 888) are on the eastern side of the waterfront.

Hydrofoil There are daily hydrofoils to Tinos, Mykonos, Paros, Naxos, Ios and Santorini; as well as one or two services a week to many of the smaller islands. There is one hydrofoil a week to Rafina on the mainland.

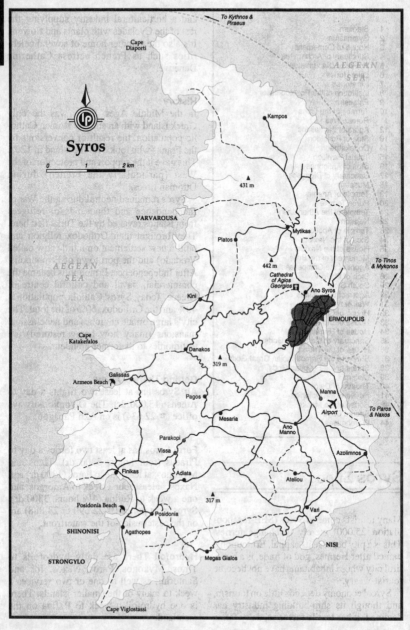

Syros

To Kythnos &
Piraeus

Cape
Diaporti

AEGEAN
SEA

Kampos

VARVAROUSA

431 m

Platos

Mytikas

442 m

Cathedral
of Agios
Georgios

To Tinos
& Mykonos

AEGEAN
SEA

Kini

Ano Syros

ERMOUPOLIS

Cape
Katakefalos

Danakos

319 m

Galissas

Armeos Beach

Pagos

Manna

To Paros
& Naxos

Mesaria

Airport

Parakopi

Ano
Manno

Vissa

Azolimnos

Finikas

Adiata

Ateliou

Posidonia Beach

317 m

Vari

SHINONISI

Posidonia

Agathopes

NISI

STRONGYLO

Megas Gialos

Cape Viglostassi

0   1   2 km

Getting Around

Frequent buses do a southern loop around the island from Ermoupolis, calling at all beaches mentioned in the text. Cars can be hired from the Team Work Agency (see Organised Tours in the Ermoupolis section, below).

ERMOUPOLIS Ερμούπολη

During the 19th century, a combination of fortuitous circumstances resulted in Ermoupolis becoming Greece's major port. It was superseded by Piraeus long ago but is still the Cyclades' largest city and its capital, with a population of 17,000. As the boat sails into Syros' port of Ermoupolis you will see the Catholic settlement of Ano Syros to the left, and the Orthodox settlement of Vrodado to the right, both set on hills. Spilling down from them both and skirting the harbour is Ermoupolis. It's an impressive sight.

Orientation & Information

All boats dock at the west of the bay. The Hoteliers' Association booth (☎ 80 356) is to the right after the wharf. The bus station is also by the quay. There are public toilets and showers (500 dr) east along the waterfront, before the port police.

To reach the central square of Plateia Miaouli from the quay, turn right and then left into El Venizelou. The tourist police (☎ 22 375) and the EOT (☎ 22 375 or 26 725), on the 2nd floor of the town hall, are both on this square. The OTE is just off it. The National Bank of Greece is on Kalomnopoulou, east of Plateia Miaouli. The post office is on Protopapadaki. Syros' postcode is 841 00 and the telephone code is 0281.

Things to See

Ano Syros (Άνω Σύρος) Vrodado and Ermoupolis merge but Ano Syros is quite different – a typical Cycladic settlement of narrow alleyways and whitewashed houses. It's a fascinating place to wander around and has splendid views of neighbouring islands. On the way up, look at the **Agios Georgios Cemetery** which has ostentatious mausoleums reminiscent of Athens' First Cemetery.

The finest of Ano Syros' Catholic churches is the baroque **Cathedral of St George**. Close by is the **Capuchin Monastery of St Jean**, founded in 1535 to minister to the poor. Ano Syros was the birthplace of Markos Vamvakaris, the celebrated rembetika singer. To reach Ano Syros, walk up Omirou.

Plateia Miaouli is the hub of bustling Ermoupolis. It's flanked by palm trees and cafés and dominated by the town hall, a magnificent neoclassical building designed by the German architect Ernst Ziller. The small **archaeological museum** in the town hall houses a mediocre collection of vases, grave steles, heads and torsos – hardly worthy of the capital of the Cyclades. It's open Tuesday to Sunday from 8.30 am to 3 pm. Admission is free.

The **Apollon Theatre**, on Plateia Vardaki, was designed by the French architect Chabeau and is a replica of La Scala in Milan. There are terrific views from the **Church of Anastasis**, on top of Vrodado hill – reached by walking up Louka Ralli.

The **Kousoulakos Gallery** on the waterfront is mostly staffed (when he's not exhibiting overseas) by the charming resident artist, Vassilis. His paintings are mainly surrealistic with mythological themes, but there are also land and seascapes.

Organised Tours

For tours of Syros, contact Team Work Agency (☎ 83 400 or 81 185) on the eastern waterfront at Plateia Kanari. It offers tours around the island by bus or boat to monasteries and deserted beaches.

Places to Stay

Syros is not as popular as most Cycladic islands so finding accommodation is usually not too difficult. The Team Work Agency (☎ 80 356) and the Hoteliers' Association have room-finding services. Domatia owners also meet ferries.

Pension Diaskouroi (☎ 22 580), on the corner of Klonos and Kyparissou Stefanou, has a colonnaded terrace and comfortable doubles with shared bathroom for 5000 dr as

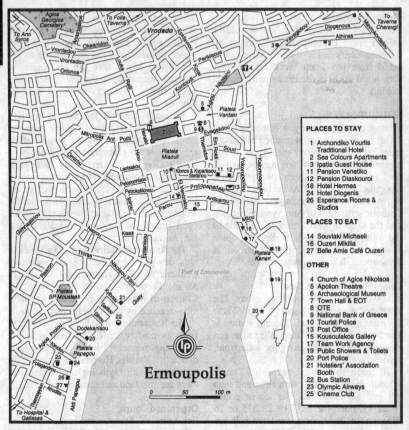

PLACES TO STAY

1 Archondiko Vourlis
  Traditional Hotel
2 Sea Colours Apartments
3 Ipatia Guest House
11 Pension Venetiko
12 Pension Diaskouroi
18 Hotel Hermes
24 Hotel Diogenis
26 Esperance Rooms &
  Studios

PLACES TO EAT

14 Souvlaki Michaeli
16 Ouzeri Mikilia
27 Belle Amie Café Ouzeri

OTHER

4 Church of Agios Nikolaos
5 Apollon Theatre
6 Archaeological Museum
7 Town Hall & EOT
8 OTE
9 National Bank of Greece
10 Tourist Police
13 Post Office
15 Kousoulakos Gallery
17 Team Work Agency
19 Public Showers & Toilets
20 Port Police
21 Hoteliers' Association
  Booth
22 Bus Station
23 Olympic Airways
25 Cinema Club

Ermoupolis

0   50   100 m

well as doubles/triples with private bathroom for 7000/9000 dr. Close by is *Pension Venetiko* (☎ 81 686), Em Roidi 2, with simple doubles with shared bathroom for 7000 dr. It has a shady rear garden.

Ipatia Guest House (☎ 83 575), Vavagiotou 3, is a wonderful 1870s neoclassical mansion. Rooms have brass bedsteads and wood-panelled ceilings. Ask to see the magnificent painted ceiling in the family quarters. Rates are 8500/10,500 dr for singles/doubles with shared facilities and 12,000 dr for doubles with bathroom. The B-class *Hotel Hermes* (☎ 83 011), Plateia

Kanari, has comfortable singles/doubles for 8000/10,600 dr.

On the waterfront, south of the bus station and quay, is the *Hotel Diogenis* (☎ 86 301/305), a restored neoclassical building with TV, minibar and hair dryer in each single/double room for 11,500/15,000 dr. Further along the waterfront is *Esperance Rooms & Studios* (☎ 81 671), which has marble surrounds with air-con and port view for 12,000 dr a double.

The luxurious *Sea Colours Apartments* (☎ 83 400 or 81 183; fax 83 508) has two-person studios for 14,000 dr and four-person apartments (with two bathrooms) for 20,000 dr. Follow the directions for Ipatia Guest House and descend the steps opposite. Sea Colours is on the right, hovering over lovely Agios Nikolaos bay. The *Archondiko Vourlis Traditional Hotel* (☎ & fax 28 440) is a well-restored neoclassical mansion overlooking Taliro bay at Mavrodkordatou 5, up and around from Sea Colours Apartments. Suites with antique furniture start at 19,500 dr a double.

Places to Eat
Ermoupolis has excellent restaurants. For basic surrounds (and prices) but top souvlaki, pitta, simple salad and Michaeli's own wine, visit *Souvlaki Michaeli* in his minuscule place on El Venizelou; there's no sign out the front, but it's the only eatery of its type left as you head towards the main square. He'll sing to you (superbly) as he polishes plates. Beneath the waterfront Esperance Rooms & Studios, *Belle Amie Café Ouzeri* is super for breakfast, snacks and mezedes (from 8 am to 2 am) which are hearty enough to make a meal. It serves shrimp salad for 900 dr.

It's worth a taxi ride (or bracing walk) to go to *Taverna Charavgi* at Agiou Dimitriou 4, a continuation of Mavrokordatou. It has fair-priced grills and staples and a share of the magical view that Catherine Deneuve enjoys. Continue on to the *Folia Taverna*, at Athanasiou Diakou 2, which has imaginatively prepared dishes, particularly rabbit and pigeon, at reasonable prices. On foot from town, walk up Omirou, turn right into Okaenidon, walk to its end, turn left then right into Athanasiou Diakou. The restaurant is on the left where the road curves.

If you've got a sweet tooth, don't miss the loukoumia (Turkish delight) that Syros is famous for. It's so popular that vendors race aboard ferries in the few minutes between arrival and departure. There is a food market on Hiou.

Entertainment
Cinema Club, Folegandrou 3, has both disco and live Greek music in a cavernous setting.

The waterfront vibrates with music in the evening as does the central square.

GALISSAS Γαλησσάς
The west-coast resort of Galissas has the island's best beach – a 900-metre crescent of sand, shaded by tamarisk trees. Armeos, a walk round the left of the bay, is an official nudist beach. Despite the fact that hotels and domatia are mushrooming at alarming rates here, Galissas still has a good laid-back feel.

Places to Stay – bottom end
Syros' two camp sites are both at Galissas. *Camping for Two* (☎ 42 052/321) has most facilities – from motorbike rental to minigolf, barbecues to bungalows. Its minibus meets the ferries. The other site is *Yianna Camping* (☎ 42 418).

Karmelina Rooms (☎ 42 320) has clean doubles which cost 8500 dr with shared bathroom and communal kitchen. The same family owns nice apartments with doubles for 9900 dr. The domatia are on the right of the main road coming from Ermoupolis (beyond the branch road to the beach). Opposite are the pleasant *Despina Studios* (☎ 42 333), with private bathroom and a communal kitchen. Rates are 8000/10,000/12,000 dr for doubles/triples/quads. Almost next door are the more luxurious *Corali Rooms* (☎ 22 265) on Vassilikosis, with rates of 8500 dr for doubles and 9900 dr for two-person apartments with private bathroom.

Dendrinos Rooms (☎ 42 469) are tastefully decorated with batik wall-hangings, Cycladic figurines and stone reliefs. Rates are 10,000/12,500 dr for doubles/triples with bathroom. The rooms are on the left side of the road to Camping for Two (signposted).

Places to Stay – middle
Hotel Benois (☎ 42 833/944/333), at the entrance to the beach, is an attractive C-class hotel. Rates are 10,200/12,400/15,000 dr for singles/doubles/triples with private bathroom.

The A-class *Dolphin Bay Hotel* (☎ 42 924; fax 42 843) is an unmissable cluster of buildings left of the beach as you face the sea. Rooms have satellite TV, private safe and other amenities. Singles/doubles are 16,500/21,000 dr.

Places to Eat

The *Café Bar* (also a minimarket), overlooking the beach, serves good, cheap meals. Three tavernas (more expensive) and a separate music bar are also in the village.

OTHER BEACHES

South of Galissas there are more beaches. All have domatia and some have hotels. The first is **Finikas**, with a small, tree-lined beach. The next, **Posidonia**, is appealing, with a sand and pebble beach shaded by tamarisk trees. Further south, **Agathopes** has a tree-bordered sandy beach. On the south coast, **Megas Gialos** is tranquil with two sand beaches. **Vari**, the next bay along, has a sandy beach but is more developed.

Naxos & the Minor Islands
Νάξος & τα Κουφονήσια

Give me again your empty boon,
Sweet Sleep – the gentle dream
How Theseus 'neath the fickle moon
Upon the Ocean stream
Took me and led me by the hand
To be his Queen in Athens land.

He slew the half-bull Minotaur
In labyrinthine ways.
But, threadless, had he come no more
From out my father's maze:
Yet I who taught his hands this guile
Am left forlorn on Naxos Isle.

Dionysiaca XLVII by Nonnos
(translated by Roger Lancelyn Green)

NAXOS

It was on Naxos (NA-xos, population 21,000), according to mythology, that Theseus abandoned Ariadne after she helped him in his efforts to slay the Minotaur on Crete. She didn't pine long; she was soon ensconced in the arms of Dionysos.

The island is the Cyclades' largest and most fertile, producing olives, citrus fruits, corn and potatoes. Its Mt Zeus (1010 metres) is the archipelago's highest peak. Rugged mountains and green valleys make it one of the most scenic Cycladic islands. Naxos is popular, although not as heavily visited as Mykonos, Santorini and Paros.

Organised Tours

The Naxos Tourist Information Centre (see Information section) offers day tours to a secluded beach by bus or caïque for about 10,000 dr, including a barbecue.

Getting There & Away

Air Daily flights to Athens are 17,000 dr. Olympic Airways is represented by Orbit Travel (☎ 22 454) on the waterfront in Naxos town and Naxos Tourist Information Centre (☎ 24 358) at the quay.

Ferry Naxos has daily ferries to Piraeus (six hours, 3600 dr), Mykonos, (1400 dr), Paros (1300 dr), Ios (1959 dr), and Santorini (1600 dr); almost daily connections with Iraklia, Shinoussa, Koufonisi and Amorgos; twice weekly ones with Folegandros, Sikinos, Donoussa and Iraklio (Crete); and a once-weekly connection with Samos. Naxos' port police (☎ 23 292) are in the town hall, south of the quay.

Hydrofoil Daily hydrofoils connect Naxos with Ios and Santorini, as well as with Paros, Mykonos and Tinos and Syros. There are five services a week to Rafina, three to Syros and occasional services to smaller islands.

Getting Around

To/From the Airport There is no shuttle bus to the airport, but you can catch the Agios Prokopios-bound bus, which passes close by.

Bus Frequent buses run to Agia Anna beach from Naxos town. There are five buses a day to Filoti (300 dr), via Halki (260 dr); four a day to Pyrgaki (174 dr), Apollonas and Apiranthos (440 dr), via Filoti and Halki; and

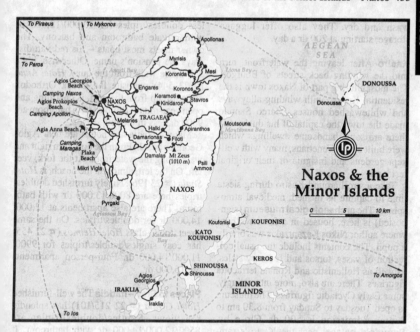

Naxos & the Minor Islands

two a day to Melanes (175 dr). Buses leave from the end of the wharf.

Car, Motorbike & Bicycle You can hire cars and motorbikes as well as 21-speed all-terrain bicycles from the outlets along the waterfront in Naxos town. Prices for the bicycles start at 2000 dr. You'll need all the gears – the roads are steep, winding and not always in good condition.

Naxos Town

Naxos town, on the west coast, is the island's port and capital. It's a large town, divided into two neighbourhoods – Bourgos, where the Greeks lived, and Kastro, on the hill above, where the Venetian Catholics lived.

A causeway to the north of the port leads to the islet of Palatia and the unfinished Temple of Apollo, Naxos' most famous landmark. Legend holds that when İstanbul is returned to Greece, the door to the temple will miraculously appear. Naxos' northern

shore is called Grotta – nicknamed Grotty by some tourists. South-west of the town is the sandy beach of Agios Georgios.

Orientation The ferry quay is at the northern end of the waterfront. The bus terminal is in front of the quay and a schedule is posted outside the bus information office to the north of the terminal.

Information There is no EOT and no tourist police. The privately owned Naxos Tourist Information Centre (☎ 24 358), opposite the quay makes up for this, thanks to the inimitable English-speaking Despina.

To reach the National Bank of Greece, walk along the quay. For OTE turn left from the quay. For the post office, turn left just beyond the OTE and take the second right. The postcode for Naxos is 843 00, and the telephone code is 0285.

There are several laundry services along the waterfront charging about 2000 dr to

CYCLADES

wash and dry. They also offer luggage storage, starting at 200 dr a day.

Kastro After leaving the waterfront, turn into the winding back streets of Bourgos. The most alluring part of Naxos town is the residential Kastro, with winding alleyways and whitewashed houses. Marco Sanudo made the town the capital of his duchy and there are some handsome dwellings which were built by the Venetians, many with well-kept gardens and insignia of their original residents.

Take a stroll around Kastro during siesta time to capture its hushed, medieval atmosphere. The **archaeological museum** (signposted) is here, housed in a former school where author Nikos Kazantzakis was briefly a pupil. The contents include the usual collection of vases, torsos and funerary steles, as well as Hellenistic and Roman terracotta figurines. There are also, more interestingly, some Early Cycladic figurines. The museum is open Tuesday to Sunday from 8.30 am to 3 pm. Admission is 500 dr. Close by, **Sanudo's palace**, near the Kastro's ramparts, and the Roman Catholic **cathedral** are worth seeing.

Places to Stay – bottom end There are three camp sites near Naxos town: *Camping Naxos* (☎ 23 500), one km south of Agios Georgios beach; *Camping Maragas* (☎ 24 552), Agia Anna beach; and *Camping Apollon* (☎ 24 417), 700 metres from Agios Prokopios beach. All sites have good facilities and minibuses usually meet the boats.

The *Dionyssos Youth Hostel* (☎ 22 331) has dorm beds for 1500 dr. Simply furnished singles/doubles are for 2000/3000 dr with shared facilities and doubles/triples with bathroom are 4000/5000 dr. The hostel is signposted from Agiou Nikodemou (also known as Market St), Bourgos' main street. The slightly dilapidated but friendly *Okeanis Hotel* (☎ 22 931), near the quay, has clean rooms for 2500/4000/6000 dr with private bathroom.

The *Pension Sofi* (☎ 25 582 or 23 077) off Neofytou, (the Grotta beach road) has spotless doubles/triples for 10,000/12,000 dr with private bathroom and balcony. The owner meets most boats – his red van displays the pension's name. Otherwise, it's a 350-metre walk from the quay. *Hotel Anna* (☎ 23 544) opposite the Greek Orthodox cathedral up from the port, is charming and open year-round. Doubles with bathroom are 9000 dr, less in the low season.

Many domatia and hotels are near Agios Georgios beach. From the port, turn right and walk along the waterfront. At the fork, veer left. On the left, almost at the beach, is *Hotel Soula* (☎ 23 196). Nicely furnished doubles/triples here are 8000/13,000 dr with bathroom. There are also apartments at 12,000/14,000 dr for doubles/triples. On the same street, the C-class *Hotel Helmos* (☎ 22 455) has cosy singles/doubles/triples for 9900/11,000/14,000 dr. Four-person apartments are 16,000 dr.

Places to Stay – middle The well-furnished *Hotel Grotta* (☎ 22 215/101) has splendid sea views. Singles/doubles/triples are 8500/12,000/14,000 dr with bathroom. If you telephone, the owner will pick you up at the quay. The *Chateau Zevgoli* (☎ 24 525/358 or 26 123 or 22 993), in Kastro, has plush, traditionally furnished rooms for 18,000/22,000 dr. The hotel is owned by Despina from the Naxos Tourist Information Centre. She also has large, restored, balconied homes for 15,000 dr for two people and 20,000 dr for four.

Back 100 metres from Agios Georgios beach, *Studios Panos* (☎ 25 582) has sparkling doubles/triples with kitchen for 12,000/15,000 dr. Right on the beach is the stylish *Hotel Nissaki* (☎ 22 876). All rooms have en suite and telephone. Facilities include a swimming pool, bar and restaurant. Singles/doubles here cost 10,000/14,000 dr and suites for four people are 25,000 dr.

Places to Eat *O Tsitas Restaurant*, up the alleyway from the waterfront Zas Travel Agency, has tasty, reasonably priced food. *Restaurant Meltemi*, at the southern end of the waterfront, offers indoor or seaside

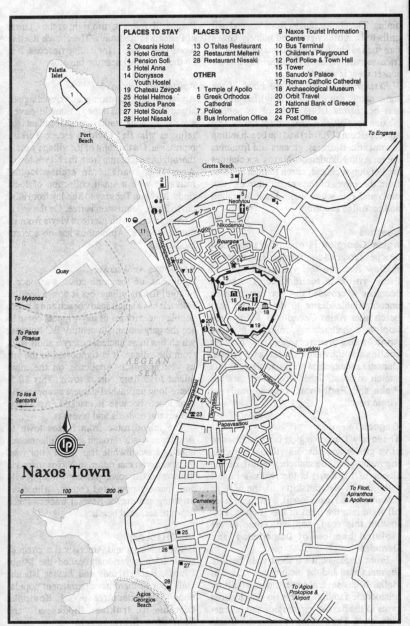

PLACES TO STAY
2 Okeanis Hotel
3 Hotel Grotta
4 Pension Sofi
5 Hotel Anna
14 Dionyssos
   Youth Hostel
19 Chateau Zevgoli
25 Hotel Helmos
26 Studios Panos
27 Hotel Soula
28 Hotel Nissaki

PLACES TO EAT
13 O Tsitas Restaurant
22 Restaurant Meltemi
28 Restaurant Nissaki

OTHER
1 Temple of Apollo
6 Greek Orthodox
   Cathedral
7 Police
8 Bus Information Office

9 Naxos Tourist Information
   Centre
10 Bus Terminal
11 Children's Playground
12 Port Police & Town Hall
15 Tower
16 Sanudo's Palace
17 Roman Catholic Cathedral
18 Archaeological Museum
20 Orbit Travel
21 National Bank of Greece
23 OTE
24 Post Office

Palatia Islet

Port Beach

To Engares

Grotta Beach

Neofytou

Agiou Nikodemou

Bourgos

Quay

To Mykonos

To Paros & Piraeus

To Ios & Santorini

AEGEAN SEA

Kastro

Ifikratidou

Prantouni

Papavasiliou

To Filoti, Apiranthos & Apollonas

Cemetery

To Agios Prokopios & Airport

Agios Georgios Beach

Naxos Town

0   100   200 m

dining. The choice ranges from seafood and grills to beautifully prepared homely Greek fare such as arni fricassee me maroulia (lamb fricassee with lettuce). Prices are fair and the sunset view is superb.

Restaurant Nissaki (in the hotel of the same name; see Places to Stay) has indoor and beachfront tables. One of its several Naxian specialties is veal with potatoes, feta and capsicum (1700 dr) and the beach setting is romantic. Bakeries, grocers and fruiterers are on Agio Nikodemou. Naxos' specialities are kefalotyri cheese, citron (a liqueur made from the leaves of the grapefruit tree), raki, ouzo and fine white wine. Look for rabbit and partridge in spring.

Beaches
Agios Georgios is one of Naxos' best beaches. You can windsurf here on water so shallow that you feel you could wade to Paros, visible in the distance. The beach becomes so crowded that you may gain an uncontrollable desire to do so. The next beach after Agios Georgios is **Agios Prokopios**, a sheltered bay, followed by **Agia Anna** – a long stretch of sand. Sandy beaches continue southwards as far as **Pyrgaki**. Domatia and tavernas are found all along this stretch of coast. Other worthy beaches are **Plaka** and **Parthenou**, known locally as Virgin beach.

Tragaea Τραγαία
The lovely Tragaea region is a vast plain of olive groves and unspoilt villages harbouring numerous little churches. **Filoti**, on the slopes of Mt Zeus, is the region's largest village. On the outskirts of the village (coming from Naxos town), a dirt road leads off right into the heart of the Tragaea. Following this road, you will come to the isolated hamlets of **Damarionas** and **Damalas**.

From Damalas, it's a short walk back to the main road and the picturesque village of **Halki**. It has several tower houses built by aristocratic families as refuges and lookout posts in the days of pirate raids and internecine feuds. The best preserved is the Grazia Pyrgos. To reach it, turn right at the Church of Panagia Protothronis. The church itself is worth checking out for its fine frescoes. It is on the main road near the bus stop.

Apiranthos Απείρανθος
Apiranthos is a handsome, austere village of stone houses and steep, marble-paved streets. Its inhabitants are descendants of refugees who fled Crete to escape Turkish repression. On the right of the village's main thoroughfare (coming from the Naxos town-Apollonas road) is an **archaeological museum** with a small collection of local finds. It's open Tuesday to Sunday from 8.30 am to 2 pm. Admission is free. On the left is a basic taverna with glorious views from its outside terrace. Apiranthos has no accommodation.

Apollonas Απόλλωνας
Apollonas, on the north coast, was once a tranquil fishing village but is now a popular resort. It has a small sandy beach and a larger pebble one. Hordes of day-trippers come to see the gargantuan 7th-century BC **kouros**, which lies in an ancient quarry a short walk from the village. It is signposted to the left as you approach Apollonas on the main inland road from Naxos town. This 10.5-metre-long unfinished statue was apparently abandoned because it cracked. Apollonas has several domatia and tavernas.

The inland route from Naxos town to Apollonas winds through spectacular mountains – a worthwhile trip. With your own transport, you can return to Naxos town via the west-coast road, passing through wild and sparsely populated country with awe-inspiring sea views. Several tracks branch down to secluded beaches.

MINOR ISLANDS
Between Naxos and Amorgos is a chain of small islands variously called the Minor Islands, Back Islands and Lesser Islands. Only four of them have permanent populations – **Donoussa** (Δονούσα), **Koufonisi** (Κουφονήσι), **Iraklia** (Ηράκλεια) and **Shinoussa** (Σχοινούσσα).

All were densely populated in antiquity, as evidenced by the large number of graves found. In the Middle Ages, the islands were uninhabited except by pirates and goats. After independence, intrepid souls from Naxos and Amorgos reinhabited them. Now, each island has a small population. Until recently, their only visitors were Greeks returning to their roots. These days they receive a few tourists, mostly backpackers looking for splendid beaches and a laid-back lifestyle.

Donoussa is the most northerly of the island group and furthest from Naxos. The others are clustered near the south-east coast of Naxos. Each has an OTE, telephone and post office, but don't depend on them for currency exchange – take drachma with you.

The island ports have domatia and tavernas, but don't expect anything fancy. Accommodation is available at Shinoussa's inland capital (also called Shinoussa).

Getting There & Away

There are two ferries a week from Piraeus to each of the minor islands; one via Syros, Paros and Naxos; and the other via Syros, Tinos and Mykonos. In summer, a local ferry links the islands about four times a week with Amorgos and Naxos. The islands are also served by hydrofoils.

Amorgos Αμοργός

Elongated Amorgos (Am-or-GOS, population 1860) is the most easterly of the Cyclades. It's too far off the beaten track for package tourists but gets overrun by latter-day hippie types who stay throughout the summer. It's also popular with the French, perhaps because Luc Besson's *The Big Blue* was filmed here. With rugged mountains and an extraordinary monastery clinging to a cliff, Amorgos is an enticing and worthwhile island for those wishing to venture off the well-worn Mykonos-Paros-Santorini route. It's also offers excellent walking.

Amorgos has two ports, Katapola and Aegiali. The capital, Amorgos town, is north-east of Katapola.

As on Ios and Paros, be wary of cheap cocktails which can pack perfidious punches.

Getting There & Away

Ferry Most ferries stop at both Katapola and Aegiali, but check if this is the case with your ferry. In summer, daily ferries link with Naxos, Koufonisi, Shinoussa, and Iraklia. Five ferries a week go to Piraeus (10 hours, 3520 dr); three a week to Paros (2390 dr), Syros, Mykonos, Tinos and Donoussa; and two to Astypalea, in the Dodecanese.

Hydrofoil Amorgos is not a major port of call on the hydrofoil network, but there are two services a week to Naxos, Paros and Syros and weekly services to Santorini, Ios and Mykonos as well as to Rafina.

Getting Around

There are frequent buses from Katapola to Amorgos town, Moni Hozoviotissas and Agia Anna beach, and one or two a day to Aegiali and Paradisi beaches. Check the frequencies of these last two because roads on Amorgos are being improved. There are also regular services from Aegiali to Langada.

KATAPOLA Κατάπολα

Katapola, the principal port, occupies a large bay in the most verdant part of the island. A smattering of remains from the ancient city of Minoa (a Cretan settlement) lie above the port. Amorgos has also yielded many finds from the Cycladic civilisation. The largest Cycladic figurine in the National Archaeological Museum in Athens was found in the vicinity of Katapola. The quay leads towards the central square and the waterfront is to the left. Katapola does not have a tourist office or tourist police. The regular police (☎ 71 210) are on the central square.

Places to Stay & Eat

Camping Amorgos (☎ 71 257) is back from

the northern end of the waterfront. Turn left from the quay (facing inland).

Domatia owners meet the ferries. *Pension Amorgos* (☎ 71 214) has spotless doubles with shared bathroom for 4500 dr and with private bathroom for 6000 dr. From the quay, walk past the central square and you'll see it on the right. The C-class *Hotel Minoa* (☎ 71 480/481) has comfortable doubles with bathroom and breakfast for 12,000 dr. The hotel is signposted from the waterfront.

A cluster of tavernas around the quay serve typical Greek fare. Try *Restaurant Minos* for a reasonably priced meal. Facing inland, turn right from the quay to reach it.

AMORGOS TOWN

Amorgos town, 400 metres above sea level and six km inland from Katapola, is a typical Cycladic village. The bus stop is on a square at the beginning of the village. The OTE is beyond it on the main road and the post office is further along. The postcode for Amorgos is 840 08 and the telephone code is 0285.

There are no hotels or pensions in Amorgos town but look for domatia signs along the main road.

AEGIALI Αιγιάλη

Aegiali is Amorgos' other port. The atmosphere is more laid-back than in Katapola and there is a good beach which stretches left of the quay.

Places to Stay & Eat

As in Katapola, domatia owners meet ferries. The C-class *Hotel Mike* (☎ 73 208), opposite the quay, was Aegiali's first hotel and opens from May to September. Doubles with private bathroom are 9500 dr. Back from the beach, *Lakki Pension* (☎ 73 253) has immaculate singles/doubles/triples with bathroom and breakfast for 6500/8100/9800 dr. The pension has a delightful garden, a taverna and bar.

The traditional Cycladic *Egialis Hotel* (☎ 73 393; fax 73 244) sits between two sandy beaches. All rooms have a telephone, radio and balcony with great views. The hotel has a sea-water pool, two bars and a restaurant. Singles/doubles cost 15,000/17,500 dr.

AROUND THE ISLAND

A visit to the 11th-century **Moni Hozoviotissas** is unreservedly worthwhile, as

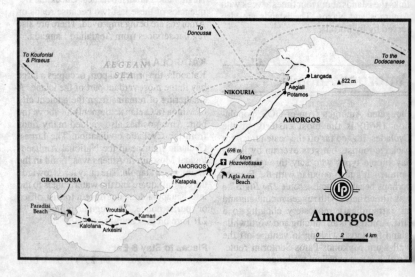

much for the spectacular scenery as for the monastery itself. The dazzling white building clings precariously to a cliff face above the east coast. A few monks still live there and one will show you around. The monastery opens at 8 am, closes at 1 pm and reopens at 5 pm, but visit early (in modest dress) or you'll miss the last bus back to Aegiali. The contents include a miracle-working icon, found in the sea below the monastery – allegedly having arrived there unaided from Asia Minor, Cyprus or Jerusalem, depending on which legend you're told. It's a splendid walk to the monastery from Amorgos town, or you can take a bus.

Pebbled **Agia Anna beach**, on the east coast south of Moni Hozoviotissas, is the nearest decent beach to both Katapola and Amorgos town. It has no facilities so take water and food. **Paradisi**, on the west coast, is a delightful, unspoilt beach. **Langada** is the most picturesque of the villages inland from Aegiali – well worth a morning's respite from the beach to explore.

Paros & Antiparos
Πάρος & Αντίπαρος

PAROS

Paros (PA-ros, population 12,000) is an attractive island, with softly contoured, terraced hills of vineyards, fruit trees and olive groves, culminating in Mt Profitis Ilias (770 metres). It is popular with backpackers and other tourists who crave style and can't afford Mykonos.

Paros is famous for its pure white marble – the Venus de Milo was created from it. Parian marble ensured the island prospered from the Early Cycladic age onwards. Trading in marble flourished during the Hellenic and Roman periods and it was occasionally used later – Napoleon's tomb is a Parian marble creation.

The island of Antiparos lies one km south-west of Paros.

Getting There & Away
Air At least eight flights daily depart for Athens (16,000 dr). The Olympic Airways office (☎ 21 900) in Paroikia is on the right side of Propona as you come from the waterfront. The airport is on the island's south-west side and served by buses to and from Aliki.

Ferry Paros is the ferry hub of the Cyclades with daily connections to Piraeus (five hours, 3300 dr), Naxos (1300 dr), Ios (2300 dr) Santorini (1500 dr), Mykonos (1550 dr) and Sifnos (2000 dr); almost daily with Syros (1300 dr), Amorgos, (2400 dr), Ikaria and Samos; and at least two a week with Sikinos (1700 dr), and Folegandros (1600 dr). The port police (☎ 21 240) are back from the northern waterfront, near the post office.

Hydrofoil There are hydrofoils every day to Naxos, Ios, Santorini, Mykonos and Tinos; continuing to Rafina three to four times weekly. There are three services a week to Syros; two to Amorgos, Iraklia, Koufonisi and Shinoussa; and one a week to Andros, Serifos and Sifnos.

Getting Around
Bus There are frequent buses from the bus station in Paroikia to Dryos (for Hrysi Akti) via Lefkes and Marpissa; Naoussa; Pounta (for Antiparos); and Aliki (for Petaloudes and the airport).

Car, Motorbike & Bicycle Parai Rent-a-Car-Motorbike (☎ 21 1771), south along the waterfront in Paroikia, rents cars, motorbikes and bicycles as well as tandem bikes. Paros Rent-a-Car (☎ 21 952) is north of the quay.

Taxi Boat Taxi boats leave from the quay at Paroikia for Antiparos and beaches around Paros.

Paroikia Παροικία
The island's capital and port is Paroikia. The waterfront conceals an attractive and typically Cycladic old quarter.

Orientation & Information The central square is straight ahead from the quay. The road on the left leads to the northern waterfront, which has modern hotels. The bus station is 50 metres left of the quay. The post office is further along on the right. Paros' postcode is 844 00.

On the left, heading inland from the quay, Propona leads to the famous Church of Ekatontapyliani. The road right of the quay follows the south-west waterfront, which is lined with cafés (and is a pedestrian precinct in high season). The OTE is on the southern waterfront. Paros' telephone code is 0284. The National Bank of Greece and the Commercial Bank of Greece are both on the central square. The street between these banks is the main thoroughfare of the old town. The regular police (☎ 23 333) are on the central square. North and south-west waterfronts are skirted by beaches.

Information and accommodation is offered by the Rooms Association located beyond the windmill (the former tourist office) at the port exit to the right (see Places to Stay).

Church of Ekatontapyliani (Our Lady of the Hundred Gates) This church is the most splendid in the Cyclades. The building is actually three distinct churches. Agios Nikolaos, the largest, is in the east of the compound with lovely columns of Parian marble and carved iconostasis. The others are the Church of Our Lady and the Baptistery. Only 99 doors have been counted. It is

said that when the 100th is found, İstanbul will return to Greece. Opening times are from 8 am to 1 pm and 4 to 9 pm.

Archaeological Museum This museum is behind the Church of the Ekatontapyliani, next to a school. It has some interesting reliefs and statues, but the most important exhibit is a fragment of the 3rd-century Parian Chronicle which lists the most outstanding artistic achievements of ancient Greece. It was discovered in the 17th century by the Duke of Arundel's cleric, and most of it ended up in the Ashmolean Museum, Oxford. The museum is open daily, except Monday and public holidays, from 8.30 am to 2.30 pm. Admission is 500 dr.

Archaeological Site On the northern waterfront there is a fenced ancient cemetery dating from the 7th century BC which was excavated in 1985. Roman graves, burial pots and sarcophagi are floodlit at night. Photographs and other finds are exhibited in an attached building but it's rarely open.

Organised Tours Tour agencies, such as Parai Rent-a-Car-Motorbike (see Getting Around), offer excursions around the area including Antiparos.

Places to Stay The nearest camp site to Paroikia is *Camping Koula* (☎ 22 081/082), 500 metres along the northern waterfront. *Parasporos Camping* (☎ 22 268) is two km south of Paroikia and has a minibus which

---

Architectural Animosity

Legend has it that St Helen, mother of Constantine the Great, had a vision of the True Cross whilst praying in a small church where the Ekatontapyliani now stands. She promised to build a magnificent church on the site, but died before fulfilling this promise.

Emperor Justinian authorised the construction of the church in the 6th century, commissioning Ignatius, an apprentice of Isidore of Miletus (architect of the Hagia Sophia in Constantinople), to design and build the church with Isidore acting as supervisor. The end product turned out to be so magnificent that Isidore was overcome with jealousy and pushed Ignatius off the roof; the tenacious Ignatius hung on to him, however, and the two fell to their deaths. A frieze depicting this sorry tale can be seen in the church's courtyard. ■

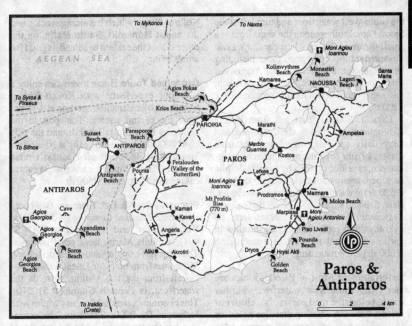

meets boats. *Krios Camping* (☎ 21 705) is on Krios beach opposite the port – take a taxi boat from Paroikia.

Across from the white windmill in front of the quay is the Rooms Association (☎ 24 528) which has information on domatia, hotels and gives out a map. For hotel details alone, call ☎ 24 555.

The D-class *Hotel Kypreou* (☎ 21 383), on Propona, has comfortable singles/doubles/triples with bathroom for 8000/10,000/12,000 dr. At the sparkling and friendly *Nikos Kypreos Apartments* (☎ 24 609) nearby, rates are 10,000/12,000/15,000 dr for doubles/triples/quads.

Mimikos Rooms (☎ 21 437) have been popular with backpackers for years. Rates are 7500/9000 dr for doubles/triples. Walk into the old town, veer left and follow the signs to Tamariska Garden Restaurant adjacent to the rooms.

The D-class *Hotel Kontes* (☎ 21 096), off the main square has nice doubles/triples for 9000/12,000 dr with bathroom. *Icarus Rooms* (☎ 21 695) has spotless doubles/triples for 11,000/13,300 dr. Walk along the northern waterfront and turn right at the Asterias Hotel. The *Hotel Stella* (☎ 21 502), 130 metres beyond the archaeological site, has doubles for 13,000 dr with bathroom.

The C-class *Hotel Argonauta* (☎ 21 440), above the Commercial Bank of Greece, has lovely doubles/triples with en suite for 14,000/16,000 dr.

The superior A-class *Yria Hotel Bungalows* (☎ 24 154/158), 2.5 km south of Paroikia, overlooking pretty Parasporos beach, has a restaurant, bar, pool and watersports. Open from April to October, it offers singles/doubles for 22,400/26,800 dr (6900 dr for an extra bed). There are also maisonettes. Take the Pounta or Aliki bus from the port and ask to be dropped off.

Places to Eat Vegetarians will find a good range of food at the *Stafedo Café*; walk along the south-west waterfront and turn left at the Salon Dior. Further along the waterfront is a small square on the left where the *Corfo Leon Restaurant* turns out a good meal, including beverage, for about 2000 dr. *Restaurant Poseidon*, signposted off the northern beach, has super staples (including kokoretsi) for 1200 dr.

Parikia Taverna, first left from Plateia Ekatontapyliani has modestly priced and tasty daily specials, including vegetarian dishes. *I Trata Taverna*, near the archaeological site, is seldom visited by tourists despite its superb seafood, not least shrimp saganaki (1500 dr) and a stimulating array of mezedes, fresh fish and salads. *Yria Hotel Bungalows' Restaurant* has more up-market fare. Its xynomyzithra (soft cheese), mushrooms in garlic sauce, and mussels as a main dish (1800 dr) are outstanding.

Entertainment Most of Paroikia's bars are along the south-west waterfront. Further south, before the road curves, is a cluster of rowdy discos. A warning that also holds for Ios and, to a lesser extent, Amorgos, is to avoid bars offering very cheap cocktails which can get players into peril. Paroikia's cinemas are *Cine Paros* back from the northern waterfront and *Cinema Rex*, on the right hand side off the road to Pounta.

Naoussa Νάουσσα
Naoussa, on the north coast, has metamorphosed from pristine fishing village to popular tourist hang-out. It's still a working harbour with piles of yellow fishing nets, brightly coloured caïques, and little ouzeria with rickety tables and raffia chairs. Behind the central square (where the bus terminates) it is a picturesque white village, with the surface of its narrow alleyways whitewashed with fish and flower motifs.

The post office is a tedious uphill walk from the central square. To the left of the harbour, domatia and posh apartment blocks have mushroomed. Despite an incursion by package tourists, Naoussa remains relaxed and its huge serrated bay has good beaches, served by taxi boats. The best beaches are

Kolimvythres, which has strange rocks, and the nudist **Monastiri**. **Santa Maria**, on the other side of the eastern headland, is good for windsurfing.

Organised Tours Horse lovers can enjoy a two-hour experience with Kokou Riding Center led by a Canadian, starting at 4.15 pm from the central square. Transport to the centre by the coast is 1000 dr, and the ride costs 7000 dr. Book with Cathy at Nissiotissa Tours (☎ 51 480), left off Naoussa's main square. The company can also organise caïque fishing trips for 2500 dr.

Places to Stay & Eat There are two camp sites. Both *Naoussa Camping* (☎ 51 398), at Kolimvythres, and *Surfing Beach* (☎ 52 491), at Santa Maria, have good facilities. The latter has a surfing and water-ski school. Minibuses from both sites meet ferries.

Left from the bus station, towards the waterfront, is *Pension Galini* (☎ 51 210). This charming place has doubles/triples with bathroom for 9000/13,000 dr. The owner also has the attractive *Spiros Apartments* at Kolimvythres beach, which cost 10,000 dr for a double.

The E-class *Hotel Madaky* (☎ 51 475), off the central square, has pleasant doubles/triples for 6100/7100 dr with shared bathroom and singles/doubles with private bathroom for 9300/10,500 dr. In the heart of Naoussa town the *Pension Stella* (☎ 51 317) has doubles with en suite for 10,800 dr. To reach it, turn left from the central square at Café Naoussa, then first right. It's past a small church on the left.

Limanaki Taverna, at the harbour, across from the National Bank, serves good fish. A meal with retsina is about 2500 dr. From the bus stop and square, take the first left towards the sea for the *Taverna Ouzeri Asteria* – the first restaurant established on Paros. It's cheap and authentic – meat balls cost 750 dr, lamb tongues are 800 dr, fried cheese is 450 dr and a Greek salad costs 700 dr. Allegedly a male aphrodisiac and hangover cure, a big serving of peppered meat is 1000 dr.

Around the Island

Marathi (Μαράθι) In ancient times, Parian marble was considered the world's finest. The **marble quarries** have been abandoned, but it's exciting to explore the three shafts by torchlight. Take the Lefkes bus and get off at Marathi village, where you'll find a signpost to the quarries.

Lefkes to Moni Agiou Antoniou Lefkes (Λεύκες), 12 km south-east of Paroikia, is the island's highest and loveliest village. It boasts the magnificent **Agias Trias cathedral**, as well as the **Museum of Popular Aegean Civilisation** (open in summer), an amphitheatre and an interesting library. The only accommodation is at the superior *Xenia-Lefkon Pension* (☎ 41 846) with appropriate B-class prices. In the Middle Ages, Lefkes was the island's capital. In its central square, a signpost points to a well-preserved Byzantine paved path which leads to the village of **Prodromos**. The walk takes about an hour through beautiful countryside.

From Prodromos, it's a short walk to either **Marmara** or **Marpissa**; from Marmara, it's a stroll to the sandy beach at **Molos**. From Marpissa you can puff your way up a steep paved path to the 16th-century **Moni Agiou Antoniou** atop a 200-metre-high hill. On this fortified summit, Paros' Venetian rulers were defeated by the Turks in 1537. Although the monastery and its grounds are usually locked, there are breathtaking views to neighbouring Naxos. After this exertion, you'll probably feel like having a swim at the nearby east-coast resort of **Piso Livadi**.

Petaloudes (Valley of the Butterflies) In summer, butterflies almost enshroud the copious foliage at Petaloudes (Πεταλούδες), eight km south of Paroikia. The butterflies are actually tiger moths, but spectacular all the same. Travel agents organise tours from Paroikia (1500 dr) and Naoussa (2000 dr), including excursions on donkeys. Otherwise, take the Aliki bus and ask to be let off at the turn-off for Petaloudes. Petaloudes is open in July and August from Monday to Saturday (9 am to 8 pm) and on Sunday

(9 am to 1 pm and 4 to 8 pm). Admission is 500 dr. If you continue to Aliki, ask the driver to stop at the **folkloric museum**, near the airport, if it appears to be open.

Beaches

Apart from the beaches already mentioned, there is a good beach at **Krios**, which is accessible by taxi boat (500 dr) from the capital. Paros' longest beach is **Hrysi Akti** (Golden beach), on the south-east coast, is popular with windsurfers. Domatia and hotels are abundant.

ANTIPAROS

Antiparos was once regarded as the quiet alternative to Paros, but development is on the increase. A permanent population of 900 lives in an attractive village (also called Antiparos), but it's hidden by all the tourist accommodation.

Orientation & Information

To reach the village centre, turn right from the quay, walk along the waterfront and turn left into the main street at the yellow ochre periptero. The post office is on the left. Antiparos' postcode is 840 07. At the top of the main street, turn left for the central square. The OTE, with currency exchange and ferry information, is just beyond, Antiparos' telephone code is 0284. There is a good bookshop and laundrette on the main street.

To reach the **kastro**, another Marco Sanudo creation, turn right at the central square and go under the stone arch. Beach bums will direct you to the island's decent beaches. Nudism is only permitted on the camp-site beach.

Cave of Antiparos

Despite previous looting of stalactites and stalagmites, the cave is still awe-inspiring. In 1673, the French ambassador Marquis de Nointel organised for Christmas Mass (enhanced by a large orchestra) to be held in the cave for 500 Parians.

The cave is open daily from 10 am to 4 pm. Admission is 500 dr. Frequent buses from the village of Antiparos go to the cave or you can take an excursion boat in summer from Antiparos village, Paroikia or Pounta. From the landing stage, it's a steep 30-minute walk – or donkey ride.

Places to Stay

The island's well-equipped camp site, *Camping Antiparos* (☎ 61 221), is on a beach 800 metres north of the quay. Signs point the way.

Domatia are prevalent and there are several hotels. Turn right from the port for the D-class *Hotel Anarghyros* (☎ 61 204) on the left. Rates are 5000/8000 dr for singles/doubles with bathroom. The renovated *Hotel Mantalena* (☎ 61 206/365) is further along. Doubles/triples with bathroom are 10,000/12,000 dr. Next door, the new *Antiparos Studios* (same telephone) charge 8,000/10,000/13,000 dr for doubles/triples/quads.

Places to Eat

The main street has many cafés. The popular *Taverna Giorgos*, on the right, serves Greek family staples, specialising in fish. Turn left at the top of the main road for *Marios Taverna* on the right. Fresh calamari is about 900 dr. Agios Georgios, in the south, has several tavernas.

Getting There & Around

In summer, frequent excursion boats depart from Paroikia on Paros for Antiparos. The trip takes 45 minutes and costs 410 dr. There is also a half-hourly car ferry from Pounta on the west coast of Paros to Antiparos (15 minutes, 150 dr; car extra). The only bus service on Antiparos runs to the cave in the centre of the island. In summer, this bus continues to Agios Georgios. Captain Yannis runs caïque trips to secluded beaches. They cost 10,000 dr for up to six people. Ask for the friendly captain at Smiles Café on the main square in Antiparos village or at the port.

Ios Ιος

Ios (EE-os, population 2300) is been regarded as the *enfant terrible* of the Greek islands, the apogee of sun, sand, sea and sex. Non-ragers should avoid the 'village' (Ios town) from June to September.

However, Ios is working hard to clean up its image. Travel agents at the port offer free luggage storage to prevent backpacks from littering the area and free use of safes to reduce thefts.

It's not only young hedonists who holiday on Ios. It's also popular with the older set – anyone over 25 – but the two groups tend to be polarised; the young staying in the village and others at Gialos port. Ios has a tenuous claims to being Homer's burial place. His tomb is supposedly in the island's north although no-one seems to know exactly where.

Getting There & Away

Ferry There are daily ferry connections with Piraeus (7½ to 9 hours, 4700 dr), Paros (2300 dr), Naxos (2000 dr), Mykonos (2700 dr) and Santorini (2400 dr). There are at least four connections a week with Sikinos and Folegandros, and two a week with Iraklio (Crete). The port police (☎ 91 264) are at the southern end of the waterfront in Gialos, just before the camp site.

Hydrofoil There are daily hydrofoil connections to Mykonos, Naxos, Paros and Santorini, as well as five a week to Rafina, three to Syros and occasional services to smaller islands.

Getting Around

In summer, crowded buses run the Gialos-Ios town-Milopotas beach route about every 15 minutes. Gialos and Ios town each have one car and motorbike-rental firm. See the warning in the Around the Island section.

GIALOS, IOS TOWN & MILOPOTAS BEACH

The capital, Ios town (the village) is two km inland from the port of Gialos. (Γυαλός). Milopotas beach (Μυλοπότας) is one km east of here. Gialos beach, at the port, is quite nice. To get there, turn left at the quay. Koumbara beach, a 20-minute walk west of Gialos, is less crowded and mainly nudist. Milopotas is a superb long curving sand beach, offering windsurfing and other water sports.

Orientation & Information

The bus terminal in Gialos is straight ahead from the ferry quay on Plateia Emirou. If you want to walk from Gialos to Ios town, turn left from Plateia Emirou, then immediately right and you'll see the stepped path leading up to the right after about 100 metres. The walk takes about 30 minutes.

The church is the main landmark in Ios town. It's uphill from the bus stop to the left. The National Bank of Greece is behind the church. To get to the post office from the church, turn right into one of the town's main thoroughfares, pass the Ios bakery, and take the second turn left. Ios' postcode is 840 01.

Continue along the main road and turn left at the junction to reach the central square of Plateia Valeta. The road straight ahead from the bus stop leads to Milopotas beach.

Ios town's OTE is signposted one street before the bus station, on the road from Gialos. It's a difficult uphill walk. The office is open from 7.30 am to 3.10 pm, closed weekends and holidays. Ios' telephone code is 0286.

In summer, there is a small municipal tourist office to the left of the quay in Gialos. The main office (☎ 91 028) is by the bus stop in Ios town. Plakiotis Travel (☎ 91 277), straight ahead from the quay, is very helpful.

American Express is represented in Gialos by Acteon Travel (☎ 91 318) on the main square. At the time of writing, a hospital was being built at the port. There is an emergency physician (☎ 91 545) in Ios town.

Places to Stay – bottom end

Ios Camping (☎ 91 329) in Gialos is reached by turning right at Plateia Emirou and walking along the waterfront. There are three camp sites on Milopotas beach: *Stars* (☎ 91 302), *Kostas Camping* (☎ 91 554) and the outstanding *Far Out Camping* (☎ 91 468/ 446), which has a restaurant, bar and swimming pool as well as volleyball, basketball and tennis courts. There's also a diving centre, water-skiing and sailboard hire. Charges are 1200 dr per person a site, and tent hire is 400 dr. New bungalows cost 4000/6000 dr for doubles/triples. Far Out has a minibus service to Ios town and Gialos.

In Gialos, domatia signs welcome you at the quay. Straight ahead from the quay are *Zorba's Rooms* (☎ 91 871), with friendly owners, neat rooms and a nice courtyard. Singles/doubles/triples with shared facilities are 3500/7000/8500 dr, or 4500/9000/ 11,000 dr with bathroom. *Irene Rooms* (☎ 91 023), signposted nearby, has balconied doubles/triples with en suite for 10,000/ 13,000 dr. The C-class *Hotel Poseidon* (☎ 91 091) has doubles/triples for 11,800/14,200 dr. From the waterfront, turn left at the Enigma Bar and climb the steps on the left. The *Golden Sun* (☎ 91 110), at the first bus

CYCLADES

stop on the road to Ios, has immaculate units complete with bath and views for 7000/9000/12,000 dr.

The best views in Ios town are from *Francesco's* (☎ 91 223), a well-restored 300-year-old house with bar and terrace. It's a lively meeting place. A dorm bed is 1900 dr, and doubles/triples with shared facilities are 4000/5500 dr, or 5000/7000 dr with private bathroom. Port transfers are free. Call from the port if the van is not there.

There are lots of domatia signs on the route towards Milopotas beach from the Ios town bus stop. *Hermes Rooms* (☎ 91 471) on the right, halfway between Ios town and the beach, charges 10,000/15,000 dr for doubles/triples with bathroom. Further along is *Petradi Rooms* (☎ 91 510), offering fine doubles/triples/quads with balcony and bathroom for 6000/7500/8500 dr. There is a bar/restaurant and a terrace with views of Milopotas beach and Santorini.

Places to Stay – middle & top end

The lovely *Far Out Hotel* (☎ 91 446/468), on the left between Ios town and Milopotas beach, is a cluster of traditional-style, white buildings with pool. Doubles/triples are 16,300/20,100 dr with air-con. The plush B-class *Ios Palace* (☎ 91 269/224), at the end of Milopotas beach closest to Ios town, has singles/doubles/triples for 15,800/19,000/21,000 dr.

Places to Eat

The *Restaurant Psarades* at Gialos has excellent fish dishes from 1000 dr. If you're into salingari (snails) or fish, try the reasonably priced *Ouzeri 33* on the waterfront. The *Talisman Restaurant* on the square offers international and Mexican cuisine.

In Ios town, *Zorba's Restaurant* is good value and friendly. *Pithari Taverna*, behind the large church, serves low-priced traditional Greek fare. Italian foodies choose *Pinocchios*, where pizzas start at 1800 dr. Look for the signs and Pinocchio standing outside.

Restaurant Polydoros on Koumbara beach is popular. *Andoni's Restaurant &* *Rooms*, at Manganari beach, serves the world's best myzithra (soft ewe's milk cheese), fabulous fish and grills.

Entertainment

The party crowd reckons the port is dull, while the older set think Ios town is crazy; so take your pick. At the port, the *Frog Club*, near Plateia Emirou is for all ages, as is the *Enigma Cocktail Bar* on the waterfront. The *Marina Bar*, overlooking Gialos beach, plays Greek music.

The scene in Ios town is so busy that it can take 30 minutes to squeeze through the tiny central square. Nearby, the *Blue Note Bar* is noisy, sociable and fun, while the *Kahlua Bar* is cosy. The *Dubliner Disco*, up from the bus stop, is a huge pub with reasonably priced imported drinks. At the *Ios Club*, you can listen to classical music at sunset – after the sun goes down the club becomes a disco. From the town bus stop, face the port and turn left at the *Sweet Irish Dream* bar where dancers take to the tables some nights. Other action places include the wild *Slammer Bar* and *Scorpion's Nightclub*, on the Milopotas road, which plays less frenetic dance music.

Warning There are signs posted around Ios town warning against alcohol abuse. The cheap locally brewed hooch used in mixed drinks and cocktails is bad news, particularly for the unwary. Beware of free shots. They may lead to fast intoxication, reckless spending and alcohol poisoning.

AROUND THE ISLAND

The beaches and nightlife are what lure travellers to Ios. From Gialos, it's 10 minutes' walk to Agia Irini for **Valmas beach. Psathi beach** on the north-east coast and **Kolitzani beach**, to the right of Ios town, down steps by the Scorpion Club, are popular.

Vying with **Milopotas** for best beach is **Manganari**, on the south coast, reached by excursion boats in summer from Gialos or by bus. There are domatia, including *Andoni's* (☎ 91 483), where doubles/triples are 7000/9000 dr. On the way to the beach is **Moni Kalamou**, which stages a religious festival in late August and a festival of music and dance on 7 September.

Agia Theodoti beach, on the north-east coast, is more remote. Neither bus nor boat go here, so it's a three-hour trek across the island or a bumpy motorbike ride. Windsurfing equipment is available for hire at many beaches, including Gialos beach.

Warning

Roads on the island are rough and steep. Don't hire an underpowered motorbike or attempt to ride on unsealed roads unless you are experienced.

Folegandros
Φολέγανδρος

The happiest man on earth is the man with fewest needs. And I also believe that if you have light, such as you have here, all ugliness is obliterated.
Henry Miller

Folegandros (Fo-LE-gan-dros, population 700) is one of Greece's most enticing islands, bridging the gap between tourist traps and small depopulated islands on the brink of total abandonment. The number of visitors is increasing, but most locals still make their living from fishing and farming.

Folegandros' tourists tend to come in search of unspoiled island life and, except for July and August, the island is uncrowded and blissful. The island has several good beaches – be prepared for strenuous walking to reach some of them – and a striking landscape of cultivated terraces which gives way to precipitous cliffs.

Courses

The Cycladic School (founded on Folegandros in 1984) offers courses in drawing, painting, Greek cookery, folk dancing and hatha yoga. For further details, contact Anne and Fotis Papadopoulos (☎ 41 137), Karavostasis 840 11.

Organised Tours

In summer, Sottovento Tourism Office operates day trips by caïque to hidden bays and the little-known **Hrysospilia caves** on the east coast, plus full island tours by bus. Commentaries are in English and Italian.

Getting There & Away

There are five ferries a week from Folegandros to Piraeus (nine to 10 hours, 4500 dr), Ios, Santorini and Sikinos. About three a week go to Paros (1600 dr), Milos, Sifnos and Serifos; and two a week to Naxos.

Getting Around

The local bus meets all boats and travels frequently between the hora and Ano Meria, stopping at the road leading to Angali beach. There are no taxis on the island. In summer, daily excursion boats leave Karavostasis for Angali, Agios Nikolaos and Livadaki beaches.

KARAVOSTASIS Καραβοστάσις

All boats dock at the small harbour of Karavostasis, on the east coast. The capital is the concealed cliff-top hora, four km inland. The only other settlement is Ano Meria, four km north-west of the hora.

Places to Stay

Camping Livadi (☎ 41 204) is at Livadi beach, one km from Karavostasis. Turn left on to the cement road skirting Karavostasis beach. It's 700 dr per person and 400 dr for tent hire.

Karavostasis has several domatia and hotels – look for the signs when you get off the ferry. The C-class *Aeolos Beach Hotel* (☎ 41 205), on the beach, has immaculate singles/doubles with bathroom for 6000/9000 dr and suites for 14,000 dr.

THE HORA Χώρα

The captivating hora is perhaps the most beautiful island capital in the Cyclades.

Orientation & Information

From the bus turnaround, facing away from the port, turn left and follow the curving road. An archway on the right leads into the kastro, the walls of which have been incorporated into dwellings. A left turn leads to three shady squares in a row. The third is the central plateia. The post office is on the left before the village on the road from the port. An OTE at this location was being planned at the time of writing. The first square has a public telephone. Folegandros' postcode is 840 11. The telephone code is 0286.

There is no bank, but Maraki Travel (☎ 41 273), by the first square, exchanges currency and sells ferry tickets, as does Sottovento Tourism Office (☎ 41 430). The office is left from the post office as you approach the hora – by the bus stop for Ano Meria and Angali.

Folegandros doesn't have an EOT or tourist police. The regular police (☎ 41 249) are west of the central plateia.

Things to See

The hora is an archetypal Cycladic village of aspirin-white churches and sugar-cube houses. The medieval **kastro**, a tangle of narrow streets, spanned by archways, dates from when Marco Sanudo ruled the island in the 13th century. The houses' wooden balconies are ablaze with bougainvillea, azaleas and hibiscus; and their external staircases are bedecked with potted geraniums and dozing cats.

The newer village, outside kastro, is just as pretty. On its first square are water troughs where donkeys drink. On the next square, the white circle painted on the ground is an old threshing floor. From the first bus stop, a steep path leads to the **Church of the Panagia**. The views are splendid.

Places to Stay

Pavlos' Rooms (☎ 41 232) are comfortable, converted stables on the main road, five minutes' walk uphill from the village. Rooms are 8000 dr a double with shared facilities and 10,000 dr with bathroom, both with breakfast. Rooftop sleeping space is

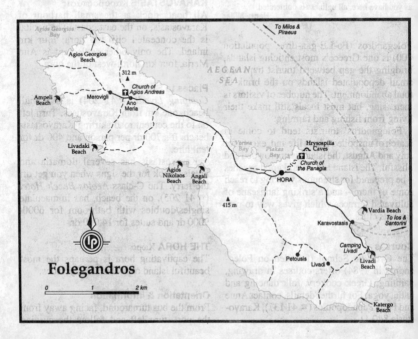

Folegandros

available in summer if there are no rooms. A bus meets boats.

There are reasonably priced domatia near the police station. The atmospheric, renovated *Hotel Kastro Danassis* (☎ 41 414) has doubles/triples with en suite for 13,000/ 17,000 dr. To get there, walk straight ahead from the entrance to the kastro and you'll find the hotel on the left. *Nikos Rooms* (☎ 41 055) has clean doubles with kitchen and bath for 10,000 dr. Turn right at Taverna Platinis on the central square. The rooms are on the right.

The C-class *Folegandros*, where the port bus terminates, has large, well-equipped apartments priced from 16,500 dr for two people. Views don't come any better than from the top-of-the-range *Anemomilos Apartments* (☎ 41 309), by the bus station. They are built in traditional Cycladic style and furnished with pottery and antiques. There is one unit for the disabled. Rates for doubles/triples/quads are 20,000/24,000/ 29,000 dr.

Places to Eat

Ouzeri Folegandros is a lively place on the central square with good mains for about 2000 dr. Prices are similar at *Taverna Nikos*, near the police station. The *Piatsa Restaurant* is the best on the island and has a small but exciting menu of daily specials such as tomato and cheese in filo with thick sauce for 800 dr. There are other vegetarian dishes and, in season, game. The restaurant is on the second square past the kastro.

Entertainment

The hora may be traditional but the Folegandriots are not killjoys. Signs in town point to music bars, including a new one next to the Sottovento Tourist Office. Karavostasis has two bars.

AROUND THE ISLAND

Ano Meria Ανω Μεριά

The settlement of Ano Meria stretches for several km. The reason for this is that while northern Folegandros is more fertile, its open landscape was too vulnerable to pirate raids.

When these threats ceased, people moved north to better farmland. Most dwellings today are surrounded by small farms. A walk from the hora to Ano Meria is rewarded by stunning sea and cliff vistas. Visit the **folkloric museum** for 400 dr. The bus fare between the two settlements is 200 dr.

Places to Stay Ano Meria has tavernas but no hotels. Ask at a kafeneio about *domatia* in family homes.

Beaches

Karavostasis has a pebbled beach (nudist and mixed). For **Livadi beach**, follow the signs for Camping Livadi. The sandy and pebbled **Angali beach**, has a lovely aspect but was in need of a clean-up at the time of writing. It has domatia and tavernas. There are other good beaches at **Agios Nikolaos** and **Livadaki**, both west of Angali. The steep path to the beach at Agios Nikolaos is only for those with strong boots and a head for heights. **Agios Georgios** is north-west of Ano Meria. A path from Ano Meria's Church of Agios Andreas leads to Agios Georgios beach. The walk takes about an hour.

Sikinos Σίκινος

For years, the neighbouring islands of Sikinos (SIK-in-os, population 390) and Folegandros were regarded as remote unspoilt islands. But while Folegandros has taken off (in the nicest way) and is now on the tourist map, Sikinos remains a backwater. Perhaps Folegandros has the edge over Sikinos, with a more dramatic landscape, better beaches and a prettier capital. If, however, a quiet unspoilt island is what you're looking for, Sikinos is a better choice.

The port of Alópronia, and the capital, Sikinos town, are the only settlements – although Sikinos town comprises the contiguous villages of the hora and the kastro. The fortified **Moni Zoödohou Pigis** stands on a hill above the town.

The town has a combined post office and

OTE. The postcode is 840 10 and the telephone code is 0286. Alopronia and Sikinos town have domatia and tavernas with basic low-priced fare. Alopronia also has the stylish B-class *Porto Sikinos* (☎ 51 220; fax 51 220) on the beach. Rates for doubles with bathroom are 10,000 dr. This establishment is in traditional Cycladic style with a bar and restaurant.

Sikinos' main excursion is a one-hour scenic trek south-west from town to Episkopi. When ruins there were investigated by 19th-century archaeologists, the Doric columns and inscriptions led them to believe it had originally been a shrine to Apollo. But remains are now believed to be those of a 3rd-century AD mausoleum. In the 7th century, the ruins were transformed into a church. In the 17th century, the church was greatly extended to become Moni Episkopis. The church and monastery are no longer used.

Getting There & Around

Sikinos has a similar ferry schedule to Folegandros. The local bus meets all ferries and makes several trips a day between Alopronia and Sikinos town.

Santorini (Thira)
Σαντορίνη (Θήρα)

Santorini (Santor-REE-nee, population 8000), also known as Thira, is regarded by many as the most spectacular of all the Greek islands. Thousands visit yearly to gaze in wonder at the caldera, a vestige of what was probably the biggest volcanic eruption in recorded history. Santorini is unique and should not be missed, although it gets crowded and is overly commercial.

Santorini's main port is Athinios. It's a functional place with a few eateries but no settlement as such. Buses meet all ferries and whisk passengers to Fira, the capital, which teeters on the lip of the caldera, high above the sea.

History

Dorians, Byzantines and Turks occupied Santorini, as they did all other Cycladic islands, but its first inhabitants were the Minoans. Its geological peculiarities make it unique. Greece is susceptible to eruptions and earthquakes – mostly minor, but on Santorini the earth movements have been so violent as to change the shape of the island several times.

The Minoans came from Crete in 3000 BC, and their settlement at Akrotiri dates from the height of their great civilisation. The island then was circular and called Stronghyle (the Round One). Around 1450 BC, a colossal volcanic eruption caused the middle of Stronghyle to sink, leaving a caldera with high cliffs – one of the world's most dramatic geological sights. Some archaeologists have speculated that this catastrophe destroyed not only Akrotiri but the whole Minoan civilisation. Another theory firing the imaginations of writers, artists and mystics since ancient times, postulates that the island was part of the mythical lost continent of Atlantis.

Major eruptions and earthquakes occurred in 236 BC, 197 BC (causing Palia Kameni island to appear), 1707 (causing Nea Kameni to appear), 1711, 1866, 1870 and 1925. The last serious earthquake was in 1956, devastating the towns of Fira and Oia.

Getting There & Away

Air There are daily flights to Athens (17,800 dr) and six a week to Mykonos (12,800 dr), as well as three flights a week to Iraklio (13,400 dr) and four flights a week to Rhodes (18,000 dr). The Olympic Airways office (☎ 22 493) is in Fira, on the road to Kamari, one block east of 25 Martiou. There's no airport shuttle bus, but enthusiastic hotel and domatia staff meet planes and some return guests to the airport.

Ferry Santorini has daily connections with Piraeus (nine hours, 4300 dr), Mykonos (2800 dr), Naxos (1600 dr), Paros (1500 dr), Ios (2400 dr) and (with the exception of Friday) Iraklio. There are also about three connections a week with Sikinos and Folegandros; and two a week with Milos, Serifos, Sifnos and Thessaloniki. Daily boats connect the town of Oia to Santorini's satellite island of Thirasia. The port police (☎ 22 239) are on the west side of 25 Martiou, north of Plateia Theotokopoulou.

Hydrofoil There are daily hydrofoils to Ios,

Naxos, Paros, Mykonos and Tinos; five a week to Rafina; two a week to Syros and weekly services to Amorgos, Iraklia, Koufonisi and Shinoussa.

Getting Around

Bus Santorini has a pretty good bus service but vehicles get crowded. In summer they leave Fira's bus station hourly for Akrotiri, Oia and Monolithos; every half-hour for Kamari and every 20 minutes for Perissa. Buses leave Fira, Kamari and Perissa for the port of Athinios 1½ hours before most ferry departures.

Car, Motorbike & Bicycle Fira has many car, motorbike and bicycle-rental firms.

FIRA Φήρα

The commercialism of Fira has not diminished its all-pervasive, dramatic aura. Walk to the edge of the caldera for spectacular

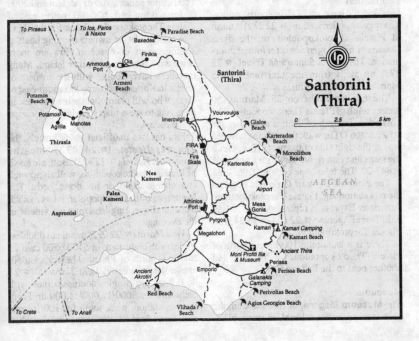

CYCLADES

views of the cliffs with their multicoloured strata of lava and pumice.

Orientation

Fira's central square is Plateia Theotokopoulou. The main road, 25 Martiou, runs north to south, intersecting the square. The main drag is packed with travel agencies.

Facing north on Plateia Theotokopoulou, turn left opposite the Commercial Bank of Greece and then right at the Hotel Tataki to reach Erythrou Stavrou, the main commercial thoroughfare. It's lined with souvenir shops, bars and restaurants. Any left turn will lead to the caldera's edge. A left turn at M Nomikou leads to the cable-car station (signposted) for Fira Skala (the port of Fira used by cruise ships and some excursion boats). Donkeys will also transport you. It costs 700 dr for a one-way donkey ride or cable-car trip, or you can opt to walk down the 600 steps.

Information

Fira doesn't have an EOT or tourist police. The regular police station (☎ 22 239) is north of Plateia Theotokopoulou, on the right. Dozens of travel agencies offer tourist information. The staff at Santorama Travel (☎ 23 177) up steps from the taxi rank on 25 Martiou, are very helpful.

The bus station is on 25 Martiou, 50 metres south of Plateia Theotokopoulou. The post office is north of the bus station on the left. For the OTE, walk through the covered way at the right side of the post office, climb the steps and turn right. Santorini's postcode is 847 00. The telephone code is 0286.

The National Bank of Greece is between the bus station and Plateia Theotokopoulou. American Express is represented by X-Ray Kilo Travel Agency (☎ 22 624 or 23 243) on Plateia Theotokopoulou.

There is a laundrette 100 metres north of Plateia Theotokopoulou, on the left, and another next to the Pelican Hotel.

Museums

The **Museum Megaro**, behind the Catholic monastery, houses local memorabilia,

including fascinating photographs of Fira before and immediately after the major earthquake of 1956. The museum is open daily from 10 am to 1.30 pm and 5 to 8 pm. Entrance is 400 dr.

The **archaeological museum**, opposite the cable-car station, houses finds from Akrotiri and ancient Thira, some Cycladic figurines and Hellenistic and Roman sculpture. It's open Tuesday to Sunday from 8.30 am to 3 pm. Admission is 500 dr.

Organised Tours

Tour agencies operate trips to Thirasia and the nearby so-called 'burnt islands', including Palea Kameni. Reaching its hot springs involves a swim of about 400 metres.

Places to Stay – bottom end

Fira's *Camping Santorini* (☎ 22 944 or 23 203) is a superb site with many facilities, including a restaurant and pool. The cost is 1400 dr per person, 700 dr per tent and 2000 dr for a dorm bed. It's 400 metres east of Plateia Theotokopoulou. Look for the sign.

Accommodation owners meeting boats at Athinios port or buses at Fira are more aggressive than on any other island. Many travellers have trouble with the owners of rooms in Karterados (three km south-east of Fira), who will claim that their rooms are in Fira. Ask to see a map showing the location of the rooms.

Fira has two unofficial youth hostels: the *Kamares Hostel* (☎ 24 472) and the *Kontonari Hostel* (☎ 22 722). Both are north of Plateia Theotokopoulou, well signposted and charge 2000 dr for dorm beds. The Kontonari is the more popular. It has a snack bar and shows English-language videos in the evening.

Villa Maria (☎ 22 092) has clean doubles/triples with bathroom for 5100/6500 dr at 25 Martiou, north of Plateia Theotokopoulou, above the laundrette. *Villa Haroula* (☎ 23 469) has airy singles/doubles/triples with bathroom for 8000/12,000/14,000 dr. From the bus station, walk south for 100 metres, and turn right at the large supermarket.

Before the road narrows, turn right again; the rooms are on the right.

The D-class *Hotel Tataki* (☎ 22 389) has a tranquil flower-filled courtyard. Balconied singles/doubles with en suite are 6400/10,000 dr. If you're facing north on Plateia Theotokopoulou, turn left opposite the Commercial Bank; the hotel is on the left.

Places to Stay – middle & top end

The *Hotel Asimina* (☎ 22 034/989/035) near the cable-car terminus on Erythrou Stavrou, beyond the archaeological museum, has nice singles/doubles/triples with facilities for 9200/13,500/15,700 dr.

The *Locos Hotel* (☎ 22 480), because of its views, charges mid-range rates. Attractive singles/doubles with bathroom and breakfast are 11,000/17,000 dr. Facing north on Plateia Theotokopoulou, turn left after the Commercial Bank, walk past the Hotel Tataki and turn

left. The *Pelican Hotel* (☎ 23 113/114) has comfortable rooms for 18,800/26,500/28,800 dr including breakfast. Facing north, turn right at the Commercial Bank on Plateia Theotokopoulou. The hotel is on the left.

The *Hotel Porto Fira* (☎ 22 849), perched on the caldera's edge, was originally a cave dwelling – some of the walls are made of volcanic rock. It charges 17,500/33,000/38,000 dr for singles/doubles/triples with en suite and there is a good restaurant. The place is open all year.

The *Santorini Palace* (☎ 22 771/781 or 22 868) has a restaurant, bar and pool. Rates are 31,000/41,400/47,200 dr for singles/doubles/triples.

Places to Eat

Fira has many tourist-trap eateries. *Nikolas Taverna*, on Erythrou Stavrou, serves good traditional fare. The *Delphi Garden* is

---

The Cats of Greece

Cats are everywhere in Greece: stalking plump pigeons around Athens' parliament house; congregating under restaurant tables in the hope of scavenging scraps; and looking cute on tourist-geared calendars and postcards. Most of the cats are strays, but sometimes you'll see a domestic cat – sporting a collar and bell – out hunting with them.

Greece is swarming with cats because of the high cost of desexing them. Even the most responsible owner will allow a female cat to produce litter after litter because the expense of having her spayed is prohibitive.

Although Greeks recognise that the mighty cat population keeps the rodent numbers down, the cats are still regarded as a major problem. To keep them at bay, some restaurateurs display signs requesting that patrons do not feed the cats. Other restaurant owners will discourage cats from bothering diners by feeding them leftovers themselves.

Travellers should take care when feeding the cats – although many of them are friendly, hunger can make them snatch at food with their paws, sometimes scratching or puncturing the skin. And people with a phobia about cats may feel very uneasy in a country which has so many!

Whatever Greeks and tourists feel about the cats, the population is likely to increase until the cost of desexing comes down. ∎

another pleasant place; turn right at the Commercial Bank and it's on the right. The *Koutouki Restaurant* specialises in grills. It's set back from the road on the left of 25 Martiou, north of Plateia Theotokopoulou. *Nefeli Restaurant*, east of the taxi rank, has quality staples such as moussaka for 800 dr and calamari for 600 dr.

The superior *Meridiana Restaurant* with both caldera and ocean views is the place for a treat. It specialises in Thai food as well as island dishes based on local baby tomatoes. Its filling cassoulet baked in clay pots is 2900 dr and tomato soup is 900 dr. The restaurant, on the next small square north of Santorama Travel and off 25 Martiou, also sells handmade ceramics and jewellery, with proceeds going to desex the island's rampant cat population.

Opposite, *Barbara's Salad Bar* has excellent pizzas priced from 1900 dr. The *Café Sante*, near the OTE, is the place to drop by for everything from a breakfast buffet to evening coffee and cake. There's soft soul music and a fire in winter.

Entertainment

The *Tithora Club* (on the steps towards Fira Skala) is a disco with a fountain in its cave interior. At sunset, sip pricey cocktails to classical music at *Franco's Bar*, opposite the archaeological museum. Continue downhill and veer right for the *Eternity Bar* and jazz. Greek music can be found at the *Apocalypse Club* signposted on the left of 25 Martiou, north of Plateia Theotokopoulou. Other bars worth trying are *Stelio's Place*, *Kira Thira Jazz Bar*, *Selene*, *Alexandria* and *Bonjour Café*.

There are four commercial wineries holding tastings in August, and a folkloric festival takes place at Canava Roussos Winery, near Kamari, around this time.

AROUND THE ISLAND

Karterados Καρτεράδος

Karterados is a pleasant village with cheaper accommodation than Fira, providing you don't mind the 20-minute walk to town.

Places to Stay *Stavros Filitsis* (☎ 23 720), at the Taverna Neraïda, has 65 rooms to choose from. Prices start at 2500/5000/6200 dr for singles/doubles/triples with shared facilities and 3500/7000/8200 dr with bathroom. Two-person apartments at a nearby beach are 10,000 to 12,000 dr. To find the Taverna Neraïda, turn left off the main approach road from Fira, and it's the last in a row of tavernas on the left.

The very comfortable *Pension George* (☎ 22 351) is owned by George and his English wife, Helen. It has singles for 10,000 dr and doubles for 14,000 dr, both with private facilities. George will collect guests from Fira, ferries or the airport if phoned. Otherwise, walk or take a bus to the village turn-off. Follow the road and turn right after a church on your left. The pension is cloaked in bougainvillea on the left.

Ancient Akrotiri Παλαιό Ακρωτήρι

Ancient Akrotiri was a Minoan outpost. Excavations were begun in 1967 by the late Professor Spyridon Marinatos, who was killed at the site in 1974. The dig uncovered an ancient city beneath the volcanic ash – the Aegean's best-preserved prehistoric settlement. Buildings, some three storeys high, date to the late 16th century BC. The absence of skeletons or treasures indicates that inhabitants were forewarned of the eruption and escaped. The most outstanding finds were the stunning frescoes now on display at the National Archaeological Museum in Athens. Site opening times are Tuesday to Sunday from 8.30 am to 3 pm. Admission is 1500 dr. On the way to Akrotiri, pause at the enchanting traditional settlement of **Megalohori**.

Ancient Thira Αρχαία Θήρα

Ancient Thira, first settled by the Dorians in the 9th century BC, has ruins from Hellenistic, Roman and Byzantine times. These include temples, houses with mosaics, an agora, a theatre and a gymnasium. The site has splendid views. It's open Tuesday to Sunday from 9 am to 3 pm. Admission is free. It takes about 30 minutes to walk to the site along the path from Perissa. If you're driving, take the road from Kamari.

Moni Profiti Ilia
Μονή Προφήτη Ηλία

This monastery crowns Santorini's highest peak, Mt Profitis Ilias (956 metres). Although the monastery now shares the peak with radio and TV pylons and a radar station, it's worth the trek for the stupendous views. The monastery has an interesting **folk museum**. You can walk there from Pyrgos (1½ hours) or from ancient Thira (one hour).

Oia Οία

The village of Oia was devastated by the 1956 earthquake and has never fully recovered, but it's dramatic, striking and quieter than Fira. Built on a steep slope of the caldera, many of its dwellings nestle in niches hewn in the volcanic rock. From the bus turnaround, go left (following signs for the youth hostel), turn immediately right, take the first left, ascend the steps and walk across the central square to the main street, Nikolaou Nomikou, which skirts the caldera.

Oia is famous for its sunsets and its narrow passageways get crowded in the evenings. There are several charming commercial **galleries**, as well as a **maritime museum**. It's open daily from 10 am to noon and from 5 to 8 pm, except Tuesday when it closes at 1 pm.

One can swim at **Ammoudi**, the tiny port with tavernas that lies 300 steps below. There are caïques from Ammoudi to Thirasia for about 1000 dr.

The last bus for Fira (220 dr) leaves Oia at 10.15 pm. After that, three to four people can bargain for a shared taxi for about 300 dr per person.

Places to Stay & Eat There are dorm beds at Oia's *youth hostel* (☎ 71 290/291/292), which opens in summer only. It is signposted from the bus stop. On the way is a sign for *Domatia/Zimmer* (no telephone) where clean doubles are 8000 dr. *Lauda Traditional Hostel* (☎ 71 204/157), on the main street overlooking the caldera, has simple singles/

doubles for 10,100/14,000 dr and two-person studios for 19,000 dr. Further along, the *Hotel Fregata* (☎ 71 221/276/ 105) has singles/doubles with breakfast for 8000/ 12,000 dr. Rooms at the *Hotel Anemones* (☎ 71 220) are 8500/9200 dr.

Blue Sky Taverna, nearby, has quite creative fare such as cheese-stuffed squid (800 dr) and a mixed-vegetable plate (395 dr).

Beaches
Black-sand beaches become so hot that using a mat is essential. The best beaches are at **Kamari** and **Perissa** on the east coast, but they get very crowded. Both have sailboards, water skis and pedal boats for hire, and both have domatia, hotels and camp sites. *Kamari Camping* (☎ 31 451/453) is one km up the main road from the beach and *Galanakis Camping* (☎ 81 343) is on Perissa beach. Note that the road along the beach at Kamari is for pedestrians only in summer.

Monolithos beach, further up the coast, is less crowded. North of here, the beaches are almost deserted.

THIRASIA & VOLCANIC ISLETS
Unspoilt Thirasia (Θηρασιά) was separated from Santorini by an eruption in 236 BC. Manolas has tavernas and domatia.

The uninhabited islets of **Palia Kameni** and **Nea Kameni** are still volcanically active. Daily boats go from Oia to Thirasia. Palia and Nea Kameni can be visited on excursions from Fira Skala. A day's excursion is about 5000 dr and a half-day about 2500 dr. Shop around Fira's travel agencies for the best deal.

Anafi Ανάφη

Unpretentious Anafi (An-AF-ee, population 300) is 30 km east of showy Santorini. Until recently, tourists were a rare sight on the island and their numbers still amount to little more than a trickle. The main attractions are the slow-paced, traditional lifestyle and the lack of commercialism – an ideal place to

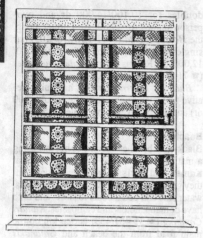

Handmade lace curtains adorn windows in traditional villages

unwind. In mythology, Anafi emerged at Apollo's command when Jason and the Argonauts were in dire need of refuge during a storm. The island's name means 'no snakes'.

Its little port is **Agios Nikolaos**, and the main town, the **hora**, is a steep 20-minute walk from the port. The hora has a post office. There are several pleasant beaches near Agios Nikolaos. The port and hora have a few domatia and tavernas. Beach camping may be tolerated. Anafi's main 'sight' is **Moni Kalamiotissas**, in the extreme east of the island near the meagre remains of a sanctuary to Apollo. The monastery is a three-hour walk from the hora.

Getting There & Away

Ferry services to Anafi are poor. There are three ferries a week from Piraeus (6400 dr) arriving at the ungodly hours of 4.30 am on Tuesday, and 2 am on Wednesday and Sunday. The usual route to Anafi from Piraeus is via Paros, Naxos, Ios and Santorini. There are occasional excursion boats to Anafi from Santorini for 1500 dr.

Milos Μήλος

Volcanic Milos (MEE-los, population 5100), the most westerly island of the Cyclades, is overlooked by most foreign tourists. It's a pity. While the island is not as visually dramatic as the volcanic islands of Santorini and Nisyros, Milos has some weird rock formations, hot springs, pleasant beaches and superb views.

The island's most celebrated asset, the beautiful Venus de Milo (a 4th-century statue of Aphrodite) is far away in the Louvre (having lost its arms on the way to Paris).

Since ancient times, the island has been quarried for minerals, resulting in huge gaps and fissures in the landscape. Obsidian (hard, black volcanic glass used for manufacturing sharp blades) was mined on the island and exported throughout the Mediterranean. These days about a third of the working population is employed in the mining industry.

Phylakope, the ancient city of Milos, was one of the oldest settlements in the Cyclades. During the Peloponnesian Wars, Milos was the only Cycladic island to take Sparta's side. It paid dearly when avenging Athenians massacred all of the island's adult males and enslaved the women and children.

Getting There & Away

Air There is at least one flight a day to Athens (12,600 dr). The Olympic Airways office (☎ 22 380) is at 25 Martiou 11 in Adamas. There are no buses to the airport, so you'll need to take a taxi.

Ferry There are daily ferries from Milos to Piraeus (seven hours, 3900 dr), almost daily to Sifnos, (1300 dr), Serifos (1300 dr) and Kythnos. Two services operate weekly to Folegandros and Santorini, and there is a direct service to Agios Nikolaos on Crete. A boat goes four times a day to the neighbouring island of Kimolos from Polonia, on Milos' east coast. Milos' port police (☎ 22

100) are on the Adamas' waterfront, near the OTE.

Getting Around
Frequent buses leave Adamas for Plaka (via Trypiti). Six a day go to Polonia, four to Paleohori and three to Provatas.

Cars, motorbikes and mopeds can be hired along the waterfront.

ADAMAS Αδάμαντας
Although Plaka is Milos' capital, the port of Adamas has most of the accommodation.

Attractive Plaka is a five-km bus ride away (180 dr).

Orientation & Information
From Adamas' quay, turn right onto the waterfront. The OTE, post office and National Bank of Greece are all on the left. Adamas' postcode is 848 01 (the rest of Milos is 848 00). The telephone code is 0287. The central square, with the bus stop and taxi rank, are at the end of this stretch of waterfront. Past the square is a major crossroad. The road to the right skirts the town beach

Milos & Kimolos

0   2.5   5 km

AEGEAN SEA

To Serifos, Kythnos & Piraeus

KIMOLOS

Paleokastro (Fortress)   Prasa

To Sifnos

KIMOLOS   Goupa

Kambana Beach   Psathi   Rematos Beach

Nerodafni Beach   Firopotamos Beach   GLARONISIA ISLET   Polonia

Plathiena Beach   Mandrakia Beach   Phylakope

Cape Vani   Areti   Agios Konstantinos   Voudia Beach

Fourkovouni   PLAKA   Voudia Bay

Trypiti   Triovasalos

Ancient Theatre &   Klima

Catacombs   Adamas   To Folegandros, Ios & Santorini

Boubarda Beach   Town Beach   MILOS

301 m   Kanava

Agios Nikolaos   Hot Springs   Zefiria   278 m

387 m   Airport   Sulphur Mine

749 m   Paleohori Beach

Kleftiko   ASPRONISI ISLET

Cape Psalida   Provatas Beach

CYCLADES

and 25 Martiou. Straight ahead is the town's main thoroughfare and the road to Plaka.

There is no EOT. Milos' municipal tourist office (☎ 22 445) is opposite the quay and open only in summer. The helpful regular police (☎ 21 378) are next to Plaka's bus station.

Organised Tours

Terry's Travel (☎ 22 640), up the steps from the quay, has a range of tours. They include a boat trip around the island (3000 dr), pausing at dramatic **Kleftiko** on the southwest coast to check out the caves, cliffs and islets. Milos Travel, on the waterfront, has a bus tour of the island for 3000 dr.

Places to Stay – bottom end

Adamas has no camp site and freelance camping is not tolerated. The many domatia include the excellent *Ethelvina's Rooms* (☎ 22 169), up from the bakery off the main square. Singles/doubles/triples, most with refrigerator and bathroom, are 9000/10,000/12,000 dr. The *Hotel Semiramis* (☎ 22 117/118) has a delightful garden and doubles/triples with facilities for 10,500/13,000 dr. Walk along 25 Martiou, take the first left and the hotel is on the left. The *Hotel Meltemi* (☎ 22 284) on 25 Martiou has singles/doubles/triples for 8500/15,000/17,000 dr.

Accommodation can be hard to find if you arrive on a night ferry in the low season. The best bet is to turn right at the quay and head for the tavernas, where you can ask for assistance.

Places to Stay – middle & top end

Follow signs off 25 Martiou for *Hotel Milos* (☎ 22 087 or 21 160) which has pleasant doubles/triples for 13,000/17,000 dr. The *Hotel Capitan Georgantas* (☎ 23 215/218), opposite Olympic Airways on 25 Martiou, has a bar, pool and sauna. It charges 24,500 dr for lovely air-con double suites with TV. If you're looking for something different, ask at Terry's Travel about staying at the restored windmill. It costs 30,000 dr per night and sleeps up to six people.

Places to Eat

On the waterfront, *Flisvos* is recommended. *Trapetselis Restaurant*, overlooking the town beach, serves reasonably priced fish dishes. *O Kimigos*, first right after the quay, offers good Greek staples.

PLAKA & TRYPITI Πλάκα & Τρυπητή

Plaka, five km uphill from Adamas, is a typical Cycladic town – dazzling white and labyrinthine. It merges with the settlement of Trypiti to the south. Both have domatia.

Things to See

Milos Folklore & Art Museum The museum is housed in a 19th-century Plaka mansion. The salon has pictures, gramophones and a stove used for heating. The bedroom is filled with fascinating items, including night attire on a four-poster bed and a child's commode. A storeroom has tools for producing wine and agricultural and fishing implements. Another room displays embroidery, appliqué work, crochet and weavings.

A sign at the bus turnaround in Plaka points to the museum. It's open daily, except Monday, from 10 am to 1 pm.

Leaving the museum, turn left for the **Church of Panagia Korfiatissa**. From its terrace there are breathtaking views of Milos' north coast and Antimilos islet, uninhabited except for goats.

Kastro At the bus turnaround, facing Adamas (south), turn right for a path which leads to the Frankish kastro, built on the ancient acropolis. Inside the walls is the 13th-century **Church of Thalassitras**. The final battle between the ancient Melians and Athenians was fought on this hill. The kastro offers panoramic views of most of the island.

Archaeological Museum This museum is in Trypiti, on the right side of the road leading from Plaka to the much signposted catacombs. Don't miss the perfectly preserved terracotta figurine of Athena (unlabelled) in the middle room. The room on the left has charming figurines from Phylakope. The museum is open Tuesday to

Sunday from 8.30 am to 3 pm. Admission is 500 dr.

AROUND PLAKA & TRYPITI
Roman Ruins
Plaka is built on the site of ancient Milos, which was destroyed by the Athenians. It was rebuilt by the Romans, and there are some Roman ruins nearby, including Greece's only Christian **catacombs**. On the road to them, a sign points right to the well-preserved **ancient theatre**. Excavations in 1964 yielded a headless statue sculpted from Naxian marble and tiles from the theatre's original ceiling. On the track to the theatre, a Greek sign points to where a farmer found the Venus de Milo in 1820. Opposite are remains of massive Doric walls. Fifty metres further along on the cement road is a sign to the 1st-century catacombs. A passage leads to a large chamber flanked by tunnels which contained the tombs. Opening times are from 8.30 am to 3 pm, closed on Wednesday and Sunday. Admission is 500 dr.

Klima Κλήμα
The village of Klima is a short stroll from the catacombs. With your back to the catacomb ticket kiosk, turn left, then right onto a path. You'll come to the steps down to Klima after 100 metres. On the way there is a chapel hewn into the rock. Klima was once the port of ancient Milos, now it's a charming unspoilt fishing village skirting a narrow beach. Whitewashed buildings, with bright blue, green and red doors and balconies, have boat houses on the ground floor and the living quarters on the 1st floor. Klima's one hotel (two km from the village) is the *Hotel Panorama* (☎ 21 623), where doubles are 10,300 dr. The hotel has a restaurant.

Plathiena Beach
Plathiena is a lovely sandy beach below Plaka. On the walk to Plathiena you can detour to the tiny fishing villages of **Areti** and **Fourkovouni**. At Plaka, walk towards the kastro path and look for the kalderimi (narrow alleyway) to the left. After five minutes, it forks. Veer left for Areti or right

for Plathiena. If you take the Areti path, after 15 minutes you'll come to a track leading down to Areti. If you take the Plathiena path, you'll see the track down to Fourkovouni after a few minutes.

Continuing along the track, the landscape becomes quite surreal, with the intense red, orange and white volcanic rock set against deep blue summer skies. The track leads to a crossroads. A left turn leads to Plathiena, while a right leads to the other branch of the kalderimi from Plaka.

AROUND THE ISLAND
The beaches of **Provatas** and **Paleohori**, on the south coast, are long and sandy. There are hot springs at Paleohori. **Polonia**, on the north coast, is a fishing village with a small beach and domatia.

The ancient **Phylakope** is two km inland from Polonia. Three levels of cities have been uncovered here – Early, Middle and Late Cycladic. The islet of **Glaronisia**, off the north coast, is a rare geological phenomenon composed entirely of hexagonal volcanic stone bars.

KIMOLOS Κίμολοσ
The small island of Kimolos is perched just to the north-east of Milos. It receives few visitors, although there are domatia, four tavernas, two bakeries, a minimarket and fine beaches lying in wait.

Those who do make the effort tend to be day-trippers arriving on the boat from Polonia, on the north-eastern tip of Milos. The boat docks at the port of Psathi and it's three km from Psathi to Kimolos town by the island's only sealed road. There's no petrol station on Kimolos – so if you're bringing a car or moped across from Milos, make sure you've got enough fuel.

Donkeys are still the principal mode of transport, and there are tracks all around the island. There are thermal springs at the settlement of **Prasa** on the north-east coast. Beaches can be reached by caïque from Psathi. At the centre of the island is the 350-metre-high cliff on which sits the fortress of **Paleokastro**.

Day-trippers should try the local food speciality, *lathenia*, a pizza-like dish with tomato, onion and cheese.

Getting There & Away
There are three ferries a week to Kimolos from Piraeus (7½ hours, 3900 dr), and daily boats from Polonia on Milos (20 minutes).

Kea Κέα

Kea (KE-a, population 1600) is the closest of the Cyclades to the mainland. The island is a popular weekend escape for Athenians in summer, but remains relatively untouched by tourism. While the island appears largely barren from a distance, it has ample water and the bare hills hide fertile valleys filled with orchards, olive groves, and almond and oak trees. The main settlements are the port of Korissia, and the capital, Ioulis, five km inland. The postcode for Kea is 840 02 and the telephone code is 0288.

Getting There & Away
Ferry Ferries to Kea (80 minutes, 1600 dr) operate from the port of Lavrio, in Attica. There are at least two ferries everyday and more at weekends. There is a one ferry a week between Kea and Kythnos.

Hydrofoil In summer, there are daily hydrofoil connections to Zea Marina at Piraeus (85 minutes, 4200 dr) and to Kythnos (45 minutes, 2500 dr).

Getting Around
You're better off forgetting about the so-called bus service. In theory, the local bus runs constantly from Korissia to Vourkari (100 dr) and then from Korissia to Ioulis (250 dr). It doesn't in practice. You're better off catching one of the taxis which hang about near the port and outside Ioulis. They can also be telephoned on ☎ 21 021/228. There are a couple of places to hire motorbikes in Korissia.

KORISSIA Κορησσία
The port of Korissia is an uninspiring place in spite of its setting on a large bay with a long, sandy beach. The tourist police (☎ 22 100) can be found one block back from the waterfront between June and September. Stefanos Lepouras, at the Flying Dolphin agency opposite the ferry and hydrofoil quay, is a good source of information about the island. He can also change money.

Places to Stay & Eat
The C-class *Hotel Karthea* (☎ 21 222) is a large concrete box at the corner of the bay with ordinary singles/doubles for 7100/8600 dr. There are better places along the road that runs behind the beach, including a couple of domatia. The *Hotel Tzia Mas* (☎ 21 305) could do with a coat of paint and a clean-up, but it has doubles that open right onto the beach for 9000 dr. The best rooms are at the *Hotel Korissia* (☎ 21 484), which has large, modern singles/doubles for 8000/10,000 dr;

and doubles/triples with kitchen for 12,000/15,000 dr. To get there, turn right off the beach road at the creek and you'll see the hotel on the right after about 150 metres. The *Restaurant O Faros*, on the waterfront in Korissia, serves good fish.

IOULIS Ιουλίδα
Ioulis is a delightful higgledy-piggledy hill-side town, full of alleyways and steps that beg to be explored. The bus turnaround is on a square at the edge of town. The post office is on the square. An archway leads to Ioulis proper, and the main thoroughfare (Ilia Malavazou) leads uphill to the right. The OTE is along here on the right. The pathway continues uphill and crosses a small square. Just beyond the square on the right is an agency of the National Bank of Greece, signposted above a minimarket.

Things to See
The **archaeological museum**, on the main thoroughfare, houses local finds, mostly from Agia Irini. Opening times are Tuesday to Sunday from 8.30 am to 3 pm. Admission is free.

The celebrated **Kea Lion**, carved from a huge chunk of granite in the 6th century BC, lies on the hillside an easy pleasant 10-minute walk north-east of town. The path to the lion leads off to the left (the main path goes sharp right) about 150 metres past the bank. There is a sign and arrow painted on the path.

Places to Stay & Eat
The *Hotel Ioulis* (☎ 22 177) has a great location, perched on an outcrop of rock just beyond the remains of the old Venetian kastro. It has spotless singles/doubles/triples for 5500/7800/8800 dr with shared bathroom, and doubles with private bathroom for 8500 dr. It's worth a visit to the terrace restaurant just for the views. To get there, turn left through the archway into Ioulis and follow the signs to the kastro.

The only other option is the friendly *Hotel Filoxenia* (☎ 22 057), a tiny place with lots

of character. Singles/doubles are 4000/6000 dr with shared bathroom.

The *Estiatorio I Piatsa*, just inside the archway, serves a generous plate of calamari for 900 dr.

AROUND THE ISLAND
The beach road from Korissia leads past **Gialiskari beach** to the trendy resort of **Vourkari**, 2.5 km away. Just north of Vourkari is the ancient site of **Agia Irini** (named after a nearby church), where a Minoan palace has been excavated. The road continues for another three km to a sandy beach at the **Otzias**. A dirt road continues beyond here for another five km to the 18th-century **Moni Panagias Kastrianis**. The monastery has a commanding position and terrific views. The island's best beach, eight km south-west of Ioulis, has the unfortunate name of **Pisses**. It is long and sandy and backed by a verdant valley of orchards and olive groves.

Places to Stay
The island's camp site, *Kea Camping* (☎ 31 332), is at Pisses beach. The site has a shop, bar and restaurant. There are also domatia and tavernas here.

The island's flashest joint is *Kea Beach Hotel & Bungalows* (☎ 22 144; fax 21 234), a package hotel occupying a headland overlooking Koundouros beach, two km south of Pisses beach. The hotel complex has a bar, restaurant, disco and swimming pool.

Kythnos Κύθνος

In contrast to Kea, Kythnos (KI-thnos), the next island south, is virtually barren. Like Kea, it is popular mainly with Athenian holiday-makers. There is little to enthuse about on Kythnos, unless you're looking for a cure for rheumatism at the island's thermal baths. The main settlements are the port of Merihas and the capital, Hora – also known as Kythnos. Merihas has an OTE, and there is an agency of the National Bank of Greece

CYCLADES

Kythnos

0   2   4 km

Milos. The *Milos Express* presses on to Kimolos, Folegandros, Sikinos, Ios and Santorini twice a week; and the *Apollo Express II* goes to Rhodes once a week via Santorini, Agios Nikolaos (Crete), Kassos, Karpathos, Halki and Symi. There is one boat a week to the port of Lavrio in Attica (3½ hours, 2200 dr), stopping at Kea.

Hydrofoil In summer, there are daily Flying Dolphins to Kea (45 minutes, 2500 dr) and Zea Marina at Piraeus (2¼ hours, 5800 dr).

Getting Around
There are regular buses from Merihas to Dryopida (200 dr) and Hora (200 dr), occasionally continuing to Loutra. The buses supposedly meet the ferries, otherwise they leave from the turn-off to Hora in Merihas. Taxis are a better bet, providing you don't want to go anywhere at siesta time. They charge 1200 dr to Dryopida and Hora and 2000 dr to Loutra. Motorbikes can be hired from the Milos Express agent next to the newsagency on the waterfront in Merihas.

MERIHAS
Merihas does not have a lot going for it other than a small sand-and-pebble beach. It is, however, a reasonable base and has most of the island's accommodation. A 10-minute walk around the port leads to a better beach and a taverna.

Places to Stay & Eat
Accommodation can be hard to find in summer. There are lots of domatia along the waterfront, but the rooms are often pre-booked. The same applies to the town's only hotel, the *Kythnos Hotel* (☎ 32 092), which is up the first set of steps you come to on the way into town from the harbour. It has pleasant singles/doubles/triples overlooking the harbour for 5000/7000/8000 dr. The *Restaurant O Gialos*, on the waterfront, has good food and a great position with tables right on the beach.

AROUND THE ISLAND
The capital, **Hora** (also known as Kythnos),

at Cava Kythnos travel agency. The agency also sells Flying Dolphin tickets. Hora has the island's post office and police station as well as an OTE. The postcode for Kythnos is 840 06 and the telephone code is 0281.

Getting There & Away
Ferry Kythnos is well served by ferries, with both the F/B *Milos Express* and the F/B *Apollo Express II* including the island on their Cycladic routes. There are boats to/from Piraeus (2½ hours, 2200 dr) five days a week. Most services from Piraeus continue to the islands of Serifos, Sifnos and

lacks the charm of other Cycladic capitals. The main reason to come here is for the walk south to **Dryopida**, a picturesque town of red-tiled roofs and winding streets that was the island's capital in the Middle Ages. It takes about 1½ hours to cover the six km. From Dryopida, you can either walk the six km back to Merihas or catch a bus or taxi. The **thermal baths** at Loutra, in the north-east, are reputedly the most potent in the Cyclades. The best beaches are on the south-west coast, near the village of Panagia Kanala.

Places to Stay

Loutra offers the only accommodation outside Merihas. There are several domatia as well as the *Hotel Porto Klaras* (☎ 31 276; fax 31 276), reportedly the best places on the island. It has doubles/triples with bathroom and kitchen facilities for 8500/11,000 dr.

Serifos Σέριφος

First impressions of Serifos (SE-rif-os, population 1250) are of a barren, rocky island. On closer inspection, a few pockets of greenery turn out to be the result of tomato and vine cultivation. Serifos' port is Livadi, on the south-east coast. The island's white-washed capital (also called Serifos) clings to a hillside two km inland.

Getting There & Around

Serifos has ferries to Piraeus (4½ hours, 2900 dr) five days a week, stopping at Kythnos. Ferries from Piraeus continue to Milos (1300 dr) via Sifnos, and three a week sail on to Folegandros, Sikinos, (1300 dr), Ios and Santorini. There is a weekly hydrofoil to Rafina (5764 dr) via Sifnos, Paros, Mykonos, Tinos and Andros. The port police (☎ 51 470) are up steps from the quay at Livadi.

There are frequent buses between Livadi and Serifos town. Motorbikes can be hired in Livadi.

LIVADI Λιβάδι

Attractive Livadi is at the top end of an elongated bay. From the ferry, walk to the quay's end and turn right to reach the waterfront and central square. Continue around the bay for the pleasant, shaded, sandy beach. Karavi beach, a 30-minute walk south, is the island's unofficial nudist beach. On the way is the crowded Livadakia beach. The OTE in Livadi opens only in summer. A branch of the National Bank of Greece is scheduled to open on the waterfront in 1996.

Places to Stay

Serifos' camp site is the excellent, shady *Coralli Camping* (☎ 51 500/073), at sandy Livadakia beach. Sites cost 1200 dr per person; tent hire is 500 dr. Bungalows cost 12,000/14,000 dr (doubles/triples). There is a restaurant, bar and minimarket.

The *Areti Hotel* (☎ 51 479) overlooks a pebbled beach and has doubles for 10,000 dr. To get there, walk to the end of the quay and turn left up the steps. *Serifos Beach Hotel* (☎ 51 209/468) is comfortable and has a restaurant. Rooms are 8,000/10,000 dr, or 11,000/16,000 with half-board (breakfast and either lunch or dinner). It's back from the

CYCLADES

waterfront, past the central square. On the waterfront, the *Maistrali Hotel* (☎ 51 381/298) has good doubles with balconies for 15,200 dr, including breakfast. Further along, the *Asteri Hotel* (☎ 51 191) has singles/doubles/triples with en suite for 13,000/20,000/23,000 dr, breakfast included.

Places to Eat
The excellent *Theofilo Taverna* at the Serifos Beach Hotel and the *Hotel Asteri Restaurant* (see Places to Stay) both offer fresh produce from the family farms on the menu. Near Theofilo's is the low-budget self-service *Cavo d'Oro. Taverna O Stamatis*, at the beach, serves good Greek dishes at reasonable prices.

Mokka's Restaurant, near the quay, is the place for the trendy set. It specialises in seafood, with most mains priced at about 2500 dr. The fish soup is a must at 1500 dr, while the shrimp saganaki with feta and tomatoes is worthwhile at 3000 dr. Those with a sweet tooth should check out the almond versions of baklava and other pastries that are an island speciality.

SERIFOS TOWN
Dazzling white Serifos town is one of the most striking of the Cycladic capitals. It can be reached either by bus or by walking up the steps from Livadi. More steps lead to a ruined 15th-century Venetian fortress above the village.

The post office is downhill from the bus stop. The OTE is further uphill, off the central square. Serifos' postcode is 840 05. The telephone code is 0281. There is no bank. A cobbler off the square makes fine leather shoes to order.

AROUND THE ISLAND
About an hour's walk north of Livadi along a track (negotiable by moped) is **Psili Ammos beach**. There's also a path to the beach from Serifos town. Another path heads north to the pretty village of **Kendarhos** (also called Kallitsos). From here, you can continue to the 17th-century fortified **Moni Taxiarhon**, which has impressive 18th-century frescoes. The walk from the town to the monastery takes about two hours. Kendarhos has various tavernas but no accommodation.

Sifnos Σίφνος

Sifnos (SEEF-nos, population 2050) coyly hides its assets from passing ferry passengers. At a glance, the island looks as barren as Serifos, but the port is in the island's most arid area. Explore and you'll find an attractive landscape of terraced olive groves, almond trees and oleanders. There are numerous dovecotes, whitewashed houses and chapels.

Sifniot olive oil is highly prized throughout Greece. Perhaps this has something to do with the island's reputation for producing some of the country's best chefs. Local specialities include *revithia* (baked chickpeas) and xynomyzithra. The island also produces superior pottery because of the quality of its clay. Many shops sell locally made ceramics.

Getting There & Around
There are ferries to Milos and Piraeus (5½ hours, 3100 dr), via Serifos and Kythnos, five days a week. There are three ferries a week to Folegandros, Sikinos, Ios and Santorini; and one a week to Agios Nikolaos on Crete. There is a weekly hydrofoil to Rafina (6200 dr) via Serifos, Paros, Mykonos, Tinos and Andros.

Frequent buses travel between Apollonia and Kamares, Kastro and Platys Gialos. Daily taxi boats go from Kamares to Vathy on the south-west coast. Cars can be hired from the Kamari Hotel in Kamares, and mopeds at Apollonia's main square.

KAMARES Καμάρες
Don't judge Sifnos by the port of Kamares, which is hard to get excited about despite the fact that it has a good sandy beach. There is municipal tourist office (☎ 31 804) opposite the quay. The helpful staff will find accommodation for you.

Places to Stay & Eat

The C-class *Stavros Hotel* (☎ 31 641), in the middle of the waterfront, has clean doubles with bathroom for 5000 dr. The *Kamari Hotel* (☎ 31 710/641/382) has attractive doubles for 6700 dr or 8500 dr with bathroom. *Captain Andreas* and *Restaurant Simos*, on the waterfront, both serve well-prepared traditional Greek fare. Full meals with retsina cost from 2000 dr. *The Dolphins' Taverna* opposite the bus stop is also recommended.

APOLLONIA Απολλώνια

Apollonia, Sifnos' modern capital, sprawls on a plateau five km uphill from the port. The bus stop is on the lively central square where the post office, OTE and the National Bank of Greece are located. The **Museum of Popular Art** is also here. Opening times are 6 to 10 pm daily. Admission is 200 dr.

Places to Stay & Eat

The C-class *Hotel Sophia* (☎ 31 238), north of the central square, has light singles/doubles with bathroom for 7000/9000 dr. Another option is the C-class *Hotel Sifnos* (☎ 31 624), which has immaculate doubles with bathroom for 12,500 dr. From the central square (facing away from Kamares), turn right beyond the museum and right again. The hotel is on the right.

The *Restaurant Sophia*, below the hotel of the same name, serves good food. Expect to pay about 2000 dr for a full meal and a beverage.

AROUND THE ISLAND

The pretty village of **Artemon** is north of Apollonia. Not to be missed is the walled, clifftop village of **Kastro**, three km from Apollonia. It was the former capital, and is a magical place of buttressed alleys and white-washed houses. The serene village of **Exambela**, south of Apollonia, is said to be the birthplace of most of Sifnos' accomplished chefs.

The resort of **Platys Gialos**, 10 km south of Apollonia, has a long sandy beach; some hotels and domatia; and the island's only camp site, *Camping Platys Gialos* (☎ 31 786), in an olive grove behind the beach. The spectacularly situated **Moni Hrysopigis**, near Platys Gialos, was built to house a miraculous icon of the Virgin, found in the sea by two fishermen. A path leads from the monastery to a beach with a taverna. **Vathy**, on the west coast, is a gorgeous unspoilt sandy bay with a few domatia and tavernas. There is no road access, but in summer there are taxi boats from Kamares.

Places to Stay

One of Sifnos' best hotels is *Platys Gialos Beach Hotel & Bungalows* (☎ 31 224/324), at Platys Gialos. All rooms have air-con, TV and minibar. Water sports are available from April to September, when B-class rates are charged.

Crete Κρήτη

Crete is Greece's largest and most southerly island. Many would argue that it is also the most beautiful. A spectacular mountain chain runs from east to west across the island, split into three mighty ranges: the Mt Dikti range in the east, the Mt Ida (also called Mt Psiloritis) range in the centre and the Lefka Ori (white mountains) in the west. The mountains are dotted with agricultural plains and plateaus, and sliced by numerous dramatic gorges. Long, sandy beaches speckle the coastline, and the east coast boasts Europe's only palm-tree forest.

Administratively, the island is divided into four prefectures: Lassithi, Iraklio, Rethymno and Hania. Apart from Lassithi, with its capital of Agios Nikolaos, the prefectures are named after their major cities. The island's capital is Iraklio with a population of 127,600. It's Greece's fifth largest city. Nearly all Crete's major population centres are on the north coast. Most of the south coast is too precipitous to support large settlements.

Crete is famous for its wild flowers. You'll find *Wild Flowers of Crete* by George Sfikas is a comprehensive field guide, but *Flowers of Crete* by Yanoukas Iatrides may be a better bet for the layperson.

Crete is visited not only for its scenery and beaches. The island was also the birthplace of Europe's first advanced civilisation, the Minoan. If you intend to spend much time at the many Minoan sites, *Palaces of Minoan Crete* by Gerald Cadogan is an excellent guide.

Due to its size and distance from the rest of Greece, a folk culture evolved on Crete independent of the mainland. Vibrant Cretan weavings can be found for sale in many of the island's towns and villages. The traditional Cretan songs differ from those heard elsewhere in Greece. Called *mantinades*, these songs are highly emotive, expressing the age-old concerns of love, death and the yearning for freedom. You will still come

across a few old men wearing the traditional dress of breeches tucked into knee-high leather boots, and black-fringed kerchiefs tied tightly around their heads. The kerchief is making a comeback as a fashion accessory these days with young Cretans.

The attractions of Crete have not gone unnoticed by tour operators, and the island has the dubious honour of playing host to almost a quarter of Greece's tourists. The result is that much of the north coast is packed solid with hastily constructed hotels for package tourists, particularly between Iraklio and Agios Nikolaos and west of Hania. The tour operators have also taken over several of the southern coastal villages that were once backpacker favourites. If you haven't visited Crete for a while, brace yourself for a shock. The wild and rugged west coast, however, remains relatively untouched.

If you want to avoid the crowds, the best times to visit are from April to June and from mid-September to the end of October. Winter is a dead loss outside the major population centres, as most hotel owners and restaurateurs choose to shut their establishments and recharge their batteries in preparation for the next tourist onslaught.

History

Although Crete has been inhabited since Neolithic times (7000 to 3000 BC), as far as most people are concerned its history begins with the Minoan civilisation. The glories of Crete's Minoan past remained hidden until British archaeologist Sir Arthur Evans made his dramatic discoveries at Knossos at the beginning of this century. The term Minoan, incidentally, was coined by Evans and derived from the King Minos of mythology. Nobody knows what the Minoans called themselves.

Of the many finds at Knossos and other sites, it is the frescoes that have captured the imagination of experts and amateurs alike. The message they communicate is of a society which was powerful, wealthy, joyful and optimistic.

Artistically the frescoes are superlative; the figures that grace them have a naturalism which is lacking in contemporary Cycladic figurines, ancient Egyptian artwork (which they resemble in certain respects), and the Archaic sculpture which came later. Compared to candle-smoke-blackened Byzantine frescoes, the Minoan frescoes, with their fresh, bright colours, look as if they were painted yesterday.

The frescoes depict a people who were physically unblemished. Gracing the frescoes are white-skinned women with elaborately coiffured glossy black locks. Proud, graceful and uninhibited, these women had hourglass figures and dressed in stylish gowns that revealed perfectly shaped breasts. The bronze-skinned men were tall, with tiny waists, narrow hips, broad shoulders and muscular thighs and biceps; and the children were slim and lithe. The Minoans also seemed to know how to enjoy themselves. They played board games, boxed and wrestled, played leap-frog over bulls and over one another, and performed bold acrobatic feats.

They were religious, as frescoes and models of people partaking in rituals testify. However, the Minoans' beliefs, like many other aspects of their society, remain an enigma. There is sufficient evidence to confirm that they worshipped bulls, but how and why is shrouded in mystery. There is, however, a suggestion that there was a dark side to Minoan society. There are hints of human sacrifice, and of a Draconian society which other races lived in fear of.

So how much of this history is fact and how much is speculation? It is known that

---

Cire Perdue

The *cire perdue* (lost wax) method of casting bronze statues was pioneered by the Cretans in preclassical times. A wax original was made and iron ducts were put into it at strategic points. These were sufficiently long to project out of the clay mould which was then put around the wax. A pouring funnel was fitted into the clay mould at a suitable place. The whole was then heated so that the wax melted and ran out through the ducts. When all the wax had escaped, the ducts were removed and the holes were plugged. Molten bronze was then poured through the funnel. When the bronze had cooled the mould was carefully chipped away.

The advantage of the cire perdue method of casting was that a high degree of detail could be achieved, and there were no joining lines on the bronze cast. The process is still used today for high-precision work.

The cire perdue method may have given rise to various legends including one which tells of Talos, a man made of bronze, who had one vein running from his neck to his leg. He was a servant of King Minos, and his duty was to help defend Crete. When the Argonauts arrived, he tried to repel them, but Medea, who had accompanied them, unplugged a pin in his ankle. He was drained of his colourless life-blood and died. ■

CRETE

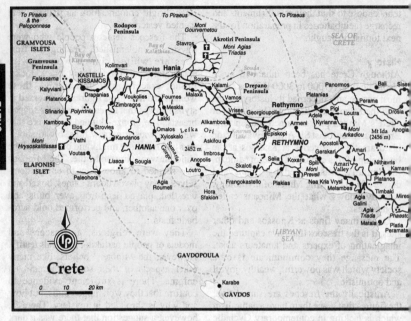

Crete

0   10   20 km

early in the 3rd millennium BC, an advanced people migrated to Crete and brought with them the art of metallurgy. Many elements of Neolithic culture lived on in the Early Minoan period (3000-2100 BC), but the Middle Minoan period (2100-1500 BC) saw the emergence of a society with unprecedented artistic, engineering and cultural achievements. It was during this time that the famous palace complexes were built at Knossos, Phaestos, Malia and Zakros.

It was also during this period that the Minoans began producing their exquisite Kamares pottery (see the Archaeological Museum entry under Iraklio) and intricate silverware, and became a maritime power that traded with Egypt and Asia Minor.

Around 1700 BC, all four palace complexes were destroyed by an earthquake. Undeterred, the Minoans built bigger and better palaces on the sites of the originals, as well as new settlements in other parts of the island.

Around 1500 BC, when the civilisation was at its peak, the palaces were destroyed again, signalling the start of the Late Minoan period (1500-1100 BC). This destruction was probably caused by Mycenaean invasions, although the massive volcanic eruption on the island of Santorini (Thira) may also have had something to do with it. The Knossos palace was the only one to be salvaged. It was finally destroyed by fire around 1400 BC.

The Minoan civilisation was a hard act to follow. The war-orientated Dorians, who arrived in 1100 BC, were pedestrian by comparison. The 5th century BC found Crete, like the rest of Greece, divided into city-states. The glorious classical age of mainland Greece had little impact on Crete, and the island was bypassed by the Persians. It was also ignored by Alexander the Great, so was never part of the Macedonian Empire.

By 67 BC Crete had fallen to the Romans. The town of Gortyn in the south became the

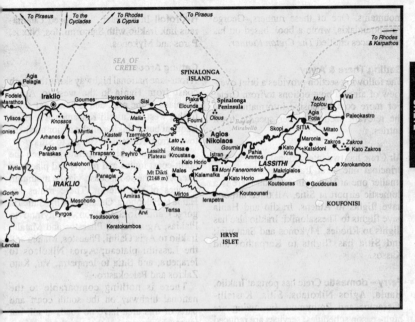

capital of Cyrenaica, a province which included large chunks of North Africa. Crete, along with the rest of Greece, became part of the Byzantine Empire in 395 AD. In 1210 the island was occupied by the Venetians, whose legacy is one of mighty fortresses, ornate public buildings and monuments, and handsome dwellings which belonged to nobles and merchants.

Despite the massive Venetian fortifications which sprang up all over the island, by 1669 the whole of the Cretan mainland was under Turkish rule. The first uprising against the Turks was led by Ioannis Daskalogiannis in 1770. This set the precedent for many more insurrections, and in 1898 the Great Powers intervened and made the island a British protectorate. It was not until the signing of the Treaty of Bucharest in 1913 that Crete officially became part of Greece, although the island's parliament had declared a de facto union in 1905.

The island saw heavy fighting during WW II. Germany wanted to use the island as an air base in the Mediterranean, and on 20 May 1941 German parachutists landed on Crete. It was the start of 10 days of fierce fighting that became known as the Battle of Crete. For two days the battle hung in the balance until Germany won a bridgehead for its air force at Maleme, near Hania. The Allied forces of Britain, Australia, New Zealand and Greece then fought a valiant rearguard action which enabled the British Navy to evacuate 18,000 of the 32,000 Allied troops trapped on the island. Most were picked up from the rugged southern coast around Hora Sfakion. The German occupation of Crete lasted until the end of WW II.

During the war, there was an active resistance movement which drew heavy reprisals from the Germans. Many mountain villages were temporarily bombed 'off the map' and their occupants shot. Among the bravest members of the resistance were the 'runners' who relayed messages on foot over the

CRETE

mountains. One of these runners, George Psychoundakis, wrote a book based on his experiences entitled *The Cretan Runner*.

Getting There & Away

The following section provides a brief overview of air and boat options to/from Crete. For more comprehensive information, see the relevant sections under specific town entries.

Air Crete has two international airports. The principal one is at Iraklio and there is a smaller one at Hania. In addition there is a domestic airport at Sitia. All three airports have flights to Athens. Iraklio and Hania have flights to Thessaloniki; Iraklio also has flights to Rhodes, Mykonos and Santorini; and Sitia has flights to Karpathos and Kassos.

Ferry – domestic Crete has ports at Iraklio, Hania, Agios Nikolaos, Sitia, Kastelli-Kissamos and Rethymno. Following are high-season schedules; services are reduced by about half in the low season.

Direct daily ferries travel to Piraeus from Iraklio and Hania, and three times a week from Rethymno. There are six ferries a week from Iraklio to Santorini, and one ferry a week from Sitia via Agios Nikolaos to Piraeus, stopping at the islands of Santorini, Sikinos, Folegandros, Milos and Sifnos. Three ferries a week go to Piraeus via Santorini, Paros and Naxos, and there are three boats a week to Thessaloniki via the Cyclades and Sporades. There are also three boats a week from Iraklio to Rhodes via Karpathos; and at least two a week from Agios Nikolaos to Rhodes via Sitia, Kassos and Karpathos. Two ferries a week sail between Piraeus and Kastelli-Kissamos via Antikythira, Kythira and the Peloponnese.

Ferry – international There are two boats a week from Iraklio to Cyprus and Israel, one via Rhodes. Between 24 June and 13 September, there are also weekly boats to Italy and Turkey.

Hydrofoil In summer, high-speed catamarans link Iraklio with Santorini, Ios, Naxos, Paros and Mykonos.

Getting Around

A four-lane national highway skirts the north coast from Hania in the west to Agios Nikolaos in the east, and is being extended further west to Kastelli-Kissamos. There are frequent buses linking all the major northern towns from Kastelli-Kissamos to Sitia.

Less frequent buses operate between the north-coast towns and resorts and places of interest on the south coast, via the mountain villages of the interior. These routes are Hania to Paleohora, Omalos (for the Samaria gorge) and Hora Sfakion; Rethymno to Plakias, Agia Galini, Phaestos and Matala; Iraklio to Agia Galini, Phaestos, Matala and the Lassithi plateau; Agios Nikolaos to Ierapetra; and Sitia to Ierapetra, Vaï, Kato Zakros and Paleokastro.

There is nothing comparable to the national highway on the south coast and parts of this area have no roads at all, but where there are roads there are bus services. There is no road between Paleohora and Hora Sfakion, the most precipitous part of the south coast; a boat (daily in summer) connects the two resorts via Sougia and Agia Roumeli.

As well as the bus schedules given in each section in this chapter, clapped out 'village buses' travel to just about every village which has a road to it. These buses usually leave in the early morning and return in the afternoon.

Central Crete

Central Crete is occupied by Iraklio prefecture, named after the island's burgeoning major city and administrative capital. The area's major attractions are the Minoan sites of Knossos, Malia and Phaestos. The north coast east of Iraklio has been heavily exploited by the package-tourism industry, particularly around Hersonisos.

IRAKLIO

The Cretan capital of Iraklio (I-RA-klee-o) is a bustling modern city of 127,600, people, the fifth largest in Greece. It has none of the charm of Hania or Rethymno, but it is a dynamic city that boasts the highest average per capita income in Greece. That wealth stems largely from its position as the island's trading capital, but also from the year-round flow of visitors who flock to Knossos.

History

The Arabs who ruled Crete from 824 to 961 AD were the first people to rule the island from the site of modern Iraklio. It was known then as El Khandak, after the moat that surrounded their fortified town, and was reputedly the slave-trade capital of the eastern Mediterranean.

El Khandak became Khandakos after Byzantine troops finally dislodged the Arabs, and then Candia under the Venetians, who ruled the island from here for more than 400 years. While the Turks quickly overran the Venetian defences at Hania and Rethymno, Candia's fortifications proved as effective as they looked – an unusual combination. They withstood a siege of 21 years before the garrison finally surrendered in 1669.

Hania became the capital of independent Crete at the end of Turkish rule in 1898, but Candia's central location soon saw it emerge as the commercial centre. Candia resumed its position as administrative centre in 1971.

The city suffered badly in WW II, when most of the old Venetian and Turkish town was destroyed by bombing.

Orientation

Iraklio's two main squares are Plateia Venizelou and Plateia Eleftherias. Plateia Venizelou, instantly recognisable by its famous Morosini fountain (better known as the Lion fountain), is the heart of Iraklio and the best place from which to familiarise yourself with the layout of the city. The city's major intersection is a few steps south of the square. From here, 25 Avgoustou runs north-east to the harbour; Dikeosynis runs south-east to Plateia Eleftherias; Kalokerinou runs west to the Hania Gate; 1866 (the market street) runs south; and 1821 runs to the south-west. To reach Plateia Venizelou from the port, turn right, walk along the waterfront and turn left onto 25 Avgoustou.

Iraklio has three intercity bus stations. Station A, on the waterfront between the port and 25 Avgoustou, serves eastern Crete. A special bus station for only Hania and Rethymno is opposite Station A. Station B, just beyond Hania Gate, serves Phaestos, Agia Galini, Matala and Fodele. To reach the city centre from Station B walk through the Hania Gate and along Kalokerinou. For details on bus schedules, see the Iraklio Getting There & Away section.

Information

Tourist Offices The EOT (☎ 22 8225/6081/8203; fax 22 6020) is at Xanthoudidou 1, just north of Plateia Eleftherias. The staff at the information desk are often work-experience students from a local tourism training college. They can give you photocopied lists of ferry and bus schedules, plus a photocopied map. Opening times are Monday to Friday from 8 am to 3 pm. The tourist police (☎ 28 3190) are open from 7 am to 11 pm at Dikeosynis 10.

Money Most of the city's banks are on 25 Avgoustou, including the National Bank of Greece at No 35. It has a 24-hour automatic-exchange machine, as does the Credit Bank at No 94. American Express (☎ 22 5906 or 34 2501) is represented by Adamis Travel Bureau, 25 Avgoustou 23. Opening hours are Monday to Saturday from 8 am to 5 pm. Thomas Cook (☎ 22 4323) is almost next door at No 27.

Post & Telecommunications The central post office is on Plateia Daskalogianni. Coming from Plateia Venizelou, turn right off Dikeosynis opposite Hotel Petra, and you will see the post office across the square in front of you. Opening hours are 7.30 am to

CRETE

Iraklio

8 pm, Monday to Friday; and 7.30 am to 2 pm on Saturday. In summer, there is a mobile post office at El Greco Park, just north of Plateia Venizelou, which is open from 8 am to 6 pm, Monday to Friday; and 8 am to 1.30 pm on Saturday. Iraklio's postcode is 710 01.

The OTE is opposite the western side of El Greco Park, and is open from 6 am to midnight every day. Iraklio's telephone code is 081.

Foreign Consulates Foreign consulates in Iraklio include:

Germany
    Zografou 7 (☎ 22 6288)
Netherlands
    25 Avgoustou 23 (☎ 24 6202)
UK
    Papalexandrou 16 (☎ 22 4012)

Bookshops The Planet International Bookshop (☎ 28 1558) is on the corner of Hortatson and Kidonias.

Laundry There is a self-service laundrette at Merabelou 25, near the archaeological museum. A wash and dry costs 2000 dr.

CRETE

PLACES TO STAY				
1	Xenia Hotel	28	Loukoumades Café	
5	Vergina Rooms	31	Lakis Taverna	
6	Hotel Rea	32	Restaurant Ionia	
8	YHA Hostel			
9	Hotel Mirabello	**OTHER**		
10	YHO Hostel			
12	Pension Atlas	2	Historical Museum of	
20	Hotel Irini		Crete	
21	Hotel Lato	4	Venetian Fortress	
27	Hotel Daedalos		(Rocca al Mare)	
30	Hotel Metropol	7	Planet International	
34	Hotel Petra		Bookshop	
35	Astoria Hotel	11	Prince Travel	
		13	OTE	
PLACES TO EAT		15	Morosini Fountain	
		16	Buses to Knossos	
3	Ippokampos Ouzeri	17	Venetian Loggia	
14	Bougatsa Serraikon	18	National Bank of	
26	Giovanni Taverna		Greece	
		19	Adamis Travel Bureau	

22	Buses to Hania & Rethymno
23	Buses to Knossos & Airport
24	Buses to Eastern Crete (Station A)
25	Laundrette
29	Agios Minos Cathedral
33	Tourist Police
36	EOT
37	Archaeological Museum
38	Buses to Airport
39	Post Office
40	Olympic Airways
41	Bembo Fountain
42	Buses to Western Crete (Station B)
43	Apollonia Hospital
44	Grave of Nikos Kazantzakis

Luggage Storage The left-luggage office at Bus Station A charges 200 dr per day and is open from 6.30 am to 8 pm every day. Prince Travel (☎ 28 2706), 25 Avgoustou 30, and the YHA hostel at Vyronos 5 both charge 300 dr.

Emergency The new University Hospital (☎ 26 9111) at Malades, five km south of Iraklio, is the city's best-equipped medical facility. The Apollonia Hospital (☎ 22 9713), inside the old walls on P Nikousiou, is more convenient.

Things to See
Archaeological Museum This superlative museum (☎ 22 6092) is second in size and importance only to the National Archaeological Museum in Athens. If you are seriously interested in the Minoan civilisation, you will want to visit the museum more than once, but even a fairly superficial perusal of the contents requires a morning or an afternoon.

The exhibits, arranged in chronological order, include pottery, jewellery, figurines, and sarcophagi as well as the famous frescoes, mostly from Knossos and Agia Triada. All testify to the remarkable imagination and advanced skills of the Minoans. Unfortu-

nately, the exhibits are not very well explained. If they were, there would be no need to part with 1500 dr for a copy of the glossy illustrated guide by the museum's director.

Room 1 is devoted to the Neolithic and Early Minoan periods. Room 2 has a collection from the Middle Minoan period. Among the most fascinating exhibits are the tiny, coloured, glazed reliefs of Minoan houses from Knossos.

Room 3 contains the famous **Phaestos disc**. The symbols inscribed on this 16-cm diameter disc have not been deciphered. Also in this room are the famous **Kamares pottery vases**, named after the sacred cave of Kamares where the pottery was first discovered. Included among this collection are many examples of the lovely 'eggshell ware' (so called because of its fragility). One of the finest examples of Kamares pottery in this room is the libation vessel decorated with dolphins and shells.

Exhibits in Room 4 are from the Middle Minoan period. Most striking is the 20-cm black stone **Bull's Head**, which was a libation vessel. The bull has a fine head of curls, from which sprout horns of gold. The eyes of painted crystal are extremely lifelike. Another fascinating exhibit in this room is the elaborate **gaming board**. Also in this room are relics from a shrine at the palace in Knossos, including two figurines of **snake goddesses**; one of the figurines is holding snakes, and another has them coiled around her. Snakes symbolised immortality for the Minoans.

Pottery, bronze figurines and seals are some of the exhibits displayed in Room 5. These include vases imported from Egypt and some Linear A and B tablets. The Mycenaean Linear B script has been deciphered, and the inscriptions on the tablets displayed here have been translated as household or business accounts from the palace at Knossos.

Room 6 is devoted to finds from Minoan cemeteries. Especially intriguing are two small clay models of groups of figures which were found in a tholos tomb. One depicts four male dancers in a circle, their arms

around each other's shoulders. The dancers may have been participating in a funeral ritual. The other model depicts two groups of three figures in a room flanked by two columns. Each group features two large seated figures, who are being offered libations by a smaller figure. It is not known whether the large figures represent gods or departed mortals. On a more grisly level, there is a display of the bones of a horse. Horses, bulls and rams were sacrificed as part of Minoan worship, which had been this particular horse's fate.

The finds in Room 7 include the beautiful bee pendant found at Malia. It's a remarkably fine piece of gold jewellery depicting two bees dropping honey into a comb. Also in this room are the three celebrated vases from Agia Triada. The **Harvester Vase**, of which only the top part remains, depicts a light-hearted scene of young farm workers

---

Linear B

The methodical decipherment of the Linear B script by English architect and part-time linguist Michael Ventris was the first tangible evidence that the Greek language had a recorded history longer than any scholar had previously believed. The decipherment demonstrated that the language disguised by these mysterious scribblings was an archaic form of Greek 500 years older than the Ionic Greek used by Homer. Linear B was written on clay tablets that had lain undisturbed for centuries until unearthed at Knossos in Crete and later on the mainland at Mycenae, Tiryns and Pylos on the Peloponnese and at Thebes in Boeotia. The clay tablets consisting of about 90 different signs dated from the 13th to the 14th century BC and were found to be mainly inventories and records of commercial transactions. Little of the social and political life of these times can be deduced from the tablets though there is enough to give a glimpse of a fairly complex and well-organised commercial structure.

For linguists, the script did not provide a detailed image of the actual language spoken, since the symbols were used primarily as syllabic clusters designed to give an approximation of the pronunciation of the underlying language. Typically, the syllabic cluster 'A-re-ka-sa-da-ra' is the woman's name Alexandra, but the exact pronunciation remains unknown. What is clear, and this is important, is that the language is undeniably Greek, thus giving the modern-day Greek language the second-longest recorded written history, after Chinese. The language of an earlier script, Linear A, remains to this day undeciphered. It is believed to be of either Anatolian or Semitic origin, though even this remains pure conjecture. ■

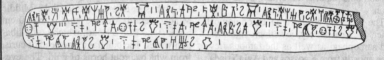

returning from olive picking. The **Boxer Vase** depicts Minoans indulging in two of their favourite pastimes – wrestling and bull grappling. The **Chieftain Cup** depicts a more cryptic scene: a chief holding a staff and three men carrying animal skins. Room 8 holds the finds from the palace at Zakros. They include a gorgeous little crystal vase and a beautiful elongated libation vessel decorated with shells and other marine life. In Room 10, case 138 has some delightful terracotta figurines, while the collection of idols in case 143 include a child (headless) on a swing. Swinging was another favourite pastime of the Minoans.

Room 13 is devoted to Minoan sarcophagi. However, the most famous and spectacular of these, the **sarcophagus from Agia Triada**, is upstairs in Room 14 (the Hall of Frescoes). This stone coffin, painted with floral and abstract designs, and ritual scenes, is regarded as one of the supreme examples of Minoan art.

The most famous of the Minoan frescoes are also displayed in Room 14. Frescoes from Knossos include the **Procession Fresco**, the **Griffin Fresco** (from the Throne Room), the **Dolphin Fresco** (from the Queen's Room) and the amazing **Bull-leaping Fresco**, which depicts a seemingly double-jointed acrobat somersaulting on the back of a charging bull. Other frescoes here include the two lovely **Frescoes of the Lilies** from Amnisos, and fragments of frescoes from Agia Triada. There are more frescoes in Rooms 15 and 16, including the famous **La Parisienne** from Knossos, so named because the young woman portrayed has an upturned nose, pretty hairstyle and elegant attire.

The museum is on Xanthoudidou, just north of Plateia Eleftherias. Opening times are Tuesday to Sunday from 8 am to 7 pm, and Monday from 12.30 to 7 pm. It closes at 5 pm from the end of October to the start of April. Admission is 1500 dr, free on Sunday.

Historical Museum of Crete The museum (☎ 28 3219) houses a fascinating range of bits and pieces from Crete's more recent past, including a collection of Venetian maps and the only El Greco painting on display in Crete. Downstairs is the large **Byzantine collection** which includes vestments, ecclesiastical ornaments, icons, coins, jewellery and a reconstruction of a chapel.

The 1st floor has a reconstruction of the **library of author Nikos Kazantzakis**, with displays of letters, manuscripts and books. Another room is devoted to Emmanual Tsouderos, who was born in Rethymno and who was prime minister in 1941. There are some dramatic photographs of a ruined Iraklio in the **Battle of Crete** section.

The outstanding **folklore collection** on the 2nd floor includes displays of embroidery, weavings, crochet, tapestry, jewellery and costumes as well as an impressive wedding loaf.

The museum, which is just back from the western waterfront, is open in summer Monday to Friday from 9 am to 4.30 pm and on Saturday from 9 am to 2 pm. In winter, it opens Monday to Saturday from 9.30 am to 2.30 pm. Admission is 800 dr.

Other Things to See Iraklio burst out of its city walls long ago but these massive **fortifications**, with seven bastions and four gates, are still very conspicuous, dwarfing the concrete structures of the 20th century. Venetians built the defences between 1462 and 1562. The 16th-century **Rocca al Mare**, another Venetian fortress, stands at the end of the Old Harbour's jetty. This fortress (☎ 24 6211) is open Tuesday to Sunday from 8.30 am to 3 pm. Entry is 500 dr.

Several other notable vestiges from Venetian times survive in the city. Most famous is the **Morosini fountain** on Plateia Venizelou, which spurts water from four lions into eight ornate U-shaped marble troughs. The fountain, built in 1628, was commissioned by Francesco Morosini while he was governor of Crete. Opposite is the three-aisled 13th-century **Basilica of San Marco**. It has been reconstructed many times and is now an exhibition gallery. A little north of here is the attractive reconstructed 17th-century **Venetian loggia**. It was a Venetian version of a gentleman's club; a place where the male aristocracy went to drink and gossip.

The delightful **Bembo fountain**, at the southern end of 1866, is shown on local maps as the Turkish fountain, but it was actually built by the Venetians in the 16th century. It was constructed from a hotchpotch of building materials including an ancient statue. The ornate edifice next to the fountain was added by the Turks, and now functions as a snack bar.

The former Church of Agia Ekaterini, next to Agios Minos Cathedral, is now a **museum** (☎ 24 2111) housing an impressive collection of icons. Most notable are the six icons painted by Mihail Damaskinos, the mentor of Domenikos Theotokopoulos (El Greco). It was closed for repairs at the time of writing, but is normally open Monday to Saturday from 10.30 am to 1 pm. In addition it opens on Tuesday, Thursday and Friday afternoons from 4.30 to 6.30 pm. Admission is 500 dr.

You can pay homage to Crete's most acclaimed contemporary writer, Nikos Kazantzakis (1883-1957), by visiting his tomb at the Martinenga Bastion (the best preserved bastion) in the southern part of town. The epitaph on his grave, 'I hope for nothing, I fear nothing, I am free', is taken from one of his works.

Trekking

The Iraklio branch of the EOS (☎ 22 7609) is at Dikeosynis 53. It owns the Prinos Refuge on Mt Ida, which is reached by walking for 1½ hours along a footpath from the village of Melisses, 25 km from Iraklio.

Organised Tours

Iraklio's travel agents run coach tours the length and breadth of Crete. Creta Travel (☎ 22 7002), Epimenidou 20-22, has a good choice of local tours. A guided tour of Knossos and Iraklio's archaeological museum costs 4100 dr. Other excursions are to Vathypetro Villa, the Arhanes villages, the Nikos Kazantzakis Museum and Thrapsano (5000 dr); Phaestos, Gortyn and Agia Triada (5500 dr); and Samaria gorge (7500 dr). Prices don't include admission fees.

Places to Stay – bottom end

The nearest camp sites are 26 km away at Hersonisos. Iraklio has two youth hostels, both charging an identical 1000 dr for a bed

---

El Greco

He may have needed to travel to Spain to earn recognition as El Greco (the Greek), one of the geniuses of the Renaissance, but Domeniko Theotokopoulos never forgot his Cretan origins.

El Greco was born in the Cretan capital of Candia (present-day Iraklio) in 1541 during a time of great artistic activity in the city. Many of the artists, writers and philosophers who fled Constantinople after it was conquered by the Turks in 1453 had settled on Crete, leading to the emergence of the Cretan school of icon painters. The painters had a formative influence upon the young El Greco, giving him the early grounding in the traditions of late Byzantine fresco painting that was to give such a powerful spiritual element to his later paintings.

Candia being a Venetian city, it was a logical step for El Greco to head to Venice to further his studies, and he set off when he was in his early 20s to join the studio of Titian. It was not, however, until he moved to Spain in 1577 that he really came into his own as a painter. His highly emotional style struck a chord with the Spanish, and the city of Toledo was to become his home until his death in 1614. To view the most famous of his works like his masterpiece *The Burial of Count Orgaz* (1586), you will have to travel to Toledo. The only El Greco work on display in Crete is *View of Mt Sinai and the Monastery of St Catherine* (1570), painted during his time in Venice. It hangs in Iraklio's Historical Museum of Crete.

A white marble bust of the painter stands in the city's Plateia El Greco, and streets are named after him throughout the island. ■

in single-sex dorms, or 3000/4500 dr for basic doubles/triples. The YHO hostel at Vyronos 5 (☎ 28 6281) is a clean, well-run place, but many people prefer the livelier atmosphere at Handakos 24 (☎ 28 0858) where the YHA hostel has a roof garden and bar. The reception area is on the roof.

Many of Iraklio's budget hotels have gone out of business in the last couple of years. Those that remain are an uninspiring lot. The best of them is the *Hotel Mirabello* (☎ 28 5052), Theotokopoulou 20, a friendly place with clean singles/doubles for 4000/6000 with shared bathroom, 5500/7500 dr with private bathroom. The *Pension Atlas* (☎ 28 8989), close to Plateia Venizelou at Kantanoleon 6, has rooms with private bathroom for 4000/6000. Theotokopoulou is just north of El Greco Park, off Kidonias.

Public relations aren't high on the agenda at *Vergina Rooms* (☎ 24 2739) at 32 Hortatson. It's a shame because the place has a bit of character – a turn-of-the-century house with a small courtyard, spacious rooms and high ceilings. Doubles/triples are 5000/6000 with shared bathroom.

The *Hotel Rea*, 50 metres away at the junction of Handakos and Kalimeraki, is nothing much to look at, but it's clean, comfortable and friendly. Singles/doubles/triples with shared bathroom are 4000/5500/7000 dr, while doubles/triples with private bathroom are 6400/8200 dr.

The *Cretan Sun Hotel* (☎ 24 3794), in the middle of the markets at No 10 Odos 1866, is not a place for late risers. The traders turn up at dawn, bellowing their greetings – better than an alarm clock if you've got an early bus to catch. It charges 5000/6000 dr for large, clean singles/doubles.

Places to Stay – middle

Several of the city's C-class hotels were being refitted at the time of writing, the *Hotel Lato* (☎ 22 8103/5001), overlooking the harbour at Epimenidou 15, was completely gutted. In the centre of town, the *Hotel Daedalos* (☎ 22 4391/2), Dedalou 15, and the *Hotel Selena* (☎ 22 6377/8), Androgeo 7, was having less radical surgery – as was the

Hotel Metropol (☎ 24 4280) on Karterou. All were previously recommended.

The absence of these four places leaves the field looking very threadbare. The supposedly B-class *Hotel Petra* (☎ 22 9912), Dikeosynis 55, looks in dire need of a refit at the very least. The 8500/11,500 dr for singles/doubles includes continental breakfast. The C-class *Hotel Irini* (☎ 22 9703), Idomeneos 4, is considerably smarter. The rooms are large and airy, but no great bargain at 10,400/14,000 dr – also with breakfast.

Places to Stay – top end

The best place in town is the A-class *Astoria Hotel* (☎ 22 9002; fax 22 9078), Plateia Eleftherias 11, where singles/doubles are 23,500/28,000. Facilities include a swimming pool.

Don't be fooled by the A-class tag attached to the dreadful *Hotel Xenia* (☎ 28 4000). This prize eyesore occupies a prime waterfront site opposite the northern end of Handakos. The crumbling concrete and flaking paint of the exterior are a fair indication of what's in store inside.

Places to Eat – inexpensive

Iraklio has some excellent restaurants, and there's something to suit all tastes and pockets.

If you're after traditional taverna food, the place to look is Theodasaki, a little street between 1866 and Evans. The choices include *Lakis Taverna*, a popular spot turning out a big bowl of tasty bean stew for 750 dr and maraconi with octopus for 1050 dr. The *Restaurant Ionia*, 20 metres away on the corner of Evans and Giannari, serves very similar food in fancier surroundings for a few drachma more.

The *Ippocampos Ouzeri*, on the waterfront just west of 25 Avgoustou, is as good as this style of eating gets. It has a huge range of mezedes on offer, priced from 400 dr. The fish dishes are especially recommended. They include grilled octopus (800 dr), calamari (800 dr) and sea urchins (900 dr). The place is always busy, so it's a good idea to get in early. It's closed between 3.30 and

7 pm. There are sea horses (ippokampos) painted over the door at the Mitsotaki entrance.

If you haven't yet tried loukoumades (fritters with syrup), then the unpretentious *Loukoumades Café* on Dikeosynis is a good place to sample this gooey confection. For a meal on the move, try the tiny *Bougatsa Serraikon*, on Idis in the city centre. It makes excellent sweet (custard-filled) and savoury (cheese-filled) bougatsa for 280 dr.

For those in need of a change, the *Curry House*, on Perdilaki, puts together a decent chicken curry for 1400 dr; or 1700 dr for lamb or beef.

Whether or not you're self catering, you'll enjoy a stroll up 1866 (the market street). This narrow street is always packed, and stalls spill over with produce of every description, including ornate Cretan wedding loaves. These loaves (smaller versions of the one on display at the Historical Museum of Crete) are not meant to be eaten, rather they make an attractive kitchen decoration.

Places to Eat – expensive

The *Giovanni Taverna* is a splendid place with elegant antique furniture and subdued lighting; in summer there is outdoor eating on a quiet pedestrian street. The food is traditional Greek, but carefully prepared with discriminating use of herbs and spices. From Platcia Venizelou walk one block up Dedalou, turn left onto Perdikari, take the first right onto Korai, and you will come to the taverna on the right. A delicious meal for two people, including a carafe of house red, costs about 9000 dr.

Getting There & Away

Air – domestic There are at least five flights a day to Athens (19,200 dr) from Iraklio's Nikos Kazantzakis Airport; six a week to Thessaloniki (27,600 dr); four a week to Rhodes (19,200 dr); and three a week to both Mykonos (18,000 dr) and Santorini (13,400 dr). The Mykonos service operates only between 11 June and 23 September. The Olympic Airways office (☎ 22 9191) is on Plateia Eleftherias.

At the time of writing, Air Greece was operating a restricted service in competition with Olympic Airways. It had three flights a week to Athens (15,000 dr), three to Thessaloniki (23,000 dr) and two to Rhodes (16,500 dr). Their office (☎ 33 0739) is at Ethnikis Antistaseos 122.

Air – international Olympic Airways has direct flights to Rome on Thursday and to Vienna on Sunday. KLM associate Transavia flies direct between Amsterdam and Iraklio on Monday and Friday, while Lufthansa flies to Frankfurt on Saturday and Sunday. Transavia is represented by Sbokos Tours (☎ 22 9712), Dimokratias 51, and Lufthansa by Plotin Travel (☎ 24 5068), Ethnikis Antistaseos 172.

Iraklio has a lot of charter flights from all over Europe. Prince Travel (☎ 28 2706), 25 Avgoustou 30, advertises cheap last-minute tickets on these flights. Sample fares include London for 28,000 dr and Munich for 38,000 dr. Grecomar Holidays (☎ 24 6672), Xanthidou 1, has flights to Paris and Zürich (both for 40,000 dr) with charter operator Venus Airlines.

Bus There are buses every half-hour (hourly in winter) to Rethymno (1½ hours, 1250 dr) and Hania (2¾ hours, 2400 dr) from the Rethymno/Hania bus station opposite Bus Station A.

Buses leave Bus Station A for:

Destination	Duration	Fare	Frequency
Agia Pelagia	30 mins	500 dr	6 daily
Agios Nikolaos	1½ hours	1150 dr	half-hourly
Arhanes	30 mins	280 dr	12 daily
Hersonisos/Malia	1 hour	600 dr	half-hourly
Ierapetra	2½ hours	1700 dr	7 daily
Lassithi plateau	2 hours	1150 dr	2 daily
Milatos	1½ hours	850 dr	2 daily
Sitia	3¼ hours	2350 dr	6 daily

Buses leave Bus Station B for:

Destination	Duration	Fare	Frequency
Agia Galini	2½ hours	1250 dr	7 daily
Anogia	1 hour	600 dr	6 daily
Fodele	1 hour	550 dr	2 daily

Destination	Duration	Fare	Frequency
Matala	2 hours	1250 dr	7 daily
Phaestos	2 hours	1050 dr	9 daily

Taxi There are long-distance taxis (☎ 21 0102) from Plateia Eleftherias, opposite the Astoria Hotel, to all parts of Crete. Sample fares include Agios Nikolaos, 7500 dr; Plakias, 13,500 dr; and Hania, 15,000 dr.

Ferry – domestic Minoan Lines and ANEK both operate ferries every evening each way between Iraklio and Piraeus (10 hours). They depart from both Piraeus and Iraklio between 6.30 and 7.30 pm. Fares are 4900 dr deck class, 6595 dr for tourist-class cabins and 8650 dr for second-class cabins. The Minoan Lines boats, the F/B *Nikos Kazantazakis* and the F/B *Knossos*, are more modern and more comfortable than their ANEK rivals. ANEK, though, is a better bet for deck-class travellers. It has dorm beds with plastic-covered mattresses, while Minoan Lines has only seats.

GA Ferries has three boats a week to Santorini (four hours, 2420 dr), continuing to Paros (7½ hours, 4200 dr) and Piraeus. Two of them also stop at Naxos. GA also has three ferries a week to Rhodes (11 hours, 5290 dr) via Karpathos (3110 dr). Nomicos Lines runs three boats a week to Thessaloniki via Santorini, Paros, Mykonos, Tinos and the Sporades. The travel agencies on 25 Avgoustou are the place to get information and buy tickets. Iraklio's port police can be contacted on ☎ 24 4912.

Ferry – international Two companies operate boats to the Israeli port of Haifa (22,500 dr for deck class, 31,500 dr for B class) via Limassol (15,000/22,500 dr). The Poseidon Lines ferry F/B *Sea Harmony* leaves Iraklio at 11 am on Tuesday and also calls at Rhodes on the way to Limassol (Wednesday noon) and Haifa (Thursday at 6.30 am). The Vergina Lines' boat F/B *Vergina* leaves at noon on Friday.

Marlines runs the F/B *Countess* on a weekly circuit from Ancona in Italy to Kuşadası in Turkey via Iraklio between 24

June and 13 September. The service leaves Ancona at 6 pm on Saturday to Iraklio (51 hours, 25,500 dr deck class), and Iraklio at 10 pm on Monday to Kuşadası (14 hours, 10,500). On the way back, it leaves Turkey at 7 pm on Wednesday and Iraklio at 10 am on Thursday, also calling at Patras en route to Ancona.

Hydrofoil From May until October, high-speed catamarans link Iraklio with Santorini (2½ hours, 4800 dr), Ios (3½ hours, 5900 dr), Naxos (4½ hours, 8800 dr), Paros (five hours, 8800 dr) and Mykonos (6½ hours, 9400 dr). The catamarans leave Iraklio at 8 am Monday to Friday, and 8.30 am on Sunday. The route varies, but always includes Santorini and Ios.

Getting Around
To/From the Airport Bus No 1 goes to/from the airport every 15 minutes between 6 am and 1 am for 140 dr. It leaves the city from outside the Astoria Hotel on Plateia Eleftherias.

To/From Knossos Local bus No 2 goes to Knossos every 15 minutes from Bus Station A. It also stops on 25 Avgoustou and 1821. The journey takes 20 minutes and costs 180 dr.

Car & Motorbike Most of Iraklio's car and motorbike-hire outlets are on 25 Avgoustou. Avis (☎ 22 5421/9402) is at No 58 and Hertz (☎ 22 9702/9802) is at No 34, but you'll get a better deal from local companies like Sun Rise (☎ 28 0428) at No 76, or from Loggeta Cars & Bikes (☎ 28 9462) at Plateia Kallergon 6, next to El Greco Park. There are car-hire outlets at the airport.

Loggeta also has a range of scooters and motorbikes.

KNOSSOS Κνωσσός
Knossos (Knos-OS), five km from Iraklio, was the capital of Minoan Crete. Nowadays it's the island's major tourist attraction.

The ruins of Knossos were uncovered in 1900 by the British archaeologist, Sir Arthur

Evans. Schliemann had had his eye on the spot (a low flat-topped mound), believing an ancient city was buried there, but had been unable to strike a deal with the local landowner.

Evans was so enthralled by his discovery that he spent 35 years and £250,000 of his own money excavating and reconstructing

sections of the palace. Some archaeologists have disparaged Evans' reconstruction, believing he sacrificed accuracy to his overly vivid imagination. However, most nonspecialists agree Sir Arthur did a good job and that Knossos is a knockout. Without these reconstructions it would be impossible to visualise what a Minoan palace looked like.

The Myth of the Minotaur

King Minos of Crete invoked the wrath of Poseidon when he failed to sacrifice a magnificent white bull sent to him for that purpose. Poseidon's revenge was to cause Pasiphae, King Minos' wife, to fall in love with the animal.

In order to attract the bull, Pasiphae asked Daedalus, chief architect at Knossos and all-round handyman, to make her a hollow, wooden cow structure. When she concealed herself inside, the bull found her irresistible. The outcome of their bizarre association was the Minotaur: a hideous monster who was half-man and half-bull.

King Minos asked Daedalus to build a labyrinth in which to confine the Minotaur and demanded that Athens pay an annual tribute of seven youths and seven maidens to satisfy the monster's huge appetite.

Theseus killing the Minotaur

Minos eventually found out that Daedalus had been instrumental in bringing about the union between his wife and the bull, and threw the architect and his son Icarus into the labyrinth. Daedalus made wings from feathers stuck together with wax and, wearing these, father and son made their getaway. As everyone knows, Icarus flew too close to the sun, the wax on his wings melted, and he plummeted into the sea off the island of Ikaria.

Athenians, meanwhile, were enraged by the tribute demanded by Minos. The Athenian hero, Theseus, vowed to kill the Minotaur and sailed off to Crete posing as one of the sacrificial youths. On arrival, he fell in love with Ariadne, the daughter of King Minos, and she promised to help him if he would take her away with him afterwards. She provided him with the ball of twine that he unwound on his way into the labyrinth and used to retrace his steps after slaying the monster. Theseus fled Crete with Ariadne. The two married but Theseus abandoned Ariadne on the island of Naxos on his way back to Athens.

On his return to Athens, Theseus forgot to unfurl the white sail that he had promised to display to announce that he was still alive. This prompted his distraught father, Aegeus, to hurl himself to his death from the Acropolis. This, incidentally, is how the Aegean Sea got its name. ∎

Knossos palace ruins

You will need to spend about four hours at Knossos to explore it thoroughly. The café at the site is expensive – you'd do better to bring a picnic along. The site (☎ 23 1940) is open every day from 8 am to 7 pm between April and October. In winter the site closes at 5 pm. Admission is 1000 dr.

History

The first palace at Knossos was built around 1900 BC. In 1700 BC it was destroyed by an earthquake and rebuilt to a grander and more sophisticated design. It is this palace which Evans reconstructed. It was partially destroyed again sometime between 1500 and 1450 BC. It was inhabited for another 50 years before it was devastated once and for all by fire.

The city of Knossos consisted of an immense palace, residences of officials and priests, the homes of ordinary people, and burial grounds. The palace consisted of royal domestic quarters, public reception rooms, shrines, workshops, treasuries and storerooms, all built around a central court. Like all Minoan palaces, it also doubled as a city hall; all the bureaucracy necessary for the smooth running of a complex society was housed within its walls.

Exploring the Site

Numerous rooms, corridors, dogleg passages, nooks and crannies, and staircases prohibit a detailed described walk around the palace. However, Knossos is not a site where you'll be perplexed by heaps of rubble, trying to fathom whether you're looking at the throne room or a workshop. Thanks to Evans' reconstruction, the most significant parts of the complex are instantly recognisable (if not instantly found). On your wanders you will come across a good number of Evans' reconstructed columns; most are painted deep brown-red with gold-trimmed black capitals. These, like all Minoan columns, taper at the bottom.

It is not only the vibrant frescoes and mighty columns which impress at Knossos; keep your eyes open for the little details which are evidence of a highly sophisticated society. Things to look out for are the drainage system; the placement of light wells; and the relationship of rooms to passages, porches, light wells and verandahs to keep rooms cool in summer and warm in winter.

The usual entrance to the palace complex is across the Western Court and along the **Corridor of the Procession Fresco**. The fresco depicted a long line of people carrying gifts to present to the king; only fragments remain. A copy of one of these fragments, called the **Priest King Fresco**, can be seen to the south of the Central Court.

An alternative is to have a look at the Corridor of the Procession Fresco, but then leave it and walk straight ahead to enter the site from the northern end. If you do this you will come to the **theatral area**, a series of steps whose function remains unknown. It could have been a theatre where spectators watched acrobatic and dance performances, or the place where people gathered to welcome important visitors arriving by the Royal Road.

The **Royal Road** leads off to the west. The road, Europe's first (Knossos has lots of firsts), was flanked by workshops and the houses of ordinary people. The **lustral basin** is also in this area. Evans speculated that this was where the Minoans performed a ritual cleansing with water before religious ceremonies.

Entering the **Central Court** from the north, you will pass the relief **Bull Fresco** which depicts a charging bull. Relief frescoes were made by moulding wet plaster, and then painting it while still wet.

Also worth seeking out in the northern section of the palace are the **giant pithoi**. Pithoi were ceramic jars used for storing olive oil, wine and grain. Evans found over 100 of these huge jars at Knossos (some were two metres high). The raised patterns decorating the jars were inspired by the ropes which were used to move them.

Once you have reached the Central Court, which in Minoan times was surrounded by the high walls of the palace, you can begin exploring the most important rooms of the complex.

CRETE

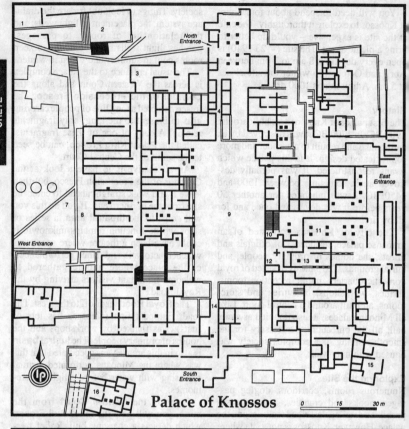

Palace of Knossos

North Entrance

East Entrance

West Entrance

South Entrance

0   15   30 m

1	Royal Road	7	Western Court	12	Water Closet
2	Theatral Area	8	Corridor of the	13	Queen's Megaron
3	Lustral Basin		Procession Fresco	14	Priest King Fresco
4	Bull Fresco	9	Central Court	15	South-East House
5	Giant Pithoi	10	Grand Staircase	16	South House
6	Throne Room	11	Hall of the Double Axes		

From the northern end of the west side of the palace, steps lead down to the **throne room**. This room is fenced off but you can still get a good view of it. The centrepiece, the simple, beautifully proportioned throne, is flanked by the **Griffin Fresco**. Griffins

were mythical beasts regarded as sacred by the Minoans.

The room is thought to have been a shrine, and the throne the seat of a high priestess, rather than a king. Certainly, the room seems to have an aura of mysticism and reverence rather than pomp and ceremony. The Minoans did not worship their deities in great temples but in small shrines, and each palace had several.

On the 1st floor of this side of the palace is the section Evans called the **Piano Nobile**, for he believed the reception and state rooms were here. A room at the northern end of this floor displays copies of some of the frescoes found at Knossos.

Returning to the Central Court, the impressive **grand staircase** leads from the middle of the eastern side of the palace to the royal apartments, which Evans called the Domestic Quarter. At the bottom of this staircase, a right turn leads eventually to the **Hall of the Double Axes**. This was the king's megaron, a spacious double room in which the ruler both slept and carried out certain court duties. The room had a light well at one end and a balcony at the other to ensure air circulation. The room is so called because of double axe marks on its light well. These marks appear in many places at Knossos. The double axe was a sacred symbol to the Minoans. *Labrys* was Minoan for 'double axe' and the origin of our word labyrinth.

A passage leads from the Hall of the Double Axes to the **queen's megaron**. Above the door is a copy of the **Dolphin Fresco**, one of the most exquisite Minoan artworks, and a blue floral design decorates the portal. Next to this room is the queen's bathroom, complete with terracotta bathtub. For most people, the *pièce de résistance* of the queen's suite is the **water closet**, touted as the first ever to work on the flush principle. Don't look for the chain – water had to be poured down by hand. This marvel of Minoan plumbing is reached by a short passage from the queen's megaron.

Getting There & Away

Regular buses operate from Iraklio. See Iraklio's Getting Around section for details.

MYRTIA Μυρτιά

Myrtia (also called Varvari), 22 km south of Iraklio, is making the most of being the village that spawned Crete's favourite literary son, Nikos Kazantzakis. Kazantzakis was born in Iraklio and lived most of his life overseas, but his father was born here – and the writer himself lived here for a time. The **Nikos Kazantzakis Museum**, on the central square of the village, has a collection of the writer's personal mementoes. A video show compiled from film clippings of the author's life is shown in Greek, German, French and English.

The museum is open Monday, Wednesday and weekends from 9 am to 1 pm and 4 to 8 pm, and on Tuesday and Friday from 9 am to 1 pm only. Admission costs 500 dr.

The journey to the village passes through lovely vineyard country. The museum is signposted from the main road. Creta Travel (see Organised Tours under Iraklio) offers a tour which includes this museum and the villages of Arhanes and Thrapsano (5000 dr, excluding museum fee).

TYLISOS Τύλισος

The minor Minoan site at the village of Tylisos (TIL-is-os), 13 km from Iraklio, is only for the insatiable enthusiast. Three villas dating from different periods have been excavated. The site (☎ 22 6092) is open Tuesday to Sunday from 8.30 am to 3 pm. Admission is 500 dr. Buses from Iraklio to Anogia go through Tylisos. They also go past another Minoan site at **Sklavokambos**, eight km closer to Anogia. The ruins date from 1500 BC and were probably the villa of a district governor.

ARHANES Αρχάνες

The attractive village of Arhanes (Ar-HAN-es), 16 km from Iraklio, lies in the heart of Crete's principal grape-producing region. Several Minoan remains have been unearthed in the vineyards surrounding the village. The most noteworthy is the elaborate **Vathypetro Villa**, the home of a prosperous Minoan noble.

The villa complex included storerooms, where wine and oil presses, a weaving loom, and a kiln were discovered. The villa is five km from Arhanes, on the road south – look for a signpost to the right. There is no entrance fee.

Getting There & Away

It's a pleasant outing from Iraklio to Arhanes if you have your own transport. Otherwise, there are 12 buses a day from Iraklio's Bus Station A to Arhanes (half an hour, 280 dr). There are no buses to Vathypetro, but Creta Travel in Iraklio has a tour which includes a visit to the villa.

GORTYN Γόρτυνα

The archaeological site of Gortyn (also called Gortina and Gortys) lies 46 km south-west of Iraklio, and 15 km from Phaestos, on the plain of Mesara. It's a vast and wonderfully intriguing site with bits and pieces from various ages strewn all over the place. The site was a settlement from Minoan to Christian times. In Roman times, Gortyn was the capital of the province of Cyrenaica.

The most significant find at the site was the massive stone tablets inscribed with the **Laws of Gortyn**, which date from the 5th century BC. The laws deal with just about every imaginable offence. The tablets are on display at the site.

The 6th-century **basilica** is dedicated to Agios Titos, who was a protégé of St Paul and the first bishop of Crete.

Other ruins at Gortyn include the 2nd-century AD **praetorin** which was the residence of the governor of the province, a **nymphaeum** and the **Temple of Pythian Apollo**. The site (☎ 081-22 6092) is open every day from 8.30 am to 3 pm. Admission is 800 dr. The ruins are on both sides of the main Iraklio-Phaestos road.

PHAESTOS Φαιστός

The Minoan site of Phaestos (Fes-TOS), 63 km from Iraklio, was the second most important palace city of Minoan Crete. Of all the Minoan sites, Phaestos has the most awe-inspiring location, with all-embracing views of the Mesara plain and Mt Ida. The layout of the palace is identical to Knossos, with rooms arranged around a central court.

In contrast to Knossos, Phaestos has yielded very few frescoes; it seems the palace walls were mostly covered with a layer of white gypsum. Perhaps, with such inspiring views from the windows, the inhabitants didn't feel any need to decorate their walls. Evans didn't get his hands on the ruins of Phaestos, so there has been no reconstruction. Like the other palatial complexes, there was an old palace here which was destroyed at the end of the Middle Minoan period. Unlike the other sites, parts of this old palace have been excavated and its ruins are partially superimposed upon the new palace.

Exploring the Site

The entrance to the new palace is by the magnificent and perfectly proportioned, 15-metre-wide **Grand Staircase**. The stairs lead to the west side of the **Central Court**. The best preserved parts of the palace complex are the reception rooms and private apartments which are to the north of the Central Court; excavations continue here. This section was entered by an imposing portal with half columns at either side, the lower parts of which are still *in situ*. Unlike the Minoan freestanding columns, these do not taper at the base. The celebrated Phaestos disc was found in a building to the north of the palace. The disc is in Iraklio's archaeological museum.

Getting There & Away

There are 10 buses a day from Iraklio's Bus Station B to Phaestos (two hours, 1050 dr), seven from Agia Galini (40 minutes, 360 dr) and six from Matala (30 minutes, 220 dr). Services are halved in winter.

AGIA TRIADA Αγία Τριάδα

Agia Triada (Ag-I-a Tri-A-da) is a small Minoan site three km west of Phaestos. Its principal building was smaller than the other royal palaces but built to a similar design. This, and the opulence of the objects found at the site, indicate that it was a royal residence, possibly a summer palace of Phaestos' rulers. To the north of the palace is a small town where remains of a stoa have been unearthed.

Finds from the palace now in Iraklio's archaeological museum include a sarcophagus, two superlative frescoes and three vases: the Harvester Vase, Boxer Vase and Chieftain Cup.

The site is open Tuesday to Sunday from 8.30 am to 3 pm. Admission is 500 dr. The road to Agia Triada takes off to the right about 500 metres from Phaestos on the road to Matala. There is no public transport to the site. You can walk there in about 30 minutes along the path around the north side of the ridge between Phaestos and Agia Triada, but only if someone has unlocked the gate giving access to the path. The path starts opposite the ruins of an old church on the roadside just west of the Phaestos car park.

MATALA Μάταλα

Matala (MA-ta-la), on the coast 11 km southwest of Phaestos, was once one of Crete's best known hippie hang-outs.

It was the old Roman caves at the northern end of the beach that made Matala famous in the 60s. There are dozens of them dotted over the cliff-face, half-a-dozen or so to each small terrace. They were originally tombs, cut out of the sandstone rock in the 1st century AD. In the 60s, they were discovered by hippies, who turned the caves into a modern troglodyte city – moving ever higher up the cliff to avoid sporadic attempts by the local police to evict them. Joni Mitchell was among the visitors, and she sang the praises of life under a Matala moon in *Carey*.

These days, Matala is another decidedly tacky tourist resort. The place is packed out in summer, bleak and deserted in winter. The sandy beach below the caves is, however, one of Crete's best, and the resort is a convenient base from which to visit Phaestos and Agia Triada.

Orientation & Information

Matala's layout is easy to fathom. The bus stop is on the central square, one block back from the waterfront. There is a mobile post office near the beach, on the right of the main road as you come into Matala. The OTE is beyond here in the beach car park. The telephone code for Matala is 0892, and the postcode is 702 00.

Places to Stay

Matala Community Camping (☎ 42 340) is a reasonable site just back from the beach. There is another camping site near Komos beach (☎ 42 596), about four km before Matala on the road from Phaestos.

If you don't mind being away from where it's all happening, there are several pleasant options along the approach road to Matala. After seeing where it's all happening you may well decide you made the right decision in staying away. The options here include *Rooms to Rent Dimitris* (☎ 42 740), where singles/doubles/triples go for 2500/3500/4500 dr.

If you decide to brave Matala proper, walk back along the main road from the bus station and turn right at the Zafiria Hotel. This street is lined with budget accommodation. One of the cheapest places is *Fantastic Rooms to Rent* (☎ 42 369), on the right. The comfortable double/triple rooms cost 4000/6000 dr with private bathroom.

The C-class *Hotel Fragiskos* (☎ 42 390), on the left as you head out of town, charges 5500/9000 dr for singles/doubles with private bathroom. It has a swimming pool.

If you don't like the sound of Matala, then **Pitsidia village**, 4.5 km inland and seven km from Phaestos, is a quieter alternative. There are no hotels but plenty of rooms.

Places to Eat

Most of the restaurants in Matala are poor value. One place that isn't is the *Taverna Giannis*, very close to the main square on the way to the southern headland. It's the only place that's open all year. A huge plate of calamari, chips and salad costs 1200 dr, while a bowl of tasty lentil soup is 600 dr. The *Restaurant Mystical View*, high above Komos beach about three km from Matala, has views which live up to its name and serves good food to boot. The restaurant is signposted off the road to Phaestos.

CRETE

Getting There & Away

There are seven buses a day between Iraklio and Matala (two hours, 1250 dr) and six a day between Matala and Phaestos (30 minutes, 220 dr).

MALIA Μάλια

The Minoan site of Malia (MAL-ee-a) is the only cultural diversion on the stretch of coast east of Iraklio, which otherwise has surrendered lock, stock and barrel to the package-tourist industry. Malia is smaller than Knossos and Phaestos, but like them consisted of a palace complex and a town. Unlike Knossos and Phaestos, the palace was built on a flat fertile plain, not on a hill.

The site (☎ 22 462) is three km east of the resort of Malia, and is open Tuesday to Sunday from 8.30 am to 3 pm. Admission is 800 dr.

Exploring the Site

Entrance to the ruins is from the **West Court**. At the extreme southern end of this court there are eight circular pits which archaeologists think were used to store grain. To the east of the pits is the main entrance to the palace which leads to the southern end of the **Central Court**. At the south-west corner of this court you will find the **Kernos Stone**, a disc with 34 holes around its edge. Archaeologists have yet to ascertain its function.

The **central staircase** is at the north end of the west side of the palace. The **loggia**, just north of the staircase, is where religious ceremonies took place.

Getting There & Away

Any bus going to/from Iraklio along the north coast can drop you at the site.

Eastern Crete

The eastern quarter of the island is occupied by the prefecture of Lassithi, named after the quaint plateau tucked high in the Mt Dikti ranges rather than its uninspiring administrative capital of Agios Nikolaos. Eastern Crete is the least fertile, the least populated and the least interesting part of the island. This hasn't prevented Agios Nikolaos from becoming something of a monument to package tourism. The main attractions are at the eastern extreme: the palm forest and beach at Vaï and the remote Minoan palace site of Zakros.

AGIOS NIKOLAOS Αγιος Νικόλαος

The manifestations of package tourism gather momentum as they advance east from Iraklio, reaching their peak at Agios Nikolaos (A-yios Nik-O-la-os). In July and August the town's permanent population of 9000 is joined by 11,000 tourists. Most of these are sun-starved Brits; the lure of the *Lotus Eaters* and *Who Pays the Ferryman* (TV series which were filmed nearby) first dragged them in over a decade ago, and they've been arriving in ever-increasing numbers since.

The result is that there is very little to attract the independent traveller. There is no point in attempting to squeeze into Agios Nikolaos in the peak season between July and mid-September, and the place just about closes down entirely in winter.

Orientation

The town centre is Plateia Venizelou, 150 metres up Sofias Venizelou from the bus station. The most interesting part of town is around the picturesque Voulismeni lake, which is ringed with tavernas and cafés. The lake is 200 metres from the central square down Koundourou. Turn left at the bottom of Koundourou and you will come to a bridge which separates the lake from the harbour. The tourist office is at the far side of the bridge.

Once over the bridge, if you turn right and follow the road as it veers left, you will come to the northern stretch of waterfront which is the road to Elounda. Most of Agios Nikolaos' large and expensive hotels are along here. If you turn right at the bottom of Koundourou you will come to a stretch of waterfront with steps leading up to the right. These lead to the streets which have the highest concentration of small hotels and pensions.

Information

The municipal tourist office (☎ 22 357; fax 26 398) is open daily from 8.30 am to 9.30 pm from 1 April to 15 November. The office has little to offer other than a map, but apparently will help to find accommodation if you are brave enough to turn up in the high season. The tourist police (☎ 26 900), Kondogianni 34, are open 24 hours.

Money The National Bank of Greece on Plastira, just off Plateia Venizelou has a 24-hour automatic-exchange machine. The tourist office also changes money.

Post & Telecommunications The post office, 28 Oktovriou 9, is open Monday to Saturday from 7.30 am to 2 pm. The OTE is on the corner of 25 Martiou and K Sfakianaki. It is open daily from 7 am to 11 pm. Agios Nikolaos' postcode is 721 00 and the telephone code is 0841.

Bookshop There is a well-stocked English-language bookshop at Koundourou 5.

CRETE

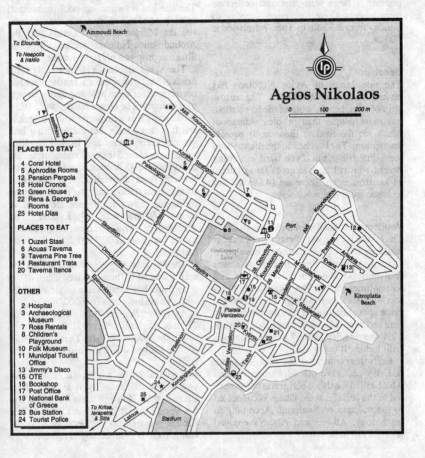

To Ammoudi Beach
To Elounda
To Neapolis & Iraklio

Agios Nikolaos

0   100   200 m

Lassithiou
Akti Koundourou
Koraka
Stratigou
Paleologou
Kontosa
Quay
Koundourou
Port
Akti
Stordilon
Dimokratias
Plastira
Voulismeni Lake
28 Oktovriou
Koundourou
25 Martiou
M Sfakianaki
Plastira
Ariadnis
Evans
Modatsou
K Sfakianaki
Kitroplatia Beach
Epimenidou
Fileninon
Plateia Venizelou
Kyprou
Kondogianni
Sofias
Venizelou
Tavla
To Kritsa, Ierapetra & Sitia
Stadium

PLACES TO STAY
4 Coral Hotel
5 Aphrodite Rooms
12 Pension Pergola
18 Hotel Cronos
21 Green House
22 Rena & George's Rooms
25 Hotel Dias

PLACES TO EAT
1 Ouzeri Stasi
6 Acuas Taverna
9 Taverna Pine Tree
14 Restaurant Trata
20 Taverna Itanos

OTHER
2 Hospital
3 Archaeological Museum
7 Ross Rentals
10 Folk Museum
11 Municipal Tourist Office
13 Jimmy's Disco
15 OTE
16 Bookshop
17 Post Office
19 National Bank of Greece
23 Bus Station
24 Tourist Police

Children's Playground

CRETE

Emergency

Agios Nikolaos' general hospital (☎ 25 221) is between Lassithiou and Paleologou.

Museums

The **folk museum**, next door to the tourist office, has a well-displayed collection of traditional handcrafts and costumes, and photographs. It's open Sunday to Friday from 10 am to 1.30 pm and 6 to 9.30 pm. Admission is 200 dr.

The **archaeological museum** (☎ 24 943), on Paleologou, is a modern building housing a large well-displayed collection from eastern Crete. It's open Tuesday to Sunday from 8.30 am to 3 pm. Admission is 500 dr.

Beaches

The popularity of Agios Nikolaos has nothing to do with its beaches. The narrow strip of town beach, south of the bus station, has more people than pebbles. Ammoudi beach, on the road to Elounda, is equally uninspiring. The beaches on the road to Sitia are a little better, but if you want something decent you will have to go as far as Istron, 11 km from town. There are 14 buses a day to Istron from Agios Nikolaos.

Voulismeni Lake Λίμνη Βουλισμένη

The lake is the subject of many stories about its depth and origins. The locals have given it various names, including Xepatomeni (bottomless), Voulismeni (sunken) and Vromolimni (dirty). The lake isn't bottomless – it is 64 metres deep. The 'dirty' tag came about because the lake used to be stagnant and gave off quite a pong in hot weather. This was rectified in 1867 when a canal was built linking it to the sea.

Early this century the lake changed colour one day and gave off sulphurous vapours which killed the fish. This bizarre occurrence led to the belief that the lake was connected to the volcano on Santorini. According to mythology, Athena and Artemis enjoyed taking a dip in its waters.

Organised Tours

Travel agencies in Agios Nikolaos offer coach outings to all Crete's top attractions, such as Knossos and the Samaria gorge, as well as trips to local attractions. The Creta Travel Bureau (☎ 28 496), on the corner of Paleologou and Katehaki, has boat trips to Spinalonga for 3000 dr, as well as guided tours of Lato and Kritsa (3000 dr) and to the Lassithi plateau (6500 dr).

Places to Stay – bottom end

The nearest camp site to Agios Nikolaos is *Gournia Moon Camping* (☎ 0842-93 243). The site has a swimming pool, restaurant, snack bar and minimarket. It is almost opposite the Minoan site of Gournia (see the Around Agios Nikolaos section). Buses to Sitia can drop you off right outside.

The Agios Nikolaos YHA hostel sign still exists at Stratigou Koraka 3, but the place has been closed for years now and shows no sign of reopening. The *Green House* (☎ 22 025), Modatsou 15, is a favourite with backpackers. It is ramshackle, but clean, with a lush garden, friendly cats and helpful English-speaking owners. Singles/doubles/triples are 2500/3500/4500 dr with shared bathroom. Walk up Tavla (a continuation of Modatsou) from the bus station, and you'll find it on the right. Just down from here are *Rena & George's Rooms* (☎ 28 059), Kyprou 15, on the corner of Tavla. The clean single/double rooms here cost 2800/3500 dr with private bathroom.

The *Pension Pergola* (☎ 28 152), on the seafront on Akti Themistokleous, east of the ferry dock, has comfortable singles/doubles with private bathroom for 6000/7000 dr.

Aphrodite Rooms (☎ 28 058), Korytsas 27, has singles/doubles with shared bathroom for 4000/6000 dr. There is a tiny rooftop kitchen where you can make tea and coffee.

If you arrive in winter, the only places you'll find officially open are the *Hotel Cronos* (☎ 28 761) on Plateia Venizelou and the *Hotel Dias* (☎ 28 263) at Latous 6. The Cronos is marginally the better of an unexciting pair. It charges slightly more, with singles/doubles for 6000/8000 dr, or 5000/6000 dr in winter.

Places to Stay – middle
The opulent B-class *Coral Hotel* (☎ 28 363/367), on the northern waterfront, is about as up-market as places get in town. It has singles/doubles for 11,000/17,300 dr. There is a swimming pool.

Places to Stay – top end
The luxury-hotel zone is just north of Agios Nikolaos on the road to Elounda. The only hotel that's open all year is the deluxe *Minos Beach Hotel & Bungalows* (☎ 22 345/349; fax 22 548), with accommodation in seaside bungalows. Swimming pool and tennis courts are among the extras for your 24,000/29,400 dr for singles/doubles.

Places to Eat
Agios Nikolaos' waterfront tavernas are expensive – head inland for better value. *Taverna Itanos*, Kyprou 1, is a lively traditional taverna, with chicken for 550 dr, lamb for 730 dr and stifado for 900 dr. *Restaurant Trata*, on the corner of Sfakianaki and Tselepi, is a cheerful restaurant with a roof garden and similar prices to the Itanos.

The *Ouzeri Stasi* is a bit out of the way at Lassithiou 23, but well worth the effort. It has an excellent selection of mezedes priced from 400 to 800 dr. The place is on the far side of the major junction at the top of Paleologou, just beyond the hospital. It opens only in the evenings.

The *Taverna Pine Tree*, next to the lake at Paleologou 18, specialises in charcoal-grilled food, such a plate of huge prawns for 1800 dr. *Aouas Taverna*, at Paleologou 50, has traditional décor and a lovely garden. A large plate of mezedes (enough for four people) is 2500 dr.

Entertainment
Discos and bars abound in Agios Nikolaos. *Lipstick Disco*, overlooking the harbour, is one of the wildest. *Jimmy's Disco*, on the corner of Evans and Tselepi, is reputed to have the cheapest drinks.

Things to Buy
Atelier Ceramica, at Paleologou 28, sells handmade copies of ceramic objects from museums throughout Greece. Items can be made to order.

Getting There & Away
Bus Destinations of buses from Agios Nikolaos' bus station are:

Destination	Duration	Fare	Frequency
Elounda	20 mins	180 dr	19 daily
Kritsa	15 mins	180 dr	12 daily
Ierapetra	1 hour	600 dr	9 daily
Iraklio	1½ hours	1150 dr	half-hourly
Istron	30 mins	250 dr	14 daily
Kroustas	20 mins	280 dr	4 daily
Lassithi plateau	3 hours	1600 dr	2 daily
Sitia	1½ hours	1200 dr	6 daily

Ferry Agios Nikolaos has the same ferry schedule as Sitia. Ferry tickets can be bought from Agios Travel (see under Organised Tours), among others. The port police (☎ 22 312) are in the same building as the tourist office.

Getting Around
Car, Motorbike & Bicycle You will find many car and motorbike-hire outlets on the northern waterfront. Ross Rentals (☎ 23 407), Koundourou 10, has a huge range of brand new motorbikes, from little runabouts up to a 1300-cc Harley (just 35,000 dr per day). It also has new mountain bikes for 2000 dr.

GOURNIA Γουρνιά
The important Minoan site of Gournia (Gour-NYA) lies just off the coast road, 19 km south-east of Agios Nikolaos. The ruins, which date from 1550 to 1450 BC, consist of a town overlooked by a small palace. Gournia's palace was far less ostentatious than the ones at Knossos and Phaestos, and was the residence of an overlord rather than a king. The town is a network of streets and stairways flanked by houses whose walls stand up to two metres in height. Trade, domestic and agricultural implements

CRETE

found on the site indicate that Gournia was a thriving little community.

The site (☎ 0841-22 462) is open Tuesday to Sunday from 8.30 am to 3 pm. Admission is free. Gournia is on the Sitia and Ierapetra bus routes from Agios Nikolaos and buses can drop you at the site.

MONI FANEROMENIS
Μονή Φανερωμένης

Just two km before Gournia, on the Agios Nikolaos-Sitia road, a five-km gravel road leads off right to the late-Byzantine Moni Faneromenis. If you have your own transport, a visit to the monastery is worthwhile for the stunning views down to the coast.

KRITSA Κριτσά

The village of Kritsa (Krit-SA), perched 600 metres up the mountainside 11 km from Agios Nikolaos, is on every package itinerary. Hordes of tourists come in busloads to the village every day in summer. The villagers exploit these invasions to the full, and craft shops of every description line the main streets.

The tiny triple-aisled **Church of Panagia Kera** is on the right one km before Kritsa on the Agios Nikolaos road. The frescoes that cover its interior walls are considered the most outstanding examples of Byzantine art on Crete. Unfortunately the church is usually packed. It's open Monday to Saturday from 9 am to 3 pm and Sunday from 9 am to 2 pm. Admission is 500 dr.

Kritsa doesn't have any hotels, but there are several domatia. They include *Rooms to Rent Argyro* (☎ 0841-51 174) on the way into the village. Rates are 3500/5000 dr for singles/doubles with shared bathroom.

There are 12 buses a day from Agios Nikolaos to Kritsa (15 minutes, 180 dr).

ANCIENT LATO Λατώ

The ancient city of Lato (La-TO), four km north of Kritsa, is one of Crete's few non-Minoan ancient sites. Lato was founded in the 7th century BC by the Dorians and at its height was one of the most powerful cities on Crete. It sprawls over the slopes of two acropolises in a lonely mountain setting, commanding stunning views down to the Gulf of Mirabello.

The city's name derived from the goddess Leto whose union with Zeus produced Artemis and Apollo, both of whom were worshipped here. Lato is far less visited than Crete's Minoan sites. It is open Tuesday to Sunday from 8.30 am to 3 pm. Admission is free.

Exploring the Site

In the centre of the site is a deep well which is cordoned off. Facing the Bay of Mirabello, to the left of the well are some steps which are the remains of a **theatre**.

Above the theatre was the **prytaneion**, where the city's governing body met. The circle of stones behind the well was a threshing floor. The columns next to it are the remains of a stoa which stood in the agora. There are remains of a pebble mosaic nearby. A path to the right leads up to the **Temple of Apollo**.

Getting There & Away

There are no buses to Lato. The road to the site is signposted to the right on the approach to Kritsa. If you don't have your own transport, it's a pleasant walk through olive groves.

SPINALONGA PENINSULA
Χερσόνησος Σπιναλόγκας

Just before Elounda (coming from Agios Nikolaos), a sign points right to **ancient Olous**, which was the port of Lato. The city stood on, and around, the narrow isthmus (now a causeway) which joined the southern end of the Spinalonga peninsula to the mainland. Most of the ruins lie beneath the water, and if you go snorkelling near the causeway you will see outlines of buildings and the tops of columns. The water around here appears to be paradise for sea urchins. The peninsula is a pleasant place to stroll and there is an early Christian mosaic near the causeway.

CRETE

SPINALONGA ISLAND
Νήσος Σπιναλόγκα

Spinalonga island lies just north of the Spinalonga peninsula. The island's massive fortress was built by the Venetians in 1579 to protect Elounda and Mirabello bays. It withstood Turkish sieges for longer than any other Cretan stronghold, finally surrendering in 1715, some 30 years after the rest of Crete. The Turks used the island as a base for smuggling. Following the reunion of Crete with Greece, Spinalonga became a leper colony. The last leper died there in 1953 and the island has been uninhabited ever since. Spinalonga is still known among locals as 'the island of the living dead'.

The island is a fascinating place to explore. It has an aura that is both macabre and poignant. The **cemetery**, with its open graves, is an especially strange place. Dead lepers came in three classes: those who saved up money from their government pension for a place in a concrete box; those whose funeral was paid for by relations and who therefore got a proper grave; and the destitute, whose remains were thrown into a charnel house.

Getting There & Away
There are regular excursion boats to the island from Agios Nikolaos for 3000 dr. Alternatively, you can negotiate with the fishermen in Elounda and Plaka (a fishing village five km further north) to take you across. The boats from Agios Nikolaos pass Bird island and Kri-Kri island, one of the last habitats of the *kri-kri*, Crete's wild goat. Both of these islands are uninhabited and designated wildlife sanctuaries.

ELOUNDA Ελούντα
There are magnificent mountain and sea views along the 11-km road from Agios Nikolaos to Elounda (El-OON-da). The place is considerably quieter than Agios Nikolaos. It also has an attractive harbour and a sheltered lagoon-like stretch of water formed by the Spinalonga peninsula.

Orientation & Information
Elounda's post office is opposite the bus stop. From the bus stop walk straight ahead to the clock tower and church which are on the central square. There is a small OTE office next to the church. Elounda's postcode is 720 53 and the telephone code is 0841. The town doesn't have a tourist office or tourist police.

Places to Stay
There's some good accommodation around, but nothing particularly cheap. *Elpis Rooms* (☎ 41 384), opposite the Church of Konstantinos, charges 6000/7000 dr for comfortable doubles/triples with private bathroom.

Self-caterers should check out *Alexandros Apartments* (☎ 41 871), above the Cava Yiannis supermarket. It has very well-equipped studio doubles for 8000 dr. The *Hotel Sofia* (☎ 41 482), on the seafront 100 metres from the town centre, has pleasantly furnished two-room apartments with kitchen for 12,000 dr among its range of options.

The deluxe hotels are just south of Elounda on the road to Agios Nikolaos. Typical of them is the *Elounda Marmin Hotel* (☎ 41 003), which has swimming pools everywhere you look, tennis courts etc. All this and half-board costs 45,000 for two people between July and September; 20,000 dr in April, May, June and October. The *Porto Elounda Mare* (☎ 41 903) is about to steal an edge on its rivals by completing its golf course.

Places to Eat
The *Marilena Restaurant* on the central square and the Hotel Calypso's restaurant are both popular and good value.

Getting There & Away
There are 19 buses a day from Agios Nikolaos to Elounda (20 minutes, 180 dr).

LASSITHI PLATEAU Οροπέδιο Λασιθίου
The first view of the mountain-fringed Lassithi (La-SITH-ee) plateau, laid out like an immense patchwork quilt, is stunning. The plateau, 900 metres above sea level, is a

vast expanse of pear and apple orchards, almond trees and fields of crops, dotted by some 7000 windmills. These are not conventional stone windmills, but slender metal constructions with white canvas sails. There are 20 villages dotted around the periphery of the plateau, the largest of which is **Tzermiado**, with 1300 inhabitants.

The plateau's rich soil has been cultivated since Minoan times. The inaccessibility of the region made it a hotbed of insurrection during Venetian and Turkish rule. Following an uprising in the 13th century, the Venetians drove out the inhabitants of Lassithi and destroyed their orchards. The plateau lay abandoned for 200 years.

Most people come to Lassithi on coach trips, but it deserves an overnight stay. Once the package tourists have departed clutching their plastic windmill souvenirs, the villages return to pastoral serenity. The telephone code for Lassithi is 0844.

Dikteon Cave Δικταίον Αντρον

Lassithi's major sight is the Dikteon cave, just outside the village of **Psyhro** (Psi-HRO). Here, according to mythology, Rhea hid the newborn Zeus from Cronos, his off-spring-gobbling father. The cave, which has both stalactites and stalagmites, was excavated in 1900 by the British archaeologist David Hogarth. He found numerous votives indicating that the cave was a place of cult worship. These finds are housed in the archaeological museum in Iraklio.

The moment you reach the parking area beneath the site, representatives from the Association of Cave Guides & Donkey Owners (still going strong despite the collapse of its booth) will be upon you. The cave guides want 2000 dr for a lantern-guided tour, while the donkey owners want the same to save you the 15-minute walk up to the cave. A guide is not essential, but a torch is. So are sensible shoes. The path to the cave is pretty rough, and the cave itself is slippery. Opening times are 10.30 am to 5 pm in summer, 8.30 am to 3 pm in winter. Admission is 500 dr.

Places to Stay & Eat

Psyhro is the nearest place to stay, but the D-class *Zeus Hotel* (☎ 31 284) is a bit on the bleak side. Doubles are 6000 dr. The rough-and-ready taverna on the right side of Psyhro's central square (as you face towards the cave) is cheap and has tasty food.

The rooms are much better places in Agios Georgios, five km away. The *Hotel Rea* (☎ 31 209), opposite the school on the main street, has much cosier singles/doubles for 2500/4000 dr with shared bathroom. The co-owned *Rent Rooms Maria* nearby has pleasant singles/doubles for 7000/8500 dr. The *Restaurant Roula-Pepi*, underneath the Hotel Rea, serves grilled food and salads.

There are also hotels and domatia in Tzermiado, but nothing very inspiring. The *Hotel Kourites* (☎ 22 194), on the left of the road in from Agios Georgios, charges 7000/9000 dr for singles/doubles with bathroom.

Getting There & Away

The bus from Agios Nikolaos to Lassithi must go via Pluto to take three hours and cost 1600 dr. It leaves Agios Nikolaos at 8.15 am and 2 pm, returning at 7 am and 2 pm. On weekends, only the morning bus from Agios Nikolaos and the afternoon bus from Lassithi operate. There are also two buses a day from Iraklio (two hours, 1150 dr), leaving at 8.30 am and 3 pm and returning at 7 am and 4.45 pm. On Sunday, only the morning service from Iraklio exists, returning at 2 pm.

All buses go through Tzermiado, Agios Georgios and Psyhro and terminate at the Dikteon cave.

SITIA Σητεία

Back on the north-coast road, Sitia (Si-TEE-a, population 8000) is a good deal quieter than Agios Nikolaos. A sandy beach skirts a wide bay to the east of town. The main part of the town is terraced up a hillside, overlooking the port. The buildings are a pleasing mixture of new and fading Venetian architecture.

Orientation & Information

The bus station is at the eastern end of

Karamanli, which runs behind the bay. The town's main square, Plateia Agnostou – recognisable by its palm trees and statue of a dying soldier – is at the western end of Karamanli. There is a mobile tourist office in the square from May to October.

There are plenty of places to change money. The Ionian Bank on the main square has a 24-hour automatic-exchange machine. The harbour near the square is for fishing boats and pleasure boats only. Ferries use the large quay further out, about 500 metres from Plateia Agnostou.

The post office is on Therissou. To get there from Plateia Agnostou, follow El Venizelou inland along the base of the hill to the next major junction. Therissou is the major road running uphill to the right. The OTE is on Kapetan Sifis, which runs uphill directly off Plateia Agnostou.

Sitia's postcode is 72 300 and the telephone code is 0843.

Archaeological Museum

Sitia's archaeological museum (☎ 23 917) houses a well-displayed collection of local finds spanning from Neolithic to Roman times, with emphasis on the Minoan. The museum is on the left side of the road to Ierapetra. It is open Tuesday to Sunday from 8.30 am to 3 pm. Admission is 500 dr.

Festivals

Sitia produces superior sultanas and a **sultana festival** is held in the town in the last week of August, during which wine flows freely and there are performances of Cretan dances.

Places to Stay – bottom end

Sitia's *youth hostel* (☎ 22 693) is at Therissou 4, on the road to Iraklio. It's a fair hike uphill from the town centre, despite assurances that it's only 400 metres from the bus station. Beds cost 1000 dr. There are hot showers and kitchen facilities. The hostel's promotional blurb says camping is allowed in the grounds, but you'd need to get to work with a scythe for that to be possible.

There's no shortage of domatia dotted around the streets overlooking the port, most of which charge 3000/4000 dr for singles/doubles.

The rooms at the D-class *Hotel Arhontiko* (☎ 28 172 or 22 993), Kondylaki 16, are beautifully maintained and the whole place is spotless. There are doubles for 5000 dr and triples for 6500 dr. There are no single rooms, but you can get a double to yourself for 4500 dr. Kondylaki is two streets up the hill from the port. The best way to get there is to walk out towards the ferry dock along El Venizelou, turn left up Filellinon and then right into Kondylaki.

Places to Stay – middle

Rooms to Let Apostolis, at Kazantzaki 27, is an up-market domatia run by the owner of the Arhontiko Hotel, Apostolis Kimalis, contactable on the same telephone numbers. The immaculate doubles/triples with private bathroom cost 6500/8000 dr. Kazantzaki runs uphill from the port, one street north of the OTE.

The *Hotel Elysee* (☎ 22 312), at Karamanli 14, has comfortable singles/doubles with bathroom for 9100/10,900. It also has a well-equipped kitchen for communal use.

Places to Eat

Meraklis Taverna, almost opposite the post office on Therissou, is not only lively, authentic and popular with the locals, but it also serves wonderful food. It's open all day and sometimes features live bouzouki music in the evenings.

There is a string of tavernas specialising in fish dishes along the quayside on El Venizelou. At No 189, *To Kyma* is less pretentious than most. It specialises in mezedes, priced from 450 dr, and serves excellent fried baby squid in crisp batter for 800 dr.

The dairy shop at Kornarou 33 specialises in sheep's milk products, including fresh milk, curdled milk, delicious yoghurt and cheese.

Getting There & Away

Air Sitia's tiny airport has flights to Athens on Tuesday and Saturday (21,000 dr), and

Saturday flights to Karpathos (7600 dr) and Kassos (7600 dr). The Olympic Airways office (☎ 22 270/596) is at El Venizelou 56.

Bus There are five buses a day to Ierapetra (1½ hours, 1000 dr); six buses to Iraklio (3¼ hours, 2350 dr) via Agios Nikolaos (1½ hours, 1200 dr); four to Vaï (one hour, 480 dr); and two to Kato Zakros (one hour, 750 dr). The buses to Vaï run only between May and October; during the rest of the year, this service terminates at Paleokastro.

Ferry The F/B *Vitsentzos Kornaros* leaves Sitia at 3.30 pm on Tuesday, Thursday and Sunday to Piraeus (6100 dr in deck class) via Agios Nikolaos and arrives at 6 am. The F/B *Georgios Express* leaves Sitia on Tuesday at 7 am for Karpathos (four hours, 2200 dr), Kassos (six hours, 2200 dr) and Rhodes.

Buy ferry tickets at Tzortzakis Travel Agency (☎ 22 631 or 28 900), El Venizelou 183.

Getting Around
To/From the Airport The airport (signposted) is one km out of town. There is no airport bus. A taxi costs about 500 dr.

Car & Motorbike Car and motorbike-hire outlets are mostly on the eastern waterfront near the bus station.

AROUND SITIA
Moni Toplou Μονή Τοπλού
The imposing Moni Toplou, 18 km from Sitia on the back road to Vaï, looks more like a fortress than a monastery. It was often treated as such, being ravaged by both the Knights of St John and the Turks. Its star attraction is an 18th-century icon by Ioannis Kornaros, one of Crete's most celebrated icon painters. The monastery is open from 9 am to 1 pm and from 2 to 6 pm.

Getting there is hard work without your own transport. The monastery is a three-km walk from the Sitia-Paleokastro road. Buses can drop you off at the junction.

Vaï Βάι
The beach at Vaï, on Crete's east coast, 24 km from Sitia, is famous for its palm forest.

There are many stories about the origin of these palms, including the theory that they sprouted from date pits spread by Roman legionaries relaxing on their way back from conquering Egypt. While these palms are closely related to the date, they are a separate species found only on Crete.

You'll need to arrive early to appreciate the setting, because the place gets packed out in summer. It's possible to escape the worst of the ballyhoo – jet skis and all – by clambering over a rocky outcrop (to the left facing the sea) to a small secluded beach. Alternatively, you can go over the hill in the other direction to a quiet beach frequented by nudists.

There are two tavernas at Vaï but no accommodation. If you're after more secluded beaches, head north for another three km to the ancient Minoan site of **Itanos**. Below the site are several good swimming spots. There are four buses a day to Vaï from Sitia (one hour, 480 dr).

ZAKROS & KATO ZAKROS
The village of Zakros (Ζάκρος), 45 km south-east of Sitia, is the nearest permanent settlement to the east-coast Minoan site of Zakros, which is seven km away.

Kato Zakros, next to the site, is a beautiful little seaside settlement that springs to life between March and October. If the weather is dry, there is a lovely two-hour walk from Zakros to Kato Zakros through a gorge known as the Valley of the Dead because of the cave tombs dotted along the cliffs. The gorge emerges close to the Minoan site.

Places to Stay
Zakros has domatia and one hotel, the bleak C-class *Hotel Zakros* (☎ 0843-93 379), where doubles with private bathroom are 6500 dr. It's much better to stay at Kato Zakros. There are a number of places dotted along the beachfront, a short walk from the end of the beachfront road. Views don't get much better than from *Popy's Rooms* and the

Pension Poseidon. Rooms to Let George (☎ 0843-93 207), 500 metres from the beach on the old dirt road to Zakros, has good rooms with cooking facilities for 6500 dr.

Getting There & Away

There are two buses a day to Zakros (via Paleokastro and Zakros) from Sitia (one hour, 650 dr). They leave Sitia at 11 am and 2 pm and return at 12.30 and 4 pm. In summer, the buses continue to Kato Zakros. The Hotel Zakros offers guests free transport to Kato Zakros.

ANCIENT ZAKROS

Ancient Zakros, the smallest of Crete's four palatial complexes, was a major port in Minoan times, with trade links with Egypt, Syria, Anatolia and Cyprus. The palace consisted of royal apartments, storerooms and workshops flanking a central courtyard.

The town occupied a low plain close to the shore. Water levels have risen over the years so that some parts of the palace complex are submerged. The ruins are not well preserved, but a visit to the site is worthwhile for its wonderfully wild and remote setting. The site is open Tuesday to Sunday from 8.30 am to 3 pm. Admission is 400 dr.

IERAPETRA Ιεράπετρα

Ierapetra (Ye-RA-pet-ra, population 11,000), on the south coast, is Crete's most southerly major town. It was a major port of call for the Romans in their conquest of Egypt. After the tourist hype of Agios Nikolaos, the unpretentiousness of Ierapetra is refreshing. Ierapetra is a town whose main business continues to be agriculture, not tourism.

Orientation

The bus station is on Lasthenous, one street back from the beachfront on the eastern side of town. Emerging from the ticket office, turn right and after about 50 metres you'll come to a roundabout. There are signposts to the beach, via Patriarhou Metaxaki, and to the city centre, via the pedestrian mall section of Lasthenous.

The mall emerges after about 200 metres onto the central square of Plateia Eleftherias. On the right of the square is the National Bank of Greece. Turn right opposite the bank to get to the OTE, which is one block inland on Koraka.

If you continue straight ahead from Plateia Eleftherias you will come to Plateia Emmanual Kothri, where you'll find the post office at Stylianou Houta 3.

Information

The tourist office has been closed since 1993, but South Crete Tours (☎ 22 892), opposite the archaeological museum on Adrianou Kostoula, can help with a map of Ierapetra. To reach it, turn right from Plateia Emmanual Kothri.

Ierapetra's postcode is 722 00 and the telephone code is 0842.

Things to See

Ierapetra's one-room **archaeological museum** is for those with a short concentration span. Pride of place is given to an exquisite statue of Demeter. Opening times are Tuesday to Sunday from 8.30 am to 3 pm. Admission is 500 dr.

If you walk south along the waterfront from the central square you will come to the **fortress**, which was built in the early years of Venetian rule and strengthened by Francesco Morosini in 1626. It's in a pretty fragile state and was closed at the time of writing. Inland from here is the labyrinthine old quarter, a delightful place to lose yourself for a while.

Beaches Ierapetra has two beaches. The main town beach is near the harbour and the other beach stretches east from the bottom of Patriarhou Metaxaki. Both beaches have coarse grey sand.

Places to Stay – bottom end & middle

The nearest camp sites to Ierapetra are two sites adjacent to one another on the beach at the coastal resort of Koutsounari, which is seven km to the east of Ierapetra. They are *Ierapetra Camping* (☎ 0842-61 351) and

Koutsounari Camping (☎ 0842-61 213). Both sites have a restaurant, snack bar and minimarket and charge identical prices. The Ierapetra-Sitia buses pass the sites.

The best places to stay are in the old quarter. Almost every other house seems to be offering rooms to let. Singles/doubles cost about 3000/5000 dr. Two places worth investigating are *Erotokritos Apartments* (☎ 28 151) and *Almyra Apartments* (☎ 24 461 or 26 081), which both have apartments with cooking facilities starting from 6000 dr. Both are close to the beachfront near the Restaurant Castello.

The *Katerina Hotel* (☎ 28 345) is much better than it looks from the outside. Doubles with private bathroom are 7000 dr. To reach the hotel from the bus station, follow Patriarhou Metaxaki to the waterfront, turn right and you'll see the hotel on the right.

Places to Stay – top end
The best hotel in town is the B-class *Astron Hotel* (☎ 25 114; fax 25 917) at the beach end of Patriarhou Metaxaki. Singles/doubles with bathroom are 9000/12,000 dr.

Places to Eat
One of the cheapest restaurants in Ierapetra is the *Restaurant Rembetiko*, on the left side of Patriarhou Metaxaki as you walk towards the sea. A large serve of moussaka will set you back 800 dr, and there is Cretan folk music most nights during summer.

For more sophisticated dining, try the *Restaurant Castello* – one of a string of tavernas along the waterfront in the old quarter. You'll have to go a long way to find better homemade dolmades (500 dr), and the squid cooked in its own ink (950 dr) is equally delicious.

Getting There & Away
In summer, there are nine buses a day to Iraklio (2½ hours, 1700 dr) via Agios Nikolaos (one hour, 600 dr), Gournia and Istron; eight to Makrigialos (30 minutes, 460 dr); six to Sitia (1½ hours, 1000 dr) via Koutsounari (for camp sites); six to Mirtos

(30 minutes, 260 dr); and two to Amiras (one hour, 480 dr).

AROUND IERAPETRA
The beaches to the east of Ierapetra tend to get crowded. For greater tranquillity, head for **Hrysi islet**, where there are good uncrowded sandy beaches. In summer an excursion boat (4000 dr) leaves for the islet every morning and returns in the afternoon. It's possible to camp on the island and there are three tavernas.

Mirtos, on the coast 17 km west of Ierapetra, is a pleasant low-key resort with a decent dark-sand beach. There are domatia and tavernas, and one hotel, the D-class *Hotel Mirtos* (☎ 0842-51 225), where doubles are 4000 dr with private bathroom. There are six buses a day from Ierapetra to Mirtos (30 minutes, 260 dr).

Western Crete

The western part of Crete comprises the prefectures of Hania and Rethymno, which take their names from the old Venetian cities which are their capitals. The two towns rank in themselves as two of the region's main attractions, although the most famous is the spectacular Samaria gorge. The south coast towns of Paleohora and Plakias are popular resorts.

RETHYMNO Ρέθυμνο
Rethymno (RETH-im-no, population 24,000) is Crete's third-largest town.

The main attractions is the old Venetian-Ottoman quarter that occupies the headland beneath the massive Venetian *fortezza* (fortress). The place is a maze of narrow streets, graceful wood-balconied houses and ornate Venetian monuments; several minarets add a touch of the Orient. The architectural similarities invite comparison with Hania, but Rethymno has a character of its own. An added attraction is a beach right in town.

The approaches to the town, especially on the road from Iraklio, could hardly be less inviting. The modern town has sprawled out along the coast, dotted with big package hotels attracted by a reasonable beach.

History

The site of modern Rethymno has been occupied since Late Minoan times – the evidence can be found in the city's archaeological museum. In the 3rd and 4th centuries BC, Rithymna emerged as an autonomous state of sufficient stature to issue its own coinage.

The town prospered once more under the Venetians, who ruled from 1210 until 1645, when the Turks took over. Turkish forces held the town until 1897, when it was taken by Russia as part of the occupation of Crete by the Great Powers.

Rethymno became an artistic and intellectual centre after the arrival of a large number of refugees from Constantinople in 1923. The city has a campus of the University of Crete, bringing a student population that keeps the town alive outside the tourist season.

Orientation

The city's old quarter occupies the headland north of Dimakopoulou, which runs from Plateia Vardinogianni on the west coast to Plateia Iroön on the east (becoming Gerakari en route).

Most of the good places to eat and sleep are to be found here, while banks and government services are just to the south on the edge of the new three-quarters of town. The beach is on the eastern side of town, curving around from the delightful old Venetian harbour in the north. El Venizelou is the beachfront street. Curving parallel one block back is Arkadiou, the main commercial street.

The old quarter's maze of twisting and curving streets make it an easy place to get lost. Coming from the south, the best way to approach is through the Porto Guora gate onto Ethnikis Antistaseos. This busy shopping street leads to the Rimondi fountain, the old quarter's best known landmark. The area around here is thick with cafés, restaurants and souvenir shops.

If you arrive in Rethymno by bus, you will be dropped at the new terminal at the western end of Igoum Gavriil, about 600 metres from Porto Guora. To get there, follow Igoum Gavriil back into the town centre. A left turn at the far end of the park will leave you facing the gate. If you arrive by ferry, the old quarter is as far away as the end of the quay.

If you are driving into town from the expressway, your final approach to the city centre is along Dimitrikaki. The parking lot opposite the park is a convenient spot to stop and check things out.

Information

Tourist Offices Rethymno's municipal tourist office (☎ 24 143) is on the beach side of El Venizelou, opposite the junction with Kalergi. It's open Monday to Friday from 9 am to 3 pm. The tourist police (☎ 28 156) occupy the same building and are open from 7 am to 10 pm every day.

Money Banks are concentrated around the junction of Dimokratias and Pavlou Kountouriotou, just outside the old quarter. The National Bank is on Dimokratias, on the far side of the square opposite the town hall. The Credit Bank, Pavlou Kountouriotou 29, and the National Mortgage Bank, next to the town hall, have 24-hour automatic-exchange machines.

Post & Telecommunications The OTE is at Kountouriotou 28, and the post office is a block south at Moatsou 21. Rethymno's postcode is 741 00 and the telephone code is 0831.

Bookshops The bookshop at Souliou 43 stocks novels in English, and has a small second-hand section.

Laundry The Laundry Mat self-service laundry at Tombazi 45, next door to the YHA hostel, charges 2000 dr for a wash and dry.

Things to See

The **archaeological museum** (☎ 29 975) is opposite the entrance to the fortress. The

CRETE

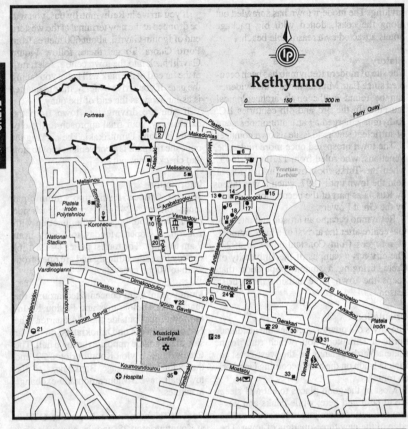

Rethymno

0   150   300 m

Ferry Quay

Fortress

Plastira
Makedonias
Mesogiou
Venetian Harbour
Kalehaki
Melissinou
Melissinou
Arabatzoglou
Vernardou
Smyrnis
Koroneou
Plateia Iroön Polytehniou
Nikiforou Foka
Paleologou
Souliou
Arkadiou
Ethnikis Antistaseos
National Stadium
Plateia Vardinoglanni
Dimakopoulou
Vlastou Sifi
Igoum Gavriil
Igoum Gavriil
Tombazi
Gerakari
Venizelou
Arkadiou
Plateia Iroön
Kountouriotou
Katatogiannidon
Alexandrou
Krari
Illiakaki
Municipal Garden
Koumoundourou
Dimitrikaki
Moatsou
Dimokratias
Hospital

PLACES TO STAY

3   Lefteris Papadakis
    Rooms
4   Pension Anna
5   Hotel Fortezza
6   Rooms to Rent
    Barbara Dolomaki
8   Rent Rooms Ergina
19 Olga's Pension
20 Rent Rooms Garden
24 YHA Hostel
26 Achillion Hotel
33 Olympic Hotel

PLACES TO EAT

9   Angela Ouzeri
10 Gounakis Restaurant &
    Bar
14 Taverna Kyria Maria
22 Taverna Ta Balkania
30 Ouzeri To Luhnari

OTHER

1   Entrance to Fortress
2   Archaeological Museum
7   Rethymniaki Lines
11 Historical & Folk Art
    Museum
12 Neradjes Mosque

13 Rimondi Fountain
15 Fortezza Disco
16 Nileas Tours
17 Loggia
18 Bookshop
21 Bus Station
23 Porto Guora
25 Happy Walker
27 Tourist Office & Police
28 Car Park
29 OTE
31 National Mortgage
    Bank
32 National Bank of
    Greece
34 Post Office
35 Olympic Airways

finds displayed here include an important coin collection. The museum is open Tuesday to Sunday from 8.30 am to 3 pm. Admission is 500 dr. Rethymno's excellent **historical & folk art museum**, Vernardou 30, is open Monday to Saturday from 9 am to 1.30 pm and 5.30 to 8 pm. Admission is 300 dr.

Rethymno's 16th-century **fortress** stands on Paleokastro hill, the site of the city's ancient acropolis. Within its massive walls once stood a great number of buildings, of which only a church and a mosque survive intact. The ramparts offer good views of the city and the coast, while the site has lots of ruins to explore. The fortress is open every day from 9 am to 4.30 pm. Admission is 300 dr.

Pride of place among the many vestiges of Venetian rule in the old quarter goes to the **Rimondi fountain** with its spouting lion heads. Just seaward of the fountain is the 16th-century **loggia**.

At the southern end of Ethnikis Anti-staseos is the well-preserved **Porto Guora** (Great Gate), a remnant of the Venetian defensive wall. Turkish legacies in the old quarter include the mosque near the Great Gate and the **Neradjes Mosque**, which was converted from a Franciscan church.

Trekking

The Happy Walker (☎ 52 920), Tombazi 56, runs a varied programme of walks along the remote mountain paths in the region. Most walks last about four hours, starting in the early morning, and finishing with lunch. Prices start at 6000 dr per person.

Rethymno's chapter of the EOS (☎ 22 710/229) is above the post office on Moatsou.

Diving

The Paradise Dive Centre (☎ 51 711; fax 29 503) has activities for all grades of divers from beginners to certified regulars. Beginners can do a four-day certification course for 75,000 dr. Courses run from Monday to Thursday.

Festivals

The city's main cultural event is the annual Renaissance Festival that runs during July and August, featuring dance, drama and films as well as art exhibitions. July is also the month of the Wine Festival, which is held in the municipal park. Admission is 750 dr. The Moni Arkadiou Festival on 7 and 8 November honours the martyrs of the monastery explosion (see Around Rethymno) with parades and church services.

Places to Stay – bottom end

The nearest camp site is *Elizabeth Camping* (☎ 28 694), near Myssiria beach, three km east of Rethymno. The site has a taverna, snack bar and minimarket. An Iraklio-bound bus can drop you at the site.

The *YHA hostel* (☎ 22 848), Tombazi 41, is friendly and well run with beds for 1000 dr and free hot showers. Breakfast is available and there's a bar in the evening. There is no curfew and an IYHF or HI card is not required. The place is open all year.

An excellent budget choice is *Olga's Pension* (☎ 29 851 or 54 896), right in the heart of town at Souliou 57. There's a wide choice of rooms which are spread about in clusters off a network of terraces – all bursting with greenery. Prices range from basic singles for 3500 dr, up to studio rooms with kitchen for 10,000 dr. In between comes a comfortable double with shower for 6000 dr. Owners George and Stella Mihalaki speak good English and run a very friendly show.

Rooms to Rent Barbara Dolomaki (☎ 24 581), Thambergi 14, is a good place for self-caterers. Doubles with shower, fridge and small stove are 7000 dr.

If you're after ocean views, *Lefteris Papadakis Rooms* (☎ 23 803), Plastira 26, has clean singles/doubles with shared bathroom for 4500/6000 dr.

Café Bar 67 (☎ 51 283) is a tiny place on the beachfront at El Venizelou 67. The four rooms include two nice clean doubles overlooking the town beach for 4000 dr.

There are a couple of outstanding domatia. *Rent Rooms Garden* (☎ 26 274), at Nikiforou Foka 82 in the heart of the old town, is an impeccably maintained 600-year-old Venetian house with many original features and a gorgeous grape-arboured garden. Doubles/triples are both 7000 dr with private bathroom. Further west in the old town, *Rent Rooms Ergina* (☎ 29 474), Smyrnis 4, has immaculate single/double/triple rooms for 6000/7500/8800 dr with private bathroom.

Right in the shadows of the fortress, *Pension Anna* (☎ 25 586), Katehaki 5, has two-person studios for 7000 dr.

The E-class *Achillion Hotel* (☎ 22 581), Arkadiou 151, is a piece of fading grandeur with huge, nicely furnished rooms. Doubles/triples/quads are 6000/7000/8000 dr with shared bathroom. It was once the only hotel in town, and claims some illustrious names on its guest list – although it's a bit hard to imagine the king of Greece sharing a bathroom.

Places to Stay – middle

The smartest hotel in town is the B-class *Hotel Fortezza* (☎ 55 551/552 or 23 828; fax 54 073), Melissinou 16, a striking crenellated building with strawberry-pink exterior walls. It has a snack bar, restaurant and swimming pool. Rates are 15,500/19,500 dr for singles/doubles. The B-class *Olympic Hotel* (☎ 24 761/762/763), on the corner of Moatsou and Dimokratias, is very ordinary by comparison. The official rates of 8000/11,500 dr are highly negotiable.

If you want to hire a villa or unit out of town, the place to ask is Nileas Tours (☎ 51 711; fax 29 503), Petihaki 1.

Places to Eat

The waterfront along El Venizelou is lined with amazingly similar tourist restaurants staffed by fast-talking waiters desperately cajoling passers-by into eating at their establishments. The situation is much the same around the Venetian Harbour, except that the setting is much better and the prices higher.

To find cheaper food and a more authentic atmosphere, wander down the little side streets back from the water. *Taverna Kyria Maria*, Diog Mesologiou 20, tucked behind

the Rimondi fountain, is a cosy, traditional taverna that also has outdoor seating along the narrow surrounding alleyways.

Gounakis Restaurant & Bar, Koroneou 6, is worth visiting for its taverna food as much as for its music (see Entertainment, below). *Angela Ouzeri*, further along Koroneou, is a rough-and-ready place serving tasty, low-priced fish dishes and mezedes.

Ouzeri To Luhnari, Gerakari 41, turns out imaginative mezes dishes priced from 400 dr. Live Greek music is sometimes featured in the evenings.

One of Rethymno's cheapest eating places is the untouristy *Taverna Ta Balkania*, at Igoum Gavriil 7. It's open 24 hours and is popular with local workers.

Entertainment

If your interests include drinking cheap wine and listening to live Cretan folk music, *Gounakis Restaurant & Bar* is the place to go. There's music and impromtu dancing most nights.

Rethymno has no shortage of discos, most of them in the streets behind the old harbour. The *Templum Club*, at the northern end of Arkadiou, caters to the heavy-metal crowd, while the *Fortezza Club* plays disco.

Things to Buy

Zaharias Theodorakis turns out a range of onyx bowls and goblets on the lathe at his small workshop opposite Pension Anna on Katehaki. Prices start at 5000 dr for a small bowl.

Getting There & Away

Bus There are numerous services to both Hania (one hour, 1200 dr) and Iraklio (1½ hours, 1250 dr). There's a bus in each direction every half-hour in summer, every hour in winter. In summer, there are also eight buses a day to Plakias (one hour, 800 dr); six to Agia Galini (1½ hours, 1000 dr); four to Moni Arkadiou (30 minutes, 380 dr); two to Omalos (two hours, 2150 dr) and two to Preveli (800 dr). The 8.30 am bus to Plakias continues to Hora Sfakion (two hours,

1500 dr). Services to these destinations are greatly reduced in winter.

Ferry Rethymniaki Lines (☎ 29 221) operates the F/B *Arkadi* on a constant shuttle between Rethymno and Piraeus. It leaves Rethymno at 7.30 pm on Tuesday, Thursday, Saturday and Sunday, returning on Monday, Wednesday and Friday at 7.30 pm and Sunday at 7.30 am.

Tickets are available from the company's office at Arkadiou 250. Deck-class tickets cost 5000 dr and a berth in a tourist-class cabin is 6500 dr. The company plans to be operating two ships by 1996, with daily sailings in each direction.

Getting Around
Car & Motorbike Most of the car-hire firms are grouped around Plateia Iroön. Motor Stavros (☎ 22 858), right in the middle of town on Paleologou, has two-wheeled transport ranging from mopeds to 400-cc trail bikes.

Bicycles Motor Stavros (see above) also rents bikes for 900 dr a day.

AROUND RETHYMNO
Moni Arkadiou Μονή Αρκαδίου
This 16th-century monastery stands in attractive hill country 23 km south-east of Rethymno. The most impressive building of the complex is the Venetian baroque church. Its striking fanade has eight slender Corinthian columns and is topped by an ornate triple-belled tower. This fanade features on the 100 dr note.

In November 1866 the Turks sent massive forces to quell insurrections which were gathering momentum throughout the island. Hundreds of men, women and children who had fled their villages used the monastery as a safe haven. When 2000 Turkish soldiers staged an attack on the building, rather than surrender, the Cretans set light to a store of gun powder. The explosion killed everyone, Turks included, except one small girl. This sole survivor lived to a ripe old age in a village nearby. A bust of this woman, and the

abbot who lit the gun powder, stand outside the monastery.

The monastery is open every day and entry is free. The small **museum** has an admission charge of 400 dr.

Getting There & Away There are buses from Rethymno to the monastery (30 minutes, 300 dr) at 6 and 10.30 am, noon and 2.30 pm, returning at 7 and 11.15 am, and 1.15 and 3.30 pm.

Amari Valley Κοιλάδα Αμαρίου
If you have your own transport you may like to explore the enchanting Amari valley, south-east of Rethymno, between mounts Ida and Kedros. This region harbours around 40 well-watered unspoilt villages set amid olive groves and almond and cherry trees.

The valley begins at the picturesque village of **Apostoli**, 25 km south-east of Rethymno. The turn-off for Apostoli is on the coast three km east of Rethymno. At Apostoli, the road forks, and then joins up again 38 km to the south, making it possible to do a circular drive around the valley; alternatively you can continue south to Agia Galini.

There is an EOS refuge on Mt Ida, a 10-km walk from the small village of **Kouroutes**, five km south of Fourfouras. For information contact the Rethymno EOS (see Rethymno section).

RETHYMNO TO PLAKIAS
Heading south from Rethymno, there is a turn-off to the right to the late Minoan cemetery of **Armeni** two km before the modern village of Armeni. The main road south continues through woodland, which gradually gives way to a bare and dramatic landscape. After 18 km there is turn-off right for **Selia**, **Rodakino** and **Frangokastello** and, a little beyond, another turn-off right for Plakias (this turn-off is referred to as the Koxare junction or Bale on timetables).

The main road continues through the mountain town of Spili (see Around Plakias), to Agia Galini. Shortly after the village of Koxare on the Plakias road, the road enters the dramatic two-km-long **Kourtaliotis gorge**, with bare cliffs towering on both sides. After Astomatis village there is a turn-off for Moni Preveli. The road continues through the village of **Lefkogia**, which has domatia and tavernas, then passes the turn-off to the right for Myrthios (two km) and enters Plakias.

PLAKIAS Πλακιάς

The south-coast town of Plakias was once a tranquil retreat for adventurous backpackers – until the package-tour operators discovered the fine beaches and dramatic mountain backdrop. It's still not a bad place to visit outside peak season.

Orientation & Information

Finding your way around is easy in this little seaside town. One street skirts the beach and another runs parallel to it one block back. The bus stop is at the middle of the water-front. Plakias doesn't have a bank, but Candia Tours Travel Agency, near the bus stop, offers currency exchange. In summer there is a mobile post office on the water-front. Plakias' postcode is 730 01 and the telephone code is 0832.

Between Plakias and Preveli beach there are several secluded coves popular with freelance campers and nudists. These coves are within walking distance of Plakias and Lefkogia (see Around Plakias).

Places to Stay

The new *Camping Apollonia*, on the right of the main approach road to Plakias, is a good site with a restaurant, minimarket, bar and swimming pool. Rates are 900 dr per person and 500 dr per tent.

There is a smart new *youth hostel* tucked away in the olive trees behind the town, about 10 minutes' walk from the bus stop. To get there from the bus stop, walk back along the waterfront into town and turn inland next to Candia Tours. Turn left at the T-junction and follow the signs for another 300 metres. Dorm beds are 1000 dr and hot showers are free. The hostel is open from 1 April until the end of October.

One of the cheapest places to stay in Plakias is *Rooms to Rent Anni & Antonis Stefanakis* (☎ 31 066). Singles/doubles/triples with bathroom are 3500/5000/6000 dr. There is a small communal kitchen. To reach the rooms walk 200 metres straight ahead from the bus stop, follow the road around to the left and they're on the right.

Morpheas Rent Rooms (☎ 31 583), next to the bus stop, are light, airy and attractively furnished. Prices are 5000/7000/9000 dr with private bathroom. If you're unhappy about anything, you can always try complaining to the tourist police in Rethymno – where you'll find owner Manolis working his day job.

There are some pleasant little pensions tucked among the olive trees behind the town. *Pension Afrodite* (☎ 31 266) has spotless doubles/triples for 7000/8400 dr with private bathroom. Head inland at Candia Tours, turn left at the T-junction and then take the first right and you will come to the pension on the left after 100 metres. A right turn at the T-junction leads to the new *Studio Emilia* (☎ 31 302), set back in the trees to the left after 100 metres. It charges 5000/6000 dr for large doubles/triples upstairs with private bathroom and access to a well-equipped communal kitchen. The downstairs rooms have private kitchen facilities.

The *Pension Paligremnos* (☎ 31 003) has a great position underneath the headland at the southern end of Plakias beach. It also has good doubles with bathroom for 5000 dr, and studio doubles for 7000 dr. The rooms are open from April to September, as is the taverna downstairs. It takes about 15 minutes to walk to the Paligremnos from the bus stop along the dirt road behind the beach.

Places to Eat

There's nothing outstanding to report on the food situation, except perhaps the bakery at the western end of the seafront. The chocolate croissants here are hard to resist.

A right turn just after the bakery leads to the *Restaurant Ariadne*, 100 metres up on the left. It's a popular place with reasonable prices and barrel wine.

There's also a good souvlaki place. *Nikos Souvlaki*, just inland from Candia Tours, has the usual favourites as well as a monster mixed grill of gyros, souvlaki, sausage, hamburger and chips for 1200 dr.

The least touristy place in Plakias has to be *Aristides Psistaria*, sporting its colourful mural out by the youth hostel. The only items on the menu are charcoal-grilled lamb (1100 dr) or chicken (1000 dr), both served with chips.

Getting There & Away

Plakias has very good bus connections in summer, but virtually none in winter. A timetable is displayed on the wall outside Morpheas Rent Rooms.

Summer services include eight buses a day to Rethymno (one hour, 800 dr), two buses to Agia Galini (1½ hours, 920 dr) and one to Hora Sfakion.

In winter, there are three buses a day to Rethymno, two at weekends. It's possible to get to Agia Galini from Plakias by catching a Rethymno bus to the Koxare junction (referred to as Bale on timetables) and waiting for a bus to Agia Galini. This works best with the 12.30 pm bus from Plakias, linking with the 12.45 pm service from Rethymno to Agia Galini.

Getting Around

Odyssia (☎ 31 596), on the waterfront next to the bridge, has cars, a large range of motorbikes and mountain bikes.

AROUND PLAKIAS
Myrthios

This pleasant village is perched on a hillside overlooking Plakias and the surrounding coast. Apart from the views, the main activity is walking, which you'll be doing a lot of unless you have your own transport.

Places to Stay & Eat Myrthios is home to the district's original *youth hostel* (☎ 31 202). The hostel is just above the square in the middle of the village. A bed here costs 800 dr, but conditions are very primitive. There are also domatia in the village, but a

much better option is *Niki's Studios & Rooms* (☎ 31 593). The rooms are just below the Restaurant Panoroma. Singles/doubles with private bathroom cost 2500/4000 dr, and a studio costs 7000 dr for two.

The *Restaurant Panorama* lives up to its name with great views. It also does good food. It's run by a couple of Austrian guys who turn out a menu that's half Greek and half Austrian. Leave room for dessert.

Moni Preveli Μονή Πρέβελη

The well-maintained Moni Preveli, 14 km east of Plakias, stands in splendid isolation high above the Libyan Sea. Like most of Crete's monasteries, it played a significant role in the islanders' rebellion against Turkish rule. It became a centre of resistance during 1866, causing the Turks to set fire to it and destroy its crops. After the Battle of Crete, many British, Australian and New Zealand soldiers were sheltered here by Abbot Agathangelos before their evacuation to Egypt. In retaliation the Germans plundered the monastery. The monastery's small **museum** contains a candelabra presented by grateful British soldiers after the war. Entry to the museum costs 500 dr.

The road to Moni Preveli leads past the ruins of the old monastery, a fascinating place to explore. It was a hippie hang-out in the 70s, and they left their mark in the shape of a large marijuana leaf on one wall and a few other cosmic decorations.

Places to Stay & Eat The nearby village of Lefkogia has several domatia and tavernas, and is a pleasant, relatively unspoilt base from which to explore the area.

Getting There & Away In summer, two buses a day from Rethymno to Plakias continue to Moni Preveli and Rethymno via Plakias.

Preveli Beach Παραλία Πρέβελης

Preveli beach is one of Crete's most photographed beaches. It has a delightful setting at the mouth of the Kourtaliotis gorge. The River Megalopotamos cuts the beach in half

CRETE

CRETE

on its way into the Libyan Sea. It's fringed with oleander bushes and palm trees and is popular with freelance campers.

The beach is not far from Moni Preveli. There is a steep path leading down to it from road to the monastery. You can get to Preveli from Plakias by caïque in summer for 3000 dr return.

Damnoni Beach
The caïques stop at Damnoni beach (1500 dr return) on the way to Preveli. It's another fine beach, even if the setting is dominated by the giant Hapimag tourist complex.

Spili Σπήλι
Spili (SPEE-lee), nine km west of the Koxare junction on the main Rethymno-Agia Galini road, is a gorgeous mountain town with cobbled streets, rustic houses and plane trees. If you are tempted to stay the night, there is the very pleasant C-class *Green Hotel* (☎ 0832-22 225/056), where singles/doubles are 4500/6000 dr with private bathroom. The hotel is signposted from the bus stop. There are also several domatia in the town.

AGIA GALINI Αγία Γαλήνη
Agia Galini (A-ya Ga-LEE-nee) is another picturesque little town which has gone down the tubes due to an overdose of tourism. Still, it does boast 340 days of sunshine a year, and some places do remain open all year. It's a convenient base from which to visit Phaestos and Agia Triada, and although the town beach is mediocre, there are boats to better beaches.

Orientation & Information
The bus station is at the top of Eleftheriou Venizelou. The central square, which overlooks the harbour, is downhill from the bus station. You'll walk past the post office on the way and the OTE is on the square. Agia Galini's postcode is 740 56 and the telephone code is 0832. Take the second turn left after the post office and you will find the agent for the National Bank of Greece. Opening times are 9 am to 1 pm and 5 to 9 pm.

Places to Stay
Agia Galini Camping (☎ 91 386/239) is next to the beach, 2.5 km east of the town. It is signposted from the Iraklio-Agia Galini road. The site is well shaded and has a restaurant, snack bar and minimarket.

Rent Rooms Pella (☎ 91 213/143) has large, clean doubles/triples with private bathroom for 5500/6000 dr. The rooms are owned by the people who run the Restaurant Megalonissis next to the bus stop – the rooms are close by.

The D-class *Hotel Selena* (☎ 91 273) is a friendly place with clean, cosy singles/doubles/triples for 3800/5000/6000 dr with private bathroom. An English breakfast is available for 900 dr. It's also open all year. Opposite the Selena is the *Hotel Ariston* (☎ 91 285), where tidy singles/doubles cost 4000/5000 dr with private bathroom. The hotel has a communal balcony, fragrant with jasmine in spring.

To reach these hotels walk downhill from the bus station, turn left after the post office, follow the road uphill and take the third turn right. The hotels are at the end of the alley, just before the steps that lead down to the harbour.

Places to Eat
The *Restaurant Megalonissis*, next to the bus stop, is one of Agia Galini's cheapest restaurants. English breakfast is 800 dr, the same price as many of the main meals. The more stylish *Acropol Taverna*, on Vasileos Ioannis, is reasonably priced with main meals for around 1500 dr. Opposite, the *Greenwich Village Restaurant* is another popular place with similar prices. Vasileos Ioannis is the second 'road' on the right heading uphill from the post office.

Getting There & Away
Bus The story is the same as at the other beach resorts: heaps of buses in summer, skeletal services in winter.

In peak season, there are eight buses a day to Iraklio (2½ hours, 1250 dr), six to Rethymno (1000 dr), six to Phaestos (40 minutes, 280 dr) and two a day to Plakias

(920 dr). You can also get to Plakias by taking a Rethymno-bound bus and changing at Koxare (Bale). To get to Matala, take an Iraklio-bound bus and change at Mires.

Taxi Boat In summer there are daily taxi boats from the harbour to the beaches of Agios Giorgios and Agios Pavlos. These beaches, which are west of Agia Galini, are difficult to get to by land. Both are less crowded and far superior to the Agia Galini beach.

RETHYMNO TO HANIA

The national highway sticks close to the coast for the first leg of the journey west from Rethymno. Much of the coastline is devoted to package tourism, intensifying on the approaches to the resort town of **Georgiou-polis**, where the Almyros River (whose source is Kournas lake) flows into the sea.

From Georgioupolis, a road (signposted Kournas) leads south to the mountain-fringed **Kournas lake**, home to a large number of water birds. The English painter and writer of limericks, Edward Lear, likened it to the English Lake District. He commented that it was 'very fine and Cumberlandish'. There are several tavernas on its shore, and pathways for strolls.

There is no bus to Kournas lake but you can take a Rethymno-Hania bus and get off at Georgioupolis, from where it's possible to hitch to the lake.

The national highway now bypasses the quaint village of **Vrises** (VRIS-ess), the junction for the road south to Hora Sfakion. There is one budget hotel and several domatia and tavernas. Vrises reputedly produces the best yoghurt in Crete.

HANIA Χανιά

Hania (Han-YA, population 65,000) is Crete's second city and former capital. The beautiful, crumbling Venetian quarter of Hania that surrounds the Old Harbour is one of Crete's best attractions. A lot of money has been spent recently on restoring the old buildings. Some of them have been con-

verted into very fine accommodation; others now house chic restaurants, bars and shops.

The Hania district gets a lot of package tourists, but most of them stick to the beach developments that stretch out endlessly to the west. Even in a town this size, many hotels and restaurants are closed from November to April.

Boats to Hania dock at the port of Souda, about seven km out of town. There are frequent buses to Hania as well as taxis.

History

Hania is the site of the Minoan settlement of Kydonia, which was centred on the hill to the east of the harbour. Little excavation work has been done, but the finding of clay tablets with Linear B script has led archaeologists to believe that Kydonia was a both a palace site and an important town.

Kydonia met the same fiery fate as most other Minoan settlements in 1450, but soon re-emerged as a force. It was a flourishing city-state during Hellenistic times and continued to prosper under Roman and Byzantine rule.

The city became Venetian at the beginning of the 13th century, and the name was changed to La Canea. The Venetians spent a lot of time constructing massive fortifications to protect their city from marauding pirates and invading Turks. This did not prove very effective against the latter, who took Hania in 1645 after a siege lasting two months.

The Great Powers made Hania the island capital in 1898 and it remained so until 1971, when the administration was transferred to Iraklio.

Hania was heavily bombed during WW II, but enough of the old town survives for it to be regarded as Crete's most beautiful city.

Orientation

The town's bus station is on Kydonias, two blocks south-west of Plateia 1866, one of the city's main squares. From Plateia 1866 to the Old Harbour is a short walk north down Halidon.

The main hotel area is to the left as you

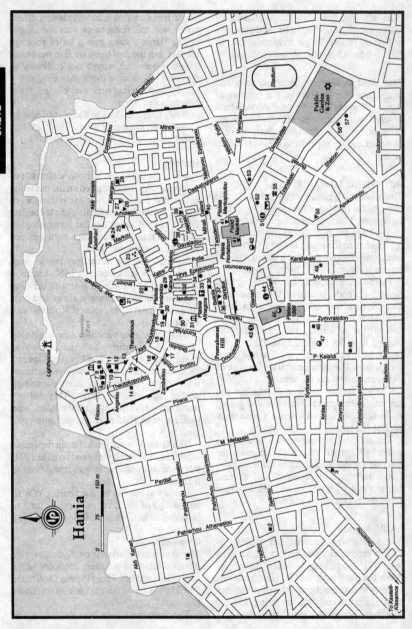

PLACES TO STAY		19	Café-Eaterie Ekstra	29	Trekking Plan
		26	Taverna Tzaki	31	Archaeological
1	Pension Ideon	27	Doloma Restaurant		Museum
2	Villa Katerina	28	Café Crete	32	Laundrette
4	Pension Lena	30	Suki Yaki Restaurant	33	Orthodox Cathedral
6	Ifigenia II	37	To Diporto Kafe Ouzeri	34	Laundrette
8	Pension Theresa	39	Well of the Turk	38	Municipal Tourist
9	Hotel Meltemi	41	Market Tavernas		Office
13	Amfora Hotel	50	Bougatsa Hanion	40	Minaret
14	Ifigenia III			42	Buses to Souda
15	Casa Delfino	**OTHER**		43	Credit Bank
16	Nostos Pension			44	EOT
18	George's Pension	3	Marinopoulos	45	Buses to Western
22	Pension Stoa		Supermarket		Beaches
24	Monastiri Pension	5	Naval Museum	47	Bus Station
25	Pension Kastelli	7	Fagotto Jazz Bar	49	Tourist Police
35	Rooms to Rent Petraki	10	Carmela's Ceramic	51	National Bank of
36	Xenia Rooms		Shop		Greece
46	Samaria Hotel	11	Top Hanas Carpet Shop	52	ANEK Lines
48	Diana Rooms	12	Angelico Rock Café	53	Minoan Lines
		20	Chaicalis Bookshop	54	Post Office
PLACES TO EAT		21	Mosque of the	55	OTE
			Janissaries	56	Olympic Airways
17	Taverna Tamam	23	Archaeological Site	57	EOS

CRETE

face the harbour, where Akti Kountourioti leads around to the old fortress on the headland. The headland separates the Old Harbour from the crowded town beach in the quarter called Nea Hora.

Zambeliou, which dissects Halidon just before the harbour, was once the town's main thoroughfare. It's a narrow, winding street, lined with craft shops, hotels and tavernas.

Information

Tourist Offices Hania's EOT (☎ 92 943) is at Kriari 40, close to Plateia 1866. It is well organised and considerably more helpful than most. The opening hours are from 8 am to 3 pm weekdays. There is also a small municipal tourist office (☎ 43 300) in the old town at Sifaka 22. It opens between May and October. The tourist police (☎ 73 333) are on Karaïaki.

Money The National Bank of Greece is on the corner of Tzanakaki and Gianari, opposite the food market. It has a 24-hour automatic exchange machine, as does the Credit Bank at the junction of Halidon and Skalidi. There are numerous places to change money outside banking hours. Most

are willing to negotiate the amount of commission, so check around.

Post & Telecommunications The central post office is at Tzanakaki 3, just up from the National Bank of Greece. It is open Monday to Friday from 7.30 am to 8 pm, and on Saturday from 7.30 am to 2 pm. Hania's postcode is 731 00. The OTE is next door to the post office at Tzanakaki 5. Opening times are 6 am to 11 pm every day. Hania's telephone code is 0821.

Bookshops The George Chaicalis Book Shop (☎ 92 838), on the square at the bottom of Halidon, sells English-language newspapers, books and maps.

Laundry There are three laundries around the old town. Laundry Express, Kanevaro 38, is the only one that charges less (1000 dr) if you hang around and do the work yourself. Otherwise it charges 1200 dr to wash and dry a load, the same rate as Laundry Fidias, Sarpaki 6, and the laundry at Ag Deka 18.

Luggage Storage Luggage can be stored at the bus station for 300 dr per day.

Things to See

Museums Hania's **archaeological museum** (☎ 24 418), Halidon 21, is housed in the 16th-century Venetian Church of San Francisco. The Turkish fountain in the grounds is a relic from the building's days as a mosque.

The museum houses a well-displayed collection of finds from western Crete dating from the Neolithic to the Roman era. Exhibits include statues, pottery, coins, jewellery and some impressive painted sarcophagi from the Late Minoan cemetery of Armeni (see the Rethymno to Plakias & Agia Galini section). The museum is open Tuesday to Friday from 8.30 am to 5 pm. Admission is 500 dr.

The **naval museum** has an interesting collection of model ships, naval instruments and paintings and photographs. Opening times are Tuesday to Sunday from 10 am to 2 pm. Admission is 500 dr. The museum is housed in the fortress on the headland overlooking the Old Harbour.

Other Things to See The area to the east of the Old Harbour, between Akti Tombazi and Karaoli Dimitriou, is the site of **ancient Kydonia**.

The search for Minoan remains began in the early 1960s and excavation work continues sporadically. The site can be seen at the junction of Kanevaro and Kandanoleu, and many of the finds are on display in the archaeological museum.

Kydonia has been remodelled by a succession of occupiers. After ejecting the Arabs, the Byzantines set about building their kastelli on the same site, on top of the old walls in some places and using the same materials. It was here, too, that the Venetians first settled. Modern Kanevaro was the Corso of their city. It was this part of town that bore the brunt of the bombing in WW II.

The massive **fortifications** built by the Venetians to protect their city remain impressive today. The best preserved section is the Western wall, running from the fortezza to the **Promahonas hill**. It was part of a defensive system begun in 1538 by

engineer Michele Sanmichele, who also designed Iraklio's defences.

The **lighthouse** at the entrance to the harbour is the most visible of the Venetian monuments. It looks in need of tender loving care these days, but the 30-minute walk around the sea wall to get there is worth it.

Whether or not you are self catering you should at least feast your eyes on Hania's magnificent covered **food market**; it makes all other food markets look like stalls at a church bazaar. Unfortunately, the central bastion of the city wall had to be demolished to make way for this fine cruciform creation, built in 1911.

Trekking

Trekking Plan (☎ 44 946), Karaoli Dimitriou 15, organises treks in the Lefka Ori. Prices for one-day treks start from 8000 dr (all inclusive) and five-day treks cost 85,000 dr (which includes meals, accommodation, transport and guide). The treks are in small groups and are all led by experienced mountaineers.

Alpin Travel (☎ 53 309), in the complex at Bonaili 11-19, offers treks through Sougia gorge and the Lefka Ori as well as rock climbing. Alpin Travel is open weekdays from 9 am to 1 pm and 5.30 to 8.30 pm.

Mountain Climbing

George Antonakakis, at Hania's chapter of the EOS (☎ 44 647), Tzanakaki 90, is the guy to talk to for information about serious climbing in the Lefka Ori and to make reservations to stay at the mountain refuge at Kallergi, near the Samaria gorge. The office is open Monday to Friday nights between 8.30 and 10.30 pm, or you can visit George at Alpin Travel (see Trekking, above).

Children's Activities

If your five-year-old has lost interest in Venetian architecture before the end of the first street, the place to head is the public garden between Tzanakaki and Dimokratias. There's a playground, a small zoo with a resident kri-kri (the Cretan wild goat) and a children's resource centre that has a small selection of books in English.

Places to Stay – bottom end

The nearest camp site is *Hania Camping* (☎ 51 090), three km west of town on the beach. It charges 900 dr for an adult and 600 dr for a tent. The site is pleasant and shaded and has a restaurant, bar and minimarket. Take a Kalamaki beach bus (every 15 minutes) from the south-east corner of Plateia 1866 and ask to be let off at the camp site.

The YHA hostel at Drakonianou 33 has been closed for a couple of years and seems unlikely to reopen. Check at the tourist information office.

Most of the cheaper rooms are to be found among the bevy of domatia on Betola. Rates at *Rooms for Rent Petraki* (☎ 43 562), at No 18, are 4000/6000 dr for singles/doubles with private bathroom. On the other side of the road, *Xenia Rooms* (☎ 53 430), at Betola 41, has tidy doubles with private bathroom for 4000 dr. The owner has two more domatia on the same street, so he should be able to fix you up with something.

The most interesting rooms are around the harbour. If it's character you're after, you can't do better than *George's Pension* (☎ 88 715), Zambeliou 30. Half the rooms in the 600-year-old house open onto the harbour, and the place is dotted with antique furniture. Singles/doubles/triples are 3000/5000/6500 dr with common bathroom.

The *Hotel Meltemi* (92 802), right next to the fortezza, charges 5000/7000 dr for singles/doubles that are a bit special. Each of the large, airy rooms is different and has been furnished stylishly. Many have harbour views.

The *Monastiri Pension* (☎ 54 776) has a great setting at Ag Markou 18, right next to the ruins of the monastery of Santa Maria de Miracolioco in the heart of the old kastelli. Double rooms are fair value at 6000 dr with outside bathroom, and there's a communal kitchen. It's open from late April to late November. Another reasonable place close to the harbour is the *Pension Stoa* (☎ 26 879), Lithinon 5, where singles/doubles are 4000/5500 dr.

If you want to hop straight out of bed and onto an early morning bus bound for the Samaria gorge, the best rooms around the bus station are at the plant-festooned *Diana Rooms* (☎ 97 888), P Kalaïdi 33. The rooms are light, airy and very clean. Singles/doubles with private bathroom are 5000/6500 dr, and triples with shared bathroom are 5000 dr.

The Nea Hora area to the west of the old town has some accommodation bargains. *Villa Katerina* (☎ 95 183 or 98 940), Selinou 78, has a range of rooms starting with attractively furnished doubles for 6000 dr. The well-kept *Pension Ideon* (☎ 70 132), on Patriarhou Ioanikeiou, is a friendly place charging 6000/8000 dr for singles/doubles.

Places to Stay – middle

Most of the places in this category are renovated Venetian houses, and there are some very stylish ones about. One of the best is *Nostos Pension* (☎ 94 740), Zambeliou 42-46, a mixture of Venetian style and modern fixtures. The 600-year-old building has been modelled into some very stylish split-level rooms/units, all with kitchen and bathroom. Rates for singles/doubles/triples are 7000/10,000/12,000 dr.

The excellent rooms and apartments run by Alex Stivanakis at the *Kasteli* (☎ 57 057; fax 45 314), Kanevaro 39, are just as good as those at the Nostos. He has spotless singles/doubles for 6000/8000 dr, and some very comfortable renovated apartments nearby priced from 10,000 dr.

There are plenty of places to choose from around Angelou, the street that runs uphill next to the fortezza. One thought to bear in mind when looking about here is the level of noise from the harbour's music clubs. If you normally go to bed after 2 am, it won't be an issue.

The *Pension Theresa* (☎ 92 798), at Angelou 2, is a place that has put some thought into furnishing its rooms. It also has a pleasant roof garden and a communal kitchen. It charges 6500/9000 dr for singles/

doubles with bathroom. It has central heating in winter.

Mihalis, at *Ifigenia II* (☎ 94 357), Angelou 18, has a range of very comfortable rooms to offer, both here and at the nearby Ifigenia III. Prices range from 5000 dr for a rare single up to 9000 dr for doubles with kitchen, all with bathroom inside or attached. The place is spotless – Mihalis always has a scrubbing brush in one hand.

Pension Lena (☎ 72 265), Theotokopoulou 60, has a washing machine and communal kitchen to complement singles/doubles with bathroom for 6000/8000 dr. To get there, follow Angelou up from the harbour and turn right.

Places to Stay – top end

The A-class *Amfora Hotel* (☎ & fax 93 224/226), just back from the harbour at Parados Theotokopolou 2, is an immaculately restored mansion with rooms around a courtyard. Unfortunately, two of the best rooms overhang the harbour's music clubs. Singles/doubles are 11,000/14,000 dr.

Nearby at Theofanous 7 is the old city's smartest accommodation, the *Casa Delfino* (☎ 93 098; fax 96 500). The Casa is the modernised former mansion of a wealthy merchant. The courtyard at the entrance features beautiful traditionally patterned cobblestones. Doubles here are 24,000 dr.

Alongside these two, the offerings of the modern B-class *Samaria Hotel* (☎ 71 271), next to the bus station at the edge of Plateia 1866, look very ordinary. It charges 16,900/24,100 dr for singles/doubles with breakfast, but rates are very negotiable.

Places to Eat – inexpensive

An old favourite with budget travellers is *To Diporto Kafe Ouzeri*, Skridlof 40, where pork chop and chips is the most expensive item on the menu at 750 dr. 'Pigs balls' (500 dr) still feature prominently, while a serve of calamari or fried small fish is also 500 dr.

The two restaurants in the *central market* are good places to seek out traditional food. Their prices are almost identical. You can get a solid chunk of swordfish with chips for 900 dr, or a bowl of fasolada for 500 dr. More adventurous eaters can tuck into a big bowl of garlic-laden snail and potato casserole for 950 dr.

You'll find very similar fare at the *Doloma Restaurant*, tucked back from the road at the western end of Kalergon. The place is a great favourite with students from the nearby Polytehnio.

The *Taverna Tzaki*, just around the corner from the Doloma on Arholeon, has an interesting small menu that includes goat soup for 950 dr and fried rabbit for 1300 dr.

One treat that's worth seeking out is the excellent bougatsa tyri at the *Bougatsa Hanion*, Apokoronou 37. This bougatsa comprises two layers of filo pastry filled with local myzithra cheese, baked in large trays and then sold by the kilo. A standard 150-gram serve costs 350 dr and comes sprinkled with a little sugar.

Places to Eat – moderate

The harbour is the place to go for seafood. The prices are not especially cheap – fresh seafood never is – but the setting is great. Expect to pay from 2500 to 3000 dr per person, plus drinks.

There are some very chic places in the streets behind the harbour. The old Turkish hammam at Zambeliou 51 has been converted into the *Taverna Tamam*, where you'll find tasty soups for about 700 dr and good range of well-prepared main dishes priced from 1500 dr. The *Café-Eaterie Ekstra*, Zambeliou 8, offers a choice of Greek and international dishes, including a delicious crêpe with shrimp and smoked trout for 2000 dr. Casual nibblers should check out the *Tsikoydadiko* mezes bar at Zambeliou 31. It has a mixed plate for two for 1500 dr.

If you fancy a change from Greek food, the *Well of the Turk* restaurant bar has a wide range of Middle Eastern dishes, as well as live music occasionally. The restaurant is in the heart of the old Turkish residential district of Splanzia at K Sarpaki 1.

The *Suki Yaki*, through the archway at Halidon 26, is a Chinese restaurant run by a

Thai family. The result is a large Chinese menu supported by a small selection of Thai favourites.

Entertainment

The *Café Crete*, Kalergon 22, is the best place in Hania to hear live Cretan music. It's a rough-and-ready joint with cheap mezedes and bulk wine, plus a lot of locals who like to reach for the instruments that line the walls once they've had a couple of drinks.

The *Ideon Adron*, next to the Suki Yaki restaurant at Halidon 26, promotes a more sophisticated atmosphere with discreet music and garden seating. *Fagotto Jazz Bar*, Angelou 16, is a stylish place with black-and-white photographs of jazz greats lining the walls. Sometimes there's live jazz in summer. The *Angelico Café*, near the Amfora Hotel on the waterfront, plays rock music at a volume that renders conversation possible only for lipreaders. The bars charge very similar prices: beer is 800 dr, spirits are 1200 dr and cocktails start at 1300 dr.

Discos are concentrated in the area behind the Mosque of the Janissaries. The action doesn't start until after midnight.

In summer, there are performances of Greek folk dancing at the fortress every Monday and Thursday night at 9 pm. Tickets cost 2000 dr, 1000 dr for children.

Things to Buy

Good-quality handmade leather goods are available from shoemakers on Skridlof, where shoes cost from 8500 dr. The old part of Hania has many craft shops. Bizzarro, at Zambeliou 19, sells exquisite handmade dolls in traditional Cretan dress. The prices start at 6500 dr. Top Hanas carpet shop, Angelou 3, specialises in the old Cretan kilims that were traditional dowry gifts. There are some beautiful pieces among them, priced from 30,000 dr. Two shops up the street, Carmela's Ceramic Shop, sells beautiful handcrafted jewellery and ceramics by young Cretan craftspeople.

Getting There & Away

Air Olympic Airways has at least three flights a day to Athens (17,400 dr) and two a week to Thessaloniki (27,600 dr). Air Greece flies to Athens (14,500 dr) at 11 am and 8.30 pm on Monday and Thursday, and at 8 am on Tuesday and Friday.

The Olympic Airways office (☎ 27 701/778) is at Tzanakaki 88. The airport is on the Akrotiri peninsula, 14 km from Hania.

Bus Buses depart from Hania's bus station for the following destinations:

Destination	Duration	Fare	Frequency
Falassarna	1½ hours	1280 dr	2 a day
Iraklio	2½ hours	2400 dr	half-hourly
Hora Sfakion	2 hours	1200 dr	4 a day
Kastelli-Kissamos	1 hour	760 dr	15 a day
Lakki	1 hour	330 dr	2 a day
Moni Agias Triadas	30 mins	360 dr	2 a day
Omalos			
(for Samaria gorge)	1 hour	1000 dr	4 a day
Paleohora	2 hours	1250 dr	6 a day
Rethymno	1 hour	1200 dr	half-hourly
Sougia	2 hours	1200 dr	2 a day
Stavros	30 mins	300 dr	6 a day

Ferry Ferries for Hania dock at Souda, about seven km east of town, There is at least one ferry a day to Piraeus. Minoan Lines operates the F/B *Knossos* from Souda on Monday, Wednesday and Friday at 7.45 pm – and ANEK has a boat every night at 8 pm – either the F/B *El Venizelou* or the F/B *Kriti*. The trip costs 4600 dr for deck class and takes about 11 hours. The ANEK office (☎ 23 636) is opposite the food market, and Minoan Lines (☎ 45 911) are nearby at El Venizelou 2.

Souda's port police can be contacted on ☎ 89 240.

Getting Around

To/From the Airport Olympic Airways buses (500 dr) leave from outside the Olympic Airways office 1½ hours before each flight.

Bus Local buses (blue) for the port of Souda leave from outside the food market; buses for the western beaches leave from Plateia 1866.

Car, Motorbike & Bicycle Hania's car-hire outlets include Avis (☎ 50 510), Tzanakaki

CRETE

58; Budget (☎ 92 788), Karaïskaki 39; and Maan (☎ 54 454), Arhontaki 10. Motorbike-hire outlets are mostly on Halidon. Mountain bicycles can be rented from Trekking Plan (☎ 44 946), Karaoli Dimitriou 15.

AKROTIRI PENINSULA
Χερσόνησος Ακρωτήρι

The Akrotiri (Ak-ro-TEE-ree) peninsula, to the east of Hania, has a few places of fairly minor interest, as well as being the site of Hania's airport, port and a military base. At Souda, there is an immaculate **military cemetery**, where about 1500 British, Australian and New Zealand soldiers who lost their lives in the Battle of Crete are buried. The buses to Souda port from outside the Hania food market can drop you at the cemetery.

If you haven't yet had your fill of Cretan monasteries, there are three on the Akrotiri peninsula. The impressive 17th-century **Moni Agias Triadas** was founded by the Venetian monks Jeremiah and Laurentio Giancarolo. The brothers were converts to the Orthodox faith. The 16th-century **Moni Gourvernetou** (Our Lady of the Angels) is four km north of Moni Agias Triadas. The church inside the monastery has an ornate sculptured Venetian fanade. Both of these monasteries are still in use.

From Moni Gourvernetou, it's a 15-minute walk on the path leading down to the coast to the ruins of **Moni Katholiko**. The monastery is dedicated to St John the Hermit who lived in the cave behind the ruins. It takes another 30 minutes to reach the sea.

There are two buses a day to Moni Agias Triadas from Hania bus station.

HANIA TO AGIA ROUMELI VIA SAMARIA GORGE

The road from Hania to the beginning of the Samaria (Sa-ma-RIA) gorge is one of the most spectacular routes on Crete. It heads through orange groves to the village of **Fournes** where a left fork leads to **Meskla**. The main road continues to the village of **Lakki** (LA-kee), 24 km from Hania. This unspoilt village in the Lefka Ori mountains affords stunning views wherever you look.

The village was a centre of resistance during the uprising against the Turks, and in WW II.

It's a beautiful walk from Lakki down to Meskla, nestled in the valley below. It's a further five km to Fournes, from where there are occasional buses back to Lakki. The *Kri-Kri Restaurant & Rooms* (☎ 67 316), in Lakki, has comfortable singles/doubles for 2500/4000 dr with shared bathroom. The restaurant serves good-value meals. There are also domatia and tavernas in Meskla.

From Lakki, the road continues to the Omalos plateau and Xyloskalo, the start of the Samaria gorge. It is possible to stay at the nearby *Kallergi Refuge*, which should be organised through the EOS in Hania (☎ 44 647). The refuge is about five km from Xyloskalo, and is a good base for climbing several peaks in the Lefka Ori range.

Samaria Gorge Φαράγγι της Σαμαριάς

It's a wonder the stones and rocks underfoot haven't worn away completely, given the number of people who trample through the Samaria gorge. Despite the crowds, a trek through this stupendous gorge is still an experience to remember.

At 18 km, the gorge is supposedly the longest in Europe. It begins below the Omalos plateau, carved out by the river that flows between the Lefka Ori and Mt Volikas. Its width varies from 150 metres to three metres and its vertical walls reach 500 metres at their highest points. The gorge has an incredible number of wild flowers, which are at their best in April and May.

It is also home to a large number of endangered species. They include the Cretan wild goat, the kri-kri, which survives in the wild only here and on the islet of Kri-Kri, off the coast of Agios Nikolaos. The gorge was made a national park in 1962 to save the kri-kri from extinction. You are unlikely to see too many of these shy animals, which show a marked aversion to trekkers.

The gorge is open most years from mid-April until the end of October. The opening date depends on the amount of water in the gorge. Visiting hours are from 6 am to 4 pm

DAVID HALL

VICKI BEALE

VICKI BEALE

Top: Dolphin frieze, Knossos, Crete
Middle: Knossos, Crete
Bottom: Knossos, Crete

DAVID HALL

MICHELLE COXALL

ANN JOUSIFFE

Top: General store, Sitia, Crete
Bottom Left: Venetian quarter, Hania, Crete
Bottom Right: Blankets drying in the sun, north coast, Crete

every day, and there's an entry fee of 1000 dr. Spending the night in the gorge is forbidden.

An early start helps to avoid the worst of the crowds, but during July and August even the early bus from Hania to the top of the gorge can be packed. The trek from Xyloskalo, the name of the steep wooden staircase that gives access to the gorge, to Agia Roumeli takes around six hours. Early on in the season it's sometimes necessary to wade through the stream. Later, as the flow drops, it's possible to use rocks as stepping stones.

The gorge is wide and open for the first six km, until you reach the abandoned village of Samaria. The inhabitants were relocated when the gorge became a national park. Just south of the village is a small church dedicated to Saint Maria of Egypt, after whom the gorge is named.

The gorge now narrows and becomes more dramatic until, at the 12-km mark, the walls are only 3.5 metres apart – the famous **Iron Gates**.

The gorge ends just north of the almost abandoned village of Old Agia Roumeli. From here the path continues to the small, messy and crowded resort of Agia Roumeli, with a much appreciated pebble beach and sparkling sea.

What to Bring Sensible footwear is essential for walking on the rocky, uneven ground. Trainers are fine. You'll also need a hat and sunscreen. There's no need to take water. While it's inadvisable to drink water from the main stream, there are plenty of springs along the way spurting delicious cool water straight from the rock. There is nowhere to buy food, so bring something to snack on.

Getting There & Away There are excursions to the Samaria gorge from every sizeable town and resort on Crete. Most travel agents have two excursions: 'Samaria Gorge Long Way' and 'Samaria Gorge Easy Way'. The first comprises the regular trek from the Omalos plateau to Agia Roumeli; the second starts at Agia Roumeli and takes you as far as the Iron Gates.

Obviously it's cheaper to trek the Samaria

gorge under your own steam. Hania is the most convenient base. There are buses to Xyloskalo (one hour, 1000 dr) at 6.15, 7.30 and 8.30 am and 1.30 pm. If you intend to stay on the south coast ask for a one-way ticket (650 dr), otherwise you'll automatically be sold a return. There also are buses to Omalos from Rethymno (two hours, 2150 dr) at 6.15 and 7 am; from Kastelli-Kissamos (1¾ hours, 1900 dr) at 5, 6 and 7 am; and from Paleohora (1½ hours, 1200 dr) at 6 am.

AGIA ROUMELI Αγία Ρούμελη
Agia Roumeli (Ag-I-a ROO-mel-ee) has little going for it, but if you have just trekked through the Samaria gorge and are too exhausted to face a journey, there is one hotel, the B-class *Hotel Agia Roumeli* (☎ 91 293), where singles/doubles are 7000/ 10,000 dr with private bathroom. There are also a number of domatia where you'll pay around 3500 dr for a double.

Getting There & Away
While the gorge is open to walkers, there are frequent boats from Agia Roumeli. There are five boats a day to Hora Sfakion (one hour, 1210 dr) via Loutro (30 minutes, 660 dr). Sometimes the last boat does not call at Loutro. It connects with the bus back to Hania, leaving you in Hora Sfakion just long enough to spend a few drachma. There are also boats from Agia Roumeli to Paleohora (1790 dr) at 3 and 4.30 pm, calling at Sougia (800 dr).

LOUTRO Λουτρό
The small but rapidly expanding fishing village of Loutro (Loo-TRO) lies between Agia Roumeli and Hora Sfakion. Loutro doesn't have a beach but there are rocks from which you can swim. There is one pension, the very comfortable *Porto Loutro* (☎ 0825-91 227), which has doubles with private bathroom for 8000 dr. There are plenty of domatia and tavernas.

An extremely steep path leads up from Loutro to the village of **Anopolis**, where there are also domatia. Alternatively, you can

CRETE

save yourself the walk by taking the Hania-Skatoli bus which calls in at Anopolis *en route*. The bus leaves Hania at 2 pm and returns the following morning, calling in at Anopolis at 7.30 am.

From Loutro it's a moderate 2½-hour walk along a coastal path to Hora Sfakion. On the way you will pass the celebrated **Sweet Water beach**, named after freshwater springs which seep from the rocks. Freelance campers spend months at a time here. Even if you don't feel inclined to join them, you won't be able to resist a swim in the translucent sea. Loutro is on the Hora Sfakion-Paleohora boat route.

HORA SFAKION Χρώα Σφακίων
Hora Sfakion (HO-ra Sfa-KI-on) is the small coastal port where the hordes of walkers from the Samaria gorge spill off the boat and onto the bus. As such, in high season it can seem like Picadilly Circus at rush hour. Most people pause only long enough to catch the next bus out – not a bad idea really because there's not much else to do.

Hora Sfakion played a prominent role during WW II when thousands of Allied troops were evacuated by sea from the town after the Battle of Crete.

Orientation & Information
The ferry quay is at the western side of the harbour. Buses leave from the square on the eastern side. The post office and OTE are on the square, and the police station overlooks it. There is no tourist office and no tourist police. Hora Sfakion's postcode is 730 01, and the telephone code is 0825.

Places to Stay & Eat
If you do wind up staying, the options aren't so exciting. The D-class *Hotel Stavros* (☎ 91 220), up the steps at the western end of the port, has clean singles/doubles with bathroom for 4500/6000 dr. Don't expect a warm welcome though.

The *Hotel Samaria* (☎ 91 261), on the waterfront, has similar rooms for similar prices. It also has a good restaurant which

turns out a very tasty plate of seafood pilaf for 1200 dr.

The best rooms are at the *Hotel Xenia* (☎ 91 202), close to the ferry dock at the western side of the harbour. Hora Sfakion is one of the few places where this government-run chain has come up with the goods. It has spacious, airy singles/doubles overlooking the sea from 6000/8000 dr.

Getting There & Away
Bus There are five buses a day from Hora Sfakion to Hania (two hours 1200 dr); two to Plakias (1¼ hours, 800 dr) via Frangokastello, leaving at 11.30 am and 5.30 pm; one to Rethymno (two hours, 1250 dr) at 7.30 pm; and one to Kastelli-Kissamos (1300 dr) which leaves at 5 pm. The 5.30 pm bus to Plakias continues to Agia Galini (2½ hours, 2050 dr).

Boat In summer there are daily boats from Hora Sfakion to Paleohora (three hours, 3000 dr) via Loutro, Agia Roumeli and Sougia. The boat leaves at 2 pm. There also are four boats a day to Agia Roumeli (one hour, 1210 dr) via Loutro (30 minutes, 660 dr).

From 1 June, there are boats to Gavdos island on Friday, Saturday and Sunday. Check the schedule with the EOT in Hania.

AROUND HORA SFAKION
The road from Vrises to Hora Sfakion cuts through the heart of the Sfakia region in the eastern Lefka Ori. The inhabitants of this region have long had a reputation for fearlessness and independence, characteristics they retain to this day. Cretans are regarded by other Greeks as being immensely proud and there are none more so than the Sfakiot.

One of Crete's most celebrated heroes, Ioannis Daskalogiannis, was from Sfakia. In 1770, Daskalogiannis led the first Cretan insurrection against Ottoman rule. When help promised by Russia failed to materialise, he gave himself up to the Turks to save his followers. As punishment the Turks skinned him alive in Iraklio. Witnesses related that Daskalogiannis suffered this excruciating death in dignified silence.

The Turks never succeeded in controlling the Sfakiots, and this rugged mountainous region was the scene of fierce fighting. The story of their resistance lives on in the form folk tales and *rizitika* (local folk songs). One of the most popular is the *Song of Daskalogiannis*.

The village of **Imbros**, 23 km from Vrises, is at the head of the 10-km-long Imbros gorge. This gorge is shorter than the Samaria gorge but reportedly its equal in beauty – and far less visited. To get there, take any bus bound for Hora Sfakion from the north coast and get off at Imbros. Walk out of the village towards Hora Sfakion and a path to the left leads down to the gorge. The gorge path ends at the village of **Komitades**, from where it is an easy walk by road to Hora Sfakion. You can of course do the trek in reverse, beginning at Komitades. The Happy Walker offers an organised trek through this gorge (see Rethymno, Organised Tours).

Frangokastello Φραγγοκάστελλο

Frangokastello (Frang-o-KAS-tel-o) is a magnificent fortress on the coast 15 km east of Hora Sfakion. It was built by the Venetians in 1371 as a defence against pirates and rebel Sfakiots, who resented the Venetian occupation as much as they did the Turkish. It was here in 1770 that Ioannis Daskalogiannis surrendered to the Turks. In 1828 many Cretan rebels, led by Hadzi Mihalis Dalanis, were killed here by the Turks. Legend has it that at dawn on 17 May (the date of the massacre) the ghosts of Hadzi Mihalis Dalanis and his followers can be seen riding along the beach.

The castle overlooks a gently shelving sandy beach. Domatia and tavernas are springing up rapidly here, but it's still a relatively unspoilt little spot.

Getting There & Away The buses between Hora Sfakion and Plakias go via Frangokastello. They leave Hora Sfakion at 11.30 am and 5.30 pm.

PALEOHORA Παλαιοχώρα

Paleohora (Pa-lee-o-HO-ra) was discovered by hippies back in the 1960s and from then on its days as a tranquil fishing village were numbered. The resort operators have not gone way over the top – yet, and the place retains a certain laidback feel. It is also the only beach resort on Crete which does not go into total hibernation in winter.

The little town lies on a narrow peninsula, with a sandy beach exposed to the wind on one side and a sheltered rocky beach on the other. On summer evenings the main street is closed to traffic and the tavernas move onto the road. The most picturesque part of Paleohora is the narrow streets huddled around the castle.

It's worth clambering up the ruins of the 13th-century **Venetian castle** for the splendid view of the sea and mountains. From Paleohora, a six-hour walk along a scenic coastal path leads to the small resort of **Sougia**, passing the ancient site of **Lissos** (five hours from Paleohora), which was a sanctuary to Asclepius.

Orientation

Paleohora's main street, El Venizelou, runs north to south. The bus stop is opposite the Hotel Lissos. Walking south along El Venizelou from the bus stop, several streets lead off left to the pebble beach. Boats leave from the old harbour at the northern end of this beach. At the southern end of El Venizelou, a right turn onto Kontekaki leads to a long, curving sandy beach which is shaded by pine trees.

Information

The municipal tourist office is in the town hall on El Venizelou. Opening times are 9 am to 2 pm and 5 to 9 pm daily between May and October.

The National Bank of Greece is on El Venizelou, north of the OTE. The post office is on the road which skirts the sandy beach. The OTE is on the west side of El Venizelou, just north of Kontekaki. Paleohora's postcode is 730 01 and the telephone code is 0823.

CRETE

Places to Stay – bottom end

Camping Paleohora (☎ 41 130/120) is 1.5 km north-east of the town, near the pebble beach. The camp site has a taverna but no minimarket.

Rooms to Rent Anonymous (☎ 41 509) is a great place for backpackers with clean, simply furnished rooms set around a small garden. Singles/doubles/triples with shared bathroom cost 2000/3000/3700 dr, and there is a communal kitchen. The owner, Manolis, is an amiable young guy who speaks good English and is full of useful information for travellers. On arrival you will probably be

greeted by Manolis' sidekick, Anonymous; a large, friendly, brown dog. To get there, walk south along El Venizelou from the bus stop and turn right at the town hall. Follow the road as it veers right, and the rooms are on the left.

The D-class *Hotel Lissos* (☎ 41 266/122), El Venizelou 12, opposite the bus stop, also has a friendly English-speaking owner called Manolis. The place doesn't look like much from the street, but it has a nice cheerful courtyard out the back with a well-loved vegetable patch and seating beneath a grape vine. Prices range from 4500 dr for doubles

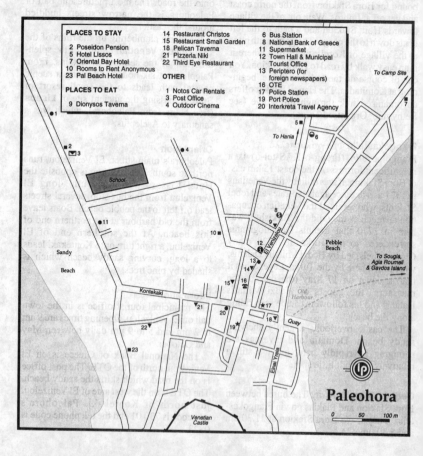

PLACES TO STAY
2 Poseidon Pension
5 Hotel Lissos
7 Oriental Bay Hotel
10 Rooms to Rent Anonymous
23 Pal Beach Hotel

PLACES TO EAT
9 Dionysos Taverna
14 Restaurant Christos
15 Restaurant Small Garden
18 Pelican Taverna
21 Pizzeria Niki
22 Third Eye Restaurant

OTHER
1 Notos Car Rentals
3 Post Office
4 Outdoor Cinema
6 Bus Station
8 National Bank of Greece
11 Supermarket
12 Town Hall & Municipal Tourist Office
13 Periptero (for foreign newspapers)
16 OTE
17 Police Station
19 Port Police
20 Interkreta Travel Agency

To Camp Site

To Hania

School

Sandy Beach

Pebble Beach

To Sougia, Agia Roumeli & Gavdos Island

Kontekaki

Ote Harbour

Quay

Venetian Castle

Paleohora

0   50   100 m

with shared bathroom to 9000 dr for well-equipped studios.

Oriental Bay Rooms (☎ 41 076) occupy the large modern building that looks like an apartment block at the northern end of the pebble beach. The owner, Thalia, is a very cheerful woman and the immaculate singles/doubles with private bathroom are good value at 4000/6000 dr.

Out of season, it's worth looking for a deal at one of the places offering self-catering apartments along the sandy beach on the other side of town. The *Poseidon Pension* (☎ 41 374/115), next to the post office, has cosy rooms for 5000/6000 dr with private bathroom. It also has studio doubles/triples for 7000/9000 dr.

Places to Stay – middle
Paleohora's smartest hotel is the C-class *Pal Beach Hotel* (☎ 41 512/556), overlooking the sandy beach. The place opens from mid-April until October and caters mainly for tour groups. It charges 9000/14,500 dr for singles/doubles.

Places to Eat
There are some good eateries. The *Restaurant Small Garden*, behind the OTE, is a fine little taverna that turns out a few treats like wild asparagus (500 dr) as well as the old favourites. The very popular *Dionysos Taverna*, on El Venizelou, also serves cheap tasty food.

Vegetarians have a treat in store at the *Third Eye*, well-signposted near the sandy beach. The menu includes curries and a range of Asian dishes, all at very reasonable prices. You can eat well and enjoy a beer for less than 1500 dr. Unfortunately the place is closed in winter.

Restaurant Christos, behind the kiosk on El Venizelou, is the place for carnivores to get their slice of the action. Charcoal-grilled lamb is 1100 dr a serve, and chicken is 1000 dr, both with chips. The more adventurous can tackle a sheep's head for 1200 dr.

The *Pelican Taverna* has a prime position overlooking the old harbour. It's a good setting for a plate of small fried fish (800 dr) or calamari (1000 dr).

Entertainment
Most visitors to Paleohora spend at least one evening at the well-signposted outdoor cinema. Another option for a night out is the *Paleohora Disco*, next to the camp site.

Getting There & Away
Bus In summer, there are six buses a day to Hania (two hours, 1250 dr); in winter, there are three – 7.30 am, noon and 3.30 pm. There's an extra daily service to Hania that goes on the back roads through the mountain villages and takes three hours. This bus leaves Paleohora at 6 am, and returns at 1.30 pm. In summer, this service goes via Omalos (1½ hours, 1200 dr) to cash in on the Samaria gorge trade.

Boat In summer there are daily boats from Paleohora to Hora Sfakion (three hours, 3000 dr) via Sougia (one hour, 800 dr), Agia Roumeli (two hours, 1790 dr) and Loutro (2½ hours, 2450 dr). The boat leaves Paleohora at 8.30 am, and returns from Hora Sfakion at 2 pm.

There is another boat operating only as far as Agia Roumeli via Sougia. It leaves Paleohora at 8 am and Agia Roumeli at 4.30 pm. This boat does the trip in half the time for the same fare. Between mid-April and mid-October, this service keeps going to the island of Gavdos (2½ hours, 2550 dr) three times a week. Tickets for all of these boats can be bought at Interkreta Tourism & Travel (☎ 41 393/888), Kontekaki 4.

Getting Around
Car, Motorbike & Bike All three can be hired from Notos Rentals (☎ 41 140), on the sandy beach next to Relax Rooms to Rent.

Excursion Boat The M/B *Elafonisos* gets cranked into action in mid-April ferrying people to the west coast beach of Elafonisi (one hour, 1140 dr). The service builds up from three times a week to twice daily in July, August and September, when boats

CRETE

CRETE

leave at 9 and 11 am. Twice a week there are boats running day trips to Anydri beach (4500 dr, children 3000 dr), calling at ancient Lissos and Sougia on the way.

AROUND PALEOHORA

Sougia Σούγια

If Paleohora is too busy for you, you may prefer quieter Sougia, the next resort east along the coast. The hotels are springing up, but it's still pretty small time. There is no bank, but you can change money at Syia Travel, 50 metres back from the beach on the main street. Buses stop by the beach.

Sougia is at the mouth of the pretty **Agia Irini gorge**. Paleohora travel agents offer guided walks through the gorge for 4000 dr. It's easy enough to organise independently – just catch the Omalos bus from Paleohora or the Hania bus from Sougia, and get off at Agia Irini. There are a couple of beautiful **Byzantine churches** tucked away in the olive groves at the start of the gorge.

The ruins of ancient **Lissos** are 1½ hours away on the coastal path to Paleohora. The path heads inland at the western end of the beach.

Places to Stay There is no camp site, but the beaches to the east are popular with freelance campers. The *Pension Maria*, just east of the bus stop, has reasonable doubles for 6000 dr. The *Hotel Santa Irene* (☎ 0823-51342), right next to the bus stop, has doubles with cooking facilities for 8000 dr, and very smart studios for 10,000 dr.

Getting There & Away There are two buses a day from Hania to Sougia (2½ hours, 1200 dr) at 8.30 am and 1.30 pm. Buses from Sougia to Hania leave at 7 am and 3.30 pm. Sougia is on the Paleohora-Hora Sfakion boat route.

Gavdos Island Νήσος Γαύδος

Gavdos island (GAV-dos, population 50), in the Libyan Sea, 65 km from Paleohora, is the most southerly place in Europe. The island has three small villages and pleasant beaches. There is a post office, OTE, one police officer and one doctor. Gavdos is an excellent choice for those craving isolation and peace. The best source of information about the island is Interkreta Tourism & Travel in Paleohora.

There are no hotels but several of the locals let rooms, and there are tavernas. There is no official camp site but camping freelance may be tolerated. Fishermen from Gavdos take tourists to the remote, uninhabited island of Gavdopoula.

Getting There & Away A small post boat operates between Paleohora and Gavdos on Monday and Thursday all year, weather permitting. It leaves Paleohora at 8 am and takes about four hours (2550 dr). It returns almost immediately. From 15 April until 15 October, the daily boats to Agia Roumeli continue to Gavdos three times a week. These boats do the journey in 2½ hours and charge the same. They leave Gavdos at 3 pm. There also are boats from Hora Sfakion to Gavdos on Friday, Saturday and Sunday.

Elafonisi Ελαφονήσι

It's hard to understand why people enthuse so much about Elafonisi, at the southern extremity of Crete's west coast, but the place is absolutely packed with day-trippers in summer. The beach is ordinary and generously littered. Opposite the beach, through about 100 metres of knee-deep water, is Elafonisi islet. The beaches here are popular with freelance campers. There is one small hotel/taverna 500 metres from the beach which opens only in summer, when there are also three cantinas operating on the beach.

There are two boats a day from Paleohora (one hour, 1140 dr) in summer, as well as daily buses from Hania (2½ hours, 1500 dr) and Kastelli-Kissamos (1½ hours, 900 dr). The buses leave Hania at 7.30 am and Kastelli-Kissamos at 8.30 am, and both depart from Elafonisi at 4 pm. The final section of road from Hrysoskalitissas to the beach is very rugged.

Moni Hrysoskalitissas

Μονή Χρυσοσκαλίτισσας

Moni Hrysoskalitissas. (Mo-NEE Hris-o-ska-LEE-tiss-as), five km north of Elafonisi, is inhabited by two nuns. It's a very beautiful monastery perched on a rock high above the sea. Hrysoskalitissas means 'golden staircase' and the name derives from a legend which claims that one of the 90 steps leading up from the sea to the monastery is made of gold. There are tavernas and domatia in the vicinity. The buses to Elafonisi drop passengers here.

KASTELLI-KISSAMOS

If you find yourself in the north-coast town of Kastelli-Kissamos (population 3000), you've probably arrived by ferry from the Peloponnese or Kythira. While there isn't anything particularly remarkable about Kastelli-Kissamos itself, there are a couple of good camp sites on the beach west of town. The town also serves as a good base from which to explore Crete's west coast.

A fair amount of confusion surrounds the name of the town. In antiquity, its name was Kissamos, the main town of the province of the same name. When the Venetians came along and built a castle here, the place became known as Kastelli. The name persisted until 1966 when authorities decided that too many people were confusing this Kastelli with Crete's other Kastelli, 40 km south-east of Iraklio. The official name reverted to Kissamos, and that's what appears on bus and shipping schedules. Local people still prefer Kastelli, and many books and maps agree with them. An alternative that is emerging is to combine the two into Kastelli-Kissamos, which leaves no room for misunderstanding.

Orientation & Information

The port is three km west of town. In summer a bus meets the boat, otherwise a taxi costs 700 dr. The bus station in Kastelli-Kissamos is to the north of the main road. The town centre is closer to the sea. With your back to the bus-station office, turn left and then take the first left onto Amerikas. Take the second right into Skalidi to reach the central square.

The post office is on the north side of the main road, beyond the bus station. The OTE is further along this road on the right. Kastelli-Kissamos' postcode is 734 00 and the telephone code is 0822. The National Bank of Greece is at the far end of Skalidi, on the left as you walk from the central square. Kastelli-Kissamos has no EOT or tourist police.

Places to Stay

There are three camp sites to choose from. *Camping Kissamos* (☎ 23 444/322), close to the city centre, is convenient for the huge supermarket next door and for the bus station, but not much else. It's got great views of the olive-processing plant next door.

A much better choice is *Camping Mithimna* (☎ 31 444/445), six km west of town. It's an excellent shady site metres from the best stretch of beach. Facilities include a restaurant, bar and shop. It charges 900 dr per person and 600 dr per tent. It also has rooms to rent nearby. Getting there involves either a four-km walk along the beach, or a bus trip to the village of Drapania – from where it's a pleasant 15-minute walk through olive groves to the site.

Camping Nopigia (☎ 31 111) is another good site, two km west of Camping Mithimna. The only drawback is that the beach is no good for swimming. It makes up for that with a swimming pool.

Back in town, one of the best deals is *Koutsounakis Rooms* (☎ 23 416), on the central square. The spotless, comfortable singles/doubles are 5000/7500 dr with private bathroom. Opposite, the C-class *Hotel Castell* (☎ 22 140) has tidy rooms for similar prices. *Argo Rooms for Rent* (☎ 23 563/322), Plateia Teloniou, has spacious rooms for 5000/7000 dr with private bathroom. From the central square, walk down to the seafront, turn left, and you will come to the rooms on the left.

In winter, the only place likely to be open is the C-class *Hotel Kissamos* (☎ 22 086),

CRETE

The Good Oil

The olive has been part of life in the eastern Mediterranean since the beginnings of civilisation. Olive cultivation can be traced back about 6000 years. It was the farmers of the Levant (modern Syria and Lebanon) who first spotted the potential of the wild European olive *(Olea europaea)* – a sparse, thorny tree that was common in the region. These farmers began the process of selection that led to the more compact, thornless, oil-rich varieties that now dominate the Mediterranean.

Whereas most Westerners think of olive oil as being just a cooking oil, to the people of the ancient Mediterranean civilisations it was very much more. It was almost indivisible from civilised life itself. As well as being an important foodstuff, it was burned in lamps to provide light, it could be used as a lubricant and it was blended with essences to produce fragant oils.

The Minoans were among the first to grow wealthy on the olive, and western Crete remains an important olive-growing area, specialising in high-quality salad oils. The region's showcase Kolymvari cooperative markets its extra-virgin oil in both the USA *(Athena* brand) and Britain *(Kydonia* brand).

Locals will tell you that the finest oil is produced from trees grown on the rocky soils of the Akrotiri peninsula, west of Hania. The oil that is prized above all others however is *agourelaio*, meaning unripe, which is pressed from green olives.

Few trees outlive the olive. Some of the fantastically gnarled and twisted olive trees that dot the countryside of western Crete are more than 1000 years old. The tree known as *dekaoktoura*, in the mountain village of Anisaraki – near Kandanos on the road from Hania to Paleohora, is claimed to be more than 1500 years old.

Many of these older trees are being cut down to make way for improved varieties. The wood is burnt in potters' kilns and provides woodturners with the raw material to produce the ultimate salad bowl for connoisseurs. The dense yellow-brown timber has a beautiful swirling grain. ■

west of the bus station on the north side of the main road. It has singles/doubles with private bathroom for 5500/7700 dr, including breakfast.

Places to Eat

The taverna next to the *Hotel Castell* turns out standard fare at reasonable prices, while the *Argo Seafood Restaurant*, opposite the Argo rooms, has a good setting overlooking the beach.

Dangerous sports enthusiasts may like to tackle a 'harmburger' (400 dr) at the bus station's *Cafe Santana*.

Getting There & Away

Bus There are 17 buses a day to Hania (760 dr), where you can change for Rethymno and Iraklio. Buses leave for Omalos (for the Samaria gorge, 1900 dr) at 5, 6 and 7 am; for Elafonisi (900 dr) via Moni Hrysoskalitissas at 8.30 am; and for Falassarna (450 dr) at 10 and 11 am, and 5 pm.

Ferry Miras Lines operates the F/B *Theseus* on a route that takes in Antikythira and Kythira and various Peloponnese ports between Kastelli-Kissamos and Piraeus. Two boats a week ply their way to Piraeus. On Sunday, the boat leaves at 9 am via

Kythira (four hours, 3300 dr), Neapolis (five hours, 3700 dr), Monemvassia and Kyparissi before finally getting to Piraeus (13 hours, 4700 dr).

On Thursday, the boat leaves at 5 pm and travels via Antikythira, Kythira, Elafonisi, Neapolis and Monemvassia. Other services from Kastelli-Kissamos are to Kalamata and Gythio. The Miras agent in town is Horeftakis Tours (☎ 23 250), Skalidi 41, five minutes' walk west of the central square.

Getting Around
Motorbikes can be hired from Rent from Antony (☎ 22 909). Walk eastwards along the main road, take the second turn left after the post office and the outlet is on the right. There are several car-hire outlets along Skalidi.

AROUND KASTELLI-KISSAMOS
Falassarna Φαλασάρνα
Falassarna, 16 km to the west of Kastelli-Kissamos, was a Cretan city-state in the 4th century BC. There's not much to see, and most people head to Falassarna for its superb beach, which is long and sandy and interspersed with boulders. There are several domatia at the beach. In summer there are three buses a day from Kastelli-Kissamos to Falassarna (450 dr) as well as buses from Hania (1250 dr).

Gramvousa Peninsula
Χερσόνησος Γραμβούσας
North of Falassarna is the wild and remote Gramvousa peninsula. There is a wide track, which eventually degenerates into a path, along the east coast side to the sandy beach of **Tigani**, on the west side of the peninsula's narrow tip. The beach is overlooked by the two islets of Agria (wild) and Imeri (tame) Gramvousa. There is a ruined castle on Agria Gramvousa. To reach the track, take a west-

bound bus from Kastelli-Kissamos and ask to be let off at the turn-off to the right for the village of Kalyviani (five km from Kastelli-Kissamos). Kalyviani is a two-km walk from the main road. The path begins at the far end of the main street. The shadeless walk takes around three hours – wear a hat and take plenty of water.

Ennia Horia Εννιά Χωριά
Ennia Horia (nine villages) is the name given to the mountainous region south of Kastelli-Kissamos, which is renowned for its chestnut trees. If you have your own transport you can drive through the region *en route* to Moni Hrysoskalitissas and Elafonisi or, with a little back tracking, to Paleohora. Alternatively, you can take a circular route, returning via the coast road. Whichever route you choose, you'll be rewarded with stunning views. The village of **Elos** stages a chestnut festival on the third Sunday of October when sweets made from chestnuts are eaten. The road to the region heads inland five km east of Kastelli-Kissamos.

Polyrrinia Πολυρρίνία
The ruins of the ancient city of Polyrrinia (Po-lee-ren-EE-a) lie seven km inland from Kastelli-Kissamos, on a hill above the village of Polyrrinia. The city was founded by the Dorians and was continuously inhabited until Venetian times. There are remains of city walls, and an aqueduct built by Hadrian. It's a scenic walk from Kastelli-Kissamos to Polyrrinia, otherwise there is a very infrequent bus service – ask at Kastelli-Kissamos' bus station. To reach the Polyrrinia road, walk east along Kastelli-Kissamos' main road, and look for the sign pointing right about 500 metres east of the bus station. The village of Polyrrinia has a taverna but no accommodation.

Dodecanese Δωδεκάνησα

Strung along the coast of western Turkey, the Dodecanese (Do-de-KA-nis-a) archipelago is much closer to Asia Minor than to mainland Greece. Because of their strategic and vulnerable position these islands have encountered an even greater catalogue of invasions and occupations than the rest of Greece.

The name means 'Twelve Islands', but a glance at the map confirms that the group has quite a few more. The name originated in 1908 when 12 of the islands united against the newly formed Young Turk-led Ottoman parliament which had retracted the liberties the Dodecanese had been granted under the sultans. The Dodecanese islanders enjoyed greater autonomy than did the rest of Greece under the sultans, and they paid less taxes.

The 12 islands were: Rhodes, Kos, Kalymnos, Karpathos, Patmos, Tilos, Symi, Leros, Astypalea, Nisyros, Kassos and Halki. The islands' vicissitudinous history has endowed them with a wealth of diverse archaeological remains, but these are not the islands' only allurements. The highly developed resorts of Rhodes and Kos have beaches and bars galore, while Lipsi and Tilos have appealing beaches, but without the crowds. The far-flung islands of Agathonisi, Arki, Kassos and Kastellorizo await Greek island aficionados in pursuit of traditional island life, while everyone boggles at the extraordinary landscape that geological turbulence has created on Nisyros.

History

The Dodecanese islands have been inhabited since pre-Minoan times; by the Archaic period Rhodes and Kos had emerged as the dominant islands of the group. Distance from Athens gave the Dodecanese considerable autonomy and they were, for the most part, free to prosper unencumbered by subjugation to imperial Athens. Following

Alexander the Great's death, Ptolemy I of Egypt ruled the Dodecanese.

The Dodecanese islanders were the first Greeks to become Christians through the tireless efforts of St Paul, who made two journeys to the archipelago, and through St John, who was banished to Patmos where he had his revelation.

The early Byzantine era was fortuitous for the islands, but by the 7th century AD they were plundered by a string of invaders. By the early 14th century it was the turn of the crusaders – the Knights of St John of Jerusalem, or Knights Hospitallers. The Knights eventually became rulers of almost all the Dodecanese, building mighty fortifications, but not mighty enough to keep out the Turks in 1522.

The Turks were ousted by the Italians in 1912 during a tussle over possession of Libya. Inspired by Mussolini's vision of a vast Mediterranean empire, they made Italian the official language and prohibited the practice of Orthodoxy. They constructed grandiose public buildings, indicative of a Fascist style which was the antithesis of

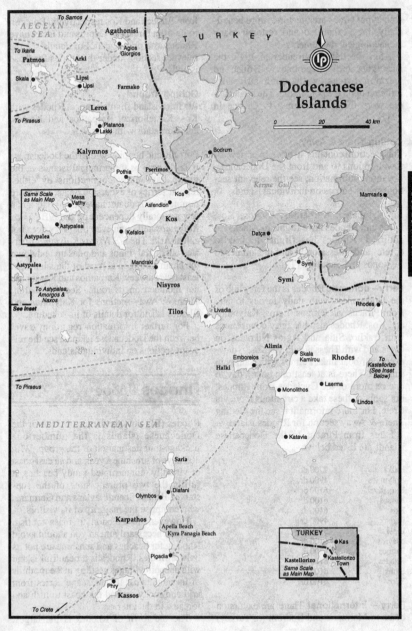

archetypal Greek architecture. More beneficially, they excavated and restored many archaeological monuments.

After the Italian surrender of 1943, the islands became battlegrounds for British and German forces, with much suffering inflicted upon the population. The Dodecanese were formally returned to Greece in 1947.

Getting There & Away

This section contains a brief overview of travel options to and from the Dodecanese. For more information, see the relevant sections under entries on individual islands.

Air Astypalea, Karpathos, Kassos, Kos, Leros and Rhodes have flights to Athens. In addition, Rhodes has flights to Iraklio (Crete) and Thessaloniki and in summer to Mykonos and Santorini (Thira).

Ferry – domestic Rhodes is the ferry hub of the Dodecanese with daily ferries to and from Piraeus via Patmos, Leros, Kalymnos and Kos. Rhodes also has ferry connections with Iraklio, Sitia and Agios Nikolaos on Crete and with Thessaloniki via Kos. A daily excursion boat links Patmos with Samos in summer. There is at least one boat a day to one or more of the Cyclades from Rhodes, but some of these take a circuitous route via Crete. For more information see the Getting There & Away section for Rhodes island.

Fares from Piraeus to the Dodecanese islands are listed below:

Halki	7700 dr
Kalymnos	4900 dr
Karpathos	6100 dr
Kassos	6100 dr
Kos	6100 dr
Leros	4900 dr
Lipsi	5100 dr
Nisyros	6100 dr
Patmos	4200 dr
Rhodes	6700 dr
Symi	6100 dr
Tilos	6100 dr

Ferry – international There are excursion boats to Marmaris and Bodrum (in Turkey)

from Rhodes and Kos respectively. Boats en route from Pireaus to Cyprus and Israel have Rhodes as a port of call. For details see the relevant sections under the entries for these islands.

Getting Around

Air Inter-island flights connect Rhodes with Kos, Kastellorizo, Karpathos and Kassos, and Karpathos with Kassos.

Ferry Island hopping within the Dodecanese is fairly easy as the principal islands in the group have daily connections by either regular ferries or excursion boats. The more remote islands do not have daily boats and a few are totally dependent on the F/B *Nissos Kalymnos*, although even this ferry does not call at Arki. The F/B *Nissos Kalymnos* operates out of Kalymnos and plies up and down the chain calling in at most of the islands, at least twice a week. Karpathos and Kassos are not included on its route. See the Getting There & Away sections for Kalymnos and Rhodes island for details of its schedule.

For further information regarding travel between the Dodecanese islands, see the relevant sections on individual islands.

Rhodes Ρόδος

Rhodes (RO-dos) the largest, by far, of the Dodecanese islands is the number-one package-tour destination of the group. With 300 days of sunshine a year, and an east coast of virtually uninterrupted sandy beaches, it fulfils the two prerequisites of the sun-starved British, Scandinavians and Germans, who comprise the majority of its visitors.

However, an aversion to mass tourism does not necessarily mean you should avoid Rhodes, for beaches and sunshine are not its only attributes. Rhodes is a beautiful island with unspoilt villages nestling in the foothills of its mountains. Its landscape varies from arid and rocky around the coast to lush and forested in the interior.

The old town of Rhodes is the largest

Rhodes & Halki

To Symi, Tilos, Nisyros & Kos

To Pireaus

To Karpathos, Kassos & Crete

AEGEAN SEA

ALIMIA

MAKRY

See Inset

HALKI

STRONGYLI

TRAGOUSA

To Marmaris
To Kastellorizo

Trianda
Ixia
RHODES
Kremasti
Paradisi
Airport
Ialyssos
Koskinou
Kalithea Thermi
Falraki
Maritsa
Fanes
Kalavarda
Kamiros
Petaloudes
Psinthos
Afandou
Salakos
Mt Profitis Ilias (790 m)
Eleousa
Kolymbia
Skala Kamirou
Platania
Epta Piges
Tsambika
Kritinia
Apollona
Church of Agios Nikolaos Fountouklis
Moni Tsambikas
Embona
Stegna Beach
Arhangelos
Mt Attavyros (1215 m)
RHODES
Agios Isidoros
Laerma
Castle of Faraklos
Haraki
Castle of Monolithos
Siana
Moni Thari
Vigla Bay
Monolithos
Istrios
Moni Agia Ipseni
Profilia
Lardos
Lindos
Bay of Apolakkia
Apolakkia
Asklipion
Pefki
Arnitha
Kiotari
Moni Skiadi
Bay of Genadi
Genadi
Messanagros
Kattavia
Plimmyri
Prasonisi
Cape Prasonisi

0   1   2 km
Areta Beach
Kania Beach
Tarpon Springs Boulevard
HALKI
EMBOREIOS
Horio
Moni Agiou Ioanni
Giali Cove
Podamos Beach
To Skala Kamirou
To Karpathos

0   5   10 km

DODECANESE

inhabited medieval town in Europe, and its mighty fortifications are the finest surviving example of defensive architecture of the time.

To water-sports buffs Rhodes will seem like heaven with the gate shut. Almost every sport is available. Windsurfing is best on the west coast and water-skiing on the east. Equipment is widely available for hire on both coasts.

Lawrence Durrell lived in Rhodes during the late 1940s and wrote his book *Reflections on a Marine Venus* as a companion to the island.

History & Mythology

As elsewhere in Greece, the early history of Rhodes is interwoven with mythology. The sun god Helios chose Rhodes as his bride and bestowed upon her light, warmth and vegetation. Their son, Cercafos, had three sons, Camiros, Ialyssos and Lindos, who each founded the cities that were named after them.

The Minoans and Mycenaeans had outposts on the islands, but it was not until the Dorians arrived in 1100 BC that Rhodes began to exert power and influence. The Dorians settled in the cities of Kamiros,

Ialyssos and Lindos and made each an autonomous state. They utilised trade routes to the East which had been established during Minoan and Mycenaean times, and the island flourished as an important centre of commerce in the Aegean. Largely through expediency and connivance, Rhodes continued to prosper until Roman times.

Rhodes was allied to Athens in the Battle of Marathon (490 BC), in which the Persians were defeated. By the time of the Battle of Salamis (480 BC), it had shifted to the Persian side. However, after the unexpected Athenian victory at Salamis, Rhodes hastily became an ally of Athens again, joining the Delian League in 478 BC. After the disastrous Sicilian Expedition (416-412 BC), when after four years of fighting at Syracuse all the Athenian soldiers were either killed, or dead from starvation, Rhodes revolted against Athens and formed an alliance with Sparta, which it aided in the defeat of the Athenians in the Peloponnesian Wars.

In 408 BC, Kamiros, Ialyssos and Lindos consolidated their p6wers for mutual protection and expansion, by co-founding the city of Rhodes. The architect Hippodamos, who came to be regarded as the father of town planning, planned the city. It was one of the most harmonious cities of antiquity, divided into four distinct parts: the acropolis, agora, harbour and residential quarter, with wide straight streets connecting them. Rhodes now became Athens' ally again, and together they defeated Sparta at the battle of Knidos, in 394 BC. Rhodes then joined forces with Persia in a battle against Alexander the Great. However, when Alexander the Great demonstrated invincibility, Rhodes hastily allied itself with him. In the skirmishes following Alexander's death, Rhodes sided with Ptolemy.

In 305 BC, Antigonus, one of Ptolemy's rivals, sent his son, the formidable Demetrius Poliorketes (the Besieger of Cities), to conquer the city. Rhodes managed to repel Demetrius after a long siege. To celebrate this victory, the 32-metre-high bronze statue of Helios Apollo (Colossus of Rhodes), one of the Seven Wonders of the Ancient World,

was built. The statue was traditionally thought to have straddled Mandraki harbour but this is now refuted. Whatever, it only stood for 65 years before collapsing during an earthquake. It lay abandoned until 653 AD when it was chopped up by the Saracens, who sold it to a merchant in Edessa. The story goes that after being shipped to Syria, it took almost 1000 camels to convey it to its final destination.

After the defeat of Poliorketes, Rhodes knew no bounds. It built up the biggest navy in the Aegean and its port became a principal Mediterranean trading centre. The arts also flourished, and the Rhodian school of sculpture supplanted that of Athens as the foremost in Greece. Its most esteemed sculptor was Pythocretes, whose works included the Victory of Samothrace, and the relief of the trireme (warship) at Lindos.

When Greece became the battleground upon which Roman generals fought for leadership of the empire, Rhodes allied itself with Julius Caesar. After Caesar's assassination in 44 BC, Cassius besieged Rhodes, destroying its ships and stripping the city of its artworks, which were then taken to Rome. This marked the beginning of Rhodes' decline. In 70 AD Rhodes became part of the Roman Empire.

In 155 AD Rhodes city was badly damaged by an earthquake, and in 269 AD the Goths invaded, rendering further damage. When the Roman Empire split, Rhodes became part of the Byzantine province of the Dodecanese. Raid upon raid followed. First it was the Persians in 620, then the Saracens in 653; the Turks followed. When the crusaders seized Constantinople, Rhodes was given independence. Later the Genoese gained control. The Knights of St John arrived in Rhodes in 1309 and ruled for 213 years until they were ousted by the Ottomans. Rhodes suffered several earthquakes during the 19th century, but greater damage was rendered in 1856 by an explosion of gunpowder which had been stored and forgotten – almost 1000 people were killed and many buildings were wrecked. After 35 years of Italian occupation, along with the

Badge of the Knights of St John

other Dodecanese islands, Rhodes became part of Greece in 1947.

Getting There & Away

Air Olympic Airways has at least five flights a day to Athens (23,000 dr); four a day to Karpathos (8800 dr); one a day to Kassos (8800 dr) and to Kastellorizo (7000 dr); four a week to Iraklio (19,000 dr); four a week to Santorini (18,000 dr); three a week to Kos (12,000 dr); and two a week to Thessaloniki (29,800 dr). These prices include the airport tax. The Olympic Airways office (☎ 24 571/572/573) is at Ierou Lohou 9. Air Greece has four flights a week to Athens (19,000 dr including airport tax). Triton Holidays (☎ 21 690; fax 31625), Plastira 9, are agents for Air Greece. The airport is 16 km south-west of the city near Paradisi.

Ferry – domestic Rhodes is the ferry hub of the Dodecanese. The following was the schedule at the time of writing, but the EOT and the municipal tourist office in Rhodes city have up-to-date schedules.

The F/B *Rodos* leaves everyday for Piraeus every day at five pm in the high season (14 hours).

The F/B *Patmos* also leaves for Piraeus every day at 5 pm in the high season, (14 hours). It sometimes sails direct to Piraeus and sometimes via Kos. This and the F/B *Rodos* are newer, cleaner and preferable to the other boats which ply between Rhodes and Piraeus. On Friday at 11.30 am the F/B *Patmos* leaves for Thessaloniki (16½ hours) via Kos (3½ hours).

The F/B *Ialyssos* leaves at noon on Monday, Wednesday and Friday and does an 18-hour run to Piraeus via Kos (3½ hours), Kalymnos (5½ hours), Leros (7½ hours) and Patmos (8½ hours). On Sunday at 10 am the F/B *Ialyssos* goes to Karpathos (Diafani, five hours; Pigadia, 6¼ hours).

The F/B *Dimitra* leaves for Piraeus (18½ hours) via Kos (3½ hours), Leros (seven hours), Lipsi (eight hours) and Patmos (8½ hours) on Tuesday at 1 pm. On Thursday at 1 pm it sails for Piraeus (17 hours) via Kos (3½ hours), Kalymnos (5½ hours) and Astypalea (eight hours). On Saturday, at 11.45 pm, it goes to Piraeus (24¼ hours) via Symi (1½ hours), Tilos (4½ hours), Nisyros (6½ hours), Kos (8½ hours), Kalymnos (10 hours), Leros (11 hours), Patmos (12½ hours), Naxos (16½ hours), Paros (17¾ hours) and Syros (19¾ hours).

The F/B *Apollon Express* leaves on Wednesday at 3 pm for Piraeus (28 hours) via Symi (1½ hours), Halki (four hours), Karpathos (Diafani, 6¼ hours; Pigadia, 7¼ hours), Kassos (8¾ hours), Agios Nikolaos (13 hours), Santorini (17 hours), Milos (21¼ hours), Sifnos (22¾ hours), Serifos (23¾ hours) and Kythnos (25 hours).

The F/B *Milena* leaves on Wednesday at 8 pm for Piraeus (25 hours) via Halki (2½ hours), Karpathos (7¼ hours), Iraklio (13 hours), Santorini (17 hours), Naxos (20 hours) and Paros (21 hours). On Saturday at 8 pm the F/B *Milena* leaves for Piraeus (22½ hours) via Karpathos (5½ hours), Kassos (7 hours), Iraklio (12 hours), Santorini (15¼ hours) and Paros (18½ hours).

The F/B *Nissos Kalymnos* leaves on Tuesday and Saturday at 9 am for Kalymnos (9¾ hours) via Symi (2½ hours), Tilos (4½ hours), Nisyros (6¼ hours) and Kos (8¼ hours). On Wednesday and Sunday it leaves Kalymnos at 7 pm for Samos (Pythagorion 7¾ hours) via Leros (two hours), Lipsi (3½ hours), Patmos (4½ hours) and Agathonisi (6½ hours). On Tuesday at 8 pm it sails for Astypalea (2½ hours) from Kalymnos. On Monday and Friday at 5 pm it goes to Kastellorizo (6 hours).

Fares from Rhodes to other Dodecanese islands are as follows:

Agathonisi	4400 dr
Halki	1750 dr
Kalymnos	3500 dr
Karpathos	3100 dr
Kassos	3100 dr
Kastellorizo	2400 dr
Kos	2800 dr
Leros	4100 dr
Lipsi	4200 dr

DODECANESE

Nisyros	2250 dr
Patmos	4200 dr
Symi	1250 dr
Tilos	2100 dr

Ferry & Hydrofoil – international The following are the schedules for international ferries from Rhodes:

To/From Cyprus & Israel In summer there are three ferries a week to Limassol (18 hours) and Haifa (30 hours). See Getting There & Away in the Piraeus section of the Athens chapter for more information. Buy tickets from Kydon Agency (☎ 23 000, 75 268), Ethelondon Dodekanision (between Amerikis and Makariou), or Kouros Travel (☎ 24 377, 22 400), Karpathou 34. Immigration and customs are on the quay.

To/From Turkey Small Turkish car ferries run between Rhodes and Marmaris daily (except Sunday) between April and October and less frequently in winter. Prices vary, so shop around.

Hydrofoils also go to Marmaris daily (weather permitting) from April to October, and are currently cheaper, as they cost 6000/12,000 dr one way/return. You can buy tickets from Triton Holidays (☎ 21 657; fax 31 625), Plastira 9 (between Mandraki and Makariou), to whom you must submit your passport on the day before your journey.

Hydrofoil The Dodecanese Hydrofoil Company and Ilio Hydrofoils service the Dodecanese. They operate from April to October but schedules vary depending on demand for the service and the weather. There is a daily service to Kos (two hours, 6665 dr); five a week to Leros (three hours 10,030 dr) and Patmos (3¼ hours); two a week to Tilos (1¼ hours, 4585 dr), Nisyros (2½ hours, 5327 dr) and Symi (50 minutes, 2675 dr); and one a week, in July and August, to Astypalea. Enquire at Kouros Travel (☎ 22 400), Karpathou 34.

Excursion Boat There are excursion boats to Symi (3500 dr return) and Lindos (4000

dr return) every day in summer, leaving Mandraki at 9 am and returning at 6 pm. You can buy tickets at most travel agencies but it is better to buy directly from the tables set up at Mandraki since you can bargain and also see the boat you will be going on. Look for shade and the size and condition of the boat, as these vary greatly. You can buy an open return if you wish to stay over on Symi, or you can buy a one-way ticket to Lindos and return by bus or taxi – many people find the return by boat, a boring and hot three hours.

Caïque For information about caïques to Halki from Rhodes, see the Getting There & Away section for Halki.

Getting Around
To/From the Airport Ten buses a day travel between the airport and the West Side bus station (250 dr). The first one leaves Rhodes at 6.50 am and the last one at 9.30 pm. From the airport the first one leaves at 7.15 am and the last one at 10.15 pm.

Bus Rhodes city has two bus stations. From the East Side bus station on Plateia Rimini there are 17 buses a day to Faliraki (250 dr), 12 to Lindos (800 dr), six to Kolymbia (450 dr), two to Genadi (1000 dr) via Lardos, and one to Psinthos (360 dr).

From the West Side station next to the New Market there are half-hourly buses to Kalithea Thermi (250 dr), 12 buses a day to Koskinou (250 dr), three to Salakos (500 dr), two to ancient Kamiros (800 dr), two to Petaloudes (800 dr), one to Monolithos (1100 dr) via Skala Kamiros, and one to Embona (900 dr). Both the EOT and municipal tourist office give out schedules.

Taxi Rhodes city's main taxi rank is east of Plateia Rimini. Meters start at 210 dr and then cost approximately 100 dr per km. There are two zones on the island for taxi meters, zone one is Rhodes city and zone two (slightly higher) is everywhere else. Rates are slightly higher between midnight and 6 am. Rip offs are rare but if you think you have been ripped-off take the taxi number and go to the tourist police.

Car & Motorbike There are many car-hire outlets in the new town. Independent (☎ 24 326), Kritis 18, and Tops (☎ 22 800), Orfanidou 44, both provide very competitive rates compared to the major companies and both are reliable. Several motorbike-hire outlets are located in the old town and 30-odd outlets are on the west side of the new town. Try several and bargain even in season because the competition is fierce.

Bicycle The Bicycle Centre (☎ 28 315), Griva 39, is an excellent bicycle-hire outlet. Daily rates are 800 dr for three-speed bikes and 1200 dr for mountain bikes.

RHODES CITY

The heart of Rhodes city is the old town, enclosed within massive walls. Much of the new town to the north is a monument to package tourism, however, it does have several places of interest to visitors.

Orientation

The old town is a mesh of Byzantine, Turkish and Latin architecture with quiet, twisting alleyways punctuated by large, lively squares. Sokratous, which runs east to west, and its easterly continuation, Aristotelous, make up the old town's bustling main commercial thoroughfare. The old town's two main squares are also along here: Plateia Martyron Evreon, with a fountain decorated with bronze sea horses, at the eastern end of Aristotelous; and Plateia Ippokratous, with the distinctive Castellania fountain, at the eastern end of Sokratous. Acquainting yourself with Sokratous and these two squares will help somewhat with orientation, but getting lost in Rhodes' old town is almost inevitable and part of the fun of exploring the place. Farther north, parallel to Sokratous, is Ippoton (Avenue of the Knights) which was the main medieval thoroughfare.

The commercial harbour, for international ferries and large inter-island ferries, is east of the old town. Excursion boats, small ferries, hydrofoils and private yachts use Mandraki harbour, to the north of the commercial harbour. When you buy a ferry ticket check which harbour the ferry is leaving from.

In Mandraki the two bronze deer (a doe and a stag) on stone pillars mark the supposed site of the Colossus of Rhodes. Mandraki's grandiose public buildings are relics of Mussolini's era. The main square of the new town is Plateia Rimini, which is just north of the old town. The tourist offices, bus stations and main taxi rank are on or near this square. If you arrive by ferry, the square is just a short walk from Mandraki, but farther from the commercial harbour.

There are eight gates into the old town. From Plateia Rimini enter through the Eleftheria Gate. Once through the gate, walk south to get to Sokratous. From the commercial harbour, enter through St Catherine's Gate. This is a narrow pedestrian gate behind the ticket offices opposite the harbour entrance.

Most of the old town is off limits to motorists but there are car parks on the periphery. Most budget accommodation for independent travellers is in the old town. Many hotels in the new town are block-booked by tour companies. However, they may have rooms available on any given day, but this is more likely in low season.

Information

Tourist Offices The EOT (☎ 23 255/655) is on the corner of Makariou and Papagou. The staff give out brochures and a map of the city, and will assist in finding accommodation. Opening times are Monday to Friday from 7.30 am to 3 pm. The same service is provided by Rhodes' municipal tourist office (☎ 35 945), on Plateia Rimini. Opening times are from 8 am to 8 pm Monday to Saturday and 8 am to noon on Sunday. It is closed in winter. From either of these offices you can pick up a copy of the *Rodos News*, a free English-language newspaper.

Tourist Police The tourist police (☎ 27 423) are next door to the EOT. The police here see

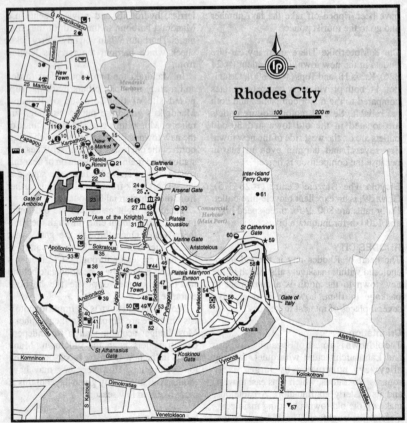

Rhodes City

their job as having to do with crime against tourists rather than tourist information and are perhaps not as helpful as the tourist police in other parts of Greece.

Money The main National Bank of Greece is on Plateia Kyprou. It has an automatic teller machine. Opening times are Monday to Thursday from 8 am to 2 pm and 6 to 8 pm, on Friday from 8 am to 1.30 pm and 3 to 8.30 pm, on Saturday from 8 am to 2 pm and on Sunday from 9 am to noon. There is also a National Bank of Greece in the old town on Plateia Moussiou and a Credit Bank on

Plateia Kyprou and a Commercial Bank of Greece on Plateia Moussiou. All have automatic teller machines.

American Express (☎ 21 010) is represented by Rhodos Tours, Ammohostou 18. Summer opening times are Monday to Saturday from 9 am to 2 pm and 5 to 9 pm. Winter opening times are Monday to Saturday from 8.30 am to 1 pm and 5 to 8 pm. There is a Thomas Cook agency (☎ 35 672) at Venizelou Sofi 6.

Post & Telecommunications The main post office is on Mandraki. Opening times

PLACES TO STAY		OTHER		24	Plateia Simi
35	Maria's Rooms			25	Temple of Aphrodite
36	Mamas Pension	1	Mosque of Murad Reis	26	Commercial Bank of
40	S Nikolis Hotel &	2	National Theatre		Greece
	Apartments	3	Olympic Airways Office	27	Museum of the
47	Pension Rena/Taverna	4	OTE		Decorative Arts
	Kostas	5	Post Office	28	National Bank of
48	Hotel Tehran	6	Port Police		Greece
51	Pension Andreos	7	Rhodos Tours	29	Byzantine Museum
52	Pension Minos	8	Oasis Swimming Pool	30	Departure Point for F/B
53	Niki's Rooms to Let	9	Tourist Police		*Nissos Kalymnos*
54	Hotel Spot	10	EOT	31	Archaeological
56	Hotel Ilianna	11	National Bank of		Museum
58	Hotel Kava d'Oro		Greece	32	Mosque of Süleyman
		12	Plateia Kyprou	33	Turkish Library
PLACES TO EAT		13	Credit Bank	37	Turkish Bath
		14	Departure Points for	39	Folk Dance Theatre
15	Patisseries		Excursion Boats &	41	Ancient Market Garden
34	Alexis Restaurant		Hydrofoils		Bar
38	Diafani Taverna	16	Bus Station (West Side)	43	Hobby Laundrette
42	Cleo's Italian	17	Kouros Travel	45	Plateia Hippocrates &
	Restaurant	18	Luggage Storage		Castellania Fountain
44	Yiannis Taverna	19	Bus Station (East Side)	50	Mosque of Retjep
46	Mythos Café Bar	20	Rhodes Municipal		Pasha
49	Popeye Bar & Grill		Tourist Office	55	Synagogue
57	Taverna Manzavino	21	Taxi Rank	59	Port Police
		22	Son et Lumiére	60	Departure Point for
		23	Palace of the Grand		Boats to Turkey
			Masters	61	Customs Office

DODECANESE

are Monday to Friday from 7.30 am to 8 pm, Saturday from 7.30 am to 2 pm and Sunday from 9 am to 1.30 pm. Rhodes' postcode is 851 00. The OTE is at Amerikis 91. It is open daily from 8 am to midnight. Rhodes' telephone code is 0241.

Foreign Consulates Foreign consulates in Rhodes include:

Germany
    Parodos Isiodou 12 (☎ 63 730)
Netherlands
    Alexandrou Diakou 27 (☎ 31 571)
Turkey
    Iroön Politehniou 12 (☎ 23 362)
UK
    25 Martiou 23 (☎ 24 963)

Bookshops The Academy Bookstore, at Dragoumi 7; and Moses Cohn, at Themeli 83D, both stock foreign-language books.

Laundry Rhodes has three self-service laundrettes: Hobby Laundrette, Platonos 31;

Lavomatique, 28 Oktovriou 32; and Express Servis, Dilberaki 97 (off Orfanidou). All charge around 1000 dr a load.

Luggage Storage The New Market Pension on Plateia Rimini has luggage storage for 500 dr a day (12 hours).

Emergency Rhodes' general hospital (☎ 25 580) is at Erythrou Stavrou. For emergency first aid and the ambulance service telephone ☎ 25 555 or 22 222.

Old Town
The town is divided into two parts. In medieval times the Knights of St John lived in the Knights' Quarter and the other inhabitants lived in the Hora. The 12-metre-thick city walls are closed to the public, but on Tuesday and Sunday at 2.45 pm you can take a guided walk along them starting at the courtyard of the Palace of the Grand Masters (1200 dr). As well as seeing the old town's sights, take time to wander in the maze of narrow,

vaulted side streets to relish the medieval aura.

Knights' Quarter The Knights of St John were a religious order of the church of Rome founded in Amalfi in the 11th century. They went to Jerusalem initially to minister to the pilgrims who arrived there, but soon extended their duties to tending the poor and sick of the Holy Land. Over the years they became increasingly militant, joining forces with the Knights Templars and the Teutonic Knights of St Mary in battles against infidels.

The Knights of St John were expelled from the Holy Land with the fall of Jerusalem. They went first to Cyprus and then to Rhodes, where they arrived in 1309. Through some wheeler-dealing with the island's ruling Genoese admiral, Viguolo de Viguoli, they became the possessors of Rhodes, transforming it into a mighty bulwark that stood at the easternmost point of the Christian West safeguarding it from the Muslim infidels of the East. The knights withstood Muslim offensives in 1444 and 1480, but in 1522 Sultan Süleyman the Magnificent staged a massive attack with 200,000 troops. After a long siege the 600 knights, with 1000 mercenaries and 6000 Rhodians surrendered – hunger, disease and death having taken their toll.

An appropriate place to begin an exploration of the old town is the imposing, cobblestone **Avenue of the Knights** which was where the knights lived. The knights were divided into seven 'tongues' or languages, according to their place of origin: England, France, Germany, Italy, Aragon, Auvergne and Provence, and each group was responsible for protecting a section of the bastion. The Grand Master, in overall charge, lived in the palace, and each tongue was under the auspices of a bailiff. The knights were divided into soldiers, chaplains and ministers to the sick.

To this day the street exudes a noble and forbidding aura, despite modern offices now occupying most of the inns. Its lofty buildings stretch in a 600-metre-long unbroken wall of honey-coloured stone blocks, and its flat façade is punctuated by huge doorways and arched windows. The inns reflect the Gothic styles of architecture of the knights' countries of origin. They form a harmonious whole in their bastion-like structure, but on closer inspection each possesses graceful and individual embellishments.

First on the right, at the eastern end of the Avenue of the Knights, is the **Inn of the Order of the Tongue of Italy** (1519); next to it is the **Palace of Villiers de l'Île Adam**. After Sultan Süleyman had taken the city, it was Villiers de l'Île who had the humiliating task of arranging the knights' departure from the island. Next along is the **Inn of France**, the most ornate and distinctive of all the inns. On the opposite side of the street is a wrought-iron gate in front of a Turkish garden. Back on the right side is the **Chapelle Française** (Chapel of the Tongue of France), embellished with a statue of the Virgin and Child. Next door is the residence of the Chaplain of the Tongue of France. Across the alleyway is the **Inn of Provence**, with four coats of arms forming the shape of a cross, and opposite is the **Inn of Spain**.

On the right is the magnificent 14th-century **Palace of the Grand Masters** (☎ 23 035). It was destroyed in the gunpowder explosion of 1856 and the Italians rebuilt it in a grandiose manner, with a lavish interior, intending it as a holiday home for Mussolini and King Emmanuel III. It is now a museum, containing sculpture, mosaics taken from Kos by the Italians, and antique furniture. The palace is open Tuesday to Sunday from 8.30 am to 3 pm. Admission is 1200 dr.

The **archaeological museum** (☎ 27 657), Plateia Moussiou, is housed in the 15th-century knights' hospital, a splendid structure built around a courtyard. Its infirmary had beds for 100 patients.

The museum's most famous exhibit is the exquisite Parian marble statuette, the *Aphrodite of Rhodes*, a 1st-century BC adaptation of a Hellenistic statue. It depicts the love goddess newly emerged from the sea, kneeling, and holding up her long hair to dry in the sun. Less charming, to most people, is the 4th-century BC *Aphrodite of Thalassia* in the next room. However, Lawrence Durrell was so enamoured by this statue that he named his *Reflections on a Marine Venus* after it. Also in this room is the 2nd-century BC marble *Head of Helios*, unearthed from near the Palace of the Grand Masters where a Temple of Helios once stood. The head belonged to a statue in the temple's pediment which depicted the sun god riding a chariot in the sky. Another renowned exhibit is the beautiful, well-preserved 4th-century BC grave stele found at Kamiros, which depicts Crito bidding farewell to her mother, Timarista. In the same room are two 6th-century BC kouroi statues, also found at Kamiros. Other exhibits include small statues from various periods, gravestones of the knights and small grave steles from the Roman period. The museum is open Tuesday to Sunday from 8.30 am to 3 pm. Admission is 800 dr.

Across the square from the archaeological museum, the 11th-century **Church of the Virgin** of the Castle was enlarged by the knights and became their cathedral. It is now the **Byzantine Museum**, with Christian artworks. It is open Tuesday to Sunday from 8.30 am to 3 pm. Admission is 600 dr.

Farther north, on the opposite side, the **Museum of the Decorative Arts** houses an interesting collection of pottery, furniture and costumes from around the Dodecanese. Opening times are Tuesday to Sunday from 8.30 am to 3 pm. Admission is 600 dr. On Plateia Simi, there are the remains of a 3rd-century BC **Temple of Aphrodite**, one of the few ancient ruins in the old town.

Hora Until this century, Rhodes had a large Jewish population who lived in the southeast district of Hora. During the Nazi occupation most of these Jews were transported to Auschwitz, never to return. The synagogue on Dosiadou has a plaque commemorating the tragedy. The remaining Jews still worship here and it is usually open in the morning. Close by, Plateia Martyron Evreon, (Square of the Jewish Martyrs) also commemorates these Jews.

The Hora also has many Ottoman legacies. During Turkish times the churches were converted to mosques, and many more were built from scratch. Most are now dilapidated. The most important one is the pink-domed **Mosque of Süleyman**, at the top of Sokratous. It was built in 1522 to commemorate the Ottoman victory against the knights. It was rebuilt in 1808. Opposite, is the 18th-century **Turkish library** where many Islamic manuscripts are kept. It is sometimes open to the public – check the times on the notice outside.

The 18th-century **Turkish bath**, on Plateia Arionos, offered a rare opportunity to have a Turkish bath in Greece, but at the time of writing it was temporarily closed. Ask at the EOT if it has re-opened.

New Town

The **Acropolis of Rhodes** (Monte Smith) was the ancient Hellenistic city of Rhodes. The alternative name is after the English admiral Sir Sydney Smith who kept watch here for Napoleon's fleet in 1802. Competitions were held in preparation for the Olympic Games in the restored 2nd-century **stadium**. The adjacent **theatre** is a reconstruction of one used for lectures by the School of Rhetoric. Steps above here lead to the **Temple of Pythian Apollo**, with four re-erected columns. From here there are superb views and you can catch some particularly good sunsets. The site is an open one. You can take city bus No 5, or walk there along Diagoridon.

North of Mandraki, at the eastern end of G Papanikolaou, is the graceful **Mosque of Murad Reis**. In its grounds are a Turkish **cemetery** and the small Villa Cleobolus, where Lawrence Durrell lived in the 1940s.

The **aquarium** is housed in a red-and-cream Italianate building at the island's northernmost point. Its exhibits include all things aquatic and some oceanography instruments. Opening times are 9 am to 9 pm daily. Admission is 600 dr.

The town **beach** begins north of Mandraki and continues around the island's northernmost point and down the west side of the new town. The best spot is on the

Windmills on the breakwater at Mandraki

northernmost point since you get both a breeze and calm water and it's not quite as crowded. Another good spot in calm weather is at the south-west end of the beach.

The Oasis **swimming pool**, in a park to the west of the EOT, charges 1000 dr (which includes a drink) and is often quite dirty. Some hotels allow public entry to their pools. Ask around.

Rodini Park, three km south of the town, is a pleasant shady park with pine, cypress and maple trees, streams, ponds and peacocks. It's believed to be the site of the Rhodes School of Rhetoric. The city bus No 3 goes there.

Activities

Scuba Diving Two diving schools operate out of Mandraki: the Waterhoppers Diving Centre (☎ 76 178; fax 20 971), Karpathou 34; and Dive Med Centre (☎ 33 654; fax 23 780). Both offer a range of courses including a One Day Try Dive for 10,000 dr. They also have a wide range of equipment for hire, advanced courses and night dives for certified divers. You can get information from the Waterhopper boat, MV *Kouros*, and the Dive Med Centre's boats *Pheonix*, *Free Spirit* and *Aurora*, at Mandraki. Diving takes place at Kalithea Thermi (currently the only area around Rhodes where diving is legal).

Tennis Many of the large hotels have tennis courts open to non-guests. The Rhodes Tennis Club (☎ 25 705) is on the waterfront north of Mandraki.

Yachting You can hire yachts from the YAR Maritime Centre (☎ 22 927; fax 23 393), Vyronos 1. For more information about yachting contact the Rodos Yacht Club (☎ 23 287).

Windsurfing The Fun Surf Center (☎ 95 819), Ialysos Beach, Ixia (six km from Rhodes city), has hourly, daily and weekly rental of sailboards. There are many other rental outlets around the coast.

Greek-Dancing Lessons The Nelly Dimoglou Dance Company (☎ 20 157 or 29 085), at the Folk Dancing Theatre, on Andronikou, gives Greek-dancing lessons.

Organised Tours

If your time on Rhodes is limited then Triton Holidays (☎ 21 690; fax 31625), Plastira 9, Mandraki, has a wide range of tours.

Places to Stay – bottom end

The old town of Rhodes is well supplied with accommodation so even in high season you should be able to find somewhere. *Mamas Pension* (☎ 25 359), Menekleous 28, has clean singles/doubles/triples for 4000/5000/6000 dr with shared bathroom.

Pension Rena (☎ 26 217), Pythagora 55, has tidy doubles for 5000 dr with shared bathroom. *Pension Minos* (☎ 31 813), at Omirou 5, has spotless, spacious rooms for 7000/10,000 dr. From the roof garden there are views of almost the entire old town. Close by, the *Pension Andreos* (☎ 34 156; fax 74 285) has pleasant rooms for 8000/9000 dr.

The E-class *Hotel Spot* (☎ 34 737), Perikleous 21, has very comfortable singles/doubles/triples for 7500/8000/9000 dr with private bathroom. Also near the Castellania fountain, *Pension Ilianna* (☎ 30 251), at Gavala 1, has singles/doubles for 3000/5000 dr with private bathroom. The immaculate and modern *Maria's Rooms* (☎ 22 169) surround a quiet courtyard just off Sokratous. Doubles/triples go for 6000/7600 dr with shared bathroom and 7500/8500 dr with private bathroom.

The *Hotel Tehran* (☎ 27 594), Sofokleous 41b, overlooking Plateia Sofokleous, has tidy rooms for 6000/7000 dr with private bathroom. Just off this square, *Niki's Rooms to Let* (☎ 25 115), Sofokleous 39, has spacious, clean singles/doubles/triples for 7000/8500/12000 dr.

The delightful D-class *Hotel Kava d'Oro* (☎ 36 980), Kistiniou 15, is in an 800-year-old house, close to the commercial harbour. It's spotlessly clean and has a friendly bar and a shady courtyard. Rates are 5000/6000/9000 dr with private bathroom. From the commercial harbour, go through St Catherine's Gate, turn left, and the hotel is 50 metres along on the left.

Places to Stay – middle

The *S Nikolis Hotel & Apartments* (☎ 34 561, 36 238; fax 32 034), Ippodamou 61, is the old town's most luxurious accommodation. The rooms, which have rough stucco walls and attractive furniture, cost 9000/14,000/17,000 dr, including breakfast. The lovely, well-equipped apartments sleep four people and cost 18,400 dr. It has a large garden and a roof terrace with terrific views.

Places to Stay – top end

The A-class *Avra Beach* (☎ 25 284/285), at the suburb resort of Ixia six km south-west of Rhodes city, has a restaurant, bar and swimming pool. Singles/doubles/triples cost 10,900/15,500/18,300 dr. The deluxe *Grand Hotel Astir Palace* (☎ 26 284) is on Akti Miaouli. The hotel has a bar, restaurant and swimming pools. Rates are 18,900/24,900 dr for singles/doubles, and 78,600 dr for suites.

The *Rodos Palace* (☎ 25 222, 26 222; fax 25 350) is also at Ixia. This vast place has loads of amenities, and the rates are 28,600/36,500 dr for singles/doubles.

Places to Eat – inexpensive

Enthusiastic touting and displays of tacky photographs of food seem to be the order of the day at many restaurants in Rhodes, with the enthusiasm of the touts not reflected in the quality of the food. However if you hunt around you will find good-value places.

The unpretentious, family-run *Taverna Manzavino*, on Kanada, south of the old town, serves well-prepared, inexpensive, traditional Greek fare. In the old town *Yiannis Taverna*, Appellou 41, is popular with locals and is also good value. Stifado is 1000 dr and souvlaki is 1300 dr. *Taverna Kostas*, Pythagora 62, is also commendable with souvlaki for 1200 dr and swordfish for 1700 dr. *Diafani Taverna*, opposite the Turkish bath serves, gratifying, reasonably priced dishes, 'cooked from the heart', as the owner says in German.

The *Popeye Bar & Grill* (see the following Entertainment section), Plateia Sofokleous, serves inexpensive snacks and barbecued meat dishes; a meze plate is 700 dr. Appropriately, this is a good place to find work on a yacht.

If you just have to have some English food then two restaurants in the new town which serve reasonably priced food as close as you'll get to home are *Mollye's*, Ionos Dragoumi 25, and *The Yorkshire Diner*, Orfanidou 45.

The suburb resort of Ixia has two restaurants of note. *Tzaki Taverna*, on the main road, just after the Ialissos beach turn-off, has around 30 different mezedes ranging from 350 to 650 dr and good barrel wine. There's live bouzouki music every evening. *Le Jardin*, just before the beach turn-off, despite the name, serves traditional Greek fare like moussaka for 800 dr and giouvetsi for 1750 dr.

The best (some say the only) cappuccino in Rhodes city can be had for 300 dr at the pleasant, relaxed *Mythos Café Bar*, Evripidou 13-15, near the Castellania fountain. The *food market* opposite Plateia Rimini has numerous fast-food outlets and fruit and vegetable stalls.

Places to Eat – moderate

Cleo's Italian Restaurant, Agiou Fanouriou

17, is a sophisticated place with a cool, elegant interior and a quiet courtyard. Set menus cost around 4000 dr. The à la carte choices here include tortellini alla crema, pomodoro mozzarella and tiramisù. *Alexis Restaurant*, on Sokratous, is a first-rate seafood restaurant, where you'll pay around 6000 dr for a meal with wine.

Feverish touting reaches its acme at the people-watching pâtisseries bordering the New Market. Nevertheless, they're convivial meeting places with a vast choice of cakes. Coffee and cake cost a pricey 1200 to 1500 dr.

Places to Eat – expensive
Palia Istoria (☎ 32421), 108 Mitropoleos, south of the old town, is popular with well-healed locals. It has a large, imaginative menu which includes delicious and unusual mezedes such as scallops with mushrooms, and artichokes in nutmeg sauce. Expect to pay 6000 to 8000 dr for a meal with wine. Reservations are recommended.

Entertainment
The son et lumière (☎ 21 922), in the Palace of the Grand Masters grounds, depicting the Turkish siege, is superior to most such efforts. The entrance is on Plateia Rimini and admission is 1000 dr. Check the times for performances in English, with the EOT.

The Nelly Dimoglou Dance Company gives first rate performances at the *Folk Dance Theatre* (☎ 20 157), on Andronikou. Performances are nightly except Saturday from May to October and begin at 9.20 pm. Admission is 1400 dr. There are classical-music recitals at the *National Theatre* (☎ 29 678).

The *Popeye Bar & Grill* (see also Places to Eat) is a lively bar with a dart board and pool table. Beers cost 350 to 500 dr and cocktails are 800 dr. The atmospheric stone-walled, wood-beamed *Ancient Market Garden Bar*, Omirou 70, built on the site of the ancient agora, is a good place for a quiet drink.

The new town has a plethora of discos and bars – over 600 at last count and rising. The two main areas are called Top Street and the Street of Bars. Top Street is Alexandrou Diakou and The Street of Bars is Orfanidou, where a cacophony of western music blares from every establishment; just take your pick. Quieter than most, is the *Red Lion*, Orfanidou 9, with the relaxed atmosphere of a British pub. Proprietors Ron and Vasilis will gladly answer any of your questions about Rhodes for the price of a drink. Beers cost from 400 to 550 dr and cocktails are 800 dr. For live rock n' roll, try the *Rock Box* at Alexandrou Diakou 65.

Things to Buy
Good buys in Rhodes old town are gold and silver jewellery, leather goods and ceramics. However, leather goods are less expensive in Turkey. Look around and be discriminating – it's quite acceptable to haggle.

Getting There & Away
See the Getting There & Away and Getting Around sections for Rhodes island at the beginning of the Rhodes section.

Getting Around
Local buses leave from Mandraki. Bus No 2 goes to Analipsi, No 3 to Rodini, No 4 to Agios Dimitrios and No 5 to Monte Smith. Buy tickets at the kiosk on Mandraki.

EASTERN RHODES
Rhodes' best beaches are on the east coast. Frequent buses go down the coast as far as Lindos, but some of the beaches are a bit of a trek from the main road, where the bus stops are.

Kalithea Thermi, 10 km from Rhodes city, is a derelict Italian-built spa. The frequent buses from Rhodes city stop on the main road opposite the short turn-off to the spa.

Walk through a colonnade to a large domed building with tiny blue-glassed star-shaped windows. Surrounding it are more buildings with crumbling colonnades, pebble-mosaic floors and domed ceilings. There is a small beach in an inlet which is used by Rhodes' diving schools (see Activities in the Rhodes city section). There's good snorkelling from the rocks to the left of here, and snorkelling gear for hire. To the right there's a small sandy beach (with a snack bar) reached along a track through pines, which veers right from the turn-off to the spa.

Kalithea is to be restored with funds awarded to Greece, under the Delors II Regional Development Programme, for improvement of its spas.

Faliraki beach, five km farther south, is the island's premiere resort and comes complete with high-rise hotels, fast-food joints and bars. Although the main stretch of beach is crowded, the bay at the extreme southern end is uncrowded and popular with nude bathers. **Aqua Adventure** (Greece's longest waterslide), is located between the Palasos and Calypso hotels at the northern end of the beach. The bus stop is close to the beach. Faliraki Camping (☎ 85 358) has a restaurant, bar, minimarket and swimming pool.

At Kolymbia, 10 km south of Faliraki, a right turn leads in over four km of pine-fringed road to the **Epta Piges** (Seven Springs), a verdant beauty spot, where a small lake fed by springs can be reached either along a path or through a tunnel. There are no buses here, so take a Lindos bus and get off at the turn-off. With your own transport you can continue for another nine km to **Eleousa** on the slopes of Profitis Ilias, and then another three km to the **Church of Agios Nikolaos** at Fountouklis, which has fine Byzantine frescoes. A dirt road continues to Salakos (see Inland Rhodes).

Back on the coast, **Kolymbia** and **Tsambikas** are good, but crowded beaches. A steep road (signposted) leads in 1.5 km to **Moni Tsambikas**, from where there are terrific views. It is a place of pilgrimage for childless women. On the 18th September, the monastery's festival day, they climb up to it on their knees and pray to conceive.

Arhangelos, four km farther on and inland, is a large agricultural village with a long tradition of carpet weaving and hand-made goatskin boots, both of which are being overtaken by tourism as the major money-earner. Just before Anchangelos there is a

turn-off to **Stegna beach**, and just after to the lovely, sandy cove of **Agathi**; both are reasonably quiet. The **Castle of Faraklos** above Agathi was a prison for recalcitrant knights and the island's last stronghold to fall to the Turks. The fishing port of **Haraki**, just south of the castle, has a pebbled beach and good fish tavernas. There are more beaches between here and Vlyha Bay, two km from Lindos.

Lindos Λίνδος

Lindos village, below the Acropolis, is an immaculate showpiece of dazzling-white, 17th-century houses, many with ornate lintels and doors, and courtyards with black-and-white *hohlakia* (pebble mosaics) floors. Once the dwellings of wealthy admirals, many have been bought and restored by foreign celebrities. The main thoroughfares are lined with tourist shops, cafés and bars, so you need to explore the labyrinthine alleyways to fully appreciate the place.

The 15th-century **Church of Agia Panagia** on Acropolis, is festooned with 18th-century frescoes of saints, and has lots of elaborately carved wood.

Orientation & Information The town is pedestrianised. All vehicular traffic terminates on the central square of Plateia Eleftherias, from where the main drag, Acropolis, begins. The donkey terminus is a little way along here. The municipal tourist information office (☎ 31 900/288/227) is on Plateia Eleftherias. It is open daily from 9 am to 11 pm. Lindos Sun Tours (☎ 31 333) and Pallas Travel (☎ 31 204), both on Acropolis, have a room-letting service and car and motorbike rental (with good rates out of high season).

The Commercial Bank of Greece is just beyond the donkey terminus and the National Bank of Greece is on the street opposite the Church of Agia Panagia. Neither has an automatic teller machine. Turn right at the donkey terminus for the post office. There is no OTE but there are cardphones on Plateia Eleftherias and the Acropolis.

DODECANESE

The privately owned Lindos Lending Library, on Acropolis, is well stocked with English books and charges 100 dr per day, per book (1500 dr deposit). The laundrette next door charges 1500 dr per load.

The Acropolis of Lindos The most famous of the Dodecanese ancient cities is Lindos, but with 500,000 visitors a year it's just a bit *too* famous.

The Acropolis of Lindos is spectacularly perched atop a 116-metre-high rock. Lindos was the most important Doric settlement, because of its excellent vantage point and good harbour. It was first established around 2000 BC and is a conglomeration of ancient, Byzantine, Frankish and Turkish remains.

After the founding of the city of Rhodes, Lindos declined in commercial importance, but remained an important place of worship. The ubiquitous St Paul landed here *en route* to Rome. The Byzantine fortress was strengthened by the knights, and also used by the Turks.

It's about a 10-minute climb to the well-signposted entrance gate. Once inside, a flight of steps leads to a large square. On the left (facing the next flight of steps) is a trireme (warship) hewn out of the rock by the sculptor Pythocretes. A statue of Hagesandros, priest of Poseidon, originally stood on the deck of the ship. At the top of the steps ahead, you enter the acropolis by a vaulted corridor. At the other side-turn sharp left through an enclosed room to reach a row of storerooms on the right. Opposite here is another rostrum. The stairway on the right leads to the remains of a 20-columned **Hellenistic stoa** (200 BC). The Byzantine **Church of Agios Ioannis** is to the right of this stairway. The wide stairway behind the stoa leads to a 5th-century BC propylaeum, beyond which is the 4th-century **Temple to Athena**, the site's most important ancient ruin (presently encased in scaffolding). Athena was worshipped on Lindos as early as the 10th century BC, so this temple has replaced earlier ones on the site. From its far side there are splendid views of Lindos

village and its packed beach, and St Paul's Beach, in an almost circular harbour.

Donkey rides to the acropolis cost 850 dr one way. The site is open Monday to Friday from 8.30 am to 4.30 pm and Saturday and Sunday from 8.30 am to 2.30 pm. Admission is 1000 dr.

Places to Stay Accommodation is expensive and reservations are essential in summer. The following options are not entirely monopolised by tour groups. *Fedra Rooms to Rent* (☎ 31 286), along the street opposite the Church of Agia Panagia, has doubles/triples for 8000/9600 dr with private bathroom.

The following recommendations are all on the street leading to the Acropolis. *Papakonstantinos Rooms* (☎ 31 369), at No 70, has doubles/triples with shared bathroom for 7000/9000 dr. *Domino Psaros* (☎ 37 322), at No 76, has doubles/triples for 8000/9600 dr with shared bathroom and kitchen. Farther along, the *Pension Electra* (☎ 31 266) has doubles with shared bathroom for 9000 dr, and double/triple studios for 14,000/20,000 dr. The *Pension Katholiki* next door has similar rates.

Getting There & Away There are 12 buses a day to and from Lindos from Rhodes city (800 dr). Buses from Genadi to Lindos leave at 7.30, 9.30 and 10.45 am and 1.45 pm (360 dr) and return to Genadi at 9 and 10.10 am, and at 3.30 and 9 pm. Buses from Pefki (via Lardos) to Lindos leave at 7.50, 8.50 and 9.50 am and at 1.50, 2.50 and 3.50 pm and return at 8.30, 9.30, 10.30 and 11.30 am and 2.30, 3.30 and 7 pm.

There are daily excursion boats from Mandraki in Rhodes city (see the Getting Around section for Rhodes city).

WESTERN RHODES

Western Rhodes is more green and forested than the east coast, but it's more exposed to winds so the sea tends to be rough, and the beaches are mostly of pebbles or stones. Nevertheless, tourist development is rampant, almost to the airport, and consists of the suburb resorts of Ixia, Trianda and Kremasti. Paradisi, despite being next to the airport, has retained some of the feel of a traditional village. If you are on Rhodes between flights or have an early morning flight you may consider staying here. There are several domatia options and decent restaurants on the main street.

Ialyssos Ιαλυσσός

Like Lindos, Ialyssos, 10 km from Rhodes, is a hotchpotch of Doric, Byzantine and medieval remains. The Doric city was built on Filerimos hill which was an excellent vantage point, and so attracted successive invaders. The only ancient remains are the foundations of a 3rd-century BC temple and a restored 4th-century BC fountain. Also at the site are the restored **Monastery of Our Lady** and the **Chapel of Agios Georgios**.

The ruined fortress was used by Süleyman the Magnificent as his headquarters during his siege of Rhodes city. The site is open Tuesday to Sunday from 8.30 am to 3 pm. Admission is 800 dr.

Getting There & Away No buses go to ancient Ialyssos. The airport bus stops at Trianda, on the coast. Ialyssos is five km inland from here.

Kamiros Κάμειρος

Many people believe this is Rhodes' best ancient site. The extensive ruins of the ancient city of Kamiros stand on an hillside above the west coast, 34 km from Rhodes city. It was a city built by the Dorians and produced figs, oil and wine. It reached its height in the 6th century BC, but by the 4th century BC it had been superseded by the city of Rhodes, and was almost totally destroyed by earthquakes in 226 and 142 BC. The site was first excavated in 1929 after locals unearthed an ancient grave. The layout of the ancient city is easily discernible.

From the entrance walk straight ahead and down the steps. The semi-circular rostrum on the right is where officials made speeches to the public. Opposite are the remains of a **Doric temple** with one standing column.

The area next to it, with a row of intact columns, was probably where the public watched priests performing rites in the temple. Ascend the wide stairway to the ancient city's main street. Opposite the top of the stairs is one of the best preserved of the **Hellenistic houses** which flanked the east side of the street. Walk along the street, ascend three flights of steps, and continue straight ahead to reach the ruins of the 3rd-century **great stoa**, which had a 206-metre portico supported by two rows of Doric columns. It was built on top of a huge 6th-century cistern which supplied the houses with rain water through an advanced drainage system. Behind the stoa, at the city's highest point, stood the **Temple to Athena**. From here there are terrific views inland to Mt Profitis Ilias and Mt Attavyros.

The site is open Monday to Friday from 8.30 am to 3.40 pm; and Saturday, Sunday and holidays from 8.30 am to 2.40 pm. Admission is 800 dr. Buses from Rhodes city to Kamiros stop on the coast road. The site is one km inland from here.

From Kamiros to Monolithos

Skala Kamiros, 16 km south of Kamiros, is touted as an 'authentic fishing village' so it's very much on the tour-bus circuit and only worth a visit to get a caïque to Halki (see the Getting There & Away section for Halki). The road south from here to Monolithos has some of the island's most impressive scenery. From Skala Kamiros the road winds uphill with great views across the sea to Halki and the islets of Alimia, Makry, Strongyli and Tragousa. This is just a taste of what's to come at the ruined 16th-century **Castle of Kastellos** that's reached along a rough road from the main road, two km beyond Skala Kamiros. Eight km farther along there is a left fork to Embona (see the Interior). The main road continues for another nine km to **Siana**, a picturesque village below Mt Akramytis (825 metres), famed for its honey and *souma*, a local firewater.

Five km beyond Siana, the village of Monolithos has the spectacularly sited

Castle of Monolithos perched on a sheer 240-metre rock and reached along a dirt track. Continuing along this track, at the fork bear right for **Moni Georgiou** and left for the very pleasant, shingled **Fourni beach**. Monolithos has rooms to rent and the *Hotel Thomas* (☎ 61 291) has singles/doubles for 6000/8000 dr.

SOUTHERN RHODES

South of Lindos, Rhodes becomes progressively less developed (see the Getting There & Away sections for Rhodes city and Lindos for information about buses to the region). **Pefki**, two km south of Lindos, was once well and truly off the beaten track, but is now package-tourist territory. However, it's still possible to get out of earshot of other tourists, away from the main beach.

Lardos

Lardos is a pleasant village six km west of Lindos, and two km inland from Lardos beach. The Tourist Information Office (☎ 0244-44 069), on the central square, has a room-finding service. Rhodes' other camping ground, *St George Camping* (☎ 0244-44 203), with a bar, restaurant, disco and swimming pool, is one km south of the village. **Lynn's Ceramic Workshop** (☎ 44 187) has some unusual pieces. Take the Laerma road out of Lardos, turn left after the playground, and look for the sign.

Around Lardos

There are two monasteries near the village worth seeing. From Lardos you can walk (or drive) to **Moni Agia Ipseni** (Monastery of Our Lady) through hilly, green countryside. Begin from the central square and with the Tourist Information Office on your right, walk along the road ahead and after 300 metres, turn sharp right. This road leads in four km to the monastery.

The well-watered village of **Laerma** is 12 km north-west of Lardos. From here it's another five km (signposted) to the beautifully sited 9th-century **Moni Thari**, which was the island's first monastery, and has recently been re-established as a monastic

community. It contains fine 13th-century frescoes.

Genadi

Genadi, 13 km south of Lardos, is another burgeoning resort, but inland from the central square and main street it's an unspoilt agricultural village. At the crossroads turn left to reach the long pebble and sand beach, and right to reach the village.

Genadi's main street is to the right (facing inland) of the central square. There is no Tourist Information Office, but Pallas Travel (☎ 43 340) on the central square organises excursions and has a room-finding service. The post office is on the right side of the main street and the OTE is on the right, just before the central square.

Places to Stay & Eat *Carrera Rooms* (☎ 43 340) has modern double studios for 7000 dr; turn right at the crossroads and the rooms are on the right. The beautiful, spacious *Betty Studios & Apartments* (☎ 43 020), 20 metres along the main street, has double/triple studios for 8600/10,000 dr and four-person apartments for 11,800 dr.

There are several restaurants along the main street. The nicest beach restaurant is *Restaurant Antonis* at the bottom of the beach road.

Around Genadi

Four km north of Genadi, **Kiotari** beach has seen recent rampant development, but with a bit of leg work secluded parts can still be found. **Asklipion**, four km inland, is an unspoilt village with the ruins of yet another castle and the 11th-century **Church of Kimisis Theotokou**.

Genadi to Prasonisi

From Genadi an almost uninterrupted beach of pebbles, shingle and sand dunes extends down to **Plimmyri**, 11 km south. Between the two, and south of Plimmyri, it's easy to find deserted beaches.

From Plimmyri the main road continues to **Kattavia**, Rhodes' most southerly village. The 11-km dirt road north to Messanagros, winds through some terrific scenery. From Kattavia there's a rough 10-km road south to the remote **Prasonisi** (Green Island) the island's southernmost point, joined to Rhodes by a narrow sandy isthmus, with rough sea on one side and calm water on the other. There are two tavernas that operate in high season. There is no formal accommodation but many people simply pitch a tent on the surrounding land.

South of Monolithos
On the west coast, the beaches south of Monolithos are prone to strong winds. From Apolakkia, an unremarkable village 10 km south of Monolithos, a road crosses the island to Genadi, passing through the unspoilt villages of Arnitha, Profilias, Istrios and Vati. Seven km south of Apolakkia, a turn-off to the left leads up to the 18th-century **Moni Skiadi**. It's a lovely, serene place with terrific views down to the coast, and there is free basic accommodation for visitors.

The coast road beyond this turn-off is unsurfaced and runs close to the sea before veering inland for Kattavia.

THE INTERIOR
Roads that cross the island between the east and west coasts have great scenery and very little traffic. If you have transport then they're well worth exploring.

Petaloudes Πεταλούδες
Petaloudes (Valley of the Butterflies), one of the 'must sees' on the package-tour itinerary, is reached along a six-km turn-off from the west coast road, 2.5 km beyond Paradisi.

The butterflies (*Callimorpha quadripunctarea*) are lured to this gorge of rustic footbridges, streams and pools by the scent of the resin exuded by the styrax trees. Regardless of what you may see other tourists doing, do not make any noises to disturb the butterflies; their numbers are declining rapidly, largely due to noise disturbance. Petaloudes is open daily from 9 am to 6 pm (from June to September), and admission is

200 dr. There are buses to Petaloudes from Rhodes city.

Around Petaloudes
From Petaloudes, a two-km dirt track leads to the 18th-century **Moni Kalopetras** built by Alexander Ypsilantas, the grandfather of the Greek freedom fighter.

Also from Petaloudes, a five-km dirt road leads to Psinthos, a pleasant village where *Artemidis Restaurant & Rooms* (☎ 51 735) serves tasty traditional Greek fare and has a swimming pool to boot. Doubles at the rooms above the restaurant cost 7000 dr. Psinthos can also be reached by a good road inland from the east coast.

Salakos & Mt Profitis Ilias
Salakos is an attractive village below Mt Profitis Ilias (790 metres) reached along an eight-km turn-off, 30 km along the west-coast road. From the village, a path leads almost to Mt Profitis Ilias' summit. Walk along Salakos' main road towards the mountains; at the curve, 60 metres beyond the Hotel Nymphi, turn left, and after 50 metres take a path to the right signposted 'Profitis Ilias'. After climbing for about 40 minutes the path levels out and proceeds through woodland towards a peak with OTE satellite dishes. After a gentle ascent, at a dirt track, turn left to reach an asphalt road and the defunct Alpine-style Elafos Hotel. The café opposite is often open.

Places to Stay & Eat The *Hotel Nymphi* (☎ 22 206/346) in Salakos has doubles for 7500 dr. It has a restaurant and there are two tavernas on the central square.

Beyond Salakos
Six km beyond Salakos the road forks. The left fork leads to the aforementioned Elafos Hotel from where a dirt road continues to the Byzantine **Church of Agios Nikolaos Fountouklis**, and Eleousa (see the Eastern Rhodes section).

The right fork leads to **Embonas** on the slopes of Mt Attavyros (1215 metres), the island's highest mountain (see Western

Rhodes). Embona is, unfortunately, touted as 'a traditional mountain village' and visited by many tourist buses. It's also renowned for its wine and is surrounded by vineyards. The wine produced is the dry white *Villaré*. It costs around 1500 dr a bottle and is produced at **The Emery Winery** (☎ 41 206), where there's free wine tasting on weekdays until 3 pm. **Agios Isidoros**, 14 km south of Embona, is a lovely unspoilt village, which you can make a detour to, *en route* to Siana (see the Western Rhodes section).

Halki Χάλκη

Halki (HAL-kee, population 250) is a small island 16 km off the west coast of Rhodes. It has escaped the tourist development of its large neighbour, however, much of the accommodation is monopolised by Laskarina for package tourists who want a holiday on an untouristy island. It's a barren, rocky island with a severe water shortage. The population has been greatly reduced by emigration. Many islanders moved to Tarpon Springs, Florida, where they have established a sponge-fishing community.

Getting There & Away
Ferry The F/B *Apollon Express* leaves Halki 10.30 am for Symi and Rhodes. On the same day it leaves Halki at 5.30 pm for Karpathos, Kassos and Agios Nikolaos, from where it continues on to Santorini, Milos, Sifnos, Serifos, Kythnos and Piraeus. Also see the Getting There & Away section for Rhodes island.

Caïque There is a caïque running from Skala Kamiros on Rhodes' west coast to and from Halki. The boat leaves Skala Kamiros every day (except Sunday) at 2.30 pm. On Sunday it leaves at 9 am. The cost is 1100 dr. To get to Skala Kamiros from Rhodes city take the 1.15 pm Monolithos bus from the West Side bus station.

Caïques from Halki to Skala Kamiros leave at 5.30 am to connect with the Rhodes city bus which arrives at Skala Kamiros at 7.30 am. There is no bus on Sunday; the Sunday boat leaves Halki at 4 pm.

Getting Around
Halki has no cars, buses or taxis. There are excursions to the island's beaches and to the nearby uninhabited islet of Alimia which has good beaches.

EMBOREIOS Εμπορείος
Halki has only one settlement, the attractive little port town of Emboreios, consisting of imposing mansions, many now derelict. The town's most prominent building is Agios Nikolaos church, with the tallest belfry in the Dodecanese.

Orientation & Information
The ferry quay is in the middle of the harbour. There is one road out of Emboreios, incongruously named Tarpon Springs Boulevard for the ex-Halkiots in Florida, who financed its construction. It begins behind the post office and passes Podamos, the island's only sandy beach.

There is a small tourist-information kiosk (☎ 57 330) between the post office (opposite the quay) and the war memorial. The staff will help you to find accommodation.

There is no OTE, but the minimarket behind the waterfront war memorial does have a metered telephone. Halki's telephone code is 0241.

Places to Stay
The nicest place to stay is the *Captain's House* (☎ 45 201), a beautiful 19th-century mansion with period furniture and a tranquil tree-shaded garden. It is owned by a retired Greek sea captain and his British wife, Christine. Rates are 7000 dr a double with shared bathroom. To reach the Captain's House, walk through the church grounds and out at the other side. Turn left and then immediately to the right to walk along a narrow alleyway. At the fork bear left to come to seven stone steps to the left. The Captain's House is at the top of these on the right.

The *Pension Cleanthi* (☎ 37 648, 57 334)

has modern rooms. The rates are 7000 dr a double with private bathroom; well-equipped studios are 7000 dr for two people and 12,000 dr for four people. The pension is on the road to Podamos beach.

Places to Eat

Several tavernas line the waterfront. *Omonoias Taverna*, to the right of the port as you face inland, has succulent spit-roast lamb for 1400 dr. At the *Ioannis Taverna*, at the far left of the waterfront, a large meal of shrimps and rice, tzatziki and beer will set you back about 2400 dr. There is also a good taverna on Podamos Beach.

AROUND THE ISLAND

Horio Χωριό

Horio, a 30-minute walk along Tarpon Springs Boulevard from Emboreios, was the 'pirate proof' inland town. Once a thriving community of 3000 people, it's now derelict and uninhabited. A path leads from Horio's churchyard to a Knights of St John castle. At Horio, if you take the left fork of Tarpon Spring Boulevard, and then take the first turn right onto a stony track, in about 30 minutes you will reach the secluded cove of **Giali**, which has a stony, often wave-lashed beach.

Moni Agiou Ioanni Μονή Αγίου Ιωάννη

This monastery is a two-hour walk from Horio. There are no monks here now, but the shepherd-cum-caretaker, Dimitris, lives here with his family. Free beds are available for tourists, but you must take your own food and water. Take the right fork of Tarpon Springs Boulevard. There are fine views of many Dodecanese islands and Turkey.

Karpathos Κάρπαθος

The elongated island of Karpathos (KAR-pa-thos), midway between Crete and Rhodes, is traversed by a mountain range which runs north-south. For hundreds of years the north and south parts of the island were isolated from one another and so they developed independently. It is even thought that the northerners and southerners have different ethnic origins. The northern village of Olymbos is of endless fascination to ethnologists for the age-old customs of its inhabitants. Karpathos has rugged mountains, numerous beaches and unspoilt villages, and despite having charter flights from northern Europe, it has not, so far, succumbed to the worst consequences of mass tourism.

Karpathos has a relatively uneventful history. Unlike almost all other Dodecanese islands, it was never under the auspices of the Knights of St John. It is a wealthy island as it receives more money from emigrants living abroad (mostly in the USA) than any other Greek island.

Getting There & Away

Air There are four flights a week to Athens (24,600 dr), four a week to Kassos (2800 dr) and four a day to Rhodes (11,800 dr). There is a flight on Tuesday to Sitia on Crete (10,600 dr). The Olympic Airways office (☎ 22 150/057) is on the central square in Pigadia. The airport is 18 km south-west of Pigadia.

Ferry The F/B *Ialyssos* is the only inter-island ferry with Diafani as a port of call (it also calls at Pigadia). The F/B *Apollon Express* and the F/B *Milena* also call in at Pigadia. See the Getting There & Away section for Rhodes island, the Getting There & Away section for Sitia (Crete) and the Getting There & Away section for Iraklio for their schedules.

Getting Around

To/From the Airport In 1995 there was no airport bus, but check with the Olympic Airways office if this is still the case. A taxi from Pigadia to the airport costs a hefty 2000 dr.

Bus Pigadia is the transport hub of the island. A schedule is pinned up at the bus station. There are four buses a day to Amopi (300 dr); four a day to Pyles (380 dr) via

Karpathos

0   2.5   5 km

MEDITERRANEAN
SEA

Cape Paraspori

SARIA ISLET

To Rhodes

Cape Vroukounda
Agios Ioannis

Avlona
Moni Agiou Konstantinou
Diafani
Olymbos

Vananda Beach

Agios Minas

Spoa

Mesohori
Agios Nikolaos

Apella Beach

KASTRO
Lefkos

KARPATHOS

Kyra Panagia Beach

Kali Limni (1215 m)
Aperi
Volada
Pyles
Othos

Ahata Beach

Cape Proni

Vronti Bay

PIGADIA

Finiki

Menetes

Amopi

Arkasa

Cape Agios Theodoros

Cape Akrotiri

Cape Liki

Airport

Cape Kastello

To Crete & Piraeus

DODECANESE

Aperi (300 dr), Volada (300 dr) and Othos (300 dr); two a day to Finiki (380 dr) via Menetes (300 dr) and Arkasa (380 dr); and only two a week to Lefkos (in 1995 on a Monday and Thursday). There is no bus between Pigadia and Olymbos or Diafani.

Car & Motorbike Next door to the post office (on the corner of 28 Oktovriou and Georgiou Loïzou in Pigadia) is a reliable, reasonably priced car and motorbike-rental outlet called By Circle (☎ 22 690/489). The 21-km road from Spoa to Olymbos is unsurfaced but driveable. However, check on its current condition with the tourist police before setting off and make sure you know where the petrol stations are – they're few and far between.

Taxi The taxi rank (☎ 22 705) is on Dimokratias, just around the corner from Karpathou. A price list is displayed.

Excursion Boat In summer there are daily excursion boats from Pigadia to Diafani for 4500 dr return. There are also frequent boats to the beaches of Ahata, Kyra Panagia and Apella for 1500 dr. Tickets can be bought from Karpathos Travel in Pigadia.

On a Sunday there is an excursion boat to the island of Kassos for 6000 dr.

PIGADIA Πηγάδια
Pigadia (population 1300) is the island's capital and main port. It's a modern town, pleasant enough, but without any eminent buildings or sites. The town is built on the edge of Vronti bay, a four-km-long sandy beach where you can rent jet skis (two people 5000 dr) and water skis (4000 dr). On the beach are the remains of the early Christian basilica of Agia Fotini.

Orientation & Information
From the quay, turn right and take the left fork onto Apodimon Karpathou, Pigadia's main thoroughfare which leads to the central square of Plateia 5 Oktovriou.

Pigadia has no EOT. The tourist police

ROSEMARY HALL

ROSEMARY HALL

ROSEMARY HALL

Top: Symi harbour, Symi, Dodecanese
Bottom Left: Autumn crocuses, Knights' Castle, Tilos, Dodecanese
Bottom Right: Moni Agiou Panteleimona, Tilos, Dodecanese

ROSEMARY HALL

ROSEMARY HALL

DAVID HALL

ROSEMARY HALL

Top Left: Enjoying the morning sun, Agathonisi, Dodecanese
Top Right: Doorway, Hora, Astypalea, Dodecanese
Bottom Left: View of the Acropolis and sea at Lindos, Rhodes, Dodecanese
Bottom Right: Bouka harbour, Kassos, Dodecanese

(☎ 22 218) are next door to the post office on Georgios Loïzou. The most helpful of the travel agencies is Karpathos Travel (☎ 22 148/754), on Dimokratias.

The OTE is on Ethnikis Anastasis. The post office is on the corner of 28 Oktovriou and Georgios Loïzou. Karpathos' telephone code is 0245 and the postcode is 857 00. The National Bank of Greece is on Apodimon Karpathou. The bus station is one block up from the waterfront, on Dimokratias. There's a laundrette, Laundro Express, on Mitr Apostolou. Stewart, a friendly guy from Halifax, sells new and second-hand books at

Carol's Corner Shop, which is on Apodimon Karpathou.

Places to Stay

There's plenty of accommodation and owners meet the boats. The E-class *Hotel Avra* (☎ 22 388/485/528), on 28 Oktovriou, has comfortable doubles for 5000 dr with shared bathroom, and 6500 dr with private bathroom. *Harry's Rooms* (☎ 22 188), just off 28 Oktovriou, has spotless singles/doubles with shared bathroom for 3300/4000 dr. Farther along 28 Oktovriou, just beyond the Karpathos Arts Centre, *To*

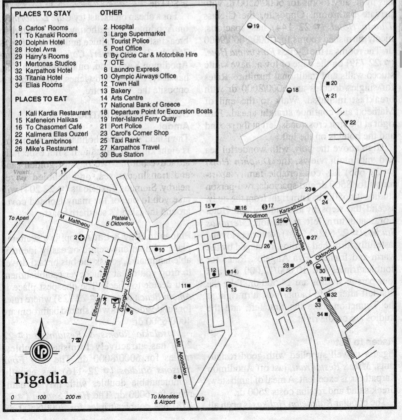

PLACES TO STAY
9 Carlos' Rooms
11 To Kanaki Rooms
20 Dolphin Hotel
28 Hotel Avra
29 Harry's Rooms
31 Mertonas Studios
32 Karpathos Hotel
33 Titania Hotel
34 Elias Rooms

PLACES TO EAT
1 Kali Kardia Restaurant
15 Kafeneion Halikas
16 To Chasomeri Café
22 Kalimera Ellas Ouzeri
24 Café Lambrinos
26 Mike's Restaurant

OTHER
2 Hospital
3 Large Supermarket
4 Tourist Police
5 Post Office
6 By Circle Car & Motorbike Hire
7 OTE
8 Laundro Express
10 Olympic Airways Office
12 Town Hall
13 Bakery
14 Arts Centre
17 National Bank of Greece
18 Departure Point for Excursion Boats
19 Inter-Island Ferry Quay
21 Port Police
23 Carol's Corner Shop
25 Taxi Rank
27 Karpathos Travel
30 Bus Station

Pigadia

0   100   200 m

Kanaki Rooms (☎ 22 908) has pleasant doubles for 6000 dr with private bathroom.

Turn left at the Arts Centre and 400 metres up the hill you will come to the delightfully kitsch and clean *Carlos' Rooms* (☎ 22 477) on the left. Rates are 2500/3500 dr for singles/doubles with shared bathroom and 3000/5000 dr with private bathroom.

The immaculate, cosy *Elias Rooms* (☎ 22 446) is in a quiet part of town with great views. Rooms with private bathroom are 4500/5000 dr. The owner, Elias Hatzigorgiou, is friendly and helpful. Ascend the steps by the Karpathos Hotel to reach the rooms.

The C-class *Karpathos Hotel* (☎ 22 347) has light, airy rooms for 6000/6500 dr with private bathroom. Opposite, the C-class *Titania Hotel* (☎ 22 144) has spacious, nicely furnished rooms for 7000/8000/9600 dr. The rooms at the C-class *Panorama Hotel* (☎ 22 739) on the edge of town, have white stucco walls and traditional furniture. Rates for singles/doubles are 6000/8000 dr with breakfast included. Walk to the end of Matheou and continue straight ahead. Turn right at the first crossroads, left at the second and the hotel is on the left.

High above the port, with wonderful sea and mountain views, the *Dolphin Hotel* (☎ 22 665) has comfortable family apartments for 8500 dr and spacious, two-person studios for 6500 dr. Turn right from the quay, ascend the steps by the side of the Hotel Coral and turn left at the top. *Mertonas Studios* (☎ 22 622, 23 074) comprises lovely, tastefully furnished studios, managed by the warm and friendly Eva Angelos. Rates for doubles/triples are 10,000/12,000 dr, and four-person studios are 14,500 dr. Take the first left after Café Lambrinos, turn right at the T-junction, take the first left, and the studios are on the right.

Places to Eat

Pigadia is well supplied with good restaurants. *Mike's Restaurant*, just off Apodimon Karpathou, is excellent. A meal of lamb stew, Greek salad and retsina costs 2500 dr.

The popular *Kafeneion Halikas* is open all day for drinks, but only serves meals in the evenings. The menu is limited; quite often it's only stifado (1200 dr) and green beans (650 dr), but both are delicious. It's a crumbling white building, just beyond the National Bank of Greece on Apodimon Karpathou. The *Kali Kardia Restaurant*, on the western side of town overlooking the beach at the beginning Vronti bay, opposite the Hotel Atlantic, serves freshly caught fish and inexpensive meat dishes.

The guys who run the atmospheric *Kalimera Ellas Ouzeri*, near the quay, come from Thessaloniki, Greece's gastronomic epicentre, and this is reflected in the delectable mezedes they serve. A mixed mezes plate is 800 dr.

For a cheap breakfast try *Café Lambrinos*, on Apodimon Karpathou, where an English breakfast with fruit juice and tea or coffee is 750 dr. *To Chasomeri Café*, farther along Apodimon Karpathou, on the opposite side, has tasty, filling, sandwiches. The *bakery* is opposite the Arts Centre.

SOUTHERN KARPATHOS
Amopi

The island's premier holiday resort, Amopi, is eight km from Pigadia. It's not especially attractive but has two bays of golden sand and translucent sea, and pebbled coves nearby. Stamatis Taxi Boats (☎ 22 204) will take you to one of the many isolated coves around the island's southern coast.

Places to Stay & Eat Amopi is a scattered place without any centre or easily identifiable landmarks, so ask the bus or taxi driver to drop you off at whichever establishment you decide to check. The cheapest place is *Amopi Beach Rooms* (☎ 22 723) where rates for singles/doubles with shared bathroom are 4000/6500 dr.

Votsalakia Rooms & Restaurant (☎ 22 204) has attractively furnished doubles/triples for 6000/8000 dr. The new *Four Seasons Studios* (☎ 22 116) has equally commendable doubles with private bathroom for 6000 dr. The *Hotel Sophia* (☎ 22 078) has doubles/triples for 7000/8500 dr,

DODECANESE

and the new *Kastelia Bay Hotel* (☎ 22 678) has light, airy singles/doubles/triples for 8000/9000/10,800 dr.

Votsalakia Restaurant below the rooms, has starters for 300 to 650 dr, calamari for 850 dr, and a mixed mezes dish for 1600 dr.

Menetes

Menetes is perched on a sheer cliff eight km above Pigadia. It's a picturesque, unspoilt village with neoclassical, pastel-coloured houses lining its main street. Behind the main street are narrow, stepped alleyways that wind between more modest white-washed dwellings. The village has a little **museum** on the right coming from Pigadia. The owner of Taverna Manolis, one block back from the main road, has the key and will open it up for you.

Places to Stay & Eat Menetes has only one place to stay: the *domatia* of friendly Greek-American Mike Rigas (☎ 81 269/255), in a traditional Karpathian house with a garden of figs and grapes. Doubles with shared bathroom are 2700 dr and triples with private bathroom are 3800 dr. Coming from Pigadia, the rooms are 150 metres down a cement road (signposted 'Lai') veering off to the right, just beyond the museum. *Taverna Manolis* serves decent, inexpensive food.

Arkasa

Arkasa, nine km farther on, is metamorphosing from traditional village to holiday resort. The old village straddles a ravine, and most of the resort development is north of here. If you turn right at the T-junction you will come to the authentic village square.

A turn-off left, just before the ravine, leads in 500 metres to the remains of the 5th-century Basilica of Agia Sophia. Two chapels stand amidst mosaic fragments and columns; one is built over a well-preserved section of mosaic. There's a nice beach just south of the ruins.

Places to Stay & Eat *Pension Philoxena* (☎ 61 341), on the left before the T-junction, has very clean singles/doubles/triples for 3500/4500/5000 dr. *Elini Rooms* (☎ 61 248), on the left along the road to Finiki, has attractive double apartments for 7000 dr.

The excellent *Taverna Petaluda*, on Arkasa's central square, has starters for 300-600 dr, moussaka and pastitsio for 850 dr and chicken souvlaki for 1000 dr.

Finiki

Turn left at the T-junction in Arkasa to reach the serene fishing village of Finiki, two km away. The little sculpture at the harbour commemorates the heroism of seven local fishers during WW II – locals will tell you the story.

Places to Stay & Eat *Fay's Paradise* (☎ 61 308), just up from the harbour, has lovely studios that cost 5000/6000/7000 dr. At the new *Finiki View Hotel* (☎ 61 309/400) spacious doubles are 7000 dr. The hotel has a swimming pool and bar, and is on the right coming from Arkasa.

Locals come from all over the island to eat the very fresh fish at *Dimitrios Fisherman's Taverna*, opposite Fay's Paradise. Lobster is 7400 a kg, and swordfish is 1500 dr a portion.

Lefkos

Lefkos, 13 km north of Finiki, is a burgeoning resort with three superb sandy beaches. In summer it gets crowded, but at other times it still has a rugged, off-the-beaten-track feel about it. It's two km from the coast road.

Places to Stay & Eat At *O Nikos Rooms* (☎ 71 003), on the left halfway down the turn-off, tidy doubles cost 5000 dr. Farther down on the right, the sparkling *Imeri Rooms* (☎ 71 375) has double/triple rooms for 4000/5500 dr with private bathroom. Enquire at *Small Paradise Taverna & Rooms* (☎ 71 171/184), farther down the road, about its Sunset Studios which overlook a beach. These immaculate, double/triple studios cost 8000/9000 dr. All of these places have tavernas.

Getting There & Away There are only two buses a week to Lefkos and a taxi costs

7000 dr. If you telephone any of the rooms' proprietors they may be able to arrange a lift from Pigadia for you, providing you intend staying with them, of course! Hitching is dicey as there is not much traffic. Backpackers sometimes do the four-hour walk to and from Pyles, which has a bus connection with Pigadia (see Mountain Villages).

East-Coast Beaches

The fine east-coast beaches of **Ahata**, **Kyra Panagia** and **Apella** can be reached along dirt roads off the east-coast road, but are most easily reached by excursion boat from Pigadia. Only Kyra Panagia has accommodation facilities and tavernas.

Mesohori & Spoa

Mesohori, four km beyond the turn-off for Lefkos, is a pretty village of whitewashed houses and stepped streets. Spoa village, five km farther on along a dirt road, is at the beginning of the 21-km dirt road to Olymbos. It overlooks the east coast and has a track down to Agios Nikolaos beach.

Mountain Villages

Aperi, Volada, Othos and Pyles, the well-watered mountain villages to the north of Pigadia, are largely unaffected by tourism. None have any accommodation for tourists, but all have tavernas and kafeneia. From Volada, Othos and Pyles are within walking distance.

Aperi was the island's capital from 1700 until 1892. Its ostentatious houses were built by wealthy returning émigrés from the USA. Like Aperi, Volada has an air of prosperity due to returning émigrés.

Othos (altitude 510 metres) is the island's highest village. Its small **ethnographic museum** is on the right as you enter the village from Volada. Yiannis Hapsis, a local artist, has the key and gives guided tours. If you would like to see Yiannis' work, his studio is on the right 200 metres beyond the museum.

From Othos the road winds downhill with good views over to Kassos. Pyles is a gorgeous village of twisting, stepped streets,

pastel houses and citrus groves. It clings to the slopes of Mt Kali Limni (1215 metres) the Dodecanese's second highest peak. Good cheese and honey are produced here.

A turn-off left is the new road to the west coast. Walk straight through Pyles to reach the old unsurfaced road which descends through a fragrant pine forest to the coast. The walk takes about one hour. The track emerges 500 metres south of Adia where there is a taverna and rooms to rent. Lefkos is 13 km farther north and Finiki, is five km south.

NORTHERN KARPATHOS
Diafani & Olymbos

Diafani is Karpathos' small northern port. There's no post office or bank, but the Nikos Travel Agency (☎ 51410), on the waterfront, has currency-exchange service. There's no OTE but there are cardphones.

Clinging to the ridge of barren Mt Profitis Ilias, four km above Diafani, Olymbos (population 340) is a living museum. Women wear bright, embroidered skirts, waistcoats and headscarves, and goatskin boots. The interiors of the houses are decorated with embroidered cloth and their façades feature brightly painted, ornate plaster reliefs. The inhabitants speak in a vernacular which contains some Doric words, and the houses have wooden locks of the kind described by Homer. Olymbos is a matrilineal society – a family's property passes down from the mother to the first-born daughter. The

Traditional embroidery of Karpathos

DODECANESE

women still grind corn in windmills and bake bread in outdoor communal ovens.

Olymbos, alas, is no longer a pristine backwater caught in a time warp. Nowadays hordes of tourists come to gape, and tourist shops are appearing everywhere. However, Olymbos is still a fascinating place, and accommodation and food are inexpensive.

The bus stops at the beginning of the village. Continue ahead along the main street to reach the central square.

Walk from Olymbos to Avlona The village of Avlona is deserted in winter, but has a small population of farmers in summer. Face the beginning of the row of windmills behind Olymbos village and go down the steps to their right, passing the windmill museum on your left. At the yellow-and-green house on the left continue straight ahead along a cement track to more steps, then a stony path. After about 10 minutes you'll pass a white church on the right. After this, cross a river bed and take the ascending path straight ahead. When the path levels out, climb the poorly defined path to the left of a ruined stone house. At the top, take the path to the left, which soon veers slightly right. To the right you will see some terraces, the river bed and the Diafani-Olymbos road.

About 30 minutes out of Olymbos the path crosses the top of a ravine. You are heading for the white, red-domed Moni Agiou Konstantinou, ahead, in the distance. In another 15 to 20 minutes the path veers slightly right and soon crosses the top of another ravine. Clamber over some rocks and veer left to go around a terraced ravine. You will reach the monastery 80 or 90 minutes after leaving Olymbos. Turn left onto the dirt road in front of the monastery (a right turn leads to the Diafani-Olymbos road). Ignore the right fork and stay on the main (downhill) track. Soon Avlona's pastel-coloured houses and neat terraces will appear. Return along the dirt road and you'll reach the Diafani-Olymbos road after about 30 minutes. The views along this road are stunning, with Olymbos and Mt Profitis Ilias to the right, and Diafani far below to the left.

Woman in traditional dress

The **Church of Agios Ioannis** at Vourgounta, a deserted village north of Avlona, is the scene of a lively, four-day festival which begins on 29 August.

Places to Stay There's an unofficial camping ground at Vananda beach, 30 minutes' walk (signposted) north of Diafani. The *Golden Beach Hotel* (☎ 51 315), opposite the quay in Diafani, has singles/ doubles/triples for 2300/4000/5000 dr with shared bathroom. *Pension Glaros* (☎ 51 259/216), back from the quay to the left, has rooms for 3000/ 4000/5000 dr with shared bathroom.

Just off the main street in Olymbos, the clean, simply furnished rooms at *Pension Olymbos* (☎ 51 252) cost 2000/3500/4500 dr with shared bathroom. One of the doubles is a traditional Karpathian room which costs 5000 dr. Just beyond the bus turnround, *Mike's Rooms* (☎ 51 304) cost 4000 dr a double.

The *Hotel Aphrodite* (☎ 51 307/454), just off the central square, has immaculate double/triple rooms for 5000/6000 dr with private bathroom.

Places to Eat In Diafani the *Golden Beach Taverna* and *Taverna Anatoli* are both good.

Makarounis (handmade noodles mixed with grated cheese and onions, and fried) is a speciality of Olymbos, served at all the restaurants. You'll eat well at *Olymbos Taverna*, below the Pension Olymbos, at *Mike's Taverna*, below his rooms, and also at *Parthenonas Restaurant*, on the central square.

Getting Around A bus meets the excursion boats from Pigadia at Diafani and transports people up to Olymbos.

From Diafani, excursion boats go to nearby beaches and occasionally to the uninhabited islet of Saria where there are some Byzantine remains.

Kassos Κάσσος

Kassos (KA-sos, population 1200), 11 km south of Karpathos, is a rocky little island with prickly pear trees, sparse olive and fig trees, dry stone walls, and sheep and goats. It is one of the least visited islands of the Dodecanese. If you tell Karparthians you're off to Kassos they'll tell you to take your knitting. However, even if you don't knit there's more to do on Kassos than contemplating your navel. It's the perfect island to see something of traditional Greek life, and it's also a great island for walking.

History

Despite being diminutive and remote, Kassos has an eventful and tragic history. During Turkish rule it flourished, and by 1820 it had 11,000 inhabitants and a large mercantile fleet. Mohammad Ali, the Turkish governor of Egypt, regarded this fleet as a impediment to his plan to establish a base on Crete from which to attack the Peloponnese and quell the uprising there. So, on 7 June 1824, Ali's men landed on Kassos and killed around 7000 inhabitants. This massacre is commemorated annually on the anniversary of the slaughter and Kassiots return from around the world to participate.

During the late 19th century, many Kassiots emigrated to Egypt and around 5000 of them helped build the Suez Canal. In this century many have emigrated to the USA.

Getting There & Away

Air There are daily flights to Rhodes (11,800 dr) and four a week to Karpathos (2800 dr). The Tuesday afternoon flight to Karpathos continues on to Sitia (10,600 dr) and Athens (24,600 dr). The Olympic Airways office (☎ 41 444) is on Kritis.

Ferry Kassos has the same ferry schedule as Pigadia (Karpathos), the F/B *Apollon Express* and the F/B *Milena* being the only ferries which use the island as a port of call. See the Getting There & Away section for Rhodes island, the Getting There & Away section for Sitia (Crete) and the Getting There & Away section for Iraklio for their schedules.

Excursion Boat There are excursion boats from Karpathos to Kassos on Sunday in summer (6000 dr). In summer there are excursion boats from Phry to the uninhabited Armathia islet (1500 dr return) where there are sandy beaches

Getting Around

To/From the Airport There is no airport bus but the airport is only 600 metres along the coast road from Phry.

Bus The island's one bus travels in a circuit to all of the villages from Phry. There is a flat fare of 150 dr.

PHRY Φρυ

Phry is the island's capital and port. The town's focal point is the picturesque old

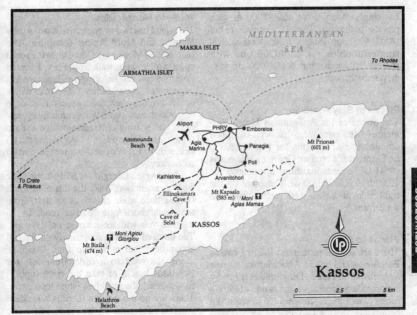

Kassos

fishing harbour of Bouka. The suburb of Emboreios is one km east of Phry.

Orientation
Turn left at the quay to reach Bouka and the Church of Agios Spyridon. Veer left towards the church, follow the road right, and then take the first left which leads to Kritis, Phry's main street. Turn left to reach the waterfront and the central square of Plateia Iroön Kassou. To reach Emboreios, turn right at the waterfront. The Poli turn-off is 120 metres along the Emboreios road.

Information
Kassos does not have an EOT or tourist police, but Emmanuel Manousos, at Kassos Maritime and Travel Agency (☎ 41 323/305), Plateia Iroön Kassou, is helpful and speaks English.

The National Bank of Greece is represented by the supermarket at the beginning of Kritis. From the waterfront, take the first turn left along Kritis to reach the post office. The OTE is behind Plateia Dimokratias – you'll see the huge satellite dishes.

Kassos' postcode is 858 00 and the telephone code is 0245.

The port police (☎ 41 288) are behind the Church of Agios Spyridon. The police (☎ 41 222) are just beyond the post office, on the opposite side. The bus terminal is on Kritis.

Places to Stay – bottom end
All of the island's accommodation (and there's not that much) is in Phry, except for the rooms at Moni Agiou Giorgiou (see Walks to Monasteries). *Ketty Markous* (☎ 41 613/498/216) rents doubles for 5000 dr with shared bathroom and kitchen. They're on the right side of the road to Emboreios. Farther along, on the opposite side, *Elias Koutlakis Rooms* (☎ 41 363), cost 5000 dr a double with private bathroom.

The *Anessis Hotel* (☎ 41 234/201), above the supermarket which represents the bank,

DODECANESE

has singles/doubles for 4000/5000 dr with private bathroom. The *Anagennisis Hotel* (☎ 41 495), on Plateia Iroön Kassou, has singles/doubles for 4350/5600 dr with shared bathroom, and 5600/8000 dr with private bathroom.

Places to Stay – middle

The owner of the Anagennisis Hotel, Emmanuel Manousos, also has well-equipped double/triple apartments for 12,000/16,000 dr. Emmanuel's brother, Georgios Manousos (☎ 41 047), rents luxurious *apartments* for 12,000/16,000/20,000 dr. These are on the right side of Kritis, 160 metres from the waterfront.

Places to Eat

There are several restaurants in Phry, two in Emboreios and one in Agia Marina. *Kassos Restaurant* on Plateia Dimokratias is run by a women's co-operative and is one of Phry's nicest places to eat. *Taverna Emborios* is the better of Emborios' two options. Phry is well supplied with supermarkets.

AROUND THE ISLAND

Kassos' best beach is the isolated, pebbled cove of **Helathros** reached along a turn-off from the Agios Georgios road (see Walks to Monasteries). The beach has no facilities. The mediocre **Ammounda** beach, just beyond the airport, is the nearest to Phry.

You can walk from Phry to all of the other villages. **Agia Marina**, one km south-west of Phry, is a pretty village with a gleaming white-and-blue church. On 17 July, the Festival of Agia Marina is celebrated here. From Agia Marina the road continues to verdant **Arvanitohori** with fig and pomegranate trees, and gardens replete with frangipani and bougainvillea.

Poli, three km south-east of Phry, is the former capital, built on the ancient acropolis. **Panagia**, between Phry and Poli, has less than 50 inhabitants. Its once grand sea-captains' and ship-owners' mansions are now derelict.

Walks to Monasteries

The island has two monasteries: **Moni Agias Mamas** and **Moni Agiou Giorgiou**. The uninhabited Moni Agias Mamas on the south coast is a 1½-hour walk from Phry. Take the Poli road and just before the village turn left (signposted 'Agia Mamas'). The road winds uphill through a dramatic, eroded landscape of rock-strewn mountains, crumbling terraces and soaring cliffs. Eventually a sharp turn right (signposted 'Agia Mamas') descends to the blue-and-white, red-domed monastery.

Moni Agiou Giorgiou is a 2½-hour walk from Arvanitohori. Take the dirt road south (with a little white church at its start) from the Avantohori-Agia Marina road. In 15 minutes you will see a house on the right. The **cave of Selai** is supposedly on the hill above here, but is hard to find. Continue along the road to a fork. Bear left for Helathros beach, or take the right (uphill) fork to reach the sparkling white monastery. There are no monks, but there is a resident caretaker for most of the year, and basic (free) accommodation for visitors.

Kastellorizo Καστελλόριζο

Tiny, rocky Kastellorizo (Kas-tel-O-ri-zo), a mere speck on the map, is 118 km east of Rhodes its nearest Greek neighbour and only 2.5 km from the southern coast of Turkey. Its official name is Megisti (the biggest), for it is the largest of a group of 14 islets. The island's remoteness has so far ensured that its tourism is low key. There are no beaches, but there are rocky inlets from where you can swim and snorkel in a crystal-clear sea.

The island featured in the Oscar-winning, Italian film *Mediterraneo* (1991) which was based on a book by an Italian army sergeant. *Castellorizo: An Illustrated History of the Island & Conquerors* by Nicholas G Pappas was published in Australia in 1994. The Australian author's parents originated from Kastellorizo.

History

The ghost town you see today is made all the more poignant by an awareness of the island's past greatness. Due to its strategic position Dorians, Romans, crusaders, Egyptians, Turks, Venetians and pirates have all landed on its shores. The 20th century has been no less traumatic with occupations by the French, British and Italians. In 1552 Kastellorizo surrendered peacefully to the Turks and so was granted special privileges. It was allowed to preserve its language, religion and traditions. Its cargo fleet became the largest in the Dodecanese and the islanders achieved a high degree of culture and education.

Kastellorizo lost all strategic and economic importance after the 1923 population exchange (a condition of the Treaty of Lausanne). In 1928 it was ceded to the Italians who severely oppressed the islanders; in contrast, Turkish rule must have seemed like the good old days. Many islanders emigrated to Perth, Australia, where today some 10,000 of them live. They call themselves 'Kassies' and refer to their homeland as 'The Rock'.

During WW II Kastellorizo suffered severe bombardment, and English commanders ordered the few remaining inhabitants to abandon their island. They fled to Cyprus, Palestine and Egypt, but were not allowed to take any belongings with them. In October 1945, 300 islanders boarded the Australian ship *Empire Control* to return to Kastellorizo. Tragically, the ship burst into flames and 35 people lost their lives. Two months later the remaining refugees returned to their island to find that most of their houses had been destroyed by bombings and the remaining ones had been ransacked by the occupying troops. Not surprisingly more islanders emigrated. Today Kastellorizo is home to only 200 inhabitants. Most of the houses that escaped the bombing in WW II stand empty. Despite this gloomy picture Kastellorizo's waterfront is very lively, with lots of local colour.

Getting There & Away

Air In July and August there are daily flights

to and from Rhodes (7000 dr), and at other times there are three a week. You can buy tickets from Dizi Tours &Travel.

Ferry The F/B *Nissos Kalymnos* is the only passenger boat that sails to Kastellorizo (six hours, 2413 dr). See the Getting There & Away section for Rhodes island for the ferry's schedule.

Excursion Boat to Turkey It is possible to visit Turkey from Kastellorizo on a day trip (4000 dr). Islanders get supplies from Turkey so you may be able to get a free lift with someone. Ask around.

Getting Around

There is one bus on the island which is used solely to transport people to and from the airport (500 dr).

KASTELLORIZO TOWN

Kastellorizo town is the only settlement. Built around a U-shaped bay, its waterfront is skirted with imposing spruced-up three-storey mansions with wooden balconies and red-tiled roofs. However, this alluring countenance fronts back streets of abandoned and derelict houses overgrown with ivy, crumbling stairways and stony pathways winding between them.

Orientation & Information

The quay is at the eastern side of the bay. The central square, Plateia Ethelonton Kastellorizou, abuts the waterfront almost halfway round the bay, next to the yachting jetty. The suburbs of Horafia and Mandraki are to the east of the bay.

The post office and police station (☎ 49 333) are on the bay's western side. There is no OTE. Kastellorizo's postcode is 851 11 and the telephone code is 0241. The National Bank of Greece is represented by Taverna International, on the waterfront beyond the central square. The port police are at the eastern tip of the bay.

Dizi Tours & Travel (☎ 49 240/241), is the island's only travel agency. Here you can buy Olympic Airways tickets, exchange travellers' cheques and get cash advances on American Express, MasterCard and Visa card.

Things to See & Do

Knights of St John Castle This castle stands above the quay. A metal staircase leads to the top from where there are splendid views of Turkey. The **museum** within the castle, houses a well-displayed eclectic collection. Opening times are erratic. Beyond the museum, steps lead down to a coastal pathway, from where there are more steps up the cliff to a **Lycian tomb** with a Doric façade. There are several of these along the

Anatolian coast, but this is the only known one in Greece.

Walk to Moni Agiou Georgiou, Paleokastro & Moni Agias Triadas Take the airport road out of Kastellorizo town and turn left onto the upper road to Horafia. Take the right fork on the outskirts of Horafia and a rough, indistinct path six metres along here on the right, leads to the steps up to Moni Agiou Georgiou. At the top the path straight ahead leads to the monastery. However 15 metres along this path look for a bomb shell to the right, then 30 metres farther on look for a path to the right. This is the path to Paleokastro. Several paths crisscross one another hereabouts, but the correct path is the widest, and flanked by two rows of rocks.

After seeing the monastery return to the Paleokastro path. After 15 minutes' walking, go through a gate and turn left (right descends to Moni Agias Triadas). After a few metres take the path to the right, and after another five minutes take the right fork. Continue along this path ignoring a turn-off left. The island's highest hill, Vikla (273 metres) with a white military look-out post on its summit, is on the right. If you ascend here you will be welcomed by the soldiers. Perhaps a breathless tourist enthusing about the views relieves the monotony of scanning the Turkish coast through binoculars. Continuing along the path below, you will soon see Paleokastro ahead. After passing between two churches continue to a stepped path and turn left to arrive at Paleokastro – a right turn leads down to the airport road.

The Woman of Ro

The Islet of Ro, one of Kastellorizo's 13 satellites, has been immortalised along with its last inhabitant, Despina Achladioti, alias the Woman of Ro, who died in 1982. Despina and her shepherd husband were the only inhabitants of Ro. When her husband died, Despina remained alone on the island, staunchly hoisting the Greek flag every morning, and lowering it in the evening, in full view of the Turkish coast. The Woman of Ro has become a symbol of the Greek spirit of indomitability in the face of adversity. There are excursion boats to the islet: look for signs along the waterfront at Kastellorizo town. There is a bust of the Woman of Ro on Plateia Horafia. ■

Paleokastro was the island's ancient acropolis. Within its Hellenistic walls are three churches, an ancient tower and a cistern with roughly hewn steps. From Paleokastro descend the stepped path to the airport road, then turn right to reach Moni Agias Triadas and Kastellorizo town.

Walk to Moni Agiou Stefanou

Moni Agiou Stefanou overlooks a bay on the north coast, about 45 minutes' walk away from Kastellorizo town. Walk towards the post office, along the track parallel to the western waterfront. Then 18 metres before the post office take a narrow path veering left. Go through a gate and continue along the path ahead. The little white monastery is usually locked but the walk is worthwhile for the views. A path leads down to the bay.

Organised Tours

Excursion boats go to the **islet of Ro**, Agios Georgios and Strogyli islets and the spectacular **Blue cave** (Parasta), which derives the name from its brilliant-blue water caused by refracted sunlight. All of these trips cost around 3000 dr.

Places to Stay – bottom end

If you are not offered a room when you disembark, the following co-owned budget options are OK and charge 4000 dr a double. *Rooms Kastraki* (☎ 29 324) and *Pension Barbara* (☎ 29 395) are both along the street to Horafia and Mandraki, beside the white-arched building; and *Rooms O Paradeisos* (☎ 29 074) is farther around the bay, behind Plateia Australias.

The *Pension Kristallo* (☎ 49 209), behind and to the right of the central square, has cosy clean doubles for 4000 dr with shared bathroom. The owner of Lazarakis Restaurant (☎ 49 370/365/357), on Plateia Ethelonton Kastellorizou, rents very pleasant singles/doubles/triples with private bathroom for 4000/5000/7000 dr, and double/triple studios for 7000/8000 dr. Beyond here, *Sydney Rooms* (☎ 49 302), above the Sydney Restaurant, has rates of 4000/7000 dr for singles/doubles with shared bathroom. The owner, Angelo, also has some lovely double rooms with private bathroom for 10,000 dr.

Pension Castelo, behind the central square, has doubles for 7000 dr and two-bedroomed family apartments for 12,000 dr. The traditionally furnished *Nektarios Apartments* (☎ 49 266), in a beautifully restored red-and-ochre mansion near the top of the harbour's west side, has rates of 15,000 dr for three people. Farther around, the island's only hotel, the B-class *Hotel Megisti* (☎ 29 072) charges 9300/15,600/19,900 dr.

Places to Stay – middle

Krystalls Apartments (☎ 49 363; fax 49 368), co-owned with Taverna International, has doubles/triples for 15,000/18,000.

Places to Eat

Restaurant Oraia Megisti, on Plateia Ethelonton Kastellorizou, is excellent. A meal of lamb cutlets and chips, green salad and retsina here costs 2000 dr. *Restaurant Eftychia*, opposite, is also highly commendable and has similar prices. *Taverna International* and *Restaurant Sydney*, beyond the square, are also good.

Restaurant Platania, on Plateia Horafian, is a nice unpretentious place, despite appearing in the film Mediterraneo. A full meal here will cost about 2000 dr.

Lazarakis Restaurant and *Restaurant Mavros*, opposite the jetty, are the yachters' haunts. They excel in seafood, but are quite expensive. The *ouzeri* behind the white-arched building is a favourite haunt of locals and serves inexpensive food.

Tilos Τήλος

Tilos (TEE-los, population 300) lies 65 km west of Rhodes. With good, uncrowded beaches, two abandoned, evocative villages, a well-kept monastery at the end of a spectacularly scenic road, and its authentic Greek island image intact, Tilos, remarkably, is still little visited. It's a terrific island for walkers, with vistas of high cliffs, rocky inlets and

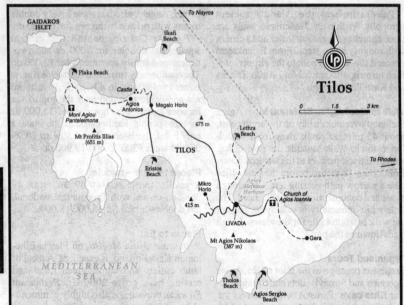

sea, and valleys of cypress, walnut and almond trees, and bucolic meadows with well-fed cattle.

Tilos' agricultural potential is not utilised, since, rather than work the land for a pittance, young Tiliots prefer to leave for the mainland or emigrate to Australia or the USA.

There are two settlements: the port of Livadia, and Megalo Horio, eight km to the north.

History

Bones of mastodons, midget elephants which became extinct around 4600 BC, were found in a cave on the island in 1974 and Irini, one of the greatest of ancient Greece's female poets, lived on Tilos in the 4th century BC.

Elephants and poetry apart, Tilos' history followed the same catalogue of invasions and occupations as the rest of the archipelago.

Getting There & Away

Ferry The F/B *Dimitra* and F/B *Nissos Kalymnos* are the only ferries with Tilos as a port of call. See the Getting There & Away section for Rhodes island for details of their schedules.

Hydrofoil There are two hydrofoils a week to and from Rhodes (4600 dr, 1¼ hours), Nisyros and Kos to Tilos, and one a week to Astypalea via Kalymnos.

Getting Around

Tilos' public transport is an orange van, which goes from Livadia to Megalo Horio and Eristos beach (both 300 dr). There are two motorbike-rental outlets in Livadia.

LIVADIA Λιβάδια

Livadia skirts around a large bay with a long pebble beach on the island's east coast. All the tourist facilities, as well as most of the accommodation, is here.

Orientation & Information

From the quay turn left, ascend the steps beside Stefanakis Travel, and continue ahead to the central square. To reach the beach, walk across the square and straight ahead; a turn to the left along here leads to the three adjacent domatia on the beach. Continuing straight ahead the road curves and turns right, passing the Church of Agios Nikolaos, to skirt the beach.

The post office and OTE are on the central square. Tilos' postcode is 850 02 and the telephone code is 0241. The port police (☎ 44 322) and the regular police (☎ 44 222) share the white Italianate building at the quay. Tilos has no EOT but the staff at both Stefanakis Travel (☎ 44 310/360/384) and Tilos Travel Agency (☎ 44 259) opposite the quay, are helpful.

Walking Tours

Lethra Beach Lethra is a long pebble beach 40 minutes' walk from Livadia. Take the Megala Horio road and in five minutes turn right onto a dirt road, which climbs steadily above Livadia Bay. This becomes a path which eventually dips as Lethra comes into view. Above the beginning of the beach take a path which veers right for 20 metres, then veers left down to a ravine. Turn right here to reach the beach.

Mikro Horio Before WW II Tilos had two villages, Megala Horio and Mikro Horio. No one lived at the port because it was vulnerable to pirates. People began to leave Mikro Horio, three km from Livadia, after the war. One elderly woman remained there alone until her death in 1974.

Two km along the Megala Horio road, turn left (signposted 'Mikro Horio'), then shortly after, turn right onto a dirt road (also signposted). The village is a lonely, evocative place. Hawks circle overhead and lizards run for cover as you wander along the overgrown pathways. There is a bar (see Entertainment), and two churches that are overlooked by a ruined tower.

Gera Gera, high above Tilos' east coast, was the summer settlement of Mikro Horio. The path begins 120 metres beyond Marina Beach Rooms (see Places to Stay). After about a 20-minute walk the path passes the Church of Agios Ioannis, and about one hour later, Gera's derelict, wooden-roofed houses appear on the left.

Places to Stay

Livadia is well provided with accommodation and freelance camping is permitted on its beaches – Plaka beach is the best spot. There are three delightful domatia right on the beach. They are *Rooms to Rent O Spiros* (☎ 44 339), *Paraskevi Rooms* (☎ 44 280) and *Pension Paradise* (☎ 44 341). All charge 5000 dr for double rooms (see Orientation & Information).

The E-class *Hotel Livadia* (☎ 44 202), behind the central square, has tidy doubles with private bathroom for 5500 dr. The *Pension Perigiali* (☎ 44 398), on the right just beyond the central square, has singles/doubles for 4400/5500 dr with private bathroom.

Both the *Casa Italiana Rooms* (☎ 44 253/259) at the quay, and *Stefanakis Studios* (☎ 44 360/384) above Stefanakis Travel, have immaculate double studios for 6000 dr.

The well-signposted, C-class *Hotel Irini* (☎ 44 293, fax 44 238) has lovely, tastefully furnished doubles for 8000 dr. The new *Eleni Hotel*, 400 metres along the beach road, did not yet have a phone number in 1995. Its double studios cost around 8000 dr. *Marina Beach Rooms* (☎ 44 354) on the bay's eastern side, one km from the quay, has immaculate but small rooms with sea-view balconies; doubles are 9000 dr.

Places to Eat

Restaurant Kostas, next to Stefanakis Travel, serves tasty Greek staples. *Sophia's Restaurant*, 20 metres along the beach road, serves delicious, low-priced food. A 'Greek plate' is 980 dr. *Restaurant Irini* nearby, and *Taverna Blue Sky* at the quay, are also good. *Kafeneion Omonoias*, next to the post office, is a favourite place for breakfast; yoghurt and

DODECANESE

honey and Nescafé is 500 dr. Tilos is well supplied with supermarkets.

Entertainment
La Luna at the quay and *Yiannis Bar* on the beach road are the local hot spots. In summer a bar at Mikro Horio blares music until the early hours.

MEGALO HORIO Μεγάλο Χωριό
Megalo Horio (population 150) is a serene whitewashed village. Crowning it is a ruined **knights' castle** which has an intact gateway, and a small chapel with frescoes. The village's main street deteriorates to a path, which passes a concrete cistern on the left, then climbs steeply to the castle.

Places to Stay & Eat
Megalo Horio has three places to stay. The *Pension Sevasti* (☎ 44 237), just beyond the Eristos beach turn-off, has singles/doubles for only 2000/3500 dr. The *Milou Rooms and Apartments* (☎ 44 204), in the village; and *Elefantakia Studios* (☎ 44 242/213), next door, have doubles for 7000 dr. *Kali Kardia Taverna*, next to Pension Sevasti, is good value.

AROUND MEGALO HORIO
Just before Megalo Horio, a turn-off to the left leads in 2.5 km to **Eristos beach**, a long swathe of tamarisk-fringed sand. A signposted turn-off to the right from this road leads to **Agios Antonios beach. Plaka beach**, three km farther west, is dotted with trees.

The 18th-century **Moni Agiou Panteleimona** is five km beyond here, along a scenic road. It is uninhabited but well-maintained with fine 18th-century frescoes. The island's minibus driver takes groups of visitors there on Sunday. A three-day festival takes place at the monastery, beginning on 25 July.

Places to Stay
The accommodation options are *Tropicana Taverna & Rooms* (☎ 44 223), on the Eristos road, with doubles/triples for 4500/5000 dr; and *Nausika Taverna & Rooms*, to the left of

Eristos beach (signposted), where rates are 3600/5000 dr.

The immaculate D-class *Hotel Australia* (☎ 44 296), overlooks Agios Antonios beach. Rates are 6000/7000 dr for singles/doubles/triples with private bathroom.

Nisyros Νίσυρος

Nisyros (NEE-see-ros, population 800), with lush vegetation combined with dramatic moonscapes, is one of the strangest and most beautiful of all Greek islands. The nucleus of the island is a dormant volcano. This creates a curious anomaly whereby the island, although waterless, is nonetheless fertile. The mineral-rich earth holds moisture and yields olives, vines, figs, citrus fruit and almonds.

It attracts a lot of day-trippers from Kos, but a relatively small number of overnight visitors.

The island's settlements are Mandraki, the capital; the fishing village of Pali; and the crater-top villages of Emboreios and Nikea.

The island's population has not suffered the drastic depletion of other small islands, because some of its men earn a living quarrying pumice.

Getting There & Away
Ferry & Hydrofoil Nisyros shares the same ferry and hydrofoil schedules as Tilos. See the Getting There & Away section for Rhodes island for details.

Excursion Boat In summer there are daily excursion boats from Kardamena and Kos town on Kos.

Getting Around
Bus There are at least two buses every day to the volcano (1000 dr), five to Pali and two on weekdays only to Nikea and Emboreios. The bus terminal is at the quay where a schedule is displayed outside Polyvotis Tours.

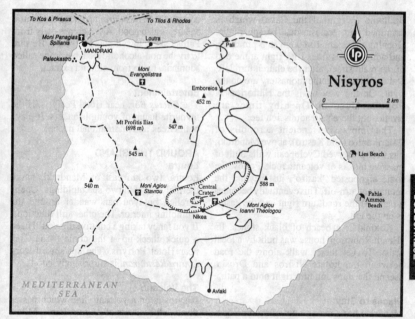

Nisyros

DODECANESE

Taxi There are two taxi companies: Bobby's Taxi (☎ 31 360) and Irene's Taxi (☎ 31 474). Tariffs to the following destinations are: the volcano (2500 dr), Emboreios (2500 dr), Nikea (3000 dr) and Pali (1200 dr).

Motorbike There are four motorbike-rental outlets on Mandraki's main street.

Taxi Boat There are occasional taxi boats to the pumice-stone islet of Giali where there is a good sandy beach (1500 dr return).

MANDRAKI Μανδράκι
Mandraki is the attractive port and capital of Nisyros. Its two-storey houses have brightly painted wooden balconies. Some are white-washed but many are painted in bright colours, predominantly ochre and turquoise. The web of streets huddled below the monastery and the central square are especially charming.

Orientation & Information
To reach Mandraki's centre walk straight ahead from the quay. At the fork bear right; the left fork leads to Hotel Porfyris. Beyond here a large square adjoins the main street, which proceeds to Plateia Aristotelous Fotiadou, then continues diagonally opposite, passing the town hall. Turn left at the T-junction for the central square of Plateia Elikiomini.

The post office, port police (☎ 31 222) and the regular police share premises opposite the quay. Both the OTE and the National Bank of Greece representative are on the right side of the main street. Nisyros' telephone code is 0242. Nisyros has no EOT or tourist police. The staff at Enetikis Travel (☎ 31 180; fax 31 168) on the main street are helpful.

Things to See
Mandraki's greatest tourist attraction is the cliff-top 14th-century **Moni Panagias**

Spilianis (Virgin of the Cave) which is crammed with ecclesiastical paraphernalia. Opening times are 10.30 am to 3 pm daily, and admission is free. Turn right at the end of the main street, after the church turn left, and the steps up to the monastery are on the right. On the way up is the **Historical & Popular Museum**. Opening times are erratic, but there's no admission fee.

The impressive ancient acropolis of **Paleokastro** (Old Kastro), above Mandraki, has well-preserved Cyclopean walls built of massive blocks of volcanic rock. Follow the route signposted 'kastro', just beyond the monastery turn-off. This eventually becomes a path. At the road turn right and the kastro is on the left.

Koklaki is a beach of black stones. Its 'Heath Robinson' house was built by a local artist. To get there, walk along the road between the hotels Nisiros and Drosia, ascend the steps and turn right onto a path.

Places to Stay

Mandraki has a fair amount of accommodation but, unusually, owners do not meet the ferries. There is no camping ground. The cheapest accommodation was always *Pension Drosia* (☎ 31 328/082), but in 1995 it was temporarily closed.

Other pleasant options are the *Hotel Romantzo* (☎ 31 340) with singles/doubles/triples for 4000/5000/7000 dr; and the *Three Brothers Hotel* (☎ 31 344) opposite, with rates of 4000/6000/7300 dr. Turn left from the quay to reach these. The C-class *Haritos Hotel* (☎ 31 322/122), farther along on the right, has comfortable rooms for 5000/7000/9000 dr. Beyond here, the immaculate *Mire Mare Apartments* (☎ 31 100) has singles/doubles/triples for 6000/10,000/14,000 dr.

The C-class *Hotel Porfyris* (☎ 31 204), with a swimming pool, has singles/doubles for 7000/9500 dr (see Orientation).

Places to Eat

Taverna Nissyros, just off the main street, is a cheery, popular little place. A meal of calamari and chips, Greek salad and ouzo costs 2000 dr. *Restaurant Irini*, on the central square, is also good. A van comes daily from Pali's bakery to sell pies and bread. Be sure to try the non-alcoholic local beverage called soumada, made from almond extract.

Entertainment

The *Cactus Bar*, near Hotel Porfyris, is the favourite haunt of young islanders. It plays both Greek and international music.

AROUND THE ISLAND
Loutra

Loutra, two km east of Mandraki, has a thermal spa, with two spa buildings. One is derelict, but you can wander around the crumbling interior. The other still functions. If you fancy taking a curative dip you'll need a quick check-up at the clinic (☎ 31 217) near Hotel Porfyris. The spa's well-worn *Loutra Restaurant* is surprisingly good.

The Volcano

Nisyros is on a volcanic line which passes through the islands of Aegina, Paros, Milos, Santorini, Nisyros, Giali and Kos. The island originally culminated in a mountain of 1400 metres, but in a violent eruption in 1552 the centre collapsed, forming the plain of Lakki. Minor eruptions occurred in 1871, 1873, 1888 and 1933. There are five craters in Lakki. A path descends into the largest one, Stefanos, where you can examine the multicoloured fumaroles, listen to their hissing and smell their sulphurous vapours. The surface is soft and hot, making sturdy footwear essential.

If you come to the crater by bus you'll be with hordes of day-trippers, who detract from the extraordinary sight. Also, the bus does not allow you long enough to wander around and savour a glass of soumada from the café near Stefanos. It's a good idea to walk either to or from the crater.

Walk from the Volcano to Mandraki via Moni Agiou Stavrou With your back to the café, walk straight ahead. Turn left at the crater, and half way around take the path which veers left up to a track. Turn right onto

DODECANESE

the track and continue ahead to reach Moni Agiou Stavrou in about 40 minutes. Shortly after the monastery, bear left at a fork. After about 40 minutes' walking the track turns sharp left. In about another 40 minutes you will reach a road, from where it's just a short walk to Mandraki along the path opposite.

Emboreios & Nikea Εμπορειός και Νίκαια
Emboreios and Nikea perch on the volcano's rim. From each, there are stunning views down into the caldera. Only 20 inhabitants linger on in Emboreios. You may encounter a few elderly women sitting on their doorsteps crocheting, and their husbands at the kafeneio. However, generally, its winding, stepped streets are empty, the silence broken only by the occasional braying of a donkey or the grunting of pigs. A stepped kalderimi, beginning on the left side of the road coming from Emboreios, leads to Pali. Halfway down you will come to the road again. Turn left, and, after two km, you will rejoin the kalderimi (recognisable by concrete steps).

In contrast to Emboreios, picturesque Nikea, with 50 inhabitants, buzzes with life. It has dazzling white houses with vibrant gardens and a central square with a lovely pebble mosaic. The bus terminates on Plateia Nikolaou Hartofili. Nikea's main street links the two squares.

The steep path down to the volcano begins from Plateia Nikolaou Hartofili. It takes about 40 minutes to walk it one way. Near the beginning you can detour to **Moni Agiou Ioanni Theologou.**

Places to Stay & Eat Emboreios has no accommodation for tourists and no tavernas – only one kafeneio.

Nikea's only accommodation is a *Community Hostel*, on Plateia Nikolaou Hartofili, which is managed by Panayiotis Mastromihalis (☎ 31 285), the owner of Nikea's only taverna, near Plateia Nikolaou Hartofili. Doubles cost 3000 dr.

Pali Πάλοι
The island's best beaches are at Pali, four km east of Mandraki, and lies five km farther on.

Pali's C-class *Hotel Hellenis* (☎ 31 453) has doubles for 6000 dr with private bathroom. Paraskevi, the owner, serves up delectable dishes in the adjoining restaurant. Her shepherd husband, the charismatic Manolis, sometimes plays the lyre in the taverna. The *Afrodite Taverna* next door is also good.

Astypalea Αστυπάλαια

Astypalea (As-ti-PA-lee-a, population 1100), the most westerly island of the archipelago, is geographically and architecturally more akin to the Cyclades. The island's two land masses are joined by a narrow isthmus.

With its wonderfully picturesque hilltop Hora, bare, gently contoured hills, high mountains, green valleys and sheltered coves, it's surprising Astypalea does not get more foreign tourists. It is, however, popular with urban Greeks.

Getting There & Away

Air There are three flights a week from Astypalea to Athens (19,000 dr). Astypalea Tours (☎ 61 588), below the Vivamare Hotel, is the agent for Olympic Airways.

Ferry Lying between the Cyclades and the Dodecanese, Astypalea misses out on the ferries that serve those groups. The F/B *Nissos Kalymnos* visits twice a week from Kalymnos (two hours, 1952 dr). Contact Central Agency (☎ 29 612) on Kalymnos for the ferry's current schedule.

The F/B *Dimitra* leaves Piraeus at 2 pm on Wednesday for Astypalea. It leaves Astypalea at 1 am on Thursday for Rhodes via Kalymnos and Kos. It leaves Rhodes at 1 pm on Thursday for Piraeus via Kos, Kalymnos and Astypalea.

Ferries sail twice a week to and from Piraeus via the Cyclades islands (16 hours): one goes via Syros, Paros, Naxos, Iraklia, Shinoussa, Koufonisi, Katapola (Amorgos), Aegiali (Amorgos) and Donoussa; and the other goes via Syros, Tinos, Mykonos,

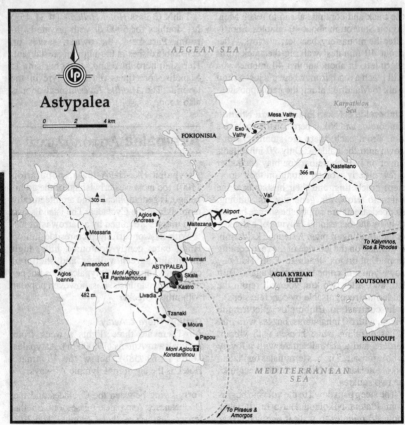

AEGEAN SEA

Astypalea

0   2   4 km

Karpathian Sea

FOKIONISIA

Mesa Vathy

Exo Vathy

▲ 305 m

Kastellano

▲ 366 m

Agios Andreas

Messaria

Vaï

✈ Airport

Maltezana

To Kalymnos, Kos & Rhodes

Armenohori

Marmari

ASTYPALEA

Moni Agiou Panteleimonos

Skala

AGIA KYRIAKI ISLET

KOUTSOMYTI

Agios Ioannis

Kastro

▲ 482 m

Livadia

Tzanaki

Moura

KOUNOUPI

Papou

Moni Agiou Konstantinou

MEDITERRANEAN SEA

To Piraeus & Amorgos

Donoussa, Katapola and Aegiali. Check the times of the ferries running to and from Astypalea with the port police or a travel agent as they are likely to change from year to year.

Paradise Travel beneath the Paradisos Hotel and Astypalea Tours (☎ 61 292/328) below the Vivamare Hotel sell ferry tickets.

Hydrofoil Between June and September there is one hydrofoil a week plying its way from Rhodes (5½ hours, 8550 dr) to Astypalea via Tilos, Nisyros, Kos and Kalymnos.

Getting Around

Bus From Skala the bus travels several times a day to Hora and Livadia (200 dr), and from Hora and Skala to Maltezana (300 dr) via Marmari.

Excursion Boat In summer Gournas Tours runs excursion boats to the island's less accessible beaches and to Agia Kyriaki islet (800 to 1500 dr).

ASTYPALEA TOWN

Astypalea town, the capital, consists of the port of Skala and the hilltop district of Hora, crowned by a fortress. Skala has a friendly pelican, Carlos, who blew in one windy day in 1992. He landed on his feet, it seems, for the local fishers throw him lots of tasty titbits.

Hora has narrow streets of dazzling-white, cubic houses with brightly painted wooden balconies, doors and banisters, some of which are ornately carved. A line of windmills completes the picture.

Orientation & Information

From Skala's quay turn right to reach the waterfront. The steep road to Hora begins beyond the white Italianate building. In Skala the waterfront road skirts around a beach and then veers right to continue along the coast to Marmari and beyond. The post office is at the top of the Skala-Hora road. The OTE is beneath the waterfront's Hotel Paradissos. Astypalea's postcode is 859 00 and the telephone code is 0243. The National Bank of Greece representative is at the Aegean Hotel, a little way up the Skala-Hora road.

A municipal tourist office adjoins the quayside café. Gournas Tours (☎ 61 334), above the beach, has a room-finding service and the owner, Louise, an English expatriate, is very helpful. The police (☎ 61 207) and port police (☎ 61 208) are in the Italianate building.

Castle

During the time of the Knights of St John, Astypalea was occupied by the Venetian Quirini family who built the imposing castle. In the Middle Ages everyone lived within its walls but gradually the settlement outgrew them. The last inhabitants left in 1948 and the stone houses are now in ruins. Above the entrance is the Church of the Our Lady of the Castle and within the walls is the Church of Agios Giorgios.

Places to Stay

The *Hotel Australia* (☎ 61 338), on the waterfront where the road veers right, has well-kept doubles/triples for 5500/6000 dr, and a friendly Greek-Australian owner.

Farther along are *Karlos Studios* (☎ 61 330), with rates of 5000/6000 dr and the *Hotel Vengalis* (☎ 61 281/114 where rooms are 6000/7000 dr and studios are 8000/9000 dr. The *Hotel Aegeon* (☎ 61 236), on the left side of the Skala-Hora road, has singles/doubles for 4000/6000 dr. The ageing but well-maintained *Hotel Paradisos* (☎ 61 224/256) has comfortable singles/doubles/triples with private bathroom for 6000/7000/8000 dr. The *Hotel Vivamare* (☎ 61 571/572), a little way up the Skala-Hora road, on the right, has new double/triple/quad studios for 8000/ 9600/15,000 dr.

Camping Astypalea (☎ 61 338) is three km east of Skala.

Places to Eat

The *Restaurant Australia*, below the Hotel Australia, has filling fish soup for 1500 dr and tasty vegetable stews for 800 dr. *Dimitrios Restaurant* on the Skala-Hora road, and *Vicki's* near the quay, are also commendable. Astypalea's *bakery* is opposite Dimitrios Restaurant. There is a *supermarket* on the waterfront, and another next to the post office in Hora.

LIVADIA Λιβάδια

The little resort of Livadia lies in a fertile valley two km from Hora. Its beach is the best on the island, but also the most crowded. Quieter beaches can be found farther south at **Tzanaki**, the island's unofficial nudist beach, and at Agios Konstantinos (see Walks to Moni Agiou Konstantinou & Moni Agiou Panteleimonos).

Walks to Moni Agiou Konstantinou & Moni Agiou Panteleimonos

From the far end of the waterfront, continue along the road as it rises above the coast. After a 30-minute walk, a track turns inland to the right for Agiou Panteleimonos. This hilly walk takes about one hour. Continuing on the road straight ahead you will soon reach Moni Agiou Konstantinou and the beach of Agios Konstantinos.

Places to Stay & Eat

There's plenty of accommodation in Livadia. A sign at the end of the beach road points to *Jim Venetos Studios & Apartments* (☎ 61 490/150) which is one of the nicest places. Double studios cost 7000 dr and four-person apartments are 12,000 dr. Tavernas line the beach road.

OTHER BEACHES

Two km north-east of Skala, **Marmari** has three bays with pebble-and-sand beaches. **Maltezana** is seven km beyond here, in a fertile valley, on the isthmus. It's a scattered, pleasantly laid-back settlement, but its two beaches are messy. There are some remains of Roman baths with mosaics on the settlement's outskirts.

The road from Maltezana is OK as far as **Vaï**, but it's atrocious beyond here. **Mesa Vathy** is a fishing hamlet with a beach at the end of a narrow inlet. It takes about 1½ hours to walk here from Vaï. From Mesa Vathy a footpath leads to **Exo Vathy**, another hamlet with a beach.

Places to Stay & Eat

There are plenty of accommodation options in Maltazena, but many only operate during the summer. There is a domatia at Exo Vathy, but check with Gournas Tours in Astypalea town if it's operating.

Getting There & Away

The bus travels between Skala and Maltez-ana several times a day. In summer Gournas Tours run excursion boats to Exo Vathy. There is also a daily excursion boat from Vaï.

Symi Σύμη

Symi (SEE-mi, population 2300) lies in the straits of Marmara, 24 km north of Rhodes, its nearest Greek neighbour, and only 10 km from the Turkish peninsula of Dorakis. The island has a scenic interior of jagged rocks, interspersed with pine and cypress woods, and a deeply indented coast with precipitous cliffs, and numerous small bays with pebbled beaches which are best reached by excursion boats or on organised walks (see the Getting Around section for Symi). Symi suffers from a severe water shortage.

Symi gets an inordinate number of day-trippers from Rhodes. Most of them don't venture any farther than the restaurants, bars and tourist shops on Gialos' waterfront; only a few make it as far as Nos beach.

History

Symi has a long tradition of both sponge diving and shipbuilding. During Ottoman times it was granted the right to fish for sponges in Turkish waters. In return Symi supplied the sultan with first-class boat builders and top-quality sponges.

These factors, and a lucrative shipbuilding industry, brought prosperity to the island. Gracious mansions were built and culture and education flourished. By the turn of the century the population was 22,500 and the island was launching some 500 ships a year. The Italian occupation, the introduction of the steamship and Kalymnos' rise as the Aegean's principal sponge producer, put an end to Symi's prosperity.

On 8 May 1945, the treaty surrendering the Dodecanese islands to the Allies was signed on Symi.

Getting There & Away

Ferry & Hydrofoil Symi shares the same ferry schedules as Tilos and Nisyros, with the addition of the F/B *Apollon Express*. See the Getting There & Away section for Rhodes island for details. There is one hydrofoil a week servicing Rhodes (50 minutes, 2675 dr), Tilos, Nisyros and Kos.

Excursion Boat There are daily excursion boats running between Symi and Rhodes' Mandraki harbour. The Symi-based and cooperatively owned *Symi I* and *Symi II* boats are the cheapest.

Getting Around

Bus & Taxi Two 12-seater vans run every half an hour between Gialos and Pedi beach

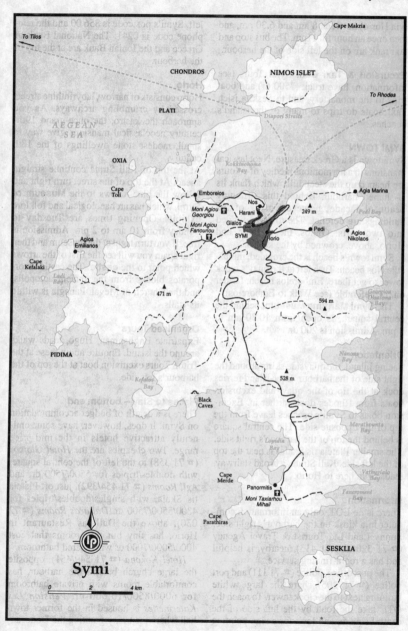

To Tilos

CHONDROS

NIMOS ISLET

To Rhodes

Diapori Straits

PLATI

AEGEAN
SEA

OXIA

Kokkinohoma
Bay

Cape
Toli

Emboreios

Moni Agiou
Georgiou

Nos

Harani

249 m

Agia Marina

Pedi Bay

Gialos

Moni Agiou
Fanouriou

SYMI

Horio

Pedi

Agios
Nikolaos

Agios
Emilianos

Cape
Kefalaki

Ladi
Bay

Georgiou
Diasloma
Bay

471 m

594 m

PIDIMA

528 m

Nanomos
Bay

Kefalos
Bay

Black
Caves

Marathounta
Bay

Lapida
Bay

Cape Merde

Vathygialo
Bay

Panormitis

Moni Taxiarhou
Mihail

Faneromeni
Bay

Cape
Parathiras

SESKLIA

Symi

0   2   4 km

Cape Makria

DODECANESE

(via Horio) between 8 am and 6.30 pm, and then once an hour till 11pm. The bus stop and taxi rank are on the left side of the harbour.

Excursion & Taxi Boat Symi Tours (see Information) have truck (7500 dr) and boat trips to the monastery, and to Sesklia islet. Taxi boats do trips to many of the island's beaches.

SYMI TOWN

Symi town is a Greek treasure. Neoclassical mansions in a harmonious medley of colours are heaped up the steep hills which flank its U-shaped harbour. Behind this strikingly beautiful façade, however, many of the buildings are derelict. The town is divided into two parts: Gialos, the harbour, and Horio, above, crowned by the kastro.

Symi town's beach is the crowded, minuscule Nos beach. Turn left at the quay's clock tower to get there. Emboreios beach, farther on, is preferable (see Walk to Emboreios).

The **Symi Maritime Museum**, behind the central square, is open from 10.30 am to 3 pm. Admission is 200 dr.

Orientation

Facing inland, the quayside skirts around the right side of the harbour. Inter-island ferries dock at the tip of the quay, and excursion boats from Rhodes dock farther in. Excursion boats to Symi's beaches leave from the top of the opposite side. The central square is behind the top of the harbour's right side. The smaller Plateia tis Skalas is near the top of the left side. Kali Strata, a broad stairway, leads from here to Horio.

Information

There is no EOT, only an information computer in a kiosk on the harbour's right side. Sunny Land Ltd Tourist & Travel Agency (☎ 71 320; fax 71 413), nearby, is helpful and has a room-finding service.

The post office, police (☎ 71 111) and port police (☎ 71 205) share the large white building next to the clock tower. To reach the OTE take the road by the left side of the central square, and look for a sign pointing

left. Symi's postcode is 856 00 and the telephone code is 0241. The National Bank of Greece and the Ionian Bank are at the top of the harbour.

Horio

Horio consists of narrow, labyrinthine streets crossed by crumbling archways. As you approach the kastro, the once-grand 19th-century neoclassical mansions give way to small, modest stone dwellings of the 18th century.

At the top of Kali Strata continue straight ahead. At the top of the street turn right and follow the blue arrows to the **Museum of Symi**, which has archaeological and folklore exhibits. Opening times are Tuesday to Sunday from 10 am to 2 pm. Admission is free. If you turn right at the museum and then right again you will see the first of the arrows which point to the **castle**. The castle incorporates blocks from the ancient acropolis, and the Church of Megali Panagia is within its walls.

Organised Tours

Expatriate Englishman, Hugo, leads walks around the island. Enquire about these at the Triton Tours excursion boat at the top of the harbour's left side.

Places to Stay – bottom end

There is a dearth of budget accommodation on Symi. It does, however, have some eminently attractive hotels in the mid-price range. Two cheapies are the *Hotel Glafkos* (☎ 71 358) to the left of the central square, with doubles/triples for 5500/7500 dr; and *Agli Rooms* (☎ 71 454/392), just off Plateia tis Skala, with singles/doubles/triples for 4300/5500/7500 dr. *Dallaras Rooms* (☎ 72 030), above the Dallaras Restaurant in Horio, has tiny but tidy rooms that cost 4000/5000/7000 dr with shared bathroom.

Hotel Kokona (☎ 71 549/451), opposite the large church behind the harbour, has comfortable rooms with private bathroom for 6000/8500/10,000 dr. *Pension Les Katerinettes* is housed in the former town hall where the treaty granting the Dodecanese to the Allies was signed. Some of its rooms have magnificent painted ceilings. Doubles here cost 9000 dr. The pension is managed by Sunny Land Ltd Tourist & Travel Agency (☎ 71 320; fax 71 413), nearby.

Places to Stay – middle

In Horio, the B-class *Hotel Village* (☎ 71 800; fax 71 802) has comfortable, carpeted doubles/triples for 12,000/15,000 dr.

The *Hotel Nireus* (☎ 72 400/403; fax 72 404) has elegant, traditional double/triple rooms for 16,000/19,300 dr and double/triple suites for 20,000/24,200 dr. Turn left at the clock tower (facing the sea) and the hotel is on the left. Farther along, the A-class *Hotel Aliki* (☎ 71 665) is another lovely, traditional-style hotel. Singles/doubles/triples are 10,000/14,000/18,00 dr.

The *Opera House Hotel* (☎ 72 034; fax 72 035) well signposted from the harbour, is a cluster of buildings in a peaceful garden. The spacious, beautiful double/triple studios are 16,000/18,000 dr.

Places to Eat

Many of Gialos' restaurants are mediocre, catering for day-trippers. Exceptions are *Vigla Restaurant* and *Vassilis Restaurant* both at the top of the harbour; *O Meraklis Taverna*, two blocks back; and *Taverna Neraida*, beyond the Hotel Glafkos.

Restaurant Les Katerinettes, below the pension, has an extensive range of well-prepared dishes. Swordfish is 1500 dr and souvlaki is 1200 dr; desserts include apple tart for 500 dr. Several supermarkets are dotted around.

In Horio try *Dallaras Restaurant*, *Taverna Georgios* or *Taverna Panorama*, all on the left at the top of Kali Strata.

AROUND THE ISLAND
Walk from Gialos to Emboreios

This is an easy, scenic walk along a paved Byzantine path. Walk along the road by the left side of the central square, and continue straight ahead. At the fork bear right and go uphill, passing a cemetery, and then a mon-

astery on either side. When the cement road turns right, take the dirt track to its left, which soon becomes a paved path passing between stone walls. After Moni Agiou Georgiou, the path drops down to Kokkinohoma bay. Turn left to reach Emboreios, or right to return to Gialos along the coast road.

Walk from Gialos to Moni Agiou Fanouriou

Walk along the road by the left side of the central square and continue straight ahead. When the road begins to ascend, turn left for the Hotel Grace. At the fork bear right, and continue uphill, passing behind the hotel. Follow this cobblestone track up the steps, and then to the left at the top. Continue to a wooden gate beyond which the path winds up to the monastery.

Pedi

Pedi is a little fishing village and burgeoning holiday resort in a fertile valley, two km downhill from Horio. It has some sandy stretches on its narrow beach.

Places to Stay & Eat Like in Symi town accommodation in Pedi is hard to find. You could try *Gallini Hotel* (☎ 71 385), inland from the jetty, where spotlessly clean, double apartments are 8000 dr. The large *Pedi Beach Hotel* (☎ 71 870/276) has singles/doubles/triples for a pricey 10,000/13,400/18,000 dr.

The waterfront *Argo Bar*, with friendly English hosts, serves well-prepared English dishes. English roast is 1700 dr, beers are 300 dr and cocktails cost 950 dr. Farther around the waterfront, *Taverna Kamares*, serves tasty Greek fare.

Moni Taxiarhou Mihail

Μονή Ταξιάρχου Μιξαήλ

The large white Moni Taxiarhou Mihail (Monastery of Michael of Panormitis) in the almost circular bay of Panormitis, is Symi's principal sight, so it's the stopping-off point for many of the day-trippers from Rhodes. A monastery was first built here in the 5th or 6th century, but the present building, with an

DODECANESE

imposing bell tower, dates from the 18th century. The **katholikon** contains an intricately carved wooden iconostasis, frescoes, and an icon of St Michael which supposedly appeared miraculously where the monastery now stands. St Michael is the patron saint of Symi, and protector of sailors.

The monastery complex comprises a museum, restaurant and basic guest rooms. Beds cost 2000 dr; you cannot make a reservation, but, except in July and August, you will have no difficulty getting a bed.

Kos Κως

Kos (population 21,000) is the third-largest island of the Dodecanese and one of its most well-watered and fertile. It lies only five km from the Turkish peninsula of Bodrum. It is second only to Rhodes in both its wealth of archaeological remains and in its tourist development, with most of its beautiful beaches wall-to-wall with sunbeds and parasols. It's a long, narrow island on a north-east south-west axis, with a mountainous spine.

Pserimos is a small island between Kos and Kalymnos. It has a good sandy beach, but unfortunately becomes overrun with day-trippers from both of its larger neighbours.

History
Kos' fertile land attracted settlers from the earliest times. So many people lived here by Mycenaean times that it was able to send 30 ships to the Trojan War. During the 7th and 6th centuries BC, Kos flourished as an ally of the powerful Rhodian cities of Ialyssos, Kamiros and Lindos. In 477 BC, after suffering an earthquake and subjugation to the Persians, it joined the Delian League, and flourished once more.

Hippocrates (460-377 BC), the father of medicine, was born and lived on the island. After Hippocrates' death, the Sanctuary of Asclepius and a medical school were built, which perpetuated his teachings, and made Kos famous throughout the Greek world.

Ptolemy II of Egypt was born on Kos, thus securing it the protection of Egypt, under which it became a prosperous trading centre. In 130 BC Kos came under Roman domination, and in the 1st century AD it was put under the administration of Rhodes, with which it came to share the same vicissitudes, right up to the tourist deluge of the present day.

Getting There & Away
Air There are at least two flights a day to Athens (18,600 dr) and three flights a week to Rhodes (12,000 dr). The Olympic Airways office (☎ 28 330/331/332, 22 833) is at Vasileos Pavlou 22, in Kos town.

Ferry – domestic Kos has good ferry connections, with daily services to Rhodes and Piraeus (6097 dr), via Kalymnos, Leros and Patmos. The F/B *Nissos Kalymnos* also calls in at Kos. See the Getting There & Away sections for Kalymnos and Rhodes island for details of its schedule.

Ferry – international There are daily ferries in summer from Kos town to Bodrum (ancient Halicarnassus) in Turkey. Boats leave at 8 am and return at 4 pm. The journey takes one hour and costs 13,000 dr return (which includes the Turkish port tax). Many travel agents around Kos town sell tickets.

Hydrofoil In high season there are daily hydrofoils running from Kos to Rhodes (two hours, 6665 dr), Patmos (1½ hours) and Samos (1¾ hours); five a week to Leros (one hour, 4300 dr); two a week to Kalymnos, Nisyros and Tilos; and one a week to Symi. Several travel agencies sell tickets.

Excursion Boat From Kos town there are many boat excursions, both around the island and to other islands. Some examples of return fares include the following: Kalymnos (3000 dr); Kálymnos and Pserimos (5000 dr); and Nisyros and Giali (5500 dr). There is also a daily excursion boat from Kardamena to Nisyros (3000 dr return) and from Mastihari to Pserimos and Kalymnos.

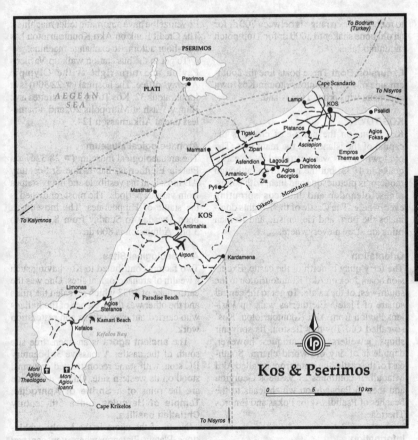

Kos & Pserimos

Check the price of the latter at For You Tourist Services (☎ 51 149) near the municipal tourist office in Mastihari.

Getting Around

To/From the Airport An Olympic Airways bus leaves the Olympic Airways office at 5.30 am and 9.40 pm (1000 dr; free to OA ticket holders). At other times take a regular bus to or from the roundabout near the airport. Buses to and from Mastihari, Kardamena and Kefalos stop here. The airport is 26 km south-west of Kos town near the village of Antimahia.

Bus The bus station is just west of the Olympic Airways office. There are five buses a day to Tigaki (200 dr); three to Mastihari (380 dr); four to Kardamena (380 dr); four to Pyli (220 dr); two to Kefalos (550 dr) via Paradise, Agios Stefanos and Kamari beaches; and two to Zia (220 dr). There are frequent local buses to the Asclepion, Lampi and Agios Fokas from Akti Kountouriotou.

Car & Motorbike There are numerous car, motorbike and moped-rental outlets.

Bicycle On Kos you'll be tripping over bikes

to rent. The price range is between 700 dr for an old bone shaker to 3000 dr for a top-notch mountain bike.

Excursion Boat These boats line the southern side of Akti Kountouriotou in Kos town and make trips around the island.

KOS TOWN

Kos town, on the north-east coast, is the capital of the island and the main port. The old town of Kos was destroyed by an earthquake in 1933; but the new town, although modern, is picturesque and lush, with palms, pines, oleander and hibiscus sprouting everywhere. The Castle of the Knights dominates the port, and Hellenistic and Roman ruins are strewn everywhere.

Orientation

The ferry quay is north of the castle. Excursion boats dock on Akti Kountouriotou to the south-west of the castle. To get to the central square of Plateia Eleftherias walk up Vasileos Pavlou from Akti Kountouriotou. Kos' so-called Old Town is Ifestou. Its souvenir shops, jewellers and boutiques, however, denude it of any old-world charm. Southeast of the castle, the waterfront is called Akti Miaouli. It continues as Vasileos Georgiou and then G Papandreou which leads to the beaches of Psalidi, Agios Fokas and Empros Thermae.

Information

Kos' municipal tourist office (☎ 24 460, 28 724; fax 21 111) is on Vasileos Georgiou. The staff are efficient and helpful. From May to October the office is open every day from 8 am to 9 pm. Both the tourist police (☎ 22 444) and regular police (☎ 22 222) are in the large yellow building, opposite the quay. The port police (☎ 28 507) can be found on the corner of Akti Kountouriotou and Megalou Alexandrou.

The post office is on El Venizelou and the OTE is close by at Vyronos 6. Kos' postcode is 853 00 and the telephone code is 0242. Both the National Bank of Greece on Antinavarhou Ioannidi, and the Ionian Bank on El Venizelou have automatic teller machines. The Credit Bank on Akti Kountouriotou has a 24-hour automatic exchange machine.

To get to the bus station walk up Vasileos Pavlou and turn right at the Olympic Airways office. The hospital (☎ 22 300) is at Ippokratous 32. Kos Town's laundrettes are: Happy Wash at Mitropolis 20, and a nameless one at Alikarnassou 124.

Archaeological Museum

The archaeological museum (☎ 28 326), on Plateia Eleftherias, has a fine 3rd-century AD mosaic in the vestibule and many statues from various periods. The most renowned is the statue of Hippocrates. The museum is open Tuesday to Sunday from 8.30 am to 3 pm. Admission is 800 dr.

Archaeological Sites

Two factors contributed to Kos having such a wealth of archaeological sites. One was the earthquake of 1933 which revealed the ruins and the other was the presence of the Italians who carried out excavations and restoration work.

The **ancient agora** is an open, free site south of the castle. A massive 3rd-century BC stoa, with some reconstructed columns, stood on its western side. On the north side are the ruins of a **Shrine of Aphrodite**, **Temple of Hercules** and a 5th-century **Christian basilica**.

North of the agora is the lovely cobblestone Plateia Platanou where you can pay your respects to the **Hippocrates Plane Tree**. Under this tree, according to the EOT brochure, Hippocrates taught his pupils. Plane trees don't usually live for more than 200 years – so much for the power of the Hippocratic oath – though in all fairness it is certainly one of Europe's oldest. This once magnificent tree is held up with scaffolding, and looks in its death throes. Beneath it is an old sarcophagus which the Turks converted into a fountain. Opposite the tree is the well-preserved, 18th-century **Mosque of Gazi Hassan Pasha**, its ground floor loggia now converted into souvenir shops.

From Plateia Platanou, a bridge leads

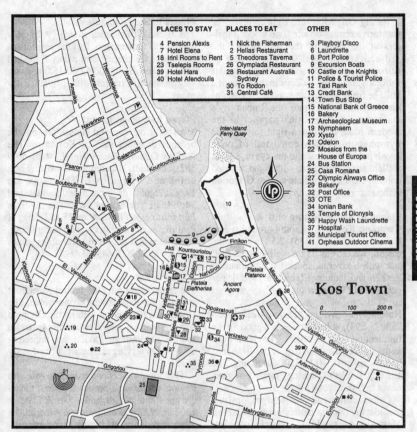

DODECANESE

PLACES TO STAY

4 Pension Alexis
7 Hotel Elena
18 Irini Rooms to Rent
23 Tselepis Rooms
39 Hotel Hara
40 Hotel Afendoulis

PLACES TO EAT

1 Nick the Fisherman
2 Hellas Restaurant
5 Theodoras Taverna
26 Olympiada Restaurant
28 Restaurant Australia
   Sydney
30 To Rodon
31 Central Café

OTHER

3 Playboy Disco
6 Laundrette
8 Port Police
9 Excursion Boats
10 Castle of the Knights
11 Police & Tourist Police
12 Taxi Rank
13 Credit Bank
14 Town Bus Stop
15 National Bank of Greece
16 Bakery
17 Archaeological Museum
19 Nymphaem
20 Xysto
21 Odeion
22 Mosaics from the
   House of Europa
24 Bus Station
25 Casa Romana
27 Olympic Airways Office
29 Bakery
32 Post Office
33 OTE
34 Ionian Bank
35 Temple of Dionysis
36 Happy Wash Laundrette
37 Hospital
38 Municipal Tourist Office
41 Orpheas Outdoor Cinema

Kos Town

across Finikon (aptly called the Avenue of Palms) to the **Castle of the Knights**. Along with the castles of Rhodes city and Bodrum this impregnable fortress was the knights' most stalwart defence against the encroaching Ottomans. The castle, which had massive outer walls and an inner keep, was built in the late 1300s. It was damaged by an earthquake in 1495 and restored by the Grand Masters d'Aubusson and d'Amboise (each a master of a 'tongue' of knights) in the 16th century. The keep was originally separated from the town by a moat, which is now Finikon. Many blocks of stone and marble from ancient buildings were used in its construction. Opening times are Monday to Saturday from 8.30 am to 3 pm. Admission is 800 dr.

The other ruins are mostly in the southern part of the town. Walk along Vasileos Pavlou to Grigoriou and cross over to the restored **Casa Romana**, an opulent 3rd-century Roman villa which was built on the site of a larger 1st-century Hellenistic house. It is open Tuesday to Sunday from 8.30 am to 2.54 pm. Admission is 500 dr. Opposite here are the scant ruins of the 3rd-century **Temple of Dionysos**.

Facing Grigoriou turn right to reach the **western excavation** site. Two wooden shelters at the back of the site protect the 3rd-century mosaics of the **House of Europa**. The best preserved mosaic depicts Europa's abduction by Zeus in the guise of a bull. In front of here an exposed section of the Dekumanus Maximus (the Roman city's main thoroughfare) runs parallel to the modern road, then turns right towards the **nymphaeum**, which consisted of once lavish public latrines, and the **xysto**, a large Hellenistic gymnasium, with some restored columns. On the opposite side of Grigoriou is the restored 3rd-century **odeion**.

Places to Stay – bottom end

Camping Kos' one camping ground is *Kos Camping* (☎ 23 910/275), 2.5 km along the eastern waterfront. It's a well-kept, shaded site with a taverna, snack bar, minimarket, kitchen and laundry. Rates are 1300 dr per person and 500 dr per tent.

Hotels The convivial *Pension Alexis* (☎ 28 798, 25 594), at Irodotou 9, is a good venue for meeting other travellers. The clean, well-kept singles/doubles/triples with shared bathroom cost 4000/6500/8000 dr. The friendly English-speaking Alexis promises never to turn anyone away.

Other commendable budget options include: the D-class *Hotel Elena* (☎ 22 986), Megalou Alexandrou 7, where doubles/triples with private bathroom are 6000/7200 dr; *Tselepis Rooms* (☎ 28 896, 23 925), El Venizelou 29, where rooms cost 6500/7200 dr with private bathroom; and *Irini Rooms to Rent* (☎ 28 298), Kolokotroni 11, where singles/doubles/triples are 4000/ 6000/7000 dr with shared bathroom.

At the other end of town the D-class *Hotel Hara* (☎ 22 500, 23 198), Halkonos 6, is a clean, well-maintained hotel, with singles/doubles/triples with private bathroom for 6500/8700/9730 dr. A little farther east, the *Hotel Afendoulis*, Evripilou 1, (☎ 25 321/ 797) has lovely, spotless and tastefully furnished rooms with private bathroom for 7000/9000 dr.

Places to Stay – middle

The B-class *Theodorou Beach* (☎ 23 363/ 364), on G Papandreou, (off the map) has a cool spacious interior, and nicely furnished rooms. Rates are 9800/14,000/16,000 dr for singles/doubles/triples with private bathroom.

Places to Stay – top end

Most of Kos' top-end hotels are on the beaches to either side of Kos town. The A-class *Dimitra Beach Hotel* (☎ 28 581/ 582), at Psalidi, is a complex consisting of a hotel and bungalows. The rates are 17,500/25,650 dr for singles/doubles and 34,900 dr for bungalows. The A-class *Platanista Hotel* (23 749 or 25 452), also at Psalidi, is an architecturally interesting, crenellated building. Singles/doubles/triples are 19,400/22,200/ 44,400 dr.

Places to Eat

The restaurants lining the central waterfront are generally expensive and poor value. The *Olympiada Restaurant*, behind the Olympic Airways office, and *Restaurant Australia Sydney*, on Vasileos Pavlou, are unpretentious places serving reasonably priced, tasty food.

The pleasant *Theodoras Taverna*, on Pindou, serves well-prepared dishes; mezedes are 400 to 600 dr, and a 'Greek Plate' is 1200 dr. *Hellas Restaurant*, on Amerikis, is more expensive but highly commendable. Mezedes dishes are 500 to 800 dr, and giouvetsi and moussaka are 1100 dr. For a fishy feast head for *Nick the Fisherman* on Averof.

The *Central Café*, Vasileos Pavlou 17, and *To Rodon*, opposite, are popular meeting places for both locals and tourists, though neither is inexpensive. There are *bakeries* on Antinavarthou Ioannidi and Vasileos Pavlou.

Entertainment

Kos has two streets of bars, Diakon and Nafklirou, that positively pulsate in high season. The discos are mostly in the north part of town. Don't miss the amazing nightly laser-light show at the *Playboy Disco* at

Kanari 2. *Orfeus* is an outdoor cinema on Vasileos Georgiou.

AROUND KOS TOWN

Asclepion Ασκληπιείον

The Asclepion (☎ 28 763), built on a pine-covered hill four km south-west of Kos town, is the island's most important ancient site. From the top there is a wonderful view of Kos town and Turkey. The Asclepion consisted of a religious sanctuary to Asclepius, the god of healing, a healing centre, and a school of medicine, where the training followed the teachings of Hippocrates.

Hippocrates was the first doctor to have a rational approach to diagnosing and treating illnesses. Up until 554 AD people came from far and wide to be treated here, as well as for medical training.

The ruins occupy three levels. The propylaia, the Roman-era public baths and the remains of guest rooms are on the first level. A wide staircase leads to the next level in the middle of which is a 4th-century BC **altar of Kyparissios Apollo**. West of this is the first **Temple of Asclepius**, which was built in the 4th century BC. To the east is the 1st-century BC **Temple to Apollo**; seven of its graceful columns have been re-erected. In the middle of the third level are the remains of the once magnificent 2nd-century BC **Temple of Asclepius**, the most important building of the Asclepion. The site is open from 8.30 am to 3 pm. Admission is 800 dr.

Getting There & Away Frequent buses go to the site, but it is pleasant to cycle or walk there via the village of Platanos, where many of the inhabitants are of Turkish origin. The village has a mosque, Turkish and Jewish cemeteries, and Taverna Arap serves good traditional Greek/Turkish fare.

AROUND THE ISLAND

The island's main road runs south-west from Kos town with turn-offs for the mountain villages, and the resorts of Tigaki and Marmari. Between Kos town and Marmari a network of quiet roads, ideal for cycling, winds through flat, agricultural land.

Antimahia (near the airport) is a major crossroads with two large roundabouts. A worthwhile detour is to the **Castle of Antimahia** along a turn-off to the left, one km before Antimahia. There's a ruined settlement within its well-preserved walls.

From Antimahia there are turn-offs to Mastihari and Kardamena. The trans-island road continues to Kefalos, the largest village in the south and gateway to the southern peninsula.

The nearest decent beach to Kos town is the crowded **Lampi beach**, four km to the north. Farther round the coast, **Tigaki**, 11 km from Kos town, has an excellent, long, pale-sand beach. **Marmari beach**, four km west of Tigaki, is slightly less crowded.

G Papandreou in Kos town leads to the three crowded beaches of **Psalidi**, three km away; **Agios Fokas**, seven km; and **Empros Thermae** 11 km from Kos town. The latter has hot mineral springs which warm the sea.

Kardamena, 27 km from Kos town, and five km south of Antimahia, is an overdeveloped, tacky resort best avoided, unless you want to take an excursion boat to Nisyros (see Getting There & Away section for Kos island).

Mastihari

Mastihari, 30 km from Kos town, retains some charm, despite recent development. It has a good sandy beach and secluded spots can be found at its extreme western end. From here there are excursion boats to Kalymnos and the small island of **Pserimos**. Buy tickets from Liza Zographou at For You Tourist Services (☎ 51 149) near the municipal tourist office.

Orientation & Information The road from Antimahia terminates at the central square at Mastihari's waterfront. There is no post office or OTE, the nearest ones are at Antimahia. There is a municipal tourist office just back from the waterfront.

Places to Stay & Eat There's loads of accommodation in Mastihari. *Fessatas Rooms to Rent* (☎ 51 261) has doubles for 5000 dr.

DODECANESE

Walk up the road by the Kali Kardia Restaurant, take the third turn to the right and the rooms are on the left. Walk inland along the main road to *Rooms to Rent Anna* (☎ 51 537), on the left, where doubles are 7000 dr. Farther up on the right, *Pension Elena* (☎ 51 282) has doubles for 6000 dr. Next door, *Rooms to Let David* (☎ 51 614) is similarly priced. The *Kali Kardia Restaurant*, on the central square, is a popular eating place.

Kamari & Kefalos

From Antimahia the main road continues south-west to the huge Kefalos bay, fringed by a five-km stretch of sand-and-pebble beaches which, although not isolated, are less crowded than most on Kos. The first is the lovely sandy Paradise beach reached down a track from the main road. The next, Agios Stefanos, is taken up by a vast Club Med complex. However, the beach, reached along a short turn-off from the main road, is still worth a visit to see the island of Agios Stefanos (named after its church), which is within swimming distance; and the ruins of two 5th-century basilicas to the left of the beach, as you face the sea. The beach continues to Kamari.

Kefalos, 43 km south of Kos town, is the sprawling village perched high above Kamari beach. It's a pleasant place with few concessions to tourism. The central square, where the bus terminates, is at the top of the two-km road from the coast.

Places to Stay Most of the accommodation options lining Kefalos bay are monopolised by tour groups, but you could try *Rooms Agios Stefanos* (☎ 71 423), opposite Agios Stefanos island, where doubles with private bathroom are 5000 dr; or *Studios Soula* (☎ 71 276/176), farther south near the Kamari fishing quay, where double studios cost 8000 dr.

Walks from Kefalos to Moni Agiou Theologou & Moni Agiou Ioanni

The southern peninsula has the island's most wild and rugged scenery. Moni Agiou Theologou is on the east coast, four km away, and

Moni Agiou Ioanni is at the end of the road, seven km south of Kefalos.

Leave Kefalos by the road signposted to both monasteries. Presently you will come to a dirt track (driveable) to the right, signposted as 'Moni Agiou Theologou'. Take this track ignoring all turn-offs, and you will reach a fork in about 30 minutes. Bear right and you will soon reach the commendable Restaurant Agiou Theologou, near a sand-and-pebble beach. Continue along the track to reach the monastery.

To get to Moni Agiou Ioanni, continue along the main road. After about 45 minutes the road curves and a dirt track ahead leads to the monastery, while the road continues to the hilltop OTE dishes.

MOUNTAIN VILLAGES

Several attractive villages are scattered on the northern slopes of the green and wooded, alpine-like Dikeos mountain range. At **Zipari**, 10 km from the capital, a road to the left (coming from Kos town) leads to **Asfendion**. From Asfendion, a turn-off to the left leads to the pristine hamlets of **Agios Georgios** and **Agios Dimitrios**. The road straight ahead leads to the village of **Zia**, which is touristy, but worth a visit for the surrounding countryside and some great sunsets. But it's not just a pretty place for it has the highly commendable Taverna Olympia, 70 metres uphill from the central square. **Lagoudi** is a small, unspoilt village to the west of Zia. From here you can continue to **Amaniou** (just before modern Pyli) where there is a left turn to the ruins of the medieval village of **Pyli** overlooked by a ruined castle.

Kalymnos Κάλυμνος

Kalymnos (KA-lim-nos, population 15,000), only 2.5 km south of Leros, is a mountainous, arid island, speckled with fertile valleys. Kalymnos is renowned as the 'sponge-fishing island', but with the demise of this industry, it has begun to exploit its

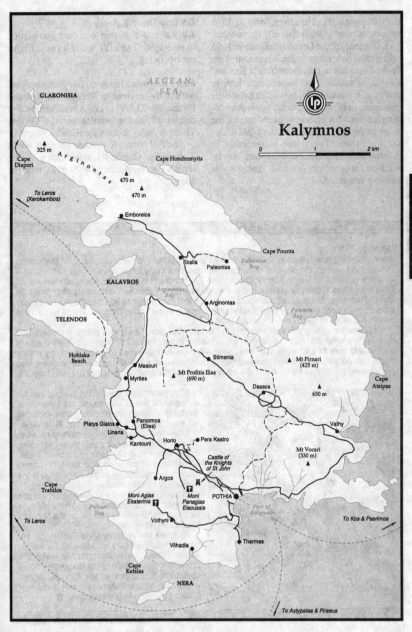

AEGEAN
SEA

Kalymnos

0   1   2 km

GLARONISIA

Cape
Diapori

325 m

Arginontas

470 m

470 m

Cape Hondromytis

To Leros
(Xerokambos)

Emboreios

Cape Pounta

Skalia

Paleonisa

*Paleonisa
Bay*

KALAVROS

*Arginontas
Bay*

Arginontas

*Patonda
Bay*

TELENDOS

Stimenia

Mt Pirnari
(425 m)

Cape
Atsipas

Hohlaka
Beach

Masouri

Mt Profitis Ilias
(690 m)

Dassos

650 m

Myrties

Vathy

Platys Gialos

Panormos
(Elies)

Linaria

Horio

Pera Kastro

Mt Vocari
(330 m)

Kantouni

*Castle of
the Knights
of St John*

Cape
Trahilos

Argos

Moni Agias
Ekaterinis

Moni
Panagias
Eleoussis

POTHIA

*Pithari
Bay*

Vothyni

*Port of
Kalymnos*

To Leros

Vlihadia

Thermes

To Kos & Pserimos

Cape
Kefalas

NERA

To Astypalea & Piraeus

tourist potential. However, out of high season its coast is still relatively uncrowded.

Kalymnos hit the Greek headlines in 1995 when local fisherman Antonis Hatziantoniou looked into his net on New Year's Eve and saw a beautiful two-metre-high bronze statue of a woman. No, he hadn't been over indulging in New Year celebrations. Archaeologists think his priceless 'catch' may be the work of the renowned 4th-century-BC sculptor Praxiteles. The statue is presently in Athens for evaluation, but a museum is to be built on Kalymnos to house it. Antonis was suitably rewarded.

Getting There & Away

Air Kalymnos' airport was near completion in mid-1995. The EOT will tell you if flights are operating.

Ferry Kalymnos has good ferry connections, with daily services to Rhodes via Kos and Piraeus (4922 dr) via Leros and Patmos. For details of their schedules see the Getting There & Away section for Rhodes island.

The F/B *Nissos Kalymnos* operates out of Kalymnos. Check its schedule with the ferry's Central Agency (☎ 29 612), near the quay.

Sponge Fishing

Sponge fishing has occupied Kalymniots since ancient times and was, until recently, their major industry. As well as the obvious one, sponges have had many other uses throughout history – everything from padding in armour to tampons. For hundreds of years the sponges were fished from the waters around Kalymnos, but as the industry grew, fishermen ventured further away. By the 19th century, divers sailed such great distances that they had to spend months at a time away from home, departing shortly after Easter and returning at the end of October. These two events were celebrated in religious and secular festivals.

Until the first diving suit was invented in the late 19th century, sponge divers were weighed down with stones and had to hold their breath under water. The early diving suits were made of rubber and canvas and were worn with a huge bronze helmet joined to an air pump by a long hose. This contraption enabled divers to stay under the water for much longer. Sponge diving was perilous work and those who didn't die young invariably became paralysed or crippled from the bends.

For many years the fishing fleets dived for sponges off the Libyan coast, but Moamar al Gadaffi proved an unwelcoming host, exacting an exorbitant tax from the divers. Nowadays, the few remaining sponge gatherers wear oxygen tanks and work much closer to home, in the north-eastern Aegean and around Crete. The demise of the sponge industry has been caused by overfishing in the Aegean and the availability of low-priced synthetic sponges.

Greeks are not ones to decline an excuse for feasting and celebration, even if the reasons for so doing have disappeared, so the festivals have been preserved.

At either the Astor Sponge Factory, or the neighbouring factory of Mike N Dovellos, behind Plateia Eleftherias, you can watch the process which transforms a disgusting black object into a nice pale-yellow sponge. It goes without saying that Kalymnos is one of the best places in Greece to buy sponges. ■

Hydrofoil From June to September, Kalymnos has daily hydrofoils to and from Leros, Patmos, Samos, Kos and Rhodes, and once a week to and from Astypalea, Lipsi, Fourni, Agathonisi, Nisyros and Tilos. The Hydrofoil Agency (☎ 29 886 or 28 502) is near the quay.

Excursion Boat There's a caïque every day at 1 pm from Myrties to Xirokambos on Leros (1500 dr, one-way). In summer there are three excursion boats a day from Pothia (two on Sunday) to Mastihari on Kos; and one daily to Pserimos (2400 dr return).

Getting Around
Bus Pothia's bus schedule at the time of writing was as follows: to Masouri (150 dr) via Myrties, every two hours between 7 am and 9 pm; to Emboreios (300 dr) on Monday, Wednesday and Friday at 8 am and 4 pm; to Vathy (200 dr) from Monday to Saturday at 6.30 am, 1.30 and 5 pm, and on Sunday at 7.30 am, 1.30 and 5 pm.

Taxi Shared taxis are an unusual feature of Kalymnos that cost around twice as much as buses. A tariff is displayed at the taxi rank on Plateia Kyprou. These taxis can also be flagged down *en route*.

Motorbike There are several motorbike-hire outlets along Pothia's waterfront.

Excursion Boat There are daily excursion boats to Emboreios (1500 dr). Every Saturday an excursion boat from Myrties does a trip around the island and to the island of Pserimos (4000 dr).

POTHIA Πόθια
Pothia, the port and capital of Kalymnos, is where the majority of the island's inhabitants live. Although it's considerably bigger and noisier than most island capitals, it's not without charm. However, a word of warning, Pothia is short in the pavement department and has more than its fair share of kamikaze motorcyclists – keep your wits about you.

Orientation
Pothia's ferry quay is at the southern side of the bay. To reach the town centre turn right at the end of the quay. Follow the waterfront around and you will come to the Cathedral of Agios Hristos. The main thoroughfare of Venizelou runs from here to Plateia Kyprou, the town's central square. Another busy street, Patriarhou Maximimou, also runs from the waterfront to this square. The settlement of Horio, three km inland, is the island's former capital.

Information
A new EOT (☎ 29 310) office is due to open on the quay in 1995. The post office and OTE are near one another north of Plateia Kyprou. Kalymnos' postcode is 852 00 and the telephone code is 0243. The National Bank of Greece is at the bottom of Patriarhou Maximimou, and the Ionian Bank is farther along the waterfront. Both have automatic teller machines.

The police (☎ 22 100) are north of Plateia Kyprou and the port police (☎ 29 304) are at the beginning of the quay. The bus station is just south of the cathedral.

Archaeological Museum
The archaeological museum (☎ 23 113), near Plateia Kyprou, is housed in a neoclassical mansion which once belonged to a wealthy sponge merchant, Mr Vouvalis. In one room there are some Neolithic and Bronze Age objects. Other rooms are reconstructed as they were when the Vouvalis family lived there. The museum is open Tuesday to Sunday from 10 am to 2 pm. Admission is free.

Places to Stay
Two pleasant, budget choices are the *Pension Greek House* (☎ 29 559 or 23 752), where cosy wood-panelled singles/doubles/triples with private bathroom cost 4000/6000/7000 dr, and *Katerina Rooms* (☎ 22 186), with rates of 3000/4000/5500 dr for rooms with shared bathroom. From the port area, go up Patriarhou Maximimou and take the first turning left. Where the road ends at

DODECANESE

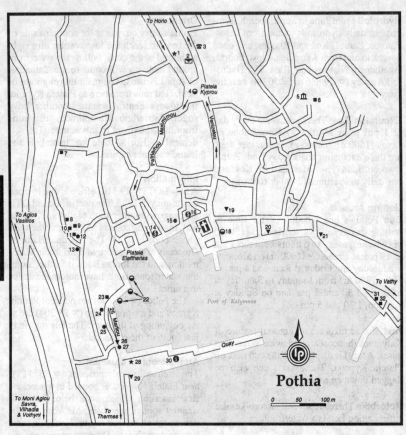

Pothia

0   50   100 m

Port of Kalymnos

To Horio

To Agios Vasilios

To Vathy

To Moni Agiou Savra, Vlihadia & Vothyni

To Thermes

Plateia Kyprou

Plateia Eleftherias

Maximilmou

Venizelou

Patriarhou

Quay

PLACES TO STAY

6   Hotel Themelina
7   Pension Stemi
8   Hotel Panorama
9   Pension Greek House
10 Katerina Rooms
11 Norma Delapoutou
23 Archontiko Hotel
31 Delphini Rooms
32 Pension Panorama

PLACES TO EAT

19 Xefteries Taverna
20 O Michalaras Special
     Cakes Café
21 Uncle Petros' Taverna
26 Flaxos Taverna
29 Yacht Club Restaurant

OTHER

1   Police Station
2   Post Office
3   OTE
4   Taxi Rank
5   Archaeological Museum
12 Astor Sponge Factory
13 Mike N Dovellos
14 National Bank of
     Greece
15 Marinos Supermarket
16 Ionian Bank
17 Cathedral of Agios
     Christos
18 Bus Station
22 Excursion Boats
24 Nissos Kalymnos
     Central Agency
25 Hydrofoil Agency
27 C & A Ferry Office
28 Port Police
30 EOT

a T-junction, turn right and then left. At the Astor Sponge Factory turn right and you'll see the Pension Greek House on the left. From its entrance continue ahead to Katerina Rooms.

Norma Delapoutou (☎ 24 054 or 48 145) rents well-kept rooms in her house adjoining the Astor Sponge Factory. Doubles with shared bathroom, kitchen and verandah are 5000 dr.

The *Pension Stemi* (☎ 28 361) has clean, modern rooms with balconies. The rate for doubles/triples with shared bathroom is 5000/6000 dr. Turn right at the aforementioned T-junction and continue straight ahead to a large square (used as a car park) on the left. Walk across here, ascend the steps, and the pension is at the top on the left.

Two pleasant neighbouring options, 400 metres along the road to Vathy, are *Delphini Rooms* (☎ 29 087), where doubles are 4000 dr, and the *Pension Panorama* (☎ 29 249), where singles/doubles/triples are 3000/5000/7000 dr.

Back in town the well-appointed C-class *Hotel Panorama* (☎ 23 138), next to Katerina Rooms, has pretty rooms and balconies with great views. Prices are 6000/9000 dr for singles/doubles with private bathroom.

The *Hotel Themelina* (☎ 22 682), opposite the archaeological museum, is a 19th-century mansion with a lush garden and a swimming pool. The spacious, traditionally furnished singles/doubles/triples cost 7000/10,000/12,000 dr with private bathroom.

The *Archontiko Hotel* (☎ 24 149/051), at the top of the quay, is a new hotel in a renovated, turn-of-the-century mansion. The immaculate rooms go for a reasonable 6000/9000/10,700 dr.

Places to Eat

The *Xefteries Taverna*, just off Venizelou, is almost a century old and serves delicious, inexpensive food; stifado is 1200 dr. Of the fish tavernas on the western waterfront, *Uncle Petros' Taverna* is the one favoured by locals. A meal and beverage will cost about

2000 dr. The well-worn, cavernous *Yacht Club Restaurant*, behind the port police, serves inexpensive food with tzatziki and taramosalata for 350 dr, Greek salad for 500 dr and calamari for 800 dr. *Flaxos Taverna*, near the quay, is a good place for a quick meal if you're waiting for a ferry. It has tasty grilled food and stewed vegetables.

O Michalaras Special Cakes Café serves galaktoboureko, a speciality of Kalymnos. A generous slice of this gooey confection is 350 dr. The *Marinos Supermarket* is well stocked.

AROUND POTHIA
Castle of the Knights of St John & Pera Kastro

The ruined Castle of the Knights of St John (or Castle Hrysoherias) looms to the left of the Pothia-Horio road. Walking, the following route avoids Pothia's heavy traffic. Follow the directions to Pension Stemi (see Places to Stay). At the pension turn right. Soon the road turns right, then left and then left again. Then it ascends. Beyond the cream, red-domed church on the left, follow the road as it turns right, then take the first turning left, and you will see three windmills ahead. Continue ahead then take the road signposted 'Vothyni and Vlihadia'. Bear right at the fork to reach the steps up to the castle.

You can take a short cut to the main Pothia-Horio road, from where you can walk to Pera Kastro. Descend the steps at the opposite side of the castle from where you entered. Clamber down the hillside, with the windmills on your right, and descend the steps to the main road. Turn left and in about 30 minutes you will come to a roundabout in Horio. Turn right here, at the fork bear left, then immediately bear right at three forks, and take the first turning left. Continue straight ahead passing a kafeneio on the left. At the top of the hill a sign points to the kastro. Follow this for 15 metres then take the steps on the left. It's a strenuous climb up to the kastro, but the splendid views make it worthwhile. Pera Kastro was a 'pirate-proof' village inhabited until the 18th century.

Within the crumbling walls are the ruins of stone houses and six tiny well-kept white churches.

Moni Agiou Savva, Vlihadia & Vothyni
Moni Agiou Savva stands above Pothia, on the left as you face inland. A large cement cross stands nearby. Climb up the stepped streets on the left side of the harbour, then take the road signposted 'Vothyni and Vlihadia'. After 700 metres, a turn-off to the right leads to the monastery. You can enter the monastery but a strict dress code is enforced: long trousers for men, and skirts (knee length or below) and blouses with sleeves for women.

The main road continues to the inland village of Vothyni and the sleepy coastal hamlet of Vlihadia, which has two nice, tree-shaded beaches.

Panormos
A tree-lined road continues from Horio to Panormos (also called Elies), a pretty village five km from Pothia. Its pre-war name of Elies (olives), derived from its abundant olive groves which were destroyed in WW II. An enterprising post-war mayor planted abundant trees and flowers to create beautiful panoramas wherever one looked – hence its present name. Kantouni, Linaria and Platys Gialos beaches are all within walking distance.

Places to Stay & Eat The *Pension Grazella* (☎ 47 314/346) has comfortable double rooms for 5000 dr, double studios for 7000 dr and five-person apartments for 10,000 dr. Popi attends the lovely garden while her husband the dynamic, English-speaking Manalos enlightens guests on the delights of Kalymnos. The pension is signposted from the main road. The *Marinos Restaurant*, on the main road, is the best eating place hereabouts.

VATHY Βαθύς
Vathy, eight km north-east of Pothia, is one of the most beautiful and peaceful parts of the island. Vathy means 'deep' in Greek and refers to the slender fjord which cuts through high cliffs into a fertile valley, where narrow roads wind between citrus orchards. There is no beach at Vathy's harbour, called Rena, but excursion boats take tourists to quiet coves nearby.

Places to Stay & Eat
Vathy has two places to stay, both at Rena. To the left as you face the sea, the C-class *Hotel Galini* (☎ 31 241), has immaculate doubles/triples are 6500/7500 dr with private bathroom and balcony.

The *Pension Manolis* (☎ 85 200, 22 641), above the right side of the harbour, has beautiful singles/doubles/triples for 5000/6000/7200 dr with private bathroom. There is a communal kitchen and terraces surrounded by a garden full of fruit trees and flowers. The English-speaking Menelaos is a tour guide and very knowledgeable about the area.

The *Harbour Taverna* serves excellent seafood.

THE WEST COAST
Myrties
The road continues to the west coast with stunning views of Telendos islet as it winds down into package-tourist territory beginning at Myrties. From Myrties there is a daily caïque to Xirokambos on Leros (see the Getting There & Away section for Kalymnos section).

Places to Stay & Eat *Pension Mikes* (☎ 47 677/318), on the final bend before Myrties, has well-kept doubles/triples for 6000/7200 dr. The *Delphini Hotel* (☎ 47 514), on the right beyond the jetty, has singles/doubles/triples with private bathroom for 4500/7000/8400 dr. The restaurant by the quay has decent food.

TELENDOS ISLET Νήσος Τέλενδος
The lovely, tranquil and traffic-free islet of Telendos (TEL-en-dos), with a little quayside hamlet, was part of Kalymnos until they were separated by an earthquake in 554 AD.

If you turn right from the quay you will

pass the ruins of a basilica. Farther on, beyond On the Rocks Café, there are several pebble-and-sand beaches. To reach Hohlaka beach, turn left from the quay, and then right at Zorba's Restaurant.

Places to Stay & Eat
Telendos has several domatia. All have pleasant clean rooms with private bathroom. Opposite the quay, *Pension & Restaurant Uncle George* (☎ 47 502, 23 855) has singles/doubles for 3000/4000 dr. Next door at *Pension Rita* (☎ 47 914) rates are 4000/5000 dr. Both *Nicky Rooms* (☎ 47 584), to the left of the quay and *Galanommatis Fotini Rooms & Restaurant* (☎ 47 401), to the right have doubles for 4000 dr.

The new *Port Potha Hotel* (☎ 47 321; fax 48 108), beyond On the Rock's Café, has rates of 5000/6000/8000 dr. The *Restaurant Uncle George* serves good seafood.

Entertainment
At the trendy *On the Rocks Café* you can hear both Greek and international music. If you can't drag yourself away from the fun to catch the last caïque back to Myrties, then George, the friendly Greek-Australian owner, will take you back in his boat free of charge.

Getting There & Away
Frequent caïques leave Myrties for Telendos (300 dr return) between 8 am and 11 pm.

FROM MYRTIES TO EMBOREIOS
Myrties blends almost imperceptibly with **Masouri**, a nondescript package-tourist resort. The road continues through spectacular scenery to the fishing villages of **Arginontas** and **Skalia**. Both have beaches, tavernas and rooms to rent.

Walk from Skalia to Paleonisa
This one-hour walk crosses the island to the remote east coast hamlet of Paleonisa where several families live on amidst the ruins. There are tremendous sea and mountain vistas along the way. From Skalia, walk north along the coast road, and after 500

metres you will come to a white church on the left. Take the dirt road opposite which winds steeply uphill. At the top take the narrow path straight ahead which leads to Paleonisa's ruined houses and abandoned terraces.

EMBOREIOS Εμπορειός
The west coast road continues to Emboreios, where there's a very pleasant tree-shaded pebble beach, which only gets crowded in July and August. One of the nicest places to stay is *Harry's Apartments* (☎ 47 434/922) where modern double/triple apartments cost 9000/10,700 dr. Harry is a dedicated chef and his adjoining *Paradise Restaurant* has a good reputation around the island.

Leros Λέρος

An infamous psychiatric institution, shabby Mussolini-inspired public buildings, a heavy military presence and, during the junta years, a prison for political dissidents, have saddled Leros (LE-ros, population 7500) with an almighty image problem. However, off-setting these flaws is the island's gentle, hilly countryside dotted with small holdings and huge, impressive almost-landlocked bays, which look more like lakes than open sea.

Lakki is the main port of Leros, but smaller ferries and some excursion boats use Agia Marina port, and the caïque from Myrties on Kalymnos docks at Xirokambos. Platanos is the capital of Leros. Lakki is one of the best natural harbours in the Aegean; and, during their occupation of the Dodecanese, the Italians chose it as their principal naval base in the eastern Mediterranean.

Getting There & Away
Air There is at least one flight a day to Athens (20,000 dr) in summer, and six a week in winter. The Olympic Airways office (☎ 22 844, 24 144) is in Platanos, just before the turn-off for Panteli. The airport is in the north of the island at Partheni.

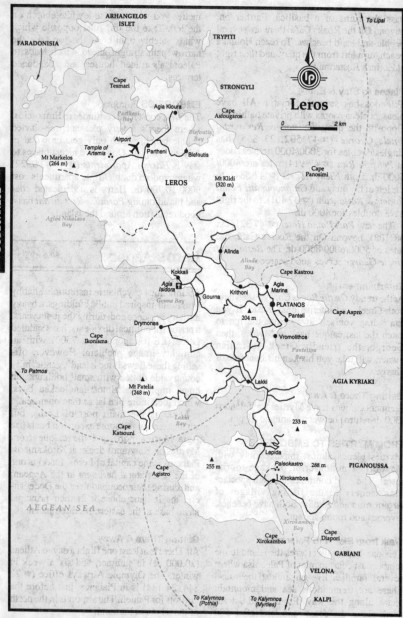

ARHANGELOS
ISLET

TRYPITI

FARADONISIA

Cape
Tesmari

STRONGYLI

Cape
Asfougaros

To Lipsi

Leros

0   1   2 km

Parthéni
Bay

Agia Kloura

Airport

Temple of
Artemis

Mt Markelos
(264 m)

Blefoutis
Bay

Partheni   Blefoutis

LEROS

Mt Klidi
(320 m)

Cape
Panosimi

Agios Nikolaos
Bay

Alinda

Alinda
Bay

Cape Kastrou

To Patmos

Kokkali

Agia
Isidora

Gourna
Bay

Gourna

Krithoni

Agia
Marina

PLATANOS

Panteli

Cape Aspro

Drymonas

Cape
Ikonisma

204 m

Vromolithos

Pantéliou
Bay

Mt Patelia
(248 m)

Lakki
Bay

Lakki

AGIA KYRIAKI

Cape
Katsouni

233 m

255 m

Cape
Agistro

Lepida

Paleokastro

Xirokambos

288 m

PIGANOUSSA

AEGEAN SEA

Xirokambos
Bay

Cape
Xirokambos

Cape
Diapori

GABIANI

To Kalymnos
(Pothia)

To Kalymnos
(Myrties)

VELONA

KALPI

DODECANESE

Ferry Leros has good ferry connections, with daily services to and from Rhodes via Kalymnos and Kos, and to and from Pireaus (4919 dr) via Patmos. For details of their schedules see the Getting There & Away section for Rhodes island. It is also the port of call for the F/B *Nissos Kalymnos*.

Tickets can be bought at either Kastis or DRM travel agencies. The telephone number of the port police in Lakki is ☎ 22 224.

Hydrofoil In summer there are hydrofoils every day to Patmos (45 minutes, 2350 dr), Lipsi (2350 dr), Samos (4300 dr), Kos (one hour, 4300 dr) and Rhodes (3¼ hours, 10,030 dr); and one a week to Agathonisi (4100 dr) via Patmos and Fourni (3800 dr). Tickets can be bought from DRM Travel & Tourism. Hydrofoils leave from Agia Marina, but are subject to cancellations.

Excursion Boat The caïque leaves Xirokambos every day at 7.30 am for Myrties on Kalymnos (1500 dr, one-way). In summer the Lipsi-based *Anna Express* (3000 dr, return) and *Captain Makis* (2500 dr, return) make daily trips between Agia Marina and Lipsi.

Getting Around
Bus The hub for Leros' buses is Platanos. There are four buses a day to Partheni via Alinda and six buses to Xirokambos via Lakki. Check the current schedule with a travel agent.

Car, Motorbike & Bicycle You can rent any one of these from John Koumoulis (☎ 24 646), on the waterfront at Alinda, and in Lakki (☎ 22 330).

LAKKI Λακκί
If you arrive on one of the large inter-island ferries, you'll disembark at Lakki. The grandiose buildings and wide tree-lined boulevards dotted around the Dodecanese reach their apogee here, for Lakki was built as a Fascist showpiece during the Italian occupation.

Places to Stay & Eat
If you must stay here the D-class *Miramare Hotel* (☎ 22 469), signposted from the waterfront, has single/double/triple rooms for 5000/5500/6600 dr with private bathroom. *Taverna O Sotos*, next to the well-signposted post office, serves hearty Greek fare.

PLATANOS Πλάτανος
Platanos, the capital of Leros, is three km north of Lakki. It's a picturesque little place which spills over a narrow hill pouring down to the port of Agia Marina to the north, with Panteli to the south, both within walking distance. On the east side of Platanos, houses are stacked up a hillside topped by a massive castle. To reach the castle you can either climb up 370 steps, or walk or drive two km along an asphalt road. A few grand neoclassical mansions have recently been restored on Xarami.

Orientation & Information
In Platanos the focus of activity is the lively central square of Plateia N Poussou. Xarami links this square with Agia Marina. The post office and OTE share premises on the right side of Xarami. Leros' postcode is 854 00 and the telephone code is 0247. The National Bank of Greece is on the central square. It has no automatic teller machine. The police station (☎ 22 222) is in Agia Marina; turn left from Xarami and it's on the right. The bus station and taxi rank are both on the Lakki-Platanos road, just before the central square.

Leros has no EOT or tourist police. Kastis Travel & Tourist Agency (☎ 22 140; fax 23 500) and DRM Travel & Tourism (☎ 23 502; fax 24 303), both near the quay in Agia Marina, are helpful.

Organised Tours
Laskarina Tours, at the Elefteria Hotel, and DRM Travel & Tourism organise island tours (1000-2500 dr).

Places to Stay
The *Pension Platanos* (☎ 22 608), on the central square, has well-kept and comfortable singles/doubles/triples with private

bathroom for 4000/6000/9000 dr. The C-class *Eleftheria Hotel* (☎ 23 550/145), near the taxi rank, has lovely rooms for 4700/5600/7000 dr with private bathroom.

Places to Eat
The quaint wood-beamed *To Kapeleio Ouzeri*, at the top of Xarami, is the 'in' place amongst trendy young locals. Its tasty mezes dishes include stuffed vine leaves, fried cheese, and octopus, which you can wash down with good barrel wine. Farther down on the right, the *Garbo Restaurant* serves well-prepared, international cuisine. The friendly owners, Frank and Kath, are English. An English breakfast is 1200 dr, vegetable curry is 1000 dr, liver and bacon casserole is 1200 dr, and chocolate gâteau with cream is 450 dr.

There's a bakery on the Lakki-Platinos road before the bus stop.

AROUND PLATANOS
The port of **Agia Marina** is a bit run-down, but a pleasant enough place with a more authentic ambience than the resort of Alinda to the north. Walking in the other direction from Platanos, you'll arrive at **Panteli**, a little fishing village-cum-resort with a sand-and-shingle beach.

Just outside of Platanos, beyond the turn-off for Panteli, a road winds steeply down to **Vromolithos** where there's a good shingle beach, superior to Pendali's.

Places to Stay
Kapiniris Miltos Rooms (☎ 22 750), just beyond the police station in Agia Marina, has spacious doubles/triples for 5000/6000 dr.

In Panteli, the waterfront *Pension Roza* (☎ 22 798) has doubles/triples for 3500/5500 dr with shared bathroom and doubles with private bathroom for 4000 dr. A bit farther along *Rooms to Rent Kavos* (☎ 23 247, 25 020) has rates of 6000/6500 dr and studios for 8000 dr. The *Pension Happiness* (☎ 23 498), on the left of the road down from Platanos, has modern, sunny rooms with private bathroom for 7000/8500 dr. There are *domatia* in Vromolithos.

Places to Eat
At Agia Marina, *Tavernaki The Meeting*, opposite the Agricultural Bank, is an authentic little place serving good, inexpensive food. Main dishes cost between 700 and 1000 dr, ouzo with mezes is 300 dr and barrel retsina is 300 dr.

Restaurant Drossia, below the Pension Roza, serves tasty fare like sardines for 800 dr and moussaka for 900 dr. *Maria's Taverna* farther along is also good. There are two tavernas on the beach at Vromolithos.

Entertainment
For a wild night of dancing (strictly Greek) on the bar top, get down to Agia Marina's *Anne's Pub*. Other lively places close by are the *Manolis Bar*, *La Playa Bar* and *Maldoro's Bar*.

Leros' two discos are *Diana Disco* on the Platinos-Pandeli road and *Cosmopolitan* in Alinda.

KRITHONI & ALINDA
Krithoni and Alinda are contiguous resorts on the wide Alinda bay, three km north-west of Agia Marina. On Krithoni's waterfront there is a poignant, well-kept **war cemetery**. After the Italian surrender in WW II, Leros saw fierce fighting between German and British forces. The cemetery contains the graves of 179 British, two Canadian and two South African soldiers.

Alinda, the island's biggest resort, has a long crescent of tree-shaded, sand-and-gravel beach, and fine views over to Agia Marina and Platanos. If you walk beyond the development you'll find some quiet coves. You can hire jet skis from John Koumoulis. (☎ 24 646), on the waterfront (2000 dr for 10 minutes).

Places to Stay
The following recommendations all have private bathrooms: Krithoni's *Hotel Costantinos* (☎ 22 337/904), on the right coming from Agia Marina, has comfortable doubles for 6000 dr. A bit farther along, the *Hotel Athena* (☎ 22 445) has agreeable singles/doubles/triples for 5500/6500/7200 dr. Just

beyond the war cemetery, a road veers left to *Hotel Gianna* (☎ 23 153, 24 135) which has nicely furnished rooms for 3000/5000/6200 dr. The sparkling, pine-furnished *Studios & Apartments Diamantis* (☎ 22 378, 23 213), behind the cemetery, has rates of 5000/6000/7000 dr.

Papafotis Pension (☎ 22 247), in a cul-de-sac at the northern end of Alinda, has light, airy rooms for 3000/5000/7000 dr.

Places to Eat

Grilled food is the speciality of *To Fanari*, a restaurant on the left 10 minutes' walk along the signposted Alinda-Partheni road. An excellent meal of grilled chicken, chips, Greek salad and retsina costs 2100 dr. Alinda's waterfront *Finikas Taverna* has an extensive menu of well-prepared Greek specialities; mezedes are 500 to 800 dr and souvlaki is 1100 dr. The *Alinda Restaurant*, at the front of the Alinda Hotel, is also highly recommended.

GOURNA

The wide bay of Gourna, on the west coast, has a similar beach to Alinda, but it is less developed. To get there, take the Alinda-Partheni road and then the first turn-off left. At the northern side of the bay, the chapel of **Agia Isidora** is on an islet reached by a causeway – it's a wonderfully tranquil spot, reached along the third turn-off left from the Alinda-Partheni road.

NORTHERN LEROS

Partheni is a scattered settlement north of the airport. Despite having a large army camp, it's an attractive area of hills, olive groves, fields of bee hives and two large bays.

Artemis, the goddess of the hunt, was worshipped on Leros in ancient times. Just before the airport there's a signposted turn to the left that leads to the **Temple of Artemis**. A dirt track (unsignposted) turns right 300 metres along. Where the track peters out, clamber up to the left. You will see the little derelict Chapel of Agia Irini where locals still tend the altar. There's little in the way of

ancient ruins but it's a strangely evocative, slightly eerie place.

Farther along the main road there is a turn to the right to **Blefoutis bay** which has a shaded, sand-and-pebble beach and the popular *Taverna Artemi*. Beyond this turn-off, the main road skirts around **Partheni bay** and its poor beach. However, if you continue straight ahead and turn right at the T-junction, go through a gate to pass the chapel of Agia Kioura, then go through another gate and bear right, you will come to a secluded pebbled cove.

XIROKAMBOS Ξερόκαμπος

Xirokambos bay, in the south of the island, is a low-key resort with a gravel-and-sand beach and some good spots for snorkelling. Just before the camping ground, on the opposite side, a signposted path leads up to the ruined fortress of **Paleokastro**.

Places to Stay & Eat

Leros' one camping ground is Xirokambos' *Camping Leros* (☎ 23 372), on the right coming from Lakki. It's pleasant and shaded, with a restaurant and bar. The owner is a qualified diving instructor who runs seven-day diving courses which cost 80,000 dr (inclusive).

Farther along on the left is *Michael Yianoukas Rooms* (☎ 23 148), which has doubles with shared bathroom for 3500 dr and double/triple apartments for 5000/7500 dr. For eating, there is a taverna opposite the camping ground, a nameless psistaria farther along the road and a taverna on the beach.

Patmos Πάτμος

Patmos (PAT-mos, population 1500) is a place of pilgrimage for both Orthodox and Western Christians, for it was here that St John wrote his divinely inspired revelation (the Apocalypse). Once a favourite venue for the pious and hippies wishing to tune into its spiritual vibes, Patmos is now just as popular with sun and sea worshippers. The only

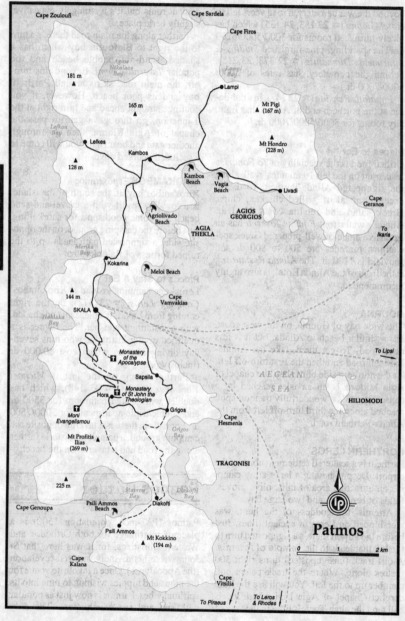

Cape Zouloufi
Cape Sardela
Cape Firos

Agios
Nikolaos
Bay

181 m

165 m

Lampi
Bay

Lampi

Mt Pigi
(167 m)

Lefkon
Bay

Lefkes

128 m

Kambos

Mt Hondro
(228 m)

Kambos Beach

Vagia
Beach

Livadi

Cape
Geranos

Agriolivado
Beach

AGIOS
GEORGIOS

AGIA
THEKLA

To
Ikaria

Merika
Bay

Kokarina

Meloi Beach

144 m

Cape
Vamvakias

Hohlaka
Bay

SKALA

Monastery
of the
Apocalypse

To Lipsi

Sapsila

Monastery
of St John the
Theologian

AEGEAN
SEA

Hora

Grigos

HILIOMODI

Moni
Evangelismou

Cape
Hesmenis

Grigos
Bay

Mt Profitis
Ilias
(269 m)

225 m

TRAGONISI

Stavros
Bay

Diakofti
Bay

Cape Genoupa

Psili Ammos
Beach

Diakofti

Psili Ammos

Mt Kokkino
(194 m)

Cape
Kalana

Cape
Vitsilia

Patmos

0   1   2 km

To Piraeus

To Leros
& Rhodes

DODECANESE

remaining vestiges of the island's exclusiveness are the umpteen signs (often ignored) that forbid topless and nude bathing. If it's contemplation or tranquillity you're after, then stay on the ferry until it gets to Lipsi or Agathonisi, or take the caïque to Arki.

History
In AD 95, St John the Divine was banished to Patmos from Ephesus by the pagan Roman emperor Dominian. Whilst residing in a cave on the island, St John wrote the *Book of Revelations*. In 1088 the Blessed Hristodoulos, an abbot who came from Asia Minor to Patmos, obtained permission from the Byzantine emperor Alexis I Comnenus to build a monastery to commemorate St John. Pirate raids necessitated sturdy fortifications, and so the monastery looks like a mighty castle.

Under the Duke of Naxos, Patmos became a semiautonomous monastic state, and achieved such wealth and influence that it was able to stand indomitable against Turkish oppression. In the early 18th century, a school of theology and philosophy school was founded by Makarios Kalogheras and it flourished until the 19th century. Gradually the island's wealth polarised into secular and monastic entities. The secular wealth was acquired through shipbuilding, an industry which diminished with the arrival of the steam ship.

Getting There & Away
Ferry Patmos has good ferry connections, with daily services to and from Rhodes via Leros, Kalymnos, and Kos, and to and from Piraeus (4900 dr). It is also the port of call for the F/B *Nissos Kalymnos*.

Hydrofoil See the Getting There & Away sections for Rhodes, Kalymnos, Leros and Kos for information about hydrofoils running to Patmos.

Excursion Boat In summer the Lipsi-based *Anna Express* (3000 dr return) and *Captain Makis* (2500 dr) sail to Patmos every day (see also the Getting There & Away section for Lipsi island). Daily Patmos-based excursion boats go to Marathi and Samos, and the caïque *Delfini* does frequent trips to Arki. if you can't see the *Delfini* at Skala's quay telephone ☎ 31 995/371 for information.

Getting Around
Bus From Skala there are seven buses a day to Hora (130 dr), five to Grigos (200 dr) and four to Kambos (170 dr). There is no bus service to Lampi.

Taxi From Skala's taxi rank tariffs are: Meloi 700 dr; Lampi 1500 dr; Grigos 1200 dr; and Hora 1000 dr.

Motorbike Theo & Giorgio Motorbikes for Rent (☎ 32 997), opposite the excursion boats, is a reliable outlet. Motorbikes are 2000 to 3500 dr a day and 18-speed mountain bikes are 1000 dr.

Excursion Boat These go to all the island's beaches from Skala, leaving about 11 am and returning about 6 pm.

SKALA Σκάλα
All boats dock at the island's port and capital of Skala. The town sprawls around a large curving bay. It's quite a glitzy place, pandering to the passengers of the many visiting cruise ships. Although it's very busy and not especially attractive, its a convenient place to stay as it's the public-transport hub and has all the tourist facilities and most of the accommodation.

Orientation
From the quay, facing inland, turn right to reach the main stretch of waterfront where excursion boats and yachts dock. The right side of the large white Italianate building opposite the quay overlooks the central square. To reach the road to Hora turn left at the quay and right at Grigori's Taverna.

Information
Patmos' municipal tourist office (☎ 31 666/235/058), post office and police station are all in the large white Italianate building.

The tourist office entrance is at the back of the building, the post office is at the right side, and the police are at the front. Patmos' port police (☎ 31 231) are behind the large quay's cafeteria/passenger-transit building. The bus terminal is at the large quay and the taxi rank (☎ 31 225) is beside the post office.

The National Bank of Greece is on the central square. Its automatic teller machine is in front of the post office. Inland from the central square is another smaller square; the OTE is on the left side of the road which proceeds inland from here. Patmos' postcode is 855 00 and the telephone code is 0247. The hospital (☎ 31 211) is two km along the road to Hora.

Places to Stay – bottom end

In Skala, enthusiastic domatia owners don't wait for passengers to disembark – they rush onto the ferry and almost knock over prospective customers.

If you are not scooped up by a domatia owner, there are several budget places along Hora road. *Pension Sofia's* (☎ 31 876), 250 metres up on the left, has doubles/triples with private bathroom and balcony for 4000/6000 dr. Farther up, *Pension Maria Paskeledi* (☎ 32 152) has singles/doubles/triples with shared bathroom for 3500/6000/8000 dr; triples with private bathroom are 10,000 dr.

The D-class *Hotel Rex* (☎ 31 242), on a narrow street opposite the cafeteria/passenger-transit building, has rooms for 4865/5947/7028 dr with private bathroom.

In the opposite direction, *Pension Sydney* (☎ 31 689) has singles/doubles/triples for 4000/7000/10,000 dr with private bathroom. The nearby *Pension Avgerinos* (☎ 32 118), run by the same family, has doubles with superb views and private bathroom for 7000 dr. For both, turn right from the quay and walk along the waterfront. Turn left past the cemetery; the Sydney is on the left and the Avgerinos is opposite.

Katina Michenni Rooms (☎ 31 327) has spotless doubles/triples for 7000/8500 dr. Ornaments and rugs add a homely touch, and there are excellent views of Skala and Hora from the communal veranda. Take the left

fork 30 metres beyond the turn-off for Pension Sydney, turn right opposite the circular traffic mirror, and the rooms are in the last house on the right.

Farther along the coast road, the C-class *Hotel Hellinos* (☎ 31 275) has immaculate doubles/triples for 7000/8500 dr with private bathroom. Co-owned with the hotel are some attractive domatia for 6000/7000 dr with shared bathroom.

Yvonne Studios (☎ 32 466, 33 066) are beautifully furnished apartments overlooking Hohlaka bay. Doubles/triples are 8000/9500 dr. Enquire about them at Yvonne's Tourist Shop, near O Pantelis Taverna.

Places to Stay – middle

The C-class *Hotel Effie* (☎ 31 298) has singles/doubles/triples for 8000/11,600/14,500 dr. Turn right at the quay, and left after the Hotel Chris and it's 120 metres up on the right.

The C-class *Hotel Delfina* (☎ 32 060; fax 32 061), to the left of the quay, has immaculate rooms for 8000/11,000/12,300 dr. Next door, the *Captain's House* (☎ 31 793) has rates of 7000/14,000/15,000 dr. Around the corner, the *Hotel Byzance* (☎ 31 052/663) has rates of 8100/12,300/15,300 dr. Triple apartments are 17,000 dr and four-person apartments are 20,400 dr.

Skala's best hotel is the B-class *Hotel Skala* (☎ 31 343/344), on the waterfront. Rates are 12,500/18,000/22,350 dr, including breakfast. The hotel has a lovely garden and a swimming pool (for Patmos' most luxurious hotel see the Kambos section).

Places to Eat – inexpensive

Skala's two most popular eateries are *Taverna Grigori's*, on the corner of the Hora road, and *O Pantelis Taverna*, behind the waterfront Café Bar Arion. *Taverna Pyrofani*, on the waterfront just beyond Hotel Skala, is a good fish restaurant.

Polar Galateria, just inland from the small square, has sweet and savoury pies and pastries for 350 to 500 dr and ice cream, in many flavours, for 700 dr. There are two excellent *bakeries* on the small square; both sell cakes, cookies and pies, as well as bread. Two well-signposted *fruit and vegetable markets* are close by.

Places to Eat – moderate

The Old Harbour is Skala's best restaurant. It's on a 1st-floor terrace just past the conspicuous Chris Hotel. A three-course meal with wine will set you back about 5000 dr.

Entertainment

The waterfront *Café Bar Arion* is a popular haunt of trendy, young locals. The *Konsolatos Dancing Bar*, to the left of the quay is the island's wildest hot spot, where you can dance until 5 am. Entrance is 1000 dr (first drink free).

MONASTERIES & HORA

The immense Monastery of St John the Theologian, with its buttressed grey walls, crowns the island of Patmos. A four-km asphalt road leads in from Skala to the monastery, but many people prefer to walk up the Byzantine path. To do this, walk up the Skala-Hora road and take the steps to the right at the far side of the football field. The path begins opposite the top of these steps.

A little way along, a dirt path to the left leads through pine trees to the **Monastery of the Apocalypse**, built around the cave where St John received his divine revelation. In the cave you can see the rock which the saint used as a pillow, and the triple fissure in the roof, from which the voice of God issued, and which supposedly symbolises the Holy Trinity. Opening times are 8.30 am to 1.30 pm on Monday, Wednesday and Thursday; 8 am to 1pm and 4 to 6 pm on Tuesday; 8.30 am to 1.50 pm on Friday; 8 am to 1pm and 3.30 to 5 pm on Saturday, and 10 am to noon and 4 to 6 pm on Sunday.

To rejoin the Byzantine path, walk across the monastery's car park and bear left onto the (uphill) asphalt road. After 60 metres, turn sharp left onto an asphalt road, and after a few metres the path veers off to the right. Soon you will reach the main road again. Cross straight over and continue ahead to reach Hora and the **Monastery of St John**

the Theologian. The finest frescoes of the monastery are those in the outer narthex, which depict significant events in St John's life. The priceless contents in the monastery's treasury include icons, ecclesiastical ornaments, embroideries and pendants made of precious stones. Opening times are the same as for the Monastery of the Apocalypse. Admission is free.

Huddled around the monastery are the immaculate whitewashed houses of **Hora**, many with handsome wooden doors. The houses are a legacy of the island's great wealth of the 18th and 19th centuries. Some of them have been bought and renovated by wealthy Greeks and foreigners.

Places to Eat – inexpensive

Vigalis Taverna, on the central square, with a garden at the back, is deservedly popular. A meal of meatballs, Greek salad and soft drink costs 1800 dr.

Places to Eat – moderate

The elegant *Patmian House* (☎ 31 180), in a restored mansion, is the island's undisputed restaurant par excellence. There's a large choice of superb mezedes: the little spinach and cheese pies are especially good. The fillet steak is also commendable. Expect to pay between 5000 and 7000 dr for a three course meal with wine. Reservations are recommended.

NORTH OF SKALA

The pleasant, tree-shaded **Meloi beach** is just two km north-east of Skala, along a turn-off from the main road.

Two km farther along the main road there's a turn-off right to the sandy and relatively quiet **Agriolivado beach**. The main road continues to the inland village of **Kambos** and then descends to the shingle beach from where you can walk to the secluded **Vagia beach**. The main road ends at **Lampi**, nine km from Skala, where there is a beautiful beach of multicoloured stones.

Places to Stay – bottom end

Next to the well-signposted Taverna Meloi

there is a basic *domatia* (☎ 31 213) where doubles are 4000 dr with shared bathroom. The owners do not speak English so telephone Taverna Meloi (☎ 31 888) to enquire about them. A new *domatia* (☎ 31 247), uphill from the taverna, was near completion in 1995, but a name had not been decided upon. Doubles/triples with private bathroom will cost around 5000/8000 dr.

At Kambos, the owners of George's Place Snack Bar (see Places to Eat) work as an unofficial room-letting agency, so if you pop in, they will put you in touch with a local domatia owner. At Lampi, *Delfini Rooms* (☎ 31 951), at Delfini Taverna, has doubles with private bathroom for 6000 dr.

Stefanos Camping (☎ 31 821), at Meloi, is a good camping ground, with bamboo-shaded pitches, minimarket, café bar and motorbike-rental facilities. The rates are 1100 dr for an adult (tent included). Buses don't go to Meloi; a taxi from Skala will cost 700 dr.

Places to Stay – top end
Patmos' best hotel is Kambos' A-class *Patmos Paradise* (☎ 32 624) which has a restaurant, tennis courts, sauna and swimming pool. Rates for singles/doubles/triples are 19,000/24,000/47,000 dr.

Places to Eat
The excellent *Taverna Meloi* has a large menu of traditional Greek dishes and is open all day long. *George's Place Snack Bar*, on Kambos beach, is owned by two friendly, laid-back, young men. Vegetable pies cost between 600 and 800 dr and superb apple pie is 600 dr. *To Kavoirakia* is commendable for Greek fare. Of the two restaurants on Lampi beach, *Leonidas* has the edge. It specialises in fish dishes but the saganaki is also very good.

SOUTH OF SKALA
Grigos, four km south-east of Skala, is a rather lifeless resort with a sandy beach. The long, sandy, tree-shaded **Psili Ammos** is the island's best, and the unofficial nudist beach.

The easiest way to get there is by excursion boat.

Most of the accommodation in Grikos is monopolised by tour groups. Try the *Restaurant O Stamatis and Rooms* (☎ 31 302), by the beach, which has comfortable doubles with private bathroom for 8000 dr. Psili Ammos has a seasonal taverna, but no accommodation.

Lipsi Λειψοί

Lipsi (Li-PSEE, population 700), 12 km east of Patmos and 11 km north of Leros, is an idyllic little island. The cheery inhabitants busy themselves with fishing, agriculture, animal husbandry and keeping happy the relatively small number of tourists who venture here. The picturesque port town of Lipsi is the only settlement. Around the coast are good beaches. Lipsi produces good cheeses and a potent wine known as Lipsi Black (see To Kohlakoura in the Walks to the Beaches from Lipsi Town section).

Getting There & Away
Ferry The F/B *Dimitra* calls in once a week at Lipsi see the Getting There & Away section for Rhodes island for its schedule. Lipsi is also a port of call for the F/B *Nissos Kalymnos*.

Excursion Boat The *Captain Makis* (2500 dr return) and *Anna Express* (3000 dr) do daily trips in summer to Agia Marina on Leros and to Skala on Patmos. The *Anna Express* and *Black Beauty* excursion boats do trips to Arki, Tiganakia bay (Arki) and Marathi islands (2000 dr return).

Getting Around
Taxi Lipsi's 'taxis' are bum-shattering Nissan trucks. They make trips to the island's beaches for around 600 dr per person.

Motorbike There is a motorbike-rental outlet at Flisvos Pension.

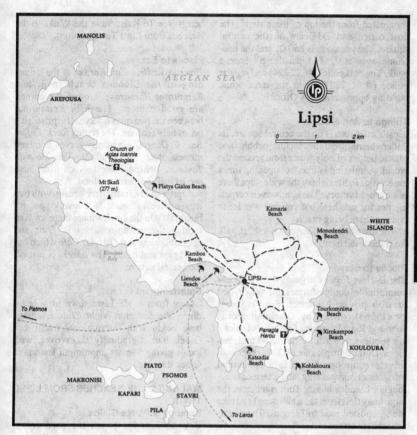

Lipsi

AEGEAN SEA

0   1   2 km

MANOLIS

AREFOUSA

Church of
Agias Ioannis
Theologias

Mt Skafi
(277 m) ▲

Platys Gialos Beach

Kimissi
Bay

Kambos
Beach

Liendos
Beach

Kamaris
Beach

Monodendri
Beach

WHITE
ISLANDS

LIPSI

Tourkomnima
Beach

Panagia
Harou

Xirokampos
Beach

KOULOURA

Katsadia
Beach

Kohlakoura
Beach

To Patmos

PIATO

MAKRONISI

PSOMOS

KAPARI

STAVRI

PILA

To Leros

Excursion Boat Various excursion boats, including the *Captain Makis* and *Anna Express*, do trips to Lipsi's beaches, and to the uninhabited White Islands (1000 dr).

LIPSI TOWN
Orientation
All boats dock at Lipsi town, where there are two quays. The Lipsi-based *Anna Express* and *Captain Makis*, dock at the small quay. All other boats and ferries dock at the large quay.

From the large quay, facing inland, turn right. Continue along the waterfront to the large Plateia Nikiforias, which is just beyond the Calypso Hotel. The small quay is opposite this hotel. Ascend the wide steps at the far side of Plateia Nikiforias and bear right to reach the central square. The left fork leads to a second, smaller square.

Information
The municipal tourist office (☎ 41 288) is on the central square, but you may find Lipsi's two privately owned tourist offices more helpful. Rena's Office is at the base of the wide steps and Lipsos Travel (☎ 41 225) run by Anna Rizos, an English woman, is

DODECANESE

signposted from the top of these steps. The post office and OTE are on the central square. The postcode is 850 01 and the telephone code is 0247. Lipsi doesn't have a bank. The port police (☎ 22 224) and regular police (☎ 41 222) are in the large white building opposite Rena's Office.

Things to See & Do

Lipsi's **museum** is on the central square. Its underwhelming exhibits include pebbles and plastic bottles of holy water from around the world. Admission is free, but opening times are erratic. To the right of the wide steps there is a **carpet factory**. The handwoven carpets are not for sale here but you can wander in and see them being made.

The town beach of **Liendos** is a short walk from the waterfront.

Places to Stay

The D-class *Hotel Calypso* (☎ 41 242) has comfortable doubles/triples for 6000/7500 dr with private bathroom. *Rena's Rooms* (☎ 41 363), owned by Greek-Americans John and Rena Paradisos (of Rena's Office), are spotless, beautifully furnished and spacious. Doubles/triples are 6000/7200 dr with private bathroom. There is a communal refrigerator and gas ring, and a terrace overlooking Liendos beach. Turn right from the large quay (left from the small quay) and take the signposted road to Liendos. The rooms are up here on the left.

Rooms Galini (☎ 41 212), opposite the large quay, have lovely, light rooms with bathroom, refrigerator, gas ring and balcony. Rates are 7000/8400 dr. Nearby, above Cafeteria Fotina, *Panorama Studios* (☎ 41235) are equally agreeable, and cost 6500/7500 dr.

Flisvos Pension (☎ 41 261), beyond the carpet factory, has singles/doubles/triples for 4000/6000/7000 dr. *Barbarosa Studios* (☎ 41 092/312), next door to Lipsos Travel, has spacious, well-equipped double/triple/quad studios for 7000/10,000/11,000 dr. The same family has doubles with shared bathroom for 5500 dr.

Lipsi does not have an official camping ground, but there is free camping at Katsadia

beach (see To Katsadia in the Walks to the Beaches from Lipsi Town section).

Places to Eat

Taverna Vasileia Kali Kardia, at the beginning of the Liendos beach road, and *Restaurant Barbarosa*, around the corner, are good choices. The *Fish Restaurant*, between the two quays, serves (surprise, surprise) only seafood. The trendy *Rock Coffee Bar & Ouzeri*, next door, serves a mixed mezes plate for 1000 dr. The *Dolphin Taverna*, behind Plateia Nikiforias, also serves well-prepared seafood.

Lipsi's shady, traffic-free square, with two inexpensive kafaneia, is a lovely spot for breakfast. On the small square there's a *fastfood outlet*, a *supermarket*, a *fruit and vegetable shop* and *O Mylos Café* which has good pies and cakes. The *bakery* is just off the central square.

Entertainment

'Away from it all' Lipsi town now has a disco, the *Scorpion Night Club*. Evenings here begin with international music but Greek music gradually takes over, with locals giving tourists impromptu lessons in Greek dancing.

WALKS TO THE BEACHES FROM LIPSI TOWN

Kambos & Platys Gialos

Beyond Liendos beach the road forks; bearing left, you will arrive at Kambos beach. If you take the right fork, after about 40 minutes you will arrive at Platys Gialos, a lovely sandy beach with a very gradual slope in the sea. There's a taverna and some friendly ducks.

Katsadia

Walk inland along the road by the cafeteria next to Restaurant Manolis and take the first turn to the right signposted 'Katsadia'. Continue straight ahead, and after passing a church on the right, take the left fork and pass another church on the right. Continue along this track and at the top of a short steep hill turn left (signposted 'Katsadia'). Soon you will see Katsadia bay. Go straight ahead then turn sharp right, passing another church on the left, to reach the sand and pebble beach.

There is free camping beside *Dilaila Restaurant*, and *Kampieris Restaurant* has some basic double rooms for 1000 dr.

Kohlakoura
Walk inland along the road by the cafeteria next to Restaurant Manolis, and take the second turn to the right signposted 'Kohlakoura'. At the fork bear right, and at the crossroads continue straight ahead. A turnoff to the right along this road leads to the **Church of Panagia Harou** (The Virgin of Death), where, according to tradition, dried flowers are resurrected on 24 August, the church's festival day. Take the next turn to the right along the road (which veers left) onto a dirt track. You will pass **Dimitris Makris' vineyard** where you can buy Lipsi Black wine (bring a container). The track becomes cement at the end of a low stone wall. Turn left here to arrive at the pebble beach of Kohlakoura. There are no facilities.

Monodendri (One Tree)
At the small square face Milos Café, turn right and take the second turn to the left. Continue along this road passing the high school on the left. At the fork bear right and keep on this track ignoring the two turnings right by a church. Soon the White Islands come into view ahead. At the next fork bear right. Continue ahead going downhill for a while, then, after going gently uphill, ignore the left turn, and continue straight ahead for another 250 metres. Then take a narrow path which veers uphill to the left. You will soon see the single tree of Monodendri (which means 'one tree') down to the left. It stands on a rocky peninsula, the neck of which is pebbled and is an unofficial nudist beach. There are no facilities.

Kimissi
This walk to Kimissi bay, on the south-west coast, is the most scenic on the island. A hermit monk lives here beside the little **Church of Our Lady**; behave appropriately with respect for his peace and holiness. In Ottoman times monks hid in a cave here, choosing death from starvation rather than capture by the Turks. A casket in the church contains their bones.

Take the Platys Gialos road. A rough track disects the road 300 metres beyond the fork. Take the track which veers left and goes uphill by a stone wall. Go through a wooden gate and continue ahead and uphill. Eventually the path levels out high above the east coast. Go through another gate and continue ahead, veering slightly left. Continue to the **Church of the Virgin of the Cross**, and pass in front of it. Soon you will see a stony track down to the right. Keep going ahead to reach this track at its summit. Turn left onto it and descend to Kimissi. You can return by this track to the Platys Gialos-Lipsi road.

Arki & Marathi
Αρκοί & Μαράθι

ARKI
Tiny Arki (population 45) five km north of Lipsi, is hilly, with shrubs, but few trees. Its one settlement, the little port on the west coast, is also called Arki. Islanders make a meagre living from fishing.

There is no post office, OTE or doctor on the island. Arki's telephone code is 0247. An islander told me that in 1994 they were promised a bi-monthly visit from a doctor, however, they are still awaiting the first visit. 'We have been forgotten' he bemoaned. One gets the feeling that this applies to all aspects of Arki, not just the medical.

Away from its little settlement, the island seems almost mystical in its peace and stillness. On the other hand, some people find it just plain dull.

Things to See & Do
Walk to the **Church of Metamorphosis** for superb views of Arki and its surrounding islets. Facing inland at the quay, turn right and then left after O Tripas Taverna. Ignore

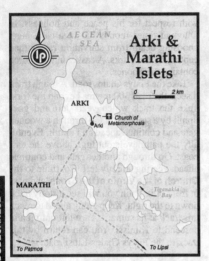

Arki & Marathi Islets

AEGEAN SEA

ARKI

Church of Metamorphosis

Arki

MARATHI

Tiganakia Bay

0   1   2 km

To Patmos

To Lipsi

DODECANESE

the cement road to the right, and take the path straight ahead. At the fork, by a telegraph pole, bear right and go through a metal gate. Turn right and climb up to a stone wall. Then turn left onto a path up to a wooden gate, beyond which is the church. Its key is kept under a stone slab to the right of the door.

Beyond the red-domed church, to the left of the port (facing the sea), there are two mediocre, rather dirty beaches. There are several other beaches around the coast. **Tiganakia bay**, which has incredibly blue water, is a superb place for swimming. It's easiest to reached by boat but it's possible to walk there along goat tracks; ask locals for directions.

Places to Stay & Eat
Arki has two tavernas, both of which also rent rooms. *Taverna Arki Katsvidis* (☎ 32 371), opposite the quay, has doubles/triples for 5500/6600 dr. To the right, *O Tripos Taverna* (☎ 32 230), has singles/doubles/triples for 3000/6000/7200 dr. The owner, Manolis, speaks good English.

Getting There & Away
No inter-island ferries call in at Arki. In

summer the Lipsi-based excursion boats go there and the caïque *Delfini* does frequent trips from Patmos (2500 dr return). There is also the possibility of 'hitching' a lift on a fishing boat or yacht, though this is not common practice, and shouldn't be taken for granted.

MARATHI
Marathi is the largest of Arki's satellite islets. Before WW II it had a dozen or so inhabitants, but is now uninhabited. However, it has two seasonal tavernas both of which rent rooms. The two tavernas, owned by Mr Pandelis and Mr Michaelis, have comfortable doubles for 6000 dr and food is exceptionally good at both places. Mr Pandelis, who was born on Arki, now lives in Australia, but spends the summer on Marathi with his family. The island has a superb beach. There is no telephone, but there's a two-way radio for emergencies.

Getting There & Away
Excursion Boat In summer the Lipsi-based *Anna Express* and *Black Beauty* do trips to Marathi. You may be able to get a lift on a fishing boat from Arki.

Agathonisi Αγαθονήσι

Agathonisi (Aga-tho-NI-si, population 110) is the most northerly island of the archipelago. It's a little gem, still only visited by adventurous backpackers and yachters. There are three villages: the port of Agios Giorgios, Megalo Horio and Mikro Horio, all less than one km apart. The island is hilly and covered with thorn bushes.

Getting There & Away
Ferry & Hydrofoil The F/B *Nissos Kalymnos* is the only passenger ferry which calls at Agathonisi. The twice-weekly supply boat from Samos also takes passengers, but its schedule is subject to change – check with the police officer or locals. A hydrofoil

running to and from Samos, Patmos, Leros and Kalymnos calls once a week.

Getting Around
The island's only motorised public transport is a spluttering three-wheeled contraption which transports people from Agios Giorgios to both Megalo Horio and Mikro Horio.

AGIOS GIORGIOS Αγιος Γεώργιος
Agios Giorgios is a delightful little place with just enough waterfront activity to stop you sinking into a state of inertia. It has a pebble beach and Spilia beach, also pebbled, is close by, reached along the track around the far side of the bay.

Orientation & Information
Boats dock at Agios Giorgios from where cement roads ascend right (facing inland) to Megalo Horio and left to Mikro Horio. There is no post office or bank or OTE, but there are cardphones. Agathonisi's telephone code is 0247.

There is no tourist information office. The one police officer, who is also the port police officer, has an office in the white building at the beginning of the Megalo Horio road.

Places to Stay
Agios Giorgios has three pensions: *Pension Maria Kamitsa* (☎ 23 650/690), *Theologis Rooms* (☎ 23 692/687) next door, and *George's Pension* (☎ 24 385) behind these. All charge 6000 dr for doubles with private bathroom. George is one of the few people on the island who speaks English.

Places to Eat
There are several eateries in Agios Giorgios, but out of high season the only place likely to be open is *George's Taverna* below the pension, where the octopus stifado is magnificent.

AROUND THE ISLAND
Megalo Horio Μεγάλο Χωριό
Megalo Horio, Aggthonisi's biggest village, has one domatia, *Mrs Katsoulieri's Rooms to*

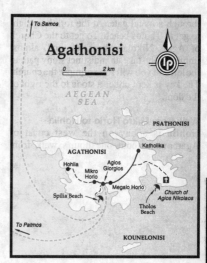

Rent (☎ 24 385). *Restaurant I Eireni* and the kafeneio/pantopoleio, both on the central square, serve inexpensive meals.

Walk from Megalo Horio to Katholika
Katholika is an abandoned fishing hamlet, 40 minutes walk from Megalo Horio. *En route* you can detour to a lookout point. From the central square turn right at Restaurant I Eireni to reach a cement road. Walk 300 metres beyond the baseball field and turn left, and then right, to reach an army lookout hut, from where there are tremendous views over to Samos and Turkey's Meandros estuary. From the hut look half-left and you will see two large olive trees – proceed towards these, then walk towards the long narrow island of Psathonisi. Ahead and half-right you will soon see an oblong enclosure: walk to this and turn right. At the road, turn left for Katholika.

Walk from Megalo Horio to the Church of Agios Nikolaos & Tholos Beach
Leave Megalo Horio on the Katholika road. After about 30 minutes, turn right onto a dirt road. At the stone building go through a wooden gate, continue along the track and

through a metal gate. At the fork bear right to get to Tholos beach. To get to the Church of Agios Nikolaos bear left and, almost immediately, take an indistinct stony path to the left and you will soon glimpse the church. The key is kept under a stone to the right of the door.

Walk from Mikro Horio to Hohlia
Hohlia is a bay on the west coast of Agathonisi, about one hour's walk from Mikro Horio. There's no beach but you can swim from the rocks. Leave Mikro Horio by the dirt road and when it turns right, you will see ahead of you a dip between two hills – Hohlia lies beyond here. Just before the track narrows to pass between two stone walls, take the path which veers off to the right and then skirts around the stone walls and an animal enclosure before ascending steeply. Keep close to the stone wall on the left, as it continues to the bay.

North-Eastern Aegean Islands
Τα Νησιά του Βορειοανατολικού Αιγαίου

The islands of the North-Eastern Aegean are grouped together more for convenience than for any historical, geographical or administrative parity. With the exceptions of Thasos and Samothraki, they are, like the Dodecanese, much closer to Turkey than to the Greek mainland, but unlike the Dodecanese they are not close to one another. This means island-hopping is not the easy matter it is within the Dodecanese and Cyclades, although, with the exceptions of Thasos and Samothraki, it is possible.

These islands are less visited than either the Dodecanese or the Cyclades. Scenically, they also differ from these groups. Mountainous, green and mantled with forests, they are ideal for hiking but most are also blessed with long stretches of delectable beaches.

Although historically diverse, a list of the islands' inhabitants from far-off times reads like a who's who of the ancient world. Some of the North-Aegean islands also boast important ancient sites. All of them became part of the Ottoman Empire and were reunited with Greece after the Balkan Wars in 1912.

There are seven major islands in the group: Chios, Ikaria, Lesvos (Mytilini), Limnos, Samos, Samothraki and Thasos. Fourni near Ikaria; Psara and Inousses near Chios; and Agios Efstratios near Limnos are small, little-visited islands in the group.

Getting There & Away
Following is a brief overview of travel options to/from and between the islands of the North-Eastern Aegean. For additional information, see the entries at the beginning of sections on individual islands.

Air Samos, Chios, Lesvos, Limnos and Ikaria have air links with Athens. In addition, Chios, Lesvos and Limnos have flights to Thessaloniki.

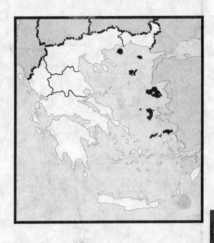

Ferry – domestic Chios, Samos, Lesvos and Ikaria have daily connections with Piraeus. Some of the ferries from Samos and Ikaria to Piraeus go via Mykonos, Naxos, Paros and Syros. Limnos has three connections a week with Piraeus, Rafina and Kavala. Chios and Lesvos have two connections a week with Thessaloniki, and Limnos has one.

Thasos and Samothraki have no connections with Piraeus, but Samothraki is linked to Limnos by both ferry and hydrofoil. Thasos has daily ferry connections with Kavala and Keramoti, both in Macedonia. There are daily connections between Samothraki and Alexandroupolis in Thrace and in summer there is a twice or thrice-weekly (depending on demand) connection with Kavala.

An excursion boat connects Samos with Patmos in the Dodecanese every day in summer. The F/B *Nissos Kalymnos* links Samos (Pythagorio) twice a week with the Dodecanese islands of Agathonisi, Lipsi, Patmos, Leros, Kalymnos, Kos, Nisyros, Tilos, Symi and Rhodes.

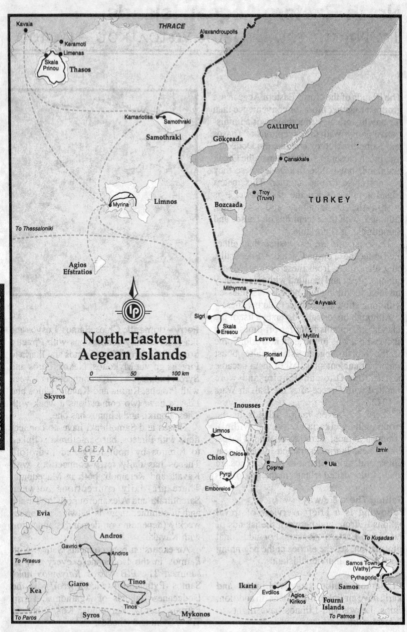

North-Eastern Aegean Islands

0   50   100 km

NORTH-EAST AEGEAN ISLANDS

Ferry – international In summer there are daily ferries from Samos to Kuşadası (for Ephesus), from Chios to Çeşme and from Lesvos to Ayvalık, all in Turkey.

Hydrofoil In summer there are extensive hydrofoil links between all the North-Eastern Aegean islands as well as with the northern mainland. Many hydrofoils ply between Thasos and Kavala every day. In summer, Samothraki is linked with four mainland ports and two islands by both ferry and hydrofoil.

Getting Around
Air Lesvos and Limnos are the only islands in the group connected by air.

Ferry There are daily ferries between Ikaria and Samos, Chios and Lesvos; ferries three times a week between Lesvos and Limnos; and twice a week between Chios and Samos.

Samos Σάμος

Samos (SA-mos, population 32,000), the most southerly island of the group, is the closest of all the Greek islands to Turkey, from which it is separated by the three-km-wide Mykale straits. The island is the most visited of all the North-Eastern Aegean group. Charter flights of tourists descend upon the island from many northern European countries. Try to avoid Samos in July and August when rooms are hard to come by.

Despite the package tourists, Samos is still worth a visit: forays into its hinterland are rewarded with unspoilt villages and mountain vistas. In summer the humid air of Samos is permeated with heavy floral scents, especially jasmine. This, and the prolific greenery of the landscape, lend Samos an exotic and tropical air. Orchids are grown here for export and an excellent table wine is made from the locally grown muscat grapes.

Samos has three ports: Samos town (Vathy) and Karlovasi on the north coast, and Pythagorio on the south coast.

History
The first inhabitants of Samos, the Pelasgian tribes, worshipped Hera, whose birthplace was Samos. Pythagoras was born on Samos in the 6th century BC. Unfortunately, his life coincided with that of the tyrant Polycrates, who in 550 BC deposed the Samiot oligarchy. As the two did not see eye to eye, Pythagoras spent much of his time in exile in Italy. Despite this, Samos became a mighty naval power under Polycrates, and the arts and sciences also flourished. 'Big is beautiful' seems to have been Polycrates' maxim; almost every construction and artwork he commissioned appears to have been ancient Greece's biggest. The historian Herodotus wrote glowingly of the tyrant's achievements, stating that the Samians had accomplished the three greatest projects in Greece at that time: the Sanctuary of Hera (one of the Seven Wonders of the Ancient World), the Evpalinos Tunnel, and a huge jetty.

After the decisive Battle of Plataea (479 BC), in which Athens had been aided by the Samians, Samos allied itself to Athens and returned to democracy. In the Battle of Mykale which took place on the same day as the Battle of Plataea, the Greek navy (with many Samian sailors) defeated the Persian fleet. However, during the Peloponnesian Wars, Samos was taken by Sparta.

Under Roman rule Samos enjoyed many privileges, but after successive occupations by the Venetians and Genoese it was conquered by the Turks in 1453. Samos played a major role in the uprising against the Turks in the early 19th century, much to the detriment of its neighbour, Chios (see Chios' History section).

Getting There & Away
Air There are at least three flights a day from Samos to Athens (14,800 dr). The Olympic Airways office (☎ 27 237) is on the corner of Kanari and Smyrnis in Samos town. There is also an Olympic Airways office (☎ 61 213) on Lykourgou Logotheti in Pythagorio. The airport is four km west of Pythagorio.

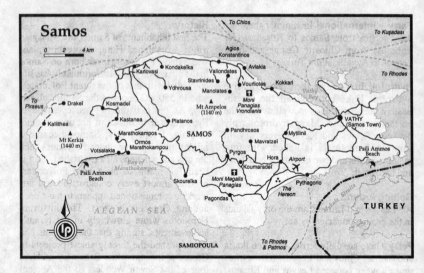

Ferry – domestic Samos is the transport hub of the North-Eastern Aegean, with ferries to the Dodecanese and Cyclades as well as to the other North-Eastern Aegean islands. Schedules are subject to seasonal changes, so consult any of the ticket offices for the latest versions. Samos Tours (☎ 27 715; fax 28 915) is the closest agency to the ferry terminal and posts a comprehensive schedule outside its offices. The following summary will give you some idea of the ferry options from Samos during summer.

Piraeus There are one to two ferries daily to Piraeus (13 hours, 4800 dr) which usually call in at Ikaria.

North-Eastern Aegean Islands There are two to three ferries daily to Ikaria (2½ hours, 1700 dr); one a day to Fourni (two hours, 1400 dr); three per week to Chios (four hours, 2100 dr); one per week to Lesvos (seven hours, 3400 dr); one per week to Limnos (11 hours, 5800 dr); and one per week to Kavala (20 hours, 7200 dr).

Cyclades There are about four ferries a week to Naxos and Paros (6½ hours,

3600 dr) with connections to Mykonos, Ios, Santorini (Thira) and Syros.

Dodecanese There are about five ferries per week to Patmos (2½ hours, 2200 dr) and one per week to Leros (3½ hours, 2200 dr), Kalymnos (five hours, 2400 dr), and Kos (seven hours, 3000 dr).

Ferry – international In summer there are two ferries daily from Samos town to Kuşadası (for Ephesus) in Turkey. From November to March there are one to two ferries a week. Tickets cost 6000/9500 dr one way/return (plus 4000 dr Greek port tax and 3000 dr Turkish port tax) and can be purchased from Samos Tours (☎ 27 715; fax 28 915), in Samos town. The fare for a small car will cost about 13,000 dr, and for a motorbike about 6000 dr. Bicycles are carried free.

Bear in mind that the ticket office will require your passport in advance for port formalities.

Hydrofoil In summer hydrofoils link Pythagorio twice a day with Patmos (one hour, 4700 dr), Leros (two hours, 4700 dr), Kos (3½ hours, 6000 dr) and Rhodes (6½ hours,

12,400 dr). There are also three services a week from Samos town to Chios (1½ hours, 4400 dr). Schedules are subject to frequent changes, so contact the tourist office in Pythagorio or the port police (☎ 61 225) for up-to-date information.

Excursion Boat In summer there are excursion boats three times a week between Pythagorio and Patmos (9000 dr) leaving at 7.30 am. There are also daily excursion boats to the little island of Samiopoula for 8000 dr including lunch.

Getting Around
To/From the Airport There are currently no Olympic Airways buses to the airport. A taxi from Samos town should cost about 2000 dr.

Bus Samos has an adequate bus service although buses stop running quite early in the evening. There are 13 buses a day from Samos town to both Kokkari (20 minutes, 200 dr) and Pythagorio (25 minutes, 260 dr); eight to Agios Konstantinos (40 minutes, 360 dr); seven to Karlovasi (via the north coast, one hour, 650 dr); six to the Hereon (25 minutes, 380 dr); five to Mytilinii (20 minutes, 220 dr); three to Psili Ammos beach (the one on the east coast, 20 minutes, 240 dr); and two buses a day to Ormos Marathokampou and Votsalakia.

In addition to frequent buses to Samos town there are six buses to the Hereon from Pythagorio and two to both Mytilinii and Karlovasi.

Car & Motorbike Samos has many car-rental outlets. They include Hertz (☎ 61 730), Lykourgou Logotheti 77; and Europcar (☎ 61 522), Lykourgou Logotheti 65, both in Pythagorio. There are also many motorbike-hire outlets on Lykourgou Logotheti. Many larger hotels can arrange bike or car hire for you.

Taxi From the taxi rank (☎ 28 404) on Plateia Pythagora in Samos town, tariffs are: Kokkari 1600 dr, Pythagorio 1800 dr, Psili Ammos 1500 dr, Avlakia 1800 dr, the airport 2000 dr, and the Hereon 2500 dr.

SAMOS TOWN (VATHY)
The island's capital is large and bustling Samos town, also called Vathy (Βαθύ), on the north-east coast. The waterfront is crowded with tourists who rarely venture to the older and extremely attractive upper town of Ano Vathy where 19th-century red-tiled houses perch on a hillside. The lower and newer town is strung out along Vathy bay and it is quite a walk from one end to the other.

Orientation
From the ferry terminal (facing inland) turn right to reach the central square of Plateia Pythagora on the waterfront. It's recognisable by its four palm trees and statue of a lion. A little further along and one block inland are the shady municipal gardens with a pleasant outdoor café. The waterfront road is called Themistokleous Sofouli.

Information
The municipal tourist office (☎ 28 530) is just north of Plateia Pythagora in a little side street, but it only operates during the summer season. The staff will assist in finding accommodation. The tourist police (☎ 27 980) are in the same building as the regular police at Themistokleous Sofouli 129 on the south side of the waterfront. The port police (☎ 27 318) are just north of the quay and one block back from the waterfront.

The post office is on Smyrnis, four blocks from the waterfront. The OTE is on Plateia Iroön, behind the municipal gardens. Samos' postcode is 831 01 (Poste Restante) and the telephone code is 0273.

The National Bank of Greece is on the waterfront just south of Plateia Pythagora and the Commercial Bank is on the east side of the square. The island's bus terminal (KTEL) is just back from the waterfront on Ioannou Lekati. The taxi rank (☎ 28 404) is on Plateia Pythagora. Samos' general hospital (☎ 27 407) is on the waterfront, north of the ferry quay.

Things to See

Apart from the charming old quarter of Ano Vathy, which is a peaceful place to stroll, and the municipal gardens which are a pleasant place to sit, the main attraction of Samos town is the **archaeological museum** (☎ 27 469). Many of the fine exhibits in this well laid out museum are a legacy of Polycrates' time. They include a gargantuan kouros statue (4.5 metres) which was found in the Hereon (Sanctuary of Hera). In true Polycrates fashion it was the largest standing kouros ever produced. The collection also includes many more statues, mostly from the Hereon; bronze sculptures; steles and pottery. The museum is east of the municipal gardens. Opening times are Tuesday to Sunday from 8.30 am to 3 pm. Admission is 800 dr, half-price for students.

Places to Stay – bottom end

Samos does not have a camp site. The cheapest hotel (classed as a pension) is the *Hotel Ionia* (☎ 28 782), on Manoli Kalomiri. Its clean and pretty rooms cost 2000/3000/4000 dr for singles/doubles/triples with shared bathroom and 3500/4500 dr with private bathroom. To get there from the quay, turn right onto the waterfront, left at Stamatiadou, then left into Manoli Kalomiri.

Close by, the traditional *Pension Avli* (☎ 22 939) is a former Roman Catholic convent, built around a lovely courtyard (*avli*). The rooms are spacious and nicely furnished. Rates are 4000/6000 dr for doubles/triples with private bathroom.

The C-class *Hotel Helen* (☎ 22 866), Grammou 2, has cosy rooms with fitted carpets and attractive furniture. Doubles are 6000 dr with private bathroom. Turn right from the quay, and left at the Roman Catholic church, veer right at the intersection and the hotel is on the right.

Close by also is the C-class *Hotel Bonis* (☎ 28 790; fax 22 501) with large rooms and TV. Rooms cost 6000/8200/12,000 dr including breakfast.

The B-class *Hotel Emily* (☎ 24 691; fax 24 692) has tastefully furnished rooms with air-con and balcony. Rooms cost 8000 dr for a double in low season and 12,500 dr in high season. The hotel is on Grammou, just up from the Hotel Helen.

Places to Stay – middle

The nearest hotel to the quay is the grand-looking C-class *Samos Hotel* (☎ 28 377; fax 23 771). It is well kept with spacious and elegant cafeteria, bar, snack bar, restaurant, breakfast room, TV room and billiard room. The comfortable rooms have fitted carpet, balcony, telephone and private bathroom. Rates are 7200/8600/11,500 dr for singles/doubles/triples. On leaving the quay turn right and you'll come to the hotel on the left.

There are many resort hotels catering for the crowds of package tourists, but if you are not travelling in this category and fancy a touch of comfort, try the *Ino Hotel* (☎ 23 241; fax 23 245) at Kalami, 500 metres past the hospital; follow the sign. There is a pool, a bar and a series of separate units scattered about the complex. Rates here are a very reasonable 9100 dr for a nice double room.

Places to Eat

Samos town has a good selection of eateries. When dining out on Samos don't forget to sample the Samian wine, extolled by Byron. One of the cheapest places for well-prepared Greek staples is *O Tasos Taverna*, just down from the bus station. The food at *To Katoï Ouzeri*, also known as Why Not, is superlative and moderately priced. The modern tastefully decorated ouzeri is tucked away on a little side street behind the municipal gardens. Just one street back from the waterfront is *Estiatorio Alekos* at Lykourgou Logotheti 49 serving ready-made staples and made-to-order dishes, at uninflated prices.

Another excellent place is *Taverna Ouzeri Ta Diodia*, also tucked away in a little side street. The taverna's sign is in Greek, but features a picture of a fish. It specialises in fish, although souvlaki and chicken are also available. Walk south along the waterfront and look for the sign just before the soldiers' sentry boxes. About 300 metres left from the ferry terminal is *La Calma* restaurant (evenings only), with perhaps the best waterside

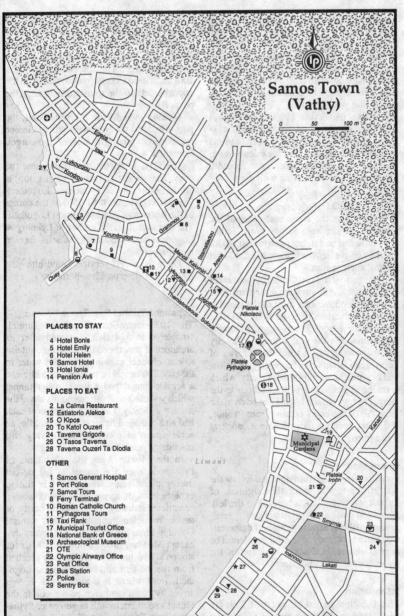

Samos Town (Vathy)

0   50   100 m

PLACES TO STAY

4 Hotel Bonis
5 Hotel Emily
6 Hotel Helen
9 Samos Hotel
13 Hotel Ionia
14 Pension Avli

PLACES TO EAT

2 La Calma Restaurant
12 Estiatorio Alekos
15 O Kipos
20 To Katoi Ouzeri
24 Taverna Grigoris
26 O Tasos Taverna
28 Taverna Ouzeri Ta Diodia

OTHER

1 Samos General Hospital
3 Port Police
7 Samos Tours
8 Ferry Terminal
10 Roman Catholic Church
11 Pythagoras Tours
16 Taxi Rank
17 Municipal Tourist Office
18 National Bank of Greece
19 Archaeological Museum
21 OTE
22 Olympic Airways Office
23 Post Office
25 Bus Station
27 Police
29 Sentry Box

Epeos
Iras
Lykourgou
Kondrou
Koundourioti
Grammou
Menoti Kalomiri
Stamatiadou
Areos
Lykourgou
Logotheti
Themistokleous Sofouli
Plateia Nikolaou
Plateia Pythagora
Municipal Gardens
Limani
Plateia Iroön
Kefali
Smyrnis
Ioannou
Lekati

NORTH-EAST AEGEAN ISLANDS

location in Samos town. The tables overlook the water and it is a very romantic spot. The food is good too.

Another commendable place is *Taverna Grigoris* on Smyrnis, near the post office. If you are here between 8.30 and 9.30 pm your table number may be drawn out of a hat, in which case you'll eat free.

For live neo kyma (1960s new wave) music and maybe some dancing, seek out *O Kipos* just off Lykourgou Logotheti (entry is from the next street up) in a garden setting. The food is commendable; try a splendid Samena Golden white wine with it.

PYTHAGORIO Πυθαγόρειο

Pythagorio, on the south-east coast of the island, is 14 km from Samos town. Today, it's a crowded and rather twee tourist resort, but it's a convenient base from which to visit Samos' ancient sites.

Pythagorio stands on the site of the ancient city of Samos. Although the settlement dates from the Neolithic age, most of the remains are from Polycrates' time (around 550 BC). The mighty jetty of Samos projected almost 450 metres into the sea, protecting the city and its powerful fleet from the vagaries of the Aegean. Remains of this jetty lie below and beyond the smaller modern jetty, which is on the opposite side of the harbour to the quay. The town beach begins just beyond the jetty. All of the boats coming from Patmos, and other points south of Samos, dock at Pythagorio.

Orientation

From the ferry quay, turn right and follow the waterfront to the main thoroughfare of Lykourgou Logotheti, a turn-off to the left. Here you will find supermarkets, greengrocers, bakers, travel agents and numerous car, motorbike and bicycle-hire outlets. The central square of Plateia Irinis is on the waterfront just beyond here.

Information

The municipal tourist office (☎ 61 389; fax 61 022) is on the south side of Lykourgou

Logotheti. The English-speaking staff are particularly friendly and helpful and give out a town map, bus timetable and information about ferry schedules. They also have a currency exchange. The tourist police (☎ 61 100) are also on Lykourgou Logotheti, on the opposite side to the tourist office, near the post office.

Walking inland from the waterfront, the post office and the National Bank of Greece are both on the right side of Lykourgou Logotheti.

The OTE is on the waterfront near the quay. The bus station (actually a bus stop) is on the south side of Lykourgou Logotheti. There is a taxi rank (☎ 61 450) on the corner of the waterfront and Lykourgou Logotheti. The newsagent on the corner of Lykourgou Logotheti and Metamorfosis sells foreign newspapers.

There is a self-service laundrette just beyond this shop on Metamorfosis.

Evpalinos Tunnel Ευπαλίνειο Ορυγμα

The 1034-metre-long Evpalinos Tunnel, completed in 524 BC, is named after its architect. It penetrated through a mountainside to channel gushing mountain water to the city. The tunnel is, in effect, two tunnels: a service tunnel and a lower water tunnel which you can see at various points along the narrow walkway. The diggers began at each end and managed to meet in the middle, an achievement of precision engineering still considered remarkable.

In the Middle Ages the inhabitants of Pythagorio used the tunnel as a hide-out during pirate raids. The tunnel is fun to explore, though access to it is via a very constricted stairway. If you are tall, portly, or suffer from claustrophobia, give it a miss! Opening times are 9 am to 2 pm, every day except Monday. Entry is 500 dr; 300 dr for students. The tunnel is most easily reached from the western end of Lykourgou Logotheti, from where it is signposted. If you arrive by car, a road sign points you to the tunnel's southern mouth as you enter Pythagorio from Samos.

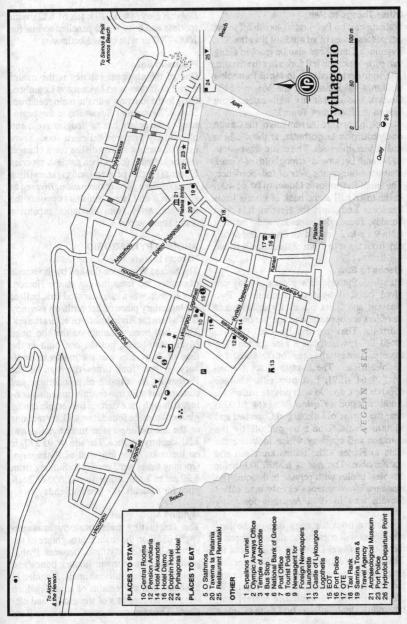

Pythagorio

To Samos & Psili
Ammos Beach

To Samos & Psili
Ammos Beach

Beach

River

Quay

Plateia
Tarsana

Plateia Irinis

Beach

AEGEAN SEA

NORTH-EAST AEGEAN ISLANDS

To Airport
& the Heraion

Streets (labelled): Polikratous, Damos, Esopou, Ergou Palaigos, Aristarhou, Evpalinou, Lykourgou Logotheti, Kanari, Melanohroos, Kyriou Despoti, Pythagora, Polikratous, Lykourgou

100 m
50
0

PLACES TO STAY
10 Central Rooms
12 Pension Arokaria
14 Hotel Alexandra
16 Hotel Damo
22 Dolphin Hotel
24 Pythagoras Hotel

PLACES TO EAT
5 O Stathmos
20 Taverna ta Platania
25 Restaurant Remataki

OTHER
1 Evpalinos Tunnel
2 Olympic Airways Office
3 Temple of Aphrodite
4 Bus Stop
6 National Bank of Greece
7 Post Office
8 Tourist Police
9 Newsagent for
   Foreign Newspapers
11 Launderette
13 Castle of Lykourgos
   Logothetis
15 EOT
16 Port Police
17 OTE
18 Taxi Rank
19 Samina Tours &
   Travel Agency
21 Archaeological Museum
23 Port Police
26 Hydrofoil Departure Point

Other Things to See

Walking east on Polykratou, a path off to the left passes traces of an **ancient theatre**. The Evpalinos Tunnel can also be reached along this path – take the left fork after the theatre. The right fork leads up to **Moni Panagias Spilianis** (Monastery of the Virgin of the Grotto). The ancient city walls extend from here to the Evpalinos Tunnel.

Back in town are the remains of the **Castle of Lykourgos Logothetis**, at the southern end of Metamorfosis. The castle was built in 1824 and became a stronghold of Greek resistance during the War of Independence. The small **Pythagorio Museum** (☎ 61 400) in the town hall at the back of Plateia Irinis has some finds from the Hereon. It is open Sunday, Tuesday, Wednesday and Thursday from 9 am to 2 pm and on Friday and Saturday from noon to 2 pm. Admission is free.

Places to Stay

Many of Pythagorio's places to stay are block-booked by tour companies. Two pleasant and quiet places for independent travellers are opposite one another on Metamorfosis. They are the *Pension Arokaria* (☎ 61 287), which has a nice garden. The lovely owner charges 6000/8000 for doubles/triples. The D-class *Hotel Alexandra* (☎ 61 429), just opposite, charges 6500 dr for a double with private bathroom. Another option is *Central Rooms* (☎ 61 032) near the corner of Lykourgou Logotheti and Metamorfosis. Don't be put off by the entrance and stairway which look like the Gate to Hades – the rooms are clean and comfortable. The rate is 6000/7200 dr for doubles/ triples with private bathroom. The manager is a courteous elderly man called Steven, who lived in Australia for many years .

Coming from the quay one of the first hotels you will come to on the waterfront is the C-class *Hotel Damo* (☎ 61 303; fax 61 745), which is above the OTE. The agreeable singles/doubles are 6000/10,000 dr and the rooms have private bathroom and telephone. Further around the waterfront, beyond the main intersection, is the C-class

Dolphin Hotel (☎ 61 205; fax 61 842), with spotless and cosy wood-panelled rooms for 7000/9700 dr with private bathroom.

Places to Eat

One of the cheapest eateries is the quaint ouzeri *O Stathmos* on Lykourgou Logotheti, close to the junction with the main road from Samos. *Restaurant Remataki*, at the beginning of the beach, has an imaginative menu of carefully prepared delicious food. Try a meal of various mezes dishes for a change: revithokeftedes (chick-pea patties), piperies Florinis (Florina peppers) and gigantes (lima beans) make a good combination. *Taverna ta Platania* is on Plateia Irinis and opposite the museum, away from the more expensive waterfront eateries.

AROUND PYTHAGORIO

Hereon Ηραίον

The Sacred Way, once flanked by thousands of statues, led from the city to the Hereon. The Hereon was a sanctuary to Hera, built at the legendary place of her birth, on swampy land where the River Imbrasos enters the sea. There had been a temple on the site since Mycenaean times, but the one built in the time of Polycrates was the most extraordinary; it was four times the size of the Parthenon. As a result of plunderings and earthquakes only one column remains standing, although the extent of the temple can be gleaned from the foundations. Other remains on the site include a stoa, more temples and a 5th-century basilica. The site (☎ 95 277) is on the coast eight km west of Pythagorio. Opening times are Tuesday to Sunday from 8.30 am to 3 pm. Admission is 800 dr, half-price for students. It's free on Sunday.

Mytilinii Μυτιληνιοί

The fascinating **paleontology museum** (☎ 52 055), on the main thoroughfare of the inland village of Mytilinii, between Pythagorio and Samos town, houses bones and skeletons of prehistoric animals. Included in the collection are remains of animals which were the antecedents of the giraffe and elephant. The museum is open daily from 9 am

NORTH-EAST AEGEAN ISLANDS

to 3 pm and on Sunday from 10.30 am to 2 pm. Admission is 500 dr, free on Sunday.

Beaches

Back on the coast, sandy **Psili Ammos** (not to be confused with a beach of the same name near Votsalakia) is the finest beach near Pythagorio. This gently sloping beach is ideal for families and is popular, so be there early to grab your spot. The beach can be reached by excursion boat (2500 dr) from Pythagorio leaving each morning at 9 am and returning at 4 pm. There are also buses from Samos town.

There is one place to stay at Psili Ammos, *Elena Apartments* (☎ 23 645; fax 28 959) right on the beach. Elena has spacious self-contained double/quad apartments for 8000/15,000 dr for bookings of at least a few days. There are four eating places, of which *Restaurant Psili Ammos* and *Sunrise* are both favourably located overlooking the beach.

SOUTH-WEST SAMOS

The south-west coast of Samos remained unspoilt for longer than the north coast, but in recent years a series of resorts have sprung up alongside the best beaches. **Ormos Marathokampou**, 55 km from Samos town, has a pebble beach. From here a road leads six km to the inland village of **Marathokampos**, which is worth a visit for the stunning view down to the immense Bay of Marathokampos. **Votsalakia**, four km west of Ormos Marathokampou and known officially as Kampos, and **Psili Ammos** (not to be confused with the Psili Ammos beach near Pythagorio), two km beyond, have long sandy beaches. There are many domatia and tavernas on this stretch of coast. The best taverna of an otherwise uninspiring bunch is *Ta Votsalakia* with tables overlooking the beach.

With your own transport you may like to continue on the dirt road from Psili Ammos which skirts Mt Kerkis, above the totally undeveloped and isolated west coast. The road passes through the village of **Kallithea**, and continues to **Drakeï** where it terminates.

WEST OF SAMOS TOWN

The road which skirts the north coast passes many beaches and resorts. The fishing village of **Kokkari**, 10 km from Samos town, is also a holiday resort with a pebble beach. The place is fairly popular with tourists, but it is exposed to the frequent summer winds and for that reason is popular with wind-surfers. Rooms, studios and tavernas abound, all offering much the same in terms of quality.

Beaches extend from here to **Avlakia**, but they are too near the road for nude bathing. Continuing west, beyond Avlakia, the road is flanked by trees, a foretaste of the alluring scenery encountered on the roads leading inland from the coast. A turn-off south along this stretch leads to the delightful mountain village of **Vourliotes**, from where you can walk another three km to **Moni Panagias Vrondianis**. Built in the 1550s, it is the island's oldest extant monastery; a sign in the village points the way.

Continuing along the coast, just before the little resort of Agios Konstantinos, a five-km road winds its way up the lower slopes of Mt Ampelos through thick, well-watered woodland of pine and deciduous trees, to the gorgeous village of **Manolates**. The area is rich in bird life, with a proliferation of nightingales, warblers and thrushes. There are no buses to Manolates so you'll have to find your own way up and walk down. In the village there are many old houses built of stone with projecting balconies. The surfaces of the narrow streets and idyllic little squares are decorated with whitewashed floral designs. There is also a sizeable community of well-fed and slightly aristocratic cats. The Samiots say that if you have not visited either Vourliotes or Manolates, then you have not seen Samos.

Back on the coast, the road continues to the quiet resort of **Agios Konstantinos**. Beyond here it winds through rugged coastal and mountain scenery to the town of **Karlovasi**, Samos' second port. The town consists of three contiguous settlements: Paleo (old), Meson (middle) and Neo (new). It once boasted a thriving tanning industry, but now it's a lacklustre town with little of interest for visitors. The nearest beach is the sand-and-pebble **Potami**, two km to the west of town.

Places to Stay

Despite the onset of package tourism, Kokkari still has many accommodation options for independent travellers. In high season an EOT (☎ 0273-92 217) operates in the village and they will assist in finding accommodation. The bus stops on the main road at a large stone church; the EOT is a little way down the street opposite the church.

The *Pension Eleni* (☎ 92 317) has immaculate tastefully furnished rooms for 6000 dr a double with private bathroom. Adjoining the pension are some pleasant domatia where rates are 4500 dr a double with shared bathroom and a communal kitchen. From the large stone church in Kokkari, continue along the main road; at the T-junction veer left and, 50 metres along on the left, next to the Taverna Dionysos, you will see a sign pointing to the pension. There are many more domatia along this stretch of road, which is just one block back from the waterfront.

Further west along the coast road, close to a beach, are the *Calypso Rooms to Rent* (☎ 94 124), named after their friendly and kind owner. The rooms are well kept and surrounded by a gorgeous garden. Rates are 5000 dr for doubles with private bathroom and use of a communal kitchen. Coming from Kokkari, turn right opposite the turn-off for Manolates (signposted) and you will come to a sign pointing right to the rooms. There are more domatia in this area. The bus stop is just before the Manolates turn-off.

There are as yet no pensions or hotels in Manolates. In the meantime a limited number of beds are available in private homes. Ask about these in the kafeneia and tavernas.

If you get stuck in Karlovasi there are several budget hotels and a domatia (☎ 32 133/707) with doubles for 5500 dr. This accommodation is signposted from the central square where the bus terminates.

Places to Eat

There are many reasonably priced restaurants in Kokkari. *Paradisos Restaurant* at the turn-off to Manolates serves delectable dishes; a full meal with wine or beer will cost around 2000 dr. *Alpha Snack Bar*, on the tiny central square in Manolates, serves low-priced tasty food. There are also a couple of small but nice eateries, on the edge of the village.

Ikaria & the Fourni Islands
Ικαρία & οι Φούρνοι

Ikaria (Ik-a-REE-a, population 9000), lying west of Samos, is a rocky and mountainous island. Like Samos it is also fertile with an abundance of cypress trees, pine forests, olive and fruit trees – Ikarian apricots are especially luscious. At present the island's tourism is low key, but the opening of the new airport may change this. Ailing Greeks have visited Ikaria since ancient times because of its therapeutic radioactive springs which they believe to be the most efficacious in Europe. One spring is so highly radioactive it was deemed unsafe and forced to close.

The name Ikaria originates from the mythical Icarus, who plummeted into the sea close to the island. While escaping from the labyrinth of King Minos on Crete, Icarus failed to heed the warning of his father, Daedalus, and flew too close to the sun. This caused the wax with which he had secured wings to his body to melt, resulting in his untimely and rapid descent. Another myth ascribes the island as the birthplace of Dionysos. Ikaria has two ports, Agios Kirykos on the south coast, and Evdilos on the north coast. The island's best beaches are on the north coast west of Evdilos.

Ikaria is a bit of an oddity as a tourist destination and clings to a very laid back

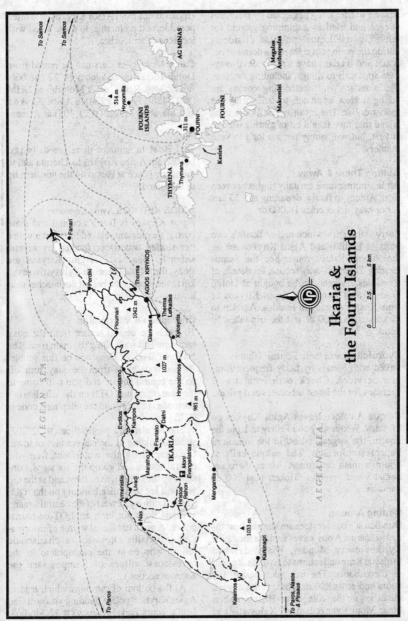

Ikaria &
the Fourni Islands

attitude to life. Long neglected by mainland Greece and used as a dumping ground for left-wing intellectual political dissidents during the periods of right-wing domination, Ikaria and Ikarians have a rather devil-may-care approach to things, including tourism. The islanders, while welcoming tourists, are taking a slow approach to cultivating the tourist dollar. The result is that Ikaria is an island that may take a bit of getting used to at first, but will surely remain long in your memory.

Getting There & Away

Air In summer there are daily flights between from Athens to Ikaria, departing at 8.35 am. A one-way ticket costs 18,000 dr.

Ferry All ferries which call at Ikaria's two ports of Evdilos and Agios Kirykos are on the Piraeus-Samos route. See the Samos Getting There & Away section for details of schedules. Tickets can be bought at Dolihi Tours Travel Agency in Agios Kirykos or from Rostas Agency in Evdilos. A ticket to Piraeus costs 3700 dr and the trip takes 10 hours.

Hydrofoil Ikaria and Fourni islands are linked with Samos by fairly frequent summer services. Check with local travel agencies for the latest schedules and prices.

Caïque A caïque leaves Agios Kirykos on Monday, Wednesday and Friday at 1 pm for Fourni, the largest island in the miniature Fourni archipelago. The caïque calls at Fourni's main settlement, where there are domatia and tavernas. Tickets cost 700 dr one way.

Getting Around

Bus Ikaria's bus services are almost as mythical as Icarus. A bus leaves Evdilos for Agios Kyrikos every Monday, Wednesday and Friday at 8 pm and returns to Evdilos at noon, or thereabouts. The trip takes about 1¼ hours and costs 800 dr. Three times a week buses go to the villages of Hristos Rahon (near Moni Evangelistrias), Xylosyrtis and

Hrysostomos from Agios Kirykos. It is often possible, and preferable, to share a taxi with locals or other tourists.

Car & Motorbike Cars can be rented from Dolihi Tours Travel Agency (☎ 22 346/068; fax 22 346), Rent Cars & Motorbikes DHM (☎ 22 426/579 or 23 230) in Agios Kirykos, and Marabou Travel (☎ 71 403) at Armenistis.

Taxi Boat In summer there are daily taxi boats from Agios Kirykos to Therma and to the sandy beach at Fanari on the northern tip of the island.

AGIOS KIRYKOS Αγιος Κήρυκος

Agios Kirykos is Ikaria's capital and main port. It's a pleasant relaxed little town with a tree-shaded waterfront flanked by several kafeneia. Beaches in Agios Kirykos are stony; the pebbled beach at Xylosyrtis, seven km to the west, is the best of the beaches near town.

Orientation & Information

To reach the central square from the quay turn right and walk along the main road. The National Bank of Greece is on this square. As you walk away from the quay, turn left on the central square and you will come to the post office and OTE on the left. Ikaria's postcode is 833 00 and the telephone code is 0275.

The regular and port police (☎ 22 207) share a building in the eastern part of town. Continue along the waterfront from the central square and go up the six steps, continue up the next flight of steps and at the top you will see the police building on the right. The bus stop is just west of the central square.

Ikaria does not have an EOT or tourist police. A good unofficial source of information is Vassilis Dionissos, a charismatic fellow who owns the pantopoleio in the north-coast village of Kampos (see the Kampos section).

At the bottom of the steps which lead to Agios Kirykos' police building you will find Dolihi Tours Travel Agency (☎ 22 346/068;

fax 22 346). The staff here have information about bus and boat schedules, and can also arrange accommodation.

Radioactive Springs
The radioactive springs are between the Hotel Akti and the police building. A dip costs 500 dr and supposedly cures a multitude of afflictions including arthritis, rheumatism, skin diseases and infertility. There are more hot springs at Therma, three km north-east of Agios Kirykos. This thriving spa community has many visitors in summer.

Archaeological Museum
Agios Kirykos' small archaeological museum houses many local finds. Pride of place is given to a large well-preserved grave stele (500 BC) depicting in low relief a mother (seated) with her husband and four children. The stele was discovered some years ago during the building of a school in a nearby village. It took a court case to prise the stele from the possessive clutches of the school.

The museum's opening times are subject to the vagaries of staffing limitations, so check at one of the tourist offices to see if it's open. The museum is west of the quay and is well signposted.

Places to Stay – bottom end
One of the cheapest places to stay in Agios Kirykos is the *Hotel Akti* (☎ 22 694), which is classed as a pension. The tidy rooms cost 4500/6500/7500 dr for singles/doubles/triples with private bathroom. The pension has great sea views from its appealing garden. To reach it, turn right facing Dolihi Tours, go up the steps to the left and follow the signs.

Pension Maria-Elena (☎ 22 835; fax 71 331) has impeccable rooms. Rates are 8000/9600 dr for doubles/triples with private bathroom. From the quay turn left at the main road, take the first right, and then first left into Artemidos – the pension is along here on the right.

Places to Stay – middle
Agios Kirykos' most luxurious hotel is the new C-class *Hotel Kastro* (☎ 23 480; fax 23 700). The rooms are beautifully furnished and have a telephone, three-channel music system, private bathroom and balcony. Rates are 8000/10,000 dr for singles/doubles, including breakfast. On a clear day you can see the islands of Amorgos, Naxos, Fourni, Patmos, Samos, Arki and Lipsi from the communal terraces. The hotel is opposite the police building.

Places to Eat
Agios Kirykos has a number of restaurants, snack bars, ouzeria and kafeneia. *Taverna Klimataria* serves tasty moderately priced Greek staples and is open all year. On the main square is *Snack Bar Dedalos* which offers delicious restaurant food as well as snacks. The fresh fish and local draught wine are recommended.

Further along the waterfront you cannot miss the looming *T'Adelfia Restaurant* that serves standard fare. *Filoti Pizzeria Restaurant* is one of the town's well-regarded restaurants. Apart from pizza and pasta, there are recommendable souvlaki and chicken dishes. The restaurant can be found at the top of the cobbled street which leads from the butcher's shop.

If you have your own transport and you fancy a change of scenery, try the little taverna *To Tzaki* in the village of Glaredes, about four km west of Agios Kyrikos.

AGIOS KIRYKOS TO THE NORTH COAST
The island's one asphalt road begins a little west of Agios Kirykos and links the capital with the north coast. As the road climbs up to the island's mountainous spine there are dramatic mountain, coastal and sea vistas. The road winds through several villages, some with traditional stone houses topped with rough-hewn slate roofs. It then descends to the island's second port of Evdilos, 41 km by road from Agios Kirykos.

This journey is worth taking for the views, but if you are based in Agios Kirykos and want to travel by bus you will more than likely have to stay overnight in Evdilos or Armenistis. A taxi back to Agios Kyrikos will cost 5000 dr. Hitching may be tricky as there is not much traffic.

EVDILOS Εύδηλος

Evdilos, the island's second port, is a small fishing town. Like Agios Kirykos it's a pleasant and relaxing place, but you may prefer to head further west to the island's best beaches. There is a reasonable beach to the east of Evdilos town, should you need to cool off in the sea. Walk 100 metres up the hill from the square and take the path downwards past the last house on the left.

Places to Stay – bottom end

If you arrive by bus in Evdilos without pre-booked accommodation, you will more than likely be directed to Pension Ioannis Spanos (☎ 31 220). The rooms are centrally located just back from the main square. Reasonable singles/doubles are 4500/6000 dr.

Facing the sea from the middle of the waterfront, the plush-looking building on the far right with black wrought-iron balconies is the domatia belonging to Spyros Rossos (☎ 31 518). Rates are 5000 dr for a double with private bathroom.

Places to Stay – middle

There are two good-quality hotels in Evdilos. The B-class Hotel Atheras (☎ 31 434; fax 31 926) is a breezy, friendly place with delightful modern rooms with balconies. There is also a small pool and bar. Singles/doubles/triples here go for 9000/10,500/12,000 dr. At the top of the hill is the small, but popular B-class Hotel Evdoxia (☎ 31 502; fax 31 571) with rooms for 10,000/11,000 dr. There is a minimarket with basic provisions, a laundry service, money exchange and restaurant (see places to eat). If you phone ahead, someone from the hotel will collect you from the boat.

For a longer-term stay you might like to consider the very tastefully self-contained Apartments Keramé (☎ 31 434; fax 31 926) one km east of Evdilos. One-bedroom apart-

ments (for up to three people) go for 12,000 dr; and two-bedroom apartments cost 16,000 dr. There are also some attic suites for between 6000 and 8000 dr. There is a wood-fired oven and BBQ facilities as well as a laundry.

Places to Eat

In season, there are a number of eateries to choose from, including the Flisvos and, next door, O Kokkos on the west side of the little harbour. On the opposite side of the harbour To Steki is an ouzeri-style place that serves a number of dishes including hamburgers and spaghetti. This is a good place for a cheap meal. Allow for about 1100 dr for spaghetti and a beer.

Hidden away slightly is Chlepas which is open all year and serves ready-made and made-to-order dishes (averaging 1000 to 1500 dr) It is on the left as you walk up the hill to the left from the square.

The well-located Hotel Evdoxia Restaurant is a good meeting place for travellers. The food is home-cooked and you can even order your own favourite dish, if you are staying at the hotel. Otherwise you will pay about 1500 dr for a meat dish and wine. It is also cheaper to eat here if you are a hotel guest. You will probably be offered the house liqueur, made to a secret recipe.

WEST OF EVDILOS
Kampos Κάμπος

Kampos, three km west of Evdilos, is an unspoilt little village with few concessions to tourism. Although it takes some believing, sleepy little Kampos was the island's ancient capital of Oinoe (etymologically derived from the Greek for wine). The name comes from the myth that the Ikarians were the first people to make wine. In ancient times Ikarian wine was considered the best in Greece. Ancient coins found in the vicinity of Kampos have a picture of the wine god, Dionysos, on them.

Information The irrepressible Vassilis Dionissos, who speaks English, is a fount of

Ancient coin depicting Dionysos, the wine god

information on Ikarian history and walking in the mountains. You will find him in his well-stocked pantopoleio – on the right as you come from Evdilos. The village's post box is outside this shop and inside there is a metered telephone. There is also a cardphone nearby.

Things to See As you enter Kampos from Evdilos, the ruins of a **Byzantine palace** can be seen up on the right. In the centre of the village there is a small **museum** housing Neolithic tools, geometric vases, fragments of classical sculpture, small figurines and a very fine 'horse head' knife sheath, carved from ivory.

Next to the museum is the 12th-century **Agia Irini**, the island's oldest church. It is built on the site of a 4th-century basilica, and columns standing in the grounds are from this original church. Agia Irini's supposedly fine frescoes are currently covered with whitewash, because of insufficient funds to pay for its removal. Vassilis Dionissos has the keys to both the museum and church.

The village is also a good base for mountain walking. A one-day circular walk along dirt roads can be made, taking in the village of **Dafni**, the remains of the 10th-century Byzantine **Castle of Koskinas**, and the villages of **Frantato** and **Maratho** and a cave (which is difficult to find).

Places to Stay & Eat There is one *domatia* in Kampos which is owned by – you guessed it – Vassilis Dionissos (☎ 31 300/688). The very pleasant rooms are 5800/6900 dr for doubles/triples with private bathroom. The optional enormous breakfasts are something to be experienced and are accompanied by tasteful Greek music. Coming from Evdilos take the dirt road to the right from near the cardphone and follow it round to the big white building. Alternatively, make your presence known at the general store. Vassilis Dionysos, in any case, meets all the ferries in Evdilos.

There are two moderately priced tavernas in the village – the *Klimataria* is the most obvious. On the east side of Kampos there is a good sandy beach with a seasonal taverna.

Armenistis Αρμενιστής
Armenistis, 15 km west of Evdilos, is the island's largest resort with two beautiful long beaches of pale golden sand, separated by a narrow headland. Although places to stay are springing up quickly here, it's still visited predominantly by independent travellers. Marabou Travel (☎ 71 403), on the road which skirts the sea, organises walking tours on the island. Just east of Armenistis a road leads inland to **Moni Evangelistrias**.

From Armenistis a 3.5-km-long dirt road continues west to the small and alluring pebbled beach of **Nas** at the mouth of a stream. This is Ikaria's unofficial nudist beach. Behind the beach are some scant remains of a **temple of Artemis**.

Places to Stay Ikaria's only camp site is *Armenistis Camping* (☎ 71 349), on the beach at Armenistis.

One of the cheapest places to stay in Armenistis is *Ikarus Rooms* (☎ 71 238) – rates are 4000 dr for a double with shared bathroom, or 5000 dr with private bathroom. The elderly owner, Dimitris Hroussis, speaks a little English and is kind and friendly. Coming from Evdilos, the road forks at the beginning of Armenistis. Take the right fork which skirts the sea, and 50 metres beyond Marabou Travel you will see a sign pointing left to the rooms.

At the approach to the village, before the road forks, you will see *Rooms Fotinos* (☎ 71 235) on the left. The rooms are light, airy and beautifully furnished. Rates are 7000/8400 dr for doubles/triples with private bathroom. Next to these rooms is a sign to the *Armena Inn* (☎ 71 320), which is 100 metres along a dirt road. The newly refurbished rooms cost 7000 dr a double with private bathroom. Family apartments with kitchens are 10,000 dr.

Armenistis' best hotels are around to the west of the village. First is the C-class *Cavos Bay Hotel* (☎ 71 381; fax 71 380), which has a cool and inviting interior. The stucco-walled rooms open out onto a large private terrace overlooking a rocky seascape. The hotel has a large restaurant and bar and a seawater swimming pool built into the rocks. Rates are 8500/11,000/15,000 dr for singles/doubles/triples, breakfast included. Next to it and similarly appointed is the C-class *Hotel Daidalos* (☎ 71 390; fax 71 393) rooms cost 14,850/15,850 dr including breakfast. The sunsets from the balconies of these hotels are poetic.

Nas has domatia and a taverna.

Places to Eat There are three restaurants along the harbourside. The *Pashalia Taverna* probably gets the nod over the other two, *To Symposio* and *Kafestiatorio o Ilios*. Wherever you eat, see if you can get to taste some of the locally made light but potent wine. Both C-class hotels have nice, but pricey, restaurants.

FOURNI ISLANDS Οι Φούρνοι
The Fourni islands are a miniature archipelago lying between Ikaria and Samos. Two of the islands are inhabited: Fourni and Thymena. The capital of the group is Fourni town (also called Kampos), which is the port of Fourni island. Fourni has one other village, tiny Hrysomilia, which is 10 km north of the port; the island's only road con-

nects the two. The islands are mountainous and a good number of beaches are dotted around the coast.

The telephone number of Fourni's port police is ☎ 51 207.

Fourni is the only island with accommodation for tourists and is ideal for those seeking a quiet retreat. Other than the settlement of Fourni itself and a beach over the headland to the south at **Kampi**, the island offers little else besides eating, sleeping and swimming. Most of the islanders make a living from fishing, and catch enough to send a large amount to the Athens fish market.

There are several domatia and tavernas in Fourni town, but no accommodation in Hrysomilia. *Snack Bar-Pension Palladio* (☎ 0275-51 436) is one option. *Taverna Nikos* or *Psarotaverna tou Miltou* on the waterfront will keep you amply supplied with fresh fish for the duration of your stay.

See the Ikaria Getting There & Away section for information about how to get to Fourni.

Chios Χίος

Chios (HEE-os, population 54,000), like its neighbours Samos and Lesvos, is a large island, covering 859 sq km. It is separated from the Turkish peninsula of Karaburun by the eight-km-wide Chios straits. It is a verdant island, although in recent years fires have destroyed many of its forests.

A large number of highly successful ship owners come from Chios and its dependencies, Inousses and Psara. This, and its mastic production, have meant that Chios has not needed to develop a tourist industry. In recent years, however, package tourism has begun to make inroads, although nothing like on the scale of what's happening in Samos.

History
In ancient times, Chios, like Samos, excelled in the arts. The island reached its height in the 7th century BC when the Chios school of

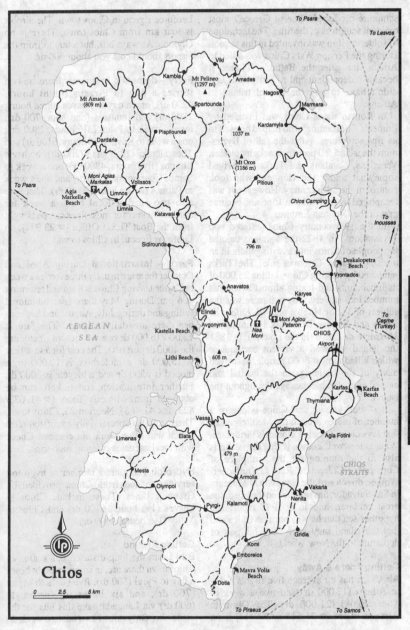

Chios

0   2.5   5 km

sculpture produced some of Greece's most eminent sculptors of the time. The technique of soldering iron was invented in this school. During the Persian Wars Chios was allied to Athens, but after the Battle of Plataea it became independent and so prospered, as it didn't have to pay the annual tribute to Athens.

In Roman times Chios was invaded by Emperor Constantine, who helped himself to its fine sculptures. After the fall of Byzantium the island fell prey to attacks by pirates, Venetians, Catalans and Turks. It revived somewhat under the Genoese who took control in the 14th century. However, it was recaptured by the Turks in 1566 and became part of the Ottoman Empire.

In the 19th century Chios suffered two devastations. In 1822 the Samians cajoled the people of Chios into assisting them in an uprising against Ottoman rule. The Turks retaliated by sacking Chios, killing 25,000 of its inhabitants and taking almost twice that number into slavery. The massacre was the subject of Victor Hugo's poem *L'Enfant de Chios* and Eugene Delacroix's painting *La Massacre de Chios* (in the Louvre). In 1881 the island suffered a violent earthquake which killed almost 6000 people, destroyed many of the buildings in the capital and caused considerable damage throughout the island.

It is well known that Chios is one of a number of places around the Mediterranean that lays claim to being Homer's birthplace. What is less well known is that the island is also in the running for the birthplace of Christopher Columbus. Ruth G Durlacher-Wolper, director of the New World Museum in San Salvador, has researched the life of the great seafarer, and in a 1982 report she hypothesised that he was born on Chios and that the island may have been his port of departure to the New World.

Getting There & Away

Air Chios has on average five flights a day to Athens (13,000 dr) and two a week to Thessaloniki (21,000 dr). The Olympic Airways office (☎ 24 515 or 22 414) is on Leoforos Egeou in Chios town. The airport is four km from Chios town. There is no Olympic Airways bus, but a taxi to/from the airport should cost you about 600 dr.

Ferry – domestic In summer there are two ferries a day to Piraeus (eight hours, 4200 dr), one a day to Lesvos (three hours, 2800 dr) and Inousses (one hour, 700 dr); three a week to Psara (3½ hours, 1800 dr); one a week to Kavala (16 hours, 6100 dr) and Thessaloniki (18 hours, 7200 dr), both via Limnos (five hours, 4800 dr); one a week to Samos (four hours, 2200 dr) and one a week to Patmos (seven hours, 3400 dr). There are also two smaller local boats a week for Samos. Tickets for most lines can be bought from the Boat Ticket Office (☎ 23 971), on Leoforos Egeou, in Chios town.

Ferry – international During April and October there are usually three ferries a week to Çeşme leaving Chios at 8 am and returning at 6 pm. During May there is an additional sailing and during July, August and September there are daily sailings. The fare is 12,000/16,000 dr one way/return (including the 4000 dr port tax). The cost for a small car is 15,000 dr, a motorbike is 10,000 dr, a moped is 6500 dr and a bicycle is 3000 dr. Further information and tickets can be obtained from Miniotis Tours (☎ 41 073/423; fax 41 468), Neorion 23, Chios town. There are also special daily excursion rates which will often work out cheaper. Check with local agencies offering such trips.

Hydrofoil There are a number of hydrofoil services to and from Chios provided by Gianmar Lines. These include Chios to Lesvos (1½ hours, 6100 dr) and Chios to Vathy (1½ hours, 4400 dr).

Getting Around

Bus From the long-distance bus station in Chios town there are, in summer, eight buses a day to Pyrgi (500 dr), five buses to Mesta (700 dr), and six buses to Kardamyla (600 dr) via Langada; take this bus for the camp site. Only one or two buses a week do the journey to Anavatos (400 dr) via Nea Moni and Avgonyma – check the schedule at the bus station, or ask for a copy of the bus timetable in English.

Car & Motorbike The numerous car-rental outlets in Chios town include Budget (☎ 41 361), on Psyhari, near the post office and Europcar (☎ 41 031; mobile 094 517 141) on Leoforos Egeou 56. Chios' ELPA representative is K Mihalakis (☎ 22 445 or 23 076), Rodokanaki 19. There are many moped and motorbike-hire outlets on and near the waterfront.

CHIOS TOWN

Chios town, on the east coast, is the island's port and capital. It's a large town, home to almost half of the island's inhabitants. Its waterfront, flanked by unattractive modern buildings and trendy coffee shops, is noisy in the extreme with an inordinate amount of cars and motorbikes careering up and down. However, things improve considerably once you begin exploring the back streets. The atmospheric old quarter, with many Turkish houses built around a Genoese castle, and the lively market area, are both worth a stroll. Chios town doesn't have a beach; the nearest one is the sandy beach at Karfas, six km south.

Orientation & Information

Most ferries dock at the northern end of the waterfront at the western end of Neorion. Bear in mind that ferries from Piraeus (to Mytilini) arrive at the very inconvenient time of 4 am – worth remembering if you are planning to find a room. The old Turkish quarter (called Kastro) is to the north of here. To reach the town centre from the ferry quay, follow the waterfront round to your left and walk along Leoforos Egeou. Turn right onto Kanari to reach the central square of Plateia Vounakiou (formerly called Plastira). To the north-west of the square are the public gardens, and to the south-east is the market area. Facing inland, the bus station for local buses (blue) is on the right side of the public

gardens and the station for long-distance buses (green) is on the left.

Continuing along the waterfront, the next turn after Kanari is Roïdou. Turn right here and then first left into Rodokanaki. The post office is two blocks along here on the right. Facing inland, take the first right along Kanari and you'll see the OTE on the left. Chios' postcode is 821 00 and the telephone code is 0271. Most banks, including the National Bank of Greece, are between Kanari and Plateia Vounakiou.

The municipal tourist office (☎ 44 389 or 44 344; fax 44 343) is at Kanari 18. The helpful staff give information on accommodation, bus and boat schedules, and have the free magazine *Chios Summertime*. The tourist police (☎ 44 428) and the port police (☎ 44 432) are near one another at the eastern end of Neorion.

Museums

Chios town's most interesting museum is the **Philip Argenti Museum** (☎ 23 463), in the same building as the **Koraïs Library**, one of the country's largest libraries. The museum, which is near the cathedral, contains exquisite embroideries, traditional costumes and portraits of the wealthy Argenti family. Both museums are open from 8 am to 2 pm on Monday to Thursday and on Friday additionally from 5 to 7 pm. On Saturday they open from 8 am to 12.30 pm. Admission is free.

The town's other museums are not so compelling. The **archaeological museum** (☎ 26 664), on Porphyra, contains sculptures, pottery and coins. However, at the time of writing, it was closed for structural repairs. The **Byzantine Museum** (☎ 26 866) is housed in a former mosque, the Medjitie Djami, on Plateia Vounakiou. Opening times are Tuesday to Sunday from 10 am to 1 pm.

Places to Stay – bottom end

With over 30 domatia to choose from, budget accommodation is plentiful in Chios town. Get a copy of the *Chios Tourist Guide* booklet from the tourist office for a full listing.

Chios has one camp site, *Chios Camping* (☎ 74 111), on the beach at Agios Isidoros,

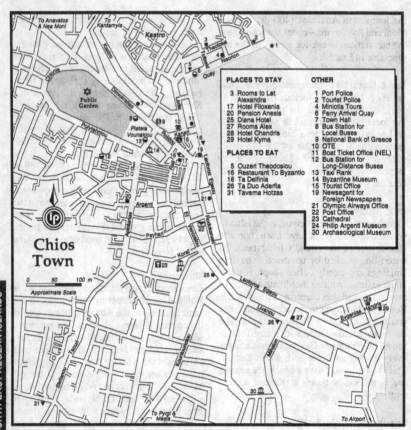

Chios Town

PLACES TO STAY
3 Rooms to Let Alexandra
17 Hotel Filoxenia
20 Pension Anesis
25 Diana Hotel
27 Rooms Alex
28 Hotel Chandris
29 Hotel Kyma

PLACES TO EAT
5 Ouzeri Theodosiou
16 Restaurant To Byzantio
18 Ta Delfinia
26 Ta Duo Aderfia
31 Taverna Hotzas

OTHER
1 Port Police
2 Tourist Police
4 Miniotis Tours
6 Ferry Arrival Quay
7 Town Hall
8 Bus Station for Local Buses
9 National Bank of Greece
10 OTE
11 Boat Ticket Office (NEL)
12 Bus Station for Long-Distance Buses
13 Taxi Rank
14 Byzantine Museum
15 Tourist Office
19 Newsagent for Foreign Newspapers
21 Olympic Airways Office
22 Post Office
23 Cathedral
24 Philip Argenti Museum
30 Archaeological Museum

NORTH-EAST AEGEAN ISLANDS

between Sykiada and Langadas, 14 km north of Chios town. The site has good facilities, a bar and restaurant. To reach it take a Kardamyla or Langadas bus.

The best and most welcoming domatia option is *Rooms Alex* (☎ 26 054) at Livanou 29. Alex has six rooms which go for 5000 dr without bathroom and 6000 dr with bathroom. There is a relaxing roof garden, festooned with flags and Alex will meet your boat, or come to pick you up, if you call him. He will also help you with car or bike rentals and will fill you in on what you need to know about Chios.

The D-class *Hotel Filoxenia* (☎ 26 559) is signposted from the waterfront and is above the Restaurant To Byzantio. The unadorned but clean rooms cost 3500/5000/6000 dr with shared bathroom and 4700/6500/7800 dr with private bathroom.

Pension Anesis (☎ 44 801), at Vasilikari 2, has B-class rooms for 4000/6000/7000 dr. To reach this place, follow Aplotarias from the main square and you will see it on your right.

In the old quarter *Rooms to Rent Alexandria* (☎ 41 815), on Theotoka, has agreeable doubles/triples for 4500/5200 dr with shared bathroom. As you walk east along Neorion, turn left onto Tsitseki, and take the first right into Theotoka – the rooms are on the left, behind the periptero.

Places to Stay – middle

The *Pension Anesis* (☎ 44 801), mentioned above, also has A-class doubles/triples with bathroom, air-con and fridge for 8000/12,000 dr. See the bottom-end section for details.

The C-class *Diana Hotel* (☎ 44 180; fax 26 748) on El Venizelou is a good mid-range hotel aimed primarily at the Greek business market. Single/doubles rates here are 8500/12,550 dr including breakfast. The C-class *Hotel Kyma* (☎ 44 500; fax 44 600) occupies a turn-of-the-century mansion and has lots of character. Rates are 11,500/15,500 dr with breakfast.

The B-class *Hotel Chandris* (☎ 44 401; fax 25 768) is considered by some to be Chios town's best hotel, though it is beginning to show its age. It has two bars, a restaurant and a swimming pool. Rates are 13,200/17,400 dr. Both of these hotels are on Evgenias Handri, on the south side of town.

Places to Eat

Restaurant To Byzantio, on the corner of Rali and Roïdou, is a bright, cheerful and unpretentious place which serves traditional Greek fare at low prices. Right opposite the ferry disembarkation point on Neorion is *Ouzeri Theodosiou*, an old-style and very popular establishment. The most original place with the freshest possible fish is *Iakovos Taverna* on the northern arm of the harbour. Blink and you'll miss it – there's no sign indicating its existence. It's wedged next to the fish terminal. Be here before 8.30 pm or you won't get a table.

Ta Delfinia is on the waterfront and is a bit touristy, with photo menus, but the food and service is good and it's a nice place to watch street life. Opposite Rooms Alex at Livanou 38 is *Ta Duo Aderfia* with a pleasant walled garden. Try the special spare ribs in BBQ sauce.

Finally, *Taverna Hotzas* (open evenings only) at the southern end of town is a bit of an institution, with cats and hens and ducks wandering around the garden. To get here, walk up Aplotarias and turn right at the fork along Stefanou Tsouri; follow it until you come across the restaurant.

AROUND THE ISLAND
Central Chios

North of Chios itself is an elongated beachside suburb leading to **Vrontados** where you can sit on the supposed stone chair of Homer, the Daskalopetra, though it is quietly accepted that it is unlikely to have been used by Homer himself. It is a serene spot though, and it would not be hard to imagine Homer and his acolytes reciting epic verses to their admiring followers.

Immediately south of Chios town is a warren of walled mansions, some restored, others crumbling, called the **Kampos**. This was the preferred place of abode for the wealthy Genoese and Greek merchant families from the 14th century onwards. You can easily get lost here so keep your wits about you. It is hard to stop your vehicle in these labyrinthine lanes to see what is over the walls, so consider riding a bicycle. Chios' main beach resort **Karfas** is here too, seven km south of Chios town. It is an OK kind of beach with some moderate development and some A-class hotels. If you like your beaches quiet, look elsewhere.

In the almost exact centre of the island is The 11th-century Nea Moni. This large monastery stands in a beautiful setting in the mountains, 14 km from Chios town. Like so many monasteries in Greece it was built to house an icon which appeared miraculously. The icon in question was of the Virgin Mary and it materialised before the eyes of three shepherds. In its heyday the monastery was one of the wealthiest in Greece and the most pre-eminent artists of Byzantium were commissioned to execute the mosaics in its katholikon.

During the 1822 atrocities the buildings were set on fire and all the resident monks were massacred. There is a macabre display of their skulls in the ossuary at the monastery's little chapel. In the earthquake of 1881

NORTH-EAST AEGEAN ISLANDS

the katholikon's dome caved in, causing quite a lot of damage to the mosaics. Nonetheless, these mosaics still rank amongst the most outstanding examples of Byzantine art in Greece. They are esteemed for the striking contrasts of their vivid colours and the fluidity and juxtapositions of the figures. A few nuns live at the monastery. Opening times are from 8 am until 1 pm and 4 to 8 pm. Admission is free. The bus service to the monastery is poor, but travel agents in Chios town have excursions here and to the village of Anavatos.

Ten km further out from Nea Moni, at the end of a road that leads to nowhere, stands the forlorn ghost-village of **Anavatos**. Its abandoned grey-stone houses stand as lonely sentinels to one of Chios' great tragedies. Nearly all the inhabitants of the village perished in the atrocities of 1822 and today only a small number of elderly people live in Anavatos, mostly in houses at the base of the village.

It is a striking village built on a precipitous cliff which the villagers chose to hurle themselves over, rather than be taken captive. Narrow stepped pathways wind between the houses to the summit of the village.

Avgonyma, further back along the road, is only slightly more populated than Anavatos, but lacks the drama of its neighbour.

The beaches on the mid-west coast are not spectacular, but they are quiet and generally undeveloped. **Lithi beach**, the southernmost, is popular with weekenders and can get busy.

Southern Chios

Southern Chios is dominated by medieval villages that look as though they were transplanted from the Levant rather than built by Genoese colonisers in the 14th century. The rolling, scrubby hills are covered in low mastic trees that for many years were the main source of income for these scattered settlements.

There are some 20 Mastihohoria (mastic villages); the two best preserved are Pyrgi and Mesta. As mastic was such a highly lucrative commodity in the Middle Ages,

many an invader cast an acquisitive eye upon the villages, necessitating sturdy fortifications. The archways spanning the streets were to prevent the houses from collapsing during earthquakes. Because of the sultan's fondness for mastic chewing gum, the inhabitants of the Mastihohoria were not included in the 1822 massacre.

Pyrgi (Πυργί) The largest of the Mastihohoria, and one of the most extraordinary villages in the whole of Greece, is Pyrgi (population 1300), 24 km south-west of Chios town. The vaulted streets of the fortified village are narrow and labyrinthine. However, what makes Pyrgi unique are the façades of its buildings, which are decorated with intricate grey and white designs. Some of the patterns are geometric and others are based on flowers, leaves and animals. The technique used is called *xysta* and is achieved by coating the walls with a mixture of cement and black volcanic sand, painting over this with white lime, and then scraping off parts of the lime to reveal the matt grey beneath. Nowadays the scraping is done with the bent prong of a fork.

From the main road, a fork to the right (coming from Chios town) leads into the heart of the village and the central square. The little 12th-century **Church of Agios Apostolos**, just off the square, is profusely decorated with well-preserved 17th-century frescoes. Ask at the taverna or kafeneio for the whereabouts of the caretaker, who will open it up for you. The façade of the larger church, on the opposite side of the square, has the most impressive xysta of all the buildings in the village.

Places to Stay & Eat The *Women's Agricultural Co-operative of Chios* (☎ 72 496) rents a number of traditionally furnished rooms in private houses throughout Pirgi. Rates are around 5000 to 7000 dr for doubles, depending on the season. The co-operative's office is near the central square of Pyrgi and is signposted. On the edge of the village are the very pleasant *Rooms to Let Nikos* (☎ 72 425) with doubles for 6000 dr.

Gum Mastic

Gum mastic is a product of the *lentisk* bush, and conditions in southern Chios are ideal for its growth. Mastic has been utilised since classical times. Many ancient Greeks, including Hippocrates, proclaimed its pharmaceutical benefits. Amongst ailments it was claimed to cure were stomach upsets, chronic coughs and diseases of the liver, intestines and bladder. It was also used as an antidote for snake bites. During Turkish rule Chios received preferential treatment from the sultans who, along with the ladies of the harem, seem to have become hooked on chewing gum made from mastic – try the stuff and you will no doubt wonder why.

Until recently, mastic was widely used in the pharmaceutical industry, as well as in the manufacture of chewing gum and certain alcoholic drinks, particularly arak, a Middle Eastern liqueur. In most cases mastic has now been replaced by other more easily available products. However, mastic production may yet have a future, as some adherents of alternative medicine claim that it stimulates the immune system and reduces blood pressure and cholesterol levels. Chewing gum made from mastic can be bought on Chios, under the brand name Elma. ■

ΓΝΗΣΙΑ **ΕΛΜΑ** ΦΥΣΙΚΗ ΜΑΣΤΙΧΑ ΧΙΟΥ NEA

THE ORIGINAL **ELMA** NATURAL CHIOS GUM MASTIC NEW

This includes the use of a kitchen and fridge and there is a handy parking area, if you have a car.

The little taverna *I Manoula* on the central square (on the right as you face the large church) is your main eating option, other than a pizza place down by the main bypass road.

Emboreios (Εμπορειός) Six km to the south of Pyrgi, Emboreios was the port of Pyrgi in the days when mastic production was big business. These days Emboreios is a quite holiday resort for people who like to relax. As you come from Chios town, a signpost points left to Emboreios, just before you arrive at Pyrgi.

There are three tavernas, the *Neptune* with the most prominent position, and to the side the *Ifestio* and the *Porto Emborios* with a marginally better ambience. If you want to stay here, call *Studio Apartments Vasiliki* (☎ 71 422), or *Themis Studios* (☎ 71 810).

Mavra Volia beach is at the end of the road and has unusual black volcanic pebbles as its main attraction. There is another more secluded beach, just over the headland along a paved track. There is good, if limited parking for both beaches.

Mesta (Μεστά) Continuing on the main road from Pyrgi you will reach the mastic village of **Olympoi** after five km. It's less immediately attractive than its two neighbours but still worth a brief stop.

Mesta, five km further on, has a very different atmosphere from that created by the striking visual impact of Pyrgi and should be on any visitor's itinerary. The village is absolutely exquisite and is completely enclosed within massive fortified walls. Entrance to the maze of streets is via one of four gates. This method of limiting entry to the settlement and its disorienting maze of streets and tunnels is a prime example of 14th-century defence architecture, as protection against pirates and marauders. The labyrinthine cobbled streets of bare stone houses and arches have a mute and melancholy aura.

The village has two churches of the Taxiarhs: the older one dates from Byzantine times and has a magnificent 17th-century iconostasis; the second one, built in the 19th century, has very fine frescoes.

Orientation Buses stop on Plateia Nikolaou Poumpaki, on the main road outside Mesta. To reach the central square of Plateia Taxiarhon, with your back to the bus shelter, turn right, and then immediately left, and you will see a sign pointing to the centre of the village.

Places to Stay The small EOT office, on Plateia Taxiarhon 51, is staffed by the Greek-Australian Dimitris Pippidis (☎ 76 319). Dimitris has a list of many of the rooms to rent in private houses in Mesta and will make a reservation for you. Most of these traditionally furnished rooms are part of the Women's Co-operative and the prices are the same as those in Pyrgi, but Dimitris may be able to find somewhere cheaper for you. One option is the accommodation belonging to *Despina Syrimis* (☎ 76 494). The room, which costs 6000 dr, will sleep up to four people, and has a kitchen and private bathroom. The room is difficult to find but Despina speaks English so you could telephone her. Otherwise you can find her in the central square's Mesaionas Restaurant where she works.

Places to Eat There are two restaurants on the Plateia Taxiarhon and both conduct their business in magical, romantic courtyard settings. Dionysios Karambelas, the affable owner of *Restaurant O Morias Sta Mesta* and originally from the Peloponnese (hence the name of the restaurant – Morias is the old name for the Peloponnese), will provide you

with some superb country cooking. Ask to try hortokeftedes (vegetable patties) and an unusual wild green, kritamos, that grows by the sea. You should also ask for a glass of souma; an ouzo made from figs.

Next door, the *Mesaionas Restaurant* will provide you with equally good food should Dionysios be full.

Northern Chios

Northern Chios is characterised by its craggy peaks (Mt Pelineo, Mt Oros and Mt Amani), deserted villages and scrawny hillsides that once sported rich pine forests. The area is mainly for the adventurous and those not phased by driving along tortuous roads. Homer's birthplace is also reputed to be here.

Volissos is the main focus for the villages of the north-western quarter. Reputedly Homer's place of birth, it is today a somewhat crumbling settlement, capped with an impressive Genoese fort. Volissos' port is **Limnia** which is a workaday fishing harbour. It's not especially appealing, but has a nice taverna. You can continue to **Limnos**, one km away, where caïques sometimes leave for Psara. The road onwards round the north end is very winding and passes some very isolated villages.

On the north-eastern side a picturesque road leads out of **Vrontados** through a landscape that is somewhat more visitor-friendly than the western side. Pretty **Langada** is the first village, wedged at the end of a bay looking out towards Inousses. **Kardamyla** and **Marmaro** are next and are the two main settlements, though Marmaro, by the sea is not geared for tourism and is mercilessly exposed to the summer meltemi winds that howl in through its narrow bay.

Most people go no further than the beach at **Nagos** which is not bad, but still exposed to the vagaries of the winds, as is all the north coast. The road onwards winds upwards, skirting craggy Mt Pelineo. The scenery is green enough, but settlements are fewer and more remote. **Armades** and **Vikio** are two villages you will traverse before hitting the last village, **Kambia**, perched high up on a ridge overlooking bare hillsides and the sea far below. From here a mostly sealed road leads you round Mt Pelineo, past a futuristic phalanx of 10 huge wind-driven generators on the opposite side of the valley, back to the cross-island route near Volissos.

Inousses Οινούσσες

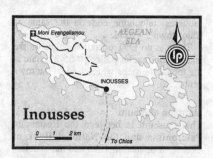

Off the north-eastern coast of Chios lie nine tiny islets, collectively called Inousses. Only one of these, also called Inousses, is inhabited. Around 400 people live here permanently, making their living from fishing and sheep farming. The island has three fish farms and exports small amounts of fish to Italy and France. Inousses is hilly and covered in scrub and has good beaches.

However, these facts apart, this is no ordinary Greek island. Small, Inousses may be, but it is the ancestral home of around 30% of Greece's ship owners. Most of these exceedingly wealthy maritime barons conduct their businesses from Athens, London and New York, but in summer return with their families to Inousses where they own luxurious mansions.

There is a rumour that these ship owners offer financial incentives to discourage people from opening tavernas or domatia on the island, because they don't want to attract foreign tourists. It may not be possible to vouch for the truth of this but certainly tourism is not encouraged on the island: no domatia owners come to meet the boat, there are no domatia signs and wandering about the streets fails to bring offers of accommodation. Several islanders have stated that Inousses has a few domatia, but they are vague as to their whereabouts.

If these quirks have not discouraged you from going to Inousses, on a more positive note the island has a picturesque town of neoclassical mansions; superb beaches; lots of opportunities for walking; stunning vistas and no package tourists – in fact not many tourists at all. In Inousses town there is a large naval boarding school. If you visit during term time you may well encounter the pupils parading around town to bellowed marching orders.

Getting There & Away

The island is only served by the local ferry boat *Oinoussai II* which plies daily between the island and Chios town. It leaves Chios town at 2 pm and Inousses at 9 am. Purchase tickets on board for 700 dr (one way). The trip takes about one hour. In summer there are sometimes excursion boats from Chios town to the island. Enquire about these at one of the travel agencies in Chios town.

Getting Around

Inousses has no public transport, but there is one taxi.

INOUSSES TOWN
Orientation & Information

The island has one settlement, the little town which is also called Inousses. From the boat quay, facing inland turn left and follow the waterfront to Plateia Antoniou P Laimou; veer slightly right here, and you will immediately come to Plateia T Naftisynis; veer right once again and you will see ahead the Restaurant & Kafeneio Pateronissa. Facing this establishment turn right and ascend the steps to reach the centre of town.

If you turn left at the Restaurant Pateronissa and then take the first right into Konstantinou Antonopoulou you will come to the National Bank of Greece, which one can surmise, is kept very busy. Next door to the bank is a combined post office and OTE.

NORTHEAST AEGEAN ISLANDS

Inousses' telephone code is the same as Chios town's – 0271.

There is no EOT or tourist police on the island. The regular police (☎ 55 222) are at the top of the steps which lead to the town centre.

Maritime Museum

This museum is between the Restaurant Pateronissa and the National Bank of Greece. It opened in 1990 and the benefactors were wealthy ship owners from the island. Many island families donated nautical memorabilia, which includes *objets d'art*, photographs, models of early ships, cannons and nautical instruments.

The museum keeps very erratic opening times. If you find it closed (which is highly likely), ask around and someone may open it up for you.

Places to Stay

There is no camp site on the island and camping freelance would definitely be frowned upon. For domatia, ask at one of the restaurants or kafeneia. Good luck!

Inousses' one hotel is the comfortable, but pricey, C-class *Hotel Thalassoporos* (☎ 55 475/476), at the top of the steps which lead to the town centre. Rates are 5800/8800 dr for singles/doubles with private bathroom. These prices drop to 4400/6500 dr in the low season. It's unlikely ever to be full, but just in case, phone ahead in July and August.

Places to Eat

Of Inousses' three restaurants, the *Restaurant Pateronissa* has been established the longest. The food is reasonably priced and well prepared.

The town has three pantopoleia: one is near the Restaurant Pateronissa and the other two are in the centre of town on the road which leads up to the prominent Agios Nikolaos church.

ISLAND WALK

This is a three-hour circular walk. Although most of the walk is along a narrow cement road, you are unlikely to meet much traffic. Take plenty of water and a snack with you as there are no refreshments available along the way. Also take your swimming gear as you will pass many of the island's beaches. You will also pass the Moni Evangelismou in the west of the island.

Just beyond the maritime museum you will see a signpost to **Moni Evangelismou**. This will take you along the cement road which skirts the west coast. Along the way you will pass several inviting beaches and coves. Only **Apiganos beach** is signposted, but there are others which are easily accessible from the road. After about one hour the road loops inland, and a little further along is the entrance to the very palatial Moni Evangelismou which stands in extensive grounds.

Within the convent is the mummified body of Irini Pateras, daughter of the late Panagos Pateras who was a multimillionaire ship owner. Irini became a nun in her late teens and died in the early 1960s when she was 20. Her distraught mother decided to build the convent in memory of her daughter. In the Greek Orthodox religion, three years after burial the body is exhumed and the bones cleaned and reburied in a casket. When Irini's body was exhumed it was found to have mummified rather than decomposed; this phenomenon is regarded in Greece as evidence of sainthood. Irini's mother is now abbess of the convent, which houses around 20 nuns. Only women may visit the convent and of course they must be appropriately (modestly) dressed.

Continuing along the cement road, beyond the entrance to the convent, you will come to two stone pillars on the left. The wide path between the pillars leads in 10 minutes to an enormous white cross which is a memorial to St Irini. This is the highest point of the island and commands stunning views over to northern Chios and the Turkish peninsula of Karaburun. About 20 minutes further along, the cement road gives way to a dirt track. Continue straight ahead to reach Inousses town.

Psara Ψαρά

Psara (Psar-A) lies off Chios' north-west coast. The island is nine km long and five km wide and is rocky with little vegetation. During Ottoman times Greeks settled on this remote island to escape Turkish oppression. By the 19th century, many of these inhabitants, like those of Chios and Inousses, had become successful ship owners. When the rallying cry for self-determination reverberated through the country, the Psariots zealously took up arms and contributed a large number of ships to the Greek cause. In retaliation the Turks stormed the island and killed all but 3000 of the 30,000 inhabitants. The island never regained its former glory and today has only around 500 inhabitants, all of whom live in the island's one settlement, also called Psara.

Places to Stay & Eat

Like Inousses, Psara sees few tourists. The old parliament building has been converted into an *EOT Guesthouse* (☎ 0274-61 293). Doubles with shared bathroom are 5500 dr and with private bathroom, 6500 dr. Exten-

sion and renovation work is currently being carried out on the building. Information may be obtained by either telephoning the guesthouse or ringing ☎ 0251-27 908 in Lesvos. There are also *domatia* in Psara.

There are a small number of eating places on the island.

Getting There & Away

Ferries leave Chios town for Psara at 7 am three times a week. Check with a local agent for current departure days since these may change from year to year.

Lesvos (Mytilini)
Λέσβος (Μυτιλήνη)

Lesvos (LES-vos, population 88,800) is the third-largest island in Greece, after Crete and Evia. It lies north of Chios and south-east of Limnos. The island is mountainous with two bottleneck gulfs penetrating its south coast. The south and east of the island are fertile, with numerous olive groves. Lesvos produces the best olive oil in Greece and has many olive-oil refineries. In contrast to the south and east, the west has rocky and barren mountains, creating a dramatic moonscape.

Lesvos is becoming a popular package-holiday destination, but is large enough to absorb tourists without seeming to be overrun. Most Greeks call the island Mytilini, which is also the name of the capital.

History

In the 6th century BC, Lesvos was unified under the rule of the tyrant Pittahos, one of ancient Greece's Seven Sages. Pittahos succeeded in dispelling the long-standing animosity between the island's two cities of Mytilini and Mithymna. This new-found peace generated an atmosphere conducive to creativity, and Lesvos became a centre of artistic and philosophical achievement. Terpander, the musical composer, and Arion the poet, were both born on Lesvos in the 7th century BC.

NORTH-EAST AEGEAN ISLANDS

Sappho

The poet Sappho is renowned chiefly for her poems that speak out in favour of lesbian relationships, though her range of lyric poetry extends beyond works of an erotic nature. She was born in 630 BC in the town of Eresos on the western side of Lesvos. Little is known about her private life other than that she was married, had a daughter and was exiled to Sicily in about 600 BC. Only fragments remain of her nine books of poems, the most famous of which are the marriage songs. Among her works were hymns, mythological poems and personal love songs. Most of these seem to have been addressed to a close inner-circle of female companions. Sappho uses sensuous images of nature to create her own special brand of erotic lyric poetry. It is a simple yet melodious style, later copied by the Roman poet Catullus. Lesvos and Eresos, in particular, are today the targets of many visits by lesbians paying homage to Sappho. ■

Arion's works influenced the tragedians of the 5th century BC such as Sophocles and Euripides. Sappho, one of the greatest poets of ancient Greece, was born on Lesvos almost a century later. Unfortunately little of her poetry is extant, but what remains reveals a genius for combining passion with simplicity and detachment, in verses of great beauty and power. In the 4th century BC, Aristotle and Epicurus taught at an exceptional school of philosophy which flourished on Lesvos.

On a more prosaic level Lesvos suffered at the hands of invaders and occupiers to the same extent as all other Greek islands. In 527 BC the Persians conquered the island, but in 479 BC it was captured by Athens and became a member of the Delian League. In the following centuries the island suffered numerous invasions, and in 70 BC it was conquered by Julius Caesar. Byzantines, Venetians, Genoese and Turks followed.

However, through all these vicissitudes the arts retained a high degree of importance. The primitive painter Theophilos (1866-1934) and the Nobel prize-winning poet Odysseus Elytis were both born on Lesvos. The island is to this day a spawning ground for innovative ideas in the arts and politics, and is the headquarters of the University of the Aegean.

Getting There & Away

Air There are three flights a day from Lesvos to Athens (14,800 dr), one a day to Thessaloniki (18,800 dr), and daily flights to Limnos (12,600 dr). There are two flights a week to Chios (9400 dr). Note that Lesvos is always referred to as Mytilini on air schedules. The Olympic Airways office (☎ 28 659/660 or 22 820) in Mytilini is at Kavetsou 44. (Kavetsou is a southerly continuation of Ermou.) The airport is eight km south of Mytilini. A taxi from/to the airport will cost 1000 dr.

Ferry – domestic In summer there is at least one ferry every day to Piraeus (12 hours, 5300 dr) via Chios and some direct services (10 hours); three a week to Kavala (11 hours, 5100 dr) via Limnos; and two a week to Thessaloniki (13 hours, 7000 dr) via Limnos. Ferry ticket offices line the eastern side of Pavlou Kountouriotou, in Mytilini. One of the most reliable places for obtaining information is the Maritime Company of Lesvos (☎ 28 480, 25 800 or 22 220), Pavlou Kountouriotou 47. The port police (☎ 28 827/647) are also on the waterfront.

Ferry – international From April to October there are ferries every day except Sunday to Ayvalık in Turkey. In winter, services drop to about three a week. Ferries leave at 8 am and the journey takes two hours. Tickets cost 14,000 dr one way/return and can be bought at the Maritime Company of Lesvos or any of the other offices that advertise this service. As is often the case when you sail from a Greek island to Turkey you must submit your passport a day in advance. Ayvalık is a coastal resort and fishing village, quite near the ruins of Pergamum.

Hydrofoil In summer, there are a number of hydrofoil routes in operation from Mytilini. The main ones are: Limnos (three hours, 6800 dr); Chios (1½ hours, 6100 dr); Samos (three hours, 7600 dr); Patmos (five hours, 9100 dr); Kavala (4½ hours direct, 10,800 dr); and Alexandroupolis (3½ hours direct, 9300 dr). Reservations and tickets can be obtained at Dimakis Tours (☎ 20 716; fax 27 865), Kountouriotou 83.

Getting Around

Bus Lesvos' transport hub is the capital, Mytilini. In summer, from the long-distance bus station there are three buses a day to Skala Eresou (2½ hours, 1600 dr) via Eresos. There are five buses a day to Mithymna (1¾ hours, 1100 dr) via Petra, and two buses to Sigri (2½ hours, 1650 dr). There are no direct buses between Eresos,

Sigri and Mithymna. If you wish to travel from one of these villages to another, change buses in the town of Kalloni, which is 48 km from Eresos and 22 km from Mithymna. There are five buses a day to the south-coast resort of Plomari (1¼ hours, 750 dr).

Car & Motorbike There are many car-hire outlets in Mytilini. They include Troho Kinisi (☎ 41 160; mobile 093 237 900), which operates from the Erato Hotel just south of the Olympic Airways office, and Lesvos Car (☎ 28 242), Pavlou Kountouriotou 47. Many motorbike-hire firms are along the same stretch of waterfront. There are also car and motorbike-hire outlets in Mithymna and Skala Eresou. Bear in mind that Lesvos is large, and a moped is not really a practical mode of transport for exploring the entire island.

MYTILINI Μυτιλήνη

Mytilini, the capital and port of Lesvos, is a

Lesvos (Mytilini)

0   5   10 km

NORTH-EAST AEGEAN ISLANDS

large workaday town. If you are enthralled by pretty and sparkling towns like Mykonos and Paros then you won't necessarily find the same ambience in Mytilini. However, this town has its own attractions including a lively harbour and nightlife, its once grand 19th-century mansions which are gradually being renovated, and its jumbled streets. All this makes Mytilini a vacation distraction its own right.

Mytilini won't enthral sun, sea and sand lovers, for its town beach is mediocre, crowded and what's more you have to pay to use it (adults, 200 dr; children, 100 dr). However, you will appreciate Mytilini if you enjoy seeking out traditional kafeneia and little back-street ouzeria, or if you simply take pleasure in wandering in unfamiliar towns.

The northern end of Ermou, the town's main commercial thoroughfare, is a wonderful ramshackle street full of character. It has old-fashioned zaharoplasteia; grocers; fruit and vegetable stores; bakers; and antique, embroidery, ceramic and jewellery shops. (The latter four are there for the benefit of discerning locals rather than spendthrift tourists.)

Orientation

Mytilini is built around two harbours (the north and south) which occupy both sides of a promontory and are linked by the main thoroughfare of Ermou. East of the harbours is a large fortress surrounded by a pine forest. All passenger ferries dock at the southern harbour. The waterfront here is called Pavlou Kountouriotou and the ferry quay is at its southern end. The northern harbour's waterfront is called Navmahias Ellis.

Information

The EOT (☎ 28 199) and tourist police (☎ 22 776) share the same office at the entrance to the quay. There is also an EOT at the airport.

The post office is on Vournazon, which is west of the southern harbour. The OTE is on the same street just west of the post office. Mytilini's postcode is 811 00; its telephone code is 0251.

Banks, including the National Bank of Greece, can be found on Pavlou Kountouriotou. There is also an automatic currency-exchange machine at the Mortgage Bank on this street, not too far from the ferry terminal.

Things to See

Mytilini's imposing **castle**, with its well-preserved walls, was built in early Byzantine times and renovated in the 14th century by Fragistco Gatelouzo. It was enlarged by the Turks. The surrounding pine forest is a pleasant place for a picnic. The castle is open daily from 8.30 am to 2.50 pm. Admission is 500 dr.

The **archaeological museum** (☎ 22 087) is housed in a neoclassical mansion one block north of the quay and has impressive finds from Neolithic to Roman times. Opening times are Tuesday to Sunday from 8.30 am to 3 pm. Admission is 500 dr.

The dome of the **Church of Agios Therapon** can be spotted from almost anywhere on the southern waterfront. The church has a highly ornate interior with a huge chandelier, an intricately carved iconostasis and priest's throne, and a frescoed dome. The **Byzantine Museum** (☎ 28 916) in the church's courtyard houses some fine icons. The museum is open from Monday to Saturday from 10 am to 1 pm. Admission is 200 dr.

Whatever you do don't miss the **Theophilos Museum** (☎ 41 644), which houses the works of the prolific primitive painter Theophilos, who was born on Lesvos. Several prestigious museums and galleries around the country now proudly display works by Theophilos. However, he lived in abject poverty painting the walls of kafeneia and tavernas in return for sustenance. The museum is open Tuesday to Sunday from 9 am to 1 pm, and 4.30 to 8 pm. Admission is 250 dr.

The **Teriade Museum** (☎ 23 372), next door, commemorates the artist and critic Stratis Eleftheriadis (he Gallicised his name to Teriade) who was born on Lesvos but lived and worked in Paris. It was largely due to the

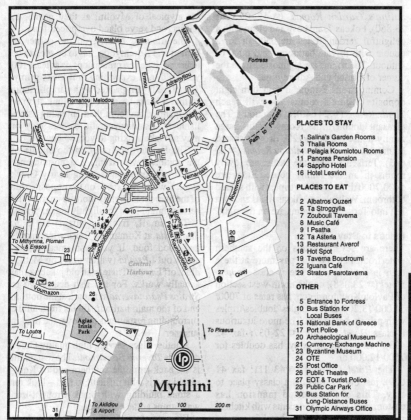

PLACES TO STAY

1 Salina's Garden Rooms
3 Thalia Rooms
4 Pelagia Koumiotou Rooms
11 Panorea Pension
14 Sappho Hotel
16 Hotel Lesvion

PLACES TO EAT

2 Albatros Ouzeri
6 Ta Stroggylia
7 Zoubouli Taverna
8 Music Café
9 I Psatha
12 Ta Asteria
13 Restaurant Averof
18 Hot Spot
19 Taverna Boudroumi
22 Iguana Café
29 Stratos Psarotaverna

OTHER

5 Entrance to Fortress
10 Bus Station for
   Local Buses
15 National Bank of Greece
17 Port Police
20 Archaeological Museum
21 Currency-Exchange Machine
23 Byzantine Museum
24 OTE
25 Post Office
26 Public Theatre
27 EOT & Tourist Police
28 Public Car Park
30 Bus Station for
   Long-Distance Buses
31 Olympic Airways Office

Mytilini

0   100   200 m

NORTH-EAST AEGEAN ISLANDS

efforts of Teriade that the works of Theophilos gained international renown. On display are reproductions of Teriade's own illustrations and his collection of works by 20th-century artists, which include such greats as Picasso, Chagall and Matisse. The museum is open Tuesday to Sunday from 9 am to 2 pm, and 5 to 8 pm. Admission is 500 dr.

These museums are four km from Mytilini in the village of **Varia** where Theophilos was born. Take a local bus from the bus station at the northernmost section of Pavlou Kountouriotou (see Information).

Places to Stay – bottom end

In Mytilini, domatia owners belong to a co-operative called *Sappho Self-Catering Rooms in Mytilini*. There are 22 establishments; if any of the ones recommended are full or don't suit, the owner will direct you to another. Most of these domatia are in little side streets off Ermou, near the northern harbour. The nearest to the quay is *Panorea Pension* (☎ 42 650), Komninaki 21. The clean and simply furnished double/triple rooms cost 5800/7500 dr with shared bathroom. Komninaki is one block behind the eastern section of Pavlou Kountouriotou.

Salina's Garden Rooms (☎ 42 073 or 23 860), Fokeas 7, are cosy and clean with a delightful garden. Rates are 6500 dr for a double with private bathroom and 6000 dr without. The rooms are signposted from the corner of Ermou and Adramytiou.

Coming from Ermou, if you turn right opposite Salina's rooms you will reach *Thalia Rooms* (☎ 24 640), at Kinikiou 1. The pleasant double/triple rooms in this large family house are 6000/7200 dr with shared bathroom. *Pelagia Koumiotou Rooms* (☎ 20 643), Tertseti 6, near the castle, are lovely rooms in an old family house. Rates are 5400/7000 dr for doubles/triples with shared bathroom. Walk along Mikras Asias and turn left into Tertseti; the rooms are on the right.

Places to Stay – middle

There are several hotels on the southern waterfront, but you will pay more at these than in the domatia. The C-class *Sappho Hotel* (☎ 28 888), on the north-west section of Pavlou Kountouriotou, has rates of 7000/11,000/13,200 dr for singles/doubles/triples with private bathroom. The more luxurious B-class *Hotel Lesvion* (☎ 22 037; fax 42 493), just two doors away, has doubles for 7500/12,000 dr.

The *Hotel Laureate* (☎ 43 111; fax 41 629), just out of town, is a classy place to stay. This old converted mansion has custom-built studio apartments with kitchen, minibar and air-con. The hotel is run by Australian-Greek couple Barbara and George Gialousis who love a yarn about Down Under. It is halfway between the airport and town, near the turn-off to the Varia museums. A room for two or three persons costs 14,000 dr, while an apartment for two to four persons costs 20,000 dr.

Places to Eat

You will eat well on Lesvos whether you enjoy fish dishes, traditional Greek food, international cuisine or vegetarian meals, and Mytilini is no exception. You might wish to avoid the restaurants on the western section of the southern waterfront where the waiters tout for customers. These restaurants are atypical of Mytilini as they pander to tourists and serve bland overpriced food.

The *Albatros Ouzeri*, on the corner of Ermou and Adramytiou, has to be seen to be believed. It has no pretensions, is at least 100 years old, and everything in it looks grimy. The place is jam-packed with paraphernalia so that it looks far more like a junk shop or disorganised museum than an eating establishment. Its idiosyncratic owners may or may not take a liking to you, so beware.

The *Restaurant Averof*, in the middle of the southern waterfront, is a no-nonsense traditional restaurant serving hearty Greek staples, while *Ta Asteria* on the opposite side of the harbour is slightly more up-market and serves similar food for slightly higher prices.

The small, friendly ouzeri-style *Ta Stroggylia* at Komninaki 9 has wine barrels and good food. If you want meat dishes, check out *I Psatha* (winter only) on Methodiou, off Ermou. There is an old jukebox that actually works. For top fish dishes, go to *Stratos Psarotaverna* at Fanari, at the bottom end of the main harbour. Tables from all the surrounding restaurants take over the road in summer.

Another place serving high quality Greek dishes is *Taverna Boudroumi*. The restaurant is set back from the southern end of Komninaki and is a bit difficult to find – look for a stone building with black wrought-iron wall lamps at the entrance.

For a great meal with a great view, drive up to *Yiannis* at the village of Taxiarhes. Take the road to the Varia museums and look for the signs.

Entertainment

The *Music Café*, on the corner of Mitropoleos and Vernardaki, is a hip place – arty without being pretentious. Drinks are in the mid-price range (around 600 dr for a beer) rather than cheap, but worth it for the terrific atmosphere. Tapes of jazz, blues and classical music are played, and there is live music on Wednesday evenings – usually jazz. The café is open from 7.30 am to 2 am. Another couple of 'in' places are the *Iguana Café* on the west side of the harbour and the *Hot Spot* on the east side. Both are popular with students and you can borrow board games, if you are feeling a tad bored yourself.

For disco life with a difference, head out to *Quebrancho* an old converted tannery, replete with all the original machinery. It is five km north of Mytilini, just before Panagiouda.

Getting There & Away

Mytilini has two bus stations: the one for long-distance buses is just beyond the southwestern end of Pavlou Kountouriotou; the bus station for buses to local villages is on the northernmost section of Pavlou Kountouriotou. For motorists, there is a large free-parking area just south of the main harbour.

AROUND THE ISLAND
Northern Lesvos

Northern Lesvos is dominated both economically and physically by the exquisitely preserved traditional town of Mithymna, a town of both historical and modern importance in Lesvos' commercial life. Its neighbouring beach resort of Petra, six km south, is affected by low-key package tourism and the villages surrounding Mt Lepetymnos are authentic, picturesque and worth a day or two of exploration.

Mithymna (Μήθυμνα) Although this town has officially reverted to its ancient name of Mithymna (Methymna) most locals still refer to it as Molyvos. It is 62 km from Mytilini and is the principal town of northern Lesvos. The one-time rival to Mytilini, Mithymna is nowadays the antithesis of the island capital, being extremely picturesque. Its impeccable stone houses with brightly coloured shutters reach down to the harbour from a castle-crowned hill. Its two main thoroughfares of Kastrou and 17 Noemvriou are winding, cobbled and shaded by vines. In contrast to Mytilini, which is quite oblivious to tourism, Mithymna's pretty streets are lined with souvenir shops.

Orientation & Information From the bus

stop, walk straight ahead towards the town. Where the road forks, take the right fork into 17 Noemvriou, which is the main street of Mithymna. Along here, at the top of the hill, the road forks again; the right fork is Kastrou and the post office is along here on the left. The left fork is a continuation of 17 Noemvriou and the OTE is almost at the end, on the left. Mithymna's postcode is 811 08 and the telephone code is 0253.

The National Bank of Greece is on the left, just past the bus stop.

There is a small tourist information office (☎ 71 347/069) on the left, between the bus stop and the fork in the road.

Things to See & Do One of the nicest things to do in Mithymna is simply to stroll along its gorgeous streets. If you have the energy, the ruined 14th-century **Genoese castle** is worth clambering up to for fine views of the coastline and over the sea to Turkey. From this castle in the 15th century, Onetta d'Oria, wife of the Genoese governor, repulsed an onslaught by the Turks by putting on her husband's armour and leading the people of Mithymna into battle. In summer the castle is the venue for a drama festival; ask for details at the tourist office.

The beach at Mithymna is pebbled and crowded, but in summer excursion boats leave daily at 10 am for the superior beaches of Eftalou, Skala Sykaminias, Petra and Anaxos (see Around Mithymna).

Places to Stay – bottom end The well-maintained camp site *Camping Mithymna* (☎ 71 169/079) is 1.5 km from town and signposted from near the tourist office. It opens in early June.

There are over 50 official domatia in Mithymna; most consist of only one or two rooms. All display domatia signs and most are of a high standard. The best street to start looking is 17 Noemvriou. As you walk up here, the first rooms you come to are those of *Eleni Vourgoutsi* (☎ 71 065), on the right. The rooms are nicely furnished and there is a terrace overlooking an attractive garden.

The cost is 5000 dr a double with shared bathroom.

The beautifully furnished double room that *Kostandina Stavrinou* (☎ 71 011) lets is on the overhanging first floor of her house. It features pine-wood panelling on both the interior and exterior walls. The cost is 5500 dr with private bathroom. From the bus stop walk towards the town and take the second right into Myrasillou. Ascend the steps, turn right and the rooms are on the left – look for the wood panelling.

Places to Stay – middle For a touch of something different, try the old converted olive-press factory *Hotel Olive Press* (☎ 71 205; fax 71 647) with half of the tasteful, modern rooms literally dangling over the water. Rooms rates, including breakfast, range from 12,200 dr for a single to 26,800 dr for a suite. Look for the chimney stack to the left as you enter Mithymna.

Places to Eat The streets 17 Noemvriou and Kastrou have a good selection of restaurants serving typical Greek fare. For more of a fishing-village ambience, head down to the far end of the little harbour where there is a clutch of eating places, including the Australian-run *Captain's Table*. Fish dishes here are as fresh as you can get them and there is live music three nights a week. Melinda and her husband Theodoros will make you more than welcome.

Petra (Πέτρα) Petra, five km south of Mithymna, is a popular coastal resort with a long sandy beach shaded by tamarisk trees. Despite tourist development it remains an attractive village retaining some traditional houses. As soon as you arrive, it will be obvious how Petra got its name, which means 'rock'. Looming over the village is an enormous almost perpendicular rock which looks as if it's been lifted from Meteora. The rock is crowned by the 18th-century Panagia Glykophilousa (Church of the Sweet Kissing Virgin). You can reach it by climbing up the 114 rock-hewn steps – worth it for the view.

Petra, like many settlements on Lesvos, is a 'preserved' village. It has not and will not make any concessions to concrete monstrosities that have so much marred tourist development elsewhere in Greece.

Petra has a post office, bank, medical facilities, and bus connections. Petra's phone code is 0253 and its postcode is 811 09.

Places to Stay Domatia and pensions line Petra's waterfront. Greece's first Women's Agricultural Tourism Collective (☎ 0253-41 238; fax 41 309) began here in 1985 and is still going strong. The women can arrange for you to stay with a family in the village; you will pay around 5000/8000 dr for a single/double. Their office is on the central square – signposted from the waterfront.

For a special treat and incomparable views, check in at the B-class *Clara Resort Hotel* (☎ 41 532; fax 41 535). Individual airy chalets built in traditional style and with seaward-facing balcony go for 11,000/15,000/20,000 dr with half-pension which includes breakfast and one other meal. The hotel is just to the west of Petra on the road to Anaxos. A booking is probably a good idea.

Places to Eat There is a veritable gamut of eateries along the waterfront, all pandering to the tourist and Greek palate alike. *To Tyhero Petalo* towards the eastern end has ready-made food at a reasonable price and attractive décor. The *Pittakos Ouzeri* is a bit more like the genuine article and is still on the seafront, while in the back street you will find a couple of places, notably *To Steki* and *To Koutouki*, which are more popular with the locals.

Driving Tour If you have your own transport – preferably a car – then you might want to explore the villages surrounding Mt Lepetymnos. **Anaxos**, three km west of Petra, is a small beach enclave with some lower key accommodation, some tavernas and a pretty good beach.

Eftalou, five km east along the coast from

NORTH-EAST AEGEAN ISLANDS

Mithymna, doesn't seem to have a lot going for it at first glance. The beach is nothing to write home about, but it is better than Mithymna's. However, a number of more up-market hotels have chosen this area for their location and they are reasonably subtly interspersed with nature and the sea, and many have pools. There are radioactive springs and a small thermal baths establishment which, at the time of research, was undergoing restoration. According to the EOT brochure the waters are a panacea for everything from gout to gynaecological problems. Eftalou was the birthplace of the writer Kleanthis Mihaelidis, who, in honour of his village, wrote under the pseudonym Argyris Eftaliotis. A bust of him stands in the centre of Mithymna town. Modern Greek novelist Ilias Venezis also lived and wrote here.

A rough but driveable dirt road will bring you to one of Lesvos' most picturesque fishing villages **Skala Sykaminias**, which has a little church on a rock overlooking the minuscule harbour. Skala Sykaminias is very laid back, has a rocky and pebbly beach, three tavernas – one of which *I Skamia* has rooms as well – and few concessions to tourism. If you do want to stay here, *Rooms to Let Gorgona*, overlooking the little square, might be worth trying. Sykaminia itself, up on the hill, is a very pretty little village and very much associated with the modern Greek writer Stratis Myrivilis.

Turning back to Petra, you will pass through the villages of **Kapi** and then **Pelopi** which proudly announces its affiliation with ex US presidential candidate, Michael Dukakis. Pelopi is his ancestral home. **Ypsilometopo** is next with its 250-year-old **Church of the Taxiarhes** and mandolin-playing Father Ignatios. If you do meet this affable old priest, he will show you around his church and his wonderful herb garden.

Stypsi is next with its narrowed cobbled streets and often visited on day trips by holiday-makers from Petra. Take care when driving through the centre. You can take an alternative route around the north flank of the mountain via Vafios and Argennos on a gradually improving road that affords some spectacular views across to Turkey.

You can drive to Mytilini from **Klio** along a much quieter and more interesting coastal road, passing through olive groves by the score and a few rather scrappy beach villages. There are some great views along the way and you'll avoid the heavy traffic which uses the main route via Kalloni.

Western Lesvos

Western Lesvos is quite different from the rest of the island and this becomes apparent almost immediately as you wind westward out of Kalloni. The landscape becomes drier and barer and there are fewer settlements, though when they do appear they look very tidy and their red-tiled roofs add vital colour to an otherwise mottled green-brown landscape. The far western end is almost devoid of trees other than the petrified kind. Here you will find Lesvos' 'petrified forest' on a windswept and barren hillside. One resort, a remote fishing village and the birthplace of Sappho are what attract people to Western Lesvos.

Eresos & Skala Eresou Eresos, 90 km from Mytilini, is a traditional inland village. It is reached via the road junction just after the hillside village of Andissa that exhorts passers-by to visit its square. The road leading down to Eresos, through what looks like a moonscape, belies what is ahead. Beyond the village of Eresos a riotously fertile agricultural plain leads to Eresos' beach annexe, Skala Eresou which is four km beyond on the west coast. It is a popular resort linked to Eresos by an attractive, very straight tree-lined road.

Skala Eresou is built over ancient Eresos where Sappho (628-568 BC) was born. Although it gets crowded in summer it has a good laid-back atmosphere. It is also a popular destination for lesbians who come on a kind of pilgrimage in honour of the poet Sappho. If you're a beach freak you should certainly visit – there is almost two km of fine silvery-brown sand.

NORTH-EAST AEGEAN ISLANDS

Orientation & Information From the bus turnaround at Skala Eresou, walk towards the sea to reach the central square of Plateia Anthis & Evristhenous abutting the waterfront. The beach stretches to the left and right of this square. Turn right at the square onto Gyrinnis and just under 50 metres along you will come to a sign pointing left to the post office; the OTE is next door. Skala Eresou's postcode is 881 05 and the telephone code is 0253. Neither Skala Eresou nor Eresos has a bank.

There is no EOT or tourist police, but Exeresis Travel (☎ 53 044), 200 metres to the right of the bus station (facing the sea), is helpful. The staff here can arrange car, motorbike and bicycle hire; and treks on foot and on horses and donkeys. They also have a currency exchange.

Archaeological Museum Eresos' archaeological museum houses Archaic, classical and Roman finds including statues, coins and grave steles. The museum, which is in the centre of Skala Eresou, stands near the remains of the early Christian Basilica of Agios Andreas. Opening times are Tuesday to Sunday from 8.30 am to 3 pm. Admission is free.

Petrified Forest of Sigri 'Petrified forest' is the EOT's hyperbolic description of the scattering of ancient tree stumps near the village of Sigri, on the west coast, north of Skala Eresou. Experts reckon the petrified wood is at least 500,000, but possibly 20 million, years old. If you're intrigued, the forest is easiest reached as an excursion from Skala Eresou; enquire at Exeresis Travel. If you're driving, the turn-off to the forest is seven km before the village of Sigri. It is signposted.

Places to Stay There is an official free *camp site* at the western end of the beach at Skala Eresou; to reach it turn right at the waterfront. The site has cold showers and toilets, but as the upkeep is minimal the latter get pretty filthy when the site is crowded. Bear in mind also that this is a de facto lesbian camp site.

There are a few domatia in Eresos but most people head for Skala Eresou, where there are many domatia, pensions and hotels. You best bet is to look around and pick and choose at you leisure. *Rooms to Let Katia,* at the eastern end of the waterfront, has nice rooms with a view.

C-class *Sappho the Eressia* (☎ 53 233; fax 53 174) is a small hotel on the waterfront with singles/doubles for 5750/9900 dr. The only problem here is possible noise pollution when the going gets busy.

Skala Eresou's best hotel is the C-class *Hotel Galini* (☎ 53 137/138 or 53 205; fax 53 155). Its light and airy rooms cost 4900/8200/10,000 dr for singles/doubles/ triples with private bathroom. The hotel has a comfortable TV room-cum-bar and an outside terrace under a bamboo shade. Follow the easy-to-spot signs to reach the Galini.

Places to Eat The shady promenade offers many eating options, most with beach and sea views across to Chios and Psara on a fine day. *Sevah o Thalassinos* is among the better establishments and has excellent fish. It is also a tad expensive. Look out for Sevah's original hand-drawn menus. *Yamas* (☎ 53 693) is a Canadian-run pancake and snack joint run by expats Nick and Linda. Here you can get home-made north American cooking, chocolate cake, and cool beer. You can also listen to 70s music, and the occasional jam takes place when the mood takes over. You can also hire bikes here. *Bennett's International & Vegetarian Restaurant* is an English-run establishment, with familiar fare, including vegetarian, at the eastern end of the waterfront.

Southern Lesvos

Southern Lesvos is dominated by 968-metre Mt Olympus and the pine forests that decorate its flanks, a large section of which have been subject to the ravages of fires in recent years – particularly the steep slopes north of the resort town of **Plomari**. A large, traditional village, popular with visitors, Plomari also has a laid-back beach settlement.

If you are touring this part of the island,

you will almost certainly want to visit the large village of **Agiasos** on the northern flank of Mt Olympus. This village features prominently in most local tourist publications and is a popular day-trip destination. Agiasos is very picturesque but not tacky, and has some fairly genuine artisan workshops making anything from handcrafted furniture to pottery. Its winding cobbled streets will eventually lead you to the church of the Panagia Vrefokratousa with its Byzantine Museum and Popular Museum in the courtyard.

In a little studio just outside the church walls, you will either hear or come across Giannis (Kakourgos) Sousamlis, a master *santouri* (hammered dulcimer) player whose family hailed originally from Kordelio in Asia Minor. He plays a mean santouri and will tell you how famous he is. He also sells cassettes of his home recordings.

A couple of restaurants near the bus stop are your best bet for eating in Agiasos. One is the *Anatoli* and the other is a nameless *psistaria* owned by Grigoris Douladellis.

Plomari on the south coast is a cramped and crumbling resort of sorts. It is not so exciting, but is very popular with Scandinavian tourists who are lured by cheap accommodation, but end up paying for it with expensive meals. Most people stay at **Agios Isidoros** three km to the east where there is a narrow overcrowded beach.

A far more superior option is the low-key family resort of **Vatera** over to the east and reached via the inland town of **Polyhnitos**. This relaxing oasis has a very good, clean nine-km-long beach, and some hotels, domatia and restaurants.

There is one camp site here: *Camping Dionysos* (☎ 0252-61 151/154; fax 61 155). It's quite good, if somewhat small, but has a pool, minimarket, restaurant, and cooking facilities. It is set back about 100 metres from the beach. Camping costs are about 2500 dr for a car, tent and one person. The site is open from 1 June to 30 September.

Your best eating and accommodation option by far is the modern C-class *Hotel Vatera Beach* (☎ 0252-61 212; fax 61 164)

with its American-Greek owners Barbara and George Ballis. They provide a relaxed environment and good Greek home cooking to cap it all off. A double room here will cost you 13,500 dr in high season.

Limnos Λήμνος

There is a saying on Limnos that when people come to the island they cry twice: once when they arrive and once when they leave. Limnos' appeal is not immediate; it's charm slowly but surely captivates.

The deeply penetrating Moudros bay almost severs the island in two. The landscape of Limnos lacks the imposing grandeur of the forested and mountainous islands and the stark beauty of the barren and rocky ones. However, gently undulating Limnos, with its little farms, has a unique understated appeal all of its own. In spring vibrant wild flowers dot the landscape, and in autumn purple crocuses sprout forth in profusion. The coastline boasts some of the best beaches in the North-Eastern Aegean group. The island is sufficiently off the beaten track to have escaped the adverse effects of mass tourism.

History

Limnos' position near the straits of the Dardanelles, midway between the Mt Athos peninsula and Turkey, has given it a traumatic history. To this day it maintains a large garrison, and jets from the huge air base loudly punctuate the daily routine.

Limnos had advanced Neolithic and Bronze Age civilisations, and during these times had contact with peoples in western Anatolia, including the Trojans. In classical times the twin sea gods, the Kabeiroi, were worshipped at a sanctuary on the island, but later the Sanctuary of the Great Gods on Samothraki became the centre of this cult.

During the Peloponnesian Wars Limnos sided with Athens and suffered many Persian attacks. After the split of the Roman Empire in 395 AD it became an important outpost of

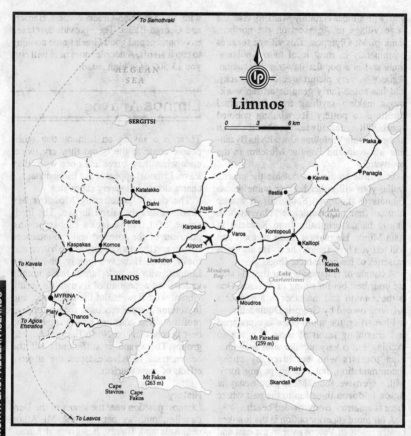

Limnos

0   3   6 km

SERGITSI

AEGEAN
SEA

To Samothraki

To Kavala

To Agios
Efstratios

To Lesvos

Katalakko
Dafni
Sardes
Kaspakas   Kornos
MYRINA
Platy
Thanos

Atsiki
Karpasi
Airport
Livadohori
LIMNOS

Varos
Moudros
Bay

Ifestia
Kontopouli
Kaviria
Lake
Alyki

Kalliopi

Keros
Beach

Lake
Chortarelimni

Moudros

Poliohni

Mt Paradisi
(259 m)

Fisini

Skandali

Plaka

Panagia

Mt Fakos
(263 m)
Cape
Stavros   Cape
Fakos

NORTH-EAST AEGEAN ISLANDS

Byzantium. In 1462 it came under the domination of the Genoese who ruled Lesvos. The Turks succeeded in conquering the island in 1478 and it remained under Turkish rule until 1912. Moudros bay, on Limnos, was the Allies' base for the disastrous Gallipoli campaign in WW I.

Getting There & Away

Air In summer there are daily flights to Limnos from Athens (12,800 dr) and Thessaloniki (13,000 dr); and daily flights from Lesvos (12,600 dr). The Olympic Airways office (☎ 22 214/215) is on Nikolaou Garou-fallidou, opposite the Hotel Kastro, in Myrina. The airport is 22 km north-east of Myrina. An Olympic Airways bus from Myrina to the airport (1000 dr) connects with all flights.

Ferry In summer there are four or five ferries a week to Kavala from Limnos (five hours, 3100 dr); three or four a week to Rafina (10 hours, 4700 dr, all via Agios Efstratios (1½ hours, 1600 dr) and one via Lesvos (six hours, 3000 dr) and Chios (11 hours, 4600 dr); three to Piraeus via Lesvos and Chios and one to Piraeus directly (13 hours,

5800 dr); and one a week to Thessaloniki (seven hours, 4200 dr).

Finally, there is one weekly service to Patmos (17 hours, 5952 dr) via Agios Efstratios, Lesvos, Chios and Samos.

Tickets can be bought at Myrina Tourist & Travel Agency (☎ 22 460; fax 23 560), next door to the Hotel Aktaion, in Myrina. The introduction of a new faster boat, the *Theofilos*, will cut the travel time on some of the services mentioned above.

Excursion Boat In July and August there are daily excursion boats to the small island of Agios Efstratios. The island is untouristy and has several beaches, tavernas and domatia. However, there are plans to introduce a regular daily return service to Agios Efstratios, which will make a day visit to the island easier to organise. For information enquire at Myrina Tourist & Travel Agency.

Getting Around

Bus The bus service on Limnos is poor. In summer there are two buses a day from Myrina to most of the villages. Check the schedule at the bus station on Plateia El Venizelou.

Car & Motorbike In Myrina, cars and jeeps can be rented from Theodoros Petrides Travel Agency (☎ 22 039; fax 22 129), on the right side of Kyda as you walk away from the harbour. There are several motorbike-hire outlets on Kyda.

MYRINA Μύρινα

Myrina is the capital and port of Limnos. Surrounded by massive hunks of volcanic rock, it is not immediately perceived as a picturesque town, but it is animated, full of character and unfettered by establishments pandering to tourism.

The main thoroughfare of Kyda is a charming paved street with shops and eating places of every description including traditional shops selling nuts and honey, and old-fashioned kafeneia. As you wander along the side streets you'll see (interspersed with modern buildings) little whitewashed stone dwellings, decaying neoclassical mansions and 19th-century wattle-and-daub houses with overhanging wooden balconies. A Genoese castle looms dramatically over the town.

Orientation & Information

From the end of the quay turn right onto Plateia Ilia Iliou. Continue along the waterfront passing the Hotel Limnos and the town hall. A little further along you will see the Hotel Aktaion, set back from the waterfront. Turn left here, then immediately veer half-left onto Kyda, the town's main street. Proceeding up here you will reach the central square where the National Bank of Greece and the OTE are located. The taxi rank (☎ 0254-23 033 or 22 348) is also on this square. Continue up Kyda and take the next turn right onto Nikolaou Garoufallidou. The post office is here on the right. Back on Kyda, continue for another 100 metres and you will come to Plateia El Venizelou where you will see the bus station.

There is a small tourist information kiosk on the quay. The tourist police (☎ 0254-22 200) are at the far end of Nikolaou Garoufallidou – on the right coming from Kyda. The port police (☎ 0254-22 225) are on the waterfront near the quay. There is a laundrette on Nikoloaou Garoufallidou, opposite the Olympic Airways office.

Limnos' telephone code is 0245 and the postcode is 800 14.

Things to See & Do

As with all Greek-island castles the one towering over Myrina is worth climbing up to for the vistas. From its vantage point there are magnificent views over the sea to Mt Athos. As you walk from the harbour, a sign at the beginning of Kyda points left to the castle.

Myrina has a lovely long sandy beach right in town. It stretches north from the castle and can be reached by walking along Kyda from the harbour, and taking any of the streets off to the left. The first part of the beach is known as **Romeïkos Yialos** and the northern end, just before the resort hotel of Akti Marina Hotel, is known as **Riha Nera**.

Myrina's **archaeological museum**, which is housed in a neoclassical mansion, is worth a visit. It contains finds from all the three sites on Limnos. The building overlooks the beach, next to the Kastro Hotel. It's open from 8.30 am to 3 pm, Tuesday to Sunday. Admission is 400 dr.

Organised Tours

In the absence of a decent bus service, Theodoros Petrides Travel Agency (see Car & Motorbike under Limnos Getting Around) organises a couple of bus excursions around the island which include a visit to ancient Poliohni. There is also a swimming stop and lunch break at Moudros. The agency also organises round-the-island boat trips which again include stops for swimming and lunch. The cost of each of these excursions is 2500 dr. Lunch is not included in the price.

Places to Stay – bottom end

Limnos doesn't have any official camp sites.

Rooms to Let Argyro (☎ 23 908 or 24 152) has spacious nicely furnished rooms with telephone, refrigerator and balcony. Rates are 10,300/13,500 dr for doubles/triples. Walk to the end of Kyda from the waterfront, at the crossroad continue straight ahead and the rooms are on the right just beyond a school and a football pitch.

Another option for budget travellers is the lovely *Apollo Pavillion* (☎ 23 712), with friendly English-speaking owners. The Pavillion is a new building in neoclassical style with ornate wrought-iron balconies; inside there is lots of cool grey marble. The rooms are spacious and clean and a variety of accommodation is offered. Cheapest are the four-bed rooms in the basement which are intended for backpackers. They cost 3500 dr per person. Studios which have private bathroom and kitchen cost 10,000/12,500 dr for doubles/triples. Two-roomed apartments with kitchens are 20,000 dr for four to five people. The Pavillion has a nice garden with a barbecue for guests' use. Walk along Nikolaou Garoufallidou from Kyda

and you will see the sign 100 metres along on the right.

The D-class *Hotel Aktaion* (☎ 22 258), on the waterfront, is the town's cheapest hotel and not all that appealing. The single/double/triple rooms are pleasant and clean and cost 4000/7000/9000 dr. The *Hotel Paris* (☎ 24 927) is a more pleasant option, with rates of 8000/9000/12,000/15,000 dr for singles/doubles/triples/quads. The hotel is on Nikolaou Garoufallidou, opposite the post office.

Places to Stay – middle

The B-class *Kastro Hotel* (☎ 22 772; fax 22 784) is built in neoclassical style. The rooms have fitted carpet, balcony, telephone, three-channel music and TV on request. Rates are 10,000/16,000/19,900/24,400 dr for singles/doubles/triples/quads with breakfast. The hotel has a restaurant, bar, snack bar, TV room and sunbathing terrace, and it overlooks the beach. It is signposted from the crossroad at the top of Kyda.

The *Hotel Ifestos* (☎ 24 960/962; fax 23 623) is another excellent B-class hotel, with tastefully furnished rooms. Doubles cost 14,000 dr. The hotel is 100 metres back from Tzitzifies Taverna on Riha Nera beach, about one km north of the harbour.

Places to Eat

Restaurants are of a high standard on Limnos. There are several fish restaurants around the waterfront. Locals give top marks to *Taverna Glaros*, which probably has the best harbourside location and somewhat expensive prices. If you're facing the waterfront the taverna is on the far left beside the small fishing boats. Further towards the middle of the harbour is the *Glaropoula* fish restaurant which is run by the same management as the Glaros. By the ferry quay is the *Avra* restaurant; handy if you are waiting for a boat to leave.

Kyda is packed with kafeneia, fast-food places and snack bars. One of its best restaurants is *O Platanos Taverna*, on the left as you walk from the waterfront. It is on a small square under a huge plane tree and makes an

NORTH-EAST AEGEAN ISLANDS

attractive alternative to the waterfront establishments.

AROUND THE ISLAND
Western Limnos

North of Myrina is the recently completed mega resort *Hotel Akti Myrina* on the south side of pristine Aspakas bay. Turn left just past the little village of **Aspakas** and a narrow road will lead you down to the beach of **Agios Yiannis**. The beach is pleasant enough, but Agios Yiannis consists of a few desultory fishing shacks, scattered beach houses and a couple of tavernas, one of which has its tables set out in the embrace of a large volcanic rock. There is only one advertised *domatia* (☎ 23 858) establishment here.

Inland from Kaspakas, the barren hilly landscape dotted with sheep and rocks (particularly on the road to Katalakko via Sardes and Dafni) reminds you more of the English Peak District than a Mediterranean island. The villages themselves have little to cause you to pause and you will certainly be an object of curiosity if you do. You can travel from Dafni to the agricultural village of Atsiki, via a reasonable dirt road.

Heading three km south from Myrina you will reach one of Limnos' best beaches below the village of **Platy**. To get to Platy beach follow the signs out of Myrina for Platy and Thanos, but turn right just before the cemetery. Look out for the signs to Villa Afroditi and Lemnos village.

As well as the huge and expensive Lemnos Village Resort Hotel, Platy beach has a couple of budget places to stay. The *rooms* belonging to Anastasia (☎ 24 127/060) are simply furnished and guests can use the kitchen area. Rates are 6500 dr a double with private bathroom. The rooms are on the right side of the road which leads from the beach to Platy village. Further along this road, you will come to *Rooms to Let* (☎ 24 142), behind Jimmy's Fish Tavern, charging 5000 dr a double. Both of the tavernas on the beach are reasonably priced.

The best accommodation option at Platy, if you are planning to stay for a few days and there are two or more of you, is *Villa Afroditi* (☎ 23 141; fax 25 031) set back about 100 metres from the beach on the road. This small but classy complex offers self-catering suites and studios. The price of rooms ranges, in high season, from 38,000 dr for a suite for four persons to 20,000 dr for two persons. A large buffet breakfast is included. There is also a pool and restaurant. Advance bookings are recommended.

If you continue along the dirt road which passes the Limnos Village Resort Hotel, you will come to a sheltered sandy cove with an islet in the bay. The beach here will probably be less crowded than Platy. **Thanos beach** is the next bay around from Platy; it is also less crowded, and long and sandy. To get there, continue on the main road from Platy village to Thanos village, where a sign points to the beach.

Central Limnos

Central Limnos is flat and agricultural with wheatfields, small vineyards, and cattle and sheep farms. There is also the island's huge air-force base, which is ominously guarded by endless barbed-wire fences. The muddy and bleak Moudros bay cuts deep into the interior, with **Moudros**, Limnos' second town in size, positioned uninvitingly on the eastern side of the bay. Moudros does not offer much for the tourist. There are a couple of small hotels with tavernas on the waterfront, but the harbour has none of the picturesque qualities of Myrina's.

One km out of Moudros on the road to Roussopouli, you will come across the **East Mudros Military Cemetery** where Commonwealth soldiers from the Gallipoli campaign are buried. Limnos with its large protected anchorage was occupied by a force of Royal Marines on 23 February 1915 and became the principal base for this ill-fated campaign. A metal plaque, just inside the gates on, gives a short history of the Gallipoli campaign and there is a regional map.

Eastern Limnos

Eastern Limnos has three archaeological sites that you may want to investigate. The

Italian School of Archaeologists has uncovered four ancient settlements at **Poliohni**, on the island's east coast. The most interesting one was a sophisticated pre-Mycenaean city, which predated Troy VI (1800-1275 BC).

The second site is that of **Kaviria** (open 9.30 am to 3.30 pm, free entry) in north-eastern Limnos on the shores of remote Tigani bay. This was originally a site for the worship of Kabeiroi gods pre-dating those of Samothraki (see Sanctuary of the Great Gods, Samothraki). There is little of the Sanctuary of Samothraki's splendour, but the layout of the site is obvious and excavations are still being carried out.

The major site, which has 11 columns, is that of a Hellenistic sanctuary. The older site is further back and is still being excavated. Of additional interest is the cave of Philoctetes where the hero of the Trojan war was abandoned while a gangrenous leg (a result of snakebite) healed. The sea cave can be reached by a path that leads down from the site.

You can reach Kaviria easily if you have your own car via a fast new road that was built for the multimillion-drachma tourist enclave Kaviria Palace. The turn-off is about five km to the left, after the village of **Kontopouli**. From Kontopouli itself you can make a detour to the third site, **Ifestia**, which was once the most important city on the island. Hephaestus was the god of fire and metallurgy and, according to mythology, was thrown here from Mt Olympus by Zeus. There is not much to see at the site and excavations are still being carried out.

The road to the northern tip of the island is worth exploring. There are some typical Limnian villages in the area and an often deserted beach at **Keros.** From the cape at the north-eastern tip of Limnos you can see the islands of Samothraki and Imvros (Gökçeada) in Turkey.

Samothraki Σαμοθράκη

The egg-shaped island of Samothraki (Sam-o-THRA-ki, population 2800) is 32 km south-west of Alexandroupolis. Scenically it is one of the most awe-inspiring of all Greek islands. It is a small island, but a great deal of diverse landscape is packed into its 176 sq km. Its natural attributes are dramatic, big and untamed; culminating in the mighty peak of Mt Fengari (1611 metres), the highest mountain in the Aegean. Homer related that Poseidon watched the Trojan War from Mt Fengari's summit.

The jagged boulder-strewn Mt Fengari looms over valleys of massive gnarled oak and plane trees, thick forests of olive trees, dense shrubbery and damp dark glades where waterfalls plunge into deep icy pools. On the gentler western slopes of the island there are corn fields studded with wild flowers. Samothraki is also rich in fauna: its springs are the habitat of a large number of frogs, toads and turtles; and in its meadows you will see swarms of butterflies and may come across the occasional lumbering tortoise. On the mountain slopes there are an inordinate number of bell-clanking goats. The island's beaches, with one exception, are stony or pebbly.

Samothraki's ancient site, the Sanctuary of the Great Gods, at Paleopolis, is one of the most evocative ancient sites in Greece. Historians have been unable to ascertain the nature of the rites performed here, and its aura of potent mysticism prevails over the whole island.

Samothraki is relatively difficult to reach and does not have any package tourism. It does, however, attract a fair number of Greek holiday-makers in July and August, so you may have some difficulty finding a room then. With the exception of the Xenia Hotel, all of Samothraki's hotels were built in the 1980s and were designed to a high standard with sensitive regard to the environment. All are extremely pleasant places to stay but none falls into the budget category. This

DAVID HALL

ROSEMARY HALL

ANN JOUSIFFE

Top: Sanctuary of the Great Gods, Samothraki, North-Eastern Aegean islands
Bottom Left: The 19th-century church of the Taxiarhs, Mesta, Chios, North-Eastern Aegean islands
Bottom Right: Packing up the nets after a day's fishing, Lesvos, North-Eastern Aegean islands

ANN JOUSIFFE

ROSEMARY HALL

Top: Beach on the island of Lesvos, North-Eastern Aegean islands
Bottom: Ancient Agora, Thasos, North-Eastern Aegean islands

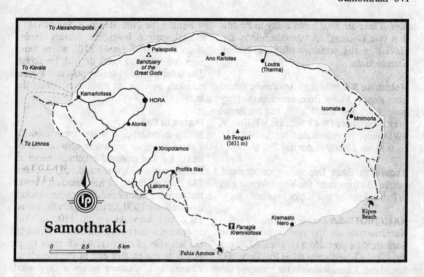

Samothraki

To Alexandroupolis
To Kavala
To Limnos

Paleopolis
Sanctuary of the Great Gods
Ano Kariotes
Loutra (Therma)
Kamariotissa
HORA
Isomata
Alonia
Mnimoria
Mt Fengari (1611 m)
Xiropotamos
Profitis Ilias
Lakoma
Kremasto Nero
Kipos Beach
Panagia Kremniotissa
Pahia Ammos

AEGEAN SEA

0   2.5   5 km

NORTH-EAST AEGEAN ISLANDS

doesn't mean budget travellers are not welcome or catered for as there are a fair number of domatia and two camp sites.

History

Samothraki was first settled around 1000 BC by Thracians who worshipped the Great gods, a cult of Anatolian origin. In 700 BC the island was colonised by inhabitants of Lesvos, who assimilated the Thracian cult into the worship of the Olympian gods.

This marriage of two cults was highly successful and by the 5th century BC Samothraki had become one of Greece's major religious centres, attracting prospective initiates from far and wide to its Sanctuary of the Great Gods. Among the luminaries initiated into the cult were King Lysander of Sparta, Philip II of Macedonia and Piso, Julius Caesar's father-in-law. One famous visitor who did not come to be initiated was St Paul, who dropped in *en route* to Philippi.

The cult survived until paganism was outlawed in the 4th century AD. After this the island became insignificant. It fell to the Turks in 1457 and became united with Greece along with the other North-Eastern

Aegean islands in 1912. During WW II Samothraki was occupied by the Bulgarians.

Getting There & Away

Ferry Samothraki has ferry connections with Alexandroupolis (two hours, 2200 dr), Kavala (four hours, 2800 dr) and Limnos (3½ hours, 2400 dr). The sailing times vary from year to year, but in summer there are usually six departures a week to Kavala, two a week to Limnos and two a day to Alexandroupolis. Tickets can be bought at Niki Tours or Saos Travel, Kamariotissa.

Hydrofoil Hydrofoil services operate from Samothraki from 1 May to 31 October. There are currently services linking Samothraki with Limnos, Thasos, Halkidiki (Stavros), Kavala, Porto Lagos and Alexandroupolis. For departure details contact Niki Tours, Kamariotissa. Ticket prices are roughly twice as much as the equivalent ferry ticket.

Getting Around

Bus In summer there are at least nine buses a day from Kamariotissa to Hora and Loutra (Therma), via Paleopolis. Some of the Loutra buses continue to the nearby camp sites. There are four buses a day to Profitis Ilias (via Lakoma). A bus schedule is displayed in the window of Saos Travel, Kamariotissa.

Motorbike & Car Motorbikes can be rented from Rent A Motor Bike, opposite the ferry quay. Cars and small jeeps can be rented from Niki Tours (☎ 41 465; fax 41 304). A 4WD jeep, recommended for Samothraki, costs about 15,000 dr per day.

Excursion Boat Depending on demand, caïques do trips from the Kamariotissa jetty to Pahia Ammos and Kipos beaches.

KAMARIOTISSA Καμαριώτισσα
Kamariotissa, on the north-west coast, is Samothraki's port. Hora (also called Samothraki), the island's capital, is five km inland from here. Kamariotissa is the transport hub of the island, so you may wish to use it as a base; otherwise it has little to offer.

Orientation & Information
The bus station is on the waterfront just east of the quay (turn left when you disembark). There is a National Bank of Greece on the waterfront, but no post office or OTE; these are in Hora. There is no EOT or tourist police and the regular police are in Hora. Opposite the bus station you will find Saos Travel (☎ 41 505) and Niki Tours (☎ 41 465; fax 41 304), both of which are reasonably helpful. The port police (☎ 41 305) are on the eastern waterfront at Kamariotissa.

Places to Stay
Domatia owners meet ferries in Kamariotissa. Otherwise, the *Pension Kyma* (☎ 41 268), at the eastern end of the waterfront, has comfortable singles/doubles for 4000/5000 dr with shared bathroom and 4500/5500 dr with private bathroom. Further along the waterfront, the C-class *Niki Beach Hotel* (☎ 41 545/461) is very modern and spacious. Room rates here are 8000/13,000/15,000 dr for singles/doubles/triples with private bathroom. The hotel is at the eastern end of the waterfront.

Behind the Niki Beach is Samothraki's most luxurious hotel, the B-class *Aeolos Hotel* (☎ 41 555; fax 41 810), where room rates are 10,000/15,000 dr with breakfast. The hotel has a swimming pool and a commanding position on a hill overlooking the sea.

Places to Eat
Eating is nothing to write home about in Kamariotissa, or anywhere else on Samothraki for that matter. Restaurants serve an unimaginative range of standard Greek fare. *The Horizon* is one of Kamariotissa's better restaurants. Main courses include chicken casserole for 1000 dr; and meatballs, moussaka, and souvlaki are all 1100 dr. The restaurant is just back from the waterfront on the left side of the road which leads up to Hora. At the eastern end of the waterfront *Klimitaria Restaurant* serves a very good gianiotiko for 1000 dr. This is a dish of diced pork, potatoes and egg baked in the oven.

HORA Χώρα
Hora, concealed in a fold of the mountains above Kamariotissa, is one of the most striking of Greek island villages. The crumbling red-tiled houses – some of grey stone, others whitewashed – are stacked up two steep adjacent mountain sides. The twisting cobbled streets resound with cockerels crowing, dogs barking and donkeys braying, rather than with the ubiquitous roar of motorbikes and honking of car horns. The village is totally authentic with no concessions to tourism. The ruined castle at the top of the main thoroughfare is fascinating to explore and from its vantage point there are sweeping vistas down to Kamariotissa. It is an open site with free entrance.

Orientation & Information
To get to Hora's narrow winding main street, follow the signs for the Kastro from the central square where the bus turns around. Here on the main street, which is nameless (as are all of Hora's streets; houses are distinguished by numbers), are the OTE, the Agricultural Bank and the post office.

Samothraki's telephone code is 0551 and the postcode is 680 02. The police (☎ 41 203) are next to the ruined castle at the top of Hora's main street. A little way up the main street, on the right, a fountain gushes refreshing mountain water.

Walk from Hora to Paleopolis

It takes between 45 minutes and one hour to walk along a dirt road from Hora to Paleopolis (Sanctuary of the Great Gods). On this walk there are tremendous views of Fengari to the right and rolling hills, corn fields and the sea to the left. To get to the road, walk up to the castle ruins in Hora and take the dirt road which leads down to the right. Alternatively, you can start the walk from the road just below the bus stop.

Follow the main track all the way down and around and look out for the Kastro Hotel to your left as you come over the rise. Bear right along a smaller track as you come down the hill and you will eventually come across the museum and ancient site. You can drive along this road (4WD recommended). Keep going straight down the hill until you hit the main road.

Places to Stay & Eat

There are no hotels in Hora. There are two reasonably priced *pensions* just off the central square but the nicest places to stay in Hora are *rooms* in private houses. Almost all of these are unofficial and do not display signs. If you ask in one of the kafeneia you will be put in touch with a room owner.

There is a *psistaria* on the square where the bus stops, and a taverna *Taverna Kastro* on the central square. Both places serve food catering for local tastes rather than for tourists. Ask for fish, if they have it. Bear in mind that these places may well be closed out of season.

SANCTUARY OF THE GREAT GODS

Το Ιερό των Μεγάλων Θεών

The Sanctuary of the Great Gods, next to the little village of Paleopolis, is six km northeast of Kamariotissa. The extensive site, lying in a valley of luxuriant vegetation between Mt Fengari and the sea, is one of the most magical in the whole of Greece. The Great gods were of greater antiquity than the Olympian gods worshipped in the official religion of ancient Greece. The principal deity was the Great Mother (Alceros Cybele), who was worshipped as a fertility goddess.

When the original Thracian religion became integrated with the state religion the Great Mother was merged with the Olympian female deities Demeter, Aphrodite and Hecate. The last of these was a mysterious goddess who was associated with darkness, the underworld and witchcraft. Other deities worshipped here were the Great Mother's consort, the virile young Kadmilos (god of the phallus), who was later integrated with the Olympian god Hermes; and the demonic Kabeiroi twins, Dardanos and Aeton, who were integrated with Castor and Pollux (known as the Dioscuri), the twin sons of Zeus and Leda. These twins were invoked by mariners to protect them against the perils of the sea. The formidable deities of Samothraki were venerated for their immense power. In comparison, the Olympian gods were a frivolous and fickle lot.

Initiates were sworn on punishment of death not to reveal what went on at the sanctuary. Consequently, there is only very flimsy knowledge of what these initiations involved. All that has been gleaned from archaeological evidence is that there were two initiations, a lower and a higher. In the first initiation, gods were invoked to bring about a spiritual rebirth within the candidate. In the second initiation the candidate was absolved of transgressions. There was no prerequisite for initiation – it was available to anyone and everyone.

The site's most celebrated relic, the Winged Victory of Samothrace, was found by Champoiseau, the French consul, at Adrianople (present-day Edirne in Turkey) in 1863. Sporadic excavations followed in the late 19th and early 20th centuries, but did not begin in earnest until just before WW II, when the Institute of Fine Arts, New York University, under the direction of Karl

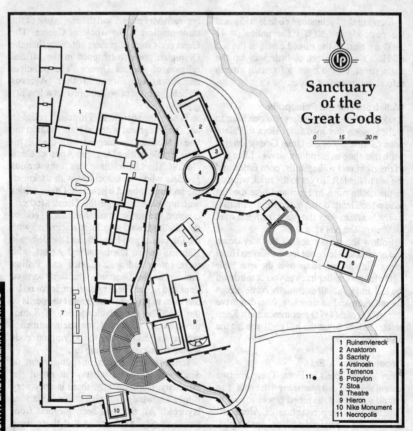

Sanctuary of the Great Gods

0   15   30 m

1 Ruinenviereck
2 Anaktoron
3 Sacristy
4 Arsinoein
5 Temenos
6 Propylon
7 Stoa
8 Theatre
9 Hieron
10 Nike Monument
11 Necropolis

Lehmann and Phyllis Williams Lehmann, began digging.

The site is open Tuesday to Sunday from 8.30 am to 3 pm. Admission is 500 dr, but is free on Sunday and public holidays.

Exploring the Site

The site is labelled in both Greek and English. If you take the path which leads south from the entrance you will arrive at the rectangular **anaktoron**, on the left. At the southern end was a **sacristy**, an antechamber where candidates put on white gowns ready for their first (lower) initiation. The

initiation ceremony took place in the main body of the anaktoron. Then one at a time each initiate entered the holy of holies, a small inner temple at the northern end of the building, where a priest instructed them in the meanings of the symbols used in the ceremony. Afterwards the initiates returned to the sacristy to receive their initiation certificate.

The **arsinoein**, which was used for sacrifices, to the south-west of the anaktoron, was built in 289 BC and was then the largest cylindrical structure in Greece. It was a gift to the Great gods from the Egyptian queen

Arsinou. To the south-east of here you will see the **sacred rock**, the site's earliest altar, which was used by the Thracians.

The initiations were followed by a celebratory feast which probably took place in the **temenos**, to the south of the arsinoein. This building was a gift from Philip II. The next building is the prominent Doric **hieron**, which is the most photographed ruin on the site; five of its columns have been reassembled. It was in this temple that candidates received the second initiation.

On the west side of the main path (opposite the hieron) are a few remnants of a **theatre**. Nearby, a path ascends to the **Nike monument** where the magnificent Winged Victory once stood. The statue was a gift from Demetrius Poliorcetes (the 'besieger of cities') to the Kabeiroi for helping him defeat Ptolemy II in battle. To the north-west of here are the remains of a massive **stoa**, which was a two-aisled portico where pilgrims to the sanctuary sheltered. Names of initiates were recorded on its walls. North of the stoa are

Winged Victory of Samothrace

the ruins of the **ruinenviereck**, a medieval fortress.

Retrace your steps to the Nike monument and walk along the path leading east; on the left is a good plan of the site. The path continues to the southern **necropolis** which is the most important ancient cemetery so far found on the island. It was used from the Bronze Age to early Roman times. North of the cemetery was the **propylon**, an elaborate Ionic entrance to the sanctuary; it was a gift from Ptolemy II.

Museum

The site's museum is well laid out with labelling in English. Exhibits include terracotta figurines, vases, jewellery and a plaster cast of the Winged Victory. It's open Tuesday to Sunday from 9 am to 3 pm. Admission is 500 dr and is free on Sunday and public holidays.

Places to Stay & Eat

There are several domatia at Paleopolis, all of which are signposted from near the museum. The B-class *Xenia Hotel* (☎ 41 230) near the museum was built 40 years ago to provide accommodation for archaeologists. Although clean and comfortable, it lacks the sophistication of Samothraki's new hotels. The double/triple rooms cost 6700/ 7800 dr with private bathroom.

Just west of Paleopolis, above the coast road, is the C-class *Kastro Hotel* (☎ 41 001/2; fax 41 000), the island's newest hotel. The rooms are simply and tastefully furnished and rates are 11,000/15,000 dr for singles/doubles, including breakfast. The hotel has a swimming pool. There are no tavernas at Paleopolis but both hotels have restaurants and if you have your own transport there are some eating places along the road towards Loutra (Therma).

AROUND THE ISLAND
Loutra (Therma) Λουτρά (Θερμά)
Loutra, also called Therma, is 13 km east of Kamariotissa and a short walk inland from the coast. It's in an attractive setting with a profusion of plane and horse-chestnut trees,

NORTH-EAST AEGEAN ISLANDS

dense greenery and gurgling creeks. It is not an authentic village, but it is the nearest Samothraki comes to having a holiday resort – most of its buildings are purpose-built domatia, and most visitors to the island seem to stay here.

The village takes both its names from its therapeutic sulphurous mineral springs. Whether or not you are arthritic you may like to take a thermal bath here. The baths are in the large white building on the right as you walk to the central square from the bus stop. Opening times are 6 to 11 am, and 5 to 7 pm. Admission is 400 dr. There is a tiny OTE in the village which, unlike the one in Hora, remains open at weekends. It is signposted from Loutra's central square.

Places to Stay Samothraki has two official camp sites; both are near Loutra, and both are signposted 'Multilary Campings'. Rest assured, the authorities mean municipal campings and not military campings. The first *Multilary Camping* (☎ 41 784) is to the left of the main road, two km beyond the turn-off for Loutra, coming from Kamariotissa. The site is very spartan, with toilets and cold showers but no other amenities. The charges are 400 dr per person, 500 dr for a caravan, 300 dr per tent, and 200 dr for a car. The second *Multilary Camping* (☎ 41 491) is two km further along the road. It has a minimarket, restaurant and hot showers. It charges 600 dr per person, 450 dr per tent, and 200 dr for a car. Both sites are open only during June, July and August.

Domatia owners meet the buses at Loutra. If you can afford something more expensive, then Loutra has two lovely hotels. The C-class *Mariva Bungalows* (☎ 98 230) are set on a hillside in a secluded part of the island, near a waterfall. The spacious rooms cost 6250/7500/8750 dr for singles/doubles/triples with private bathroom. To reach the hotel take the first turn left along the road which leads from the coast up to Loutra. Follow the signs to the hotel which is 600 metres along this road.

The B-class *Kaviros Hotel* (☎ 98 277; fax 98 278) is bang in the middle of Loutra, just beyond the central square. It is a very pleasant family-run hotel with single/double rates of 9000/13,000 dr. The hotel is surrounded by a pretty garden and draped in copious greenery.

Places to Eat In Loutra there is little difference between the four or five restaurants; choose the place with the most people eating there. Look out for *Restaurant O Thodoros*, just beyond the central square, which is probably the cheapest. *Feggari Restaurant*, next to the OTE, is slightly more expensive, but the food is no better. The *Paradeisos Taverna* might be your best choice. Facing inland, take the first turn right after the central square to reach the taverna.

Other Villages

The small villages of **Profitis Ilias**, **Lakoma** and **Xiropotamos** in the south-west, and **Alonia** near Hora, are serene unspoilt villages all worth a visit. The hillside Profitis Ilias, with many trees and springs, is particularly delightful and has several tavernas. Asphalt roads lead to all of these villages.

Beaches

The Great Gods did not overendow Samothraki with good beaches. However, its one sandy beach, **Pahia Ammos**, on the south coast, is superb. You can reach this 800-metre stretch of fine white sand by walking along an eight-km winding road from Lakoma. In summer there are caïques from Kamariotissa to the beach. Around the headland is the equally superb **Vatos beach**, used mainly by nudists. Opposite Pahia Ammos, on a good day, you can see the mass of the former Greek island of Imvros (Gökçeada), which was ceded to the Turks under the Treaty of Lausanne in 1923.

There is now a restaurant and domatia at Pahia Ammos, but bookings are recommended for July and August, since there are only six rooms. Call *Taverna Pahia Ammos* (☎ 94 235), or write to Nikolaos Kapelas, Profitis Ilias, Samothraki. You will probably be able to camp (unofficially) at Pahia Ammos too.

Samothraki's other decent beach is the pebbled **Kipos beach** on the south-east coast. It can be reached on the unsealed road which is the easterly continuation of the road skirting the north coast. However, there are no facilities here other than a shower and a freshwater fountain, and there is no shade. It also pales in comparison to Pahia Ammos beach. Kipos beach can also be reached by caïque from Kamariotissa.

Thasos Θάσος

Thasos (THA-sos, population 13,300) lies 10 km south-east of Kavala. It is almost circular in shape and although its scenery is not as awesome as Samothraki's it has some pleasing mountain vistas. The EOT brochures tout it as the 'emerald isle', but like so many other Greek islands it has suffered bad fires which have destroyed much of its forest. The main attractions of Thasos are its excellent beaches and the many archaeological remains in and around the capital of Limenas. A good asphalt road goes around

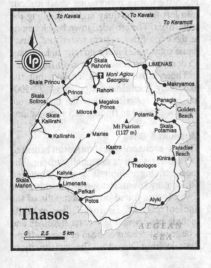

the island so all the beaches are easily accessible.

There are still enough rooms for everyone even in high season and Thasos has no less than eight camp sites dotted around its coast. A notice opposite the bus station in Limenas lists the town's hotels, and also, very helpfully, indicates which hotels remain open in the winter – if only all Greek islands did this.

History
Thasos has been continuously inhabited since the Stone Age. Its ancient city was founded by Parians in 700 BC who were led there by a message from the Delphic oracle. The oracle told them to 'Find a city in the Isle of Mists'. From Thasos the Parians established settlements in Thrace where they mined for gold in Mt Pangaion.

Gold was also mined on Thasos, and the islanders were able to develop a lucrative export trade based on ore, marble, timber and wine, as well as gold. As a result Thasos built a powerful navy and culture also flourished. Famous ancient Thassiots included the painters Polygnotos, Aglafon, Aristofon and the sculptors Polyclitos and Sosicles. The merchants of Thasos traded with Asia Minor, Egypt and Italy.

After the Battle of Plataea, Thasos became an ally of Athens, but when Athens attempted to curtail Thasos' trade with Egypt and Asia Minor war broke out between the two cities. The islanders were defeated and forced into becoming part of the Delian League; the heavy tax this imposed crippled its economy. Decline set in and continued through Macedonian and Roman times. Heavy taxes were imposed by the Turks, many inhabitants left the island and during the 18th century the population dropped from 8000 to 2500.

Thasos revived in the 19th century when Mohammed Ali Pasha of Egypt became governor of Kavala and Thasos. Ali allowed the islanders to govern themselves and exempted them from paying taxes. The revival was, however, short-lived. The Egyptian governors who superseded Ali Pasha usurped the island's natural resources and imposed heavy taxes. In 1912, along with the other

NORTH-EAST AEGEAN ISLANDS

islands of the group, Thasos was united with Greece. Like Samothraki, Thasos was occupied by Bulgaria in WW II.

In recent years Thasos has once again struck 'gold'. This time it's 'black gold', in the form of off-shore oil which has been found in the sea around the island.

Getting There & Away

Ferry There are ferries every hour between Kavala, on the mainland, and Skala Prinou (1½ hours, 400 dr). There is only one ferry a day between Kavala and Limenas. Ferries direct to Limenas leave every 45 minutes (30 minutes, 280 dr) from Keramoti, 46 km south-east of Kavala.

Hydrofoil There are six hydrofoils every day between Limenas and Kavala (30 minutes, 1400 dr).

Getting Around

Bus Limenas is the transport hub of the island. There are many buses a day to Limenaria (via the west-coast villages) and to Golden beach via Panagia and Potamia. There are six buses to Theologos and three to Aliki. Two or three buses a day journey in a clockwise direction all the way around the island. The cost of a complete circuit of the island by bus is 6350 dr.

Car, Motorbike & Bicycle Cars can be hired from Avis Rent a Car (☎ 22 535 or 23 081) on the central square in Limenas. They also have offices in Skala Prinou (☎ 71 202) and Potamia (☎ 61 506). Motorbikes and mopeds can be hired from Billy's Bikes (☎ 22 490) opposite the foreign-language newspapers' agency; and motorbikes, mopeds and bicycles from Babi's Bikes (☎ 22 129) which is on a side street between 18 Oktovriou and the central square, in Limenas.

Excursion Boat The *Eros 2* excursion boat does daily trips around the island, with stops for swimming and a barbecue. The boat leaves from the old harbour at 9.30 am and returns at 5.30 pm. The price is 5000 dr.

LIMENAS Λιμένας

Limenas, on the north-east coast, is the main port and capital of the island. Confusingly, it is also called Thasos town and Limin. The island's other port is Skala Prinou on the west coast. Limenas is built on top of the ancient city, so ruins are scattered all over the place. It is also the island's transport hub, with a reasonable bus service to the coastal resorts and villages.

Orientation & Information

The quay for both ferries and hydrofoils is at the centre of the waterfront. The central square is straight ahead from the waterfront. The main thoroughfare is 18 Oktovriou, which is parallel to the waterfront and north of the central square. Turn left into 18 Oktovriou from the quay to reach the OTE on the right. Take the next turn right into Theogenous and the second turn right to reach the post office, which is on the left. Thasos' telephone code is 0593 and the postcode is 640 04.

The National Bank of Greece is on the waterfront opposite the quay. The newsagent on Theogenous sells English-language newspapers. The bus station is on the waterfront; to reach it turn left from the quay. To reach the town's picturesque small harbour turn left from the quay and walk along the waterfront. The crowded town beach begins at the end of the western waterfront. Street name signs are a bit of a novelty in Limenas, so don't be surprised if you can't find one.

There is no EOT on Thasos, but the extremely helpful tourist police (☎ 22 500) are on the waterfront near the bus station. They will assist in finding accommodation.

Museum & Sites

Thasos' **archaeological museum** is next to the ancient agora at the small harbour. The most striking exhibit is a very elongated 6th-century kouros statue which stands in the foyer. It was found on the acropolis of the ancient city of Thasos. Other exhibits include pottery and terracotta figurines and a large well-preserved head of a very effeminate-looking Dionysos. The ancient city of

Thasos was excavated by the French School of Archaeology, so the museum's labelling is in French and Greek.

The **ancient agora** next to the museum was the bustling market place of ancient and Roman Thasos – the centre of its civic, social and business life. It's a pleasant, verdant site with the foundations of stoas, shops and dwellings. Entrance is free.

The **ancient theatre**, in a lovely wooded setting, has been fitted with wooden seats (now a bit dilapidated), and performances of ancient dramas are staged here annually.

(See under Festivals below.) The theatre is signposted from the small harbour.

From the theatre a path leads up to the **acropolis of ancient Thasos** where there are substantial remains of a medieval fortress which was built on the foundations of the ancient walls which encompassed the entire city. From the topmost point of the acropolis there are magnificent views. From the far side of the acropolis, steps carved into the rock (with a dodgy-looking metal handrail) lead down to the foundations of the ancient wall. From here it's a short walk to the

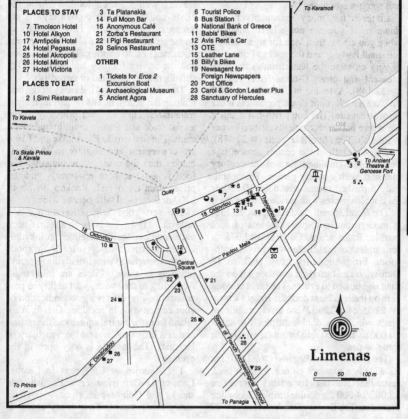

PLACES TO STAY

7 Timoleon Hotel
10 Hotel Alkyon
17 Amfipolis Hotel
24 Hotel Pegasus
25 Hotel Akropolis
26 Hotel Mironi
27 Hotel Victoria

PLACES TO EAT

2 I Simi Restaurant

3 Ta Platanakia
14 Full Moon Bar
16 Anonymous Café
21 Zorba's Restaurant
22 I Pigi Restaurant
29 Selinos Restaurant

OTHER

1 Tickets for *Eros 2* Excursion Boat
4 Archaeological Museum
5 Ancient Agora

6 Tourist Police
8 Bus Station
9 National Bank of Greece
11 Babis' Bikes
12 Avis Rent a Car
13 OTE
15 Leather Lane
18 Billy's Bikes
19 Newsagent for Foreign Newspapers
20 Post Office
23 Carol & Gordon Leather Plus
28 Sanctuary of Hercules

To Keramoti

To Kavala

To Skala Prinou & Kavala

Old Harbour

To Ancient Theatre & Genoese Fort

Quay

18 Oktovriou

18 Oktovriou

Central Square

Pavlou Mela

Theologou

Street of French Archaeological School

K. Dimitradou

To Prinos

To Panagia

Limenas

0   50   100 m

NORTH-EAST AEGEAN ISLANDS

Limenas-Panagia road at the southern edge of town.

Festivals

In July and August, performances of ancient dramas are held at Limenas' ancient theatre, as part of the Kavala Festival of Drama. Information and tickets can be obtained from the EOT in Kavala or the tourist police on Thasos.

Places to Stay – bottom end

The nearest camp site to Limenas is *Nysteri Camping*, just west of the town. With the exception of the camp site on Golden beach all of Thasos' other camp sites are on the west and south-west coasts.

Limenas has many reasonably priced *domatia*. If you are not offered anything when you arrive, then look for signs around the small harbour and the road to Prinos.

Very close to the waterfront is the very pleasant and clean C-class *Hotel Alkyon* (☎ 22 148). A double will cost about 8000 dr. Take a back room if you prefer less noise from street life. The hotel also has a snack bar where tea is the speciality; the co-owner is English. The *Hotel Akropolis* (☎ 22 488), one block south of the central square, is a very well-maintained turn-of-the-century mansion, with a lovely garden. The beautifully furnished rooms cost 8500/10,200 dr for doubles/triples with private bathroom.

The *Hotel Mironi* (☎ 23 256; fax 22 132) is modern and spacious with lots of cool marble. Rates are 8,000/10,000/12,975 dr for singles/doubles/triples with private bathroom. From the ferry quay walk to 18 Oktovriou and turn right and then left on the road signposted to Prinos. The hotel is along here on the left. Next door the *Hotel Victoria* (☎ 22 556; fax 22 132) is a lovely traditional place which has doubles/triples for 8500/10,000 dr. Both establishments are run by the same owner.

The B-class *Hotel Pegasus* (☎ 22 061; fax 22 373) is a pleasant choice. It has a pool, restaurant and bar. Its quality rooms are 12,000/14,000 for doubles/triples, including breakfast. The B-class *Timoleon Hotel* (☎ 22 177; fax 23 277) has clean spacious rooms with balcony. Rates are 10,800/14,000/17,500 dr with private bathroom; the price includes breakfast. The hotel is on the water-front just beyond the bus station.

Places to Stay – middle

The A-class *Amfipolis Hotel* (☎ 23 101; fax 22 110), on the corner of 18 Oktovriou and Theogenous, is an attractive mock castle complete with turrets. Rates are 13,000/17,800 dr including breakfast. The hotel has a swimming pool.

Places to Eat & Drink

Limenas has a good selection of restaurants serving well-prepared food. Perhaps the chefs could give their counterparts on Samothraki a few lessons. *I Pigi Restaurant*, on the central square, is a nice unpretentious restaurant next to a spring. The food is good and the service friendly and attentive. Try stifado, mussel saganaki or swordfish.

The old harbour, and the area just beyond it along the beach, boasts no less than eight restaurants. They all cater primarily to the tourist trade and feature multilingual menu cards. The first two *Ta Platanakia* and *I Simi* are convenient and slightly more down-market than the other establishments. The food is good at both restaurants and the prices aren't too bad. Reckon on about 2200 dr for a meal with beer or wine.

The very good *Selinos Restaurant* is a little out of town, but is worth a visit. Check out a couple of their specialities: kolokytho-keftedes (zucchini rissoles), ohtapodi krasato (octopus in wine), or mydia saganaki (mussels in sauce). Prices are mid-range. According to the owner, your ability to pronounce the first dish is a good indication of your competence in speaking Greek. Walk inland from the central square and the restaurant is a little way beyond the Sanctuary of Hercules. The taverna is only open in the evening.

The *Anonymous Café* next to Leather Lane on 18 Oktovriou serves English-style snacks and Guinness in a can, as well as many other beers. Two doors along is another popular watering hole, the *Full Moon*, which has an Australian owner.

Things to Buy

Limenas has two excellent leather shops, both of which sell high-quality leather bags. They are Carol & Gordon Leather Plus on the central square and Leather Lane on 18 Oktovriou. The latter also has a used-book exchange (with mostly English and German titles).

EAST COAST

The neighbouring hillside villages of **Panagia** and **Potamia** are quite touristy but picturesque. Both are four km west of Golden beach. The Greek-American artist Polygnotos Vagis was born in Potamia in 1894 and some of his work can be seen in a small museum in the village. It is open from Tuesday to Saturday from 9 am to 1 pm and 6 to 9 pm and on Sunday from 10 am to 2 pm. (The municipal museum in Kavala also has a collection of Vagis' work.)

The long and mostly sandy **Golden beach** is the island's best beach and roads from both Panagia and Potamia lead down to it. These roads are very pleasant to walk along, but if you prefer, the bus from Limenas calls at both villages before continuing to the southern end of the beach.

The next beach south is at the village of **Kinira**, and just south of here is the very pleasant **Paradise beach**. The little islet just off the coast here is also called Kinira. **Alyki**, on the south-east coast, consists of two idyllic beaches back to back on a headland. There is a small archaeological site near the beach and a marble quarry. The road linking the east side with the west side runs high across the cliffs and bays at the bottom of the island and offers some great views. You can complete the island circuit (110 km) by motorbike in about 3½ hours if you only take a few breaks.

Places to Stay & Eat

Hrysi Ammoudia (☎ 61 207/472/473), on Golden beach, is the only camp site on this side of the island. The *Hotel Emerald* (☎ 61

979), on Golden beach, has self-contained studios for two to four persons for 11,400 to 14,000 dr.

In Panagia, *Hotel Elvetia* (☎ 61 231) has pleasant double rooms costing 9500 dr. With your back to the fountain in the central square of Panagia (where the bus stops), turn left and take the first main road to the left and the hotel is on the left. Just beyond here on the right, the *Hotel Chrysalis* (☎ 61 451) has doubles and triples for 9500 dr with private bathroom. There are domatia at both Kinira and Aliki.

There are reasonably priced restaurants in Panagia. *Restaurant Vigli*, overlooking the northern end of Golden beach, has superb views and food to match. There are tavernas on the beach at Kinira and Aliki.

WEST COAST

The west coast consists of a series of seaside villages with Skala (by the sea) before their names. Roads lead from each of these to inland villages with the same name (minus the 'skala'). Beaches along the west coast are uniformly pebbly and exposed. Travelling from north to south the first village is **Skala Rahonis**. This is Thasos' latest development, having recently been discovered by the package-tour companies. It has an excellent camp site and the inland village of Rahoni remains unspoilt. Just before Rahoni there is a turn-off left to Moni Agiou Georgiou.

Skala Prinou, the next coastal village, and Thasos' second port, is crowded and unattractive. **Skala Sotirou** and **Skala Kallirahis** are more pleasant and both have small beaches. Kallirahi, two km inland from Skala Kallirahis, is a peaceful village with steep narrow streets and old stone houses. It has a large population of skinny anxious-looking cats and, judging by the graffiti, a lot of communists.

Skala Marion is a delightful fishing village and one of the least touristy places around the coast. It was from here, earlier this century, that the German Speidel Metal Company exported ore from Thasos to Europe. There are beaches at both sides of the village, and between here and Limenaria there are stretches of uncrowded beach.

Limenaria (42 km from Limenas) is Thasos' second largest town and a very crowded resort with a narrow sandy beach. The town was built in 1903 by the Speidel Metal Company which mined ore in the area. There are slightly less crowded beaches around the coast at **Pefkari** and **Potos**. From Potos a scenic 10-km road leads inland to **Theologos** which was the capital of the island in medieval and Turkish times. This is the island's most beautiful village and the only mountain settlement served by public transport. The village houses are of whitewashed stone with slate roofs. It's a serene place, unblemished by tourism.

Places to Stay

Camping Perseus (☎ 81 352), at Skala Rahonis, is an excellent camp site in a pretty setting of flowers and olive and willow trees. The cook at the site's taverna will prepare any Greek dish you wish if you place your order a day in advance. The next camp site along is *Camping Ioannidis* (☎ 71 377), between Skala Rahonis and Skala Prinou. It's also pleasant and has a minimarket, restaurant and bar. The EOT-owned *Camping*

Prinos (☎ 71 171/270), at Skala Prinou, is well maintained but like most EOT sites is rather regimented.

The next camp site, *Camping Daidalos* (☎ 71 365/766), is just north of Skala Sotirou. It has a minimarket, restaurant and bar. The next site, *Pefkari Camping* (☎ 51 190/595), at Pefkari beach, is south of Limenaria. All the sites charge around 850 dr per person and 600 dr per tent.

All of the seaside villages have hotels and domatia and the inland villages have rooms in private houses. For information about these enquire at kafeneia. The *rooms* of Stelios Kontogeorgiadis, overlooking the harbour at Skala Marion, are clean and attractive and cost 4500/6500/8000 dr for singles/doubles/triples with shared bathroom and kitchen.

Places to Eat

All of the coastal villages have tavernas. *Taverna Drosia*, in Rahoni, features live bouzouki music on Friday and Saturday evenings. *Taverna Orizontes*, in Theologos, features rembetika nights. *Kostas Taverna*, on the main street in Theologos, has an outdoor terrace with wonderful views of the surrounding mountains.

NORTH-EAST AEGEAN ISLANDS

Ionian Islands Τα Επτάνησα

The Ionian group consists of seven main islands anchored in the Ionian Sea – Corfu, Paxoi, Kefallonia, Zakynthos, Ithaki, Lefkada and Kythira; this last one is more accessible from the Peloponnese. The islands differ from other island groups and, geographically, are less quintessentially Greek. More reminiscent of Corfu's neighbour Italy, not least in light, their colours are mellow and green compared with the stark, dazzling brightness of the Aegean. These islands receive a great amount of rain and consequently, the vegetation, with the exception of the more exposed Kythira, is more luxuriant. Corfu has the nation's highest rainfall. Overall, vegetation combines elements of the tropical with forests that could be northern European: exotic orchids with wild flowers emerging below spring snowlines and eucalypts and acacias sharing soil with plane, oak and maple trees. The islands do not experience the meltemi wind, and as a result they can be extremely hot in summer. No island is really undiscovered except Antikythira, left in the rough tidal wash of larger Kythira. However, as throughout all of Greece, island hinterlands yield rewards of unspoiled, small villages.

The culture and cuisine of each Ionian island is unique and differs from the Aegean islands and Crete. Influences from Mediterranean Europe and Britain have also been stronger yet have developed with special individuality on each island.

Accommodation prices in this chapter are for the high season (July and August). They are lower at other times. Farm holidays in rural village homes are available in Lefkada, Preveza, (close to Lefkada on the mainland), Kefallonia and Kythira. Properties are listed in the brochure *Agrotourism: Holidays in the Countryside*, available from main EOT offices.

History & Mythology

The origin of the name Ionian is obscure but

is thought to derive from the goddess Io. Yet another one of Zeus' countless paramours, Io, while fleeing the wrath of a jealous Hera, happened to pass through the waters now known as the Ionian Sea.

If we are to believe Homer, the islands were important during Mycenaean times; however, no magnificent palaces or even modest villages from that period have been revealed although Mycenaean tombs have been unearthed. Ancient history lies buried beneath tonnes of earthquake rubble. Seismic activity has been constant on all Ionian islands, including Kythira.

According to Homer, Odysseus' kingdom consisted not only of Ithaca (Ithaki) but also encompassed Kefallonia, Zakynthos and Lefkada. Ithaca has long been controversial. Classicists and archaeologists in the 19th century concluded that Homer's Ithaca was modern-day Ithaki, his Sami was Sami on Kefallonia, and his Zakynthos was today's Zakynthos, which sounded credible. But early this century German archaeologist Wilhelm Dorpfeld put a spanner in the works by claiming that Lefkada was ancient Ithaca,

Ionian Islands

modern Ithaki was ancient Sami and Kefallonia was ancient Doulichion. His theories have now fallen from favour with everyone except the people of Lefkada.

By the 8th century BC, the Ionian islands were in the clutches of mighty Corinth which regarded them of value as stepping stones on the route to Sicily and Italy. A century later, Corfu staged a successful revolt against Corinth, which was allied to Sparta, and became an ally of Sparta's archenemy, Athens. This alliance provoked Sparta into challenging Athens, thus precipitating the Peloponnesian Wars. The wars left Corfu depleted as they did all participants and Corfu became little more than a staging post for whoever happened to be holding sway in Greece. By the end of the 3rd century, Corfu, along with the other Ionian islands, had become Roman. Following the decline of the Roman Empire, the islands saw the usual waves of invaders that Greece suffered. After the fall of Constantinople, the islands became Venetian.

Corfu was never part of the Ottoman Empire. Paxoi, Kefallonia, Zakynthos, Ithaki and Kythira were variously occupied by the Turks, but the Venetians held them the longest. The exception was Lefkada, which was Turkish for 200 years. The Ionian islands fared better under the Venetians than their counterparts in the Cyclades. They benefited culturally through contact with Italy and the tradition of icon-painting was allowed to continue. In Turkish-occupied Greece, icon-painting was driven underground as Islamic law prohibited portrayal of the human form.

Venice fell to Napoleon in 1797. Two years later in the Treaty of Campo Formio, the Ionian islands were allotted to France. In 1799 Russian forces wrested the islands from Napoleon, but by 1807 they were his again. By then, the all-powerful British couldn't resist meddling. As a result, in 1815, after Napoleon's downfall, the islands became a British protectorate under the jurisdiction of a series of Lords High Commissioner. These reportedly ranged from being eccentric to downright nutty.

British rule was oppressive but, on a more positive note, the British constructed roads, bridges, schools and hospitals, established trade links and developed agriculture and industry. However, the fervour of nationalism in the rest of Greece soon reached the Ionian islands.

The call for enosis (union with Greece) was realised in 1862 when Britain relinquished the islands to Greece. In WW II the Italians invaded Corfu as part of Mussolini's plan to resurrect the mighty Roman Empire. Italy surrendered to the Allies in September 1943 and, in revenge, the Germans massacred thousands of Italians who had occupied the island. The Germans also sent some 5000 Corfiot Jews to Auschwitz.

A severe earthquake shook the Ionian islands in 1953. It did considerable damage, particularly on Zakynthos and Kefallonia.

Getting There & Away

Air Corfu, Kefallonia, Zakynthos and Kythira have airports. Corfu has a weekly Olympic Airways scheduled flight to/from Rome. In addition, many charter flights to Corfu come from northern Europe and the UK. Kefallonia and Zakynthos also receive flights. These islands have frequent flights to Athens and one connection a week between Kefallonia and Zakynthos.

Bus Lefkada is joined to the mainland by a causeway and can be reached by bus from Athens and Patras. Buses go from Athens and Thessaloniki to Corfu and from Athens to Kefallonia and Zakynthos.

Ferry – domestic The Peloponnese has several ports of departure for the Ionian islands: Patras for ferries to Kefallonia, Ithaki, Paxoi and Corfu; Kyllini for ferries to Kefallonia and Zakynthos, and Monemvassia, Neapoli and Gythio for Kythira which is also served from Crete. Epiros has one port, Igoumenitsa, for Corfu; and Sterea Ellada has two, Astakos for Ithaki and Kefallonia, and Mytikas for Lefkada.

Ferry – international From Corfu, ferries

depart for Brindisi, Bari, Ancona, Ortona, Otranto, Trieste and Venice in Italy. At least three times weekly, a ferry goes from Kefallonia to Brindisi via Ithaki, Igoumenitsa and Corfu. Ferries also go to Albania.

Corfu Κέρκυρα

Corfu (population 100,000) is the second-largest, greenest Ionian island and the best known. In Greek, the island is called Kerkyra (KER-kee-ra). It was Homer's 'beautiful and rich land', and Odysseus' last stop on his journey home to Ithaca. Shakespeare reputedly used it as a background for *The Tempest*. This century, the Durrell brothers, among others, have extolled its virtues. With its beguiling landscape of vibrant wild flowers and slender cypress trees rising out of shimmering olive groves, Corfu is considered by many as Greece's most beautiful island. With the highest rainfall, it's also the nation's major vegetable garden and produces scores of herbs. The mountain air is heavily scented. In autumn, the night sky over the sea is a spectacular sight.

Getting There & Away

Air Corfu has three daily flights to Athens and four on Tuesday, Thursday and Saturday (18,000 dr). The Olympic Airways office (☎ 38 694/695/696) is at Kapodistriou 24.

Bus Two daily buses go to Athens (11 hours, 7450 dr including ferry), at 8.30 am and 6.30 pm, and one to Thessaloniki. Tickets must be bought in advance.

Ferry – domestic From Corfu, hourly ferries go to Igoumenitsa (1½ hours, 700 dr). One daily ferry goes to Paxoi (two hours, 1630 dr). In summer, fast boats take 90 minutes. These leave from the old port. For details on ferries to Patras, see the following section. Corfu's port police can be contacted on ☎ 32 655.

IONIAN ISLANDS

To Brindisi,
Otranto, Bari,
Ortona &
Ancona (Italy)

Pelekito

Roda

Sidhari

Kassiopi

Karoussades

Perithia

Agios
Stefanos

Mt
▲Pantokrator
(906 m)

ALBANIA

Strinila

Agrilla

Pyrgi

Makrades

Ypos

Krini

Lakones

Kato Koriakiana

Dassia

Paleokastritsa

Liapades

Danilia Village

Gouvia

PITHIA

Giannades

Ropa Valley

CORFU
(KERKYRA)

Ermones

Kanoni
Peninsula

Vatos

Myrtiotissa

Pelekas

Glyfada

Perama

Ionian
Sea

Sinarades

Gastouri

GREECE

Agios
Gordios

Agioi
Deka

Benitses

Strongyli

Paramonas

Agios
Matheos

Skala

Prasouda

Messongi

To Igoumenitsa

Gardiki

Boukari

Petriti

Panagia
Messavrisi

Lefkimmi

Corfu

Agios
Giorgios

Marathias

Vitalades

Kritika

Kavos

Paleohori

Spartera

0   5   10 km

Asprokavos

To Paxoi,
Kefallonia
& Patras

Ferry – international Corfu is on the Patras-Igoumenitsa ferry route to Italy (Brindisi, Bari, Ancona, Ortona, Otranto, Trieste, Venice). Some Ancona ferries go direct from Igoumenitsa, but others go via Corfu (10 hours, 6000 dr), where some lines allow a free stopover. About six ferries a day go to Brindisi (9½ hours); at least one a day to Bari and Ancona; five a week to Otranto; three a week to Ortona and one daily to Venice in summer.

Brindisi-bound ferries leave Corfu's new port between 8.30 and 9.30 am. For ticket prices see the Igoumenitsa Getting There &

Away section in the Northern Greece chapter. Agencies selling tickets are mostly on Xenofondos Stratigou. Shop around for the best deal. You can take one of the frequent international ferries to Patras (10 hours, 4500 dr), daily in summer.

Summer excursions to Albania (☎ 31 649 or 39 293 for details) leave the new port daily (4000 dr from Corfu and 5000 dr return from Albania). No visa is required but a passport must be produced.

Getting Around
To/From the Airport There is no Olympic

Airways shuttle bus between Corfu town and the airport. City bus No 3 from Plateia San Rocco stops on the main road 500 metres from the airport.

Bus Destinations of buses (green and cream) from Corfu town's long-distance bus station are as follows:

Destination	Duration	Fare	Frequency
Agios Stefanos			
(via Sidhari)	1½ hours	650 dr	5 daily
Glyfada (via Vatos)	45 mins	260 dr	4 daily
Kassiopi			
(via Loutses)	1 hour	550 dr	4 daily
Kavos			
(via Lefkimmi)	1½ hours	500 dr	8 daily
Messongi	45 mins	320 dr	4 daily
Paleokastritsa	45 mins	360 dr	6 daily
Pyrgi (via Ipsos)	30 mins	220 dr	4 daily
Roda (via Aharavi)	1½ hours	550 dr	4daily
Sinarades			
(via Agios Gordios)	45 mins	225 dr	4 daily

Numbers and destinations of buses (dark blue) from the bus station at Plateia San Rocco, Corfu town, are:

Destination	Bus No	Duration	Frequency
Ahillion			
(via Gastouri)	No 10	20 mins	6 daily
Afra	No 8	30 mins	8 daily
Agios Ioannis			
(via Pelekas)	No 11	30 mins	9 daily
Kastellani			
(via Kourmades)	No 5	25 mins	14 daily
Kontokali			
(via Gouvia & Dassia)	No 7	30 mins	hourly
Perama			
(via Benitses)	No 6	30 mins	12 daily
Potamos			
(via Evropouli & Tembloni)	No 4	45 mins	12 daily

The local bus flat fare is 110 dr. Tickets can be bought on board or on Plateia San Rocco.

Car & Motorbike Car-hire companies in Corfu town include Autorent (☎ 44 623/ 624/625), Xenofondos Stratigou 34; Avis (☎ 24 042), Ethnikis Antistaseos 42; Budget (☎ 22 062), Donzelot 5; and Europcar (☎ 46 931/932/933), Xenofondos Stratigou 32.

Several motorbike-hire outlets are on Xenofondos Stratigou.

CORFU TOWN

The island capital is Corfu town (Kerkyra), built on a promontory. It is a harmonious, gracious medley of numerous occupying influences, which never included the Turks. The Spianada (esplanade) is green, gardened and boasts Greece's only cricket ground, a legacy of the British. After a match, spectators may join players in drinking ginger beer made to an old Victorian recipe or, typically, tea or gin and tonic.

The Liston, a row of arcaded buildings flanking the north-western side of the Spianada, was built during the French occupation and modelled on Paris' Rue de Rivoli. The buildings function as up-market cafés, lamplit by night. Georgian mansions and Byzantine churches complete the picture. The Venetian influence prevails, particularly in the enchanting old town, wedged between two fortresses. Narrow alleyways of 18th-century shuttered tenements in muted ochres and pinks are more reminiscent of Venice or Naples than Greece.

Orientation

The town is separated into northern and southern sections. The old town is in the northern section between the Spianada and the New Fortress. The Palaio Frourio (Old Fortress) is east of the northern section and projects out to sea, cut off from the town by a moat. The Neo Frourio (New Fortress) is west. The Spianada separates the Old Fortress from the town. The southern section is the new town.

The old port is north of the old town. The new port is west. Between them is the hulking New Fortress. The long-distance bus station is on Avrami, inland from the new port and west of the Neo Frourio. The local bus station is on Plateia San Rocco. Local buses serve the town and nearby villages.

Information

Tourist Offices The EOT (☎ 37 520/638) is on Rizospaston Voulefton, between the post

IONIAN ISLANDS

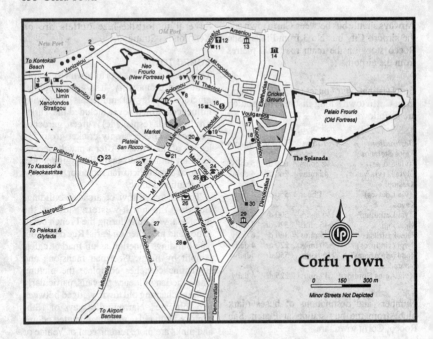

Corfu Town

0   150   300 m

Minor Streets Not Depicted

office and the OTE. The tourist police (☎ 30 265) are on Plateia Neou Frouriou 1, near Plateia Solomou. From the EOT, take a free copy of the summer-published *Corfu News*, Corfu's English-language newspaper.

Money The National Bank of Greece is in the old town at the junction of Voulgareos and G Theotoki. American Express is represented by Greek Skies Tours (☎ 32 469 or 30 883) at Kapodistriou 20a.

Post & Telecommunications The main post office is on the right side of Alexandras as you walk from Plateia San Rocco (the site of the local bus station). It is open Monday to Friday from 7.30 am to 8 pm; on Saturday from 7.30 am to 2 pm; and on Sunday from 9 am to 1.30 pm. The postcode for Corfu town is 491 00.

The main OTE office is nearby at Mantzarou 9 and is open from 6 am to midnight daily. The telephone code for Corfu town and

all villages on Corfu island except Paleokastritsa is 0661. Paleokastritsa's code is 0663.

Foreign Consulates Foreign consulates in Corfu include that for the Netherlands (☎ 39 900) at Idromenon 2 and the UK (☎ 30 055) at Menekratous 1.

Emergency The Corfu General Hospital (☎ 45 811) is on Polihroni Kostanda.

Museums

Archaeological Museum The star exhibit of this museum is the Gorgon Medusa sculpture, one of the best preserved pieces of Archaic sculpture in Greece. It was part of the west pediment of the 6th-century Temple of Artemis at Corcyra (the ancient capital), which stood on the peninsula south of the town. The petrifying Medusa is depicted in the instant before she was beheaded by Perseus. This precipitated the birth of her

PLACES TO STAY		OTHER		18	Olympic Airways
				19	Indoor Cinema
3	Hotel Ionian	1	Agents for Boat Tickets	20	Greek Skies Tours
4	Hotel Europa		to Italy	21	Local Bus Station
5	Hotel Atlantis	2	Departure Points for	23	Hospital
11	Hotel Astron		boats to Igoumenitsa	24	OTE
15	Hotel Cyprus	6	Long Distance Bus	25	EOT
17	Hotel Arcadian		Station	26	Post Office
30	Corfu Palace Hotel	7	Shell Museum	27	British Cemetery
		12	Church of Agios	28	Outdoor Cinema
PLACES TO EAT			Spiridon	29	Archaeological
		13	Byzantine Museum		Museum
8	Gistakis Restaurant	14	Palace of St Michael &		
9	Naftikon Restaurant		St George		
10	Restaurant Dionysos	16	National Bank of		
22	Taverna Stamatis		Greece		

sons, Chrysaor and Pegasus (the winged horse), who emerged from her headless body.

Also impressive is the 7th-century crouching lion, found near the Tomb of Menecrates. Archaeologists ascertained that it stood on top of the tomb. The museum (☎ 30 680) is on Vraili. Opening times are Tuesday to Saturday from 8.45 am to 3 pm and Sunday from 9.30 am to 2.30 pm. Admission is 800 dr.

Museum of Asiatic Art At the time of writing, this museum was moving. Ask the EOT where you can see the outstanding collection, bequeathed by the Greek diplomats Grigoris Manos and Nikolaos Hatzivasiliou. It includes Chinese and Japanese porcelain, bronzes, screens, sculptures, theatrical masks, armour, books and prints from Nepal, Tibet, India, Thailand, Korea and Japan. The museum was previously housed in the Palace of St Michael & St George, built in 1819 as the British Lord High Commissioner's residence. Stroll north along Eleftherias to see the palace.

Shell Museum On Plateia Neou Frouriou, relocated from Solomou, this museum (☎ 28 568) reputedly contains the best private shell collection in Europe. It's a fascinating dive without equipment. Exhibits include sharks' jaws from Australia where the informative owner, whose name is Napoleon, has also collected coral. Fossils, crabs, lobsters, sponges, even snakes are displayed. The museum is open daily from 10 am to 9 pm. Admission is 800 dr.

Byzantine Museum This museum (☎ 38 313), overlooking the sea on Arseniou, is housed in the Church of Our Lady of Antivouniotissa with icons well representative of the Byzantine period. It's open Tuesday to Saturday, 8.45 am to 3 pm and Sunday from 9.30 pm to 2.30 pm.

Other Things to See

Apart from the pleasure of wandering the narrow streets of the old town and the gardens of the Spianada, you can't miss the two fortresses, Corfu town's most dominant landmarks. The **Neo Frourio**, built between 1576 and 1588, is closed to the public. The promontory on which it stands was first fortified in the 12th century. Existing remains date from 1588. You can walk around the ruins of **Palaio Frourio**, which dates from the mid-12th century; it is open from 8 am to 7 pm (free entry).

In Corfu, a disproportionate number of males are christened Spyros after the island's miracle-working patron St Spyridon. His mummified body is in a silver glass-fronted coffin in the 16th-century **Church of Agios Spyridon**. He's not a pretty sight, but what can you expect of someone over 1000 years old? He is paraded on Palm Sunday, Easter

IONIAN ISLANDS

Sunday, 11 August and the first Sunday in November.

The well-kept **British cemetery** is a fitting resting-place for soldiers and civilians who died during the British occupation and WW II. Wild orchids, indigenous to the island, grow here, as do fine trees including araucarias, cypresses, Californian sequoias and jacarandas. The cemetery is at the northern end of Kolokotroni.

Festivals
The Corfu festival of dance and music is held in August and September.

Activities
The Ionian University offers courses in modern Greek and Greek civilisation in July and August. For details, contact the secretariat (☎ 22 993/994) on Megaron Kapodistria in Corfu or, in Athens (☎ 522 9770), at Deligiorgi 55-59.

Go yachting with a crew or bareboat in fabled waters. Corfu's biggest charterer is Corfu Yachting Centre, Theotokou 120, near the new port.

Places to Stay – bottom end
The nearest camp site to Corfu town is *Camping Kontokali Beach* (☎ 91 170/202), next to the youth hostel. Take bus No 7 from Plateia San Rocco bus station.

Corfu's *YHA hostel* (☎ 91 292) is at Kontokali beach, next to the camp site.

Out of high season, domatia owners meet ferries at both ports. This is often the easiest way of securing budget accommodation. Be wary of booking rooms for Greece in advance in Italy before arrival. A few unscrupulous agencies may suggest your preferred choice is closed or full – and reap a tidy commission from the place(s) booked through them.

The D-class *Hotel Cyprus* (☎ 30 032 or 40 675), Agios Paterou 13, has spotless rooms with character. Rates are 5500/6000 dr for doubles/triples with shared bathroom. Go up Agios Paterou, opposite the western end of Voulgareos, turn left at the top of the short, steep hill and you'll see the hotel.

The D-class *Hotel Europa* (☎ 39 304), at the new port on Neos Limin, offers clean singles/doubles for 5500/6000 dr with shared bathroom. Doubles with private bathroom are 7000 dr. Walk to customs at the new port, take Venizelou which forks left and soon you will see a sign pointing to the hotel.

The *Hotel Arcadian* (☎ 37 6670/6671/6672), Kapodistriou 44, has small, comfortable rooms for 6000/8000 dr with private bathroom. Another good value C-class place is the *Hotel Ionian* (☎ 30 628), on Xenofondos Stratigou, opposite the new port, with singles/doubles for 7500/10,200 dr, including breakfast.

Places to Stay – middle
The *Hotel Atlantis* (☎ 35 560/561/562) has pleasant singles/doubles/triples for 12,500/16,000/19,800 dr. The hotel is on Xenofondos Stratigou, near the Hotel Ionian.

The B-class *Hotel Astron* (☎ 39 505/986), Donzelot 15, has an old neoclassical ambience, friendly owner and several balconied rooms (all with facilities) with port-facing views. Rates here are 12,600/16,600/20,700/24,900 dr, with breakfast.

Places to Stay – top end
The *Corfu Palace* (☎ 39 485/486/487; fax 31 749) on Dimokratias, is the town centre's only deluxe hotel, the choice of Monaco's Prince Rainier and the late Princess Grace when staying off their yacht. Refurbished since, it has two bars, two restaurants and pools. Rates are 36,700/50,900 dr for singles/doubles.

The deluxe *Corfu Hilton* (☎ 36 540/541/542; fax 36 551) is at Kanoni, four km from Corfu town. Facilities include two restaurants, two bars, a health club, two pools, tennis courts, a jogging track and Corfu's casino. Rates are 43,000/52,000 dr.

Places to Eat
As it was not conquered by the Turks, Corfu maintains a distinctive cuisine influenced by other parts of Europe, including Russia, in a few places. (See the food section in Facts for the Visitor.) *Gistakis Restaurant*, Solomou

20, is unpretentious and has delicious food. *Naftikon Restaurant*, 152 N Theotoki, has fair prices and Corfiot food. *Restaurant Dionysos*, on Dona, is also commendable. These restaurants are close to the old port. Prices for main dishes in all three restaurants start at about 850 dr. *Taverna Stamatis*, on Dimoulitsa, is a cheap and popular with locals.

Entertainment

Corfu town has an outdoor cinema, halfway down Marasli, on the right towards the sea. The indoor cinema is at the *Pallas*, north of Plateia San Rocco. The old town has many bars but discos are at the tourist ghettos. The nearest to town are on the coast to the north.

Opposite *Disco Apocalypsis* towards the new port, try summer bungy jumping if you're game. Otherwise, take the kids to an amusement park on Plateia Spilia, or join high rollers at the *casino* in the Hilton Hotel. Take your passport. You may need to produce it to enter.

AROUND THE ISLAND
North of Corfu Town

Most of the coast of northern Corfu is package-tourist saturated, and thoroughly de-Greeked. Camp sites along the north-east coast include: *Karda Beach* (☎ 93 595) and *Kormarie* (93 587) at Dassia; *Kerkira Camping* (☎ 93 246) and *Ipsos Ideal* (☎ 93 243) at Ipsos; and *Paradise Camping* (☎ 93 282) at Pyrgi.

Out of Gouvia is **Danilia village**, a reconstructed settlement, totally tourist-orientated yet not without the charm of the past. Visit to stroll, shop and enjoy the food, wine and dance. At **Kato Korakiana** there is an annexe of the National Art Gallery, part of the Corfu National Art Gallery. Inland, towards Paleokastritsa, 13 km from Corfu on the edge of **Felekas** village, is the island's oldest distillery, Mavromatis. Yes, it's geared for tour groups but also highlights the quality of five Corfiot spirits, reserve brandy and cumquat liqueur as well as preserved fruits. Tastings are free.

At **Pyrgi**, 16 km north of Corfu town, a road continues around the base of the mighty **Mt Pantokrator** (906 metres), the island's highest peak. At this point, where the island protrudes as if to accommodate the mountain, the 2000-metre-high mountains of Albania are less than two km away. The writers Lawrence and Gerald Durrell spent their idyllic childhoods in this region. Back at Pyrgi, another road snakes inland over the western flank of the mountain to the north coast. A detour can be made to the picturesque village of **Strinila** from where a road leads through stark terrain to the summit and monastery of Mt Pantokrator and stupendous views. The coast road continues to the large resort of Kassiopi, 36 km from Corfu town, above which there is a ruined fortress.

The **Church of Our Lady of Kassiopi** stands on what may have been the site of the Roman Temple of Jupiter, where the showoff Emperor Nero is supposed to have sung while accompanying himself on the lyre. Beyond Kassiopi is a turn-off for the remote and half-derelict but delightful village of **Perithia**, high up on Mt Panokrator. Several of the Corfu town-Kassiopi buses continue to Perithia. The coast road continues west through the resort of **Roda**, with a camp site *Roda Beach* (☎ 0663-63 120), and on to Sidhari.

South of Corfu Town

The Kanoni peninsula, four km from Corfu town, was the site of the ancient capital; however, it retains little evidence. Its greatest attractions are two pretty islets. On one is **Moni Vlahernas**, reached by a causeway. On the other, **Mouse Island**, there is a 13th-century church. Caïques ply back and forth.

The **Ahillion Palace** (☎ 56 245/251), near the hillside village of Gastouri, eight km from Corfu town was, in the 1890s, the summer palace of Austria's Empress Elisabeth. King Otho of Greece was her uncle. She dedicated the villa to Achilles. The beautifully landscaped garden is guarded by kitsch statues of the empress' other mythological heroes.

The palace is an astonishing farrago of excessive elements of styles fashionable in

IONIAN ISLANDS

the late 19th century, and definitely worth a visit. A few rooms are open to the public. After the empress' assassination, the palace was bought by Kaiser Wilhelm II. It is open Monday to Sunday from 11 am to 4 pm. Admission is 700 dr but is free on Sunday.

If you thought the development north of Corfu was bad then the once tranquil fishing village of **Benitses** will break your heart. This is the playground of holiday hooligans (ie British lager louts). If you can fight your way through this lot, head for the ruins of a 3rd-century AD Roman villa, inland. It's also a delightful 30-minute walk to an old water-works, built during the time of the British protectorate. A better option is to visit **Perama beach**, which is much closer to Corfu town. Here *Aeolos Beach Bungalows'* chef has a reputation for serving some of the island's best food. Rates for singles/doubles with breakfast are 14,000/19,000 dr, and half-board (breakfast and either lunch or dinner) is 18,000/26,000 dr. **Messongi**, 20 km south of Corfu town, is marginally quieter. The town was founded by Cretan refugees fleeing the Turks. The sea is shallow for a long way so swimming is safe for children. Further south, development decreases and quieter beaches can be found.

Western Corfu

Paleokastritsa, 26 km west of Corfu, is the west coast's largest resort. Built around several sandy and pebbled coves with a green mountain backdrop, it's incredibly beautiful. Once it must have been paradise, but it too has been a victim of rampant development. **Moni Theotokou** perches on the rocky promontory at Paleokastritsa, above the shimmering turquoise sea. The monastery was founded in the 13th century but the present building dates from the 18th century. A small museum contains 17th-century icons. It is open from 7 am to 1 pm and 3 to 8 pm. Admission is free but a donation is expected.

Paleokastritsa Camping (☎ 0663-41 104) is on the main approach road to the resort. The bus will drop you at the entrance. The resort also has many hotels and domatia.

Explore mountain villages above Paleokastritsa. **Lakones**, five km inland from Paleokastritsa, is relatively unspoilt. From here the Makrades road leads to **Krini**. Use this as a base to visit the ruins of the 13th-century Byzantine fortress of **Angelokastro** where the inhabitants of Paleokastritsa took refuge from attackers. The ruins offer superb views. A village bus goes twice daily to Krini from the long-distance bus station in Corfu town.

Further south, the beach at **Ermones** is a short distance from the **Corfu Golf Course**, the largest in Europe. Golfers can find spotless rooms as well as self-catering units at *Magdalena Apartments & Studios* (☎ 94 096), five minutes' stroll away in the Ropa Valley, with a pool, barbecue, bar, restaurant and weekend live Greek music shows. Prices for doubles/triples/quads start at 8000/10,000/11,500 dr. The blue bus for **Giannades** will leave you at the entrance. **Glyfada**, on the west coast, has a sandy beach. It's another resort crowded with package tourists.

Hilltop **Pelekas**, four km away, is no less busy, but is laid back and popular with young, independent travellers. Tourists come to watch the sunset from here, supposedly the best spot on Corfu to do so. A track leads from the village to a sandy beach. The village has domatia. **Myrtiotissa** is an unofficial nudist beach, north of Glyfada. Take a Glyfada bus and ask to be left by the track which leads to this beach.

The nearest official camp site in the area is *Vatos Camping* (☎ 94 505) near the village of Vatos.

There is also nudist bathing on one section of **Agios Gordios beach**, about eight km south of Glyfada. This beach lies beneath the extraordinary *Pink Palace* (☎ 53 103/104), a pink-painted, 14-building pleasure complex charging 4500 dr for a room with shared bathroom, cooked breakfast, three-course dinner and use of a pool, volleyball and basketball courts, disco, bar and roof for night dancing. Guests can also stay in quiet hillside or beach villas. Facilities include a pool-sized jacuzzi, weight room and indoor games. Jet and water-skiing, snorkelling and scuba diving are also available. Moped hire is from 2500 dr. Tours around the island are 2500 dr. Ebullient Magda, who runs the complex with her brother George, meets the boats from 1 March to 30 November. Alternatively, take a **Sinarades** bus from town (225 dr).

At **Gardiki**, further south, there is the castle cave of Grava which has tools and bones from Palaeolithic times. In the southwest, true Corfiot food is served at *Skidi Restaurant* in **Prasouda**, and at *Alonaki Restaurant* in **Panagia Messavrisi**.

Paxoi & Antipaxoi
Παξοί & Αντίπαξοι

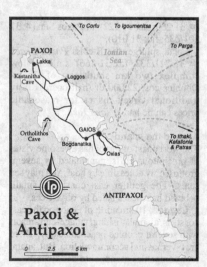

Paxoi & Antipaxoi

PAXOI

Low-lying, olive-tree-covered Paxoi (population 2650), 10 km long and four km wide, is the smallest main Ionian island. Olives are the main industry and tiny Paxoi vies with mighty Lesvos as producer of Greece's best olive oil. It's a pretty island although no longer an unspoilt idyll. It was ferreted out long ago by the UK-based Greek Islands Touring Club which has a windsurfing and sailing centre in Lakka. (See the Yacht section in the Getting Around chapter for the UK address.)

Package tourism has hit Paxoi. Small, discerning companies send clients to Paxoi. But when they are joined by day-trippers from Corfu and mainland Parga, the island becomes extremely crowded. It has three main coastal settlements – Gaios, Loggos and Lakka, and a few inland villages. For tranquillity, dismiss the beaches and stroll in the olive groves of the interior.

Getting There & Away
At least one regular ferry a day connects Paxoi and Corfu (2½ hours, 1600 dr). Daily excursion boats also come from Corfu and Parga on the mainland. Paxoi's port police can be contacted on ☎ 31 222

Getting Around
The island's one bus links Gaios and Lakka via Loggos up to five times a day.

Gaios Γάιος
Gaios, on a wide, east coast bay, is the capital and largest settlement. It's an attractive place with crumbling 19th-century red-tiled pink, cream and whitewashed buildings. Agios Nikolaos islet (also called Kastro), with a 15th-century Venetian fortress and a ruined windmill, almost fills its harbour. The islet at the entrance to the bay is Moni Panagias, named after its monastery. On 15 August, a lively day-long festival ends with dancing in Gaios' central square.

Information The post office and OTE are near the central square. Paxoi's postcode is 490 82. The telephone code is 0622. There is no tourist office. The tourist police (☎ 32 222) are off the waterfront.

Places to Stay & Eat In summer, most accommodation is filled by package tourists. The tourist police or travel agents may help you find a room. Try Gaios Travel (☎ 31 823/151; fax 31 975), Paxoi Holiday Agency

IONIAN ISLANDS

(☎ 31 269; fax 31 122), or Paxos Sun (☎ 31 201/035; fax 31 010).

For a splurge, the B-class *Paxos Beach* (☎ 31 211/333; fax 31 166) is a bungalow complex two km south-east of Gaios. Doubles cost 22,000 dr (half-board). Tasty traditional Greek dishes for reasonable prices can be had at *Taka Taka*.

Around the Island

The west coast of Paxoi has awesome vistas of precipitous cliffs, punctuated by several grottos, only accessible by boat. You may see seals. The gentler east coast has small, pebbled beaches, shaded by olive trees.

Loggos, 10 km north of Gaios on the east coast, is a small fishing village-cum-resort with several pebbled beaches nearby. There are tavernas and accommodation. But, again, tour companies monopolise bookings.

Lovely **Lakka**, at the end of a deep, narrow bay on the north coast, is a favourite location for Greek Islands Touring Club members who fill the bay with bright boats and sailboards. If you want to stay in Lakka, contact Planos Travel Office (☎ 31 108/821/010; fax 31 010).

The islet of **Mogonissi**, joined by a causeway to the southern tip of Paxoi, has a small sand beach and a taverna.

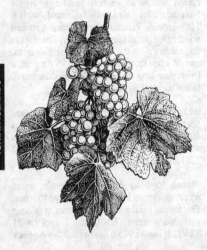

ANTIPAXOI

The diminutive island of Antipaxoi, a little over two km south of Paxoi, is covered with grapevines from which notable wine is produced. The beaches of Antipaxoi are superb. Best is the pale sand beach at Voutoumi on the east coast. There is no accommodation but a few tavernas cater for tourists.

In summer, small boats ply frequently between Gaios and Antipaxoi.

Lefkada & Meganisi
Λευκάδα & Μεγανήσι

LEFKADA

Lefkada (Lef-KAD-ha, population 23,000), between Corfu and Kefallonia, is the fourth-largest island in the Ionian group. Joined to the mainland by a narrow isthmus until the occupying Corinthians dug a canal in the 8th century BC, its 25-metre strait is spanned from the mainland by a causeway. Lefkada has 10 satellite islets – Meganisi, Madouri, Kastos, Kalamos, Sparti, Skorpidi, Skorpios, Thilia, Petalou and Kythros. Lefkada is mountainous with two peaks over 1000 metres. It is also fertile, well-watered by underground streams, with cotton fields, acres of dense olive groves, vineyards, fir and pine forests. Once a very poor island, Lefkada's beauty is also in its people, who display intense pride in their island. An International Festival of Literature & Art is held on the island in the last two weeks of August.

Getting There & Away

Air Lefkada has no airport but Aktion, near Preveza on the mainland, is a 30-minute bus journey away. Daily flights to Athens are 11,800 dr. Lefkada's Olympic Airways office (☎ 22 881) is at Dorpfeld 1. Preveza's (☎ 0682-28 674) is on Spiliadou 5.

Bus From Lefkada town there are four buses a day that go to Patras (2250 dr), Athens (5½ hours, 5100 dr) and Aktion airport (30 minutes, 300 dr).

IONIAN ISLANDS

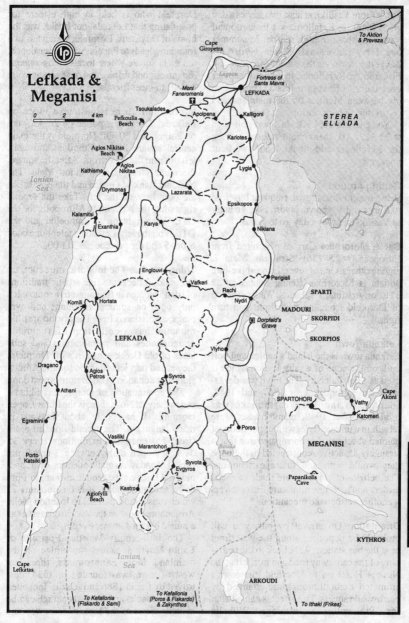

Lefkada & Meganisi

0   2   4 km

- Cape Giropetra
- Lagoon
- Fortress of Santa Mavra
- Moni Faneromenis
- LEFKADA
- Tsoukalades
- Apolpena
- Kalligoni
- STEREA ELLADA
- To Aktion & Preveza
- Pefkoulia Beach
- Kariotes
- Agios Nikitas Beach
- Kathisma
- Agios Nikitas
- Lygia
- Ionian Sea
- Drymonas
- Lazarata
- Epsikopos
- Kalamitsi
- Exanthia
- Karya
- Nikiana
- Englouvi
- Vafkeri
- Perigiali
- Rachi
- SPARTI
- Komili
- Hortata
- Nydri
- MADOURI
- Dorpfeld's Grave
- SKORPIDI
- SKORPIOS
- LEFKADA
- Vlyho
- Dragano
- Agios Petros
- Syvros
- SPARTOHORI
- Vathy
- Cape Akoni
- Athani
- Katomeri
- Egremini
- Vasiliki
- Poros
- MEGANISI
- Porto Katsiki
- Marantohori
- Rouda Bay
- Syvota
- Evgyros
- Papanikolis Cave
- Kastro
- Agiofylli Beach
- Ionian Sea
- KYTHROS
- Cape Lefkatas
- ARKOUDI
- To Kefallonia (Fiskardo & Sami)
- To Kefallonia (Poros & Fiskardo) & Zakynthos
- To Ithaki (Frikes)

IONIAN ISLANDS

Ferry From Vasiliki, at least two ferries a day go to Sami on Kefallonia via Fiskardo and Vathy on Ithaki in high season. In summer one ferry leaves daily from Nydri for Zakynthos town via the islet of Meganisi and Fiskardo on Kefallonia. In summer another goes daily to Frikes on Ithaki. Ferries also ply between Mytikas on the mainland and Nydri during high season.

You can contact Lefkada's port police on ☎ 22 322. Ask them about caïques leaving for Kefallonia and Ithaki, both two-hour voyages.

Getting Around

Bus From Lefkada town, frequent buses go to Karya and Vlyho via Nydri. Four go daily to Vasiliki and two a day go to Poros.

Car & Motorbike Cars can be hired from Europcar (☎ 25 726), Stratigou Mela 7, among others. One of several motorbike-hire outlets is Motorbike Rental Santas (☎ 22 371), on Aristotelis Valoritis. Walk to the top of Dorpfeld from the waterfront and turn right.

Lefkada Town

Lefkada town is the island's capital and port built on the edge of a salty lagoon which is used as a fish hatchery. The town was devastated by earthquakes in 1867 and 1948. Damage in the 1953 earthquake was minimal. After 1948, many houses were rebuilt in a unique style, with upper floors of painted sheet metal or corrugated iron that is strangely attractive, constructed in the hope they would withstand future earthquakes. The belfries of churches are made of metal girders and look like miniature Eiffel towers – another earthquake precaution.

Orientation On arrival by bus, you will probably be deposited along the waterfront or at the bus station. Walk back to the beginning of the causeway road and turn left at the Nirikos Hotel on to Dorpfeld, the town's animated main thoroughfare, flanked by narrow side streets. This street is named after the 19th-century archaeologist Wilhelm

Dorpfeld who is held in high esteem for postulating that Lefkada, not Ithaki, was the home of Odysseus. Dorpfeld, which has two fountains, leads to Plateia Agiou Spyridonos, the main square where locals enjoy *soumadia* (an almond drink), and the evening volta (stroll) to meet friends.

Information There is no tourist office on Lefkada. The tourist police (☎ 26 450) are on Politehniou 30. Off Dorpfeld is the main central square Plateia Ethnikis Antistasis, left up from the waterfront. After the square, the name changes to Ioannou Mela. The National Bank of Greece and the post office are both here on the left. Take the second right after the bank on to Mitropolis for the OTE. Veer right on to Zambelou and the OTE is on the left. Lefkada's telephone code is 0645 and the postcode is 311 00.

Things to See The **folkloric museum**, up Dorpfeld, reflects the fine artistic traditions of island women in four attractive rooms. It's only open on summer mornings and evenings; admission is free. The **phonographic museum** has a collection of venerable gramophones and memorabilia and sells tapes of old Greek songs. It's off Dorpfeld, the second turn left after the square. Admission is by donation. A book store is next door.

The continuation of Dorpfeld is Skiadaresis where, at No 1, there is the library, open mornings. It has books about Lefkada in many languages. The ground-floor art room (free) has changing exhibitions every 15 days. It's open daily between 7 and 9 pm except Monday. A small collection of archaeological finds can be seen from 9 am to 1 pm daily, except Monday, at Pefaneromenis 21 which runs almost parallel to Ioannou Mela. An anchored boat on the waterfront serves as a music bar on summer evenings.

The 14th-century Venetian **Fortress of Santa Mavra** is across the bridge on the mainland. **Moni Fanerominis**, three km west of town, was founded in 1634, destroyed by fire in 1886 and rebuilt. Inhabited by a few monks and nuns, its church can be visited. Views of the lagoon, causeway and

IONIAN ISLANDS

town are worth the ascent. West of the lagoon, past windmills, is **Agios Ioannis beach** where, at sunset, clouds are neon-lit islands in the sky. In summer, you may be lucky enough to see nesting turtles, also seals, on this section of coast. The nearest beaches to town are at the northern side of the lagoon, about a two-km walk away.

Eastern coastal beaches are pebbled, while most on the west are white sand. You can go round the whole island on a 75-km trip. Lefkada is famous for its embroideries. A small museum is at **Karya**, the island's core, west of **Nikiana**.

Places to Stay – bottom end The nearest camp site to Lefkada town is *Episkopos Camping* (☎ 23 043, 92 410 or 71 388), halfway to Nydri. See the Around the Island section for Lefkada's other camp sites. Lefkada also has farm-holiday accommodation in eight different locations.

The C-class *Hotel Santa Maura* (☎ 22 342) has pleasant singles/doubles for 6000/ 9000 dr. It is on the left of Dorpfeld, beyond the Hotel Byzantio.

The D-class *Hotel Byzantio* (☎ 22 629), Dorpfeld 4 has a pine theme. Rates are 8000/10,000 dr with bathroom. The hotel is just off the waterfront, on the right side of Dorpfeld.

Places to Stay – middle The comfortable B-class *Hotel Niricos* (☎ 24 132/133), on the corner of the waterfront and Dorpfeld, has singles/doubles/triples for 9200/12,700/ 17,700 dr (half-board). Close by, the palatial, balconied, port-facing and efficient B-class *Hotel Lefkas* (☎ 23 916/917/918), Panagou 2, has rates of 10,000/13,700/16,500 dr with breakfast.

Places to Stay – top end *Porto Galini* (☎ 22 548), two km north of Nikiana, is a charming seaside village resort of studios and two-storeyed apartments, some self-catering. It has a restaurant. High-season bed and breakfast prices start from 30,400 dr. Half-board is available.

Places to Eat *Taverna I Kato Vrisi* on the left side of Dorpfeld, opposite the fountain, serves tasty Greek food. Lefkada has some distinctive dishes and produces fine wines. In Lefkada town, *Karaboulia's Restaurant* east on the waterfront offers traditional fare with flair. The intimate *Karfakis Taverna* has hearty, inexpensive food, including agria salad, a mixture of wild greens such as radikia (dandelion). The walls are graced by watercolours by Pagagos. Turn right at the second fountain on Dorpfeld and walk up a lane to find the taverna. *Zorba's* at the village of Nikiana on the east coast offers specialties of savoro (a preserved, tuna-like fish), skylopsaro (dogfish with garlic sauce) and pina (abalone) at reasonable prices. On the waterfront at Nydri, *Nick the Greek* was one of Jackie Onassis' favourite eateries. Home-style food is served and a huge 3000-dr seafood platter can be shared.

Around the Island
The road south of Lefkada town follows the coast and 16 km later reaches Nydri, a busy, commercialised but fun town from where one can cruise around the islets of **Madouri**, **Sparti**, **Skorpidi** and **Skorpios**, from 2500 dr or 6000 dr if a barbecue and unlimited drinks are included. You sail on vessels operated by the brothers Ktenas (☎ 92 685). The family-owned Madouri Islet, where the Greek poet Aristotelis Valoritis (1824-79) spent his last 10 years, is off-limits. But it's usually possible to land on Skorpios, where Ari, sister Artemis and children Alexander and Christina Onassis are buried in a cemetery visible from the sea. You can swim off a pebbled beach spread with sand if Christina's daughter Athina is not holidaying there.

Windsurfing, waterskiing, parasailing, sailing (bare-boating with licence or crewed yachts), speed boating and jet-skiing out of Nydri can be organised by Nikos Thermes' Sport Boat Charter, Nikiana (☎ 92 431; mobile 093 233 164). He is also the only operator to conduct full-day boat trips that visit several caves along the coast and **Papanikolis cave** on Meganisi – 40,000 dr

IONIAN ISLANDS

for six people. Englishman Andy Fenna runs the island's only Padi School of Diving (☎ 92 286) from Nydri for beginners to experienced divers. He will show divers typical Mediterranean rock walls, underwater caves, rock reefs, fish and sponges.

MEGANISI

The large islet of Meganisi can be reached by daily ferry from Nydri. It has two ports, Vathy and Spartohori, the capital, one km inland. From here, a road leads via Katomeri to Vathy. There are domatia and tavernas. Cape Akoni offers safe anchorage to yachts.

Papanikolis cave, in the south, is an incredible cavern where the Nazis hid a submarine from which WW II operations were conducted against Allied forces. Caïques sometimes take travellers to the cave.

Back on Lefkada, the quiet village of **Vlyho** is three km south of Nydri. Beyond here, a road leads left to a peninsula where Wilhelm Dorpfeld is buried. There are Bronze Age ruins which he excavated, leading him to believe Lefkada was Homer's Ithaca. *Desimi Beach Camping* (☎ 95 223/ 225) is south of the peninsula. Further south and then west is **Vasiliki**. Detour to *Poros Beach Camping & Bungalows* (☎ 95 452 or 23 203) or to the village of **Poros**. Its pebbled beach is on **Rouda bay**.

Vasiliki is a pretty fishing village, purported to be *the* best windsurfing location in Europe. Amateurs should stick to Nydri as appointments with the wind can be taxing for all but the professional at Vasiliki. Windsurfing at both locations, through Sport Boat Charter, Nikiana, is 2500 dr per hour or 5000 dr a day. A week's hire will yield two free days. Vasiliki has both sand and pebbled beaches, a couple of hotels and domatia. It's crowded in summer so prepare to commute.

Caïques will take visitors from Vasiliki (from 1500 dr, more if a barbecue is included), to swim at the best sand beaches on the west coast, **Porto Katsiki**, **Egremini**, and **Kathisma**. All are signposted on the west coast off the road leading to the island's south-west promontory. A boat will also take you to **Agiofylli beach**. It's sandy, pebbled

and unspoiled. A Sanctuary to Apollo once stood at **Cape Lefkatas**. From this high-cliffed cape, Sappho supposedly leapt, distraught over her unrequited love for Phaon. This seems to have set a precedent for further suicides throughout the ages; however, most people now come here to see dramatic sunsets.

Kefallonia & Ithaki
Κεφαλλονιά & Ιθάκη

KEFALLONIA

Kefallonia (population 30,000) is the largest of the Ionian islands. It has rugged, towering mountains, the highest of which is Mt Enos in the south. It is the Mediterranean's only mountain with a unique fir forest species, *Abies kefallia*. While not as tropical as Corfu, Kefallonia has hundreds of species of wild flowers, including 60 different orchids and, when you approach it by sea on a windy summer's day, the scents of thyme, oregano, bay leaves and flowers will reach you before you land. This unspoiled garden island also receives package tourists, but not on the same scale as Corfu and Zakynthos. It is also a nesting ground for loggerhead turtles which lay their eggs on southern beaches in June. Turtle numbers ashore have remained stable, unlike on Zakynthos. A Marine Turtle Project monitors the turtles. If you would like more details, write to Marine Turtle Project, Care for the Wild, 1 Ashfolds, Horsham Rd, Rusper, West Sussex RH12 4QX, UK. Monk seals may also be seen on the north-west coasts of Kefallonia and Ithaki.

Kefallonia's capital is Argostoli but the main port is Sami. As the island is so big and mountainous, travelling between towns is time consuming. Consider this when planning your itinerary. In summer there are art exhibitions in major towns. In August and September an international choral festival is held in Argostoli and Lixouri.

Kefallonia & Ithaki

0   5   10 km

Ionian Sea

To Lefkada   To Lefkada   To Italy

ATOKOS

Fiskardo
Ventourata   Mazoukata
Vassiliklades   Mesovounia
Plagia
Assos   Karya
Ath128 Beach
Myrtos   Anomeria
Divarata
Zola   Agonas
Nifi
Kardakata   Riza   Dendrinata
Petani Beach   Agia Evthymia
Vilatoria
Delaportata   Farsa   Dilinata
Koronatou   Mellisani Cave
Lixouri   Drogarati Cave   Sami
Chaliotata
ARGOSTOLI   Faraklata
Razata
Megas Lakos   Lepeda Beach   Lassi   Agios Georgios Castle   Frangata
Makrys Gialos   Mitakata   Digaleto
Platys Gialos   Karavados   Poriarata
Minies Beach   Peratata   Poros
Svorotata   Metaxata   Viahata   Mt Enos (1520 m)   Tzanata
Avythos Beach   Spartia   Pesada   Lourdata
Lourdata Beach   Pastra   Spathi
Markopoulo   Skala
Kato Katelios

Frikes   Stavros   Kioni   Anogi
ITHAKI
Agios Ioannis   Gulf of Molos
Cave of the Nymphs   ITHAKI   Perachori
Pissoaetos
Fountain of Arethusa

KEFALLONIA

To Patras
To Killini
To Killini   To Zakinthos

Ionian Sea

Getting There & Away

Air Daily flights operate from Kefallonia and Athens (two in summer, 15,800 dr). There is one flight a week (low season) to Zakynthos (3300 dr). The Olympic Airways office (☎ 28 808/881) in Argostoli is at Rokou Vergoti 1.

Ferry Kefallonia has seven ports (the telephone numbers of the port police are in brackets): Sami (☎ 0674-22 091), Argostoli (☎ 0671-22 224), Poros (☎ 0674-72 460), Lixouri (☎ 0671-91 205), Pesada, Fiskardo and Agia Evthymia.

Domestic From Fiskardo, at least two ferries a day leave for Vasiliki (800 dr). At least one a day goes from Sami to Patras (four hours, 2500 dr). From Poros (90 minutes, 1450 dr), and Argostoli (2¾ hours, 2200 dr), at least two ferries ply daily to Kyllini in the Peloponnese. From Agia Evthymia, at least one ferry goes daily to Vathy on Ithaki and Astakos on the mainland. From Pesada, near Spartia, there is a high-season service to Skinari on Zakynthos. Daily ferries go from Fiskardo to Ithaki (Frikes) and Lefkada (Nydri). The latter voyage is 90 minutes, (870 dr). In summer, small boats leave Sami at 6.30 am to go to Fiskardo via Pissoaetos on Ithaki. From Fiskardo they continue to Vasiliki on Lefkada to return to Kefallonia later in the day. Frequent ferries take 30 minutes to reach Lixouri from Argostoli. The 200-dr tickets are sold on board. In the high season, daily ferries connect Fiskardo with Sami. Ferries to Italy sail via Corfu.

International A daily ferry leaves Sami for Italy's Brindisi via Ithaki, Igoumenitsa and Corfu.

Getting Around
To/From the Airport The airport is nine km south of Argostoli. A shuttle bus runs between it and the Olympic Airways office.

Bus From Argostoli, frequent buses go to Platys Gialos, to Sami, three daily to Poros (via Peratata, Vlahata and Markopoulo), three a day to Skala and two a day to Fiskardo. But in the off season, only one return service daily connects Fiskardo with Argostoli. Daily return buses leave Athens' A terminal for Argostoli (eight hours via ferry to Poros, 6200 dr).

Car & Motorbike Reliable transport can be hired from Ainos Tours (☎ 22 333), Kilipsous Vergoti 5, west of the main square where other firms are also located. Vehicle hire is recommended off season because of the infrequency of buses.

Argostoli Αργοστόλι
Unlike Zakynthos, also devastated by the 1953 earthquake, Argostoli, was not restored to its former Venetian splendour. But it's a modern, lively port set on a peninsula. Its harbour is divided from Koutavos lagoon by a British-built causeway connecting it with the rest of Kefallonia. There is a colourful, fresh-produce market on the waterfront on Saturday morning. The town's closest sandy beaches are **Makrys Gialos** and **Platys Gialos**, five km south. Here a partly pebbled road leads to the beach with rocky outcrops and a kiosk. The island's most expensive

accommodation is in this exclusive area although domatia can be found.

Orientation & Information The bus station (☎ 22 276) is on the waterfront at Ioannou Metaxa. The post office is on Diad Konstantinou and the OTE is on Georgiou Vergoti, a block up and north of, the post office. Plateía Valianou is the palm-treed central square up from the waterfront off 21 Maiou. Argostoli's postcode is 281 00. The telephone code is 0671. The National Bank of Greece is on a street south-west of the bus station (next door is a bookstore). Other banks are on the waterfront. The ferry quay is at the waterfront's northern end.

The EOT (☎ 22 248) is on the waterfront, south of the quay for ferries to Lixouri. The helpful municipal tourist office (☎ 22 230) is on the main square beside which is a children's park.

Museums The **archaeological museum** (☎ 28 300) has a small collection of island relics including Mycenaean finds from tombs. Walk up Rokou Vergoti from the waterfront. Opening times are Tuesday to Sunday from 8.30 am to 3 pm. Admission is 500 dr.

The **historical & cultural museum** (☎ 28 835), further up Rokou Vergoti, has a collection of traditional costumes, furniture and tools, items which belonged to British occupiers, and photographs of Argostoli before it was devastated by an earthquake. The museum is open Monday to Saturday from 9 am to 2 pm. Admission is 500 dr. In the same building is the **library** which houses more than 53,000 old, rare and new books; thousands of manuscripts written between 1535 and 1900; and a collection of icons.

Places to Stay *Argostoli Camping* (☎ 23 487) is a nice site with a restaurant, bar and minimarket. It's on the coast, under two km north of town. Relaxing farm holidays can be taken out of 16 village locations. Argostoli's D-class *Hotel Allegro* (☎ 22 268 or 28 684), Andrea Choida 2, has pleasant rooms with balconies. Doubles with shared bath-

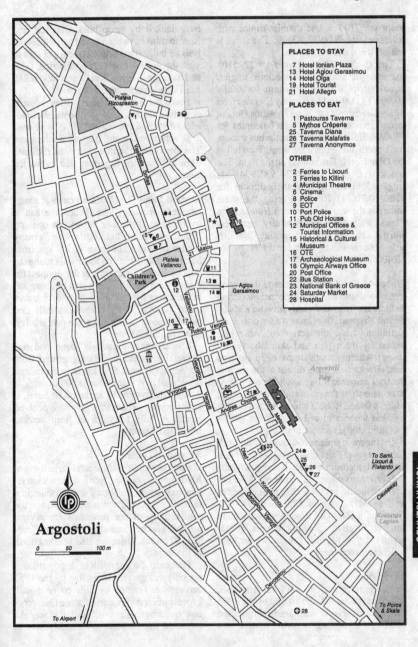

PLACES TO STAY

- 7 Hotel Ionian Plaza
- 13 Hotel Agiou Gerasimou
- 14 Hotel Olga
- 19 Hotel Tourist
- 21 Hotel Allegro

PLACES TO EAT

- 1 Pastouras Taverna
- 5 Mythos Crêperie
- 25 Taverna Diana
- 26 Taverna Kalafatis
- 27 Taverna Anonymos

OTHER

- 2 Ferries to Lixouri
- 3 Ferries to Killini
- 4 Municipal Theatre
- 6 Cinema
- 8 Police
- 9 EOT
- 10 Port Police
- 11 Pub Old House
- 12 Municipal Offices & Tourist Information
- 15 Historical & Cultural Museum
- 16 OTE
- 17 Archaeological Museum
- 18 Olympic Airways Office
- 20 Post Office
- 22 Bus Station
- 23 National Bank of Greece
- 24 Saturday Market
- 28 Hospital

Argostoli

0   50   100 m

room are 7100 dr and doubles/triples with bathroom are 9600/12,700 dr. The street is left off the waterfront.

The C-class *Hotel Tourist* (☎ 22 510), Ioannou Metaxa 94, has spacious singles/doubles/triples with bathroom for 6000/10,000/12,000 dr. The friendly C-class *Hotel Agios Gerasimos* (☎ 28 697), Agios Gerasimou 6, has cosy rooms with balconies for 9300/10,700/11,700 dr. From the bus station, walk north along the waterfront. Turn left at the Olga Hotel. The hotel is on the right. The spacious *Olga Hotel* (☎ 24 981/984) has singles/doubles/triples with bathroom for 9300/10,700/11,700 dr. Facing the main square is the marble-decorated *Hotel Ionian Plaza* (☎ 25 581), which is airy, near new and has a bar and Italian restaurant. Comfortable air-con suites with breakfast go for 10,400/16,400/20,300 dr.

Places to Eat & Drink Opposite the waterfront food market are three neighbouring restaurants *Taverna Diana*, *Taverna Kalafatis* and *Taverna Anonymos* – all worth a try. Kefallonia has a distinctive cuisine, represented by meat pies and skordalia (garlic sauce) which accompanies eggplant and fish. Greeks find these dishes at the simple, family *Patsouras Taverna* on Plateia Rizospaston north of the main square. Ask for the island's famed Robola wine, which is expensive but wonderful and comes from grapes grown in stony, mountainous soil.

Off the main square, *Restaurant Captain's Table* serves pie and many spaghetti and fish dishes at medium prices. Nearby, *Mythos Crêperie Restaurant* has no Greek food but a wide, middle-priced selection of crêpes as well as Mexican and Chinese dishes. At Argostoli's *Pub Old House*, off the main square, English-speaking expats gather nightly, by a roaring fire in winter, and welcome newcomers.

Sami Σάμη

Sami, the main port, 25 km from Argostoli, was, like the capital, devastated by the 1953 earthquake. Now with undistinguished buildings, its setting is pretty, nestled in a bay, flanked by steep hills. Classical and Roman ruins have been found and a museum is to be built. It's worth an overnight stay to visit the nearby caves. A post office, OTE and bank are in town. Sami's postcode is 280 82. The telephone code is 0674.

Buses for Argostoli meet ferries. Mostly, domatia owners meet the boats. *Karavomilos Beach Camping* (☎ 22 480) is well kept with a restaurant, bar and minimarket. The site is less than one km west of Sami. Turn left from the tiny quay and follow the coast.

Around Sami The **Mellisani cave** is a subterranean seawater lake. When the sun is overhead its rays shine through an opening in the cave ceiling, lighting the water's many shades of blue. The cave is 2.5 km from Sami. To get there from Sami walk along the Argostoli road. Turn right at the signpost for Agia Evthymia. There is a sign pointing left to the caves beyond the village of Karavomilos (which has a lake, windmill and pebbled beach). The cave is open all day. Admission is 700 dr.

The **Drogarati cave** is large and has impressive stalactites. It's signposted from the Argostoli road, four km from Sami, and is open all day. Admission is 700 dr.

Agia Evthymia, 10 km north of Sami, is a picturesque fishing village with a pebbled beach. A daily ferry leaves from here to Ithaki and Astakos.

Around the Island

Lixouri is Kefallonia's second-largest town. It's an unremarkable place but has ecclesiastical exhibits in its library and museum in a restored mansion. Between the town and the southern tip of the peninsula are several unspoilt beaches, including **Lepeda** and red-sand **Xi beach**. There are also beaches north of the town.

Fiskardo, 50 km north of Argostoli, was the only village not devastated by the 1953 earthquake. Framed by hills covered with cypress trees, and featuring some fine Venetian buildings, it's a delightful place. An extended Roman cemetery and Mycenaean

IONIAN ISLANDS

Coast near Alykes, Zakynthos, Ionian islands

DAVID HALL

DAVID HALL

DAVID HALL

Top: Lalaria Beach, Skiathos, Sporades islands
Middle: The end of the bay, Skopelos town, Sporades islands
Bottom: Beach at Ormos Milia Gialos, Alonnisos, Sporades islands

pottery have been found. Fiskardo is popular and it's hard to get accommodation. You can get there by ferry from Lefkada and Ithaki or take a day trip from Argostoli. Two buses run daily (one in the off season).

Assos village, between Argostoli and Fiskardo, is a gem straddling the isthmus of a peninsula on which stands a Venetian fortress. Assos was damaged in the earthquake but sensitively restored with the help of a donation from the city of Paris. Its whitewashed and pastel houses are offset by vibrant flowers and poplar and plane trees. There are domatia and a pebbled beach. You'll find an outstanding white sandy beach at **Myrtos**, three km south of Assos. If you explore by boat, you'll find nearby hidden coves between tall limestone cliffs.

Kastro, above the village of Peratata, nine km south-east of Argostoli, was the island's capital in the Middle Ages. Ruined houses stand beneath the 13th-century castle of San Giorgio which affords magnificent views. Peratata has domatia as has **Vlahata**, a pleasant village east along the road which branches to **Lourdata beach** where you can go horse-riding. Above it, each vegetable garden has its own well. On a 2½-hour circular walk from Lourdata with its spring, you pass a barrier of cypress trees, carob trees, orchards, olive groves, oak and pine forests with flowers and birds, and return along the coast. A free Lourdata trail walk guide is available from the municipal tourist office.

South of Peratata, at **Metaxata**, palms appear incongruous against white winter slopes of Mt Enos. No wonder Lord Byron found inspiration. Near it, **Moni Agiou Andreou** dates from the 13th century with restored frescoes from the 14th to 16th century. The church, said to house a bone of St Andrew's foot, is an ecclesiastical museum, its Byzantine icons soon to be moved next door. It's open daily from 9 am to 1 pm and 3 to 6 pm. Admission is 300 dr. Two weeks before Easter, hymn-singing reaches its epitome in the church and on 15 August and 20 October, festivals are held. Only 500 metres from the convent are Mycenaean tombs, discovered in 1993.

More tombs, carved from rock, are at nearby **Mazarakata**. Spartia operates a summer sailing school off its small, sandy beach.

At **Markopoulo** an extraordinary event creeps up on 15 August (the Feast of the Assumption). The village church becomes infested with harmless snakes with crosses on their heads. They are said to bring good luck.

Poros is overdeveloped but has a nice pebbled beach. **Skala**, on the southern tip, is a preferable resort with a large, fine gravel beach on either side of the village. There are domatia and hotels. Three buses a day go from Argostoli to Skala.

ITHAKI Ιθάκη

Ithaki (ancient Ithaca) was Odysseus' long-lost home, the island where the stoical Penelope sat patiently, weaving a shroud for her father-in-law. She told her suitors, who believed Odysseus was dead, that she would choose one of them for her husband once she had completed the shroud. Cunningly, she unravelled it every night in order to keep her suitors at bay, as she awaited Odysseus' return. Less well known is that Ithaki, lying amidst the tourist ghettos of the Ionian islands, remains relatively unspoilt.

Ithaki is separated from Kefallonia by a strait, only two to four km wide. The island is one of contrasts, with a harsh precipitous east coast and a soft green west coast. The interior is mountainous and rocky with pockets of pine forest, stands of cypresses, olive groves and vineyards.

Getting There & Away

From Ithaki there are daily ferries to Sami (one hour), Agia Evthymia and Fiskardo on Kefallonia; Patras (six hours, 3050 dr); Vasiliki on Lefkada; and Astakos (1¾ hours) on the mainland. A ferry goes three or four times a week to Brindisi in Italy via Igoumenitsa and Corfu. In high season, a daily ferry sails between Frikes (Ithaki) and Fiskardo (Kefallonia).

The telephone number of Ithaki's port police is ☎ 32 909.

Getting Around

The island's one bus runs two or three times a day to Kioni (via Stavros and Frikes) from Vathy.

Ithaki Town (Vathy)

Ithaki town is small with a few twisting streets, a central square, nice cafés and restaurants and a few tourist shops, grocers and hardware stores. Old mansions rise up from the seafront.

Orientation & Information The ferry quay is on the west side of the bay. To reach the central square of Plateia Efstathiou Drakouli, turn left and follow the waterfront. The main thoroughfare, Kallinikou, is parallel to, and one block inland from, the waterfront.

Ithaki has no tourist office. The tourist police (☎ 32 205) are on the right side of Evmeou, which runs south from the middle of the waterfront. The National Bank of Greece is south-west of the central square. The post office is on the central square and the OTE is further around the waterfront. Ithaki's postcode is 283 00. The telephone code is 0674.

Things to See The town's modest **archaeological museum** is on Kallinikou. Entrance is free but opening times are erratic. There is a **library**. Archives include manuscripts from Venetian times.

A summer music & theatre festival is held in Ithaki town.

Places to Stay Domatia owners meet the ferries if they're not busy. Otherwise, look for signs on Odysseos and Pinelopis which (appropriately) lie parallel to the west of the quay. Polyctor Tours (☎ 33 120/130; fax 33 130) on the central square will assist with finding domatia or an apartment.

The *Hotel Odysseus* (☎ 32 381), classed as a pension and closed in the low season, has pleasant doubles for 9000 dr. The hotel overlooks the bay from its western side. Turn right from the quay.

The *Hotel Mentor* (☎ 32 433/293), on the waterfront beyond the central square, has a bar, restaurant and roof garden. Attractive rooms with bathroom and breakfast are 9100/12,900/16,000 dr for singles/doubles/triples.

Places to Eat *Taverna Trehantiri*, a long-established place west of the central square, serves quality traditional Greek dishes. Set in a restored waterfront mansion, *Restaurant Dracoulis* is a place for a special treat. Several *zaharoplasteia* are found along the waterfront. One of the local specialities is ravani, a sweet, gooey pudding.

Around the Island

Ithaki has a few sites associated with Homer's *Odyssey*. Though none is impressive, you may enjoy (or endure) the scenic walks to them. The most renowned is the **Fountain of Arethusa**, where Odysseus' swineherd, Eumaeus, brought his pigs to drink and where Odysseus, on his return to Ithaca, went to meet him disguised as a beggar after receiving directions from the goddess Athena. Lesser mortals have to deal with inadequate signposting. The walk takes between 1½ to two hours, depending on your stamina.

Take Evmeou which leads south from town and becomes an uphill track. After about an hour, you'll see a sign pointing left to the fountain. It indicates a narrow downhill footpath which almost disappears at one point and would probably be rejected by any self-respecting mountain goat. Eventually, you'll see a big rocky crag above a spring. This is the Koraka (raven's) crag (mentioned in the *Odyssey*). Take plenty of water as the spring shrinks in summer.

A shorter trek is to the **Cave of the Nymphs**, where Odysseus concealed the splendid gifts of gold, copper and fine fabrics that the Phaeacians had given him. Below the cave is the Bay of Dexia, thought to be ancient Phorkys where the Phaeacians disembarked and laid the sleeping Odysseus on the sand. The cave is signposted from the town. The location of Odysseus' palace has been much disputed and archaeologists have been unable to find conclusive evidence.

IONIAN ISLANDS

Schliemann erroneously believed it was near Ithaki town whereas present-day archaeologists speculate it was on a hill near Stavros.

Beaches Beaches on Ithaki are mostly pebbled. The village of **Stavros**, 17 km north-west of Ithaki town, is unspectacular but with rooms and tavernas and five roads radiating out, it makes a good base from which to explore the north. One road leads in around one km to the **Bay of Polis**, which has a stony beach. **Frikes**, 1.5 km in the opposite direction, is a charming fishing village with wind-swept cliff faces patterned like well-used brooms. It has low-key development (including a centre of the Greek Islands Touring Club). Attractive **Kioni**, four km south of Frikes, is a popular yacht anchorage. There are pretty, pebbled coves in, and between, these villages. Caïques take people from Ithaki town to inaccessible beaches in summer.

Zakynthos Ζάκυνθος

The island of Zakynthos (ZAK-een-thos) (population 35,000) has inspired many superlatives. The Venetians called it Fior' di Levante (flower of the orient). The poet Dionysios Solomos wrote 'Zakynthos could make one forget the Elysian Fields'. Indeed, it is an island of exceptional natural beauty and outstanding beaches. But it is disheartening that its coastline has been the victim of the most unacceptable manifestations of package tourism. Even worse, tourism is endangering the loggerhead turtle *(Caretta caretta)*.

Getting There & Away
Air Two daily summer flights operate from Zakynthos to Athens (15,400 dr). The Olympic Airways office (☎ 28 611) in Zakynthos town is at Alexandrou Roma 16. You can call the airport on ☎ 28 322.

Bus Four buses a day leave Zakynthos town for Athens (seven hours, 3930 dr) via Patras.

Ferry Depending on the season, between three and seven ferries a day operate from Zakynthos town to Kyllini, in the Peloponnese (1½ hours, 1040 dr).

From Skinari, one ferry a day goes to Pesada on Kefallonia, high season only. There is no bus from Pesada to anywhere else on Kefallonia. Check with the port police (☎ 42 417) for the times of the high-season crossing from Zakynthos town to Nydri, on Lefkada.

Getting Around
To/From the Airport There is no shuttle service between Zakynthos town and the airport, six km to the south-west. A taxi is about 1000 dr.

Bus Frequent buses go from Zakynthos town to Alykes (220 dr), Tsilivi (175 dr), Argasi (175 dr) and Laganas. Bus services to other villages are poor, one or two a day. Check the current schedule at the bus station.

Car & Motorbike Car-hire outlets include Hertz (☎ 45 706) at Lombardou 38, in Zakynthos town. A reliable motorbike-hire outlet is Moto Stakis, at Demokratias 3, near Plateia Solomou.

ZAKYNTHOS TOWN
Zakynthos town is the capital and port of Zakynthos. The town was devastated by an earthquake in 1953 but was reconstructed with its former layout preserved in wide arcaded streets, imposing squares and gracious neoclassical public buildings. Unless you have seen the beautiful pre-earthquake town or photographs of it, you should be impressed.

Orientation & Information
The central Plateia Solomou is on the waterfront of Lombardou, opposite the ferry quay. Another large square, Plateia Agiou Markou, is a short distance away. The bus station is on Filitia, one block back from the waterfront and south of the quay. The main thoroughfare is Alexandrou Roma, parallel to the waterfront several blocks inland.

IONIAN ISLANDS

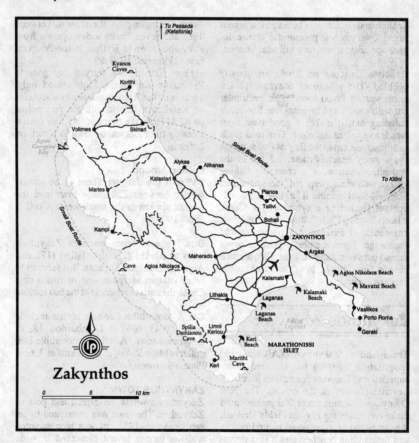

Zakynthos

0   5   10 km

To Pessada
(Kefallonia)

Kyanos
Caves
Korithi
Volimes
Skinari
Ionian
Sea
Agios
Georgiou
Bay
Alykes
Alikanas
Katastari
Pianos
Tsilivi
Maries
Bohali
Kampi
ZAKYNTHOS
Argasi
Cave
Maherado
Agios Nikolaos
Agios Nikolaos Beach
Kalamaki
Mavatzi Beach
Kalamaki
Beach
Lithakia
Laganas
Vasilikos
Porto Roma
Laganas
Beach
Geraki
Spilia
Damianou
Cave
Limni
Keriou
Bay of
Laganas
Keri
Beach
MARATHONISSI
ISLET
Marithi
Cave
Keri
Small Boat Route
Small Boat Route
To Killini

IONIAN ISLANDS

Zakynthos town has no tourist office. The helpful tourist police (☎ 22 367), at Lombardou 62, are on the waterfront. They will provide information about accommodation.

The National Bank of Greece is west of Plateia Solomou. The post office is at Tertseti 27, one block west of Alexandrou Roma. The OTE is on the northern side of Plateia Solomou. Zakynthos' postcode is 291 00 and the telephone code is 0695. Zakynthos' hospital (☎ 22 514) is west of town.

Museums
The **Museum of Solomos** is dedicated to Dionysios Solomos (1798-1857), who was born on Zakynthos. His work, *Hymn to Liberty*, became the stirring Greek national anthem. Solomos is regarded as the father of modern Greek poetry, because he was the first Greek poet to use demotic Greek, rather than katharevousa. This museum houses a collection of memorabilia associated with his life, as well as displays pertaining to the poets Andreas Kalvos (1792-1869) and Ugo Foskolo (1778-1827), who were also born on Zakynthos. The museum is on Plateia Agiou Markou. Opening times are 9 am to 2 pm every day. Entrance is free.

The **neo-Byzantine museum**, on Plateia Solomou, houses a collection of ecclesiastical art (mostly icons) which was rescued from the churches that were razed in the 1953 earthquake. Opening times for the museum are Tuesday to Sunday from 8.30 am to 3 pm.

Churches

At the southern end of town, the **Church of Agios Dionysios** is named after the island's patron saint and contains the saint's relics in a silver coffer. This is paraded around the streets during the festivals held in his honour

on 24 August and 17 December. The church also has notable frescoes.

The 16th-century **Church of Agios Nikolaos**, on Plateia Solomou, was built in Italian Renaissance style. Partially destroyed in the earthquake, it has been carefully reconstructed.

Organised Tours

Zante Tours (☎ 42 845), Lombardou 18, is one travel agent offering tours. An island tour (including the Kyanos (blue) caves and shipwreck) is 4000 dr. The tour including the beached shipwreck near Skinari, Keri caves

PLACES TO STAY
10 Hotel Ionian
11 Hotel Apollon
12 Rooms

PLACES TO EAT
3 Carissimo Café
15 Village Inn
16 Tyler's Place

OTHER
1 Church of Agios Nikolaos
2 Museum of Solomos
4 OTE
5 Neo-Byzantine Museum
6 Church of Agios Nikolaos Molu
7 National Bank of Greece
8 Port Police
9 Olympic Airways Office
13 Post Office
14 Zante Tours
17 Bus Station
18 Hospital
19 Tourist Police

Zakynthos Town

0   150   300 m

IONIAN ISLANDS

and Porto Roma with lunch is 6000 dr. A bus tour to south-west Kampi – magic if the sun descends spectacularly – includes lunch and Greek dancing for 4000 dr. Longer day trips can include mainland Olympia. *Hello Zakynthos* is a boat which offers 1½ hours' swimming on lesser known beaches. A 9 am to 7.30 pm circumnavigation including lunch and wine is 7000 dr. Enquire at the quay.

Places to Stay – bottom end
The nearest camp site to Zakynthos town is *Zante Camping* (☎ 24 754 or 61 710) at Tsilivi, five km away while eight km south-west of the port is *Camping Lagonas* (☎ 29 100) by the sea at Agios Sostis. It costs 2000 dr each and 600 dr per tent.

The clean, nameless rooms (☎ 26 012), at Alexandrou Roma 40, are 7000/10,000 dr. The D-class *Hotel Ionian* (☎ 42 511), Alexandrou Roma 18, has tidy singles/doubles/triples for 5000/7000/8000 dr. The C-class *Hotel Apollon* (☎ 42 838), Tertseti 30, has pleasant singles/doubles/triples for 6000/8,500/12,000 dr with private facilities.

Places to Stay – middle
The B-class *Hotel Palatino* (☎ 45 400), on the corner of Kolokotroni and Koliva, is of neoclassical style with comfortable modern rooms. Rates are 11,500/13,800/16,500 dr for singles/doubles/triples with private bathroom.

Places to Eat
Plenty of fast-food places and zaharoplasteia, featuring madelato, a local nougat sweet, are on Alexandrou Roma. *Carissimo Café* near the main square has good selections from 300 dr for soup. *Village Inn* on the waterfront at Lombardou 20 features rabbit stifado in season and Odysseus Plate (gyros, souvlaki, lamb chop, hamburger and tzatziki to share for 1690 dr) – food such as Odysseus never knew. Try *Tyler's Place*, on the waterfront, for British food: breakfast and stuffed potatoes from 600 dr and apple pie and custard for 700 dr.

AROUND THE ISLAND
The huge Bay of Laganas extends across Zakynthos' south coast. It is fringed with beaches of golden sand where loggerhead turtles come ashore to lay their eggs. Before reaching this shore, you can organise a ride with Nana's Horses (☎ 23 196) at **Kteo**. **Laganas** is the most developed resort on the island. Spacious, with pool, indoor games, bar, good restaurant and children's area, the *Hotel Alexander Laganas* (☎ 51 580/583) has doubles/triples/quads/quins for 15,000/20,000/26,000/30,000 dr, with bathroom and breakfast. The two main drags have Asian restaurants, full Brit breakfasts for 800 dr and several cycle and motorbike-hire outlets. **Kalamaki** is not much quieter and even **Geraki**, where the highest number of turtles lay their eggs, has not been spared water sports. The turtles also nest on nearby **Marathonissi** islet. You may decide to avoid these beaches for the turtles' sakes and to ignore the commercialism.

IONIAN ISLANDS

Vassilikos and **Porto Roma**, south of Zakynthos town, have crowded, sand beaches but are less developed than those of the Bay of Laganas. The best beach north of Zakynthos town is at **Alykes**. It's a long swathe of sand.

The **Kyanos (blue) caves** and grottos, on the northern tip of the island, should not be missed. They are second only to their namesake on Kastellorizo. Various travel agencies offer excursions to the caves, which can only be reached by boat. Several continue to the beached shipwreck, beneath sheer cliffs at **Agios Georgios sta Gremna** (St George of the Cliffs), one of the island's most photographed scenes.

You can escape from the tourist hype of Zakynthos by going inland to the farming villages. The village of **Maherado** has a 14th-century church, Agia Mavra, which is one of the most impressive on the island. It has an elaborate interior, a valuable icon and a lovely iconostasis. **Agios Nikolaos** is an attractive village. The drive north from here to **Maries** is through splendid hilly country.

Kythira & Antikythira
Κύθηρα & Αντικύθηρα

KYTHIRA
The island of Kythira (KI-thi-ra, population 2800, swelling to about 4000 in summer), south-west of Neapoli, is about 30 km long and 18 km wide. Its north-east coast faces the sometimes turbulent meeting of the Ionian and Aegean seas. This anomalous island of 600 churches is geographically an extension of the Peloponnese, historically part of the Ionian archipelago and administered from Piraeus. It survives economically mainly on remittances from many islanders who have emigrated to 'big Kythira', as these expats call Australia. Kythira supplied Australia with its first Greek settlers in 1850s gold rush days when sailors jumped ship.

Mythology records the island was the birthplace of Aphrodite, who rose magnificent from the foam where Zeus had thrown Cronos' sex organ after castrating him. The goddess of love then re-emerged in Cyprus, so both islands haggle over her birthplace.

Until recently, Kythira was little visited by foreign tourists because of uncertain shipping schedules and local indifference to tourism. It was also wiped off the tourist map under the military junta which exiled political dissidents to this island about which no visitor information was available. The EOT has begun encouraging tourists to visit Kythira but it's still an island for those who want to get away from it all. However, don't turn up in July or August without a hotel reservation, as accommodation, particularly in the low-budget range, is not abundant. Domatia owners don't meet boats as they do on most islands.

Kythira's plateau of rolling hills is above high cliffs. Once denuded of timber, Kythira is responding to a pine re-afforestation programme. The two ports are Agia Pelagia on the north-east coast and Kapsali in the south below the capital, Hora (also called Kythira). The island's main road cuts through the centre, joining the ports and several settlements between.

Getting There & Away
Air There is at least one flight a day to Athens (50 minutes, 12,800 dr), two or three a day in summer. The Olympic Airways office (☎ 33 362) is on the central square in the town of Potamos, 10 km south of Agia Pelagia. Book also at Conomos Travel, (☎ 33 490/890), opposite the quay at Agia Pelagia or Kythira Travel (☎ 31 390) in Hora's square. The airport is 10 km east of Potamos.

Ferry The F/B *Martha* sails at least daily from Agia Pelagia to Neapoli (850 dr) and goes to Gythio on Monday, Wednesday and Sunday (900 dr). The F/B *Theseus* leaves Piraeus for Kyparissi, Monemvassia, Neapoli, Elafonisi, Agia Pelagia, sometimes Antikythira, and Kastelli-Kissamos (Crete). On return to Piraeus, it stops at Gythio. It no longer calls at Kapsali. Schedules and times

IONIAN ISLANDS

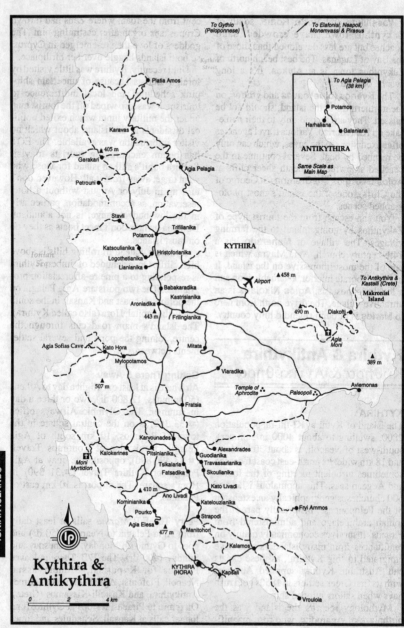

To Gythio
(Peloponnese)

To Elafonisi, Neapoli,
Monamvassi & Piraeus

Kythira
Strait

To Agia Pelagia
(38 km)

Potamos

Harhaliana   Galaniana

ANTIKYTHIRA

Same Scale as
Main Map

Platia Amos

Karavas

405 m

Gerakari

Petrouni

Stavli

Potamos   Trifilianika

KYTHIRA

Katsoulianika
                    Hristoforianika
Logothetianika
Lianianika

Airport   458 m

To Antikythira &
Kastelli (Crete)

Babakaradika
                    Kastrisianika
Aroniadika
      443 m   Frilingianika

490 m   Diakofti

Makronisi
Island

Agia Sofias Cave   Kato Hora

Mylopotamos

507 m

Mitata

Viaradika

Agia
Moni

389 m

Temple of
Aphrodite

Paleopoli

Avlemonas

Fratsia

Karvounades

Kalokerines   Pitsinianika

Moni
Myrtidion

Alexandrades

Guodianika
Travassarianika
Skoulianika

Tsikalaria
Fatsadika

Kato Livadi

Ano Livadi

Kominianika
          Pourko

Katelouzianika

Fryi Ammos

Agia Elesa

477 m

Strapodi

Manitohori

Kalamos

KYTHIRA
(HORA)   Kapsali

Vrouloia

Kythira &
Antikythira

0   2   4 km

IONIAN ISLANDS

are often subject to delays so check at Agia Pelagia's Conomos Travel, which sells ferry and hydrofoil tickets.

In summer, caïques connect Agia Pelagia with Elafonisi. Ask the port police (☎ 33 280) at Agia Pelagia on the waterfront. .

Hydrofoil In summer, hydrofoils leave Agia Pelagia daily (except Friday and Sunday) for Piraeus (five hours, 9000 dr) via Monemvassia, Geraki, Kyparissi, Spetses and Hydra.

Getting Around
Bus Kythira's bus service is deplorable. In summer, a bus leaves Agia Pelagia at 8 am, stopping at all the main-road villages and arrives at Kapsali at 9.30 am to begin the return trip at 11.30 am. In school terms, buses are more frequent but are monopolised by children. On Sunday, buses usually operate between Agia Pelagia and Potamos and Hora and Potamos. There is no airport bus. Not surprisingly, Kythira has many taxis (which meet flights also). Hitching is fairly easy.

Car & Motorbike Cars can be hired from Tserigo Rent Car (☎ 31 363/030/836), on Hora's main street. Panayiotos, at Moto Rent (☎ 31 600) on Kapsali's waterfront, rents mopeds for 1300 to 1700 dr, motorbikes for 3500 to 4000 dr, also cars and jeeps.

Agia Pelagia Αγία Πελαγία
Kythira's northern port of Agia Pelagia has more places to stay than the more attractive Hora. However, it's a simple, friendly waterfront village strung to the right of the quay. It's advisable to book accommodation in advance as the *Theseus* arrives from Piraeus in the wee small hours. At the top of the quay is a room-finding office (no telephone) operating in July and August. Lia at Conomos Travel happily assists newcomers.

Pebbled beaches are to either side of the quay but behind an outcrop past Pari Gerakiti's Rooms is a secluded, grainy red-sand beach.

Places to Stay – bottom end Agia Pelagia's cheapest accommodation is *Pari Gerakiti's Rooms* (☎ 33 462), which is on the seafront. Clean double/triple rooms with bathroom and kitchen have rates of 6000/6500 dr. Turn left from the quay and walk along the shore road to a large white building with green shutters. Opposite the quay above the Faros Taverna, *Alexandra Megalopoulou's Rooms* (☎ 33 282) are tidy, simply furnished and with bathroom for 7700 dr a double. The welcoming D-class *Hotel Kytherea*(☎ 33 321), owned by helpful Mike and Freda from Australia, has very comfortable, spotless singles/doubles with bathroom for 7500/ 10,500 dr. The hotel is opposite the quay above a well-stocked souvenir shop next to Conomos Travel.

Places to Stay – middle The new *Hotel Romantica* (telephone to be connected) to the right of the quay and signposted up a dirt road, has charming self-contained apartments for four (18,000 dr) and double/triple air-con studios with TV for 12,000/ 14,000 dr.

Places to Stay – top end The attractive *Filoxenia Apartments* (☎ 33 100) each have a bedroom, lounge and kitchen. Rates for doubles/quads are 15,000/20,000 dr. Two-bedroom units for four/six people are 22,000/26,000 dr. Turn left then right from the quay. Look for a white building with blue shutters. Kythira's sole A-class hotel, *Hotel Marou* (☎ 33 466/496), with the island's only tennis court, a bar, snack bar, laundry and a wheelchair-accessible unit, is above the north-west end of the village. Doubles are 20,900 dr.

Places to Eat & Drink *Faros Taverna*, opposite the quay, serves good, economical Greek staples. To the far right, *Ouzerie Moustakias*, next to a tempting patisserie, serves food ranging from snacks to seafood all year round and excels on Easter Sunday with continual lamb on the spit. Next door is Kapsani's minimarket. For an aperitif or nightcap, drop in to the *Mouragio* bar, snugly located between the two eateries.

Potamos

About 10 km uphill from Agia Pelagia is Potamos, the island's commercial hub, even though Hora is the capital. Its small, shady, central square is typical of an untouristed village, particularly on Sunday when it magnetises almost every islander to market. The National Bank of Greece is on the square. The post office, the OTE and police are south of it, also the only hotel, *Hotel Porfyra* (☎ 33 329). Self-contained units with TV surround an internal courtyard. Doubles/triples/quads are 10,000/12,000/13,000 dr. Off the square, which has tavernas, the best eateries are on the road leading from Agia Pelagia and are open Sunday for lunch.

The well-equipped hospital (☎ 33 203) and pharmacy next door are off the road curving towards the airport.

Mylopotamos Μυλοπόταμος

Mylopotamos is an alluring bougainvillea-draped village. It has no accommodation. Its central square is flanked by a much-photographed church and kafeneia. Stroll to the **Neraïda** (water nymph) waterfall. From the square, continue along the road and take the right fork. After 100 metres, a path on the right leads to the waterfall. It's magical, with luxuriant greenery, shady maple, plane and poplar trees and a picnic bench.

To reach the abandoned **kastro** of Mylopotamos, take the left fork after the church and follow the sign for Kato Hora (lower village). The road leads to the centre of Kato Hora, from where a portal with the insignia of St Mark leads into the slightly spooky kastro, with derelict houses and well-preserved little churches (locked). Like the kastro in Hora, this one also ends abruptly at a precipice.

The **Cave of Agia Sophia** was first explored by Ioannis and Anna Patrochilos of Diros cave fame. In the 12th century, the cave was converted into a chapel and dedicated to Agia Sophia. Legend says she visited the cave with her daughters Pistis, Elpis and Agape (Faith, Hope and Charity). At the entrance are well-preserved frescoes. The cave is reached by a two-km road and a

steep path from Mylopotamas. Irregular opening times are pinned on a signpost to the cave beyond Mylopotamos' square. Admission is 500 dr and includes a guided tour.

Hora (Kythira)

Hora, the capital of Kythira, and also known by the island's name, perches on a long slender ridge, two km uphill from Kapsali. It's a pretty settlement, with white, blue-shuttered houses and a central square planted with hibiscus, bougainvillea and palms.

Orientation & Information The central square is Plateia Dimitriou Stati. The main street runs south of it. The post office is on the left, at its southern end. For the OTE, climb the steps by the side of Kythira Travel on the central square and follow the signs. Kythira's postcode is 802 00. Its telephone code is 0735.

The National Bank of Greece is on the central square. The police station (☎ 31 206) is signposted from the southern end of the main street.

Kythira has no tourist office or tourist police but English-speaking Panáyiotis offers information to tourists at his Moto Rent office (☎ 31 600) on the waterfront in Kapsali. The staff at Kythira Travel (☎ 31 390/490) on Hora's central square are also helpful.

Kastro Hora's Venetian kastro is at the southern end of town. It contains early cannons. If you walk to its southern extremity, passing the Church of Panagia, you will come to a sheer cliff. From here there is a stunning view of Kapsali's twin bays and the hills and coast beyond. On a clear day you may see Crete.

Museum The town's interesting museum is north of the central square. It features gravestones of British soldiers and their infants who died on the island in the 19th century. The Potamos bridge is a British legacy. (Kythira was part of Britain's Ionian Protectorate from 1815 to 1864.) A large stone lion is exhibited and a sweet terracotta figurine of a woman and child. The museum is open Tuesday to Saturday from 8.45 am to 3 pm and Sunday from 8.30 am to 2.30 pm. Admission is free.

Places to Stay – bottom end Hora's cheapest accommodation is *Georgiou Pissi Rooms* (☎ 31 070/210), where singles/doubles are 3000/4000 dr with shared bathroom. Walk south along the main street and look for the sign on the left. The *Castelli Rooms* (☎ 31 869) are spacious, have kitchens, bathrooms and shared terraces with breathtaking views. Rates are 8000 dr a double. There's a sign south of the main street, before the road forks.

Places to Stay – middle The B-class *Hotel Margarita* (☎ 31 694/695) is an authentically renovated 19th-century mansion. Rates are 15,200/19,300/26,000 dr for singles/doubles/triples with breakfast. Air-con rooms have TV, telephone and bathroom. The hotel is down the steps opposite Zorba's.

Places to Eat On the main street, *Zorba's Psistaria* serves tasty grilled food. *Restaurant Mirtoön* is one of Kythira's best, but only open in summer. It is on the main Kapsali-Hora road but can be reached through Hora's narrow streets. Locals will direct you. *To Apaggio Snack Bar* serves summer evening snacks on the central square. *Crêperie* on the main street has a French cook.

Kapsali Καψάλι

Kapsali, Kythira's southern harbour, is an appealing village with two beaches separated by a headland. The larger beach is skirted by the road to Hora. The third beach is secluded. On the Hora road, take the first left along a dirt track. Steps descend to the beach. An inland road and one parallel to the waterfront is also signposted Hora. The two merge outside Kapsali. Canoes (300 dr per hour), pedal boats and surf boards (both 800 dr per hour) and water-skis (3000 dr per hour) can be hired from Panayiotis at Moto Rent, on the waterfront. Kapsali's port police (☎ 31 222) are next door.

Places to Stay – bottom end Kythira's one camp site, *Camping Kapsali* (☎ 31 580), is pine-shaded and open in summer only. Rates are 800 dr per person and tent. The site is 400 metres from Kapsali's quay and signposted from the inland road to Hora.

Kapsali has little accommodation. Try *Irene Megaloudi's Rooms* (☎ 31 340); clean doubles/triples with bathroom cost 9000/11,000 dr. They are at the far end of the road around the large beach, fronted by a bamboo-shaded terrace with cacti.

Places to Stay – top end The B-class *Raikos Hotel* (☎ 31 629), a striking white complex with a pool on a hill between Kapsali and Hora, has air-con rooms with balcony, radio, minibar and kitchen. Rates are 16,500/25,500/34,400 dr for singles/doubles/triples including breakfast.

Places to Eat Kapsali has few tavernas. The most popular local choice is *Restaurant Zerbas* at the quay. Friendly *Grosso Ponta* serves drinks and meal-sized snacks to a young crowd.

Around the Island

If you have transport, a tour round the island will reward you. See the map for locations of the monasteries of Agia Moni and Agia Elesa, both mountain refuges with superb views. Moni Mirtidion is a beautiful monastery surrounded by trees. From Hora, drive north-east to the picturesque village of **Avlemonas** via **Paleopoli** with its wide, pebbled beach. Here, archaeologists spent years searching for temple evidence of Aphrodite's birthplace. Avlemonas is a tiny fishing port with palms and some remains of Venetian settlement. Mainland Greeks in the know go to O Sotiros Restaurant for outstanding seafood fresh off the boats. The once bustling central village of **Aroniadika**, near the airport, has comfortable domatia and is reputedly full of ghosts.

ANTIKYTHIRA

The tiny island of Antikythira (population 70), 38 km south-east of Kythira, is the most remote island in the Ionian group – one for the reclusive. It has only one settlement (Potamos), one doctor, one police officer, one teacher (with five pupils), one metered telephone and a monastery. It has no post office or bank. Antikythira's telephone code is 0735.

Places to Stay & Eat The only accommodation for tourists is 10 basic rooms in two purpose-built blocks, open in summer only. Potamos has a kafeneio. A restaurant should open soon.

Getting There & Away The F/B *Theseus* calls at least weekly in the early hours on the way to Crete, returning the same day towards Kythira, Gythio, Neapoli and Monemvassia. If the sea is choppy, the ferry does not stop so this is not an island for tourists on a tight schedule. Check conditions in Piraeus if you intend to come direct or with Conomos Travel in Kythira's Agia Pelagia.

Evia & the Sporades
Εύβοια & οι Σποράδες

Evia, Greece's second-largest island, is so close to the mainland historically, physically and topographically that one tends not to regard it as an island at all. Athenians regard Evia as a convenient destination for a weekend break, so consequently it gets packed, although, except for the resort of Eretria, it is not much visited by foreign tourists.

The Sporades lie to the north and east of Evia and to the east and south-east of the Pelion peninsula, to which they were joined in prehistoric times. With their dense vegetation and mountainous terrain, they seem like a continuation of this peninsula. There are 11 islands in the archipelago, four of which are inhabited: Skiathos, Skopelos, Alonnisos and Skyros. The first two have a highly developed tourist industry, whereas Alonnisos and Skyros, although by no means remote, are far less visited and retain more local character.

Getting There & Away

Air Skiathos airport receives charter flights from northern Europe and there are also domestic flights to Athens. Skyros airport has flights to Athens only.

Bus From Athens' Terminal B bus station there are buses every half-hour to Halkida from 5.45 am to 9.45 pm (1½ hours, 1120 dr), six a day to Kymi from 6 am to 7 pm (3½ hours, 2440 dr) and three a day to Edipsos (for Loutra Edipsou; 3½ hours, 2250 dr). From the Mavromateon terminal in Athens, there are buses every 45 minutes to Rafina (for Karystos; one hour, 380 dr).

Train There are hourly trains each day from Athens' Larisis station to Halkida. The journey takes 1½ hours and costs 880 dr. The Halkida train station is on the mainland side of the bridge. To get there, walk over the bridge, turn left and you will find Leoforos Venizelou, Halkida's main drag, off to the right.

Ferry There are six ferry crossings from the mainland to Evia. They are from north to south: eight a day from Glyfa to Agiokambos (30 minutes, 330 dr); 12 a day from Arkitsa to Loutra Edipsou (one hour, 650 dr); every half-hour from Oropou to Eretria (30 minutes, 260 dr); five a day from Agia Marina to Nea Styra (40 minutes, 540 dr); three a day from Rafina to Marmari (1¼ hours, 920 dr); and two a day from Rafina to Karystos (one hour, 1420 dr).

There are two ferries a day from Kymi to Skyros (2½ hours, 1800 dr). To Volos there are two ferries a week (eight hours, 6900 dr) via Alonnisos (three hours), Skopelos (3½ hours) and Skiathos (4½ hours).

Mainland ports serving Skiathos, Skopelos (Glossa and Skopelos town) and Alonnisos are Volos and Agios Konstantinos, in the Thessaly and Sterea Ellada regions, respectively. Less frequent ferries go to these three islands from Kymi on Evia.

Evia & the Sporades Islands

There are hourly buses from Athens' Terminal B bus station to Agios Konstantinos (2½ hours, 2240 dr) and six a day to Kymi (3½ hours, 2440 dr).

Note that Skopelos has two ports – Glossa and Skopelos town. All ferries stop at Skopelos town and almost all at Glossa, but check to determine where your ferry is headed. To complicate matters further the port referred to on timetables as Glossa is not Glossa at all but Loutraki; Glossa is a village three km uphill from the port.

Skyros, to the south-east of the other Sporades islands, is served by at least two ferries and one hydrofoil every day from Kymi.

Hydrofoil There are hydrofoils every day from Agios Konstantinos and Volos (via Platanias on the Pelion peninsula) to Skiathos, Glossa (Skopelos), Skopelos town and Alonnisos. Five times a week the hydrofoil from Volos continues from Alonnisos to Skyros. There are daily services in summer from Thessaloniki to Skiathos, Skopelos and Alonnisos.

For full details, get the latest version of the Ceres timetable for the Sporades, from Ceres

Hydrofoil Joint Service (☎ 01-428 0001; fax 01-428 3526), Akti Themistokleous 8, Piraeus GR-185 36, or from local hydrofoil booking offices.

Getting Around

Bus Halkida is the transport hub of Evia. There are nine buses a day to the port of Kymi (2½ hours, 1350 dr) via Eretria and Kymi town; six to Steni (¾ hour, 480 dr); and three to Karystos (3½ hours, 1850 dr) via Eretria. There are four buses a day to Limni (2½ hours, 1250 dr). Buses to Athens run almost half-hourly. For some strange reason, the timetables are not displayed, so be prepared for communication problems unless you speak Greek.

Hydrofoil In summer there are daily hydrofoils from Halkida to Loutra Edipsou (one hour, 3480 dr) via Limni. These hydrofoils continue on to the Sporades islands.

Evia Εύβοια

Evia (EV-ia) will probably never be a prime destination for foreign tourists, but if you're based in Athens with a few days to spare, and (preferably) your own transport, a foray into Evia is worthwhile for its scenic mountain roads, pristine inland villages, and a look at some resorts which cater for Greeks (including one for ailing Greeks), rather than foreign tourists.

A mountainous spine runs north-south through the island; the east coast consists of precipitous cliffs, whereas the gentler west coast has a string of beaches and resorts. The island is reached overland by a bridge over the Euripous channel to the island's capital, Halkida. At the mention of Evia, most Greeks will eagerly tell you that the current in this narrow channel changes direction around seven times a day, which it does, if you are prepared to hang around to watch it. The next bit of the story, that Aristotle became so perplexed at not finding an explanation for this mystifying occurrence that he

threw himself into the channel and drowned, can almost certainly be taken with a grain of salt.

HALKIDA Χαλκίδα

Halkida (Hal-KEED-a, population 45,000) was an important city-state in ancient times and it had several colonies dotted around the Mediterranean. The name derives from the bronze which was manufactured here in antiquity (Halkos means 'bronze' in Greek). Today it's a lively industrial and agricultural town, but with nothing of sufficient note to warrant an overnight stay. However, if you have an hour or two to spare between buses, then the **archaeological museum**, Leoforos Venizelou 13, is worth a mosey around. It houses finds from Evia's three ancient cities of Halkida, Eretria and Karystos, including a chunk of the pediment of the Temple of Dafniforos Apollo at Eretria. The museum is open Tuesday to Sunday from 8.30 am to 3 pm. Admission is 500 dr.

The phone number of the Haldiki tourist police is ☎ 0221-83 333.

CENTRAL EVIA

Steni Στενή

From Halkida it's 31 km to the lovely mountain village of Steni, with gurgling springs and plane trees. The village has two hotels, both C class. The *Hotel Dirfys* (☎ 0228-51 217) has singles/doubles for 3250/6000 dr. The *Hotel Steni* (☎ 0228-51 221; fax 51 325) has singles/doubles for 6000/8000 dr with private bathroom.

Steni is the starting point for the climb up Mt Dirfys (1743 metres), which is Evia's highest mountain. The EOS-owned *Dirfys Refuge* (☎ 0228-51 285), at 1120 metres, can be reached along a nine-km dirt road, or after a two-hour walk along a forest footpath. From the refuge it's two hours to the summit. For further information contact the EOS (☎ 0221-25 230), Angeli Gyviou 22, Halkida.

A rough road continues from Steni to **Hiliadou**, on the east coast, where there is a fine beach. There are six buses a day from Halkida to Steni (one hour, 480 dr).

Kymi Κύμη

Kymi is a picturesque town built on a cliff 250 metres above the sea. The port of Kymi (called Paralia Kymis), four km downhill, is the only natural harbour on the precipitous east coast, and the departure point for ferries to Skyros. Kymi's postcode is 340 03 and the telephone code is 0222.

The **folklore museum**, on the road to Paralia Kymis, has an impressive collection of local costumes and memorabilia, and a display commemorating Dr George Papanikolaou, the inventor of the Pap smear test, who was born in Kymi. Opening times are 10 am to 1 pm and 5 to 7.30 pm every day.

Kymi has three hotels: the E-class *Hotel Krineion* (☎ 22 287), on the central square, has doubles for 6300 dr; the C-class *Hotel Beis* (☎ 22 604), at Paralia Kymis, has singles/doubles for 7000/8500 dr; and the C-class *Hotel Korali* (☎ 22 212) has rooms for 6500/10,000 dr.

NORTHERN EVIA

From Halkida a road heads north to **Psahna**, the gateway to the highly scenic mountainous interior of northern Evia. The road climbs through pine forests to the beautiful agricultural village of **Prokopi**, 52 km from Halkida. The inhabitants are descended from refugees who came from Prokopion (present day Ürgüp) in Turkey in 1923, bringing with them the relics of St John the Russian. On 27 May (St John's festival), hordes of pilgrims come to worship his relics in the Church of Agios Ioannis Rosses.

At **Strofylia**, 14 km beyond Prokopi, a road heads west to **Limni**, a pretty (but pretty crowded) fishing village with whitewashed houses and a beach. With your own transport or a penchant for walking, you can visit the 16th-century **Convent of Galataki**, eight km south-east of Limni. Its katholikon (main church) has fine frescoes. Limni has limited places to stay, with only two hotels and some domatia. There's one camp site, *Rovies Camping* (☎ 0227-71 120), on the coast, 13 km north-west of Limni.

The road continues to the sedate spa resort of **Loutra Edipsou** (119 km from Halkida) whose therapeutic sulphur waters have been celebrated since antiquity. Many luminaries, including Aristotle, Plutarch, Strabo and Plinius sang their praises. The waters are reputed to cure many ills, mostly of a rheumatic, arthritic or gynaecological nature. Today the town has the most up-to-date hydrotherapy-physiotherapy centre in Greece. If you're interested contact any EOT or the EOT Hydrotherapy-Physiotherapy Centre (☎ 0226-23 500), Loutra Edipsou. Even if you don't rank amongst the infirm you may enjoy a visit to this resort which has an attractive setting, a beach and many domatia and hotels.

SOUTHERN EVIA

Eretria Ερέτρια

Heading south from Halkida, Eretria is the first major place of interest. It has metamorphosed from Evia's major archaeological site into a tacky resort patronised by British package tourists. Ancient Eretria was a major maritime power and also had an eminent school of philosophy. The city was destroyed in 87 AD during the Mithridatic War. This war was fought between Mithridates (King of Pontos) and the Roman commander, Sulla. The modern town was founded in the 1820s by islanders from Psara fleeing the Turkish.

Things to See From the top of the **ancient acropolis**, at the northern end of town, there are splendid views over to the mainland. West of the acropolis are the remains of a palace, temple, and a theatre with a subterranean passage which was used by actors. Close by, the **Museum of Eretria** (☎ 0221-62 206) contains well-displayed finds from ancient Eretria. Opening times are Tuesday to Sunday from 8.30 am to 3 pm. Admission is 500 dr. In the centre of town are the remains of the **Temple of Dafniforos Apollo** and a mosaic from an ancient bath.

Places to Stay Eretria has loads of hotels and domatia, and the *Eva Camping* (☎ 61 081/024) camp site is just north on the coast.

Karystos Κάρυστος

Continuing south, the road branches at Lepoura: the left leads to Kymi, and the right, to Karystos (KAR-is-tos, population 4500). Set in the wide Karystian bay, below Mt Ohi (1398 metres), Karystos is the most attractive of southern Evia's resorts. The town was designed on a grid system by the Bavarian architect Bierbach, who was commissioned by King Otho. If you turn right from the quay you will come to the **Bourtzi**, the remains of a 14th-century Venetian castle, which has marble from a temple to Apollo incorporated into its walls. Beyond this there is a sandy beach. There is also a beach at the other end of the waterfront.

Karystos' postcode is 340 01 and the telephone code is 0224.

Places to Stay

Look for domatia signs along the waterfront or there are three C-class hotels in town, on streets which run inland from the centre of the waterfront. The *Hotel Als* (☎ 22 202) and *Hotel Karystion* (☎ 22 391; fax 22 727) are both on Kriezotou and the *Hotel Plaza* (☎ 22 337) is at Ioannou Kotsika 9. All three hotels have rates of around 7500 dr for a double room.

Around Karystos

The ruins of the 13th-century Frankish fortress of **Castello Rossa** (red castle) is a short walk from **Myli**, a delightful well-watered village, four km inland from Karystos. The aqueduct behind the castle once carried water from the mountain springs and a tunnel led from this castle to the Bourtzi in Karystos. A little beyond Myli there is an **ancient quarry** scattered with fragments of the once prized Karyston marble.

With your own transport you can explore the sleepy villages nestling in the southern foothills of Mt Ohi. The rough road winds through citrus groves and pine trees high above the south coast. At **Platanistos**, a charming village named for its plane trees, a five-km dirt road (drivable) leads to the coastal village of **Potami** with its sand and pebble beach. The 'main road' continues to the east coast.

Skiathos Σκιάθος

The good news is that much of the coast of pine-covered Skiathos (Skee-ATH-os, population 4100) consists of exquisite beaches of golden sand. The bad news is that the island is overrun with package tourists, and is very expensive. Despite the large presence of sun-starved northern Europeans and its ensuing tourist excess, Skiathos is still a pretty island and not surprisingly is one of Greece's premier resorts.

The island has only one settlement, the port and capital of Skiathos town, on the south-east coast. The rest of the south coast is one long chain of holiday villas and hotels. The north coast is precipitous and less accessible. Most people come to the island for the beaches and nightlife – if you've come for anything else you may depart quickly.

Getting There & Away

Air As well as the numerous charter flights from northern Europe to Skiathos, in summer there are up to five flights a day to Athens (14,600 dr). The Olympic Airways office (☎ 22 229/200) is on the right side of Papadiamanti, Skiathos town, walking inland.

Ferry In summer, there are three to four daily ferries from Skiathos to Volos (three to four hours, 2300 dr), one or two to Agios Konstantinos (3½ hours, 3000 dr), four to six a day to Alonnisos (two hours, 1450 dr) via Glossa (Skopelos) and Skopelos town (1½ hours, 1300 dr). There are one or two ferries a week from Skiathos to Kymi (five hours, 4600 dr). There are many agencies on the waterfront selling ferry tickets. The telephone number of the port police is ☎ 22 017.

Hydrofoil In summer, there is a bewildering array of hydrofoils from Skiathos and around the Sporades in general. Among the main services, there are three or four hydrofoils daily from Skiathos to Volos (1¼ hours,

4600 dr), and eight or 10 to Alonnisos (one hour, 2350 dr) via Glossa (Skopelos) and Skopelos town (35 minutes, 1800 dr). There are also two or three daily hydrofoils to Agios Konstantinos (1½ hours, 5300 dr). Three to five times a week there is a hydrofoil to Skyros (2¼ hours, 5800 dr) and Kymi (three hours, 9300 dr). There are five or six hydrofoils a week to Thessaloniki (3½ hours, 10,000 dr). In addition, there are also services to the Pelion peninsula, Halkidiki, to various ports in Evia and to Stylida near Lamia. Hydrofoil tickets may be purchased from Skiathos Holidays (☎ 22 018/033; fax 22 771) in the middle of the new harbour waterfront.

Getting Around

Bus Crowded buses leave Skiathos town for Koukounaries beach every half-hour between 7.30 am and 10.30 pm. The buses stop at all the access points to the beaches along the south coast. There are a couple of private buses to Megali Aselinos beach, on the north coast.

Car & Motorbike There are heaps of motorbike-hire outlets along the waterfront in

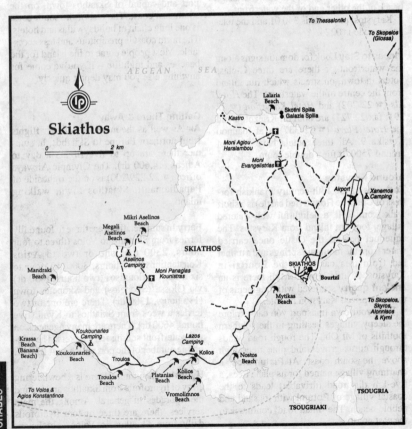

Skiathos

Skiathos town. Car-hire outlets include Autorent (☎ 21 797) and Eurocar (☎ 21 124), both of which are on the waterfront.

Excursion Boat As well as the bus, there are excursion boats to most of the south-coast beaches. There are also excursion boats which do around-the-island trips (2500 dr). These include a visit to Kastro, Lalaria beach, and the three caves of Halkini Spilia, Skotini Spilia and Galazia Spilia, which are only accessible by boat. Excursion boats leave from the old harbour.

SKIATHOS TOWN

Skiathos town, with red-roofed, white-washed houses, built on two low hills, is picturesque enough, although it's not as pretty as Skopelos or Skyros towns. The islet of Bourtzi (reached by a causeway) between the two harbours is covered with pine forest. Inevitably, hotels, souvenir shops, travel agents and bars dominate the waterfront and main thoroughfares.

Orientation

The quay is in the middle of the waterfront, just north of Bourtzi islet. To the right (as you face inland) is the straight new harbour; to the left, and with more character, is the curving old harbour used by local fishermen and excursion boats. The main thoroughfare of Papadiamanti strikes inland from opposite the quay. The central square of Plateia Trion Ierarhon is just back from the middle of the old harbour and has a large church in the middle.

Information

The tourist police (☎ 23 172) is opposite the regular police about halfway along Papadiamanti, next to the high school. It operates from 8 am to 9 pm every day during the summer season.

The post office and OTE are on the right side of Papadiamanti, and the National Bank of Greece is on the left. Skiathos' postcode is 370 02 and the telephone code is 0427. The bus terminus is at the northern end of the new harbour.

Museum

Skiathos was the birthplace of the Greek short-story writer and the poet Alexandros Papadiamantis, and novelist Alexandros Moraïtidis. Alexandros Papadiamantis' house is now a museum with a small collection documenting the writer's life.

The museum's opening times are 4 to 7 pm; it's closed on Monday. It is just off the right side of Papadiamanti coming up from the harbour.

Organised Tours

Various local operators run excursion-boat trips around the island. See the Getting Around section for Skiathos island.

Places to Stay – bottom end

Skiathos has four camp sites: *Koukounaries Camping* (☎ 49 250), at the east end of the beach with the same name; *Lazos Camping* (☎ 49 206), at Kolios beach, seven km west of Skiathos town (take the Koukounaries beach bus from Skiathos town); *Aselinos Camping* (☎ 49 312), on the north coast, at Megali Aselinos beach; and *Xanemos Camping*, close to the airport. Of the four, Koukounaries Camping is probably the best. Xanemos Camping is too close to the airport for comfort.

Most accommodation is booked solid from July to September by package-tour operators, and in the July to August bracket prices are often double those in low season. Outside these months you may be offered a room when you get off the ferry – if not, look up Papadiamanti and around Plateia Trion Ierarhon for domatia signs. If you're brave enough to arrive during the summer rush then just about any travel agent will endeavour to fix you up with somewhere. Worth trying are Alkyon Travel (☎ 22 029/948), at the bottom of Papadiamanti; Meridian (☎ 21 309/477), Papadiamanti 8; or Mare Nostrum Holidays (☎ 21 463/464), Papadiamanti 21.

The E-class *Hotel Karafelas* (☎ 21 235) is one of the town's best-value hotels. The comfortable singles/doubles are 4000/6000 dr (low season), or 7000/10,000 dr (high season) with private bathroom. The hotel is at the far end of Papadiamanti, on the left. Also worth a try is the slightly more expensive E-class *Australia Hotel* (☎ 22 488), which has tidy singles/doubles for 6500/8700 dr (low season) and 12,000/15,000 dr (high season) with private bathroom. Walk up Papadiamanti to the post office, turn right and take the first left.

If you would like a nice quiet domatio within walking distance of Skiathos town (1.5 km), try *Villa Meroulas* (☎ 21 154). This place has comfortable rooms with large balconies and is set back from the Koukounaries road among olive groves. A double room here costs 7000 to 11,000 dr, depending on the season.

Places to Stay – middle

The *Hotel Morfo* (☎ 21 737; fax 23 222) has nicely furnished single/double rooms for 8700/9700 dr (low season), or 12,200/14,000 dr (high season) with private bathroom. From the waterfront take M Ananiou (parallel, and to the right of, Papadiamanti), and you'll come to the hotel on the left. The B-class *Hotel Alkyon* (☎ 22 981; fax 21 643), at the far end of the new harbour waterfront, is a large plush place. Rates are 7100/9900 dr for singles/doubles (low season) or 15,100/19,900 dr (high season) with private bathroom.

Places to Stay – top end

Most of the island's top-end hotels are on the coast to the west of Skiathos town. The A-class *Hotel Paradise* (☎ 21 939; fax 21 939), three km west of Skiathos town, is one of the newest and smallest of these hotels. It has tastefully furnished air-con rooms and a restaurant and bar. Doubles are 20,700 dr (low season).

The A-class *Nostos Bungalows* (☎ 22 420; fax 22 525) is a well-designed bungalow complex at Nostos beach, five km west of town. The complex has bars, a restaurant, taverna, pool and tennis court. Bungalows cost 27,000 dr. The *Atrium Hotel* (☎ 49 345/376; fax 49 444) is an attractive place with a bar, restaurant, pool and gymnasium.

Singles/doubles are 19,000/23,000 dr. The hotel is seven km west of town.

Places to Eat

The good news is that there is a wide choice of eateries in Skiathos; the bad news is that they all tend to gear their cuisine to the tourist trade and they are more expensive than elsewhere. Finding some real Greek cuisine is a matter of trial and error. There is a swathe of restaurants just down from Plateia Trion Ierarhon, overlooking the old harbour. Of these, *Taverna Stamatis* does a good job and seems to draw most of the customers. The service is fast and the food is good and reasonably Greek.

Taverna Ouzeri Kambourelis on the waterfront of the old harbour also rates well and *Psarotaverna to Aigaio* has reasonable prices and ready-made dishes as well as fish, but is in a less attractive location on the new harbourfront. Finally, if you can't cope with the hit and miss of finding authentic Greek food you can always settle for an expensive curry at the *Lemon Tree* English/Indian restaurant in a side street off Papadiamanti. A curry dish here costs about 2500 dr.

Entertainment

Scan Papadiamanti and Polytehniou (parallel, and to the left of Papadiamanti) and see which disco or bar takes your fancy. The *Adagio Bar* is one of the most civilised, playing classical music and jazz. Walk up Papadiamanti, turn left at the post office and it's on the left. In contrast, the *Banana Bar*, on Polytehniou, is one of the rowdiest and wildest, if that's your scene. *Borzoï* and *Spartakus* are reputed to play Greek music. Both are on Polytehniou.

AROUND THE ISLAND
Beaches

With some 65 beaches to choose from on Skiathos, beach-hopping can become a full-time occupation. Many are really only accessible by caïque and the ones that are more easily accessible tend to get crowded.

Buses ply the south coast stopping at the access points to the beaches. The ones nearest town are extremely crowded; the first one worth getting off the bus for is the pine-fringed, long and sandy **Vromolimnos beach**. **Platanias** and **Troulos**, the next two beaches along, are also nice but both, alas, are very popular. The bus continues to **Koukounaries beach**, backed by pine trees and a lagoon and touted as the best beach in Greece. It's best nowadays viewed from a distance from where the wide sweep of pale gold sand does indeed look beautiful.

Krassa beach, at the other side of a narrow headland, is more commonly known as **Banana beach**, though you can't be sure whether this is because everything's peeled (it's nudist) or because of what's revealed when everything's peeled (it's predominantly male). The north coast's beaches are less crowded but exposed to the meltemi.

From Troulos a road heads inland to sandy **Megali Aselinos beach** (with a camp site). Turn left onto a dirt road to reach this beach. A right fork from this road leads to **Mikri Aselinos beach**. **Lalaria**, on the northern coast, is a striking beach of pale grey pebbles, easiest reached by excursion boat from Skiathos town and is the one that features in most of the tourist brochures depicting Skiathos.

Kastro Κάστρο
Kastro, perched dramatically on a rocky headland above the north coast, was the fortified pirate-proof capital of the island from 1540 to 1829. It consisted of some 300 houses and 20 churches and the only access was by a drawbridge. Now it's in ruins except for two of its churches, and access is by steps. The views from Kastro are tremendous. Excursion boats do the trip to the beach below Kastro, from where it's an easy clamber up to the ruins.

Moni Evangelistrias
Μονή Ευαγγελίστριας
The 18th-century Moni Evangelistrias is the most appealing of the island's monasteries. It is in a delightful setting, poised above a gorge, 450 metres above sea level, and sur-rounded by pine and cypress trees. The monastery, like many in Greece, was a refuge for freedom fighters during the War of Independence, and the islanders claim the first Greek flag was raised here in 1807.

The monastery is an hour's walk from town or you can drive there. Take the road out of town towards the airport and there is a signpost pointing left to the monastery.

Skopelos Σκόπελος

Skopelos (SKO-pel-os, population 5000) is less commercialised than Skiathos, but following hot on its trail. Like Skiathos, the north-west coast is exposed, with high cliffs. The sheltered south-east coast harbours many beaches although, unlike Skiathos, most are pebbled. The island is heavily pine-forested and has agricultural pockets of vineyards, olive groves and fruit orchards. There are two large settlements: the capital and main port of Skopelos town on the east coast; and the lovely unspoilt hill village of Glossa, three km from Loutraki, the island's second port, on the west coast.

Skopelos has yielded an exciting archaeological find. In ancient times the island was an important Minoan outpost ruled by Staphylos, who according to mythology was the son of Ariadne and Dionysos. *Staphylos* means grape in Greek and the Minoan ruler is said to have introduced wine-making to the island. In the 1930s a tomb containing gold treasures, and believed to be that of Staphylos, was unearthed at Staphylos, now a resort.

Getting There & Away
Ferry Skopelos' second port is called Glossa. However, boats actually depart from Loutraki, on the coast. Glossa is three km inland. In summer there are three ferries a day from Glossa and Skopelos town to Alonnisos (30 minutes, 950 dr); four to Volos (4½ hours, 2800 dr); two to Agios Konstantinos (4½ hours, 3500 dr); and four or five to Skiathos

Skopelos

0   2   4 km

(1½ hours, 1300 dr). Additionally, there are two boats a week to Kymi (3½ hours, 4100 dr) and two a week to Thessaloniki (six hours, 3700 dr). The times given are for Skopelos town; Glossa is one hour less. Tickets are available from Lemonis Agents (☎ 22 363; fax 22 363)

The telephone number of Skopelos' port police is ☎ 22 180.

Hydrofoil Like Skiathos, Skopelos is linked to a large number of destinations by hydrofoil. Among the main services during the summer period are the following: eight or nine per day to Alonnisos (20 minutes, 1500 dr); 10 or 12 to Skiathos (one hour, 1800 dr); five a day to Volos (two hours 20 minutes, 6000 dr); three a day to Agios Konstantinos (2½ hours, 7100 dr); four or six a week to Skyros (two hours 20 minutes, 4600 dr); and one a day to Thessaloniki (4¾ hours, 11,200 dr). Cheaper return fares apply on most of these services. In addition, there are also services to the Pelion peninsula, Halkidiki, to various ports in Evia and to Stylida, which is near Lamia. Hydrofoil tickets may be purchased from Madro Travel (☎ 22 145; fax 22 941).

Getting Around

Bus There are eight buses a day all the way to Glossa/Loutraki (one hour, 600 dr), a further three that go only as far as Milia (35 minutes, 420 dr) and another two that go only as far as Agnontas (15 minutes, 180 dr).

Car & Motorbike There are a fair number of rental outlets for cars and bikes, mostly at the eastern end of the waterfront. Among them is Motor Tours (☎ 22 986), on the waterfront near the Hotel Eleni.

SKOPELOS TOWN

Skopelos town is one of the most captivating of the island's towns. It skirts a semicircular bay and clambers in tiers up a hillside, culminating in a ruined fortress. Dozens of churches are interspersed amongst tall dazzling white houses with brightly shuttered windows and flower-adorned balconies. Traditionally, roofs in Skopelos town were tiled with beautiful rough-hewn bluestone, but these are gradually being replaced with mass-produced red tiles.

Orientation

Skopelos town's quay is on the west side of the bay. From the ferry turn left to reach the bustling waterfront lined with cafés, souvenir shops and travel agencies. The bus station is to the left of the quay at the end of the excursion boat moorings.

Information

The post office lurks in an obscure alleyway; walk up the road opposite the bus station, take the first left, the first right and the first left and it's on the right. To reach the OTE turn left at the quay, right at the Armoloï craft shop and you'll come to it on the left at the first crossroad. Skopelos' postcode is 370 03 and the telephone code is 0424.

The National Bank of Greece is on the waterfront near the quay. To reach Skopelos' laundrette go up the street opposite the bus station, turn right at Platanos Taverna and it's on the left.

There is no tourist office or tourist police on Skopelos. To reach the regular police

station (☎ 22 235) go up the steps to the right of the National Bank of Greece, turn left and it's on the left.

Museum

Strolling around town and sitting at the waterside cafés will probably be your chief occupations in Skopelos town, but there is also a small **folk-art museum** on Hatzistamati. It is open daily from 7 to 10 pm and admission is free. Walk up the steps to the left of the pharmacy on the waterfront, take the first right, the first left, the first right and it's on the right.

Places to Stay – bottom end

Skopelos town is still a place where you have a good chance of renting a room in a family house. People with rooms to offer meet the ferries, but be aware that many of these rooms are in the labyrinthine streets high above the waterfront, so getting to them initially, and finding them again afterwards, tests stamina and powers of orientation to the limit.

One of the most pleasant domatia is *Pension Soula* (☎ 22 930/032). This lovely place is owned by an elderly couple who don't speak English but are very hospitable. The rates are 7500/8000 dr for doubles/triples with private bathroom; there is a communal kitchen and a tranquil garden. To find the pension, turn left at the Hotel Amalia and follow this road, bearing right after about 200 metres. You will find the house on your right. There are no camp sites on Skopelos.

Places to Stay – middle

The D-class *Hotel Eleni* (☎ 22 393; fax 22 936) has lovely traditionally furnished rooms with balconies. The cost is 3800/4300 dr (low season) and 9200/11,400 dr (high season) for singles/doubles with private bathroom. Turn left from the quay and the hotel is on the right, two buildings before the Dolphin Hotel.

On the road leading eastwards along the bay you will find the small but very comfortable C-class *Hotel Agnanti* (☎ 22 722) which has doubles/triples facing the harbour for

8000/9600 dr (low season) and 15,000/18,000 dr (high season).

Places to Stay – top end
The B-class *Dolphin Hotel* (☎ 23 015; fax 23 016) is a striking pastel-coloured building with an ultramodern, luxurious interior and an extensive garden with a swimming pool and an ornamental pond. The rooms have a minibar, telephone, radio and balcony. Rates are 10,200/12,800 dr (low season) and 15,300/19,000 dr (high season) for singles/doubles. Apartments for three or four people cost 25,000 dr.

Places to Eat
Like Skiathos, finding a good Greek restaurant can be a hit-and-miss affair. However, there is hope; the following are among the better ones. *O Platanos* is cheap, basic and popular. Its speciality is souvlaki. You will find it if you follow the instructions (above) for finding the post office. It has tables underneath a large plane tree.

There are two reasonable Greek restaurants next to each other on the waterfront near the ferry quay. The *Klimataria* and the *Molos* serve a range of good food and are in the mid-price range.

Two more expensive, but very pleasant restaurants catering mainly for better-heeled visitors are the *Taverna Finikas* and the *Taverna Alexander*. Look for the signs to this first place from the OTE. It has a mixed cuisine and the restaurant is set round an enormous palm tree. In the Taverna Alexander, apart from good food, you get to eat in a walled garden. Follow the signs from the OTE.

For a special treat in summer only, head to the *Ouzeri Anatoli* high up above the town. Here in summer, from 11 pm onwards, you will hear rembetika music sung by Skopelos' own rembetis Georgos Xindaris to accompany your mezedes. To get there by road, turn right at the road junction as you head out of town and follow the ring road to the end. To walk there, put your trust in your sense of direction and head upwards and to the right. Ask for help if you get lost.

Entertainment
The *Platanos Jazz Club*, opposite the quay, is a long-time favourite hang-out with backpackers. New-age music is played at breakfast time, and jazz and blues in the evenings. The *Costa Bar* is the liveliest place for disco music. It's is at the eastern end of the waterfront, just past the bus station.

GLOSSA Γλώσσα
Glossa, Skopelos' other major settlement, is another whitewashed delight and considerably quieter than the capital. It manages to combine being a pristine Greek village with having most of the amenities that visitors require.

The bus stops at a large church at a T-junction. Facing the church, the left road winds down to Loutraki and the right to the main thoroughfare of Agiou Riginou. Along here you'll find a bank and a shop with a metered telephone.

Skopelos' beaches are just as accessible by bus from Glossa as they are from Skopelos town; Milia, the island's best beach, is actually closer to Glossa. There are also places to stay and tavernas at Loutraki, but it's an uninteresting and unattractive place.

Places to Stay & Eat
In summer, if accommodation gets tight in Skopelos town, you can try the *Hotel Atlantes* (☎ 33 223), at the T-junction in Glossa. The clean, attractive single/double/triple rooms are 5000/6500/8500 dr. Just before you enter Glossa, you will find *Rooms Kerasia* (☎ 33 373) in a newish building set back from the road to the left. Rates here are around 6000 dr a double. Glossa also has a few other rooms in private houses – enquire at kafeneia.

Taverna Agnanti serves well-prepared, reasonably priced Greek fare. It's on the left side of Agiou Riginou as you walk from the T-junction. Just before you enter Glossa from Skopelos you'll find the *Kali Kardia* taverna, which has very nice views down to Loutraki.

SPORADES

AROUND THE ISLAND
Monasteries

Skopelos has many monasteries, several of which can be visited on a scenic, although quite strenuous, one-day trek from Skopelos town. Facing inland from the waterfront turn left and follow the road which skirts the bay and then climbs inland (signposted Hotel Aegeon). Continue beyond the hotel and you will come to a fork. Take the left fork for the 18th-century **Moni Evangelismou** (now a convent). From here there are breathtaking views of Skopelos town, four km away. The monastery's prize piece is a beautiful and highly ornate carved and gilded iconostasis in which there is an 11th-century icon of the Virgin Mary.

The right fork leads to the uninhabited 16th-century **Moni Metamorphosis**, which is the island's oldest monastery. From here the track continues to the 18th-century **Moni Prodromou** (now a nunnery), eight km from Skopelos town.

Beaches

Skopelos' beaches are almost all on the sheltered south-west coast. All the buses stop at the beginning of paths which lead down to them. The first beach along is the crowded sand and pebble **Staphylos beach** (site of Staphylos' tomb), four km from Skopelos town. There is a nice taverna here with romantic views when there is a full moon. From the eastern end of the beach a path leads over a small headland to the quieter **Velanio beach**, the island's official nudist beach. **Agnontas**, which is three km west of Staphylos, has a small pebble beach and from here caïques ply to the superior and sandy **Limnonari beach** (you can also walk here along a path from Agnontas, or along a track from the main road). There are four waterside tavernas at Agnontas. From Agnontas the road cuts inland through pine forests and re-emerges at sheltered **Panormos beach**. **Milia**, the next beach along, is considered the island's best – a long swathe of tiny pebbles.

All of these beaches have tavernas or cantinas, and there are hotels and domatia at Staphylos, Limnonari, Panormos and Milia.

Alonnisos Αλόννησος

Alonnisos (Al-ON-is-os, population 3000) is still a serene island despite having been ferreted out by 'high-quality' package-tour companies. Package tourism would no doubt have taken off in a bigger way had the airport (erroneously and optimistically shown on island maps) materialised. This project was begun in the mid-1980s, but the rocks of Alonnisos proved unyielding and the politics Byzantine, making the construction of a runway impossible.

Alonnisos once had a flourishing wine industry, but in 1950 the vines were struck with disease and, robbed of their livelihood, many islanders moved away. Fate struck another cruel blow in 1965 when a violent earthquake destroyed the hilltop capital of Alonnisos town (now called Old Alonnisos or Hora). The inhabitants abandoned their hilltop homes and were subsequently rehoused in hastily assembled concrete dwellings at Patitiri. In recent years many of the derelict houses in the capital have been bought for a song from the government and renovated by northern Europeans.

Alonnisos is a green island with pine and oak trees, mastic and arbutus bushes, and fruit trees. The west coast is mostly precipitous cliffs but the east coast is speckled with many pebbled beaches. The water around Alonnisos has been declared a marine park, and consequently is the cleanest in the Aegean. Every house has a cesspit, so no sewage goes into the sea.

Getting There & Away

Ferry There are two or three daily ferries from Alonnisos to Volos (six hours, 3200 dr); five a day to both Skopelos (30 minutes, 900 dr) and Skiathos (two hours, 1450 dr); and two a day to Agios Konstantinos (six hours, 3850 dr). Additionally, there are two ferries a week to Kymi (2¼ hours, 3800 dr) and one or three a week to Thessaloniki (6½ hours, 2500 dr). Tickets can be purchased from Alonnisos Travel (☎ 65 198; fax 65 511). The port police (☎ 65 595) are on the left side of Ikion Dolopon.

Hydrofoil There are, as with Skiathos and Skopelos, a large number of connections in summer. The more important ones are as follows: two or three services a day to Volos (2¾ hours, 6700 dr); seven or 11 services a day to both Skopelos town (20 minutes, 1500 dr) and Skiathos (40 minutes, 2350 dr); two or three a day to Agios Konstantinos

(2½ hours, 7400 dr); one or two a day to Skyros (1¼ hours, 4400 dr); and one a day to Thessaloniki (5¼ hours, 11,200 dr).

Cheaper return fares apply on most of these services. In addition, there are also services to the Pelion peninsula, Halkidiki, to various ports in Evia and to Stylida near Lamia. Hydrofoil tickets may be purchased from Ikos Travel (☎ 65 230; fax 65 321) in Patitiri.

Getting Around
If you'd prefer to leave the travel arrangements up to someone else, Ikos Travel in

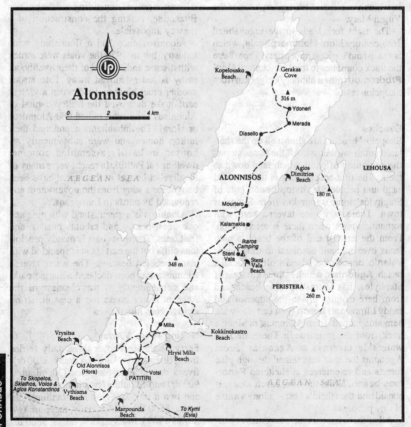

Alonnisos

Patitiri operates various excursions. See Organised Tours under the Patitiri entry.

Bus In summer, Alonnisos' one bus plies more or less hourly between Patitiri (from opposite the quay) and Old Alonnisos. The ticket costs 200 dr each way.

Motorbike There are several motorbike-hire outlets on Pelasgon, in Patitiri. There are not many surfaced roads in Alonnisos, so exercise extra caution when venturing away from the main settlements.

Taxi Boat The easiest way to get to the east-coast beaches is by the taxi boats which leave from the quay every morning.

PATITIRI Πατητήρι

Patitiri sits between two high sandstone cliffs at the southern end of the east coast. Not surprisingly, considering its origins, it's not a traditionally picturesque place, but nevertheless makes a convenient base and has a very relaxed atmosphere.

Orientation

Finding your way around Patitiri is easy. The quay is in the centre of the waterfront and two roads lead inland. Facing away from the sea, turn left and then right for Pelasgon and right and then left for Ikion Dolopon.

Information

There is no tourist office or tourist police. The regular police (☎ 65 205) are just east of the southern end of Ikion Dolopon.

The post office is on the right side of Ikion Dolopon and the OTE is on the waterfront to the right of the quay. The postcode is 370 05 and the telephone code is 0424.

The National Bank of Greece is on Ikion Dolopon. There is a laundrette on the left side of Pelasgon.

Walk to Old Alonnisos

From Patitiri to Old Alonnisos there is a delightful path which winds through shrubbery and orchards. Walk up Pelasgon and, 40 metres beyond Pension Galini, a battered

blue and white sign points left to Old Alonnisos. Take this path and after 10 minutes turn right at a water tap (not functioning), then after about 15 minutes the path is intersected by a dirt road. Continue straight ahead on the path and after about 25 minutes you will come to the main road. Walk straight along this road and you will see Old Alonnisos ahead.

Organised Tours

Ikos Travel (☎ 65 320/575; fax 65 321), opposite the quay, has several excursions. These include: Kyra Panagia, Psathoura and Peristera islets (7000 dr, including a picnic on a beach, snacks and drinks) and a round-the-island excursion (6500 dr).

Places to Stay – bottom end

Alonnisos has two camp sites. The nearest one to the port is the semi-official *Camping Rocks* (☎ 65 410). Don't be put off by the name; it doesn't refer to the site's surface but to the nearest rocky beach (which is nudist). The site is a 700-metre uphill slog from the quay (signposted from the 4X4 Disco on Pelasgon); however, the owner meets all the ferries in his jeep. The other site is *Ikaros Camping* (☎ 65 258), on Steni Vala beach.

Accommodation standards are good (and cheaper than on Skiathos and Skopelos) on Alonnisos and, except for the first two weeks of August, you shouldn't have any difficulty finding a room. The Rooms to Let service (☎ 65 577), opposite the quay, will endeavour to find a room for you on any part of the island.

The *domatia* of Eleni Alexiou (☎ 65 149) are a pleasant place to stay in Alonnisos. If you call ahead, you will be met at the quay. Rates are 6000/7200 dr for doubles/triples. The rooms are high up and a bit back from the harbour. Ask at Rooms to Let for more detailed instructions on how to get there. Along Pelasgon, on the left at No 27, are the prettily furnished *rooms* of Magdelini Bassini (☎ 65 451). They cost 8000/9600 dr with private bathroom. *Pension Galini* (☎ 65 573; fax 65 094) is beautifully furnished and has a flower-festooned terrace. Doubles/triples are 6000/7200 dr with private bathroom, and well-equipped apartments for five/six people are 13,000/16,000 dr. The pension can be found on the left 400 metres up Pelasgon.

Eleni Athanasiou (☎ 65 240) rents lovely *rooms* in a sparkling white, blue-shuttered building high above the harbour. Rates are 6500/7000 dr for doubles/triples with private bathroom, and five-person apartments are 14,000 dr. The rooms are reached by taking the first left off Ikion Dolopon and following the path upwards until you come across them on your right. The C-class *Alkyon Guest House* (☎ 65 220; fax 65 195), on the waterfront, has comfortable singles/doubles for 7500/9700 dr with private bathroom.

The attractive rooms in the C-class *Liadromia Hotel* (☎ 65 521) have stucco walls, stone floors, balcony and traditional carved-wood furniture. Walk inland up Ikion Dolopon and take the first turn right, follow the road around and the hotel is on the left. Doubles are 8500 dr.

Places to Stay – middle

Alonnisos' classiest hotel is the C-class *Galaxy Hotel* (☎ 65 254; fax 65 110), where luxurious balconied single/double/triple rooms cost 7500/10,500/13,500 dr. The hotel is built on a hill to the left of the bay if you're facing inland. Turn left at the port and beyond the waterfront tavernas take the steps up to the right; turn left at the top to reach the hotel.

Places to Eat

If you feel you can't stomach another moussaka, pastitsio or souvlaki, then Alonnisos will come as a revelation, for the island has some of Greece's best eateries. Most specialise in imaginatively prepared fish dishes. At *To Kamaki Ouzeri*, on the left side of Ikion Dolopon, try mussels in cream sauce or other delicious saganaki dishes.

Another superlative little ouzeri is *Ouzeri Lefteris*, on the right side of Pelasgon, which has stuffed cuttlefish as well as lobster with tomatoes and peppers. The *Argo Restaurant* has wonderful views of the sea from its

terrace and the food is good, with main meals for about 1700 dr. Face the sea, walk to the extreme left of the harbour and the restaurant is signposted. The waterfront restaurants are all much of a muchness: take your pick and hope for the best.

OLD ALONNISOS

Nowadays, Old Alonnisos (Hora) has a strange appearance. Its narrow streets are made of mud and stone but it is dominated by highly renovated stone villas. These dwellings are owned by wealthy northern Europeans hankering after the simple life.

Old Alonnisos is a tranquil, picturesque place with lovely views. From the main road just outside Old Alonnisos a path leads down to Vrisitsa beach, and paths lead south to Vythisma and Marpounda beaches.

Places to Stay

There are no hotels in Old Alonnisos, but there are a few domatia. One agreeable place is the *Rooms & Studios* of John Tsoukanas (☎ 65 135/469), with rates of 5000/7000/9000 dr for singles/doubles/triples with private bathroom. The domatia are on the central square of Plateia Hristou, which is named after its 17th-century church. Nearby is the newer *Fadasia House* (☎ 65 186) with lovely rooms for 7000 dr and a studio with fridge and cooker for 12,000 dr. There is also a little snack bar and garden.

Places to Eat

Old Alonnisos has three tavernas, all on the main street. All are good but the one with the nicest view is the *Paraport Taverna*, which has main meals for around 1700 dr. On Plateia Hristou the snack bar below John Tsoukanas' rooms has tasty small souvlaki sticks and Greek salad at a good price. There are a couple of other tavernas on the upper thoroughfare.

BEACHES

Most of Alonnisos' beaches are on the east coast. Apart from the Patitiri-Old Alonnisos road, the only road is one which goes north to the tip of the island. It is driveable all the way but only has tarmac for a few km out of Patitiri. Dirt tracks lead off the road to the beaches. The first beach is the gently shelving **Hrysi Milia beach**. The next beach up is **Kokkinokastro**. Kokkinokastro is the site of the city of Ikos (the capital in ancient times) and there are remains of city walls and a necropolis under the sea. **Steni Vala** is a small fishing village with a permanent population of 30, three tavernas and 30-odd rooms in domatia as well as the *Ikaros Camping* camp site. **Kalamakia**, further north, also has rooms and tavernas. **Agios Dimitrios**, further up, is an unofficial nudist beach.

ISLETS AROUND ALONNISOS

Alonnisos is surrounded by seven uninhabited islets, all of which have rich flora & fauna. The monk seal *(Monachus monachus)* is a Mediterranean sea mammal threatened with extinction, and the largest existing population lives in the waters around the Sporades. These factors were the incentive behind the formation of the marine park in 1983. The park encompasses the sea and the islets around Alonnisos. Its research station is on Alonnisos, near Gerakas cove.

Piperi, to the north-east of Alonnisos, is a refuge for the monk seal and it is forbidden to set foot there without a licence to carry out research.

Gioura, also north-east of Alonnisos, has many rare plants and a rare species of wild goat. **Skantzoura**, to the south-east of Alonnisos, is the habitat of falcons and the rare Aegean seagull. **Peristera**, just off Alonnisos' east coast, has several sandy beaches and the remains of a castle.

Kyra Panagia also has good beaches and two abandoned monasteries. **Psathoura** has the submerged remains of an ancient city and the brightest lighthouse in the Aegean. Both of these islands are to the north of Alonnisos.

The seventh islet is tiny **Adelphi**, between Peristera and Skantzoura.

Skyros Σκύρος

Skyros (SKEE-ros, population 2800) is some distance from the rest of the group and differs from them topographically. Almost bisected, its northern half is pine forested, but the south is barren and rocky.

There are only two settlements on the island: the small port of Linaria, and Skyros town, the capital, 10 km away on the east coast. Skyros is visited by poseurs rather than package tourists – and as many of these are wealthy young Athenians as foreigners. Skyros also has quite a different atmosphere to other islands in this region, reminding you more of the Cyclades than the Sporades, especially the stark, cubist architecture of Skyros town.

Some visitors come to Skyros to attend courses at the Skyros Institute, a centre for holistic health and fitness. See under Skyros town for details.

Skyros' factual history was mundane in comparison to its mythological origins until Byzantine times, when rogues and criminals from the mainland were exiled there. When pirates invaded, these opportunist exiles, rather than driving them away, entered into a mutually lucrative collaboration with them. The exiles became the elite of Skyriot society, furnishing and decorating their houses with elaborately hand-carved furniture; and plates and copper ornaments from Europe, the Middle East and Far East. Some of these items were brought by seafarers and some were simply looted by pirates from merchant ships. The peasants soon began to emulate the elite in their choice of décor, so local artisans cashed in by making copies of the furniture and plates, a tradition which continues to this day. Almost every Skyriot house is festooned with plates, copperware and hand-carved furniture.

Other traditions also endure. Many elderly Skyriot males still dress in the traditional baggy pantaloons and *trohadia* (multi-thonged footwear unique to the island). The Skyros Carnival is Greece's weirdest and most wonderful festival, and is the subject of Joy Coulentianou's book *The Goat Dance of Skyros*.

Another special feature of Skyros which shouldn't go unmentioned, although it will probably go unseen, is the wild Skyrian pony, a breed unique to Skyros. The ponies used to roam freely in the southern half of the island, but are now almost extinct.

Finally, Skyros was the last port of call of the English poet Rupert Brooke (1887-1915), who died of septicaemia on a ship off the coast of Skyros in 1915, *en route* to Gallipoli.

Getting There & Away

Air In summer there are at least five flights a week between Athens and Skyros (50 minutes, 13,800 dr) on all days except Friday and Monday. Olympic Airways is represented by Skyros Travel & Tourism Agency, in Skyros town.

Ferry & Hydrofoil There are ferries at least twice a day, including the F/B *Lykomidis* to and from the port of Kymi (Evia) and Skyros (2½ hours, 1800 dr). There are three hydrofoils a week to Volos (4¼ hours, 10,200 dr) via Alonnisos (4400 dr), Skopelos town

Skyros Carnival

In this pre-Lenten festival, which takes place on the last two Sundays before *Kathara Deftera* (Clean Monday – the first Monday in Lent), young men don goat masks, hairy jackets and dozens of copper goat bells. They then proceed to clank and dance around town, each with a partner (another man), dressed up as a Skyriot bride but also wearing a goat mask. Women and children also wear fancy dress. During these revelries there is singing and dancing, performances of plays, recitations of satirical poems and drinking and feasting. These riotous goings-on are overtly pagan, with elements of Dionysian festivals, goat worship (in ancient times Skyros was renowned for its excellent goat meat and milk), and the cult of Achilles, the principal deity worshipped here. The transvestism evident in the carnival may derive from the fact that Achilles hid on Skyros dressed as a girl to escape the oracle's prophecy that he would die in battle at Troy. ■

(4600 dr), Glossa (Skopelos) and Skiathos (5800 dr), and six per week to Kymi (45 minutes, 4000 dr).

You can buy ferry tickets from Lykomidis Ticket Office (☎ 91 789; fax 91 791), on Agoras in Skyros town. The hydrofoil ticket office is on Agoras, 40 metres north of Skyros Travel & Tourism. There are also ferry and hydrofoil ticket offices at Linaria. The port police telephone no is ☎ 91 475.

Getting Around

In addition to the options listed below, it is also possible to join a boat trip to sites around the island. See Organised Tours under the Skyros town entry.

Bus There are five buses a day from Skyros town to Linaria (200 dr), Molos (via Magazia) and the airport. Buses for both Skyros town and Molos meet the boats and hydrofoils at Linaria. Bus services to other parts of the island are lousy. The bus time-table is published in the window of Skyros Travel & Tourism, but any further information must be obtained from the bus drivers themselves.

Car & Motorbike Cars can be rented from Skyros Travel & Tourism Agency (see under Organised Tours). Cheap & Nice Motorbikes (☎ 92 022) are hardly cheap (3500 dr for 50 cc and 4000 dr for 80 cc), but they claim the bikes are the best maintained on the island because 'the mechanic is English'. To

find the outlet, walk north and take the second turn right past Skyros Travel & Tourism Agency.

SKYROS TOWN

Skyros' capital is a striking, dazzling white town of flat-roofed Cycladic-style houses draped over a high rocky bluff, topped by a 13th-century fortress and the monastery of Agios Georgios. It is a gem of a place and a wander around its labyrinthine whitewashed streets is more than likely to produce an invitation to admire a traditional Skyrian house by its proud and hospitable owner.

Orientation

The bus terminal is at the southern end of town on the main thoroughfare of Agoras, an animated street lined with tavernas, snack bars and grocery shops, flanked by narrow winding alleyways. To reach the central square of Plateia Iroön walk straight ahead up the hill.

Walk along Agoras, beyond Plateia Iroön, and eventually you will come to a fork in the road. The right fork leads up to the fortress and Moni Agiou Georgiou (with fine frescoes), from where there are breathtaking views. The left fork leads to Plateia Rupert Brooke, which is dominated by a disconcerting nude bronze statue; the effigy of the real Rupert Brooke is on the pedestal. This statue caused an outcry among the islanders when it was first installed in the 1930s. From this square a cobbled, stepped path leads in 15 minutes to Magazia beach.

Information

Skyros does not have a tourist office or tourist police. The regular police (☎ 91 274) are just beyond Cheap & Nice Motorbikes (see the Skyros island Getting Around section).

To get to the post office, take the first turn right after the bus terminal and it's on the left. The OTE is on the main road, a little way back towards Linaria, on the right as you walk from the bus terminal. Skyros' postcode is 340 07 and the telephone code is 0222. The National Bank of Greece is on Agoras, a little way up from the bus terminal on the left.

Museums

There are three museums in Skyros town. The **archaeological museum** features an impressive collection of artefacts from Mycenaean to Roman times, as well as a traditional Skyrian house interior, transported in its entirety from the home of the benefactor. It is open Tuesday to Sunday from 8.30 am to 3 pm. Admission is 500 dr.

The **Faltaïts Museum** is a private museum housing the outstanding collection of Manos Faltaïts, a Skyriot ethnologist. The contents include costumes, furniture, books, ceramics and photographs and is a truly admirable collection. Opening times are from 10 am to 1 pm, and 5.30 to 8 pm. Admission is free. Both museums are just off Plateia Rupert Brooke.

The little-known **Traditional Skyrian House** is just what its name implies. It's difficult to find, but worth the effort. Take the steps which lead up to the fortress. When you come to a crossroad with house No 993 straight ahead, turn left and the museum is a little way along on the left. Opening times are Monday to Saturday from 11 am to noon and 6 to 8 pm. Admission is 400 dr.

Courses

The Skyros Institute runs courses on a whole range of subjects, from yoga and dancing, to massage and windsurfing. The emphasis is on learning to develop a holistic approach to life. The main centre is in Skyros town, and there is a branch at Atsitsa beach, on the west coast. For more information contact The Skyros Centre (☎ 0171-267 4424/284 3065; fax 0171-284 3063), 92 Prince of Wales Rd, London NW5 3NE, UK.

Organised Tours

Skyros Travel & Tourism Agency (☎ 91 600; fax 92 123), on the left, north of the central square, has two boat excursions: one to the Nyfi spring, Tris Boukes, Rupert Brooke's grave and Kalamitsa beach; and the other to Sarakino islet and the sea caves of Pendekali and Gerania. Both excursions cost 3000 dr.

Places to Stay – bottom end

In Skyros town there are many rooms (decorated with traditional plates) to rent in private houses; the owners meet the buses from Linaria, but there is a dearth of organised hotel-style rooms. If there are two of you, the best bet is for one person to look after the luggage while the other goes to inspect a room, because quality varies enormously.

The cheapest hotel is the E-class *Hotel Eleni* (☎ 91 738), next to the post office, with tidy singles/doubles for 3500/7000 dr with bathroom. The luxurious *Lykomedes House* (☎ 91 697) has spacious rooms with terraces affording fine hill vistas. There is an ultramodern communal kitchen and dining area; doubles are 7000 dr. Walk north along Agoras and turn sharp left at the Flying Dolphin Agency, turn right at the Pegasus Restaurant, and the rooms are a little beyond Kabanera Restaurant, on the left.

Maria Emmanouil-Fregadi (☎ 91 582) has a couple of traditional *rooms* to rent. She also has a wonderful traditional home of her own, including a 300-year-old loom. Her house is to the left of the Megali Strata – the little street leading to Plateia Rupert Brooke. Ask for directions once you are within shouting distance.

Places to Stay – middle

Moraïtis Houses (☎ 92 123) is a small

number of delightful apartments in one of the nicest parts of town, high up above the town. A traditional double room here goes for 12,000 dr. Contact Skyros Travel & Tourism for bookings and directions.

The B-class *Hotel Nefeli* (☎ 91 964; fax 92 061) is one of the best hotels in Skyros town. The lovely rooms have enlarged black and white photographs depicting traditional Skyrian life. Rates are 11,300/16,100 dr for doubles/triples with private bathroom. The hotel is on the left just before you enter Skyros town.

The same hotel can organise your stay in *Skyriana Spitia*, an apartment complex made up of new, self-contained units in traditional Skyrian style. It costs 26,800 dr for an apartment for two to four people.

Places to Eat

With a few exceptions, Skyros town lacks memorable eating establishments. The most exceptional is *Kristina's Restaurant* in a delightful walled garden. Kristina is an Australian who conjures up delectable local and international dishes. The kasseri cheese and sac cheese (local specialities), chicken fricassee and cheesecake are recommended. The restaurant is open only in the evenings. Walk south along the main street, beyond the OTE where the road forks, continue straight ahead, bear right and the restaurant is on the left. The unpretentious *Glaros Restaurant*, on Agoras, near the central square, serves the best Greek food in town. The restaurant is next door to the *Sibosio* ouzeri and its sign is only in Greek.

O Pigasos restaurant is more expensive, has a chic ambience and is for that special meal. It has a mixed Greek and European menu. Turn left after Skyros Travel & Tourism and you will find it 20 metres down on your right.

The Sweets Workshop, on Agoras, has a vast array of mouth-watering traditional cakes, chocolates, nuts and Turkish delight.

Entertainment

The popularity enjoyed by particular bars in Skyros is ephemeral, but flavours of the month at the time of research were the stylish *Artistico*, the *Apokalypsis*, *Kalipso* and the *Renaissance Pub*, all on or just off Agoras. *Borio*, just south of Skyros town, was an 'in' disco. At Linaria *To Kastro* is another 'in' disco club, as is *O Kavos* for drinks and evening gossip. Both overlook the harbour.

MAGAZIA & MOLOS Μαγαζιά & Μώλος

The resort of Magazia is at the southern end of a splendid long sandy beach, a short distance east of Skyros town; quieter Molos is at the northern end, although there is not much to physically distinguish between the two communities these days.

Places to Stay – bottom end & middle

Skyros has one camp site, *Skyros Camping* (☎ 92 458), at Magazia. It's a scruffy run-down place with a few thirsty-looking olive trees offering shade. Freelance campers stake out without hassle at Atsitsa among the pines, and at nearby Kyra Panagia, both on the west coast (see Beaches).

Efrosyni Varsamou Rooms (☎ 91 142), above the family ceramics shop, in Magazia, are spacious and beautifully furnished. Rates are 9600/11,000 dr for doubles/triples. If you're walking, go down the cobbled path from Skyros town, turn right at the bottom, and then right at the camp site (signposted Magazia and the Xenia Hotel) and the rooms are on the left. If you get the bus, get off at the camp site.

If you turn left at the Xenia Hotel, in just under 150 metres you will come to the *Alekos Domatia* (☎ 91 828), on the right, overlooking the beach. Pleasant and comfortable doubles/triples are 12,000/14,000 dr with private bathroom.

At Molos, the *Motel Hara* (☎ 91 763) has clean, pine-furnished double/triple rooms for 11,000/13,200 dr. It also has some newer self-contained apartments. If you arrive by bus look for the motel on the right. *Angela's Bungalows* (☎ 91 764; fax 92 030), set in a lovely garden, has clean, spacious single/double/triple rooms with bathroom, balcony and telephone for 10,000/13,000/15,600 dr, including breakfast. The bungalows are signposted from the Molos bus terminal. The C-class *Hotel Paradise* (☎ 91 220; fax 92 030), next to the bus terminal, is an attractive hotel with cream marble floors and white walls. Rates here are 12,000/14,400 dr for doubles/triples.

Places to Stay – top end
The island's most luxurious hotel is the A-class *Skyros Palace* (☎ 91 994; fax 92 070), a complex of attractive apartments, which stands in splendid isolation just north of Molos. The apartments have air-con, verandas and music channels. The complex has a café, bar, restaurant, TV lounge and swimming pool, and is 50 metres from a beach. Ask for a mosquito zapper: these little nasties can be a problem here. Singles/doubles go for 14,000/18,900 dr in high season.

Things to Buy
A good selection of ceramics is on sale at Efrosyni Varsamou's shop below the domatia of the same name at Magazia (see Places to Stay). It's hard to imagine any non-Skyriot wanting to wear the multi-thonged trohadia, but maybe they'd appeal to someone with a foot fetish who is into bondage. They can be bought at the Argo Shop, on the street which leads to Plateia Rupert Brooke.

AROUND THE ISLAND
Beaches
At **Atsitsa**, on the west coast, there's a tranquil pebble beach shaded by pines. The beach attracts freelance campers and there's a branch of the Skyros Institute and a taverna/domatia here. Just to the north is the even less crowded beach of **Kyra Panagia** (also with freelance campers). At **Pefkos**, 10 km south of Atsitsa, there is another good beach. If you don't have transport take a Skyros town-Linaria bus and ask to be let off at the turn-off. Further south, the pebble-and-sand beach at **Kalamitsa** is rated as one of the island's best.

Rupert Brooke's Grave
Rupert Brooke's well-tended grave is in an olive grove on the east side of Tris Boukes bay in the south of the island. The grave stone is inscribed with the apt epitaph:

> If I should die think only this of me:
> That there's some corner of a foreign field
> That is forever England.

No buses go to this corner of the island. You can take an excursion boat, or drive or walk along a rough scenic road from Kalamitsa that is currently being upgraded . If you walk it will take about 1½ hours; take food and water.

Language Guide

The Greek language is probably the oldest European language, with an oral tradition of 4000 years, and a written tradition of approximately 3000 years. Its evolution was characterised by its strength during the golden age of Athens; its use as a lingua franca throughout the Middle Eastern world, spread by Alexander the Great and his successors as far as India during the Hellenistic period (330 BC-100 AD); its adaptation as the language of the new religion, Christianity; its use as the official language of the Eastern Roman Empire; and its eventual proclamation as the language of the Byzantine Empire (380-1453 AD).

Greek maintained its status and prestige during the rise of the European Renaissance and was employed as the linguistic perspective for all contemporary sciences and terminologies during the period of Enlightenment. Today, Greek constitutes a large part of the vocabulary of any Indo-European language, and much of the lexicon of any scientific repertoire.

The modern Greek language is a southern Greek dialect which is now used by most Greek speakers in Greece, Cyprus and abroad. It is the result of an intralinguistic influence and synthesis of the ancient vocabulary combined with lexemes from Greek regional dialects – namely Cretan, Cypriot and Macedonian.

Greek is spoken throughout Greece and Cyprus by a population of around 11 million, and by some five million Greeks who live abroad.

For a more detailed guide to the Greek language, check out Lonely Planet's *Greek Phrasebook*.

Stress

All Greek words of two or more syllables have an acute accent which indicates where the stress falls. For instance, άγαλμα (statue) is pronounced A-ghal-ma, and αγάπη (love) is pronounced a-GHA-pi.

Greetings & Civilities

Hello.
YA sas	Γειά σας.
YA sou (informal)	Γειά σου.

Goodbye.
and-I-o	Αντίο.

Good morning.
kali-ME-ra	Καλημέρα.

Good afternoon.
HE-ret-e	Χαίρετε.

Good evening.
kali-SPE-ra	Καλησπέρα.

Good night.
kali-NIH-ta	Καληνύχτα.

Please.
para-ka-LO	Παρακαλώ.

Thank you.
ef-hari-STO	Ευχαριστώ.

Yes.
ne	Ναι.

No.
O-hi	Οχι.

Sorry. (excuse me, forgive me)
sigh-NO-mi	Συγνώμη.

How are you?
ti KA-nete	Τι κάνετε;
ti KA-nis (informal)	Τι κάνεις;

Well, thanks.
ka-LA ef-hari-STO	Καλά ευχαριστώ.

Essentials

I (don't) understand.
(dhen) katala-VE-no	(Δεν) καταλαβαίνω.

Do you speak English?
mi-LA-te angli-KA	Μιλάτε Αγγλικά;

Where is...?
pou I-ne	Πού είναι...;

How much?
PO-so KA-ni	Πόσο κάνει;

When?
PO-te	Πότε;

Where are the toilets?
pou I-ne i toua-LE-tez	Πού είναι οι τουαλέτες;

Greek Alphabet & Pronunciation

Greek	Pronunciation Guide		Example		
Α α	a	like the *a* in 'father'	αγάπη	a-GHA-pi	love
Β β	v	as in 'vine'	βήμα	VI-ma	step
Γ γ	gh	like a rough *g*	γάτα	GHA-ta	cat
	y	as in 'yes'	για	ya	for
Δ δ	dh	as in 'there'	δέμα	DHE-ma	parcel
Ε ε	e	as in 'egg'	ένας	E-nas	one (m)
Ζ ζ	z	as in 'zoo'	ζώο	ZO-o	animal
Η η	i	as in 'feet'	ήταν	IT-an	was
Θ θ	th	as in 'throw'	θέμα	THE-ma	theme
Ι ι	i	as in 'feet'	ίδιος	I-dhy-os	same
Κ κ	k	as in 'kite'	καλά	ka-LA	well
Λ λ	l	as in 'leg'	λάθος	LA-thos	mistake
Μ μ	m	as in 'man'	μαμά	ma-MA	mother
Ν ν	n	as in 'net'	νερό	ne-RO	water
Ξ ξ	x	as in 'ox'	ξύδι	KSI-dhi	vinegar
Ο ο	o	as in 'hot'	όλα	O-la	all
Π π	p	as in 'pup'	πάω	PA-o	I go
Ρ ρ	r	as in 'road'	ρέμα	RE-ma	stream
		a slightly trilled *r*	ρόδα	RO-dha	tyre
Σ σ, ς	s	as in 'sand'	σημάδι	si-MA-dhi	mark
Τ τ	t	as in 'tap'	τόπι	TO-pi	ball
Υ υ	i	as in 'feet'	ύστερα	IS-ter-a	after
Φ φ	f	as in 'find'	φύλλο	FI-lo	leaf
Χ χ	h	like the *ch* in the Scottish loch, or	χάνω	HA-no	I lose
		like a rough *h*	χέρι	HE-ri	hand
Ψ ψ	ps	as in 'lapse'	ψωμί	pso-MI	bread
Ω ω	o	as in 'hot'	ώρα	O-ra	time

Help!
vo-I-thya   Βοήθεια!
Go away!
FI-ye   Φύγε!
Doctor!
ya-TRO   γιατρό!
Police!
astino-MI-a   Αστυνομία!

There's been an accident.
E-yine a-TI-hima
Εγινε ατύχημα.

Small Talk

What is your name?
pos sas LE-ne   Πώς σας λένε;
My name is...
me LE-ne...   Με λένε...

Where are you from?
a-PO pou I-ste   Από πού είστε;
I am from...
I-me a-PO   Είμαι από...
Australia
af-stra-LI-a   Αυστραλία
England
ang-LI-a   Αγγλία
New Zealand
NE-a zilan-DHI-a   Νέα Ζηλανδία
America
amer-i-KI   Αμερική

How old are you?
PO-son hro-NON I-ste
Πόσων χρονών είστε;

I am...years old.
I-me...hro-NON   Είμαι...χρονών.

Combinations of Letters

The combinations of letters shown here are pronounced as follows:

Greek		Pronunciation Guide	Example		
ει	i	as in 'feet'	είδα	I-dha	I saw
οι	i	as in 'feet'	οικόπεδο	i-KO-pe-dho	land
αι	e	as in 'bet'	αίμα	E-ma	blood
ου	u	as in 'mood'	πού	pou	where
μπ	b	as in 'beer'	μπάλα	BA-la	ball
	mb	as in 'amber'	κάμπος	KAM-bos	forest
ντ	d	as in 'dot'	ντουλάπα	dou-LA-pa	wardrobe
	nd	as in 'bend'	πέντε	PEN-de	five
γκ	g	as in 'God'	γκάζι	GA-zi	gas
γγ	ng	as in 'angle'	αγγελία	an-ge-LI-a	classified
γξ	ks	as in 'minks'	σφιγξ	sfinks	sphynx
τζ	dz	as in 'hands'	τζάκι	DZA-ki	fireplace

The pairs of vowels shown above are pronounced separately if the first has an acute accent, or the second a dieresis, as in the examples below:

γαϊδουράκι	ga-i-dhou-RA-ki	little donkey
Κάιρο	KA-i-ro	Cairo

Some Greek consonant sounds have no English equivalent. The υ of the groups αυ, ευ and ηυ is generally pronounced *v*.

The Greek question mark is represented with the English equivalent of a semicolon ;.

Getting Around

How do I get to...
pos tha PA-o sto/sti
Πώς θα πάω στο/στη...

I'd like...
tha I-thela
Θα ήθελα...

a one-way ticket
mo-NO isi-TI-rio
μονό εισιτήριο

a return ticket
isi-TI-rio me epistro-FI
εισιτήριο με επιστροφή

two tickets
DHI-o isi-TI-ria
δύο εισιτήρια

a student's fare
fiti-ti-KO isi-TI-rio
φοιτητικό εισιτήριο

1st class
PRO-ti THE-si
πρώτη θέση

economy
touristi-KI THE-si
τουριστική θέση

railway station
sidhirodromi-KOS stath-MOS
σιδηροδρομικός σταθμός

timetable
dhromo-LO-gio
δρομολόγιο

What time does the boat leave/arrive?
ti O-ra FEV-yi/FTA-ni to ka-RA-vi
Τι ώρα φεύγει/φτάνει το καράβι;

plane
aero-PLA-no
αεροπλάνο

boat
ka-RA-vi
καράβι

bus (city)
asti-KO
αστικό

bus (intercity)
  leofor-I-o   λεωφορείο
train
  TRE-no   τραίνο
taxi
  ta-XI   ταξί

Where can I hire a car?
  pou bo-RO na ni-kiA-so E-na afto-KI-nito
  Πού μπορώ να νοικιάσω ένα αυτοκίνητο;

Directions
I am lost.
  E-ho ha-THI   Έχω χαθεί.
Where is...?
  pou I-ne   Πού είναι ...;
Is it near?
  I-ne makri-A   Είναι μακριά;
Is it far?
  I-ne kon-DA   Είναι κοντά;
straight ahead
  ef-THI-a   ευθεία
left
  ari-ste-RA   αριστερά
right
  dhe-ksi-A   δεξιά
behind
  PI-so   πίσω
in front of
  bro-STA a-PO   μπροστά από
far
  makri-A   μακριά
near
  kon-DA   κοντά
opposite
  a-PE-nandi   απέναντι

Can you show me on the map?
  bo-RI-te na mou DHI-ksete sto HAR-ti
  Μπορείτε να μου δείξετε στο χάρτη;

Useful Signs
ΕΙΣΟΔΟΣ	ENTRY
ΓΥΝΑΙΚΩΝ	WOMEN (toilets)
ΑΝΔΡΩΝ	MEN (toilets)
ΝΟΣΟΚΟΜΕΙΟ	HOSPITAL
ΠΛΗΡΟΦΟΡΙΕΣ	INFORMATION
ΑΠΑΓΟΡΕΥΕΤΑΙ	
ΤΟ ΚΑΠΝΙΣΜΑ	NO SMOKING
ΑΣΤΥΝΟΜΙΑ	POLICE
ΑΠΑΓΟΡΕΥΕΤΑΙ	PROHIBITED
ΕΙΣΙΤΗΡΙΑ	TICKETS
ΕΚΔΟΤΗΡΙΑ	TICKET
ΕΙΣΙΤΗΡΙΩΝ	OFFICE

Around Town
I'm looking for...
  PSA-hno   Ψάχνω...
bank
  TRA-peza   τράπεζα
the...embassy
  tin...pres-VI-a   την...πρεσβεία
market
  ago-RA   αγορά
museum
  mou-SI-o   μουσείο
police
  astino-MI-a   αστυνομία
post office
  tahi-dhro-MI-o   ταχυδρομείο
tourist office
  touristi-KO gra-FI-o   τουριστικό
                         γραφείο
beach
  para-LI-a   παραλία
castle
  KA-stro   κάστρο
church
  ekli-SI-a   εκκλησία
ruins
  e-RI-pia   ερείπια

I want to exchange some money.
  THE-lo si-NA-laghma
  Θέλω συνάλλαγμα.

Accommodation
Where is...?
  pou I-ne   Πού είναι...;
a cheap hotel
  E-na fti-NO xenodo-HI-o
  ένα φτηνό ξενοδοχείο

a good hotel
  E-na ka-LO xenodo-HI-o
  ένα καλό ξενοδοχείο
a youth hostel
  E-nas xe-NO-nas ne-O-itos
  ένας ξενώνας νεότητος

a camp site
  E-na KAM-ping   ένα κάμπιγκ

I'd like a...
  THE-lo E-na   Θέλω ένα...
single
  mo-NO   μονό
double
  dhi-PLO   διπλό
room
  dho-MA-tio   δωμάτιο
with bathroom
  me BA-nio   με μπάνιο

How much is it... ?
  PO-so KA-ni   Πόσο κάνει...;
per night
  ti vra-dhy-A   τη βραδυά
for...nights
  ya...vradhy-EZ   για...βραδυές

Is breakfast included?
  simberi-lam-VA-nike pro-i-NO
  Συμπεριλαμβάνει και πρωϊνό;

Can I see it?
  bo-RO na to dho   Μπορώ να το δω;
Where is the bathroom?
  pou I-ne to BA-nio   Πού είναι το
                         μπάνιο;
It's expensive.
  I-ne po-LI akri-VO   Είναι πολύ
                         ακριβό.
I'm leaving today.
  FEV-gho SI-mera   Φεύγω σήμερα.
key
  kli-DHI   κλειδί

Food
I'd like...
  tha I-thela   Θα ήθελα...
breakfast
  pro-i-NO   πρωϊνό
lunch
  mes-im-vri-NO   μεσημβρινό
dinner
  DHI-pno   δείπνο
wine
  kras-I   κρασί

beef
  vodhi-NO   βοδινό
bread
  pso-MI   ψωμί
beer
  BI-ra   μπύρα
cheese
  ti-RI   τυρί
chicken
  ko-TO-poulo   κοτόπουλο
Greek coffee
  elini-KOS ka-FES   ελληνικός καφές
iced coffee
  frap-PE   φραππέ
lamb
  ar-NI   αρνί
milk
  GHA-la   γάλα
mineral water
  metali-KO ne-RO   μεταλλικό νερό
tea
  TSA-i   τσάι
wine
  kra-SI   κρασί

I am a vegetarian.
  I-me horto-FA-ghos   Είμαι
                         χορτοφάγος.

Shopping
How much is it?
  PO-so KA-ni   Πόσο κάνει;
I'm just looking.
  a-PLOS ki-TA-zo   απλώς κοιτάζω.

I'd like to buy...
  THE-lo na-gho-RA-so...
  Θέλω να'γοράσω...

Do you accept credit cards?
  PER-nete pistoti-KEZ KAR-tez
  παίρνετε πιστωτικές κάρτες;

Could you lower the price?
  bo-RI-te na mou KA-nete mya
  ka-LI-teri ti-MI?
  Μπορείτε να μου κάνετε μια
  καλύτερη τιμή;

Time & Dates

What time is it?		
ti O-ra I-ne	Τι ώρα είναι;	
It's...		
I-ne	Είναι...	
1 o'clock		
MI-a i O-ra	μία η ώρα	
2 o'clock		
DHI-o i O-ra	δύο η ώρα	
7.30		
ef-Ta ke mi-SI	εφτά και μισή	
am		
to pro-I	το πρωί	
pm		
to a-PO-yevma	το απόγευμα	

Sunday		
kiria-KI	Κυριακή	
Monday		
dhef-TE-ra	Δευτέρα	
Tuesday		
TRI-ti	Τρίτη	
Wednesday		
te-TA-rti	Τετάρτη	
Thursday		
PEMP-ti	Πέμπτη	
Friday		
para-ske-VI	Παρασκευή	
Saturday		
SA-va-to	Σάββατο	

January		
yanou-A-rios	Ιανουάριος	
February		
fevrou-A-rios	Φεβρουάριος	
March		
MAR-tios	Μάρτιος	
April		
a-PRIL-ios	Απρίλιος	
May		
MA-ios	Μάιος	
June		
YOUN-ios	Ιούνιος	
July		
YOUL-ios	Ιούλιος	
August		
AV-ghoust-os	Αύγουστος	
September		
sep-TEM-vrios	Σεπτέμβριος	

October		
ok-TO-vrios	Οκτώβριος	
November		
no-EM-vrios	Νοέμβριος	
December		
dhe-KEM-vrios	Δεκέμβριος	

today		
SI-mera	σήμερα	
tonight		
a-PO-pse	απόψε	
now		
TO-ra	τώρα	
yesterday		
hthes	χθες	
tomorrow		
AV-rio	αύριο	

Numbers & Amounts

0	mi-DHEN	μηδέν	
1	E-nas	ένας (m)	
	MI-a	μία (f)	
	E-na	ένα (neuter)	
2	DHI-o	δύο	
3	tris	τρεις (m&f)	
	TRI-a	τρία (neuter)	
4	TE-sera	τέσσερα (neuter)	
	TE-seris	τέσσερεις (m&f)	
5	PEN-de	πέντε	
6	EX-i	έξη	
7	ep-TA	επτά	
8	oh-TO	οχτώ	
9	e-NE-a	εννέα	
10	DHE-ka	δέκα	
11	EN-dheka	ένδεκα	
20	I-kosi	είκοσι	
30	tri-AN-da	τριάντα	
40	sa-RAN-da	σαράντα	
50	pe-NIN-da	πενήντα	
60	ex-IN-da	εξήντα	
70	evdho-MIN-da	εβδομήντα	
80	og-DHON-da	ογδόντα	
90	ene-NIN-da	ενενήντα	
100	eka-TO	εκατό	
1000	HI-lia	χίλια (neuter)	
	HI-li-i	χίλιοι (m)	
	HI-li-es	χίλιες (f)	
one million			
E-na ekato-MI-rio		ένα εκατομμύριο	

Health

I need a doctor.
hri-A-zome ya-TRO Χρειάζομαι
       γιατρό.

I want something for...
the-lo KA-ti ya Θέλω κάτι για...

insect bites
tsim-BI-mata a-PO EN-doma
τσιμπήματα από έντομα

travel sickness
naf-TI-a taxidhi-OU
ναυτία ταξιδιού

diarrhoea
dhi-A-ria   διάρροια

aspirin
aspi-RI-ni   ασπιρίνη

condoms
profilakti-KA (ka-PO-tez)
προφυλακτι (κάκαπότες)

contact lenses
fa-KI epa-FIS φακοί επαφής

medical insurance
yatri-KI as-FA-lya ιατρική
       ασφάλεια

Can you take me to hospital?
bo-RI-te na me PA-te sto nosoko-MI-o
Μπορείτε να με πάτε στο νοσοκομείο;

Glossary

Achaean Civilisation – see *Mycenaean civilisation*

acropolis – highest point of an ancient city

AEK – Athens football club

agia (f), **agios** (m) – saint

agora – commercial area of an ancient city; shopping precinct in modern Greece

amphora – large two-handled vase in which wine or oil was kept

ANEK – Anonymi Naftiliaki Eteria Kritis; main shipping line to Crete

Archaic period (800-480 BC) – period in which the city-states emerged from the 'dark age' and traded their way to wealth and power; the city-states were unified by a Greek alphabet and common cultural pursuits, engendering a sense of national identity; also known as the Middle Age

architrave – part of the *entablature* which rests on the columns of a temple

arhontika – 17th and 18th-century AD mansions which belonged to archons, the leading citizens of a town

Arvanites – Albanian-speakers of northwestern Greece

Asia Minor – the Aegean litoral of Turkey centred around İzmir but also including İstanbul; formerly populated by Greeks

askitiria – mini-chapels; places of solitary worship

baglamas – miniature bouzouki with a tinny sound

basilica – early Christian church

bouleuterion – council house

bouzouki – stringed lute-like instrument associated with rembetika music

bouzoukia – 'bouzoukis'; used to mean any nightclub where the bouzouki is played and low-grade blues songs are sung; see *skyladika*

buttress – support built against the outside of a wall

Byzantine Empire – characterised by the merging of Hellenistic culture and Christianity and named after Byzantium, the city on the Bosporus which became the capital of the Roman Empire in 324 AD; when the Roman Empire was formally divided in 395 AD, Rome went into decline and the eastern capital, renamed Constantinople after Emperor Constantine I, flourished; the Byzantine Empire dissolved after the fall of Constantinople to the Turks in 1453

capital – top of a column

cella – room in a temple where the cult statue stood

choregos – wealthy citizen who financed choral and dramatic performances

chryselephantine statue – ivory and gold statue

city-states – states comprising a sovereign city and its dependencies; the city-states of Athens and Sparta were famous rivals

classical Greece – period in which the city-states reached the height of their wealth and power after the defeat of the Persians in the 5th century BC; ended with the decline of the city-states as a result of the Peloponnesian Wars, and the expansionist aspirations of Philip II, King of Macedon (ruled 359-336 BC), and his son, Alexander the Great (ruled 336-323 BC)

Corinthian – order of Greek architecture recognisable by columns with bell-shaped *capitals* with sculpted elaborate ornaments based on acanthus leaves

cornice – the upper part of the *entablature*, extending beyond the frieze

crypt – lowest part of a church, often a burial chamber

Cycladic civilisation (3000-1100 BC) – civilisation which emerged following the settlement of Phoenician colonists on the Cycladic islands

cyclopes – mythical one-eyed giants

dark age (1200 - 800 BC) – period in which Greece was under *Dorian* rule

delfini – dolphin; common name for hydrofoil

diglossy – the existence of two forms of one language within a country; has existed in Greece for most of its modern history

dimarhio – town hall

Dimotiki – demotic Greek language; the official spoken language of Greece

domatio (s), **domatia** (pl) – room; a cheap accommodation option available in most tourist areas

Dorians – Hellenic warriors who invaded Greece around 1200 BC, demolishing the city-states and destroying the Mycenaean civilisation; heralded Greece's 'dark age', when the artistic and cultural advancements of the Mycenaeans and Minoans were abandoned; the Dorians later developed into land-holding aristocrats which encouraged the resurgence of independent city-states led by wealthy aristocrats

Doric – order of Greek architecture characterised by a column which has no base, a *fluted* shaft and a relatively plain capital, when compared with the flourishes evident on *Ionic* and *Corinthian* capitals

ELPA – Elliniki Leshi Periigiseon & Aftokinitou; Greek motoring and touring club

ELTA – Ellinika Tahydromia; Greek post office

entablature – part of a temple between the tops of the columns and the roof

EOS – Ellinikos Orivatikos Syllogos; Greek alpine club

EOT – Ellinikos Organismos Tourismou-national tourism organisation which has offices in most major towns

Epitaphios – picture on cloth of Christ on his bier

estiatorio – restaurant serving ready-made food as well as à la carte dishes

ET – Elliniki Tileorasi; state television company

evzones – famous border guards from the northern Greek village of Evzoni; they also guard the Parliament building

Filiki Eteria – friendly society; a group of Greeks in exile; formed during Ottoman rule to organise an uprising against the Turks

fluted – vertical indentations on the shaft of some columns

frappé – iced coffee

frieze – part of the *entablature* which is above the *architrave*

galaktopoleio (s), **galaktopoleia** (pl) – a shop which sells dairy products

Geometric period (1200-800 BC) – period characterised by pottery decorated with geometric designs; sometimes referred to as Greece's 'dark age'

GESEE – Greek trade union association

giouvetsi - casserole of meat and pasta

Hellas, Ellas or **Ellada** – the Greek name for Greece

Helots – original inhabitants of Lakonia whom the Spartans used as slaves

hora – main town (usually on an island)

ikonostasis – altar screen embellished with icons

Ionic – order of Greek architecture characterised by a column with truncated flutes and capitals with ornaments resembling scrolls

kafeneio (s), **kafeneia** (pl) – traditionally a male-only coffee house where cards and backgammon are played

kafeteria – up-market kafeneio, mainly for younger people

kalderimi – cobbled footpath

kasseri – mild, slightly rubbery sheep's milk cheese

kastro – walled-in town

Katharevousa – purist Greek; very rarely used these days

katholikon – principal church of a monastic complex

kefi – an undefinable feeling of good spirit, without which no Greek can have a good time

KKE – Kommounistiko Komma Elladas; Greek communist party

Koine – Greek language used in pre-Byzantine times; the language of the church liturgy

kore – female statue of the Archaic period; see *kouros*

kouros – male statue of the Archaic period,

characterised by a stiff body posture and enigmatic smile

KTEL – Kino Tamio Ispraxeon Leoforion; national bus cooperative; runs all long-distance bus services

Kypriako – the 'Cyprus issue'; politically sensitive and never forgotten by Greeks and Greek Cypriots

libations – in ancient Greece, wine or food which was offered to the gods

libation vessel – utensil from which the wine offered to the gods was poured; see *rhyton*

Linear A – Minoan script; so far undeciphered

Linear B – Mycenaean script; has been deciphered

lyra – small violin-like instrument, played on the knee; common in Cretan and Pontian music

malakas – literally 'wanker'; used as a familiar term of address, or as an insult, depending on context

mangas – 'wide boy' or 'dude'; originally a person of the underworld, now any streetwise person

mayiria – cook houses

megaron – central room of a Mycenaean palace

meltemi – north-easterly wind which blows throughout much of Greece during the summer

metope – sculpted section of a Doric frieze

meze (s), **mezedes** (pl) – appetiser

Middle Age – see *Archaic period*

Minoan civilisation (3000-1100 BC) – Bronze Age culture of Crete named after the mythical King Minos and characterised by pottery and metalwork of great beauty and artisanship

moni – monastery or convent

Mycenaean civilisation (1900-1100 BC) – first great civilisation of the Greek mainland, characterised by powerful independent city-states ruled by kings; also known as the Achaean civilisation

myzithra – soft sheep's milk cheese

narthex – porch of a church

nave – aisle of a church

Nea Dimokratia – New Democracy; conservative political party

necropolis – literally 'city of the dead'; ancient cemetery

nefos – cloud; usually used to refer to pollution in Athens

NEL – Naftiliaki Eteria Lesvou; Lesvos shipping company

neo kyma – 'new wave'; left-wing music of the boîtes and clubs of 1960s Athens

nomarhia – prefecture building

nomos – prefectures into which the regions and island groups of Greece are divided

nymphaeum – in ancient Greece, building containing a fountain and often dedicated to nymphs

OA – Olympiaki Aeroporia or Olympic Airways; Greece's national airline and major domestic air carrier

odeion – ancient Greek indoor theatre

odos – street

ohi – 'no'; what the Greeks said to Mussolini's ultimatum when he said surrender or be invaded; the Italians were subsequently repelled and the event is celebrated on October 28

omphalos – sacred stone at Delphi which the ancient Greeks believed marked the centre of the world

OSE – Organismos Sidirodromon Ellados; Greek railways organisation

OTE – Organismos Tilepikinonion Ellados; Greece's major telecommunications carrier

oud – a bulbous, stringed instrument with a sharply raked-back head

ouzeri (s), **ouzeria** (pl) – place which serves *ouzo* and light snacks

ouzo – a distilled spirit made from grapes and flavoured with aniseed

Panagia – Mother of God; name frequently used for churches

Pantokrator – painting or mosaic of Christ in the centre of the dome of a Byzantine church

pantopoleio – general store

PAO – official initials for Panathinaïkos football club

PAOK – main Thessaloniki football club

paralia – waterfront

PASOK – Panellinio Sosialistiko Komma; Greek socialist party

pediment – triangular section (often filled with sculpture) above the columns, found at the front and back of a classical Greek temple

periptero (s), **periptera** (pl) – streek kiosk

peristyle – columns surrounding a building (usually a temple) or courtyard

pinakotheke – picture gallery

pithos (s), **pithoi** (pl) – large Minoan storage jar

plateia – square

Politiki Anixi – Political Spring; centrist political party

Pomaks – minority, non-Turkic Muslim people from northern Greece

Pontians – Greeks whose ancestral home was on the Black Sea coast of Turkey

PRO-PO – Prognostiko Podosferou; Greek football pools

propylon (s), **propylaia** (pl) – elaborately built main entrance to an ancient city or sanctuary; a propylon had one gateway and a propylaia more than one

psistaria – restaurant serving grilled food

rembetika – blues songs commonly associated with the underworld of the 1920s

retsina – resinated white wine

rhyton – another name for a *libation vessel*

rizitika – traditional, patriotic songs of Crete

sacristy – room attached to a church were sacred vessels etc are kept

sandouri – hammered dulcimer from Asia Minor

Sarakatsani – Greek-speaking nomadic shepherd community from northern Greece

SEO – Syllogos Ellinon Orivaton; Greek mountaineers' association

skites (s), **skiti** (pl) – hermit's dwelling

Skopia – what the Greeks call the Former Yugoslav Republic of Macedonia (FYROM)

skyladika – literally 'dog songs'; popular, but not lyrically challenging, blues songs most often sung in *bouzoukia* nightclubs

spilia – cave

stele – grave stone which stands upright

stoa – long colonnaded building, usually in an *agora*; used as a meeting place and shelter in ancient Greece

taverna – traditional restaurant which serves food and wine

temblon - votive screen

tholos – Mycenaean tomb shaped like a beehive

toumberleki – small lap drum played with the fingers

triglyph – sections of a *Doric frieze* between the *metopes*

trireme – ancient Greek galley with three rows of oars on each side

tsikoudia – Cretan version of *tsipouro*

Tsingani – Gypsies or Romanies

tsipouro – distilled spirit made from grapes

vaulted – having an arched roof, normally of brick or stone

velenza – flokati rug

Vlach – traditional, seminomadic shepherds from northern Greece who speak a latin-based dialect

volta – promenade; evening stroll

volute – spiral decoration on *Ionic* capitals

xythomyzithra – soft sheep's milk cheese

zaharoplasteio (s), **zaharoplasteia** (pl) – pâtisserie; shop which sells cakes, chocolates, sweets and, sometimes, alcoholic drinks

Appendix – Climate Charts

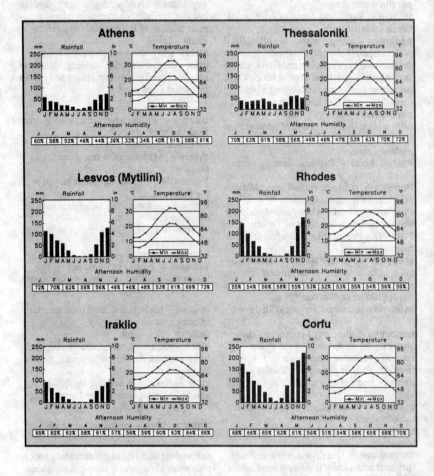

Athens

Rainfall / Temperature

Afternoon Humidity

J	F	M	A	M	J	J	A	S	O	N	D
60%	58%	52%	46%	44%	39%	33%	34%	40%	51%	58%	61%

Thessaloniki

Rainfall / Temperature

Afternoon Humidity

J	F	M	A	M	J	J	A	S	O	N	D
70%	63%	61%	58%	56%	49%	46%	47%	53%	63%	70%	72%

Lesvos (Mytilini)

Rainfall / Temperature

Afternoon Humidity

J	F	M	A	M	J	J	A	S	O	N	D
72%	70%	62%	59%	56%	49%	46%	48%	53%	61%	69%	73%

Rhodes

Rainfall / Temperature

Afternoon Humidity

J	F	M	A	M	J	J	A	S	O	N	D
55%	54%	56%	58%	55%	53%	52%	53%	55%	54%	56%	59%

Iraklio

Rainfall / Temperature

Afternoon Humidity

J	F	M	A	M	J	J	A	S	O	N	D
65%	62%	62%	58%	61%	57%	56%	59%	60%	63%	64%	66%

Corfu

Rainfall / Temperature

Afternoon Humidity

J	F	M	A	M	J	J	A	S	O	N	D
68%	66%	65%	63%	61%	56%	51%	54%	58%	65%	68%	70%

Index

ABBREVIATIONS

Ath – Athens
Att – Attica
Cen – Central Greece
Cre – Crete
Cyc – Cyclades

Dod – Dodecanese
Evi – Evia
Ion – Ionian Islands
NEA – North-Eastern Aegean Islands

NG – Northern Greece
Pel – Peloponnese
SG – Saronic Gulf Islands
Spo – Sporades

MAPS

Aegina (SG) 397
Agathonisi (Dod) 595
Agios Nikolaos (Cre) 487
Alexandroupolis (NG) 386
Alonnisos (Spo) 698
Amorgos (Cyc) 438
Ancient Delphi (Cen) 280
Ancient Olympia (Pel) 264
Andros (Cyc) 414
Argostoli (Ion) 671
Arki & Marathi Islets (Dod) 594
Astypalea (Dod) 562
Athens (Ath) 140
  Acropolis 154
  Ancient Agora 161
  Ancient Athens 156
  Around Athens 197
  National Archaeological
    Museum 166
  Omonia & Train Station Area
    178
  Plaka, Syntagma & Monastiraki
    150
  Veïkou & Koukaki 177
Attica 204

Chios (NEA) 615
Chios Town (NEA) 618
Citadel of Mycenae (Pel) 222
Corfu (Ion) 656
Corfu Town (Ion) 658
Corinth (Pel) 214
Crete 468-9
Cyclades 412

Delos (Cyc) 426
Dodecanese Islands 523

Epiros (NG) 315
Ermoupolis (Cyc) 430
Evia & the Sporades Islands 686

Folegandros (Cyc) 448

Greece
  colour map, between 16 & 17
  Main Ferry Routes 131

Hania (Cre) 506
Hydra (SG) 403

Ikaria & the Fourni Islands
  (NEA) 609
Inousses (NEA) 623
Ioannina (NG) 317
Ionian Islands 654
Ios (Cyc) 445
Iraklio (Cre) 472

Kalamata (Pel) 254
Kalymnos (Dod) 575
Karpathos (Dod) 544
Karyes (NG) 373
Kassos (Dod) 551
Kastellorizo (Dod) 553
Kastoria (NG) 364
Kavala (NG) 376
Kea (Cyc) 460
Kefallonia & Ithaki (Ion) 669
Kos & Pserimos (Dod) 569
Kos Town (Dod) 571
Kythira (Ion) 680
Kythnos (Cyc) 462

Lamia (Cen) 290
Larisa (Cen) 295
Lefkada & Meganisi (Ion) 665
Leros (Dod) 582
Lesvos (Mytilini) (NEA) 627
Limenas (NEA) 649
Limnos (NEA) 636
Lipsi (Dod) 591

Macedonia (NG) 336
Meteora (Cen) 311
Milos & Kimolos (Cyc) 457
Mt Athos Peninsula (NG) 369

Mt Olympus (NG) 352
Mykonos (Cyc) 420
Mystras (Pel) 239
Mytilini (NEA) 629

Nafplio (Pel) 227
Naxos & the Minor Islands
  (Cyc) 433
Naxos Town (Cyc) 435
Nisyros (Dod) 559
North-Eastern Aegean Islands
  598

Palace of Knossos (Cre) 482
Paleohora (Cre) 516
Parga (NG) 329
Paros & Antiparos (Cyc) 441
Patmos (Dod) 586
Patras (Pel) 268
Paxoi & Antipaxoi (Ion) 663
Pelion Peninsula (Cen) 301
Peloponnese 210-211
  Prefectures 211
Pigadia (Dod) 545
Piraeus (Ath) 199
Poros (SG) 400
Pothia (Dod) 578
Prespa Lakes (NG) 361
Preveza (NG) 332
Psara (NEA) 625
Pythagorio (NEA) 605

Rethymno (Cre) 498
Rhodes & Halki (Dod) 525
Rhodes City (Dod) 530

Samos (NEA) 600
Samos Town (Vathy) (NEA) 603
Samothraki (NEA) 641
Sanctuary of Apollo (Cen) 282
Sanctuary of the Great Gods
  (NEA) 644
Santorini (Thira) (Cyc) 451

Saronic Gulf Islands (SG) 396
Serifos (Cyc) 463
Sifnos (Cyc) 465
Sikinos (Cyc) 450
Skiathos (Spo) 690
Skopelos (Spo) 694
Skyros (Spo) 702
Spetses (SG) 408

Sterea Ellada (Cen) 276
Symi (Dod) 565
Syros (Cyc) 428

Thasos (NEA) 647
Thessaloniki (NG) 340
Thessaly (Cen) 293
Thrace (NG) 381

Tilos (Dod) 556
Tinos (Cyc) 417

Volos (Cen) 297

Zakynthos (Ion) 676
Zakynthos Town (Ion) 677

TEXT

Map references are in **bold** type.

accommodation 75, 97-9
  IYHF 75
Achaïa (Pel) 266-74
Achaïa Clauss winery (Pel) 267
acid rain 153
Acrocorinth (Pel) 215-6
Acropolis (Ath) 58-60, 152, **154**
  Museum 159
Acropolis of Ancient Thasos
  (NEA) 649
Acropolis of Lindos (Dod) 538
Adamas (Cyc) 457-8
Adelphi (Spo) 701
Aegiali (Cyc) 438
Aegina (SG) 396-9, **397**
Aegina Town (SG) 397-8
Aeschylus (Ath) 44, 142
Afyssos (Cen) 305
Agamemnon (Pel) 223
Agathi (Dod) 537
Agathonisi (Dod) 594-6, **595**
Agathopes (Cyc) 432
Agia Anna (Cyc) 436
Agia Anna (NG) 373
Agia Anna beach (Cyc) 439
Agia Evthymia (Ion) 672
Agia Galini (Cre) 501, 504-5
Agia Irini (Cyc) 461
Agia Kyriaki (Cen) 305-6
Agia Maria (NG) 365
Agia Marina (Dod) 552, 584
Agia Marina (Dod) 399, 410
Agia Paraskevi (SG) 410
Agia Pelagia (Ion) 681
Agia Roumeli (Cre) 513
Agia Theodoti beach (Cyc) 447
Agia Triada (Cre) 484-5
Agias Trias cathedral (Cyc) 443
Agiasos (NEA) 634
Agiofylli beach (Ion) 668
Agion Oros (NG) 368-75
Agios Ahillios (NG) 360
Agios Andreas (Pel) 256
Agios Dimitrios (Dod) 574
Agios Dimitrios (Spo) 701

Agios Fokas (Dod) 573
Agios Georgios (Spo) 703
Agios Georgios (Cyc) 436, 449
Agios Georgios (Cre) 492
Agios Georgios (Dod) 574
Agios Georgios Sta Gremna
  (Ion) 679
Agios Germanos (NG) 361
Agios Giorgios (Dod) 595
Agios Gordios beach (Ion) 662
Agios Ioannis (Cen) 303
Agios Ioannis beach (Ion) 667
Agios Isidoros (NEA) 635
Agios Kirykos (NEA) 610-1
Agios Konstantinos (Cen) 292
Agios Konstantinos (NEA) 607
Agios Kyprianos (Cyc) 416
Agios Kyprianos (Pel) 250
Agios Nikolaos (Cen) 285
Agios Nikolaos (Cyc) 449
Agios Nikolaos (Cre) 486-9, **487**
Agios Nikolaos (Ion) 679
Agios Petros tower (Cyc) 416
Agios Prokopios (Cyc) 436
Agios Stefanos (Cyc) 423
Agios Yiannis (Cyc) 423
Agios Yiannis (NEA) 639
Agnontas (Spo) 697
Agora (Ath) 160-2, **161**
Agora, Roman (Ath) 163
Agrari beach (Cyc) 424
Agria (Cen) 303
Agria Gramvousa (Cre) 521
Agrinio (Cen) 286-7
Agriolefkes (Cen) 302
Agriolivado beach (Dod) 589
Ahata (Dod) 548
Aheloös River (Cen) 308
Aheron River (NG) 328
Ahillion Palace (Ion) 661
air travel
  departure tax 121
  glossary 110-1
  inter-island flights 124
  mainland flights 122
  mainland to island flights 123-4
  to/from Athens 190

to/from Greece 109-16
travellers with special needs
  112
within Greece 122-4
Akrotiri (Cyc) 454
Akrotiri peninsula (Cre) 512
Alcaeus 49
alcohol 105-6
Alexander the Great 22-3, 142,
  277
Alexandroupolis (NG) 385-9,
  386
Ali Pasha 320, 647
Alinda (Dod) 584-5
Alipa (Pel) 250
Alonia (NEA) 646
Alonnisos (Spo) 697-701, **698**
Alykes (Ion) 679
Alyki (NEA) 651
Amaniou (Dod) 574
Amari valley (Cre) 501
Amfilohia (Cen) 287
Ammoudi (Cyc) 455
Ammounda (Dod) 552
Amopi (Dod) 546-7
Amorgos (Cyc) 437-9, **438**
Anafi (Cyc) 455-6
Anakasia (Cen) 301
Anargyrios, Sotirios 407
Anargyris (SG) 410
Anastenaria (NG) 348
Anatoliki (Cen) 289
Anavatos (NEA) 620
Anaxos (NEA) 632
ancient sites
  Acropolis (Ath) 58-60, 152-9,
    154
  Acropolis (Cen) 294
  Acropolis of Lindos (Dod) 538
  Agia Irini (Cyc) 461
  Agia Triada (Cre) 484-5
  Agios Petros tower (Cyc) 416
  Agora (Ath) 160-2, **161**
  Agora, Roman (Ath) 163
  Akrotiri (Cyc) 454
  Andros (Cyc) 416, **414**
  Arch of Galerius (NG) 343

Argos (Pel) 225
Asclepion (Ath) 160
Asclepion (Dod) 573
Asini (Pel) 230
Athens **156**
Corinth (Pel) 215-6
Dafni (Att) 201-3
Delos (Cyc) 425
Delphi (Cen) 279-83, **280**
Dion (NG) 353-4
Dodoni (NG) 321
Eleusis (Att) 202-3
Epidaurus (Pel) 230-1
Evpalinos tunnel (NEA) 604
Figalia (Pel) 260
Gortyn (Cre) 484
Gortys (Pel) 234
Gournia (Cre) 489-90
Hereon (NEA) 606
Ialyssos (Dod) 539
Ifestia (NEA) 640
Isthmia (Pel) 217
Itanos (Cre) 494
Kamiros (Dod) 539
Kaviria (NEA) 640
Kea Lion (Cyc) 461
Keramikos (Ath) 162-3
Knossos (Cre) 479-83, **482**
Kos (Dod) 570-2
Kydonia (Cre) 508
Lato (Cre) 490
Likosoura (Pel) 233
Limenas (NEA) 648-51
Lissos (Cre) 515
Macedonian tomb, Vergina (NG) 356
Malia (Cre) 486
Marathon tomb (Att) 207
Mycenae (Pel) 219-24
Mystras (Pel) 238-41
Nekromanteio of Aphyra (NG) 328
Nemea (Pel) 218
Nikopolis (NG) 333-4
Olympia (Pel) 209, 262-5, **264**
Paleokastro (Dod) 555
Paleopolis (NEA) 640, 643-5
Pella (NG) 348-9
Phaestos (Cre) 484
Philippi (NG) 379-80
Phylakope (Cyc) 459
Plataea (Cen) 275
Poliohni (NEA) 639
Polyrrinia (Cre) 521
Pyramid of Helenekion (Pel) 225
Roman ruins (Cyc) 459
Roman stadium (Ath) 164

Sanctuary of Apollo (Cen) 281-2
Sanctuary of Hera (NEA) 599
Sanctuary of Poseidon & Amphitrite (Cyc) 419
Sanctuary of the Great Gods (NEA) 643-5
Sanctuary to Hera (NEA) 606
Sikyon (Pel) 218
Sparta (Pel) 237-8
Stoa of Eumenes (Ath) 160
Tegea (Pel) 233
Temple of Aphaia (SG) 398-9
Temple of Aphrodite (Dod) 533
Temple of Apollo (SG) 398
Temple of Olympian Zeus (Ath) 164
Temple of Poseidon (SG) 402
Temple of Pythian Apollo (Dod) 533
Temple of Vasses (Pel) 235
Theatre of Dionysos (Ath) 159-60
Theatre of Herodes Atticus (Ath) 160
Thira (Cyc) 454-5
Tower of the Winds (Ath) 163
Troizen (Pel) 231
Tiryns (Pel) 230
Zakros (Cre) 495
Andissa (NEA) 633
Andritsena (Pel) 235-6
Andros (Cyc) 413-16, **414**
Aneroussa (Cyc) 416
Angali beach (Cyc) 449
Angelokastro (Ion) 662
Angelopoulos, Theodoros 44, 358
Angistri Islet (SG) 399
Ano Boutari (Pel) 249
Ano Mera (Cyc) 424
Ano Meria (Cyc) 449
Ano Syros (Cyc) 429
Ano Volos (Cen) 301
Anopolis (Cre) 513
Antikythira (Ion) 683-4
Antiparos (Cyc) 443-4, **441**
Antipaxoi (Ion) 664, **663**
antiques 108
Antony, Mark 379
Aoös River (NG) 322, 324
Apella (Dod) 548
Aperi (Dod) 548
Aphrodite 35, 37
Apiganos beach (NEA) 624
Apiranthos (Cyc) 436
Apollo 35, 37
Apollonas (Cyc) 436
Apollonia (Cyc) 465

Apostoli (Cre) 501
Arahova (Cen) 283-4
Arcadia (Pel) 232-6
Arch of Galerius (NG) 343
Arch of Hadrian (Ath) 164
Archaeological Museum, Iraklio (Cre) 473-5
Archaeological Museum of Piraeus (Att) 198
Archaic period 18-20, 58
architecture 53-68
Areopagus hill (Ath) 171
Areopoli (Pel) 246-7
Areos Park (Ath) 172
Ares 35-6
Areti (Cyc) 459
Argalasti (Cen) 305
Arginontas (Dod) 581
Argolis (Pel) 218-31
Argonauts 38
Argos (Pel) 224-6
Argostoli (Ion) 670-2, **671**
Arhanes (Cre) 483-4
Arhangelos (Dod) 537
Ariadne (Cre) 480
Arion (NEA) 625
Aristi (NG) 322
Aristotle 47-8, 142, 626
Arkasa (Dod) 547
Arki (Dod) 593-4, **594**
Armades (NEA) 622
Armeni (Cre) 501
Armenistis (NEA) 613
Aroniadika (Ion) 683
art 53-68
Arta (Cen) 308
Arta (NG) 334-5
Artemis 35, 37
Artemon (Cyc) 465
Arvanitohori (Dod) 552
Asclepion (Ath) 160
Asclepion (Dod) 573
Asclepius (Pel) 230
Asfendion (Dod) 574
Asini (Pel) 229
Asklipion (Dod) 540
Aspakas (NEA) 639
Assos (Ion) 673
Astakos (Cen) 287-8
Astros (Pel) 236
Astypalea (Dod) 561-4, **562**
Atatürk, Kemal 29, 342
Athena 35, 37
Athens 139-208, **140, 150, 177, 178, 197**
  Acropolis 141, 152-9, **154**
  banks 145-6
  Byzantine Athens 164
  entertainment 187-90

Athens *cont*
  festivals 174
  getting around 193-6
  getting there & away 190-3
  history 141-3
  museums 164-71
  orientation 143-5
  places to eat 181-7
  places to stay 174-81
  postal services 146
  Roman Athens 163-4
  safety 147-8
  shopping 144, 190
  son et lumière 188
  tourist offices 145
  tours, organised 173
  travel agencies 146-7
  walking tour 148-52
Athos peninsula (NG) 367-8
Atlas 35
Atsitsa (Spo) 706
Attica 203-8, **204**
automobile associations 75
Avgonyma (NEA) 620
Avlakia (NEA) 607
Avlemonas (Ion) 683
Avlona (Dod) 549

Balkan wars 28
Banana beach (Spo) 693
bargaining 72
banks 71
bars 93
Basilica of San Marco (Cre) 475
Batsi (Cyc) 415
Battle of Crete 469, 475, 503
Battle of Khaironeia 281
Battle of Leuctra 22
Battle of Marathon 526
Battle of Navarino 258
Battle of Salamis 526
Bay of Nikopolis (NG) 334
Bay of Polis (Ion) 675
beaches 97
Benaki Museum (Ath) 169
Benitses (Ion) 662
bicycling, *see* cycling
Bird Island (Cre) 491
birdwatching 40, 173
Blefoutis bay (Dod) 585
Blue cave (Dod) 555
boat travel 133-4, *see also* ferry
  travel, hydrofoil
books 80-4
  botanical field guides 83
  children's books 83
  history 81-2
  mythology 81-2
  novels 82

people & society 80-1
poetry 82
travel books & guides 82-3
bookshops 83-4
Botanical Museum (Ath) 172
Bouboulina, Lascarina 409
Bourtzi (Evi) 689
Bourtzi (Spo) 691
Bouzianis, George 68
Brauron, *see* Vravrona
Bridge of Arta (NG) 334
Bronze Age 15-17
bus travel
  to/from Athens 191
  to/from Greece 116-17
  within Athens 193
  within Greece 124
business hours 76
Byron, Lord George 285-6
Byzantine art 62-5
Byzantine Empire 24
Byzantine Museum (Ath) 169-70
Byzantines (Pel) 209

Caesar, Julius 526
camping 97-8
canoeing 306, *see also* kayaking
canyoning 288, 324
Cape Lefkatas (Ion) 668
Cape Sounion (Att) 203-6
car travel, *see* driving
Cassius (Dod) 526
Castello Rossa (Evi) 689
Castle of Antimahia (Dod) 573
Castle of Faraklos (Dod) 537
Castle of Kastellos (Dod) 539
Castle of Monolithos (Dod) 540
Castle of the Knights of St John
  (Dod) 579-80
catamarans 134
Cathedral, Athens 152
Cathedral of St George (Cyc)
  429
Catherine the Great 26
Cavafy, Constantine 49, 82
Cave of Agia Sophia (Ion) 682
Cave of Philoctetes (NEA) 640
Cave of Selai (Dod) 552
Cave of the Nymphs (Ion) 674
Cecrops 208
Cemetery, Athens' First (Ath)
  172
Central Greece 275-313
Centre of Folk Arts & Traditions
  (Ath) 170
ceramics 57-8, 68, 108, 141
  Museum of Traditional Greek
  Ceramics (Ath) 152
Charon (NG) 330

chestnut festival (Cre) 521
children
  activities in Athens 174
  activities in Crete 508-9
  air travel with 112
  children's books 83
Chios (NEA) 614-23, **615**
Chios town (NEA) 617-9, **618**
Christianity 379
churches
  Agia Panagia (Dod) 537
  Agia Sofia (NG) 343
  Agia Sophia (Pel) 242
  Agios Dimitrios (NG) 342
  Agios Dionysios (Ion) 677
  Agios Eleftherios (Ath) 152
  Agios Georgios (NG) 343
  Agios Ioannis Rosses (Evi) 688
  Agios Nikolaos (Dod) 595
  Agios Nikolaos (Ion) 677
  Agios Pavlos (Pel) 242
  Agios Spyridon (Ion) 659
  Cathedral of Christ in Chains
    (Pel) 242
  Dodeka Apostoloi (NG) 343
  Ekatontapyliani (Cyc) 440
  Holy Apostles (Ath) 162
  Metamorphosis (Ath) 149
  Mirtidiotissa (Pel) 242
  Nikolaos Orfanos (NG) 343
  Osios David (NG) 343
  Our Lady of Kassiopi (Ion) 661
  Panagia Ahiropoiitos (NG) 343
  Panagia Evangelistria (Cyc)
    417-18
  Panagia Kera (Cre) 490
  Panagia Paraportiani (Cyc) 422
  St John the Theologian (NG) 365
  the Virgin (Dod) 533
cinema, *see* film
Citadel of Mycenae (Pel) 223,
  222
City of Athens Museum (Ath)
  170-1
civil war 30-1
classical period 20, 59-60
Cleopatra 23
climate 39-40
codeine 86
Communist Party 30
Constantine II 28, 31-2
Constantine the Great 52
Corfu (Ion) 655-63, **656**
Corfu town (Ion) 657-61, **658**
Corinth (Pel) 213-5, **214**
Corinth Canal (Pel) 209, 216-7
Corinthia (Pel) 213-8
courses
  language 95, 173

Skyros Institute (Spo) 704
Cycladic School (Cyc) 447
credit cards 71
Crete 466-521, **468-9**
Archaeological Museum 473-5
getting around 470
getting there & away 470
history 467-70
Cronos 35
Crusades 24-5
cultural events 76-8
Easter 77
culture 51-2
cultural considerations 51-2
traditional lifestyle 51
currency 72
customs regulations 70-1
Cyclades 411-65, **412**
Cycladic art 55-7
Cycladic civilisation 15
cycling 128, 196
Cyclopes 35
Cyprus 31

Daedalus (Cre) 480
Dafni (Att) 201-3
Dafni (NEA) 613
Dalaras, Georgos 50
Damalas (Cyc) 436
Damarionas (Cyc) 436
Damaskinos, Mikhail 476
Damnoni beach (Cre) 504
dance 49-51, 174, 534
Athens 188
ballet 188
folk 49, 107
Danilia village (Ion) 661
Daphne (NG) 373
Daskalogiannis, Ioannis 469, 514
Delavoia (Cyc) 416
Delian League 20, 526
Delos (Cyc) 424-5, **426**
Delphi (Cen) 278-83, **280**
Delphic oracle (Cen) 277, 281
Demeter 35, 37
Democratic Army 30
Dhamala (Pel) (SG) 402
Diafani (Dod) 548
Diakofto (Pel) 271-2
Diakofto-Kalavryta railway
(Pel) 271-2
Diastavrosi (NG) 353
Didymotiho (NG) 389-90
Dikteon cave (Cre) 35, 492
Dimitsana (Pel) 234-5
Dion (NG) 353-4
Dionysos 38
Ancient Theatre of Dionysos 44
Diros caves (Pel) 248

disabled travellers 75-6
diving 94, 253, 499, 534, 668
Dodecanese 522-96, **523**
getting around 524
getting there & away 524
Dodoni (NG) 321
domatia 98
Donoussa (Cyc) 436
Dorians 17-8, 468
Drakeï (NEA) 607
drama 44
Drepano (Pel) 229
Drepanos (NG) 327
drinks 105-7
driving 70
Athens 192-6
rentals 127-8
road rules 126-7
road tolls 126
to/from Greece 116-8
within Greece 126-8
Drogarati cave (Ion) 672
Drugs 93
Dryopida (Cyc) 463
Durrell, Lawrence 82
Dytiki Frangista (Cen) 289

Easter 77
Ecclesiastical Art Museum of
Alexandroupolis (NG) 387
economy 42-3
Edessa (NG) 356-8
Edirne (NG) 391
education 43-4
Eftalou (NEA) 632
Egremini (Ion) 668
El Greco 169, 170, 476
Elafonisi (Cre) 518
Elafonisi (Pel) 243
electricity 80
Elefsina (Att) 203
Eleousa (Dod) 537
Eleusis, see Elefsina
Elgin Marbles 33, (Ath) 158
Elia beach (Cyc) 424
Elia (Pel) 260-6
Elos (Cre) 521
Elounda (Cre) 491
Elpa 75
Elytis, Odysseus 49, 82, 626
embassies 69-70
foreign embassies in Greece 70
Greek embassies abroad 69
Embonas (Dod) 541
Emboreios (Dod) 542-3, 561,
567, 581, 621
emergency 712
Emperor Michael VIII
Paleologus 211, 238

employment, see work
Empros Thermae 573
Enipeas River (NG) 349
Ennia Horia (Cre) 521
entertainment 106-8
environmental issues
acid rain 153
Aheloös dam 308
deforestation 39
olive trees 39, see also flora
traffic congestion 195
EOS, see Greek Alpine
Association
EOT, see tourist offices
Epicurus (NEA) 626
Epidavros (Pel) 230-1
Epiros (NG) 314-35, **315**
Episkopi (SG) 406
Epta Piges (Dod) 537
Erechtheion (Ath) 158
Eresos (NEA) 633-4
Eretria (Evi) 688
Eristos beach (Dod) 558
Ermones (Ion) 662
Ermoupolis (Cyc) 429-31, **430**
Erodotus 49
Euripides 44, 142
Evans, Sir Arthur 56, 481
Evdilos (NEA) 612
Evia 685-9, **686**
'evil eye' 51, 418
Evros delta (NG) 389
Evzones (Ath) 148
Exambela (Cyc) 465
exchange rates, see money
Exo Vathy (Dod) 564

Falassarna (Cre) 521
Faliraki (Dod) 537
Faltaïts Museum (Spo) 704
farmstays 98-9
fauna 40-2, 308, 322, 372, 382,
389, 640
loggerhead turtle 42, 668
monk seal 41, 668, 701
fax services 79
Felekas (Ion) 661
ferry travel 128, 132-3
routes & fares 130-1, **131**
to/from Cyclades 413, 528
to/from Cyprus 120-1
to/from Israel 121, 528
to/from Italy 119-20, 328,
670
to/from Turkey 119, 528, 568
to/from Volos (Cen) 300
festivals
Festival of Agios Georgios
(Cen) 283

festivals *cont*
  festival of ancient drama (NG)
    318
  see also cultural events
film 44
Filopappos hill (Ath) 171
Filoti (Cyc) 436
Finikas (Cyc) 432
Finiki (Dod) 547
Finikoundas (Pel) 257
Fira (Cyc) 451-4
fire-walking 348
Fiskardo (Ion) 672
flea markets
  Athens 190
  Piraeus (Att) 200
flokati rugs 190, 319
flora 40-2, 372
  forests 322, 349
  olives 39, 520
  plane tree 303
  wild flowers of Crete 466
Florina (NG) 358-60
Folegandros (Cyc) 447-9, **448**
folk art 68
Folk Art, Museum of (Ath) 170
Folkloric & Ethnological
  Museum of Macedonia (NG)
    341-2
food 99-105
Fortress of Santa Mavra (Ion)
  666
Fountain of Arethusa (Ion) 674
Fourkovouni (Cyc) 459
Fournes (Cre) 512
Fourni (NEA) 614
Fourni beach (Dod) 540
Fourni islands (NEA) 614, **609**
Fourth Sacred War 281
Frangokastello (Cre) 501, 515
Frantato (NEA) 613
frescoes 55, 62, 168, 467, 475,
  481
Frikes (Ion) 675

Gaea 35, 281
Gaios (Ion) 663-4
Galaktopoleia 100
Galataki, Convent of (Evi) 688
Galatas (Pel) 402
Galaxidi (Cen) 284
Galissas (Cyc) 431-2
Gardiki (Ion) 663
Gastouni (Pel) 266
Gavdos island (Cre) 518
Gavrio (Cyc) 415
gay travellers 75
  bars (Ath) 189
Gefyra (Pel) 241-3

Genadi (Dod) 540
geography 39
Geometric Age 17-18
George I 28
George II 29, 30
Georgioupolis (Cre) 505
Gera (Dod) 557
Geraki (Ion) 678
Geraki (Pel) 241
Gerolimenas (Pel) 249
Gialiskari beach (Cyc) 461
Gialos (Cyc) 445-6
Gialos (Dod) 567
Giannades (Ion) 662
Gios Antonios beach (Dod) 558
Giossos Apostolides (NG) 352-3
Gioura (Spo) 701
Glaronisia (Cyc) 459
Glossa (Spo) 696
Glyfada (Ion) 662
Glyfada (Att) 203
Golden Age (Ath) 141
Golden beach (Cyc) 443
Golden beach (NEA) 651
Gortyn (Cre) 468, 484
Gortys (Pel) 234
Goths 24
Goulandris Museum of Cycladic
  & Ancient Greek Art (Ath)
    169
Gourna (Dod) 585-9
Gournia (Cre) 489-90
government 42
Gramvousa (Cre) 521
Gramvousa peninsula (Cre) 521
Great Mother (NEA) 643
Greek Alpine Association (EOS)
  94
Greek language, *see* language
Greek Orthodox Church 52
Green beach (Cyc) 416
Grigos (Dod) 590
Gypsies 43
Gythio (Pel) 243-5

Hades 35, 38, 330
Hadrian 142, 163
Hadrian's library (Ath) 163-4
Halki (Cyc) 436
Halki (Dod) 542-3
Halkida (Evi) 687
Halkidiki peninsula (NG) 366-75
handcrafts 190
Hania (Cen) 302
Hania (Cre) 505-12, **506**
Haraki (Dod) 537
Haviaras, Stratis 82
health 85-92
  HIV/AIDS 90

insurance 86
medical problems & treatment
  87-92
Hebe 35
Helathros (Dod) 552
Hellenistic period 61
Hephaestus 35-6
Hera 35-6
Heracles 38
Hereon (NEA) 606
Hermes 36-7
Herodotus (Ath) 142
Hersonisos (Cre) 476
Hestia 36-7
hiking, *see* trekking
Hiliadou (Evi) 687
Hios, *see* Chios
Hippocrates (Dod) 568
Hippodamos (Dod) 526
history 15-34
  Archaic Age 18-20
  Athens 141-3
  Balkan wars 28
  books 83
  Bronze Age 15-17
  Byzantine Empire 24
  civil war 30-1
  classical period 20-2
  Crusades 24-5
  Cycladic civilisation 15
  Geometric Age 17-18
  Minoan civilisation 15-17
  Mycenaean civilisation 17
  Ottoman Empire 25-6
  Roman rule 23-4
  Stone Age 15
  War of Independence 26-7
  WW I 28-9
  WW II 30
hitching 117, 128, 193
HIV/AIDS 90
Hlemoutsi Castle (Pel) 266
Hogarth, David 492
Hohlia (Dod) 596
holidays, *see* public holidays
Homer 49, 219, 223, 619
Hora (Cyc) 447-9, 456, 462
Hora (Dod) 589
Hora (NEA) 642-3
Hora (Pel) 260
Hora (Kythira) (Ion) 682
Hora (Old Alonnisos) (Spo)
  699-700
Hora Sfakion (Cre) 469, 514
Horefto (Cen) 302
Horio (Dod) 543, 566
horse racing 190
Horto (Cen) 305
hostels 98-9

Hrani (Pel) 256
Hrysi Akti (Cyc) 443
Hrysi islet (Cre) 496
Hrysi Milia beach (Spo) 701
Hrysomilia (NEA) 614
Hrysospilia caves (Cyc) 447
Hydra (SG) 402-6, **403**
Hydra town (SG) 404-6
hydrofoil 133-4, 201
    to/from Cyprus & Israel 528

Ialyssos (Dod) 539
Icarus 480
icons 63
Ierapetra (Cre) 495-6
Ierissos (NG) 368
Ifestia (NEA) 640
Igoumenitsa (NG) 327-8
Ikaria (NEA) 608-14, **609**
Ikos (Spo) 701
Imbros (Cre) 515
Imbros gorge (Cre) 515
Imeri (Cre) 521
Inousses (NEA) 623-4, **623**
insurance
    health 86
    travel 109
International Student & Youth
    Travel Service 75
International Student Identity
    Card 73
international transfers, *see*
    money
Ioannina (NG) 316-20, **317**
Ionian islands 653-84, **654**
Ios (Cyc) 444-7, **445**
Ioulis (Cyc) 461
Iraklia (Cyc) 436
Iraklio (Cre) 471-9, **472**
Iria (Pel) 229
Islet of Ro (Dod) 555
Isthmia (Pel) 217
Isthmus of Corinth (Pel) 213
Istron (Cre) 488
Itanos (Cre) 494
Itea (Cen) 284
Ithaki (Ion) 673-5, **669**
Iti National Park (Cen) 42
Itilo (Pel) 247-8
Iviron (NG) 373
IYHF, *see* accommodation

Jason 38
jewellery 108
Jewish Museum (Ath) 171
Jews 43

Kabeiroi twins 643
Kadia (Pel) 229

kafeneia 100-1
Kala Nera (Cen) 303
Kalamaki (Ion) 678
Kalamaki (Pel) 256
Kalamakia (Spo) 701
Kalamata (Pel) 252-6, **254**
Kalambaka (Cen) 308-10
Kalamitsa (Spo) 706
Kalavryta (Pel) 272-4
Kaleas, Konstantinos 68
Kalithea Thermi (Dod) 536
Kallithea (NEA) 607
Kalvos, Andreas 49
Kalymnos (Dod) 574-81, **575**
Kalyviani (Cre) 521
kamakia 92
Kamares (Cyc) 464-5
Kamares pottery 473
Kamari (Cyc) 455
Kamari (Dod) 574
Kamari (Pel) 217
Kamariotissa (NEA) 642
Kambia (NEA) 622
Kambos (Dod) 589, 592
Kamini (SG) 406
Kamiros (Dod) 539
Kampi (NEA) 614
Kampos (NEA) 612-14, 619
Kanali beach (SG) 402
Kanellopoulos Museum (Ath)
    170
Kapi (NEA) 633
Kapsali (Ion) 683
Karamanlis, Konstantinos 31
Karathona beach (Pel) 229
Karavomilos (Ion) 672
Karavostasis (Cyc) 447
Kardamena (Dod) 573
Kardamyla (NEA) 622
Kardamyli (Pel) 251-2
Karfas (NEA) 619
Karitena (Pel) 234
Karlovasi (NEA) 607
Karpathos (Dod) 543-50, **544**
Karpenisi (Cen) 288
Karterados (Cyc) 454
Karya (Ion) 667
Karyes (NG) 373, **373**
Karystos (Evi) 689
Kassandra peninsula (NG) 366
Kassos (Dod) 550-2, **551**
Kastanies (NG) 391
Kastelli-Kissamos (Cre)
    519-21
Kastellorizo (Dod) 552-5, **553**
Kastoria (NG) 363-6, **364**
Kastorian Museum of Folklore
    (NG) 364
Kastra (NG) 343

Kastraki (Cen) 312-3
Kastro (Cyc) 434-6, 448, 458,
    465
Kastro (Ion) 673
Kastro (NG) 330
Kastro (Spo) 693
Kastrosykia (NG) 334
Katapola (Cyc) 437-8
Kathisma (Ion) 668
Katholika (Dod) 595
Kato Boutari (Pel) 249
Kato Gatzea (Cen) 303
Kato Korakiana (Ion) 661
Kato Lehonia (Cen) 303
Kato Livadi (Cyc) 424
Kato Zakros (Cre) 494
Katsadia (Dod) 592-3
Kattavia (Dod) 541
Kavala (NG) 375-9, **376**
Kaviria (NEA) 640
kayaking 288, 308, 323-4, *see*
    also canoeing
Kazantzakis, Nikos 49, 82-3,
    251, 476, 483
Kea (Cyc) 460-1, **460**
Kefalari (Pel) 225
Kefallonia (Ion) 668-73, **669**
Kefalos (Dod) 574
Kendarhos (Cyc) 464
Keramikos (Ath) 162-3
Kerasia (NG) 373
Keros (NEA) 640
Kiato (Pel) 217
Kimissi (Dod) 593
Kimolos (Cyc) 459-60, **457**
Kinira (NEA) 651
Kioni (Ion) 675
Kionia (Cyc) 419
Kiotari (Dod) 540
Kipos beach (NEA) 647
Kira (Cen) 284
Kissamos, *see* Kastelli-
    Kissamos
Kissos (Cen) 303
KKE *see* Communist Party
Kleftiko (Cyc) 458
klephts 26, 49
Klio (NEA) 633
Knights of St John 526, 532, 563
    Castle (Dod) 554
Knossos (Cre) 55, 467-8, 479-83
Kohlakoura (Dod) 593
Kokala (Pel) 250
Kokkari (NEA) 607
Kokkinokastro (Spo) 701
Koklaki (Dod) 560
Kolimvythres (Cyc) 442
Kolitzani beach (Cyc) 446
Kolymbia (Dod) 537

Kolymvythra bay (Cyc) 419
Komitades (Cre) 515
Komotini (NG) 384-5
Konitsa (NG) 323-4
Kontopouli (NEA) 640
Korissia (Cyc) 460-1
Kornaros, Ioannis 494
Koroni (Pel) 256-7
Koropi (Att) 205
Korthion (Cyc) 416
Kos (Dod) 568-74, **569**
Kos town (Dod) 570-3, **571**
Kosmas (Pel) 236
Kotronas (Pel) 250
Koufonisi (Cyc) 436
Koufos (NG) 367
Koukounaries beach (Spo) 693
Koundouriotis, Georgios 403
Kournas lake (Cre) 505
Kouroutas (Pel) 260
Koursoun Tzami (Cen) 307
Kourtaliotis gorge (Cre) 502-3
Koutouki cave (Att) 205
Koxare (Cre) 501
Krassa beach (Spo) 693
Kri-Kri island (Cre) 491, 512
Kriezis, Andreas 67
Krikellos (Cen) 287
Krini (Ion) 662
Krios (Cyc) 443
Krithoni (Dod) 584-5
Kritsa (Cre) 490
Kteo (Ion) 678
Kyanos (blue) caves (Iøn) 677, 679
Kydonia (Cre) 508
Kyllini (Pel) 265-6
Kymi (Evi) 688
Kyra Panagia (Dod) 548
Kyra Panagia (Spo) 701, 706
Kythira (Ion) 679-83, **680**
Kythnos (Cyc) 461-3, **462**

Laerma (Dod) 540
Laganas (Ion) 678
Lagia (Pel) 249
Lagoudi (Dod) 574
Lake Koronia (NG) 366
Lake Kremasta (Cen) 289
Lake Marathon (Att) 207-8
Lake Orestiada (NG) 363
Lake Pamvotis (NG) 316
Lake Volvi (NG) 366
Lakka (Ion) 664
Lakki (Cre) 512
Lakki (Dod) 583
Lakoma (NEA) 646
Lakones (Ion) 662
Lakonia (Pel) 236-45

Lakonian Mani (Pel) 246-50
Lakos (Pel) 236
Lalaria (Spo) 693
Lamia (Cen) 289-91, **290**
Lampi (Dod) 573, 589
Langada (Cyc) 439
Langada (NEA) 622
Langada pass (Pel) 256
Langadas (NG) 348
language 12, 707-13
    courses 95, 173
Lardos (Dod) 540
Larisa (Cen) 292-6, **295**
Lassithi plateau (Cre) 491-2
Lato (Cre) 490
laundry 80
Lavrio (Att) 206
leather work 108
Lefka Ori (Cre) 514
Lefka Ori mountains (Cre) 512
Lefkada (Ion) 664-8, **665**
Lefkes (Cyc) 443
Lefkogia (Cre) 502
Lefkos (Dod) 547-8
Lemonodasos (Pel) 402
Leonidio (Pel) 236
Lepeda (Ion) 672
Lepoura (Evi) 689
Leros (Dod) 581-5, **582**
lesbian travellers 75
Lesvos (Mytilini) (NEA) 625-35, **627**
Lethra (Dod) 557
lightning 88
Ligoneri (SG) 410
Limenaria (NEA) 652
Limenas (NEA) 648-51, **649**
Limeni (Pel) 247
Limni (Evi) 688
Limni Kastrion cave (Pel) 274
Limnia (NEA) 622
Limnonari beach (Spo) 697
Limnos (NEA) 622, 635-40, **636**
Linaria (Spo) 701
Lindos (Dod) 537-8
Linear A 17, 474
Linear B 17, 260, 474, 505
Lipsi (Dod) 590-3, **591**
Lissos (Cre) 515
literature 49
Lithi beach (NEA) 620
Litohoro (NG) 349-51
Livadaki (Cyc) 449
Livadi (Cyc) 463-4
Livadi beach (Cyc) 449
Livadia (Cen) 278
Livadia (Dod) 556-8, 563-4
Lixouri (Ion) 672
Loggos (Ion) 664

Lourdata beach (Ion) 673
Loutra (Dod) 560
Loutra (NEA) 645-6
Loutraki (Pel) 217
Loutraki(Pel) 693
Loutro (Cre) 513-4
Lykavittos hill (Ath) 171
Lytras, Nikiphoros 67

Macedonia (NG) 335-80, **336**
Macedonian tomb (NG) 356
Madouri (Ion) 667
Magazia (Spo) 705-6
magazines 84-5
Maherado (Ion) 679
Makrynitsa (Cen) 302
Makrys Gialos (Ion) 670
Malakio (Cen) 303
Malaliamos (Cyc) 423
Malia (Cre) 486
Maltezana (Dod) 564
Mandraki (Dod) 559-60
Mandraki (SG) 406
Manganari (Cyc) 446
Mani (Pel) 245-52
Manolates (NEA) 607
Mantinades (Cre) 466
maps 84
Marathi (Cyc) 443
Marathi (Dod) 593-4, **594**
Maratho (NEA) 613
Marathokampos (NEA) 607
Marathon (Att) 207-8
Marathonisi islet (Pel) 244
Marathonissi (Ion) 678
Maries (Ion) 679
Marine Turtle Project 668
Maritime Museum of Piraeus (Att) 198
Markopoulo (Att) 205
Markopoulo (Ion) 673
Marlas (Cyc) 419
Marmara (Cyc) 443
Marmari (Dod) 564
Marmari beach (Dod) 573
Marmaro (NEA) 622
Marpissa (Cyc) 443
Marpounda beach (Spo) 700
Masouri (Dod) 581
Mastihari (Dod) 573-4
Matala (Cre) 485-6
Mavri Petra (Cen) 305
Mavroneri waterfall (Pel) 274
Mazarakata (Ion) 673
media 84-5
medical problems, *see* health
Megali Aselinos beach (Spo) 693
Megali Idea 28-9
Megali Prespa (NG) 360

Megalo Horio (Cen) 288
Megalo Horio (Dod) 558, 595
Megalo Papingo (NG) 322
Megalohori (Cyc) 454
Megalopoli (Pel) 233
Meganisi (Ion) 668, **665**
Megas Gialos (Cyc) 432
Mehmet Ali (NG) 375
Mellisani cave (Ion) 672
Meloi beach (Dod) 589
Meltemi 40
Menelaus 236
Menetes (Dod) 547
Merihas (Cyc) 462
Mesa Vathy (Dod) 564
Meskla (Cre) 512
Mesohora (Cen) 308
Mesohori (Dod) 548
Messinia (Pel) 252-60
Messinian Mani (Pel) 250-2
Messolongi (Cen) 285-6
Messongi (Ion) 662
Mesta (NEA) 621-2
Metaxas, Ioannis 29
Metaxata (Ion) 673
Meteora (Cen) 308, 310-12, **311**
Methoni (Pel) 257-8
metro 135, 194
Metsovo (NG) 324-7
Miaoulis, Andreas 403
Mikines, *see* Mycenae
Mikri Aselinos beach (Spo) 693
Mikri Prespa (NG) 360
Mikro Horio (Cen) 288
Mikro Horio (Dod) 557, 596
Mikro Papingo (NG) 322
Milia (Spo) 696
Milies (Cen) 303-4
Milina (Cen) 305
Miller, Henry 230
Milopotas (Cyc) 446
Milopotas beach (Cyc) 445-6
Milos (Cyc) 456-9, **457**
Mineralogical Museum (Att) 206
Minoan art 55-7
Minoan civilisation 15-7, 209, 466-8
Minos 480
Minor islands (Cyc) 436-7, **433**
Mirtos (Cre) 496
Mithymna (NEA) 631-2
Mitsotakis, Konstantinos 34
Mogonissi (Ion) 664
Molai (Pel) 236
Molos (Cyc) 443
Molos (SG) 406
Molos (Spo) 705-6
Molyvos, *see* Methymna

monasteries
Agia Triada (Cen) 312
Capuchin Monastery of St Jean (Cyc) 429
Convent of Pantanassa (Pel) 240
Monastery of Agios Nikolaos Anapafsas (Cen) 311
Metamorphosis (Cen) 311
Monastery of Dekoulou (Pel) 247
Monastery of Koutloumoussiou (NG) 373
Monastery of Megisti Lavra (NG) 373
Monastery of Perivleptos (Pel) 240
Monastery of St John the Theologian (Dod) 589
Monastery of the Apocalypse (Dod) 589
Monastery of the Saviour (Pel) 252
Monastery of the Virgin of Proussiotissa (Cen) 288
Moni Agia Ipseni (Dod) 540
Moni Agias Lavras (Pel) 274
Moni Agias Mamas (Dod) 552
Moni Agias Paraskevis (NG) 322
Moni Agias Triadas (Cre) 512
Moni Agias Triadas (Dod) 554
Moni Agiou Andreou (Ion) 673
Moni Agiou Antoniou (Cyc) 443
Moni Agiou Georgiou (Dod) 554
Moni Agiou Giorgiou (Dod) 552
Moni Agiou Ioanni (Dod) 543, 574
Moni Agiou Konstantinou (Dod) 563
Moni Agiou Nektariou (SG) 399
Moni Agiou Nikolaou (NG) 326
Moni Agiou Nektariou(SG) 407, 409
Moni Agiou Panteleimona (Dod) 558
Moni Agiou Panteleimonos (Dod) 563
Moni Agiou Savva (Dod) 580
Moni Agiou Stefanou (Dod) 555
Moni Agiou Theologou (Dod) 574
Moni Arkadiou (Cre) 501
Moni Arkadiou Festival (Cre) 499
Moni Dafniou (Att) 201-2
Moni Dionysiou (NG) 374
Moni Dohiariou (NG) 374
Moni Efpraxias (SG) 406
Moni Evangelismou (NEA) 624

Moni Evangelismou (Spo) 697
Moni Evangelistrias (Spo) 693
Moni Faneromenis (Cre) 490
Moni Faneromini (Ion) 666
Moni Filotheou (NG) 373
Moni Gourvernetou (Cre) 512
Moni Grigoriou (NG) 374
Moni Hiliandariou (NG) 374
Moni Hozoviotissas (Cyc) 438
Moni Hrysoleontissas (SG) 399
Moni Hrysopigis (Cyc) 465
Moni Hrysoskalitissas (Cre) 519
Moni Inlet (SG) 399
Moni Kaissarianis (Att) 203
Moni Kalamiotissas (Cyc) 456
Moni Kalamou (Cyc) 446
Moni Karakallou (NG) 373
Moni Katholiko (Cre) 512
Moni Mavriotissas (NG) 365
Moni Megalou Spileou (Pel) 272
Moni Metamorphosis (Spo) 697
Moni Osiou Louka (Cen) 284
Moni Panagias (SG) 404
Moni Panagias Spilianis (Dod) 560
Moni Panagias Vrondianis (NEA) 607
Moni Panteleimonos (NG) 320
Moni Preveli (Cre) 503
Moni Prodromou (Spo) 697
Moni Profiti Ilia (SG) 406
Moni Profiti Ilia (Cyc) 455
Moni Roussanou (Cen) 311
Moni Skiadi (Dod) 541
Moni Simonas Petras (NG) 374
Moni Taxiarhon (Cyc) 464
Moni Taxiarhou Mihail (Dod) 567-8
Moni Thari (Dod) 540
Moni Theotokou (Ion) 662
Moni Toplou (Cre) 494
Moni Vatopediou (NG) 374
Moni Vlahernas (Ion) 661
Moni Xiropotamou (NG) 374
Moni Zografou (NG) 374
Moni Zoödohou Pigis (SG) 402
Mt Athos (NG) 368, 370-5
Stomio Monastery (NG) 324
Varlaam (Cen) 311
Vrontokhion Monastery (Pel) 240
Monastiraki Square (Ath) 144
Monastiri (Cyc) 442
Monemvassia (Pel) 236, 241-3
money 71-2
banks 71
bargaining 72

money cont
credit cards 71
post offices 71
tipping 72
travellers' cheques 71
Monodendri (Dod) 593
Monodendri (NG) 322
Monolithi (NG) 334
Monolithos (Dod) 539
Monolithos beach (Cyc) 455
Monument of Lysicrates (Ath) 149
Moraïtidis, Alexandros 691
Morosini fountain (Cre) 475
mosaics 61, 63, 348, 353, 356
Moudros (NEA) 639
mountain refuges 98
Kallergi (Cre) 508
mountaineering 94, 349, 351-3, 373-4, 508
clubs 75
Mouse island (Ion) 661
Mt Astraka (NG) 323
Mt Athos (NG) 339, 367-8, 370-5, 369, 373
Mt Attavyros (Dod) 541
Mt Dirfys (Evi) 687
Mt Fengari (NEA) 640
Mt Gamila (NG) 322-3
Mt Grammos (NG) 363
Mt Helmos (Pel) 274
Mt Ida (Cre) 476
Mt Iti (Cen) 291
Mt Kali Limni (Dod) 548
Mt Lepetymnos (NEA) 632
Mt Ohi (Evi) 689
Mt Olympus (NG) 35, 335, 349-54, 352, 634-5
Mt Orthys (Cen) 289
Mt Pangaion (NEA) 647
Mt Pantokrator (Ion) 661
Mt Parnassos (Cen) 283
Mt Profitis Ilias (Cyc) 455,
Mt Profitis Ilias (Dod) 541
Mt Taÿgetos (Pel) 238, 252
Mt Vitsi (NG) 363
Museum of Traditional Greek Ceramics (Ath) 152
music 49-51
classical 174, 188
instruments of ancient Greece 50
jazz 188
live 189
opera 188
rembetika 50, 189
Muslim minorities 384
Mycenae (Pel) 219-24
Mycenaean art 57
Mycenaean civilisation 17

Mykonos (Cyc) 419-24, 420
Myli (Pel) 236
Myli (Evi) 689
Mylopotamos (Cen) 303
Mylopotamos (Ion) 682
Mylos (Cen) 305
Myron (Ath) 142
Myrthios (Cre) 503
Myrtia (Cre) 483
Myrties (Dod) 580-1
Myrtiotissa (Ion) 662
Myrtos (Ion) 673
Mystras (Pel) 238-41, 239
mythology 34-8
books 81-2
Mytikas (Cen) 287
Mytikas (NG) 352
Mytilini (NEA) 627-31, 629
see also Lesvos
Mytilinii (NEA) 606-7

Nafpaktos (Cen) 284
Nafplio (Pel) 226-9, 227
Nagos (NEA) 622
Naoussa (Cyc) 442
Nas (NEA) 613
National Archaeological Museum (Ath) 164-9, 166
National Art Gallery (Ath) 170
National Gardens (Ath) 172
National Historical Museum (Ath) 170
National Marine Park (Spo) 42
naval museum, Hania (Cre) 508
Naxos (Cyc) 432-6, 433
Naxos town (Cyc) 433-4, 435
Nea Figalia (Pel) 260
Nea Kameni (Cyc) 455
Neapoli (Pel) 243
Nekromanteio of Aphyra (NG) 328
Nemea (Pel) 218
Neo Itilo (Pel) 247-8
neoclassical architecture 66-8
Neorion beach (SG) 402
Neos Marmaras (NG) 366
Neradjes Mosque (Cre) 499
Neraïda (Ion) 682
Nestor's Palace (Pel) 259-60
New Democracy Party 32-4
newspapers 84-5
Nikea (Dod) 561
Nikiana (Ion) 667
Nikitas (NG) 366
Nikopolis (NG) 333-4
Nisyros (Dod) 558-61, 559
North-Eastern Aegean islands 597-652, 598

Northern Greece 314-91
novels 82
Nyfi (Pel) 250

Octavian 380
Odysseus 38
Oedipus 277
Oia (Cyc) 455
Olymbos (Dod) 548-50
Olympia (Pel) 209, 260-5, 264
Olympic Airways 122
Olympic Games 263
Olympoi (NEA) 621
Olympus Festival (NG) 353
Olympus National Park (NG) 42
Omalos plateau (Cre) 512
Omonia Square (Ath) 144
Oracle of Trophonios (Cen) 278
Orestiada (NG) 390
Ormos Marathokampou (NEA) 607
Ornos (Cyc) 423
OTE, see telephone services
Otho 27-8, 143
Othos (Dod) 548
Ottoman Empire 25-6, 143
Otzias (Cyc) 461
Ouranopolis (NG) 368
ouzeria 100, 299
overland travel, see bus travel, train travel

Pahia Ammos (NEA) 646
Paleohora (Cre) 515-8, 516
Paleohora (SG) 399
Paleohori (Cyc) 459
Paleokastritsa (Ion) 662
Paleokastro (Cyc) 459
Paleokastro (Dod) 555
Paleokastro hill (Cre) 499
Paleonisa (Dod) 581
Paleopoli (Ion) 683
Paleopolis (Cyc) 416
Paleopolis (NEA) 640, 643-5
Paleos Astros (Pel) 236
Pali (Dod) 561
Palia Kameni (Cyc) 455
Palio Trikeri (Cen) 306
Pan 38
Panagia (Dod) 552
Panagia (NEA) 651
Panagia (NG) 376-7
Panagia Hrysospiliotissa (Ath) 160
Panagia Kanala (Cyc) 463
Panathenaic Way (Ath) 155
Panhellenic Socialist Union 32-4
Panormos (Cyc) 419
Panormos (Dod) 580

Panormos bay (Cyc) 419
Panormos beach (Cyc) 424
Panormos beach (Spo) 697
Panteli (Dod) 584
Papadiamantis, Alexandros 691
Papandreou, Georgos 31-4
Papanikolis cave (Ion) 667
Paradise beach (Cyc) 424
Paradise beach (NEA) 651
Paradisi beach (Cyc) 439
Paradisos (NG) 367
paragliding 324
Paralia Kymis (Evi) 688
Paralia Tyrou (Pel) 236
parasailing 667
Parga (NG) 328-31, 329
parliament building (Ath) 148
Parnassos National Park (Cen) 42
Parnitha National Park (Att) 42
Paroikia (Cyc) 439-42
Paros (Cyc) 439-43, 441
Partenis, Konstantinos 67
Partheni bay (Dod) 585
Parthenon (Ath) 157-9
Parthenou (Cyc) 436
PASOK, see Panhellenic
    Socialist Union
Patitiri (Spo) 699-700
Patmos (Dod) 585-90, 586
Patras (Pel) 266-71, 268
Patras Carnival (Pel) 269
Paxoi (Ion) 663-4, 663
Peania (Att) 205
Pedi (Dod) 567-8
Pefkari (NEA) 652
Pefki (Dod) 540
Pefkos (Spo) 706
Peisistratos (Ath) 141, 164
Pelekas (Ion) 662
Pelion peninsula (Cen) 300-6,
    301
Pella (NG) 348-9
Pelopi (NEA) 633
Peloponnese 209-74, 210-11
Peloponnesian Wars 20-1, 233
Pelops 209, 212
Pera Kastro (Dod) 579-80
Perahora (Pel) 217
Perama beach (Ion) 662
Perama cave (NG) 321
Pergamum 23
Pericles (Ath) 142, 152-3
Perissa (Cyc) 455
Peristera (Spo) 701
Perithia (Ion) 661
Persian Empire 22
Persian Wars 19-20
Pertouli (Cen) 308
Petalidi (Pel) 256

Petaloudes (Cyc) 443
Petaloudes (Dod) 541
Petra (NEA) 632
Petralona cave (NG) 366
Phaestos (Cre) 484
Phaestos disc 473
Pheidias 142, 157-8
Philip II 22, 142, 280, 336-8,
    379, 382, 641
Philippi (NG) 379-80
photography 85
Phry (Dod) 550-2
Phylakope (Cyc) 459
Pigadia (Dod) 544-6, 545
Pindar 49
Pindos mountains (NG) 41, 314
Piperi (Spo) 701
Piraeus (Att) 196-201, 199
Pisses beach (Cyc) 461
Pitsidia (Cre) 485
Plaka (Ath) 144
Plaka (Cyc) 436, 458-9
Plaka (Pel) 229, 236
Plaka beach (Dod) 558
Plakias (Cre) 501-3
Plataea (Cen) 275
Platanias (Cen) 306
Platanias (Spo) 693
Platanidia (Cen) 303
Platanistos (Evi) 689
Platanos (Dod) 583-4
Plateia Monastirakiou (Ath) 144
Plateia Omonias (Ath) 144
Plateia Syntagmatos (Ath) 143-4
Plathiena beach (Cyc) 459
Plato 46-7, 142
Platy (NEA) 639
Platys Gialos (Cyc) 423, 465
Platys Gialos (Dod) 592
Platys Gialos (Ion) 670
Plethon, Gemistos 239
Plimmyri (Dod) 540
Plomari (NEA) 634
poetry
    history 49
    books 82
    poets, Greek 49
Poli (Dod) 552
Poliohni (NEA) 639
Polonia (Cyc) 459
Polycrates (NEA) 599
Polyhnitos (NEA) 635
Polyrrinia (Cre) 521
population 43
Poros (SG) 399-402, 400
Poros (Ion) 668, 673
Port Kagio (Pel) 249
Portaria (Cen) 301
Porto (Cyc) 419

Porto Germeno (Cen) 275
Porto Katsiki (Ion) 668
Porto Roma (Ion) 679
Poseidon 35, 37, 480
Posidonia (Cyc) 432
postal services 78-9, see also
    money
poste restante 79
Potami (NEA) 608
Potami (Evi) 689
Potamia (NEA) 651
Potamos (Ion) 682
Pothia (Dod) 577-9, 578
Potos (NEA) 652
pottery, see ceramics
Poulithra (Pel) 236
Pouri (Cen) 303
Prasa (Cyc) 459
Prasonisi (Dod) 541
Prespa National Park (NG) 42
Prespa lakes (NG) 360-3, 361
Preveli beach (Cre) 503-4
Preveza (NG) 331-3, 332
Prinos Refuge (Cre) 476
Prionia (NG) 351
Proastio (Pel) 252
Prodromos (Cyc) 443
Profitis Ilias (NEA) 646
Prokopi (Evi) 688
Proussos (Cen) 288
Provatas (Cyc) 459
Psahna (Evi) 688
Psalidi (Dod) 573
Psara (NEA) 625, 625
Psarades (NG) 361-3
Psathi beach (Cyc) 446
Psathoura (Spo) 701
Pserimos (Dod) 573, 569
Psili Ammos (Dod) 590
Psili Ammos (NEA) 607
Psili Ammos beach (Cyc) 464
Psychoundakis, George 470
Psyhro (Cre) 492
Ptolemaic dynasty 23
Ptolemy II 568
public holidays 76, see also
    cultural events
Pyles (Dod) 548
Pyli (Cen) 308
Pyli (Dod) 574
Pylos (Pel) 258-9
Pyramid of Helenekion (Pel) 225
Pyrgaki (Cyc) 436
Pyrgi (NEA) 620-1
Pyrgi (Ion) 661
Pyrgos (Pel) 260-1
Pyrgos Dirou (Pel) 248-9
Pythagoras 599
Pythagorio (NEA) 604-6, 605

radio 85
radioactive springs (NEA) 611
Rafina (Att) 206-7
rafting 288, 324
Ramnous (Att) 208
Rea (Pel) 262
rembetika 50-1
Renaissance Festival (Cre) 499
restaurants 100
Rethymno (Cre) 496-501, **498**
retsina 107
Rhea 35
Rhodes (Dod) 524-42, **525**
Rhodes city (Dod) 529-36, **530**
Riha Nera (NEA) 637
Ritsos, Yiannis 49
River Arahthos (NG) 334
River Evros (NG) 382, 389
River Litheos (Cen) 306
River Sperhios (Cen) 292
Ro (Dod) 555
road accidents 126
Rocca al Mare (Cre) 475
rock climbing 312, 323
rock paintings 362
Roda (Ion) 661
Rodakino (Cre) 501
Roman Catholicism 43
Roman Empire 23-4
Roman period 62
Romeïkos Yialos (NEA) 637
Rouda bay (Ion) 668
Russian bay (SG) 402

safety 89, 93
sailing 667, *see also* yachting
Salakos (Dod) 541
Samaria (Cre) 513
Samaria gorge (Cre) 512-3
Samaria National Park (Cre) 42
Sami (Ion) 672
Samos (NEA) 599-608, **600**
Samos town (NEA) 601-4, **603**
Samothraki (NEA) 640-7, **641**
Sanctuary of Apollo (Cen) **282**
Sanctuary of Artemis (Att) 208
Sanctuary of Asclepius (Dod) 568
Sanctuary of Demeter (Att) 203
Sanctuary of Hera (NEA) 599
Sanctuary of Poseidon and Amphitrite (Cyc) 419
Sanctuary of the Great Gods (NEA) 640-1, 643-5, **644**
Sanctuary to Hera (NEA) 606
Santa Maria (Cre) 475
Santorini (Cyc) 55, 450-5, **451**
Sappho 49, 82, 626

Sarcophagus of Agia Triada (Cre) 475
Saronic Gulf islands 395-410, **396**
Sarti (NG) 367
Schliemann, Heinrich 57, 219-21, 480
sculpture 54-62
    classical 167-8
    late classical & Hellenistic 167-8
Seferis, George 49, 82
Selia (Cre) 501
Serifos (Cyc) 463-4, **463**
Shakespeare, William 655
Shinias (Att) 208
Shinoussa (Cyc) 436
shopping 108
Siana (Dod) 539
Sifnos (Cyc) 464-5, **465**
Sigri (NEA) 634
Sikelianos, Angelos 49
Sikia (NG) 367
Sikinos (Cyc) 449-50, **450**
Sikyon (Pel) 218
Sithonian peninsula (NG) 366-7
Sitia (Cre) 492-4
Skala (Dod) 587-9
Skala (Ion) 673
Skala Eresou (NEA) 633-4
Skala Kallirahis (NEA) 651
Skala Marion (NEA) 651
Skala Prinou (NEA) 651
Skala Rahonis (NEA) 651
Skala Sotirou (NEA) 651
Skala Sykaminias (NEA) 633
Skalia (Dod) 581
Skantzoura (Spo) 701
Skiathos (Spo) 689-93, **690**
skiing 95, 172-3, 274, 283, 302, 308, 326, 358, *see also* waterskiing
Sklavokambos (Cre) 483
Skopelos (Spo) 693-7, **694**
Skorpidi (Ion) 667
Skorpios (Ion) 667
Skyros (Spo) 701-6, **702**
Skyros Carnival (Spo) 701, 703
snake goddesses 474
snorkelling, *see* diving
soccer 108, 189-90
Socrates 45-6, 142
Solomos, Dionysios 49
Solon 18, 39, 141
Sophocles 44, 142
Soufli (NG) 389
Sougia (Cre) 515, 518
Sounion (Att) 205
Sparta (Pel) 236-8

history 19-22, 142
Sparti (Ion) 667
Spetses (SG) 406-10, **408**
Spetsopoula (SG) 410
Spili (Cre) 504
Spilios Agapitos (NG) 351-2
Spinalonga island (Cre) 491
Spinalonga peninsula (Cre) 490
Spoa (Dod) 548
Sporades 685-6, 689-706, **686**
sport 52, 108, 173
St Pandeleimon (NG) 374
St Paul (NG) 380
Staphylos beach (Spo) 697
Stavronikita (NG) 373
Stavros (Ion) 675
Stegna beach (Dod) 537
Stemnitsa (Pel) 234
Steni (Evi) 687
Steni Vala (Spo) 701
Sterea Ellada (Cen) 275-92, **276**
Sthmus of Corinth (Pel) 209
Stoa of Eumenes (Ath) 160
Stone Age 15
Stoupa (Pel) 251
Strinila (Ion) 661
Strofylia (Evi) 688
student travellers 75
Stymfalia (Pel) 218
Stypi (NEA) 633
Stypalea (Dod) 562-3
Stypsi (NEA) 633
Süleyman the Magnificent 25
sultana festival (Cre) 493
Super Paradise beach (Cyc) 424
superstition 51
Sweet Water beach (Cre) 514
Sykia (Pel) 236
Symi (Dod) 564-8, **565**
Syntagma Square (Ath) 143-4
Syros (Cyc) 427-32, **428**

tavernas 100
taxi boats 133
Taxiarhia of the Metropolis (NG) 363
taxis 126, 135, 194
Taÿgetos gorge (Pel) 252
Taÿgetos mountains (Pel) 250
telegraph services 79
Telendos islet (Dod) 580-1
telephone services 79
television 85
telex services 79
Temple of Aphaia (SG) 398-9
Temple of Apollo (SG) 398
Temple of Athena Nike (Ath) 155-7
Temple of Dafniforos Apollo (Evi) 688

Temple of Nemesis (Att) 208
Temple of Olympian Zeus (Ath) 164
Temple of Poseidon (SG) 402
Temple of Poseidon (Att) 205-6
Teriade (NEA) 628
Terpander (NEA) 625
Thanos beach (NEA) 639
Thasos (NEA) 647-52, **647**
theatre 187
Theatre Museum (Ath) 171
Theatre of Dionysos (Ath) 159-60
Theatre of Herodes Atticus (Ath) 160
Thebes (Cen) 277-8
theft 93
Theologos (NEA) 652
Theophilos 301, 626, 628
Therma (NEA) 611, 645-6
Thermopylae (Cen) 289
Theseus 38, 402
Thessaloniki (NG) 335-48, **340**
    Archaeological Museum 339-41
Thessaly (Cen) 292-313, **293**
Thira, see Santorini
Thirasia (Cyc) 455
Third Sacred War 280
Thiva (Cen) 277-8
Tholos (Pel) 260
Tholos beach (Dod) 595
Thrace (NG) 380-91, **381**
Thucydides 49, 142
Thymena (NEA) 614
Tigaki (Dod) 573
Tiganakia bay (Dod) 594
Tigani (Cre) 521
Tilos (Dod) 555-8, **556**
time 80
Tinos (Cyc) 416-9, **417**
tipping, see money
Tiryns 57
Titans 35
Tolo (Pel) 229
Toroni (NG) 367
tourist offices 74-5
    abroad 74-5
    local 74
tourist police 74
Tourlos (Cyc) 423
tours 121, 135
Tower of the Winds (Ath) 163
traditional settlements 99
Tragaea (Cyc) 436
train travel
    Diakofto-Kalavryta railway (Pel) 271-2

to/from Athens 192
to/from Greece 116-18
within Greece 125
travel books & guides, see books
travellers' cheques, see money
Treaty of Bucharest 469
Treaty of Lausanne 143
trekking 94-5, 288, 291, 322-4, 350-3, 372-5, 476, 499, 508, clubs 75
    mountain refuges 98
    organised expeditions 121
    organised treks 135
Tria Potamia (Cen) 308
Trikala (Cen) 306-8
Trikeri (Cen) 305
Trikoupis, Harilaos 28
Triple Alliance 212
Tripolis (Pel) 232-3
Trizin (Pel) 231
Troizen (Pel) 402
Troulos (Spo) 693
Troy (Pel) 221
Trypiti (Cyc) 458-9
Tsambikas (Dod) 537
Tsepelovo (NG) 323
Tsipouro (Cen) 299
Tsokos, Dionysios 68
Turkish architecture 66
Tylisos (Cre) 483
Tymfristos (Cen) 292
Tyrosapounakia (Pel) 236
Tzanaki (Dod) 563
Tzermiado (Cre) 492

University Museum (Ath) 151

Vagia beach (Dod) 589
Vagis, Polygnotos 377
Vaï (Cre) 494
Vaï (Dod) 564
Valley of the Butterflies (Cyc) 443
Valley of the Butterflies (Dod) 541
Valley of the Dead (Cre) 494
Valmas beach (Cyc) 446
Valtos beach (NG) 330
Vari beach (Cyc) 432
Varia (NEA) 629
Varkiza (Att) 204
Varvari, see Myrtia
Vasiliki (Ion) 668
Vasses (Pel) 235
Vassilikos (Ion) 679
Vatera (NEA) 635
Vathy (Cyc) 465
Vathy (Dod) 580
Vathy (Ion) 674

Vathy (NEA), see Samos town
Vathypetro Villa (Cre) 483
Vatos beach (NEA) 646
vegetarian food 104, 182-3, 186, 517
Velanio beach (Spo) 697
Venetians 25
Venizelos, Eleutherios 29
Vergina (NG) 356
Veria (NG) 354-6
Viglafia (Pel) 243
Vikio (NEA) 622
Vikos gorge (NG) 322-3
Vikos-Aoös National Park (NG) 42, 314, 316, 322
Villehardouin, Guillaume de 238
visas 69-70
Vlahata (Ion) 673
Vlahiotis (Pel) 236
Vlasios (Cen) 303
Vlihadia (Dod) 580
Vlyho (Ion) 668
Vlyhos (SG) 406
Voïdomatis River (NG) 322
Volada (Dod) 548
Volanakis, Theodoros 67
Volissos (NEA) 622
Volos (Cen) 296, 299-300, **297**
Vonitsa (Cen) 287
Vorres Museum (Att) 205
Vothyni (Dod) 580
Votsalakia (NEA) 607
Voula (Att) 204
Voulismeni lake (Cre) 488
Vourkari (Cyc) 461
Vourliotes (NEA) 607
Vravrona (Att) 208
Vrises (Cre) 505
Vrisitsa beach (Spo) 700
Vromolimnos beach (Spo) 693
Vromolithos (Dod) 584
Vrontados (NEA) 619, 622
Vythisma beach (Spo) 700
Vyzitsa (Cen) 304-5

walking 128
War Museum (Ath) 170
War of Independence 26-7, 143, 211, 232, 285-6, 403
water 87
waterskiing 667
weights & measures 80
White Tower (NG) 342
wild flowers, see flora
windsurfing 94, 534, 667-8
wine 106
Wine Festival (Cre) 499

women travellers 923
work
  permits 93
  teaching 93

Xanthi (NG) 382-4
XEN, see YWCA
Xenofondos (NG) 374
Xenophon 142
Xi (Ion) 672
Xinara (Cyc) 419
Xirokambos (Dod) 585

Xiropotamos (NEA) 646
Xylokastro (Pel) 217

yachting 534, see also sailing
  charter companies 134
Ypati (Cen) 291
Ypsilometopo (NEA) 633
YWCA (Ath) 176

Zaga (Pel) 256
Zagora (Cen) 302
Zagorohoria (NG) 314, 321-3

zaharoplasteia 100
Zahlorou (Pel) 272-3
Zakros (Cre) 494
Zakynthos (Ion) 675-9, 676
Zakynthos town (Ion) 675-8,
  677
Zappeio gardens (Ath) 172
Zea Marina (Att) 196
Zeus 35-6
Zia (Dod) 574
Zipari (Dod) 574
Zographos, Panayiotis 68

LONELY PLANET JOURNEYS

FULL CIRCLE: A South American Journey by Luis Sepúlveda (translated by Chris Andrews)

Full Circle invites us to accompany Chilean writer Luis Sepúlveda on 'a journey without a fixed itinerary'. Extravagant characters and extraordinary situations are memorably evoked: gauchos organising a tournament of lies, a scheming heiress on the lookout for a husband, a pilot with a corpse on board his plane . . . Part autobiography, part travel memoir, *Full Circle* brings us the distinctive voice of one of South America's most compelling writers.

THE GATES OF DAMASCUS by Lieve Joris (translated by Sam Garrett)

This best-selling book is a beautifully drawn portrait of contemporary Syria. Through her intimate contact with local people, Lieve Joris explores women's lives and family relationships – the hidden world that lies behind the gates of Damascus.

IN RAJASTHAN by Royina Grewal

Indian travel writer Royina Grewal takes us behind the exotic facade of this fabled destination: here is an insider's perceptive account of India's most colourful state. *In Rajasthan* discusses folk music and architecture, feudal traditions and regional cuisine . . . Most of all, it focuses on people – from maharajahs to itinerant snake charmers – to convey the excitement and challenges of a region in transition.

ISLANDS IN THE CLOUDS: Travels in the Highlands of New Guinea by Isabella Tree

This is the fascinating account of a journey to the remote and beautiful Highlands of Papua New Guinea and Irian Jaya. The author travels with a PNG Highlander who introduces her to his intriguing and complex world. *Islands in the Clouds* is a thoughtful, moving book, full of insights into a region that is rarely noticed by the rest of the world.

KINGDOM OF THE FILM STARS: Journey into Jordan by Annie Caulfield

With honesty and humour, Annie Caulfield writes of travelling in Jordan and falling in love with a Bedouin. Her book offers fascinating insights into the country and unpicks some of the tight-woven Western myths about the Arab world within the intimate framework of a compelling love story.

LOST JAPAN by Alex Kerr

Lost Japan draws on the author's personal experiences of Japan over a period of 30 years. Alex Kerr takes his readers on a backstage tour: friendships with Kabuki actors, buying and selling art, studying calligraphy, exploring rarely visited temples and shrines . . . The Japanese edition of this book was awarded the 1994 Shincho Gakugei Literature Prize for the best work of non-fiction.

SEAN & DAVID'S LONG DRIVE by Sean Condon

Sean and David are young townies who have rarely strayed beyond city limits. One day, for no good reason, they set out to discover their homeland, and what follows is a wildly entertaining adventure that covers half of Australia. Sean Condon has written a hilarious, offbeat road book that mixes sharp insights with deadpan humour and outright lies.

SHOPPING FOR BUDDHAS by Jeff Greenwald

Shopping for Buddhas is Jeff Greenwald's story of his obsessive search for the perfect Buddha statue. In the backstreets of Kathmandu, he discovers more than he bargained for . . . and his souvenir-hunting turns into an ironic metaphor for the clash between spiritual riches and material greed. Politics, religion and serious shopping collide in this witty account of an enlightening visit to Nepal.

LONELY PLANET TRAVEL ATLASES

Lonely Planet has long been famous for the number and quality of its guidebook maps. Now we've gone one step further and in conjunction with Steinhart Katzir Publishers produced a handy companion series: Lonely Planet travel atlases – maps of a country produced in book form.

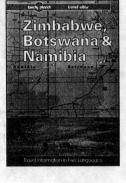

Unlike other maps, which look good but lead travellers astray, our travel atlases have been researched on the road by Lonely Planet's experienced team of writers. All details are carefully checked to ensure the atlas corresponds with the equivalent Lonely Planet guidebook.

The handy atlas format means no holes, wrinkles, torn sections or constant folding and unfolding. These atlases can survive long periods on the road, unlike cumbersome fold-out maps. The comprehensive index ensures easy reference.

- full-colour throughout
- maps researched and checked by Lonely Planet authors
- place names correspond with Lonely Planet guidebooks
  – no confusing spelling differences
- legend and travelling information in English, French, German, Japanese and Spanish
- size: 230 x 160 mm

Available now:
Chile; Egypt; India & Bangladesh; Israel & the Palestinian Territories; Jordan, Syria & Lebanon; Laos; Thailand; Vietnam; Zimbabwe, Botswana & Namibia

---

LONELY PLANET TV SERIES & VIDEOS

Lonely Planet travel guides have been brought to life on television screens around the world. Like our guides, the programmes are based on the joy of independent travel, and look honestly at some of the most exciting, picturesque and frustrating places in the world. Each show is presented by one of three travellers from Australia, England or the USA and combines an innovative mixture of video, Super-8 film, atmospheric soundscapes and original music.

Videos of each episode – containing additional footage not shown on television – are available from good book and video shops, but the availability of individual videos varies with regional screening schedules.

Video destinations include: Alaska; Australia (Southeast); Brazil; Ecuador & the Galápagos Islands; Indonesia; Israel & the Sinai Desert; Japan; La Ruta Maya (Yucatán, Guatemala & Belize); Morocco; North India (Varanasi to the Himalaya); Pacific Islands; Vietnam; Zimbabwe, Botswana & Namibia.

Coming soon: The Arctic (Norway & Finland); Baja California; Chile & Easter Island; China (Southeast); Costa Rica; East Africa (Tanzania & Zanzibar); Great Barrier Reef (Australia); Jamaica; Papua New Guinea; the Rockies (USA); Syria & Jordan; Turkey.

The Lonely Planet TV series is produced by:
Pilot Productions
Duke of Sussex Studios
44 Uxbridge St
London W8 7TG UK

Lonely Planet videos are distributed by:
IVN Communications Inc
2246 Camino Ramon
California 94583, USA

107 Power Road, Chiswick
London W4 5PL UK

Music from the TV series is available on CD & cassette.
For ordering information contact your nearest Lonely Planet office.

PLANET TALK

Lonely Planet's FREE quarterly newsletter

We love hearing from you and think you'd like to hear from us.

*When...*is the right time to see reindeer in Finland?
*Where...*can you hear the best palm-wine music in Ghana?
*How...*do you get from Asunción to Areguá by steam train?
*What...*is the best way to see India?

For the answer to these and many other questions read PLANET TALK.

Every issue is packed with up-to-date travel news and advice including:

- a letter from Lonely Planet co-founders Tony and Maureen Wheeler
- go behind the scenes on the road with a Lonely Planet author
- feature article on an important and topical travel issue
- a selection of recent letters from travellers
- details on forthcoming Lonely Planet promotions
- complete list of Lonely Planet products

To join our mailing list contact any Lonely Planet office.

Also available: Lonely Planet T-shirts. 100% heavyweight cotton..

LONELY PLANET ONLINE

Get the latest travel information before you leave or while you're on the road

Whether you've just begun planning your next trip, or you're chasing down specific info on currency regulations or visa requirements, check out the Lonely Planet World Wide Web site for up-to-the-minute travel information.

As well as travel profiles of your favourite destinations (including interactive maps and full-colour photos), you'll find current reports from our army of researchers and other travellers, updates on health and visas, travel advisories, and the ecological and political issues you need to be aware of as you travel.

There's an online travellers' forum (the Thorn Tree) where you can share your experiences of life on the road, meet travel companions and ask other travellers for their recommendations and advice. We also have plenty of links to other Web sites useful to independent travellers.

With tens of thousands of visitors a month, the Lonely Planet Web site is one of the most popular on the Internet and has won a number of awards including GNN's Best of the Net travel award.

http://www.lonelyplanet.com

LONELY PLANET PRODUCTS

Lonely Planet is known worldwide for publishing practical, reliable and no-nonsense travel information in our guides and on our web site. The Lonely Planet list covers just about every accessible part of the world. Currently there are eight series: *travel guides*, *shoestring guides*, *walking guides*, *city guides*, *phrasebooks*, *audio packs*, *travel atlases* and *Journeys* – a unique collection of travellers' tales.

EUROPE

Austria • Baltic States & Kaliningrad • Baltic States phrasebook • Britain • Central Europe on a shoestring • Central Europe phrasebook • Czech & Slovak Republics • Denmark • Dublin city guide • Eastern Europe on a shoestring • Eastern Europe phrasebook • Finland • France • Greece • Greek phrasebook • Hungary • Iceland, Greenland & the Faroe Islands • Ireland • Italy • Mediterranean Europe on a shoestring • Mediterranean Europe phrasebook • Paris city guide • Poland • Prague city guide • Russia, Ukraine & Belarus • Russian phrasebook • Scandinavian & Baltic Europe on a shoestring • Scandinavian Europe phrasebook • Slovenia • St Petersburg city guide • Switzerland • Trekking in Greece • Trekking in Spain • Ukrainian phrasebook • Vienna city guide • Walking in Switzerland • Western Europe on a shoestring • Western Europe phrasebook

NORTH AMERICA

Alaska • Backpacking in Alaska • Baja California• California & Nevada • Canada • Florida • Hawaii • Honolulu city guide • Los Angeles city guide • Mexico • Miami city guide • New England • New Orleans city guide • Pacific Northwest USA • Rocky Mountain States • San Francisco city guide • Southwest USA • USA phrasebook

CENTRAL AMERICA & THE CARIBBEAN

Bermuda • Central America on a shoestring • Costa Rica • Cuba • Eastern Caribbean • Guatemala, Belize & Yucatán: La Ruta Maya • Jamaica

SOUTH AMERICA

Argentina, Uruguay & Paraguay • Bolivia • Brazil • Brazilian phrasebook • Buenos Aires city guide • Chile & Easter Island • Chile & Easter Island travel atlas • Colombia • Ecuador & the Galápagos Islands • Latin American Spanish phrasebook • Peru • Quechua phrasebook • Rio de Janeiro city guide • South America on a shoestring • Trekking in the Patagonian Andes • Venezuela

Travel Literature: Full Circle: A South American Journey

ANTARCTICA

Antarctica

ISLANDS OF THE INDIAN OCEAN

Madagascar & Comoros • Maldives & Islands of the East Indian Ocean • Mauritius, Réunion & Seychelles

AFRICA

Arabic (Moroccan) phrasebook • Africa on a shoestring • Cape Town city guide • Central Africa • East Africa • Egypt • Egypt travel atlas• Ethiopian (Amharic) phrasebook • Kenya • Morocco • North Africa • South Africa, Lesotho & Swaziland • Swahili phrasebook • Trekking in East Africa • West Africa • Zimbabwe, Botswana & Namibia • Zimbabwe, Botswana & Namibia travel atlas

ALSO AVAILABLE:

Travel with Children • Traveller's Tales

MAIL ORDER

Lonely Planet products are distributed worldwide. They are also available by mail order from Lonely Planet, so if you have difficulty finding a title please write to us. North American and South American residents should write to Embarcadero West, 155 Filbert St, Suite 251, Oakland CA 94607, USA; European and African residents should write to 10 Barley Mow Passage, Chiswick, London W4 4PH; and residents of other countries to PO Box 617, Hawthorn, Victoria 3122, Australia.

NORTH-EAST ASIA

Beijing city guide • Cantonese phrasebook • China • Hong Kong, Macau & Guangzhou• Hong Kong city guide • Japan • Japanese phrasebook • Japanese audio pack • Korea • Korean phrasebook • Mandarin phrasebook • Mongolia • Mongolian phrasebook • North-East Asia on a shoestring • Seoul city guide • Taiwan • Tibet • Tibet phrasebook • Tokyo city guide

Travel Literature: Lost Japan

INDIAN SUBCONTINENT

Bangladesh • Bengali phrasebook • Delhi city guide • Hindi/Urdu phrasebook • India • India & Bangladesh travel atlas • Indian Himalaya • Karakoram Highway • Nepal • Nepali phrasebook • Pakistan • Rajasthan • Sri Lanka • Sri Lanka phrasebook • Trekking in the Indian Himalaya • Trekking in the Karakoram & Hindukush • Trekking in the Nepal Himalaya

Travel Literature: In Rajasthan • Shopping for Buddhas

SOUTH-EAST ASIA

Bali & Lombok • Bangkok city guide • Burmese phrasebook • Cambodia • Ho Chi Minh city guide • Indonesia • Indonesian phrasebook • Indonesian audio pack • Jakarta city guide • Java • Laos • Lao phrasebook • Laos travel atlas • Malay phrasebook • Malaysia, Singapore & Brunei • Myanmar (Burma) • Philippines • Pilipino phrasebook • Singapore city guide • South-East Asia on a shoestring •South-East Asia phrasebook • Thailand • Thailand travel atlas • Thai phrasebook • Thai audio pack • Thai Hill Tribes phrasebook • Vietnam • Vietnamese phrasebook • Vietnam travel atlas

AUSTRALIA & THE PACIFIC

Australia • Australian phrasebook • Bushwalking in Australia • Bushwalking in Papua New Guinea • Fiji • Fijian phrasebook • Islands of Australia's Great Barrier Reef • Melbourne city guide • Micronesia • New Caledonia • New South Wales & the ACT • New Zealand • Northern Territory • Outback Australia • Papua New Guinea • Papua New Guinea phrasebook • Queensland • Rarotonga & the Cook Islands • Samoa • Solomon Islands • South Australia • Sydney city guide • Tahiti & French Polynesia • Tasmania • Tonga • Tramping in New Zealand • Vanuatu • Victoria • Western Australia

Travel Literature: Islands in the Clouds • Sean & David's Long Drive

MIDDLE EAST & CENTRAL ASIA

Arab Gulf States • Arabic (Egyptian) phrasebook • Central Asia • Iran • Israel & the Palestinian Territories • Israel & the Palestinian Territories travel atlas • Istanbul city guide • Jerusalem city guide • Jordan & Syria • Jordan, Syria & Lebanon travel atlas • Middle East • Turkey • Turkish phrasebook • Trekking in Turkey • Yemen

Travel Literature: The Gates of Damascus • Kingdom of the Film Stars: Journey into Jordan

THE LONELY PLANET STORY

Lonely Planet published its first book in 1973 in response to the numerous 'How did you do it?' questions Maureen and Tony Wheeler were asked after driving, bussing, hitching, sailing and railing their way from England to Australia.

Written at a kitchen table and hand collated, trimmed and stapled, *Across Asia on the Cheap* became an instant local bestseller, inspiring thoughts of another book.

Eighteen months in South-East Asia resulted in their second guide, *South-East Asia on a shoestring*, which they put together in a backstreet Chinese hotel in Singapore in 1975. The 'yellow bible', as it quickly became known to backpackers around the world, soon became *the* guide to the region. It has sold well over half a million copies and is now in its 8th edition, still retaining its familiar yellow cover.

Today there are over 180 titles, including travel guides, walking guides, language kits & phrasebooks, travel atlases and travel literature. The company is one of the largest travel publishers in the world. Although Lonely Planet initially specialised in guides to Asia, we now cover most regions of the world, including the Pacific, North America, South America, Africa, the Middle East and Europe.

The emphasis continues to be on travel for independent travellers. Tony and Maureen still travel for several months of each year and play an active part in the writing, updating and quality control of Lonely Planet's guides.

They have been joined by over 70 authors and 170 staff at our offices in Melbourne (Australia), Oakland (USA), London (UK) and Paris (France). Travellers themselves also make a valuable contribution to the guides through the feedback we receive in thousands of letters each year.

The people at Lonely Planet strongly believe that travellers can make a positive contribution to the countries they visit, both through their appreciation of the countries' culture, wildlife and natural features, and through the money they spend. In addition, the company makes a direct contribution to the countries and regions it covers. Since 1986 a percentage of the income from each book has been donated to ventures such as famine relief in Africa; aid projects in India; agricultural projects in Central America; Greenpeace's efforts to halt French nuclear testing in the Pacific; and Amnesty International.

'I hope we send the people out with the right attitude about travel. You realise when you travel that there are so many different perspectives about the world, so we hope these books will make people more interested in what they see. These are guidebooks, but you can't really guide people. All you can do is point them in the right direction.'
– Tony Wheeler

LONELY PLANET PUBLICATIONS

Australia
PO Box 617, Hawthorn 3122, Victoria
tel: (03) 9819 1877 fax: (03) 9819 6459
e-mail: talk2us@lonelyplanet.com.au

USA
Embarcadero West, 155 Filbert St, Suite 251,
Oakland, CA 94607
tel: (510) 893 8555 TOLL FREE: 800 275-8555
fax: (510) 893 8563
e-mail: info@lonelyplanet.com

UK
10 Barley Mow Passage, Chiswick,
London W4 4PH
tel: (0181) 742 3161 fax: (0181) 742 2772
e-mail: 100413.3551@compuserve.com

France:
71 bis rue du Cardinal Lemoine, 75005 Paris
tel: 1 44 32 06 20 fax: 1 46 34 72 55
e-mail: 100560.415@compuserve.com

World Wide Web: http://www.lonelyplanet.com